THE ESSENTIAL
FRENCH
DICTIONARY

THE ESSENTIAL
FRENCH
DICTIONARY

CHANCELLOR PRESS

First published in Great Britain in 1976 by
The Hamlyn Publishing Group Limited under the title
French Dictionary

This edition published in 1988 by
Chancellor Press
Michelin House
81 Fulham Road
London SW3 6RB

Compiled by Laurence Urdang Associates Limited
Aylesbury, Bucks

ISBN 1 85152 082 1

Printed in Yugoslavia

Foreword

This dictionary aims to give concise and accurate definitions of 24,000 of the most important words in use in the English and French languages today.

A pronunciation system based on the International Phonetic Alphabet is used (see *Key to symbols used in pronunciation*). Pronunciation is given for all headwords in both sections of the dictionary, and also for selected subentries in the French-English section.

Modern technical, commercial, and informal usage is given particular attention, in preference to outmoded terms or other expressions not in common contemporary use. Definitions are numbered in order to distinguish senses, and abbreviations are used to indicate use in specific technical, scientific, or commercial fields (see *Abbreviations used in the Dictionary*). An additional feature is the inclusion of idiomatic expressions and phrases, so necessary for the understanding and use of the foreign language.

This dictionary, with its emphasis on modernity, together with its compact form and clear typeface, should prove indispensable in the home, at school, in the office, and abroad.

Abbreviations used in the Dictionary

adj	adjective	*indef art*	indefinite article	*poss*	possessive
adv	adverb	*inf*	informal	*pref*	prefix
anat	anatomy	*infin*	infinitive	*prep*	preposition
arch	architecture	*interj*	interjection	*pron*	pronoun
aux	auxiliary	*invar*	invariable	*rel*	religion
aviat	aviation	*lit*	literature	*s*	singular
bot	botany	*m*	masculine	*sci*	science
cap	capital	*math*	mathematics	*sl*	slang
comm	commerce	*med*	medical	*suff*	suffix
conj	conjunction	*mil*	military	*tab*	taboo
cul	culinary	*min*	minerals	*Tdmk*	trademark
def art	definite article	*mod*	modal	*tech*	technical
derog	derogatory	*mot*	motoring	*Th*	theatre
dom	domestic	*mus*	music	*US*	United States
educ	education	*n*	noun	*v*	verb
fam	familiar	*naut*	nautical	*vi*	intransitive verb
fml	formal	*neg*	negative	*v imp*	impersonal verb
game	cards, chess, etc.	*pers*	person	*vr*	reflexive verb
gram	grammar	*phot*	photography	*vt*	transitive verb
geog	geography	*pol*	politics	*zool*	zoology

Key to symbols used in pronunçiation

English

Vowels						Consonants	
iː	m*ee*t	u	p*u*t	ai	fl*y*	θ	*th*in
i	b*i*t	uː	sh*oo*t	au	h*ow*	ð	*th*en
e	g*e*t	ʌ	c*u*t	ɔi	b*oy*	ŋ	si*ng*
æ	h*a*t	ə	*a*go	iə	h*ere*	j	*y*es
ɑː	h*ear*t	əː	s*ir*	ɛə	*air*	ʃ	*sh*ip
ɔ	h*o*t	ei	l*a*te	uə	p*oor*	ʒ	mea*s*ure
ɔː	*ough*t	ou	g*o*			tʃ	*ch*in
						dʒ	*g*in

ˈ indicates that the following syllable is stressed, as in *ago* (əˈgou).

ˌ placed under an *n* or *l* indicates that the *n* or *l* is pronounced as a syllable, as in *button* (ˈbʌtn̩) and *flannel* (ˈflænl̩).

French

Vowels						Consonants	
iː	*i*l	uː	*ou*	ɑ̃	bl*anc*	j	*h*i*e*r
eː	*été*	y	t*u*	ɥ	l*u*i	ʃ	*ch*at
ɛ	*e*lle	œ	s*oeu*r	iːj	f*ille*	ʒ	*j*e
a	p*a*tte	ə	l*e*	ɛj	sol*eil*	ɲ	a*gn*eau
ɑ	*â*ge	ɛ̃	v*in*	ɑj	trav*ail*		
ɔ	m*o*rt	œ̃	*un*	œj	f*euille*		
o	r*ô*le	ɔ̃	b*on*				

ˈ indicates that the following syllable is stressed, as in *été* (eːˈteː).

Notes on the use of the Dictionary

Irregular plural forms of French nouns and adjectives are shown in the headword list of the French-English section and in the text of the English-French section: for example, *journal, -aux*; *jeu, jeux*; *ail, aulx*. A plural is considered to be irregular if it is not formed by adding *-s* to the singular. Exceptions are nouns and adjectives ending in *-x*, such as *vieux*, which do not vary in the plural.
The abbreviation *invar* means that a noun or adjective does not vary in the plural.

Irregular feminine forms are shown in the same way: for example, *lion, lionne*; *sec, sèche*; *relatif, -ive*. A feminine is considered to be irregular if it is not formed by adding *-e* to the masculine. Exceptions are nouns and adjectives ending in *-e*, such as *brave*, which do not vary in the feminine.

Variant masculine forms of adjectives used before an initial vowel sound are shown in the French-English section: for example, *vieux, vieil, vieille* (as in *un vieil homme*); *beau, bel, belle, beaux, belles* (as in *un bel arbre*).

Irregular verbs are marked with an asterisk in the headword lists of both sections of the dictionary. The principal parts of these verbs are shown in the verb tables. For compounds, see the base form in the table; for example, for *comprendre*, see *prendre*. Verbs ending in *-e + consonant + er*, such as *appeler* and *mener*, which either double the consonant or take a grave accent before mute endings, are not considered to be irregular.

Adverbs derived from adjectives are not shown in either section of the dictionary unless a separate translation is required, or unless the formation is not regular. French adverbs are considered regular if they add the suffix *-ment* to the feminine singular of the adjective; English adverbs are considered regular if they add *-ly* to the adjective.

When the same word may be both an adjective and a noun, the gender of the noun is given only when it is fixed. Thus, **coopératif, -ive** . . . *adj,nf* . . . (cooperative) indicates that the word may be an adjective or a feminine noun (*la coopérative*); **métis, -isse** . . . *adj,n* . . . (half-breed) indicates that the word may be an adjective and a masculine or feminine noun (*le métis, la métisse*).

A swung dash (~) before a change of part of speech indicates that the part of speech refers to the headword, not the preceding subentry in heavy type.

English irregular verbs

Infinitive	Past Tense	Past Participle
abide	abode *or* abided	abode *or* abided
arise	arose	arisen
awake	awoke *or* awaked	awoke *or* awaked
be	was	been
bear[1]	bore	borne *or* born
beat	beat	beaten
become	became	become
begin	began	begun
bend	bent	bent
bet	bet	bet
beware[2]		
bid	bid	bidden *or* bid
bind	bound	bound
bite	bit	bitten *or* bit
bleed	bled	bled
blow	blew	blown
break	broke	broken
breed	bred	bred
bring	brought	brought
build	built	built
burn	burnt *or* burned	burnt *or* burned
burst	burst	burst
buy	bought	bought
can	could	
cast	cast	cast
catch	caught	caught
choose	chose	chosen
cling	clung	clung
come	came	come
cost	cost	cost
creep	crept	crept
crow	crowed *or* crew	crowed
cut	cut	cut
deal	dealt	dealt
dig	dug *or* digged	dug *or* digged
do	did	done
draw	drew	drawn
dream	dreamed *or* dreamt	dreamed *or* dreamt
drink	drank	drunk
drive	drove	driven
dwell	dwelt	dwelt
eat	ate	eaten
fall	fell	fallen
feed	fed	fed
feel	felt	felt
fight	fought	fought
find	found	found
flee	fled	fled
fling	flung	flung
fly	flew	flown
forbid	forbade *or* forbad	forbidden *or* forbid
forget	forgot	forgotten *or* forgot
forgive	forgave	forgiven
forsake	forsook	forsaken
freeze	froze	frozen
get	got	got
give	gave	given
go	went	gone
grind	ground	ground
grow	grew	grown
hang[3]	hung *or* hanged	hung *or* hanged
have	had	had
hear	heard	heard
hide	hid	hidden *or* hid
hit	hit	hit
hold	held	held
hurt	hurt	hurt
keep	kept	kept
kneel	knelt	knelt
knit	knitted *or* knit	knitted *or* knit
know	knew	known

English irregular verbs

Infinitive	Past Tense	Past Participle	Infinitive	Past Tense	Past Participle
lay	laid	laid	**shear**	sheared	sheared *or* shorn
lead	led	led	**shed**	shed	shed
lean	leant *or* leaned	leant *or* leaned	**shine**	shone	shone
leap	leapt *or* leaped	leapt *or* leaped	**shoe**	shod	shod
learn	learnt *or* learned	learnt *or* learned	**shoot**	shot	shot
leave	left	left	**show**	showed	shown
lend	lent	lent	**shrink**	shrank *or* shrunk	shrunk *or* shrunken
let	let	let	**shut**	shut	shut
lie	lay	lain	**sing**	sang	sung
light	lit *or* lighted	lit *or* lighted	**sink**	sank	sunk
lose	lost	lost	**sit**	sat	sat
make	made	made	**sleep**	slept	slept
may	might		**slide**	slid	slid
mean	meant	meant	**sling**	slung	slung
meet	met	met	**slink**	slunk	slunk
mow	mowed	mown	**slit**	slit	slit
must			**smell**	smelt *or* smelled	smelt *or* smelled
ought			**sow**	sowed	sown *or* sowed
panic	panicked	panicked	**speak**	spoke	spoken
pay	paid	paid	**speed**	sped *or* speeded	sped *or* speeded
picnic	picnicked	picnicked	**spell**	spelt *or* spelled	spelt *or* spelled
put	put	put	**spend**	spent	spent
quit	quitted *or* quit	quitted *or* quit	**spill**	spilt *or* spilled	spilt *or* spilled
read	read	read	**spin**	spun	spun
rid	rid *or* ridded	rid *or* ridded	**spit**	spat *or* spit	spat *or* spit
ride	rode	ridden	**split**	split	split
ring	rang	rung	**spread**	spread	spread
rise	rose	risen	**spring**	sprang	sprung
run	ran	run	**stand**	stood	stood
saw	sawed	sawn *or* sawed	**steal**	stole	stolen
say	said	said	**stick**	stuck	stuck
see	saw	seen	**sting**	stung	stung
seek	sought	sought	**stink**	stank *or* stunk	stunk
sell	sold	sold	**stride**	strode	stridden
send	sent	sent	**strike**	struck	struck
set	set	set			
sew	sewed	sewn *or* sewed			
shake	shook	shaken			
shall	should				

Infinitive	Past Tense	Past Participle
string	strung	strung
strive	strove	striven
swear	swore	sworn
sweep	swept	swept
swell	swelled	swollen *or* swelled
swim	swam	swum
swing	swung	swung
take	took	taken
teach	taught	taught
tear	tore	torn
tell	told	told
think	thought	thought
throw	threw	thrown
thrust	thrust	thrust
traffic	trafficked	trafficked
tread	trod	trodden *or* trod
wake	woke	woken
wear	wore	worn
weave	wove	woven *or* wove
weep	wept	wept
will	would	
win	won	won
wind	wound	wound
wring	wrung	wrung
write	wrote	written

[1] when *bear* means *give birth to,* the past participle is always *born*.

[2] used only in the infinitive or as an imperative.

[3] the preferred form of the past tense and past participle when referring to death by hanging is *hanged*.

French irregular verbs

Infinitive	Present Indicative	Present Participle	Imperfect	Past Participle	Future
absoudre	absous	absolvant	absolvais	absous	absoudrai
acquérir	acquiers	acquérant	acquérais	acquis	acquerrai
aller	vais	allant	allais	allé	irai
apercevoir[1]	aperçois	apercevant	apercevais	aperçu	apercevrai
assaillir	assaille	assaillant	assaillais	assailli	assaillirai
asseoir	assieds *or* assois	asseyant	asseyais *or* assoyais	assis	assiérai *or* assoirai
atteindre[2]	atteins	atteignant	atteignais	atteint	atteindrai
avoir	ai	ayant	avais	eu	aurai
battre	bats	battant	battais	battu	battrai
boire	bois	buvant	buvais	bu	boirai
bouillir	bous	bouillant	bouillais	bouilli	bouillirai
circoncire	circoncis	circoncisant	circoncisais	circoncis	circoncirai
clore	clos	closant		clos	clorai
conclure	conclus	concluant	concluais	conclu	conclurai
conduire[3]	conduis	conduisant	conduisais	conduit	conduirai
confire	confis	confisant	confisais	confit	confirai
conquérir	conquiers	conquérant	conquérais	conquis	conquerrai
contraindre	contrains	contraignant	contraignais	contraint	contraindrai
coudre	couds	cousant	cousais	cousu	coudrai
courir	cours	courant	courais	couru	courrai
couvrir	couvre	couvrant	couvrais	couvert	couvrirai
craindre	crains	craignant	craignais	craint	craindrai
croire	crois	croyant	croyais	cru	croirai
croître	crois	croissant	croissais	crû	croîtrai
cueillir	cueille	cueillant	cueillais	cueilli	cueillerai
cuire	cuis	cuisant	cuisais	cuit	cuirai
devoir	dois	devant	devais	dû	devrai
dire	dis	disant	disais	dit	dirai
dissoudre	dissous	dissolvant	dissolvais	dissous	dissoudrai
dormir	dors	dormant	dormais	dormi	dormirai
échoir	il échoit *or* échet	échéant		échu	il échoira *or* écherra
écrire[4]	écris	écrivant	écrivais	écrit	écrirai
envoyer	envoie	envoyant	envoyais	envoyé	enverrai
être	suis	étant	étais	été	serai
exclure	exclus	excluant	excluais	exclu	exclurai
faillir		faillant		failli	faillirai
faire	fais	faisant	faisais	fait	ferai
falloir	il faut		il fallait	fallu	il faudra
férir				féru	
frire	fris			frit	frirai

Infinitive	Present Indicative	Present Participle	Imperfect	Past Participle	Future
fuir	fuis	fuyant	fuyais	fui	fuirai
gésir	gis	gisant	gisais		
haïr	hais	haïssant	haïssais	haï	haïrai
importer	il importe	important		importé	
inclure	inclus	incluant	incluais	inclus	inclurai
joindre	joins	joignant	joignais	joint	joindrai
lire	lis	lisant	lisais	lu	lirai
luire	luis	luisant	luisais	lui	luirai
maudire	maudis	maudissant	maudissais	maudit	maudirai
mentir	mens	mentant	mentais	menti	mentirai
messeoir	il messied	messéant	il messeyait		il messiéra
mettre	mets	mettant	mettais	mis	mettrai
moudre	mouds	moulant	moulais	moulu	moudrai
mourir	meurs	mourant	mourais	mort	mourrai
mouvoir	meus	mouvant	mouvais	mû	mouvrai
naître	nais	naissant	naissais	né	naîtrai
nuire	nuis	nuisant	nuisais	nui	nuirai
offrir	offre	offrant	offrais	offert	offrirai
ouïr		oyant		ouï	ouïrai
ouvrir	ouvre	ouvrant	ouvrais	ouvert	ouvrirai
paître	pais	paissant	paissais		paîtrai
paraître[5]	parais	paraissant	paraissais	paru	paraîtrai
partir	pars	partant	partais	parti	partirai
plaindre	plains	plaignant	plaignais	plaint	plaindrai
plaire	plais	plaisant	plaisais	plu	plairai
pleuvoir	il pleut	pleuvant	il pleuvait	plu	il pleuvra
pourvoir	pourvois	pourvoyant	pourvoyais	pourvu	pourvoirai
pouvoir	peux *or* puis	pouvant	pouvais	pu	pourrai
prendre	prends	prenant	prenais	pris	prendrai
repaître	repais	repaissant	repaissais	repu	repaîtrai
se repentir	me repens	se repentant	me repentais	repenti	me repentirai
requérir	requiers	requérant	requérais	requis	requerrai
résoudre	résous	résolvant	résolvais	résolu	résoudrai
rire	ris	riant	riais	ri	rirai
saillir	il saillit *or* saille	saillissant *or* saillant	il saillissait *or* saillait	sailli	il saillira *or* saillera
savoir	sais	sachant	savais	su	saurai
sentir	sens	sentant	sentais	senti	sentirai
seoir	il sied	séant *ou* seyant	il seyait	sis	il siéra
servir	sers	servant	servais	servi	servirai
sortir	sors	sortant	sortais	sorti	sortirai

French irregular verbs

Infinitive	Present Indicative	Present Participle	Imperfect	Past Participle	Future
souffrir	souffre	souffrant	souffrais	souffert	souffrirai
suffire	suffis	suffisant	suffisais	suffi	suffirai
suivre	suis	suivant	suivais	suivi	suivrai
surseoir	sursois	sursoyant	sursoyais	sursis	surseoirai
taire	tais	taisant	taisais	tu	tairai
tenir	tiens	tenant	tenais	tenu	tiendrai
traire	trais	trayant	trayais	trait	trairai
tressaillir	tressaille	tressaillant	tressaillais	tressailli	tressaillirai
vaincre	vaincs	vainquant	vainquais	vaincu	vaincrai
valoir	vaux	valant	valais	valu	vaudrai
venir	viens	venant	venais	venu	viendrai
vêtir	vêts	vêtant	vêtais	vêtu	vêtirai
vivre	vis	vivant	vivais	vécu	vivrai
voir	vois	voyant	voyais	vu	verrai
vouloir	veux	voulant	voulais	voulu	voudrai

[1] All other verbs ending in *-cevoir* are conjugated like *apercevoir*.
[2] All other verbs ending in *-eindre* are conjugated like *atteindre*.
[3] All other verbs ending in *-uire* are conjugated like *conduire*.
[4] All other verbs ending in *-crire* are conjugated like *écrire*.
[5] All other verbs ending in *-aître* are conjugated like *paraître*.

A

a (a) *v* see **avoir.**

à (a) *prep* **1** to. **2** at. **3** in. **4** by. **5** from. **6** for. **7** according to.

abaisser (abɛ'se:) *vt* **1** lower, let down. **2** reduce. **s'abaisser** *vr* **1** humble oneself. **2** decrease. **abaissement** *nm* **1** humiliation, degradation. **2** lowering.

abandon (abɑ̃'dɔ̃) *nm* **1** desertion. **2** surrender. **3** neglect. **à l'abandon** uncared for.

abandonner (abɑ̃dɔ'ne:) *vt* **1** abandon, desert. **2** give up, surrender. **3** let go. **s'abandonner à** *vr* **1** give way to. **2** indulge in.

abasourdir (abazu:r'di:r) *vt* **1** astound, dumbfound. **2** bewilder.

abats (a'ba) *nm pl* offal.

abattoir (aba'twar) *nm* abattoir, slaughterhouse.

abattre* (a'batr) *vt* **1** knock or pull down. **2** slaughter. **3** lay. **4** shoot down. **s'abattre** *vr* **1** fall, collapse. **2** abate. **3** become depressed. **abat-jour** *nm invar* lampshade. **abattu** *adj* depressed, disheartened.

abbaye (abɛ'ji:) *nf* abbey, monastery.

abbé (a'be:) *nm* **1** abbot. **2** priest. **abbesse** (a'bɛs) *nf* abbess.

abcès (ap'sɛ) *nm* abscess.

abdiquer (abdi:'ke:) *vt* **1** abdicate. **2** renounce.

abdomen (abdɔ'mɛn) *nm* abdomen.

abeille (a'bɛj) *nf* bee.

abhorrer (abɔ're:) *vt* abhor, loathe.

abîmer (abi:'me:) *vt* **1** spoil, damage. **2** injure. **s'abîmer** *vr* **1** be engulfed. **2** get damaged. **abîme** *nm* abyss.

abnégation (abnɛga'sjɔ̃) *nf* self-sacrifice.

aboi (a'bwa) *nm* bark. **aux abois** in a desperate situation. **aboiement** *nm* **1** barking. **2** bark.

abolir (abɔ'li:r) *vt* abolish. **abolition** *nf* **1** abolition. **2** repeal.

abominable (abɔmi:'nabl) *adj* abominable.

abonder (abɔ̃'de:) *vi* abound, be plentiful. **abondamment** *adv* abundantly. **abondance** *nf* **1** abundance. **2** wealth. **abondant** *adj* abundant, plentiful.

s'abonner (sabɔ'ne:) *vr* subscribe. **abonnement** *nm* **1** subscription. **2** season ticket.

abord (a'bɔr) *nm* access, approach. **d'abord** *adv* at first.

aborder (abɔr'de:) *vi* land. *vt* **1** approach, accost. **2** collide with. **3** deal with. **abordable** *adj* **1** approachable. **2** accessible. **3** reasonable.

aborigène (abɔri:'ʒɛn) *adj* **1** Aboriginal. **2** native. *nm,f* Aborigine.

abortif, -ive (abɔr'ti:f, -'ti:v) *adj* abortive.

aboutir (abu:'ti:r) *vi* **1** end. **2** lead, result. **3** succeed.

aboyer (abwa'je:) *vi* bark.

abrasif, -ive (abra'zi:f, -'zi:v) *adj,nm* abrasive.

abréger (abre:'ʒe:) *vt* **1** abbreviate. **2** abridge, cut down. **abrégé** *nm* precis, summary.

abreuver (abrœ've:) *vt* **1** water (animals). **2** soak. **s'abreuver** *vr* quench one's thirst.

abréviation (abre:vja'sjɔ̃) *nf* abbreviation.

abri (a'bri:) *nm* shelter. **à l'abri** **1** sheltered, under cover. **2** safe.

abriter (abri:'te:) *vt* shelter, protect. **s'abriter** *vr* take cover or shelter.

abricot (abri:'ko) *nm* apricot. **abricotier** *nm* apricot tree.

abrutissant (abryti:'sɑ̃) *adj* **1** stunning. **2** extremely tedious.

absence (ap'sɑ̃s) *nf* absence. **absent** *adj* absent, missing.

abside (ap'si:d) *nf* apse.

absinthe (ap'sɛ̃t) *nf* absinthe.

absolu (apsɔ'ly) *adj* absolute, complete, utter. **absolument** *adv* absolutely.

absolvant (apsɔl'vɑ̃) *v* see **absoudre.**

absorber (apsɔr'be:) *vt* **1** absorb. **2** engross, occupy.

absoudre* (ap'su:dr) *vt* absolve, forgive.

absous (ap'su:) *v* see **absoudre.**

s'abstenir (sapstə'ni:r) *vr* **s'abstenir de** abstain or refrain from. **abstention** *nf* abstention. **abstinence** *nf* abstinence.

abstrait (ap'strɛ) *adj* abstract.
absurde (ap'syrd) *adj* absurd, ridiculous.
abus (a'by) *nm* **1** abuse, misuse. **2** error.
Abyssinie (abi:si:'ni:) *nf* Abyssinia. **abyssinien, -ienne** (abi:si:'njɛ̃, -'njɛn) *adj,n* Abyssinian.
académie (akade:'mi:) *nf* **1** academy. **2** college, school. **académique** *adj* academic.
acajou (aka'ʒu:) *nm* mahogany.
accabler (akɑ'ble:) *vt* **1** overwhelm. **2** overload. **accablé** *adj* **1** overwhelmed, overcome. **2** tired out.
accaparer (akapa're:) *vt* **1** monopolize, take possession of. **2** hoard.
accéder (akse:'de:) *vi* **accéder à 1** agree to, comply with. **2** have access to.
accélérer (akse:le:'re:) *vt* accelerate, quicken. **accélérateur** (akse:lɛra'tœr) *nm* accelerator.
accent (ak'sɑ̃) *nm* **1** accent. **2** stress. **3** pronunciation. **4** expression.
accentuer (aksɑ̃'tɥe:) *vt* stress, accentuate, emphasize.
accepter (aksɛp'te:) *vt* accept. *vi* agree. **acceptable** *adj* **1** acceptable, reasonable. **2** welcome.
accès (ak'sɛ) *nm* **1** access. **2** fit, attack.
accessoire (aksɛ'swar) *adj,nm* accessory.
accident (aksi:'dɑ̃) *nm* accident, mishap. **accidenté** *adj* **1** uneven. **2** eventful. **accidentel, -elle** *adj* accidental.
acclamer (akla'me:) *vt* acclaim, applaud, cheer. **acclamation** *nf* **1** acclamation. **2** *pl* cheers.
acclimater (akli:ma'te:) *vt* acclimatize. **s'acclimater** *vr* get acclimatized.
accommoder (akɔmɔ'de:) *vt* **1** suit. **2** cook. **3** adapt. **s'accommoder à** *vr* **1** adapt oneself to. **2** come to an agreement with. **s'accommoder de** *vr* put up with. **accommodant** *adj* easygoing.
accompagner (akɔ̃pa'ɲe:) *vt* accompany. **accompagnement** *nm* **1** accompaniment. **2** *pl* trimmings.
accomplir (akɔ̃'pli:r) *vt* **1** complete. **2** accomplish, achieve. **3** fulfil. **accompli** *adj* **1** accomplished, perfect. **2** finished.
accord (a'kɔr) *nm* **1** agreement. **2** *mus* chord. **d'accord!** agreed! **être d'accord** agree.
accorder (akɔr'de:) *vt* grant. **s'accorder** *vr* **1** agree. **2** correspond, tally.
accordéon (akɔrde:'ɔ̃) *nm* accordion.
accoucher (aku'ʃe:) *vi* give birth.
accoutumer (aku:ty'me:) *vt* accustom. **s'accoutumer à** *vr* get used to.
accrocher (akrɔ'ʃe:) *vt* **1** hook, catch. **2** hang up. **3** collide with. **s'accrocher** *vr* cling or hang on. **accrocheur, -euse** (akrɔ'ʃœr, -'ʃœz) *adj* **1** tenacious. **2** eye-catching.
accroître* (a'krwatr) *vt* **1** increase. **2** add to.
s'accroupir (sakru:'pi:r) *vr* crouch, squat.
accueil (a'kœj) *nm* **1** reception. **2** welcome.
accueillir* (akœ'ji:r) *vt* **1** receive. **2** welcome. **3** greet.
accumuler (akymy'le:) *vt* **1** accumulate, amass. **2** hoard.
accuser (aky'ze:) *vt* **1** accuse. **2** accentuate. **3** indicate. **accuser réception de** acknowledge receipt of. **accusation** *nf* accusation, charge. **accusé** *adj* prominent. *nm* accused (person).
acerbe (a'sɛrb) *adj* **1** harsh. **2** bitter.
s'acharner (saʃar'ne:) *vr* persist. **s'acharner à** keep at. **acharné** *adj* **1** eager, keen. **2** desperate. **acharnement** (aʃarnə'mɑ̃) *nm* **1** eagerness. **2** relentlessness.
achat (a'ʃa) *nm* purchase. **faire des achats** go shopping.
acheminer (aʃəmi:'ne:) *vt* dispatch, forward. **s'acheminer** *vr* make one's way.
acheter (aʃ'te:) *vt* buy.
achever (aʃ've:) *vt* complete, finish. **achevé** *adj* accomplished. **achèvement** (aʃɛv'mɑ̃) *nm* completion.
acide (a'si:d) *adj* **1** acid. **2** sour, sharp. *nm* acid.
acier (a'sje:) *nm* steel.
acné (ak'ne:) *nf* acne.
acompte (a'kɔ̃t) *nm* instalment.
acoustique (aku:'sti:k) *adj* acoustic. *nf* acoustics.
acquérir* (ake:'ri:r) *vt* **1** acquire. **2** secure, get.
acquiers (aki'ɛr) *v* see **acquérir.**
acquiescer (akjɛ'se:) *vt* acquiesce, agree.
acquis (a'ki:) *v* see **acquérir.**
acquit (a'ki:) *nm comm* receipt.
acquitter (aki:'te:) *vt* **1** acquit. **2** pay off. **3** receipt. **s'acquitter de** *vr* fulfil, carry out.
âcre (ɑkr) *adj* **1** bitter, sharp. **2** pungent.
acrilique (akri:'li:k) *adj* acrylic.
acrimonie (akri:mɔ'ni:) *nf* acrimony, bitterness.
acrobate (akrɔ'bat) *nm,f* acrobat. **acrobatique** *adj* acrobatic.
acte[1] (akt) *nm* **1** act, action, deed. **2** record. **acte de décès/mariage/naissance** death/marriage/birth certificate.
acte[2] (akt) *nm Th* act.
acteur, -trice (ak'tœr, -'tri:s) *nm,f* actor, actress.

actif, -ive (ak'ti:f, -'ti:v) *adj* **1** active, busy. **2** brisk. *nm comm* credit.
action (ak'sjɔ̃) *nf* **1** action, act. **2** effect. **3** *comm* share.
activer (akti:'ve:) *vt* **1** stir up, activate. **2** quicken. **activiste** *nm* activist. **activité** *nf* activity, industry.
actuaire (ak'tɥɛr) *nm* actuary.
actualité (aktɥali:'te:) *nf* **1** reality. **2** topical event or question. **3** *pl* news, current events.
actuel, -elle (ak'tɥɛl) *adj* **1** current, present, topical. **2** real. **à l'heure actuelle** at the present time.
acuponcture (akypɔ̃k'tyr) *nf* acupuncture.
adapter (adap'te:) *vt* **1** adjust, fit. **2** adapt.
addenda (adɛ̃'da) *nm invar* addendum.
addition (adi:'sjɔ̃) *nf* **1** addition. **2** bill.
additionner (adi:sjɔ̃'ne:) *vt* add up.
adénoïde (ade:nɔ'i:d) *adj* adenoidal. **végétations adénoïdes** *nf pl* adenoids.
adhérer (ade:'re:) *vi* adhere, stick. **adhérer à** join (a party). **adhérent** *adj* adherent, sticky.
adhésion (ade:'zjɔ̃) *nf* **1** adhesion. **2** membership. **adhésif, -ive** (ade:'zi:f, -'zi:v) *adj* adhesive.
adieu, -eux (a'djœ) *interj* goodbye! farewell! *nm* farewell. **faire ses adieux à** say goodbye to, take one's leave of.
adjacent (adʒa'sɑ̃) *adj* adjacent.
adjectif, -ive (adʒɛk'ti:f, -'ti:v) *nm* adjective. *adj* adjectival.
adjoint (a'dʒwɛ̃) *nm* assistant, deputy.
adjudication (adʒydi:ka'sjɔ̃) *nf* adjudication, award. **mettre en adjudication** put up for auction.
adjuger (adʒy'ʒe:) *vt* **1** award. **2** allocate. **une fois! deux fois! trois fois! adjugé!** going! going! gone!
admettre* (ad'mɛtr) *vt* **1** admit. **2** allow. **3** suppose. **4** acknowledge.
administrer (admi:ni:'stre:) *vt* administer, manage. **administrateur** *nm* administrator, manager. **administratif, -ive** (admi:ni:stra-'ti:f, -'ti:v) *adj* administrative. **administration** *nf* **1** administration, management. **2** civil service.
admirer (admi:'re:) *vt* **1** admire. **2** wonder at. **admirable** *adj* admirable, wonderful. **admiration** *nf* admiration.
admission (admi:'sjɔ̃) *nf* admission. **admissible** (admi:'si:bl) *adj* **1** allowable. **2** eligible.
adolescence (adɔlɛs'sɑ̃s) *nf* adolescence. **adolescent** *adj* teenage, adolescent. *nm* teenager, adolescent.
s'adonner (sadɔ'ne:) *vr* **s'adonner à** **1** devote oneself to, go in for. **2** become addicted to.
adopter (adɔp'te:) *vt* **1** adopt. **2** take up. **3** *pol* pass, carry. **adopté** *nm* adopted child.
adorer (adɔ're:) *vt* **1** adore. **2** worship.
adoucir (adu:'si:r) *vt* **1** soften. **2** alleviate. **3** pacify, calm.
adrénaline (adrɛna'li:n) *nf* adrenaline.
adresser (adrɛ'se:) *vt* address, direct. **s'adresser à** *vr* **1** apply to. **2** speak to. **adresse** *nf* **1** address. **2** skill.
adriatique (adri:a'ti:k) *adj* Adriatic. (**Mer**) **Adriatique** *nf* Adriatic (Sea).
adroit (a'drwa) *adj* **1** skilful, dexterous, adroit. **2** shrewd.
adulation (adyla'sjɔ̃) *nf* adulation, flattery.
adulte (a'dylt) *adj,n* adult.
adultère (adyl'tɛr) *nm* adultery.
adultérer (adylte:'re:) *vt* adulterate.
advenir* (advə'ni:r) *v imp* **1** occur to. **2** happen to.
adverbe (ad'vɛrb) *nm* adverb. **adverbial, -aux** (advɛr'bjal, -'bjo) *adj* adverbial.
adverse (ad'vɛrs) *adj* **1** adverse. **2** opposite. **adversaire** *nm* **1** opponent. **2** enemy.
aérer (ae:'re:) *vt* ventilate, air. **aérien, -ienne** (ae:'rjɛ̃, -'rjɛn) *adj* aerial, air.
aérodynamique (ae:rɔdi:na'mi:k) *adj* aerodynamic. *nf* aerodynamics.
aéroglisseur (ae:rɔgli:'sœr) *nm* hovercraft.
aéronautique (ae:rɔno'ti:k) *adj* aeronautical. *nf* aeronautics.
aéroport (ae:rɔ'pɔr) *nm* airport.
aéroporté (ae:rɔpɔr'te:) *adj* airborne.
aérosol (e:rɔ'sɔl) *nm* aerosol.
affable (a'fabl) *adj* affable.
affaiblir (afɛ'bli:r) *vt* **1** weaken. **2** impair. **3** reduce. **s'affaiblir** *vr* become weak, flag.
affaire (a'fɛr) *nf* **1** business. **2** matter. **3** trouble. **4** *pl* belongings, things. **avoir affaire à** have to do with. **faire l'affaire de** suit. **affairé** *adj* busy.
s'affaisser (safɛ'se:) *vr* **1** subside. **2** collapse.
affamer (afa'me:) *vt* starve. **affamé** *adj* hungry, ravenous.
affecter[1] (afɛk'te:) *vt* **1** feign, affect. **2** be partial to. **3** assume.
affecter[2] (afɛk'te:) *vt* allocate.
affecter[3] (afɛk'te:) *vt* move, touch, affect.
affecter[4] (afɛk'te:) *vt* concern.
affection (afɛk'sjɔ̃) *nf* **1** affection, liking. **2**

ailment. **affectueux, -euse** (afɛkˈtɥœ, -ˈtɥœz) *adj* loving, affectionate.

affiche (aˈfi:ʃ) *nf* **1** placard. **2** poster, bill.

affilier (afi:ˈlje:) *vt* affiliate. **s'affilier à** *vr* affiliate oneself to, join.

affinité (afi:ni:ˈte:) *nf* **1** affinity. **2** resemblance.

affirmer (afi:rˈme:) *vt* **1** affirm. **2** assert. **affirmatif, -ive** (afi:rmaˈti:f, -ˈti:v) *adj* **1** affirmative. **2** positive. **affirmation** *nf* affirmation, assurance.

affliction (afli:kˈsjɔ̃) *nf* affliction, grief.

affliger (afli:ˈʒe:) *vt* **1** afflict. **2** distress. **s'affliger** *vr* grieve.

affluence (aflyˈɑ̃s) *nf* **1** abundance, plenty. **2** crowd.

affoler (afɔˈle:) *vt* **1** distract. **2** drive crazy. **s'affoler** *vr* **1** panic. **2** be infatuated. **affolé** *adj* crazy, frantic.

affranchir (afrɑ̃ˈʃi:r) *vt* **1** (set) free. **2** stamp.

affréter (afre:ˈte:) *vt* charter (a ship).

affreux, -euse (aˈfrœ, -ˈfrœz) *adj* **1** horrible, dreadful. **2** atrocious.

affront (aˈfrɔ̃) *nm* affront, insult.

Afghanistan (afgani:ˈstɑ̃) *nm* Afghanistan. **afghan** *adj,n* Afghan.

afin (aˈfɛ̃) **afin de** *prep* to, in order to. **afin que** *conj* so that, in order that.

Afrique (aˈfri:k) *nf* Africa. **Afrique du Sud** South Africa. **africain** *adj,n* African.

agacer (agaˈse:) *vt* **1** annoy. **2** jar, set on edge. **agaçant** *adj* annoying.

âge (ɑʒ) *nm* **1** age. **2** period. **d'un certain âge** middle-aged. **quel âge avez-vous?** how old are you? **âgé** *adj* aged, elderly.

agence (aˈʒɑ̃s) *nf* agency. **agence de voyages** travel agency. **agent** *nm* agent. **agent de change** stockbroker. **agent de police** policeman. **agent immobilier** estate agent.

s'agenouiller (saʒnuˈje:) *vr* kneel down.

agglomération (aglɔmɛraˈsjɔ̃) *nf* **1** built-up area. **2** mass.

aggraver (agraˈve:) *vt* **1** aggravate. **2** worsen. **3** increase.

agile (aˈʒi:l) *adj* **1** agile, nimble. **2** quick.

agir (aˈʒi:r) *vi* **1** act, do. **2** behave. **3** influence. **s'agir de** *v imp* concern, be a question of. **de quoi s'agit-il?** what's it all about?

agiter (aʒi:ˈte:) *vt* **1** wave, shake. **2** agitate. **3** discuss. **s'agiter** *vr* fidget.

agneau, -aux (aˈɲo) *nm* lamb.

agnostique (agnɔˈsti:k) *adj,n* agnostic.

agonie (agɔˈni:) *nf* death agony. **à l'agonie** dying.

agrafe (aˈgraf) *nf* **1** hook, clasp. **2** clamp. **3** staple.

agraire (aˈgrɛr) *adj* agrarian.

agrandir (agrɑ̃ˈdi:r) *vt* **1** enlarge. **2** increase, magnify.

agréer (agre:ˈe:) *vt* **1** accept. **2** approve. **3** please. **agréable** *adj* **1** agreeable, pleasant. **2** comfortable. **agrément** *nm* **1** pleasure. **2** consent, approval. **3** amenities.

agression (agrɛˈsjɔ̃) *nf* agression. **agressif, -ive** (agrɛˈsi:f, -ˈsi:v) *adj* aggressive.

agricole (agri:ˈkɔl) *adj* agricultural.

agriculture (agri:kylˈtyr) *nf* agriculture. **agriculteur** *nm* farmer.

agrumes (aˈgrym) *nm pl* citrus fruits.

aguets (aˈgɛ) *nm pl* **aux aguets** watchful.

ahurir (ayˈri:r) *vt* **1** astound, flabbergast. **2** bewilder.

ai (ɛ) *v* see **avoir.**

aider (ɛˈde:) *vt* help, assist, aid. **aide** *nf* **1** help, aid. **2** assistant. **3** relief. **à l'aide!** help! **venir en aide à** come to the help of.

aïeul (aˈjœl) *nm* **1** *pl* **aïeuls** grandfather. **2** *pl* **aïeux** forefather.

aigle (ɛgl) *nm* **1** eagle. **2** genius. **3** lectern.

aiglefin (ɛgləˈfɛ̃) *nm* haddock.

aigrir (ɛˈgri:r) *vt* **1** sour. **2** embitter. *vi* turn sour. **aigre** *adj* **1** sour, tart. **2** shrill. **aigreur** *nf* **1** sourness. **2** bitterness.

aigu, -uë (e:ˈgy) *adj* **1** sharp, pointed. **2** acute. **3** shrill.

aiguille (e:ˈgɥi:j) *nf* **1** needle. **2** hand (of a clock). **aiguille à tricoter** knitting needle.

aiguillon (e:gɥi:ˈjɔ̃) *nm* **1** incentive. **2** sting.

aiguiser (e:gɥi:ˈze:) *vt* **1** sharpen, point. **2** stimulate.

ail (aj) *nm, pl* **aulx** garlic.

aile (ɛl) *nf* **1** wing (of bird, building, car, or aircraft). **2** aisle. **ailé** *adj* winged. **aileron** (ɛlˈrɔ̃) *nm* fin.

ailleurs (aˈjœr) *adv* elsewhere. **d'ailleurs** besides.

aimant (ɛˈmɑ̃) *nm* magnet.

aimer (ɛˈme:) *vt* **1** like, care for. **2** love. **aimer mieux** prefer. **aimable** *adj* amiable, kind.

aine (ɛn) *nf* groin.

aîné (ɛˈne:) *adj* **1** elder. **2** eldest. **3** senior.

ainsi (ɛ̃ˈsi:) *adv* thus, in this way. **et ainsi de suite** and so on. **pour ainsi dire** so to speak. ~*conj* so. **ainsi que 1** just as. **2** as well as.

air[1] (ɛr) *nm* **1** air, atmosphere. **2** wind.

air[2] (ɛr) *nm* **1** look, appearance. **2** way. **avoir l'air** look, seem.

air[3] (ɛr) *nm* tune, melody.
airain (ɛ'rɛ̃) *nm* brass.
aire (ɛr) *nf* area.
aise (ɛz) *nf* ease, comfort. **être à l'aise 1** be comfortable. **2** be well off. ~*adj* glad, pleased. **aisé** *adj* easy.
aisselle (ɛ'sɛl) *nf* armpit.
ajonc (a'ʒɔ̃) *nm* gorse.
ajourner (aʒu:r'ne:) *vt* **1** adjourn. **2** postpone.
ajouter (aʒu:'te:) *vt* **1** add. **2** add up.
ajuster (aʒy'ste:) *vt* **1** adjust, fit. **2** put in order.
alarme (a'larm) *nf* **1** alarm. **2** fear.
Albanie (alba'ni:) *nf* Albania. **albanais** *adj,n* Albanian.
albatros (alba'trɔs) *nm* albatross.
album (al'bɔm) *nm* album.
alcali (alka'li:) *nm* alkali.
alchimie (alʃi:'mi:) *nf* alchemy.
alcool (al'kɔl) *nm* **1** alcohol. **2** spirits. **alcoolique** *adj,n* alcoholic.
aléatoire (ale:a'twar) *adj* **1** contingent. **2** risky.
alentour (alɑ̃'tu:r) *adv* around, about. **alentours** *nm pl* **1** neighbourhood. **2** surroundings.
alerte (a'lɛrt) *adj* alert, agile. *nf* alarm, warning. **fin d'alerte** *nf* all clear.
algèbre (al'ʒɛbr) *nf* algebra.
Algérie (alʒe:'ri:) *nf* Algeria. **algérien, -ienne** (alʒe:'rjɛ̃, -'rjɛn) *adj,n* Algerian.
algue (alg) *nf* seaweed.
alibi (ali:'bi:) *nm* alibi.
aliéner (alje:'ne:) *vt* alienate. **aliénable** *adj* transferable. **aliéné** *adj* mad, mentally ill.
aligner (ali:'ɲe:) *vt* align, put in a row.
aliment (ali:'mɑ̃) *nm* food. **alimentaire** *adj* alimentary. **alimentation** *nf* **1** nourishment, feeding. **2** foodstuffs.
alinéa (ali:ne:'a) *nm* paragraph.
aliter (ali:'te:) *vt* confine to bed.
allée (a'le:) *nf* garden path.
alléger (ale:'ʒe:) *vt* **1** relieve, alleviate. **2** lighten.
allégorie (alle:gɔ'ri:) *nf* allegory.
allègre (al'lɛgr) *adj* **1** lively. **2** cheerful, lighthearted. **3** brisk.
alléguer (ale:'ge:) *vt* **1** allege. **2** plead, urge.
alléluia (ale:ly'ja) *nm* hallelujah.
Allemagne (al'maɲ) *nf* Germany. **allemand** (al'mɑ̃) *adj,n* German. *nm* German (language).
aller* (a'le:) *vi (aux* être) **1** go. **2** suit, fit. **aller chercher** fetch. **ça va!** OK! **comment allez-vous?** how are you? **vas-y! allez-y!** go on! **y aller de** stake, be at stake. **s'en aller** *vr* go away, depart. ~*nm* **1** single ticket. **2** outward journey. **au pis aller** if the worst comes to the worst.
allergie (alɛr'ʒi:) *nf* allergy. **allergique** *adj* allergic.
allier (a'lje:) *vt* **1** unite. **2** mix, blend. **alliage** *nm* alloy. **alliance** *nf* **1** alliance. **2** marriage. **3** wedding ring. **allié** *adj* **1** allied. **2** related by marriage. *nm* ally.
alligator (ali:ga'tɔr) *nm* alligator.
allitération (alli:tɛra'sjɔ̃) *nf* alliteration.
allô (a'lo) *interj* (on the telephone) hello!
allocation (allɔka'sjɔ̃) *nf* **1** allocation. **2** allowance.
allocution (allɔky'sjɔ̃) *nf* address, short speech.
allonger (alɔ̃'ʒe:) *vt* **1** lengthen. **2** thin (a sauce). **3** stretch out. **allonger une gifle à** slap.
allouer (a'lwe:) *vt* **1** grant. **2** allocate.
allumer (aly'me:) *vt* **1** light. **2** excite. **s'allumer** *vr* catch fire. **allumé** *adj* alight. **allume-feu** *nm invar* firelighter. **allumette** *nf* match.
allure (a'lyr) *nf* **1** pace, speed. **2** gait. **3** behaviour. **4** look. **à toute allure** at top speed.
allusion (ally'zjɔ̃) *nf* allusion. **faire allusion à** refer to.
almanach (alma'na) *nm* almanac.
aloi (a'lwa) *nm* quality. **de bon aloi** genuine.
alors (a'lɔr) *adv* **1** then, at that time. **2** so, in that case. **alors même que** even when. **alors que** when.
alouette (a'lwɛt) *nf* lark.
alourdir (alu:r'di:r) *vt* **1** make heavy. **2** make stupid.
aloyau, -aux (alwa'jo) *nm* sirloin.
Alpes (alp) *nf pl* Alps. **alpestre** *adj* alpine. **alpin** *adj* alpine. **alpiniste** *nm* mountaineer.
alphabet (alfa'bɛ) *nm* alphabet. **alphabétique** (alfabe:'ti:k) *adj* alphabetical.
altercation (altɛrka'sjɔ̃) *nf* dispute, squabble.
altérer (alte:'re:) *vt* **1** alter. **2** adulterate, corrupt. **3** make thirsty.
alterner (altɛr'ne:) *vi* alternate, take turns. *vt* alternate. **alternatif, -ive** (altɛrna'ti:f, -'ti:v) alternative, alternate. *nf* alternative.
Altesse (al'tɛs) *nf* Highness.
altier, -ière (al'tje:, -'tjɛr) *adj* haughty, arrogant.
altitude (alti:'tyd) *nf* altitude.
alto (al'to) *nm* **1** alto. **2** viola.
aluminium (alymi'njɔm) *nm* aluminium.
amadouer (ama'dwe:) *vt* coax.
amaigrir (amɛ'gri:r) *vt* make thin, emaciate.

amalgamer (amalga'me:) *vt* amalgamate, blend.
amande (a'mɑ̃d) *nf* almond.
amant (a'mɑ̃) *nm* lover.
amarrer (ama're:) *vt* **1** moor. **2** tie up.
amas (a'mɑ) *nm* pile, heap, mass. **amasser** (ɑma'se:) *vt* **1** pile up. **2** amass.
amateur, -trice (ama'tœr, -'tri:s) *nm,f* **1** enthusiast. **2** patron. **3** amateur.
ambassade (ɑ̃ba'sad) *nf* embassy. **ambassadeur** *nm* ambassador.
ambiance (ɑ̃'bjɑ̃s) *nf* **1** surroundings. **2** atmosphere.
ambidextre (ɑ̃bi:'dɛkstr) *adj* ambidextrous.
ambigu, -uë (ɑ̃bi:'gy) *adj* ambiguous. **ambiguïté** *nf* ambiguity.
ambition (ɑ̃bi:'sjɔ̃) *nf* ambition. **ambitieux, -euse** (ɑ̃bi:'sjœ, -'sjœz) *adj* ambitious.
ambivalent (ɑ̃bi:va'lɑ̃) *adj* ambivalent.
ambre (ɑ̃br) *nm* amber.
ambulance (ɑ̃by'lɑ̃s) *nf* ambulance.
ambulant (ɑ̃by'lɑ̃) *adj* **1** wandering. **2** travelling.
âme (ɑm) *nf* **1** soul. **2** spirit. **3** mind. **4** feeling. **5** person. **6** core. **7** bore (of a gun).
améliorer (ame:ljɔ're:) *vt* improve. **amélioration** *nf* improvement.
aménager (amɛna'ʒe:) *vt* arrange, lay out. **aménagement** *nm* **1** fittings. **2** development.
amender (amɑ̃'de:) *vt* **1** improve. **2** amend. **amende** *nf* fine.
amener (am'ne:) *vt* **1** bring. **2** lead. **3** induce.
amer, -ère (a'mɛr) *adj* bitter. **amertume** *nf* bitterness.
Amérique (ame:'ri:k) *nf* America. **Amérique du Nord/Sud** North/South America. **américain** *adj,n* American.
améthyste (ame:'ti:st) *nf* amethyst.
ameublement (amœblə'mɑ̃) *nm* **1** furnishing. **2** furniture.
ami (a'mi:) *nm* **1** friend. **2** boyfriend. *adj* friendly. **amiable** *adj* amicable, friendly. **amical, -aux** (ami:'kal, -'ko) *adj* friendly. **amitié** *nf* **1** friendship. **2** kindness, favour.
amiante (a'mjɑ̃t) *nm* asbestos.
amibe (a'mi:b) *nf* amoeba.
amidon (ami:'dɔ̃) *nm* starch.
amiral, -aux (ami:'ral, -'ro) *nm* admiral. **amirauté** *nf* admiralty.
ammoniaque (amɔ'njak) *nf* ammonia.
amnistie (amni:'sti:) *nf* amnesty.
amoindrir (amwɛ̃'dri:r) *vt* reduce, diminish.
amollir (amɔ'li:r) *vt* **1** soften. **2** weaken.
amonceler (amɔ̃'sle:) *vt* heap up. **s'amonceler** *vr* gather. **amoncellement** *nm* **1** heap. **2** accumulation.
amont (a'mɔ̃) **en amont** *adv* upstream. **en amont de** above.
amoral, -aux (amɔ'ral, -'ro) *adj* amoral.
amorcer (amɔr'se:) *vt* **1** bait. **2** begin. **amorce** *nf* **1** bait. **2** beginning.
amorphe (a'mɔrf) *adj* amorphous.
amortir (amɔr'ti:r) *vt* **1** deaden, soften. **2** pay off. **amortissement** *nm* **1** deadening. **2** redemption. **amortisseur** *nm* shock absorber.
amour (a'mu:r) *nm* love, affection. **amoureux, -euse** (amu'rœ, -'rœ:z) *adj* loving. **être amoureux de** be in love with. **amour-propre** *nm* **1** self-respect. **2** vanity.
ampère (ɑ̃'pɛr) *nm* ampere.
amphétamine (ɑ̃fe:ta'mi:n) *nf* amphetamine.
amphibie (ɑ̃fi:'bi:) *adj* amphibious. *nm* amphibian.
ample (ɑ̃pl) *adj* **1** ample. **2** full. **3** spacious. **ampleur** *nf* fullness.
amplifier (ɑ̃pli:'fje:) *vt* **1** amplify. **2** magnify. **amplificateur** (ɑ̃pli:fi:ka'tœr) *nm* amplifier.
ampoule (ɑ̃'pu:l) *nf* **1** bulb. **2** blister.
amputer (ɑ̃py'te:) *vt* **1** amputate. **2** cut, reduce.
amuser (amy'ze:) *vt* amuse, entertain. **s'amuser** *vr* enjoy oneself. **amusement** *nm* **1** pastime. **2** recreation.
amygdale (ami:'dal) *nf* tonsil. **amygdalite** *nf* tonsillitis.
an (ɑ̃) *nm* year. **avoir six ans** be six years old. **tous les ans** every year.
anachronisme (anakrɔ'ni:sm) *nm* anachronism.
anal, -aux (a'nal, -'no) *adj* anal.
analogie (analɔ'ʒi:) *nf* analogy.
analphabète (analfa'bɛt) *adj* illiterate.
analyser (anali:'ze:) *vt* analyse. **analyse** *nf* analysis.
ananas (ana'nɑ) *nm* pineapple.
anarchie (anar'ʃi:) *nf* anarchy. **anarchiste** *adj,n* anarchist.
anatomie (anatɔ'mi:) *nf* anatomy.
ancêtre (ɑ̃'sɛtr) *nm,f* **1** ancestor. **2** forefather.
anchois (ɑ̃'ʃwa) *nm* anchovy.
ancien, -ienne (ɑ̃'sjɛ̃, -'sjɛn) *adj* **1** ancient. **2** old, past. **3** former. **4** senior. **ancienneté** *nf* **1** antiquity. **2** seniority.
ancre (ɑ̃kr) *nf* anchor.
Andorre (ɑ̃'dɔr) *nm* Andorra. **andorran** *adj,n* Andorran.
âne (ɑn) *nm* **1** donkey, ass. **2** fool.
anéantir (ane:ɑ̃'ti:r) *vt* annihilate, destroy.

s'anéantir *vr* **1** come to nothing. **2** humble oneself. **anéanti** *adj* **1** exhausted. **2** prostrate.
anecdote (anɛk'dɔt) *nf* anecdote.
anémie (ane:'mi:) *nf* anaemia. **anémique** *adj* anaemic.
anémone (ane:'mɔn) *nf* anemone.
anesthésier (anɛste:'zje:) *vt* anaesthetize. **anesthésique** *adj,nm* anaesthetic.
anfractueux, -euse (ɑ̃frak'tɥœ, -'tɥœz) *adj* **1** winding. **2** irregular, rugged.
ange (ɑ̃ʒ) *nm* angel.
angélique[1] (ɑ̃ʒe:'li:k) *adj* angelic.
angélique[2] (ɑ̃ʒe:'li:k) *nf* angelica.
angine (ɑ̃'ʒi:n) *nf* sore throat, tonsillitis.
angle (ɑ̃gl) *nm* **1** angle. **2** corner. **3** point of view. **angle droit** right angle.
Angleterre (ɑ̃glə'tɛr) *nf* England. **anglais** (ɑ̃'glɛ) *adj* English. *nm* **1** Englishman. **2** English (language).
anglican (ɑ̃gli:'kɑ̃) *adj,n* Anglican.
angoisse (ɑ̃'gwas) *nf* **1** anguish. **2** distress. **angoissant** (ɑ̃gwa'sɑ̃) *adj* **1** distressing. **2** alarming.
anguille (ɑ̃'gi:j) *nf* eel.
anguleux, -euse (ɑ̃gy'lœ, -'lœz) *adj* **1** angular. **2** bony.
anhydride (ani:'dri:d) *nm* **anhydride carbonique** carbon dioxide.
animal, -aux[1] (ani:'mal, -'mo) *nm* animal.
animal, -aux[2] (ani:'mal, -'mo) *adj* **1** animal. **2** brutal. **3** sensual.
animer (ani:'me:) *vt* **1** animate. **2** prompt. **3** brighten. **s'animer** *vr* **1** come to life. **2** become excited. **animé** *adj* **1** lively. **2** bright.
animosité (ani:mɔzi:'te:) *nf* spite.
anis (a'ni:) *nm* aniseed.
annales (an'nal) *nf pl* annals.
anneau, -aux (a'no) *nm* **1** ring. **2** link. **3** ringlet.
année (a'ne:) *nf* year. **bonne année!** Happy New Year!
annexer (anɛk'se:) *vt* **1** annex. **2** attack. **annexe** *nf* annexe.
annihiler (ani:i:'le:) *vt* annihilate, destroy.
anniversaire (ani:vɛr'sɛr) *adj* anniversary. *nm* **1** birthday. **2** anniversary.
annoncer (anɔ̃'se:) *vt* **1** announce. **2** advertise. **3** indicate. **s'annoncer bien** *vr* look promising. **annonce** *nf* **1** announcement. **2** advertisement. **petites annonces** *nf pl* classified advertisements.
annoter (anɔ'te:) *vt* annotate.
annuaire (a'nɥɛr) *nm* **1** almanac. **2** annual. **3** telephone directory.
annuel, -elle (a'nɥɛl) *adj* annual.
annuler (any'le:) *vt* annul, cancel.
anode (a'nɔd) *nf* anode.
anomalie (anɔma'li:) *nf* anomaly.
anonyme (anɔ'ni:m) *adj* anonymous. *nm* anonymity.
anormal, -aux (anɔr'mal, -'mo) *adj* **1** abnormal. **2** irregular.
anse (ɑ̃s) *nf* **1** handle. **2** cove.
antagonisme (ɑ̃tagɔ'ni:sm) *nm* antagonism. **antagoniste** *adj* antagonistic. *nm* opponent.
antarctique (ɑ̃tar'ti:k) *adj* antarctic. *nm cap* Antarctic.
antenne (ɑ̃'tɛn) *nf* **1** aerial. **2** antenna. **3** horn.
antérieur (ɑ̃te:'rjœr) *adj* **1** former, previous, prior. **2** fore.
anthologie (ɑ̃tɔlɔ'ʒi:) *nf* anthology.
anthropologie (ɑ̃trɔpɔlɔ'ʒi:) *nf* anthropology.
anti-aérien, -ienne (ɑ̃ti:ae:'rjɛ̃, -'rjɛn) *adj* anti-aircraft.
antialcoolique (ɑ̃ti:alkɔ'li:k) *adj* teetotal. *nm,f* teetotaller.
antibiotique (ɑ̃ti:bjɔ'ti:k) *adj, nm* antibiotic.
anticiper (ɑ̃ti:si:'pe:) *vt,vi* anticipate. **anticipation** *nf* anticipation.
anticonceptionnel, -elle (ɑ̃ti:kɔ̃sɛpsjɔ'nɛl) *adj* contraceptive.
anticorps (ɑ̃ti:'kɔr) *nm* antibody.
anticyclone (ɑ̃ti:si:'klon) *nm* anticyclone.
antidater (ɑ̃ti:da'te:) *vt* backdate.
antidote (ɑ̃ti:'dɔt) *nm* antidote.
anti-gel (ɑ̃ti:'ʒɛl) *nm invar* antifreeze.
Antilles (ɑ̃'ti:j) *nf pl* West Indies. **antillais** *adj,n* West Indian.
antilope (ɑ̃ti:'lɔp) *nf* antelope.
antique (ɑ̃'ti:k) *adj* **1** ancient. **2** antique. *nf* antique. **antiquaire** *nm* antique dealer. **antiquité** *nf* **1** antiquity. **2** *pl* antiques.
antisémitique (ɑ̃ti:se:mi:'ti:k) *adj* anti-Semitic.
antiseptique (ɑ̃ti:sɛp'ti:k) *adj,nm* antiseptic.
antisocial, -aux (ɑ̃ti:sɔ'sjal, -'sjo) *adj* antisocial.
antithèse (ɑ̃ti:'tɛz) *nf* antithesis.
antonyme (ɑ̃tɔ'ni:m) *nm* antonym.
antre (ɑ̃tr) *nm* **1** cave. **2** den.
anus (a'nys) *nm* anus.
anxiété (ɑ̃ksje:'te:) *nf* anxiety, worry. **anxieux, -euse** (ɑ̃k'sjœ, -'sjœz) *adj* anxious, concerned.
août (u:) *nm* August.
apaiser (apɛ'ze:) *vt* **1** calm, appease. **2** alleviate. **3** quench. **s'apaiser** *vr* **1** calm down. **2** abate.
apathie (apa'ti:) *nf* apathy. **apathique** *adj* apathetic.
apercevoir* (apɛrsə'vwar) *vt* **1** perceive. **2** catch

sight of. **s'apercevoir** *vr* **1** notice. **2** realize. **aperçu** *nm* **1** glimpse. **2** outline.

apéritif (ape:ri'ti:f) *nm* aperitive.

aphis (a'fi:s) *nm* greenfly.

aplanir (apla'ni:r) *vt* **1** smooth, plane. **2** level.

aplatir (apla'ti:r) *vt* flatten. **s'aplatir** *vr* **1** go flat. **2** grovel.

aplomb (a'plɔ̃) *nm* **1** equilibrium. **2** uprightness. **3** self-assurance. **d'aplomb** upright, vertical.

apogée (apɔ'ʒe:) *nm* apex, climax.

apologie (apɔlɔ'ʒi:) *nf* **1** defence. **2** justification.

apostrophe (apɔ'strɔf) *nf* apostrophe.

apôtre (a'potr) *nm* apostle.

apparaître* (apa'rɛtr) *vi* (*aux* être) appear, become visible.

apparat (apa'ra) *nm* pomp, show. **d'apparat** formal.

appareil (apa'rɛj) *nm* **1** display. **2** apparatus. **3** machine, appliance. **4** *inf* phone. **appareil photo** camera.

apparence (apa'rɑ̃s) *nf* appearance, look. **en apparence** apparently. **apparent** *adj* **1** visible. **2** obvious. **3** apparent.

apparenter (aparɑ̃'te:) *vt* connect (by marriage).

appartement (apartə'mɑ̃) *nm* flat.

appartenir* (apartə'ni:r) *vi* **appartenir à** belong to. *v imp* concern.

appas (a'pa) *nm pl* charm, attraction.

appât (a'pɑ) *nm* bait.

appel (a'pɛl) *nm* **1** appeal. **2** call. **appel d'incendie** fire alarm.

appeler (ap'le:) *vt* **1** call. **2** summon. **3** appeal. **4** ring, telephone. **faire appeler** send for. **s'appeler** *vr* be called.

appendice (apɛ̃'di:s) *nm* appendix. **appendicite** *nf* appendicitis.

appentis (apɑ̃'ti:) *nm* **1** penthouse. **2** shed, outhouse.

appétit (ape:'ti:) *nm* **1** appetite. **2** desire. **bon appétit!** enjoy your meal!

applaudir (aplo'di:r) *vt* **1** applaud. **2** commend. **3** praise. **applaudissement** *nm* applause.

appliquer (apli:'ke:) *vt* **1** apply. **2** enforce. **application** *nf* **1** application. **2** diligence. **applicable** *adj* **1** applicable. **2** appropriate. **appliqué** *adj* **1** applied. **2** studious.

appointements (apwɛ̃t'mɑ̃) *nm pl* salary.

apporter (apɔr'te:) *vt* **1** bring. **2** provide.

apposer (apo'ze:) *vt* affix.

apprécier (apre:'sje:) *vt* **1** appreciate. **2** appraise, value. **appréciable** *adj* appreciable. **appréciation** *nf* **1** estimate. **2** appreciation.

appréhender (apre:ɑ̃'de:) *vt* **1** seize. **2** apprehend, fear. **apprehensif, -ive** (apre:ɑ̃si:f, -'si:v) *adj* apprehensive, timid.

apprendre* (a'prɑ̃dr) *vt* **1** learn. **2** teach. **3** inform.

apprenti (aprɑ̃'ti:) *nm* apprentice.

apprivoiser (apri:vwa'ze:) *vt* **1** tame. **2** domesticate. **s'apprivoiser** *vr* grow tame.

approbation (aprɔba'sjɔ̃) *nf* consent, approval.

approcher (aprɔ'ʃe:) *vt* approach, bring near. *vi* approach, draw near. **s'approcher de** *vr* approach, come near to. **approche** *nf* approach.

approfondir (aprɔfɔ̃'di:r) *vt* **1** make deeper. **2** examine thoroughly. **approfondi** *adj* **1** deep. **2** thorough.

approprier (aprɔpri:'e:) *vt* **1** appropriate. **2** fit. **s'approprier à** *vr* adapt oneself to.

approuver (apru:'ve:) *vt* **1** approve. **2** agree to.

approximatif, -ive (aprɔksi:ma'ti:f, -'ti:v) *adj* approximate, rough.

appui (a'pɥi:) *nm* prop, support.

appuyer (apɥi:'je:) *vt* **1** support. **2** rest. **3** hold. **appuyer sur 1** lean or press on. **2** emphasize. **s'appuyer sur** *vr* **1** lean on. **2** rely on.

âpre (ɑpr) *adj* **1** rough, harsh. **2** sharp. **3** keen. **4** greedy.

après (a'prɛ) *prep* after. **d'après** according to. ~*adv* afterwards, later. **après que** after, when. **et après?** what then? **après-demain** *adv* the day after tomorrow. **après-midi** *nm invar* afternoon.

à-propos (aprɔ'po) *nm* aptness.

apte (apt) *adj* **1** suited. **2** capable. **aptitude** *nf* **1** aptitude. **2** capacity.

aquarelle (akwa'rɛl) *nf* watercolour.

aquarium (akwa'rjɔm) *nm* aquarium.

aquatique (akwa'ti:k) *adj* aquatic.

aqueux, -euse (a'kœ, -'kœz) *adj* watery.

Arabie (ara'bi:) *nf* Arabia. **Arabie Séoudite** Saudi Arabia. **arabe** *adj* **1** Arab. **2** Arabic. *nm* **1** Arab. **2** Arabic (language).

arable (a'rabl) *adj* arable.

arachide (ara'ʃi:d) *nf* peanut.

araignée (arɛ'ɲe:) *nf* spider.

arbitre[1] (ar'bi:tr) *nm* umpire, referee.

arbitre[2] (ar'bi:tr) *nm* **libre arbitre** free will.

arbitrer (arbi:'tre:) *vt* **1** arbitrate. **2** umpire. **arbitraire** (arbi:'trɛr) *adj* arbitrary.

arbre (arbr) *nm* **1** tree. **2** shaft, axle. **arbre de Noël** Christmas tree. **arbre vert** evergreen.

arbuste (ar'byst) *nm* **1** bush. **2** shrub.

arc (ark) *nm* **1** bow. **2** arc. **3** arch. **arc-en-ciel** *nm, pl* **arcs-en-ciel** rainbow.

arcade (ar'kad) *nf* **1** archway. **2** arcade.

archaïque (arka'i:k) *adj* archaic.

arche[1] (arʃ) *nf* ark.

arche[2] (arʃ) *nf* **1** arch. **2** hoop.

archéologie (arke:ɔlɔ'ʒi:) *nf* archaeology. **archéologique** *adj* archaeological. **archéologue** *nm,f* archaeologist.

archet (ar'ʃɛ) *nm mus* bow.

archevêque (arʃə'vɛk) *nm* archbishop.

archi- (arʃi:) *pref* **1** arch. **2** utterly. **archibondé** (arʃi:bɔ̃'de:) *adj* crammed full. **archifou** (arʃi:'fu:) *adj* stark mad. **archiplein** (arʃi:'plɛ̃) *adj* packed.

archiduc (arʃi:'dyk) *nm* archduke.

archipel (arʃi:'pɛl) *nm* archipelago.

architecte (arʃi:'tɛkt) *nm,f* architect. **architecture** *nf* architecture.

archives (ar'ʃi:v) *nf pl* **1** archives. **2** public records.

arctique (ark'ti:k) *adj* arctic. *nm cap* Arctic.

ardent (ar'dɑ̃) *adj* **1** burning. **2** ardent, keen. **ardemment** (arda'mɑ̃) *adv* ardently, eagerly.

ardeur (ar'dœr) *nf* **1** heat. **2** ardour, eagerness.

ardoise (ar'dwaz) *nf* slate.

ardu (ar'dy) *adj* **1** steep. **2** difficult, arduous.

are (ar) *nm* unit of measure, equal to 100 square metres.

arène (a'rɛn) *nf* arena, ring.

arête (a'rɛt) *nf* **1** fish bone. **2** edge. **3** ridge.

argent (ar'ʒɑ̃) *nm* **1** silver. **2** money. **argent comptant** cash. **argent liquide** ready money. **argenté** *adj* silvered. **argenterie** *nf* plate.

Argentine (arʒɑ̃'ti:n) *nf* Argentina. **argentin** *adj* Argentine, Argentinian. *nm* Argentinian.

argile (ar'ʒi:l) *nf* clay.

argot (ar'go) *nm* slang.

argument (argy'mɑ̃) *nm* **1** argument. **2** synopsis.

aride (a'ri:d) *adj* **1** arid, dry. **2** barren.

aristocratie (ari:stɔkra'si:) *nf* aristocracy. **aristocrate** *nm,f* aristocrat. **aristocratique** *adj* aristocratic.

arithmétique (ari:tme:'ti:k) *nf* arithmetic.

armer (ar'me:) *vt* **1** arm. **2** strengthen. **3** equip. **4** load (a gun). **arme** *nf* **1** arm, weapon. **2** *pl* coat of arms. **armée** *nf* army. **armée de l'air** air force. **armure** *nf* armour.

armoire (ar'mwar) *nf* **1** wardrobe. **2** cupboard.

arome (a'rom) *nm* aroma.

arpenter (arpɑ̃'te:) *vt* **1** measure. **2** pace up and down.

arquer (ar'ke:) *vt* arch, bend. *vi* become bent, sag. **arqué** *adj* bent, curved.

arracher (ara'ʃe:) *vt* **1** tear away. **2** snatch, seize. **d'arrache-pied** *adv* steadily.

arranger (arɑ̃'ʒe:) *vt* **1** arrange. **2** settle. **3** accommodate. **s'arranger** *vr* **1** manage. **2** come to an agreement. **arrangement** *nm* **1** arrangement. **2** agreement.

arrérages (arɛ'raʒ) *nm pl* arrears.

arrestation (arɛsta'sjɔ̃) *nf* arrest.

arrêt (a'rɛ) *nm* **1** stop. **2** decree.

arrêter (arɛ'te:) *vt* **1** stop. **2** restrain. **3** arrest. **4** fix. *vi* stop. **s'arrêter** *vr* stop, halt. **s'arrêter sur** dwell on. **arrêté** *adj* fixed. *nm* **1** decision. **2** decree.

arrhes (ar) *nf pl* deposit (of money).

arrière (a'rjɛr) *nm invar* **1** back, back part of. **2** *sport* back. **en arrière** **1** behind. **2** arrears. **3** backwards. ~*adj invar* back, rear. **arriéré** *adj* **1** backward. **2** old-fashioned. **arrière-garde** *nf, pl* **arrière-gardes** rearguard. **arrière-plan** *nm, pl* **arrière-plans** background.

arriver (ari:'ve:) *vi* (*aux* être) **1** arrive. **2** come. **3** succeed. **4** happen. **arrivée** *nf* arrival. **arriviste** *nm,f* social climber.

arrogance (arɔ'gɑ̃s) *nf* arrogance. **arrogant** *adj* arrogant, haughty.

arrondissement (arɔ̃di:s'mɑ̃) *nm* **1** district of a town. **2** division of a French department.

arroser (aro'ze:) *vt* **1** water. **2** sprinkle. **arrosoir** *nm* watering-can.

arsenic (arsə'ni:k) *nm* arsenic.

art (ar) *nm* **1** art. **2** skill.

artère (ar'tɛr) *nf* **1** artery. **2** thoroughfare. **tension artérielle** *nf* blood pressure.

arthrite (ar'tri:t) *nf* arthritis.

artichaut (arti:'ʃo) *nm* globe artichoke.

article (ar'ti:kl) *nm* **1** article. **2** item, commodity. **article-réclame** *nm, pl* **articles-réclame** special offer. **articles de Paris** fancy goods.

articuler (arti:ky'le:) *vt* articulate. **articulation** *nf* **1** *anat* joint. **2** link. **3** articulation. **articulation du doigt** knuckle. **articulé** *adj* articulate, distinct.

artifice (arti:'fi:s) *nm* **1** guile. **2** deceit.

artificiel, -elle (arti:fi:'sjɛl) *adj* **1** artificial. **2** imitation.

artillerie (arti:j'ri:) *nf* artillery.

artisan (arti'zɑ̃) *nm* craftsman.

artiste (ar'ti:st) *nm,f* **1** artist. **2** performer. **3** actor. **artistique** *adj* artistic.

as[1] (ɑs) *nm* **1** ace. **2** expert, first-rate performer.

as[2] (a) *v* see **avoir.**

asbeste (az'bɛst) *nm* asbestos.
ascendance (asɑ̃'dɑ̃s) *nf* **1** ascent. **2** ancestry. **ascendant** *adj* upward.
ascenseur (asɑ̃'sœr) *nm* lift.
Asie (a'zi:) *nf* Asia. **asiatique** *adj* Asiatic, Asian. *nm* Asian.
asile (a'zi:l) *nm* **1** refuge. **2** asylum. **sans asile** homeless.
aspect (a'spɛ) *nm* **1** sight. **2** appearance. **3** point of view. **4** aspect.
asperge (a'spɛrʒ) *nf* asparagus.
asphalte (as'falt) *nm* asphalt.
aspirer (aspi:'re:) *vt* **1** aspire. **2** inhale. **aspirant** *nm* candidate. **aspirateur** *nm* vacuum cleaner.
aspirine (aspi:'ri:n) *nf* aspirin.
assaillir (asa'ji:r) *vt* attack.
assainir (asɛ'ni:r) *vt* **1** make healthier. **2** cleanse.
assaisonner (asɛzɔ'ne:) *vt* season.
assassin (asa'sɛ̃) *nm* murderer, assassin. **assassinat** *nm* assassination, murder.
assassiner (asasi:'ne:) *vt* assassinate, murder.
assaut (a'so) *nm* attack, assault.
assembler (asɑ̃'ble:) *vt* **1** assemble. **2** gather, collect. **3** put together. **assemblage** *nm* assembling. **assemblée** *nf* assembly. **Assemblée Nationale** Lower Chamber of French Parliament.
assentiment (asɑ̃ti:'mɑ̃) *nm* assent.
asseoir* (a'swar) *vt* **1** seat, set. **2** establish. **s'asseoir** *vr* sit down.
assez (a'se:) *adv* **1** enough, sufficient. **2** fairly, rather. **j'en ai assez!** I'm fed up with it!
asseyant (asɛ'jɑ̃) *v* see **asseoir.**
assidu (asi:'dy) *adj* **1** industrious, diligent. **2** regular. **assidûment** *adv* **1** diligently. **2** constantly.
assieds (a'sjɛ) *v* see **asseoir.**
assiéger (asje:'ʒe:) *vt* **1** besiege. **2** surround.
assiette (a'sjɛt) *nf* **1** plate. **2** seat, position. **3** situation. **4** base. **assiette creuse** soup plate. **assiette plate** dinner plate.
assigner (asi:'ɲe:) *vt* **1** assign. **2** appoint. **3** summon. **assignation** *nf* **1** assignment. **2** summons.
assimiler (asi:mi:'le:) *vt* assimilate, digest.
assis (a'si:) *v* see **asseoir.** *adj* seated. **assises** *nf pl* assizes.
assister (asi:'ste:) *vt* help, assist. **assister à** attend, be present. **assistance** *nf* **1** audience. **2** congregation. **3** assistance. **assistant** *nm* **1** onlooker. **2** assistant.
associer (asɔ'sje:) *vt* associate, connect. **s'associer à** *vr* **1** join in. **2** go into partnership with. **association** *nf* **1** association. **2** society, company. **3** partnership. **associé** *nm* **1** partner. **2** associate member.
assommer (asɔ'me:) *vt* **1** knock senseless, overpower. **2** *inf* bore. **assommant** *adj* **1** overwhelming. **2** boring.
assortir (asɔr'ti:r) *vt* **1** assort. **2** match. **3** stock. **assorti** *adj* **1** assorted. **2** matched. **assortiment** *nm* **1** assortment. **2** set.
assoupir (asu:'pi:r) *vt* **1** make sleepy. **2** allay. **s'assoupir** *vr* doze off.
assourdir (asu:r'di:r) *vt* **1** make deaf. **2** deaden. **3** muffle.
assujettir (asyʒe:'ti:r) *vt* **1** subdue. **2** subject. **3** fasten.
assurer (asy're:) *vt* **1** assure. **2** make secure. **3** affirm. **4** insure. **assurance** *nf* **1** assurance. **2** insurance. **assuré** *adj* **1** sure. **2** safe. **3** certain. **4** confident. **5** insured.
astérisque (aste:'ri:sk) *nm* asterisk.
asthme (asm) *nm* asthma.
astre (astr) *nm* star.
astreindre* (a'strɛ̃dr) *vt* **1** force. **2** subject. **s'astreindre à** *vr* keep to.
astrologie (astrɔlɔ'ʒi:) *nf* astrology. **astrologique** *adj* astrological.
astronomie (astrɔnɔ'mi:) *nf* astronomy. **astronomique** *adj* astronomical.
astronaute (astrɔ'not) *nm* astronaut.
astucieux, -euse (asty'sjœ, -'sjœz) *adj* **1** astute. **2** artful.
atelier (atə'lje:) *nm* **1** workshop. **2** studio.
athée (a'te:) *nm* atheist. **athéisme** *nm* atheism.
Athènes (a'tɛn) *nf* Athens.
athlète (at'lɛt) *nm* athlete. **athlétique** *adj* athletic. **athlétisme** *nm* athletics.
atlantique (atlɑ̃'ti:k) *adj* Atlantic. (**Océan**) **Atlantique** *nm* Atlantic (Ocean).
atlas (at'lɑs) *nm* atlas.
atmosphère (atmɔ'sfɛr) *nf* atmosphere. **atmosphérique** *adj* atmospheric.
atome (a'tom) *nm* atom. **atomique** (atɔ'mi:k) *adj* atomic.
atout (a'tu:) *nm* trump.
âtre (ɑtr) *nm* hearth.
atroce (a'trɔs) *adj* **1** atrocious. **2** terrible. **atrocité** *nf* atrocity.
s'attabler (sata'ble:) *vr* sit down to table.
attacher (ata'ʃe:) *vt* **1** attach. **2** fasten. **s'attacher** *vr* **1** cling. **2** apply oneself. **attache** *nf* **1** fastening. **2** tie. **3** leash. **attaché** *adj* attached. *nm pol* attaché.

attaquer (ata'ke:) *vt* **1** attack. **2** assault. **3** begin. **s'attaquer à** *vr* **1** attack, tackle. **2** grapple with. **attaque** *nf* **1** attack. **2** bout, fit. **3** stroke.

attarder (atar'de:) *vt* keep late. **s'attarder** *vr* linger, delay.

atteignant (atɛ'ɲɑ̃) *v* see **atteindre.**

atteindre* (a'tɛ̃dr) *vt* **1** reach. **2** touch, hit. **3** attain.

atteint (a'tɛ̃) *v* see **atteindre. atteinte** (a'tɛ̃t) *nf* **1** reach. **2** blow, hit, attack. **hors d'atteinte** out of reach.

attenant (at'nɑ̃) *adj* adjacent, next.

attendre (a'tɑ̃dr) *vt* **1** wait for. **2** expect. **en attendant** in the meantime. **faire attendre** keep waiting. **s'attendre** *vr* expect. **attendu** *adj* expected. *prep* considering. **attendu que** seeing that.

attendrir (atɑ̃'dri:r) *vt* **1** make tender, soften. **2** move. **s'attendrir** *vr* **1** become tender. **2** be moved. **attendrissement** *nm* **1** emotion. **2** pity.

attentat (atɑ̃'ta) *nm* **1** criminal attempt. **2** outrage.

attente (a'tɑ̃t) *nf* **1** waiting. **2** expectation.

attention (atɑ̃'sjɔ̃) *nf* **1** attention. **2** care. **faire attention à** pay attention to. ~*interj* look out! **attentif, -ive** (atɑ̃'ti:f, -'ti:v) *adj* **1** attentive. **2** careful.

atténuer (ate'nɥe:) *vt* **1** weaken, lessen. **2** make allowance for.

atterrer (atɛ're:) *vt* overwhelm.

atterrir (atɛ'ri:r) *vi* land. **atterrissage** *nm* landing.

attester (atɛ'ste:) *vt* testify.

attirail (ati'raj) *nm* **1** apparatus, outfit. **2** show. **3** *inf* stuff, rubbish.

attirer (ati:'re:) *vt* **1** attract. **2** bring on. **3** lure. **attirant** *adj* **1** attractive. **2** engaging.

attitré (ati:'tre:) *adj* **1** appointed. **2** regular.

attitude (ati:'tyd) *nf* **1** attitude. **2** posture.

attraction (atrak'sjɔ̃) *nf* attraction. **attractif, -ive** (atrak'ti:f, -'ti:v) *adj* attractive.

attrait (a'trɛ) *nm* **1** attraction. **2** charm.

attraper (atra'pe:) *vt* **1** catch. **2** trap. **3** trick. **4** seize. **attrape** *nm* **1** trap. **2** trick. **attrape-nigaud** *nm, pl* **attrape-nigauds** practical joke.

attrayant (atrɛ'jɑ̃) *adj* attractive.

attribuer (atri'bɥe:) *vt* **1** assign. **2** attribute. **s'attribuer** *vr* **1** assume. **2** claim. **attribut** (atri'by) *nm* attribute.

au, aux (o) contraction of **à le, à les.**

aubaine (o'bɛn) *nf* windfall, piece of good luck.

aube[1] (ob) *nf* dawn.

aube[2] (ob) *nf* paddle.

aubépine (obe:'pi:n) *nf* hawthorn.

auberge (o'bɛrʒ) *nf* inn. **auberge de la jeunesse** youth hostel.

aubergine (obɛr'ʒi:n) *nf* aubergine, eggplant.

aucun (o'kœ̃) *pron,adj* any. **ne...aucun 1** none, no. **2** no-one. **aucunement** *adv* in no way, not at all.

audace (o'das) *nf* **1** audacity. **2** impudence. **audacieux, -euse** (oda'sjœ, -'sjœz) *adj* **1** audacious, bold. **2** impudent.

au-delà (o'dla) *adv* beyond. *nm* next world. **au-delà de** beyond, on the other side of.

au-dessous (od'su:) *adv* below, underneath. **au-dessous de** below, under.

au-dessus (od'sy) *adv* above, over. **au-dessus de** above, over, beyond.

au-devant (od'vɑ̃) *adv* **aller au-devant** go to meet.

audible (o'di:bl) *adj* audible.

audience (o'djɑ̃s) *nf* **1** audience, hearing. **2** session.

auditeur (odi:'tœr) *nm* listener.

audition (odi:'sjɔ̃) *nf* **1** audition. **2** hearing.

auditoire (odi:'twar) *nm* **1** auditorium **2** audience.

auge (oʒ) *nf* trough.

augmenter (ɔgmɑ̃'te:) *vt,vi* **1** increase. **2** raise. **augmentation** *nf* **1** increase. **2** rise.

aujourd'hui (oʒu:r'dɥi) *adv* **1** today. **2** nowadays. **d'aujourd'hui en huit** today week.

aumône (o'mon) *nf* alms. **aumônier** *nm* chaplain.

auparavant (opara'vɑ̃) *adv* **1** before, first. **2** previously.

auprès (o'prɛ) *adv* close by, near. **auprès de 1** close to, near. **2** beside. **3** in comparison with.

auquel, auxquels (o'kɛl) contraction of **à lequel, à lesquels.**

aurai (ɔ'rɛ) *v* see **avoir.**

aurais (ɔ'rɛ) *v* see **avoir.**

auréole (ɔre:'ɔl) *nf* **1** halo. **2** glory.

aurore (ɔ'rɔr) *nf* dawn, daybreak.

aussi (o'si:) *adv* **1** as, so. **2** also, too. *conj* therefore, consequently. **aussi bien que** as well as. **aussitôt** (osi:'to) *adv* immediately, at once. **aussitôt que** as soon as.

austère (ɔ'stɛr) *adj* **1** austere, severe. **2** stern.

Australie (ɔstra'li:) *nf* Australia. **australien, -ienne** (ɔstra'ljɛ̃, -'ljɛn) *adj,n* Australian.

autant (o'tɑ̃) *adv* **1** as much. **2** as many. **autant**

que 1 as much as. **2** as far as. **d'autant plus/moins** the more/less. **d'autant que** more especially as.
autel (o'tɛl) *nm* altar.
auteur (o'tœr) *nm* **1** author. **2** inventor, maker.
authentique (otɑ̃'ti:k) *adj* authentic, genuine.
autistique (oti:'sti:k) *adj also* **autiste.** autistic.
auto (ɔ'to) *nf* car. **auto-école** *nf, pl* **auto-écoles** driving school. **faire de l'auto-stop** hitchhike.
autobiographie (otɔbjɔgra'fi:) *nf* autobiography. **autobiographique** *adj* autobiographical.
autobus (otɔ'bys) *nm* bus. **autobus à impériale** double-decker bus.
autographe (otɔ'graf) *nm* autograph.
automatique (otɔma'ti:k) *adj* automatic.
automatisation (ɔtɔmati:za'sjɔ̃) *nf* automation.
automne (o'tɔn) *nm* autumn.
automobile (otɔmɔ'bi:l) *nf* motor car. **automobiliste** *nm* motorist.
autonome (otɔ'nɔm) *adj* autonomous.
autopsie (otɔp'si:) *nf* post-mortem.
autoriser (otɔri:'ze:) *vt* authorize.
autorité (otɔri:'te:) *nf* authority. **autoritaire** *adj* domineering.
autoroute (ɔtɔ'ru:t) *nf* motorway.
autour (o'tu:r) *adv* round, about. **autour de** around, about.
autre (otr) *adj* **1** other. **2** different. *pron* other. **autre chose** something else. **autre part** elsewhere. **d'autre part** on the other hand. **d'un moment à l'autre** from one moment to the next. **l'un et l'autre** both. **quelqu'un d'autre** someone else. **tout autre** quite different. **autrement** (otrə'mɑ̃) *adv* otherwise.
autrefois (otrə'fwa) *adv* formerly, in the past.
Autriche (o'tri:ʃ) *nf* Austria. **autrichien, -ienne** (otri'ʃjɛ̃, -ʃjɛn) *adj,n* Austrian.
autruche (o'tryʃ) *nf* ostrich.
autrui (o'trɥi:) *pron invar* others, other people.
aux (o) see **au.**
auxiliaire (ɔksi:'ljɛr) *adj* auxiliary. *nm* **1** auxiliary. **2** assistant.
avais (a'vɛ) *v* see **avoir.**
aval (a'val) *nm* lower part. **en aval** downstream.
avalanche (ava'lɑ̃ʃ) *nf* avalanche.
avaler (ava'le:) *vt* swallow.
avancer (avɑ̃'se:) *vt* advance, put forward. *vi* advance. **s'avancer** *vr* **1** move forward. **2** progress. **avance** *nf* **1** advance. **2** loan. **à l'avance** or **d'avance** beforehand. **être en avance 1** be early. **2** be fast. **avancement** *nm* **1** promotion. **2** progress.
avant[1] (a'vɑ̃) *prep* before. *adv* **1** before. **2** far, deep. **en avant** forward, in front.
avant[2] (a'vɑ̃) *nm* **1** *naut* bow. **2** *sport* forward. *adj invar* fore. *In the following compounds* **avant** *is invar; the noun or adjective takes the plural.* **avant-bras** *nm* forearm. **avant-centre** *nm sport* centre-forward. **avant-cour** *nf* forecourt. **avant-coureur** *nm* forerunner. **avant-dernier, -ière** *adj* last but one. **avant-goût** *nm* foretaste. **avant-hier** *adv* day before yesterday. **avant-main** *nm sport* forehand. **avant-propos** *nm* preface.
avantage (avɑ̃'taʒ) *nm* advantage. **avantageux, -euse** (avɑ̃ta'ʒœ, -'ʒœz) *adj* advantageous.
avare (a'var) *adj* miserly. *nm,f* miser.
avarie (ava'ri:) *nf* damage.
avec (a'vɛk) *prep* with. *adv* with it.
avènement (avɛn'mɑ̃) *nm* **1** coming. **2** accession.
avenir (av'ni:r) *nm* future. **à l'avenir** in future, henceforth.
Avent (a'vɑ̃) *nm* Advent.
aventure (avɑ̃'tyr) *nf* **1** adventure. **2** chance. **à l'aventure** at random. **dire la bonne aventure** tell fortunes. **aventureux, -euse** (avɑ̃ty'rœ, -'rœz) *adj* **1** adventurous. **2** risky.
avenue (av'ny) *nf* avenue.
averse (a'vɛrs) *nf* downpour.
aversion (avɛr'zjɔ̃) *nf* aversion, dislike.
avertir (avɛr'ti:r) *vt* **1** warn. **2** notify. **avertissement** *nm* **1** warning. **2** notice.
aveu, aveux (a'vœ) *nm* confession.
aveugler (avœ'gle:) *vt* **1** blind. **2** dazzle. **s'aveugler sur** *vr* shut one's eyes to. **aveugle** (a'vœgl) *adj* blind. *nm,f* blind person.
avez (a'vɛ) *v* see **avoir.**
aviateur (avja'tœr) *nm* airman. **aviation** *nf* aviation.
avide (a'vi:d) *adj* **1** greedy, avid. **2** grasping.
avilir (avi:'li:r) *vt* **1** degrade. **2** depreciate. **s'avilir** *vr* disgrace oneself.
avion (a'vjɔ̃) *nm* **1** aircraft. **2** plane. **par avion** by airmail.
aviron (avi:'rɔ̃) *nm* **1** oar. **2** rowing. **faire de l'aviron** row.
avis ('avi:) *nm* **1** opinion. **2** advice. **3** notice. **changer d'avis** change one's mind.
aviser (avi:'ze:) *vt* **1** perceive, catch a glimpse of. **2** *comm* advise, inform. **aviser à** see

about. **s'aviser de** *vr* take it into one's head to. **avisé** *adj* **1** prudent. **2** shrewd.
avocat[1] (avɔ'ka) *nm* barrister.
avocat[2] (avɔ'ka) *nm* avocado.
avoine (a'vwan) *nf* oats.
avoir*[1] (a'vwar) *vt* **1** have, possess. **2** get. *v aux* have. **en avoir à** or **contre** bear a grudge against. **il y a 1** there is, are. **2** ago. **il n'y a pas de quoi** don't mention it. **qu'est ce-qu'il y a?** what's the matter?
avoir[2] (a'vwar) *nm* **1** possession. **2** property.
avoisiner (avwazi:'ne:) *vt* be near, border on.
avons (a'vɔ̃) *v* see **avoir.**
avorter (avɔr'te:) *vi* **1** miscarry. **2** fail. **avortement** *nm* abortion.
avouer (a'vwe:) *vt* **1** admit. **2** acknowledge. **avoué** *nm* solicitor.
avril (a'vri:l) *nm* April.
axe (aks) *nm* **1** axis. **2** axle.
ayant (ɛ'jɑ̃) *v* see **avoir.**
ayez (a'je:) *v* see **avoir.**
ayons (ɛ'jɔ̃) *v* see **avoir.**
azalée (aza'le:) *nf* azalea.
azote (a'zɔt) *nm* nitrogen.

B

babiller (babi:'je:) *vi* **1** chatter, prattle. **2** babble. **babillage** *nm* chatter, prattle. **babillard** *adj* talkative.
bâbord (ba'bɔr) *nm naut* port (side).
babouin (ba'bwɛ̃) *nm* baboon.
bac (bak) *nm* **1** ferry. **2** ferryboat.
baccalauréat (bakalɔre:'a) *nm* school leaving examination.
bâche (bɑʃ) *nf* **1** canvas cover. **2** tank, cistern.
bachelier, -ière (baʃə'lje:, -'ljɛr) *nm,f* one who has passed the school leaving examination.
bâcler (bɑ'kle:) *vt* **1** bar, bolt. **2** do in a slapdash way.
bactérie (bakte:'ri:) *nf* bacteria.
badigeonner (badi:ʒɔ'ne:) *vt* **1** whitewash. **2** paint.
badiner (badi:'ne:) *vi* trifle, joke. **badinage** *nm* **1** jest. **2** play. **badine** *nf* cane.
bafouiller (bafu:'je:) *vi,vt* **1** stammer. **2** splutter.
bagage (ba'gaʒ) *nm* **1** baggage. **2** *pl* luggage. **bagages à main** *nm pl* hand luggage. **bagages non accompagnés** *nm pl* luggage in advance.
bagarre (ba'gar) *nf* brawl, scuffle.
bagatelle (baga'tɛl) *nf* trifle.
bagne (baɲ) *nm* prison.
bagnole (ba'ɲɔl) *nf inf* old car.
bague (bag) *nf* (jewellery) ring.
baguette (ba'gɛt) *nf* **1** rod, stick. **2** wand. **3** long thin loaf of French bread.
bahut (ba'y) *nm* **1** cupboard. **2** *sl* school.
bai (bɛ) *adj* bay.
baie[1] (bɛ) *nf geog* bay.
baie[2] (bɛ) *nf arch* bay. **fenêtre en baie** *nf* bay window.
baie[3] (bɛ) *nf* berry.
baigner (bɛ'ɲe:) *vt* **1** bathe. **2** wash. *vi* soak, steep. **se baigner** *vr* **1** have a bath. **2** bathe. **baigneur, -euse** (bɛ'ɲœr, -'ɲœz) *nm,f* bather. **baignoire.** *nf* bath.
bail (baj) *nm, pl* **baux** lease.
bâiller (bɑ'je:) *vi* **1** yawn. **2** be ajar. **bâillement** *nm* yawn.
bâillon (bɑ'jɔ̃) *nm* gag.
bâillonner (bɑjɔ'ne:) *vt* gag.
bain (bɛ̃) *nm* **1** bath. **2** bathe. **prendre un bain** have a bath.
baïonnette (bajɔ'nɛt) *nf* bayonet.
baiser (bɛ'ze:) *vt* kiss. *nm* kiss.
baisser (bɛ'se:) *vt* **1** lower. **2** bend. *vi* go down, decline. **se baisser** *vr* bend down. **baisse** *nf* **1** fall. **2** decline. **3** ebb.
bal (bal) *nm* ball, dance. **bal travesti** fancy-dress ball.
balader (bala'de:) *vi* saunter. **se balader** *vr* stroll. **se balader en auto** go for a drive.
balafrer (bala'fre:) *vt* gash. **balafre** *nf* **1** gash. **2** scar. **balafré** *adj* scarred.
balai (ba'lɛ) *nm* broom, brush.
balancer (balɑ̃'se:) *vt* **1** balance. **2** swing, rock. *vi* **1** swing. **2** hesitate. **se balancer** *vr* sway, swing. **balance** *nf* **1** balance. **2** pair of scales. **3** *cap* Libra. **4** hesitation. **être en balance** be in suspense. **balancier** *nm* **1** pendulum. **2** beam. **balançoire.** *nf* **1** swing. **2** seesaw.
balayer (balɛ'je:) *vt* sweep.
balbutier (balby'sje:) *vi,vt* stammer, mumble.
balcon (bal'kɔ̃) *nm* **1** balcony. **2** *Th* dress circle.
baldaquin (balda'kɛ̃) *nm* canopy.
baleine (ba'lɛn) *nf* whale.
balise (ba'li:z) *nf* **balise flottante** buoy.
balistique (bali:'sti:k) *adj* ballistic.
baliverne (bali:'vɛrn) *nf* **1** idle story. **2** nonsense.
ballade (ba'lad) *nf* ballad.
balle (bal) *nf* **1** ball. **2** bullet. **3** bale. **à l'épreuve des balles** bullet-proof. **balle de golf** golfball.

ballet (ba'lɛ) *nm* ballet.
ballon (ba'lɔ̃) *nm* **1** balloon. **2** football.
ballotter (balɔ'te:) *vt* toss about, shake. *vi* **1** rattle. **2** toss.
balnéaire (balne:'ɛr) *adj* bathing. **station balnéaire** *nf* seaside resort.
Baltique (bal'ti:k) *adj* Baltic. (**Mer**) **Baltique** *nf* Baltic (Sea).
balustrade (baly'strad) *nf* handrail.
balustre (ba'lystr) *nm* banister.
bambou (bɑ̃'bu:) *nm* bamboo.
ban (bɑ̃) *nm* **1** ban. **2** proclamation. **3** *pl* banns. **4** banishment.
banal, -aux (ba'nal, -'no) *adj* **1** common, banal. **2** commonplace, trite.
banane (ba'nan) *nm* banana. **bananier** *nm* banana tree.
banc (bɑ̃) *nm* **1** bench. **2** pew. **3** bed. **4** bank. **banc des prévenus** *law* dock. **bancal** *adj* **1** bandy-legged. **2** wobbly.
bandage (bɑ̃'daʒ) *nm* **1** bandage. **2** tyre.
bande[1] (bɑ̃d) *nf* band, strip. **bande magnétique** recording tape. **bande sonore** soundtrack.
bande[2] (bɑ̃d) *nf* party, gang, group.
bander (bɑ̃'de:) *vt* **1** bandage, bind. **2** tighten. **bander les yeux à** blindfold. **bandé** *adj* **1** bandaged. **2** taut.
bandit (bɑ̃'di:) *nm* **1** bandit. **2** ruffian.
banlieue (bɑ̃'ljœ) *nf* **1** suburb. **2** outskirts.
banne (ban) *nf* **1** hamper. **2** awning.
bannière (ba'njɛr) *nf* banner.
bannir (ba'ni:r) *vt* **1** banish, exile. **banni** *adj* banished, outlawed. *nm* exile, outlaw.
banque (bɑ̃k) *nf* **1** bank. **2** banking. **banquier, -ière** (bɑ̃'kje:, -'kjɛr) *adj* banking. *nm* banker.
banqueroute (bɑ̃k'ru:t) *nf* bankruptcy. **faire banqueroute** go bankrupt.
banquet (bɑ̃'kɛ) *nm* banquet, feast.
banquette (bɑ̃'kɛt) *nf* **1** seat. **2** bench.
baptême (ba'tɛm) *nm* baptism, christening.
baptiser (bati:'ze:) *vt* baptize, christen.
bar (bar) *nm* **1** public bar. **2** pub.
baragouiner (baragwi:'ne:) *vi,vt* gabble.
baraque (ba'rak) *nf* **1** hut, shanty. **2** stall, booth.
baratte (ba'rat) *nf* churn.
barbare (bar'bar) *adj* **1** barbaric. **2** barbarous, cruel. *nm,f* barbarian. **barbarie** *nf* barbarity.
barbe (barb) *nf* **1** beard. **2** whiskers (of an animal). **quelle barbe!** what a nuisance! **se faire la barbe** shave. **barbu** *adj* bearded.
barbecue (barbə'kju:) *nm* barbecue.
barbier (bar'bje:) *nm* barber.
barbiturate (barbity'rat) *nm* barbiturate.
barboter (barbɔ'te:) *vi* **1** paddle. **2** bubble. **3** *inf* get confused. *vt sl* steal.
barbouiller (barbu:'je:) *vt* **1** smear. **2** blot. **3** scribble.
barème (ba'rɛm) *nm* scale, schedule.
bariolé (barjɔ'le:) *adj* gaudy.
baromètre (barɔ'mɛtr) *nm* barometer.
baron (ba'rɔ̃) *nm* baron.
baronnet (barɔ'nɛ) *nm* baronet.
baroque (ba'rɔk) *adj* odd, quaint.
barque (bark) *nf* boat.
barrage (ba'raʒ) *nm* **1** obstruction. **2** dam.
barrer (bɑ're:) *vt* **1** fasten with bars. **2** bar, obstruct. **3** *naut* steer. **4** cross. **5** cross out. **barre** *nf* **1** bar, rod. **2** tiller, helm. **3** stroke. **barreau, -aux** **1** small wooden or metal bar. **2** prison bar. **3** *law* bar. **barrière** *nf* **1** barrier. **2** tollgate.
barricade (bari:'kad) *nf* barricade.
baryton (bari:'tɔ̃) *adj,nm* baritone.
bas, basse (bɑ, bɑs) *adj* **1** low. **2** deep. **3** mean, base. **bas** *adv* **1** low. **2** quietly. *nm* **1** bottom, lower part. **2** stocking. **à bas** down. **en bas 1** below. **2** downstairs. **en bas de** at the foot of. **mettre bas** lay down. **basse** *nf mus* bass. **basse-cour** *nf* farmyard.
basculer (basky'le:) *vi,vt* **1** rock. **2** tip. **bascule** *nf* seesaw.
base-ball (bas'bal) *nm* baseball.
baser (bɑ'ze:) *vt* **1** base. **2** ground. **se baser** *vr* **1** be founded. **2** rely. **base** *nf* **1** base. **2** basis.
basilic (bazi:'li:k) *nm* basil.
basket-ball (baskɛt'bal) *nm also* **basket** basketball.
bassin (ba'sɛ̃) *nm* **1** basin. **2** dock. **3** ornamental pond. **4** *anat* pelvis.
basson (bɑ'sɔ̃) *nm* bassoon.
bastille (ba'sti:j) *nf* small fortress.
bataclan (bata'klɑ̃) *nm inf* belongings.
bataille (ba'tɑj) *nf* battle. **bataillon** *nm* battalion.
bâtard (bɑ'tar) *adj,n* bastard.
bateau, -aux (ba'to) *nm* boat. **bateau à vapeur** steamship. **bateau à voiles** sailing boat. **bateau de sauvetage** lifeboat.
bâtir[1] (bɑ'ti:r) *vt* build, construct. **bâti** *nm* frame. **bien bâti** well-built. **bâtiment** *nm* **1** building, construction. **2** building trade. **3** ship. **bâtisse** *nf* ramshackle building.
bâtir[2] (bɑ'ti:r) *vt* (sewing) tack.

bâton (ba'tɔ̃) *nm* stick. **à bâtons rompus** by fits and starts.

batterie (ba'tri:) *nf* **1** fight. **2** *mil* battery. **3** set. **4** drums.

battre* (batr) *vt* **1** beat, thrash. **2** shuffle. *vi* beat. **se battre** *vr* fight. **battant** *adj* **1** beating. **2** pelting. **à dix heures battant** on the stroke of ten. **tout battant neuf** brand-new. ~*nm* **1** leaf (of a table). **2** clapper (of a bell). **battement** *nm* **1** banging. **2** throbbing. **3** interval. **battement de paupières** blink.

battu (ba'ty) *v* see **battre.**

bavard (ba'var) *adj* talkative.

bavarder (bavar'de:) *vi* **1** chatter. **2** gossip. **bavardage** *nm* chatter.

baver (ba've:) *vi* dribble. **bave** *nf* dribble. **bavette** *nf* bib.

béant (be:'ɑ̃) *adj* open, gaping.

béat (be:'a) *adj* complacent, smug.

beau, bel, belle, beaux, belles (bo, bɛl, bɛl, bo, bɛl) *adj* **1** beautiful, handsome, good-looking. **2** fine. **au beau milieu** right in the middle. **bel et bien** well and truly. **beauté** *nf* beauty.

beaucoup (bo'ku:) *adv* **1** much. **2** many **3** a great deal, a lot. **de beaucoup** by far

beau-fils *nm, pl* **beaux-fils** **1** son-in-law. **2** stepson.

beau-frère *nm, pl* **beaux-frères** brother-in-law.

beau-père *nm, pl* **beaux-pères** **1** father-in-law. **2** stepfather.

beaux-arts *nm pl* fine arts.

bébé (be:'be:) *nm* baby.

bec (bɛk) *nm* **1** beak. **2** spout. **3** mouthpiece. **bec de plume** pen nib. **prise de bec** *nf* argument, row.

bécane (bɛ'kan) *nf inf* bicycle.

bécasse (bɛ'kas) *nf* woodcock. **bécassine** *nf* snipe.

bêcher (bɛ'ʃe:) *vt* dig. **bêche** *nf* spade.

becqueter (bɛk'te:) *vt* **1** peck at. **2** *inf* kiss.

bedaine (bə'dɛn) *nf* paunch.

bée (be:) *adj* **bouche bée** open-mouthed.

beffroi (bɛ'frwa) *nm* belfry

bégayer (be:gɛ'je:) *vi* stutter, stammer.

bégueule (be:'gœl) *nf* prude.

béguin (be:'gɛ̃) *nm* hood. **avoir un béguin pour** have a fancy for.

beige (bɛʒ) *adj* **1** beige. **2** natural coloured. *nf* beige.

beignet (bɛ'ɲɛ) *nm* **1** fritter. **2** doughnut.

bel (bɛl) *adj* see **beau.**

bêler (bɛ'le:) *vi* bleat.

belette (bə'lɛt) *nf* weasel.

Belgique (bɛl'ʒi:k) *nf* Belgium. **belge** *adj,n* Belgian.

bélier (be:'lje:) *nm* **1** ram. **2** *cap* Aries.

belle (bɛl) *adj* see **beau.**

belle-fille *nf, pl* **belles-filles** **1** daugher-in-law. **2** stepdaughter.

belle-mère *nf, pl* **belles-mères** **1** mother-in-law. **2** stepmother.

belle-sœur *nf, pl* **belles-sœurs** sister-in-law.

bémol (be:'mɔl) *nm mus* flat.

bénédicité (be:ne:di:si:'te:) *nm* grace (before meals). **bénédiction** *nf* blessing.

bénéficier (be:ne:fi:'sje:) *vi* **1** benefit. **2** make a profit. **bénéfice** *nm* **1** profit. **2** benefit.

bénévole (be:ne:'vɔl) *adj* **1** benevolent, kind. **2** voluntary.

benin, -igne (be'nɛ̃, -'ni:ɲ) *adj* **1** kindly. **2** mild, gentle.

bénir (be:'ni:r) *vt* **1** bless. **2** consecrate. **bénit** *adj* consecrated, holy.

béquille (be:'ki:j) *nf* crutch.

bercer (bɛr'se:) *vt* **1** rock. **2** lull. **se bercer** *vr* delude oneself. **berceau, -aux** *nm* cradle. **berceuse** *nf* lullaby.

berger, -ère (bɛr'ʒe:, -'ʒɛr) *n* shepherd, shepherdess.

besogne (bə'zɔɲ) *nf* **1** work. **2** task. **besogneux, -euse** (bəzɔ'ɲœ, -'ɲœz) *adj* needy, poor.

besoin (bə'zwɛ̃) *nm* **1** want, need **2** necessity. **au besoin** if necessary. **avoir besoin de** need.

bétail (be:'taj) *nm, pl* **bestiaux** (bɛ'stjo) **1** cattle. **2** livestock.

bête (bɛt) *nf* **1** beast, animal. **2** fool. *adj* stupid. **bête à bon Dieu** ladybird. **bête noire** pet aversion. **bêtise** (be:'ti:z) *nf* **1** stupidity. **2** stupid remark. **3** trifle. **4** blunder. **5** *pl* nonsense.

béton (be:'tɔ̃) *nm* concrete.

betterave (bɛ'trav) *nf* beet. **betterave rouge** beetroot. **betterave sucré** sugarbeet.

beugler (bœ'gle:) *vi* **1** low. **2** bellow. *vt* bellow.

beurre (bœr) *nm* butter.

bévue (be:'vy) *nf* blunder.

biais (bjɛ) *adj* **1** sloping. **2** askew. **3** oblique. *nm* **1** slant. **2** bias. **3** expedient. **de biais** sideways. **en biais.** on the slant.

bibelot (bi:'blo) *nm* knick-knack.

biberon (bi:'brɔ̃) *nm* feeding bottle.

Bible (bi:bl) *nf* Bible. **biblique** *adj* biblical

bibliographie (bi:bli:ɔgra'fi:) *nf* bibliography. **bibliographique** *adj* bibliographical.
bibliothécaire (bi:bli:ɔte:'kɛr) *nm,f* librarian.
bibliothèque (bi:bli:ɔ'tɛk) *nf* **1** library. **2** bookcase.
biceps (bi:'sɛps) *adj,nm* biceps.
biche (bi:ʃ) *nf* **1** *zool* hind. **2** *inf* darling.
bicyclette (bi:si:'klɛt) *nf* bicycle.
bidon (bi:'dɔ̃) *nm* can, drum.
bien (bjɛ̃) *adv* **1** well. **2** properly. **3** good. **4** very. **5** many. **6** quite. **eh bien!** well then! **bien que** although. ~*nm* **1** good. **2** property. **3** *pl* belongings.
bien-aimé *adj* or *n, pl* **bien-aimés** darling.
bien-être *nm* well-being.
bienfaisant (bjɛ̃fɛ'zɑ̃) *adj* charitable, kind.
bienheureux, -euse (bjɛ̃nœ'rœ, -'rœz) *adj* **1** happy. **2** fortunate.
biennal, -aux (bi:ɛ'nal, -'no) *adj* biennial.
bienséance (bjɛ̃se:'ɑ̃s) *nf* propriety. **bienséant** *adj* proper, seemly.
bientôt (bjɛ̃'to) *adv* soon, before long. **à bientôt!** so long!
bienveillance (bjɛ̃vɛ'jɑ̃s) *nf* goodwill. **bienveillant** *adj* kind, benevolent.
bienvenu (bjɛ̃və'ny) *adj* welcome. **bienvenue** *nf* welcome.
bière[1] (bjɛr) *nf* beer. **bière à la pression** draught beer. **bière blonde** **1** pale ale. **2** lager.
bière[2] (bjɛr) *nf* coffin.
biffer (bi:'fe:) *vt* delete.
bifteck (bi:f'tɛk) *nm* steak.
bifurcation (bi:fyrka'sjɔ̃) *nf* fork (in a road).
bigamie (bi:ga'mi:) *nf* bigamy.
bigorneau, -aux (bi:gɔr'no) *nm* winkle.
bigot (bi:'go) *adj* **1** devout. **2** bigoted.
bijou, -oux (bi:'ʒu:) *nm* **1** jewel. **2** *inf* darling. **bijouterie** *nf* **1** jewellery. **2** jeweller's shop. **bijoutier** *nm* jeweller.
bikini (bi:ki:'ni:) *nm* bikini.
bilan (bi:'læ̃) *nm comm* balance sheet.
bile (bi:l) *nf* **1** bile. **2** anger. **se faire de la bile** fret.
bilingue (bi'lɛ̃g) *adj* bilingual.
billard (bi:'jar) *nm* billiards.
bille (bi:j) *nf* **1** marble. **2** billiard ball.
billet (bi'jɛ) *nm* **1** note. **2** ticket. **billet d'aller et retour** return ticket. **billet de banque** banknote. **billet de faveur** free ticket. **billet simple** single ticket.
billot (bi:'jo) *nm* block (of wood).
binaire (bi:'nɛr) *adj* binary.
biner (bi:'ne:) *vt* hoe. **binette** *nf* hoe.
biographie (bi:ɔgra'fi:) *nf* biography. **biographique** *adj* biographical.
biologie (bi:ɔlɔ'ʒi:) *nf* biology. **biologique** *adj* biological.
bis (bi:s) *adv* **1** twice. **2** repeat. *interj* encore!
bisannuel, -elle (bi:za'nɥɛl) *adj* biennial.
biscornu (bi:skɔr'ny) *adj* **1** irregular. **2** *inf* odd, queer.
biscotte (bi:'skɔt) *nf* French toast, rusk.
biscuit (bi:'skɥi:) *nm* biscuit.
bise[1] (bi:z) *nf* north wind.
bise[2] (bi:z) *nf inf* kiss.
bisque (bi:sk) *nf* shellfish soup.
bissextile (bi:sɛk'sti:l) **année bissextile** *nf* leap year.
bistro (bi:'stro) *nm also* **bistrot** **1** French cafe. **2** pub.
bizarre (bi:'zar) *adj* **1** peculiar. **2** strange.
blafard (bla'far) *adj* **1** dim. **2** pale.
blaguer (bla'ge:) *vi* **1** tell lies. **2** tease. **blague** *nf* **1** hoax. **2** joke. **sans blaque?** really?
blaireau, -aux (blɛ'ro) *nm* **1** badger. **2** shaving brush.
blâmer (blɑ'me:) *vt* blame. **blâme** *nm* blame.
blanc, blanche (blɑ̃, blɑ̃ʃ) *adj* **1** white. **2** clean. **3** pale. **4** blank. *nm* white. *nf mus* minim. **blancheur** *nf* whiteness.
blanchir (blɑ̃'ʃi:r) *vt* **1** whiten. **2** bleach. **3** wash. **4** whitewash. *vi* turn white. **blanchissage** *nm* washing. **blanchisserie** *nf* laundry.
blanquette (blɑ̃'kɛt) *nf* veal stew.
blaser (blɑ'ze:) *vt* **1** blunt. **2** surfeit. **se blaser** *vr* become indifferent.
blason (blɑ'zɔ̃) *nm* **1** coat of arms. **2** heraldry.
blasphémer (blasfe:'me:) *vi,vt* blaspheme.
blatte (blat) *nf* cockroach.
blé (ble:) *nm* **1** corn. **2** wheat.
blêmir (ble:'mi:r) *vi* turn pale. **blême** (blɛm) *adj* very pale.
blesser (blɛ'se:) *vt* **1** wound. **2** injure. **3** hurt. **blessé** *adj* wounded. *nm* casualty. **blessure** *nf* **1** wound. **2** injury.
blet, blette (blɛ, blɛt) *adj* (of fruit) soft, over-ripe.
bleu (blœ) *adj* blue. *nm* **1** blue. **2** bruise. **3** novice. **bleu clair/foncé** light/dark blue. **bleuet** *nm also* **bluet** cornflower.
blindé (blɛ̃'de:) *adj* armour-plated.
bloc (blɔk) *nm* **1** block. **2** lump. **3** *pol* coalition. **à bloc** thoroughly. **en bloc** in one piece.
blocus (blɔ'kys) *nm* blockade.
blond (blɔ̃) *adj* **1** fair, blond. **2** light.

blondir (blɔ̃'di:r) *vi* turn yellow. *vt* bleach.
bloquer (blɔ'ke:) *vt* **1** block up. **2** obstruct. **3** jam.
se blottir (blɔ'ti:r) *vr* **1** squat, crouch. **2** nestle.
blouse (blu:z) *nf* **1** blouse. **2** overall.
bluff (blœf, blyf) *nm* bluff.
bobine (bɔ'bi:n) *nf* **1** reel, spool. **2** coil.
bocage (bɔ'kaʒ) *nm* grove.
bock (bɔk) *nm* glass of beer.
bœuf (bœf) *nm* **1** bullock **2** beef.
bohème (bɔ'ɛm) *adj* unconventional, bohemian. *nf* group of artists.
boire* (bwar) *vt* **1** drink. **2** absorb. **boire à petits coups** sip.
bois (bwɑ) *nm* **1** wood, woodland **2** timber, wood. **3** *pl* antlers. **4** woodwind instruments. **bois contre-plaqué** plywood. **de** or **en bois** wooden. **boiserie** (bwɑz'ri:) *nf* woodwork.
boisson (bwa'sɔ̃) *nf* drink, beverage.
boîte (bwat) *nf* **1** box. **2** tin. **3** *inf* nightclub, discotheque. **boîte aux lettres** letter-box. **boîte d'allumettes** matchbox. **boîte de vitesses** gearbox.
boiter (bwa'te:) *vi* **1** limp. **2** be lame. **boiteux, -euse** (bwa'tœ, -'tœz) *adj* lame. *nm,f* cripple.
bol (bɔl) *nm* bowl, basin.
bombarder (bɔ̃bar'de:) *vt* **1** bombard. **2** bomb. **bombardier** *nm aviat* bomber
bombe (bɔ̃b) *nf* bomb. **bombe atomique** atom bomb.
bomber (bɔ̃'be:) *vt* **1** stick out. **2** arch. *vi* bulge. **bombé** *adj* bulging.
bon, bonne (bɔ̃, bɔn) *adj* **1** good. **2** kind. **3** right. **4** nice. *nm* **1** good. **2** voucher. **3** *comm* bond. **à quoi bon?** what's the use? **pour de bon** for good. ~*interj* right!
bonasse (bɔ'nas) *adj* **1** simple. **2** silly.
bonbon (bɔ̃'bɔ̃) *nm* sweet.
bond (bɔ̃) *nm* **1** leap, jump. **2** bounce.
bondé (bɔ̃'de:) *adj* packed, crowded.
bondir (bɔ̃'di:r) *vi* **1** jump, leap. **2** bounce.
bonheur (bɔ'nœr) *nm* **1** happiness. **2** good fortune. **au petit bonheur** in a haphazard way. **par bonheur** fortunately.
bonhomie (bɔnɔ'mi:) *nf* good nature.
bonhomme (bɔ'nɔm) *nm* **1** good-humoured man. **2** old man.
boni (bɔ'ni:) *nm* **1** surplus. **2** profit.
bonjour (bɔ̃'ʒu:r) *interj, nm* good morning, good afternoon.
bonne (bɔn) *nf* housemaid.
bonne-maman *nf, pl* **bonnes-mamans** granny.
bonnet (bɔ'nɛ) *nm* **1** cap. **2** bonnet. **c'est bonnet blanc et blanc bonnet** it's six of one and half a dozen of the other. **gros bonnet** *inf* bigwig. **bonneterie** *nf* hosiery. **bonnetier** *nm* hosier.
bon-papa *nm, pl* **bons-papas** grandad.
bonsoir (bɔ̃'swar) *interj, nm* good evening.
bonté (bɔ̃'te:) *nf* **1** kindness. **2** goodness.
bord (bɔr) *nm* **1** edge. **2** rim. **3** hem. **4** bank. **5** side. **à bord** on board, aboard. **au bord de la mer** at the seaside. **bordure** *nf* **1** border. **2** edging. **3** kerb.
bordeaux (bɔr'do) *nm* **1** Bordeaux wine. **2** *cap* Bordeaux. **bordeaux rouge** *nm* claret.
bordel (bɔr'dɛl) *nm* brothel.
border (bɔr'de:) *vt* **1** line. **2** edge, skirt.
bordereau, -aux (bɔrdə'ro) *nm* **1** memorandum. **2** account, statement.
borgne (bɔrɲ) *adj* **1** blind in one eye. **2** (of a cafe, hotel, etc.) disreputable.
borner (bɔr'ne:) *vt* **1** mark out the boundary. **2** limit. **borne** *nf* boundary, limit. **borne milliaire** milestone. **borné** *adj* **1** limited. **2** narrow-minded.
bosquet (bɔ'skɛ) *nm* grove.
bosse (bɔs) *nf* **1** bump. **2** hump. **avoir la bosse de** have a gift for.
bosseler (bɔ'sle:) *vt* **1** emboss. **2** dent. **bosselure** *nf* dent.
bossu (bɔ'sy) *adj* hunchbacked. *nm* hunchback.
bot (bo) **pied bot** *nm* **1** club foot. **2** club-footed person.
botanique (bɔta'ni:k) *nf* botany. *adj* botanical.
botte[1] (bɔt) *nf* bunch.
botte[2] (bɔt) *nf* high boot. **bottier** *nm* shoemaker.
botte[3] (bɔt) *nf* (fencing) thrust.
botteler (bɔt'le:) *vt* put in bunches.
botter (bɔ'te:) *vt* **1** put boots on. **2** kick.
Bottin (bɔ'tɛ̃) *nm Tdmk* French street and trade directory.
bouc (bu:k) *nm* billy-goat. **bouc émissaire** scapegoat.
boucaner (bu:ka'ne:) *vt cul* cure.
bouche (bu:ʃ) *nf* **1** mouth. **2** opening. **bouchée** *nf* mouthful.
boucher[1] (bu:'ʃe:) *vt* **1** stop or fill up. **2** cork.
boucher[2] (bu:'ʃe:) *nm* butcher. **boucherie** *nf* butcher's shop.
bouchon (bu:'ʃɔ̃) *nm* **1** cork, stopper. **2** wisp (of straw).
boucler (bu:'kle:) *vt* **1** buckle, fasten. **2** curl. *vi* be curly. **boucle** *nf* **1** buckle **2** loop. **3** ring. **4**

curl. **boucle d'oreille** earring. **bouclier** *nm* shield.

bouddhisme (bu:'di:sm) *nm* Buddhism. **bouddhiste** *adj,n* Buddhist.

bouder (bu:'de:) *vi* sulk. **boudeur, -euse** (bu:'dœr, -'dœz) *adj* sulky.

boudin (bu:'dɛ̃) *nm* black pudding.

boue (bu:) *nf* **1** mud. **2** filth, dirt. **boueur** *nm* **1** dustman. **2** roadsweeper. **boueux, -euse** (bu:'œ, -'œz) *adj* muddy.

bouée (bu:'e:) *nf* buoy. **bouée de sauvetage** lifebuoy.

bouffer (bu:'fe:) *vi,vt* **1** puff out. **2** eat greedily. **bouffant** *adj* **1** puffed. **2** baggy. **bouffée** *nf* **1** puff. **2** gust. **3** whiff.

bouffir (bu:'fi:r) *vi,vt* swell. **bouffissure** *nf* swelling.

bouffon, -onne (bu:'fɔ̃, -'fɔn) *adj* comical. *nm,f* clown, fool.

bouger (bu:'ʒe:) *vi* move, stir. *vt* move.

bougie (bu:'ʒi:) *nf* candle. **bougeoir** *nm* candlestick.

bouillabaisse (bu:ja'bɛs) *nf* Provençal fish stew.

bouillir* (bu:'ji:r) *vi* boil. **bouillant** *adj* **1** boiling. **2** hot-tempered. **bouilloire** *nf* kettle.

bouillon *nm* **1** bubble. **2** soup. **3** stock.

bouillonner (bu:jɔ'ne:) *vi* **1** bubble. **2** seethe.

bouillotte (bu:'jɔt) *nf* hot-water bottle.

boulangerie (bu:lɑ̃ʒ'ri:) *nf* **1** bakery. **2** baking. **boulanger** *nm* baker.

boule (bu:l) *nf* **1** ball. **2** bulb. **3** *sl* face. **partie de boules** *nf* game of bowls.

bouleau, -aux (bu:'lo) *nm* birch tree.

bouledogue (bu:l'dɔg) *nm* bulldog.

boulevard (bu:l'var) *nm* avenue.

bouleverser (bu:lvɛr'se:) *vt* **1** overturn. **2** upset. **3** astound. **bouleversement** *nm* **1** overturning. **2** confusion, upheaval.

boulon (bu:'lɔ̃) *nm* bolt.

boulot[1], **-otte** (bu:'lo, -'lot) *adj* chubby, plump. *nm inf* food.

boulot[2] (bu:'lo) *nm inf* job, work.

boulotter (bu:lɔ'te:) *vi* jog along. *vt inf* eat.

bouquet (bu:'kɛ) *nm* **1** bunch. **2** clump. **3** aroma.

bouquin (bu:'kɛ̃) *nm* **1** old book. **2** *inf* book. **bouquiniste** *nm* second-hand bookseller.

bourbe (bu:rb) *nf* mud.

bourdon (bu:r'dɔ̃) *nm* **1** *mus* drone. **2** bumble bee.

bourdonner (bu:rdɔ'ne:) *vi* **1** buzz. **2** hum. **bourdonnement** *nm* buzz.

bourg (bu:r) *nm* **1** market town. **2** borough.

bourgeois (bu:r'ʒwa) *adj* **1** middle-class. **2** plain. **3** common. *nm* citizen. **bourgeoisie** *nf* middle class.

bourgeon (bu:r'ʒɔ̃) *nm* bud.

bourgeonner (bu:rʒɔ'ne:) *vi* come into bud.

Bourgogne (bu:r'gɔɲ) *nf* Burgundy. **(vin de) Bourgogne** *nm* Burgundy wine.

bourrade (bu:'rad) *nf* blow, thump.

bourrage (bu:'raʒ) *nm* padding, stuffing.

bourrasque (bu:'rask) *nf* gust of wind.

bourreau, -aux (bu:'ro) *nm* **1** executioner. **2** torturer.

bourrelet (bu:r'lɛ) *nm* **1** pad. **2** fold, swelling.

bourrer (bu:'re:) *vt* **1** stuff. **2** cram.

bourriche (bu:'ri:ʃ) *nf* hamper.

bourru (bu:'ry) *adj* **1** surly. **2** gruff.

bourse (bu:rs) *nf* **1** purse. **2** scholarship. **3** *cap* Stock Exchange.

boursoufler (bu:rsu:'fle:) *vt* **1** swell. **2** blister. **boursouflure** *nf* swelling.

bousculer (bu:sky'le:) *vt* **1** jostle. **2** upset, knock over. **bousculade** *nf* scuffle.

bousiller (bu:zi:'je:) *vt* **1** hurry through. **2** *inf* smash.

boussole (bu:'sɔl) *nf* compass.

bout (bu:) *nm* **1** end. **2** tip. **3** bit. **à bout de forces** exhausted. **à bout portant** pointblank. **au bout de 1** at the end of. **2** after. **au bout du compte** after all. **de bout en bout** through and through. **venir à bout 1** manage. **2** overcome. **boutade** *nf* **1** whim. **2** outburst. **3** flash of wit.

bouteille (bu:'tɛj) *nf* bottle. **bouteille Thermos** *Tdmk* Thermos flask.

boutique (bu:'ti:k) *nf* shop. **boutiquier, -ière** (bu:ti:'kje:, -'kjɛr) *n* shopkeeper.

bouton (bu:'tɔ̃) *nm* **1** button. **2** bud. **3** handle. **4** spot, pimple. **bouton à pression** press-stud. **bouton de col** stud. **bouton d'or** buttercup. **boutons de manchettes** cufflinks. **boutonnière** *nf* buttonhole.

boutonner (bu:tɔ'ne:) *vt* button.

bouvier (bu:'vje:) *nm* cowhand.

boxer (bɔk'se:) *vi,vt sport* box. **boxe** *nf* boxing.

boyau, -aux (bwa'jo) *nm* **1** bowel, guts. **2** passage, trench.

boycotter (bɔjkɔ'te:) *vt* boycott.

bracelet (bra'slɛ) *nm* **1** bracelet, bangle. **2** (watch) strap.

braconner (brakɔ'ne:) *vi,vt* poach. **braconnier** *nm* poacher.

braguette (bra'gɛt) *nf* fly (of trousers).

braille (braj) *nm* braille.
brailler (bra'je:) *vi* bawl, shout.
braire (brɛr) *vi* bray.
braise (brɛz) *nf* embers.
braiser (brɛ'ze:) *vt* braise.
brancard (brɑ̃'kar) *nm* **1** stretcher. **2** shaft.
brancher (brɑ̃'ʃe:) *vi* perch. *vt tech* connect, plug in. **branche** *nf* **1** branch. **2** division.
brandir (brɑ̃'di:r) *vt* flourish, wave.
branler (brɑ̃'le:) *vi,vt* **1** shake. **2** move. **branle** *nm* motion.
braquer (bra'ke:) *vt* aim, point.
bras (bra) *nm* **1** arm. **2** handle. **3** *pl* labour. **bras dessus bras dessous** arm in arm.
brasier (bra'zje:) *nm* fire, blaze.
brasse (bras) *nf* **1** *naut* fathom. **2** stroke. **3** breaststroke.
brassée (bra'se:) *nf* armful.
brasser (bra'se:) *vt* **1** brew, mash. **2** stir. *nf* **1** brewery. **2** restaurant, café.
braver (bra've:) *vt* brave, face. **brave** *adj* **1** brave. **2** honest. **3** good. **bravoure** *nf* bravery, courage.
brebis (brə'bi:) *nf* **1** ewe. **2** sheep.
brèche (brɛʃ) *nf* **1** breach. **2** gap.
bredouiller (brədu:'je:) *vt,vi* mumble, stammer.
bref, brève (brɛf, brɛv) *adj* brief, short. **bref** *adv* briefly. **en bref** in short.
breloque (brə'lɔk) *nf* charm, trinket.
Bretagne (brə'taɲ) *nf* Brittany. **breton, -onne** (brə'tɔ̃, -'tɔn) *adj,n* Breton.
bretelle (brə'tɛl) *nf* **1** strap. **2** *pl* braces.
breuvage (brœ'vaʒ) *nm* drink, beverage.
brevet (brə'vɛ) *nm* **1** patent. **2** certificate.
breveter (brəv'te:) *vt* **1** grant a patent to. **2** patent.
bribes (bri:b) *nf pl* scraps, fragments.
bricoler (bri:kɔ'le:) *vi* do odd jobs, tinker about. *vt* arrange.
brider (bri:'de:) *vt* **1** bridle. **2** check. **3** fasten. **bride** *nf* **1** bridle. **2** rein. **3** strap. **à bride abattue** at full speed.
bridge (bri:dʒ) *nm game* bridge.
brièvement (brjɛv'mɑ̃) *adv* briefly.
brigade (bri:'gad) *nf* **1** brigade. **2** gang.
brigand (bri:'gɑ̃) *nm* **1** robber. **2** rascal.
brigue (bri:g) *nf* intrigue.
briller (bri:'je:) *vi* shine, sparkle. **brillamment** *adv* brilliantly. **brillant** *adj* **1** brilliant. **2** shining. *nm* **1** brilliance. **2** shine.
brin (brɛ̃) *nm* **1** blade. **2** sprig. **3** strand. **brindille** *nf* **1** twig. **2** sprig.
brioche (bri:'ɔʃ) *nf cul* bun.
brique (bri:k) *nf* brick. **briquet** *nm* cigarette lighter.
brise (bri:z) *nf* breeze.
briser (bri:'ze:) *vt* break, smash.
britannique (bri:ta'ni:k) *adj* British.
broc (brɔ) *nm* jug.
brocanter (brɔkɑ̃'te:) *vi* deal in second-hand goods. *vi* **1** barter. **2** sell. **brocanteur** *nm* second-hand dealer.
broche (brɔʃ) *nf* **1** *cul* spit. **2** peg. **3** brooch.
broché (brɔ'ʃe:) *adj* stitched. **livre broché** *nm* hardback book.
brochet (brɔ'ʃɛ) *nm zool* pike.
brochette (brɔ'ʃɛt) *nf* **1** skewer. **2** kebab.
brochure (brɔ'ʃyr) *nf* brochure, leaflet.
brocoli (brɔkɔ'li:) *nm* broccoli.
broder (brɔ'de:) *vt* **1** embroider. **2** embellish. **broderie** *nf* **1** embroidery. **2** embellishment.
broncher (brɔ̃'ʃe:) *vt* **1** stumble. **2** shy. **3** falter.
bronchite (brɔ̃'ʃi:t) *nf* bronchitis.
bronzer (brɔ̃'ze:) *vt* **1** bronze. **2** tan. **bronze** *nm* bronze.
brosser (brɔ'se:) *vt* brush. **brosse** *nf* brush. **brosse à cheveux/dents/habits** hairbrush/toothbrush/clothes brush. **brosse dure** *nf* scrubbing brush.
brouette (bru:'ɛt) *nf* wheelbarrow.
brouhaha (bru:a'a) *nm* uproar, din.
brouillard (bru:'jar) *nm* fog, mist.
brouiller (bru:'je:) *vt* **1** mix up. **2** confuse. **se brouiller** *vr* **1** get confused. **2** quarrel, fall out. **brouille** *nf* quarrel.
brouillon (bru:'jɔ̃) *nm* rough copy.
broussaille (bru:'saj) *nf* undergrowth.
brouter (bru:'te:) *vt* graze.
broyer (brwa'je:) *vt* **1** pound. **2** pulverize.
bru (bry) *nf* daughter-in-law.
bruiner (brɥi:'ne:) *v imp* drizzle.
bruire (brɥi:r) *vi* rustle.
bruit (brɥi:) *nm* **1** noise, din. **2** rumour. **3** fuss.
brûler (bry'le:) *vi* **1** be on fire, burn. **2** be eager. *vt* **1** burn. **2** scorch. **brûlure** *nf* **1** burn. **2** scald.
brume (brym) *nf* mist, fog. **brumeux, -euse** (bry'mœ, -'mœz) *adj* foggy.
brun (brœ) *adj* **1** brown. **2** dark. *nm* brown. **brune** *nf* dusk.
brunir (bry'ni:r) *vi* become dark. *vt* brown, darken, tan.
brusque (brysk) *adj* **1** abrupt, brusque. **2** sudden. **3** sharp.
brut (bryt) *adj* **1** raw. **2** rough. **3** *comm* gross. **brute** *nf* brute, beast.

brutal, -aux (bry'tal, -'to) *adj* **1** brutal. **2** coarse. **3** rough. **4** blunt. **brutalité** *nf* brutality.
brutaliser (brytali:'ze:) *vt* **1** ill-treat. **2** bully.
Bruxelles (bry'sɛl) *nf* Brussels.
bruyant (bry'jɑ̃) *adj* noisy.
bruyère (bry'jɛr) *nf* **1** heather. **2** heath.
bu (by) *v* see **boire.**
bucarde (by'kard) *nf* cockle.
buccin (byk'sɛ̃) *nm* whelk.
bûche (byʃ) *nf* **1** log. **2** idiot.
bûcher[1] (by'ʃe:) *nm* **1** woodshed. **2** stake. **bûcheron** *nm* lumberjack.
bûcher[2] (by'ʃe:) *vi,vt inf* work hard, swot.
budget (by'dʒɛ) *nm* budget.
buée (bɥe:) *nf* steam, vapour.
buffet (by'fɛ) *nm* **1** sideboard. **2** refreshment room. **buffet de cuisine** dresser.
buffle (byfl) *nm* buffalo.
buisson (bɥi:'sɔ̃) *nm* **1** bush. **2** thicket. **faire l'école buissonnière** play truant.
bulbe (bylb) *nf bot* bulb.
Bulgarie (bylga'ri:) *nf* Bulgaria. **bulgare** *adj,n* Bulgarian.
bulle (byl) *nf* bubble.
bulletin (byl'tɛ̃) *nm* **1** bulletin. **2** report. **3** ticket. **bulletin de vote** voting paper. **bulletin météorologique** weather forecast.
bungalow (bɛ̃ga'lo) *nm* bungalow.
bureau, -aux (by'ro) *nm* **1** desk. **2** office. **3** board, committee. **bureau de poste** post office.
bureaucratie (byrokra'si:) *nf* **1** bureaucracy. **2** *inf* red tape. **bureaucrate** (byro'krat) *nm* bureaucrat.
buriner (byri:'ne:) *vt* engrave.
burlesque (byr'lɛsk) *adj* comical, ludicrous.
buste (byst) *nm* bust.
but (byt) *nm* **1** aim. **2** purpose. **3** target. **4** goal.
buter (by'te:) *vi* **1** knock. **2** strike. **3** stumble. **se buter** *vr* **1** prop oneself up. **2** be set on.
butin (by'tɛ̃) *nm* plunder, loot.
butoir (by'twar) *nm* buffer.
butte (byt) *nf* mound. **être en butte à** be exposed to.
buvant (by'vɑ̃) *v* see **boire.**
buvard (by'var) *adj* **papier buvard** *nm* blotting paper.
buvette (by'vɛt) *nf* refreshment bar.
buveur (by'vœr) *nm* drinker.
byzantin (bi:zɑ̃'tɛ̃) *adj* Byzantine.

C

c' *pron* see **ce**[1].
ça (sa) *pron inf* contraction of **cela.**
çà (sa) *adv* here. **çà et là** here and there.
cabale (ka'bal) *nf* intrigue, plot.
cabane (ka'ban) *nf* hut.
cabaret (kaba'rɛ) *nm* **1** public house. **2** restaurant. **3** cabaret.
cabillaud (kabi:'jo) *nm* fresh cod.
cabine (ka'bi:n) *nf* **1** cabin. **2** callbox. **3** cab (of a lorry). **cabine d'essayage** cubicle, fitting room. **cabinet** *nm* **1** closet. **2** office. **3** collection. **4** *pol* cabinet. **5** lavatory. **cabinet de toilette** dressing-room. **cabinet de travail** study.
câbler (kɑ'ble:) *vt* **1** cable. **2** wire up. **câble** *nm* cable, rope. **câblogramme** *nm* cable.
cabosser (kabɔ'se:) *vt* **1** bump. **2** dent.
se cabrer (kɑ'bre:) *vr* **1** rear. **2** revolt against.
cabriole (kabri:'ɔl) *nf* **1** leap. **2** somersault.
cacahouette (kaka'wɛt) *nf also* **cacahuète** peanut.
cacao (kaka'o) *nm* cocoa.
cachemire (kaʃ'mi:r) *nm* cashmere.
cacher (ka'ʃe:) *vt* hide, conceal. **se cacher de** *vr* hide from. **cache-cache** *nm* hide-and-seek. **cache-nez** *nm invar* scarf.
cachet (ka'ʃɛ) *nm* **1** seal. **2** stamp. **3** mark. **4** style.
cacheter (kaʃ'te:) *vt* seal.
cachette (ka'ʃɛt) *nf* hiding place. **en cachette** on the quiet.
cachot (ka'ʃo) *nm* dungeon.
cactus (kak'tys) *nm* cactus.
cadavre (ka'dɑvr) *nm* **1** corpse. **2** carcass.
cadeau, -aux (ka'do) *nm* present, gift.
cadenas (kad'nɑ) *nm* padlock.
cadence (ka'dɑ̃s) *nf* **1** cadence. **2** rhythm. **cadencé** *adj* rhythmical.
cadet, -ette (ka'dɛ, -'dɛt) *adj* **1** younger. **2** junior. *nm* cadet.
cadran (ka'drɑ̃) *nm* dial. **cadran solaire** sundial.
cadrer (kɑ'dre:) *vi* agree, tally. **cadre** *nm* **1** frame. **2** framework. **3** executive. **4** limits. **5** plan.
caduc, -uque (ka'dyk) *adj* **1** decayed. **2** infirm.
cafard (ka'far) *adj* hypocritical. *nm* **1** cockroach. **2** *inf* sneak, telltale. **avoir le cafard** be fed up.

café (ka'fe:) *nm* 1 coffee. 2 cafe. **café crème** or **au lait** white coffee. **café nature** or **noir** black coffee.
caféine (kafe:'i:n) *nf* caffeine.
cafetier, -ière (kaf'tje:, -'tjɛr) *nm,f* owner of a cafe. *nf* coffee pot.
cage (kaʒ) *nf* 1 cage. 2 casing. **cage à poules** coop.
cagnotte (ka'ɲɔt) *nf game* kitty.
cagoule (ka'gu:l) *nf* hood.
cahier (ka'je:) *nm* exercise book.
cahin-caha (kaɛ̃ka'a) *adv* so-so.
cahot (ka'o) *nm* 1 jolt. 2 bump.
cahoter (kaɔ'te:) *vi,vt* 1 jolt. 2 bump.
caille (kaj) *nf* quail.
cailler (ka'je:) *vt* 1 clot. 2 curdle. 3 congeal. **caillot** *nm* clot.
caillou, -oux (ka'ju:) *nm* pebble, stone.
caisse (kɛs) *nf* 1 case. 2 box. 3 tub. 4 till, cash desk. 5 *mus* drum. **caisse d'épargne** savings bank. **caissier, -ière** (kɛ'sje:, -'sjɛr) *nm,f* cashier.
cajoler (kaʒɔ'le:) *vt* coax.
calamité (kalami:'te:) *nf* disaster.
calcaire (kal'kɛr) *adj* chalky. *nm* limestone.
calcium (kal'sjɔm) *nm* calcium.
calcul (kal'kyl) *nm* 1 calculation. 2 arithmetic.
calculer (kalky'le:) *vt* 1 calculate. 2 reckon. **calculé** *adj* 1 premeditated. 2 deliberate.
cale (kal) *nf* 1 *naut* hold. 2 chock, wedge.
caleçon (kal'sɔ̃) *nm* men's pants. **caleçon de bain** bathing trunks.
calembour (kalɑ̃'bu:r) *nm* pun.
calendrier (kalɑ̃dri:'je:) *nm* 1 calendar. 2 diary.
calepin (kal'pɛ̃) *nm* notebook.
caler (ka'le:) *vt* 1 wedge. 2 stall. 3 adjust. *vi* stall.
calfeutrer (kalfœ'tre:) *vt* block up.
calibre (ka'li:br) *nm* 1 calibre. 2 bore (of a gun). 3 size.
califourchon (kali:fu:r'ʃɔ̃) **à califourchon** *adv* astride.
câlin (ka'lɛ̃) *adj* 1 caressing. 2 winning.
câliner (kali:'ne:) *vt* caress, fondle.
calleux, -euse (ka'lœ, -'lœz) *adj* horny, callous.
calmar (kal'mar) *nm* squid.
calmer (kal'me:) *vt* 1 calm. 2 quiet. 3 soothe. **se calmer** *vr* calm down. **calmant** *nm* sedative. **calme** *adj* 1 calm. 2 still. *nm* 1 calm. 2 peace.
calomnier (kalɔm'nje:) *vt* slander. **calomnie** *nf* libel, slander.
calorie (kalɔ'ri:) *nf* calorie.
calorifère (kalɔri:'fɛr) *nm* 1 central heating apparatus. 2 stove.
calorifuger (kalɔri:fy'ʒe:) *vt* insulate.
calquer (kal'ke:) *vt* trace.
calvitie (kalvi:'si:) *nf* baldness.
camarade (kama'rad) *nm,f* comrade, mate, friend.
Cambodge (kɑ̃'bɔdʒ) *nm* Cambodia. **cambodgien, -ienne** (kɑ̃bɔ'dʒjɛ̃, -'dʒjɛn) *adj,n* Cambodian.
cambrer (kɑ̃'bre:) *vt* 1 bend. 2 arch. **se cambrer** *vr* brace oneself.
cambrioler (kɑ̃bri:ɔ'le:) *vt* burgle. **cambriolage** *nm* burglary. **cambrioleur, -euse** (kɑ̃bri:ɔ'lœr, -'lœz) *nm,f* burglar.
caméléon (kame:le:'ɔ̃) *nm* chameleon.
camelote (kam'lɔt) *nf* rubbish, junk.
camembert (kamɑ̃'bɛr) *nm* a French cheese.
caméra (kame:'ra) *nf* cinecamera.
camion (ka'mjɔ̃) *nm* lorry. **camionnette** *nf* van.
camoufler (kamu:'fle:) *vt* disguise, camouflage. **camouflage** *nm* camouflage.
camp (kɑ̃) *nm* 1 camp. 2 side.
campagne (kɑ̃'paɲ) *nf* 1 country, countryside. 2 campaign. **en rase campagne** in the heart of the country. **campagnard** *adj* 1 rustic. 2 country.
camper (kɑ̃'pe:) *vt* camp. **camping** *nm* 1 camping. 2 camping ground.
campus (kɑ̃'pys) *nm* campus.
Canada (kana'da) *nm* Canada. **canadien, -ienne** (kana'djɛ̃, -'djɛn) *adj,n* Canadian.
canaille (ka'naj) *nf inf* 1 rabble. 2 scoundrel. *adj* vulgar, coarse.
canal, -aux (ka'nal, -'no) *nm* 1 canal. 2 channel. 3 pipe.
canapé (kana'pe:) *nm* couch, sofa.
canard (ka'nar) *nm* 1 duck. 2 drake. 3 false report.
canari (kana'ri:) *nm* canary.
Canaries (kana'ri:) **îles Canaries** *nf pl* Canary Islands.
cancan (kɑ̃'kɑ̃) *nm* 1 gossip. 2 *pl* scandal.
cancer (kɑ̃'sɛr) *nm* 1 cancer. 2 *cap* Cancer.
cancre (kɑ̃kr) *nm* 1 crab. 2 dunce.
candeur (kɑ̃'dœr) *nf* 1 frankness. 2 artlessness.
candidat (kɑ̃di:'da) *nm* 1 candidate. 2 applicant.
candide (kɑ̃'di:d) *adj* 1 frank. 2 open.
cane (kan) *nf* duck. **caneton** *nm* duckling.
canevas (kan'va) *nm* 1 canvas. 2 outline.
caniche (ka'ni:ʃ) *nm,f* poodle.
canif (ka'ni:f) *nm* penknife.

canin (ka'nɛ̃) *adj* canine.
caniveau, -aux (kani:'vo) *nm* gutter.
canne (kan) *nf* **1** cane. **2** walking stick. **canne à pêche** fishing rod. **canne à sucre** sugar cane.
canneler (kan'le:) *vt* **1** groove. **2** flute. **cannelure** *nf* groove, channel.
cannelle (ka'nɛl) *nm* cinnamon.
canon[1] (ka'nɔ̃) *nm mil* **1** cannon. **2** barrel.
canon[2] (ka'nɔ̃) *nm* canon.
cañon (ka'ɲɔ̃) *nm* canyon.
canoniser (kanɔni:'ze:) *vt* canonize.
canot (ka'no) *nm* **1** canoe. **2** boat. **canot de sauvetage** lifeboat. **canot glisseur** speedboat. **canotage** *nm* boating. **faire du canotage** row. **canotier** *nm* **1** oarsman. **2** straw hat.
cantatrice (kɑ̃ta'tri:s) *nf* singer.
cantine (kɑ̃'ti:n) *nf* canteen.
canton (kɑ̃'tɔ̃) *nm* district, canton. **cantonade** *nf Th* wings.
cantonnier (kɑ̃tɔ'nje:) *nm* road mender.
caoutchouc (kau:'tʃu:) *nm* **1** rubber. **2** mackintosh.
cap (kap) *nm geog* cape.
capable (ka'pabl) *adj* able, fit, capable.
capacité (kapasi:'te:) *nf* **1** capacity. **2** ability.
cape (kap) *nf* cape, cloak.
capitaine (kapi:'tɛn) *nm* captain.
capital, -aux (kapi:'tal, -'to) *adj* **1** capital. **2** principal. *nm comm* capital. *nf* capital (city). **capitalisme** *nm* capitalism.
capitaliser (kapi:tali:'ze:) *vt* **1** capitalize. **2** save.
capiteux, -euse (kapi:'tœ, -'tœz) *adj* **1** (of wine) strong. **2** sensuous.
capitonner (kapi:tɔ'ne:) *vt* pad. **capitonnage** *nm* upholstery.
caporal, -aux (kapɔ'ral, -'ro) *nm* corporal.
capot (ka'po) *nm* **1** cover. **2** bonnet.
capote (ka'pɔt) *nf* **1** overcoat. **2** *mot* hood.
câpre (kɑpr) *nf* caper.
caprice (ka'pri:s) *nm* whim. **capricieux, -euse** (kapri:'sjœ, -'sjœz) *adj* **1** capricious. **2** temperamental. **3** wayward.
Capricorne (kapri:'kɔrn) *nm* Capricorn.
capsule (kap'syl) *nf* capsule.
capter (kap'te:) *vt* **1** obtain by fraud. **2** win over. **3** tune in. **captieux, -euse** (kap'sjœ, -'sjœz) *adj* **1** cunning. **2** insidious.
captif, -ive (kap'ti:f, -'ti:v) *adj,n* captive. **captivité** *nf* captivity.
captiver (kapti:'ve:) *vt* captivate, charm.
capuchon (kapy'ʃɔ̃) *nm* **1** hood. **2** cap.
capucine (kapy'si:n) *nf* nasturtium.
caquet (ka'kɛ) *nm* cackle.
caqueter (kak'te:) *vi* **1** cackle. **2** *inf* chatter.
car[1] (kar) *conj* because, for, as.
car[2] (kar) *nm* bus.
carabine (kara'bi:n) *nf* rifle.
caractère (karak'tɛr) *nm* **1** character. **2** nature. **3** type. **4** letter. **d'un caractère facile** good-humoured. **caractéristique** *adj* **1** characteristic. **2** typical. *nm* characteristic.
carafe (ka'raf) *nf* decanter.
caramel (kara'mɛl) *nm* caramel. **caramel au beurre** butterscotch.
carapace (kara'pas) *nf* shell.
carat (ka'ra) *nm* carat.
caravane (kara'van) *nf* caravan.
carbone (kar'bɔn) *nm* carbon.
carboniser (karbɔni:'ze:) *vt* **1** char. **2** carbonize.
carburant (karby'rɑ̃) *nm* motor fuel.
carburateur (karbyra'tœr) *nm* carburettor.
carcasse (kar'kas) *nf* **1** carcass. **2** framework.
cardiaque (kar'djak) *adj* cardiac.
cardinal, -aux (kardi:'nal, -'no) *adj* cardinal. *nm rel* cardinal.
carême (ka'rɛm) *nm* Lent.
carène (ka'rɛn) *nf naut* hull.
caresser (karɛ'se:) *vt* **1** caress. **2** cherish. **caresse** *nf* caress.
cargaison (kargɛ'zɔ̃) *nf* **1** cargo. **2** freight.
caricaturer (kari:katy're:) *vt* caricature. **caricature** *nf* caricature.
carier (ka'rje:) *vt* rot. **carie** *nf* decay.
carillon (kari:'jɔ̃) *nm* **1** chime. **2** peal of bells.
carillonner (kari:jɔ'ne:) *vi* **1** chime. **2** peal. **carillonneur** *nm* bellringer.
carnage (kar'naʒ) *nm* slaughter.
carnassier, -ière (karna'sje:, -'sjɛr) *adj* carnivorous.
carnaval (karna'val) *nm* carnival.
carnet (kar'nɛ) *nm* notebook. **carnet de chèques** chequebook.
carnivore (karni:'vɔr) *adj* carnivorous.
carotte (ka'rɔt) *nf* **1** carrot. **2** *inf* trick.
carpette (kar'pɛt) *nf* rug.
carquois (kar'kwa) *nm sport* quiver.
carreau, -aux (ka'ro) *nm* **1** small square. **2** tile. **3** pane. **4** *game* diamonds.
carrefour (kar'fu:r) *nm* **1** crossroads. **2** square.
carreler (kɑr'le:) *vt* **1** pave. **2** tile. **3** draw squares. **carrelage** *nm* tiling. **carrelé** *adj* checked.
carrelet (kɑr'lɛ) *nm* plaice.
carrer (kɑ're:) *vt* square. **se carrer** *vr* swagger.

carré *adj* **1** square. **2** plain. *nm* **1** square. **2** landing. **carrément** *adv* **1** squarely. **2** bluntly, straightforwardly.
carrière[1] (ka'rjɛr) *nf* quarry.
carrière[2] (ka'rjɛr) *nf* career.
carrosse (ka'rɔs) *nm* coach. **carrosserie** *nf mot* body.
carrousel (karu:'zɛl) *nm* **1** tournament. **2** merry-go-round.
carrure (ka'ryr) *nf* **1** breadth (across shoulders). **2** stature.
cartable (kar'tąbl) *nm* satchel.
carte (kart) *nf* **1** map. **2** card. **3** playing card. **4** list. **5** menu. **carte à jouer** playing card. **carte d'abonnement** season ticket. **carte de crédit** credit card. **carte d'identité** identity card. **carte postale** postcard. **donner carte blanche à** give a free hand to.
cartilage (karti:'laʒ) *nm* **1** cartilage. **2** gristle.
carton (kar'tɔ̃) *nm* **1** cardboard. **2** cardboard box. **3** cartoon. **carton-pâte** *nm invar* papier-mâché.
cartouche (kar'tu:ʃ) *nf* **1** cartridge. **2** carton. **3** refill.
carvi (kar'vi:) *nm* caraway.
cas (ka) *nm* **1** case. **2** matter. **3** circumstance. **cas urgent** emergency. **faire cas de** value. **le cas échéant** should the occasion arise.
cascade (ka'skad) *nf* **1** cascade. **2** waterfall.
caser (ka'ze:) *vt* **1** put away. **2** *inf* find a place for. **se caser** *vr* settle down. **case** *nf* **1** hut. **2** compartment.
caserne (ka'zɛrn) *nf* barracks.
casino (kazi:'no) *nm* casino.
casque (kask) *nm* helmet. **casque protecteur** crash-helmet. **casque téléphonique** headphones. **casquette** *nf* cap.
casse (kas) *nf* breakage, damage.
casser (ka'se:) *vt* **1** break. **2** cashier. **3** quash. **se casser la tête** rack one's brains. **cassant** *adj* **1** brittle. **2** crisp. **3** abrupt. **cassé** *adj* **1** broken. **2** worn out. **casse-cou** *nm invar* **1** reckless fellow. **2** danger spot. **casse-croûte** *nm invar* snack. **casse-noisette** *nm invar* nutcrackers. **cassure** *nf* **1** break. **2** fracture.
casserole (ka'srɔl) *nf* **1** saucepan. **2** stew.
cassette (ka'sɛt) *nf* **1** case. **2** moneybox.
cassis (ka'si:s) *nm* **1** blackcurrant. **2** blackcurrant bush.
cassonade (kasɔ'nad) *nf* brown sugar.
castagnettes (kasta'ɲɛt) *nf pl* castanets.
caste (kast) *nf* caste.
castor (ka'stɔr) *nm* beaver.
casuel, -elle (ka'zɥɛl) *adj* **1** accidental. **2** casual.
cataloguer, (katalɔ'ge:) *vt* catalogue, list. **catalogue** *nm* **1** catalogue. **2** list.
catamaran (katama'rɑ̃) *nm* catamaran.
Cataphote (kata'fɔt) *nm Tdmk mot* cat's eye.
cataplasme (kata'plasm) *nm* poultice.
cataracte (kata'rakt) *nf* cataract.
catarrhe (ka'tar) *nm* catarrh.
catastrophe (kata'strɔf) *nf* catastrophe, disaster.
catéchisme (kate:'ʃism) *nm* catechism.
catégoriser (kate:gɔri:'ze:) *vt* categorize. **catégorie** *nf* category. **catégorique** *adj* **1** categorical. **2** explicit.
cathédrale (kate:'dral) *nf* cathedral.
cathode (ka'tɔd) *nf* cathode.
catholique (katɔ'li:k) *adj* **1** catholic. **2** orthodox. *adj,n* Roman Catholic.
cauchemar (kɔ'ʃmar) *nm* nightmare.
causer[1] (ko'ze:) *vt* cause, bring about. **cause** *nf* **1** cause. **2** *law* brief, suit. **à cause de** on account of. **et pour cause** for a very good reason.
causer[2] (ko'ze:) *vi* chat, talk. **causerie** *nf* chat.
caustique (ko'sti:k) *adj* **1** caustic. **2** cutting. *nm sci* caustic.
cauteleux, -euse (kot'lœ, -'lœz) *adj* cunning, sly.
caution (ko'sjɔ̃) *nf* **1** security. **2** guarantee.
cautionnement (kosjɔn'mɑ̃) *nm* **1** *comm* guarantee. **2** deposit. **cautionnement judiciaire** bail.
cavalerie (kaval'ri:) *nf* cavalry. **cavalier, -ière** (kava'lje:, -'ljɛr) *adj* offhand. *nm* **1** horseman. **2** partner. **3** *game* knight.
cave[1] (kav) *adj* hollow.
cave[2] (kav) *nf* cellar. **caveau, -aux** (ka'vo) *nm* **1** small cellar. **2** vault. **caverne** *nf* **1** cave. **2** den.
caviar (ka'vjar) *nm* caviar.
cavité (kavi:'te:) *nf* cavity, hollow.
cayenne (ka'jɛn) *nf* cayenne.
ce[1] (sə) *pron* he, she, it. **ce que** what, which. **pour ce qui est de** as regards. **sur ce** thereupon.
ce[2]**, cet, cette** (sə, sɛt, sɛt) *adj* this, that. **ce dernier** the latter. **ceci** *pron* this.
cécité (se:si:'te:) *nf* blindness.
céder (se:'de:) *vt* **1** give up, surrender. **2** make over. *vi* yield. **le céder à** be inferior to.
cédille (se:'di:j) *nf* cedilla.
cèdre (sɛdr) *nm* cedar.
ceindre* (sɛ̃dr) *vt* **1** encircle. **2** put on.

ceinture (sɛ̃'tyr) *nf* **1** belt. **2** girdle. **3** sash. **4** waist. **ceinture de securité** safety belt.
cela (sə'la, sla) *pron also inf* **ça 1** that. **2** it. **3** so. **c'est ça** that's right. **comme ci comme ça** so-so. **où ça?** where?
célèbre (se:'lɛbr) *adj* famous. **célébrité** *nf* celebrity.
célébrer (se:le:'bre:) *vt* **1** celebrate. **2** observe.
celer (sə'le:) *vt* conceal.
céleri (se:l'ri:) *nm* celery.
céleste (se:'lɛst) *adj* celestial, heavenly.
célibataire (se:li:ba'tɛr) *adj* celibate, single. *nm* bachelor.
celle (sɛl) *pron* see **celui.**
Cellophane (sɛlɔ'fan) *nf Tdmk* Cellophane.
cellule (sɛ'lyl) *nf* cell.
celte (sɛlt) *nm,f* Celt.
celui, celle (sə'lɥi:, sɛl) *pron* **1** he, she. **2** the one. **celui-ci, celle-ci 1** this one. **2** the latter. **celui-là, celle-là 1** that one. **2** the former.
cendre (sɑ̃dr) *nf* **1** ash. **2** cinder. **cendrier** *nm* ashtray.
cène (sɛn) *nf* Last Supper.
censé (sɑ̃'se:) *adj* supposed.
censeur (sɑ̃'sœr) *nm* **1** critic. **2** censor.
censurer (sɑ̃sy're:) *vt* **1** censure. **2** censor. **censure** *nf* censure, blame.
cent (sɑ̃) *adj* one hundred. *nm* **1** hundred. **2** cent. **faire les cent pas** walk up and down. **centaine** *nf* about a hundred. **centième** *adj* hundredth.
centenaire (sɑ̃t'nɛr) *nm* centenary.
centigrade (sɑ̃ti:'grad) *adj* centigrade.
centime (sɑ̃'ti:m) *nm* centime.
centimètre (sɑ̃ti:'mɛtr) *nm* **1** centimetre. **2** *inf* tape measure.
central, -aux (sɑ̃'tral, -'tro) *adj* **1** central, middle. **2** principal.
centraliser (sɑ̃trali:'ze:) *vt* centralize.
centre (sɑ̃tr) *nm* centre, middle.
cep (sɛp) **cep de vigne** *nm* vine plant.
cependant (səpɑ̃'dɑ̃) *adv* meanwhile. *conj* however, still, yet.
céramique (sɛra'mi:k) *adj* ceramic. *nf* ceramics.
cerceau, -aux (sɛr'so) *nm* hoop.
cercle (sɛrkl) *nm* **1** circle. **2** club.
cercueil (sɛr'kœj) *nm* coffin.
céréale (se:re:'al) *adj* cereal. **céréales** *nf pl* cereals, corn.
cérébral, -aux (se:rɛ'bral, -'bro) *adj* of the brain.
cérémonie (se:re:mɔ'ni:) *nf* ceremony. **sans cérémonie** informally. **cérémonieux, -euse** (se:re:mo'njœ, -'njœz) ceremonious, formal.
cerf (sɛr) *nm* stag. **cerf-volant** *nm, pl* **cerfs-volants** kite.
cerise (sə'ri:z) *nf* cherry. **cerisier** *nm* cherry tree.
cerner (sɛr'ne:) *vt* encircle, surround. **avoir les yeux cernés** have bags under one's eyes.
certain (sɛr'tɛ̃) *adj* **1** certain, sure. **2** fixed. *pron pl* some, certain.
certes (sɛrt) *adv* indeed, most certainly.
certifier (sɛrti:'fje:) *vt* **1** certify. **2** witness. **certificat** *nm* certificate.
certitude (sɛrti:'tyd) *nf* certainty.
cerveau, -aux (sɛr'vo) *nm* **1** brain. **2** mind. **3** intellect.
cervelle (sɛr'vɛl) *nf anat* brain. **avoir une cervelle de lièvre** have a brain like a sieve.
Cervin (sɛr'vɛ̃) **Mont Cervin** *nm* Matterhorn.
ces (se:, sɛ) *adj pl* these, those.
cesser (sɛ'se:) *vi,vt* cease, stop. **faire cesser** put a stop to. **cesse** *nf* cease, respite.
cet (sɛt) *adj* see **ce**[2].
cette (sɛt) *adj* see **ce**[2].
ceux (sœ) *pron pl* those. **ceux-ci 1** these. **2** the latter. **ceux-là 1** those. **2** the former.
Ceylan (se:'lɑ̃) *nm* Ceylon.
chacal (ʃa'kal) *nm* jackal.
chacun (ʃa'kœ̃) *pron* **1** each. **2** everybody, everyone.
chagrin[1] (ʃa'grɛ̃) *adj* **1** sad, downcast. **2** peevish.
chagrin[2] (ʃa'grɛ̃) *nm* **1** grief, sorrow. **2** worry.
chagriner (ʃagri:'ne:) *vt* **1** grieve. **2** vex.
chahut (ʃa'y) *nm* row, uproar.
chaîne (ʃɛn) *nf* **1** chain. **2** cable. **3** channel (television). **4** *pl* fetters. **chaîne de montage** assembly line.
chair (ʃɛr) *nf* **1** flesh. **2** meat. **3** pulp. **4** skin (of a person).
chaire (ʃɛr) *nf* **1** pulpit. **2** *educ* chair.
chaise (ʃɛz) *nf* chair, seat. **chaise à bascule** rocking chair. **chaise-longue** *nf* couch.
chaland (ʃa'lɑ̃) *nm* barge.
châle (ʃɑl) *nm* shawl.
chalet (ʃa'lɛ) *nm* chalet, cottage.
chaleur (ʃa'lœr) *nf* **1** heat, warmth. **2** ardour. **chaleureux, -euse** (ʃalœ'rœ, -'rœz) *adj* **1** warm. **2** cordial.
chaloupe (ʃa'lu:p) *nf* launch.
chalumeau, -aux (ʃaly'mo) *nm* **1** straw. **2** *mus* pipe.

chaluter (ʃaly'te:) *vi* trawl. **chalutier** *nm* trawler.

se chamailler (ʃamɑ'je:) *vr* squabble.

chambellan (ʃɑ̃bɛ'lɑ̃) *nm* chamberlain.

chambranle (ʃɑ̃'brɑ̃l) *nm* **1** frame. **2** mantelpiece.

chambre (ʃɑ̃br) *nf* **1** room, bedroom. **2** chamber. **chambre d'ami** spare room. **chambre d'enfants** nursery. **Chambre des Communes/Lords** House of Commons/Lords. **Chambre des Députés** French equivalent of the House of Commons.

chameau, -aux (ʃa'mo) *nm* **1** camel. **2** *sl* scoundrel.

chamois (ʃa'mwa) *nm* chamois.

champ (ʃɑ̃) *nm* field. **sur le champ** immediately. **champ d'aviation** airfield. **champ de courses/foire** racecourse/fairground. **champêtre** *adj* rustic, rural.

champagne (ʃɑ̃'paɲ) *nf* champagne.

champignon (ʃɑ̃pi:'ɲɔ̃) *nm* mushroom.

champion, -ionne (ʃɑ̃'pjɔ̃, -'pjɔn) *nm,f* champion. **championnat** *nm* championship.

chance (ʃɑ̃s) *nf* **1** luck. **2** chance. **pas de chance!** bad luck! **chanceux, -euse** (ʃɑ̃'sœ, 'sœz) *adj* **1** hazardous. **2** fortunate.

chanceler (ʃɑ̃'sle:) *vi* **1** stagger. **2** totter. **chancelant** *adj* **1** staggering, unsteady. **2** delicate.

chancelier (ʃɑ̃sə'lje:) *nm* chancellor.

chandail (ʃɑ̃'daj) *nm* sweater.

chandelle (ʃɑ̃'dɛl) *nf* **1** candle. **2** prop, support. **3** *sport* lob. **chandelier** *nm* candlestick.

changer (ʃɑ̃'ʒe:) *vt* **1** change, exchange. **2** alter. *vi* change. **change** *nm* exchange. **changeant** *adj* changing, fickle. **changement** *nm* change, alteration.

chanoine (ʃan'wan) *nm rel* canon.

chanson (ʃɑ̃'sɔ̃) *nf* **1** song. **2** *pl* nonsense. **chanson d'enfants** nursery rhyme. **chanson populaire** folksong.

chant (ʃɑ̃) *nm* **1** singing. **2** song. **3** chant. **chant de Noël** carol.

chanter (ʃɑ̃'te:) *vt* **1** sing. **2** chirp. **faire chanter** blackmail. **chantage** *nm* blackmail. **chanteur, -euse** (ʃɑ̃'tœr, -'tœz) *nm,f* singer.

chantier (ʃɑ̃'tje:) *nm* yard. **chantier naval** shipyard.

chantonner (ʃɑ̃tɔ'ne:) *vi,vt* hum.

chanvre (ʃɑ̃vr) *nm* hemp.

chaos (ka'o) *nm* chaos. **chaotique** *adj* chaotic.

chape (ʃap) *nf* **1** *rel* cope. **2** covering.

chapeau, -aux (ʃa'po) *nm* **1** hat. **2** cover.

chapelain (ʃa'plɛ̃) *nm* chaplain.

chapelet (ʃa'plɛ) *nm* rosary, beads.

chapelle (ʃa'pɛl) *nf* chapel.

chapelure (ʃa'plyr) *nf* breadcrumbs.

chapitre (ʃa'pi:tr) *nm* **1** chapter. **2** subject.

chaque (ʃak) *adj* each, every.

char (ʃar) *nm* **1** chariot. **2** wagon. **char de combat** *mil* tank. **char funèbre** hearse.

charabia (ʃara'bja) *nm* gibberish, double dutch.

charbon (ʃar'bɔ̃) *nm* **1** coal. **2** carbon. **charbon de bois** charcoal.

charcuterie (ʃarky'tri:) *nf* **1** pork butcher's shop. **2** delicatessen.

chardon (ʃar'dɔ̃) *nm* thistle.

chardonneret (ʃardɔn'rɛ) *nm* goldfinch.

charger (ʃar'ʒe:) *vt* **1** load. **2** charge. **3** instruct. **se charger de** *vr* undertake. **charge** *nf* **1** load. **2** burden. **3** responsibility. **4** office. **5** expense. **6** charge. **à charge de** on condition that. **chargement** *nm* **1** loading. **2** cargo.

chariot (ʃa'rjo) *nm* **1** wagon. **2** trolley.

charisme (ʃa'ri:sm) *nm* charisma.

charité (ʃari:'te:) *nf* charity, alms.

charivari (ʃari:va'ri:) *nm inf* din, racket.

charlatan (ʃarla'tɑ̃) *nm* quack.

charmer (ʃar'me:) *vt* **1** charm. **2** delight. **charme** *nm* **1** charm. **2** spell. **3** attraction.

charnel, -elle (ʃar'nɛl) *adj* carnal, sensual.

charnière (ʃar'njɛr) *nf* hinge.

charnu (ʃar'ny) *adj* fleshy, plump.

charpente (ʃar'pɑ̃t) *nf* framework.

charrette (ʃa'rɛt) *nf* cart. **charrette à bras** barrow.

charrue (ʃa'ry) *nf* plough.

charte (ʃart) *nf* charter.

châsse (ʃɑs) *nf* shrine.

chasser (ʃa'se:) *vt* **1** chase. **2** hunt. **3** shoot. **4** drive out. **5** dismiss. *vi* hunt. **chasse** *nf* **1** hunting. **2** shooting. **3** hunt. **4** shoot. **5** chase. **chasse d'eau** flush. **chasse-neige** *nm invar* snowplough. **chasseur** *nm* huntsman.

châssis (ʃɑ'si:) *nm* **1** frame. **2** chassis.

chaste (ʃast) *adj* pure, chaste.

chat, chatte (ʃa, ʃat) *nm,f* cat. **chaton** *nm* kitten. *nm* catkin.

châtaigne (ʃɑ'tɛɲ) *nf* chestnut. **châtaignier** *nm* sweet-chestnut tree.

châtain (ʃɑ'tɛ̃) *adj invar* auburn, chestnut-brown.

château, -aux (ʃɑ'to) *nm* **1** castle. **2** mansion.

châteaubriant (ʃɑtobri:'ɑ̃) *nm* grilled steak.

châtier (ʃɑ'tje:) *vt* **1** punish, chastise. **2** correct. **châtiment** *nm* punishment, chastisement.

chatouiller (ʃatu:'je:) *vt* tickle. **chatouilleux, -euse** (ʃatu:'jœ, -'jœz) *adj* **1** ticklish. **2** sensitive.

chatoyer (ʃatwa'je:) *vi* **1** shimmer. **2** sparkle. **chatoiement** *nm* **1** shimmer. **2** glistening.

châtrer (ʃɑ'tre:) *vt* castrate.

chaud (ʃo) *adj* hot, warm. *nm* warm. **avoir chaud** (of a person) be hot. **tenir au chaud** keep in a warm place. **chaudière** *nf* boiler.

chauffer (ʃo'fe:) *vt* **1** heat, warm. **2** stoke. **3** swot. *vi* get hot. **chauffage** *nm* heating. **chauffage central** central heating. **chauffe-assiette** *nm, pl* **chauffe-assiettes** hotplate. **chauffeur** *nm* **1** stoker. **2** chauffeur.

chaume (ʃom) *nm* **1** thatch. **2** stubble. **chaumière** *nf* thatched cottage.

chaussée (ʃo'se:) *nf* **1** causeway. **2** road.

chausser (ʃo'se:) *vt* **1** put on (shoes). **2** supply with shoes. **se chausser** *vr* put on one's shoes. **chaussette** *nf* sock. **chausson** *nm* slipper. **chaussure** *nf* **1** footwear. **2** shoe, boot.

chauve (ʃov) *adj* bald. **chauve-souris** *nf, pl* **chauves-souris** *zool* bat.

chauvinisme (ʃovi:'ni:sm) *nm* chauvinism.

chaux (ʃo) *nf* lime. **blanchir à la chaux** whitewash. **lait** or **blanc de chaux** *nm* whitewash.

chavirer (ʃavi:'re:) *vi* capsize. *vt* turn upside down, upset.

chef (ʃɛf) *nm* **1** head. **2** chief. **3** leader. **chef de bande** ringleader. **chef de cuisine** chef. **chef d'équipe** *sport* captain. **chef de gare** stationmaster. **chef d'orchestre** conductor.

chef-d'œuvre (ʃɛ'dœvr) *nm, pl* **chefs-d'œuvre** masterpiece.

chef-lieu (ʃɛf'ljœ) *nm, pl* **chefs-lieux** chief town.

cheik (ʃɛk) *nm* sheikh.

chelem (ʃlɛm) *nm* (in bridge, etc.) slam.

chemin (ʃmɛ̃) *nm* **1** way. **2** road, path. **à moitié chemin** halfway. **chemin de fer** railway. **chemin faisant** on the way. **grand chemin** highway. **se mettre en chemin** set off.

chemineau, -aux (ʃmi:'no) *nm* tramp.

cheminée (ʃmi:'ne:) *nf* **1** fireplace. **2** mantelpiece. **3** chimney. **4** funnel.

cheminer (ʃmi:'ne:) *vi* tramp, walk.

chemise (ʃmi:z) *nf* **1** shirt. **2** folder, jacket. **chemise de nuit** nightdress, nightgown.

chêne (ʃɛn) *nm* oak.

chenille (ʃə'ni:j) *nf* caterpillar.

chèque (ʃɛk) *nm* cheque. **chèque de voyage** traveller's cheque.

cher, chère (ʃɛr) *adj* **1** dear. **2** expensive. *adv* at a high price, dearly.

chercher (ʃɛr'ʃe:) *vt* look for, seek. **chercher à** attempt to.

chérir (ʃe:'ri:r) *vt* cherish. **chéri** *adj,n* dear, darling.

chérubin (ʃe:ry'bɛ̃) *nm* cherub.

chétif, -ive (ʃe:'ti:f, -'ti:v) *adj* **1** weak, sickly. **2** miserable, poor.

cheval, -aux (ʃə'val, -'vo) *nm* horse. **à cheval** on horseback. **cheval à bascule** rocking horse. **cheval de course** racehorse. **cheval pur sang** thoroughbred. **chevaux de bois** *nm pl* merry-go-round.

chevalet (ʃəva'lɛ) *nm* **1** support. **2** trestle. **chevalet de peintre** easel.

chevalier (ʃəva'lje:) *nm* **1** knight. **2** horseman. **chevalerie** *nf* chivalry. **cheval-vapeur** *nm, pl* **chevaux-vapeur** horsepower.

chevaucher (ʃəvo'ʃe:) *vi,vt* ride. *vt* overlap.

chevelu (ʃə'vly) *adj* hairy. **chevelure** *nf* hair, head of hair.

chevet (ʃə'vɛ) *nm* bedside.

cheveu, -eux (ʃə'vœ) *nm* **1** hair. **2** *pl* (head of) hair.

cheville (ʃə'vi:j) *nf* **1** peg, pin. **2** bolt. **3** ankle.

chèvre (ʃɛvr) *nf* goat. **chevreau, -aux** (ʃə'vro) *nm zool* kid.

chèvrefeuille (ʃɛvrə'fœj) *nm* honeysuckle.

chevron (ʃə'vrɔ̃) *nm* **1** rafter. **2** stripe.

chez (ʃe:) *prep* **1** at. **2** care of. **3** with. **4** among. **5** in. **6** at the house of. **chez soi** at home.

chic (ʃi:k) *nm* **1** skill. **2** style. *adj invar* **1** smart, elegant. **2** first-rate.

chicaner (ʃi:ka'ne:) *vi* quibble. *vt* wrangle with.

chiche (ʃi:ʃ) *adj* **1** poor. **2** mean.

chicorée (ʃi:kɔ're:) *nf* **chicorée sauvage** chicory. **chicorée frisée** endive.

chien, chienne (ʃjɛ̃, ʃjɛn) *nm,f* dog, bitch. **chien de berger/garde** sheepdog/watchdog. **entre chien et loup** in the twilight.

chiffe (ʃi:f) *nf* rag.

chiffon (ʃi:'fɔ̃) *nm* **1** rag. **2** scrap. **3** duster. **4** chiffon.

chiffonner (ʃi:fɔ'ne:) *vt* **1** crumple. **2** annoy.

chiffrer (ʃi:'fre:) *vi* calculate. *vt* **1** number. **2** code. **3** work out. **chiffre** *nm* **1** figure, number. **2** code. **chiffre d'affaires** *comm* turnover.

chignon (ʃi'ɲɔ̃) *nm* bun, coil of hair.

Chili (ʃi:'li:) *nm* Chile. **chilien, -ienne** (ʃi:'ljɛ̃, -'ljɛn) *adj,n* Chilean.
chimère (ʃi:'mɛr) *nf* illusion. **chimérique** *adj* fanciful.
chimie (ʃi:'mi:) *nf* chemistry. **chimique** *adj* chemical. **chimiste** *nm,f sci* chemist.
chimpanzé (ʃɛ̃pɑ̃'ze:) *nm* chimpanzee.
Chine (ʃi:n) *nf* China. **chinois** *adj,n* Chinese. *nm* Chinese (language).
chiot (ʃjo) *nm* puppy.
chiper (ʃi:'pe:) *vt inf* **1** pinch. **2** scrounge.
chipoter (ʃi:pɔ'te:) *vi* waste time. *vt* nibble.
chiquenaude (ʃi:k'nod) *nf* flick (of fingers).
chiromancie (ki:rɔmɑ̃'si:) *nf* palmistry.
chiropracteur (ki:rɔprak'tœr) *nm* osteopath.
chirurgie (ʃi:ryr'ʒi:) *nf* surgery. **chirurgie plastique** plastic surgery. **chirurgien, -ienne** (ʃi:ryr'ʒjɛ̃, -'ʒjɛn) *nm,f* surgeon. **chirurgique** *adj* surgical.
chlore (klɔr) *nm* chlorine.
chlorophylle (klɔrɔ'fi:l) *nf* chlorophyll.
choc (ʃɔk) *nm* **1** shock. **2** impact. **3** clash.
chocolat (ʃɔkɔ'la) *nm* chocolate. *adj invar* chocolate-coloured.
chœur (kœr) *nm* **1** chorus. **2** choir.
choir* (ʃwar) *vi* fall.
choisir (ʃwa'zi:r) *vt* choose, select. **choisi** *adj* **1** selected. **2** choice.
choix (ʃwa) *nm* **1** choice. **2** selection. **de tout premier choix** first-class, best quality.
choléra (kɔlɛ'ra) *nm* cholera.
chômer (ʃo'me:) *vi* **1** be unemployed. **2** take a holiday. **chômage** *nm* unemployment. **chômeur** *nm* unemployed person.
chope (ʃɔp) *nf* tankard.
chopine (ʃɔ'pi:n) *nf* half-pint.
choquer (ʃɔ'ke:) *vt* **1** shock. **2** offend. **3** strike. **se choquer** *vr* **1** be shocked. **2** collide. **se choquer de** take offence at.
choral (kɔ'ral) *adj* choral.
chorégraphie (kɔre:gra'fi:) *nf* choreography. **chorégraphe** *nm* choreographer.
chose (ʃoz) *nf* **1** thing. **2** matter. **être tout chose** feel queer.
chou, choux (ʃu:) *nm* **1** cabbage. **2** rosette. **chou de Bruxelles** Brussels sprout. **chou-fleur** *nm, pl* **choux-fleurs** cauliflower. **mon petit chou** my dear.
choucas (ʃu:'kɑ) *nm* jackdaw.
choucroute (ʃu:'kru:t) *nf* sauerkraut.
chouette (ʃwɛt) *nf* owl. *adj,interj* fine, excellent.
choyer (ʃwa'je:) *vt* **1** pet. **2** cherish.
chrétien, -ienne (kre:'tjɛ̃, -'tjɛn) *adj,n* Christian.
Christ (kri:st) *nm* Christ.
christianisme (kri:stja'ni:sm) *nm* Christianity.
chrome (krom) *nm* **1** chromium. **2** chrome. **chromatique** *adj* chromatic. **chromé** *adj* chrome.
chromo (krɔ'mo) *nm inf* colour photo.
chromosome (kromo'zom) *nm* chromosome.
chronique[1] (krɔ'ni:k) *nf* **1** history. **2** report.
chronique[2] (krɔ'ni:k) *adj* chronic.
chronologique (krɔnɔlɔ'ʒi:k) *adj* chronological.
chronométrer (krɔnɔme:'tre:) *vt* time, keep the time. **chronomètre** *nm* stopwatch.
chrysalide (kri:za'li:d) *nf* chrysalis.
chrysanthème (kri:zɑ̃'tɛm) *nm* chrysanthemum.
chuchoter (ʃyʃɔ'te:) *vi,vt* whisper.
chuinter (ʃɥɛ̃'te:) *vi* (of an owl) hoot.
chut (ʃyt) *interj* hush!
chute (ʃyt) *nf* **1** fall. **2** downfall. **chute d'eau** waterfall.
Chypre (ʃi:pr) *nf* Cyprus. **chypriot** *adj,n* Cypriot.
ci[1] (si:) *adv* here.
ci[2] (si:) *pron invar* this. **ci-après** *adv* further on. **ci-contre** *adv* opposite, on the other side. **ci-dessous** *adv* below. **ci-dessus** *adv* above. **ci-devant** *adv* formerly, previously. **ci-inclus** *adj* enclosed. **ci-joint** *adj* attached.
cible (si:bl) *nf* target.
ciboule (si:'bu:l) *nf* spring onion. **ciboulette** *nf* chives.
cicatrice (si:ka'tri:s) *nf* scar.
cidre (si:dr) *nm* cider.
ciel (sjɛl) *nm, pl* **ciels** or **cieux** **1** sky. **2** heaven. **3** climate.
cierge (sjɛrʒ) *nm rel* candle.
cigale (si:'gal) *nf* cicada.
cigare (si:'gar) *nm* cigar. **cigarette** *nf* cigarette.
cigogne (si:'gɔɲ) *nf* stork.
cil (si:l) *nm* eyelash.
cime (si:m) *nf* summit, top.
ciment (si:'mɑ̃) *nm* cement.
cimenter (si:mɑ̃'te:) *vt* cement.
cimetière (sim'tjɛr) *nf* churchyard, graveyard, cemetery.
cinéaste (si:ne:'ast) *nm* film producer.
cinéma (si:nɛ'mɑ) *nm* cinema. **cinématographique** *adj* film.
cinétique (si:ne:'ti:k) *adj* kinetic.
cingalais (sɛ̃ga'lɛ) *adj,n* Ceylonese.
cingler (sɛ̃'gle:) *vt* whip, lash. **cinglant** *adj* biting, cutting, scathing.
cinq (sɛ̃k) *adj,nm* five. **cinquième** *adj* fifth.

cinquante (sɛ̃'kɑ̃t) *adj,nm* fifty. **cinquantième** *adj* fiftieth.
cintrer (sɛ̃'tre:) *vt* **1** arch. **2** bend. **cintre** *nm* **1** curve. **2** arch. **3** coat-hanger.
circoncire* (si:rkɔ̃'si:r) *vt* circumcise. **circoncision** *nf* circumcision.
circonférence (si:rkɔ̃fɛ'rɑ̃s) *nf* circumference, perimeter.
circonflexe (si:rkɔ̃'flɛks) *adj* circumflex.
circonscrire* (si:rkɔ̃'skri:r) *vt* **1** circumscribe. **2** encircle. **3** limit. **circonscription** *nf pol* division, district. **circonscription électorale** constituency.
circonstance (si:rkɔ̃'stɑ̃s) *nf* **1** circumstance. **2** event.
circuit (si:r'kɥi:) *nm* circuit. **circuit touristique** organized tour.
circuler (si:rky'le:) *vi* circulate. **circulaire** *adj,nf* circular. **circulation** *nf* **1** circulation. **2** traffic.
cirer (si:'re:) *vt* **1** wax. **2** polish. **cire** *nf* wax. **ciré** *adj* **1** waxed. **2** polished. *nm* oilskin.
cirque (si:rk) *nm* circus.
cisaille (si:'zɑj) *nf* shears.
ciseau, -aux (si:'zo) *nm* **1** chisel. **2** *pl* scissors.
ciseler (si:'zle:) *vt* **1** engrave. **2** chisel.
cité (si:'te:) *nf* city. **cité universitaire** student's hall of residence.
citer (si:'te:) *vt* quote, cite. **citation** *nf* quotation.
citerne (si:'tɛrn) *nf* cistern, tank.
cithare (si:'tar) *nf* zither.
citoyen, -enne (si:twa'jɛ̃, -'jɛn) *nm,f* citizen.
citron (si:'trɔ̃) *nm* **1** *bot* lemon. **2** citrus. **3** lemon (colour). **citron pressé** lemon juice. **citronnier** *nm* lemon tree.
citrouille (si:'tru:j) *nf* pumpkin.
civette (si:'vɛt) *nf* chives.
civière (si:'vjɛr) *nf* stretcher.
civil (si:'vi:l) *adj* **1** civil. **2** civilian. **3** polite. *nm* civilian. **en civil** in plain clothes.
civiliser (si:vi:li:'ze:) *vt* civilize. **civilisation** *nf* civilization.
civique (si:'vi:k) *adj* civic.
clair (klɛr) *adj* **1** clear. **2** obvious, plain. **3** bright. **4** pale. *adv* clearly, plainly. *nm* light. **clair de lune** moonlight.
clairon (klɛ'rɔ̃) *nm* bugle.
clairsemé (klɛrsə'me:) *adj* **1** scattered. **2** thinly sown.
clairvoyant (klɛrvwa'jɑ̃) *adj* shrewd.
clameur (kla'mœr) *nf* clamour, outcry.
clan (klɑ̃) *nm* **1** clan. **2** set.
clandestin (klɑ̃dɛ'stɛ̃) *adj* secret, clandestine, underground.
claquer (kla'ke:) *vi* **1** clap. **2** bang. **3** snap. **4** *sl* die. *vt* smack. **claque** *nf* smack, slap.
clarifier (klari:'fje:) *vi* clarify.
clarinette (klari:'nɛt) *nf* clarinet.
clarté (klar'te:) *nf* **1** clarity. **2** light, brightness.
classer (klɑ'se:) *vt* **1** class. **2** sort out. **3** file. **classe** *nf* **1** class. **2** form. **aller en classe** go to school. **de première classe** first-class. **faire la classe** teach. **classeur** *nm* **1** rack. **2** filing cabinet.
classifier (klasi:'fje:) *vt* classify.
classique (kla'si:k) *adj* **1** classic. **2** classical. **3** academic. *nm pl* classics.
claustrophobie (klɔstrɔfɔ'bi:) *nf* claustrophobia.
clavecin (klav'sɛ̃) *nm* harpsichord.
clavicule (klavi:'kyl) *nf* collarbone.
clavier (kla'vje:) *nm* keyboard.
claxon (klak'sɔ̃) *nm* hooter.
claxonner (klaksɔ'ne:) *vi* hoot.
clef (kle:) *nf also* **clé** **1** key. **2** clue. **3** *mus* clef. **sous clef** under lock and key.
clémence (klɛ'mɑ̃s) *nf* mercy. **clément** *adj* **1** lenient, merciful. **2** mild.
cleptomanie (klɛptoma'ni:) *nf* kleptomania. **cleptomane** *nm,f* kleptomaniac.
clerc (klɛr) *nm* **1** clerk. **2** scholar. **faire un pas de clerc** make a blunder.
clergé (klɛr'ʒe:) *nm* clergy, priesthood.
clérical, -aux (kle:ri:'kal, -'ko) *adj rel* clerical.
cliché (kli:'ʃe:) *nm* **1** *phot* negative. **2** stock phrase.
client (kli:'ɑ̃) *nm* client, patient, customer. **clientèle** *nf* **1** customers. **2** *med* practice.
cligner (kli:'ɲe:) *vi,vt* blink, screw up one's eyes. **clignement** *nm* **1** blink. **2** flicker.
clignoter (kli:ɲɔ'te:) *vi* **1** blink. **2** twitch. **3** twinkle. **clignotant** *nm* indicator.
climat (kli:'ma) *nm* climate. **climatisation** *nf* air-conditioning.
clin d'œil (klɛ̃) *nm* wink.
clinique (kli:'ni:k) *adj* clinical. *nf* nursing home.
clinquant (klɛ̃'kɑ̃) *nm* **1** tinsel. **2** glitter. *adj* flashy.
cliqueter (kli:k'te:) *vi* rattle, clank.
cliquette (kli:'kɛt) *nf* pair of castanets.
clitoris (kli:tɔ'ri:s) *nm* clitoris.
clochard (klɔ'ʃar) *nm* tramp.
cloche (klɔʃ) *nf* **1** bell. **2** cover.
clocher[1] (klɔ'ʃe:) *nm* **1** belfry. **2** steeple.
clocher[2] (klɔ'ʃe:) *vi* limp, hobble.

cloison (klwa'zɔ̃) *nf* partition.
cloître (klwɑtr) *nm* **1** cloister. **2** monastery. **3** close.
clopin-clopant (klɔpɛ̃klɔ'pɑ̃) *adv* **aller clopin-clopant** limp along.
clore* (klɔr) *vt* **1** close. **2** end. **clos** *adj* **1** closed. **2** finished. *nm* enclosure.
clôture (klo'tyr) *nf* **1** fence. **2** closing.
clou (klu:) *nm* **1** nail. **2** boil. **3** *Th* main attraction. **4** old car. **clou de girofle** *cul* clove.
clouer (klu.'e:) *vt* **1** nail. **2** hold fast. **être cloué au lit** be bedridden.
clouter (klu:'te:) *vt* stud.
clovisse (klɔ'vi:s) *nf* clam.
clown (klu:n) *nm* clown.
club (klɔb) *nm* **1** club. **2** golf club.
coaguler (koagy'le:) *vt* congeal.
coalition (koali:'sjɔ̃) *nf* coalition, union.
coasser (koa'se:) *vi* croak.
cobaye (kɔ'baj) *nm* guineapig.
cobra (kɔ'bra) *nm* cobra.
cocarde (kɔ'kard) *nf* rosette.
cocasse (kɔ'kas) *adj* funny, humorous.
coccinelle (kɔksi:'nɛl) *nf* ladybird.
cocher[1] (kɔ'ʃe:) *nm* coachman, driver.
cocher[2] (kɔ'ʃe:) *vt* mark off. **coche** *nf* notch.
cochon, -onne (kɔ'ʃɔ̃, -'ʃɔn) *adj* **1** *inf* indecent. **2** dirty. *nm* **1** pig. **2** swine. **cochon d'Inde** guineapig. **cochonnerie** *nf inf* **1** filthiness. **2** rubbish. **3** dirty trick.
cocktail (kɔk'tɛl) *nm* **1** cocktail. **2** cocktail party.
coco (kɔ'ko) **noix de coco** *nm* coconut. **cocotier** *nm* coconut palm.
cocon (kɔ'kɔ̃) *nm* cocoon.
cocotte[1] (kɔ'kɔt) *nf* **1** child's word for chicken. **2** *sl* tart.
cocotte[2] (kɔ'kɔt) *nf* stewpan.
code (kɔd) *nm* **1** law. **2** code. **code de la route** highway code.
codéine (kɔde:'i:n) *nf* codeine.
coéducation (koe:dyka'sjɔ̃) *nf* co-education.
cœur (kœr) *nm* **1** heart. **2** mind. **3** courage. **4** middle. **5** *game* hearts. **au cœur léger** light-hearted. **de bon/mauvais cœur** willingly/reluctantly.
coexister (koe:gzi:'ste:) *vi* coexist.
coffre (kɔfr) *nm* **1** chest, box. **2** *mot* boot. **coffre-fort** *nm, pl* **coffres-forts** safe.
cognac (kɔ'ɲak) *nm* brandy.
cogner (kɔ'ɲe:) *vt* hammer, hit. *vi,vt* **1** knock. **2** bump. **cognée** *nf* hatchet, axe.
cohabiter (koabi:'te:) *vi* cohabit, live together.
cohérent (kɔɛ'rɑ̃) *adj* coherent.
cohue (kɔ'y) *nf* crowd, mob.
coiffer (kwa'fe:) *vt* **1** cover. **2** put on (a hat). **se coiffer** *vr* **1** put on one's hat. **2** do one's hair. **coiffeur, -euse** (kwa'fœr, -'fœz) *nm,f* hairdresser. *nf* dressing table. **coiffure** *nf* **1** hairdressing. **2** hairstyle.
coin (kwɛ̃) *nm* **1** corner. **2** spot. **3** wedge.
coincer (kwɛ̃'se:) *vt* wedge. *vi* jam, stick.
coïncider (kɔɛ̃si:'de:) *vi* coincide. **coïncidence** *nf* coincidence.
coing (kwɛ̃) *nm* quince.
col (kɔl) *nm* **1** neck. **2** collar. **3** pass (of a mountain).
coléoptère (kɔle.ɔp'tɛr) *nm* beetle.
colère (kɔ'lɛr) *nf* anger. **coléreux, -euse** (kɔle:'rœ, -'rœz) *adj* quick-tempered.
colimaçon (kɔli:ma'sɔ̃) *nm* snail. **en colimaçon** spiral.
colique (kɔ'li:k) *nf* stomach ache.
colis (kɔ'li:) *nm* **1** parcel, package. **2** piece of luggage. **par colis postal** by parcel post.
collaborer (kɔlabɔ're:) *vi* collaborate. **collaborateur** *nm* **1** collaborator. **2** contributor.
collant (kɔ'lɑ̃) *adj* **1** sticky. **2** close-fitting. *nm* tights.
colle (kɔl) *nf* paste, glue.
collectif, -ive (kɔlɛk'ti:f, -'ti:v) *adj* collective. **collectivité** *nf* **1** group. **2** community.
collection (kɔlɛk'sjɔ̃) *nf* collection.
collectionner (kɔlɛksjɔ'ne:) *vt* collect.
collège (kɔ'lɛʒ) *nm* **1** college. **2** school. **collège d'enseignement général** secondary modern school. **collège privé** public school. **collégien, -ienne** (kɔle:'ʒjɛ̃, -'ʒjɛn) *nm,f* schoolboy, schoolgirl.
collègue (kɔl'lɛg) *nm,f* colleague.
coller (kɔ'le:) *vt* paste, glue. *vi* stick, cling. **se coller** *vr* stick or cling close. **colle** *nf* glue, paste.
collet (kɔ'lɛ) *nm* collar. **collet monté** *adj invar* prim, prudish.
collier (kɔ'lje:) *nm* **1** necklace. **2** collar.
colline (kɔ'li.n) *nf* hill.
collision (kɔli:'zjɔ̃) *nf* **1** collision. **2** clash.
colombe (kɔ'lɔ̃b) *nf* pigeon, dove. **colombier** *nm* dovecote.
Colombie (kɔlɔ̃'bi:) *nf* Columbia. **colombien, -ienne** *adj,n* Columbian.
colonel (kɔlɔ'nɛl) *nm* colonel.
colonie (kɔlɔ'ni:) *nf* colony. **colonie de vacances** children's holiday camp. **colonial, -aux** (kɔlɔ'njal, -'njo) *adj,n* colonial.

colonne (kɔ'lɔn) *nf* **1** column. **2** pillar. **colonne vertébrale** backbone.
colorer (kɔlɔ're:) *vt* **1** colour. **2** stain.
coloris (kɔlɔ'ri:) *nm* colouring.
colossal, -aux (kɔlɔ'sal, -'so) *adj* colossal, huge.
colporter (kɔlpɔr'te:) *vt* **1** peddle. **2** spread (news). **colporteur** *nm* pedlar.
coma (kɔ'ma) *nm* coma.
combat (kɔ̃'ba) *nm* **1** combat, fight. **2** conflict. **hors de combat** disabled.
combattre (kɔ̃'batr) *vt* fight, combat. *vi* fight, struggle.
combien (kɔ̃'bjɛ̃) *adv* how much, how many. **le combien sommes-nous?** what day of the month is it?
combiner (kɔ̃bi:'ne:) *vt* **1** combine. **2** contrive. **combinaison** *nf* **1** combination. **2** plan.
comble[1] (kɔ̃bl) *nm* **1** heap. **2** top, summit. **3** roof. **ça, c'est le comble!** that's the limit!
comble[2] (kɔ̃bl) *adj* **1** heaped. **2** full, crowded.
combler (kɔ̃'ble:) *vt* **1** fill, fill to overflowing. **2** make good.
combustion (kɔ̃by'stjɔ̃) *nf* combustion. **combustible** *adj* combustible. *nm* fuel.
comédie (kɔme:'di:) *nf* **1** comedy. **2** play. **jouer la comédie** act a part. **comédien, -ienne** (kɔme:'djɛ̃, -'djɛn) *nm,f* **1** comedian. **2** actor, actress.
comestible (kɔmɛ'sti:bl) *adj* edible. *nm* **1** article of food. **2** *pl* provisions.
comète (kɔ'mɛt) *nf* comet.
comique (kɔ'mi:k) *adj* **1** comic. **2** comical. *nm* **1** comedy. **2** comedian.
comité (kɔmi:'te:) *nm* committee, board.
commander (kɔmɑ̃'de:) *vt* **1** order, command. **2** govern. **3** control. **commandant** *nm mil* officer in command, major. **commande** *nf* order. **de commande** forced. **fait sur commande** made to order. **commandement** *nm* **1** command. **2** commandment.
commanditer (kɔmɑ̃di:'te:) *vt* finance.
comme (kɔm) *adv* **1** as, like. **2** in the way of. **3** how. *conj* as.
commémorer (kɔmme:mɔ're:) *vt* commemorate.
commencer (kɔmɑ̃'se:) *vi,vt* begin, commence. **commençant** *nm* beginner. **commencement** *nm* beginning.
comment (kɔ'mɑ̃) *adv* **1** how. **2** what. **3** *interj* what! why!
commenter (kɔmɑ̃'te:) *vi,vt* **1** comment. **2** annotate. **commentaire** *nm* **1** commentary. **2** comment. **commentateur, -trice** (kɔmɑ̃ta'tœr, -'tri:s) *nm,f* commentator.
commérage (kɔmɛ'raʒ) *nm* gossip.
commerce (kɔ'mɛrs) *nm* commerce, trade. **commerçant** *adj* business, mercantile. *nm* tradesman. **commercial, -aux** (kɔmɛr'sjal, -'sjo) *adj* commercial. **commerciale** *nf* estate car.
commettre* (kɔ'mɛtr) *vt* **1** commit. **2** entrust.
commis (kɔ'mi:) *nm* **1** clerk. **2** assistant.
commissaire (kɔmi:'sɛr) *nm* commissioner. **commissaire de police** police superintendent. **commissaire-priseur** *nm, pl* **commissaires-priseurs** auctioneer.
commissariat (kɔmi:sa'rja) *nm* police station.
commission (kɔmi:'sjɔ̃) *nf* **1** commission. **2** message, errand. **3** board, committee.
commissionnaire (kɔmi:sjɔ'nɛr) *nm* messenger.
commode (kɔ'mɔd) *adj* **1** convenient. **2** comfortable. **3** accommodating. *nf* chest of drawers. **commodité** *nf* **1** convenience. **2** comfort.
commotion (kɔmo'sjɔ̃) *nf* **1** commotion. **2** concussion.
commun (kɔ'mœ̃) *adj* **1** common. **2** general. **3** usual. **4** vulgar. **peu commun** unusual.
commune (kɔ'myn) *nf* **1** commune. **2** parish. **communal, -aux** (kɔmy'nal, -'no) *adj* **1** common. **2** communal. **communauté** *nf* community.
communiant (kɔmy'njɑ̃) *nm* communicant.
communication (kɔmyni:ka'sjɔ̃) *nf* **1** communication. **2** connection. **3** telephone call. **4** message.
communion (kɔmy'njɔ̃) *nf* communion.
communiquer (kɔmyni:'ke:) *vt* **1** communicate. **2** convey. *vi* communicate. **se communiquer** *vr* **1** be communicative. **2** spread.
communisme (kɔmy'ni:sm) *nm* communism. **communiste** *nm,f* communist.
compact (kɔ̃'pakt) *adj* **1** compact. **2** close.
compagnie (kɔ̃pa'ɲi:) *nf* **1** company. **2** party, group. **compagnon, compagne** *nm,f* companion.
comparer (kɔ̃pa're:) *vt* compare. **comparable** *adj* comparable. **comparaison** *nf* comparison. **comparatif, -ive** (kɔ̃para'ti:f, -'ti:v) *adj* comparative. **comparé** *adj* comparative.
compartiment (kɔ̃parti:'mɑ̃) *nm* compartment.
compas (kɔ̃'pɑ) *nm* **1** pair of compasses. **2** scale.
compassion (kɔ̃pa'sjɔ̃) *nf* compassion, pity. **avoir compassion de** take pity on.
compatible (kɔ̃pa'ti:bl) *adj* compatible.
compatir (kɔ̃pɑ'ti:r) *vi* **compatir à** **1** sympathize

with. **2** be indulgent with. **compatissant** *adj* **1** soft-hearted. **2** indulgent.

compenser (kɔ̃pɑ̃'se:) *vt* compensate.

compère (kɔ̃'pɛr) *nm* **1** accomplice. **2** comrade.

compétent (kɔ̃pɛ'tɑ̃) *adj* competent. **avec compétence** *adv* competently.

compétition (kɔ̃pe:ti:'sjɔ̃) *nf* **1** competition. **2** race.

compiler (kɔ̃pi'le:) *vt* compile.

complaisance (kɔ̃plɛ'zɑ̃s) *nf* **1** kindness. **2** self-satisfaction. **complaisant** *adj* **1** obliging. **2** self-satisfied, complacent.

complément (kɔ̃ple:'mɑ̃) *nm* complement.

complet, -ète (kɔ̃'plɛ, -'plɛt) *adj* **1** complete, entire. **2** full. *nm* suit.

compléter (kɔ̃ple:'te:) *vt* complete.

complexe (kɔ̃'plɛks) *adj* **1** complex. **2** intricate. *nm* complex. **complexité** *nf* complexity.

complice (kɔ̃'pli:s) *adj* **1** accessory. **2** accomplice. *nm,f* accomplice.

compliment (kɔ̃pli:'mɑ̃) *nm* **1** compliment. **2** *pl* compliments. **3** *pl* congratulations.

complimenter (kɔ̃pli:mɑ̃'te:) *vt* **1** compliment. **2** congratulate.

compliquer (kɔ̃pli:'ke:) *vt* complicate

complot (kɔ̃'plo) *nm* plot, conspiracy.

comploter (kɔ̃plɔ'te:) *vt* plot, scheme.

comporter (kɔ̃pɔr'te:) *vt* **1** allow. **2** require. **3** comprise. **4** involve. **se comporter** *vr* behave.

composer (kɔ̃po'ze:) *vt* **1** compose. **2** arrange. **composer avec** come to terms with. **se composer de** *vr* consist of. **composé** *adj* **1** compound. **2** composed. *nm* compound. **compositeur, -trice** (kɔ̃pɔzi:'tœr, -'tri:s) *nm,f* composer. **composition** *nf* **1** composition. **2** arrangement.

compote (kɔ̃'pɔt) *nf* stewed fruit.

compréhensif, -ive (kɔ̃pre:ɑ̃'si:f, -'si:v) *adj* **1** comprehensive. **2** intelligent.

comprendre* (kɔ̃'prɑ̃dr) *vt* **1** include, comprise. **2** understand, comprehend. **se faire comprendre** make oneself understood. **y compris** including.

comprimer (kɔ̃pri:'me:) *vt* **1** compress. **2** restrain. **comprimé** *adj* compressed. *nm* tablet.

compromettre* (kɔ̃prɔ'mɛtr) *vi,vt* compromise. **compromis** *nm* compromise.

comptable (kɔ̃'tabl) *adj* **1** of bookkeeping. **2** responsible. *nm,f* accountant. **comptabilité** *nf* bookkeeping.

compter (kɔ̃'te:) *vt* **1** count, reckon. **2** charge. **3** expect. *vi* rely. **comptant** *nm* cash. **compte** *nm* **1** account. **2** calculation. **compte à rebours** countdown. **compte rendu 1** report. **2** review. **en fin de compte** all things considered.

compteur (kɔ̃'tœr) *nm* **1** counter. **2** meter. **compteur de stationnement** parking meter.

comptoir (kɔ̃t'war) *nm* counter.

comte (kɔ̃t) *nm* (title) count. **comtesse** *nf* countess.

comté (kɔ̃'te:) *nm* county.

concave (kɔ̃'kav) *adj* concave.

concéder (kɔ̃se:'de:) *vt* **1** concede. **2** grant. **3** admit.

concentrer (kɔ̃sɑ̃'tre:) *vt* **1** concentrate. **2** focus. **3** repress. **concentration** *nf* concentration. **concentré** *adj* **1** concentrated. **2** reserved. *nm* extract, concentrate.

concentrique *adj* concentric.

concept (kɔ̃'sɛpt) *nm* concept.

conception (kɔ̃sɛp'sjɔ̃) *nf* **1** conception. **2** idea. **conception dirigée** birth control.

concerner (kɔ̃sɛr'ne:) *vt* concern, affect.

concert (kɔ̃'sɛr) *nm* **1** concert. **2** harmony.

concerto (kɔ̃sɛr'to) *nm* concerto.

concession (kɔsɛ'sjɔ̃) *nf* concession.

concevoir* (kɔ̃sə'vwar) *vt* **1** conceive. **2** imagine. **3** understand.

concierge (kɔ̃'sjɛrʒ) *nm,f* **1** caretaker. **2** porter.

concilier (kɔ̃si:'lje:) *vt* **1** settle. **2** reconcile.

concis (kɔ̃'si:) *adj* concise.

conclure* (kɔ̃'klyr) *vt* **1** conclude. **2** finish. **conclusion** *nf* **1** conclusion, decision. **2** end.

concombre (kɔ̃'kɔ̃br) *nm* cucumber.

concourir* (kɔ̃ku:'ri:r) *vi* **1** converge. **2** unite. **3** compete.

concours (kɔ̃'ku:r) *nm* **1** gathering. **2** assistance. **3** competition. **4** show

concret, -ète (kɔ̃'krɛ, -'krɛt) *adj* **1** concrete. **2** solid.

concurrence (kɔ̃ky'rɑ̃s) *nf* competition. **concurrent** *adj* **1** competitive. **2** rival. *nm* **1** competitor. **2** candidate. **3** contestant.

condamner (kɔ̃da'ne:) *vt* **1** condemn. **2** sentence. **3** reprove. **4** block up. **condamnation** *nf* **1** condemnation. **2** *law* sentence.

condenser (kɔ̃dɑ̃'se:) *vt* condense. **condensation** *nf* condensation.

condescendre (kɔ̃dɛ'sɑ̃dr) *vi* condescend.

condition (kɔ̃di:'sjɔ̃) *nf* **1** condition, proviso. **2** position. **3** *pl* terms. **à condition** on approval. **à condition de** provided that. **conditionnel, -elle** *adj* conditional

conditionner (kɔ̃di:sjɔ'ne:) *vt* **1** condition. **2** *comm* package.

condoléance (kɔ̃dɔle:ˈɑ̃s) *nf* condolence.
conducteur, -trice (kɔ̃dykˈtœr, -ˈtri:s) *nm,f* **1** driver. **2** leader. *adj* conducting.
conduire* (kɔ̃ˈdɥi:r) *vt* **1** conduct. **2** lead. **3** drive. **4** manage. **se conduire** *vr* behave. **conduit** *nm* **1** passage. **2** pipe. **conduite** *nf* **1** behaviour. **2** management. **3** driving. **4** leading. **conduite intérieure** saloon car.
cône (kon) *nm* cone.
confectionner (kɔ̃fɛksjɔˈne:) *vt* **1** make up. **2** manufacture. **confectionné** *adj* ready-made.
confédérer (kɔ̃fe:de:ˈre:) *vt* confederate. **confédération** *nf* confederation.
conférer (kɔ̃fe:ˈre:) *vt* **1** compare. **2** award. *vi* confer. **conférence** *nf* **1** conference. **2** lecture. **conférencier, -ière** (kɔ̃fe:rɑ̃ˈsje:, -ˈsjɛr) *nm,f* lecturer.
confesser (kɔ̃fɛˈse:) *vt* confess.
confetti (kɔ̃fɛtˈti:) *nm pl* confetti.
confidentiel, -ielle (kɔ̃fi:dɑ̃ˈsjɛl) *adj* confidential.
confier (kɔ̃ˈfje:) *vt* **1** trust. **2** confide. **se confier à** *vr* put one's trust in. **confiance** *nf* confidence, trust. **digne de confiance** reliable, trustworthy. **confiant** *adj* **1** confiding. **2** confident, assured.
confire* (kɔ̃ˈfi:r) *vt cul* preserve (food).
confirmer (kɔ̃fi:rˈme:) *vt* confirm. **confirmation** *nf* confirmation.
confiserie (kɔ̃fi:ˈzri:) *nf* **1** confectioner's shop. **2** confectionery. **confiseur** *nm* confectioner.
confisquer (kɔ̃fi:ˈske:) *vt* confiscate, seize.
confiture (kɔ̃fi:ˈtyr) *nf* jam. **confiture d'oranges** marmalade.
conflagration (kɔ̃flagraˈsjɔ̃) *nf* blaze, fire.
conflit (kɔ̃ˈfli:) *nm* **1** conflict. **2** clash.
confluer (kɔ̃flyˈe:) *vi* join, meet.
confondre (kɔ̃ˈfɔ̃dr) *vt* **1** confound, baffle. **2** confuse, mistake. **se confondre** *vr* blend. **confondu** *adj* **1** overwhelmed. **2** confused.
conforme (kɔ̃ˈfɔrm) *adj* **conforme à** **1** according to. **2** consistent with. **conformément** *adv* accordingly.
conformer (kɔ̃fɔrˈme:) *vt* **1** shape. **2** conform. **se conformer à** *vr* comply with.
confort (kɔ̃ˈfɔr) *nm* comfort. **confortable** *adj* comfortable, cosy.
confrère (kɔ̃ˈfrɛr) *nm* **1** colleague. **2** *rel* brother.
confus (kɔ̃ˈfy) *adj* **1** confused. **2** vague. **3** obscure. **confusion** *nf* confusion, muddle.
congé (kɔ̃ˈʒe:) *nm* **1** leave, holiday. **2** notice.
congédier (kɔ̃ʒe:ˈdje:) *vt* **1** dismiss. **2** discharge.
congeler (kɔ̃ˈʒle:) *vt* **1** freeze. **2** congeal. **congélateur** *nm* deep-freeze. **congélation** *nf* freezing.
congestion (kɔ̃ʒɛsˈtjɔ̃) *nf* congestion. **congestion cérébrale** *med* stroke. **congestion pulmonaire** pneumonia. **congestionné** *adj* flushed, red in the face.
congrès (kɔ̃ˈgrɛ) *nm* congress.
conifère (kɔni:ˈfɛr) *nm* conifer.
conique (kɔˈni:k) *adj* conical.
conjoint (kɔ̃ˈʒwɛ̃) *adj* **1** joined. **2** married. **conjoints** *nm pl* husband and wife.
conjonction (kɔ̃ʒɔ̃kˈsjɔ̃) *nf* **1** union. **2** conjunction.
conjugal, -aux (kɔ̃ʒyˈgal, -ˈgo) *adj* conjugal.
conjuguer (kɔ̃ʒyˈge:) *vt* conjugate. **conjugaison** *nf* conjugation.
connaissance (kɔnɛˈsɑ̃s) *nf* **1** knowledge. **2** acquaintance. **3** consciousness. **4** *pl* learning. **sans connaissance** unconscious. **connaisseur** *nm* connoisseur, expert. *adj* expert.
connaître* (kɔˈnɛtr) *vt* **1** know. **2** be acquainted with. **3** have a thorough knowledge of. **4** distinguish. **se connaître en** *vr* know all about.
connu (kɔˈny) *v* see **connaître.**
conquérir* (kɔ̃ke:ˈri:r) *vt* **1** conquer. **2** win over.
conquête (kɔ̃ˈkɛt) *nf* conquest.
conquis (kɔ̃ˈki:) *v* see **conquérir.**
consacrer (kɔ̃saˈkre:) *vt* **1** consecrate. **2** devote. **consacré** *adj* sacred.
consanguin (kɔ̃sɑ̃ˈgɛ̃) **frère consanguin** *nm* half-brother. **sœur consanguine** *nf* half-sister.
conscience (kɔ̃ˈsjɑ̃s) *nf* **1** conscience. **2** consciousness. **avoir conscience de** be aware of. **consciencieux, -euse** (kɔ̃sjɑ̃ˈsjœ, -ˈsjœz) *adj* conscientious. **conscient de** *adj* conscious of.
conscription (kɔ̃skri:pˈsjɔ̃) *nf* conscription.
conscrit (kɔ̃ˈskri:) *nm* conscript.
consécutif, -ive (kɔ̃se:kyˈti:f, -ˈti:v) *adj* consecutive.
conseil (kɔ̃ˈsɛj) *nm* **1** advice. **2** counsel. **3** council. **conseil d'administration** board of directors. **conseil de guerre** court-martial. **conseil des ministres** *pol* cabinet. **conseil général** county council.
conseiller (kɔ̃sɛˈje:) *vt* advise, counsel.
consentir (kɔ̃sɑ̃ˈti:r) *vi* consent, agree. **consentement** *nm* consent.
conséquence (kɔsɛˈkɑ̃s) *nf* **1** consequence. **2** importance. **conséquent** *adj* **1** consistent. **2** following. **par conséquent** consequently.

conservatoire (kɔ̃sɛrva'twar) *nm* school, academy (of music).

conserver (kɔ̃sɛr've:) *vt* **1** preserve. **2** keep. **conservateur, -trice** (kɔ̃sɛrva'tœr, -'tri:s) *nm,f* **1** curator, warden. **2** *pol* conservative.

considérer (kɔ̃si:de:'re:) *vt* **1** consider. **2** contemplate. **3** regard. **considérable** *adj* **1** considerable. **2** large. **3** eminent, important. **considération** *nf* **1** consideration. **2** reason. **3** respect.

consigner (kɔ̃si:'ɲe:) *vt* **1** deposit. **2** consign. **3** record. **4** confine to barracks. **non consigné** non-returnable. **consignation** *nf* **1** deposit. **2** consignment. **consigne** *nf* **1** order. **2** cloakroom.

consister (kɔ̃si:'ste:) *vi* consist. **consistance** *nf* consistency. **consistant** *adj* firm, solid.

consoler (kɔ̃sɔ'le:) *vt* console, comfort.

consolider (kɔ̃sɔli:'de:) *vt* consolidate. **se consolider** *vr* **1** become firm. **2** heal.

consommer (kɔ̃sɔ'me:) *vt* **1** consume. **2** accomplish. **consommateur, -trice** (kɔ̃sɔma'tœr, -'tri:s) *nm,f* **1** consumer. **2** customer (in restaurant). **consommation** *nf* **1** consumption. **2** accomplishment. **3** drink. **consommé** *nm* clear soup.

consonne (kɔ̃'sɔn) *nf* consonant.

conspirer (kɔ̃spi:'re:) *vi,vt* conspire, plot. **conspiration** *nf* plot.

conspuer (kɔ̃'spɥe:) *vt* to shout down.

constant (kɔ̃'stɑ̃) *adj* **1** constant, steadfast. **2** firm. **constamment** *adv* constantly.

constater (kɔ̃sta'te:) *vt* **1** ascertain. **2** state. **3** certify.

constellation (kɔ̃stɛlla'sjɔ̃) *nf* constellation.

consterner (kɔ̃stɛr'ne:) *vt* dismay.

constipation (kɔ̃sti:pa'sjɔ̃) *nf* constipation.

constituer (kɔ̃sti'tɥe:) *vt* **1** constitute. **2** form. **3** assign. **4** *comm* incorporate. **constituant** *adj* constituent. *nm* **1** component. **2** constituent. **constitution** *nf* **1** constitution. **2** composition.

construction (kɔ̃stryk'sjɔ̃) *nf* **1** construction. **2** building. **construction mécanique** mechanical engineering.

construire* (kɔ̃'stryi:r) *vt* **1** construct. **2** build.

consul (kɔ̃'syl) *nm* consul.

consulat (kɔ̃sy'la) *nm* consulate.

consulter (kɔ̃syl'te:) *vt* consult. **se consulter** *vr* consider. **consultation** *nf* **1** consultation. **2** advice, opinion.

consumer (kɔ̃sy'me:) *vt* **1** consume. **2** destroy. **3** use up. **se consumer** *vr* burn up.

contact (kɔ̃'takt) *nm* contact, touch.

contagieux, -euse (kɔ̃ta'ʒjœ, -'ʒjœz) *adj* contagious, catching.

contaminer (kɔ̃tami:'ne:) *vt* **1** contaminate. **2** infect.

conte (kɔ̃t) *nm* story, tale. **conte de fées** fairytale.

contempler (kɔ̃tɑ̃'ple:) *vt* **1** contemplate. **2** meditate. **3** gaze at.

comtemporain (kɔ̃tɑ̃pɔ'rɛ̃) *adj,n* contemporary.

contenance (kɔ̃t'nɑ̃s) *nf* **1** look. **2** content. **faire bonne contenance** put on a brave face.

contenir* (kɔ̃t'ni:r) *vt* **1** contain. **2** restrain. **contenu** *adj* **1** restrained. **2** reserved. *nm* **1** contents. **2** subject.

content (kɔ̃'tɑ̃) *adj* **1** content, satisfied. **2** pleased.

contenter (kɔ̃tɑ̃'te:) *vt* **1** content, satisfy. **2** gratify. **contentement** *nm* contentment, satisfaction.

conter (kɔ̃'te:) *vt* tell, relate. **conteur** *nm* narrator.

contester (kɔ̃tɛs'te:) *vi,vt* contest, dispute. **contestable** *adj* debatable. **contestation** *nf* debate.

contexte (kɔ̃'tɛkst) *nm* context.

contigu, -uë (kɔ̃ti:'gy) *adj* adjoining, adjacent.

continent (kɔ̃ti:'nɑ̃) *nm* continent. **continental, -aux** (kɔ̃tl:na'tal, -'to) *adj* continental.

contingent (kɔ̃tɛ̃'ʒɑ̃) *nm* quota, allowance.

continuer (kɔ̃ti:'nɥe:) *vi,vt* continue. **continu** *adj* continuous. **continuel, -elle** (kɔ̃ti:'nɥɛl) *adj* continual. **continuité** *nf* continuity.

contour (kɔ̃'tu:r) *nm* **1** outline. **2** contour.

contourner (kɔ̃tu:r'ne:) *vt* **1** shape. **2** skirt. **3** twist. **route de contournement** *nf* bypass.

contraception (kɔ̃trasɛp'sjɔ̃) *nf* contraception.

contracter[1] (kɔ̃trak'te:) *vt* **1** contract, incur. **2** catch.

contracter[2] (kɔ̃trak'te:) *vt* contract, draw together.

contractuel, -elle (kɔ̃trak'tɥɛl) *nm,f* traffic warden.

contradiction (kɔ̃tradi:k'sjɔ̃) *nf* **1** contradiction. **2** discrepancy. **contradictoire** *adj* contradictory, conflicting.

contraindre* (kɔ̃'trɛ̃dr) *vt* **1** compel. **2** restrain. **contrainte** *nf* **1** constraint. **2** compulsion.

contraire (kɔ̃'trɛr) *adj* **1** contrary, opposite. **2** adverse. *nm* contrary, reverse.

contrarier (kɔ̃tra'rje:) *vt* **1** oppose. **2** annoy.

contraster (kɔ̃tras'te:) *vi,vt* contrast. **contraste** *nm* contrast.

contrat (kɔ̃'tra) *nm* contract, agreement.

contravention (kɔ̃travɑ̃'sjɔ̃) *nf* **1** infringement, minor offence. **2** fine.
contre (kɔ̃tr) *prep* **1** against. **2** for. **3** from. **4** to. **5** by. *adv* **1** against. **2** close to. **le pour et le contre** the pros and cons.
contre-amiral, -aux *nm* rear admiral.
contre-attaque *nf* counterattack.
contre-avion *adj* anti-aircraft.
contrebande (kɔ̃trə'bɑ̃d) *nf* **1** contraband. **2** smuggling. **faire la contrebande** smuggle. **contrebandier** *nm* smuggler.
contrebasse (kɔ̃trə'bɑs) *nf* double bass.
contre-boutant *nm* buttress.
contrecarrer (kɔ̃trəkɑ're:) *vt* thwart, cross.
contre-cœur (kɔ̃trə'kœr) **à contre-cœur** *adv* reluctantly.
contre-coup *nm* **1** repercussion. **2** reaction.
contredire* (kɔ̃trə'di:r) *vt* contradict.
contrée (kɔ̃'tre:) *nf* region.
contrefaçon (kɔ̃trəfa'sɔ̃) *nf* counterfeit, forgery.
contrefaire* (kɔ̃trə'fɛr) *vt* **1** forge, counterfeit. **2** feign. **3** imitate.
contre-interroger *vt* cross-question, cross-examine.
contremaître (kɔ̃trə'mɛtr) *nm* foreman.
contremander (kɔ̃trəmɑ̃'de:) *vt* **1** cancel. **2** call off.
contre-pied *nm* opposite view. **à contre-pied** contrary to.
contre-plaqué *nm* plywood.
contre-poil *adv* **à contre-poil** the wrong way.
contre-poison *nm* antidote.
contre-sens *nm* **1** misunderstanding. **2** wrong way. **à contre-sens** in the wrong direction.
contretemps (kɔ̃trə'tɑ̃) *nm* **1** mishap. **2** hitch.
contre-torpilleur *nm naut* destroyer.
contrevenir (kɔ̃trə'vni:r) *vt (aux* avoir) contravene.
contrevent (kɔ̃trə'vɑ̃) *nm* shutter.
contre-voie *adv* **à contre-voie** **1** in the wrong direction. **2** on the wrong side.
contribuer (kɔ̃tri:'bɥe:) *vi* **contribuer à** contribute to. **contribuable** *nm,f* taxpayer. **contribution** *nf* **1** contribution. **2** tax.
contrôler (kɔ̃tro'le:) *vt* **1** inspect. **2** check. **3** control. **4** hallmark. **contrôle** *nm* **1** inspection, checking. **2** control. **3** list. **contrôleur** *nm* **1** inspector. **2** ticket collector.
controverse (kɔ̃trɔ'vɛrs) *nf* controversy.
contusionner (kɔ̃tyzjɔ'ne:) *vt* bruise.
convaincre* (kɔ̃'vɛ̃kr) *vt* **1** convince. **2** convict.
convalescence (kɔ̃valɛs'sɑ̃s) *nf* convalescence. **convalescent** *adj,n* convalescent.
convenir* (kɔ̃'vni:r) *vi (aux* avoir) **1** suit. **2** agree. **3** admit. **convenable** *adj* **1** suitable, appropriate. **2** proper. **convenance** *nf* **1** agreement. **2** suitability. **3** convenience. **4** propriety. **5** *pl* convention. **convenu** *adj* **1** agreed. **2** appointed.
convention (kɔ̃vɑ̃'sjɔ̃) *nf* **1** convention. **2** agreement. **3** condition. **conventionnel, -elle** (kɔ̃vɑ̃sjɔ'nɛl) *adj* conventional.
converger (kɔ̃vɛr'ʒe:) *vi* converge.
convers (kɔ̃'vɛr) *adj* **1** *rel* lay. **2** converse.
conversation (kɔ̃vɛrsa'sjɔ̃) *nf* conversation, talk.
conversion (kɔ̃vɛr'zjɔ̃) *nf* conversion.
convertir (kɔ̃vɛr'ti:r) *vt* convert. **converti** *nm* convert.
convexe (kɔ̃'vɛks) *adj* convex.
conviction (kɔ̃vi:k'sjɔ̃) *nf* conviction.
convier (kɔ̃'vje:) *vt* **1** invite. **2** urge.
convive (kɔ̃'vi:v) *nm,f* guest.
convocation (kɔ̃vɔka'sjɔ̃) *nf* summons.
convoi (kɔ̃'vwa) *nm* convoy, train.
convoiter (kɔvwa'te:) *vt* desire.
convoquer (kɔ̃vɔ'ke:) *vt* summon, call together.
coopérer (koɔpe:'re:) *vi* cooperate. **coopératif, -ive** (koɔpe:ra'ti:f, -'ti:v) *adj,nf* cooperative. **coopération** *nf* cooperation.
coordonner (koɔrdɔ'ne:) *vt* coordinate.
copain (kɔ'pɛ̃) *nm inf* friend, pal.
Copenhague (kɔpɛ'nag) *nf* Copenhagen.
copier (kɔ'pje:) *vt* **1** copy. **2** imitate. **copie** *nf* **1** copy. **2** reproduction.
copine (kɔ'pi:n) *nf inf* friend.
coq (kɔk) *nm* **1** cock. **2** weathercock. **coq-à-l'âne** *nm invar* cock-and-bull story.
coque (kɔk) *nf* **1** shell (of an egg). **2** *naut* hull. **3** cockle. **coquetier** *nm* eggcup.
coquelicot (kɔkli:'ko) *nm* poppy.
coqueluche (kɔ'klyʃ) *nf* whooping cough.
coquet, -ette (kɔ'kɛ, -'kɛt) *adj* **1** coy. **2** smart. **3** trim. *nf* flirt.
coquille (kɔ'ki:j) *nf* **1** shell. **2** misprint. **coquille d'œuf** *nf* eggshell. **coquillage** *nm* **1** shellfish. **2** shell.
coquin (kɔ'kɛ̃) *adj* naughty. *nm* rascal.
cor (kɔr) *nm* **1** *mus* horn. **2** *med* corn.
corail, -aux (kɔ'raj, -'ro) *nm* coral.
corbeau, -aux (kɔr'bo) *nm* crow.
corbeille (kɔr'bɛj) *nf* **1** basket. **2** flowerbed. **corbeille à papier** wastepaper basket.
corbillard (kɔrbi:'jar) *nm* hearse.
corder (kɔr'de:) *vt* **1** twist. **2** rope. **3** string. **cordage** *nm naut* **1** rope. **2** rigging. **corde** *nf* **1** rope, cord. **2** *mus* chord. **3** string. **4** note.

corde à linge clothes line. **corde de remorque** towrope. **corde tendue** tightrope. **cordée** *nf sport* line, group.

cordial, -aux (kɔr'djal, -'djo) *adj* cordial, hearty. *nm* cordial.

cordon (kɔr'dɔ̃) *nm* **1** strand. **2** cord, rope. **3** ribbon. **4** row, cordon. **cordonnier** *nm* cobbler.

coriace (kɔ'rjas) *adj* **1** tough. **2** (of a person) hard.

corne (kɔrn) *nf* horn. **cornet** *nm* **1** small horn. **2** cornet.

corneille (kɔr'nɛj) *nf* crow.

cornemuse (kɔrnə'myz) *nf* bagpipes.

cornichon (kɔrni:'ʃɔ̃) *nm* gherkin.

cornu (kɔr'ny) *adj* horned.

corporation (kɔrpɔra'sjɔ̃) *nf* **1** corporation. **2** guild.

corporel, -elle (kɔrpɔ'rɛl) *adj* corporal.

corps (kɔr) *nm* **1** body. **2** corpse. **3** main part. **4** corps. **corps à corps** hand to hand.

corpulent (kɔrpy'lɑ̃) *adj* stout, fat.

correct (kɔ'rɛkt) *adj* **1** correct. **2** proper. **correction** *nf* **1** correction. **2** accuracy. **3** punishment.

correspondre (kɔrɛ'spɔ̃dr) *vi* **1** agree, tally. **2** correspond, match. **correspondance** *nf* **1** correspondence. **2** connection (train, etc.). **correspondant** *adj* corresponding. *nm* **1** correspondent. **2** penfriend.

corrida (kɔri:'da) *nf* bullfight.

corridor (kɔri:'dɔr) *nm* corridor, passage.

corriger (kɔri:'ʒe:) *vt* **1** correct. **2** punish.

corroder (kɔrrɔ'de:) *vt* corrode.

corrompre (kɔ'rɔ̃pr) *vt* **1** corrupt. **2** bribe. **3** taint. **corrompu** *adj* **1** corrupt. **2** tainted.

corsage (kɔr'saʒ) *nm* bodice.

Corse (kɔrs) *nf* Corsica. **corse** *adj,n* Corsican.

corset (kɔr'sɛ) *nm* corset.

cortège (kɔr'tɛʒ) *nm* **1** procession. **2** train.

corvée (kɔr've:) *nf* drudgery, unpleasant task.

cosmétique (kɔsme:'ti:k) *adj,nm* cosmetic.

cosmique (kɔs'mi:k) *adj* cosmic.

cosmopolite (kɔsmɔpɔ'li:t) *adj,n* cosmopolitan.

cosmos ('kɔsmɔs) *nm* cosmos.

cosse (kɔs) *nf* pod, husk, hull.

cossu (kɔ'sy) *adj* well-off, rich.

costaud (kɔ'sto) *adj* **1** strong. **2** well-built.

costume (kɔ'stym) *nf* **1** costume. **2** dress. **3** suit (of clothes).

cote (kɔt) *nf* **1** share. **2** number. **3** *comm* quotation.

côte (kot) *nf* **1** rib. **2** coast. **3** hill. **côte à côte** side by side. **côtier, -ière** (ko'tje:, -'tjɛr) *adj* coastal.

côté (ko'te:) *nm* **1** side. **2** way. **3** direction. **à côté de** beside. **à côté l'un de l'autre** or **côte à côte** side by side. **de côté** sideways. **de l'autre côté** on the other side or hand.

coteau, -aux (kɔ'to) *nm* hillside.

côtelette (kot'lɛt) *nf* cutlet, chop.

coter (kɔ'te:) *vt* **1** assess. **2** classify. **3** *comm* quote.

se cotiser (kɔti:'ze:) *vr* **1** subscribe. **2** club together. **cotisation** *nf* **1** subscription. **2** contribution, share.

coton (kɔ'tɔ̃) *nm* **1** cotton. **2** cottonwool.

côtoyer (kotwa'je:) *vt* coast along.

cou (ku:) *nm* neck. **cou-de-pied** *nm, pl* **cous-de-pied** instep.

coucher (ku:'ʃe:) *vt* **1** put to bed. **2** lay down. *vi* sleep. **se coucher** *vr* **1** go to bed. **2** lie down. **coucher** *nm* setting. **coucher du soleil** sunset. **couchant** *adj* setting. *nm* **1** west. **2** decline. **couche** *nf* **1** couch. **2** *pl med* labour. **3** nappy. **4** layer. **couché sociale** social class. **fausse couche** miscarriage. **couché** *adj* **1** lying. **2** in bed. **couchette** *nf* **1** cot. **2** berth.

coucou (ku:'ku:) *nm* cuckoo.

coude (ku:d) *nm* **1** elbow. **2** bend.

coudre* (ku:dr) *vt* sew, stitch.

coudrier (ku:'drje:) *nm* hazel tree.

couenne (kwen) *nf* rind.

couic (kwi:k) *nm* **1** chirp. **2** squeak.

couin-couin (kwɛ̃'kwɛ̃) *nm* quack.

couler (ku:'le:) *vt* **1** pour. **2** strain. **3** sink. **4** cast. *vi* **1** flow, run. **2** leak. **3** sink. **se couler** *vr* slip, glide. **coulant** *adj* running, flowing. **coulé** *adj* (of metal) cast. *nm mus* slur

couleur (ku:'lœr) *nf* **1** colour. **2** paint. **3** *game* suit.

couleuvre (ku:'lœvr) *nf* grass snake.

coulisse (ku:'li:s) *nf* **1** slot. **2** *pl Th* wings. **à coulisse** sliding.

couloir (ku:l'war) *nm* **1** corridor, passage. **2** *pol* lobby.

coup (ku:) *nm* **1** blow. **2** knock. **3** stroke. **4** attempt. **coup de bec** peck. **coup de coude** nudge. **coup de feu** shot. **coup de froid** chill. **coup d'envoi** kick-off. **coup de pied** kick. **coup de soleil** sunstroke. **coup d'œil** glance. **coup illicite** *sport* foul. **du coup** now at last. **du premier coup** at the first attempt. **tout à coup** suddenly.

coupable (ku:'pabl) *adj* guilty. *nm* culprit.

coupe[1] (ku:p) *nf* cup.
coupe[2] (ku:p) *nf* cutting, cut.
couper (ku:ˈpe:) *vt* **1** cut. **2** cross. **3** interrupt, stop. **4** dilute. **se couper** *vr* **1** cut oneself. **2** intersect. **3** contradict oneself. **coupant** *adj* cutting, sharp. **coupure** *nf* **1** cut, gash. **2** cutting.
couperose (ku:pˈroz) *nf* acne.
coupler (ku:ˈple:) *vt* **1** couple. **2** connect. **couple** *nm* pair, couple. *nf* couple, brace.
couplet (ku:ˈplɛ) *nm* verse.
coupon (ku:ˈpɔ̃) *nm* **1** coupon, warrant. **2** piece cut off or detached. **3** *pl* remnants.
cour (ku:r) *nf* **1** court. **2** courtyard. **3** courtship. **4** playground. **cour de ferme** farmyard.
courage (ku:ˈraʒ) *nm* courage, pluck. **courageux, -euse** (ku:raˈʒœ, -ˈʒœz) *adj* brave.
couramment (ku:raˈmɑ̃) *adv* **1** fluently, easily. **2** generally, currently.
courant (ku:ˈrɑ̃) *v* see **courir.** *adj* **1** running. **2** current, present. *nm* **1** current. **2** stream. **3** course. **courant d'air** draught. **être au courant de** know all about. **mettre au courant** inform.
courbature (ku:rbaˈtyr) *nf* **1** stiffness. **2** tiredness. **courbaturé** *adj* **1** stiff. **2** aching.
courber (ku:rˈbe:) *vt* bend, curve. *vi* sag. **se courber** *vr* stoop. **courbe** *nf* curve, bend. **courbé** *adj* curved.
courge (ku:rʒ) *nf* gourd. **courge à la moelle** marrow. **courgette** *nf* courgette.
courir* (ku:ˈri:r) *vi* **1** run. **2** race. **3** be current. *vt* **1** run. **2** hunt. **3** roam. **coureur, -euse** (ku:ˈrœr, -ˈrœz) *nm,f* **1** runner. **2** wanderer.
couronner (ku:rɔˈne:) *vt* **1** crown. **2** cap. **3** award. **couronne** *nf* **1** crown. **2** wreath. **couronnement** *nm* **1** coronation. **2** crowning.
courrier (ku:ˈrje:) *nm* **1** mail, letters. **2** post. **3** messenger. **4** courier.
courroie (ku:rˈwa) *nf* strap.
courroux (ku:ˈru:) *nm* anger.
cours (ku:r) *nm* **1** course. **2** path. **3** circulation. **4** quotation. **5** lesson. **cours de change** rate of exchange. **en cours** in progress, current.
course (ku:rs) *nf* **1** run. **2** race. **3** journey. **4** errand. **5** path. **faire des courses 1** go shopping. **2** run errands.
court[1] (ku:r) *adj* short, brief. *adv* short. **à court de** short of. **tout court** simply, merely.
court[2] (ku:r) *nm* tennis court.
courtier (ku:rˈtje:) *nm* broker.
courtisan (ku:rti:ˈzɑ̃) *nm* courtier.
courtois (ku:rˈtwa) *adj* courteous, polite. **courtoisie** *nf* courtesy.
cousant (ku:sɑ̃) *v* see **coudre.**
cousin[1] (ku:ˈzɛ̃) *nm* cousin. **cousin germain** first cousin.
cousin[2] (ku:ˈzɛ̃) *nm* gnat.
coussin (ku:ˈsɛ̃) *nm* cushion. **coussinet** *nm* pad.
cousu (ku:ˈzy) *v* see **coudre.**
coût (ku:) *nm* cost.
couteau, -aux (ku:ˈto) *nm* knife. **couteau à découper** carving-knife.
coutellerie (ku:tɛlˈri:) *nf* cutlery.
coûter (ku:ˈte:) *vi* cost. **coûter cher/peu** be expensive/cheap. **coûteux, -euse** (ku:ˈtœ, -ˈtœz) *adj* expensive, dear.
coutume (ku:ˈtym) *nf* custom, habit.
couture (ku:ˈtyr) *nf* **1** needlework. **2** seam. **couturier, -ière** (ku:tyˈrje:, -ˈrjɛr) *nm,f* dressmaker.
couvent (ku:ˈvɑ̃) *nm* convent.
couver (ku:ˈve:) *vt* **1** sit on. **2** hatch. **3** brood. *vi* **1** smoulder. **2** brew, be imminent **couvée** *nf* clutch, brood. **couveuse artificielle** *nf* incubator.
couvercle (ku:ˈvɛrkl) *nm* **1** lid. **2** cover.
couvrir* (ku:ˈvri:r) *vt* **1** cover. **2** conceal. **se couvrir** *vr* **1** put on one's hat. **2** become overcast. **couvert** *adj* **1** covered. **2** overcast. *nm* **1** shelter. **2** place at table. **mettre/ôter le couvert** lay/clear the table. **couverture** *nf* **1** cover. **2** rug. **3** blanket. **4** *pl* bedclothes. **couverture de lit** bedspread. **couvre-feu** *nm invar* curfew. **couvre-lit** *nm, pl* **couvre-lits** bedspread.
crabe (krab) *nm* crab.
crac (krak) *interj,nm* **1** crack. **2** snap.
cracher (kraˈʃe:) *vi* spit. *vt* **1** spit out. **2** *sl* cough up. **crachat** *nm* spit.
crachiner (kraʃi:ˈne:) *vi* drizzle.
craie (krɛ) *nf* chalk.
craignant (kreˈɲɑ̃) *v* see **craindre.**
craindre* (krɛ̃dr) *vt* **1** fear, dread. **2** be afraid of.
craint (krɛ̃) *v* see **craindre.**
crainte (krɛ̃t) *nf* fear, dread. **craintif, -ive** (krɛ̃ˈti:f, -ˈti:v) *adj* **1** timid. **2** afraid.
cramoisi (kramwaˈzi:) *adj,nm* crimson.
crampe (krɑ̃p) *nf* cramp.
crampon (krɑ̃ˈpɔ̃) *nm* **1** clamp. **2** stud (for a boot).
cramponner (krɑ̃pɔˈne:) *vt* **1** clamp. **2** *inf* buttonhole. **se cramponner à** *vr* hang on to.
cran (krɑ̃) *nm* **1** notch. **2** catch. **3** *inf* pluck.

crâner (krɑ'ne:) *vi* swagger, swank. **crâne** *nf* skull. *adj* **1** swaggering. **2** plucky.
crapaud (kra'po) *nm* toad.
crapuleux, -euse (krapy'lœ, -'lœz) *adj* **1** lewd. **2** filthy.
craquer (kra'ke:) *vi* **1** crack. **2** crackle. **craquelure** *nf* crack.
crasse (kras) *adj f* gross. *nf* **1** dirt. **2** meanness. **crasseux, -euse** (kra'sœ, -'sœz) *adj* **1** filthy. **2** squalid.
cratère (kra'tɛr) *nm* crater.
cravate (kra'vat) *nf* scarf, necktie.
crayon (krɛ'jɔ̃) *nm* **1** pencil. **2** stick. **3** sketch.
crayonner *vt* **1** make a pencil sketch. **2** note.
créance (kre:'ɑ̃s) *nf* **1** belief. **2** trust. **3** credit.
créateur, -trice (kre:a'tœr, -'tri:s) *adj* creative. *nm,f* **1** creator. **2** inventor.
création (kre:a'sjɔ̃) *nf* creation.
créature (kre:a'tyr) *nf* creature.
crèche (krɛʃ) *nf* **1** crib, manger. **2** day nursery.
crédence (krɛ'dɑ̃s) *nf* sideboard.
crédit (kre:'di:) *nm* **1** credit. **2** trust. **3** influence. **créditeur, -trice** (kre:di:'tœr, -'tri:s) *nm,f* creditor. *adj* credit.
créer (kre:'e:) *vt* **1** create. **2** found.
crémaillère (krɛma'jɛr) *nf* **pendre la crémaillère** have a house-warming.
crématoire (krɛma'twar) **four crématoire** *nm* crematorium.
crème (krɛm) *nf* **1** cream. **2** custard. **3** best.
crémer (kre:'me:) *vi* cream. **crémerie** *nf* dairy.
crénelé (krɛn'le:) *adj* **1** notched. **2** toothed.
crêpe (krɛp) *nf* pancake.
crêper (krɛ'pe:) *vt* fizz. **crépu** *adj* **1** crisp. **2** crinkled.
crépiter (kre:pi:'te:) *vi* crackle.
crépuscule (kre:py'skyl) *nm* dusk, twilight.
cresson (krə'sɔ̃) *nm* cress.
crête (krɛt) *nf* **1** *zool* crest. **2** ridge.
creuser (krœ'ze:) *vt* **1** hollow out. **2** excavate. **3** go deeply into.
creux, creuse (krœ, krœz) *adj* **1** hollow. **2** empty. **3** slack. **4** sunken. *nm* **1** hollow. **2** pit.
crevaison (krəvɛ'zɔ̃) *nf* puncture.
crevasser (krəva'se:) *vt* **1** crack. **2** chap. **crevasse** *nf* **1** crack. **2** crevice.
crever (krə've:) *vi* **1** burst. **2** split. **3** *sl* die. *vt* burst, puncture.
crevette (krə'vɛt) *nf* **1** shrimp. **2** prawn.
cri (kri:) *nm* **1** cry. **2** shout. **3** shriek. **le dernier cri** the latest fashion.
criailler (kri:ɑ'je:) *vi* **1** bawl. **2** whine.
cribler (kri:'ble:) *vt* **1** riddle. **2** sift. **crible** *nm* **1** sieve. **2** riddle.
cric (kri:k) *nm* jack.
cricri (kri:'kri:) *nm zool* cricket.
cricket (kri:'kɛ) *nm sport* cricket.
criée (kri:'e:) *nf* auction.
crier (kri:'e:) *vi* **1** cry. **2** shout. **3** scream. *vt* shout. **criant** *adj* flagrant, gross. **criard** *adj* **1** crying. **2** shrill. **3** loud, flashy.
crime (kri:m) *nm* crime. **criminel, -elle** (kri:mi:'nɛl) *adj* **1** guilty. **2** criminal. *nm,f* criminal. **incendie criminel** *nm* arson.
crin (krɛ̃) *nm* horsehair. **crinière** *nf* mane.
crique (kri:k) *nf* cove.
criquet (kri:'kɛ) *nm* **1** locust. **2** *zool* cricket.
crise (kri:z) *nf* **1** crisis. **2** attack, fit. **3** shortage. **crise cardiaque** heart attack.
crisper (kri'spe:) *vt* **1** contract. **2** clench. **se crisper** *vr* **1** contract. **2** shrivel up. **crispé** *adj* on edge.
crisser (kri:'se:) *vi,vt* **1** grate. **2** grind.
cristal, -aux (kri:'stal, -'sto) *nm* crystal. **cristal taillé** cut glass.
cristalliser (kri:stali:'ze:) *vi,vt* crystallize.
critère (kri:'tɛr) *nm also* **critérium** criterion.
critiquer (kri:ti:'ke:) *vt* **1** criticize. **2** censure. **critique** *adj* **1** critical. **2** crucial. *nf* **1** criticism. **2** censure. *nm* critic.
croasser (krɔa'se:) *vi* croak.
croc (kro) *nm* **1** hook. **2** fang. **3** tusk. **faire** or **donner un croc-en-jambe à** trip.
croche (krɔʃ) *nf mus* quaver.
crochet (krɔ'ʃɛ) *nm* **1** hook. **2** crochet. **3** swerve. **4** *pl* square brackets. **faire du crochet** crochet.
crochu (krɔ'ʃy) *adj* **1** hooked. **2** crooked.
crocodile (krɔkɔ'di:l) *nm* crocodile.
crocus (krɔ'kys) *nm* crocus.
croire* (krwar) *vt* **1** believe. **2** think. **croire à** or **en** believe in.
croisade (krwa'zad) *nf* crusade.
croiser (krwa'ze:) *vt* **1** cross. **2** pass. *vi* **1** fold over. **2** cruise. **croisée** *nf* crossing. **croisement** *nm* **1** crossing. **2** intersection. **croisière** *nf* cruise.
croissance (krwa'sɑ̃s) *nf* growth.
croissant (krwa'sɑ̃) *v see* **croître.** *adj* **1** growing. **2** increasing. **3** rising. *nm* **1** crescent. **2** bread roll in a crescent shape.
croître* (krwatr) *vi* **1** grow. **2** increase. **3** rise.
croix (krwa) *nf* cross. **croix gammée** swastika.
croquer (krɔ'ke:) *vt* **1** crunch. **2** munch. **3**

sketch. **croquant** *adj* crisp. *nm* **1** gristle. **2** crackling.
croquet (krɔ'kɛ) *nm* croquet.
croquis (krɔ'ki:) *nm* sketch.
crosse (krɔs) *nf* **1** crook. **2** *sport* stick, club. **3** butt (of a rifle). **crosse de golf** golf club.
crotter (krɔ'te:) *vt* dirty, soil. **crotte** *nf* **1** dirt. **2** mud. **3** dung. **une crotte de chocolat** a chocolate.
crouler (kru:'le:) *vi* **1** collapse. **2** totter. **3** crumble. **croulement** *nm* collapse.
croupe (kru:p) *nf* **1** rump. **2** ridge. **3** *pl zool* buttocks.
croupir (kru:'pi:r) *vi* **1** wallow. **2** stagnate.
croustiller (kru:sti:'je:) *vi* crunch. **croustillant** *adj* **1** crisp. **2** spicy.
croûte (kru:t) *nf* **1** crust. **2** rind. **3** scab. **casser une croûte** have a snack. **croûton** *nm* piece of crust.
croyance (krwa'jɑ̃s) *nf* belief. **croyable** *adj* **1** credible. **2** trustworthy.
croyant (krwa'jɑ̃) *v* see **croire.** *adj* believing. *nm* believer.
cru [1] (kry) *adj* **1** raw. **2** coarse. **3** crude.
cru [2] (kry) *nm* **1** wine-growing district. **2** vintage.
cru [3] (kry) *v* see **croire.**
crû (kry) *v* see **croire.**
cruauté (kryo'te:) *nf* cruelty.
crucifier (krysi:'fje:) *vt* crucify.
crucifix (krysi:'fi:) *nm* crucifix.
crudité (krydi:'te:) *nf* **1** rawness. **2** crudeness. **3** coarseness.
crue (kry) *nf* **1** rising. **2** flood.
cruel, -elle (kry'ɛl) *adj* cruel.
crûment (kry'mɑ̃) *adv* **1** crudely. **2** roughly.
crustacés (krysta'se:) *nm pl* shellfish.
crypte (kri:pt) *nf* crypt.
cube (kyb) *nm* cube. **cubique** *adj* cubic.
cueillir* (kœ'ji:r) *vt* **1** gather. **2** pick.
cuiller (kyi:'je:) *nf also* **cuillère** spoon. **cuiller à bouche/dessert/pot/thé** tablespoon/dessertspoon/ladle/teaspoon. **cuillerée** *nf* spoonful.
cuir (kɥi:r) *nm* **1** leather. **2** hide. **3** skin. **cuir chevelu** scalp. **cuir verni** patent leather.
cuirasse (kɥi:'ras) *nf* armour. **cuirassé** *adj* armoured, armour-plated. *nm* battleship.
cuire* (kɥi:r) *vt* **1** cook. **2** fire, bake. *vi* **1** cook. **2** smart. **cuire au four** roast, bake. **cuit à point** done to a turn. **cuisant** *adj* **1** burning. **2** smarting. **3** bitter.
cuisine (kɥi:'zi:n) *nf* **1** kitchen. **2** cookery. **3** cooking. **faire la cuisine** cook. **cuisinier, -ière** (kɥi:zi:'nje:, -'njɛr) *nm,f* cook. *nf* cooker.
cuisse (kɥi:s) *nf* thigh. **cuisses de grenouille** *nf pl* frogs' legs.
cuivre (kɥi:vr) *nm* copper. **cuivre jaune** brass.
cul (kyl) *nm* **1** bottom. **2** behind. **3** rump. **cul-de-sac** *nm, pl* **culs-de-sac** dead end, blind alley.
culbuter (kylby'te:) *vi* somersault. *vt* **1** overthrow. **2** tip. **culbute** *nf* **1** somersault. **2** tumble.
culinaire (kyli:'nɛr) *adj* culinary.
culminant (kylmi:'nɑ̃) *adj* highest.
culot (ky'lo) *nm* **1** bottom, base. **2** *sl* cheek.
culotte (ky'lɔt) *nf* **1** shorts. **2** pants.
culpabilité (kylpabi:li:'te:) *nf* guilt.
culte (kylt) *nm* **1** worship. **2** cult.
cultiver (kylti:'ve:) *vt* **1** farm. **2** cultivate. **cultivateur** *nm* farmer. **cultivé** *adj* **1** cultivated. **2** cultured.
culture (kyl'tyr) *nf* **1** culture. **2** cultivation. **culturel, -elle** (kylty'rɛl) *adj* cultural.
cupide (ky'pi:d) *adj* greedy. **cupidité** *nf* greed.
cure (kyr) *nf* **1** care. **2** cure.
curé (ky're:) *nm* parish priest.
curer (ky're:) *vt* **1** pick. **2** clean out. **cure-dents** *nm invar* toothpick.
curieux, -euse (ky'rjœ, -'rjœz) *adj* **1** curious. **2** interested. **3** inquisitive. **4** odd.
curiosité (kyrjɔzi:'te:) *nf* **1** curiosity. **2** peculiarity.
cuver (ky've:) *vi,vt* ferment. **cuve** *nf* **1** vat. **2** tub. **cuve à lessive** copper. **cuvette** *nf* **1** washbasin. **2** basin.
cycle [1] (si:kl) *nm* cycle.
cycle [2] (si:kl) *nm* bicycle. **cycliste** *nm,f* cyclist.
cyclomoteur (si:klomɔ'tœr) *nm* moped.
cyclone (si:'klon) *nm* cyclone.
cygne (si:ɲ) *nm* swan.
cylindre (si:'lɛ̃dr) *nm* cylinder. **cylindre compresseur** steamroller.
cymbale (sɛ̃'bal) *nf* cymbal.
cynique (si:'ni:k) *adj* **1** cynical. **2** brazen. *nm* cynic.
cyprès (si:'prɛ) *nm* cypress.
cypriote (si:pri:'ɔt) *adj,n* Cypriot.

D

dactylographier (dakti:lɔgra'fje:) *vt* type. **dactylographe** *nm,f* typist.
dague (dag) *nf* dagger.

daigner (dɛ'ɲe) *vt* condescend.
daim (dɛ̃) *nm* **1** deer. **2** buck. **3** suede.
dais (dɛ) *nm* canopy.
daller (da'le:) *vt* pave, flag. **dalle** *nf* tile.
daltonien, -ienne (daltɔ'njɛ̃, -'njɛn) *adj* colour-blind. **daltonisme** *nm* colour-blindness.
damas (da'mɑ) *nm* damson.
dame[1] (dam) *interj* **1** indeed! **2** rather!
dame[2] (dam) *nf* **1** lady. **2** *game* queen. **3** *pl* draughts.
damier (da'mje:) *nm* chessboard.
damner (dɑ'ne:) *vt* damn. **damnable** *adj* **1** damnable. **2** frightful.
dandiner (dɑ̃di:'ne:) *vi* strut. **se dandiner** *vr* waddle.
Danemark (dan'mɑrk) *nm* Denmark. **danois** *adj* Danish. *nm* **1** Dane. **2** Danish (language).
danger (dɑ̃'ʒe:) *nm* **1** danger, peril. **2** risk. **dangereux, -euse** (dɑ̃ʒ'rœ, -'rœz) *adj* dangerous.
dans (dɑ̃) *prep* **1** in. **2** within. **3** into. **4** during.
danser (dɑ̃'se:) *vi,vt* dance. **danse** *nf* **1** dance. **2** dancing. **danseur, -euse** (dɑ̃'sœr, -'sœz) *nm,f* dancer.
dard (dar) *nm* **1** dart. **2** sting.
darder (dar'de:) *vt* **1** hurl. **2** dart. **3** shoot out.
dater (da'te:) *vi,vt* date. **date** *nf* date.
datte (dat) *nf bot* date. **dattier** *nm* date palm.
daube (dob) *nf* stew.
dauphin (do'fɛ̃) *nm* **1** dolphin. **2** eldest son of the French king.
davantage (davɑ̃'taʒ) *adv* more, any more.
de (də) *prep* **1** from. **2** of. **3** by. **4** with. **5** in. **6** made of. **7** some.
dé (de:) *nm* **1** dice. **2** tee. **dé (à coudre)** thimble.
débâcle (de:'bɑkl) *nf* **1** collapse, downfall. **2** breaking up.
déballer (de:ba'le:) *vt* unpack.
débander[1] (de:bɑ̃'de:) *vt* **1** relax. **2** unbend.
débander[2] (de:bɑ̃'de:) *vt* disband. **se débander** *vr* disperse. **débandade** *nf* stampede.
débarbouiller (de:barbu:'je:) *vt* wash, clean. **se débarbouiller** *vr* wash one's face.
débarcadère (de:barka'dɛr) *nm* wharf, landing stage.
débardeur (de:bar'dœr) *nm* docker.
débarquer (de:bar'ke:) *vi,vt* **1** land. **2** disembark. *vt* unload. **débarquement** *nm* **1** landing. **2** arrival.
débarras (de:ba'rɑ) *nm* riddance.
débarrasser (de:bara'se:) *vt* **1** rid. **2** free. **3** clear. **se débarrasser de** *vr* get rid of.

débat (de:'ba) *nm* **1** debate. **2** discussion. **3** dispute.
débattre* (de:'batr) *vt* **1** debate. **2** discuss. **se débattre** *vr* struggle.
débaucher (de:bo'ʃe:) *vt* **1** lead astray. **2** discharge. **se débaucher** *vr* go astray, misbehave.
débile (de:'bi:l) *adj* weak, feeble.
débit[1] (de:'bi:) *nm* **1** sale. **2** retail shop. **3** cutting up. **4** delivery. **5** output. **débit de boissons** public house.
débit[2] (de:'bi) *nm* debit.
débiter[1] (de:bi:'te:) *vt* **1** retail. **2** cut up. **3** supply. **4** recite.
débiter[2] (de:bi:'te:) *vt* debit.
déblai (de:'blɛ) *nm* **1** clearing. **2** excavation. **3** rubbish.
déblayer (de:blɛ'je:) *vt* **1** clear. **2** remove.
déboîter (de:bwa'te:) *vt* **1** dislocate. **2** disconnect.
débonnaire (de:bɔ'nɛr) *adj* easygoing.
déborder (de:bɔr'de:) *vi,vt* overflow. *vt* project, protrude. **débordé** *adj* **1** overflowing. **2** busy.
déboucher[1] (de:bu:'ʃe:) *vt* **1** clear. **2** open.
déboucher[2] (de:bu:'ʃe:) *vi* **1** emerge. **2** come from. **débouché** *nm* **1** outlet. **2** opening.
débourser (de:bu:r'se:) *vt* spend.
debout (də'bu:) *adj* **1** upright. **2** standing.
déboutonner (de:bu:tɔ'ne:) *vt* unbutton.
débraillé (de:brɑ'je:) *adj* **1** untidy. **2** slovenly. **3** improper.
débrayer (de:brɛ'je:) *vt* disconnect. *vi* declutch. **débrayage** *nm* **1** disconnecting. **2** *mot* clutch.
débris (de:'bri:) *nm pl* **1** remains. **2** rubbish.
débrouiller (de:bru:'je:) *vt* **1** sort out. **2** extricate. **se débrouiller** *vr* manage.
débuter (de:by'te:) *vi* begin, start. **début** *nm* **1** beginning. **2** first appearance. **débutant** *nm* beginner.
deçà (də'sa) *adv* on this side. **deçà delà** here and there.
décade (dɛ'kad) *nf* decade.
décadent (de:ka'dɑ̃) *adj* **1** decadent. **2** in decay. **décadence** *nf* **1** decline. **2** decay.
décaler (de:ka'le:) *vt* shift, displace. **décalé** *adj* off balance.
décamper (de:kɑ̃'pe:) *vi* **1** *inf* clear off. **2** bolt.
décanter (de:kɑ̃te:) *vt* decant.
décéder (de:se:'de:) *vi* decease, die.
déceler (de:s'le:) *vt* **1** disclose. **2** reveal.
décembre (de:'sɑ̃br) *nm* December.
décent (de:'sɑ̃) *adj* **1** decent. **2** proper.

déception (de:sɛp'sjɔ̃) *nf* **1** deception. **2** disappointment.
décerner (de:sɛr'ne:) *vt* **1** award. **2** confer.
décès (de:'sɛ) *nm* decease, death.
décevoir* (de:sə'vwar) *vt* **1** deceive. **2** disappoint.
déchaîner (de:ʃɛ'ne:) *vt* let loose, loose. **se déchaîner** *vr* break out, rage.
décharger (de:ʃar'ʒe:) *vt* **1** unload. **2** discharge, let off. **décharge** *nf* **1** unloading. **2** discharge. **3** rebate.
décharné (de:ʃar'ne:) *adj* emaciated, skinny.
se déchausser (de:sho'se:) *vr* take off one's shoes.
déchéance (de:ʃe:'ɑ̃s) *nf* **1** fall. **2** downfall. **3** loss.
déchet (de:'ʃɛ) *nm* **1** loss. **2** *pl* waste, scraps.
déchiffrer (de:ʃi:'fre:) *vt* **1** decipher. **2** sight-read.
déchiqueter (de:ʃi:k'te:) *vt* **1** slash. **2** tear. **3** cut.
déchirer (de:ʃi:'re:) *vt* tear. **déchirure** *nf* tear, slit.
déchoir* (de:'ʃwar) *vi* (*aux* être) fall.
décibel (de:si:'bɛl) *nm* decibel.
décider (de:si:'de:) *vt* **1** decide. **2** settle. **3** persuade. **se décider à** *vr* make up one's mind to.
décimale (de:si:'mal) *nf* decimal. **decimal, -aux** (de:si:'mal, -'mo) *adj* decimal.
décisif, -ive (de:si:'si:f, -'si:v) *adj* **1** decisive. **2** critical.
décision (de:si:'zjɔ̃) *nf* **1** decision. **2** determination.
déclarer (de:kla're:) *vt* **1** declare. **2** make known. **déclaration** *nf* declaration.
déclencher (de:klɑ̃'ʃe:) *vt* **1** release. **2** launch.
déclin (de:'klɛ̃) *nm* **1** decline. **2** close. **3** end.
décliner (de:kli:'ne:) *vi,vt* decline. *vt* refuse. **déclinaison** *nf* declension.
décoiffé (de:kwa'fe:) *adj* dishevelled.
décoller (de:kɔ'le:) *vt* loosen. *vi* take off. **se décoller** *vr* work loose. **décollage** *nm* take-off. **décolleté** *adj* low-necked. *nm* neckline.
décolorer (de:kɔlɔ're:) *vt* **1** fade. **2** bleach.
décombres (de:'kɔ̃br) *nm pl* **1** rubbish. **2** ruins.
décommander (de:kɔmɑ̃'de:) *vt* cancel.
décomposer (de:kɔ̃po'ze:) *vt* **1** rot. **2** distort.
décompte (de:'kɔ̃t) *nm* **1** deduction. **2** disappointment.
déconcerter (de:kɔ̃sɛr'te:) *vt* **1** confound. **2** baffle.
décongeler (de:kɔ̃ʒ'le:) *vt* thaw.
déconseiller (de:kɔ̃sɛ'je:) *vt* dissuade.
décontracter (de:kɔ̃trak'te:) *vt* relax.
déconvenue (de:kɔ̃və'ny) *nf* disappointment.
décor (de:'kɔr) *nm* **1** decoration. **2** arrangement. **3** *pl Th* scenery.
décorer (de:kɔ're:) *vt* decorate. **décoration** *nf* **1** medal. **2** decoration.
découper (de:ku:'pe) *vt* **1** cut up. **2** carve. **3** cut out.
décourager (de:ku:ra'ʒe:) *vt* **1** discourage. **2** deter.
décousu (de:ku:'zy) *adj* **1** undone. **2** disconnected. **3** disjointed.
découverte (de:ku:'vɛrt) *nf* discovery.
découvrir (de:ku:'vri:r) *vt* **1** discover. **2** uncover.
décrasser (de:kra'se:) *vt* **1** clean. **2** scour.
décret (de:'krɛ) *nm* decree.
décrire* (de:'kri:r) *vt* describe.
décrocher (de:krɔ'ʃe:) *vt* **1** take down. **2** disconnect.
décroître* (de:'krwatr) *vi* **1** decrease. **2** diminish. **décroissance** *nf* **1** decrease. **2** decline.
dédaigner (de:dɛ'ɲe:) *vt* scorn. **dédaigneux, -euse** (de:dɛ'ɲœ, -'ɲœz) *adj* scornful.
dédain (de:'dɛ̃) *nm* **1** scorn. **2** contempt.
dédale (de:'dal) *nm* maze, labyrinth.
dedans (də'dɑ̃) *adv* inside, within. *nm* **1** inside. **2** interior.
dédier (de:'dje:) *vt* dedicate. **dédicace** *nf* dedication.
dédit (de:'di:) *nm* **1** forfeit. **2** retraction.
dédommager (de:dɔma'ʒe:) *vt* compensate.
déduction (de:dyk'sjɔ̃) *nf* deduction.
déduire* (de:'dɥi:r) *vt* **1** deduce. **2** deduct. **3** infer.
déesse (de:'ɛs) *nf* goddess.
défaillir* (de:fa'ji:r) *vi* **1** grow weak. **2** fail. **3** faint. **défaillance** *nf* **1** lapse. **2** weakness. **3** faint.
défaire* (de:'fɛr) *vt* **1** undo. **2** untie. **3** defeat. **défaite** *nf* defeat.
défalquer (de:fal'ke:) *vt* deduct.
défaut (de:'fo) *nm* **1** defect. **2** fault. **3** lack.
défection (de:fɛk'sjɔ̃) *nf* defection. **defectueux, -euse** (de:fɛk'tɥœ, -'tɥœz) *adj* **1** defective. **2** deficient.
défendre (de:'fɑ̃dr) *vt* **1** defend. **2** protect. **3** forbid.
défense (de:'fɑ̃s) *nf* **1** defence. **2** tusk. **défense de fumer** no smoking.

déférer (de:fɛ'reː) *vt* **1** refer. **2** hand over. **3** confer. *vi* defer. **déférent** *adj* deferential.
défi (de:'fiː) *nm* **1** challenge. **2** defiance.
déficeler (de:fiː'sleː) *vt* untie.
déficit (de:fiː'siː) *nm* **1** deficit. **2** shortage.
défier (de:'fjeː) *vt* **1** challenge. **2** defy. **se défier** *vr* mistrust. **défiance** *nf* **1** mistrust, distrust. **2** suspicion. **défiant** *adj* **1** wary. **2** suspicious.
défigurer (de:fi:gy'reː) *vt* **1** disfigure. **2** distort. **3** deface.
défilé (de:fiː'leː) *nm* **1** pass. **2** procession.
définir (de:fiː'niːr) *vt* define. **défini** *adj* definite. **définitif, -ive** (de:fi:niː'tiːf, -'tiːv) *adj* **1** final. **2** permanent. **définition** *nf* **1** definition. **2** clue.
défoncer (de:fɔ̃'seː) *vt* break up. **se défoncer** *vr* collapse.
déformer (de:fɔr'meː) *vt* **1** deform. **2** distort.
défraîchi (de:frɛ'ʃiː) *adj* **1** faded. **2** soiled.
défricher (de:friː'ʃeː) *vt* **1** clear. **2** reclaim (land).
défunt (de:'fœ̃) *adj* **1** deceased. **2** defunct.
dégager (de:ga'ʒeː) *vt* **1** redeem. **2** clear. **3** release. **dégagé** *adj* **1** free. **2** easy. **3** offhand.
dégarnir (de:gar'niːr) *vt* strip off.
dégât (de:'gɑ) *nm* damage.
dégel (de:'ʒɛl) *nm* thaw.
dégeler (de:'ʒleː) *vi,vt* thaw.
dégénérer (de:ʒe:ne:'reː) *vi* degenerate. **dégénéré** *adj* degenerate.
dégivrer (de:ʒiː'vreː) *vt* defrost.
dégonfler (de:gɔ̃'fleː) *vt* **1** deflate. **2** reduce. **se dégonfler** *vr* **1** collapse. **2** subside. **3** *inf* back down.
dégorger (de:gɔr'ʒeː) *vt* free, clear. *vi* overflow.
dégourdir (de:guːr'diːr) *vt* **1** revive. **2** remove stiffness. **dégourdi** *adj* sharp, astute.
dégoûter (de:guː'teː) *vt* **1** disgust. **2** sicken.
dégrader (de:gra'deː) *vt* **1** degrade. **2** deface. **se dégrader** *vr* lower oneself.
dégrafer (de:gra'feː) *vt* undo.
dégraisser (de:grɛ'seː) *vt* **1** clean. **2** skim the fat off.
degré (də'greː) *nm* **1** degree. **2** step.
dégringoler (de:grɛ̃gɔ'leː) *vi,vt* tumble down. **dégringolade** *nf* **1** tumble. **2** collapse.
dégriser (de:griː'zeː) *vt* sober.
déguenillé (de:gniː'jeː) *adj* ragged, in rags.
déguerpir (de:gɛr'piːr) *vi* **1** move out. **2** clear out or off.
déguiser (de:giː'zeː) *vt* disguise. **déguisement** *nm* **1** disguise. **2** fancy dress.
déguster (de:gy'steː) *vt* taste, sample.
dehors (də'ɔr) *adv* out, outside, outdoors. *nm* outside, exterior.
déité (de:iː'teː) *nf* deity.
déjà (dɛ'ʒa) *adv* **1** already. **2** before. **3** yet.
déjeuner (de:ʒœ'neː) *vi* **1** have lunch. **2** breakfast. *nm* lunch. **petit déjeuner** breakfast.
delà (də'la) *prep* beyond. **par delà** beyond. **au delà de** beyond. **par delà** on the other side. **en delà** further away.
délabré (de:la'breː) *adj* **1** dilapidated. **2** in ruins.
délai (de:'lɛ) *nm* **1** delay. **2** notice.
délaisser (de:lɛ'seː) *vt* **1** forsake, desert. **2** relinquish.
délasser (de:la'seː) *vt* **1** rest. **2** refresh. **délassement** *nm* relaxation.
délateur (dɛla'tœr) *nm* informer.
délavé (de:la'veː) *adj* faded, washed out.
délayer (de:lɛ'jeː) *vt* **1** mix with water. **2** dilute. **3** spin out.
déléguer (de:leː'geː) *vt* **1** delegate. **2** assign. **délégation** *nf* delegation. **délégué** *nm* **1** delegate. **2** deputy.
délibérer (de:liːbeː'reː) *vi* deliberate, ponder. *vt* discuss. **délibération** *nf* **1** discussion. **2** reflection.
délicat (de:liː'ka) *adj* **1** delicate. **2** dainty. **3** sensitive. **4** tricky. **délicatesse** *nf* delicacy.
délice (de:'liːs) *nm* delight. **délicieux, -euse** (de:liː'sjœ, -'sjœz) *adj* delicious.
délier (de:'ljeː) *vt* **1** untie. **2** release. **se délier** *vr* come undone. **délié** *adj* **1** slender. **2** thin.
délinquance (de:lɛ̃'kɑ̃s) *nf* delinquency.
délit (de:'liː) *nm* offence.
délivrer (de:liː'vreː) *vt* **1** deliver. **2** rescue. **délivrance** *nf* rescue.
déloyal, -aux (de:lwa'jal, -'jo) *adj* **1** unfaithful, disloyal. **2** false. **3** unfair.
delta (dɛl'ta) *nm* delta.
déluge (de:'lyʒ) *nm* **1** flood. **2** downpour.
déluré (de:ly'reː) *adj* astute, sharp.
se démailler (de:mɑ'jeː) *vr* (of a stocking) ladder.
demain (də'mɛ̃) *adv,nm* tomorrow. **à demain!** see you tomorrow! **demain en huit** tomorrow week.
demander (dəmɑ̃'deː) *vt* **1** ask. **2** ask for. **3** enquire. **4** want. **5** require. **se demander** *vr* wonder. **demande** *nf* **1** request. **2** question. **3** application. **4** *comm* demand.
démanger (de:mɑ̃'ʒeː) *vi* itch.
démaquiller (de:makiː'jeː) *vt* remove make-up.
démarche (de:'marʃ) *nf* **1** gait, walk. **2** step. **3** proceedings.

démarrer (de:ma're:) *vt* start (a car). *vi* drive off.
démêler (de:me:'le:) *vt* unravel.
démembrer (de:mã'bre:) *vt* cut up.
déménager (de:mɛna'ʒe:) *vi* move house. **déménagement** *nm* removal.
démence (dɛ'mãs) *nf* lunacy.
se démener (de:m'ne:) *vr* struggle.
démentir* (de:mã'ti:r) *vt* **1** contradict. **2** deny. **démenti** *nm* **1** denial. **2** contradiction.
démesuré (de:mzy're:) *adj* **1** huge. **2** excessive.
démettre* (de:'mɛtr) *vt* **1** dislocate. **2** dismiss. **se démettre** *vr* resign.
demeurer (dəmœ're:) *vi (aux* être) **1** live. **2** remain, stay. **au demeurant** *adv* after all. **demeure** *nf* **1** abode. **2** delay. **à demeure** permanent.
demi (də'mi:) *adj,n* half. **à demi** half.
demi-arrière *nm* half-back.
demi-cercle *nm* semicircle.
demi-douzaine *nf* half-a-dozen.
demi-finale *nf* semifinal.
demi-frère *nm* **1** half-brother. **2** stepbrother.
demi-heure *nf* half-hour.
demi-sœur *nf* **1** half-sister. **2** stepsister.
démission (de:mi:'sjɔ̃) *nf* resignation. **donner sa démission** resign.
demi-teinte *nf* halftone.
demi-tour *nm* **1** half-turn. **2** U-turn.
démocratie (de:mɔkra'si:) *nf* democracy. **démocratique** *adj* democratic.
démodé (de:mɔ'de:) *adj* old-fashioned.
demoiselle (dəmwa'zɛl) *nf* **1** young lady. **2** spinster.
démolir (de:mɔ'li:r) *vt* **1** demolish. **2** pull down.
démon (de:'mɔ̃) *nm* demon, fiend.
démonter (de:mɔ̃'te:) *vi* **1** dismantle. **2** upset. **se démonter** *vr* **1** come apart. **2** *inf* get upset.
démontrer (de:mɔ̃'tre:) *vt* **1** demonstrate. **2** prove.
démoraliser (de:mɔrali:'ze:) *vt* **1** demoralize. **2** dishearten.
démordre (de:'mɔrdr) *vi* **1** let go. **2** give up.
démuni (de:my'ni:) *adj*. **démuni de** short, out of.
dénaturé (de:naty're:) *adj* unnatural.
dénégation (de:nega'sjɔ̃) *nf* denial.
dénicher (de:ni:'ʃe:) *vt* find, discover.
denier (də'nje:) *nm* small coin, penny.
dénigrer (de:ni:'gre:) *vt* disparage.
dénombrement (de:nɔ̃brə'mã) *nm* **1** census. **2** count.
dénominateur (de:nɔmi:na'tœr) *nm* denominator.
dénomination (de:nɔmi:na'sjɔ̃) *nf* denomination.
dénommer (de:nɔ'me:) *vt* name.
dénoncer (de:nɔ̃'se:) *vt* **1** denounce. **2** declare. **3** betray.
dénoter (de:nɔ'te:) *vt* denote.
dénouer (de:'nwe:) *vt* **1** undo, untie. **2** untangle. **se dénouer** *vr* **1** come undone. **2** end. **dénouement** *nm* **1** end. **2** outcome.
denrée (dã're:) *nf* commodity.
densité (dãsi:'te:) *nf* density.
dent (dã) *nf* **1** tooth. **2** prong. **3** cog. **avoir une dent contre** bear a grudge against. **dentaire** *adj* dental. **dental, -aux** (dã'tal, -'to) *adj* dental.
denteler (dãt'le:) *vt* **1** notch. **2** indent.
dentelle *nf* lace.
dentier (dã'tje:) *nm* denture.
dentifrice (dãti:'fri:s) *nm* toothpaste.
dentiste (dã'ti:st) *nm,f* dentist.
dénuder (de:ny'de:) *vt* **1** strip. **2** lay bare.
dénuer (de:'nɥe:) *vt* strip. **se dénuer de** *vr* part with. **dénué** *adj* **1** devoid. **2** destitute.
dépanner (de:pa'ne:) *vt* **1** repair. **2** help out.
dépaqueter (de:pak'te:) *vt* unpack.
dépareillé (de:parɛ'je:) *adj* **1** odd. **2** ill-assorted.
départ (de:'par) *nm* **1** departure. **2** start.
département (de:partə'mã) *nm* department.
départir (de:par'ti:r) *vt* **1** divide. **2** allot. **se départir de** *vr* **1** deviate from. **2** part with.
dépasser (de:pa'se:) *vt* **1** pass beyond. **2** exceed. **3** overtake.
dépaysé (de:pe:i:'ze:) *adj* **1** lost. **2** bewildered.
dépêcher (de:pe:'ʃe:) *vt* dispatch. **se dépêcher** *vr* hurry, make haste. **dépêche** *nf* **1** dispatch. **2** telegram.
dépeindre* (de:'pɛ̃dr) *vt* **1** depict. **2** describe.
dépendre[1] (de:'pãdr) *vi* **dépendre de** **1** depend on. **2** be subject to. **3** belong to.
dépendre[2] (de:'pãdr) *vt* take down.
dépens (de:'pã) *nm pl law* costs.
dépenser (de:pã'se:) *vt* spend. **dépense** *nf* **1** expense. **2** expenditure. **dépensier, -ière** (de:pã'sje', -'sjɛr) *adj* extravagant. *nm,f* spendthrift.
dépérir (de:pe:'ri:r) *vi* **1** waste away. **2** decay.
dépêtrer (de:pe:'tre:) *vt* extricate.
dépister (de:pi:'ste:) *vt* **1** track down. **2** outwit.
dépit (de:'pi:) *nm* **1** spite. **2** resentment.
déplacer (de:pla'se:) *vt* **1** displace. **2** take the

place of. **se déplacer** *vr* **1** move. **2** travel. ~*nm* **1** displacement. **2** transfer. **3** travelling.

déplaire* (de:'plɛr) *vt* **1** displease. **2** offend. **se déplaire à** *vr* dislike.

déplantoir (de:plan'twar) *nm* trowel.

déplier (de:pli:'e:) *vt* unfold.

déplorer (de:'plɔre:) *vt* **1** deplore. **2** regret. **3** mourn.

déployer (de:plwa'je:) *vt* **1** spread out. **2** display.

déplumer (de:ply'me:) *vt* pluck. **se déplumer** *vr* moult.

déporter (de:pɔr'te:) *vt* deport.

déposer[1] (de:po'ze:) *vt* **1** lay down. **2** deposit.

déposer[2] (de:po'ze:) *vt* depose.

dépositaire (de:pɔzi:'tɛr) *nm* trustee. **dépositaire de journaux** newsagent.

dépot (de:'po) *nm* **1** deposit. **2** trust. **3** store, depot. **4** sediment.

dépouiller (de:pu:'je:) *vt* **1** skin, strip. **2** deprive. **se dépouiller** *vr* cast off, shed. **dépouille** *nf* **1** skin, hide. **2** remains.

dépourvu (de:pu:r'vy) *adj* **1** destitute. **2** devoid. **au dépourvu** unawares.

dépraver (de:pra've:) *vt* deprave.

déprécier (de:pre:'sje:) *vt* **1** depreciate. **2** underrate. **3** disparage.

dépression (de:prɛ'sjɔ̃) *nf* **1** depression. **2** fall. **3** hollow. **4** gloom. **dépression nerveuse** nervous breakdown.

déprimer (de:pri:'me:) *vt* depress.

depuis (də'pɥi:) *prep* **1** since. **2** for. **3** from. **depuis lors** ever since. **depuis que** since.

députation (de:pyta'sjɔ̃) *nf* deputation.

député (de:py'te:) *nm* **1** deputy. **2** member of parliament.

déraciner (de:rasi:'ne:) *vt* uproot.

dérailler (de:ra'je:) *vi* become derailed.

déraisonnable (de:rɛzɔ'nabl) *adj* **1** unreasonable. **2** irrational.

déranger (de:rɑ̃ʒe:) *vt* **1** disturb. **2** trouble. **3** upset. **se déranger** *vr* **1** make way. **2** put oneself out.

déraper (de:ra'pe:) *vi* skid.

derechef (dəre:'ʃɛf) *adv* a second time, once more.

dérégler (de:re:'gle:) *vt* **1** upset. **2** put out of order. **déréglé** *adj* **1** out of order. **2** irregular. **3** immoral.

dérision (de:ri:'zjɔ̃) *nf* ridicule, mockery. **dérisoire** *adj* ridiculous.

dériver[1] (de:ri:'ve:) *vt* **1** divert. **2** derive. *vi* be diverted.

deriver[2] (de:ri:'ve:) *vi* drift. **dérive** *nf* drift.

dernier, -ière (dɛr'nje:, -'njɛr) *adj* **1** last, latest. **2** latter. **3** utmost. **4** extreme.

dérober (de:rɔ'be:) *vt* **1** steal. **2** hide. **se dérober** *vr* **1** escape. **2** evade. **3** give way. **dérobé** *adj* **1** secret. **2** hidden.

dérogatoire (de:rɔga'twar) *adj* derogatory.

dérouiller (de:ru:'je:) *vt* rub the rust off. **se dérouiller** *vr* brush up.

dérouler (de:ru:'le:) *vt* **1** unwind. **2** unfold. **se dérouler** *vr* **1** unfold. **2** happen.

dérouter (de:ru:'te:) *vt* **1** lead astray. **2** baffle. **3** divert. **déroute** *nf* rout, defeat.

derrière (dɛr'jɛr) *prep* behind. *adv* behind, at the back. *nm* **1** rear. **2** *inf* behind.

des (de:) contraction of **de les.**

dès (dɛ) *prep* **1** from. **2** since. **dès lors** ever since. **dès que 1** as soon as. **2** when.

désabuser (de:zaby'ze:) *vt* disillusion.

désaccord (de:za'kɔr) *nm* **1** disagreement. **2** clash **3** *mus* discord.

désagréable (de:zagre:'abl) *adj* **1** disagreeable. **2** unpleasant. **3** offensive.

désagréger (de:zagre:'ʒe:) *vt* disintegrate.

désagrément (de:zagre:'mɑ̃) *nm* trouble.

se désaltérer (de:zalte:'re:) *vr* quench one's thirst.

désappointer (de:zapwɛ̃'te:) *vt* disappoint.

désapprobation (de:zaprɔba'sjɔ̃) *nf* disapproval.

désapprouver (de:zapru:'ve:) *vt* disapprove of.

désarmer (de:zar'me:) *vt* disarm.

désarroi (de:za'rwa) *nm* disorder, confusion.

désassocier (de:zasɔ'sje:) *vt* dissociate.

désassorti (de:zasɔr'ti:) *adj* made up of odd pieces.

désastre (de:'zastr) *nm* disaster.

désavantage (de:zavɑ̃'taʒ) *nm* disadvantage, drawback.

désaveu, -eux (de:za'vœ) *nm* denial.

désavouer (de:za'vwe:) *vt* **1** repudiate. **2** disown.

désaxé (de:zak'se:) *adj* eccentric.

descendre (dɛ'sɑ̃dr) *vi* (*aux* être) **1** descend. **2** come or go down. **3** alight. *vt* **1** go down. **2** take or bring down. **descendant** *adj* descending, downward. *nm* descendant.

descente (dɛ'sɑ̃t) *nf* **1** descent. **2** slope. **3** raid. **descente de lit** bedside rug.

description (de:skrip'sjɔ̃) *nf* description.

désembarquer (de:zɑ̃bar'ke:) *vi,vt* disembark.

désemparer (de:zɑ̃pa're:) *vt* **1** disable. **2** undo.

sans désemparer without stopping. **désemparé** *adj* 1 in distress. 2 crippled.
désencombrer (de:zɑ̃kɔ̃'bre:) *vt* 1 clear. 2 free.
désenfler (de:zɑ̃'fle:) *vt* deflate. *vi* go down.
désengager (de:zɑ̃ga'ʒe:) *vt* release, free.
désert (de:'zɛr) *adj* 1 deserted. 2 lonely. *nm* 1 desert. 2 wilderness.
déserter (de:zɛr'te:) *vt* desert.
désespérer (de:zɛspe:'re:) *vi* despair. *vt* drive to despair. **désespéré** *adj* 1 desperate. 2 hopeless.
désespoir (de:zɛ'spwar) *nm* despair.
déshabiller (de:zabi:'je:) *vt* undress.
déshériter (de:ze:ri:'te:) *vt* disinherit.
déshonnête (de:zɔ'nɛt) *adj* indecent, improper.
déshonneur (de:zɔ'nœr) *nm* 1 disgrace. 2 dishonour.
déshonorer (de:zɔnɔ're:) *vt* 1 dishonour, disgrace. 2 disfigure.
déshydrater (de:zi:dra'te:) *vt* dehydrate.
désigner (de:zi'ɲe:) *vt* 1 designate, show. 2 appoint. **désignation** *nf* 1 designation. 2 description. 3 appointment.
désinfecter (de:zɛ̃fɛk'te:) *vt* disinfect. **désinfectant** *adj,nm* disinfectant.
désintégrer (de:zɛ̃te'gre:) *vt* disintegrate.
désinvolte (de:zɛ̃'vɔlt) *adj* 1 easy. 2 casual. 2 cheeky.
désir (de:'zi:r) *nm* desire, wish. **désireux, -euse** (de:zi:'rœ, -'rœz) *adj* eager, anxious.
désirer (de:zi:'re:) *vt* desire, wish.
désobéir (de:zɔbe:'i:r) *vt* disobey. **désobéissant** *adj* disobedient.
désodorisant (de:zɔdɔri:'zɑ̃) *nm* deodorant.
désœuvré (dezœ'vre:) *adj* idle.
désoler (de:zɔ'le:) *vt* 1 distress, grieve. 2 desolate. 3 devastate. **se désoler** *vr* grieve. **désolé** *adj* 1 desolate, dreary. 2 grieved, sad, sorry.
désordonné (de:zɔrdɔ'ne:) *adj* 1 untidy. 2 wild, extravagant.
désordre (de:'zɔrdr) *nm* 1 disorder. 2 *pl* riots.
désorganisé (de:zɔrgani:'ze:) *adj* disorganized.
désorienter (de:zɔrjɑ̃'te:) *vt* bewilder. **se désorienter** *vr* 1 lose one's bearings. 2 get confused.
désormais (de:zɔr'mɛ) *adv* from now on.
désosser (de:zo'se:) *vt* bone.
dessécher (de:se:'ʃe:) *vt* 1 dry. 2 wither. **se déssecher** *vr* wither, dry up.
dessein (dɛ'sɛ̃) *nm* 1 plan, scheme. 2 intention.
desserrer (de:sɛ're:) *vt* 1 loosen. 2 unscrew.
dessert (de:'sɛr) *nm* dessert.
desservir (de:sɛr'vi:r) *vt* 1 clear (the table). 2 do a bad turn. 3 serve, connect.
dessin (de:'sɛ̃) *nm* 1 drawing. 2 design. **dessin animé** (cinema) cartoon. **dessinateur** *nm* 1 designer. 2 draughtsman.
dessiner (de:si:'ne:) *vt* 1 draw, sketch. 2 design. 3 outline. **se dessiner** *vr* stand out.
dessous (də'su:) *prep,adv* below, beneath, underneath. *nm* 1 underneath. 2 lower part. **avoir le dessous** get the worst of it. **dessous de plat** tablemat.
dessus (də'sy) *prep,adv* 1 above, over. 2 on. **de dessus** from, off. **en dessus** on top. *~nm* top. **avoir le dessus** have the upper hand. **dessus de cheminée** mantelpiece.
destin (dɛ'stɛ̃) *nm* destiny, fate.
destiner (dɛsti:'ne:) *vt* 1 destine. 2 intend. **destination** *nf* destination. **destinée** *nf* destiny.
destituer (dɛsti:'tɥe:) *vt* dismiss.
destruction (dɛstryk'sjɛ̃) *nf* destruction.
désuet, -ète (de:'sɥɛ, -'sɥɛt) *adj* obsolete.
désunir (de:zy'ni:r) *vt* 1 divide. 2 detach.
détacher[1] (de:ta'ʃe:) *vt* 1 detach. 2 untie, undo. **se détacher** *vr* come undone. **se détacher de** *vr* break away from.
détacher[2] (de:ta'ʃe:) *vt* remove stains from.
détail (de:'taj) *nm* 1 detail. 2 retail.
détailler (de:ta'je:) *vt* 1 cut up. 2 retail. 3 relate in detail.
détective (de:tɛk'ti:v) *nm* detective.
déteindre* (de:'tɛ̃dr) *vi* lose colour, run.
détendre (de:'tɑ̃dr) *vt* slacken, relax. **se détendre** *vr* 1 relax. 2 spring out.
détenir (de:t'ni:r) *vt* 1 hold. 2 detain. 3 withhold. **détenu** *nm* prisoner.
détente (de:'tɑ̃t) *nf* 1 relaxation. 2 easing (of a political situation). 3 trigger.
détergent (de:tɛr'ʒɑ̃) *nm* detergent.
détériorer (de:te:rjɔ're:) *vt* damage, spoil. **se détériorer** *vr* deteriorate.
déterminer (de:tɛrmi:'ne:) *vt* 1 determine. 2 fix. 3 bring about. **déterminer de** decide to. **se déterminer** *vr* make up one's mind. **détermination** *nf* determination. **déterminé** *adj* 1 resolute. 2 specific.
déterrer (de:tɛ're:) *vt* 1 dig up. 2 discover.
détester (de:tɛ'ste:) *vt* detest.
détoner (de:tɔ'ne:) *vi* detonate. **détonant** *adj,nm* explosive.
détonner (de:tɔ'ne:) *vi* 1 be out of tune. 2 clash.
détour (de:'tu:r) *nm* 1 detour. 2 curve.

détourner (de:tu:r'ne:) *vt* **1** divert. **2** turn away. **3** embezzle. **4** hijack. **détournement** *nm* diversion.

détraqué (de:tra'ke:) *adj* **1** out of order. **2** crazy.

détremper (de:trã'pe:) *vt* **1** moisten. **2** soak.

détresse (de:'trɛs) *nf* distress.

détritus (de:tri:'tys) *nm* refuse.

détruire* (de:'trɥi:r) *vt* **1** demolish. **2** destroy. **3** overthrow.

dette (dɛt) *nf* debt.

deuil (dœj) *nm* mourning.

deux (dœ) *adj,nm* two. **tous les deux** both. **tous les deux jours** every other day. **deux-points** *nm* colon. **deuxième** *adj* second.

dévaler (de:va'le:) *vi,vt* rush down. *vi* descend.

dévaliser (de:vali:'ze:) *vt* rob, burgle.

dévaluer (de:va'lɥe:) *vt* devalue.

devancer (dəvã'se:) *vt* precede. **2** leave behind. **3** forestall. **devancier, -ière** (dəvã'sje:, -'sjɛr) *nm,f* predecessor.

devant (də'vã) *prep* before, in front of. *adv* in front, ahead. *nm* front. **devanture** *nf* **1** front. **2** window.

dévaster (de:va'ste:) *vt* devastate.

développer (de:viɔ'pe:) *vt* **1** develop. **2** spread out. **3** explain.

devenir* (dəv'ni:r) *vi* (*aux* être) become, grow, get.

dévers (de:'vɛr) *nm* **1** slope. **2** warp.

déverser (de:vɛr'se:) *vt* **1** pour. **2** dump.

dévêtir (de:ve:'ti:r) *vt* strip, undress.

dévier (de:'vje:) *vi* **1** deviate. **2** swerve. **déviation** *nf* **1** deviation. **2** diversion. **3** bypass.

deviner (dəvi:'ne:) *vt* guess. **devinette** *nf* riddle.

devis (də'vi:) *nm* estimate.

dévisager (de:vi:za'ʒe:) *vt* stare at.

devise (də'vi:z) *nf* **1** motto. **2** slogan. **3** currency.

dévisser (de:vi:'se:) *vt* unscrew.

dévoiler (de:vwa'le:) *vt* reveal.

devoir* (də'vwar) *vt* **1** have to, must. **2** owe. *nm* **1** duty. **2** task. **3** exercise. **4** *pl* homework.

dévorer (de:vɔ're:) *vt* devour.

dévot (de:'vo) *adj* devout, religious. *nm* religious person. **faux dévot** hypocrite.

dévouer (de:'vwe:) *vt* **1** dedicate. **2** devote. **dévouement** *nm* devotion.

dextérité (dɛkste:ri:'te:) *nf* skill.

diabète (dja'bɛt) *nm* diabetes.

diable (djabl) *nm* devil. **diablerie** *nf* mischief, fun.

diagonal, -aux (djagɔ'nal, -'no) *adj* diagonal. **diagonale** *nf* diagonal.

dialecte (dja'lɛkt) *nm* dialect.

dialogue (dja'lɔg) *nm* dialogue.

diamant (dja'mã) *nm* diamond.

diamètre (dja'mɛtr) *nm* diameter.

diaphragme (dja'fragm) *nm* diaphragm.

diapositive (diapɔzi:'ti:v) *nf phot* slide.

diaprer (dja'pre:) *vt* mottle.

diarrhée (dja're:) *nf* diarrhoea.

dictateur (di:kta'tœr) *nm* dictator. **dictature** *nf* dictatorship.

dicter (di:k'te:) *vt* dictate. **dictée** *nf* dictation.

dictionnaire (di:ksjɔ'nɛr) *nm* dictionary.

dicton (di:k'tɔ̃) *nm* maxim, saying.

dièse (djɛz) *nm mus* sharp.

diète (djɛt) *nm pol* diet.

dieu, dieux (djœ) *nm* god.

diffamer (di:ffa'me:) *vt* **1** slander. **2** libel.

différence (di:fe:'rãs) *nf* difference. **à la différence de** contrary to. **différent** *adj* different.

différencier (di:fɛrã'sje:) *vt* differentiate.

différend (di:fe:'rã) *nm* difference, dispute.

différentiel, -elle (di:fe:rã'sjɛl) *adj,nf* differential.

différer (di:fe:'re:) *vt* **1** defer. **2** put off. *vi* differ.

difficile (di:fi:'si:l) *adj* difficult. **difficulté** *nf* difficulty.

difforme (di:'fɔrm) *adj* deformed.

diffuser (di:fy'ze:) *vt* **1** spread. **2** broadcast.

digérer (di:ʒe:'re:) *vt* **1** digest. **2** assimilate.

digestion (di:ʒɛs'tjɔ̃) *nf* digestion.

digitale (di:ʒi:'tal) **digitale pourprée** *nf* foxglove.

digne (di:ɲ) *adj* **1** worthy. **2** dignified. **digne d'éloges** praiseworthy. **digne de remarque** noteworthy.

dignité (di:ɲi:'te:) *nf* dignity.

digue (di:g) *nf* **1** embankment. **2** dam. **3** jetty. **4** obstacle.

dilapider (di:lapi:'de:) *vt* squander.

dilater (di:la'te:) *vt* expand.

dilemme (di:'lɛm) *nm* dilemma.

diligent (di:li:'ʒã) *adj* **1** diligent. **2** industrious. **3** busy.

diluer (di:'lɥe:) *vt* dilute.

dimanche (di:'mãʃ) *nm* Sunday. **dimanche des rameaux** Palm Sunday.

dimension (dimã'sjɔ̃) *nf* **1** dimension, size. **2** *pl* measurements.

diminuer (di:mi:'nɥe:) *vt* **1** diminish. **2** reduce

vi **1** decrease. **2** abate. **diminutif, -ive** (di:mi:ny'ti:f, -'ti:v) *adj,nm* diminutive. **diminution** *nf* decrease.
dindon (dɛ̃'dɔ̃) *nm* turkey.
dîner (di:'ne:) *vi* dine, have dinner. *nm* dinner.
dingue (dɛ̃g) *adj inf* daft, mad.
dinosaure (di:nɔ'sɔr) *nm* dinosaur.
diocèse (djɔ'sɛz) *nm* diocese.
diphtongue (di:f'tɔ̃g) *nf* diphthong.
diplomatie (di:plɔma'si:) *nf* diplomacy. **diplomate** *nm* diplomat. **diplomatique** *adj* diplomatic.
diplôme (di:'plom) *nm* diploma. **diplômé** *nm* graduate.
dire* (di:r) *vt* **1** say. **2** tell. **c'est à dire** that is to say.
direct (di:rɛkt) *adj* **1** direct. **2** straight.
directeur (di:rɛk'tœr) *nm* **1** director. **2** manager. **3** headmaster. **4** governor.
direction (di:rɛk'sjɔ̃) *nf* **1** direction. **2** management. **3** steering.
diriger (di:ri:'ʒe:) *vt* **1** manage. **2** direct. **3** aim. **se diriger vers** *vr* go towards.
discerner (di:sɛr'ne:) *vt* discern, distinguish.
disciple (di:'si:pl) *nm* disciple.
discipline (di:si'pli:n) *nf* discipline, order.
discontinuer (di:skɔ̃ti:'nɥe:) *vi,vt* discontinue.
discorde (di:s'kɔrd) *nf* discord.
discothèque (diskɔ'tɛk) *nf* **1** discotheque. **2** record library.
discours (di:'sku:r) *nm* **1** talk. **2** speech.
discret, -ète (di'skrɛ, -skrɛt) *adj* **1** discreet. **2** quiet. **discrétion** *nf* discretion.
discriminer (di:skrimi:'ne:) *vt* discriminate.
discussion (di:sky'sjɔ̃) *nf* **1** discussion. **2** debate.
discuter (di:sky'te:) *vt* **1** discuss. **2** question.
disette (di:'zɛt) *nf* scarcity. **disette d'eau** drought.
disgrâce (di:z'grɑs) *nf* disgrace.
disgracieux, -euse (di:zgra'sjœ, -'sjœz) *adj* **1** awkward. **2** uncouth. **3** unsightly.
disloquer (di:slɔ'ke:) *vt* dislocate. **se disloquer** *vr* break up.
disparaître* (di:spa'rɛtr) *vi* (*aux* être or avoir) **1** disappear. **2** vanish. **disparu** *adj* **1** missing. **2** extinct.
disparate (di:spa'rat) *adj* dissimilar.
dispendieux, -euse (di:spɑ̃'djœ, -'djœz) *adj* expensive.
dispenser (di:spɑ̃'se:) *vt* **1** exempt. **2** dispense. **se dispenser de** *vr* get out of, excuse oneself. **dispensaire** *nm* dispensary.
disperser (di:spɛr'se:) *vt* scatter, disperse.
disponible (di:spɔ'ni:bl) *adj* **1** available. **2** free. **3** vacant.
dispos (di:'spo) *adj* fit, active.
disposer (di:spo'ze:) *vt* **1** dispose. **2** arrange. **disposer de** have at one's disposal. **se disposer à** *vr* be ready to. **disposition** *nf* **1** disposition. **2** arrangement. **3** disposal. **4** tendency. **5** *pl* provisions.
dispositif (di:spozi:'ti:f) *nm* apparatus, device.
disputer (di:spy'te:) *vt* **1** discuss. **2** dispute, argue. *vi* quarrel. **se disputer** *vr* argue, quarrel. **dispute** *nf* dispute, quarrel.
disqualifier (di:skali:'fje:) *vt* disqualify.
disque (di:sk) *nf* **1** disc. **2** record.
dissemblable (di:sɑ̃'blabl) *adj* dissimilar, different.
disséminer (di:se:mi:'ne:) *vt* scatter, spread.
dissentiment (di:sɑ̃ti:'mɑ̃) *nm* dissent.
disséquer (di:se:'ke:) *vt* dissect.
dissimuler (di:si:my'le:) *vt* **1** conceal. **2** disguise. **se dissimuler** *vr* hide. **dissimulation** *nf* deceit.
dissiper (di:si:'pe:) *vt* **1** waste. **2** dispel.
dissoudre* (di:'su:dr) *vt* dissolve. **se dissoudre** *vr* **1** melt. **2** break up.
dissuader (di:sɥa'de:) *vt* dissuade. **forces de dissuasion** *nf pl mil* deterrent.
distance (di:'stɑ̂s) *nf* distance. **distant** *adj* **1** distant. **2** aloof.
distiller (di:sti:'le:) *vt* distil.
distinct (di:'stɛ̃) *adj* **1** distinct, clear. **2** separate. **distinctif, -ive** (di:stɛ̃k'ti:f, -'ti:v) *adj* distinctive. **distinction** *nf* **1** distinction. **2** honour. **3** rank.
distinguer (di:stɛ̃'ge:) *vt* **1** distinguish. **2** discern. **3** honour. **distingué** *adj* **1** eminent. **2** refined.
distraire* (di'strɛr) *vt* **1** divert, take out. **2** distract. **3** entertain. **se distraire** *vr* amuse oneself. **distrait** *adj* absent-minded.
distribuer (di:stri:'bɥe:) *vt* **1** distribute. **2** give out. **3** deliver. **distribution** *nf* **1** distribution. **2** delivery.
divaguer (di:va'ge:) *vi* **1** wander. **2** ramble.
divan (di:'vɑ̃) *nm* **1** divan. **2** couch.
diverger (di:vɛr'ʒe:) *vi* diverge.
divers (di:'vɛr) *adj* **1** changing. **2** diverse, sundry. **3** varied.
divertir (di:vɛr'ti:r) *vt* entertain. **divertissement** *nm* entertainment, recreation.
dividende (di:vi:'dɑ̃d) *nm* dividend.
divin (di:'vɛ̃) *adj* divine, holy.

diviser (di:vi:'ze:) *vt* divide. **divisible** *adj* divisible. **division** *nf* **1** division. **2** department. **3** discord.
divorcer (di:vɔr'se:) *vi* divorce. **divorce** *nm* divorce.
divulguer (di:vyl'ge:) *vt* divulge, disclose.
dix (di:s, di:) *adj,nm* ten. **dixième** *adj* tenth.
dix-huit *adj,nm* eighteen. **dix-huitième** *adj* eighteenth.
dix-neuf *adj,nm* nineteen. **dix-neuvième** *adj* nineteenth.
dix-sept *adj,nm* seventeen. **dix-septième** *adj* seventeenth.
dizaine (di:'zɛn) *nf* about ten.
docile (dɔ'si:l) *adj* docile, manageable.
docte (dɔkt) *adj* learned.
docteur (dɔk'tœr) *nm* doctor.
doctrine (dɔk'tri:n) *nf* doctrine.
document (dɔky'mɑ̃) *nm* document. **documentaire** *adj,nm* documentary.
documenter (dɔkymɑ̃'te:) *vt* document.
dodo (dɔ'do) *nm inf* sleep. **faire dodo** go to sleep.
dodu (dɔ'dy) *adj* plump.
dogmatique (dɔgma'ti:k) *adj* dogmatic.
dogme (dɔgm) *nm* dogma.
doigt (dwa) *nm* **1** finger. **2** digit. **doigt de pied** toe. **doigté** *nm* **1** *inf* tact. **2** *mus* fingering.
dois (dwa) *v* see **devoir.**
doit (dwa) *nm* debit.
dol (dɔl) *nm* fraud.
doléances (dɔle:'ɑ̃s) *nf pl* complaints.
dollar (dɔ'lar) *nm* dollar.
Dolomites (dɔlɔ'mi:t) *nf pl* Dolomites.
domaine (dɔ'mɛn) *nm* **1** domain, estate. **2** scope, field.
dôme (dom) *nm* dome.
domestiquer (dɔmɛsti:'ke:) *vt* domesticate. **domestique** *adj* domestic. *nm,f* servant.
domicile (dɔmi:'si:l) *nm* residence, abode.
dominer (dɔmi:'ne:) *vi* rule. *vt* **1** dominate. **2** master. **3** overlook. **dominant** *adj* **1** ruling. **2** dominant. **domination** *nf* rule.
dominion (dɔmi:'njɔ̃) *nm* dominion.
dommage (dɔ'maʒ) *nm* damage, harm. **quel dommage!** what a pity! **dommages-intérêts** *nm pl* damages.
dompter (dɔ̃'te:) *vt* **1** tame. **2** subdue.
don (dɔ̃) *nm* **1** gift, present. **2** talent.
donc (dɔ̃k) *conj* therefore, so. *adv* **1** well. **2** just.
donner (dɔ'ne:) *vt* **1** give. **2** donate. **3** *game* deal. **4** provide. **donner contre** run into. **donner dans** fall into. **donner sur** look out onto. **s'en donner** *vr* enjoy oneself. **donne** *nf game* deal. **donnée** *nf* **1** fundamental idea. **2** *pl* data.
dont (dɔ̃) *pron* **1** of whom or which. **2** by, with, from whom or which. **3** whose.
dorénavant (dɔre:na'vɑ̃) *adv* from now on.
dorer (dɔ're:) *vt* **1** gild. **2** brown.
dorloter (dɔrlɔ'te:) *vt* **1** fondle, cuddle. **2** pamper.
dormir* (dɔr'mi:r) *vi* sleep, be asleep. **dormant** *adj* **1** sleeping. **2** dormant. **3** stagnant.
dors (dɔr) *v* see **dormir.**
dortoir (dɔr'twar) *nm* dormitory.
dorure (dɔ'ryr) *nf* gilt, gilding.
dos (do) *nm* back.
dose (doz) *nf* dose. **dosage** *nm* dosage.
dossier (do'sje:) *nm* **1** file. **2** record. **3** back (of a chair).
dot (dɔt) *nf* dowry.
doter (dɔ'te:) *vt* endow.
douane (dwan) *nf* customs.
doubler (du:'ble:) *vt* **1** double. **2** line. **3** overtake. **4** quicken. **5** understudy. **double** *adj,nm* double, duplicate. **doublure** *nf* **1** lining. **2** understudy.
douceur (du:'sœr) *nf* **1** sweetness. **2** softness. **3** comfort. **4** gentleness.
douche (du:ʃ) *nf* shower (bath).
douer (dwe:) *vt* endow. **doué** *adj* gifted.
douille (du:j) *nf* **1** socket. **2** case, casing. **3** sleeve.
douillet, -ette (du:'jɛ, -'jɛt) *adj* **1** soft. **2** delicate.
douleur (du:'lœr) *nf* **1** pain. **2** sorrow. **douloureux, -euse** (du:lu:'rœ, -'rœz) *adj* **1** sore, painful. **2** sad, distressing.
douter (du:'te:) *vi* doubt. **se douter de** *vr* suspect. **doute** *nm* **1** doubt. **2** misgiving. **mettre en doute** question. **douteux, -euse** (du:'tœ, -'tœz) *adj* **1** uncertain. **2** dubious.
douve (du:v) *nf* **1** ditch. **2** moat.
Douvres (du:vr) *nf* Dover.
doux, douce (du:, du:s) *adj* **1** sweet. **2** soft. **3** gentle. **4** pleasant. **5** mild.
douze (du:z) *adj,nm* twelve. **douzaine** *nf* dozen. **douzième** *adj* twelfth.
doyen, -enne (dwa'jɛ̃, -'jɛn) *nm,f* **1** dean. **2** senior.
drachme (drakm) *nf* drachma.
dragée (dra'ʒe:) *nf* **1** sugared almond. **2** lozenge.
dragon (dra'gɔ̃) *nm* dragon.
draguer (dra'ge:) *vt* dredge, drag.

dramatiser (dramati:'ze:) *vt* dramatize. **dramatique** *adj* dramatic.

dramaturge (drama'tyrʒ) *nm,f* dramatist.

drame (dram) *nm* **1** drama. **2** play.

drap (dra) *nm* **1** cloth. **2** sheet. **drapeau, -aux** (dra'po) *nm* **1** flag. **2** *mil* colours.

draper (dra'pe:) *vt* **1** drape. **2** hang. **draperie** *nf* drapery. **drapier, -ière** (dra'pje:, -'pjɛr) *nm,f* draper.

drelin (drə'lɛ̃) *nm* tinkle.

dresser (drɛ'se:) *vt* **1** raise. **2** set, lay. **3** draw up. **4** train. **dresser les oreilles** prick one's ears. **se dresser** *vr* stand up, rise. **dressage** *nm* breaking in, training. **dressoir** *nm* dresser.

drogue (drɔg) *nf* **1** drug. **2** chemical.

droit[1] (drwa) *adj* **1** straight. **2** upright. **3** right (side, etc.). **4** honest. *adv* **1** straight. **2** directly. **tout droit** straight on.

droit[2] (drwa) *nm* **1** right. **2** charge, tax. **3** law. **droit d'auteur** copyright. **droits d'auteur** *nm pl* royalties. **droit de passage** right of way. **exempt de droit** duty-free.

droite (drwat) *nf* right, right-hand side.

drôle (drol) *adj* **1** funny, comic. **2** odd. *nm* rascal.

dromadaire (drɔma'dɛr) *nm* dromedary.

dru (dry) *adj* **1** thick. **2** strong. **3** dense. *adv* **1** thickly. **2** heavily.

du (dy) contraction of **de le.**

dû, due (dy) *v* see **devoir.** *adj* **1** due. **2** owing. **3** proper. *nm* due.

duc (dyk) *nm* duke. **duchesse** (dy'ʃɛs) *nf* duchess.

duel (dɥɛl) *nm* duel.

dûment (dy'mɑ̃) *adv* duly.

dune (dyn) *nf* dune.

Dunkerque (dœ̃'kɛrk) *nf* Dunkirk.

duo (dyo) *nm mus* duet.

duper (dy'pe:) *vt* trick, take in.

dur (dyr) *adj* **1** hard. **2** tough. **3** difficult. **4** harsh. *adv* hard. **durcir** (dyr'si:r) *vi,vt* harden.

durer (dy're:) *vi* **1** last. **2** endure. **durant** *prep* during. **durée** *nf* **1** duration. **2** life, wear.

duvet (dy'vɛ) *nm* **1** down, fluff. **2** quilt.

dynamique (di:na'mi:k) *adj* dynamic.

dynamite (di:na'mi:t) *nf* dynamite.

dynastie (di:na'sti:) *nf* dynasty.

dysenterie (di:sɑ̃'tri:) *nf* dysentery.

E

eau, eaux (o) *nf* water. **eau douce 1** soft water. **2** freshwater. **eau-de-vie** *nf, pl* **eaux-de-vie 1** spirits. **2** brandy. **eau minérale** mineral water. **eaux d'égout** *nf pl* sewage. **faire eau** leak.

ébahir (e:ba'i:r) *vt* astound, flabbergast. **s'ébahir de** *vr* be amazed at. **ébahissement** *nm* astonishment.

ébats (e:'ba) *nm pl* sport, frolics.

ébaucher (e:bo'ʃe:) *vt* **1** sketch. **2** outline. **ébauche** *nf* **1** rough sketch. **2** outline.

ébène (e:'bɛn) *nf* ebony. **ébéniste** *nm* cabinet-maker.

éberlué (e:bɛr'lɥe:) *adj* flabbergasted.

éblouir (e:blu:'ir) *vt* dazzle. **éblouissement** *nm* **1** dazzle. **2** fit of dizziness.

éboulement (e:bu:l'mɑ̃) *nm* landslide.

ébouriffer (e:bu:ri:'fe:) *vt* **1** ruffle. **2** amaze.

ébranler (e:brɑ̃'le:) *vt* **1** shake. **2** loosen. **3** disturb. **s'ébranler** *vr* **1** totter. **2** move off. **ébranlement** *nm* **1** shaking. **2** shock. **3** commotion.

ébrécher (e:bre:'ʃe:) *vt* **1** notch. **2** chip.

ébrouer (e:bru:'e:) *vi* snort. **ébrouement** *nm* snort.

ébullition (e:byli:'sjɔ̃) *nf* **1** boiling. **2** turmoil.

écailler (e:kɑ'je:) *vt* scale. **s'écailler** *vr* flake off. **écaille** *nf* **1** scale. **2** shell. **3** flake.

écaler (e:ka'le:) *vt* shell, husk. **écale** *nf* shell, pod.

écarlate (e:kar'lat) *adj,nf* scarlet.

écarquiller (e:karki:'je:) *vt* open wide.

écart (e:'kar) *nm* **1** distance apart. **2** deviation, swerve. **3** remote place. **à l'écart** aside, on one side. **faire le grand écart** do the splits. **faire un écart** shy.

écarter (e:kar'te:) *vt* **1** separate. **2** keep off. **3** divert. **s'écarter** *vr* **1** move aside. **2** diverge. **s'écarter de** stray from. **écarté** *adj* **1** isolated, remote. **2** apart.

ecclésiastique (ɛkle:zja'sti:k) *adj* ecclesiastical. *nm* clergyman.

écervelé (e:sɛrvə'le:) *adj* **1** thoughtless. **2** crazy. **3** light-headed.

échafaud (e:ʃa'fo) *nm* scaffold. **échafaudage** *nm* scaffolding.

échalote (e:ʃa'lɔt) *nf* shallot.

échancrer (e:ʃɑ̃'kre:) *vt* **1** cut out. **2** indent.

échanger (e:ʃɑ̃'ʒe:) *vt* exchange.

échantillon (e:ʃɑ̃ti:'jɔ̃) *nm* **1** sample, specimen. **2** pattern.
échapper (e:ʃa'pe:) *vi* (*aux* être or avoir) escape. **s'échapper** *vr* **1** break free. **2** escape. **3** leak. **échappatoire** *nf* loophole, way out. **échappement** *nm* **1** escape. **2** leakage. **3** exhaust.
écharde (e:'ʃard) *nf* splinter.
écharpe (e:'ʃarp) *nf* **1** scarf. **2** sash. **3** sling.
échasse (e:'ʃɑs) *nf* stilt.
échauder (e:ʃo'de:) *vt* scald.
échauffer (e:ʃo'fe:) *vt* **1** overheat. **2** heat. **3** rouse. **s'échauffer** *vr* **1** get overheated. **2** warm up. **échauffé** *adj* **1** overheated. **2** excited.
échéance (e:ʃe:'ɑ̃s) *nf* **1** date (of payment). **2** maturity. **3** expiration. **échéant** *adj* payable, falling due.
échec (e:'ʃɛk) *nm* **1** check. **2** failure, setback. **3** *pl* chess. **échec et mat** checkmate.
échelle (e:'ʃɛl) *nf* **1** ladder. **2** scale.
échelon (e:ʃ'lɔ̃) *nm* **1** rung. **2** step. **3** level.
échelonner (e:ʃlɔ'ne:) *vt* space out.
échevelé (e:ʃɛv'le:) *adj* **1** dishevelled. **2** wild.
échine (e:'ʃi:n) *nf* spine, backbone.
échiquier (e:ʃi:'kje:) *nm* chessboard.
écho (e:'ko) *nm* echo.
échoir* (e:'ʃwar) **1** fall. **2** mature. **3** expire.
échoppe (e:'ʃɔp) *nf* booth, stall.
échouer (e:'ʃwe:) *vi,vt* ground. *vi* **1** be stranded. **2** fail.
éclabousser (e:klabu:'se:) *vt* splash.
éclair (e:'klɛr) *nm* **1** flash. **2** *pl* lightning. **3** eclair.
éclaircir (e:klɛr'si:r) *vt* **1** clear up. **2** lighten. **3** explain. **s'éclaircir** *vr* **1** clear up. **2** thin out. **éclaircie** *nf* **1** break, opening. **2** clearing
éclairer (e:klɛ're:) *vt* **1** light. **2** enlighten. **s'éclairer** *vr* **1** light up. **2** clear. **éclairage** *nm* **1** lighting. **2** illumination. **éclaireur** *nm* scout.
éclat (e:'kla) *nm* **1** splinter. **2** chip. **3** burst. **4** flash. **5** brightness.
éclater (e:kla'te:) *vi,vt* **1** burst. **2** splinter. *vi* **1** explode. **2** break out. **éclater de rire** burst out laughing. **éclatant** *adj* **1** bright. **2** brilliant. **3** loud.
éclipser (e:kli:p'se:) *vt* **1** eclipse. **2** obscure. **éclipse** *nf* eclipse.
éclisse (e:'kli:s) *nf* **1** wedge. **2** *med* splint.
éclopé (e:klɔ'pe:) *adj* lame. *nm* cripple.
éclore* (e:'klɔr) *vi* (*aux* être) **1** hatch. **2** open, blossom.
écluse (e:'klyz) *nf* **1** sluice. **2** lock.
écœurer (e:kœ're:) *vt* **1** disgust. **2** nauseate.
école (e:'kɔl) *nf* school. **école maternelle/primaire** nursery/primary school.
écologie (e:kɔlɔ'ʒi:) *nf* ecology.
éconduire* (e:kɔ̃'dɥi:r) *vt* **1** show out. **2** reject.
économe (e:kɔ'nɔm) *adj* economical. **économie** *nf* **1** economy. **2** *pl* savings. **faire des économies** save. **économique** *adj* economic.
économiser (e:kɔnɔmi:'ze:) *vt* economize, save.
écoper (e:kɔ'pe:) *vt naut* bail out.
écorcer (e:kɔr'se:) *vt* skin, peel. **écorce** *nf* **1** rind, peel. **2** bark.
écorcher (e:kɔr'ʃe:) *vt* **1** skin. **2** graze. **3** fleece. **écorchure** *nf* **1** graze. **2** scratch.
écornifler (e:kɔrni:'fle:) *vt* scrounge, sponge.
Ecosse (e:'kɔs) *nf* Scotland. **écossais** *adj* Scottish, Scotch, Scots. *nm* Scot.
écot (e'ko) *nm* share, quota.
écouler (e:ku:'le:) *vt* get rid of. **s'écouler** *vr* **1** flow out. **2** pass, elapse. **écoulement** *nm* **1** flow. **2** discharge. **3** sale.
écouter (e:ku:'te:) *vt* **1** listen to. **2** pay attention to. **écouter à la porte** eavesdrop. **écouteur** *nm* **1** listener. **2** receiver. **3** headphone
écran (e:'krɑ̃) *nm* screen.
écraser (e:krɑ'ze:) *vt* **1** crush. **2** overcome. **3** flatten. **4** run over. **se faire écraser** get run over. **s'écraser** *vr* **1** collapse. **2** crash. **écrasant** *adj* **1** crushing. **2** overwhelming.
écrémer (e:kre:'me:) *vt* skim.
écrevisse (e:krə'vi:s) *nf* crayfish.
s'écrier (se:'krje:) *vr* **1** exclaim. **2** cry out.
écrin (e:'krɛ̃) *nm* (jewel) case.
écrire* (e:'kri:r) *vt* **1** write. **2** note down. **s'écrire** *vr* be written. **écrit** *adj* written. *nm* **1** writing. **2** written examination. **écriteau, -aux** (e:kri:'to) *nm* placard. **écriture** *nf* writing.
écrit (e:'kri:) *v see* **ecrire.**
écrivain (e:kri:'vɛ̃) *nm* author, writer.
écrivant (e:kri:'vɑ̃) *v see* **écrire.**
écrivasser (e:kri:va'se:) *vt* scribble.
écrou (e:'kru:) *nm tech* nut.
s'écrouler (se:kru:'le:) *vr* collapse, fall in. **écroulement** *nm* **1** collapse. **2** ruin.
écru (e:'kry) *adj* **1** natural. **2** raw.
écu (e:'ky) *nm* **1** shield. **2** crown (money).
écueil (e:'kœj) *nm* **1** reef, rock. **2** snag.
écuelle (e:'kɥɛl) *nf* bowl.
écumer (e:ky'me:) *vi* foam, froth. *vt* skim. **écume** *nf* **1** foam, froth. **2** scum.
écureuil (e:ky'rœj) *nm* squirrel.
écurie (e:ky'ri:) *nf* stable.

écuyer (e:kɥi:ˈje:) *nm* **1** squire. **2** horseman.
édenté (e:dɑ̃ˈte:) *adj* toothless.
édifier (e:di:ˈfje:) *vt* **1** build, erect. **2** enlighten. **édifice** *nm* **1** building. **2** structure.
Edimbourg (edɛ̃ˈbu:r) *nm* Edinburgh.
édit (e:ˈdi:) *nm* decree.
éditer (e:di:ˈte:) *vt* **1** edit. **2** publish. **éditeur** *nm* **1** editor. **2** publisher. **édition** *nf* edition, issue. **éditorial, -aux** (e:di:tɔˈrjal, -ˈrjo) *adj* editorial. *nm* newspaper leader.
édredon (e:drəˈdɔ̃) *nm* eiderdown.
éducation (e:dykaˈsjɔ̃) *nf* **1** education. **2** upbringing. **3** breeding.
éduquer (e:dyˈke:) *vt* **1** bring up. **2** train.
effacer (ɛfaˈse:) *vt* erase, rub out. **s'effacer** *vr* **1** wear away. **2** fade. **3** stand aside.
effarer (ɛfaˈre:) *vt* **1** scare. **2** bewilder.
effaroucher (ɛfaru:ˈʃe:) *vt* **1** scare away. **2** startle. **s'effaroucher** *vr* be startled.
effectif, -ive (e:fɛkˈti:f, -ˈti:v) *adj* **1** effective. **2** actual.
effectuer (e:fɛkˈtɥe:) *vt* effect, carry out.
efféminé (e:fe:mi:ˈne:) *adj* effeminate.
effervescence (e:fɛrvɛˈsɑ̃s) *nf* effervescence.
effet (eˈfɛ) *nm* **1** effect, result. **2** impression. **3** *pl* bills. **4** *pl* belongings. **en effet** indeed.
s'effeuiller (e:fœˈje:) *vr* shed its leaves or petals.
efficace (e:fi:ˈkas) *adj* **1** effective. **2** efficient.
effigie (e:fi:ˈʒi:) *nf* effigy.
effiler (e:fi:ˈle:) *vt* **1** unravel. **2** taper.
effleurer (e:flœˈre:) *vt* **1** skim, touch lightly. **2** touch on.
effondrer (e:fɔ̃ˈdre:) *vt* break in. **s'effondrer** *vr* **1** cave in. **2** collapse. **3** slump. **effondrement** *nm* **1** collapse. **2** subsidence.
s'efforcer (se:fɔrˈse:) *vr* **s'efforcer de** strive to.
effort (e:ˈfɔr) *nm* **1** effort. **2** strain.
effrayer (e:frɛˈje:) *vt* frighten, scare.
effréné (e:fre:ˈne:) *adj* frantic.
effroi (e:ˈfrwa) *nm* fear, dread. **effroyable** *adj* **1** dreadful. **2** awful.
effronté (e:frɔ̃ˈte:) *adj* **1** bold. **2** impudent, cheeky. **effronterie** *nf* impudence, cheek.
égal, -aux (e:ˈgal, -ˈgo) *adj* **1** equal. **2** level. **3** even. **4** regular. **cela m'est égal** it's all the same to me. **également** *adv* **1** equally. **2** likewise. **3** also. **égalité** *nf* **1** equality. **2** regularity.
égaler (e:gaˈle:) *vt* **1** equal. **2** match.
égaliser (e:gali:ˈze:) *vi,vt* equalize. *vt* smooth.
égard (e:ˈgar) *nm* **1** respect. **2** regard. **3** consideration.
égarer (e:gaˈre:) *vt* **1** lead astray. **2** mislay. **3** bewilder. **s'égarer** *vr* lose one's way. **égaré** *adj* **1** stray. **2** distracted.
égayer (e:gɛˈje:) *vt* **1** cheer up. **2** amuse.
égée (e:ˈʒe:) *adj* Aegean. (**Mer**) **Egée** *nf* Aegean (Sea).
église (e:ˈgli:z) *nf* church.
ego (ˈe:go) *nm* ego. **égocentrique** (e:gɔsɑ̃ˈtri:k) *adj* self-centred, egocentric. **égoïste** (e:gɔˈi:st) *adj* selfish. **égoïsme** *nm* selfishness, egoism.
égorger (e:gɔrˈʒe:) *vt* **1** cut the throat of. **2** massacre. **3** ruin.
égout (e:ˈgu:) *nm* **1** drain. **2** sewer. **3** gutter.
égoutter (e:gu:ˈte:) *vt* **1** drain. **2** drip.
égratigner (e:grati:ˈɲe:) *vt* scratch. **égratignure** *nf* scratch.
égrener (e:grəˈne:) *vt* **1** shell. **2** pick.
Egypte (ˈe:ʒi:pt) *nf* Egypt. **égyptien, -ienne** (e:ʒi:pˈsjɛ̃, -ˈsjɛn) *adj,n* Egyptian.
éjaculer (e:ʒakyˈle:) *vt* ejaculate.
éjecter (e:ʒɛkˈte:) *vt* eject.
élaborer (e:labɔˈre:) *vt* **1** elaborate. **2** work out.
élaguer (e:laˈge:) *vt* **1** prune. **2** cut down.
élan (e:ˈlɑ̃) *nm* **1** spring, bound. **2** dash. **3** impetus. **4** burst.
s'élancer (se:lɑ̃ˈse:) *vr* **1** spring. **2** rush. **élancé** *adj* slender. **élancement** *nm* **1** throb. **2** twinge.
élargir (e:larˈʒi:r) *vt* **1** widen. **2** enlarge. **3** extend. **4** release.
élastique (e:laˈsti:k) *adj* elastic. *nm* **1** elastic. **2** rubber band.
élection (e:lɛkˈsjɔ̃) *nf* **1** election. **2** choice.
électoral, -aux (e:lɛktɔˈral, -ˈro) *adj* electoral. **électorat** *nm* electorate.
électricité (e:lɛktri:si:ˈte:) *nf* electricity.
électrifier (e:lɛktri:ˈfje:) *vt* electrify.
électrique (e:lɛkˈtri:k) *adj* electric.
électriser (e:lɛktri:ˈze:) *vt* **1** electrify. **2** excite.
électrocuter (e:lɛktrɔkyˈte:) *vt* electrocute.
électrode (e:lɛkˈtrɔd) *nf* electrode.
électron (e:lɛkˈtrɔ̃) *nm* electron.
électronique (e:lɛktrɔni:k) *adj* electronic. *nf* electronics.
élégant (e:le:ˈgɑ̃) *adj* **1** elegant. **2** smart.
élément (e:le:ˈmɑ̃) *nm* **1** element. **2** unit. **3** *pl* rudiments. **élémentaire** *adj* **1** elementary. **2** elemental.
éléphant (e:le:ˈfɑ̃) *nm* elephant.
élevage (ɛlˈvaʒ) *nm* stockbreeding.
élévation (e:le:vaˈsjɔ̃) *nf* **1** elevation. **2** rise. **3** raising. **4** height. **élévateur** *nm* elevator.

élève (e:'lɛv) *nm,f* pupil. **élevé** *adj* **1** high. **2** raised. **bien/mal élevé** well/ill-bred.
élever (e:l've:) *vt* **1** raise. **2** elevate. **3** erect. **4** bring up. **s'élever** *vr* rise up.
elfe (ɛlf) *nm* elf.
éligible (e:li:'ʒi:bl) *adj* eligible.
éliminer (e:li:mi:'ne:) *vt* **1** eliminate. **2** get rid of.
élire* (e:'li:r) *vt* **1** elect. **2** choose.
élite (e:'li:t) *nf* **1** elite. **2** cream. **d'élite** crack.
elle (ɛl) *pron 3rd pers fs* **1** she. **2** her. **3** it. **elle-même** *pron 3rd pers fs* **1** herself. **2** itself.
elles (ɛl) *pron 3rd pers f pl* **1** they. **2** them. **elles-mêmes** *pron 3rd pers f pl* themselves.
ellipse (ɛl'li:ps) *nf* ellipse.
élocution (e:lɔky'sjɔ̃) *nf* elocution.
éloge (e:'lɔʒ) *nm* praise.
éloigner (e:lwa'ɲe:) *vt* **1** remove. **2** send away. **3** postpone. **s'éloigner** *vr* **1** go away. **2** stand back. **éloigné** *adj* **1** distant. **2** remote. **éloignement** *nm* **1** removal. **2** distance. **3** absence. **4** aversion.
éloquent (e:lɔ'kɑ̃) *adj* eloquent.
élu (e:'ly) *adj* **1** chosen. **2** successful.
élucider (e:lysi:'de:) *vt* elucidate.
éluder (e:ly'de:) *vt* elude, evade.
émail, -aux (e:'maj, -'mo) *nm* **1** enamel. **2** glaze.
émailler (e:ma'je:) *vt* **1** enamel. **2** glaze. **3** dot.
émanciper (e:mɑ̃si:'pe:) *vt* emancipate.
émaner (e:ma'ne:) *vi* **émaner de** emanate or come from.
emballer (ɑ̃ba'le:) *vt* **1** pack. **2** wrap up. **3** excite. **s'emballer** *vr* **1** bolt, run away. **2** get carried away. **emballage** *nm* wrapping, packing.
embarcadère (ɑ̃barka'dɛr) *nm* **1** quay, wharf. **2** platform.
embargo (ɑ̃bar'go) *nm* embargo
embarquer (ɑ̃bar'ke:) *vi,vt* embark. *vt* **1** ship. **2** *inf* arrest. **s'embarquer** *vr* embark.
embarras (ɑ̃ba'ra) *nm* **1** obstacle. **2** embarrassment, confusion. **3** difficulty. **4** *pl* fuss.
embarrasser (ɑ̃bara'se:) *vt* **1** embarrass. **2** encumber. **3** obstruct. **4** perplex. **5** confuse. **s'embarrasser** *vr* burden oneself.
embaucher (ɑ̃bo'ʃe:) *vt* engage, take on.
embaumer (ɑ̃bo'me:) *vt* **1** embalm. **2** perfume.
embellir (ɑ̃bɛ'li:r) *vt* **1** embellish. **2** improve in looks.
embêter (ɑ̃bɛ'te:) *vt inf* **1** annoy. **2** bother.
emblée (ɑ̃'ble:) **d'emblée** *adv* straightaway.
emblème (ɑ̃'blɛm) *nm* emblem.
emboîter (ɑ̃bwa'te:) *vt* **1** pack in boxes. **2** fit together.
embouchure (ɑ̃bu:'ʃyr) *nf* **1** mouthpiece. **2** *geog* mouth.
embouteiller (ɑ̃bu:tɛ'je:) *vt* **1** bottle. **2** block up. **embouteillage** *nm* **1** bottling. **2** traffic jam.
emboutir (ɑ̃bu:'ti:r) *vt* collide with.
embrancher (ɑ̃brɑ̃'ʃe:) *vt* join up. **embranchement** *nm* **1** branch, fork. **2** junction.
embraser (ɑ̃bra'ze:) *vt* set on fire. **s'embraser** *vr* catch fire.
embrasser (ɑ̃bra'se:) *vt* **1** embrace. **2** hug. **3** kiss. **4** include. **embrassement** *nm* embrace.
embrayer (ɑ̃brɛ'je:) *vt* **1** connect. **2** let in the clutch. **embrayage** *nm* **1** connecting. **2** *mot* clutch.
embrouiller (ɑ̃bru:'je:) *vt* **1** tangle. **2** confuse, muddle.
embryon (ɑ̃'brjɔ̃) *nm* embryo.
embuscade (ɑ̃by'skad) *nf* ambush.
éméché (e:me:'ʃe:) *adj* tipsy.
émeraude (ɛm'rod) *adj,nf* emerald.
émerger (e:mɛr'ʒe:) *vi* emerge.
émerveiller (e:mɛrvɛ'je:) *vt* amaze. **s'émerveiller de** *vr* marvel at.
émettre* (e:'mɛtr) *vt* **1** emit. **2** utter. **3** broadcast. **4** issue. **émetteur** *nm* transmitter.
émou (e:'mœ) *nm* emu.
émeute (e:mœt) *nf* riot.
émietter (e:mjɛ'te:) *vt* crumble.
émigrer (e:mi:'gre:) *vi* **1** emigrate. **2** migrate. **émigrant** *nm* emigrant. **émigré** *nm* refugee.
éminent (e:mi:'nɑ̃) *adj* eminent.
émission (e:mi:'sjɔ̃) *nf* **1** emission. **2** broadcast. **3** issue.
emmagasiner (ɑ̃magazi:'ne:) *vt* **1** store. **2** store up.
emmancher (ɑ̃mɑ̃'ʃe:) *vt* **1** put a handle on. **2** fit together. **3** begin.
emmanchure (ɑ̃mɑ̃'ʃyr) *nf* armhole.
emmêler (ɑ̃mɛ'le:) *vt* entangle, mix up.
emménager (ɑ̃mɛna'ʒe:) *vi* move into a new house.
emmener (ɑ̃m'ne:) *vt* take or lead away.
emmitoufler (ɑ̃mi:tu'fle:) *vt* muffle up.
émoi (e:mwa) *nm* **1** emotion. **2** agitation.
émonder (e:mɔ̃'de:) *vt* prune.
émotion (e:mo'sjɔ̃) *nf* **1** emotion. **2** excitement.
émousser (e:mu:'se:) *vt* **1** blunt. **2** deaden.
émouvoir* (e:mu:'vwar) *vt* **1** move, touch. **2** rouse. **émouvant** *adj* **1** moving. **2** stirring.

empailler (ãpa'je:) *vt* **1** pack in straw. **2** stuff.
empaqueter (ãpak'te:) *vt* pack up.
s'emparer (sãpa're:) *vr* **s'emparer de 1** seize. **2** take possession of.
empâter (ãpɑ'te:) *vt* **1** paste. **2** make sticky. **3** fatten.
empêcher (ãpe:'ʃe:) *vt* **1** prevent. **2** hinder. **n'empêche que** nevertheless. **s'empêcher de** *vr* refrain from.
empereur (ãp'rœr) *nm* emperor.
empeser (ãpə'ze:) *vt* starch.
empester (ãpɛ'ste:) *vt* **1** stink. **2** infect.
empêtrer (ãpɛ'tre:) *vt* entangle.
empiéter (ãpje:'te:) *vi* **1** encroach. **2** infringe.
empiffrer (ãpi:'fre:) *vt inf* stuff.
empiler (ãpi:'le:) *vt* stack.
empire (ã'pi:r) *nm* **1** empire. **2** dominion.
empirer (ãpi:'re:) *vi* worsen. *vt* make worse, aggravate.
empirique (ãpi:'ri:k) *adj* empirical.
emplacement (ãplas'mã) *nm* **1** site. **2** place.
emplâtre (ã'plɑtr) *nm* plaster.
emplette (ã'plɛt) *nf* purchase.
emplir (ã'pli:r) *vt* fill, fill up.
emploi (ã'plwa) *nm* **1** use. **2** employment.
employer (ãplwa'je:) *vt* **1** use. **2** employ. **s'employer** *vr* occupy oneself. **employé** *nm* clerk, employee. **employeur** *nm* employer.
empoigner (ãpwa'ɲe:) *vt* **1** grasp. **2** arrest. **3** grip.
empoisonner (ãpwazɔ'ne:) *vt* **1** poison. **2** infect. **3** corrupt. **4** bore.
emporter (ãpɔr'te:) *vt* carry, take away. **l'emporter sur** get the better of. **s'emporter** *vr* lose one's temper, get very annoyed. **emporté** *adj* quick-tempered, hot-tempered.
empourpré (ãpu:r'pre:) *adj* crimson.
empreindre* (ã'prɛ̃dr) *vt* imprint, stamp.
empreinte (ã'prɛ̃t) *nf* impression, mark. **empreinte de pas** footprint. **empreinte digitale** fingerprint.
s'empresser (sãprɛ'se:) *vr* hurry. **s'empresser à** be eager to. **empressé** *adj* eager, fervent.
emprisonner (ãpri:zɔ'ne:) *vt* put in prison.
emprunt (ã'prœ̃) *nm* loan.
emprunter (ãprœ̃'te:) *vt* **1** borrow. **2** assume.
ému (e:'my) *adj* moved, touched.
émulsion (e:myl'sjɔ̃) *nf* emulsion.
en[1] (ã) *prep* **1** in. **2** into. **3** to. **4** as. **5** while. **6** by. **en-tête** *nm, pl* **en-têtes 1** heading. **2** headline.
en[2] (ã) *adv* **1** from there. **2** because of that. *pron invar* **1** of it or them. **2** about it or them. **3** some, any. **4** for that.
encadrer (ãka'dre:) *vt* frame. **encadrement** *nm* **1** frame. **2** framework.
encaisser (ãkɛ'se:) *vt* **1** pack in boxes. **2** collect. **3** cash. **encaisse** *nf* cash in hand.
enceinte[1] (ã'sɛ̃t) *nf* **1** surrounding wall. **2** *sport* ring.
enceinte[2] (ã'sɛ̃t) *adj* pregnant.
encens (ã'sã) *nm* incense.
encercler (ãsɛr'kle:) *vt* encircle.
enchaîner (ãʃɛ'ne:) *vt* **1** chain up. **2** curb. **3** connect.
enchanter (ãʃã'te:) *vt* **1** enchant. **2** delight. **enchantement** *nm* **1** magic. **2** charm. **3** delight.
enchère (ã'ʃɛr) *nf* **1** bid. **2** auction.
enchérir (ãʃe:'ri:r) *vi* **1** go up in price. **2** make a higher bid. **enchérissement** *nm* increase, rise.
enchevêtrer (ãʃvɛ'tre:) *vt* **1** mix up, confuse. **2** entangle.
enclin (ã'klɛ̃) *adj* **enclin à** inclined or prone to.
enclore* (ã'klɔr) *vt* enclose, fence in. **enclos** *nm* **1** enclosure. **2** paddock.
enclume (ã'klym) *nf* anvil.
encoche (ã'kɔʃ) *nf* notch.
encoignure (ãkɔ'ɲyr) *nf* corner.
encolure (ãkɔ'lyr) *nf* **1** neck. **2** neck size.
encombrer (ãkɔ̃'bre:) *vt* **1** encumber. **2** crowd. **3** litter. **encombrant** *adj* **1** cumbersome. **2** clumsy. **sans encombre** *adv* without a hitch. **encombrement** *nm* **1** obstruction. **2** litter.
encontre (ã'kɔ̃tr) **à l'encontre** *adv* to the contrary. **à l'encontre de 1** against. **2** contrary to.
encore (ã'kɔr) *adv* **1** still. **2** yet. **3** again. **4** more.
encorner (ãkɔr'ne:) *vt* gore.
encourager (ãku:ra'ʒe:) *vt* encourage. **encouragement** *nm* encouragement.
encourir* (ãku:'ri:r) *vt* **1** incur. **2** bring upon onself.
encrasser (ãkra'se:) *vt* **1** dirty, soil. **2** clog.
encre (ãkr) *nf* ink.
encroûter (ãkru:'te:) *vt* cake.
encyclopédie (ãsi:klɔpe:'di:) *nf* encyclopedia.
endémique (ãde:'mi:k) *adj* endemic.
s'endetter (sãdɛ'te:) *vr* get into debt.
endiablé (ãdja'ble:) *adj* **1** reckless. **2** wild.
s'endimancher (ãdi:mã'ʃe:) *vr* dress in one's Sunday best.
endive (ã'di:v) *nf* endive.

endolori (ãdɔlɔ'ri:) *adj* **1** sore. **2** tender.
endommager (ãdɔma'ʒe:) *vt* damage.
endormir* (ãdɔr'mi:r) *vt* **1** send to sleep. **2** deaden. **s'endormir** *vr* fall asleep. **endormi** *adj* asleep.
endosser (ãdo'se:) *vt* **1** put on. **2** endorse.
endroit (ã'drwa) *nm* **1** place. **2** spot. **3** part. **4** right side.
enduire* (ã'dɥi:r) *vt* coat, smear. **enduit** *nm* layer, coat.
endurcir (ãdyr'si:r) *vt* harden.
endurer (ãdy're:) *vt* endure, bear.
énergie (enɛr'ʒi:) *nf* **1** energy, drive. **2** force. **énergie atomique** atomic energy.
énerver (enɛr've:) *vt* get on someone's nerves. **s'énerver** *vr* get irritable or excited.
enfance (ã'fãs) *nf* **1** childhood. **2** infancy. **3** children. **enfant** *nm,f* **1** child. **2** infant. **d'enfant** *adj* childish. **enfant de chœur** choirboy. **enfantin** *adj* **1** childlike. **2** childish.
enfanter (ãfã'te:) *vt* give birth to.
enfer (ã'fɛr) *nm* hell.
enfermer (ãfɛr'me:) *vt* **1** shut up. **2** shut in. **3** surround.
enfiler (ãfi:'le:) *vt* **1** thread. **2** string. **3** go along. **4** slip on. **enfilade** *nf* succession.
enfin (ã'fɛ̃) *adv* **1** finally. **2** in fact. **3** at last.
enflammer (ãfla'me:) *vt* **1** inflame. **2** ignite. **s'enflammer** *vr* **1** catch fire. **2** become inflamed.
enfler (ã'fle:) *vi,vt* swell. *vt* puff out.
enfoncer (ãfɔ̃'se:) *vt* **1** drive in. **2** break in. *vi* sink. **s'enfoncer** *vr* plunge, go deep.
enfouir (ã'fwi:r) *vt* **1** bury. **2** hide under the ground.
enfreindre* (ã'frɛ̃dr) *vt* infringe.
s'enfuir* (sã'fɥi:r) *vr* **1** flee. **2** run away. **3** elope. **4** leak.
engager (ãga'ʒe:) *vt* **1** pledge. **2** engage. **3** begin. **4** urge. **s'engager** *vr* **1** undertake. **2** enlist. **engagement** *nm* engagement, commitment.
engelure (ãʒ'lyr) *nf* chilblain.
engendrer (ãʒã'dre:) *vt* **1** breed. **2** produce.
engin (ã'ʒɛ̃) *nm* **1** engine. **2** device. **3** missile. **4** *pl* tackle, equipment.
englober (ãglɔ'be:) *vt* **1** include. **2** unite.
engloutir (ãglu:'ti:r) *vt* **1** gulp down. **2** engulf.
engorger (ãgɔr'ʒe:) *vt* block up.
engouffrer (ãgu:'fre:) *vt* **1** engulf. **2** swallow up.
engourdir (ãgu:r'di:r) *vt* **1** numb. **2** dull.
engrais (ã'grɛ) *nm* **1** manure. **2** fertilizer.
engraisser (ãgrɛ'se:) *vt* **1** fatten. **2** manure.
engrenage (ãgrɛ'naʒ) *nm* **1** gearing. **2** intricacy.
engueuler (ãgœ'le:) *vt sl* **1** blow up, shout at. **2** abuse.
enhardir (ãar'di:r) *vt* encourage. **s'enhardir** *vr* pluck up courage.
énigme (e:'ni:gm) *nf* **1** enigma. **2** riddle.
enivrer (ãni:'vre:) *vt* intoxicate. **s'enivrer** *vr* get drunk.
enjamber (ãʒã'be:) *vt* step over.
enjeu, -eux (ã'ʒœ) *nm game* stake.
enjôler (ãʒo'le:) *vt* coax.
enjoué (ã'ʒwe:) *adj* **1** lively. **2** cheerful.
enlaidir (ãle:'di:r) *vt* disfigure. *vi* grow ugly.
enlever (ãl've:) *vt* **1** remove. **2** carry or take off. **3** abduct. **4** kidnap. **s'enlever** *vr* **1** come off. **2** rise. **enlèvement** (ãlɛv'mã) *nm* **1** removal. **2** kidnapping.
enliser (ãli:'ze:) *vt* suck in. **s'enliser** *vr* get bogged down.
ennemi (ɛn'mi:) *nm* enemy, foe. *adj* hostile.
ennui (ã'nɥi:) *nm* **1** worry, anxiety. **2** boredom.
ennuyer (ãnɥi:'je:) *vt* **1** worry. **2** annoy. **3** bore. **s'ennuyer** *vr* be bored. **ennuyant** *adj* annoying. **ennuyeux, -euse** (ãnɥi:'jœ, 'jœz) *adj* tedious, boring.
énoncer (e:nɔ̃'se:) *vt* **1** state. **2** enunciate.
s'enorgueillir (sãnɔrgœ'ji:r) *vr* become proud.
énorme (e:'nɔrm) *adj* enormous, huge. **énormément** *adj* enormously, tremendously.
s'enquérir (sãke:'ri:r) *vr* inquire.
enquête (ã'kɛt) *nf* **1** inquiry. **2** investigation. **3** inquest.
enraciné (ãrasi:'ne:) *adj* deep-seated.
enrager (ãra'ʒe:) *vt* **1** enrage. **2** excite. **enragé** *adj* **1** mad. **2** keen. *nm* fan.
enrayer (ãrɛ'je:) *vt* **1** lock. **2** jam. **3** check.
enregistrer (ãrəʒi:'stre:) *vt* **1** register. **2** record.
s'enrhumer (ãry'me:) *vr* catch a cold.
enrichir (ãri:'ʃi:r) *vt* enrich.
enrôler (ãro'le:) *vt* **1** enrol. **2** enlist.
enroué (ã'rwe:) *adj* **1** hoarse. **2** husky.
enseigne[1] (ã'sɛɲ) *nf* sign, mark.
enseigne[2] (ã'sɛɲ) *nf mil* ensign.
enseigner (ãsɛ'ɲe:) *vt* teach. **enseignement** *nm* **1** teaching. **2** education.
ensemble (ã'sãbl) *adv* together. *nm* **1** whole. **2** general effect. **3** set. **dans l'ensemble** on the whole.
ensemencer (ãsmã'se:) *vt* sow.
ensevelir (ãsə'vli:r) *vt* **1** bury. **2** shroud. **ensevelissement** *nm* burial.

ensoleillé (ɑ̃sɔlɛ'je:) *adj* sunny.
ensorceler (ɑ̃sɔrsə'le:) *vt* **1** put a spell on. **2** captivate.
ensuite (ɑ̃'sɥi:t) *adv* **1** then. **2** afterwards. **3** next.
s'ensuivre* (sɑ̃'sɥi:vr) *vr* follow.
entaille (ɑ̃'taj) *nf* **1** notch. **2** slash.
entamer (ɑ̃ta'me:) *vt* **1** cut into. **2** start.
entasser (ɑ̃tɑ'se:) *vt* **1** accumulate. **2** heap up. **3** pack.
entendre (ɑ̃'tɑ̃dr) *vt* **1** hear. **2** understand. **3** mean. **entendre parler de** hear of. **s'entendre** *vr* **1** agree. **2** understand one another. **entendu** *adj* **1** capable. **2** sensible. **3** agreed. **bien entendu** certainly, of course.
entente (ɑ̃'tɑ̃t) *nf* **1** understanding. **2** agreement.
enterrer (ɑ̃tɛ're:) *vt* bury. **enterrement** *nm* **1** burial. **2** funeral.
entêté (ɑ̃tɛ'te:) *adj* **1** obstinate. **2** headstrong.
enthousiasme (ɑ̃tu:'zjasm) *nm* enthusiasm. **enthousiaste** *nm,f* enthusiast. *adj* enthusiastic.
s'enticher (sɑ̃ti:'ʃe:) *vr* **s'enticher de** become infatuated with.
entier, -ière (ɑ̃'tje:, -'tjɛr) *adj* entire, whole. **en entier** in full.
entité (ɑ̃ti:'te:) *nf* entity.
entonnoir (ɑ̃tɔ'nwar) *nm* funnel.
entorse (ɑ̃'tɔrs) *nf* **1** sprain. **2** twist.
entortiller (ɑ̃tɔrti:'je:) *vt* **1** twist. **2** wind. **3** get round. **s'entortiller** *vr* coil, twine.
entourer (ɑ̃tu:'re:) *vt* surround, encircle. **entourage** *nm* **1** setting. **2** circle of friends.
entracte (ɑ̃'trakt) *nm* **1** *Th* interval. **2** interlude.
entrailles (ɑ̃'traj) *nf pl* entrails.
entrain (ɑ̃'trɛ̃) *nm* spirit, vigour, zest.
entraîner (ɑ̃trɛ'ne:) *vt* **1** drag away. **2** involve. **3** lead astray. **4** bring about. **5** train.
entraver (ɑ̃tra've:) *vt* **1** fetter. **2** hinder. **entrave** *nf* **1** fetter. **2** obstacle.
entre (ɑ̃tr) *prep* **1** between. **2** among. **entretemps** *adv* in the meantime. *nm* interval.
entrebâillé (ɑ̃trəbɑ'je:) *adj* ajar.
s'entrechoquer (sɑ̃trəʃɔ'ke:) *vr* collide.
entrecôte (ɑ̃trə'kot) *nf* rib steak.
entrecouper (ɑ̃trəku:'pe:) *vt* **1** intersect. **2** interrupt.
s'entrecroiser (sɑ̃trəkrwa'ze:) *vr* **1** cross each other. **2** intersect.
entrefaite (ɑ̃trə'fɛt) *nf* interval. **sur ces entrefaites** **1** at this moment. **2** meanwhile.
entrefilet (ɑ̃trəfi:'lɛ) *nm* paragraph.
entregent (ɑ̃trə'ʒɑ̃) *nm* tact.
entremets (ɑ̃trə'mɛ) *nm* dessert, sweet.
s'entremettre* (sɑ̃trə'mɛtr) *vr* intervene.
entrepôt (ɑ̃trə'po) *nm* **1** warehouse. **2** store.
entreprendre* (ɑ̃trə'prɑ̃dr) *vt* **1** undertake. **2** attempt. **3** contract for.
entrepreneur (ɑ̃trəprə'nœr) *nm* contractor. **entrepreneur de pompes funèbres** undertaker.
entreprise (ɑ̃trə'pri:z) *nf* **1** enterprise. **2** venture. **3** firm.
entrer (ɑ̃'tre:) *vi* (*aux* être) **1** enter. **2** begin. **faire entrer** show in. **entrée** *nf* **1** entrance. **2** entry. **3** admission. **4** beginning. **5** first course.
entretenir* (ɑ̃trət'ni:r) *vt* **1** maintain, keep up. **2** support. **s'entretenir** *vr* converse. **entretien** *nm* **1** upkeep. **2** conversation. **3** interview.
entrevoir* (ɑ̃trə'vwar) *vt* catch a glimpse of.
entrevue (ɑ̃trə'vy) *nf* interview.
entrouvert (ɑ̃tru:'vɛr) *adj* ajar.
envahir (ɑ̃va'i:r) *vt* **1** invade. **2** overrun.
envelopper (ɑ̃vlɔ'pe:) *vt* **1** envelop. **2** wrap up. **3** cover. **4** shroud. **enveloppe** *nf* **1** cover. **2** envelope.
envenimer (ɑ̃vni:'me:) *vt* **1** poison. **2** embitter. **s'envenimer** *vr* fester.
envergure (ɑ̃vɛr'gyr) *nf* span, spread.
envers[1] (ɑ̃'vɛr) *prep* **1** towards. **2** to.
envers[2] (ɑ̃'vɛr) *nm* **1** wrong side. **2** reverse. **à l'envers** **1** inside out. **2** upside down.
envier (ɑ̃'vje:) *vt* **1** envy. **2** begrudge. **envie** *nf* **1** desire. **2** envy. **3** birthmark. **avoir envie de** feel like, fancy.
environ (ɑ̃vi:'rɔ̃) *adv* about. **environs** *nm pl* **1** outskirts. **2** neighbourhood.
environnement (ɑ̃vi:rɔn'mɑ̃) *nm* environment.
envisager (ɑ̃viza'ʒe:) *vt* **1** envisage. **2** consider. **3** anticipate.
envoi (ɑ̃'vwa) *nm* **1** dispatch, sending. **2** parcel.
s'envoler (sɑ̃vɔ'le:) *vr* **1** fly away. **2** take off.
envoyer* (ɑ̃vwa'je:) *vt* **1** send. **2** dispatch. **envoyer chercher** send for. **envoyer en chandelle** lob. **envoyé** *nm* **1** messenger. **2** envoy. **envoyé spécial** correspondent.
enzyme (ɑ̃'zi:m) *nf* enzyme.
épagneul (e:pa'ɲœl) *nm* spaniel.
épais, -aisse (e:'pɛ, -'pɛs) *adj* **1** thick. **2** dense. **épaisseur** *nf* **1** thickness. **2** density.
épaissir (e:pɛ'si:r) *vt* thicken.
épancher (e:pɑ̃'ʃe:) *vt* pour out.
épandre (e:'pɑ̃dr) *vt* spread.
s'épanouir (e:pa'nwi:r) *vr* **1** open out. **2** bloom. **3** beam. **épanoui** *adj* in full bloom.

épargner (e:par'ɲe:) *vt* **1** save. **2** economize. **3** spare. **épargne** *nf* **1** saving. **2** economy.
éparpiller (e:parpi:'je:) *vt* **1** scatter. **2** disperse.
épars (e:'par) *adj* **1** scattered. **2** stray.
épater (e:pa'te:) *vt* stagger, amaze.
épaule (e:'pol) *nf* shoulder. **épaulette** *nf* epaulet.
épave (e:'pav) *nf* **1** wreck. **2** waif. **3** debris.
épée (e:'pe:) *nf* sword.
épeler (e:'ple:) *vt* spell.
éperdu (e:pɛr'dy) *adj* **1** distracted, distraught. **2** wild, mad. **3** desperate.
éperon (e:'prɔ̃) *nm* spur.
éphémère (e:fe:'mɛr) *adj* ephemeral.
épi (e:'pi:) *nm* **1** ear (of corn). **2** cluster.
épice (e:'pi:s) *nf* spice. **épicerie** *nf* grocer's shop. **épicier** *nm* grocer.
épicrâne (e:pi:'kran) *nm* scalp.
épidémie (e:pi:de:'mi:) *nf* epidemic.
épier (e:'pje:) *vt* **1** spy. **2** watch for.
épilepsie (e:pi:lɛp'si:) *nf* epilepsy. **épileptique** *adj* epileptic.
épilogue (e:pi:'lɔg) *nm* epilogue.
épiloir (e:pi:'lwar) *nm* tweezers.
épinards (e:pi:'nar) *nm pl* spinach.
épine (e:'pi:n) *nf* thorn. **épine dorsale** spine.
épingler (e:pɛ̃'gle:) *vt* pin. **épingle** *nf* pin. **épingle à cheveux** hairgrip. **épingle de nourrice** or **sûreté** safety pin.
Epiphanie (e:pi:fa'ni:) *nf* Epiphany.
épique (e:'pi:k) *adj* epic.
épiscopal, -aux (e:pi:skɔ'pal, -'po) *adj* episcopal.
épisode (e:pi:'zɔd) *nm* episode.
épitaphe (e:pi:'taf) *nf* epitaph.
épitomé (e:pi:tɔ'me:) *nm* epitome.
éploré (e:plɔ're:) *adj* in tears, weeping.
éplucher (e:ply'ʃe:) *vt* **1** clean. **2** peel. **3** examine.
éponger (e:pɔ̃'ʒe:) *vt* **1** sponge. **2** mop. **éponge** *nf* sponge.
épopée (e:pɔ'pe:) *nf* epic.
époque (e:'pɔk) *nf* **1** epoch, age. **2** time, period.
épouser (e:pu:'ze:) *vt* marry. **épousée** *nf* bride.
épousseter (e:pu:'ste:) *vt* dust, clean.
épouvanter (e:pu:vɑ̃'te:) *vt* terrify. **épouvantable** *adj* dreadful, frightful. **épouvantail** *nm* scarecrow. **épouvante** *nf* terror, dread.
époux, -ouse (e:'pu:, -'pu:z) *nm,f* husband, wife.
s'éprendre (se:'prɑ̃dr) *vr* **s'éprendre de** fall in love with.
épreuve (e:'prœv) *nf* **1** test. **2** trial. **3** proof. **4** print.
éprouver (e:pru:'ve:) *vt* **1** try, test. **2** experience, suffer. **éprouvette** *nf* test tube.
épuiser (e:pɥi:'ze:) *vt* **1** exhaust. **2** empty. **3** use up. **épuisé** *adj* **1** exhausted. **2** worn out.
épurer (e:py're:) *vt* **1** purify. **2** refine.
équateur (e:kwa'tœr) *nm* **1** equator. **2** *cap* Ecuador. **équatorial, -aux** (e:kwatɔ'rjal, -'rjo) *adj* equatorial.
équation (e:kwa'sjɔ̃) *nf* equation.
équerre (e:'kɛr) *nf* **1** square. **2** right angle.
équestre (e:'kɛstr) *adj* equestrian.
équilatéral, -aux (e:kɥi:late:'ral, -'ro) *adj* equilateral.
équilibrer (e:ki:li:'bre:) *vt* balance. **équilibre** *nm* **1** balance. **2** equilibrium.
équinoxe (e:ki:'nɔks) *nm* equinox.
équiper (e:ki:'pe:) *vt* **1** equip. **2** fit out. **équipage** *nm* **1** crew. **2** equipment. **équipe** *nf* **1** gang. **2** *sport* team, side.
équitable (e:ki:'tabl) *adj* fair, just.
équitation (e:ki:ta'sjɔ̃) *nf* riding.
équité (e:ki:'te:) *nf* equity.
équivaloir* (e:ki:va'lwar) *vi* be equivalent or equal. **équivalent** *adj,nm* equivalent.
équivoque (e:ki:'vɔk) *adj* **1** ambiguous. **2** dubious.
érable (ɛ'rabl) *nm* maple tree.
érafler (e:rɑ'fle:) *vt* **1** graze. **2** scratch. **éraflure** *nf* graze.
eraillé (e:'raj) *adj* **1** frayed. **2** scratched. **3** raucous.
ère (ɛr) *nf* **1** era. **2** epoch.
éreinter (e:rɛ̃'te:) *vt inf* **1** exhaust. **2** smash. **3** *inf* slate, severely criticize. **s'éreinter** *vr* tire oneself out. **s'éreinter à** slave at
ériger (e:ri:'ʒe:) *vt* **1** erect. **2** set up.
ermite (ɛr'mi:t) *nm* hermit.
éroder (e:rɔ'de:) *vt* **1** erode. **2** eat away.
érotique (e:rɔ'ti:k) *adj* erotic.
errer (ɛ're:) *vi* **1** wander, roam. **2** stray. **3** err. **erreur** *nf* **1** error. **2** mistake. **3** fallacy.
éruption (e:ryp'sjɔ̃) *nf* **1** eruption. **2** *med* rash.
es (ɛ) *v* see **être.**
ès (ɛs) *prep* contraction of **en les. licencié ès lettres/sciences** Bachelor of Arts/Science.
escabeau, -aux (ɛska'bo) *nm* **1** stool. **2** stepladder.
escadre (ɛs'kadr) *nf naut* squadron. **escadrille** *nf aviat* squadron. **escadron** *nm mil* troop
escale (ɛs'kal) *nf* **1** port of call. **2** stop.
escalier (ɛska'lje:) *nm* **1** staircase. **2** stairs.

escalier roulant escalator. **escalier tournant** spiral staircase.
escalope (ɛska'lɔp) *nf* escalope.
escamoter (ɛskamɔ'te:) *vt* **1** make disappear. **2** *inf* swipe. **escamoteur** *nm* conjuror.
escarbilles (ɛskar'bi:j) *nf pl* ashes, cinders.
escargot (ɛskar'go) *nm* snail.
escarmouche (ɛskar'mu:ʃ) *nf* skirmish.
escarpé (ɛskar'pe:) *adj* steep, sheer.
escarpolette (ɛskarpɔ'lɛt) *nf* swing.
escient (ɛ'sjɑ̃) *nm* knowledge. **à bon escient** deliberately.
esclandre (ɛs'klɑ̃dr) *nm* scandal.
esclave (ɛ'sklav) *nm,f* slave.
escompter (ɛskɔ̃'te:) *vt* **1** discount. **2** *inf* anticipate. **escompte** *nm* **1** discount. **2** rebate.
escorte (ɛ'skɔrt) *nf* **1** escort. **2** *naut* convoy.
escrime (ɛ'skri:m) *nf* fencing. **faire de l'escrime** fence.
escroc (ɛ'skro) *nm* crook, swindler.
escroquer (ɛskrɔ'ke:) *vt* **1** cheat. **2** swindle. **escroquerie** *nf* swindle.
espace (ɛ'spas) *nm* space.
espadon (ɛspa'dɔ̃) *nm* swordfish.
Espagne (ɛ'spaɲ) *nf* Spain. **espagnol** *adj* Spanish. *nm* **1** Spaniard. **2** Spanish (language).
espèce (ɛ'spɛs) *nf* **1** kind, sort. **2** species.
espérer (ɛspe:'re:) *vt* **1** hope. **2** trust. **espérance** *nf* **1** hope. **2** expectation.
espiègle (ɛ'spjɛgl) *adj* mischievous.
espion, -onne (ɛ'spjɔ̃, -'spjɔn) *nm,f* spy.
espionner (ɛspjɔ'ne:) *vt* spy on. **espionnage** *nm* espionage.
esplanade (ɛspla'nad) *nf* esplanade, promenade.
espoir (ɛ'spwar) *nm* hope.
esprit (ɛ'spri:) *nm* **1** spirit. **2** ghost. **3** soul. **4** mind. **5** wit. **à l'esprit étroit/large** narrow/broad-minded. **faible d'esprit** weak-minded.
esquimau, -aude, -aux (ɛski:'mo, -'mod, -'mo) *adj,n* Eskimo.
esquisser (ɛski:'se:) *vt* **1** sketch. **2** outline. **esquisse** *nf* **1** sketch. **2** outline. **3** draft.
esquiver (ɛski:'ve:) *vt* dodge, evade. **s'esquiver** *vr* slip off.
essai (e:'sɛ) *nm* **1** trial, test. **2** attempt. **3** essay. **4** *sport* try. **à l'essai** on approval or trial.
essaim (ɛ'sɛ̃) *nm* swarm.
essaimer (e:sɛ'me:) *vi* swarm.
essayer (e:sɛ'je:) *vt* **1** try, test. **2** try on.
essence (ɛ'sɑ̃s) *nf* **1** essence. **2** petrol. **3** extract.
essentiel, -elle (ɛsɑ̃'sjɛl) *adj* essential. *nm* main point.
essieu, -ieux (e:'sjœ) *nm* axle.
essor (ɛ'sɔr) *nm* **1** flight. **2** scope. **3** rise.
essorer (e:sɔ're:) *vt* wring out. **essoreuse** *nf* **1** spin-dryer. **2** mangle.
essoufflé (e:su:'fle:) *adj* out of breath.
essuyer (e:sɥi:'je:) *vt* **1** wipe. **2** dry. **3** suffer. **essuie-glace** *nm, pl* **essuie-glaces** windscreen wiper. **essuie-main** *nm invar also* **essuie-mains** towel. **essuie-pieds** *nm invar* doormat.
est[1] (ɛst) *nm* east. *adj invar* east, eastern. **à l'est** in the east. **d'est** easterly. **vers l'est** eastward, eastwards.
est[2] (ɛ) *v see* **être.**
estaminet (ɛstami:'nɛ) *nm* public house.
estamper (ɛstɑ̃'pe:) *vt* **1** print, engrave. **2** stamp.
estampille (ɛstɑ̃'pi:j) *nf* **1** official stamp. **2** trademark.
esthétique (ɛste:'ti:k) *adj* aesthetic. *nf* aesthetics.
estimer (ɛsti:'me:) *vt* **1** estimate. **2** consider. **3** esteem. **estime** *nf* esteem.
estivant (ɛsti:'vɑ̃) *nm* holiday-maker.
estomac (ɛstɔ'ma) *nm* stomach.
estomper (ɛstɔ̃'pe:) *vt* blur.
estrade (ɛ'strad) *nf* platform, stage.
estragon (ɛstra'gɔ̃) *nm* tarragon.
estropier (ɛstrɔ'pje:) *vt* **1** cripple. **2** maim. **3** ruin.
estuaire (ɛs'tɥɛr) *nm* estuary.
esturgeon (ɛstyr'ʒɔ̃) *nm* sturgeon.
et (e:) *conj* and. **et...et** both...and.
établir (e:ta'bli:r) *vt* **1** establish. **2** set up. **3** draw up. **4** lay down. **s'établir** *vr* establish oneself, settle. **établissement** *nm* **1** establishment. **2** institution.
étage (e:'taʒ) *nm* floor, storey. **étagère** *nf* **1** shelf. **2** set of shelves.
étai (e:'tɛ) *nm* stay, prop.
étain (e:'tɛ̃) *nm* **1** tin. **2** pewter.
étais (e:'tɛ) *v see* **être.**
étaler (e:ta'le:) *vt* **1** display. **2** set out. **3** spread out. **4** *inf* show off. **s'étaler** *vr* stretch oneself out. **étalage** *nm* **1** display. **2** window-dressing. **faire étalage de** show off.
étalon[1] (e:ta'lɔ̃) *nm* stallion.
étalon[2] (e:ta'lɔ̃) *nm* standard.
étancher (e:tɑ̃'ʃe:) *vt* **1** stop, staunch. **2** quench. **3** make watertight or airtight. **étanche** *adj* **1** watertight. **2** airtight.

étang (e:'tɑ̃) *nm* pond.
étant (e:'tɑ̃) *v* see **être.**
étape (e:'tap) *nf* **1** stage. **2** halt.
état (e:'ta) *nm* **1** state. **2** condition. **3** statement. **4** profession. **faire état de 1** take into account. **2** depend on. **étatisme** *nm* state control. **état-major** *nm, pl* **états-major 1** *mil* staff. **2** management.
Etats-Unis *nm pl* United States of America.
étayer (e:tɛ'je:) *vt* **1** prop up. **2** support.
été[1] (e:'te:) *nm* summer.
été[2] (e:'te:) *v* see **être.**
éteindre* (e:'tɛ̃dr) *vi* **1** extinguish, put out. **2** turn off. **3** soften. **s'éteindre** *vr* die out. **éteint** *adj* **1** extinguished. **2** extinct. **3** dim.
étendard (e:tɑ̃'dar) *nm* standard, flag.
étendre (e:'tɑ̃dr) *vt* **1** stretch. **2** spread. **3** extend, enlarge. **s'étendre** *vr* **1** stretch oneself out. **2** spread. **étendu** *adj* **1** extensive. **2** wide. **3** far-reaching. **étendue** *nf* **1** extent. **2** expanse.
éternel, -elle (e:tɛr'nɛl) *adj* **1** eternal. **2** everlasting.
éternité (e:tɛrni:'te:) *nf* eternity.
éternuer (e:tɛr'nɥe:) *vi* sneeze. **éternuement** *nm* **1** sneeze. **2** sneezing.
êtes (ɛt) *v* see **être.**
éther (e:'tɛr) *nm* ether. **éthéré** *adj* ethereal.
Ethiopie (e:tjɔ'pi:) *nf* Ethiopia. **éthiopien, -ienne** (e:tjɔ'pjɛ̃, -'pjɛn) *adj,n* Ethiopian.
éthique (e:'ti:k) *adj* ethical. *nf* ethics.
ethnique (ɛt'ni:k) *adj* ethnic.
étinceler (e:tɛ̃'sle:) *vi* **1** sparkle. **2** glitter. **étincelle** *nf* spark.
étiquette (e:ti:'kɛt) *nf* **1** label. **2** tag. **3** etiquette. **4** ceremony.
étirer (e:ti:'re:) *vt* **1** stretch. **2** draw out.
étoffe (e:'tɔf) *nf* **1** material, fabric. **2** stuff, potential.
étoile (e:'twal) *nf* **1** star. **2** decoration. **3** fate. **étoile polaire** Pole Star.
étole (e:'tɔl) *nf* stole.
étonner (e:tɔ'ne:) *vt* astonish, amaze. **s'étonner** *vr* **1** be astonished. **2** wonder.
étouffer (e:tu:'fe:) *vi,vt* **1** suffocate. **2** choke. *vt* **1** stifle. **2** smother. **3** hush up. **étouffant** *adj* **1** stifling. **2** stuffy. **3** sultry. **cuire à l'étouffée** braise.
étourdir (e:tu:r'di:r) *vt* **1** stun. **2** daze. **3** make dizzy. **4** deafen. **étourderie** *nf* **1** thoughtlessness. **2** blunder. **étourdi** *adj* **1** giddy. **2** thoughtless. **3** light-headed. **à l'étourdie** thoughtlessly.
étourneau, -aux (e:tu:r'no) *nm* starling.
étrange (e:'trɑ̃ʒ) *adj* **1** strange. **2** odd. **3** peculiar. **4** weird. **étranger, -ère** (e:trɑ̃'ʒe:, -'ʒɛr) *adj* **1** foreign. **2** unfamiliar. **3** irrelevant. *nm,f* **1** stranger. **2** foreigner. **à l'étranger** abroad.
étrangler (e:trɑ̃gle:) *vt* **1** strangle. **2** throttle. **3** choke. **étranglé** *adj* **1** choked. **2** narrow.
étrave (e:'trav) *nf naut* bow.
être* (ɛtr) *vi* **1** be. **2** exist. *v aux* be. **être à 1** belong to. **2** be in or at. ~*nm* **1** existence. **2** being. **3** individual. **être humain** human being.
étreindre* (e:'trɛ̃dr) *vt* **1** embrace. **2** grasp. **3** clasp. **4** wring. **étreinte** *nf* **1** grasp. **2** hug.
étrenne (e:'trɛn) *nf* New Year's present.
étrier (e:tri:'e:) *nm* stirrup.
étriqué (e:tri:'ke:) *adj* tight.
étroit (e:'trwa) *adj* **1** narrow. **2** tight. **3** confined. **4** strict. **étroitesse** *nf* **1** narrowness. **2** tightness.
étude (e:'tyd) *nf* **1** study. **2** research. **3** chambers.
étudier (e:ty'dje:) *vt* **1** study. **2** investigate. **s'étudier à** *vr* endeavour to. **étudiant** *nm* **1** student. **2** undergraduate.
étui (e:'tɥi:) *nm* case, box.
étuver (e:ty've:) *vt* **1** dry. **2** heat. **3** steam.
étymologie (e:ti:mɔlɔ'ʒi:) *nf* etymology.
eu (y) *v* see **avoir.**
eucalyptus (œkali:p'tys) *nm* eucalyptus.
eucharistie (œkari:'sti:) *nf* Eucharist.
eunuque (œ'nyk) *nm* eunuch.
euphémisme (œfe:'mi:sm) *nm* euphemism.
euphorie (œfɔ'ri:) *nf* euphoria.
Europe (œ'rɔp) *nf* Europe. **européen, -enne** (œrɔpe:'ɛ̃, -'ɛn) *adj,n* European.
eus (y) *v* see **avoir.**
euthanasie (œtana'zi:) *nf* euthanasia.
eux (œ) *pron 3rd pers m pl* **1** they. **2** them. **eux-mêmes** *pron 3rd pers m pl* themselves.
évacuer (e:va'kɥe:) *vt* **1** evacuate. **2** empty. **3** vacate.
s'évader (se:va'de:) *vr* escape.
évaluer (e:va'lɥe:) *vt* **1** value. **2** assess. **3** estimate.
évangélique (e:vɑ̃ʒe:'li:k) *adj* **1** Evangelical. **2** Protestant. **évangéliste** *nm* Evangelist.
évangile (e:vɑ̃'ʒi:l) *nm* gospel.
s'évanouir (se:va'nwi:r) *vr* **1** vanish. **2** faint. **évanouissement** *nm* **1** disappearance. **2** faint.
évaporer (e:vapɔ're:) *vt* evaporate.
évasion (e:va'zjɔ̃) *nf* escape.

éveil (e:'vɛj) *nm* **1** awakening. **2** alert. **3** alarm.
éveiller (e:vɛ'je:) *vt* **1** wake up, waken. **2** arouse. **s'éveiller** *vr* awake, wake up.
événement (e:vɛn'mɑ̃) *nm* **1** event. **2** incident. **3** outcome.
éventail (e:vɑ̃'taj) *nm* fan.
éventer (e:vɑ̃'te:) *vt* **1** air. **2** fan. **3** get wind of. **s'éventer** *vr* **1** spoil. **2** go flat or stale. **éventé** *adj* stale, flat.
éventrer (e:vɑ̃'tre:) *vt* **1** gut. **2** rip open.
éventuel, -elle (e:vɑ̃'tɥɛl) *adj* **1** possible. **2** eventual. **éventualité** *nf* contingency.
évêque (e:'vɛk) *nm* bishop.
s'évertuer (se:vɛr'tɥe:) *vr* do one's utmost.
évidence (e:vi:'dɑ̃s) *nf* **1** obviousness. **2** evidence. **évidemment** (e:vi:da'mɑ̃) *adv* evidently. **évident** *adj* evident, clear.
évider (e:vi:'de:) *vt* hollow out.
évier (e:'vje:) *nm* sink.
évincer (e:vɛ̃'se:) *vt* evict.
éviter (e:vi:'te:) *vt* **1** avoid. **2** shun.
évoluer (e:vɔ'lɥe:) *vi* **1** manoeuvre. **2** evolve.
évoquer (e:vɔ'ke:) *vt* **1** evoke. **2** conjure up.
exact (ɛg'zakt) *adj* **1** exact. **2** accurate. **3** true. **4** punctual. **5** strict.
exagérer (ɛgzaʒe:'re:) *vt* exaggerate. **exagération** *nf* exaggeration.
exalter (ɛgzal'te:) *vt* **1** exalt. **2** excite.
examen (ɛgza'mɛ̃) *nm* **1** examination. **2** inspection.
examiner (ɛgzami:'ne:) *vt* **1** examine. **2** inspect.
exaspérer (ɛgzaspe:'re:) *vt* **1** aggravate. **2** exasperate.
exaucer (ɛgzo'se:) *vt* **1** grant. **2** hear. **3** fulfil.
excaver (ɛkska've:) *vt* excavate.
excédant (ɛkse:'dɑ̃) *adj* surplus, excess.
excellent (ɛksɛ'lɑ̃) *adj* excellent. **excellence** *nf* **1** excellence. **2** *cap* Excellency.
exceller (ɛksɛ'le:) *vi* excel.
excentrique (ɛksɑ̃'tri:k) *adj* eccentric.
excepter (e:ksɛp'te:) *vt* exclude. **excepté** *prep* except, save, but. **exception** *nf* exception. **exceptionnel, -elle** (e:ksɛpsjɔ'nɛl) *adj* exceptional.
excès (e:k'sɛ) *nm* excess. **excessif, -ive** (e:ksɛ'si:f, -'si:v) *adj* excessive.
exciter (e:ksi:'te:) *vt* **1** excite. **2** arouse. **3** animate. **4** inflame. **s'exciter** *vr* get excited.
s'exclamer (sɛkskla'me:) *vr* exclaim. **exclamation** *nf* exclamation.
exclure* (ɛks'klyr) *vt* exclude. **exclusif, -ive** (ɛkskly'si:f, -'si:v) *adj* **1** exclusive. **2** sole.
excommunier (ɛkskɔmy'nje:) *vt* excommunicate.
excursion (ɛkskyr'zjɔ̃) *nf* **1** excursion. **2** tour. **3** trip.
excuser (ɛksky'ze:) *vt* **1** excuse. **2** pardon. **s'excuser** *vr* apologize. **excuse** *nf* **1** excuse. **2** *pl* apology.
exécrer (e:gze:'kre:) *vt* loathe. **exécrable** (e:gzɛ'krabl) *adj* abominable.
exécuter (e:gze:ky'te:) *vt* **1** execute. **2** carry out. **3** perform. **exécutif, -ive** (e:gze:ky'ti:f, -'ti:v) *adj* executive.
exemple (e:g'zɑ̃pl) *nm* **1** example. **2** lesson. **3** precedent. **par exemple** **1** for instance. **2** indeed. **exemplaire** *nm* **1** copy. **2** sample.
exempt (e:g'zɑ̃) *adj* exempt, free.
exempter (e:gzɑ̃'te:) *vt* exempt.
exercer (e:gzɛr'se:) *vt* **1** exercise. **2** train. **3** exert. **4** practise, pursue.
exercice (e:gzɛr'si:s) *nm* **1** exercise. **2** *mil* drill. **3** use. **4** practice.
exhaler (ɛgza'le:) *vt* **1** exhale. **2** emit. **3** vent.
exhiber (e:gzi:'be:) *vt* **1** show. **2** exhibit. **exhibition** *nf* exhibition, display.
exiger (egzi:'ʒe:) *vt* **1** exact. **2** demand. **3** require.
exigu, -uë (e:gzi:'gy) *adj* **1** tiny. **2** slender.
exil (e:g'zi:l) *nm* exile.
exiler (e:gzi:'le:) *vt* **1** exile. **2** banish.
existentialisme (e:gzi:stɑ̃sja'li:sm) *nm* existentialism.
exister (e:gzi:'ste:) *vi* **1** exist. **2** live.
exorbitant (ɛgzɔrbi:'tɑ̃) *adj* **1** exorbitant. **2** outrageous.
exorciser (ɛgzɔrsi:'ze:) *vt* exorcize.
exotique (ɛgzɔ'ti:k) *adj* exotic.
expatrier (ɛkspatri:'e:) *vt* expatriate. **expatrié** *adj,n* expatriate.
expédier (ɛkspe'dje:) *vt* **1** dispatch. **2** hurry through. **3** send off. **expédient** *adj,nm* expedient. **expéditeur** *nm* sender. **expédition** *nf* **1** expedition. **2** copy. **3** forwarding. **4** consignment.
expérience (ɛkspe:'rjɑ̃s) *nf* **1** experience. **2** experiment. **3** test.
expérimenter (ɛkspe:ri:mɑ̃'te:) *vt* **1** test. **2** try. *vi* experiment. **expérimenté** *adj* **1** experienced. **2** skilled.
expert (ɛk'spɛr) *adj* **1** skilled. **2** expert. *nm* expert.
expier (ɛk'spje:) *vt* atone for.
expirer (ɛkspi:'re:) *vt* breathe out. *vi* **1** die. **2** expire.

explétif, -ive (ɛksple:'ti:f, -'ti:v) *adj,nm* expletive.
explication (ɛkspli:ka'sjɔ̃) *nf* explanation.
explicite (ɛkspli'si:t) *adj* **1** explicit. **2** clear.
expliquer (ɛkspli'ke:) *vt* **1** explain. **2** account for.
exploit (ɛk'splwa) *nm* **1** exploit. **2** feat. **3** writ.
exploiter (ɛksplwa'te:) *vt* **1** exploit. **2** cultivate. **3** take advantage of.
explorer (ɛksplɔ're:) *vt* explore. **explorateur** *nm* explorer.
exploser (ɛksplo'ze:) *vi* explode. **explosif, -ive** (ɛksplo'si:f, -'si:v) *adj,nm* explosive.
exporter (ɛkspɔr'te:) *vt* export. **exportation** *nf* export.
exposer (ɛkspo'ze:) *vt* **1** show. **2** exhibit. **3** explain. **4** expose. **exposé** *nm* **1** account. **2** short talk. **exposition** *nf* **1** exhibition. **2** exposure.
exprès, -esse (ɛk'sprɛ, -'sprɛs) *adj* **1** express. **2** explicit. **exprès** *adv* on purpose.
express (ɛk'sprɛs) *nm* express train.
expression (ɛksprɛ'sjɔ̃) *nf* expression.
exprimer (ɛkspri:'me:) *vt* **1** express. **2** squeeze out
expulser (ɛkspyl'se:) *vt* **1** expel. **2** turn out.
exquis (ɛk'ski:) *adj* exquisite.
extase (ɛk'stɑz) *nf* ecstasy.
extension (ɛkstɑ̃'sjɔ̃) *nf* **1** extension. **2** spread. **3** extent.
exténuer (ɛkste:'nɥe:) *vt* exhaust.
extérieur (ɛkste:'rjœr) *adj* **1** exterior. **2** outer. **3** foreign. *nm* **1** exterior. **2** outside. **à l'extérieur** **1** outside. **2** abroad.
exterminer (ɛkstɛrmi:'ne:) *vt* exterminate.
externe (ɛk'stɛrn) *adj* external. *nm* **1** day pupil. **2** outpatient. **externat** *nm* day school.
extirper (ɛksti:r'pe:) *vt* **1** uproot. **2** eradicate.
extra (ɛk'stra) *nm invar* extra. *adj invar inf* first-class, excellent.
extraire* (ɛk'strɛr) *vt* **1** extract. **2** pull out. **extrait** *nm* **1** extract. **2** excerpt. **3** certificate.
extraordinaire (ɛkstrɔrdi:'nɛr) *adj* **1** extraordinary. **2** unusual.
extravagant (ɛkstrava'gɑ̃) *adj* **1** extravagant. **2** foolish. **3** exorbitant.
extraverti (ɛkstravɛr'ti:) *adj,n* extrovert.
extrême (ɛk'strɛm) *adj* **1** extreme **2** farthest. **3** utmost. **4** intense. *nm* extreme limit. **extrémité** *nf* **1** extremity. **2** end. **3** tip. **4** limit.
Extrême-Orient *nm* Far East.
exubérant (egzybɛ'rɑ̃) *adj* exuberant.

F

fable (fabl) *nf* **1** fable. **2** story.
fabricant (fabri:'kɑ̃) *nm* manufacturer.
fabriquer (fabri:'ke:) *vt* **1** manufacture. **2** make. **fabriquer en série** mass-produce. **fabrique** *nf* **1** manufacture. **2** factory.
fabuleux, -euse (faby'lœ, -'lœz) *adj* fabulous.
façade (fa'sad) *nf* **1** facade. **2** front.
face (fas) *nf* **1** face. **2** front. **3** aspect. **en face** opposite. **face à** facing.
facétie (fase:'si:) *nf* joke. **facétieux, -euse** (fase:'sjœ, -'sjœz) *adj* facetious.
fâcher (fɑ'ʃe:) *vt* make angry. **se fâcher** *vr* get angry. **fâché** *adj* **1** angry, cross. **2** sorry. **fâcheux, -euse** (fɑ'ʃœ, -'ʃœz) *adj* **1** annoying. **2** unfortunate.
facile (fa'si:l) *adj* **1** easy. **2** facile, ready. **3** weak.
faciliter (fasi:li:'te:) *vt* facilitate. **facilité** *nf* **1** easiness. **2** gift, talent. **3** facility.
façon (fa'sɔ̃) *nf* **1** manner. **2** way. **3** making. **4** make. **5** *pl* fuss. **à façon** made to measure. **de façon à** so as to. **de toute façon** anyway, in any case.
façonner (fasɔ'ne:) *vt* **1** shape. **2** fashion. **3** mould.
fac-similé (faksi:mi:'le:) *nm, pl* **fac-similés** facsimile.
facteur (fak'tœr) *nm* **1** postman. **2** factor. **3** agent.
factice (fak'ti:s) *adj* **1** artificial. **2** imitation. **3** dummy.
faction (fak'sjɔ̃) *nf* **1** faction. **2** guard.
facture (fak'tyr) *nf* invoice.
facultatif, -ive (fakylta'ti:f, -'ti:v) *adj* optional.
faculté (fakyl'te:) *nf* **1** option. **2** right. **3** ability. **4** faculty. **5** *pl* resources.
fadaise (fa'dɛz) *nf* **1** silly remark. **2** *pl* nonsense.
fade (fad) *adj* **1** dull. **2** tasteless.
fagot (fa'go) *nm* bundle.
fagoter (fagɔ'te:) *vt* dress without taste.
faiblir (fɛ'bli:r) *vi* **1** grow weaker. **2** fail. **faible** (fɛbl) *adj* **1** weak. **2** feeble. *nm* failing. **faiblesse** *nf* **1** weakness. **2** failing.
faïence (fa'jɑ̃s) *nf* **1** crockery. **2** earthenware.
faillible (fa'ji:bl) *adj* fallible.
faillir* (fa'ji:r) *vi* fail. **faillir tomber** nearly fall. **failli** *adj,n* bankrupt. **faillite** *nf* bankruptcy. **faire faillite** go bankrupt.
faim (fɛ̃) *nf* hunger. **avoir faim** be hungry.

fainéant (fɛne:ˈɑ̃) *adj* idle, lazy.
faire* (fɛr) *vt* **1** make. **2** do. **3** matter. **4** be. **5** arrange. **6** cause. **7** *sport* go in for. **ça ne fait rien** that doesn't matter. **faire faire** have made or done. **faire voir** show. **faites attention!** be careful! **il n'y a rien à faire** nothing can be done about it. **que faire?** what is to be done? **se faire** *vr* **1** develop. **2** become. **3** accustom oneself. **4** be. **se faire fort de** undertake to. **faire-part** *nm invar* announcement.
faisable (fəˈzabl) *adj* feasible.
faisan (fɛˈzɑ̃) *nm* pheasant.
faisant (fɛˈzɑ̃) *v* see **faire.**
faisceau, -aux (fɛˈso) *nm* bundle.
fait[1] (fɛ) *v* see **faire.** *adj* **1** done. **2** made. **3** fully grown. **4** ripe.
fait[2] (fɛ) *nm* **1** act. **2** deed. **3** fact. **4** exploit. **5** incident. **au fait** after all. **de** or **en fait** actually, in actual fact. **de son fait** of one's own accord. **fait-divers** *nm* news item.
faîte (fɛt) *nm* **1** top, summit. **2** ridge.
faix (fɛ) *nm* **1** burden. **2** load.
falaise (faˈlɛz) *nf* cliff.
falloir* (faˈlwar) *v imp* **1** need. **2** be necessary. **3** must. **comme il faut 1** proper. **2** properly. **s'en falloir** *vr* **1** be lacking. **2** be far from.
falsifier (falsi:ˈfje:) *vt* **1** falsify. **2** forge.
famé (faˈme:) *adj* **bien/mal famé** of good/evil repute.
fameux, -euse (faˈmœ, -ˈmœz) *adj* **1** famous. **2** *inf* great, excellent.
familial, -aux (fami:ˈljal, -ˈljo) *adj* family.
familier, -ière (fami:ˈlje:, -ˈljɛr) *adj* **1** domestic. **2** of the family. **3** familiar.
famille (faˈmi:j) *nf* **1** family. **2** household. **3** relations. **en famille** informally.
famine (faˈmi:n) *nf* famine.
fanal, -aux (faˈnal, -ˈno) *nm* lantern.
fanatique (fanaˈti:k) *adj* fanatical. *nm,f* fanatic.
faner (faˈne:) *vt* **1** make hay. **2** cause to fade. **se faner** *vr* **1** droop. **2** wilt. **3** fade.
fanfare (fɑ̃ˈfar) *nf* **1** *mus* flourish. **2** brass band.
fange (fɑ̃ʒ) *nf* **1** mud. **2** filth.
fantaisie (fɑ̃tɛˈzi:) *nf* **1** imagination. **2** fantasy. **3** fancy. **4** whim.
fantasmagorique (fɑ̃tasmagɔˈri:k) *adj* **1** weird. **2** fantastic.
fantastique (fɑ̃taˈsti:k) *adj* **1** fantastic. **2** *inf* incredible.
fantoche (fɑ̃ˈtɔʃ) *nm* puppet.
fantôme (fɑ̃ˈtom) *nm* **1** ghost. **2** phantom.
faon (fɑ̃) *nm zool* fawn.
farce (fars) *nf* **1** farce. **2** prank.
farcir (farˈsi:r) *vt cul* stuff.
fard (far) *nm* **1** make-up. **2** rouge. **3** disguise.
fardeau, -aux (farˈdo) *nm* burden.
farder (farˈde:) *vt* **1** make up. **2** disguise.
farfouiller (farfu:ˈje:) *vi* rummage.
farine (faˈri:n) *nf* **1** flour. **2** meal. **farine d'avoine** oatmeal. **farine de maïs** cornflour.
farouche (faˈru:ʃ) *adj* **1** wild. **2** savage. **3** sullen. **4** shy. **5** cruel.
fart (far) *nm* wax.
fasciner (fassi:ˈne:) *vt* fascinate.
fascisme (faˈsi:sm) *nm* fascism. **fasciste** *adj,n* fascist.
faste (fast) *nm* **1** pomp. **2** display.
fastidieux, -euse (fasti:ˈdjœ, -ˈdjœz) *adj* **1** tedious. **2** boring.
fastueux, -euse (faˈstɥœ, -ˈstɥœz) *adj* **1** ostentatious. **2** pompous.
fatal (faˈtal) *adj* **1** fatal. **2** inevitable. **fatalité** *nf* **1** fatality. **2** fate.
fatiguer (fati:ˈge:) *vt* **1** tire. **2** overwork. **3** bore. *vi mot* labour. **se fatiguer** *vr* get tired. **fatigue** *nf* fatigue, tiredness.
fatras (faˈtrɑ) *nm* **1** jumble. **2** rubbish.
faubourg (foˈbu:r) *nm* suburb.
faucher (foˈʃe:) *vt* **1** reap, cut. **2** *inf* pinch, steal. **fauché** *adj* **1** cut. **2** *inf* broke.
faucon (foˈkɔ̃) *nm* **1** falcon. **2** hawk.
faudra (fo:ˈdra) *v* see **falloir.**
faufiler (fofi:ˈle:) *vt* **1** (sewing) tack. **2** baste. **3** insert. **se faufiler** *vr* creep.
faune (fon) *nf* fauna.
fausser (foˈse:) *vt* **1** falsify. **2** *mus* put out of tune. **3** pervert. **4** bend.
faut (fo:) *v* see **falloir.**
faute (fot) *nf* **1** fault. **2** error. **3** lack. **faute de** for want of. **sans faute** without fail.
fauteuil (foˈtœj) *nm* **1** armchair. **2** *educ* chair.
fauve (fov) *adj* fawn. *nm* **1** fawn (colour). **2** *pl* wild beasts.
faux[1]**, fausse** (fo, fos) *adj* **1** false. **2** untrue. **3** wrong. **4** counterfeit. *nm* **1** falsehood. **2** forgery. **à faux** wrongly. **faux-filet** *nm, pl* **faux-filets** sirloin.
faux[2] (fo) *nf* scythe.
faveur (faˈvœr) *nf* favour. **en faveur de** on behalf of. **favorable** *adj* favourable.
favori, -ite (favɔˈri:, -ˈri:t) *adj,n* favourite.
favoriser (favɔri:ˈze:) *vt* **1** favour. **2** assist. **3** patronize. **4** promote.
fébrile (fe:ˈbri:l) *adj* feverish.
fécond (fe:ˈkɔ̃) *adj* **1** fertile. **2** prolific.

fédérer (fe:de:'re:) *vt* federate. **fédéral, -aux** (fe:de:'ral, -'ro) *adj* federal.
fée (fe:) *nf* fairy.
feindre* (fɛ̃dr) *vt* feign. **feindre de** pretend to. **feinte** *nf* feint, pretence.
fêler (fɛ'le:) *vt* crack. **fêlure** *nf* crack.
féliciter (fe:li:si'te:) *vt* congratulate. **félicitations** *nf pl* congratulations.
félin (fe:'lɛ̃) *adj* feline.
femelle (fə'mɛl) *adj,nf* female, she.
féminin (fe:mi:'nɛ̃) *adj* **1** feminine. **2** female.
femme (fam) *nf* **1** woman. **2** wife. **femme de chambre 1** chambermaid. **2** housemaid. **femme de charge/ménage** housekeeper/charwoman.
fémur (fe:'myr) *nm* thighbone.
fendre (fɑ̃dr) *vt* split.
fenêtre (fə'nɛtr) *nf* window.
fenouil (fə'nu:j) *nm* fennel.
fente (fɑ̃t) *nf* **1** crack. **2** crevice. **3** split. **4** slit. **5** slot.
féodal, -aux (fe:ɔ'dal, -'do) *adj* feudal.
fer (fɛr) *nm* **1** iron. **2** sword. **3** *pl* chains. **fer à cheval** horseshoe. **fer à repasser** *dom* iron. **fer blanc** tin. **fer forgé** wrought iron.
ferai (fə're) *v see* **faire.**
férié (fe:'rje:) **jour férié** *nm* **1** holiday. **2** bank holiday.
férir* (fe:'ri:r) *vt* strike.
ferme[1] (fɛrm) *adj* **1** firm. **2** steady. **3** steadfast. *adv* **1** firmly. **2** hard. **fermeté** *nf* firmness.
ferme[2] (fɛrm) *nf* **1** farm. **2** farmhouse. **fermier** (fɛr'mje:) *nm* farmer.
fermenter (fɛrmɑ̃'te:) *vi* **1** ferment. **2** rise.
fermer (fɛr'me:) *vi,vt* **1** close. **2** shut. *vt* **1** turn or switch off. **2** fasten. **fermer à clef** lock. **fermeture** *nf* **1** closing. **2** shutting. **Fermeture Eclair** *nf Tdmk* zip.
féroce (fe:rɔs) *adj* **1** wild. **2** ferocious.
ferraille (fɛ'rɑj) *nf* scrap iron.
ferré (fɛ're:) *adj* **1** fitted with iron. **2** hobnailed.
ferroviaire (fɛrrɔ'vjɛr) *adj* railway.
fertile (fɛr'ti:l) *adj* **1** fertile. **2** fruitful.
fertiliser (fɛrti:li:'ze:) *vt* fertilize.
fervent (fɛr'vɑ̃) *adj* **1** fervent. **2** ardent. *nm* enthusiast.
ferveur (fɛr'vœr) *nf* fervour.
fesser (fɛ'se:) *vt* spank. **fesse** *nf* **1** buttock. **2** *pl inf* bottom. **fessée** *nf* spanking.
festin (fɛ'stɛ̃) *nm* **1** banquet. **2** feast.
feston (fɛ'stɔ̃) *nm* **1** festoon. **2** scallop.
festonner (fɛstɔ'ne:) *vt* **1** festoon. **2** scallop.
fêter (fɛ'te:) *vt* **1** celebrate. **2** keep as a holiday.
fête *nf* **1** feast. **2** festival. **3** holiday. **4** entertainment. **5** festivity.
fétiche (fe:'ti:ʃ) *nm* **1** fetish. **2** mascot.
fétide (fe:'ti:d) *adj* fetid.
feu[1], **feux** (fœ) *nm* **1** fire. **2** heat. **3** passion. **4** light. **feu d'artifice** fireworks, firework display. **feu de joie** bonfire. **feu de position** sidelight. **feux de circulation** *n pl* traffic lights.
feu[2] (fœ) *adj* late, deceased.
feuille (fœj) *nf* **1** leaf. **2** sheet (of paper). **feuillage** *nm* foliage. **feuillet** *nm* leaf (of a book). **feuilleton** *nm* serial story.
feuilleter (fœj'te:) *vt* flip through (a book).
feutre (fœtr) *nm* felt.
fève (fɛv) *nf* bean. **grosse fève** broad bean.
février (fe:vri:'e:) *nm* February.
fiacre (fjakr) *nm* cab.
se fiancer (fjɑ̃'se:) *vr* get engaged. **fiançailles** (fjɑ̃'saj) *nf pl* engagement. **fiancé** *nm* fiancé.
fiasco (fja'sko) *nm invar* fiasco, wash-out.
fibre (fi:br) *nf* **1** fibre. **2** grain.
ficeler (fi:'sle:) *vt* tie up. **ficelle** *nf* string.
ficher (fi:'ʃe:) *vt* **1** drive in. **2** *sl* stick. **3** give. **4** do. **fiche-moi la paix!** clear off! **se ficher de** *vr* make fun of. **je m'en fiche** I don't care. **fiche** *nf* **1** peg. **2** plug. **3** slip of paper. **4** voucher. **5** form. **fichu** *adj sl* **1** awful. **2** done for.
fiction (fi:k'sjɔ̃) *nf* fiction. **fictif, -ive** (fi:k'ti:f, -'ti:v) *adj* fictitious.
fidèle (fi:'dɛl) *adj* **1** faithful. **2** loyal. **fidélité** *nf* **1** loyalty. **2** fidelity.
fiel (fjɛl) *nm* gall, bile.
fiente (fjɑ̃t) *nf* droppings.
fier[1], **fière** (fjɛr) *adj* **1** proud. **2** haughty. **fierté** *nf* pride.
se fier[2] (fje:) *vr* trust.
fièvre (fjɛvr) *nf* **1** fever, temperature. **2** excitement.
figer (fi:'ʒ:e) *vt* **1** congeal, clot. **2** fix.
figue (fi:g) *nf* fig. **figuier** *nm* fig tree.
figurer (fi:gy're:) *vt* **1** represent. **2** appear. **se figurer** *vr* imagine. **figure** *nf* **1** shape. **2** figure. **3** face. **figuré** *adj* **1** figured. **2** figurative.
fil (fi:l) *nm* **1** thread. **2** yarn. **3** edge. **4** grain. **5** current. **fil de fer** wire.
filament (fi:la'mɑ̃) *nm* **1** filament. **2** fibre.
filer (fi:'le:) *vt* **1** spin. **2** prolong. **3** shadow. *vi* **1** flow smoothly. **2** slip by. **3** ladder. **4** slip off. **filer à l'anglaise** take French leave. **file** *nf* **1** line. **2** row. **filé** *nm* thread.

filet[1] (fi:'lɛ) *nm* **1** thin thread. **2** streak. **3** trickle.
filet[2] (fi:'lɛ) *nm* fillet.
filet[3] (fi:'lɛ) *nm* net.
filial, -aux (fi:'ljal, -'ljo) *adj* filial. **filiale** *nf* **1** subsidiary company. **2** *comm* branch.
fille (fi:j) *nf* **1** daughter. **2** girl. **jeune fille** young woman or girl. **vieille fille** spinster. **fillette** *nf* little girl.
filleul (fi:'ljœl) *nm* **1** godchild. **2** godson. **filleule** *nf* goddaughter.
film (fi:lm) *nm* film.
filou (fi:'lu:) *nm* **1** pickpocket. **2** cheat.
filouter (fi:lu:'te:) *vt* **1** rob. **2** swindle.
fils (fi:s) *nm* **1** son. **2** boy.
filtrer (fi:l'tre:) *vi,vt* **1** filter. **2** strain. *vi* percolate. **filtre** *nm* filter.
fin[1] (fɛ̃) *nf* **1** end. **2** close. **3** aim. **4** purpose. **en fin de compte** finally.
fin[2] (fɛ̃) *adj* **1** fine. **2** choice. **3** delicate. **4** shrewd. **5** expert. **6** slender. **7** semiprecious.
final (fi:'nal) *adj* **1** final. **2** last. **3** ultimate. **finale** *nf sport* final.
finance (fi:'nɑ̃s) *nf* **1** finance. **2** *pl* resources. **financier, -ière** (fi:nɑ̃'sje:, -'sjɛr) *adj* financial. *nm* financier.
finaud (fi:'no) *adj* cunning, sly.
finesse (fi:'nɛs) *nf* **1** delicacy. **2** shrewdness.
finir (fi:'ni:r) *vt* **1** finish. **2** end. **3** complete. *vi* come to an end. **fini** *adj* **1** finished. **2** accomplished. **3** finite.
Finlande (fɛ̃'lɑ̃d) *nf* Finland. **finlandais** *adj* Finnish. **finnois** (fi:'nwa) *adj* Finnish. *nm* **1** Finn. **2** Finnish (language).
fisc (fi:sk) *nm* **1** treasury. **2** exchequer. **3** Inland Revenue. **fiscal, -aux** (fi:'skal, -'sko) *adj* fiscal.
fission (fi:'sjɔ̃) *nf* fission.
fissure (fi:'syr) *nf* fissure, crack.
fixer (fi:k'se:) *vt* **1** fix. **2** determine. **3** settle. **fixe** *adj* **1** fixed, immovable. **2** firm. **3** regular. **4** settled.
fjord (fjɔr) *nm also* **fiord** fiord.
flacon (fla'kɔ̃) *nm* bottle.
flageller (flaʒɛl'le:) *vt* flog.
flagrant (fla'grɑ̃) *adj* **1** flagrant. **2** obvious.
flair (flɛr) *nm* **1** scent. **2** gift, flair.
flairer (flɛ're:) *vt* **1** scent, smell out. **2** sniff.
flamand (fla'mɑ̃) *adj* Flemish. *nm* **1** Fleming. **2** Flemish (language).
flamant (fla'mɑ̃) *nm* flamingo.
flamber (flɑ̃'be:) *vi* **1** blaze. **2** burn. *vt* singe. **flambeau, -aux** (flɑ̃'bo) *nm* **1** torch. **2** light. **3** candlestick.
flamboyant (flɑ̃bwa'jɑ̃) *adj* **1** blazing. **2** gaudy.
flamme (flɑm) *nf* **1** flame. **2** blaze. **3** passion. **flammèche** (fla'mɛʃ) *nf* spark.
flan (flɑ̃) *nm* custard tart.
flanc (flɑ̃) *nm* **1** flank. **2** side.
flanelle (fla'nɛl) *nf* flannel.
flâner (flɑ'ne:) *vi* **1** stroll. **2** dawdle.
flanquer (flɑ̃'ke:) *vt* **1** flank. **2** chuck, throw.
flaque (flak) *nf* puddle, pool.
flasque (flask) *adj* **1** flabby. **2** limp. **3** weak.
flatter (fla'te:) *vt* **1** stroke, pat. **2** delude. **3** flatter.
fléau, -aux (fle:'o) *nm* **1** scourge. **2** pest.
flèche (flɛʃ) *nf* **1** arrow. **2** spire.
fléchir (fle:'ʃi:r) *vt* **1** bend. **2** move to pity. *vi* **1** give way. **2** sag.
flegme (flɛgm) *nm* calmness.
flet (flɛ) *nm zool* flounder.
flétan (fle:'tɑ̃) *nm* halibut.
flétrir[1] (fle:'tri:r) *vt* **1** wither. **2** fade. **3** spoil.
flétrir[2] (fle:'tri:r) *vt* **1** brand. **2** disgrace.
fleur (flœr) *nf* **1** flower. **2** bloom. **3** blossom. **4** prime. **fleuriste** *nm,f* florist.
fleurir (flœ'ri:r) *vi* **1** flower, bloom. **2** prosper. *vt* decorate with flowers. **fleuri** *adj* **1** in bloom or flower. **2** flowery.
fleuve (flœv) *nm* river.
flexible (flɛk'sibl) *adj* flexible.
flibustier (fli:by'stje:) *nm* **1** pirate. **2** rogue.
flic (fli:k) *nm inf* copper, policeman.
flirter (flœr'te:) *vi* flirt.
flocon (flɔ'kɔ̃) *nm* **1** flake. **2** tuft.
flore (flɔr) *nf* flora.
florissant (flɔri:'sɑ̃) *adj* prosperous.
flot (flo) *nm* **1** wave. **2** flood. **3** surge. **à flot** afloat. **à flots** in torrents.
flotter (flɔ'te:) *vi,vt* float. *vi* **1** waft. **2** waver. **3** wander. **flotte** *nf* **1** fleet. **2** float.
flou (flu:) *adj* **1** blurred. **2** woolly.
fluctuer (flyk'tɥe:) *vi* fluctuate.
fluet, -ette (fly'ɛ, -'ɛt) *adj* thin, slender.
fluide (fly'i:d) *adj,nm* fluid.
flûte (flyt) *nf* **1** flute. **2** long thin loaf of bread. **3** tall champagne glass.
flux (fly) *nm* **1** flow. **2** flux.
focal, -aux (fɔ'kal, -'ko) *adj* focal.
fœtus (fe:'tys) *nm* foetus.
foi (fwa) *nf* **1** faith. **2** trust. **3** belief.
foie (fwa) *nm* liver.
foin (fwɛ̃) *nm* hay.
foire (fwar) *nf* fair.
fois (fwa) *nf* **1** time. **2** occasion. **à la fois** at the same time. **une fois** once.

foison (fwa'zɔ̃) *nf* plenty.
foisonner (fwazɔ'ne:) *vi* **1** abound. **2** increase.
fol (fɔl) *adj* see **fou.**
folâtre (fɔ'lɑtr) *adj* **1** playful. **2** lively.
folie (fɔ'li:) *nf* **1** madness. **2** folly.
folle (fɔl) *adj* see **fou.**
follet, -ette (fɔ'lɛ, -'lɛt) *adj* merry.
follicule (fɔli:'kyl) *nm* follicle.
foncer (fɔ̃'se:) *vi* **1** rush. **2** charge. *vt* sink. **se foncer** *vr* get darker. **foncé** *adj* dark.
foncier, -ière (fɔ̃'sje:, -'sjɛr) *adj* **1** of the land. **2** fundamental.
fonction (fɔ̃k'sjɔ̃) *nf* **1** function. **2** office. **fonctionnaire** *nm* **1** official. **2** civil servant.
fonctionner (fɔ̃ksjɔ'ne:) *vi* **1** function. **2** work. **3** run.
fond (fɔ̃) *nm* **1** bottom. **2** depth. **3** back. **4** background. **5** foundation. **à fond** thoroughly. **de fond** basic, fundamental.
fondamental, -aux (fɔ̃damɑ̃'tal, -'to) *adj* basic, fundamental.
fonder (fɔ̃'de:) *vt* **1** found. **2** establish. **3** base. **se fonder sur** *vr* **1** be based on. **2** rely on.
fondre (fɔ̃dr) *vi,vt* **1** melt. **2** dissolve. *vt* **1** cast. **2** blend. *vi* pounce.
fondrière (fɔ̃dri:'ɛr) *nf* **1** bog. **2** hollow.
fonds (fɔ̃) *nm* **1** land. **2** business. **3** fund. **4** funds. **5** *pl* cash.
font (fɔ̃) *v* see **faire.**
fontaine (fɔ̃'tɛn) *nf* **1** spring. **2** fountain. **3** cistern.
fonts (fɔ̃) *nm pl* font.
football (fu:t'bal) *nm* football.
for (fɔr) **for intérieur** *nm* conscience.
forain (fɔ'rɛ̃) *adj* travelling.
forçat (fɔr'sa) *nm* convict.
forcené (fɔrsə'ne:) *adj* **1** furious. **2** frantic.
forcer (fɔr'se:) *vt* **1** force. **2** break open. **3** compel. **force** *nf* **1** strength. **2** force. **3** power. *adj invar* a lot of. **à force de** by means of. **forcé** *adj* **1** forced. **2** compulsory. **forcément** *adv* **1** necessarily. **2** forcibly.
forer (fɔ're:) *vt* **1** drill. **2** bore.
forêt (fɔ'rɛ) *nf* forest.
forfait[1] (fɔr'fɛ) *nm* serious crime.
forfait[2] (fɔr'fɛ) *nm* contract.
forfait[3] (fɔr'fɛ) *nm* forfeit.
forficule (fɔrfi:'kyl) *nf* earwig.
forger (fɔr'ʒe:) *vt* **1** forge. **2** counterfeit. **3** fabricate. **forge** *nf* forge.
formaliser (fɔrmali:'ze:) *vt* offend. **se formaliser** *vr* take offence.
former (fɔr'me:) *vt* **1** form. **2** create. **3** train. **4** develop. **5** constitute. **se former** *vr* take shape. **formalité** *nf* **1** formality. **2** ceremony. **formation** *nf* **1** formation. **2** structure. **3** education, training. **4** development, growth. **forme** *nf* **1** form. **2** figure. **3** method. **4** *pl* manners. **être en forme** be fit. **formel, -elle** (fɔr'mɛl) *adj* **1** formal. **2** explicit. **3** definite.
formidable (fɔrmi:'dabl) *adj* **1** formidable. **2** *inf* tremendous, terrific.
formuler (fɔrmy'le:) *vt* **1** formulate. **2** state. **3** express. **formule** *nf* **1** formula. **2** prescription. **3** form.
fors (fɔr) *prep* except, but.
fort[1] (fɔr) *adj* **1** strong. **2** large, stout. **3** loud. **4** clever. **5** thick. **6** violent. *nm* **1** strong part. **2** height. **3** fort.
fort[2] (fɔr) *adv* **1** hard. **2** much. **3** very.
forteresse (fɔrtə'rɛs) *nf* fortress.
fortifier (fɔrti:'fje:) *vt* **1** strengthen. **2** fortify.
fortuit (fɔr'tɥi) *adj* **1** chance. **2** accidental. **3** casual.
fortune (fɔr'tyn) *nf* **1** chance. **2** luck. **3** fortune. **4** wealth. **fortuné** *adj* **1** fortunate. **2** happy. **3** rich.
fosse (fos) *nf* **1** hole. **2** pit. **3** grave. **fossé** *nm* **1** ditch. **2** moat. **fossette** *nf* dimple.
fossile (fɔ'si:l) *adj,nm* fossil.
fou, fol, folle (fu:, fɔl, fɔl) *adj* **1** mad. **2** foolish, silly. **3** insane. *nm,f* **1** lunatic. **2** fool.
foudre (fu:dr) *nm* lightning. **coup de foudre** *nm* **1** flash of lightning. **2** love at first sight.
foudroyer (fu:drwa'je:) *vt* **1** strike by lightning. **2** overwhelm. **foudroyant** *adj* **1** terrifying. **2** overwhelming. **3** terrific.
fouet (fwɛ) *nm* **1** whip. **2** lash.
fouetter (fwɛ'te:) *vt* **1** whip. **2** flog. **3** beat. **4** whisk.
fougère (fu:'ʒɛr) *nf* fern.
fougue (fu:g) *nf* **1** ardour. **2** spirit. **fougueux, -euse** (fu:'gœ, -'gœz) *adj* **1** ardent. **2** fiery. **3** impetuous.
fouiller (fu:'je:) *vt* **1** excavate. **2** dig. **3** search. *vi* rummage. **fouille** *nf* **1** excavation. **2** search.
fouillis (fu:'ji:) *nm* muddle, jumble.
fouir (fwi:r) *vt* burrow, dig.
foulard (fu:'lar) *nm* **1** silk handkerchief. **2** scarf.
fouler (fu:'le:) *vt* **1** crush. **2** trample. **3** sprain. **foule** *nf* crowd, mob. **foulure** *nf* sprain.
four (fu:r) *nm* **1** oven. **2** kiln. **3** furnace.
fourbe (fu:rb) *adj* crafty. *nm* **1** cheat. **2** rogue. **fourberie** (fu:rbə'ri:) *nf* **1** swindle. **2** deceit.

fourche (fu:rʃ) *nf* fork, pitchfork. **fourchette** *nf cul* fork.
fourgon[1] (fu:r'gɔ̃) *nm* poker.
fourgon[2] (fu:r'gɔ̃) *nm* **1** van. **2** wagon.
fourmi (fu:r'mi:) *nf* ant. **avoir des fourmis** have pins and needles.
fourmiller (fu:rmi:'je:) *vi* **1** swarm. **2** tingle.
fourneau, -aux (fu:r'no) *nm* **1** furnace. **2** stove.
fournir (fu:r'ni:r) *vt* **1** supply. **2** provide. **fourni** *adj* **1** thick. **2** bushy. **fournisseur** (fu:rni:-'sœr) *nm* tradesman. **fourniture** *nf pl* materials.
fourrer (fu:'re:) *vt* **1** stuff, cram. **2** shove. **3** line with fur. **fourreau, -aux** (fu:'ro) *nm* **1** sheath. **2** case, cover. **fourre-tout** *nm invar* holdall. **fourreur** *nm* furrier. **fourrure** *nf* **1** fur, skin. **2** lining.
foutre* (fu:tr) *vt* **1** *tab* have sexual intercourse with. **2** *sl* do. **je m'en fous** I don't give a damn.
foyer (fwa'je:) *nm* **1** hearth, fireplace. **2** centre. **3** home. **4** focus. **5** *Th* entrance hall.
fracas (fra'kɑ) *nm* **1** uproar. **2** din.
fracasser (fraka'se:) *vt* **1** smash. **2** shatter.
fraction (frak'sjɔ̃) *nf* fraction.
fracturer (frakty're:) *vt* **1** break. **2** fracture. **fracture** *nf* fracture.
fragile (fra'ʒi:l) *adj* **1** fragile. **2** delicate.
fragment (frag'mɑ̃) *nm* **1** fragment. **2** scrap.
frai (frɛ) *nm* spawn.
frais[1], **fraîche** (frɛ, frɛʃ) *adj* **1** fresh. **2** cool. **3** new. **fraîcheur** *nf* **1** coolness. **2** freshness.
frais[2] (frɛ) *nm pl* **1** expenses. **2** cost.
fraise[1] (frɛz) *nf* strawberry.
fraise[2] (frɛz) *nf* ruff.
framboise (frɑ̃'bwaz) *nf* raspberry.
franc[1] (frɑ̃) *nm* franc.
franc[2], **franche** (frɑ̃, frɑ̃ʃ) *adj* **1** free. **2** frank, candid, honest. **3** aboveboard.
France (frɑ̃s) *nf* France. **français** *adj* French. *nm* **1** Frenchman. **2** French (language).
franchir (frɑ̃'ʃi:r) *vt* **1** jump over. **2** cross.
franchise (frɑ̃'ʃi:z) *nf* **1** franchise. **2** freedom. **3** exemption. **4** frankness.
franco (frɑ̃'ko) *adv* free of charge.
frange (frɑ̃ʒ) *nf* fringe.
frapper (fra'pe:) *vt* **1** hit. **2** mint. **3** knock. **frappe** *nf* **1** striking. **2** stamp, mark.
fraternel, -elle (fratɛr'nɛl) *adj* fraternal. **fraternité** *nf* **1** fraternity. **2** brotherhood.
fraterniser (fratɛrni:'ze:) *vi* fraternize.
fraude (frod) *nf* **1** fraud. **2** deceit. **3** false pretences. **passer en fraude** smuggle through.
frayer (frɛ'je:) *vt* **1** rub, scrape. **2** clear or open up. *vi* **1** spawn. **2** associate.
fredaine (frə'dɛn) *nf* prank.
fredonner (frədɔ'ne:) *vt* hum.
frein (frɛ̃) *nm* **1** brake. **2** curb. **3** horse's bit.
freiner (frɛ'ne:) *vi* brake. *vt* check.
frêle (frɛl) *adj* **1** frail. **2** delicate.
frelon (frə'lɔ̃) *nm* hornet.
frémir (fre:'mi:r) *vi* **1** quiver. **2** rustle. **3** tremble. **4** shudder.
frêne (frɛn) *nm* ash tree.
frénésie (fre:ne:'zi:) *nf* frenzy. **frénétique** *adj* frantic.
fréquence (frɛ'kɑ̃s) *nf* **1** frequence. **2** frequency. **fréquent** *adj* frequent.
fréquenter (frɛkɑ̃'te:) *vt* **1** visit. **2** associate.
frère (frɛr) *nm* brother.
fresque (frɛsk) *nf* fresco.
fret (frɛ) *nm* freight.
fréter (fre:'te:) *vt* **1** freight. **2** charter.
frétiller (fre:ti:'je:) *vi* **1** wriggle. **2** wag.
freux (frœ) *nm invar* rook.
friand (fri:'ɑ̃) *adj* **1** fond of delicacies. **2** fond.
fricoter (fri:kɔ'te:) *vi,vt inf* cook.
friction (fri:k'sjɔ̃) *nf* friction.
frictionner (fri:ksjɔ'ne:) *vt* rub.
Frigidaire (fri:ʒi:'dɛr) *nm Tdmk* refrigerator **frigo** (fri:'go) *nm* fridge.
frigide (fri:'ʒi:d) *adj* frigid.
frileux, -euse (fri:'lœ, -'lœz) *adj* chilly, sensitive to cold.
frimas (fri:'mɑ) *nm* frost.
friper (fri:'pe:) *vt* **1** crumple. **2** crush.
fripon, -onne (fri:'pɔ̃, -'pɔn) *nm,f* rogue, rascal.
frire* (fri:r) *vi,vt* fry.
frise (fri:z) *nf* frieze.
friser (fri:'ze:) *vi,vt* curl. *vt* skim.
frisson (fri:'sɔ̃) *nm* shiver.
frissonner (fri:sɔ'ne:) *vi* **1** shiver. **2** shudder.
frit (fri:) *v* see **frire.**
frivole (fri:'vɔl) *adj* **1** frivolous. **2** empty.
froid (frwa) *adj* **1** cold. **2** cool. **3** indifferent. **avoir froid** feel cold. ~*nm* cold, coldness. **froideur** *nf* coldness.
froisser (frwa'se:) *vt* **1** crumple. **2** crease. **3** hurt. **se froisser** *vr* take offence.
frôler (fro'le:) *vt* touch lightly, brush.
fromage (frɔ'maʒ) *nm* cheese.
froment (frɔ'mɑ̃) *nm* wheat.
froncer (frɔ̃'se:) *vt* wrinkle. **froncer les sourcils** frown. **fronce** *nf* crease.

fronde (frɔ̃d) *nf* sling.
front (frɔ̃) *nm* **1** forehead. **2** front. **3** brow. **frontal, -aux** (frɔ̃'tal, -'to) *adj* front, frontal. **frontière** *nf* frontier.
frotter (frɔ'te:) *vt* **1** rub. **2** strike. **3** scrub. **frottoir** *nm* **1** polisher. **2** scrubbing brush.
fructueux, -euse (fryk'tɥœ, -'tɥœz) *adj* fruitful.
frugal, -aux (fry'gal, -'go) *adj* frugal.
fruit (frɥi:) *nm* fruit.
fruste (fryst) *adj* **1** worn. **2** defaced. **3** rough.
frustrer (fry'stre:) *vt* **1** frustrate. **2** disappoint. **frustration** *nf* frustration.
fuir* (fɥi:r) *vi* **1** flee. **2** recede. **3** leak. *vt* **1** avoid. **2** shun. **fuite** *nf* **1** flight. **2** leak.
fumer (fy'me:) *vi,vt* smoke. *vi* steam. **fumée** *nf* smoke.
fumier (fy'mje:) *nm* manure, dung.
funèbre (fy'nɛbr) *adj* **1** funereal. **2** dismal.
funérailles (fynɛ'rɑj) *nf pl* funeral.
funeste (fy'nɛst) *adj* fatal, deadly.
fur (fyr) **au fur et à mesure** *adv* **1** as. **2** gradually.
furet (fy'rɛ) *nm* ferret.
fureter (fyr'te:) *vi* **1** ferret, rummage. **2** pry.
fureur (fy'rœr) *nf* **1** fury, rage. **2** mania. **furibond** *adj* furious. **furie** *nf* fury, rage. **furieux, -euse** (fy'rjœ, -'rjœz) *adj* furious.
furoncle (fy'rɔ̃kl) *nm* boil.
furtif, -ive (fyr'ti:f, -'ti:v) *adj* furtive.
fusée (fy'ze:) *nf* **1** rocket. **2** fuse.
fusil (fy'zi:) *nm* gun. **fusil rayé** rifle.
fusiller (fyzi:'je:) *vt* shoot, execute.
fusion (fy'zjɔ̃) *nf* **1** fusion. **2** melting.
fusionner (fyzjɔ'ne:) *vi,vt* **1** blend. **2** unite.
fustiger (fysti:'ʒe:) *vt* thrash, flog.
fût (fy) *nm* **1** shaft. **2** handle. **3** barrel.
futaie (fy'tɛ) *nf* forest.
futaille (fy'tɑj) *nf* barrel.
futile (fy'ti:l) *adj* **1** futile. **2** trivial
futur (fy'tyr) *adj,nm* future.
fuyant (fy'jɑ̃) *v* see **fuir.**

G

gâche (gɑʃ) *nf tech* staple.
gâcher (gɑ'ʃe:) *vt* **1** spoil. **2** bungle. **3** waste. **gâchis** *nm* **1** mud, slush. **2** mess.
gâchette (gɑ'ʃɛt) *nf* trigger.
gaffe (gaf) *nf* **1** boathook. **2** blunder.
gager (ga'ʒe:) *vt* **1** bet. **2** hire. **gage** *nm* **1** pledge. **2** token. **3** forfeit. **4** *pl* wages.
gagner (ga'ɲe:) *vt* **1** earn. **2** gain. **3** win. **4** reach. **gagne-pain** *nm invar* breadwinner.
gai (ge:) *adj* **1** gay. **2** merry. **3** bright. **gaieté** *nf* gaiety, mirth.
gaillard[1] (ga'jar) *adj* **1** strong. **2** healthy. **3** merry. **4** free. *nm* chap, fellow.
gaillard[2] (ga'jar) **gaillard arrière** *nm* quarterdeck.
gain (gɛ̃) *nm* **1** gain. **2** profit.
gaine (gɛn) *nf* **1** sheath. **2** cover. **3** case.
galant (ga'lɑ̃) *adj* **1** gallant. **2** courteous, polite. **galamment** *adv* gallantly.
galaxie (galɔk'si:) *nf* galaxy.
galbe (galb) *nm* **1** contour. **2** outline. **3** figure.
gale (gal) *nf* mange.
galère (ga'lɛr) *nf* galley.
galerie (gal'ri:) *nf* gallery.
galet (ga'lɛ) *nm* pebble. **gros galet** boulder.
Galles (gal) **pays de Galles** Wales. **gallois** (gal'wa) *adj* Welsh. *nm* **1** Welshman. **2** Welsh (language).
gallon (ga'lɔ̃) *nm* gallon.
galon (ga'lɔ̃) *nm* **1** braid. **2** stripe.
galop (ga'lo) *nm* gallop. **petit galop** canter.
galoper (galɔ'pe:) *vi* gallop.
galvaniser (galvani:'ze:) *vt* galvanize.
gambade (gɑ̃'bad) *nf* leap, gambol.
gamin (ga'mɛ̃) *n* **1** *inf* rascal. **2** youngster.
gamme (gam) *nf* **1** *mus* scale. **2** range.
gangster (gɑ̃g'stɛr) *nm* gangster.
gant (gɑ̃) *nm* glove. **gant de toilette** facecloth.
garage (ga'raʒ) *nm* **1** garage. **2** shed. **3** storage.
garant (ga'rɑ̃) *nm* **1** guarantor. **2** bail.
garantir (garɑ̃'ti:r) *vt* **1** guarantee. **2** vouch for. **3** protect. **4** insure. **garantie** *nf* guarantee.
garce (gars) *nf inf* bitch.
garçon (gar'sɔ̃) *nm* **1** boy. **2** lad. **3** bachelor. **4** waiter. **garçon d'honneur** best man.
garde-boue (gardə'bu:) *nm invar* mudguard.
garde-chasse (gardə'ʃas) *nm, pl* **gardes-chasse(s)** gamekeeper.
garde-côte (gardə'kot) *nm, pl* **gardes-côte(s)** coastguard.
garde-feu (gardə'fœ) *nm invar* fireguard.
garde-malade (gardma'lad) *nm or f,pl* **gardes-malades** nurse.
garde-manger (gardmɑ̃'ʒe:) *nm invar* larder, pantry.
garder (gar'de:) *vt* **1** guard. **2** take care of. **3** watch. **4** keep. **garder les bébés** baby-sit. **se garder** *vr* protect oneself. **se garder de** beware of. **garde** *nf* **1** care. **2** custody. **3** guard. **prendre garde à/de** take care to/not

to. ~*nm* **1** keeper. **2** warder. **garde du corps** bodyguard. **guardien, -ienne** (gar'djɛ̃, -'djɛn) *nm,f* guardian. **guardien de but** goalkeeper.
garde-robe (gardə'rɔb) *nf, pl* **gardes-robes** wardrobe.
gare[1] (gar) *nf* railway station.
gare[2] (gar) *interj* look out!
garenne (ga'rɛn) *nf* warren.
garer (ga're:) *vt* **1** dock. **2** park. **3** shunt. **se garer** *vr* get out of the way.
se gargariser (gargari:'ze:) *vr* gargle.
gargouiller (gargu:'je:) *vi* **1** gurgle. **2** rumble. **gargouille** *nf* **1** gargoyle. **2** spout.
garnir (gar'ni:r) *vt* **1** strengthen. **2** provide. **3** decorate. **4** garnish. **garnison** *nf* garrison. **garniture** *nf* **1** fittings. **2** *cul* trimmings.
gars (gɑ) *nm inf* lad.
gaspiller (gaspi:'je:) *vt* **1** waste. **2** squander. **gaspillage** *nm* **1** waste. **2** wastefulness.
gastrique (ga'stri:k) *adj* gastric.
gastronomique (gastrɔnɔ'mi:k) *adj* gastronomic.
gâteau, -aux (gɑ'to) *nm* cake.
gâter (gɑ'te:) *vt* **1** spoil. **2** harm. **gâte-tout** *nm invar* spoilsport.
gauche (goʃ) *adj* **1** left. **2** clumsy, gauche. *nf* left. **gaucher, -ère** (go'ʃe:, -'ʃɛr) *adj* left-handed.
gaufre (gofr) *nf* waffle. **gaufrette** (go'fret) *nf* wafer.
gaz (gɑz) *nm* gas.
gaze (gɑz) *nf* gauze.
gazéifier (gɑze:i:'fje:) *vt* aerate.
gazelle (ga'zɛl) *nf* gazelle.
gazon (gɑ'zɔ̃) *nm* **1** lawn. **2** turf.
gazouiller (gazu:'je:) *vi* **1** twitter. **2** babble.
géant (ʒe:'ɑ̃) *nm* giant. *adj* gigantic.
geindre* (ʒɛ̃dr) *vi* **1** whine. **2** whimper.
gel (ʒɛl) *nm* **1** frost. **2** freezing.
gélatine (ʒɛla'ti:n) *nf* gelatine.
geler (ʒə'le:) *vt* freeze. *vi* become frozen. *v imp* freeze. **gelé** *adj* frozen. **gelée** *nf* **1** frost. **2** jelly.
gélignite (ʒe:li:g'ni:t) *nf* gelignite.
Gémeaux (ʒe:'mo) *nm pl* Gemini.
gémir (ʒe:'mi:r) *vi* **1** groan. **2** moan. **3** wail. **gémissement** *nm* **1** groan. **2** moan.
gemme (ʒɛm) *nf* gem.
gencive (ʒɑ̃'si:v) *nf anat* gum.
gendarme (ʒɑ̃'darm) *nm* policeman.
gendre (ʒɑ̃dr) *nm* son-in-law.
gène (ʒɛn) *nm* gene.
généalogie (ʒe:ne:alɔ'ʒi:) *nf* genealogy. **généalogique** *adj* genealogical.
gêner (ʒe:'ne:) *vt* **1** hinder, obstruct. **2** embarrass, inconvenience. **se gêner** *vr* put oneself out. **gênant** (ʒɛ'nɑ̃) *adj* **1** awkward. **2** embarrassing. **gêne** (ʒɛn) *nf* **1** difficulty. **2** embarrassment. **3** need.
général, -aux (ʒe:nɛ'ral, -'ro) *adj,nm* general. **général de brigade/division** brigadier/ major general.
généraliser (ʒe:nɛrali:'ze:) *vt* generalize.
génération (ʒe:nɛra'sjɔ̃) *nf* generation.
généreux, -euse (ʒe:ne:'rœ, -'rœz) *adj* generous. **générosité** *nf* generosity.
générique (ʒe:ne:'ri:k) *adj* generic.
génétique (ʒe:ne:'ti:k) *adj* genetic. *nf* genetics.
Genève (ʒə'nɛv) *nf* Geneva.
génie (ʒe:'ni:) *nm* **1** spirit. **2** genius. **génial, -aux** (ʒe:'njal, -'njo) *adj* inspired, brilliant.
genièvre (ʒə'njɛvr) *nf* **1** juniper berry. **2** gin.
génital, -aux (ʒe:ni:'tal, -'to) *adj* genital.
genou, -oux (ʒə'nu:) *nm* knee.
genre (ʒɑ̃r) *nm* **1** kind, sort, type. **2** genus, family. **3** gender. **4** style. **genre humain** mankind.
gens (ʒɑ̃) *nm,f pl* people, folk.
gentiane (ʒɑ̃'sjan) *nf* gentian.
gentil[1], **-ille** (ʒɑ̃'ti:, -'ti:j) *adj* **1** nice. **2** kind. **3** pretty. **4** good. **gentilhomme** *nm* **1** nobleman. **2** gentleman. **gentillesse** *nf* **1** kindness. **2** prettiness. **gentiment** *adv* **1** nicely. **2** kindly. **3** prettily.
gentil[2] (ʒɑ̃'ti:) *nm* Gentile.
génuflexion (ʒe:nyflɛk'sjɔ̃) *nf* genuflection.
géographie (ʒe:ɔgra'fi:) *nf* geography. **géographique** *adj* geographic.
geôle (ʒol) *nf* jail, prison.
géométrie (ʒe:ɔme:'tri:) *nf* geometry. **géométrique** *adj* geometric.
géranium (ʒɛra'njɔm) *nm* geranium.
gerbe (ʒɛrb) *nf* **1** sheaf. **2** bunch.
gercer (ʒɛr'se:) *vt* **1** crack. **2** chap. **gerçure** *nf* **1** crack. **2** fissure.
gérer (ʒe:'re:) *vt* manage, run. **gérance** (ʒɛ'rɑ̃s) *nf* management. **gérant** (ʒɛ'rɑ̃) *nm* **1** manager. **2** director.
germanique (ʒɛrma'ni:k) *adj* Germanic.
germer (ʒɛr'me:) *vi* **1** germinate. **2** sprout, shoot. **germe** *nm* **1** germ. **2** sprout.
gérondif (ʒe:rɔ̃'di:f) *nm* gerund.
gésir* (ʒe:'zi:r) *vi* lie. **ci-gît** here lies.
geste (ʒɛst) *nm* **1** gesture. **2** movement. **3** sign.
gesticuler (ʒɛsti:ky'le:) *vi* gesticulate.

gestion (ʒɛ'stjɔ̃) *nf* **1** management. **2** administration.
geyser (ʒi:'zɛr) *nm* geyser.
ghetto (gɛ'to) *nm* ghetto.
gibet (ʒi:'bɛ) *nm* gallows.
gibier (ʒi:'bje:) *nm* (hunting) game.
giboulée (ʒi:bu:'le:) *nf* shower (of rain).
gicler (ʒi:'kle:) *vi* squirt out. **giclée** *nf* squirt.
gifler (ʒi:'fle:) *vt* **1** slap. **2** smack. **gifle** *nf* slap.
gigantesque (ʒi:gɑ̃'tɛsk) *adj* gigantic, huge.
gigot (ʒi:'go) *nm* leg of mutton.
gigue (ʒi:g) *nf* jig.
gilet (ʒi:'lɛ) *nm* **1** waistcoat. **2** cardigan. **gilet de sauvetage** lifejacket.
gin (dʒi:n) *nm* gin.
gingembre (ʒɛ̃'ʒɑ̃br) *nm* ginger.
girafe (ʒi:'raf) *nf* giraffe.
girofle (ʒi:'rɔfl) *nm bot* clove. **giroflée jaune** *nf* wallflower.
giron (ʒi:'rɔ̃) *nm* lap.
gisement (ʒi:z'mɑ̃) *nm* layer, bed. **gisement petrolifère** oilfield.
gît (ʒi:) *v* see **gésir.**
gitan (ʒi:'tɑ̃) *nm* Gipsy.
gîte (ʒi:t) *nm* **1** shelter, refuge. **2** home.
givre (ʒi:vr) *nm* hoarfrost.
glabre (glabr) *adj* smooth.
glacer (gla'se:) *vt* **1** freeze. **2** chill. **3** ice. **4** glaze. **glace** *nf* **1** ice. **2** ice-cream. **3** glass. **4** mirror. **glacé** *adj* **1** frozen. **2** icy. **glaçon** *nm* icicle.
glacier (gla'sje:) *nm* glacier.
glaise (glɛz) *nf* clay.
gland (glɑ̃) *nm* **1** acorn. **2** tassel.
glande (glɑ̃d) *nf* gland.
glaner (gla'ne:) *vt* glean.
glapir (gla'pi:r) *vi* yelp, yap.
glisser (gli:'se:) *vi* **1** slide. **2** skid. **3** glide. *vt* slip. **se glisser** *vr* creep. **glissade** *nf* **1** slip. **2** slide. **glissière** *nf* **1** groove. **2** chute.
globe (glɔb) *nm* **1** globe. **2** sphere. **globe de l'œil** eyeball. **global, -aux** (glɔ'bal, -'bo) *adj* **1** total. **2** inclusive.
gloire (glwar) *nf* **1** glory. **2** pride. **3** honour. **4** halo. **glorieux, -euse** (glɔ'rjœ, -'rjœz) *adj* glorious.
glorifier (glɔri:'fje:) *vt* **1** glorify. **2** praise. **se glorifier** *vr* boast.
gloser (glo'ze:) *vt* **1** gloss. **2** criticize. **glose** *nf* **1** gloss. **2** comment.
glossaire (glɔs'sɛr) *nm* glossary.
glouglou (glu:'glu:) *nm* gurgle.
glouglouter (glu:glu:'te:) *vi* gurgle.
glouton, -onne (glu:'tɔ̃, -'tɔn) *adj* greedy. *nm,f* glutton.
gluant (gly'ɑ̃) *adj* sticky.
glucose (gly'koz) *nm* glucose.
glycine (gli:'si:n) *nf* wisteria.
gnome (gnom) *nm* gnome.
go (go) **tout de go** *adv inf* **1** all of a sudden. **2** without a hitch.
gobelet (gɔ'blɛ) *nm* tumbler, mug.
gobelin (gɔ'blɛ̃) *nm* goblin.
gober (gɔ'be:) *vt* **1** swallow, gulp down. **2** *sl* believe. **se gober** *vr* fancy oneself.
godasse (gɔ'das) *nf sl* shoe.
godet (gɔ'dɛ) *nm* **1** mug. **2** bowl.
godiche (gɔ'di:ʃ) *adj inf* **1** awkward. **2** simple.
goéland (gɔɛ'lɑ̃) *nm* seagull.
goélette (gɔɛ'lɛt) *nf* schooner.
goémon (gɔɛ'mɔ̃) *nm* seaweed.
gogo (gɔ'go) **à gogo** *adv inf* galore.
golf (gɔlf) *nm* golf.
golfe (gɔlf) *nm* gulf, bay.
gommer (gɔ'me:) *vt* **1** gum. **2** rub out. **gomme** *nf* **1** gum. **2** eraser.
gond (gɔ̃) *nm* hinge.
gondole (gɔ̃'dɔl) *nf* gondola. **gondolier** *nm* gondolier.
gonfler (gɔ̃'fle:) *vt* **1** inflate, blow up. **2** swell.
gong (gɔ̃) *nm* gong.
gorge (gɔrʒ) *nf* **1** throat. **2** breast. **3** gorge. **4** (mountain) pass. **5** groove. **gorgée** *nf* mouthful. **petite gorgée** sip.
gorille (gɔ'ri:j) *nm* gorilla.
gosier (go'zje:) *nm* **1** gullet. **2** throat.
gosse (gɔs) *nm,f inf* kid, youngster.
gothique (gɔ'ti:k) *adj* Gothic.
goudron (gu:'drɔ̃) *nm* tar.
gouffre (gu:fr) *nm* gulf, abyss.
goulot (gu:'lo:) *nm* neck (of a bottle).
goulu (gu:'ly) *adj* greedy. *nm* glutton.
gourde (gu:rd) *nf* **1** gourd. **2** flask. **3** *inf* fool.
gourmand (gu:r'mɑ̃) *adj* greedy. *nm* glutton.
gousse (gu:s) *nf* pod, shell, husk. **gousse d'ail** clove of garlic.
goût (gu:) *nm* **1** taste. **2** flavour. **3** liking. **4** style.
goûter (gu:'te:) *vt* **1** taste. **2** enjoy. **goûter à** taste, try. ~*nm* afternoon tea.
goutte (gu:t) *nf* **1** drop. **2** spot. **gouttière** *nf* **1** gutter. **2** spout.
gouvernail (gu:vɛr'naj) *nm* **1** rudder. **2** helm.
gouverner (gu:vɛr'ne:) *vt* **1** govern, rule. **2** control. **3** steer. **gouvernante** *nf* governess.

gouvernement (gu:vɛrnə'mɑ̃) *nm* government. **gouverneur** *nm* governor.
grâce (grɑs) *nf* **1** grace. **2** charm. **3** favour. **4** pardon. **de bonne grâce** willingly. **grâce à** thanks to. **gracieux, -euse** (gra'sjœ, -'sjœz) *adj* **1** gracious. **2** kind. **3** free.
gracile (gra'si:l) *adj* **1** slender. **2** slim.
grade (grad) *nm* **1** grade. **2** rank. **3** degree. **gradient** *nm* gradient.
gradin (gra'dɛ̃) *nm* **1** tier. **2** step.
graduer (gra'dɥe:) *vt* **1** graduate. **2** grade. **graduel, -elle** (gra'dɥɛl) *adj* gradual.
graffitti (graffi:'ti:) *nm pl* graffiti.
grain (grɛ̃) *nm* **1** grain. **2** corn. **3** bean. **4** particle. **5** bead. **grain de café** coffee bean. **grain de poivre** peppercorn. **grain de raisin** grape.
graine (grɛn) *nf* seed. **graine de lin** linseed.
graisser (grɛ'se:) *vt* **1** grease. **2** oil. **graisse** *nf* **1** grease. **2** fat. **graisse de porc/rognon** lard/suet.
grammaire (gram'mɛr) *nf* grammar. **grammatical, -aux** (gramati:'kal, -'ko) *adj* grammatical.
gramme (gram) *nm* gram.
grand (grɑ̃) *adj* **1** big. **2** tall. **3** chief, main. **4** great. **5** grand. **grandeur** *nf* **1** size. **2** height. **3** importance. **4** grandeur. **5** *cap* (title) Grace.
grand-chose *nm invar* much.
Grande-Bretagne *nf* Great Britain.
grandiose (grɑ̃'djoz) *adj* grand, imposing.
grandir (grɑ̃'di:r) *vi* **1** grow, grow up. **2** increase. *vt* **1** exaggerate. **2** enlarge.
grand-maman *nf, pl* **grands-mamans** granny.
grand-mère *nf, pl* **grands-mères** grandmother.
grand-parent *nm, pl* **grands-parents** grandparent.
grand-père *nm, pl* **grands-pères** grandfather.
grand-route *nf, pl* **grands-routes** highroad.
grand-voile *nf, pl* **grands-voiles** mainsail.
grange (grɑ̃ʒ) *nf* barn.
granit (gra'ni:) *nm* granite.
graphique (gra'fi:k) *adj* graphic. *nm* **1** graph. **2** diagram.
grappe (grap) *nf* **1** bunch. **2** cluster.
gras, grasse (grɑ, grɑs) *adj* **1** fat. **2** rich. **3** thick. *nm* fat. **grassouillet, -ette** (grɑsu:'jɛ, -'jɛt) *adj* plump, chubby.
gratifier (grati:'fje:) *vt* **1** confer. **2** give.
gratin (gra'tɛ̃) *nm* burnt part. **au gratin** cooked with breadcrumbs and grated cheese.
gratitude (grati:'tyd) *nf* gratitude.
gratter (gra'te:) *vt* **1** scratch. **2** scrape. **gratte-ciel** *nm invar* skyscraper.

gratuit (gra'tɥi:) *adj* free.
grave (grav) *adj* **1** grave, serious. **2** severe. **3** important. **4** *mus* low. **gravité** *nf* gravity.
graver (gra've:) *vt* **1** engrave. **2** carve. **gravure** *nf* **1** engraving. **2** etching.
gravier (gra'vje:) *nm* gravel.
gravir (gra'vi:r) *vt* climb.
gré (gre:) *nm* **1** will. **2** liking.
Grèce (grɛs) *nf* Greece. **grec, grecque** *adj* Greek, Grecian. *nm* **1** Greek. **2** Greek (language).
gredin (grə'dɛ̃) *nm* scoundrel.
gréer (gre:'e:) *vt naut* rig.
greffer (grɛ'fe:) *vt* graft. **greffe** *nf* graft.
greffier (grɛ'fje:) *nm* registrar.
grégaire (gre:'gɛr) *adj* gregarious.
grêle[1] (grɛl) *nf* hail. **grêlon** *nm* hailstone.
grêle[2] (grɛl) *adj* slender, thin.
grêler (grɛ'le:) *v imp* hail.
grelotter (grəlɔ'te:) *vi* **1** tremble, shiver. **2** jingle.
grenade[1] (grə'nad) *nf* **1** pomegranate. **grenadier** *nm* pomegranate tree. **grenadine** *nf* syrup made of pomegranate juice.
grenade[2] (grə'nad) *nf* grenade. **grenade à main** hand grenade.
grenier (grə'nje:) *nm* **1** granary. **2** loft.
grenouille (grə'nu:j) *nf* frog.
grès (grɛ) *nm* grit, sandstone.
grésil (gre:'zi:) *nm* sleet.
grésiller[1] (gre:zi:'je:) *v imp* sleet.
grésiller[2] (gre:zi:'je:) *vi* **1** crackle. **2** sizzle.
grève[1] (grɛv) *nf* bank, shore.
grève[2] (grɛv) *nf* strike. **grève de la faim** hunger-strike. **grève de zèle** work to rule. **se mettre en grève** go on strike.
grever (grə've:) *vt* **1** mortgage. **2** encumber.
grief (gri:'ɛf) *nm* grievance.
griffer (gri:'fe:) *vt* scratch. **griffe** *nf* **1** claw. **2** signature. **griffe à papiers** paperclip.
griffonner (gri:fɔ'ne:) *vt* scrawl, scribble. **griffonnage** *nm* scrawl, scribble.
grignoter (gri:ɲɔ'te:) *vt* nibble (at).
gril (gri:) *nm* grill.
grille (gri:j) *nf* **1** grille. **2** gate.
griller (gri:'je:) *vt* **1** grill. **2** toast. **3** burn. **grille-pain** *nm invar* toaster.
grillon (gri:'jɔ̃) *nm zool* cricket.
grimacer (gri:ma'se:) *vi* **1** grimace. **2** grin. **grimace** *nf* **1** grimace. **2** grin.
grimer (gri:'me:) *vt Th* make up.
grimper (grɛ̃'pe:) *vi* climb up. *vt* climb.
grincer (grɛ̃'se:) *vi* **1** grate. **2** gnash. **3** creak.

grincheux, -euse (grɛ̃'ʃœ, -'ʃœz) *adj* 1 bad-tempered. 2 grumpy.
grippe (gri:p) *nf* influenza.
gris (gri:) *adj* 1 grey. 2 tipsy. *nm* grey.
grive (gri:v) *nf* thrush.
Groenland (grɔɛn'lɑ̃d) *nm* Greenland. **groenlandais** *adj* of Greenland. *nm* Greenlander.
grogner (grɔ'ɲe:) *vi* 1 grunt. 2 growl. 3 grumble. 4 groan.
groin (grwɛ̃) *nm* snout (of a pig).
grommeler (grɔm'le:) *vi* grumble. *vt* mutter.
gronder (grɔ̃'de:) *vt* scold. *vi* 1 growl. 2 rumble.
gros, grosse (gro, gros) *adj* 1 big. 2 stout. 3 thick. 4 coarse. 5 gross. 6 pregnant. **gros** *adv* much. *nm* 1 bulk. 2 wholesale. **en gros** 1 wholesale. 2 on the whole. **grosse** *nf* gross. **grossesse** *nf* pregnancy. **grosseur** *nf* 1 size. 2 thickness. **grossier, -ière** (gro'sje:, -'sjɛr) *adj* 1 coarse, rough. 2 vulgar, rude.
groseille (gro'zɛj) *nf* currant. **groseille à maquereau** gooseberry. **groseille rouge** redcurrant. **groseillier** *nm* currant bush.
grossir (gro'si:r) *vi* 1 increase. 2 grow bigger. *vt* 1 enlarge. 2 magnify. **grossissant** *adj* 1 growing. 2 magnifying.
grotesque (grɔ'tɛsk) *adj* 1 grotesque. 2 absurd, ludicrous. *nm* grotesque.
grotte (grɔt) *nf* grotto.
grouiller (gru:'je:) *vi* crawl.
grouper (gru:'pe:) *vt* group, arrange. **groupe** *nf* 1 group, party. 2 clump.
grue (gry) *nf zool,tech* crane.
grumeau, -aux (gry'mo) *nm* clot, lump.
se grumeler (grym'le:) *vr* clot.
gué (ge:) *nm* ford.
guenille (gə'ni:j) *nf* rag.
guépard (gɛ'par) *nm* cheetah.
guêpe (gɛp) *nf* wasp.
guère (gɛr) *adv* 1 hardly, scarcely. 2 not much or many.
guérilla (ge:ri:l'la) *nf* band of guerillas.
guérillero (ge:ri:llɛ'ro) *nm* guerilla.
guérir (ge:'ri:r) *vt* 1 cure. 2 heal. *vi* recover. **guérison** *nf* 1 cure. 2 recovery.
Guernesey (gɛrnə'zɛ) *nm* Guernsey.
guerre (gɛr) *nf* 1 war. 2 warfare. **guerrier** *nm* warrior.
guerroyer (gɛrwa'je:) *vi* war, wage war.
guet (gɛ) *nm* watch, guard. **guet-apens** *nm invar* 1 ambush. 2 trap.
guetter (gɛ'te:) *vt* 1 lie in wait for. 2 watch for.
gueuler (gœ'le:) *vi* bawl, yell. **gueule** *nf* 1 mouth (of animals). 2 jaws. 3 *sl* mouth (of humans). 4 large opening. **avoir la gueule de bois** have a hangover. **ta gueule!** shut up!
gueux, -euse (gœ, gœz) *nm,f* beggar. *adj* poor.
gui (gi:) *nm* mistletoe.
guichet (gi:'ʃɛ) *nm* 1 barrier. 2 box office. 3 counter. 4 grille.
guide[1] (gi:d) *nm* 1 guide. 2 guidebook.
guide[2] (gi:d) *nf* rein.
guider (gi:'de:) *vt* 1 guide. 2 direct. 3 lead.
guidon (gi:'dɔ̃) *nm* handlebar.
guigne (gi:ɲ) *nf* bad luck.
guillemets (gi:j'mɛ) *nm pl* quotation marks. **entre guillemets** in inverted commas.
guilleret, -ette (gi:j'rɛ, -'rɛt) *adj* lively, gay.
guillotine (gi:jɔ'ti:n) *nf* guillotine.
guimauve (gi:'mo:v) *nf* marshmallow.
guindé (gɛ̃'de:) *adj* stiff, formal.
guindeau, -aux (gɛ̃'do) *nm* windlass.
guinée (gi:'ne:) *nf* guinea.
guingan (gɛ̃'gɑ̃) *nm* gingham.
guingois (gɛ̃'gwa) **de guingois** *adv* askew, lopsided.
guirlande (gi:r'lɑ̃d) *nf* 1 garland. 2 wreath.
guise (gi:z) *nf* manner, way.
guitare (gi:'tar) *nf* guitar.
gymnase (ʒi:m'nɑz) *nm* gymnasium. **gymnaste** *nm,f* gymnast. **gymnastique** *adj* gymnastic.
gynécologie (ʒi:ne:kɔlɔ'ʒi:) *nf* gynaecology. **gynécologiste** *nm,f also* **gynécologue** gynaecologist.

H

(The asterisk denotes that the initial h is aspirate and that there is therefore no liaison or elision.)
habile (a'bi:l) *adj* 1 clever. 2 able. 3 cunning. **habileté** *nf* 1 ability, skill. 2 cleverness.
habiller (abi:'je:) *vt* 1 dress. 2 clothe. 3 prepare. **s'habiller** *vr* dress. **habillement** *nm* 1 clothing. 2 clothes.
habit (a'bi:) *nm* 1 dress. 2 coat. 3 evening dress. 4 *pl* clothes.
habiter (abi:'te:) *vi* live, reside. *vt* dwell or live in. **habitable** *adj* habitable. **habitant** *nm* 1 inhabitant. 2 resident. **habitation** *nf* 1 dwelling. 2 abode.
habituer (abi:'tɥe:) *vt* accustom. **s'habituer à** *vr* get used to. **habitude** *nf* 1 habit. 2 custom. 3 knack. 4 practice. **comme d'habitude**

as usual. **d'habitude** usually. **habitué** *nm* regular customer. **habituel, -elle** (abi:'tɥɛl) *adj* **1** usual. **2** habitual.
***hâbler** (ɑ'ble:) *vi* boast, brag.
***hacher** (a'ʃe:) *vt* **1** chop. **2** hack. **3** mince. ***hache** *nf* axe. ***hachette** *nf* hatchet. ***hachis** *nm* mince. ***hachoir** *nm* chopper.
***hagard** (a'gar) *adj* haggard, drawn.
***haie** (ɛ) *nf* **1** hedge. **2** hurdle. **3** line.
***haillon** (a'jɔ̃) *nm* rag.
haïr (a'i:r) *vt* hate, detest. ***haine** *nf* **1** hatred, hate. **2** spite.
***halage** (ɑ'laʒ) *nm* towing.
***hâle** (ɑl) *nm* **1** sunburn. **2** tan.
haleine (a'lɛn) *nf* breath.
***haler** (ɑ'le:) *vt* **1** tow. **2** haul.
***haleter** (al'te:) *vi* **1** pant. **2** gasp (for breath).
***hall** (al) *nm* **1** hall. **2** hotel lounge.
***halle** (al) *nf* covered market. **Les Halles** *nf pl* old site of markets in Paris.
hallucination (alysi:na'sjɔ̃) *nf* hallucination.
***halte** (alt) *nm* stop, halt. **faire halte** halt.
haltérophilie (alte:rɔfi:'li:) *nf* weight-lifting.
***hamac** (a'mak) *nm* hammock.
***hameau, -aux** (a'mo) *nm* hamlet.
hameçon (am'sɔ̃) *nm* **1** (fish) hook. **2** bait.
***hampe** (ɑ̃p) *nf* **1** shaft. **2** handle. **3** pole.
***hamster** (am'stɛr) *nm* hamster.
***hanche** (ɑ̃ʃ) *nf* **1** hip. **2** haunch.
***handicap** (ɑ̃di:'kap) *nm sport* handicap.
***handicaper** (ɑ̃di:ka'pe:) *vt sport* handicap.
***hangar** (ɑ̃'gar) *nm* **1** shed. **2** outhouse.
***hanter** (ɑ̃'te:) *vt* haunt. ***hantise** *nf* obsession.
***happer** (a'pe:) *vt* seize, snatch, snap up. ***happe** *nf* staple.
***haras** (a'rɑ) *nm zool* stud.
***harasser** (ara'se:) *vt* **1** tire out. **2** harass.
***harceler** (arsə'le:) *vt* **1** harass. **2** worry. **3** pester.
***harde** (ard) *nf* herd, flock.
***hardes** (ard) *nf pl inf* clothes.
***hardi** (ar'di:) *adj* **1** bold. **2** daring. **3** rash. **4** impudent. *interj* courage! ***hardiesse** *nf* **1** daring. **2** pluck.
***hareng** (a'rɑ̃) *nm* herring. **hareng salé et fumé** kipper. **hareng saur** red herring.
***hargneux, -euse** (ar'ɲœ, -'ɲœz) *adj* **1** peevish. **2** cross. **3** surly.
***haricot** (ari:'ko) *nm* kidney bean. **haricot vert** French bean.
harmonica (armɔni:'ka) *nm* harmonica.
harmoniser (armɔni:'ze:) *vt* **1** *mus* harmonize. **2** match. **s'harmoniser avec** *vr* **1** be in keeping with. **2** tone in with. **harmonie** *nf* **1** harmony. **2** agreement. **harmonieux, -euse** (armɔ'njœ, -'njœz) *adj* harmonious. **harmonique** *adj,nm mus* harmonic.
***harnais** (ar'nɛ) *nm* harness.
***harpe** (arp) *nf* harp.
***harpon** (ar'pɔ̃) *nm* harpoon.
***hasard** (a'zar) *nm* **1** chance. **2** luck. **3** accident. **4** risk. **5** hazard.
***hasarder** (azar'de:) *vt* **1** risk. **2** venture.
***haschich** (a'ʃi:ʃ) *nm* hashish.
***hâter** (ɑ'te:) *vt* hasten, quicken. ***hâte** *nf* haste, hurry.
***hausser** (o'se:) *vt* **1** raise. **2** lift. *vi* rise. **hausser les épaules** shrug one's shoulders. ***hausse** *nf* rise.
***haut** (o) *adj* **1** high. **2** tall. **3** lofty. **4** loud. **5** upper. *nm* **1** height. **2** top. **3** head. **de haut en bas 1** downwards. **2** from top to bottom. **en haut 1** upstairs. **2** above.
***haut-de-forme** *nm, pl* **hauts-de-forme** top-hat.
***haut-parleur** *nm, pl* **haut-parleurs** loud-speaker.
***hautain** (o'tɛ̃) *adj* haughty.
***hautbois** (o'bwɑ) *nm* oboe.
***hâve** (ɑv) *adj* **1** haggard. **2** hollow. **3** sunken.
***hâvre** (ɑvr) *nm* **1** harbour. **2** haven.
***havresac** (ɑvrə'sak) *nm* haversack.
***Haye, La** (ɛ) *nf* The Hague.
hebdomadaire (ɛbdɔma'dɛr) *adj* weekly.
héberger (e:bɛr'ʒe:) *vt* **1** lodge. **2** shelter.
hébéter (e:be:'te:) *vt* **1** dull. **2** daze.
hébraïque (e:bra'i:k) *adj* Hebrew.
hébreu, -eux (e:'brœ) *adj* Hebrew. *nm* **1** Hebrew. **2** Hebrew (language).
hectare (ɛk'tar) *nm* French measurement equivalent to 2.47 acres.
hélas (e:'lɑs) *interj* alas!
***héler** (e:'le:) *vt* hail, call.
hélice (ɛ'li:s) *nf* screw, propeller.
hélicoptère (e:li:kɔp'tɛr) *nm* helicopter.
helvétique (ɛlve:'ti:k) *adj* Swiss.
hémisphère (e:mi:'sfɛr) *nm* hemisphere.
hémorragie (e:mɔra'ʒi:) *nf* haemorrhage.
hémorroïde (e:mɔrɔ'i:d) *nf med* pile.
***henné** (ɛn'ne:) *nm* henna.
***hennir** (ɛ'ni:r) *vi* neigh.
***héraut** (e:'ro) *nm* herald.
herbe (ɛrb) *nf* **1** grass. **2** herb. **3** plant. **fines herbes** *nf pl* herbs used for seasoning. **mauvaise herbe** weed. **herbicide** *nm* weedkiller.

hérédité (e:re:di:'te:) *nf* heredity. **héréditaire** *adj* hereditary.
hérésie (e:re:'zi:) *nf* heresy.
***hérisser** (e:ri:'se:) *vt* **1** bristle up. **2** ruffle. **se hérisser** *vr* **1** bristle. **2** (of hair) stand on end. ***hérisson** *nm* hedgehog.
hériter (e:ri:'te:) *vt* inherit. **héritage** *nm* **1** inheritance, heritage. **2** legacy. **héritier, -ière** (e:ri:'tje:, -'tjɛr) *nm,f* heir, heiress.
hermétique (ɛrme:'ti:k) *adj* **1** airtight. **2** watertight.
hermine (ɛr'mi:n) *nf* **1** stoat. **2** ermine.
héroïne[1] (e:rɔ'i:n) *nf* heroine.
héroïne[2] (e:rɔ'i:n) *nf* heroin.
***héron** (e:'rɔ̃) *nm* heron.
***héros** (e:'ro) *nm* hero. **héroïque** *adj* heroic. **héroïsme** *nm* heroism.
hésiter (e:zi:'te) *vi* **1** hesitate. **2** falter. **3** waver.
hétéroclite (e:te:rɔ'kli:t) *adj* **1** irregular. **2** strange, odd.
***hêtre** (ɛtr) *nm* beech tree. **hêtre rouge** copper beech tree.
heure (œr) *nf* **1** hour. **2** time. **3** o'clock. **à tout à l'heure** see you later. **de bonne heure** early. **dernière heure** latest news. **être à l'heure** be punctual. **heures d'affluence** or **de pointes** *nf pl* rush hour. **heures supplémentaires** *nf pl* overtime. **tout à l'heure** just now.
heureux, -euse (œ'rœ, -'rœz) *adj* **1** happy. **2** lucky, fortunate. **3** successful.
***heurt** (œr) *nm* **1** shock. **2** bump. **sans heurt** smoothly.
***heurter** (œr'te:) *vi,vt* **1** knock (against). **2** run (into). *vt* **1** shock. **2** offend. **se heurter** *vr* collide. **heurtoir** *nm* doorknocker.
hexagone (ɛgza'gɔn) *nm* hexagon. *adj* hexagonal.
hiberner (i:bɛr'ne:) *vi* hibernate.
***hibou, -oux** (i:'bu:) *nm* owl.
***hideux, -euse** (i:'dœ, -'dœz) *adj* hideous.
hier (i:'ɛr) *adv,nm* yesterday.
***hiérarchie** (jɛrar'ʃi:) *nf* hierarchy.
hippique (i:p'pi:k) *adj* of horses.
hippodrome (i:pɔ'drɔm) *nm* racecourse.
hippopotame (i:pɔpɔ'tam) *nm* hippopotamus.
hirondelle (i:rɔ̃'dɛl) *nf* swallow.
***hisser** (i:'se:) *vt* hoist. **se hisser** *vr* pull oneself up.
histoire (i:'stwar) *nf* **1** history. **2** story, tale. **faire des histoires** make a fuss. **historien, -ienne** (i:stɔ'rjɛ̃, -'rjɛn) *nm,f* historian.
hiver (i:'vɛr) *nm* winter.
hiverner (i:vɛr'ne:) *vi* hibernate.
***hocher** (ɔ'ʃe:) *vt* **1** shake. **2** toss. **3** nod.
***hockey** (ɔ'kɛ) *nm* hockey. **hockey sur glace** ice hockey.
***Hollande** (ɔ'lɑ̃d) *nf* Holland. ***hollandais** *adj* Dutch. *nm* **1** Dutchman. **2** Dutch (language).
***homard** (ɔ'mar) *nm* lobster.
hommage (ɔ'maʒ) *nm* **1** homage. **2** token. **3** *pl* respects.
homme (ɔm) *nm* **1** man. **2** mankind. **homme de loi** lawyer. **homme d'état** statesman. **homme politique** politician.
homonyme (ɔmɔ'ni:m) *nm* **1** homonym. **2** namesake.
homosexuel, -elle (ɔmɔsɛk'sɥɛl) *adj,n* homosexual.
***Hongrie** (ɔ̃'gri:) *nf* Hungary. ***hongrois** *adj,n* Hungarian. *nm* Hungarian (language).
honnête (ɔ'nɛt) *adj* **1** honest, upright. **2** honourable. **3** decent. **4** well-bred. **5** reasonable. **honnêteté** *nf* **1** honesty. **2** fairness.
honneur (ɔ'nœr) *nm* **1** honour. **2** credit.
honoraire (ɔnɔ'rɛr) *adj* honorary.
honorer (ɔnɔ're:) *vt* **1** honour. **2** respect. **honorable** *adj* **1** honourable. **2** respectable.
***honte** (ɔ̃t) *nf* **1** shame. **2** disgrace. **avoir honte** be ashamed. **faire honte à** put to shame. ***honteux, -euse** (ɔ'tœ, -'tœz) *adj* **1** ashamed. **2** shamefaced. **3** shameful.
hôpital, -aux (ɔpi:'tal, -'to) *nm* hospital.
***hoquet** (ɔ'kɛ) *nm* **1** hiccup. **2** gasp.
horaire (ɔ'rɛr) *nm* timetable.
***horde** (ɔrd) *nf* horde.
horizon (ɔri:'zɔ̃) *nm* horizon.
horizontal, -aux (ɔri:zɔ̃'tal, -'to) *adj* horizontal.
horloge (ɔr'lɔʒ) *nf* clock.
***hormis** (ɔr'mi:) *prep* except, but, save.
hormone (ɔr'mɔn) *nf* hormone.
horoscope (ɔrɔ'skɔp) *nm* horoscope.
horreur (ɔr'rœr) *nf* **1** horror. **2** disgust. **3** *pl* atrocities. **avoir en horreur** **1** hate. **2** have a horror of.
horrible (ɔr'ri:bl) *adj* **1** horrible. **2** awful.
horrifier (ɔrri:'fje:) *vt* horrify.
***hors** (ɔr) *prep* **1** outside. **2** out of. **3** beyond. **4** except. **hors de** outside, out of. **être hors de soi** be beside oneself. ***hors-bord** *nm invar* speedboat. **hors de combat** out of action, disabled. ***hors-d'œuvre** *nm invar* a dish served as the first course of a meal. ***hors-jeu** *adj invar* offside. ***hors-la-loi** *nm invar* outlaw.

horticulture (ɔrti:kyl'tyr) *nf* horticulture. **horticulteur** *nm* horticulturist.
hospice (ɔ'spi:s) *nm* **1** home, institution. **2** asylum.
hospitalier, -ière (ɔspi:ta'lje:, -'ljɛr) *adj* hospitable. **hospitalité** *nf* hospitality.
hostile (ɔ'sti:l) *adj* **1** hostile. **2** adverse.
hôte, hôtesse (ot, o'tɛs) *nm,f* **1** host, hostess. **2** landlord, landlady. **3** guest. **hôtesse de l'air** air-hostess.
hôtel (o'tɛl) *nm* **1** hotel. **2** mansion. **hôtel de ville** town hall. **hôtel des Postes** General Post Office.
***houblon** (u:'blɔ̃) *nm bot* hop.
***houer** (u:'e:) *vt* hoe. ***houe** *nf* hoe.
***houille** (u:j) *nf* coal. ***houille blanche** hydro-electric power. ***houillère** *nf* coalmine. ***houilleur** *nm* coal-miner.
***houle** (u:l) *nf* swell (of the sea). **houleux, -euse** (u:'lœ, -'lœz) *adj* rough.
***houppe** (u:p) *nf* **1** tuft. **2** bunch. **3** crest.
***hourra** (u:'rɑ) *interj,nm* hurrah.
***houspiller** (u:spi:'je:) *vt* **1** hustle. **2** jostle. **3** abuse. **4** reprimand.
***houx** (u:) *nm* holly.
***hublot** (hy'blo) *nm* porthole.
***huer** (y'e:) *vi* **1** shout, boo. **2** (of an owl) hoot.
huiler (ɥi:'le:) *vt* oil, grease. **huile** (ɥi:l) *nf* oil.
huis (ɥi:) **à huis clos** *adv* behind closed doors, in camera.
huissier (ɥi:'sje:) *nm* bailiff.
***huit** (ɥi:t) *adj,nm* eight. ***huitaine** *nf* **1** about eight. **2** week. ***huitième** *adj* eighth.
huître (ɥi:tr) *nf* oyster.
humain (y'mɛ̃) *adj* **1** human. **2** humane. **humanisme** *nm* humanism. **humanitaire** *adj* **1** humanitarian. **2** humane. **humanité** *nf* **1** humanity. **2** mankind. **3** kindness.
humble (œ̃bl) *adj* **1** humble. **2** lowly.
humecter (ymɛk'te:) *vt* dampen, moisten.
humer (y'me:) *vt* breathe in, sniff.
humeur (y'mœr) *nf* humour, mood. **avoir l'humeur vive** be quick-tempered. **de mauvaise humeur** bad-tempered. **d'humeur égale** even-tempered.
humide (y'mi:d) *adj* **1** humid. **2** damp. **3** watery. **humidité** *nf* **1** moisture. **2** dampness. **3** humidity.
humilier (ymi:'lje:) *vt* humiliate. **humilité** *nf* humility.
humour (y'mu:r) *nm* humour. **humoriste** *adj* humorous. *nm* humorist. **humoristique** *adj* humorous.
***huppe** (yp) *nf zool* crest.
***hurler** (yr'le:) *vi* **1** yell. **2** howl. ***hurlement** (yrlə'mɑ̃) *nm* **1** yell. **2** howl.
***hussard** (y'sar) *nm* hussar.
***hutte** (yt) *nf* hut, shed.
hybride (i:'bri:d) *adj,nm* hybrid.
hydrate (i:'drat) **hydrate de carbone** *nm* carbohydrate.
hydraulique (i:dro'li:k) *adj* hydraulic. *nf* hydraulics.
hydro-électrique (i:drɔe:lɛk'tri:k) *adj* hydro-electric.
hydrofuge (i:drɔ'fyʒ) *adj* waterproof.
hydrogène (i:drɔ'ʒɛn) *nm* hydrogen.
hydrophile (i:drɔ'fi:l) *adj* absorbent.
hyène (jɛn) *nf* hyena.
hygiène (i:'ʒjɛn) *nf* hygiene. **hygiénique** *adj* **1** hygienic. **2** healthy. **3** sanitary.
hymne (i:m) *nm* **1** song, anthem. **hymne national** national anthem. ~*nf* hymn. **hymnaire** *nm* hymnbook.
hypnose (i:p'noz) *nf* hypnosis. **hypnotisme** *nm* hypnotism.
hypocondrie (i:pɔkɔ̃'dri:) *nf* hypochondria. **hypocondriaque** *adj,n* hypochondriac.
hypocrisie (i:pɔkri:'zi:) *nf* hypocrisy. **hypocrite** *adj* hypocritical. *nm,f* hypocrite.
hypodermique (i:pɔdɛr'mi:k) *adj* hypodermic.
hypothéquer (i:pɔte:'ke:) *vt* mortgage. **hypothèque** *nf* mortgage.
hypothèse (i:pɔ'tɛz) *nf* hypothesis. **hypothétique** *adj* hypothetical.
hystérectomie (i:ste:rɛktɔ'mi:) *nf* hysterectomy.
hystérie (i:ste:'ri:) *nf* hysteria. **hystérique** *adj* hysterical.

I

Ibérie (i:be:'ri:) *nf* Iberia. **ibère** *adj,n* Iberian.
iceberg (i:s'bɛrk) *nm* iceberg.
ici (i:'si:) *adv* **1** there. **2** now. **d'ici là** between now and then. **d'ici peu** before long. **ici et là** here and there.
icône (i:'kon) *nf* icon.
idéal, -als or **-aux** (i:de:'al, -'al, -'o) *adj,nm* ideal. **idéaliste** *adj* idealistic. *nm,f* idealist.
idéaliser (i:de:ali:'ze:) *vt* idealize.
idée (i:'de:) *nf* **1** idea. **2** thought, notion. **3** opinion. **4** mind. **idée fixe/lumineuse** obsession/brainwave.

identifier (i:dɑ̃ti:ˈfje:) *vt* identify. **identique** *adj* identical. **identité** *nf* identity.
idéologie (i:de:ɔlɔˈʒi:) *nf* ideology. **idéologique** *adj* ideological.
idiome (i:ˈdjom) *nm* **1** idiom. **2** dialect.
idiosyncrasie (i:djɔsɛ̃kraˈzi:) *nf* idiosyncrasy.
idiot (i:ˈdjo) *adj* **1** idiotic. **2** absurd. *nm* idiot.
idiotisme (i:djɔˈti:sm) *nm* idiom.
idolâtrer (i:dɔlɑˈtre:) *vt* idolize. **idolâtrie** *nf* idolatry.
idole (i:ˈdɔl) *nf* idol.
idyllique (i:di:ˈli:k) *adj* idyllic.
if (i:f) *nm* yew.
igloo (i:ˈglu:) *nm* igloo.
ignorer (i:ɲɔˈre:) *vt* not to know, be unaware of.
il (i:l) *pron 3rd pers ms* **1** he. **2** it. **3** there. **il y a** there is or are.
île (i:l) *nf* island, isle. **îles Anglo-Normandes** *nf pl* Channel Islands.
illégal, -aux (i:llɛˈgal, -ˈgo) *adj* illegal, unlawful.
illégitime (i:lle:ʒi:ˈti:m) *adj* illegitimate.
illettré (i:llɛˈtre:) *adj* illiterate.
illicite (i:lli:ˈsi:t) *adj* illicit, unlawful.
illimité (i:lli:mi:ˈte:) *adj* **1** boundless. **2** indefinite.
illisible (i:lli:ˈzi:bl) *adj* illegible.
illuminer (i:lymi:ˈne:) *vt* **1** illuminate. **2** enlighten. **illumination** *nf* illumination, lighting.
illusion (i:llyˈzjɔ̃) *nf* illusion.
illustrer (i:llyˈstre:) *vt* illustrate. **illustration** *nf* illustration. **illustre** *adj* famous.
ils (i:l) *pron 3rd pers m pl* they.
image (i:maʒ) *nf* **1** image. **2** picture. **3** likeness. **4** reflection. **5** simile, metaphor. **imagé** (i:ma ˈʒe:) *adj* vivid. **imagerie** *nf* imagery.
imaginer (i:maʒi:ˈne:) *vt* **1** imagine. **2** conceive. **3** invent. **4** suppose. **s'imaginer** *vr* think, fancy. **imaginaire** *adj* imaginary. **imaginatif, -ive** (i:maʒi:naˈti:f, -ˈti:v) *adj* imaginative. **imagination** *nf* **1** imagination. **2** fancy.
imbécile (ɛ̃be:ˈsi:l) *adj* silly. *nm,f* idiot, halfwit.
imbiber (ɛ̃bi:ˈbe:) *vt* **1** soak. **2** steep. **3** absorb. **s'imbiber** *vr* **1** absorb. **2** become saturated.
imbrisable (ɛ̃bri:ˈsabl) *adj* unbreakable.
imiter (i:mi:ˈte:) *vt* **1** imitate. **2** mimic. **3** copy. **4** forge.
immaculé (i:mmakyˈle:) *adj* immaculate.
immanquable (ɛ̃mɑ̃ˈkabl) *adj* **1** inevitable. **2** infallible.
immatriculer (i:mmatri:kyˈle:) *vt* register.
immaturité (i:mmatyri:ˈte:) *nf* immaturity.
immédiat (i:mme:ˈdjat) *adj* **1** immediate. **2** near. **3** urgent.
immense (i:mˈmɑ̃s) *adj* huge, vast, immense.
immerger (i:mmɛrˈʒe:) *vt* **1** immerse. **2** plunge.
immeuble (i:mˈmœbl) *adj law* real, fixed. *nm* block of flats.
immigrer (i:mmi:ˈgre:) *vi* immigrate. **immigrant** *nm* immigrant. **immigration** *nf* immigration.
imminent (i:mmi:ˈnɑ̃) *adj* imminent.
immiscer (i:mmi:ˈse:) *vt* involve. **s'immiscer dans** *vr* interfere with.
immobile (i:mmɔˈbi:l) *adj* immobile, still. **immobilier, -ière** (i:mmɔbi:ˈlje:, -ˈljɛr) *adj* of land, property.
immobiliser (i:mmɔbi:li:ˈze:) *vt* immobilize.
immonde (i:mˈmɔ̃d) *adj* **1** filthy. **2** foul.
immortel, -elle (i:mmɔrˈtɛl) *adj* immortal, everlasting. **immortalité** *nf* immortality.
immuniser (i:mmyni:ˈze:) *vt* immunize.
impair (ɛ̃ˈpɛr) *adj* odd, uneven.
imparfait (ɛ̃parˈfɛ) *adj* imperfect. *nm* imperfect tense.
impartial, -aux (ɛ̃parˈsjal, -ˈsjo) *adj* impartial.
impasse (ɛ̃ˈpɑs) *nf* **1** deadlock. **2** dead end.
impassible (ɛ̃paˈsi:bl) *adj* **1** unmoved. **2** callous.
impatience (ɛ̃paˈsjɑ̃s) *nf* impatience. **impatient** *adj* **1** impatient. **2** eager.
impatienter (ɛ̃pasjɑ̃ˈte:) *vt* annoy. **s'impatienter** *vr* lose one's patience.
impeccable (ɛ̃pɛˈkabl) *adj* faultless, impeccable.
imper (ɛ̃ˈpɛr) *nm inf* mac.
impératif, -ive (ɛ̃pɛraˈti:f, -ˈti:v) *adj,nm* imperative.
impératrice (ɛ̃pɛraˈtri:s) *nf* empress.
impérial, -aux (ɛ̃pɛˈrjal, -ˈro) *adj* imperial. **impériale** *nf* top deck (of a bus).
imperméable (ɛ̃pɛrme:ˈabl) *adj* waterproof. *nm* mackintosh.
impersonnel, -elle (ɛ̃pɛrsɔˈnɛl) *adj* impersonal.
impétueux, -euse (ɛ̃pe:ˈtɥœ, -ˈtɥœz) *adj* impetuous.
impitoyable (ɛ̃pi:twaˈjabl) *adj* **1** ruthless. **2** cruel.
implicite (ɛ̃pli:ˈsi:t) *adj* **1** implicit. **2** absolute.
impliquer (ɛ̃pli:ˈke:) *vt* **1** involve. **2** imply.
impopulaire (ɛ̃pɔpyˈlɛr) *adj* unpopular.
implorer (ɛ̃plɔˈre:) *vt* implore, entreat.
importer[1] (ɛ̃pɔrˈte:) *vt* import.
importer*[2] (ɛ̃pɔrˈte:) *vi* matter, be important. **n'importe** never mind. **n'importe comment/quand/qui/quoi** anyhow/anytime/anyone/

anything. **importance** *nf* importance. **important** *adj* **1** important. **2** large. **3** considerable.

importuner (ɛ̃pɔrty'ne:) *vt* **1** pester. **2** trouble, inconvenience.

imposer (ɛ̃po'ze:) *vt* **1** impose. **2** inflict. **3** tax. **imposant** *adj* imposing, grand.

impossible (ɛ̃pɔ'si:bl) *adj* impossible.

imposteur (ɛ̃pɔ'stœr) *nm* imposter.

impôt (ɛ̃'po) *nm* tax, duty.

impotent (ɛ̃pɔ'tɑ̃) *adj* **1** helpless. **2** infirm. *nm* cripple.

imprécis (ɛ̃pre:'si:) *adj* **1** vague, indefinite. **2** inaccurate.

impression (ɛ̃prɛ'sjɔ̃) *nf* **1** impression. **2** printing. **3** print.

impressionner (ɛ̃prɛsjɔ'ne:) *vt* **1** impress. **2** move. **impressionnant** *adj* **1** impressive. **2** sensational.

imprévu (ɛ̃pre:'vy) *adj* unexpected.

imprimer (ɛ̃pri:'me:) *vt* **1** print. **2** imprint. **3** publish. **4** stamp. **imprimé** *nm* **1** printed matter. **2** form. **imprimeur** *nm* printer.

improbable (ɛ̃prɔ'babl) *adj* improbable, unlikely.

impromptu (ɛ̃prɔ̃'ty) *adj,adv* without preparation, impromptu.

improviser (ɛ̃prɔvi:'ze:) *vt* **1** improvise. **2** ad-lib. **à l'improviste** *adv* unexpectedly, without warning.

imprudent (ɛ̃pry'dɑ̃) *adj* imprudent, rash.

impudent (ɛ̃py'dɑ̃) *adj* cheeky, impudent.

impuissant (ɛ̃pɥi:'sɑ̃) *adj* **1** impotent. **2** helpless. **3** incapable.

impulsion (ɛ̃pyl'sjɔ̃) *nf* **1** impulse. **2** impetus. **impulsif, -ive** (ɛ̃pyl'si:f, -'si:v) *adj* impulsive.

impur (ɛ̃'pyr) *adj* **1** impure. **2** indecent, lewd.

imputer (ɛ̃py'te:) *vt* **1** attribute. **2** charge.

inadapté (i:nadap'te:) *nm* (social) misfit.

inadéquat (i:nade:'kwa) *adj* inadequate.

inadvertance (i:nadvɛr'tɑ̃s) *nf* oversight.

inalliable (i:na'ljabl) *adj* incompatible.

inappréciable (i:napre:'sjabl) *adj* **1** not perceptible. **2** invaluable.

inapte (i:'napt) *adj* unfit, not suited.

inarticulé (i:narti:ky'le:) *adj* inarticulate.

inaugurer (i:nogy're:) *vt* inaugurate, open. **inaugural, -aux** (i:nogy'ral, -'ro) *adj* **1** opening. **2** maiden.

incapable (ɛ̃ka'pabl) *adj* **1** incapable, unable. **2** unfit.

incapacité (ɛ̃kapasi:'te:) *nf* inability.

incendier (ɛ̃sɑ̃'dje:) *vt* set fire to. **incendiaire** *adj* incendiary. **incendie** *nm* fire. **incendie volontaire** arson.

incertain (ɛ̃sɛr'tɛ̃) *adj* **1** uncertain, unsettled. **2** doubtful. **incertitude** *nf* uncertainty, doubt.

incessant (ɛ̃sɛ'sɑ̃) *adj* ceaseless, incessant. **incessamment** *adv* immediately.

inceste (ɛ̃'sɛst) *nm* incest.

incident (ɛ̃si:'dɑ̃) *nm* **1** incident. **2** hitch, difficulty. *adj* incidental. **incidemment** (ɛ̃si:da'mɑ̃) *adv* incidentally. **incidentel, -elle** (ɛ̃si:dɑ̃'tɛl) *adj* incidental.

incinérer (ɛ̃si:ne:'re:) *vt* cremate. **incinération** (ɛ̃si:nɛra'sjɔ̃) *nf* cremation.

inciter (ɛ̃si:'te:) *vt* incite, urge.

incliner (ɛ̃kli:'ne:) *vt* **1** slope, slant. **2** tilt. **3** bend. **incliner à** be inclined to. **s'incliner** *vr* bow. **inclinaison** *nf* **1** slope. **2** nod.

inclure* (ɛ̃'klyr) *vt* include. **inclusif, -ive** (ɛ̃kly'zi:f, -'zi:v) *adj* inclusive.

incohérent (ɛ̃kɔɛ'rɑ̃) *adj* incoherent.

incolore (ɛ̃kɔ'lɔr) *adj* colourless.

incommoder (ɛ̃kɔmɔ'de:) *vt* **1** inconvenience. **2** annoy. **3** upset. **incommode** *adj* **1** inconvenient. **2** uncomfortable. **incommodité** *nf* inconvenience.

incompatible (ɛ̃kɔ̃pa'ti:bl) *adj* incompatible, inconsistent.

incompétent (ɛ̃kɔ̃pɛ'tɑ̃) *adj* incompetent.

inconnu (ɛ̃kɔ'ny) *adj* unknown. *nm* stranger.

inconscience (ɛ̃kɔ̃'sjɑ̃s) *nf* unconsciousness. **inconscient** *adj,nm* unconscious.

inconséquent (ɛ̃kɔ̃sɛ'kɑ̃) *adj* **1** inconsistent. **2** irresponsible.

inconstant (ɛ̃kɔ̃'stɑ̃) *adj* **1** fickle. **2** erratic.

incontestable (ɛ̃kɔ̃tɛ'stabl) *adj* undeniable.

inconvenant (ɛ̃kɔ̃v'nɑ̃) *adj* improper, indecent.

inconvénient (ɛ̃kɔ̃ve:'njɑ̃) *nm* drawback, disadvantage.

incorporer (ɛ̃kɔrpɔ're:) *vt* incorporate.

incriminer (ɛ̃kri:mi:'ne:) *vt* **1** incriminate. **2** accuse.

incroyable (ɛ̃krwa'jabl) *adj* incredible, unbelievable.

incuber (ɛ̃ky'be:) *vt* **1** incubate. **2** hatch. **incubateur** *nm* incubator.

inculper (ɛ̃kyl'pe:) *vt* *law* charge.

inculte (ɛ̃'kylt) *adj* **1** wild. **2** untidy.

Inde (ɛ̃d) *nf* India. **indien, -ienne** (ɛ̃'djɛ̃, -'djɛn) *adj,n* Indian.

indéchiffrable (ɛ̃de:ʃi:'frabl) *adj* illegible.

indécis (ɛ̃de:'si:) *adj* **1** undecided. **2** vague. **3** uncertain.

indéfini (ɛ̃de:fi:'ni:) *adj* indefinite.

indemne (ɛ̃'dɛmn) *adj* unhurt. **indemnité** *nf* **1** compensation. **2** allowance.

indemniser (ɛ̃dɛmni:'ze:) *vt* compensate.

indépendant (ɛ̃de:pɑ̃'dɑ̃) *adj* **1** independent. **2** free. **3** self-contained. **indépendance** *nf* independence.

index (ɛ̃'dɛks) *nm* **1** forefinger, index finger. **2** index.

indication (ɛ̃di:ka'sjɔ̃) *nf* **1** indication. **2** information. **3** sign. **4** *pl* instructions. **indicateur, -trice** (ɛ̃di:ka'tœr, -'tri:s) *adj* indicating. *nm* **1** indicator. **2** timetable. **3** gauge. **indicatif, -ive** (ɛ̃di:ka'ti:f, -'ti:v) *adj* indicative. *nm* indicative mood.

indice (ɛ̃'di:s) *nm* **1** sign. **2** indication. **3** index.

indifférent (ɛ̃di:fɛ'rɑ̃) *adj* indifferent.

indigence (ɛ̃di:'ʒɑ̃s) *nf* poverty. **indigent** *adj* poor, needy.

indigène (ɛ̃di:'ʒɛn) *adj,n* native.

indigestion (ɛ̃di:ʒɛ'stjɔ̃) *nf* indigestion.

indigner (ɛ̃di:'ɲe) *vt* make indignant. **s'indigner** *vr* become indignant. **indigné** *adj* indignant.

indiquer (ɛ̃di:'ke:) *vt* **1** indicate. **2** point out. **3** show.

indiscipliné (ɛ̃di:si:pli:'ne:) *adj* unruly.

indispensable (ɛ̃di:spɑ̃'sabl) *adj* essential.

indisposé (ɛ̃di:spo'ze:) *adj* unwell.

individu (ɛ̃di:vi:'dy) *nm* **1** individual. **2** *inf* fellow. **individuel, -elle** (ɛ̃di:vi:'dɥɛl) *adj* **1** individual. **2** personal, private.

indolent (ɛ̃dɔ'lɑ̃) *adj* indolent, lazy.

indolore (ɛ̃dɔ'lɔr) *adj* painless.

induire* (ɛ̃'dɥi:r) *vt* **1** induce. **2** infer.

indulgence (ɛ̃dyl'ʒɑ̃s) *nf* indulgence. **indulgent** *adj* **1** indulgent. **2** lenient.

industrie (ɛ̃dy'stri:) *nf* **1** industry. **2** trade. **3** activity. **industriel, -elle** (ɛ̃dystri:'ɛl) *adj* industrial. **industrieux, -euse** (ɛ̃dy'strɥœ, -'strɥœz) *adj* industrious.

inébranlable (i:ne:brɑ̃'labl) *adj* **1** firm, solid. **2** resolute, steadfast.

inégal, -aux (i:ne:'gal, -'go) *adj* **1** unequal. **2** uneven. **3** irregular. **inégalité** *nf* inequality.

inéluctable (i:ne:lyk'tabl) *adj* inevitable.

inepte (i:'nɛpt) *adj* inane, idiotic.

inestimable (i:nɛsti:'mabl) *adj* invaluable.

inévitable (i:ne:vi:'tabl) *adj* unavoidable, inevitable.

inexact (i:nɛg'zakt) *adj* **1** incorrect. **2** inaccurate. **3** unreliable.

infaillible (ɛ̃fa'ji:bl) *adj* **1** infallible. **2** sure.

infâme (ɛ̃'fɑm) *adj* **1** infamous. **2** vile, foul.

infanterie (ɛ̃fɑ̃'tri:) *nf* infantry.

infatuer (ɛ̃fa'tɥe:) *vt* infatuate. **s'infatuer** *vr* become infatuated.

infécond (ɛ̃fe:'kɔ̃) *adj* barren, sterile.

infect (ɛ̃'fɛkt) *adj* foul, putrid.

infecter (ɛ̃fɛk'te:) *vt* **1** infect. **2** pollute. **s'infecter** *vr* turn septic. **infectieux, -euse** (ɛ̃fɛk'sjœ, -'sjœz) *adj* infectious. **infection** *nf* **1** infection. **2** stink.

inférieur (ɛ̃fe:'rjœr) *adj* **1** inferior. **2** lower. **3** poor. *nm* inferior.

infester (ɛ̃fɛ'ste:) *vt* **1** infest. **2** overrun.

infidèle (ɛ̃fi:'dɛl) *adj* **1** unfaithful, disloyal. **2** false. **3** faithless. **infidélité** *nf* infidelity.

s'infiltrer (ɛ̃fi:l'tre:) *vr* **1** infiltrate, seep. **2** filter in.

infime (ɛ̃fi:m) *adj* minute.

infini (ɛ̃fi:'ni:) *adj* infinite. **infinité** *nf* infinity. **infinitif, -ive** (ɛ̃fi:ni:'ti:f, -'ti:v) *adj,nm* infinitive.

infirme (ɛ̃'fi:rm) *adj* **1** disabled. **2** crippled. **3** infirm. **infirmier, -ière** (ɛ̃fi:r'mje:, -'mjɛr) *nm,f* nurse. **infirmité** *nf* disability.

inflammable (ɛ̃fla'mabl) *adj* inflammable.

inflation (ɛ̃fla'sjɔ̃) *nf* inflation.

inflexion (ɛ̃flɛk'sjɔ̃) *nf* inflection.

infliger (ɛ̃fli:'ʒe:) *vt* inflict.

influencer (ɛ̃flyɑ̃'se:) *vt* influence. **influence** *nf* influence.

influenza (ɛ̃flyɑ̃'za) *nf* influenza.

influer (ɛ̃fly'e:) *vi* **influer sur** influence, have an effect upon.

informer (ɛ̃fɔr'me:) *vt* inform. **s'informer** *vr* make enquiries. **information** *nf* **1** information. **2** inquiry. **3** *pl* news.

infortune (ɛ̃fɔr'tyn) *nf* misfortune. **infortuné** *adj* unfortunate.

infraction (ɛ̃frak'sjɔ̃) *nf* **1** infringement. **2** breach.

infroissable (ɛ̃frwa'sabl) *adj* crease-resistant.

ingénieur (ɛ̃ʒe:'njœr) *nm* engineer.

ingénieux, -euse (ɛ̃ʒe:'njœ, -'njœz) *adj* ingenious.

ingénu (ɛ̃ʒe:'ny) *adj* **1** simple, naive. **2** candid.

s'ingérer (sɛ̃ʒe:'re:) *vr* **1** interfere. **2** meddle.

ingrat (ɛ̃'gra) *adj* **1** ungrateful. **2** thankless. **3** unpleasant.

ingrédient (ɛ̃gre:'djɑ̃) *nm* ingredient.

inhabile (i:na'bi:l) *adj* **1** clumsy. **2** unfit. **3** incompetent.

inhaler (i:na'le:) *vt* inhale.

inhérent (i:nɛ'rɑ̃) *adj* inherent.

inhiber (i:ni:'be:) *vt* inhibit. **inhibition** *nf* inhibition.
inhumain (i:ny'mɛ̃) *adj* inhuman.
initial, -aux (i:ni:'sjal, -'sjo) *adj* initial, starting. *nf* initial.
initier (i:ni:'sje:) *vt* initiate. **initiative** *nf* initiative.
injecter (ɛ̃ʒɛk'te:) *vt* inject. **injection** *nf* injection.
injurier (ɛ̃ʒy'rje:) *vt* insult, abuse. **injure** *nf* **1** insult. **2** *pl* abuse. **3** wrong. **injurieux, -euse** (ɛ̃ʒy'rjœ, -'rjœz) *adj* **1** abusive. **2** offensive.
injuste (ɛ̃'ʒyst) *adj* unfair. **injustice** *nf* **1** injustice. **2** wrong.
inné (i:n'ne:) *adj* innate.
innocent (i:nɔ'sɑ̃) *adj* **1** innocent, pure. **2** simple. **3** harmless. *nm* idiot. **innocence** *nf* innocence.
innovation (i:nnɔva'sjɔ̃) *nf* innovation.
inoccupé (i:nɔky'pe:) *adj* **1** idle. **2** vacant.
inoculer (i:nɔky'le:) *vt* **1** inoculate. **2** inject.
inonder (i:nɔ̃'de:) *vt* **1** flood. **2** inundate. **inondation** *nf* flood.
inopiné (i:nɔpi:'ne:) *adj* **1** sudden. **2** unexpected.
inouï (i:'nwi:) *adj* **1** extraordinary, incredible. **2** outrageous.
inquiet, -iète (ɛ̃'kjɛ, -'kjɛt) *adj* anxious, worried.
inquiéter (ɛ̃kje:'te:) *vt* **1** alarm. **2** disturb, trouble. **s'inquiéter** *vr* worry. **inquiétude** *nf* **1** anxiety. **2** concern.
inquisition (ɛ̃ki:zi:'sjɔ̃) *nf* inquisition, inquiry.
insciemment (ɛ̃sja'mɑ̃) *adv* unconsciously.
inscription (ɛ̃skri:'psjɔ̃) *nf* **1** registration. **2** inscription.
inscrire* (ɛ̃'skri:r) *vt* **1** inscribe, write down. **2** enrol. **3** register. **4** inscribe. **s'inscrire** *vr* **1** enrol. **2** register.
insecte (ɛ̃'sɛkt) *nm* insect. **insecticide** *nm* insecticide.
inséminer (ɛ̃se:mi:'ne:) *vt* inseminate.
insensé (ɛ̃sɑ̃'se:) *adj* **1** mad, insane. **2** wild. **3** ridiculous.
insensible (ɛ̃sɑ̃'si:bl) *adj* **1** insensitive. **2** indifferent. **3** callous.
insérer (ɛ̃se:'re:) *vt* insert.
insidieux, -euse (ɛ̃si:'djœ, -'djœz) *adj* insidious.
insigne (ɛ̃'si:ɲ) *adj* **1** remarkable. **2** notorious. *nm* **1** badge. **2** emblem. **3** medal.
insinuer (ɛ̃si:'nɥe:) *vt* **1** insinuate. **2** hint at, suggest. **s'insinuer** *vr* **1** creep in. **2** slip in.
insister (ɛ̃si:'ste:) *vi* insist. **insister sur** lay stress on.
insolation (ɛ̃sɔla'sjɔ̃) *nf* sunstroke.
insolent (ɛ̃sɔ'lɑ̃) *adj* insolent, cheeky.
insomnie (ɛ̃sɔm'ni:) *nf* insomnia.
insonore (ɛ̃sɔ'nɔr) *adj* soundproof.
insouciant (ɛ̃su:'sjɑ̃) *adj* carefree. **insoucieux, -euse** (ɛ̃su:'sjœ, -'sjœz) *adj* heedless.
inspecter (ɛ̃spɛk'te:) *vt* inspect, examine. **inspecteur, -trice** (ɛ̃spɛk'tœr, -'tri:s) *nm,f* inspector.
inspirer (ɛ̃spi:'re:) *vt* **1** inspire. **2** breathe in. **inspiration** *nf* **1** inspiration. **2** suggestion.
instabilité (ɛ̃stabi:li:'te:) *nf* instability.
installer (ɛ̃sta'le:) *vt* **1** install. **2** equip. **s'installer** *vr* **1** settle down. **2** move in. **installation** *nf* **1** installation. **2** fittings. **3** *tech* plant.
instant (ɛ̃'stɑ̃) *adj* **1** urgent. **2** imminent. *nm* moment, instant. **à l'instant 1** a moment ago. **2** at once. **par instants** on and off. **instantané** *adj* instantaneous. *nm* snapshot.
instar (ɛ̃'star) **à l'instar de** *prep* like, after the fashion of.
instiller (ɛ̃sti:'le:) *vt* instil.
instinct (ɛ̃'stɛ̃) *nm* instinct. **instinctif, -ive** (ɛ̃stɛ̃k'ti:f, -'ti:v) *adj* instinctive.
instituer (ɛ̃sti:'tɥe:) *vt* **1** set up, institute. **2** appoint. **institut** *nm* **1** institute. **2** institution. **instituteur, -trice** (ɛ̃sti:ty'tœr, -'tri:s) *nm,f* **1** primary school teacher. **2** founder. **institution** *nf* **1** establishment, institution. **2** boarding school.
instruire* (ɛ̃'strɥi:r) *vt* **1** inform. **2** teach, instruct. **3** train. **instruction** *nf* **1** instruction. **2** education. **3** *pl* directions.
instrument (ɛ̃stry'mɑ̃) *nm* **1** instrument. **2** tool, implement. **instrumental, -aux** (ɛ̃strymɑ̃'tal, -'to) *adj* instrumental.
insu (ɛ̃'sy) **à l'insu de** *prep* unknown to.
insubordonné (ɛ̃sybɔrdɔ'ne:) *adj* insubordinate.
insuccès (ɛ̃syk'sɛ) *nm* failure.
insuffisant (ɛ̃syfi:'zɑ̃) *adj* **1** inadequate. **2** incompetent.
insulaire (ɛ̃sy'lɛr) *adj* insular.
insuline (ɛ̃sy'li:n) *nf* insulin.
insulter (ɛ̃syl'te:) *vt* insult. **insulte** *nf* insult.
insupportable (ɛ̃sypɔr'tabl) *adj* unbearable.
s'insurger (sɛ̃syr'ʒe:) *vr* **1** rebel. **2** revolt. **insurgé** *nm* rebel.
intact (ɛ̃'takt) *adj* whole, intact.
intégrer (ɛ̃te:'gre:) *vt* integrate. **intégral, -aux** (ɛ̃tɛ'gral, -'gro) *adj* entire, whole, integral **intégrant** (ɛ̃tɛ'grɑ̃) *adj* integral. **intègre** *adj* honest, upright. **intégrité** *nf* **1** integrity, honesty. **2** entirety.

intellect (ɛ̃tɛl'lɛkt) *nm* intellect. **intellectuel, -elle** (ɛ̃tɛlɛk'tɥɛl) *adj,n* intellectual.

intelligence (ɛ̃tɛli:'ʒɑ̃s) *nf* **1** intelligence, intellect. **2** understanding. **intelligent** *adj* clever, intelligent. **intelligible** *adj* intelligible, clear.

intendant (ɛ̃tɑ̃'dɑ̃) *nm* **1** steward. **2** administrator.

intensifier (ɛ̃tɑ̃si:'fje:) *vt* intensify. **intense** *adj* intense, severe. **intensif, -ive** (ɛ̃tɑ̃'si:f, -'si:v) *adj* intensive. **intensité** *nf* intensity, strength.

intention (ɛ̃tɑ̃'sjɔ̃) *nf* intention, purpose. **à l'intention de** for, in honour of. **avoir l'intention de** intend to.

intercepter (ɛ̃tɛrsɛp'te:) *vt* intercept.

interdire* (ɛ̃tɛr'di:r) *vt* **1** forbid, prohibit. **2** bewilder

intéresser (ɛ̃te:rɛ'se:) *vt* **1** interest. **2** concern. **s'intéresser à** *vr* be interested in.

intérêt (ɛ̃te:'rɛ) *nm* **1** interest. **2** advantage. **3** profit. **4** share. **avoir intérêt à** be in one's interest to.

intérieur (ɛ̃te:'rjœr) *adj* **1** interior. **2** inner. **3** internal. **4** domestic. *nm* interior, inside. **à l'intérieur** inside.

intérim (ɛ̃te:'ri:m) *nm* interim.

interjection (ɛ̃tɛrʒɛk'sjɔ̃) *nf* interjection.

interloquer (ɛ̃tɛrlɔke:) *vt* disconcert.

intermède (ɛ̃tɛr'mɛd) *nm* interlude. **intermédiaire** *adj* intermediate. *nm* intermediary.

intermission (ɛ̃tɛrmi:'sjɔ̃) *nf* intermission.

intermittent (ɛ̃tɛrmi:t'tɑ̃) *adj* irregular, intermittent.

international, -aux (ɛ̃tɛrnasjɔ'nal, -'no) *adj* international.

interner (ɛ̃tɛr'ne:) *vt* intern, confine. **internat** *nm* boarding school. **interne** *adj* **1** internal. **2** interior. *nm* **1** boarder. **2** medical student.

interpeller (ɛ̃tɛrpɛ'le:) *vt* **1** challenge. **2** heckle. **interpellation** *nf* **1** question. **2** challenge.

interposer (ɛ̃tɛrpo'ze:) *vt* interpose. **s'interposer** *vr* intervene.

interpréter (ɛ̃tɛrpre:'te:) *vt* interpret. **interprétation** (ɛ̃tɛrprɛta'sjɔ̃) *nf* interpretation. **interprète** *nm,f* interpreter

interroger (ɛ̃tɛrɔ'ʒe:) *vt* question, examine, interrogate. **interrogatif, -ive** (ɛ̃tɛrɔga'ti:f, -'ti:v) *adj* interrogative. **interrogation** *nf* **1** interrogation, questioning. **2** question.

interrompre (ɛ̃tɛ'rɔ̃pr) *vt* **1** interrupt. **2** stop. **3** break, cut short.

interruption (ɛ̃tɛryp'sjɔ̃) *nf* interruption. **interrupteur** *nm* switch

intervalle (ɛ̃tɛr'val) *nm* **1** interval. **2** gap. **3** period. **dans l'intervalle** in the meantime.

intervenir* (ɛ̃tɛrvə'ni:r) *vi* (*aux* être) **1** intervene. **2** interfere. **3** happen.

intervertir (ɛ̃tɛrvɛr'ti:r) *vt* invert.

interview (ɛ̃tɛr'vju:) *nm,f* interview.

intestin (ɛ̃tɛ'stɛ̃) *adj* internal. *nm* **1** intestine. **2** gut. **3** *pl* bowels.

intime (ɛ̃'ti:m) *adj* **1** intimate, close. **2** private. **3** interior.

intimider (ɛ̃ti:mi:'de:) *vt* intimidate, frighten.

intituler (ɛ̃ti:ty'le:) *vt* **1** entitle, give a title to. **intitulé** *nm* title.

intolérable (ɛ̃tɔlɛ'rabl) *adj* intolerable, unbearable.

intonation (ɛ̃tɔna'sjɔ̃) *nf* intonation.

intoxiquer (ɛ̃tɔksi:'ke:) *vt* poison.

intransitif, -ive (ɛ̃trɑ̃zi:'ti:f, -'ti:v) *adj* intransitive.

intrépide (ɛ̃tre:'pi:d) *adj* bold, daring.

intriguer (ɛ̃tri:'ge:) *vt* **1** puzzle. **2** intrigue. *vi* plot. **intrigue** *nf* plot, scheme.

intrinsèque (ɛ̃trɛ̃'sɛk) *adj* intrinsic.

introduire* (ɛ̃trɔ'dɥi:r) *vt* **1** introduce. **2** insert. **3** show in. **s'introduire** *vr* get in, enter. **introduction** *nf* **1** introduction. **2** admission. **3** preface.

introverti (ɛ̃trɔvɛr'ti:) *nm* introvert.

intrusion (ɛ̃try'zjɔ̃) *nf* intrusion. **faire intrusion** intrude.

intuition (ɛ̃tɥi:'sjɔ̃) *nf* intuition. **intuitif, -ive** (ɛ̃tɥi:'ti:f, -'ti:v) *adj* intuitive.

inutile (i:ny'ti:l) *adj* **1** useless. **2** unnecessary. **3** vain.

invaincu (ɛ̃vɛ̃'ky) *adj* unbeaten.

invalide (ɛ̃va'li:d) *adj* **1** infirm, invalid. **2** *law* invalid, null. *nm,f med* invalid.

invariable (ɛ̃va'rjabl) *adj* invariable.

invasion (ɛ̃va'zjɔ̃) *nf* invasion.

inventer (ɛ̃vɑ̃'te:) *vt* **1** invent. **2** discover. **inventaire** *nm* **1** inventory. **2** stocktaking. **invention** *nf* **1** invention. **2** device.

inverser (ɛ̃vɛr'se:) *vt* reverse. **inverse** *adj* **1** opposite. **2** reverse. **3** inverted. *nm* opposite, reverse.

invertébré (ɛ̃vɛrte:'bre:) *adj* invertebrate.

invertir (ɛ̃vɛr'ti:r) *vt* invert, reverse.

investir (ɛ̃vɛ'sti:r) *vt* invest. **investissement** *nm* investment.

invisible (ɛ̃vi:'zi:bl) *adj* invisible.

inviter (ɛ̃vi:'te:) *vt* **1** invite. **2** ask, request. **invitation** *nf* invitation. **invité** *nm* guest.

invoquer (ɛ̃vɔ'ke:) *vt* **1** plead, call upon. **2** bring forward.
invraisemblable (ɛ̃vrɛsɑ̃'blabl) *adj* **1** unlikely, improbable. **2** unbelievable.
iode (i:'ɔd) *nm* iodine.
ion (i:'ɔ̃) *nm* ion.
iouler (ju:'le:) *vi* yodel.
irai (i:'rɛ) *v* see **aller.**
Irak (i:'rak) *nm* Iraq. **irakien, -ienne** (i:ra'kjɛ̃, -'kjɛn) *adj,n* Iraqi.
Iran (i:'rɑ̃) *nm* Iran. **iranien, -ienne** (i:ra'njɛ̃, -'njɛn) *adj,n* Iranian.
iris (i:'ri:s) *nm anat,bot* iris.
Irlande (i:r'lɑ̃d) *nf* Ireland. **irlandais** *adj* Irish. *nm* Irishman.
ironie (i:rɔ'ni:) *nf* irony. **ironique** *adj* ironic.
irrationnel, -elle (irrasjɔ'nɛl) *adj* irrational.
irréfléchi (irre:fle:'ʃi:) *adj* **1** thoughtless. **2** rash.
irrégulier, -ière (i:rre:gy'lje:, -'ljɛr) *adj* irregular.
irrésistible (i:rre:zi:'stabl) *adj* irresistible.
irrespect (i:rrɛ'spɛ) *nm* disrespect. **irrespectueux, -euse** (i:rrɛspɛk'tɥœ, -'tɥœz) *adj* disrespectful.
irresponsable (i:rrɛspɔ̃'sabl) *adj* irresponsible.
irrévocable (i:rre:vɔ'kabl) *adj* irrevocable.
irriguer (i:rri:'ge:) *vt* irrigate. **irrigation** *nf* irrigation.
irriter (i:rri:'te:) *vt* **1** annoy, provoke. **2** irritate. **s'irriter** *vr* **1** get angry. **2** become inflamed.
irruption (i:ryp'sjɔ̃) *nf* **1** raid, attack. **2** flood. **faire irruption dans** burst or rush into.
Islam (i:'slam) *nm* Islam. **islamique** *adj* Islamic.
Islande (i:'slɑ̃d) *nf* Iceland. **islandais** *adj* Icelandic. *nm* **1** Icelander. **2** Icelandic (language).
isoler (i:zɔ'le:) *vt* **1** isolate. **2** insulate. **isolé** *adj* **1** isolated, remote. **2** lonely. **3** detached.
Isorel (i:zɔ'rɛl) *nm Tdmk* hardboard.
Israël (i:zra'ɛl) *nm* Israel. **israélien, -ienne** (i:zrae:'ljɛ̃, -'ljɛn) *adj,n* Israeli.
issu (i:'sy) **issu de** *adj* descended from.
issue (i:'sy) *nf* **1** exit. **2** escape. **3** end, result.
Italie (i:ta'li:) *nf* Italy. **italien, -ienne** (i:ta'ljɛ̃, -'ljɛn) *adj,n* Italian. *nm* Italian (language).
italique (i:ta'li:k) *adj* italic. *nm* italics.
itinéraire (i:ti:ne:'rɛr) *nm* **1** route, itinerary. **2** guidebook.
ivoire (i:'vwar) *nm* ivory.
ivre (i:vr) *adj* drunk, drunken. **ivrogne** *nm* drunkard.

J

jabot (ʒa'bo) *nm* **1** *zool* crop. **2** frill.
jacasser (ʒaka'se:) *vt* chatter. **jacasse** *nf inf* **1** magpie. **2** chatterbox.
jachère (ʒa'ʃɛr) *nf* fallow.
jacinthe (ʒa'sɛ̃t) *nf* hyacinth. **jacinthe des bois** or **près** *nf* bluebell.
jade (ʒad) *nm* jade.
jadis (ʒa'di:s) *adv* **1** formerly. **2** once.
jaguar (ʒa'gwar) *nm* jaguar.
jaillir (ʒa'ji:r) *vi* **1** squirt, gush out. **2** run, spread. **3** flash. **4** spring up.
jais (ʒɛ) *nm min* jet.
jalonner (ʒalɔ'ne:) *vt* **1** mark out. **2** set out.
jaloux, -ouse (ʒa'lu:, -'lu:z) *adj* **1** jealous. **2** anxious, keen. **jalousie** *nf* jealousy.
Jamaïque (ʒama'i:k) *nf* Jamaica. **jamaïquain** *adj,n* Jamaican.
jamais (ʒa'mɛ) *adv* ever. **à tout jamais** for ever and ever. **ne...jamais** never.
jambe (ʒɑ̃b) *nf* **1** leg. **2** prop, stay.
jambon (ʒɑ̃'bɔ̃) *nm* ham.
janséniste (ʒɑ̃se:'ni:st) *adj,n* Jansenist.
jante (ʒɑ̃t) *nf* rim (of a wheel).
janvier (ʒɑ̃'vje:) *nm* January.
Japon (ʒa'pɔ̃) *nm* Japan. **japonais** *adj,n* Japanese. *nm* Japanese (language).
japper (ʒa'pe:) *vi* yap, yelp.
jaquette (ʒa'kɛt) *nf* **1** (lady's) jacket. **2** morning coat.
jardin (ʒar'dɛ̃) *nm* garden. **jardin d'enfants** kindergarten. **jardin maraîcher** market garden.
jardiner (ʒardi:'ne:) *vi* garden. **jardinage** *nm* gardening. **jardinier, -ière** (ʒardi:'nje:, -'njɛr) *adj* garden. *nm,f* gardener. *nf* window box. **jardiniste** *nm* landscape gardener.
jargon (ʒar'gɔ̃) *nm* **1** jargon. **2** slang.
jarret (ʒa'rɛ) *nm* **1** bend of the knee. **2** *zool* hock. **3** *cul* knuckle, shin.
jars (ʒar) *nm* gander.
jaser (ʒɑ'ze:) *vi* **1** chatter. **2** gossip.
jasmin (ʒa'smɛ̃) *nm* jasmine.
jatte (ʒat) *nf* bowl, basin.
jauger (ʒo'ʒe:) *vt* **1** gauge. **2** measure. **jauge** *nf* gauge.
jaune (ʒon) *adj* yellow. *nm* **1** yellow. **2** yolk (of an egg). **3** blackleg. **jaunir** *vt* make or turn yellow. *vi* turn yellow. **jaunisse** *nf* jaundice.
javelot (ʒa'vlo) *nm* javelin.

jazz (ʒaz) *nm* jazz.
je, j' (ʒə) *pron 1st pers m,f s* I.
jeep (dʒi:p) *nf* jeep.
jersey (ʒɛr'zɛ) *nm* jersey, jumper.
Jersey (ʒɛr'zɛ) *nm* Jersey.
Jérusalem (ʒɛryza'lɛm) *nf* Jerusalem.
jésuite (ʒe:'zɥi:t) *nm* Jesuit. **jésuitique** *adj* **1** Jesuit. **2** hypocritical.
Jésus (ʒe:'zy) *nm* Jesus.
jet (ʒɛ) *nm* **1** throw. **2** cast. **3** jet, stream, ray, spurt.
jeter (ʒə'te:) *vt* throw, fling. **jetée** *nf* jetty. **jeton** *nm* **1** counter. **2** token.
jeu, jeux (ʒœ) *nm* **1** game. **2** play. **3** set. **4** gambling. **jeu de cartes** pack of cards. **jeu de mots** pun. **prendre du jeu** work loose.
jeudi (ʒœ'di:) *nm* Thursday. **jeudi saint** Maundy Thursday.
jeun (ʒœ̃) **à jeun** *adv* fasting.
jeune (ʒœn) *adj* **1** young. **2** juvenile. **3** junior, younger. **jeunesse** *nf* **1** youth. **2** childhood, boyhood, girlhood. **3** young people.
jeûner (ʒœ'ne:) *vi* fast. **jeûne** *nm* fast.
joaillier, -ière (ʒwa'je:, -'jɛr) *nm,f* jeweller. **joaillerie** *nf* **1** jewellery. **2** jeweller's shop.
jockey (ʒɔ'kɛ) *nm* jockey.
joie (ʒwa) *nf* joy, delight.
joindre* (ʒwɛ̃dr) *vt* **1** join. **2** combine. **3** add. **4** clasp. *vi* fit. **se joindre** *vr* join, unite. **joint** *adj* joined, united. *nm* join, joint. **jointure** *nf* joint. **jointure du doigt** knuckle.
joli (ʒɔ'li:) *adj* **1** pretty. **2** good-looking. **3** pleasant, nice. **joliment** *adv* **1** prettily. **2** nicely. **3** *inf* very, awfully.
jonc (ʒɔ̃) *nm bot* rush. **jonc à balais** reed.
joncher (ʒɔ̃'ʃe:) *vt* scatter, litter.
jonction (ʒɔ̃k'sjɔ̃) *nf* junction.
jongler (ʒɔ̃'gle:) *vi* juggle. **jongleur** *nm* juggler.
jonquille (ʒɔ̃'ki:j) *nm* daffodil.
Jordanie (ʒɔrda'ni:) *nf* Jordan. **jordanien, -ienne** (ʒɔrda'njɛ̃, -'njɛn) *adj,n* Jordanian.
joue (ʒu:) *nf anat* cheek.
jouer (ʒwe:) *vi* **1** play. **2** gamble. **3** be loose. *vt* **1** stake. **2** play. **3** perform. **4** trick. **se jouer de** *vr* make fun of. **jouet** *nm* toy. **joueur, -euse** (ʒwœr, ʒwœz) *nm,f* **1** player. **2** gambler. **joujou, -oux** (ʒu:'ʒu:) *nm inf* toy.
joufflu (ʒu:'fly) *adj* chubby.
joug (ʒu:g) *nm* yoke.
jouir (ʒwi:r) *vi* **jouir de** enjoy. **jouissance** *nf* **1** enjoyment. **2** possession.
jour (ʒu:r) *nm* **1** day. **2** daylight. **3** light. **4** hole, gap. **au jour le jour 1** from day to day. **2** from hand to mouth. **de nos jours** nowadays. **jour de semaine** weekday. **journée** *nf* **1** day. **2** day's work. **toute la journée** all day long.
journal, -aux (ʒu:r'nal, -'no) *nm* **1** newspaper. **2** diary. **3** journal. **journalier, -ière** (ʒu:rna'lje:, -'ljɛr) *adj* daily. **journalisme** *nm* journalism. **journaliste** *nm,f* journalist.
jovial, -aux (ʒɔ'vjal, -'vjo) *adj* jolly, jovial.
joyau, -aux (ʒwa'jo) *nm* jewel.
joyeux, -euse (ʒwa'jœ, -'jœz) *adj* **1** merry. **2** glad.
jubilé (ʒybi:'le:) *nm* jubilee.
jucher (ʒy'ʃe:) *vi* **1** perch. **2** roost.
judaïsme (ʒyda'i:sm) *nm* Judaism.
judiciaire (ʒydi:'sjɛr) *adj* **1** judicial. **2** legal.
judicieux, -euse (ʒydi:'sjœ, -'sjœz) *adj* judicious.
juger (ʒy'ʒe:) *vt* **1** judge. **2** *law* try. **3** adjudicate. **4** consider, think. **au jugé** *adv* **1** by guesswork. **2** at random. **juge** *nm* **1** judge. **2** umpire. **jugement** *nm* **1** judgment. **2** *law* trial.
juif, juive (ʒɥi:f, ʒɥi:v) *nm,f* Jew. *adj* Jewish.
juillet (ʒɥi:'jɛ) *nm* July.
juin (ʒɥɛ̃) *nm* June.
jumeler (ʒym'le:) *vt* pair, arrange in pairs. **jumeau, -elle, -aux, -elles** (ʒy'mo:, -'mɛl, -'mo, -'mɛl) *adj,n* twin. **jumelles** *nf pl* binoculars.
jument (zy'mɑ̃) *nf* mare.
jungle (ʒɔ̃gl) *nf* jungle.
junte (ʒɔ̃t) *nf* junta.
jupe (ʒyp) *nf* skirt. **jupon** *nm* petticoat.
Jupiter (ʒypi:'tɛr) *nm* Jupiter.
jurer (ʒy're:) *vt* swear, vow. *vi* **1** curse, use bad language. **2** clash. **juré** *adj* sworn. *nm* **1** juror. **2** *pl* jury. **juron** *nm* **1** oath. **2** swearword. **jury** *nm* jury.
juridique (ʒyri:'di:k) *adj* **1** judicial. **2** legal.
jus (ʒy) *nm* **1** juice. **2** gravy.
jusant (ʒy'zɑ̃) *nm* ebb.
jusque (ʒysk) *prep* **1** as far as. **2** up to. **3** till, until. **4** even. **jusqu'à ce que** until. **jusqu'ici** so far, up to now. **jusqu'où?** how far?
juste (ʒyst) *adj* **1** just, fair. **2** right, exact. **3** upright. **4** tight. *adv* **1** just. **2** exactly. **3** barely. **justesse** *nf* **1** accuracy. **2** correctness.
justice (ʒy'sti:s) *nf* **1** justice. **2** law.
justifier (ʒysti:'fje:) *vt* **1** justify. **2** clear.
jute (ʒyt) *nm* jute.
juteux, -euse (ʒy'tœ, -'tœz) *adj* juicy.
juvénile (ʒyve:'ni:l) *adj* juvenile.

juxtaposer (ʒykstapo'ze:) *vt* juxtapose, put side by side.

K

kaki (ka'ki:) *adj invar,nm* khaki.
kaléidoscope (kale:i:dɔ'skɔp) *nm* kaleidoscope.
kangourou (kɑ̃gu:'ru:) *nm* kangaroo.
karaté (kara'te:) *nm* karate.
képi (ke:'pi:) *nm mil* cap.
kermesse (kɛr'mɛs) *nf* village fair.
kérosène (ke:rɔ'zɛn) *nm* paraffin oil.
kibboutz (ki:'bu:ts) *nm* kibbutz.
kilo (ki:'lo) *nm inf* kilo.
kilogramme (ki:lɔ'gram) *nm* kilogram.
kilomètre (ki:lɔ'mɛtr) *nm* kilometre. **kilométrique** *adj* kilometric.
kilowatt (ki:lɔ'wat) *nm* kilowatt.
kimono (ki:mɔ'no) *nm* kimono.
kiosque (kjɔsk) *nm* **1** kiosk. **2** newspaper stall. **3** summerhouse.
kiwi (ki:'wi:) *nm* kiwi.
klaxon (klak'sɔ̃) *nm* hooter, horn.
klaxonner (klaksɔ'ne:) *vi* blow one's horn, hoot.
kleptomanie (klɛptɔma'ni:) *nf* kle omania. **kleptomane** *adj,n* kleptomaniac.

L

l' *def art* see **le** and **la.**
la, l' (la) *def art f* **1** the. **2** a. *pron 3rd pers fs* **1** her. **2** it.
là (la) *adv* **1** there. **2** then. **3** that. **là-bas** *adv* **1** over there, yonder. **2** down there. **là-dedans** *adv* **1** in there. **2** within, in it or them. **là-dessous** *adv* **1** under there. **2** under it, that, or them. **3** underneath. **là-dessus** *adv* **1** on that. **2** thereupon. **là-haut** *adv* up there.
laboratoire (labɔra'twar) *nm* laboratory.
labourer (labu:'re:) *vt* till, plough. **laborieux, -euse** (labɔ'rjœ, -'rjœz) *adj* **1** hard-working. **2** arduous. **labourable** *adj* arable.
labyrinthe (labi:'rɛ̃t) *nm* labyrinth, maze.
lac (lak) *nm* lake, loch.
lacer (la'se:) *vt* lace (up). **lacet** *nm* **1** lace, shoelace. **2** noose. **en lacet** winding.
lacérer (lasɛ're:) *vt* **1** slash. **2** tear.
lâcher (lɑ'ʃe:) *vt* **1** let go, release. **2** drop. **3** slacken. **4** divulge. **lâcher pied** give way. **lâche** *adj* **1** cowardly, faint-hearted. **2** loose, slack. *nm* coward. **lâcheté** *nf* cowardice.
lacrymogène (lakri:mɔ'ʒɛn) **gaz lacrymogène** *nm* tear-gas.
lacté (lak'te:) *adj* milky.
lacune (la'kyn) *nf* **1** gap. **2** break. **3** blank.
ladre (lɑdr) *adj* mean. *nm* miser.
laid (lɛ) *adj* **1** ugly, plain. **2** unsightly. **laideur** *nf* ugliness.
laine (lɛn) *nf* wool. **de laine 1** woollen. **2** woolly. **laine filée** yarn. **laineux, -euse** (lɛ'nœ, -'nœz) *adj* woolly.
laïque (la'i:k) *adj* lay, secular. *nm* **1** layman. **2** *pl* laity.
laisser (lɛ'se:) *vt* **1** let, allow. **2** leave. **laisse** *nf* lead, leash. **laisser-aller** *nm invar* **1** carefreeness. **2** neglect. **laisser-passer** *nm invar* pass, permit.
lait (lɛ) *nm* milk. **laiterie** *nf* dairy. **laitier, -ière** (lɛ'tje:, -'tjɛr) *adj* dairy. *nm* milkman.
laiton (lɛ'tɔ̃) *nm* brass.
laitue (lɛ'ty) *nf* lettuce.
lama (la'ma) *nm* llama.
lambeau, -aux (lɑ̃'bo) *nm* **1** scrap. **2** shred.
lambrequin (lɑ̃brə'kɛ̃) *nm* pelmet.
lame (lam) *nf* **1** blade. **2** strip, sheet. **3** *naut* wave.
se lamenter (lamɑ̃'te:) *vr* wail, lament, bewail. **lamentation** *nf* lament.
lampe (lɑ̃p) *nf* lamp.
lamper (lɑ̃'pe:) *vt inf* swig. **lampée** *nf* swig, gulp.
lancer (lɑ̃'se:) *vt* **1** throw, fling, hurl. **2** start, set going. **3** launch. **se lancer** *vr* rush, dash. **lance** (lɑ̃s) *nf* spear. **lance-pierre** *nm invar* catapult.
lanciner (lɑ̃si:'ne:) *vi* throb.
landau (lɑ̃'do) *nm* pram.
lande (lɑ̃d) *nf* heath.
landier (lɑ̃'dje:) *nm* gorse.
langage (lɑ̃'gaʒ) *nm* **1** language. **2** speech. **3** talk.
langouste (lɑ̃'gu:st) *nf* crayfish. **langoustines** *nf pl* scampi.
langue (lɑ̃g) *nf* **1** *anat* tongue. **2** language. **langue maternelle** mother tongue.
languir (lɑ̃'gi:r) *vi* pine, yearn. **languissant** *adj* **1** listless. **2** dull.
lanterne (lɑ̃'tɛrn) *nf* lantern.
laper (la'pe:) *vt* lap.
lapin (la'pɛ̃) *nm* rabbit.
Laponie (lapɔ'ni:) *nf* Lapland. **lapon** *adj,n* Lapp.
laque (lak) *nm* lacquer. **laquer** *vt* lacquer.
larcin (lar'sɛ̃) *nm* larceny.

lard (lar) *nm* bacon.
larder (lar'de:) *vt* **1** lard. **2** cover.
large (larʒ) *adj* **1** broad. **2** wide. **3** ample. **4** generous. **5** big. *nm* **1** width. **2** room, space. **3** sea. *adv* **1** largely. **2** broadly. **3** loosely. **largeur** *nf* breadth, width.
larme (larm) *nf* tear, teardrop.
larmoyer (larmwa'je:) *vi* **1** weep. **2** snivel. **larmoyant** *adj* tearful.
larron (la'rɔ̃) *nm* thief.
larve (larv) *nf* larva, grub.
laryngite (larɛ̃'ʒi:t) *nf* laryngitis.
larynx (la'rɛ̃ks) *nm* larynx.
las, lasse (lɑ, lɑs) *adj* tired, weary.
lascif, -ive (la'si:f, -'si:v) *adj* lewd.
lasser (lɑ'se:) *vt* **1** tire. **2** exhaust. **se lasser** *vr* grow, get tired.
lasso (la'so) *nm* lasso. **prendre au lasso** lasso.
latent (la'tɑ̃) *adj* latent, hidden.
latin (la'tɛ̃) *adj,nm* Latin.
latitude (lati:'tyd) *nf* **1** latitude. **2** scope.
laurier (lɔ'rje:) *nm* laurel.
lavabo (lava'bo) *nm* **1** washbasin. **2** lavatory.
lavande (la'vɑ̃d) *nf* lavender.
lave (lav) *nf* lava.
laver (la've:) *vt* **1** wash. **2** bathe. **se laver** *vr* wash oneself, have a wash. **laverie** *nf* laundry. **lavette** *nf* dishcloth.
laxatif, -ive (laksa'ti:f, -'ti:v) *adj,nm* laxative.
le, l' (lə) *def art m* **1** the. **2** a. *pron 3rd pers ms* **1** him. **2** it. *pron* so.
lécher (le:'ʃe:) *vt* **1** lick. **2** polish, refine. **lèche-vitrines** *nm* windowshopping. **faire du lèche-vitrines** windowshop.
leçon (lə'sɔ̃) *nf* lesson.
lecteur, -trice (lɛk'tœr, -'tri:s) *nm,f* **1** reader. **2** foreign language assistant (in a university). **lecture** *nf* reading.
ledit, ladite (lə'di:, la'di:t) *adj, pl* **lesdits, lesdites** aforesaid.
légal, -aux (le'gal, -'go) *adj* **1** legal, lawful. **2** statutory.
légaliser (le:gali:'ze:) *vt* **1** legalize. **2** certify
légataire (lɛga'tɛr) *nm,f* heir.
légende (lɛ'ʒɑ̃d) *nf* legend, myth, fable. **légendaire** *adj* legendary.
léger, -ère (le:'ʒe:, -'ʒɛr) *adj* **1** light. **2** slight. **3** agile. **4** loose, fast. **5** mild. **6** weak. **à la légère** lightly. **légèreté** *nf* lightness.
légiférer (le:ʒi:fe:'re:) *vi* legislate.
légion (le:'ʒjɔ̃) *nf* **1** legion. **2** crowd, host.
légitime (le:ʒi:'ti:m) *adj* legitimate, lawful.
legs (lɛ) *nm* legacy.
léguer (le:'ge:) *vt* leave, bequeath.
légume (le:'gym) *nm* vegetable.
lendemain (lɑ̃d'mɛ̃) *nm* next day, day after.
lent (lɑ̃) *adj* slow. **lenteur** *nf* slowness.
lentille (lɑ̃'ti:j) *nf* **1** lentil. **2** lens. **3** freckle. **lentilles de contact** *nf pl* contact lenses.
léopard (le:ɔ'par) *nm* leopard.
lèpre (lɛpr) *nf* leprosy. **lépreux, -euse** (le:'prœ, -'prœz) *nm,f* leper.
lequel, laquelle (lə'kɛl, la'kɛl) *pron, pl* **lesquels, lesquelles** **1** who, whom. **2** which.
les (lɛ) *def art m,f pl* the. *pron 3rd pers m,f pl* them.
lesbien (lɛs'bjɛ̃) *adj* lesbian. **lesbienne** (lɛs-'bjɛn) *nf* lesbian.
léser (le:'ze:) *vt* **1** wrong, wound. **2** injure.
lésiner (le:zi:'ne:) *vi* **1** be mean. **2** haggle.
lessive (lɛ'si:v) *nf* **1** washing. **2** detergent.
lest (lɛst) *nm* ballast.
leste (lɛst) *adj* **1** lively, nimble, agile. **2** sharp, smart. **3** free, brazen.
léthargie (lɛtar'ʒi:) *nf* **1** lethargy. **2** apathy. **léthargique** *adj* lethargic.
lettre (lɛtr) *nf* **1** letter (of the alphabet). **2** letter, note. **3** *pl* literature, letters. **4** *pl* arts. **lettré** *adj* **1** literate. **2** learned. *nm* scholar.
leu (lœ) **à la queue leu leu** *adv* in single file.
leucémie (lœse:'mi:) *nf* leukaemia.
leur (lœr) *poss adj 3rd pers pl* their. *poss pron 3rd pers m,f pl* **le** or **la leur** **1** theirs. **2** their own. **3** to them.
leurrer (lœ're:) *vt* **1** lure. **2** bait. **3** entice. **se leurrer** *vr* delude oneself. **leurre** *nm* **1** lure. **2** bait. **3** decoy.
lever (lə've:) *vt* **1** lift, raise. **2** collect. **3** levy. **4** adjourn. **se lever** *vr* **1** rise. **2** get up. **3** stand up. ~*nm* rising. **lever du soleil** *nm* sunrise. **levant** *adj* rising. *nm* east. **levé** *adj* raised. *nm* survey. **levée** *nf* **1** lifting. **2** levy. **3** collection. **4** embankment. **5** *game* trick. **levier** *nm* lever.
lèvre (lɛvr) *nf* lip.
lévrier (le:vri:'e:) *nm* greyhound.
levure (lə'vyr) *nf* yeast.
lézard (lɛ'zar) *nm* lizard.
lézarder (lɛzar'de:) *vt* crack, split. *vi inf* **1** bask in the sun. **2** lounge. **lézarde** *nf* **1** crack. **2** crevice.
liaison (ljɛ'zɔ̃) *nf* **1** joining, liaison. **2** connection. **3** relationship. **4** *mus* slur.
liasse (ljas) *nf* **1** bundle, wad. **2** file.
Liban (li:'bɑ̃) *nm* Lebanon. **libanais** *adj,n* Lebanese.

libelle (liː'bɛl) *nf* libel.
libellule (liːbɛl'lyl) *nf* dragonfly.
libérer (liːbeː'reː) *vt* **1** free, liberate. **2** release. **3** discharge. **libéral, -aux** (liːbɛ'ral, -'ro) *adj* **1** broad, wide. **2** free. **3** generous. **4** *pol* liberal. **liberté** *nf* liberty, freedom.
librairie (liːbrɛ'riː) *nf* **1** bookshop. **2** publishing house. **libraire** *nm,f* bookseller.
libre (liːbr) *adj* **1** free. **2** clear, open. **3** independent. **4** exempt. **5** vacant. **libre-service** *nm, pl* **libres-services** self-service (shop or restaurant, etc.).
Libye (liː'biː) *nf* Libya. **libyen, -enne** (liː'bjɛ̃, -'bjɛn) *adj,n* Libyan.
licence (liː'sɑ̃s) *nf* **1** licence. **2** leave, permission. **3** *educ* degree. **4** excessive liberty. **licencié** *nm* **1** graduate. **2** licensee.
licorne (liː'kɔrn) *nf* unicorn.
licou (liː'kuː) *nm* halter.
lie (liː) *nf* dregs.
liège (ljɛʒ) *nm* cork.
lier (ljeː) *vt* **1** fasten, bind. **2** link, connect. **3** *cul* thicken. **lien** *nm* **1** tie, bond. **2** link. **3** fetter. **4** strap.
lierre (ljɛr) *nm* ivy.
lieu, -eux (ljœ) *nm* **1** place. **2** spot. **3** reason. **4** *pl* premises. **au lieu de** instead of. **au lieu que** whereas. **avoir lieu** take place. **donner lieu à** give rise to. **lieux d'aisances** *nm pl* lavatory.
lieutenant (ljœt'nɑ̃) *nm* lieutenant. **lieutenant-colonel** *nm, pl* **lieutenants-colonels** **1** lieutenant colonel. **2** wing commander.
lièvre (ljɛvr) *nm* hare.
ligne (liɲ) *nf* **1** line. **2** row. **3** cord. **4** formation. **à la ligne** new paragraph. **hors ligne** outstanding. **soigner sa ligne** watch one's figure.
ligoter (liːgɔ'teː) *vt* bind, tie.
ligue (liːg) *nf* league, alliance.
lilas (liː'lɑ) *nm* lilac. *adj invar* lilac.
limace (liː'mas) *nf* slug. **limaçon** (liːma'sɔ̃) *nm* snail.
limaille (liː'maj) *nf* filings.
limer (liː'meː) *vt* file. **lime** *nf* file. **lime à ongles** nailfile.
limiter (liːmiː'teː) *vt* **1** limit, restrict. **2** mark the bounds of. **limite** (liː'miːt) *nf* **1** boundary. **2** limit. **3** *pl* bounds.
limon[1] (liː'mɔ̃) *nm* silt, mud.
limon[2] (liː'mɔ̃) *nm* lime.
limonade (liːmɔ'nad) *nf* lemonade.
lin (lɛ̃) *nm* **1** flax. **2** linen.
linceul (lɛ̃'sœj) *nm* shroud.
linéaire (liːneː'ɛr) *adj* linear.
linge (lɛ̃ʒ) *nm* **1** linen. **2** household linen. **linge de corps** underwear. **lingerie** *nf* lingerie, underwear.
linguiste (lɛ̃'gɥiːst) *nm,f* linguist. **linguistique** *adj* linguistic. *nf* linguistics.
lino (liː'no) *nm inf* lino.
linoléum (liːnɔleː'ɔm) *nm* linoleum.
lion (ljɔ̃) *nm* **1** lion. **2** *cap* Leo.
liqueur (liː'kœr) *nf* **1** liquor. **2** liqueur. **3** drink.
liquider (liːkiː'deː) *vt* **1** liquidate. **2** settle. **3** realize. **liquide** *adj,nm* liquid.
lire*[1] (liːr) *vt* read. **lire à vue** sightread. **lisible** *adj* legible.
lire[2] (liːr) *nf* lira.
lis[1] (liː) *v* see **lire**[1].
lis[2] (liːs) *nm* lily.
lisière (liː'zjɛr) *nf* edge, border.
lisser (liː'seː) *vt* **1** smooth, gloss. **2** polish.
liste (liːst) *nf* **1** list. **2** register. **liste des abonnés** mailing list.
lit (liː) *nm* **1** bed. **2** layer. **3** bottom. **lit d'enfant** cot, crib. **lit de camp** or **de sangle** camp bed.
litanies (liːta'niː) *nf pl* litany.
litée (liː'teː) *nf* litter.
litre (liːtr) *nm* litre.
littéraire (liːteː'rɛr) *adj* literary.
littéral, -aux (liːtɛ'ral, -'ro) *adj* literal.
littérature (liːtɛra'tyr) *nf* literature.
littoral, -aux (liːtɔ'ral, -'ro) *adj* coastal. *nm* coastline.
livide (liː'viːd) *adj* **1** livid. **2** ghastly, pale.
livre[1] (liːvr) *nm* book. **livre à succès** or **à fort tirage** bestseller. **livre de poche** paperback. **livret** *nm* **1** booklet. **2** handbook.
livre[2] (liːvr) *nf* **1** pound (weight). **2** pound (money). **livre sterling** pound sterling.
livrer (liː'vreː) *vt* **1** surrender, give up. **2** deliver. **3** confide. **se livrer** *vr* give oneself up. **se livrer à** give way to, indulge in. **livraison** *nf* **1** delivery. **2** instalment.
lobe (lɔb) *nm* lobe.
local, -aux (lɔ'kal, -'ko) *adj* local. *nm* **1** building. **2** premises. **localité** *nf* **1** place. **2** area.
localiser (lɔkaliː'zeː) *vt* **1** localize. **2** locate.
locataire (lɔka'tɛr) *nm,f* tenant.
location (lɔka'sjɔ̃) *nf* **1** hiring. **2** renting. **3** booking. **en location** on hire.
locomotive (lɔkɔmɔ'tiːv) *nf* locomotive, engine.
locuste (lɔ'kyst) *nf* locust.
locution (lɔky'sjɔ̃) *nf* expression, saying.

logarithme (lɔga'ri:tm) *nm* logarithm.

loger (lɔ'ʒe:) *vi* **1** lodge, stay. **2** live. *vt* **1** accommodate, house. **2** put, plant. **loge** *nf* **1** hut. **2** lodge. **3** cabin. **4** *Th* box. **5** dressing-room. **logement** *nm* **1** accommodation, housing. **2** lodgings. **logeur, -euse** (lɔ'ʒœr, -'ʒœz) *nm,f* landlord, landlady. **logis** *nm* dwelling.

logique (lɔ'ʒi:k) *nf* logic. *adj* logical.

loi (lwa) *nf* **1** law. **2** authority. **3** *pol* act.

loin (lwɛ̃) *adv* **1** far. **2** distant. **au loin** in the distance. **de loin 1** by far. **2** from afar. **plus loin** further. **lointain** *adj* distant, remote. *nm* **1** distance. **2** background.

loir (lwar) *nm* dormouse.

loisir (lwa'zi:r) *nm* leisure.

lombric (lɔ̃'bri:k) *nm* earthworm.

Londres (lɔ̃dr) *nm* London.

long, longue (lɔ̃, lɔ̃g) *adj* **1** long. **2** lengthy. **3** slow. **longue-vue** *nf, pl* **longues-vues** telescope. ~*nm* length. **de long en large** up and down, to and fro. **le long de** along, alongside. **tout au long de** throughout. **tout le long du jour** all day long. **longueur** *nf* length. **longueur d'onde** wavelength.

longer (lɔ̃'ʒe:) *vt* **1** walk along. **2** skirt round.

longévité (lɔ̃ʒe:vi:'te:) *nf* longevity.

longitude (lɔ̃ʒi:'tyd) *nf* longitude.

longtemps (lɔ̃'tɑ̃) *adv* long, a long time.

loque (lɔk) *nf* rag.

loquet (lɔ'kɛ) *nm* latch.

lorgner (lɔr'ɲe:) *vt* **1** make eyes at. **2** leer at.

lors (lɔr) *adv* **1** even. **2** at the time, when.

lorsque (lɔrsk) *conj* when.

lot (lo) *nm* **1** share, portion. **2** batch, lot. **3** prize.

loterie (lɔ'tri:) *nf* **1** lottery. **2** raffle.

lotion (lɔ'sjɔ̃) *nf* lotion.

lotus (lɔ'tys) *nm* lotus.

louche[1] (lu:ʃ) *adj* **1** cross-eyed. **2** suspicious.

louche[2] (lu:ʃ) *nf* ladle.

loucher (lu:'ʃe:) *vi* squint.

louer[1] (lwe:) *vt* praise, commend. **louable** *adj* praiseworthy. **louange** *nf* praise.

louer[2] (lwe:) *vt* **1** let. **2** rent, hire. **3** reserve.

loufoque (lu:'fɔk) *adj* mad, eccentric.

loup (lu:) *nm* wolf. **loup-cervier** *nm, pl* **loups-cerviers** lynx.

loupe (lu:p) *nf* magnifying glass.

louper (lu:'pe:) *vt inf* **1** bungle, fluff. **2** fail. **3** miss.

lourd (lu:r) *adj* **1** heavy. **2** clumsy. **3** stupid, dull. **4** close, sultry. **lourdeur** *nf* **1** heaviness. **2** clumsiness. **3** dullness.

loutre (lu:tr) *nm* **1** otter. **2** sealskin.

loyal, -aux (lwa'jal, -'jo) *adj* **1** loyal, faithful. **2** honest. **3** fair. **loyauté** *nf* **1** loyalty. **2** honesty.

loyer (lwa'je:) *nm* rent.

lu (ly) *v* see **lire**[1].

lubie (ly'bi:) *nf* whim.

lucarne (ly'karn) *nf* attic window.

lucide (ly'si:d) *adj* lucid, clear.

lucratif, -ive (lykra'ti:f, -'ti:v) *adj* lucrative.

lueur (lɥœr) *nf* **1** glimmer. **2** flash.

luge (lyʒ) *nf* toboggan.

lugubre (ly'gybr) *adj* dismal, gloomy.

lui (lɥi:) *pron 3rd pers ms* **1** he. **2** it. **3** him. **4** to him, her, or it. **lui-même** *pron 3rd pers ms* himself.

luire* (lɥi:r) *vi* **1** shine. **2** glimmer, glitter. **luisant** *adj* **1** shining, bright. **2** glossy. *nm* **1** shine. **2** gloss.

lumière (ly'mjɛr) *nf* **1** light. **2** *pl* knowledge. **lumineux, -euse** (lymi:'nœ, -'nœz) *adj* **1** luminous. **2** lucid.

lundi (lœ̃'di:) *nm* Monday.

lune (lyn) *nf* moon. **lune de miel** honeymoon. **lunaire** *adj* lunar.

lunette (ly'nɛt) *nf* **1** telescope. **2** *pl* spectacles. **lunettes protectrices** *nf pl* goggles. **lunettes de soleil** *nf pl* sunglasses.

luron (ly'rɔ̃) *nm inf* jolly fellow.

lustrer (ly'stre:) *vt* **1** polish. **2** gloss. **lustre** *nm* **1** lustre, polish. **2** chandelier.

luth (lyt) *nm* lute.

lutin (ly'tɛ̃) *nm* **1** imp. **2** *inf* mischievous child. *adj* mischievous.

lutrin (ly'trɛ̃) *nm* lectern.

lutter (ly'te:) *vi* **1** struggle, fight. **2** compete. **3** wrestle. **lutte** *nf* **1** struggle, fight. **2** contest. **3** wrestling.

luxe (lyks) *nm* luxury. **luxueux, -euse** (lyk'sɥœ, -'sɥœz) *adj* luxurious.

Luxembourg (lyksɑ̃'bu:r) *nm* Luxembourg.

lycée (li:'se:) *nm* grammar school.

lyncher (lɛ̃'ʃe:) *vt* lynch.

lynx (lɛ̃ks) *nm* lynx.

Lyon (ljɔ̃) *nm* Lyons.

lyre (li:r) *nf* lyre.

lyrique (li:'ri:k) *adj* lyrical.

M

ma (ma) *poss adj* see **mon.**

macabre (ma'kɑbr) *adj* gruesome, macabre.

macédoine (mase:'dwan) *nf* **1** salad. **2** miscellany.

mâcher (mɑ'ʃe:) *vt* **1** chew. **2** munch. **mâchoire** (mɑ'ʃwar) *nf* jaw.

machin (ma'ʃɛ̃) *nm inf* gadget, thing.

machine (ma'ʃi:n) *nf* **1** machine. **2** engine. **3** device, apparatus. **4** *pl* machinery. **machine á calculer** calculator. **machine à coudre** sewing machine. **machine à écrire** typewriter. **machine à sous** fruit machine. **machinal, -aux** (maʃi:'nal, -'no) *adj* mechanical, unconscious.

macis (ma'si:) *nm cul* mace.

maçon (ma'sɔ̃) *nm* mason.

maçonner (masɔ'ne:) *vt* build. **maçonnerie** *nf* masonry.

maculer (maky'le:) *vt* stain, spot. **macule** *nf* **1** stain, spot. **2** blemish.

madame (ma'dam) *nf, pl* **mesdames** **1** madam. **2** *cap* Mrs.

mademoiselle (madmwa'zɛl) *nf, pl* **mesdemoiselles** **1** miss. **2** young lady. **3** *cap* Miss.

madone (ma'dɔn) *nf* madonna.

madrier (madri:'e) *nm* **1** beam. **2** joist.

magasin (maga'zɛ̃) *nm* **1** shop. **2** warehouse. **3** stock. **grand magasin** store. **magasin à succursales multiples** chain-store.

magazine (maga'zi:n) *nm* magazine.

magie (ma'ʒi:) *nf* magic. **magicien** *nm* magician, wizard. **magique** *adj* magic.

magistrat (maʒi:'stra) *nm* magistrate. **magistral, -aux** (maʒi:'stral, -'stro) *adj* **1** authoritative, magisterial. **2** brilliant.

magnat (mag'na) *nm* magnate, tycoon.

magnétiser (maɲe:ti:'ze:) *vt* **1** magnetize. **2** mesmerize. **magnétique** *adj* magnetic. **magnétisme** (maɲe:'ti:sm) *nm* **1** magnetism. **2** mesmerism. **3** attraction.

Magnétophone (maɲe:tɔ'fɔn) *nm Tdmk* tape-recorder.

magnifique (maɲi:'fi:k) *adj* magnificent, splendid.

magnitude (magni:'tyd) *nf* magnitude.

mai (mɛ) *nm* **1** May. **2** Maypole. **le premier mai** May Day.

maigrir (mɛ'gri:r) *vi* slim, lose weight. **maigre** *adj* **1** thin, skinny. **2** lean. **3** meagre. **4** frugal. **maigreur** *nf* thinness.

maille (maj) *nf* **1** mesh. **2** (knitting) stitch. **3** link.

maillet (ma'jɛ) *nm* mallet.

maillot (ma'jo) *nm* **1** *sport* vest. **2** tights. **maillot de bain** swimming costume.

main (mɛ̃) *nf* **1** hand. **2** handwriting. **3** *game* deal. **à main** by hand. **main-d'œuvre** *nf* manpower, labour. **sous la main** to or at hand.

maint (mɛ̃) *adj* many a.

maintenant (mɛ̃t'nɑ̃) *adv* now.

maintenir* (mɛ̃t'ni:r) *vt* **1** uphold. **2** support. **3** maintain, hold. **se maintenir** *vr* **1** hold one's own. **2** continue. **maintien** *nm* **1** maintenance. **2** deportment.

maire (mɛr) *nm* mayor. **mairie** *nf* town hall.

mais (mɛ) *conj* **1** but. **2** why.

maïs (ma'i:s) *nm* maize.

maison (mɛ'zɔ̃) *nf* **1** house. **2** home. **3** household. **maison de commerce** firm. **maison de santé** nursing home.

maître, -esse (mɛtr, mɛ'trɛs) *nm,f* master, mistress. **maître de chapelle** choirmaster. **maître d'hôtel** **1** butler. **2** head waiter. ~*adj* chief, principal.

maîtriser (mɛtri:'ze:) *vt* **1** master. **2** control. **maîtrise** *nf* command, control.

majesté (maʒɛ'ste:) *nf* **1** majesty. **2** dignity. **3** grandeur. **majestueux, -euse** (maʒɛ'stɥœ, -'stɥœz) *adj* majestic.

majeur (ma'ʒœr) *adj* **1** major, greater. **2** chief, main. **3** *law* of age.

majorer (maʒɔ're:) *vt* raise or increase the price of. **majorité** *nf* **1** majority. **2** coming of age.

majuscule (maʒy'skyl) *adj* large, capital. *nf* capital letter.

mal[1]**, maux** (mal, mo) *nm* **1** evil. **2** wrong, ill. **3** harm. **4** pain, ache. **5** difficulty. **avoir le mal de mer** be seasick. **avoir le mal du pays** be homesick. **avoir mal à l'oreille** have earache. **mal de dents** toothache. **mal de tête** headache. **se donner du mal à** take pains to.

mal[2] (mal) *adv* **1** badly. **2** ill. **3** amiss. **4** uncomfortably. **pas mal de** a good many, a lot of.

malade (ma'lad) *adj* ill, unwell, sick. *nm* invalid. **maladie** *nf* **1** illness. **2** disease. **3** ailment.

maladresse (mala'drɛs) *nf* **1** awkwardness. **2** blunder.

maladroit (mala'drwa) *adj* **1** clumsy, awkward. **2** tactless.

malaise (ma'lɛz) *nm* **1** uneasiness. **2** indisposition.

Malaisie (malɛ'zi:) *nf* **1** Malaya. **2** Malaysia. **malais** (ma'lɛ) *adj,n* Malay. *nm* Malay (language).

malappris (mala'pri:) *adj* **1** ill-bred. **2** uncouth.
malavisé (malavi:'ze:) *adj* rash, unwise.
malchance (mal'ʃɑ̃s) *nf* bad luck. **malchanceux, -euse** (malʃɑ̃'sœ, -'sœz) *adj* unfortunate, unlucky.
malcommode (malkɔ'mɔd) *adj* inconvenient.
mâle (mɑl) *nm* male. *adj* **1** male, cock, dog. **2** virile.
malédiction (male:di:k'sjɔ̃) *nf* curse.
malentendu (malɑ̃tɑ̃'dy) *nm* misunderstanding.
malfaisant (malfə'zɑ̃) *adj* **1** harmful. **2** evil.
malgré (mal'gre:) *prep* in spite of.
malheur (ma'lœr) *nm* **1** misfortune. **2** accident. **malheureux, -euse** (malœ'rœ, -'rœz) *adj* **1** unfortunate. **2** unhappy, wretched. **3** poor.
malhonnête (malɔ'nɛt) *adj* **1** dishonest. **2** rude. **3** improper.
malice (ma'li:s) *nf* **1** mischievousness. **2** prank. **3** spite, malice.
malin, -igne (ma'lɛ̃, -'li:ɲ) *adj* **1** mischievous. **2** shrewd, sly. **3** malignant.
malingre (ma'lɛ̃gr) *adj* sickly.
malle (mal) *nf* **1** (luggage) trunk. **2** *mot* boot.
malmener (malmə'ne:) *vt* maltreat, manhandle.
malotru (malɔ'try) *adj* **1** vulgar. **2** uncouth.
malpropre (mal'prɔpr) *adj* **1** grubby, dirty. **2** immoral. **3** dishonest.
malsain (mal'sɛ̃) *adj* unhealthy.
malséant (malse:'ɑ̃) *adj* improper.
malt (malt) *nm* malt.
Malte (malt) *nf* Malta. **maltais** *adj,n* Maltese. *nm* Maltese (language).
maltraiter (maltrɛ'te:) *vt* **1** ill-treat. **2** misuse.
maman (ma'mɑ̃) *nf inf* mummy.
mamelle (ma'mɛl) *nf* **1** breast. **2** udder. **mamelon** *nm* **1** nipple. **2** teat.
mammifère (mammi:'fɛr) *nm* mammal.
mammouth (mam'mu:t) *nm* mammoth.
manche[1] (mɑ̃ʃ) *nf* **1** sleeve. **2** *cap* English Channel. **manchette** *nf* **1** cuff. **2** headline. **manchon** *nm* muff.
manche[2] (mɑ̃ʃ) *nm* handle.
manchot (mɑ̃'ʃo) *adj* one-armed. *nm* penguin.
mandarine (mɑ̃da'ri:n) *nf* mandarin, tangerine.
mander (mɑ̃'de:) *vt* **1** order. **2** summon. **3** report. **mandat** *nm* **1** mandate. **2** warrant. **mandat-poste** *nm, pl* **mandats-postes** postal or money order.
mandoline (mɑ̃dɔ'li:n) *nf* mandolin.
manège (ma'nɛʒ) *nm* **1** horsemanship. **2** *inf* trick. **3** behaviour. **manège (de chevaux de bois)** roundabout, merry-go-round.
manette (ma'nɛt) *nf* handle.
manger (mɑ̃'ʒe:) *vt* **1** eat. **2** squander. *nm* food. **mangeable** *adj* edible.
mangue (mɑ̃g) *nf* mango. **manguier** *nm* mango tree.
manie (ma'ni:) *nf* **1** mania. **2** craze.
manier (ma'nje:) *vt* **1** feel. **2** handle. **3** control.
manière (ma'njɛr) *nf* **1** manner, way. **2** style. **3** kind, sort. **4** *pl* manners. **d'une manière ou d'une autre** somehow or other. **maniéré** *adj* affected. **maniérisme** *nm* mannerism.
manifeste[1] (mani:'fɛst) *adj* evident, obvious, manifest.
manifeste[2] (mani:'fɛst) *nm* manifesto.
manifester (mani:fɛ'ste:) *vt* **1** reveal, manifest. **2** demonstrate. **manifestation** *nf* **1** demonstration. **2** manifestation.
manipuler (mani:py'le:) *vt* **1** manipulate. **2** handle. **3** operate.
manivelle (mani'vɛl) *nf* crank, handle.
manne (man) *nf* hamper, basket.
manœuvrer (manœ'vre:) *vt* operate, work. *vi* **1** manoeuvre. **2** *inf* scheme. **manœuvre** *nf* **1** working. **2** *mil* drill. **3** manoeuvre. *nm* labourer.
manoir (ma'nwar) *nm* manor.
manquer (mɑ̃'ke:) *vi* **1** lack. **2** fail. **3** be missing. *vt* miss. **elle a manqué (de) tomber** she nearly fell. **ne pas manquer de** be sure to. **manque** (mɑ̃k) *nm* lack, want.
mansarde (mɑ̃'sard) *nf* attic.
manteau, -aux (mɑ̃'to) *nm* **1** coat. **2** cloak.
manuel, -elle (ma'nɥɛl) *adj* manual. *nm* manual, handbook.
manuscrit (many'skri:) *nm* manuscript.
manutention (manytɑ̃'sjɔ̃) *nf* **1** administration. **2** handling.
manxois (mɑ̃k'swɑ) *adj* Manx.
maori (maɔ'ri:) *adj,n* Maori.
maquereau, -aux[1] (ma'kro) *nm* mackerel.
maquereau, -aux[2] (ma'kro) *nm* pimp.
maquette (ma'kɛt) *nf Art* model.
maquiller (maki:'je:) *vt* **1** make up (the face). **2** fake. **maquillage** *nm* make-up.
maquis (ma'ki:) *nm* scrub, bush.
maraîcher (marɛ'ʃe:) *nm* market gardener.
marais (ma'rɛ) *nm* marsh, bog.
marathon (mara'tɔ̃) *nm* marathon.
marâtre (ma'rɑtr) *nf* stepmother.
marbre (marbr) *nm* marble.
marchand (mar'ʃɑ̃) *nm* **1** shopkeeper. **2** dealer. **3** merchant. **4** tradesman. **marchand de poisson** fishmonger. **marchand en détail**

retailer. **marchand en gros** wholesaler. ~*adj* commercial, market.

marchander (marʃɑ̃'de:) *vt* haggle, bargain. **marchandise** *nf* merchandise, goods.

marché (mar'ʃe:) *nm* **1** market. **2** deal, contract. **bon marché** cheap. **marché commun** Common Market.

marcher (mar'ʃe:) *vi* **1** walk. **2** tread. **3** go, move. **4** work, run. **5** march. **marche** *nf* **1** step, stair. **2** walk. **3** march. **4** progress, development. **marche arrière** *mot* reverse. **mettre en marche** start, set going. **marche-pied** *nm* **1** step. **2** step-ladder.

mardi (mar'di:) *nm* Tuesday. **mardi gras** Shrove Tuesday.

mare (mar) *nf* **1** pool. **2** pond.

marécage (marɛ'kaʒ) *nm* **1** bog, swamp. **2** marsh.

maréchal, -aux (marɛ'ʃal, -'ʃo) *nm* **1** marshal. **2** field marshal. **maréchal-ferrant** *nm, pl* **maréchaux-ferrants** blacksmith.

marée (ma're:) *nf* tide.

margarine (marga'ri:n) *nf* margarine.

marge (marʒ) *nf* **1** margin. **2** edge, border.

marguerite (margə'ri:t) *nf* daisy.

mari (ma'ri:) *nm* husband.

marier (mar'je:) *vt* **1** marry. **2** blend. **se marier** *vr* marry, get married. **mariage** (mar'jaʒ) *nm* **1** marriage. **2** wedding. **nouveau marié** *nm* bridegroom. **nouvelle mariée** *nf* bride.

marihuana (mariwa'na) *nf* marijuana.

marin (ma'rɛ̃) *adj* **1** marine. **2** nautical. *nm* sailor, seaman.

marine (ma'ri:n) *nf* seamanship. **marine de guerre** navy. **marine marchande** merchant navy.

mariner (mari:'ne:) *vt* pickle. *vi* marinate. **marinade** *nf* **1** pickle. **2** marinade.

marionnette (marjɔ'nɛt) *nf* puppet.

marital, -aux (mari:'tal, -'to) *adj* marital.

maritime (mari:'ti:m) *adj* maritime.

marjolaine (marʒɔ'lɛn) *nf* marjoram.

mark (mark) *nm comm* mark.

marmite (mar'mi:t) *nf* saucepan, pot.

marmonner (marmɔ'ne:) *vt* mumble.

marmot (mar'mo) *nm inf* child, brat.

marmotter (marmɔ'te:) *vt* mumble, mutter.

Maroc (ma'rɔk) *nm* Morocco. **marocain** (marɔ'kɛ̃) *adj,n* Moroccan.

marotte (ma'rɔt) *nf* hobby.

marquer (mar'ke:) *vt* **1** mark. **2** note down. **3** score. **4** indicate. *vi* stand out. **marque** *nf* **1** mark. **2** brand, make. **3** score. **4** token. **marque de fabrique** trademark. **marque de standing** status symbol.

marquis (mar'ki) *nm* marquess.

marquise (mar'ki:z) *nf* **1** marchioness. **2** marquee. **3** porch.

marraine (ma'rɛn) *nf* godmother.

marrant (ma'rɑ̃) *adj inf* **1** funny. **2** strange, odd.

marron (mɑ'rɔ̃) *nm* chestnut. **marron d'Inde** horse chestnut. ~*adj* maroon. **marronnier** *nm* chestnut tree. **maronnier d'Inde** horse chestnut tree.

mars (mars) *nm* **1** March. **2** *cap* Mars.

Marseille (mar'sɛj) *nf* Marseilles. **marseillaise** *nf* French national anthem.

marsouin (mar'swɛ̃) *nm* porpoise.

marsupial, -aux (marsy'pjal, -'pjo) *adj,nm* marsupial.

marteau, -aux (mar'to) *nm* **1** hammer. **2** door-knocker. **marteau pneumatique** pneumatic drill.

marteler (martə'le:) *vt* hammer.

martial, -aux (mar'sjal, -'sjo) *adj* martial.

martinet (marti:'nɛ) *nm* swift.

martin-pêcheur (martɛ̃pɛ'ʃœr) *nm, pl* **martins-pêcheurs** kingfisher.

martre (martr) *nf* **martre du Canada** mink. **martre zibeline** sable.

martyr (mar'ti:r) *nm* martyr. **martyre** *nm* martyrdom.

marxisme (mark'si:sm) *nm* Marxism. **marxiste** *adj,n* Marxist.

mascara (maska'ra) *nm* mascara.

mascarade (maska'rad) *nf* masquerade.

mascotte (ma'skɔt) *nf* mascot.

masculin (masky'lɛ̃) *adj* masculine, male. *nm* masculine gender.

masochisme (mazɔ'ʃi:sm) *nm* masochism. **masochiste** *nm,f* masochist.

masquer (mas'ke:) *vt* **1** mask. **2** hide. **3** disguise. **masque** *nm* **1** mask. **2** expression. **3** pretence. **masque anti-rides** *nm* face-pack.

massacrer (masa'kre:) *vt* **1** massacre. **2** spoil. **massacre** *nm* massacre.

masse[1] (mas) *nf* **1** mass. **2** bulk.

masse[2] (mas) *nf* **1** sledge-hammer. **2** mace.

massepain (mas'pɛ̃) *nm* marzipan.

masser[1] (ma'se:) *vt* mass. **se masser** *vr* mass together.

masser[2] (ma'se:) *vt* massage. **massage** *nm* massage.

massif, -ive (ma'si:f, -'si:v) *adj* **1** massive. **2** solid. **3** heavy. *nm* **1** clump, bed (of flowers). **2** mountain range.

massue (ma'sy) *nf* club.
mastic (ma'sti:k) *nm* putty.
mastiquer[1] (masti:'ke:) *vt* chew, masticate.
mastiquer[2] (masti:'ke:) *vt* fill with cement.
se masturber (mastyr'be:) *vr* masturbate.
mat[1] (mat) *adj invar* checkmated. *nm* checkmate.
mat[2] (mat) *adj* **1** dull, matt. **2** heavy.
mât (mɑ) *nm* **1** mast. **2** pole.
matelas (mat'lɑ) *nm* mattress.
matelot (mat'lo) *nm* sailor, seaman.
matérialiser (mate:rjali:'ze:) *vt* materialize. **matérialiste** *nm,f* materialist. *adj* materialistic.
matériaux (mate:'rjo) *nm pl tech* materials.
matériel, -elle (mate:'rjɛl) *adj* **1** material. **2** physical. *nm* **1** *tech* plant. **2** equipment.
maternel, -elle (matɛr'nɛl) *adj* maternal. **maternité** *nf* maternity, motherhood.
mathématique (mate:ma'ti:k) *adj* mathematical. *nf* mathematics.
matière (ma'tjɛr) *nf* **1** matter, substance. **2** material. **3** subject. **matières grasses** *nf pl* fats. **matières premières** *nf pl* raw materials.
matin (ma'tɛ̃) *nm* morning. **de bon matin** early in the morning. **le matin** in the morning. **matinal, -aux** (mati:'nal, -'no) *adj* **1** morning. **2** early. **matinée** *nf* **1** morning. **2** *Th* afternoon performance.
matois (ma'twa) *adj* sly, crafty.
matriarcal, -aux (matri:ar'kal, -'ko) *adj* matriarchal.
matrice (ma'tri:s) *nf* **1** matrix. **2** womb.
matriculer (matri:ky'le:) *vt* register.
matrimonial, -aux (matri:mɔ'njal, -'njo) *adj* matrimonial.
maturité (matyri:'te:) *nf* maturity.
maudire* (mo'di:r) *vt* curse.
maure (mɔr) *nm,f* Moor. *adj* Moorish.
Maurice (mɔ'ri:s) **île Maurice** *nm* Mauritius.
mausolée (mozɔ'le:) *nm* mausoleum.
maussade (mo'sad) *adj* **1** sullen. **2** surly. **3** dismal.
mauvais (mɔ'vɛ) *adj* **1** evil, wicked. **2** bad. **3** poor. **4** unpleasant. *adv* bad.
mauve (mov) *adj, nm* mauve.
maxime (mak'si:m) *nf* maxim.
maximum (maksi:'mɔm) *adj,nm* maximum.
mayonnaise (majɔ'nɛz) *nf* mayonnaise.
mazout (ma'zu) *nm* fuel oil.
me, m' (mə) *pron 1st pers m,f s* **1** me. **2** to me. **3** myself. **4** to myself.
méandre (me:'ɑ̃dr) *nm* meander, bend.
mec (mɛk) *nm sl* bloke, fellow.
mécaniser (mɛkani:'ze:) *vt* mechanize. **mécanicien** *nm* **1** mechanic. **2** engineer. **mécanique** *adj* mechanical. *nf* mechanics.
mécanisme (mɛka'ni:sm) *nm* **1** mechanism. **2** machinery.
méchant (mɛ'ʃɑ̃) *adj* **1** wicked, evil. **2** naughty. **3** spiteful. **4** vicious. **5** miserable. **méchanceté** *nf* **1** wickedness. **2** spite, malice.
mèche (mɛʃ) *nf* **1** lock (of hair). **2** wisp. **être de mèche avec** be in league with.
mécompte (me:'kɔ̃t) *nm* **1** error. **2** disappointment.
mécontent (me:kɔ̃'tɑ̃) *adj* dissatisfied.
mécontenter (me:kɔ̃tɑ̃'te:) *vt* displease.
médaille (mɛ'daj) *nf* medal.
médecin (mɛt'sɛ̃) *nm* doctor, physician. **médecin chirurgien** surgeon. **médecin de médecine générale** general practitioner. **médecine** *nf* medicine.
médial, -aux (me:'djal, -'djo) *adj* medial.
médian (me:'djɑ̃) *adj* median.
médical, -aux (me:di:'kal, -'ko) *adj* medical.
médicament (me:di:ka'mɑ̃) *nm* medicine.
médication (me:di:ka'sjɔ̃) *nf* medication.
médiéval, -aux (me:dje:'val, -'vo) *adj* medieval.
médiocre (me:'djɔkr) *adj* **1** moderate, mediocre. **2** second-rate, indifferent.
médire* (me:'di:r) *vi* slander.
méditer (me:di:'te:) *vt* contemplate, have in mind. *vi* **1** meditate. **2** muse.
méditerrané (me:di:tɛra'ne:) **(Mer) Méditerranée** *nf* Mediterranean (Sea). **méditerranéen, -enne** (me:di:tɛrane:'ɛ̃, -'ɛn) *adj* Mediterranean.
méduse (me:dyz) *nf* jellyfish.
méfait (me:'fɛ) *nm* **1** misdeed. **2** *pl* damage.
se méfier (me:'fje:) *vr* **se méfier de** **1** distrust, mistrust. **2** beware of. **méfiance** *nf* distrust, mistrust. **méfiant** *adj* **1** suspicious. **2** timid.
mégaphone (mɛga'fɔn) *nm* megaphone.
mégarde (me'gard) **par mégarde** *adv* inadvertently.
mégère (me:'ʒɛr) *nf* shrew.
mégot (me:'go) *nm. sl* fag-end, stub (of a cigarette).
meilleur (mɛ'jœr) *adj* better. **le meilleur** best. ~*adv* better.
mélancolie (mɛlɑ̃kɔ'li:) *nf* melancholy, gloom.
mélanger (mɛlɑ̃'ʒe:) *vt* mix, mingle, blend. **mélange** *nm* **1** mixture, blend. **2** jumble. **3** miscellany.
mélasse (mɛ'las) *nf* treacle.

mêler (me:ˈle:) *vt* **1** mix. **2** tangle. **3** involve. **4** shuffle. **mêlée** *nf* fray, scuffle.

mélèze (me:ˈlɛz) *nm* larch.

mélodie (me:lɔˈdi:) *nf* melody, tune.

mélodrame (me:lɔˈdram) *nm* melodrama. **mélodramatique** *adj* melodramatic.

melon (məˈlɔ̃) *nm* **1** melon. **2** bowler hat.

membrane (mɑ̃ˈbran) *nf* **1** membrane. **2** web.

membre (mɑ̃br) *nm* **1** member. **2** limb.

même (mɛm) *adj* **1** same. **2** very. **3** self. *pron* same thing. *adv* even. **de même** in the same way. **tout de même** all the same.

mémento (me:mɛ̃ˈto) *nm* **1** note, memento. **2** notebook.

mémoire[1] (me:ˈmwar) *nf* **1** memory. **2** recollection.

mémoire[2] (me:ˈmwar) *nm* **1** statement. **2** bill, account. **3** thesis. **4** *pl* memoirs.

mémorable (me:mɔˈrabl) *adj* **1** memorable. **2** eventful.

mémorandum (me:mɔrɑ̃ˈdɔm) *nm* **1** memorandum. **2** notebook.

menacer (mənaˈse:) *vt* threaten. **menace** *nf* threat, menace.

ménager (me:naˈʒe:) *vt* **1** save. **2** be sparing. **3** manage. **4** arrange. **ménage** *nm* **1** housekeeping. **2** household. **3** married couple. **faire le ménage** do the housework. **ménagement** *nm* **1** consideration. **2** tact. **3** care. **ménager, -ère** (menaˈʒe:, -ˈʒɛr) *adj* **1** domestic. **2** thrifty. *nf* housewife.

mendier (mɑ̃dje:) *vi* beg. *vt* beg for. **mendiant** *nm* beggar.

mener (məˈne:) *vt* **1** lead. **2** conduct. **3** drive. **4** manage. **menée** *nf* intrigue, plot. **meneur** *nm* **1** leader. **2** ringleader.

ménestrel (me:nɛˈstrɛl) *nm* minstrel.

ménopause (me:nɔˈpoz) *nf* menopause.

menottes (məˈnɔt) *nf pl* handcuffs.

mensonge (mɑ̃ˈsɔ̃ʒ) *nm* lie, falsehood. **petit mensonge** fib.

menstruel, -elle (mɑ̃stryˈɛl) *adj* menstrual.

mensuel, -elle (mɑ̃ˈsyɛl) *adj* monthly.

mensurer (mɑ̃syˈre:) *vt* measure. **mensuration** (mɑ̃syraˈsjɔ̃) *nf* measurement.

mental, -aux (mɑ̃ˈtal, -ˈto) *adj* mental. **mentalité** *nf* mentality.

menthe (mɑ̃t) *nf* mint. **menthe anglaise** or **poivrée** peppermint.

menthol (mɛ̃ˈtɔl) *nm* menthol.

mention (mɑ̃ˈsjɔ̃) *nf* **1** mention. **2** (on a letter) reference. **faire mention de** refer to.

mentionner (mɑ̃sjɔˈne:) *vt* mention.

mentir* (mɑ̃ˈti:r) *vi* lie, tell lies. **menteur, -euse** (mɑ̃ˈtœr, -ˈtœz) *nm,f* liar. *adj* **1** false. **2** deceptive.

menton (mɑ̃ˈtɔ̃) *nm* chin.

menu (məˈny) *adj* **1** small, fine. **2** slender, slight. **3** petty. *adv* small, finely. *nm cul* menu.

menuisier (mənɥi:ˈzje:) *nm* carpenter, joiner. **menuiserie** *nf* woodwork, carpentry.

se méprendre (me:ˈprɑ̃dr) *vr* make a mistake.

mépris (me:ˈpri:) *nm* scorn, contempt.

méprise (me:ˈpri:z) *nf* mistake, error.

mépriser (me:pri:ˈze:) *vt* despise, scorn.

mer (mɛr) *nf* sea. **en/sur mer** at sea/afloat.

mercantile (mɛrkɑ̃ˈti:l) *adj* commercial.

mercenaire (mɛrsəˈnɛr) *adj* mercenary. *nm* mercenary.

merci (mɛrˈsi:) *nf* mercy. *nm* thanks. *adv* **1** thank you. **2** no thank you. **merci bien** thank you very much.

mercier, -ière (mɛrˈsje:, -ˈsjɛr) *nm,f* haberdasher. **mercerie** *nf* haberdashery.

mercredi (mɛrkrəˈdi:) *nm* Wednesday. **mercredi des cendres** Ash Wednesday.

mercure (mɛrˈkyr) *nm* mercury.

mère (mɛr) *nf* **1** mother. **2** *zool* dam. **3** source. **mère nourricière** fostermother. **mère supérieure** mother superior.

méridien (me:ri:ˈdjɛ̃) *nm* meridian. **méridienne** *nf* **1** meridian line. **2** *inf* siesta.

méridional, -aux (me:ri:djɔˈnal, -ˈno) *adj* southern.

meringue (məˈrɛ̃g) *nf* meringue.

mériter (me:ri:ˈte:) *vt* **1** deserve, merit. **2** earn, gain. **mérite** *nm* **1** merit, credit. **2** worth. **3** talent.

merlan (mɛrˈlɑ̃) *nm* whiting.

merle (mɛrl) *nm* blackbird.

merveille (mɛrˈvɛj) *nf* marvel, wonder. **à merveille** excellently. **merveilleux, -euse** (mɛrvɛˈjœ, -ˈjœz) *adj* marvellous, wonderful.

mes (mɛ) *poss adj* see **mon.**

mésaventure (me:zavɑ̃ˈtyr) *nf* mishap.

mesquin (mɛˈskɛ̃) *adj* **1** shabby. **2** petty. **3** mean.

message (mɛˈsaʒ) *nm* message. **messager, -ère** (mɛsaˈʒe:, -ˈʒɛr) *nm, f* messenger. **messagerie** (mɛsaʒˈri:) *nf* **1** parcels office. **2** goods department.

messe (mɛs) *nf rel* mass.

messeoir* (me:ˈswar) *vi* be unbecoming.

mesurer (məzyˈre:) *vt* **1** measure. **2** calculate. **3** distribute. **mesure** *nf* **1** measure. **2** measurement. **3** gauge. **4** limit. **5** size. **6** *mus* time. **à**

mesure que (in proportion) as. **dépasser la mesure** overstep the mark. **fait sur mesure** made to measure. **mesuré** *adj* **1** measured. **2** moderate, restrained.

mésuser (me:zy'ze:) *vt* **mésuser de 1** misuse. **2** abuse. **mésusage** *nm* misuse.

métabolisme (mɛtabɔ'li:sm) *nm* metabolism.

métal, -aux (me:'tal, -'to) *nm* metal.

métallurgie (me:tallyr'ʒi:) *nf* metallurgy.

métamorphose (mɛtamɔr'foz) *nf* metamorphosis.

métaphore (mɛta'fɔr) *nf* metaphor. **métaphorique** *adj* metaphorical.

métaphysique (mɛtafi:'zi:k) *adj* metaphysical. *nf* metaphysics.

météore (me:te:'ɔr) *nm* meteor.

météorologie (me:te:ɔrɔlɔ'ʒi:) *nf* meteorology. **météorologique** *adj* meteorological. **météorologiste** *nm* meteorologist.

méthane (mɛ'tan) *nm* methane.

méthode (me:'tɔd) *nf* **1** method, system. **2** way. **méthodique** *adj* methodical, systematic. **méthodologie** *nf* methodology.

méthodiste (me:tɔ'di:st) *adj,n* Methodist.

méticuleux, -euse (me:ti:ky'lœ, -'lœz) *adj* meticulous, particular.

métier (me:'tje:) *nm* trade, profession, craft. **métier à tisser** loom.

métis, -isse (me:'ti:, -'ti:s) *adj,n* half-breed, hybrid, mongrel.

métrage (mɛ'traʒ) *nm* **1** measure. **2** length.

mètre (mɛtr) *nm* **1** metre. **2** rule. **mètre à ruban** tape-measure. **métrique** *adj* metric.

métro (me:'tro) *nm* underground, tube.

métropole (me:trɔ'pɔl) *nf* **1** metropolis. **2** capital. **métropolitain** (me:trɔpɔli:'tɛ̃) *adj* metropolitan.

mets (mɛ) *nm* **1** dish (of food). **2** food.

mettre* (mɛtr) *vt* **1** put, set, place. **2** wear. **3** contribute. **mettre les pieds dans le plat** put one's foot in it. **se mettre** *vr* **1** go. **2** dress. **se mettre à** begin, set about. **metteur en scène** *nm* **1** *Th* producer. **2** director (of films).

meubler (mœ'ble:) *vt* **1** furnish. **2** stock. **meuble** *adj* movable. *nm* **1** piece of furniture. **2** *pl* furniture.

meugler (mœ'gle:) *vi* low, moo. **meuglement** *nm* lowing.

meule (mœl) *nf* **1** millstone. **2** stack, pile. **meule de foin** haystack.

meurs (mœr) *v* see **mourir.**

meurtre (mœrtr) *nm* murder. **meurtrier, -ière** (mœrtri:'e:, -'ɛr) *nm, f* murderer, murderess. *adj* deadly, murderous.

meurtrir (mœr'tri:r) *vt* bruise. **meurtrissure** *nf* bruise.

meute (mœt) *nf* **1** *zool* pack. **2** *inf* mob.

Mexique (mɛk'si:k) *nm* Mexico. **mexicain** *adj,n* Mexican.

mi (mi:) *pref* **1** half. **2** mid. **3** semi. **à mi-chemin** *adv* halfway. **à mi-corps** *adv* to the waist. **à mi-côte** *adv* halfway up or down. **mi-matin** *nf* midmorning. **mi-temps** *nf* half-time, interval. **à mi-temps** part-time.

miaou (mjau) *nm* miaow.

miauler (mjo'le:) *vi* miaow.

miche (mi:ʃ) *nf* round loaf.

micro (mi:'kro) *nm inf* microphone, mike.

microbe (mi:'krɔb) *nm* **1** microbe. **2** germ.

microphone (mi:krɔ'fɔn) *nm* microphone.

microscope (mi:krɔ'skɔp) *nm* microscope. **microscopique** *adj* microscopic.

microsillon (mi:krosi:'jɔ̃) *nm* long-playing record.

midi (mi:'di:) *nm* **1** midday, noon. **2** south. **3** *cap* South of France.

mie (mi:) *nf* crumb.

miel (mjɛl) *nm* honey.

mien, mienne (mjɛ̃, mjɛn) *poss pron 1st pers s* **le mien, la mienne 1** mine. **2** my own.

miette (mjɛt) *nf* soft part of bread.

mieux (mjœ) *adj,adv* better. **le mieux** best.

mièvre (mjɛvr) *adj* **1** affected. **2** delicate.

mignard (mi:'ɲar) *adj* affected, mincing.

mignon, -onne (mi:'ɲɔ̃, -'ɲɔn) *adj* **1** dainty, delicate. **2** sweet. *nm,f* darling.

migraine (mi:'grɛn) *nf* migraine.

mijoter (mi:ʒɔ'te:) *vi,vt* **1** stew. **2** simmer. *vt* plot.

mil (mi:l) *adj* thousand.

milieu, -eux (mi:'ljœ) *nm* **1** middle, midst. **2** environment. **3** class, circle. **4** mean. **au (beau) milieu de** (right) in the middle of. **juste milieu** happy medium.

militaire (mi:li:'tɛr) *adj* military. *nm* soldier. **militant** *adj* militant.

mille[1] (mi:l) *adj,nm* thousand. **millénium** *nm* millennium. **millième** *adj* thousandth. **millier** *nm* about a thousand.

mille[2] (mi:l) *nm* mile. **mille-feuille** *nf* pastry filled with cream and jam. **mille-pattes** *nm invar* centipede.

milligramme (mi:lli:'gram) *nm* milligram.

millilitre (mi:lli:'li:tr) *nm* millilitre.

millimètre (mi:lli:'mɛtr) *nm* millimetre.

million (mi:ˈljɔ̃) *nm* million. **milliard** *nm* **1** one thousand million. **2** *US* billion. **millionième** *adj* millionth.

mimer (mi:ˈme:) *vt* **1** mimic. **2** imitate. **mime** *nm* **1** mime. **2** mimic.

minable (mi:ˈnabl) *adj* **1** shabby. **2** miserable, wretched.

minauder (mi:noˈde:) *vi* smirk.

mince (mɛ̃s) *adj* **1** thin. **2** slim. **3** scanty. *interj* blast! **minceur** *nf* thinness.

mine[1] (mi:n) *nf* **1** appearance, look. **2** expression. **avoir bonne/mauvaise mine** look well/ill.

mine[2] (mi:n) *nf* **1** mine, pit. **2** *mil* mine. **3** lead (of a pencil). **mine de houille** coalmine. **mine d'or** goldmine.

minérai (mi:nˈrɛ) *nm* ore.

minéral, -aux (mi:ne:ˈral, -ˈro) *adj,nm* mineral.

mineur[1] (mi:ˈnœr) *adj* **1** minor. **2** under age. *nm law* minor, infant.

mineur[2] (mi:ˈnœr) *nm* miner.

miniature (mi:njaˈtyr) *nf* miniature.

minimiser (mi:ni:mi:ˈze:) *vt* minimize. **minime** *adj* **1** very small. **2** trivial. **minimum** *adj,nm* minimum.

ministère (mi:ni:ˈstɛr) *nm* **1** ministry. **2** agency. **3** government office, department. **ministre** *nm* **1** *pol* minister, secretary. **2** clergyman. **premier ministre** prime minister.

minorité (mi:nɔri:ˈte:) *nf* minority.

Minorque (mi:ˈnɔrk) *nf* Minorca. **minorquin** *adj,n* Minorcan.

minuit (mi:ˈnɥi:) *nm* midnight.

minuscule (mi:ni:ˈskyl) *adj* **1** minute, tiny. **2** small.

minute (mi:ˈnyt) *nf* **1** minute. **2** moment. **3** record, draft.

minutieux, -euse (mi:nyˈsjœ, -ˈsjœz) *adj* **1** scrupulous, extremely careful. **2** thorough, detailed.

mioche (mjɔʃ) *nm,f inf* brat, small child.

miracle (mi:ˈrakl) *nm* miracle. **miraculeux, -euse** (mi:rakyˈlœ, -ˈlœz) *adj* miraculous, marvellous.

mirage (mi:ˈraʒ) *nm* mirage.

mirer (mi:ˈre:) *vt* aim at. **se mirer** *vr* look at oneself.

miroir (mi:rˈwar) *nm* mirror.

miroiter (mi:rwaˈte:) *vi* **1** gleam, shimmer. **2** flash.

mis (mi:) *v* see **mettre.**

miscellanées (mi:sɛllaˈne:) *nf pl* miscellany.

mise (mi:z) *nf* **1** placing. **2** dress, appearance. **3** *game* stake. **4** bid. **être de mise** be the done thing. **mise en scène** *Th* production.

miser (mi:ˈze:) *vt* **1** *game* stake. **2** bid.

misérable (mi:zɛˈrabl) *adj* **1** miserable, unhappy. **2** wretched, destitute. *nm* wretch, rogue.

misère (mi:ˈzɛr) *nf* **1** misery, distress. **2** poverty. **3** *inf* trifle. **crier misère** plead poverty. **dans la misère** poverty-stricken. **faire des misères à 1** tease. **2** worry.

miséricorde (mi:ze:ri:ˈkɔrd) *nf* mercy.

mission (mi:ˈsjɔ̃) *nf* mission. **missionnaire** *nm* missionary.

mistral (mi:ˈstral) *nm* cold north wind.

mitaine (mi:ˈtɛn) *nf* mitten.

mite (mi:t) *nf* moth. **mité** *adj* moth-eaten. **miteux, -euse** (mi:ˈtœ, -ˈtœz) *adj* shabby.

mitoyen, -enne (mi:twaˈjɛ̃, -ˈjɛn) *adj* intermediate, middle, dividing.

mitrailleuse (mi:traˈjœz) *nf* machine-gun. **mitraillette** *nf* submachine gun.

mitre (mi:tr) *nf* **1** mitre. **2** chimneypot.

mixte (mi:kst) *adj* mixed.

mobile (mɔˈbi:l) *adj* **1** mobile, movable. **2** changeable. **3** detachable. *nm* **1** motive. **2** mobile. **mobilier, -ière** (mɔbi:ˈlje:, -ˈljɛr) *adj* **1** personal. **2** movable. *nm* furniture.

mobiliser (mɔbi:li:ˈze:) *vt* mobilize.

moche (mɔʃ) *adj sl* **1** ugly. **2** rotten, lousy.

mode[1] (mɔd) *nf* **1** fashion. **2** manner. **à la mode** in fashion.

mode[2] (mɔd) *nm* **1** *gram* mood. **2** method, mode. **mode d'emploi** directions for use.

modeler (mɔdˈle:) *vt* model, mould. **modèle** *nm* **1** model. **2** pattern.

modérer (mɔde:ˈre:) *vt* moderate, restrain. **se modérer** *vr* control oneself. **modéré** *adj* **1** moderate. **2** temperate.

moderne (mɔˈdɛrn) *adj* modern.

moderniser (mɔdɛrni:ˈze:) *vt* modernize.

modeste (mɔˈdɛst) *adj* unassuming, humble.

modifier (mɔdi:ˈfje:) *vt* **1** modify. **2** alter.

modique (mɔˈdi:k) *adj* **1** modest, slender. **2** moderate, reasonable.

module (mɔˈdyl) *nm* **1** module. **2** unit.

moduler (mɔdyˈle:) *vt* modulate.

moelle (mwal) *nf* **1** *anat* marrow. **2** pith. **moelleux, -euse** (mwaˈlœ, -ˈlœz) *adj* **1** mellow. **2** soft.

mœurs (mœrs) *nf pl* **1** customs. **2** manners. **3** morals.

mohair (mɔˈɛr) *nm* mohair.

moi (mwa) *pron 1st pers m,f s* **1** I. **2** me. *nm*

ego, self. **moi-même** *pron 1st pers m,f s* myself.
moindre (mwɛ̃dr) *adj* **1** less, minor. **2** least.
moine (mwan) *nm* monk, friar.
moineau, -aux (mwa'no) *nm* sparrow.
moins (mwɛ̃) *adv* **1** less. **2** under. **3** least. **à moins de** unless, barring. **à moins que** unless. **au moins** at least, not less than. **de moins en moins** less and less. **du moins** at least. **moins de** less than. ~*prep* minus.
mois (mwa) *nm* month.
moisir (mwa'zi:r) *vi* go mouldy. **moisissure** *nf* mildew, mould.
moisson (mwa'sɔ̃) *nf* **1** harvest. **2** crop.
moissonner (mwasɔ'ne:) *vt* harvest, reap. **moissonneuse-batteuse** *nf, pl* **moissonneuses-batteuses** combine harvester.
moite (mwat) *adj* moist, clammy.
moitié (mwa'tje:) *nf* half. **à moitié** half. **moitié moitié** half-and-half.
molécule (mɔle:'kyl) *nf* molecule.
molester (mɔlɛ'ste:) *vt* molest.
mollasse (mɔ'las) *adj* **1** flabby. **2** apathetic, lazy.
mollesse (mɔ'lɛs) *nf* **1** softness. **2** slackness. **3** apathy.
mollet, -ette (mɔ'lɛ, -'lɛt) *adj* soft. *nm anat* calf.
mollir (mɔ'li:r) *vt* slacken. *vi* **1** soften. **2** abate. **3** slacken.
mollusque (mɔ'lysk) *nm* mollusc.
môme (mom) *nm,f sl* kid.
moment (mɔ'mɑ̃) *nm* **1** moment. **2** time, instant. **3** occasion.
momie (mɔ'mi:) *nf* mummy (dead body).
mon, ma, mes (mɔ̃, ma, mɛ) *poss adj 1st pers s* my.
monarque (mɔ'nark) *nm* monarch.
monastère (mɔna'stɛr) *nm* monastery. **monastique** *adj* monastic.
monceau, -aux (mɔ̃'so) *nm* pile, heap.
monde (mɔ̃d) *nm* **1** world. **2** people. **3** society. **tout le monde** everybody, everyone. **mondain** *adj* **1** worldly. **2** mundane. **mondial, -aux** (mɔ̃'djal, -'djo) *adj* worldwide.
monétaire (mɔne:'tɛr) *adj* monetary.
moniteur, -trice (mɔni:'tœr, -'tri:s) *nm,f* **1** monitor. **2** instructor. **3** *sport* coach.
monnayer (mɔnɛ'je:) *vt* **1** coin, mint. **2** *inf* cash in on. **monnaie** *nf* **1** money. **2** currency. **3** change. **petite monnaie** small change.
monogamie (mɔnɔga'mi:) *nf* monogamy.
monologue (mɔnɔ'lɔg) *nm* monologue.
monopole (mɔnɔ'pɔl) *nm* monopoly.
monopoliser (mɔnɔpɔli:'ze:) *vt* monopolize.
monosyllabe (mɔnɔsi:l'lab) *adj* monosyllabic. *nm* monosyllable.
monotone (mɔnɔ'tɔn) *adj* monotonous.
monseigneur (mɔ̃sɛ'ɲœr) *nm* **1** *pl* **nosseigneurs** His or Your Royal Highness, His Grace. **2** *pl* **messeigneurs** Your Grace, His or Your Lordship.
monsieur (mə'sjœ) *nm, pl* **messieurs** **1** sir. **2** master. **3** gentleman. **4** *cap* Mr.
monstre (mɔ̃str) *nm* monster. *adj* huge, enormous. **monstrueux, -euse** (mɔ̃stry'œ, -'œz) *adj* **1** monstrous. **2** huge. **3** scandalous.
mont (mɔ̃) *nm* mount, mountain.
montagne (mɔ̃'taɲ) *nf* mountain. **montagnard** *adj* mountain, highland. *nm* highlander, person living in the mountains. **montagneux, -euse** (mɔ̃ta'ɲœ, -'ɲœz) *adj* mountainous.
monter (mɔ̃'te:) *vi (aux usu* être*)* **1** climb. **2** go up. **3** ride. **4** mount. **5** rise. *vt* **1** climb, ascend. **2** carry or take up. **3** erect. **4** *Th* produce. **monter à cheval** ride. **montant** *adj* **1** rising. **2** uphill. *nm* **1** upright. **2** rise. **3** (total) amount. **monté** *adj* **1** mounted. **2** equipped. **montée** *nf* **1** rise. **2** step. **monture** *nf* **1** mount (a horse, etc.). **2** setting. **3** frame. **4** handle.
montrer (mɔ̃'tre:) *vt* **1** show. **2** display. **3** point out. **4** teach. **se montrer** *vr* appear. **montre** *nf* **1** watch. **2** show, display. **montre-bracelet** *nf, pl* **montres-bracelets** wristwatch.
monument (mɔny'mɑ̃) *nm* monument.
se moquer (mɔ'ke:) *vr* **se moquer de** mock, make fun of. **moquerie** *nf* mockery, ridicule.
moral, -aux (mɔ'ral, -'ro) *adj* **1** moral. **2** ethical. **3** mental. **morale** *nf* **1** morals. **2** ethics. **3** moral. **moralité** *nf* **1** morality. **2** moral.
moraliser (mɔrali:'ze:) *vi* moralize. *vt* lecture.
morbide (mɔr'bi:d) *adj* morbid.
morceau, -aux (mɔr'so) *nm* **1** piece. **2** bit, scrap.
mordre (mɔrdr) *vt* **1** bite. **2** nip. **mordant** *adj* **1** biting, caustic. **2** sarcastic. **mordu** *adj sl* mad, keen.
morgue (mɔrg) *nf* **1** mortuary. **2** pride.
moribond (mɔri:'bɔ̃) *adj* dying.
morne (mɔrn) *adj* **1** gloomy. **2** dreary, dull.
morose (mɔ'roz) *adj* morose, sullen.
morphine (mɔr'fi:n) *nf* morphine.
mors (mɔr) *nm* bit (of a bridle).
morse[1] (mɔrs) *nm* walrus.
morse[2] (mɔrs) *nm* morse code.
morsure (mɔr'syr) *nf* bite.

mort[1] (mɔr) *v* see **mourir.** *adj* **1** dead. **2** stagnant. **3** neutral. **mort-né** *adj, pl* **mort-nés** stillborn. **morte-saison** *nf, pl* **mortes-saisons** off-season.

mort[2] (mɔr) *nf* death.

mortalité (mɔrtali:'te:) *nf* **1** mortality. **2** death rate.

mortel, -elle (mɔr'tɛl) *adj* **1** mortal. **2** fatal. **3** deadly.

mortier (mɔr'tje:) *nm* mortar.

mortifier (mɔrti:'fje:) *vt* **1** mortify, hurt. **2** *cul* hang.

mortuaire (mɔr'tɥɛr) *adj* mortuary.

morue (mɔ'ry) *nf* cod.

morveux, -euse (mɔr'vœ, -'vœz) *nm,f* brat, child.

mosaïque (mɔza'i:k) *adj,nf* mosaic.

mosquée (mɔ'ske:) *nf* mosque.

mot (mo) *nm* **1** word. **2** saying. **3** hint. **gros mot** swearword. **mots croisés** crossword.

motel (mɔ'tɛl) *nm* motel.

moteur, -trice (mɔ'tœr, -'tri:s) *adj* motive, driving. *nm* motor, engine. **moteur-fusée** *nm, pl* **moteurs-fusées** rocket.

motif (mɔ'ti:f) *nm* **1** motive, reason. **2** pattern. **3** *mus* theme.

motion (mɔ'sjɔ̃) *nf* motion, proposal.

motiver (mɔti:'ve:) *vt* **1** give the reason for. **2** warrant.

motocyclette (mɔtɔsi:'klɛt) *nf* motorcycle.

motte (mɔt) *nf* **1** mound. **2** lump. **3** *cul* pat, roll.

mou, mol, molle (mu:, mɔl, mɔl) *adj* **1** soft. **2** weak. **3** slack. **4** limp. *nm* **1** slack. **2** *zool* lungs.

mouche (mu:ʃ) *nf* **1** fly. **2** spot, stain.

moucher (mu:'ʃe:) *vt* **1** wipe (the nose of). **2** snuff. **se moucher** *vr* blow one's nose.

moucheter (mu:ʃ'te:) *vt* speckle, spot. **moucheture** *nf* speckle, fleck, spot.

mouchoir (mu:'ʃwar) *nm* handkerchief.

moudre* (mu:dr) *vt* grind.

moue (mu:) *nf* pout. **faire la moue** pout, sulk.

mouette (mwɛt) *nf* gull.

moufette (mu:'fɛt) *nf* skunk.

moufle (mu:fl) *nf* mitten.

mouiller (mu:'je:) *vt* **1** dampen, moisten. **2** anchor. **se mouiller** *vr* get wet.

moule[1] (mu:l) *nm* mould.

moule[2] (mu:l) *nf* mussel.

mouler (mu:'le:) *vt* **1** cast. **2** mould.

moulin (mu:'lɛ̃) *nm* mill. **moulin à eau** watermill. **moulin à poivre** peppermill. **moulin à vent** windmill. **moulinet** *nm sport* reel.

moulu (mu:'ly) *v* see **moudre.** *adj* ground.

mourir* (mu:'ri:r) *vi (aux* être) die. **se mourir** *vr* **1** be dying. **2** die out.

mousse[1] (mu:s) *nf* **1** moss. **2** foam, froth. **3** lather. **4** mousse.

mousse[2] (mu:s) *nm* cabin boy.

mousseline (mu:s'li:n) *nf* muslin.

mousser (mu:'se:) *vi* **1** froth, foam. **2** lather. **3** sparkle.

mousson (mu:'sɔ̃) *nf* monsoon.

moustache (mu:'staʃ) *nf* **1** moustache. **2** *zool* whiskers.

moustique (mu:'sti:k) *nm* mosquito.

moutarde (mu:'tard) *nf* mustard.

mouton (mu:'tɔ̃) *nm* **1** sheep. **2** mutton.

mouvoir* (mu:'vwar) *vt* **1** move. **2** drive. **3** prompt, activate. **se mouvoir** *vr* move. **mouvant** *adj* **1** moving. **2** mobile. **3** fickle. **mouvement** *nm* **1** movement. **2** change. **3** impulse. **4** emotion. **mouvementé** *adj* **1** lively. **2** thrilling.

moyen[1]**, -enne** (mwa'jɛ̃, -'jɛn) *adj* **1** middle. **2** average. **3** medium. **moyen âge** Middle Ages. ~*nf* average.

moyen[2] (mwa'jɛ̃) *nm* **1** means. **2** way. **3** *pl* ability.

moyennant (mwajɛ'nɑ̃) *prep* for, at (a price). **moyennant que** on condition that.

Moyen Orient *nm* Middle East.

moyeu, -eux (mwa'jœ) *nm* hub.

muer (mɥe:) *vi* **1** moult. **2** (of the voice) break.

muet, -ette (mɥɛ, mɥɛt) *adj* **1** dumb, mute. **2** silent.

mufle (myfl) *nm* **1** muzzle. **2** *sl* mug, face. **3** *sl* swine.

muge (myʒ) *nm* mullet.

mugir (my'ʒi:r) *vi* **1** moo. **2** bellow. **3** roar.

muguet (my'gɛ) *nm* lily-of-the-valley.

mule[1] (myl) *nf* mule.

mule[2] (myl) *nf* slipper.

multiplier (mylti:pli:'e;) *vi,vt* multiply. **multiple** *adj* multiple, manifold. *nm* multiple.

multitude (mylti:'tyd) *nf* multitude, crowd.

municipal, -aux (myni:si:'pal; -'po) *adj* municipal. **municipalité** *nf* **1** municipality. **2** town hall. **3** town council.

munir (my'ni:r) *vt* **munir de 1** provide, supply. **2** equip. **munitions** *nf pl* **1** ammunition. **2** supplies.

mur (myr) *nm* wall.

mûr (myr) *adj* **1** ripe. **2** mature. **3** mellow.

mural, -aux (my'ral, -'ro) *adj* mural.

mûre (myr) *nf* mulberry. **mûre sauvage** blackberry. **mûrier** *nm* mulberry tree or bush.
mûrir (my'ri:r) *vi,vt* **1** ripen. **2** mature.
murmurer (myrmy're:) *vi* **1** murmur. **2** grumble. *vt* whisper. **murmure** *nm* murmur.
musc (mysk) *nm* musk.
muscade (my'skad) *nf* nutmeg.
muscle (myskl) *nm* muscle. **musclé** *adj* muscular.
museau, -aux (my'zo) *nm* muzzle, snout.
musée (my'ze:) *nm* museum. **musée de peinture** or **beaux arts** art gallery.
museler (my'zle:) *vt* muzzle. **muselière** *nf* muzzle.
muser (my'ze:) *vi* dawdle, loiter.
muséum (myze:'ɔm) *nm* natural history museum.
musique (my'zi:k) *nf* **1** music. **2** *mil* band. **musique de chambre** chamber music. **musical, -aux** (myzi'kal, -'ko) *adj* musical. **musicien, -ienne** (myzi:'sjɛ̃, -'sjɛn) *nm,f* musician. *adj* musical.
musulman (myzyl'mɑ̃) *adj,n* Muslim.
mutiler (myti:'le:) *vt* **1** maim. **2** mutilate, deface. **mutilé** *adj* maimed, disabled.
mutin (my'tɛ̃) *adj* insubordinate, disobedient.
se mutiner (myti:'ne:) *vr* mutiny, revolt. **mutinerie** *nf* mutiny, rebellion.
mutisme (my'ti:sm) *nm* dumbness.
mutuel, -elle (my'tɥɛl) *adj* mutual.
myope (mjɔp) *adj* short-sighted. **myopie** *nf* short-sightedness.
myrrhe (myr) *nf* myrrh.
myrte (mi:rt) *nm* myrtle.
myrtille (mi:r'ti:j) *nf* bilberry.
mystère (mi:'stɛr) *nm* mystery. **mystérieux, -euse** (mi:ste:'rjœ, -'rjœz) *adj* mysterious.
mystifier (mi:sti:'fje:) *vt* **1** hoax, fool. **2** mystify.
mystique (mi:'sti:k) *adj,n* mystic. *nf* mystique.
mythe (mi:t) *nm* myth, legend.
mythologie (mi:tɔlɔ'ʒi:) *nf* mythology. **mythologique** *adj* mythological.

N

nabot (na'bo) *nm* dwarf, midget.
nacré (na'kre:) *adj* pearly.
nager (na'ʒe:) *vi* **1** swim. **2** float. **3** row. **nager debout** tread water. **nage** *nf* **1** rowing. **2** swimming. **3** stroke. **nageoire** *nf* fin.
naguère (na'gɛr) *adv* not long ago.
naïf, -ïve (na'i:f, -'i:v) *adj* **1** naive, simple. **2** innocent.
nain (nɛ̃) *adj,n* dwarf.
naissance (nɛ'sɑ̃s) *nf* **1** birth. **2** descent. **3** source.
naître* (nɛtr) *vi* (*aux* être) **1** be born. **2** originate, rise. **faire naître** provoke, arouse.
nappe (nap) *nf* **1** tablecloth. **2** cloth. **3** cover. **4** sheet.
naquis (na'ki:) *v* see **naître.**
narcotique (narkɔ'ti:k) *adj,nm* narcotic.
narine (na'ri:n) *nf* nostril.
narquois (nar'kwa) *adj* sneering, mocking.
narrer (na're:) *vt* narrate, relate. **narratif, -ive** (narra'ti:f, -'ti:v) *adj* narrative. **narration** *nf* **1** narration. **2** narrative.
nasal, -aux (na'zal, -'zo) *adj* nasal. **naseau, -aux** (na'zo) *nm zool* nostril.
natal (na'tal) *adj* native (country, town, etc.). **natalité** *nf* birthrate.
natation (nata'sjɔ̃) *nf* swimming.
natif, -ive (na'ti:f, -'ti:v) *adj* **1** native. **2** natural.
nation (na'sjɔ̃) *nf* nation. **national, -aux** (nasjɔ'nal, -'no) *adj* national. **nationalité** *nf* nationality.
nationaliser (nasjɔnali:'ze:) *vt* nationalize.
nativité (nati:vi:'te:) *nf* nativity.
natter (na'te:) *vt* plait. **natte** *nf* **1** mat. **2** plait.
naturaliser (natyrali:'ze:) *vt* naturalize.
nature (na'tyr) *nf* **1** nature. **2** character. **3** temperament. **4** kind. **nature morte** still life. ~*adj invar* plain, natural. **naturaliste** *nm,f* naturalist.
naturel, -elle (naty'rɛl) *adj* **1** natural. **2** unaffected. **3** illegitimate. *nm* disposition.
naufrage (no'fraʒ) *nm* shipwreck.
nauséabond (noze:a'bɔ̃) *adj* **1** nauseating. **2** foul. **nausée** *nf* nausea.
nautique (no'ti:k) *adj* nautical.
naval (na'val) *adj* naval, nautical.
navet (na'vɛ) *nm* **1** turnip. **2** *inf* rubbish.
naviguer (navi:'ge:) *vi* **1** sail. **2** navigate. **navigateur** *nm* navigator.
navire (na'vi:r) *nm* ship, vessel.
navrer (na'vre:) *vt* grieve. **navré** *adj* sad, distressed, sorry.
ne, n' (nə) *adv* not.
né (ne:) *v* see **naître.** *adj* born.
néanmoins (ne:ɑ̃'mwɛ̃) *adv* nevertheless, yet.
néant (ne:'ɑ̃) *nm* nought, nothing.
nébuleux, -euse (ne:by'lœ, -'lœz) *adj* **1** nebulous. **2** cloudy. **3** vague, obscure.
nécessité (ne:sɛsi:'te:) *nf* **1** necessity. **2** need,

want. **nécessaire** *adj* **1** necessary. **2** essential.

nécrologie (ne:krɔlɔ'ʒi) *nf* obituary notice, deaths column.

néerlandais (ne:ɛrlɑ̃'dɛ) *adj* Dutch. *nm* Dutchman.

nef (nɛf) *nf* nave. **nef latérale** aisle.

néfaste (ne:'fast) *adj* **1** baneful. **2** evil.

nèfle (nɛfl) *nf* medlar. **néflier** *nm* medlar tree.

négatif, -ive (ne:ga'ti:f, -'ti:v) *adj* negative. *nm phot* negative. *nf* negative, refusal.

négliger (ne:gli:'ʒe:) *vt* **1** neglect. **2** disregard. **négligé** *adj* **1** neglected. **2** careless. **négligence** *nf* **1** carelessness. **2** neglect. **négligent** *adj* negligent, careless.

négocier (ne:gɔ'sje:) *vt* negotiate. **négoce** *nm* trade. **négociant** *nm* merchant. **négociateur** *nm* negotiator. **négotiation** *nf* **1** negotiation. **2** transaction.

nègre, négresse (nɛgr, ne:'grɛs) *nm,f* Negro, Negress. **parler petit nègre** speak pidgin French. ~*adj* Negro.

neiger (ne:'ʒe:) *v imp* snow. **neige** (nɛʒ) *nf* snow.

nénuphar (ne:ny'far) *nm* waterlily.

néon (ne:'ɔ̃) *nm* neon.

néo-Zélandais (ne:oze:lɑ̃'dɛ) *adj* New Zealand. *nm* New Zealander.

nerf (nɛrf) *nm* **1** nerve. **2** energy. **3** sinew. **nerveux, -euse** (nɛr'vœ, -'vœz) *adj* **1** *med* nervous. **2** vigorous. **3** excitable, hysterical. **nervosité** (nɛrvozi:'te:) *nf* nerves, irritability.

net, nette (nɛt) *adj* **1** clean. **2** clear. **3** distinct. **4** net. *adv* **1** plainly. **2** clearly. **3** outright. **netteté** *nf* **1** cleanness. **2** clearness.

nettoyer (nɛtwa'je:) *vt* **1** clean. **2** scour. **3** wipe. **4** clear out. **nettoyer à fond** spring-clean. **nettoyer à sec** dry-clean. **nettoiement** *nm also* **nettoyage** **1** cleaning. **2** clearing.

neuf[1] (nœf) *adj,nm* nine. **neuvième** *adj* ninth.

neuf[2]**, neuve** (nœf, nœv) *adj* new. **à neuf** again.

neutraliser (nœtrali:'ze:) *vt* neutralize.

neutralité (nœtrali:'te:) *nf* neutrality.

neutre (nœtr) *adj* **1** neutral. **2** neuter. *nm* neuter.

neveu, -eux (nə'vœ) *nm* nephew.

névrose (ne:'vroz) *nf* neurosis. **névrosé** *adj,n* neurotic.

nez (ne:) *nm* **1** nose. **2** scent.

ni (ni:) *conj* nor, or. **ni...ni** neither...nor.

niais (ni:'ɛ) *adj* **1** simple, foolish. **2** inane. *nm* fool.

nicher (ni:'ʃe:) *vi* **1** nest. **2** lodge. **se nicher** *vr* nestle. **niche** *nf* **1** recess. **2** kennel.

nickel (ni:'kɛl) *nm* nickel.

nicotine (ni:kɔ'ti:n) *nf* nicotine.

nid (ni:) *nm* nest.

nièce (njɛs) *nf* niece.

nier (ni:'e:) *vt* deny.

nigaud (ni:'go) *adj* simple, stupid. *nm* idiot.

Nigeria (ni:ʒɛ'rja) *nf* Nigeria. **nigérien, -ienne** (ni:ʒɛ'rjɛ̃, -'rjɛn) *adj,n* Nigerian.

Nil (ni:l) *nm* Nile.

nimbe (nɛ̃b) *nm* halo.

nitouche (ni:'tu:ʃ) **sainte nitouche** *nf inf* little hypocrite.

niveau, -aux (ni:'vo) *nm* **1** level. **2** standard.

niveler (ni:v'le:) *vt* level.

noble (nɔbl) *adj* **1** noble. **2** lofty. *nm* nobleman. **noblesse** *nf* nobility.

noce (nɔs) *nf* wedding.

nocif, -ive (nɔ'si:f, -'si:v) *adj* harmful.

nocturne (nɔk'tyrn) *adj* nocturnal.

Noël (nɔ'ɛl) *nm* Christmas.

nœud (nœ) *nm* **1** knot. **2** bow. **3** bond. **nœud coulant** noose.

noir (nwar) *adj* **1** black. **2** dark. **3** gloomy. **4** dirty. **5** base. *nm* **1** black. **2** *cap* Black. *nf mus* crotchet. **noirceur** *nf* **1** blackness. **2** darkness. **3** baseness. **noircir** *vi* turn black, darken. *vt* blacken.

noisette (nwa'zɛt) *nf* hazelnut. *adj invar* hazel. **noisetier** *nm* hazel tree.

noix (nwa) *nf* **1** nut. **2** walnut. **noix de coco** coconut.

nom (nɔ̃) *nm* **1** name. **2** noun. **nom de famille** surname. **nom de jeune fille** maiden name.

nomade (nɔ'mad) *adj* nomadic. *nm* nomad.

nombre (nɔ̃br) *nm* number. **nombreux, -euse** (nɔ̃'brœ, -'brœz) *adj* **1** numerous. **2** many.

nombril (nɔ̃'bri:) *nm* navel.

nominal, -aux (nɔmi:'nal, -'no) *adj* nominal.

nommer (nɔ'me:) *vt* **1** call, name. **2** mention by name. **3** appoint.

non (nɔ̃) *adv* **1** no. **2** non-. *nm invar* no. **non-être** *nm* nonentity.

nonne (nɔn) *nf* nun.

nonobstant (nɔnɔp'stɑ̃) *prep* notwithstanding. *adv* nevertheless.

nord (nɔr) *nm* north. *adj invar* north, northern. **au nord** in the north. **du nord 1** northern. **2** northerly. **vers le nord** northward, northwards. **nord-est** *nm* north-east. *adj invar* north-east. **du nord-est 1** north-eastern. **2** north-easterly. **nord-ouest** *nm* north-west. *adj* *invar* north-west. **du nord-ouest 1** north-western. **2** north-westerly.

normal, -aux (nɔr'mal, -'mo) *adj* **1** normal. **2** standard. **école normale** *nf* teacher-training college.

Normandie (nɔrmɑ̃'di:) *nf* Normandy. **normand** *adj, n* Norman.

norme (nɔrm) *nf* norm, standard.

Norvège (nɔr'vɛʒ) *nf* Norway. **norvégien, -ienne** (nɔrve:'ʒjɛ̃, -'ʒjɛn) *adj,n* Norwegian. *nm* Norwegian (language).

nos (no) *poss adj* see **notre.**

nostalgie (nɔstal'ʒi:) *nf* nostalgia, homesickness. **nostalgique** (nɔstal'ʒi:k) *adj* homesick.

notable (nɔ'tabl) *adj* **1** notable, considerable. **2** eminent.

notaire (nɔ'tɛr) *nm* lawyer.

notamment (nɔta'mɑ̃) *adv* in particular.

notation (nɔta'sjɔ̃) *nf* notation.

noter (nɔ'te:) *vt* **1** note, observe. **2** make a note of. **note** *nf* **1** note. **2** notice. **3** *educ* mark. **4** bill. **5** *mus* note.

notice (nɔ'ti:s) *nf* **1** account. **2** *lit* review. **3** directions (for use).

notifier (nɔti:'fje:) *vt* notify, inform.

notion (no'sjɔ̃) *nf* notion, idea.

notoire (nɔ'twar) *adj* **1** well-known. **2** evident. **notoriété** *nf* **1** notoriety. **2** repute. **notoriété publique** common knowledge.

notre, nos (nɔtr, no) *poss adj 1st pers pl* our.

nôtre (notr) *poss pron 1st pers pl* **le** *or* **la nôtre** **1** ours. **2** our own.

nouer (nu:'e:) *vt* **1** tie. **2** knot. **3** establish. **noueux, -euse** (nu:'œ, -'œz) *adj* **1** knotted. **2** gnarled.

nouilles (nu:j) *nf pl* noodles.

nounou (nu:'nu:) *nf inf* nanny.

nounours (nu:'nu:rs) *nm inf* teddy.

nourrice (nu:'ri:s) *nf* nurse. **nourricier, -ière** (nu:ri:'sje:, -'sjɛr) *adj* **1** nutritious. **2** foster.

nourrir (nu:'ri:r) *vt* **1** nourish, feed. **2** rear. **3** foster, harbour. **nourrisson, -onne** (nu:ri:'sɔ̃, -'sɔn) *nm,f* fosterchild. **nourriture** *nf* **1** food. **2** board, keep.

nous (nu) *pron 1st pers m,f pl* **1** we. **2** us. **3** to us. **4** ourselves. **5** each other. **nous-mêmes** *pron 1st pers m,f pl* ourselves.

nouveau, -el, -elle, -aux (nu:'vo, -'vɛl, -'vɛl, -'vo) *adj* **1** new. **2** recent. **3** fresh. **4** another. **à/de nouveau** afresh/again. **nouvel an** *nm* New Year. **nouveauté** *nf* **1** novelty. **2** change.

nouvelle[1] (nu:'vɛl) *adj* see **nouveau.**

nouvelle[2] (nu:'vɛl) *nf* **1** piece of news. **2** news. **3** short story.

Nouvelle-Zélande (ze:'lɑ̃d) *nf* New Zealand.

novateur, -trice (nɔva'tœr, -'tri:s) *nm,f* innovator. *adj* innovating.

novembre (nɔ'vɑ̃br) *nm* November.

novice (nɔ'vi:s) *nm,f* novice.

noyau, -aux (nwa'jo) *nm* **1** stone (of fruit). **2** kernel. **3** nucleus.

noyer[1] (nwa'je:) *vt* **1** drown. **2** swamp. **3** flood. **noyade** *nf* drowning.

noyer[2] (nwa'je:) *nm* walnut tree.

nu (ny) *adj* **1** naked, nude. **2** bare. **3** plain. *nm* nude. **à nu** bare, exposed.

nuage (nɥaʒ) *nm* **1** cloud. **2** haze. **nuageux, -euse** (nɥa'ʒœ, -ʒœz) *adj* cloudy.

nuancer (nɥɑ̃'se:) *vt* **1** blend. **2** vary. **nuance** *nf* **1** shade. **2** nuance.

nucléaire (nykle:'ɛr) *adj* nuclear.

nuée (nɥe:) *nf* **1** cloud. **2** swarm. **3** host, crowd.

nuire* (nɥi:r) *vt* **nuire à** **1** harm. **2** prejudice. **nuisible** *adj* harmful.

nuit (nɥi:) *nf* **1** night. **2** darkness. **bonne nuit!** good night! **cette nuit** **1** tonight. **2** last night.

nul, nulle (nyl) *adj* **1** no, not one. **2** worthless. **nul et non avenu** null and void. **nulle part** nowhere.

numéral, -aux (nymɛ'ral, -'ro) *adj, nm* numeral.

numéro (nyme:'ro) *nm* **1** number. **2** *lit* issue.

numéroter (nyme:rɔ'te:) *vt* number.

nuptial, -aux (nyp'sjal, -'sjo) *adj* bridal.

nutrition (nytri:'sjɔ̃) *nf* nutrition.

nylon (ni:'lɔ̃) *nm* nylon.

nymphe (nɛ̃f) *nf* nymph.

O

oasis (oa'zi:s) *nf* oasis.

obéir (ɔbe:'i:r) *vi* **obéir à** **1** obey. **2** yield. **obéissance** *nf* **1** obedience. **2** submission. **obéissant** *adj* **1** obedient. **2** docile. **3** dutiful.

obèse (ɔ'bɛz) *adj* obese, fat.

obituaire (ɔbi:'tɥɛr) *nm* obituary.

objecter (ɔbʒɛk'te:) *vt* object.

objectif (ɔbʒɛk'ti:f) *adj* objective. *nm* **1** aim, objective. **2** target. **3** lens.

objection (ɔbʒɛk'sjɔ̃) *nf* objection.

objet (ɔb'ʒɛ) *nm* **1** object, thing. **2** aim, purpose. **3** *gram* object. **objet d'art** work of art. **objets trouvés** *pl* lost property

obliger (ɔbli:'ʒe:) *vt* **1** oblige, compel. **2** help. **obligation** *nf* **1** obligation, duty. **2** *law* agreement. **3** *comm* bond. **obligatoire** *adj* obligatory.

oblique (ɔ'bli:k) *adj* **1** oblique. **2** underhand.

oblitérer (ɔbli:te:'re:) *vt* **1** obliterate. **2** cancel.

oblong, -ongue (ɔb'lɔ̃, -'lɔ̃g) *adj* oblong.

obscène (ɔp'sɛn) *adj* obscene.

obscur (ɔp'skyr) *adj* **1** dark, gloomy. **2** obscure. **3** humble. **obscurité** *nf* obscurity.

obscurcir (ɔpskyr'si:r) *vt* **1** darken. **2** dim. **3** obscure.

obséder (ɔpse:'de:) *vt* **1** haunt. **2** obsess. **3** worry.

obsèques (ɔp'sɛk) *nf pl* funeral.

observer (ɔpsɛr've:) *vt* **1** observe, comply with. **2** watch. **3** note. **s'observer** *vr* be careful. **observance** *nf* observance. **observateur, -trice** (ɔpsɛrva'tœr, -'tri:s) *nm,f* observer. *adj* observant. **observatoire** *nm* observatory.

obsession (ɔpsɛ'sjɔ̃) *nf* obsession.

obstacle (ɔp'stakl) *nm* obstacle, hindrance.

s'obstiner (sɔpsti:'ne:) *vr* **s'obstiner à** persist in. **obstination** *nf* obstinacy. **obstiné** *adj* obstinate, stubborn.

obstruer (ɔpstry'e:) *vt* obstruct, block.

obtenir* (ɔptə'ni:r) *vt* **1** obtain, get. **2** achieve.

obtus (ɔp'ty) *adj* **1** obtuse. **2** blunt. **3** dull.

obus (ɔ'bys) *nm mil* shell.

occasion (ɔka'zjɔ̃) *nf* **1** opportunity. **2** bargain. **3** cause. **d'occasion** second-hand. **occasionnel, -elle** (ɔkazjɔ'nɛl) *adj* occasional.

occident (ɔksi:'dɑ̃) *nm* **1** west. **2** Occident. **occidental, -aux** (ɔksi:dɑ̃'tal, -'to) *adj* western.

occulte (ɔ'kylt) *adj* **1** occult. **2** hidden.

occuper (ɔky'pe:) *vt* **1** occupy. **2** live in. **3** take up. **s'occuper de** *vr* attend to. **occupant** *nm* occupant. **occupation** *nf* **1** occupation. **2** employment. **3** profession. **occupé** *adj* **1** busy. **2** engaged, taken.

océan (ɔse:'ɑ̃) *nm* ocean.

ocre (ɔkr) *nf* ochre.

octane (ɔk'tan) *nm* octane.

octave (ɔk'tav) *nf* octave.

octobre (ɔk'tɔbr) *nm* October.

octogone (ɔktɔ'gɔn) *nm* octagon. **octogonal, -aux** (ɔktɔgɔ'nal, -'no) *adj* octagonal.

octroi (ɔk'trwa) *nm* concession.

octroyer (ɔktrwa'je:) *vt* grant, concede.

oculiste (ɔky'li:st) *nm* oculist. **oculaire** *adj* ocular. **témoin oculaire** *nm* eyewitness.

ode (ɔd) *nf* ode.

odeur (o'dœr) *nf* **1** smell, odour. **2** scent. **odorant** *adj* fragrant. **odorat** *nm* sense of smell.

odieux, -euse (ɔ'djœ, -'djœz) *adj* **1** odious. **2** hateful.

œil (œj) *nm, pl* **yeux** **1** eye. **2** sight. **3** look. **œil poché** black eye. **œillade** *nf* **1** glance. **2** leer. **œillet** *nm* **1** eyelet. **2** *bot* pink, carnation.

œstre (ɛstr) *nm* oestrus.

œuf (œf) *nm* **1** egg. **2** *pl* roe, spawn. **œuf à la coque** boiled egg. **œuf dur/poché** hard-boiled/poached egg. **œufs brouillés** scrambled eggs. **œuf sur le plat** fried egg.

œuvre (œvr) *nf* **1** work. **2** act. *nm* works (of an artist, etc.).

offenser (ɔfɑ̃'se:) *vt* **1** offend. **2** shock. **offensant** *adj* offensive. **offense** *nf* **1** offence. **2** sin. **offensif, -ive** (ɔfɑ̃'si:f, -'si:v) *adj* offensive. *nf mil* offensive.

offert (ɔ'fɛr) *v* see **offrir.**

office (ɔ'fi:s) *nm* **1** office, duty. **2** help. **3** *rel* service. **4** office. *nf* pantry. **officiel, -elle** (ɔfi:'sjɛl) *adj* **1** official. **2** formal. *nm* official. **officier** *nm* officer.

officieux, -euse (ɔfi:'sjœ, -'sjœz) *adj* **1** officious. **2** unofficial.

officine (ɔfi:'si:n) *nf* dispensary.

offrir* (ɔ'fri:r) *vt* **1** offer. **2** give. **3** bid. **4** afford, present. **offrande** *nf* **1** offering. **2** present. **offre** *nf* **1** offer. **2** proposal. **3** tender. **4** bid.

offusquer (ɔfy'ske:) *vt* **1** veil, obscure. **2** shock.

ogre, ogresse (ɔgr, ɔ'grɛs) *nm,f* ogre, ogress.

oie (wa) *nf* goose.

oignon (ɔ'ɲɔ̃) *nm* **1** onion. **2** *bot* bulb.

oindre* (wɛ̃dr) *vt* **1** oil. **2** anoint.

oiseau, -aux (wa'zo) *nm* bird.

oisif, -ive (wa'zi:f, -'zi:v) *adj* **1** idle. **2** lazy.

oison (wa'zɔ̃) *nm* gosling.

olive (ɔ'li:v) *nf* olive. **olivier** *nm* olive tree.

ombrage (ɔ̃'braʒ) *nm* **1** shade. **2** offence.

ombre (ɔ̃br) *nf* **1** shadow. **2** shade. **3** darkness.

omettre* (ɔ'mɛtr) *vt* **1** omit, fail. **2** leave out. **omission** *nf* omission.

omnibus (ɔmni:'bys) *nm* **1** omnibus. **2** slow train. *adj invar* general, blanket.

omnipotent (ɔmni:pɔ'tɑ̃) *adj* omnipotent, almighty.

omoplate (ɔmɔ'plat) *nf* shoulder-blade.

on (ɔ̃) *indef pron s* one, people, they, we, you. **on demande** wanted. **on dit** it is said. **on y va?** shall we go?

once (ɔ̃s) *nf* ounce.

oncle (ɔ̃kl) *nm* uncle.

onde (ɔ̃d) *nf* wave. **grande onde** long wave. **onde courte** short wave. **ondée** *nf* heavy shower.

on-dit *nm invar* rumour.

ondoyer (ɔ̃dwa'je:) *vi* wave, ripple.

onduler (ɔ̃dy'le:) *vi* ripple. *vt* wave, curl.

ongle (ɔ̃gl) *nm* **1** fingernail. **2** claw. **3** talon.

onguent (ɔ̃'gɑ̃) *nm* ointment.

ont (ɔ̃) *v* see **avoir.**

onze (ɔ̃z) *adj,nm* eleven. **onzième** *adj* eleventh.

opale (ɔ'pal) *nf* opal.

opaque (ɔ'pak) *adj* opaque.

opéra (ɔpɛ'ra) *nm* **1** opera. **2** opera house.

opérer (ɔpe:re:) *vt* **1** operate. **2** work. **3** effect. **se faire opérer** undergo an operation. **opération** *nf* **1** operation. **2** process. **3** transaction.

s'opiniâtrer (sɔpi:njɑ'tre:) *vr* be stubborn, obstinate. **opiniâtre** *adj* **1** stubborn, obstinate. **2** headstrong. **3** persistent.

opinion (ɔpi:'njɔ̃) *nf* opinion, view.

opportun (ɔpɔr'tœ̃) *adj* **1** opportune, favourable. **2** expedient. **opportunité** *nf* **1** timeliness. **2** favourable occasion. **3** expediency.

opposer (ɔpo'ze:) *vt* **1** oppose. **2** place opposite. **opposer à** compare with. **s'opposer à** *vr* oppose; be opposed to. **opposé** *adj* **1** opposed. **2** opposite. **3** contrary. **opposite** *nm* opposite, contrary. **opposition** *nf* **1** opposition. **2** contrast.

opprimer (ɔpri:'me:) *vt* oppress.

opprobre (ɔ'prɔbr) *nm* shame, disgrace.

opter (ɔp'te:) *vi* opt, choose. **option** *nf* option, choice.

opticien (ɔpti:'sjɛ̃) *nm* optician.

optimisme (ɔpti:'mi:sm) *nm* optimism. **optimiste** *adj* optimistic. *nm,f* optimist.

optique (ɔp'ti:k) *adj* **1** optical. **2** optic. *nf* optics.

opulent (ɔpy'lɑ̃) *adj* **1** opulent. **2** abundant.

or[1] (ɔr) *nm* gold. **d'or** *adj* golden.

or[2] (ɔr) *conj* **1** now. **2** well. **3** but.

orage (ɔ'raʒ) *nm* thunderstorm. **orageux, -euse** (ɔra'ʒœ, -'ʒœz) *adj* stormy.

oraison (ɔrɛ'zɔ̃) *nf* **1** oration. **2** prayer.

oral, -aux (ɔ'ral, -'ro) *adj* **1** oral. **2** verbal. *nm* oral examination.

orange (ɔ'rɑ̃ʒ) *nf* **1** *bot* orange. **2** orange (colour). *adj invar* orange. **oranger** *nm* orange tree.

orateur (ɔra'tœr) *nm* orator.

orbite (ɔr'bi:t) *nf* orbit.

Orcades (ɔr'kad) *nf pl* Orkneys.

orchestrer (ɔrkɛ'stre:) *vt* orchestrate. **orchestre** *nm* orchestra.

orchidée (ɔrki:'de:) *nf* orchid.

ordinaire (ɔrdi:'nɛr) *adj* **1** ordinary. **2** usual. **3** common. *nm* habit.

ordinal, -aux (ɔrdi:'nal, -'no) *adj* ordinal.

ordinateur (ɔrdi:na'tœr) *nm* computer.

ordonner (ɔrdɔ'ne:) *vt* **1** arrange. **2** order. **3** ordain. **ordonnance** *nf* **1** arrangement. **2** order. **3** prescription. **ordonné** *adj* **1** orderly. **2** tidy.

ordre (ɔrdr) *nm* **1** order. **2** discipline. **3** sequence. **4** class, category. **5** *pl* holy orders. **ordre du jour** agenda.

ordure (ɔr'dyr) *nf* **1** filth, dirt. **2** filthiness. **3** *pl* refuse.

oreille (ɔ'rɛj) *nf* ear. **oreiller** *nm* pillow. **oreillons** *nm pl* mumps.

ores (ɔr) *adv* **d'ores et déjà** here and now.

orfèvre (ɔr'fɛvr) *nm* goldsmith.

organe (ɔr'gan) *nm* **1** organ. **2** voice. **3** agency, means. **4** mouthpiece.

organique (ɔrga'ni:k) *adj* organic.

organiser (ɔrgani:'ze:) *vt* **1** organize. **2** arrange. **3** set up. **organisation** *nf* **1** organization. **2** structure. **3** system. **organisé** *adj* **1** organic. **2** organized. **organisme** *nm* organism.

orge (ɔrʒ) *nf* barley.

orgie (ɔr'ʒi:) *nf* orgy.

orgue (ɔrg) *nm mus* organ.

orgueil (ɔr'gœj) *nm* pride. **orgueilleux, -euse** (ɔrgœ'jœ, -'jœz) *adj* **1** proud. **2** arrogant.

orient (ɔ'rjɑ̃) *nm* **1** Orient. **2** east. **oriental, -aux** (ɔrjɑ̃'tal, -'to) *adj* **1** eastern. **2** oriental.

orienter (ɔrjɑ̃'te:) *vt* **1** orientate. **2** direct.

origan (ɔri:'gɑ̃) *nm* oregano.

originaire (ɔri:ʒi:'nɛr) *adj* **1** native. **2** original.

origine (ɔri:'ʒi:n) *nf* **1** origin. **2** beginning. **3** source. **4** descent. **à l'origine** originally. **original, -aux** (ɔri:zi:'nal, -'no) *adj* **1** original. **2** novel. **3** eccentric. **originalité** *nf* **1** originality. **2** eccentricty.

orme (ɔrm) *nm* elm tree.

ornement (ɔrnə'mɑ̃) *nm* ornament. **ornemental, -aux** (ɔrnəmɑ̃tal, -'to) *adj* ornamental.

orner (ɔr'ne:) *vt* **1** decorate. **2** adorn.

ornière (ɔr'njɛr) *nf* **1** rut. **2** groove.

ornithologie (ɔrni:tɔlɔ'ʒi:) *nf* ornithology.

orphelin (ɔrfə'lɛ̃) *nm* orphan. **orphelinat** *nm* ophanage.

orteil (ɔr'tɛj) *nm* toe.

orthodoxe (ɔrtɔ'dɔks) *adj* orthodox, conventional.

orthographe (ɔrtɔ'graf) *nf* orthography, spelling.

orthopédique (ɔrtɔpe:ˈdi:k) *adj* orthopaedic.
ortie (ɔrˈti:) *nf* nettle.
os (ɔs) *nm* bone. **os à moelle** marrowbone.
osciller (ɔsi:ˈje:) *vi* **1** sway. **2** waver. **3** fluctuate.
oser (oˈze:) *vt* dare. **osé** *adj* bold.
ossature (ɔssaˈtyr) *nf* **1** skeleton. **2** framework.
ostentation (ɔstɑ̃taˈsjɔ̃) *nf* ostentation, show.
ostraciser (ɔstrasi:ˈze:) *vt* ostracize.
otage (ɔˈtaʒ) *nm* hostage.
ôter (oˈte:) *vt* **1** remove. **2** take away.
ou (u:) *conj* **1** or. **2** either. **3** else. **ou bien** or else. **ou...ou** either...or.
où (u:) *adv* **1** where. **2** when.
ouater (waˈte:) *vt* pad, wad. **ouate** *nf* **1** cotton-wool. **2** wadding.
oubli (u:ˈbli:) *nm* **1** forgetfulness. **2** oblivion. **3** oversight. **oublie** *nf* wafer.
oublier (u:bli:ˈe:) *vt* **1** forget. **2** overlook. **oublieux, -euse** (u:bli:ˈœ, -ˈœz) *adj* **1** forgetful. **2** oblivious.
ouest (wɛst) *nm* west. *adj invar* west, western. **à l'ouest** westward. **de l'ouest** westerly. **vers l'ouest** westward, westwards.
oui (wi:) *adv,nm invar* yes.
ouïr* (wi:r) *vt* hear. **ouï-dire** *nm invar* hearsay. **ouïe** *nf* **1** sense of hearing. **2** *pl zool* gill.
ouragan (u:raˈgɑ̃) *nm* hurricane.
ourler (u:rˈle:) *vt* hem. **ourlet** *nm* hem.
ours (u:rs) *nm* bear. **ours blanc** polar bear.
outil (u:ˈti:) *nm* **1** tool. **2** implement. **outillage** *nm* **1** set of tools. **2** equipment. **3** *tech* plant.
outiller (u:ti:ˈje:) *vt* equip with tools.
outrager (u:traˈʒe:) *vt* **1** insult. **2** outrage. **outrage** *nm* **1** outrage. **2** insult, affront.
outrance (u:ˈtrɑ̃s) *nf* excess.
outre (u:tr) *prep* **1** beyond. **2** in addition to. *adv* further. **en outre 1** besides. **2** moreover. **outre-mer** *adv* abroad, overseas.
outrer (u:ˈtre:) *vt* **1** carry to excess, overdo. **2** exaggerate. **3** exasperate.
ouvert (u:ˈvɛr) *v see* **ouvrir.** *adj* **1** open. **2** frank. **3** exposed. **ouverture** *nf* **1** opening. **2** hole. **3** overture.
ouvrable (u:ˈvrabl) **jour ouvrable** *nm* weekday.
ouvrage (u:ˈvraʒ) *nm* **1** work. **2** piece of work. **3** workmanship.
ouvrier, -ière (u:vri:ˈe:, -ˈɛr) *adj* **1** working. **2** labour, industrial. *nm* **1** worker. **2** workman.
ouvrir* (u:ˈvri:r) *vt* **1** open. **2** turn on. **3** cut through. **4** begin, start. *vi* open. **ouvre-boîte** *nm invar* tin-opener. **ouvre-bouteille** *nm, pl* **ouvre-bouteilles** bottle-opener.
ovaire (ɔˈvɛr) *nm* ovary.
ovale (ɔˈval) *adj,nm* oval.
ovation (ɔvaˈsjɔ̃) *nf* ovation.
oxygène (oksi:ˈʒɛn) *nm* oxygen.

P

pacage (paˈkaʒ) *nm* **1** pasture. **2** grazing.
pacifier (pasi:ˈfje:) *vt* **1** pacify. **2** appease. **se pacifier** *vr* calm down. **pacifisme** *nm* pacifism.
pacifique (pasi:ˈfi:k) *adj* peaceful. (**Océan**) **Pacifique** *nm* Pacific (Ocean).
pacte (pakt) *nm* pact, agreement.
pagaie (paˈgɛ) *nf* paddle (for a canoe).
pagaïe (paˈgaj) *nf* disorder, confusion, chaos.
pagayer (pagɛˈje:) *vi,vt* paddle (a boat).
page[1] (paʒ) *nf* page.
page[2] (paʒ) *nm* page (boy).
pagode (paˈgɔd) *nf* **1** pagoda. **2** temple.
paie (pɛ) *nf* **1** pay. **2** wages. **paiement** *nm* payment.
païen, -ïenne (paˈjɛ̃, -jɛn) *adj,n* pagan.
paillasson (pajaˈsɔ̃) *nm* **1** mat. **2** doormat.
paille (pɑj) *nf* **1** straw. **2** flaw. **paillette** *nf* **1** grain. **2** flake. **3** flaw.
pain (pɛ̃) *nm* **1** bread. **2** loaf. **pain d'épice** gingerbread. **pain de savon** cake of soap. **pain grillé** toast. **petit pain** roll.
pair[1] (pɛr) *adj* **1** equal. **2** even.
pair[2] (pɛr) *nm* peer. **pairesse** *nf* peeress.
paire (pɛr) *nf* pair, brace.
paisible (pɛˈzi:bl) *adj* **1** peaceful, calm. **2** quiet.
paître* (pɛtr) *vt* **1** graze (cattle). **2** feed upon. *vi* **1** graze. **2** feed.
paix (pɛ) *nf* **1** peace. **2** quiet.
Pakistan (paki:ˈstɑ̃) *nm* Pakistan. **pakistanais** *adj,n* Pakistani.
palace (paˈlas) *nm* luxury hotel.
palais[1] (paˈlɛ) *nm* palace. **palais de justice** law courts.
palais[2] (paˈlɛ) *nm* **1** palate. **2** sense of taste.
pâle (pɑl) *adj* **1** pale. **2** faint. **pâleur** *nf* paleness.
palefrenier (palfrəˈnje:) *nm* groom.
Palestine (palɛˈsti:n) *nf* Palestine. **palestinien, -ienne** *adj,n* Palestinian.
palette (paˈlɛt) *nf* **1** bat. **2** blade (of an oar). **3** palette.
palier (palˈje:) *nm* (of stairs) landing.
pâlir (pɑˈli:r) *vi* **1** turn or grow pale. **2** grow dim. **3** fade. *vt* make pale.

palissader (pali:sa'de:) *vt* enclose, fence in. **palissade** *nf* fence.
palmarès (palma'rɛs) *nm* prize list.
palme (palm) *nf* **1** palm (branch). **2** victory. **palmier** *nm* palm tree.
palombe (pa'lɔ̃b) *nf* woodpigeon.
palourde (pa'lu:rd) *nf* clam.
palper (pal'pe:) *vt* **1** feel. **2** finger.
palpiter (palpi:'te:) *vi* **1** quiver. **2** throb.
paludisme (paly'di:sm) *nm* malaria.
pâmer (pɑ'me:) *vi* faint. **se pâmer de** *vr* be overcome with.
pamphlet (pɑ̃'flɛ) *nm* pamphlet.
pamplemousse (pɑ̃plə'mu:s) *nm* grapefruit.
pan (pɑ̃) *nm* **1** flap (of a garment). **2** section. **3** side.
panache (pa'naʃ) *nm* **1** plume. **2** tuft. **avoir du panache** have style or dash. **panaché** *adj* **1** mixed. **2** plumed. *nm* shandy.
panais (pa'nɛ) *nm* parsnip.
pancarte (pɑ̃'kart) *nf* **1** placard. **2** poster, bill.
pancréas (pɑ̃kre:'ɑs) *nm* pancreas.
panda (pɑ̃'da) *nm* panda.
panier (pa'nje:) *nm* basket. **gros panier** hamper.
panique (pa'ni:k) *adj,nf* panic.
panne (pan) *nf* **1** breakdown. **2** failure.
panneau, -aux (pa'no) *nm* **1** snare. **2** trap. **3** panel. **4** board. **panneau-réclame** *nm, pl* **panneaux-réclames** hoarding.
panorama (panɔra'ma) *nm* panorama. **panoramique** *adj* panoramic.
panse (pɑ̃s) *nf* **1** *inf* belly. **2** paunch.
panser (pɑ̃'se:) *vt* **1** *med* dress. **2** groom (a horse). **pansement** *nm med* dressing.
pantalon (pɑ̃ta'lɔ̃) *nm* trousers.
panteler (pɑt'le:) *vi* **1** pant. **2** gasp.
panthère (pɑ̃'tɛr) *nf* panther.
pantomime (pɑ̃tɔ'mi:m) *nf* **1** pantomime. **2** mime.
pantoufle (pɑ̃'tu:fl) *nf* slipper.
paon (pɑ̃) *nm* peacock.
papa (pa'pa) *nm inf* dad.
pape (pap) *nm* pope. **papal, -aux** (pa'pal, -'po) *adj* papal. **papauté** *nf* papacy.
papeterie (pap'tri:) *nf* **1** stationer's shop. **2** stationery. **papetier** *nm* stationer.
papier (pa'pje:) *nm* **1** paper. **2** document. **papier à écrire** notepaper. **papier buvard** blotting paper. **papier de verre** sandpaper. **papier ministre** foolscap. **papier teint** wallpaper.
papillon (papi:'jɔ̃) *nm* **1** butterfly. **2** moth. **3** leaflet. **4** ticket.
paquebot (pak'bo) *nm* **1** liner. **2** steamer.
pâquerette (pɑk'rɛt) *nf* daisy.
Pâques (pak) *nf pl* Easter. **pâque** *nf* Passover.
paquet (pa'kɛ) *nm* **1** parcel. **2** packet. **3** bundle.
paqueter (pak'te:) *vt* parcel up.
par (par) *prep* **1** by. **2** through. **3** in. **4** out of, for the sake of. **par-ci par-là** here and there. **par-dessous** *prep,adv* under, underneath. **par-dessus** *prep,adv* over. **par ici/là** this/that way.
parabole (para'bɔl) *nf* parable.
parachuter (paraʃy'te:) *vt* parachute. **parachute** *nm* parachute. **parachutiste** *nm* **1** parachutist. **2** paratrooper.
parade (pa'rad) *nf* **1** parade. **2** show, display.
paradigme (para'di:gm) *nm* paradigm.
paradis (para'di:) *nm* **1** paradise. **2** *inf Th* gallery.
paradoxe (para'dɔks) *nm* paradox. **paradoxal, -aux** (paradɔk'sal, -'so) *adj* paradoxical.
paraffine (para'fi:n) *nf* paraffin.
parages (pa'raʒ) *nm pl* district, area.
paragraphe (para'graf) *nm* paragraph.
paraître* (pa'rɛtr) *vi* **1** appear. **2** show, be visible. **3** seem. **4** be published. *v imp* seem. **faire paraître** publish.
parallèle (paral'lɛl) *adj* parallel.
paralyser (parali:'ze:) *vt* paralyse. **paralysie** *nf* paralysis.
paraphraser (parafrɑ'ze:) *vt* paraphrase. **paraphrase** *nf* paraphrase.
parapluie (para'plɥi:) *nm* umbrella.
parasite (para'zi:t) *nm* **1** parasite. **2** *pl tech* interference. *adj* parasitic.
parc (park) *nm* **1** park. **2** pen. **parc de stationnement** car park.
parcelle (par'sɛl) *nf* **1** particle. **2** plot, patch.
parce que (pars kə) *conj* because.
parchemin (parʃə'mɛ̃) *nm* parchment.
parcomètre (parkɔ'mɛtr) *nm* parking meter.
parcourir* (parku:'ri:r) *vt* **1** travel through. **2** wander. **3** glance through.
parcours (par'ku:r) *nm* **1** distance. **2** route. **3** course.
pardessus (pardə'sy) *nm* overcoat.
pardon (par'dɔ̃) *nm* **1** forgiveness. **2** pardon. **pardonner** (pardɔ'ne:) *vt* **1** pardon. **2** forgive. **3** excuse.
pareil, -eille (pa'rɛj) *adj* **1** like, similar. **2** same. **3** such.

parement (par'mɑ̃) *nm* **1** ornament. **2** facing. **3** cuff (of a coat, etc.).
parent (pa'rɑ̃) *nm* **1** parent. **2** relative.
parenthèse (parɑ̃'tɛzʃ *nf* **1** parenthesis. **2** bracket.
parer[1] (pa're:) *vt* **1** decorate. **2** adorn. **3** prepare. **se parer de** *vr* dress oneself in.
parer[2] (pa're:) *vt* **1** ward off. **2** avoid. **pare-boue** *nm invar* mudguard. **pare-brise** *nm invar* windscreen. **pare-choc** *nm invar* bumper.
paresseux, -euse (parɛ'sœ, -'sœz) *adj* lazy.
parfait (par'fɛ) *adj* **1** perfect. **2** complete.
parfois (par'fwa) *adv* sometimes, occasionally.
parfum (par'fœ̃) *nm* **1** perfume. **2** scent. **3** flavour.
parfumer (parfy'me:) *vt* **1** scent, perfume. **2** flavour.
pari (pa'ri:) *nm* bet. **parier** *vt* bet.
Paris (pa'ri:) *nm* Paris. **parisien, -ienne** (pari:-'zjɛ̃, -'zjɛn) *adj,n* Parisian.
parité (pari:'te:) *nf* parity, equality.
parjure (par'ʒyr) *nm* perjury.
parking (par'ki:ɲ) *nm* car park.
parlement (parlə'mɑ̃) *nm* parliament.
parler (par'le:) *vi* **1** speak. **2** talk. **tu parles!** you can say that again! ~*nm* speech. **parleur, -euse** ((par'lœr,-'lœz) *nm,f* speaker. **parloir** *nm* parlour.
parmi (par'mi:) *prep* among, amid.
parodie (parɔ'di:) *nf* parody.
paroi (par'wa) *nf* **1** partition. **2** wall. **3** lining.
paroisse (par'was) *nf* parish.
parole (pa'rɔl) *nf* **1** word. **2** remark. **3** parole. **4** speech.
parquet (par'kɛ) *nm* **1** floor. **2** *cap* magistrate.
parrain (pa'rɛ̃) *nm* **1** godfather. **2** patron.
parrainer (parɛ'ne:) *vt* sponsor.
pars (par) *v* see **partir.**
parsemer (parsə'me:) *vt* sprinkle, scatter.
part (par) *nf* **1** share, portion. **2** participation. **3** part. **à part** apart. **autre/nulle/quelque part** elsewhere/nowhere/somewhere. **d'autre part** moreover.
partager (parta'ʒe:) *vt* **1** divide. **2** share. **partage** *nm* **1** division. **2** sharing. **3** share.
partance (par'tɑ̃s) *nf* departure. **en partance pour** bound for.
partenaire (partə'nɛr) *nm,f* partner.
parterre (par'tɛr) *nm* **1** flowerbed. **2** *Th* stalls.
parti (par'ti:) *nm* **1** party. **2** side, part. **3** decision. **4** advantage. **parti pris** bias.
partial, -aux (par'sjal, -'sjo) *adj* partial, biased. **partialité** *nf* partiality, bias.
participe (parti:'si:p) *nm* participle. **participe passé** past participle.
participer (parti:si:'pe:) *vi* **participer à 1** participate in. **2** take part in. **participer de** partake of. **participant** *nm* participant. **participation** *nf* **1** participation. **2** interest, share.
particulariser (parti:kylari:'ze:) *vt* specify.
particule (parti:'kyl) *nf* particle.
particulier, -ière (parti:ky'lje:, -'ljɛr) *adj* **1** particular. **2** special. **3** characteristic. **4** private. *nm* private individual.
partie (par'ti:) *nf* **1** part. **2** party. **3** game. **4** client. **partie carrée** foursome. **partie nulle** *sport* draw. **partiel, -elle** (par'sjɛl) *adj* partial, part.
partir* (par'ti:r) *vi* (*aux* être) **1** depart. **2** leave. **3** set off. **4** start. **à partir de** as from.
partisan (parti:'zɑ̃) *nm* partisan, supporter.
partout (par'tu:) *adv* everywhere. **partout où** wherever. **un peu partout** all over the place.
paru (pa'ry) *v* see **paraître.**
parure (pa'ryr) *nf* **1** ornament. **2** dress. **3** set (of clothing, etc.).
parvenir* (parvə'ni:r) *vi* (*aux* être) **parvenir à 1** reach. **2** succeed. **parvenu** *nm* self-made man.
pas[1] (pɑ) *nm* **1** pace, stride. **2** step. **3** footstep. **4** doorstep. **5** pass. **à pas de loup** slyly.
pas[2] (pɑ) *adv* not. **ne...pas** not. **pas du tout** not at all.
passage (pɑ'saʒ) *nm* **1** passage. **2** crossing. **3** way. **passage à niveau** level crossing. **passage clouté** pedestrian crossing. **passage interdit** no thoroughfare. **passage souterrain** subway. **passager, -ère** (pɑsa'ʒe:, -'ʒɛr) *adj* **1** migratory. **2** momentary. **3** busy. *nm,f* passenger. **passager clandestin** stowaway.
passer (pɑ'se:) *vi* (*aux* avoir or être) **1** go by or through. **2** pass. **3** call. **4** cease. **5** become. *vt* **1** cross. **2** pass. **3** show. **4** spend. **5** surpass. **6** filter, strain. **en passant** by the way. **passer un examen** sit an exam. **se passer** *vr* **1** happen. **2** decay. **se passer de** do without. **passe** *nf* **1** passing. **2** permit. **3** pass. **passé** *adj,nm* past. *prep* after, beyond.
passeport (pɑs'pɔr) *nm* passport.
passerelle (pɑs'rɛl) *nf* footbridge. **passerelle de service** *naut* gangway.
passe-temps *nm invar* pastime.
passif, -ive (pa'si:f, -'si:v) *adj* passive.
passion (pɑ'sjɔ̃) *nf* passion.

passionner (pasjɔ'ne:) *vt* **1** interest greatly. **2** thrill, exite. **se passionner pour** *vr* become very fond of. **passionnant** (pasjɔ'nɑ̃) *adj* thrilling. **passionné** *adj* **1** passionate. **2** ardent. *nm* enthusiast.

pastel (pa'stɛl) *nm* **1** crayon. **2** pastel.

pastèque (pa'stɛk) *nf* watermelon.

pasteuriser (pastœri:'ze:) *vt* pasteurize.

pastille (pa'sti:j) *nf* pastille.

pastis (pa'sti:s) *nm* **1** aniseed aperitif. **2** *inf* muddle.

pat (pat) *nm invar* stalemate.

pataud (pa'to) *adj* clumsy.

patauger (pato'ʒe:) *vi* **1** paddle. **2** flounder.

pâte (pɑt) *nf* **1** paste. **2** dough. **3** *pl* pasta. **pâte à modeler** Plasticine *Tdmk*. **pâte dentifrice** toothpaste. **pâte lisse** batter.

pâté (pɑ'te:) *nm* **1** meat paste. **2** blot. **3** block (of houses). **pâté en croûte** pie.

patelin (pat'lɛ̃) *adj* **1** glib. **2** wheedling. *nm inf* place, locality.

patelle (pa'tɛl) *nf* limpet.

patenôtre (pat'notr) *nf* Lord's Prayer.

patent (pa'tɑ̃) *adj* **1** patent. **2** obvious.

patenter (patɑ̃'te:) *vt* license. **patente** *nf* **1** licence. **2** tax.

patère (pa'tɛr) *nf* peg (for coats, etc.).

paterne (pa'tɛrn) *adj* benevolent, kind.

paternel, -elle (patɛr'nɛl) *adj* paternal.

pâteux, -euse (pɑ'tœ, -'tœz) *adj* **1** pasty. **2** thick. **3** dull.

pathétique (pate:'ti:k) *adj* **1** pathetic. **2** touching. *nm* pathos.

pathologie (patɔlɔ'ʒi:) *nf* pathology. **pathologique** *adj* pathological. **pathologiste** *nm,f* pathologist.

patience (pa'sjɑ̃s) *nf* patience. **patiemment** *adv* patiently. **patient** *adj* **1** patient. **2** long-suffering. *nm med* patient.

patin (pa'tɛ̃) *nm* skate. **patin à roulette** roller-skate.

patiner (pati:'ne:) *vi* **1** skate. **2** skid. **patinage** *nm* skating. **patinoire** *nf* skating rink.

pâtir (pɑ'ti:r) *vi* suffer.

pâtisserie (pɑti:s'ri:) *nf* **1** pastry. **2** cake. **3** cake shop.

patois (pa'twa) *nm* **1** dialect. **2** jargon.

patouiller (patu:'je:) *vi* splash, flounder. *vt* **1** finger. **2** meddle with.

patrie (pa'tri:) *nf* fatherland, native country.

patrimoine (patri:'mwan) *nm* heritage.

patriote (patri:'ɔt) *nm,f* patriot. *adj* patriotic.

patriotique *adj* patriotic. **patriotisme** *nm* patriotism.

patron (pa'trɔ̃) *nm* **1** patron. **2** proprietor. **3** patron saint. **4** employer. **5** skipper. **6** *inf* boss. **7** pattern (for a dress). **patronage** *nm* **1** patronage. **2** club. **patronat** *nm* **1** body of employers. **2** management.

patrouiller (patru:'je:) *vi* patrol. **patrouille** *nf* patrol.

patte (pat) *nf* **1** *zool* paw, foot, leg. **2** flap. **patte de derrière** hindleg. **patte de devant** foreleg. **patte de mouche** scrawl.

pâture (pɑ'tyr) *nf* **1** pasture. **2** food.

paume (pom) *nf anat* palm.

paupière (po'pjɛr) *nf* eyelid.

pause (poz) *nf* **1** pause. **2** rest. **pause café** tea-break.

pauvre (povr) *adj* **1** poor. **2** unfortunate. **3** wretched. **pauvreté** *nf* poverty.

se pavaner (pava'ne:) *vr* strut about.

paver (pa've:) *vt* pave. **pavé** *nm* **1** pavement. **2** highway. **3** slab,flagstone.

pavillon (pavi:'jɔ̃) *nm* **1** pavilion. **2** tent. **3** flag.

pavot (pa'vo) *nm* poppy.

payer (pɑ'je:) *vt* pay.

pays (pe:'i:) *nm* **1** land, country. **2** district. **3** nation. **4** home. **pays chauds** *nm pl* tropics. **paysage** *nm* **1** landscape. **2** scenery. **paysan, -anne** (pe:i:'zɑ̃, -'zan) *adj,n* **1** peasant. **2** rustic.

Pays-Bas *nm pl* Netherlands.

péage (pe:'aʒ) *nm* toll.

peau, peaux (po) *nf* **1** *anat* skin. **2** *zool* fur, hide, pelt. **3** peel. **peau de mouton** sheepskin. **peau-rouge** *nm, pl* **peaux-rouges** Red Indian.

pêche[1] (pɛʃ) *nf* peach.

pêche[2] (pɛʃ) *nf* **1** fishing. **2** catch (of fish). **aller à la pêche** go fishing.

pécher (pe:'ʃe:) *vi* sin. **péché** *nm* sin. **pécheur, -eresse** (pe:'ʃœr, pɛʃ'rɛs) *nm,f* **1** sinner. **2** offender. *adj* sinful.

pêcher[1] (pe:'ʃe:) *nm* peach tree.

pêcher[2] (pe:'ʃe:) *vt* fish for. **pêcher à la ligne** angle. **pêcheur** *nm* fisherman.

pédaler (pɛda'le:) *vi* **1** pedal. **2** *inf* cycle. **pédale** *nf* pedal.

pédéraste (pe:dɛ'rast) *nm* homosexual.

pédicure (pe:di:'kyr) *nm,f* chiropodist.

peignant (pɛ'ɲɑ̃) *v* see **peindre.**

peigner (pɛ'ɲe:) *vt* comb. **peigne** *nm* **1** comb. **2** *zool* scallop. **bien/mal peigné** trim/slovenly. **peignoir** *nm* dressing-gown.

peindre* (pɛ̃dr) *vt* **1** paint. **2** depict. **3** describe.

peine (pɛn) *nf* **1** punishment. **2** sorrow. **3** trouble. **4** difficulty. **à peine** hardly, scarcely.
peiner (pɛ'ne:) *vt* **1** grieve. **2** tire. *vi* toil.
peint (pɛ̃) *v* see **peindre.**
peintre (pɛ̃tr) *nm* **1** painter. **2** decorator. **peinture** *nf* **1** painting. **2** picture. **3** paint.
péjoratif, -ive (pe:ʒɔra'ti:f, -'ti:v) *adj* pejorative, disparaging.
pelage (pə'laʒ) *nm* coat, fur (of an animal).
pêle-mêle (pɛl'mɛl) *adv* pell-mell. *nm invar* jumble.
peler (pə'le:) *vi,vt* peel. *vt* skin.
pèlerin (pɛl'rɛ̃) *nm* pilgrim. **pèlerinage** *nm* pilgrimage. **pèlerine** *nf* cloak.
pélican (pe:li:'kɑ̃) *nm* pelican.
pelle (pɛl) *nf* **1** shovel. **2** scoop. **pelle à poussière** dustpan.
pelleter (pɛl'te:) *vt* shovel.
pelletier (pɛl'tje:) *nm* furrier.
pellicule (pɛlli:'kyl) *nf* **1** film, layer. **2** *phot* film. **3** *pl* dandruff.
pelote (plɔt) *nf* **1** ball (of wool). **2** wad. **pelote à épingles** pincushion.
peloton (plɔ'tɔ̃) *nm* **1** ball (of wool). **2** group. **3** squad.
pelotonner (plɔtɔ'ne:) *vt* wind into a ball. **se pelotonner** *vr* **1** curl up. **2** crowd together.
pelouse (plu:z) *nf* lawn.
pelu (pə'ly) *adj* hairy.
pelure (plyr) *nf* **1** peel. **2** rind.
pénal, -aux (pe:'nal, -'no) *adj* penal.
pénaliser (pe:nali:'ze:) *vt* penalize. **pénalité** *nf* penalty.
penaud (pə'no) *adj* shamefaced.
pencher (pɑ̃'ʃe:) *vi* **1** lean. **2** slope. **3** incline. *vt* tilt. **se pencher** *vr* **1** bend. **2** lean. **penchant** *adj* sloping. *nm* **1** slope. **2** tendency. **3** taste.
pendant[1] (pɑ̃'dɑ̃) *adj* **1** hanging. **2** flabby. *nm* **1** pendant. **2** pair, match.
pendant[2] (pɑ̃'dɑ̃) *prep,adv* during. **pendant que** *conj* whilst.
pendiller (pɑ̃di:'je:) *vi* dangle.
pendre (pɑ̃dr) *vt* hang (up). *vi* **1** hang. **2** sag. **se pendre à** *vr* cling to. **pendule** *nm* pendulum.
pêne (pɛn) *nm* bolt, latch.
pénétrer (pe:ne:'tre:) *vi* **1** enter. **2** break into. *vt* **1** penetrate. **2** fathom. **pénétrant** *adj* **1** penetrating. **2** sharp. **3** keen.
pénible (pe:'ni:bl) *adj* **1** hard. **2** laborious. **3** painful. **4** *inf* annoying.
péniche (pe:'ni:ʃ) *nf* barge.
pénicilline (pe:ni:si:'li:n) *nf* penicillin.
péninsule (pe:nɛ̃'syl) *nf* peninsula.
pénis (pe:'ni:s) *nm* penis.
pénitent (pe:ni:'tɑ̃) *adj,n* penitent. **pénitence** *nf* **1** repentance. **2** penance.
penser (pɑ̃'se:) *vi,vt* think. *vt* **1** imagine. **2** believe. **penser à** think about. **penser de** think of, have an opinion of. **penser faire** expect to do. ~*nm* thought. **pensée** *nf* **1** thought. **2** *bot* pansy.
pension (pɑ̃'sjɔ̃) *nf* **1** pension. **2** board and lodging. **3** boarding school. **pension de famille** boarding house. **pensionnat** *nm* boarding school.
pentagone (pɛ̃ta'gɔn) *nm* pentagon. *adj* pentagonal.
pente (pɑ̃t) *nf* **1** slope. **2** gradient.
Pentecôte (pɑ̃t'kot) *nf* **1** Whitsun. **2** Pentecost.
pénurie (pe:ny'ri:) *nf* **1** scarcity. **2** lack. **3** poverty.
pépier (pe:'pje:) *vi* chirp.
pépin (pe:'pɛ̃) *nm* **1** pip. **2** *bot* stone. **3** *inf* hitch. **pepinière** *nf bot* nursery.
pépite (pe:'pi:t) *nf* nugget.
perception (pɛrsɛp'sjɔ̃) *nf* **1** collection. **2** tax-office. **3** perception. **percepteur, -trice** (pɛrsɛp'tœr, -'tri:s) *adj* discerning. *nm* tax-collector. **perceptible (à l'oreille)** *adj* audible. **perceptif, -ive** (pɛrsɛp'ti:f, -'ti:v) *adj* perceptive.
percer (pɛr'se:) *vt* **1** pierce. **2** break through. **3** penetrate. *vi* come through. **perçant** *adj* **1** piercing. **2** sharp. **3** shrill. **perce-neige** *nm invar* snowdrop. **perce-oreille** *nm, pl* **perce-oreilles** earwig.
percevoir* (pɛrsə'vwar) *vt* **1** perceive. **2** collect.
perche[1] (pɛrʃ) *nf zool* perch.
perche[2] (pɛrʃ) *nf* pole.
percher (pɛr'ʃe:) *vi* **1** perch. **2** roost. **perchoir** *nm* **1** perch. **2** roost.
perclus (pɛr'kly) *adj* **1** crippled. **2** stiff.
percussion (pɛrky'sjɔ̃) *nf* **1** impact. **2** *mus* percussion.
perdre (pɛrdr) *vt* **1** lose. **2** ruin. **3** waste. **4** leak. *vi* **1** deteriorate. **2** leak. **se perdre** *vr* **1** get lost. **2** disappear.
perdrix (pɛr'dri:) *nf* partridge.
père (pɛr) *nm* father.
perfection (pɛrfɛk'sjɔ̃) *nf* perfection.
perfide (pɛr'fi:d) *adj* treacherous.
perforer (pɛrfɔ're:) *vt* **1** perforate. **2** punch. **3** drill. **4** puncture. **perforation** *nf* **1** perforation. **2** hole.
péril (pe:'ri:l) *nm* peril, danger.

périmé (pe:ri:'me:) *adj* out-of-date.
périmètre (pe:ri:'mɛtr) *nm* **1** perimeter. **2** area.
période (pe:'rjɔd) *nf* **1** period. **2** era. **périodique** *adj* periodical. *nm* periodical (magazine).
périphérie (pe:ri:fe:'ri:) *nf* **1** periphery. **2** outskirts. **boulevard périphérique** *nm* ring-road.
périr (pe:'ri:r) *vi* **1** perish. **2** be destroyed. **3** die. **périssable** *adj* perishable.
périscope (pe:ri:'skɔp) *nm* periscope.
périssoire (pe:ri:'swar) *nf* canoe.
perle (pɛrl) *nf* **1** pearl. **2** bead.
permanent (pɛrma'nɑ̃) *adj* **1** permanent. **2** continuous. **permanence** *nf* permanence.
perméable (pɛrme:'abl) *adj* porous.
permettre* (pɛr'mɛtr) *vt* **1** permit. **2** allow. **3** enable.
permis (pɛr'mi:) *adj* **1** allowed. **2** permissible. *nm* **1** permit. **2** licence. **permis de conduire** *nm* driving licence.
permission (pɛrmi:'sjɔ̃) *nf* **1** permission. **2** *mil* leave.
permutation (pɛrmyta'sjɔ̃) *nf* **1** exchange. **2** permutation.
pernicieux, -euse (pɛrni:'sjœ, -'sjœz) *adj* **1** injurious. **2** harmful.
peroxyde (pɛrɔk'si:d) *nm* peroxide.
perpendiculaire (pɛrpɑ̃di:ky'lɛr) *adj,nf* perpendicular.
perpétuer (pɛrpe:'tɥe:) *vt* perpetuate. **se perpétuer** *vr* **1** endure. **2** survive. **perpétuel, -elle** (pɛrpe:'tɥɛl) *adj* **1** perpetual. **2** constant. **perpétuité** *nf* endlessness. **à perpétuité** for ever, for life.
perplexe (pɛr'plɛks) *adj* perplexed, puzzled.
perquisition (pɛrki:zi:'sjɔ̃) *nf* house search.
perron (pɛ'rɔ̃) *nm* flight of steps.
perroquet (pɛrɔ'kɛ) *nm* parrot.
perruque (pɛ'ryk) *nf* wig.
persécuter (pɛrse:ky'te:) *vt* **1** persecute. **2** harass. **persécution** *nf* persecution.
persévérer (pɛrse:ve:'re:) *vi* **1** persevere. **2** persist. **persévérance** (pɛrse:vɛ'rɑ̃s) *nf* perseverance. **persévérant** (pɛrse:vɛ'rɑ̃) *adj* **1** persevering. **2** steadfast.
persienne (pɛr'sjɛn) *nf* shutter.
persifler (pɛrsi:'fle:) *vt* mock.
persil (pɛr'si:l) *nm* parsley.
persister (pɛrsi:'ste:) *vi* **persister à** persist in. **persistance** *nf* persistance. **persistant** *adj* **1** persistent **2** lasting.
personne (pɛr'sɔn) *nf* **1** person. **2** individual. *pron* anyone, anybody. **ne...personne** no one, nobody. **personnage** *nm* **1** person. **2** *lit* character. **personnalité** *nf* **1** personality. **2** important person. **3** personal remark. **personnel, -elle** (pɛrsɔ'nɛl) *adj* personal. *nm* personnel, staff.
personnifier (pɛrsɔni:'fje:) *vt* **1** personify. **2** impersonate.
perspective (pɛrspɛk'ti:v) *nf* **1** outlook. **2** prospect. **3** perspective.
perspicace (pɛrspi:'kas) *adj* shrewd. **perspicacité** *nf* **1** insight. **2** shrewdness.
persuader (pɛrsɥa'de:) *vt* **1** persuade. **2** convince. **3** induce. **persuasif, -ive** (pɛrsɥa'zi:f, -'zi:v) *adj* **1** persuasive. **2** convincing. **persuasion** *nf* **1** persuasion. **2** belief.
perte (pɛrt) *nf* **1** loss. **2** waste. **3** ruin. **4** death. **à perte de vue** as far as the eye can see.
pertinent (pɛrti:'nɑ̃) *adj* pertinent, relevant. **pertinemment** (pɛrti:na'mɑ̃) *adv* pertinently. **pertinence** *nf* relevance.
perturbateur, -trice (pɛrtyrba'tœr, -'tri:s) *adj* disturbing. *nm,f* agitator. **perturbation** *nf* disturbance.
pervers (pɛr'vɛr) *adj* **1** perverse. **2** depraved.
pervertir (pɛrvɛr'ti:r) *vt* **1** pervert. **2** corrupt. **perverti** *nm* pervert.
peser (pə'ze:) *vt* weigh. *vi* be heavy. **pesage** *nm* **1** weighing. **2** *sport* paddock. **pesant** *adj* **1** heavy. **2** clumsy. *nm* weight. **pesanteur** *nf* **1** weight. **2** *sci* gravity. **3** heaviness. **4** dullness.
pessimisme (pɛsi:'mi:sm) *nm* pessimism. **pessimiste** *adj* pessimistic. *nm,f* pessimist.
peste (pɛst) *nf* **1** plague. **2** *inf* pest.
pet (pɛ) *nm sl* fart.
pétale (pɛ'tal) *nm* petal.
pétanque (pe:'tɑ̃k) *nf* game of bowls.
pétarader (pe:tara'de:) *vi* backfire.
pétard (pɛ'tar) *nm* **1** blast. **2** firework, banger. **3** *inf* row, noise.
pet-de-nonne (pɛdə'nɔn) *nm, pl* **pets-de-nonne** *cul* fritter.
pétiller (pe:ti:'je:) *vi* **1** crackle. **2** sparkle.
petit (pə'ti:) *adj* **1** small, little. **2** petty, insignificant. **en petit** in miniature. **petit-enfant** *nm, pl* **petits-enfants** grandchild. **petite-fille** *nf, pl* **petites-filles** granddaughter. **petit-fils** *nm, pl* **petits-fils** grandson. **petitesse** *nf* **1** smallness. **2** pettiness.
pétition (pe:ti:'sjɔ̃) *nf* petition.
pétrifier (pe:tri:'fje:) *vt* petrify.
pétrir (pe:'tri:r) *vt* **1** knead. **2** mould.

pétrole (pe:'trɔl) *nm* petroleum. **pétrole brut** crude oil. **pétrolier, -ière** (pe:trɔ'lje:, -'ljɛr) *adj* oil. *nm* tanker. **pétrolifère** *adj* oil-producing.

pétulant (pe:ty'lɑ̃) *adj* lively.

peu (pœ) *adv* **1** little. **2** few. **3** not very. *nm* little, bit. **à peu près** almost, more or less.

peupler (pœ'ple:) *vt* people, populate. **peuple** *nm* **1** people. **2** nation. **3** masses.

peuplier (pœpli:'e:) *nm* poplar tree.

peur (pœr) *nf* **1** fear. **2** fright. **3** dread. **peureux, -euse** (pœ'rœ, -'rœz) *adj* **1** timid. **2** shy. **3** nervous.

peut (pœ) *v* see **pouvoir.**

peut-être (pœ'tɛtr) *adv* **1** perhaps. **2** maybe. **3** possibly.

peux (pœ) *v* see **pouvoir.**

phallus (fal'lys) *nm* phallus.

phare (far) *nm* **1** lighthouse. **2** headlamp.

pharmacie (farma'si:) *nf* **1** pharmacy. **2** chemist's shop. **pharmacien, -ienne** (farma'sjɛ̃, -'sjɛn) *nm,f* **1** chemist. **2** pharmacist.

pharynx (fa'rɛ̃ks) *nm* pharynx.

phase (fɑz) *nf* **1** phase. **2** stage.

phénix (fe:'ni:ks) *nm* **1** phoenix. **2** paragon.

phénomène (fe:nɔ'mɛn) *nm* **1** phenomenon. **2** *inf* freak. **phénoménal, -aux** (fe:nɔmɛ'nal, -'no) *adj* **1** phenomenal. **2** extraordinary.

philanthropie (fi:lɑ̃trɔ'pi:) *nf* philanthropy. **philanthrope** *nm,f* philanthropist.

philatélie (fi:late:'li:) *nf* philately. **philatéliste** *nm,f* philatelist.

philistin (fi:li:'stɛ̃) *adj,nm* Philistine.

philosophie (fi:lɔzɔ'fi:) *nf* philosophy. **philosophe** *nm,f* philosopher. *adj* philosophical. **philosophique** *adj* philosophical.

phobie (fɔ'bi:) *nf* phobia.

phonétique (fɔne:'ti:k) *adj* phonetic. *nf* phonetics.

phonographe (fɔnɔ'graf) *nm* gramophone.

phoque (fɔk) *nm* seal.

phosphate (fɔs'fat) *nm* phosphate.

phosphore (fɔs'fɔr) *nm* phosphorus.

photo (fɔ'to) *nf* photo.

photocopier (fɔtɔkɔ'pje:) *vt* photocopy. **photocopie** *nf* photocopy.

photographier (fɔtɔgra'fje:) *vt* photograph. **photographe** *nm,f* photographer. **photographie** *nf* **1** photography. **2** photograph. **photographique** *adj* photographic.

phrase (frɑz) *nf* **1** sentence. **2** phrase.

physiologie (fi:zjɔlɔ'ʒi:) *nf* physiology. **physiologique** *adj* physiological. **physiologiste** *nm,f* physiologist.

physiothérapie (fi:zjɔte:ra'pi:) *nf* physiotherapy. **physiothérapiste** *nm,f* physiotherapist.

physique[1] (fi:'zi:k) *adj* physical. *nm* physique.

physique[2] (fi:'zi:k) *nf* physics. **physicien, -ienne** (fi:zi:'sjɛ̃, -'sjɛn) *nm,f* physicist.

piaffer (pja'fe:) *vi* **1** prance. **2** paw the ground.

piailler (pjɑ'je:) *vi* **1** chirp. **2** squeal.

piano (pja'no) *nm* piano. **piano à queue** grand piano. **pianiste** *nm,f* pianist.

piauler (pjo'le:) *vi* whine.

pic[1] (pi:k) *nm* woodpecker.

pic[2] (pi:k) *nm* pick.

pic[3] (pi:k) *nm* peak. **à pic** sheer. **tomber à pic** **1** fall sheer. **2** happen just in time.

picoter (pi:kɔ'te:) *vt* **1** peck (at). **2** prick. **3** sting. *vi* **1** smart. **2** tingle.

pie (pi:) *nf* magpie.

pièce (pjɛs) *nf* **1** piece. **2** part. **3** room (in a house). **4** fragment. **5** chessman. **à la pièce** separately. **pièce de monnaie** coin. **pièce de théâtre** play.

pied (pje:) *nm* **1** foot. **2** leg (of a chair, etc.). **3** stem. **à pied** on foot. **en pied** full-length. **mettre sur pied** establish, start. **pied bot** club foot. **pied-noir** *nm, pl* **pieds-noirs** Algerian of French origin. **pied plat** flat-footed.

piédestal, -aux (pje:dɛ'stal, -'sto) *nm* pedestal.

piéger (pje:'ʒe:) *vt* trap. **piège** *nm* trap.

pierre (pjɛr) *nf* stone. **pierre à briquet** flint. **pierre à chaux** limestone. **pierre précieuse** gem. **pierres de gué** *nf pl* stepping stones.

piété (pje:'te:) *nf* **1** piety. **2** devotion.

piétiner (pje:ti:'ne:) *vt* **1** trample. **2** tread under foot. **3** stamp.

piéton (pje:'tɔ̃) *nm* pedestrian.

pieu, pieux (pjœ) *nm* stake, pole.

pieuvre (pjœvr) *nf* octopus.

pieux, pieuse (pjœ, pjœz) *adj* pious, devout.

pigeon (pi:'ʒɔ̃) *nm* pigeon.

pigment (pi:g'mɑ̃) *nm* pigment.

pignon (pi:'ɲɔ̃) *nm* **1** gable. **2** pinion.

pile[1] (pi:l) *nf* **1** pile, heap. **2** battery.

pile[2] (pi:l) *nf* reverse (of a coin). **pile ou face** heads or tails.

piler (pi:'le:) *vt* **1** pound. **2** crush. **3** grind.

pilier (pi:l'je:) *nm* **1** pillar. **2** column.

piller (pi:'je:) *vt* plunder, pillage. **pillage** *nm* pillage, looting.

piloter (pi:lɔ'te:) *vt* **1** pilot. **2** fly. **pilote** *nm* pilot.

pilule (pi:'lyl) *nf* **1** pill. **2** contraceptive pill.

piment (pi:'mɑ̃) *nm* **1** pimento. **2** capsicum.

pimenter (pi:mɑ̃'te:) *vt* season with spices.

pimpant (pɛ̃'pɑ̃) *adj* smart.

pin (pɛ̃) *nm* pine.

pinacle (pi:'nakl) *nm* pinnacle.

pinceau, -aux (pɛ̃'so) *nm* paintbrush.

pincer (pɛ̃'se:) *vt* **1** pinch. **2** nip. **3** *mus* pluck. **4** catch (a thief). **pince** *nf* **1** grip. **2** pincers. **3** forceps. **4** clip. **5** claw. **6** dart (in clothes). **pince à épiler** tweezers. **pince à linge** clothes peg. **pincé** *adj* **1** affected. **2** prim. **pincée** *nf* pinch.

pingouin (pɛ̃'gwɛ̃) *nm* penguin.

Ping-pong (pi:ɲ'pɔɲ) *nm invar Tdmk* table-tennis.

pinson (pɛ̃'sɔ̃) *nm* chaffinch.

piocher (pjɔ'ʃe:) *vt* **1** dig (with a pick). **2** *sl* swot. **3** *game* pick up (a card, etc.). **pioche** *nf* pick.

pion (pjɔ̃) *nm* **1** *educ* junior master. **2** *game* pawn.

pionnier (pjɔ'nje:) *nm* pioneer.

pipe (pi:p) *nf* **1** pipe. **2** tube.

pipette (pi:'pɛt) *nf* pipette.

piquant (pi:'kɑ̃) *adj* **1** stinging. **2** cutting. **3** tart. **4** piquant. *nm* **1** point, pith. **2** sting. **3** quill.

pique[1] (pi:k) *nf mil* pike. *nm game* spade.

pique[2] (pi:k) *nf* pique, spite.

piquer (pi:'ke:) *vt* **1** prick. **2** sting. **3** offend. **4** excite. **5** stitch. **piqué** *adj* **1** quilted. **2** padded. **3** spotted. **4** vertical. **piqûre** *nf* **1** sting, bite. **2** prick. **3** small hole. **4** injection. **pique-nique** *nm, pl* **pique-niques** picnic.

piquet (pi:'kɛ) *nm* **1** peg. **2** stake. **3** picket.

pirate (pi:'rat) *nm* pirate.

pire (pi:r) *adj* worse. **le pire** worst.

pis[1] (pi:) *nm* udder.

pis[2] (pi:) *adv* worse. **de pis en pis** worse and worse. **le pis** worst. **tant pis!** too bad! it can't be helped! **pis-aller** *nm invar* makeshift.

piscine (pi:s'si:n) *nf* swimming pool.

pissenlit (pi:sɑ̃'li:) *nm* dandelion.

pistache (pi:'staʃ) *nf* pistachio.

piste (pi:st) *nf* **1** track. **2** trail. **3** scent. **piste cavalière** bridlepath. **piste d'envol** runway.

pistolet (pi:stɔ'lɛ) *nm* pistol.

piston (pi:'stɔ̃) *nm* **1** piston. **2** influence.

pitié (pi:'tje:) *nf* **1** pity. **2** compassion. **piteux, -euse** (pi:'tœ, -'tœz) *adj* pitiful, sorry. **pitoyable** *adj* **1** wretched. **2** pitiful. **3** contemptible.

pitre (pi:tr) *nm* clown.

pittoresque (pi:ttɔ'rɛsk) *adj* picturesque.

pivot (pi:'vo) *nm* **1** pivot. **2** axis. **3** centre.

pivoter (pi:vɔ'te:) *vi* **1** pivot. **2** revolve. **3** swivel. **pivoter sur** hinge on.

plaçage (pla'saʒ) *nm* veneer.

placard (pla'kar) *nm* **1** poster. **2** placard. **3** wall cupboard.

placer (pla'se:) *vt* **1** place. **2** invest. **3** sell. **4** find a job for. **se placer** *vr* **1** take one's place. **2** sit. **3** find a job. **place** *nf* **1** place. **2** seat. **3** room. **4** job. **5** spot. **6** square. **rester sur place** stay put.

placide (pla'si:d) *adj* placid, calm.

plafond (pla'fɔ̃) *nm* ceiling.

plage (plaʒ) *nf* **1** beach. **2** shore. **3** seaside resort.

plagier (pla'ʒje:) *vt* plagiarize. **plagiaire** *nm,f* plagiarist. **plagiat** *nm* plagiarism.

plaider (plɛ'de:) *vi,vt* plead.

plaie (plɛ) *nf* **1** wound. **2** sore. **3** evil, misfortune.

plaignant (plɛ'ɲɑ̃) *v* see **plaindre.**

plaindre* (plɛ̃dr) *vt* pity. **se plaindre de** *vr* complain about.

plaine (plɛn) *nf geog* plain.

plain-pied (plɛ̃'pje:) **de plain-pied** *adv* **1** on a level. **2** easily.

plaint (plɛ̃) *v* see **plaindre.**

plainte (plɛ̃t) *nf* **1** complaint. **2** groan.

plaire* (plɛr) *vt* **plaire à** **1** please. **2** suit. **s'il vous plaît** please. **se plaire** *vr* be happy. **se plaire à** enjoy.

plaisance (plɛ'zɑ̃s) *nf* pleasure. **plaisancier** *nm* **1** yacht. **2** yachtsman.

plaisant (plɛ'zɑ̃) *adj* **1** attractive. **2** agreeable. **3** amusing.

plaisanter (plɛzɑ̃'te:) *vi* joke, jest. *vt* tease. **plaisanterie** *nf* joke, jest.

plaisir (plɛ'zi:r) *nm* **1** pleasure. **2** delight. **3** amusement.

plan[1] (plɑ̃) *adj* **1** flat. **2** level. **3** even. *nm* **1** plane. **2** sphere. **premier plan** *nm* foreground.

plan[2] (plɑ̃) *nm* **1** plan. **2** project. **3** draft. **4** model.

planche (plɑ̃ʃ) *nf* **1** board. **2** plank. **3** shelf. **faire la planche** float on one's back.

plancher (plɑ̃'ʃe:) *nm* floor.

plancton (plɑ̃k'tɔ̃) *nm* plankton.

planer[1] (pla'ne:) *vt* plane, smooth.

planer[2] (pla'ne:) *vi* **1** soar. **2** hover. **3** *aviat* glide. **planeur** *nm* glider.

planète (pla'nɛt) *nf* planet.
plant (plɑ̃) *nm* **1** plantation. **2** sapling. **jeune plant** *nm* seedling.
plantation (plɑ̃ta'sjɔ̃) *nf* **1** plantation. **2** planting.
plante[1] (plɑ̃t) *nf anat* sole.
plante[2] (plɑ̃t) *nf* plant. **plante verte** evergreen.
planter (plɑ̃'te:) *vt* **1** plant. **2** set, place. **planter là** jilt. **se planter** *vr* stand.
planton (plɑ̃'tɔ̃) *nm* **1** *mil* orderly. **2** usher.
plaque (plak) *nf* **1** sheet (of metal). **2** slab. **3** plaque. **4** badge. **plaque chauffante** hot-plate. **plaque tournante** turntable.
plaquer (pla'ke:) *vt* **1** veneer. **2** plate. **3** plaster. **4** *sport* tackle. **5** *inf* abandon. **se plaquer** *vr* lie flat.
plastique (pla'sti:k) *adj,nm* plastic.
plat (pla) *adj* **1** flat. **2** level. **3** dull. *nm* **1** flat (of the hand). **2** dish. **3** course. **à plat 1** flat. **2** *inf* exhausted. **plate-bande** *nf, pl* **plates-bandes** flowerbed. **plate-forme** *nf, pl* **plates-formes** platform.
plateau, -aux (pla'to) *nm* **1** tray. **2** plateau. **3** platform. **4** stage. **plateau à thé** teatray.
platine (pla'ti:n) *nm* platinum.
platonique (platɔ'ni:k) *adj* **1** platonic. **2** futile.
plâtrer (plɑ'tre:) *vt* **1** plaster. **2** patch up. **plâtre** *nm* **1** plaster. **2** plaster cast. **plâtre de moulage** plaster of Paris. **plâtrier** *nm* plasterer.
plausible (plo'zi:bl) *adj* likely, probable.
plectre (plɛktr) *nm* plectrum.
plein (plɛ̃) *adj* **1** full. **2** complete. **3** solid. **4** (of animals) with young. *adv* full. **en plein air/jour** in the open air/in broad daylight. **faire le plein** fill up.
pleurer (plœ're:) *vi* **1** cry, weep. **2** water. **3** drip. *vt* mourn for. **pleurard** *adj* tearful.
pleurnicher (plœrni:'ʃe:) *vi* **1** whine. **2** snivel.
pleuvoir* (plœ'vwar) *v imp* rain.
pli (pli:) *nm* **1** fold. **2** pleat. **3** crease. **4** bend. **5** envelope. **6** note. **petit pli** tuck.
plie (pli:) *nf* plaice.
plier (pli:'e:) *vt* **1** fold. **2** bend. *vi* **1** bend. **2** submit. **pliant** *adj* **1** flexible. **2** collapsible. *nm* folding chair.
plisser (pli:'se:) *vt* **1** crease. **2** pleat.
plomb (plɔ̃) *nm* lead. **à plomb** vertically. **plombier** *nm* plumber.
plomber (plɔ̃'be:) *vt* **1** cover with lead. **2** stop, fill (a tooth). **3** seal.
plonger (plɔ̃'ʒe:) *vi* **1** dive. **2** plunge. *vt* **1** immerse. **2** thrust. **plonge** *nf* washing-up. **plongée** *nf* **1** dive. **2** plunge. **3** slope. **plongée autonome** skin diving. **plongeoir** *nm* diving board. **plongeur, -euse** (plɔ̃'ʒœr, -'ʒœz) *nm,f* **1** diver. **2** washer-up.
ployer (plwa'je:) *vt* bend. *vi* bow, give way.
plu[1] (ply) *v see* **plaire.**
plu[2] (ply) *v see* **pleuvoir.**
pluie (plɥi:) *nf* rain. **pluie battante** downpour.
plumer (ply'me:) *vt* **1** pluck. **2** *sl* fleece. **plume** *nf* **1** feather. **2** pen. **3** nib.
plupart (ply'par) *nf* **1** most. **2** the greater part. **pour la plupart** mostly.
pluriel, -elle (ply'rjɛl) *adj,nm* plural.
plus (ply) *adv* **1** more. **2** most. **3** plus, in addition. *nm* **1** more. **2** most. **de plus 1** more. **2** besides. **en plus** in addition. **(tout) au plus** at most or best. **plus-que-parfait** *nm* pluperfect.
plusieurs (ply'zjœr) *adj,pron pl* several.
Pluton (ply'tɔ̃) *nm* Pluto.
plutôt (ply'to) *adv* **1** rather. **2** on the whole.
pluvieux, -euse (ply'vjœ, -'vjœz) *adj* rainy, wet.
pneu (pnœ) *nm* tyre.
pneumatique (pnœma'ti:k) *adj* pneumatic. *nm* **1** tyre. **2** express letter (in Paris).
pneumonie (pnœmɔ'ni:) *nf* pneumonia.
pochard (pɔ'ʃar) *nm* drunkard.
poche (pɔʃ) *nf* **1** pocket. **2** bag. **pochette** *nf* **1** small pocket. **2** handbag. **3** fancy handkerchief.
pocher (pɔ'ʃe:) *vt* **1** *cul* poach. **2** sketch. **pochade** *nf* sketch.
poêle[1] (pwɑl) *nm* stove, cooker.
poêle[2] (pwɑl) *nf* frying pan.
poème (pɔ'ɛm) *nm* poem. **poésie** *nf* **1** poetry. **2** poem. **poète** *nm* poet. **poétique** *adj* poetic.
poids (pwɑ) *nm* **1** weight. **2** importance. **3** burden. **poids léger** lightweight. **poids lourd 1** heavyweight. **2** heavy goods vehicle.
poignant (pwa'ɲɑ̃) *adj* poignant, gripping.
poignard (pwa'ɲar) *nm* dagger.
poignarder (pwaɲar'de:) *vt* stab.
poigne (pwaɲ) *nf* **1** grip. **2** energy. **3** will. **poignée** *nf* **1** handful. **2** handle. **poignée de main** handshake. **poignet** *nm* **1** wrist. **2** cuff (of a garment).
poil (pwal) *nm* **1** hair, fur (of animals). **2** hair (of humans). **3** nap (of material). **4** *inf* mood. **à poil 1** hairy. **2** *inf* naked. **poilu** *adj* hairy.
poinçon (pwɛ̃'sɔ̃) *nm* **1** *tech* punch. **2** stamp, mark. **3** hallmark.
poinçonner (pwɛ̃sɔ'ne:) *vt* **1** stamp. **2** hallmark. **3** punch, clip.

poindre* (pwɛ̃dr) *vi* **1** dawn. **2** sprout.

poing (pwɛ̃) *nm* fist.

point[1] (pwɛ̃) *nm* **1** point. **2** stitch. **3** dot. **4** extent. **5** full stop. **6** score, mark. **à point** perfect, to a turn. **mettre au point 1** focus. **2** perfect. **deux points** colon. **point d'exclamation** exclamation mark. **point d'interrogation** question mark. **point du jour** daybreak. **point-virgule** *nm* semicolon.

point[2] (pwɛ̃) *adv* **1** not. **2** no. **3** not at all. **ne...point** not any.

pointe (pwɛ̃t) *nf* **1** point. **2** tip. **3** touch, hint. **4** peak.

pointer[1] (pwɛ̃'te:) *vt* **1** check. **2** tick off. **3** aim, train.

pointer[2] (pwɛ̃'te:) *vt* **1** prick. **2** stab. **3** point. *vi* **1** appear. **2** sprout. **3** rise. **4** soar. **pointu** *adj* pointed.

pointiller[1] (pwɛ̃ti:'je:) *vt* dot. **pointillé** *adj* dotted. *nm* dotted line.

pointiller[2] (pwɛ̃ti:'je:) *vi* bicker.

pointilleux, -euse (pwɛ̃ti:'jœ, -'jœz) *adj* **1** touchy. **2** fastidious.

pointure (pwɛ̃'tyr) *nf* size (in clothes).

poire (pwar) *nf* **1** pear. **2** *sl* mug, face. **3** *sl* fool, dupe. **poirier** *nm* pear tree.

poireau, -aux (pwa'ro) *nm* leek.

pois (pwa) *nm* **1** pea. **2** spot. **petits pois** *nm pl* green peas. **pois de senteur** sweet pea.

poison (pwa'zɔ̃) *nm* poison.

poisson (pwa'sɔ̃) *nm* **1** fish. **2** *cap pl* Pisces. **poisson d'avril** April fool. **poisson rouge** goldfish. **poissonnerie** *nf* fish shop. **poissonnier, -ière** (pwasɔn'je:, -'jɛr) *nm,f* fishmonger.

poitrine (pwa'tri:n) *nf* **1** chest. **2** breast, bosom.

poivrer (pwa'vre:) *vt* season with pepper. **poivre** *nm* pepper. **poivre de Cayenne** Cayenne pepper. **poivré** *adj* **1** peppery. **2** spicy. **poivron** *nm* sweet pepper.

poix (pwa) *nf* pitch. **poix liquide** tar.

polaire (pɔ'lɛr) *adj* polar.

polariser (pɔlari:'ze:) *vt* polarize.

pôle (po:l) *nm* pole. **pôle nord** North Pole. **pôle sud** South Pole.

polémique (pɔle:'mi:k) *adj,nf* polemic.

poli[1] (pɔ'li:) *adj* **1** polite. **2** courteous. **poliment** *adv* politely.

poli[2] (pɔ'li:) *adj* **1** polished. **2** glossy. *nm* **1** polish. **2** gloss.

police[1] (pɔ'li:s) *nf* police. **faire la police** keep order. **policier, -ière** (pɔli:'sje:, -'sjɛr) *adj* **1** police. **2** detective. *nm* policeman.

police[2] (pɔ'li:s) *nf comm* policy.

polir (pɔ'li:r) *vt* **1** polish. **2** perfect.

polisson, -onne (pɔli:'sɔ̃, -'sɔn) *adj* **1** naughty. **2** depraved. *nm,f* rascal, rogue. **polissonnerie** *nf* **1** mischievousness. **2** depravity.

politesse (pɔli:'tɛs) *nf* **1** politeness. **2** courtesy.

politique (pɔli:'ti:k) *adj* **1** political. **2** diplomatic. *nf* **1** politics. **2** policy. **politicien, -ienne** (pɔli:ti:'sjɛ̃, -'sjɛn) *nm,f* politician.

pollen (pɔl'lɛn) *nm* pollen.

polliniser (pɔli:ni:'ze:) *vt* pollinate.

polluer (pɔl'lɥe:) *vt* pollute. **pollution** *nf* pollution.

Pologne (pɔ'lɔɲ) *nf* Poland. **polonais** *adj* Polish. *nm* **1** Pole. **2** Polish (language).

poltron, -onne (pɔl'trɔ̃, -'trɔn) *adj* **1** timid. **2** cowardly. **poltronnerie** *nf* cowardice.

polygamie (pɔli:ga'mi:) *nf* polygamy. **polygame** *adj* polygamous. *nm,f* polygamist.

polygone (pɔli:'gɔn) *nm* polygon. **polygonal, -aux** (pɔl:gɔn'al, -'no) *adj* polygonal.

polytechnique (pɔli:tɛk'ni:k) *adj* polytechnic.

polythène (pɔli:'tɛn) *nm* polythene.

pommade (pɔ'mad) *nf* ointment.

pomme (pɔm) *nf* apple. **pomme d'Adam** Adam's apple. **pomme de pin** pine cone. **pomme de terre** potato. **pommé** *adj* **1** rounded. **2** *inf* utter, complete. **pommelé** *adj* mottled. **pommier** *nm* apple tree.

pommeau, -aux (pɔ'mo) *nm* pommel.

pommette (pɔ'mɛt) *nf* cheekbone.

pompe[1] (pɔ̃p) *nf* pomp, ceremony. **pompeux, -euse** (pɔ̃'pœ, -'pœz) *adj* **1** pompous. **2** stately.

pompe[2] (pɔ̃p) *nf* pump. **pompe à incendie** fire-engine. **pompier** *nm* fireman.

pomper (pɔ̃'pe:) *vt* **1** pump. **2** suck up.

ponce (pɔ̃s) *nf* pumice stone.

ponctuel, -elle (pɔ̃k'tɥɛl) *adj* punctual. **ponctualité** *nf* punctuality.

ponctuer (pɔ̃k'tɥe:) *vt* **1** punctuate. **2** emphasize. **ponctuation** *nf* punctuation.

pondéré (pɔ̃de:'re:) *adj* **1** level-headed. **2** calm.

pondre (pɔ̃dr) *vt* **1** lay (eggs). **2** produce. **pondaison** *nf* laying (of eggs).

poney (pɔ'ni:) *nm* pony.

pont (pɔ̃) *nm* **1** bridge. **2** *naut* deck. **3** axle. **4** public holiday. **pont à bascule** weighbridge. **pont aérien** airlift. **pont-levis** *nm, pl* **ponts-levis** drawbridge. **pont suspendu** suspension bridge.

populace (pɔpy'las) *nf* rabble.

populaire (pɔpy'lɛr) *adj* **1** popular. **2** *pol* people's. **popularité** *nf* popularity. **populeux, -euse** (pɔpy'lœ, -'lœz) *adj* densely populated.

population (pɔpyla'sjɔ̃) *nf* population.

porc (pɔr) *nm* **1** pig. **2** pork. **3** *sl* swine. **porc-épic** *nm, pl* **porcs-épics** porcupine.

porcelaine (pɔrsə'lɛn) *nf* **1** porcelain. **2** china.

porche (pɔrʃ) *nm* porch.

porcherie (pɔrʃə'ri:) *nf* pigsty.

pore (pɔr) *nm* pore. **poreux, -euse** (pɔ'rœ, -'rœz) *adj* porous.

pornographie (pɔrnɔgra'fi:) *nf* pornography. **pornographique** *adj* pornographic.

port[1] (pɔr) *nm* **1** port. **2** harbour.

port[2] (pɔr) *nm* **1** carriage. **2** transport. **3** bearing.

porte (pɔrt) *nf* **1** door. **2** doorway. **3** entrance. **4** gate. **5** *pl geog* pass.

porte-affiches *nm invar* notice board.

porte-bagages *nm invar* luggage rack.

porte-bébé *nm invar* carrycot.

porte-bonheur *nm invar* **1** mascot. **2** charm.

porte-clefs *nm invar* keyring.

porte-fenêtre *nf, pl* **portes-fenêtres** French window.

portefeuille (pɔrtə'fœj) *nm* **1** portfolio. **2** wallet.

porte-monnaie *nm invar* purse.

porte-parole *nm invar* spokesman.

porter (pɔr'te:) *vt* **1** carry. **2** wear. **3** bear. **4** enter. **5** induce. *vi* **1** rest. **2** hit, strike home. **se porter** *vr* proceed. **se porter bien/mal** be in good/bad health. **portable** *adj* wearable. **portatif, -ive** (pɔrta'ti:f, -'ti:v) *adj* portable. **porté** *adj* inclined, prone. **portée** *nf* **1** span. **2** litter. **3** reach, range. **4** significance. **5** *mus* scale. **porteur, -euse** (pɔr'tœr, -'tœz) *nm, f* porter, carrier, bearer.

porte-vêtements *nm invar* coat-hanger.

porte-voix *nm invar* megaphone.

portière (pɔr'tjɛr) *nf* door (of a car, train, etc.).

portion (pɔr'sjɔ̃) *nf* **1** portion, helping. **2** part.

portique (pɔr'ti:k) *nm* porch.

porto (pɔr'to) *nm* port (wine).

portrait (pɔr'trɛ) *nm* **1** portrait. **2** likeness.

Portugal (pɔrty'gal) *nm* Portugal. **portugais** *adj,n* Portuguese. *nm* Portuguese (language).

poser (po'ze:) *vt* **1** set, put. **2** place. **3** fix up. **4** suppose. *vi* **1** rest, lie. **2** pose. **se poser** *vr* alight. **se poser en** set oneself up as. **pose** *nf* **1** pose. **2** attitude. **3** affectation. **4** laying. **posé** *adj* **1** sedate. **2** steady. **3** staid.

positif, -ive (pɔzi:'ti:f, -'ti:v) *adj* **1** positive. **2** certain. **3** actual. **4** practical.

position (pɔzi:'sjɔ̃) *nf* **1** position. **2** posture. **3** status. **4** job.

posséder (pɔse:'de:) *vt* possess, own. **possédé** *adj* possessed. *nm* madman.

possessif, -ive (pɔsɛ'si:f, -'si:v) *adj* possessive. **possession** *nf* possession.

possible (pɔ'si:bl) *adj* possible. **possibilité** *nf* possibility.

poste[1] (pɔst) *nf* **1** post. **2** post office. **mettre à la poste** post (a letter). **postal, -aux** (pɔ'stal, -'sto) *adj* postal.

poste[2] (pɔst) *nm* **1** post, station. **2** position. **3** *inf* television set. **4** (telephone) extension. **poste de police** local police station. **poste d'incendie** fire station.

poster (pɔ'ste:) *vt* post, station.

postérieur (pɔste:'rjœr) *adj* **1** subsequent. **2** hind. *nm inf* bottom, posterior. **postérité** *nf* posterity.

posthume (pɔ'stym) *adj* posthumous.

postiche (pɔ'sti:ʃ) *adj* **1** false. **2** imitation. *nm* wig.

postscolaire (pɔstskɔ'lɛr) *adj* after-school.

post-scriptum (pɔstskri:p'tɔm) *nm invar* postscript.

postuler (pɔsty'le:) *vt* **1** apply for. **2** postulate. **postulant** *nm* applicant.

posture (pɔ'styr) *nf* **1** posture. **2** position.

pot (po) *nm* **1** pot. **2** jug. **3** can. **pot-au-feu** *nm invar* beef and vegetable stew. **pot-de-vin** *nm, pl* **pots-de-vin** *inf* bribe. **pot en étain** tankard. **prendre un pot** *inf* have a drink.

potable (pɔ'tabl) *adj* drinkable.

potage (pɔ'taʒ) *nm* soup.

potager, -ère (pɔta'ʒe:, -'ʒɛr) *adj* for cooking. *nm* kitchen garden.

poteau, -aux (pɔ'to) *nm* stake, post.

potelé (pɔt'le:) *adj* **1** plump. **2** chubby.

potence (pɔ'tɑ̃s) *nf* **1** gallows. **2** support.

potentiel, -elle (pɔtɑ̃'sjɛl) *adj,nm* potential.

poterie (pɔ'tri:) *nf* pottery. **potier, -ière** (pɔ'tje:, -'tjɛr) *nm,f* potter.

potin (pɔ'tɛ̃) *nm* **1** *pl* gossip. **2** row, noise.

potiner (pɔti:'ne:) *vi* gossip.

potion (pɔ'sjɔ̃) *nf med* potion, mixture.

potiron (pɔti:'rɔ̃) *nm* pumpkin.

pou, poux (pu:) *nm* louse.

poubelle (pu:'bɛl) *nf* dustbin.

pouce (pu:s) *nm* **1** thumb. **2** big toe. **3** inch. **manger sur le pouce** have a snack.

poudrer (pu:'dre:) *vt* powder. **poudre** *nf* **1** powder. **2** explosive. **poudre à canon** gunpowder. **poudreux, -euse** (pu:'drœ, -'drœz) *adj* dusty.

pouffer (pu:'fe:) *vi* burst out laughing.

poulain (pu:'lɛ̃) *nm* **1** foal. **2** colt.

poule (pu:l) *nf* **1** hen. **2** fowl. **3** *sl* tart. **poulet** *nm* **1** chicken. **2** *inf* cop, policeman.

pouliche (pu:'li:ʃ) *nf* filly.

poulie (pu:'li:) *nf* pulley.

poulpe (pu:lp) *nm* octopus.

pouls (pu) *nm* pulse.

poumon (pu:'mɔ̃) *nm* lung.

poupe (pu:p) *nf naut* stern.

poupée (pu:'pe:) *nf* **1** doll. **2** puppet.

pour (pu:r) *prep* **1** for. **2** instead of. **3** for the sake of. **4** as to. **5** to. **pour que** in order that.

pourboire (pu:r'bwar) *nm* tip, gratuity.

pourceau, -aux (pu:r'so) *nm* swine, pig.

pour-cent *nm invar* per cent. **pourcentage** *nm* percentage.

pourchasser (pu:rʃa'se:) *vt* pursue.

pourpre (pu:rpr) *nf* purple. *adj,nm* crimson.

pourquoi (pu:r'kwa) *adv,conj* why. **pourquoi faire?** what for?

pourrai (pu:'rɛ) *v* see **pouvoir.**

pourrir (pu:'ri:r) *vi,vt* rot. *vi* **1** decay. **2** go bad. **pourriture** *nf* **1** rot. **2** decay.

poursuivre (pu:r'sɥi:vr) *vt* **1** pursue, chase. **2** *law* prosecute. **3** continue. **poursuite** *nf* **1** pursuit. **2** chase. **3** *pl law* proceedings.

pourtant (pu:r'tɑ̃) *adv* **1** however. **2** yet. **3** still.

pourtour (pu:r'tu:r) *nm* **1** circumference. **2** precincts.

pourvoir* (pu:r'vwar) *vt* **1** supply. **2** equip. **pourvoir à** provide.

pourvu (pu:r'vy) *v* see **pourvoir.**

pourvu que (pu:r'vy) *conj* provided that.

pousser (pu:'se:) *vt* **1** push. **2** thrust. **3** urge. **4** utter. **5** shoot out. *vi* **1** grow. **2** push forward or on. **pousser du coude** nudge. **pousse** *nf* **1** growth. **2** *bot* shoot. **poussé** *adj* **1** elaborate. **2** thorough. **poussée** *nf* **1** push, shove. **2** thrust. **3** growth. **poussette** *nf* pushchair.

poussière (pu:'sjɛr) *nf* **1** dust. **2** powder. **3** spray. **poussiéreux, -euse** (pu:sje:'rœ, -'rœz) *adj* dusty.

poussin (pu:'sɛ̃) *nm* chick.

poutre (pu:tr) *nf* **1** beam. **2** girder.

pouvoir* (pu:'vwar) *vt* **1** be able. **2** be allowed. *v imp* be possible. **n'en plus pouvoir** be tired out. **on n'y peut rien** nothing can be done about it. ~*nm* **1** power. **2** command.

pragmatique (pragma'ti:k) *adj* pragmatic.

prairie (prɛ'ri:) *nf* **1** meadow. **2** prairie.

praticable (prati:'kabl) *adj* **1** practicable. **2** feasible. **3** passable.

pratique[1] (pra'ti:k) *nf* **1** practice. **2** application. **3** custom. **4** habit.

pratique[2] (pra'ti:k) *adj* **1** practical. **2** useful.

pratiquer (prati:'ke:) *vt* **1** practise. **2** employ. **3** do.

pré (pre:) *nm* meadow.

préalable (pre:a'labl) *adj* **1** previous. **2** preliminary. **au préalable** to begin with.

préavis (pre:a'vi:) *nm* (previous) notice.

précaire (pre:'kɛr) *adj* **1** precarious. **2** uncertain. **3** delicate. **précarité** *nf* precariousness.

précaution (pre:ko'sjɔ̃) *nf* **1** precaution. **2** care.

précéder (pre:se:'de:) *vt* precede. **précédement** *adv* previously, already. **précédence** *nf* precedence, priority. **précédent** *adj* **1** preceding, previous. **2** former. *nm* precedent.

précepteur, -trice (pre:sɛp'tœr, -'tri:s) *nm,f* tutor, governess.

prêcher (pre:'ʃe:) *vt* preach. **prêche** (prɛʃ) *nm* sermon.

précieux, -euse (pre:'sjœ, -'sjœz) *adj* **1** precious. **2** valuable. **3** affected.

précipiter (pre:si:pi:'te:) *vt* **1** precipitate. **2** rush. **3** throw down. **précipitamment** *adv* **1** headlong. **2** in a hurry. **précipité** *adj* **1** precipitate. **2** hasty. **3** headlong.

précis (pre:'si:) *adj* **1** precise. **2** accurate. **3** clear. *nm* summary, precis.

préciser (pre:si:'ze:) *vt* **1** state precisely. **2** specify. **se préciser** *vr* become clear. **précisément** *adv* precisely, just. **précision** *nf* **1** precision. **2** accuracy. **3** *pl* full details.

précoce (pre:'kɔs) *adj* **1** precocious. **2** early. **3** advanced, forward.

préconcevoir* (pre:kɔ̃sə'vwar) *vt* preconceive.

préconiser (pre:kɔni:'ze:) *vt* **1** recommend. **2** praise.

prédateur, -trice (pre:da'tœr, -'tri:s) *adj* predatory. *nm* beast of prey.

prédécesseur (pre:de:sɛ'sœr) *nm* predecessor.

prédestiner (pre:dɛsti:'ne:) *vt* predestine.

prédicat (pre:di:'ka) *nm* predicate.

prédicateur (pre:di:ka'tœr) *nm* preacher.

prédire* (pre:'di:r) *vt* predict, foretell.

prédominer (pre:dɔmi:'ne:) *vi* predominate, prevail. **prédominance** *nf* predominance. **prédominant** *adj* **1** predominant. **2** prevalent.

prééminent (pre:e:mi:'nɑ̃) *adj* pre-eminent.

préfabriquer (pre:fabri:'ke:) *vt* prefabricate.

préface (prɛ'fas) *nf* preface.

préfecture (pre:fɛk'tyr) *nf* headquarters of the prefect of a French department. **préfecture de police** headquarters of the Paris police.
préférer (pre:fe:'re:) *vt* prefer. **préféré** *adj,n* favourite. **préférence** *nf* preference. **préférentiel, -elle** (pre:fɛrɑ̃'sjɛl) *adj* preferential.
préfet (pre:'fɛ) *nm* prefect. **préfet de police** chief commissioner of Paris police.
préfixe (pre:'fi:ks) *nm* prefix.
préhistorique (pre:i:stɔ'ri:k) *adj* prehistoric.
préjudice (pre:ʒy'di:s) *nm* **1** wrong. **2** detriment. **3** prejudice.
préjugé (pre:ʒy'ʒe:) *nm* prejudice, bias.
prélever (pre:l've:) *vt* levy. **prélèvement** *nm* levy, tax.
préliminaire (pre:li:mi:'nɛr) *adj* preliminary.
prélude (pre:'lyd) *nm* prelude.
prématuré (pre:maty're:) *adj* premature.
préméditer (pre:me:di:'te:) *vt* premeditate. **préméditation** *nf* premeditation. **prémédité** *adj* deliberate.
premier, -ière (prə'mje:, -'mjɛr) *adj* **1** first. **2** original. **3** foremost. **4** maiden (voyage, speech, etc.). *nf* first class.
prémisse (pre:'mi:s) *nf* premise.
prenant (prə'nɑ̃) *v* see **prendre.**
prénatal (pre:na'tal) *adj* antenatal.
prendre* (prɑ̃dr) *vt* **1** take. **2** seize. **3** assume. *vi* **1** set, congeal. **2** take, catch on. **se prendre** *vr* catch, get caught. **s'en prendre à** blame. **se prendre à 1** cling to. **2** begin. **s'y prendre** set about.
prénom (pre:'nɔ̃) *nm* Christian name.
prénuptial, -aux (pre:nyp'sjal) *adj* premarital.
préoccupé (pre:ɔky'pe:) *adj* **1** preoccupied. **2** engrossed. **3** anxious. **préoccupation** *nf* **1** preoccupation. **2** anxiety. **3** obsession.
préparer (prɛpa're:) *vt* **1** prepare. **2** get ready. **se préparer à** *vr* get ready for. **préparatifs** *nm pl* preparations. **préparation** *nf* preparation. **préparatoire** *adj* preparatory.
préposition (pre:pɔzi:'sjɔ̃) *nf* preposition.
prérogative (pre:rɔga'ti:v) *nf* prerogative.
près (prɛ) *adv* near. **à cela près** with that exception. **à peu près 1** approximately. **2** nearly. **de près** closely, near to. **près de** *prep* near to.
présager (prɛza'ʒe:) *vt* **1** predict. **2** foresee. **3** signify. **présage** *nm* omen.
presbyte (prɛz'bi:t) *adj* long-sighted.
presbytère (prɛzbi:'tɛr) *nm* vicarage.
prescrire* (prɛ'skri:r) *vt* **1** prescribe. **2** order. **3** demand. **prescription** *nf* **1** prescription. **2** instruction. **3** *med* directions for use.
préséance (pre:se:'ɑ̃s) *nf* **1** precedence. **2** priority.
présence (pre:'zɑ̃s) *nf* presence.
présent[1] (pre:'zɑ̃) *adj* present. *nm* present (time or tense). **à présent** now. **jusqu'à présent** as yet, up to now.
présent[2] (pre:'zɑ̃) *nm* present, gift.
présenter (pre:zɑ̃'te:) *vt* **1** present. **2** offer. **3** introduce. **se présenter** *vr* **1** present oneself. **2** occur. **présentateur, -trice** (pre:zɑ̃ta'tœr, -'tri:s) *nm,f* **1** presenter. **2** disc jockey. **présentation** (pre:zɑ̃ta'sjɔ̃) *nf* **1** presentation. **2** introduction.
préserver (pre:zɛr've:) *vt* **1** preserve. **2** protect. **préservateur, -trice** (pre:zɛrva'tœr, -'tri:s) *adj* preserving. **préservatif, -ive** (pre:zɛrva'ti:f, -'ti:v) *adj* **1** preservative. **2** protective. *nm* contraceptive sheath.
présider (pre:zi:'de:) *vt* preside over. *vi* be in the chair. **président** *nm* **1** president. **2** chairman. **présidentiel, -elle** (pre:zi:dɑ̃'sjɛl) *adj* presidential.
presque (prɛsk) *adv* **1** almost, nearly. **2** hardly.
presqu'île (prɛ'ski:l) *nf* peninsula.
presser (prɛ'se:) *vt* **1** press. **2** squeeze. **3** hurry. **se presser** *vr* **1** hurry. **2** crowd. **pressant** *adj* urgent. **presse** *nf* **1** press. **2** press, newspapers. **3** pressure. **4** crowd. **pressé** *adj* **1** crowded. **2** hurried. **3** urgent. **pression** *nf* pressure.
preste (prɛst) *adj* **1** quick. **2** nimble. **3** alert.
prestidigitateur (prɛsti:di:ʒi:ta'tœr) *nm* conjurer. **prestidigitation** *nf* conjuring.
prestige (prɛ'sti:ʒ) *nm* **1** prestige. **2** attraction. **prestigieux, -euse** (prɛsti:'ʒjœ, -'ʒjœz) *adj* marvellous.
présumer (pre:zy'me:) *vt* presume, assume.
prêt[1] (prɛ) *adj* **1** ready. **2** prepared. **prêt à porter** ready-made (clothes).
prêt[2] (prɛ) *nm* loan.
prétendre (prɛ'tɑ̃dr) *vt* **1** claim. **2** require. **3** maintain. **prétendant** (prɛtɑ̃'dɑ̃) *nm* **1** applicant. **2** candidate. **prétendu** (prɛtɑ̃'dy) *adj* **1** alleged. **2** so-called.
prétention (prɛtɑ̃'sjɔ̃) *nf* **1** pretension. **2** claim. **prétentieux, -euse** (prɛtɑ̃'sjœ, -'sjœz) *adj* **1** pretentious. **2** conceited.
prêter (prɛ'te:) *vt* **1** lend. **2** attribute. *vi* stretch. **prête-nom** *nm, pl* **prête-noms** figurehead. **prêter attention** pay attention. **prêteur,**

-euse (prɛ'tœr, -'tœz) *nm,f* lender. **prêteur sur gages** *nm* pawnbroker.
prétexte (pre:'tɛkst) *nm* pretext, excuse.
prêtre (prɛtr) *nm* priest. **prêtrise** *nf* priesthood.
preuve (prœv) *nf* **1** proof. **2** evidence.
prévaloir* (prɛval'war) *vi* prevail. **se prévaloir de** *vr* take advantage of.
prévenir* (pre:v'ni:r) *vt* **1** warn. **2** forestall. **3** prevent. **4** prejudice. **prévenance** *nf* **1** attention. **2** kindness. **prévenant** *adj* **1** attentive. **2** considerate. **3** pleasing.
préventif, -ive (pre:vɑ̃'ti:f, -'ti:v) *adj* preventive. **prévention** *nf* **1** prejudice. **2** imprisonment. **3** prevention.
prévenu (pre:v'ny) *adj* prejudiced. *nm law* accused.
prévision (pre:vi:'zjɔ̃) *nf* **1** forecast. **2** expectation.
prévoir* (pre:'vwar) *vt* **1** foresee. **2** provide for. **prévoyance** *nf* **1** foresight. **2** precaution.
prévu (pre:'vy) *v* see **prévoir.**
prier (pri:'e:) *vt* **1** pray. **2** ask. **3** invite. **je vous en prie** don't mention it. **prière** *nf* **1** prayer. **2** request.
prieuré (pri:œ're:) *nm* priory.
primaire (pri:'mɛr) *adj* primary.
prime[1] (pri:m) *adj* first. **de prime abord** at first.
prime[2] (pri:m) *nf* **1** premium. **2** bonus.
primer[1] (pri:'me:) *vt* excel.
primer[2] (pri:'me:) *vt* award a prize to. **primé** *adj* **1** prized. **2** subsidized.
primerose (pri:m'roz) *nf* hollyhock.
primesautier, -ière (pri:mso'tje:, -'tjɛr) *adj* **1** impulsive. **2** spontaneous.
primeur (pri:'mœr) *nf* **1** newness. **2** freshness. **3** *pl* early vegetables.
primevère (pri:m'vɛr) *nf* primrose.
primitif, -ive (pri:mi:'ti:f, -'ti:v) *adj* **1** primitive. **2** original.
primordial, -aux (pri:mɔr'djal, -'djo) *adj* **1** prime. **2** primeval.
prince (prɛ̃s) *nm* prince.
princesse (prɛ̃'sɛs) *nf* princess.
principal, -aux (prɛ̃si:'pal, -'po) *adj* principal, chief, main. *nm* **1** chief. **2** headmaster. **3** main thing. **principauté** *nf* principality.
principe (prɛ̃'si:p) *nm* principle.
printanier, -ière (prɛ̃ta'nje:, -'njɛr) *adj* spring.
printemps (prɛ̃'tɑ̃) *nm* spring, springtime.
priorité (pri:ɔri:'te:) *nf* priority.
pris (pri:) *v* see **prendre.** *adj* **1** engaged, occupied. **2** busy.
prise (pri:z) *nf* **1** hold. **2** grip. **3** solidification. **4** capture. **5** pinch. **en prise** in gear. **lâcner prise** let go. **prise de courant 1** (electric) socket. **2** plug.
priser (pri:'ze:) *vt* **1** value. **2** prize.
prisme (pri:sm) *nm* prism.
prison (pri:'zɔ̃) *nf* **1** prison, jail. **2** imprisonment. **prisonnier, -ière** (pri:zɔ'nje:, -'njɛr) *nm,f* prisoner.
privé (pri:'ve:) *adj* **1** private. **2** privy.
priver (pri:'ve:) *vt* deprive. **se priver** *vr* deny oneself. **privation** *nf* deprivation.
privilège (pri:vi:'lɛʒ) *nm* **1** privilege. **2** licence. **privilégié** *adj* **1** privileged. **2** licensed.
prix (pri:) *nm* **1** price. **2** cost. **3** worth. **4** prize. **à tout prix** at all costs.
prix-courant *nm, pl* **prix-courants** price-list.
probable (prɔ'babl) *adj* probable, likely. **probabilité** *nf* probability, likelihood.
probe (prɔb) *adj* honest. **probité** *nf* integrity.
problème (prɔ'blɛm) *nm* problem.
procéder (prɔse:'de:) *vi* **1** proceed. **2** originate. **procédé** *nm* **1** dealing. **2** process. **3** behaviour. **procédure** *nf law* procedure.
procès (prɔ'sɛ) *nm law* **1** case. **2** trial. **procès-verbal** *nm, pl* **procès-verbaux 1** official report. **2** minutes. **3** *law* particulars.
procession (prɔsɛ'sjɔ̃) *nf* procession.
processus (prɔsɛs'sys) *nm* **1** process. **2** method.
prochain (prɔ'ʃɛ̃) *adj* **1** next. **2** nearest. **3** immediate. *nm* neighbour. **prochainement** *adv* soon.
proche (prɔʃ) *adv* near. *adj* near, close.
Proche Orient *nm* Near East.
proclamer (prɔkla'me:) *vt* **1** proclaim. **2** announce. **3** declare. **proclamation** *nf* proclamation.
procréer (prɔkre:'e:) *vt* procreate.
procurer (prɔky're:) *vt* **1** procure, get. **2** obtain. **procuration** (prɔkyra'sjɔ̃) *nf* power of attorney. **procureur** *nm* attorney. **procureur général** Attorney General.
prodige (prɔ'di:ʒ) *nm* prodigy, marvel.
produire* (prɔ'dɥi:r) *vt* **1** produce. **2** bring about. **3** yield. **productif, -ive** (prɔdyk'ti:f, -'ti:v) *adj* productive. **production** *nf* **1** production. **2** product. **produit** *nm* product.
proéminence (prɔe:mi:'nɑ̃s) *nf* prominence. **proéminent** *adj* protruding.
profane (prɔ'fan) *adj* **1** profane. **2** secular. *nm* layman.
professer (prɔfɛ'se:) *vt* **1** profess. **2** teach.

professeur *nm* **1** professor. **2** teacher. **3** instructor.

profession (prɔfɛ'sjɔ̃) *nf* profession, trade. **professionnel, -elle** (prɔfɛsjɔ'nɛl) *adj* **1** professional. **2** vocational. *nm,f* professional.

profil (prɔ'fi:l) *nm* profile.

profit (prɔ'fi:) *nm* **1** profit, gain. **2** advantage.

profiter (prɔfi:'te:) *vi* **1** profit. **2** make a profit. **profiter de** take advantage of.

profond (prɔ'fɔ̃) *adj* **1** deep. **2** profound. **3** deep-seated. **profondeur** *nf* depth.

profus (prɔ'fy) *adj* profuse, abundant.

programme (prɔ'gram) *nm* **1** programme. **2** syllabus. **3** plan.

progrès (prɔ'grɛ) *nm* **1** progress. **2** improvement.

progressif, -ive (prɔgrɛ'si:f, -'si:v) *adj* **1** progressive. **2** gradual.

prohiber (prɔi:'be:) *vt* prohibit, forbid.

proie (prwa) *nf* prey.

projecteur (prɔʒɛk'tœr) *nm* **1** projector. **2** searchlight. **3** floodlight. **projectile** *nm* **1** missile. **2** projectile. **projection** *nf* **1** projection. **2** slide, film.

projet (prɔ'ʒɛ) *nm* **1** project, scheme. **2** (rough) plan. **projet de loi** *pol* bill.

prolétariat (prɔlɛta'rja) *nm* proletariat.

prolifique (prɔli:'fi:k) *adj* prolific.

prolonger (prɔlɔ̃'ʒe:) *vt* prolong, extend.

promener (prɔm'ne:) *vt* take for a walk. **se promener** *vr* **1** go for a walk. **2** wander. **promenade** *nf* **1** walk. **2** walking. **3** outing. **4** promenade.

promesse (prɔ'mɛs) *nf* promise.

promettre* (prɔ'mɛtr) *vt* **1** promise. **2** make a promise.

promouvoir* (prɔmu:'vwar) *vt* promote. **promotion** *nf* promotion.

prompt (prɔ̃) *adj* **1** quick, prompt. **2** hasty.

prône (pron) *nm* sermon.

pronom (prɔ'nɔ̃) *nm* pronoun.

prononcer (prɔnɔ̃'se:) *vt* **1** pronounce. **2** deliver (a speech). **se prononcer** *vr* express one's opinion. **prononciation** *nf* pronunciation.

propagande (prɔpa'gɑ̃d) *nf* **1** propaganda. **2** publicity. **faire de la propagande** advertise.

propager (prɔpa'ʒe:) *vt* **1** propagate. **2** spread.

prophète, prophétesse (prɔ'fɛt, prɔfe:'tɛs) *nm,f* prophet, prophetess. **prophétie** (prɔfe:'si:) *nf* prophecy. **prophétique** *adj* prophetic.

prophétiser (prɔfe:ti:'ze:) *vt* prophesy.

propice (prɔ'pi:s) *adj* favourable.

proportion (prɔpɔr'sjɔ̃) *nf* **1** proportion. **2** ratio. **3** *pl* size. **proportionnel, -elle** (prɔpɔrsjɔ'nɛl) *adj* proportional.

propos (prɔ'po) *nm* **1** purpose. **2** subject. **3** remark. **4** *pl* gossip. **à propos 1** by the way. **2** at the right moment. **à propos de** with regard to, concerning.

proposer (prɔpo'ze:) *vt* propose. **se proposer** *vr* **1** offer oneself. **2** intend. **proposition** *nf* **1** proposal. **2** proposition.

propre (prɔpr) *adj* **1** proper. **2** own. **3** appropriate. **4** clean. **propre à 1** suitable to. **2** peculiar to. **propreté** *nf* **1** cleanness. **2** tidiness.

propriétaire (prɔpri:e:'tɛr) *nm,f* **1** proprietor, proprietress. **2** landlord, landlady. **propriété** *nf* **1** property. **2** ownership. **3** propriety.

propulser (prɔpyl'se:) *vt* propel. **propulseur** *nm* propeller. **propulsion** *nf* propulsion, drive.

proscrire* (prɔ'skri:r) *vt* banish. **proscrit** *nm* outlaw.

prose (proz) *nf* prose.

prospectif, -ive (prɔspɛk'ti:f, -'ti:v) *adj* prospective.

prospérer (prɔspe:'re:) *vi* prosper, do well. **prospère** *adj* **1** prosperous. **2** thriving. **prospérité** *nf* prosperity.

se prosterner (prɔstɛr'ne:) *vr* **1** bow down. **2** *inf* grovel. **prosterné** *adj* prostrate.

prostituée (prɔsti:ty'e:) *nf* prostitute. **prostitution** *nf* prostitution.

protagoniste (prɔtagɔ'ni:st) *nm* protagonist.

protecteur, -trice (prɔtɛk'tœr, -'tri:s) *nm,f* **1** protector. **2** patron, patroness. *adj* protective. **protection** *nf* **1** protection. **2** patronage.

protéger (prɔte:'ʒe:) *vt* **1** protect. **2** shelter. **3** patronize. **protégé** *nm* dependant.

protéine (prɔte:'i:n) *nf* protein.

protester (prɔtɛ'ste:) *vt* declare. *vi* protest. **protestant** *adj,n* Protestant. **protestation** *nf* protest.

protocole (prɔtɔ'kɔl) *nm* protocol.

proton (prɔ'tɔ̃) *nm* proton.

proue (pru:) *nf naut* bow, prow.

prouesse (pru:'ɛs) *nf* prowess, bravery.

prouver (pru:'ve:) *vt* prove.

provençal, -aux (prɔvɑ̃'sal, -'so) *adj,nm* Provençal.

provenir* (prɔv'ni:r) *vi* **provenir de 1** arise from. **2** originate in or from. **provenance** *nf* **1** source. **2** origin. **en provenance de** coming from.

proverbe (prɔ'vɛrb) *nm* proverb. **proverbial, -aux** (prɔvɛr'bjal, -'bjo) *adj* proverbial.
province (prɔ'vɛ̃s) *nf* province. **provincial, -aux** (prɔvɛ̃'sjal, -'sjo) *adj* provincial.
proviseur (prɔvi:'zœr) *nm* headmaster.
provision (prɔvi:'zjɔ̃) *nf* **1** provision. **2** stock. **3** funds.
provisoire (prɔvi:'zwar) *adj* **1** provisional. **2** temporary. **à titre provisoire** provisionally.
provoquer (prɔvɔ'ke:) *vt* **1** provoke. **2** challenge. **3** arouse. **4** cause. **provocant** *adj* **1** provocative. **2** aggressive. **provocateur, -trice** (prɔvɔka'tœr, -'tri:s) *adj* provocative. **provocation** *nf* provocation.
proximité (prɔksi:mi:'te:) *nf* proximity.
prude (pryd) *nf* prude. *adj* prudish.
prudent (pry'dɑ̃) *adj* **1** prudent, wise. **2** discreet. **prudemment** (pryda'mɑ̃) *adv* prudently. **prudence** *nf* prudence, carefulness.
prune (pryn) *nf* plum. **prune de damas** damson. **pruneau, -aux** (pry'no) *nm* prune. **prunelle** *nf* **1** *anat* pupil. **2** sloe. **prunier** *nm* plum tree.
psaume (psom) *nm* psalm.
pseudonyme (psœdɔ'ni:m) *nm* pseudonym.
psychanalyse (psi:kana'li:z) *nf* psychoanalysis.
psychédélique (psi:ke:de:'li:k) *adj* psychedelic.
psychiatrie (psi:kja'tri:) *nf* psychiatry. **psychiatre** *nm,f* psychiatrist. **psychiatrique** *adj* psychiatric.
psychique (psi:'ʃi:k) *adj* psychic.
psychologie (psi:kɔlɔ'ʒi:) *nf* psychology. **psychologique** *adj* psychological. **psychologue** *nm,f* psychologist.
psychopathique (psi:kɔpa'ti:k) *adj* psychopathic.
psychosomatique (psi:kosɔma'ti:k) *adj* psychosomatic.
pu (py) *v* see **pouvoir.**
puanteur (pɥɑ̃'tœr) *nf* stink.
puberté (pybɛr'te:) *nf* puberty.
public, -ique (py'bli:k) *adj* **1** public. **2** common. *nm* public. **grand public** general public.
publicité (pybli:si:'te:) *nf* **1** publicity. **2** advertising. **publicitaire** *adj* advertising.
publier (pybli:'e:) *vt* **1** publish. **2** proclaim. **publication** *nf* **1** publication. **2** publishing.
puce (pys) *nf* flea. **puceron** *nm* greenfly.
pudeur (py'dœr) *nf* modesty, decency.
pudique (py'di:k) *adj* **1** modest. **2** chaste.
puer (pɥe:) *vi* stink.
puéril (pɥe:'ri:l) *adj* childish.
pugilat (pyʒi:'la) *nm* boxing. **pugiliste** *nm* boxer.
puîné (pɥi:'ne:) *adj* younger.
puis[1] (pɥi:) *adv* **1** then. **2** afterwards. **3** besides.
puis[2] (pɥi:) *v* see **pouvoir.**
puiser (pɥi:'ze:) *vt* **1** draw (water). **2** derive.
puisque (pɥi:sk) *conj* since, as.
puissance (pɥi:'sɑ̃s) *nf* **1** power. **2** authority. **puissant** *adj* **1** powerful. **2** strong. **3** potent.
puits (pɥi:) *nm* **1** well. **2** shaft.
pull-over (pu:lo'vɛr) *nm* pullover.
pulluler (pylly'le:) *vi* swarm.
pulpe (pylp) *nf* pulp.
pulsation (pylsa'sjɔ̃) *nf* throb. **pulsation du cœur** heartbeat.
pulvériser (pylve:ri:'ze:) *vt* **1** pulverize. **2** grind.
punaise (py'nɛz) *nf* **1** bug. **2** drawing pin.
punch[1] (pɔ̃ʃ) *nm* (drink) punch.
punch[2] (pœnʃ) *nm sport* punch.
punir (py'ni:r) *vt* punish. **punition** *nf* **1** punishment. **2** forfeit.
pupille[1] (py'pi:l) *nm,f law* ward.
pupille[2] (py'pi:l) *nf anat* pupil.
pupitre (py'pi:tr) *nm* desk.
pur (pyr) *adj* **1** pure. **2** genuine. **3** clear. **4** innocent. **pur-sang** *nm invar* thoroughbred. **pureté** *nf* purity.
purée (py're:) *nf* **1** mash. **2** thick soup.
purgatoire (pyrga'twar) *nm* purgatory.
purger (pyr'ʒe:) *vt* **1** purge. **2** cleanse. **3** clear. **purge** *nf* **1** purge. **2** cleaning.
purifier (pyri:'fje:) *vt* **1** purify. **2** refine.
puritain (pyri:'tɛ̃) *nm* Puritan.
pus (py) *nm med* pus.
pusillanime (pyzi:lla'ni:m) *adj* faint-hearted.
pustule (py'styl) *nf* pimple.
putain (py'tɛ̃) *nf sl* prostitute.
putride (py'tri:d) *adj* putrid.
puzzle (pyzl) *nm* jigsaw.
pygmée (pi:g'me:) *adj,n* pygmy.
pyjama (pi:ʒa'ma) *nm* pyjamas.
pyramide (pi:ra'mi:d) *nf* pyramid.
Pyrénées (pi:re:'ne:) *nf pl* Pyrenees.

Q

quadrant (ka'drɑ̃) *nm* quadrant.
quadrilatéral, -aux (kwadri:latɛ'ral, -'ro) *adj* quadrilateral.
quadrilatère (kwadri:la'tɛr) *nm* **1** quadrilateral. **2** quadrangle.
quadrillé (kadri:'je:) *adj* squared, checked.

quadrupède (kwadry'pɛd) *nm* quadruped.
quadrupler (kwadry'ple:) *vi,vt* quadruple. **quadruplés** *nm pl* quadruplets.
quai (ke:) *nm* **1** quay, wharf. **2** platform. **3** embankment. **Quai d'Orsay** French Foreign Office.
quaker, -eresse (kwa'kɛr, -'krɛs) *nm,f* Quaker.
qualifier (kali:'fje:) *vt* **1** call, term. **2** qualify. **qualification** *nf* **1** qualification. **2** title.
qualité (kali:'te:) *nf* **1** quality. **2** excellence. **3** property. **4** qualification. **5** title. **6** rank. **en qualité de** as, in the capacity of.
quand (kɑ̃) *conj, adv* when. **quand même 1** all the same. **2** even if.
quant (kɑ̃t) *prep* **quant à** with regard to.
quantifier (kɑ̃ti:'fje:) *vt* quantify.
quantité (kɑ̃ti:'te:) *nf* quantity, amount.
quarante (ka'rɑ̃t) *adj,nm* forty. **quarantaine** *nf* **1** about forty. **2** quarantine. **faire quarantaine** be in quarantine. **quarantième** *adj* fortieth.
quart (kar) *nm* quarter, fourth part. **quart de finale** quarterfinal. **quart d'heure** quarter of an hour. **trois quarts** *nm pl* threequarters.
quartier (kar'tje:) *nm* **1** quarter. **2** piece. **3** district. **bas quartier** slum. **quartier général** *mil* headquarters.
quartz (kwarts) *nm* quartz.
quasi (ka'zi:) *adv* almost.
quatorze (ka'tɔrz) *adj,nm* fourteen. **quatorzième** *adj* fourteenth.
quatre (katr) *adj,nm* four. **à quatre pattes** on all fours. **quatrième** *adj* fourth.
quatre-vingt-dix *adj,nm* ninety. **quatre-vingt-dixième** *adj* ninetieth.
quatre-vingts *adj,nm* eighty. **quatre-vingtième** *adj* eightieth.
quatuor (kwa'tɥɔr) *nm* quartet.
que[1] (kə) *conj* **1** that. **2** lest, in case. **3** but. **4** as. **5** than. **à ce que** or **de ce que** that. **ne...que** only. **que...ou non** whether...or not. **que...que** whether...or.
que[2] (kə) *adv* **1** how. **2** how much or many.
que[3] (kə) *pron* **1** that. **2** whom. **3** which. **4** what. **qu'est-ce que** or **qui?** what?
quel, quelle (kɛl) *adj,pron* **1** what. **2** which. **quel que 1** whatever. **2** whoever. **quelconque** *adj* **1** any (whatever). **2** some kind of. **3** ordinary, commonplace. **quelque** *adj* **1** some. **2** *pl* some, a few. *adv* **1** about. **2** some. **quelque chose** *pron m invar* something, anything. **quelquefois** *adv* sometimes. **quelque part** *adv* somewhere. **quelque...que** or **qui 1** whatever, whatsoever. **2** however. **quelqu'un, quelqu'une** (kɛl'kœ̃, kɛl'kyn) *pron, pl* **quelques-uns, quelques-unes** one.
quémander (ke:mɑ̃'de:) *vi* beg. *vt* beg for.
quenelle (kə'nɛl) *nf* fish or mincemeat ball.
quereller (kərɛ'le:) *vt* quarrel with. **se quereller** *vr* quarrel. **querelle** *nf* quarrel. **querelleur, -euse** (kərɛ'lœr, -'lœz) *adj* quarrelsome.
quérir (ke:'ri:r) *vt* **1** fetch. **2** send for.
question (kɛ'stjɔ̃) *nf* **1** question, query. **2** matter, issue. **question pour la forme** rhetorical question. **questionnaire** *nm* questionnaire.
questionner (kɛstjɔ'ne:) *vt* **1** question. **2** ask questions.
quêter (kɛte:) *vt* **1** collect (money, etc.). **2** look for. **quête** (kɛt) *nf* **1** search, quest. **2** *rel* collection.
queue (kœ) *nf* **1** tail. **2** end. **3** queue. **4** *sport* cue. **faire la queue** queue up.
qui (ki:) *pron* **1** who. **2** whom. **3** which. **4** that. **qui est-ce qui/que?** who/whom? **qui...que** whoever. **quiconque** *pron* **1** whoever. **2** anyone.
quiche (ki:ʃ) *nf* flan filled with cheese, eggs, cream, and bacon, etc.
quignon (ki:'ɲɔ̃) *nm* hunk (of bread, etc.).
quille[1] (ki:j) *nf* **1** skittle. **2** *pl sl* pins, legs.
quille[2] (ki:j) *nf* keel.
quincaillerie (kɛ̃kɑj'ri:) *nf* **1** ironmongery. **2** hardware shop. **quincaillier** *nm* ironmonger.
quintal, -aux (kɛ̃'tal, -'to) *nm* (approx.) hundredweight.
quinte (kɛ̃t) *nf* **1** fit, bout. **2** *mus* fifth.
quintessence (kɛ̃tɛs'sɑ̃s) *nf* quintessence.
quintette (kɛ̃'tɛt) *nm* quintet.
quinze (kɛ̃z) *adj,nm* fifteen. **quinze jours** *nm pl* fortnight. **quinzaine** *nf* **1** fortnight. **2** about fifteen. **quinzième** *adj* fifteenth.
quiproquo (ki:prɔ'ko) *nm* **1** mistake. **2** misunderstanding.
quittance (ki:'tɑ̃s) *nf* receipt.
quitter (ki:'te:) *vt* leave, quit. **quitte** *adj* **1** quit. **2** free, rid. **quitte à quitte** quits.
quoi (kwa) *pron* **1** what. **2** which. **à quoi bon?** what's the use? **avoir de quoi** be well-off. **quoi que** or **qui** whatever. **sans quoi** otherwise. **quoique** *conj* although, though.
quote-part (kot'par) *nf* quota.
quotidien, -ienne (kɔti:'djɛ̃, -'djɛn) *adj* **1** daily. **2** everyday. *nm* daily newspaper.

R

rabâcher (rabɑ'ʃe:) *vi* keep repeating the same thing.
rabais (ra'bɛ) *nm* **1** reduction. **2** discount.
rabaisser (rabɛ'se:) *vt* **1** lower. **2** disparage.
rabattre* (ra'batr) *vt* **1** fold back. **2** lower, bring down. **3** reduce. **4** *sport* beat. *vi* turn off. **rabat-joie** *nm,f invar* spoil-sport.
rabbin (ra'bɛ̃) *nm* rabbi.
rabot (ra'bo) *nm tech* plane.
raboter (rabɔ'te:) *vt* **1** plane. **2** file down. **raboteux, -euse** (rabɔ'tœ, -'tœz) *adj* **1** uneven, rough. **2** rugged.
rabougrir (rabu:'gri:r) *vt* stunt.
racaille (ra'kɑj) *nf* rabble.
raccommoder (rakɔmɔ'de:) *vt* **1** mend, repair. **2** darn. **3** reconcile. **raccommodage** *nm* **1** mending. **2** mend.
raccorder (rakɔr'de:) *vt* join, connect.
raccourcir (raku:r'si:r) *vt* **1** shorten. **2** abridge. *vi* grow shorter, shorten. **raccourci** *nm* **1** abridgment. **2** short cut.
raccrocher (rakrɔ'ʃe:) *vt* **1** hang up again. **2** ring off. **3** get hold of again. **se raccrocher à** *vr* clutch, cling to.
race (ras) *nf* **1** race. **2** breed. **3** descent. **racial, -aux** (ra'sjal, -'sjo) *adj* racial. **racisme** *nm* racialism.
rachat (ra'ʃa) *nm* **1** repurchase. **2** atonement. **3** ransom.
racheter (raʃ'te:) *vt* **1** buy back. **2** atone for. **3** redeem. **4** ransom.
racine (ra'si:n) *nf* root.
racler (rɑ'kle:) *vt* scrape. **se racler la gorge** clear one's throat. **raclée** *nf inf* thrashing, hiding. **raclure** *nf* scrapings.
racoler (rakɔ'le:) *vt* recruit.
raconter (rakɔ̃'te:) *vt* tell, relate. **racontar** *nm inf* gossip. **raconteur, -euse** (rakɔ̃'tœr, -'tœz) *nm,f* narrator, storyteller.
radar (ra'dar) *nm* radar.
radeau, -aux (ra'do) *nm* raft.
radial, -aux (ra'djal, -'djo) *adj* radial.
radiateur (radja'tœr) *nm* radiator.
radiation[1] (radja'sjɔ̃) *nf* **1** crossing out. **2** cancellation.
radiation[2] (radja'sjɔ̃) *nf* radiation.
radical, -aux (radi:'kal, -'ko) *adj* radical.
radier (ra'dje:) *vt* **1** erase. **2** cross out.
radieux, -euse (ra'djœ, -'djœz) *adj* **1** radiant. **2** brilliant.
radin (ra'dɛ̃) *adj inf* mean, miserly.
radio (ra'djo) *nf* **1** radio. **2** X-ray. **passer à radio** X-ray. **radioactif, -ive** (radjoak'ti:f, -'ti:v) *adj* radioactive. **radioactivité** *nf* radioactivity.
radiodiffuser (radjodi:ffy'ze:) *vt* broadcast.
radis (ra'di:) *nm* radish.
radium (ra'djɔm) *nm* radium.
radoter (radɔ'te:) *vi* talk nonsense, ramble. **radotage** *nm* nonsense.
radoucir (radu:'si:r) *vt* **1** calm down. **2** soften. **se radoucir** *vr* grow softer or milder.
rafale (ra'fal) *nf* gust, blast (of wind).
raffermir (rafɛr'mi:r) *vt* **1** harden. **2** strengthen. **3** restore. **se raffermir** *vr* **1** improve. **2** recover.
raffiner (rafi:'ne:) *vt* refine. **raffinage** *nm* refining. **raffiné** *adj* **1** refined. **2** subtle. **3** delicate.
raffoler (rafɔ'le:) *vi* **raffoler de** rave about, love madly.
raffut (ra'fy) *nm inf* din, uproar.
rafistoler (rafi:stɔ'le:) *vt inf* patch up, mend.
rafle (rafl) *nf* raid (by police).
rafraîchir (rafrɛ'ʃi:r) *vt* **1** cool. **2** refresh. **3** revive. **rafraîchissement** *nm* **1** cooling. **2** refreshing, brushing up. **3** *pl* refreshments.
rager (ra'ʒe:) *vi* be in a rage. **rage** (raʒ) *nf* **1** rage, fury. **2** mania. **3** rabies. **rageur, -euse** (ra'ʒœr, -'ʒœz) *adj* **1** passionate. **2** hot-tempered.
ragot (ra'go) *nm* gossip, scandal.
ragoût (ra'gu:) *nm* stew.
raidir (rɛ'di:r) *vt* **1** stiffen. **2** tighten. **se raidir** *vr* **1** stiffen. **2** brace oneself. **raide** *adj* **1** stiff, rigid. **2** taut. **3** steep. **4** *inf* hard. *adv* hard. **raideur** *nf* **1** stiffness. **2** steepness.
raie[1] (rɛ) *nf* **1** line. **2** streak, stripe. **3** parting (of hair).
raie[2] (rɛ) *nf zool* skate.
raifort (rɛ'fɔr) *nm* horseradish.
rail (rɑj) *nm* rail (of a railway track).
railler (rɑ'je:) *vt* **1** jeer at. **2** tease. **raillerie** (rɑj'ri:) *nf* jest, joke.
rainure (rɛ'nyr) *nf* groove, channel.
raisin (rɛ'zɛ̃) *nm* grape. **raisin de Corinthe/Smyrne** currant/sultana. **raisin sec** raisin.
raison (rɛ'zɔ̃) *nf* **1** reason. **2** reasoning. **3** satisfaction. **4** ratio. **avoir raison** be right. **raisonnable** *adj* **1** reasonable. **2** rational.
raisonner (rɛzɔ'ne:) *vi* **1** reason. **2** argue. *vt* **1**

consider. **2** reason with. **raisonnement** *nm* **1** reasoning. **2** argument.

rajeunir (raʒœ'ni:r) *vt* **1** rejuvenate. **2** renovate. *vi* get younger.

rajuster (raʒy'ste:) *vt* **1** readjust. **2** put straight.

ralentir (ralɑ̃'ti:r) *vt,vi* slow down, slacken. **ralenti** *adj* slow.

rallier (ral'je:) *vt* **1** rally, assemble. **2** win over.

rallonger (ralɔ̃'ʒe:) *vt* lengthen, let down. *vi* draw out. **rallonge** *nf* extension.

ramas (ra'mɑ) *nm* **1** heap. **2** collection

ramasser (ramɑ'se:) *vt* **1** gather together. **2** collect. **3** pick up. **se ramasser** *vr* pick oneself up. **ramassé** *adj* **1** thickset. **2** squat. **3** concise. **ramasse-poussière** *nm invar* dust-pan.

rame[1] (ram) *nf* oar.

rame[2] (ram) *nf* stick, prop. **rameau, -aux** (ra'mo) *nm* branch.

rame[3] (ram) *nf* train.

ramener (ram'ne:) *vt* **1** bring back or round. **2** restore.

ramer (ra'me:) *vi* row. **rameur** *nm* oarsman.

ramier (ra'mje:) *nm* woodpigeon.

se ramifier (rami:'fje:) *vr* branch out.

ramollir (ramɔ'li:r) *vt* **1** soften. **2** weaken.

ramoner (ramɔ'ne:) *vt* sweep (a chimney). **ramoneur** *nm* chimneysweep.

ramper (rɑ̃'pe:) *vi* **1** creep. **2** trail. **3** grovel. **rampe** *nf* **1** slope. **2** banister, handrail. **3** *Th* footlights.

rancart (rɑ̃'kar) *nm* **mettre au rancart** cast aside.

rance (rɑ̃s) *adj* **1** rancid. **2** rank.

rançon (rɑ̃'sɔ̃) *nf* ransom.

rançonner (rɑ̃sɔ'ne:) *vt* ransom, hold to ransom.

rancune (rɑ̃'kyn) *nf* **1** spite. **2** malice. **3** grudge.

rang (rɑ̃) *nm* **1** row, line. **2** rank. **3** status. **de premier rang** first-rate.

ranger (rɑ̃ʒe:) *vt* **1** arrange. **2** put away. **3** tidy. **se ranger** *vr* **1** draw up. **2** settle down. **rangé** *adj* **1** tidy, orderly. **2** staid. **rangée** *nf* row, line.

ranimer (rani:'me:) *vt* **1** revive. **2** stir up.

rapace (ra'pas) *adj* **1** rapacious. **2** predatory.

rapatrier (rapatri:'e:) *vt* repatriate. **rapatrié** *nm* repatriate.

râper (rɑ'pe:) *vt* **1** *cul* grate. **2** grind. **3** wear out. **râpé** *adj* **1** shabby. **2** grated.

rapetisser (rapti:'se:) *vt* **1** make smaller. **2** shrink. *vi* **1** shorten. **2** become smaller.

raphia (ra'fja) *nm* raffia.

rapide (ra'pi:d) *adj* rapid, swift. *nm* express train. **rapidité** *nf* rapidity.

rapiécer (rapje:'se:) *vt* patch (a garment).

rapin (ra'pɛ̃) *nm inf* art student.

rappel (ra'pɛl) *nm* **1** recall. **2** repeal. **3** reminder.

rappeler (ra'ple:) *vt* **1** recall. **2** remind. **3** repeal. **se rappeler** *vr* remember.

rapport (ra'pɔr) *nm* **1** return, yield. **2** report. **3** connection. **4** relations, relationship. **par rapport à 1** with regard to. **2** in comparison with.

rapporter (rapɔr'te:) *vt* **1** bring back. **2** yield. **3** report. **4** *inf* tell tales. **se rapporter** *vr* **1** tally. **2** refer. **s'en rapporter à** rely on. **rapporteur, -euse** (rapɔr'tœr, -'tœz) *nm,f* sneak. *nm* **1** reporter. **2** chairman.

rapprocher (raprɔ'ʃe:) *vt* **1** bring nearer. **2** bring together. **3** compare. **se rapprocher de** *vr* **1** draw nearer to. **2** reconcile with. **rapprochement** *nm* **1** nearness. **2** comparison. **3** reconciliation.

raquette (ra'kɛt) *nf sport* racket.

rare (rɑr) *adj* **1** rare. **2** unusual. **3** exceptional. **4** sparse.

ras (rɑ) *adj* **1** short, cropped. **2** smooth, level. **3** bare. **au ras de** on a level with. **avoir ras le bol de** be sick of. **faire table rase** make a clean sweep.

raser (rɑ'ze:) *vt* **1** shave. **2** brush, skim. **3** *sl* bore. **rasoir** *nm* **1** razor. **2** *inf* bore.

rassasier (rasa'zje:) *vt* satisfy (hunger). **se rassasier** *vr* eat one's fill.

rassembler (rasɑ̃'ble:) *vt* assemble.

se rasséréner (rase:re:'ne:) *vr* **1** (of weather) clear up. **2** brighten up.

rassir (ra'si:r) *vi* get stale. **rassis** *adj* **1** stale. **2** staid. **3** sedate.

rassurer (rasy're:) *vt* **1** reassure. **2** strengthen.

rat (ra) *nm* rat.

ratatiner (ratati:'ne:) *vt* **1** shrivel up. **2** shrink.

râteau, -aux (rɑ'to) *nm* rake.

râteler (rɑt'le:) *vt* rake up. **râtelier** *nm* **1** rack. **2** denture.

rater (ra'te:) *vi* **1** misfire. **2** fail. *vt* miss.

ration (ra'sjɔ̃) *nf* ration, allowance.

rationaliser (rasjɔnali:'ze:) *vt* rationalize. **rationnel, -elle** (rasjɔ'nɛl) *adj* rational.

rationner (rasjɔ'ne:) *vt* ration.

ratisser (rati:'se:) *vt* **1** rake. **2** *inf* raid. **ratissoire** *nm* hoe.

rattacher (rata'ʃe:) *vt* **1** fasten. **2** bind. **3** link. **se rattacher à** *vr* **1** be fastened to. **2** be connected with.

rattraper (ratra'pe:) *vt* **1** catch again. **2** catch up. **3** recover. **se rattraper** *vr* save oneself.
rauque (rok) *adj* raucous, hoarse.
ravager (rava'ʒe:) *vt* **1** devastate. **2** ruin. **3** ravage. **ravages** *nm pl* havoc.
ravauder (ravo'de:) *vt* mend, patch.
ravir (ra'vi:r) *vt* **1** ravish, delight. **2** carry off. **ravi de** *adj* **1** overjoyed at. **2** delighted to. **ravissant** *adj* lovely. **ravisseur** *nm* kidnapper.
se raviser (ravi:'ze:) *vr* change one's mind.
rayer (rɛ'je:) *vt* **1** rule. **2** stripe. **3** scratch. **4** delete.
rayon[1] (rɛ'jɔ̃) *nm* **1** ray. **2** beam. **3** radius. **4** spoke (of a wheel). **rayon X** X-ray.
rayon[2] (rɛ'jɔ̃) *nm* **1** shelf. **2** department (in a shop). **3** counter (of a shop). **rayon de miel** honeycomb.
rayon[3] (rɛ'jɔ̃) *nm* **1** drill (for seed). **2** row.
rayonne (rɛ'jɔn) *nf* rayon.
rayonner (rɛjɔ'ne:) *vi* **1** radiate. **2** beam. **rayonnant** *adj* **1** radiant. **2** beaming. **rayonnement** *nm* **1** radiation. **2** radiance. **3** influence.
rayure (rɛ'jyr) *nf* **1** stripe, streak. **2** scratch. **3** deletion.
razzia (rad'zja) *nf* raid.
réaction (re:ak'sjɔ̃) *nf* reaction. **réacteur** *nm* reactor. **reactionnaire** *adj* reactionary.
réagir (re:a'ʒi:r) *vi* react.
réaliser (re:ali:'ze:) *vt* **1** realize. **2** carry out. **3** sell out.
réalité (re:ali:'te:) *nf* reality. **en réalité** really. **réalisme** *nm* realism. **réaliste** *adj* realistic. *nm,f* realist.
rébarbatif, -ive (re:barba'ti:f, -'ti:v) *adj* **1** grim. **2** surly.
rebattu (rəba'ty) *adj* hackneyed, trite.
rebelle (rə'bɛl) *adj* **1** rebellious. **2** stubborn. **3** opposed. *nm,f* rebel. **rébellion** *nf* rebellion, revolt.
rebondir (rəbɔ̃'di:r) *vi* **1** rebound. **2** bounce.
rebord (rə'bɔr) *nm* **1** edge. **2** rim. **3** hem.
rebours (rə'bu:r) *nm* **1** wrong way. **2** reverse. **à rebours 1** the wrong way. **2** against the grain.
rebrousser (rəbru:'se:) *vt* brush up (hair or nap). *vi* turn back. **rebrousser chemin** retrace one's steps. **à rebrousse-poil** *adv* the wrong way. **à rebrousse-poil** *adv* the wrong way.
rebuffade (rəby'fad) *nf* snub.
rebut (rə'by) *nm* **1** waste. **2** scrap. **3** *pl* rejects.
rebutant (rəby'tɑ̃) *adj* **1** tedious. **2** repulsive.
recéler (rase:'le:) *vt* **1** receive. **2** contain.
récemment (re:sa'mɑ̃) *adv* recently.
recensement (rəsɑ̃s'mɑ̃) *nm* census.
récent (re:'sɑ̃) *adj* recent, fresh.
récepteur, -trice (re:sɛp'tœr, -'tri:s) *adj* receiving. *nm* receiver. **réception** *nf* **1** receipt. **2** welcome. **3** reception.
récession (re:sɛ'sjɔ̃) *nf* recession, slump.
recette (rə'sɛt) *nf* **1** takings. **2** receipt. **3** recipe.
recevable (rəsə'vabl) *adj* allowable.
receveur, -euse (rəsə'vœr, -'vœz) *nm,f* **1** receiver. **2** collector. **3** (bus) conductor.
recevoir* (rəsə'vwar) *vt* **1** receive. **2** entertain. **3** accept. **être reçu à un examen** pass an exam.
rechange (rə'ʃɑ̃ʒ) *nm* replacement, refill, spare. **de rechange** *adj* spare.
réchapper (re:ʃa'pe:) *vi* (*aux* être or avoir) **réchapper de 1** escape from. **2** recover from.
recharge (rə'ʃarʒ) *nf* refill.
réchaud (re:'ʃo) *nm* **1** portable stove. **2** hotplate.
réchauffer (re:ʃo'fe:) *vt* **1** reheat. **2** warm up.
rêche (rɛʃ) *adj* **1** harsh. **2** rough.
rechercher (rəʃɛr'ʃe:) *vt* **1** search for. **2** inquire into. **recherche** *nf* **1** search. **2** research. **3** affectation. **recherché** *adj* **1** in demand. **2** choice. **3** affected.
rechute (rə'ʃyt) *nf* relapse.
récif (re:'si:f) *nm* reef.
récipient (re:si:'pjɑ̃) *nm* container, receptacle.
réciproque (re:si:'prɔk) *adj* reciprocal, mutual.
récit (re:'si:) *nm* **1** narrative, story. **2** account.
réciter (re:si:'te:) *vt* recite. **récital** *nm mus* recital. **récitant** *adj,n mus* solo.
réclame (re:'klam) *nf* **1** publicity, advertising. **2** advertisement. **3** sign. **en réclame** on offer. **faire de la réclame** advertise. **réclamation** *nf* complaint.
recoin (rə'kwɛ̃) *nm* recess.
reçois (rə'swa) *v* see **recevoir.**
récolter (re:kɔl'te:) *vt* **1** harvest. **2** gather. **récolte** *nf* **1** crop. **2** harvest. **3** harvesting.
recommander (rəkɔmɑ̃'de:) *vt* **1** recommend. **2** advise. **3** register (mail).
recommencer (rəkɔmɑ̃'se:) *vt,vi* begin again.
récompenser (re:kɔ̃pɑ̃'se:) *vt* recompense, reward. **récompense** *nf* reward.
réconcilier (re:kɔ̃si:'lje:) *vt* reconcile.
reconduire (rəkɔ̃'dɥi:r) *vt* **1** accompany back. **2** escort home. **3** see out.
réconforter (re:kɔ̃fɔr'te:) *vt* **1** cheer up. **2** fortify.
reconnaissant (rəkɔnɛ'sɑ̃) *adj* **1** grateful. **2**

thankful. **reconnaissance** *nf* **1** recognition. **2** acknowledgment. **3** gratitude. **4** thankfulness.
reconnaître* (rəkɔ'nɛtr) *vt* **1** recognize. **2** acknowledge, admit. **3** explore.
reconstituer (rəkɔ̃sti:'tɥe:) *vt* restore.
record (rə'kɔr) *nm* record.
recours (rə'ku:r) *nm* recourse, resort.
récréation (re:kre:a'sjɔ̃) *nf* **1** recreation, amusement. **2** *educ* break.
recrue (rə'kry) *nf* recruit.
recruter (rəkry'te:) *vt* **1** recruit. **2** enlist.
rectangle (rɛk'tɑ̃g) *adj* right-angled. *nm* rectangle. **rectangulaire** *adj* rectangular.
recteur (rɛk'tœr) *nm* **1** *educ* vice-chancellor. **2** rector.
rectifier (rɛkti:'fje:) *vt* **1** straighten. **2** rectify. **3** correct. **4** adjust.
rectitude (rɛkti:'tyd) *nf* **1** straightness. **2** correctness. **3** integrity.
reçu (rə'sy) *v* see **recevoir.** *adj* **1** received. **2** recognized. *nm* **1** receipt. **2** voucher.
recueil (rə'kœj) *nm* **1** collection. **2** selection. **recueil d'expressions** phrasebook.
recueillir* (rəkœ'ji:r) *vt* **1** gather. **2** pick up, obtain. **3** take in. **se recueillir** *vr* collect one's thoughts. **recueillement** *nm* **1** meditation. **2** composure. **recueilli** *adj* meditative.
recul (rə'kyl) *nm* **1** retreat. **2** setback.
reculer (rəky'le:) *vi* **1** move back. **2** draw back. *vt* **1** move back. **2** postpone. **reculé** *adj* remote. **à reculons** *adv* backwards.
récupérer (re:kype:'re:) *vt* **1** recover. **2** retrieve. **3** make up. **4** *inf* scrounge.
récurer (re:ky're:) *vt* scour, clean.
récurrent (re:kyr'rɑ̃) *adj* recurrent.
rédacteur, -trice (re:dak'tœr, -'tri:s) *nm,f* **1** writer. **2** editor. **rédacteur en chef** editor (of a newspaper, etc.). **rédaction** *nf* **1** writing. **2** editing. **3** editorial staff.
rédiger (re:di:'ʒe:) *vt* **1** draft. **2** write. **3** edit.
redire* (rə'di:r) *vt* repeat. **trouver à redire à** find fault with.
redondant (rədɔ̃'dɑ̃) *adj* superfluous. **redondance** *nf* superfluity.
redouter (rədu:'te:) *vt* fear, dread. **redoutable** *adj* **1** formidable. **2** dangerous.
redresser (rədrɛ'se:) *vt* **1** set upright again. **2** straighten. **3** rectify.
réduire* (re:'dɥi:r) *vt* reduce. **se réduire à** *vr* **1** amount to. **2** confine oneself to. **réduction** *nf* reduction, cut. **réduit** *nm* **1** retreat. **2** nook.
réel, réelle (re:ɛl) *adj* **1** real. **2** actual. **3** true. *nm* reality.
refaire* (rə'fɛr) *vt* **1** do or make again. **2** repair. **se refaire** *vr* recover.
réfectoire (re:fɛk'twar) *nm* refectory.
référendum (re:fe:rɛ̃'dɔm) *nm* referendum.
référer (re:fe:'re:) *vt* **1** refer. **2** ascribe. **se référer à** *vr* refer to. **référence** *nf* reference.
réfléchir (re:fle:'ʃi:r) *vt* reflect. *vi* think, ponder. **réfléchir à** consider. **réfléchi** *adj* **1** thoughtful. **2** deliberate. **3** reflexive.
réflecteur (re:flɛk'tœr) *nm* reflector.
reflet (rə'flɛ) *nm* reflection.
refléter (rəfle:'te:) *vt* reflect.
réflexe (re:'flɛks) *adj,nm* reflex.
réflexion (re:flɛk'sjɔ̃) *nf* **1** reflection. **2** thought.
reflux (rə'fly) *nm* ebb (tide).
réformer (re:fɔr'me:) *vt* **1** reform. **2** discharge. **réformation** *nf* reformation. **réforme** *nf* **1** reform. **2** discharge.
refouler (rəfu:'le:) *vt* **1** drive back. **2** repress.
refrain (rə'frɛ̃) *nm* **1** refrain. **2** chorus.
réfrigérer (re:fri:ʒe:'re:) *vt* refrigerate. **réfrigérateur** *nm* refrigerator.
refroidir (rəfrwa'di:r) *vt* cool, chill. *vi* cool down. **refroidissement** *nm* **1** cooling. **2** *med* chill.
refuge (rə'fyʒ) *nm* refuge, shelter.
se réfugier (re:fy'ʒje:) *vr* take refuge. **réfugié** *nm* refugee.
refus (rə'fy) *nm* refusal.
refuser (rəfy'ze:) *vt* **1** refuse. **2** decline. **3** deny. **4** reject. **être refusé** fail.
réfuter (re:fy'te:) *vt* refute, disprove.
regagner (rəgɑ'ɲe:) *vt* **1** recover, regain. **2** catch up. **3** return to.
regain (rə'gɛ̃) *nm* **1** aftermath. **2** renewal.
régal (re:'gal) *nm* **1** feast. **2** treat.
régaler (re:ga'le:) *vt* **1** entertain. **2** treat.
regard (rə'gar) *nm* **1** look. **2** gaze. **3** glance. **4** manhole. **regard fixe** stare.
regarder (rəgar'de:) *vt* **1** look at. **2** consider. **3** concern. **regarder fixement** stare at.
régent (re:'ʒɑ̃) *nm* regent. **régence** (re:'ʒɑ̃s) *nf* regency.
régie (re:'ʒi:) *nf* administration.
régime (re:'ʒi:m) *nm* **1** regime. **2** system. **3** diet.
régiment (re:ʒi:'mɑ̃) *nm* regiment. **régimentaire** *adj* regimental.
région (re:'ʒjɔ̃) *nf* **1** region. **2** territory. **régional, -aux** (re:ʒjɔ'nal, -'no) *adj* **1** regional. **2** local.
régir (re:'ʒi:r) *vt* **1** govern. **2** manage. **régisseur** *nm* **1** manager. **2** agent. **3** stage manager.
registre (rə'ʒi:str) *nm* register.

régler (re:'gle:) *vt* **1** rule (paper, etc.). **2** regulate. **3** adjust. **4** settle. **règle** *nf* **1** rule. **2** ruler. **3** *pl med* period. **en règle** in order. **règle à calcul** *nf* slide rule. **réglé** *adj* **1** ruled. **2** regular. **3** methodical. **règlement** *nm* **1** regulation. **2** settlement. **réglementaire** (rɛgləmɑ̃'tɛr) *adj* **1** regulation. **2** compulsory, statutory.

réglisse (re:'gli:s) *nf* liquorice.

régner (rɛ'ɲe:) *vi* reign. **règne** *nm* **1** reign. **2** kingdom.

regret (rə'grɛ) *nm* regret.

regretter (rəgrɛ'te:) *vt* regret, be sorry.

régulier, -ière (re:gy'lje:, -'ljɛr) *adj* **1** regular. **2** steady. **3** even. **régularité** *nf* regularity.

réhabiliter (re:abi:li:'te:) *vt* rehabilitate.

rehausser (re:o'ze:) *vt* **1** raise. **2** accentuate. **3** enhance.

rein (rɛ̃) *nm* **1** kidney. **2** *pl* back.

réincarnation (re:ɛ̃karna'sjɔ̃) *nf* reincarnation.

reine (rɛn) *nf* queen. **reine-claude** *nf, pl* **reines-claude** greengage.

réintégrer (re:ɛ̃te:'gre:) *vt* **1** reinstate. **2** resume.

rejeter (rəʒə'te:) *vt* **1** throw back. **2** cast aside. **3** reject. **se rejeter sur** *vr* fall back on.

rejoindre* (rə'ʒwɛ̃dr) *vt* **1** rejoin. **2** connect. **3** catch up. **se rejoindre** *vr* meet.

réjouir (re:'ʒwi:r) *vt* **1** amuse. **2** please. **se réjouir** *vr* **1** be delighted. **2** rejoice.

relâcher (rəlɑ'ʃe:) *vt* **1** slacken. **2** relax. **3** release. **se relâcher** *vr* **1** become slack. **2** abate. **relâche** *nm* **1** relaxation. **2** respite. *nf* port of call.

relais (rə'lɛ) *nm* **1** relay. **2** shift (in a factory, etc.). **relais d'essence** filling station.

relatif, -ive (rəla'ti:f, -'ti:v) *adj* relative.

relation (rəla'sjɔ̃) *nf* **1** relation. **2** communication, contact. **3** statement

relativité (rəlati:vi:'te:) *nf* relativity.

relayer (rəlɛ'je:) *vt* **1** relay. **2** relieve.

relever (rəl've:) *vt* **1** raise. **2** pick up. **3** point out. **4** relieve. **relever de** be dependent on. **relève** *nf* **1** relief. **2** changing of the guard. **relevé** *adj* **1** raised. **2** high. *nm* **1** abstract. **2** summary. **relevé de compte** bank statement.

relief (rə'ljɛf) *nm Art* relief.

religion (rəli:'ʒjɔ̃) *nf* religion. **religieux, -euse** (rəli:'ʒjœ, -'ʒjœz) *adj* **1** religious. **2** sacred. *nm* monk. *nf* nun.

relique (rə'li:k) *nf* relic.

relire* (rə'li:r) *vt* re-read.

reluire (rə'lɥi:r) *vi* **1** shine. **2** glitter.

remanier (rəma'nje:) *vt* adapt, alter.

remarquer (rəmar'ke:) *vt* notice. **faire remarquer** point out. **se faire remarquer** attract attention. **remarque** *nf* remark.

remblai (rɑ̃'blɛ) *nm* embankment.

rembourrer (rɑ̃bu:'re:) *vt* stuff, pad.

rembourser (rɑ̃bu:r'se:) *vt* reimburse, refund. (rɑ̃bu:rsə'mɑ̃) *nm* repayment.

remédier (rəme:'dje:) *vi* **remédier à** remedy. **remède** *nm* remedy, cure.

remercier (rəmɛr'sje:) *vt* **1** thank. **2** dismiss. **remerciement** *nm* thanks.

remettre* (rə'mɛtr) *vt* **1** put back. **2** hand over **3** recollect. **4** postpone.

remise (rə'mi:z) *nf* **1** delivery. **2** remittance. **3** discount. **4** garage.

rémission (re:mi:'sjɔ̃) *nf* remission.

remonter (rəmɔ̃'te:) *vi* (*aux* être) **1** go up again. **2** go back. *vt* **1** climb up again. **2** carry or pull up, raise. **3** wind up. **remontant** *nm* tonic. **remontée** *nf* climb. **remontée du visage** facelift.

remords (rə'mɔr) *nm* remorse.

remorquer (rəmɔr'ke:) *vt* tow. **remorque** *nf* **1** towing. **2** towrope. **3** trailer.

remous (rə'mu:) *nm naut* swirl, wash

rempart (rɑ̃'par) *nm* rampart.

remplacer (rɑ̃pla'se:) *vt* **1** replace **2** substitute. **3** succeed. **remplaçant** *nm* substitute.

rempli (rɑ̃'pli:) *nm* tuck (in a dress).

remplir (rɑ̃'pli:r) *vt* **1** refill. **2** fill up or in. **3** fulfil.

remporter (rɑ̃pɔr'te:) *vt* **1** take away. **2** carry off. **3** win.

remuer (rə'mɥe:) *vt* **1** move. **2** stir. *vi* fidget.

rémunérer (re:myne:'re:) *vt* **1** remunerate. **2** reward. **rémunérateur, -trice** (re:myne:ra'tœr, -'tri:s) *adj* remunerative.

renâcler (rənɑ'kle:) *vi* snort.

renaissance (rənɛ'sɑ̃s) *nf* renaissance.

renard (rə'nar) *nm* fox.

renchérir (rɑ̃ʃe:'ri:r) *vi* increase in price.

rencontrer (rɑ̃kɔ̃'tre:) *vt* **1** meet. **2** encounter. **se rencontrer** *vr* **1** meet. **2** collide. **3** agree. **rencontre** *nf* **1** meeting. **2** encounter. **3** occasion

se rendormir (rɑ̃dɔr'mi:r) *vr* go back to sleep.

rendre (rɑ̃dr) *vt* **1** give back. **2** render. **3** restore. **4** yield. **5** deliver. **6** surrender. **7** make. **se rendre** *vr* **1** go. **2** surrender. **rendez-vous** *nm invar* **1** appointment. **2** meeting place.

rêne (rɛn) *nf* rein.

renfermer (rɑ̃fɛr'me:) *vt* **1** shut up. **2** contain, comprise. **renfermé** *adj* uncommunicative, reserved.

renforcer (rɑ̃fɔr'se:) *vt* **1** reinforce. **2** strengthen. **3** intensify. *vi* grow stronger.

renfort (rɑ̃'fɔr) *nm* reinforcement(s).

se renfrogner (rɑ̃frɔ'ɲe:) *vr* **1** scowl. **2** frown. **renfrogné** *adj* sullen.

rengaine (rɑ̃'gɛn) *nf* hackneyed story.

renier (rə'nje:) *vt* **1** disown. **2** repudiate, deny. **reniement** *nm* **1** repudiation, denial.

renifler (rəni:'fle:) *vi,vt* sniff.

renne (rɛn) *nm* reindeer.

renommée (rənɔ'me:) *nf* renown, fame. **renommé** *adj* famous.

renoncer (rənɔ̃'se:) *vt* **1** renounce. **2** give up.

renoncule (rənɔ̃'kyl) *nf* buttercup.

renouer (rə'nwe:) *vt* **1** tie up again. **2** resume.

renouveler (rənu:'vle:) *vt* renew. **se renouveler** *vr* recur.

rénover (re:nɔ've:) *vt* **1** renovate. **2** restore.

renseigner (rɑ̃sɛ'ɲe:) *vt* inform. **se renseigner sur** *vr* make enquiries about. **renseignement** *nm* information.

rente (rɑ̃t) *nf* **1** private income. **2** pension. **3** rent.

rentrer (rɑ̃'tre:) *vi* (*aux* être) **1** return. **2** come in again. **3** go home. *vt* take or bring in. **rentrée** *nf* **1** return. **2** reopening. **3** beginning of school term.

renverser (rɑ̃vɛr'se:) *vt* **1** turn upside down. **2** knock over. **3** invert. **4** *inf* amaze. **se renverser** *vr* overturn. **renverse** *nf* **1** turn. **2** change. **renversement** *nm* **1** reversal, inversion. **2** overthrow.

renvoi (rɑ̃'vwa) *nm* **1** return. **2** dismissal. **3** postponement.

renvoyer* (rɑ̃vwa'je:) *vt* **1** send back. **2** dismiss. **3** postpone. **4** refer.

réorganiser (re:ɔrgani:'ze:) *vt* reorganize.

repaire (rə'pɛr) *nm* **1** den. **2** refuge.

répandre (re:'pɑ̃dr) *vt* **1** spill. **2** spread. **3** scatter. **se répandre** *vr* be spread. **répandu** *adj* **1** widespread. **2** well-known.

reparaître* (rəpa'rɛtr) *vi* reappear.

réparer (re:pa're:) *vt* **1** repair. **2** make amends. **réparation** *nf* **1** repair. **2** amends.

repartie (rəpar'ti:) *nf* **1** repartee. **2** retort.

répartir (re:par'ti:r) *vt* **1** distribute. **2** divide. **3** allocate. **répartition** *nf* **1** distribution. **2** allocation.

repas (rə'pa) *nm* meal.

repasser (rəpɑ'se:) *vi* (*aux* être) pass again. *vt* **1** pass over. **2** go over. **3** sharpen. **4** iron. **repassage** *nm* **1** sharpening. **2** ironing.

se repentir* (rəpɑ̃'ti:r) *vr* repent, be sorry. **repenti** *adj* repentant. **repentir** *nm* repentance.

répercussion (re:pɛrky'sjɔ̃) *nf* repercussion.

répercuter (re:pɛrky'te:) *vt* **1** reverberate. **2** reflect.

repérer (rəpe:'re:) *vt* spot, locate. **repère** *nm* reference. **point de repère** *nm* landmark.

répertoire (re:pɛr'twar) *nm* **1** index, catalogue. **2** repertoire. **3** repertory.

répéter (re:pe:'te:) *vt* **1** repeat. **2** rehearse. **répétiteur, -trice** (re:pe:ti:'tœr, -'tri:s) *nm,f* tutor. **répétition** *nf* **1** repetition. **2** rehearsal. **répétition générale** dress rehearsal.

répit (re:'pi:) *nm* respite.

replacer (rəpla'se:) *vt* **1** put back. **2** reassign.

repli (rə'pli:) *nm* **1** fold, crease. **2** coil.

replier (rəpli:'e:) *vt* **1** fold up. **2** turn back.

répliquer (re:pli:'ke:) *vi* retort. **réplique** *nf* **1** retort. **2** *Th* cue. **3** *Art* replica.

répondre (re:'pɔ̃dr) *vt* **1** reply, answer. **2** respond. **répondre de** answer for.

réponse (re:'pɔ̃s) *nf* **1** answer, reply. **2** response.

reporter[1] (rəpɔr'te:) *vt* **1** carry back. **2** defer. **se reporter** *vr* refer.

reporter[2] (rəpɔr'te:) *nm* reporter. **reportage** *nm* **1** report. **2** reporting.

repos (rə'po) *nm* **1** rest. **2** peace.

reposer[1] (rəpo'ze:) *vt* put back, replace.

reposer[2] (rəpo'ze:) *vt* rest. *vi* **1** lie. **2** be based. **se reposer** *vr* **1** rest. **2** settle. **3** rely.

repousser (rəpu:'se:) *vt* **1** push back. **2** repulse. **3** reject.

reprendre* (rə'prɛ̃dr) *vt* **1** take back. **2** resume. **3** reply. **4** reprimand. *vi* recommence. **se reprendre** *vr* **1** pull oneself together. **2** correct oneself.

représailles (rəprɛ'zaj) *nf pl* retaliation, reprisal. **user de représailles** retaliate.

représenter (rəpre:zɑ̃'te:) *vt* **1** represent. **2** depict. **3** act for. **4** *Th* perform. **représentant** *adj,n* representative. **représentation** *nf* **1** representation. **2** agency. **3** *Th* performance.

répressif, -ive (re:prɛ'si:f, -'si:v) *adj* repressive. **répression** *nf* repression.

réprimander (re:pri:mɑ̃'de:) *vt* reprimand, censure. **réprimande** *nf* reprimand.

réprimer (re:'pri:'me:) *vt* **1** repress. **2** quell.

reprise (rə'pri:z) *nf* **1** renewal. **2** revival. **3**

repetition. **4** darning. **5** *sport* round. **à plusieurs reprises** again and again.
reprocher (rəprɔ'ʃe:) *vt* **1** reproach. **2** grudge. **reproche** *nm* reproach.
reproduction (rəprɔdyk'sjɔ̃) *nf* reproduction.
reproduire (rəprɔ'dɥi:r) *vt* reproduce. **se reproduire** *vr* recur.
reptile (rɛp'ti:l) *adj,nm* reptile.
répu (re:'py) *adj* well fed, sated.
républicain (re:pybli:'kɛ̃) *adj,n* republican.
république (re:py'bli:k) *nf* republic.
répudier (re:py'dje:) *vt* repudiate.
répulsif, -ive (re:pyl'si:f, -'si:v) *adj* repulsive. **répulsion** *nf* repulsion.
réputation (re:pyta'sjɔ̃) *nf* reputation, repute. **réputé** *adj* famous, well-known.
requérir* (rəke:'ri:r) *vt* **1** ask, request. **2** demand.
requête (rə'kɛt) *nf* **1** request. **2** petition.
requiem (re:kɥi:'ɛm) *nm invar* requiem.
requin (rə'kɛ̃) *nm* shark.
requis (rə'ki:) *adj* necessary.
rescapé (rɛska'pe:) *nm* survivor.
réseau, -aux (re:'zo) *nm* network, system.
réserver (re:zɛr've:) *vt* reserve. **réserve** *nf* **1** reservation. **2** reserve. **3** caution. **4** store. **réservé** *adj* **1** reserved. **2** cautious. **3** secretive. **réservoir** *nm* **1** reservoir. **2** tank.
résider (re:zi:'de:) *vi* **1** reside, live. **2** consist. **résidence** *nf* residence. **résident** *nm* resident. **résidentiel, -elle** (re:zi:dɑ̃'sjɛl) *adj* residential.
résidu (re:si:'dy) *nm* residue.
se résigner (re:zi:'ɲe:) *vr* resign oneself.
résilier (re:zi:l'je:) *vt* cancel, annul.
résille (re:'zi:j) *nf* hairnet.
résine (re:'zi:n) *nf* resin.
résister (re:zi:'ste:) *vi* (of colours) be fast. **résister à** **1** resist. **2** withstand. **3** oppose. **résistance** *nf* **1** resistance. **2** strength.
résolu (re:zɔ'ly) *v* see **résoudre.** *adj* determined, resolute. **résolution** *nf* **1** solution (of a problem). **2** resolution. **3** resolve.
résolvant (re:zɔl'vɑ̃) *v* see **résoudre.**
résonner (re:zɔ'ne:) *vi* resound, reverberate.
résoudre* (re:'zu:dr) *vt* **1** dissolve. **2** solve, settle. **3** resolve.
respect (rɛ'spɛ) *nm* respect. **respect de soi** self-respect.
respecter (rɛspɛk'te:) *vt* **1** respect. **2** abide by. **respectable** *adj* respectable. **respectueux, -euse** (rɛspɛk'tɥœ, -'tɥœz) *adj* respectful. **respectueux des lois** law-abiding.
respectif, -ive (rɛspɛk'ti:f, -'ti:v) *adj* respective.
respirer (rɛspi:'re:) *vi,vt* breathe. **respiration** *nf* breathing. **respiration artificielle** artifical respiration.
resplendir (rɛsplɑ̃'di:r) *vi* **1** glitter. **2** glow.
responsable (rɛspɔ̃'sabl) *adj* responsible. **responsabilité** *nf* responsibility.
resquiller (rɛski:'je:) *vi* gatecrash. *vt inf* wangle.
ressaisir (rəsɛ'zi:r) *vt* seize again. **se ressaisir** *vr* pull oneself together.
ressembler (rəsɑ̃'ble:) *vt* resemble. **se ressembler** *vr* be alike. **ressemblance** *nf* resemblance.
ressentir* (rəsɑ̃'ti:r) *vt* feel. **ressentiment** *nm* resentment.
ressort[1] (rə'sɔr) *nm* **1** spring. **2** energy. **3** elasticity.
ressort[2] (rə'sɔr) *nm* scope, province.
ressortir* (rəsɔr'ti:r) *vi* (*aux* être) **1** come or go out again. **2** stand out. *vt* bring out again. **ressortir de** follow from.
ressource (rə'su:rs) *nf* **1** resource. **2** expedient. **3** *pl* means.
ressusciter (re:sysi:'te:) *vt* restore to life. *vt,vi* revive.
restaurer (rɛstɔ're:) *vt* **1** restore. **2** refresh. **restauration** *nf* restoration.
rester (rɛ'ste:) *vi* (*aux* être) **1** remain, stay. **2** be left. **restant** *adj* remaining. *nm* remainder. **reste** *nm* **1** remainder. **2** *pl* remains. **du reste** moreover.
restituer (rɛsti:'tɥe:) *vt* **1** restore. **2** return.
restreindre* (rɛ'strɛ̃dr) *vt* restrict, limit.
restriction (rɛstri:k'sjɔ̃) *nf* restriction.
résulter (re:zyl'te:) *vi* (*aux* être) result, follow. **résultat** *nm* **1** result. **2** outcome.
résumer (re:zy'me:) *vt* summarize. **résumé** *nm* summary, résumé.
résurrection (re:zyrɛk'sjɔ̃) *nf* resurrection.
rétablir (re:ta'bli:r) *vt* **1** re-establish. **2** restore. **3** reinstate. **rétablissement** *nm* **1** restoration. **2** recovery.
retard (rə'tar) *nm* delay. **en retard** **1** late, behindhand. **2** backward.
retarder (rətar'de:) *vt* retard, delay. *vi* be late. **retardataire** *adj* **1** late. **2** backward.
retenir* (rət'ni:r) *vt* **1** hold back. **2** detain. **3** secure. **4** retain. **5** book, reserve. **se retenir** *vr* **1** restrain oneself. **2** cling.
retentir (rətɑ̃'ti:r) *vi* **1** resound. **2** reverberate. **3** echo. **retentissement** *nm* **1** repercussion. **2** reverberation.

retenue (rət'ny) *nf* **1** discretion. **2** withholding. **3** detention. **retenu** *adj* prudent.
réticent (re:ti:'sɑ̃) *adj* reticent, reserved.
rétif, -ive (re:'ti:f, -'ti:v) *adj* obstinate.
rétine (re:'ti:n) *nf* retina.
retirer (rəti:'re:) *vt* **1** withdraw. **2** pull out. **3** remove. **se retirer** *vr* retire, withdraw.
retomber (rətɔ̃'be:) *vi* (*aux* être) **1** fall back. **2** hang down.
retors (rə'tɔr) *adj* **1** twisted. **2** cunning.
retoucher (rətu:'ʃe:) *vt* touch up, improve. **retouche** *nf* small alteration.
retour (rə'tu:r) *nm* return. **être de retour** be back.
retourner (rətu:r'ne:) *vt* **1** turn (inside out). **2** turn round or back. **3** return. *vi* (*aux* être) go back. **se retourner** *vr* turn round or back.
rétracter[1] (re:trak'te:) *vt* retract, withdraw.
rétracter[2] (re:trak'te:) *vt* retract, draw in.
retraite (rə'trɛt) *nf* **1** retreat. **2** *mil* tattoo. **3** retirement. **4** refuge. **prendre sa retraite** retire. **retraité** *nm* pensioner.
retrancher (rətrɑ̃'ʃe:) *vt* **1** cut off or down. **2** entrench.
rétrécir (re:tre:'si:r) *vi,vt* **1** narrow. **2** contract, shrink. **rétrécissement** *nm* shrinkage.
rétribuer (re:tri:'bɥe:) *vt* remunerate, pay.
rétroaction (re:troak'sjɔ̃) *nf* feedback.
rétrograder (re:trɔgra'de:) *vi* retrogress, go backwards. **rétrograde** *adj* retrograde, backward.
rétrospectif, -ive (re:trɔspɛk'ti:f, -'ti:v) *adj* retrospective.
retrousser (rətru:'se:) *vt* **1** turn up. **2** tuck up. **3** roll up.
retrouver (rətru:'ve:) *vt* **1** find again. **2** regain.
rétroviseur (re:trɔvi:'zœr) *nm* driving mirror.
réunir (re:y'ni:r) *vt* reunite. **se réunir** *vr* gather together. **réunion** *nf* reunion, meeting.
réussir (re:y'si:r) *vi* succeed. **réussi** *adj* successful. **réussite** *nf* **1** success. **2** *pl game* patience.
revanche (rə'vɑ̃ʃ) *nf* **1** revenge. **2** return match. **en revanche 1** in return. **2** on the other hand.
rêvasser (rɛva'se:) *vi* daydream.
rêve (rɛv) *nm* dream.
revêche (rə'vɛʃ) *adj* **1** perverse, difficult. **2** harsh, churlish.
réveiller (re:vɛ'je:) *vt* wake, awaken. **se réveiller** *vr* awake, wake up. **réveille-matin** *nm invar* alarm clock.
révéler (re:ve:'le:) *vt* **1** reveal, disclose. **2** show. **révélateur, -trice** (re:ve:la'tœr, -'tri:s) *adj* revealing, telltale.
revendiquer (rəvɑ̃di:'ke:) *vt* **1** claim, demand. **2** assume. **revendication** *nf* demand.
revenir* (rəv'ni:r) *vi* (*aux* être) **1** return, come back. **2** go back on. **3** cost. **4** amount. **revenir de** recover. **en revenir** get over it. **revenant** *adj* pleasing. *nm* ghost. **revenu** *nm* revenue, income.
rêver (rɛ've:) *vi* **1** dream. **2** muse.
réverbérer (re:vɛrbe:'re:) *vt* reflect. *vi* reverberate. **réverbère** *nm* **1** streetlamp. **2** reflector.
révérence (re:vɛ'rɑ̃s) *nf* **1** reverence. **2** bow, curtsy.
revers (rə'vɛr) *nm* **1** reverse. **2** wrong side. **3** lapel.
revêtir* (rəvɛ'ti:r) *vt* **1** clothe, dress. **2** coat, case.
revirement (rəvi:r'mɑ̃) *nm* sudden change.
reviser (rəvi:'ze:) *vt* revise, modify. **revision** *nf* **1** revision. **2** inspection.
revivre* (rə'vi:vr) *vi* relive. **faire revivre** revive.
revoir* (rə'vwar) *vt* **1** see again. **2** revise. **au revoir!** *interj* goodbye!
révolter (re:vɔl'te:) *vt* **1** rouse, stir up. **2** disgust. **révolte** *nf* revolt. **révolté** *nm* rebel.
révolution (re:vɔly'sjɔ̃) *nf* revolution. **révolutionnaire** *adj* revolutionary.
revolver (re:vɔl'vɛr) *nm* revolver.
révoquer (re:vɔ'ke:) *vt* **1** revoke. **2** dismiss.
revue (rə'vy) *nf* **1** inspection. **2** review. **3** revue.
rez-de-chaussé (re:dʃo'se:) *nm invar* ground floor.
rhétorique (re:tɔ'ri:k) *nf* rhetoric.
Rhin (rɛ̃) *nm* Rhine.
rhinocéros (rinɔse:'rɔs) *nm* rhinoceros.
Rhodésie (rɔde:'zi:) *nf* Rhodesia. **rhodésien, -ienne** (rɔde:'zjɛ̃, -'zjɛn) *adj,n* Rhodesian.
Rhône (ron) *nm* Rhone.
rhubarbe (ry'barb) *nf* rhubarb.
rhum (rɔm) *nm* rum.
rhumatisme (ryma'ti:sm) *nm* rheumatism.
rhume (rym) *nm med* cold. **rhume des foins** hayfever.
ri (ri:) *v* see **rire.**
riant (ri:'ɑ̃) *v* see **rire.**
ricaner (ri:ka'ne:) *vi* sneer.
riche (ri:ʃ) *adj* **1** rich, wealthy. **2** valuable. **3** fertile. **richesse** *nf* **1** wealth. **2** richness.
rider (ri:'de:) *vt* **1** wrinkle. **2** shrivel. **se rider** *vr* **1** wrinkle. **2** shrivel. **3** ripple. **ride** *nf* **1**

wrinkle. 2 ripple. **ridé** *adj* 1 wrinkled. 2 corrugated.
rideau, -aux (ri:'do) *nm* 1 curtain. 2 screen. **Rideau de Fer** Iron Curtain.
ridectomie (ri:dɛktɔ'mi:) *nf* facelift.
ridicule (ri:di:'kyl) *adj* ridiculous. *nm* 1 absurdity. 2 ridicule.
rien (rjɛ̃) *pron* anything: **ne...rien** nothing. **cela ne fait rien** that doesn't matter. **il n'y a rien à faire** it can't be helped. ~*nm* trifle, trivial thing or affair.
rigide (ri:'ʒi:d) *adj* 1 rigid. 2 stiff. 3 tense. **rigidité** *nf* rigidity.
rigole (ri:'gɔl) *nf* drain, gutter.
rigoler (ri:gɔ'le:) *vi inf* 1 laugh. 2 enjoy oneself. 3 joke. **rigolo, -ote** *adj* funny, comical.
rigoureux, -euse (ri:gu:'rœ, -'rœz) *adj* 1 rigorous. 2 harsh. 3 strict.
rigueur (ri:'gœr) *nf* 1 rigour, strictness. 2 severity. 3 hardship. **à la rigueur** 1 strictly. 2 if need be. **de rigueur** compulsory.
rimer (ri:'me:) *vi* rhyme. **rime** *nf* rhyme.
rincer (rɛ̃'se:) *vt* rinse.
riposter (ri:pɔ'ste:) *vi* retort. **riposte** *nf* retort.
rire* (ri:r) *vi* 1 laugh. 2 joke. **rire nerveusement** giggle. **rire tout bas** chuckle. **se rire de** *vr* laugh at. ~*nm* 1 laughter. 2 laugh. **petit rire nerveux** giggle. **rire étouffé** chuckle.
ris (ri:) **ris de veau** *nm* sweetbread.
risquer (ri:'ske:) *vt* risk. **se risquer** *vr* take a risk. **risque** *nm* risk.
ristourne (ri:'stu:rn) *nf* 1 refund, rebate. 2 discount.
rite (ri:t) *nm* rite. **rituel, -elle** (ri:'tɥɛl) *adj,nm* ritual.
rival, -aux (ri:'val, -'vo) *adj,n* rival.
rivaliser (ri:vali:'ze:) *vi* 1 rival. 2 compete. **rivalité** *nf* rivalry.
rive (ri:v) *nf* 1 bank (of a river). 2 shore. 3 riverside. 4 edge. **rivage** *nm* 1 bank (of a river). 2 shore.
river (ri:'ve:) *vt* rivet. **rivet** *nm* rivet.
rivière (ri:'vjɛr) *nf* 1 river. 2 stream.
rixe (ri:ks) *nf* brawl, scuffle.
riz (ri:) *nm* rice.
robe (rɔb) *nf* 1 dress. 2 gown. 3 robe. 4 skin (of an onion, etc.). **robe de chambre** dressing-gown. **robe du soir** evening dress.
robinet (rɔbi:'nɛ) *nm* tap.
robot (ro'bo) *nm* robot.
robuste (rɔ'byst) *adj* 1 robust. 2 sturdy. 3 hardy.
roche (rɔʃ) *nf* rock, boulder. **rocher** *nm* rock.
rôder (ro'de:) *vi* prowl.
rogner (rɔ'ɲe:) *vt* clip, trim.
rognon (rɔ'ɲɔ̃) *nm cul* kidney.
rogue (rɔg) *adj* arrogant.
roi (rwa) *nm* king.
roitelet (rwat'lɛ) *nm* wren.
rôle (rol) *nm* 1 roll. 2 part, role.
romain (rɔ'mɛ̃) *adj,n* Roman.
roman[1] (rɔ'mɑ̃) *nm* 1 novel. 2 *pl* fiction. **roman policier** detective novel. **romancier, -ière** (rɔmɑ̃'sje:, -'sjɛr) *nm,f* novelist.
roman[2] (rɔ'mɑ̃) *adj* 1 romance. 2 Romanesque.
romanesque (rɔma'nɛsk) *adj* romantic.
romantique (rɔmɑ̃'ti:k) *adj* romantic.
romarin (rɔma'rɛ̃) *nm* rosemary.
Rome (rɔm) *nf* Rome.
rompre (rɔ̃pr) *vt* 1 break. 2 snap. 3 break off or up. *vi* break. **rompu** *adj* broken.
ronce (rɔ̃s) *nf* 1 blackberry bush. 2 *pl* thorns.
rond (rɔ̃) *adj* 1 round. 2 plump. 3 *sl* drunk. *nm* 1 ring, circle. 2 washer. 3 disc. **rond-de-cuir** *nm, pl* **ronds-de-cuir** *inf* 1 clerk. 2 bureaucrat. **rond-point** *nm, pl* **ronds-points** roundabout. **ronde** *nf* 1 round, inspection. 2 semibreve.
ronfler (rɔ̃'fle:) *vi* 1 snore. 2 (of a fire) roar. 3 hum. **ronflement** *nm* 1 snore. 2 snoring. 3 buzzing.
ronger (rɔ̃'ʒe:) *vt* 1 gnaw. 2 corrode. 3 erode. **rongeur, -euse** (rɔ̃'ʒœr, -'ʒœz) *adj* gnawing. *nm* rodent.
ronron (rɔ̃'rɔ̃) *nm* purr.
ronronner (rɔ̃rɔ'ne:) *vi* purr.
roquet (rɔ'kɛ) *nm* mongrel.
roquette (rɔ'kɛt) *nf* rocket.
rosaire (ro'zɛr) *nm* rosary.
rosbif (rɔs'bi:f) *nm* roast beef.
rose (roz) *nf* rose. **rose trémière** hollyhock. *adj* pink, rosy. *nm* pink. **rosé** *adj* pink. *nm* rosé wine. **rosier** *nm* rose bush or tree.
roseau, -aux (ro'zo) *nm* reed.
rosée (ro'ze:) *nf* dew.
roselet (ro'zlɛ) *nm* ermine.
rosette (ro'zɛt) *nf* 1 bow (of ribbon). 2 rosette.
rosser (rɔ'se:) *vt* give a beating. **rossée** *nf inf* thrashing.
rossignol (rɔsi:'ɲɔl) *nm* 1 nightingale. 2 *inf* piece of junk.
rotatif, -ive (rɔta'ti:f, -'ti:v) *adj* rotary. **rotation** *nf* rotation.
rôtir (ro'ti:r) *vt,vi* 1 roast. 2 toast. 3 scorch. **rôti** *nm* roast (meat). **rôtisserie** *nf* grillroom.
rotor (rɔ'tɔr) *nm* rotor.

rotule (rɔ'tyl) *nf* kneecap.
rouage (rwaʒ) *nm* **1** works, machinery. **2** wheel.
roublard (ru:'blar) *adj inf* sly, artful.
rouble (ru:bl) *nm* rouble.
roue (ru:) *nf* wheel. **faire la roue 1** strut. **2** do a cartwheel.
roué (rwe:) *adj* cunning.
rouelle (rwɛl) *nf* round slice, round.
rougeole (ru:'ʒɔl) *nf* measles.
rougir (ru:'ʒi:r) *vt* redden. *vi* **1** turn red. **2** blush. **rouge** *adj* red. **rouge-gorge** *nm, pl* **rouges-gorges** robin. *nm* **1** red. **2** rouge. **rougeur** *nf* **1** redness. **2** blush, flush.
rouiller (ru:'je:) *vi* **1** rust. **2** mildew. **rouille** *nf* **1** rust. **2** mildew.
rouler (ru:'le:) *vt* **1** roll. **2** *inf* take in, swindle. **3** turn over. *vi* **1** roll (over or down). **2** rumble. **3** roam. **4** turn. **se rouler** *vr* roll. **roulage** *nm* carriage, haulage. **roulant** *adj* **1** sliding, moving. **2** smooth. **3** *sl* hilarious. **rouleau, -aux** (ru:'lo) *nm* **1** roller. **2** roll. **3** spool. **4** rolling pin. **rouleau compresseur** steam-roller. **rouleau de papier hygiénique** toilet roll. **roulette** *nf* **1** castor, small wheel. **2** roulette.
roulotte (ru:'lɔt) *nf* (gipsy) caravan.
roupiller (ru:pi:'je:) *vi inf* sleep, snooze. **roupillon** *nm* snooze.
rouquin (ru:'kɛ̃) *adj inf* red-haired, ginger.
rouspéter (ru:spe:'te:) *vi* **1** protest. **2** grumble.
roussir (ru:'si:r) *vi,vt* turn brown. *vi* singe, get scorched. **rousseur** *nf* redness (of hair).
route (ru:t) *nf* **1** road, track. **2** route. **route nationale** main road, trunk road.
routine (ru:'ti:n) *nf* routine.
roux, rousse (ru:, ru:s) *adj* **1** red-haired. **2** reddish.
royal, -aux (rwa'jal, -'jo) *adj* royal, regal.
royaume (rwa'jom) *nm* **1** kingdom. **2** realm. **royauté** (rwajo'te:) *nf* royalty.
Royaume-Uni *nm* United Kingdom.
ruban (ry'bɑ̃) *nm* **1** ribbon. **2** band.
rubéole (rybe:'ɔl) *nf* German measles.
rubis (ry'bi:) *nm* ruby.
rubrique (ry'bri:k) *nf* heading, title.
ruche (ryʃ) *nf* beehive.
rude (ryd) *adj* **1** hard. **2** rough. **3** harsh. **4** uncouth. **5** gruff. **rudement** *adv inf* very. **rudesse** *nf* **1** harshness. **2** severity. **3** roughness.
rudiment (rydi:'mɑ̃) *nm* rudiment.
rudoyer (rydwa'je:) *vt* **1** treat roughly. **2** bully.
rue (ry) *nf* street, thoroughfare. **rue à sens unique** one-way street. **ruelle** *nf* alley, lane.
ruer (rɥe:) *vi* (of a horse, etc.) kick (out). **se ruer** *vr* **1** fling oneself. **2** rush. **ruée** *nf* rush.
rugir (ry'ʒi:r) *vi* **1** roar. **2** howl. **rugissement** *nm* **1** roar. **2** roaring.
rugueux, -euse (ry'gœ, -'gœz) *adj* **1** rough. **2** rugged. **3** wrinkled.
ruiner (rɥi:'ne:) *vt* ruin. **se ruiner** *vr* **1** go to ruin. **2** ruin oneself. **ruine** *nf* **1** ruin. **2** downfall. **3** destruction.
ruisseau, -aux (rɥi:'so) *nm* **1** gutter. **2** brook. **3** stream.
ruisseler (rɥi:'sle:) *vi* **1** trickle, drip. **2** stream, flow.
rumeur (ry'mœr) *nf* **1** murmur, distant noise. **2** din. **3** rumour.
rupture (ryp'tyr) *nf* **1** breaking. **2** rupture.
rural, -aux (ry'ral, -'ro) *adj* rural.
ruse (ryz) *nf* trick, stratagem. **rusé** *adj* sly.
Russie (ry'si:) *nf* Russia. **russe** *adj,n* Russian. *nm* Russian (language).
rustique (ry'sti:k) *adj* **1** rustic. **2** rural.
rutabaga (rytaba'ga) *nm* swede.
rythme (ri:tm) *nm* **1** rhythm. **2** *mus* beat. **rythmique** *adj* rhythmical.

S

sa (sa) *poss adj* see **son.**
sabbat (sa'ba) *nm* Sabbath.
sable[1] (sɑbl) *nm* sand. **sables mouvants** *nm pl* quicksand. **sableux, -euse** (sa'blœ, -'blœz) *adj* sandy. **sablière** (sɑbli:'ɛr) *nf* sandpit.
sable[2] (sɑbl) *nm* sable.
sabot (sa'bo) *nm* **1** clog. **2** hoof.
sabotage (sabɔ'taʒ) *nm* sabotage.
sabre (sabr) *nm* **1** sabre. **2** swordfish.
sac (sak) *nm* **1** sack. **2** bag. **sac à dos** rucksack. **sac à main** handbag. **sac de couchage** sleeping-bag.
saccade (sa'kad) *nf* jolt, jerk. **par saccades** by fits and starts.
saccager (saka'ʒe:) *vt* **1** pillage. **2** ransack, cause havoc.
saccharine (sakka'ri:n) *nf* saccharin.
sacerdoce (sasɛr'dɔs) *nm* priesthood.
sachant (sə'ʃɑ̃) *v* see **savoir.**
sachet (sa'ʃɛ) *nm* **1** small bag. **2** sachet.
sacoche (sa'kɔʃ) *nf* **1** saddlebag. **2** satchel.
sacrement (sakrə'mɑ̃) *nm* sacrament.
sacrer (sa'kre:) *vt* anoint, crown. *vi* swear.

sacre *nm* **1** coronation. **2** consecration. **sacré** *adj* **1** holy, sacred. **2** *sl* damned, cursed.
sacrifier (sakri:'fje:) *vt* **1** sacrifice. **2** give up. **sacrifice** *nm* sacrifice.
sacrilège (sakri:'lɛʒ) *nm* sacrilege. *adj* sacrilegious.
sacristie (sakri:'sti:) *nf* vestry.
sadisme (sa'di:sm) *nm* sadism. **sadique** *adj* sadistic. *nm,f* sadist.
safran (sa'frɑ̃) *nm* **1** saffron. **2** crocus.
sagace (sa'gas) *adj* shrewd.
sage (saʒ) *adj* **1** wise. **2** discreet. **3** well-behaved. **4** chaste. **sois sage!** be good! **sage-femme** *nf, pl* **sages-femmes** midwife. **sagesse** *nf* **1** wisdom. **2** prudence.
Sagittaire (saʒi:t'tɛr) *nm* Sagittarius.
sagou (sa'gu:) *nm* sago.
saigner (sɛ'ɲe:) *vi,vt* bleed. **saignant** *adj* **1** bleeding. **2** *cul* underdone, rare.
saillir* (sa'ji:r) *vi* **1** gush out. **2** protrude. **3** stand out. **saillant** *adj* **1** prominent, protruding. **2** outstanding. **saillie** *nf* **1** spurt. **2** bound. **3** flash of wit. **4** ledge.
sain (sɛ̃) *adj* **1** healthy. **2** sound. **3** wholesome. **sain et sauf** safe and sound.
saindoux (sɛ'du:) *nm* lard.
saint (sɛ) *adj* **1** holy. **2** saintly. **3** hallowed. *nm* saint. **sainteté** *nf* holiness.
Saint-Esprit *nf* Holy Ghost.
sais (sɛ) *v see* **savoir.**
saisir (sɛ'zi:r) *vt* **1** seize, grab. **2** understand. **se saisir de** *vr* **1** seize upon. **2** lay hands on. **saisie** *nf* seizure. **saisissant** *adj* **1** striking. **2** piercing. **3** thrilling. **saisissement** *nm* **1** shock. **2** shiver.
saison (sɛ'zɔ̃) *nf* season. **de saison** in season. **saisonnier, -ière** (sɛzɔ'nje:, -'njɛr) *adj* seasonal.
salade (sa'lad) *nf* **1** salad. **2** lettuce. **3** *sl* mess.
salaire (sa'lɛr) *nm* **1** wages, salary. **2** reward.
salamandre (sala'mɑ̃dr) *nf* salamander. **salamandre aquatique** newt.
sale (sal) *adj* **1** dirty, filthy. **2** offensive, obscene. **saleté** *nf* **1** dirt. **2** trash. **3** obscenity. **4** dirty trick.
saler (sa'le:) *vt* **1** salt. **2** *cul* cure. **3** *inf* overcharge. **salaison** *nf cul* curing. **salé** *adj* **1** salted. **2** *inf* spicy. **3** *sl* exorbitant. **salière** *nf* salt-cellar.
salir (sa'li:r) *vt* **1** dirty, soil. **2** sully.
saliver (sali:'ve:) *vi* salivate. **salive** *nf* saliva.
salle (sal) *nf* **1** room. **2** *Th* house. **3** *pol* lobby. **salle à manger** dining room. **salle d'attente** waiting room. **salle de bain** bathroom. **salle de bal** ballroom. **salle de classe** classroom. **salle de séjour** living room. **salle de spectacle** theatre. **salle d'hôpital** *med* ward. **salle d'opérations** *med* theatre.
salon (sa'lɔ̃) *nm* **1** drawing room. **2** saloon. **3** salon.
saloperie (salɔ'pri:) *nf* **1** filthiness. **2** *inf* rubbish. **3** dirty trick.
salopette (salɔ'pɛt) *nf* **1** overalls. **2** dungarees.
saltimbanque (saltɛ̃'bɑ̃k) *nm* **1** showman. **2** charlatan.
salubre (sa'lybr) *adj* **1** healthy. **2** wholesome.
saluer (sal'ɥe:) *vt* **1** greet. **2** salute. **3** bow.
salut (sa'ly) *nm* **1** safety. **2** salvation. **3** bow. **4** greeting. **5** salute. *interj* hello! **salutation** *nf* **1** greeting. **2** bow.
salutaire (saly'tɛr) *adj* **1** beneficial. **2** healthy.
samedi (sam'di:) *nm* Saturday.
sanctifier (sɑ̃kti:'fje:) *vt* hallow.
sanction (sɑ̃k'sjɔ̃) *nf* **1** sanction, approval. **2** *law* penalty.
sanctionner (sɑ̃ksjɔ'ne:) *vt* **1** sanction, approve. **2** penalize.
sanctuaire (sɑ̃k'tɥɛr) *nm* sanctuary.
sandale (sɑ̃'dal) *nf* sandal.
sandwich (sɑ̃'dwi:tʃ) *nm* sandwich.
sang (sɑ̃) *nm* **1** blood. **2** relationship. **à sang chaud/froid** warm/cold-blooded. **sang-froid** *nm* composure, coolness. **sang-mêlé** *nm invar* half-caste.
sanglant (sɑ̃'glɑ̃) *adj* **1** covered in blood. **2** scathing.
sangler (sɑ̃'gle:) *vt* **1** strap, tie up. **2** thrash. **sangle** *nf* **1** strap. **2** girth.
sanglier (sɑ̃gli:'e:) *nm* wild boar.
sanglot (sɑ̃'glo) *nm* sob. **sangloter** *vi* sob.
sangsue (sɑ̃'sy) *nf* leech.
sanguin (sɑ̃'gɛ̃) *adj* blood. **sanguinaire** *adj* bloodthirsty.
sanitaire (sani:'tɛr) *adj* sanitary.
sans (sɑ̃) *prep* **1** without. **2** but for. **sans que** without. **sans-abri** *nm invar* homeless person. **sans-façon** *adj* homely. *nm* straightforwardness. **sans-gêne** *adj* offhand, blunt. *nm inf* cheek. **sans-souci** *adj invar* carefree, easygoing.
sansonnet (sɑ̃sɔ'nɛ) *nm* starling.
santé (sɑ̃'te:) *nf* health. **à votre santé!** cheers!
saper (sa'pe:) *vt* undermine.
sapeur (sa'pœr) *nm mil* pioneer, scout. **sapeur-**

pompier *nm, pl* **sapeurs-pompiers 1** fireman. **2** *pl* fire brigade.
saphir (sa'fi:r) *nm* sapphire.
sapin (sa'pɛ̃) *nm* fir.
sarcasme (sar'kasm) *nm* sarcasm. **sarcastique** *adj* sarcastic.
sarcler (sar'kle:) *vt* **1** weed. **2** hoe.
Sardaigne (sar'dɛɲ) *nf* Sardinia. **sarde** *adj,n* Sardinian.
sardine (sar'di:n) *nf* **1** pilchard. **2** sardine.
sardonique (sardɔ'ni:k) *adj* sardonic.
Satan (sa'tɑ̃) *nm* Satan.
satin (sa'tɛ̃) *nm* satin.
satire (sa'ti:r) *nf* satire. **satirique** *adj* satirical.
satisfaction (sati:sfak'sjɔ̃) *nf* satisfaction.
satisfaire* (sati:s'fɛr) *vt* **1** satisfy, content. **2** meet, fulfil. **satisfaisant** *adj* satisfactory.
saturer (saty're:) *vt* saturate.
Saturne (sa'tyrn) *nm* Saturn.
sauce (sos) *nf* **1** sauce. **2** gravy.
saucée (so'se:) *nf sl* **1** downpour. **2** telling-off
saucisse (so'si:s) *nf* sausage. **saucisson** *nm* large dry sausage.
sauf, sauve (sof, sov) *adj* safe, intact. **sauf** *prep* save, except, but.
sauge (soʒ) *nf bot* sage.
saugrenu (sogrə'ny) *adj* absurd, ridiculous.
saule (sol) *nm* willow.
saumon (so'mɔ̃) *nm* salmon.
saumure (so'myr) *nf* pickle.
sauna (so'na) *nm* sauna.
saupoudrer (sopu:'dre:) *vt* sprinkle, dust.
saurai (so:'rɛ) *v* see **savoir.**
saut (so) *nm* leap, jump. **saut-de-lit** *nm, pl* **sauts-de-lit** bedside rug. **saut-de-mouton** *nm, pl* **sauts-de-mouton** *mot* flyover. **saute-mouton** *nm* leapfrog. **saut périlleux** somersault.
sauter (so'te:) *vi* **1** jump, leap. **2** skip. **3** explode. **4** (of a fuse) blow. *vt* jump over. **sauterelle** *nf* grasshopper. **sauterie** *nf* **1** jumping. **2** private party.
sautiller (soti:'je:) *vt* **1** hop. **2** skip.
sauvage (so'vaʒ) *adj* **1** savage, wild. **2** primitive. **3** shy. *nm,f* savage. **sauvagerie** *nf* **1** brutality. **2** unsociability.
sauvegarder (sovgar'de:) *vt* safeguard, protect. **sauvegarde** *nf* **1** safeguard, protection. **2** bodyguard.
sauver (so've:) *vt* **1** save, rescue. **2** protect. **se sauver** *vr* **1** escape. **2** run away. **sauve-qui-peut** *nm invar* stampede, panic. **sauvetage** *nm* **1** rescue. **2** salvage. **sauveur** *nm* **1** saviour. **2** rescuer.
savant (sa'vɑ̃) *adj* **1** learned, scholarly. **2** able. **3** skilful. *nm* **1** scientist. **2** scholar. **savamment** *adv* **1** knowingly. **2** skilfully.
savate (sa'vat) *nf* **1** old shoe. **2** French boxing. **savetier** *nm* cobbler.
saveur (sa'vœr) *nf* **1** taste, flavour. **2** piquancy.
savoir* (sa'vwar) *vt* **1** know. **2** be aware of. **3** be able. **c'est à savoir** that remains to be seen. **faire savoir à** inform. **savoir-faire** *nm invar* **1** ability. **2** tact. **savoir-vivre** *nm invar* breeding, good manners. ~*nm* knowledge.
savon (sa'vɔ̃) *nm* soap. **savon en poudre** soap powder.
savonner (savɔ'ne:) *vt* soap, lather.
savourer (savu:'re:) *vt* **1** relish. **2** enjoy. **savoureux, -euse** (savu:'rœ, -'rœz) *adj* **1** tasty. **2** *inf* juicy.
scabreux, -euse (skɑ'brœ, -'brœz) *adj* **1** difficult, ticklish. **2** indecent.
scandale (skɑ̃'dal) *nm* **1** scandal. **2** disgrace.
scandaliser (skɑ̃dali:'ze:) *vt* shock, offend.
Scandinavie (skɑ̃di:na'vi:) *nf* Scandinavia. **scandinave** *adj,n* Scandinavian.
scaphandrier (skafɑ̃'dri:'e:) *nm* diver.
sceau, sceaux (so) *nm* **1** seal. **2** stamp, mark.
scélérat (ske:lɛ'ra) *adj* wicked, criminal. *nm* **1** scoundrel. **2** villain.
sceller (sɛ'le:) *vt* **1** seal. **2** confirm. **scellé** *nm* seal.
scène (sɛn) *nf* **1** stage. **2** scene. **3** *inf* quarrel, scene.
sceptique (sɛp'ti:k) *nm,f* sceptic. *adj* sceptical. **scepticisme** *nm* scepticism.
schéma (skɛ'ma) *nm* diagram.
schizophrénie (ski:zɔfre:'ni:) *nf* schizophrenia. **schizophrène** *adj* schizophrenic.
scie (si:) *nf* **1** saw. **2** *inf* bore.
sciemment (sja'mɑ̃) *adv* knowingly.
science (sjɑ̃s) *nf* **1** knowledge, learning. **2** science. **sciences naturelles** *nf pl* natural science.
scientifique (sjɑ̃ti:'fi:k) *adj* scientific. *nm,f* scientist.
scier (sje:) *vt* **1** saw (off). **2** *inf* bore. **scierie** *nf* sawmill. **sciure de bois** *nf* sawdust.
scintiller (sɛ̃ti:'je:) *vi* **1** sparkle. **2** twinkle. **3** flicker.
scolaire (skɔ'lɛr) *adj* scholastic.
scooter (sku:'tɛr) *nm* scooter.
scorpion (skɔr'pjɔ̃) *nm* **1** scorpion. **2** *cap* Scorpio.

scrupuleux, -euse (skrypy'lœ, -'lœz) *adj* scrupulous.
scruter (skry'te:) *vt* scrutinize.
scrutin (skry'tɛ̃) *nm* **1** poll. **2** ballot. **3** voting.
sculpter (skyl'te:) *vt* **1** sculpt. **2** carve. **sculpteur** *nm* sculptor. **sculpture** *nf* sculpture.
se, s' (sə) *pron 3rd pers m,f s,pl* **1** oneself, himself, herself, itself, themselves. **2** each other, one another.
séance (se:'ɑ̃s) *nf* **1** meeting. **2** *pol* session. **3** sitting. **4** *Th* performance.
séant (se:'ɑ̃) *adj* fitting, seemly. *nm inf* bottom.
seau, sceaux (so) *nm* bucket.
sec, sèche (sɛk, sɛʃ) *adj* **1** dry. **2** dried. **3** curt. **4** harsh. *nf sl* fag, cigarette.
sécher (se:'ʃe:) *vt,vi* dry. **sécheresse** (se:ʃ'rɛs) *nf* **1** dryness. **2** drought. **3** harshness.
second (sə'gɔ̃) *adj* second. *nm* second in command. **en second** in second place. **seconde** *nf* **1** second, moment. **2** second class. **secondaire** *adj* secondary, subordinate.
secouer (sə'kwe:) *vt* **1** shake. **2** jolt. **3** shake off.
secourir* (səku:'ri:r) *vt* help. **secours** *nm* help, assistance. **au secours!** help! **premiers secours** *nm pl* first aid.
secousse (sə'ku:s) *nf* **1** jolt, jerk. **2** shock.
secret[1], -ète (sə'krɛ, -'krɛt) *adj* **1** secret, confidential. **2** hidden.
secret[2] (sə'krɛ) *nm* **1** secret. **2** secrecy.
secrétaire (səkre:'tɛr) *nm,f* **1** secretary. **2** clerk. *nm* bureau, desk.
sécréter (se:kre:'te:) *vt* secrete.
secte (sɛkt) *nf* sect, group. **sectaire** *adj,n* sectarian.
secteur (sɛk'tœr) *nm* **1** sector. **2** area, district.
section (sɛk'sjɔ̃) *nf* **1** section. **2** branch, division. **3** stage (on a bus route).
séculaire (se:ky'lɛr) *adj* **1** occurring once in a century. **2** venerated.
séculier, -ière (se:ky'lje:, -'ljɛr) *adj* secular. *nm* layman.
sécurité (se:kyri:'te:) *nf* **1** security. **2** safety.
sédatif, -ive (sɛda'ti:f, 'ti:v) *adj,nm* sedative.
sédiment (se:di:'mɑ̃) *nm* sediment.
séduire* (se:'dɥi:r) *vt* **1** seduce. **2** lead astray. **3** charm. **séduisant** *adj* **1** seductive. **2** attractive.
segment (sɛg'mɑ̃) *nm* segment.
ségrégation (se:grɛga'sjɔ̃) *nf* segregation.
seigle (sɛgl) *nm* rye.
seigneur (sɛ'ɲœr) *nm* lord.
sein (sɛ̃) *nm* breast, bosom.
séisme (se:'i:sm) *nm* earthquake.
seize (sɛz) *adj,nm* sixteen. **seizième** *adj* sixteenth.
séjour (se:'ʒu:r) *nm* **1** stay. **2** residence.
séjourner (se:ʒu:r'ne:) *vi* **1** stay. **2** reside.
sel (sɛl) *nm* **1** salt. **2** wit.
sélection (se:lɛk'sjɔ̃) *nf* selection, choice. **sélectif, -ive** (se:lɛk'ti:f, -'ti:v) *adj* selective.
sélectionner (se:lɛksjɔ'ne:) *vt* select, choose.
selle (sɛl) *nf* **1** saddle. **2** stool. **sellier** *nm* saddler.
selon (sə'lɔ̃) *prep* according to.
Seltz (sɛls) **eau de Seltz** *nm Tdmk* soda-water.
semaine (sə'mɛn) *nf* week.
sémantique (se:mɑ̃'ti:k) *adj* semantic. *nf* semantics.
sémaphore (sɛma'fɔr) *nm* semaphore.
sembler (sɑ̃'ble:) *vi* seem, appear. **semblable** *adj* **1** similar, alike. **2** such. **semblant** *nm* appearance, show. **faire semblant de** pretend.
semelle (sə'mɛl) *nf* sole (of a shoe).
semence (sə'mɑ̃s) *nf* seed.
semer (sə'me:) *vt* **1** sow. **2** scatter.
semestre (sə'mɛstr) *nm* **1** term. **2** half-year.
séminaire (se:mi:'nɛr) *nm* **1** seminary. **2** seminar.
semi-voyelle (səmi:vwa'jɛl) *nf* semivowel.
semoule (sə'mu:l) *nf* semolina.
sénat (sɛ'na) *nm* senate. **sénateur** *nm* senator.
sénile (se:'ni:l) *adj* senile.
sens (sɑ̃s) *nm* **1** sense. **2** judgment. **3** meaning. **4** direction. **bon sens** commonsense. **dans le sens des aiguilles d'une montre** clockwise. **sens dessus dessous** upside down. **sens interdit** no entry.
sensation (sɑ̃sa'sjɔ̃) *nf* **1** sensation. **2** feeling. **sensationnel, -elle** (sɑ̃sasjɔ'nɛl) *adj* **1** sensational. **2** *inf* superb.
sensé (sɑ̃'se:) *adj* sensible.
sensible (sɑ̃'si:bl) *adj* **1** sensitive. **2** susceptible. **3** sympathetic. **4** tender. **5** apparent. **sensibilité** *nf* **1** sensibility. **2** sensitivity. **3** feeling. **4** tenderness.
sensuel, -elle (sɑ̃'sɥɛl) *adj* sensual, sensuous.
sentence (sɑ̃'tɑ̃s) *nf* **1** *law* sentence. **2** maxim.
sentier (sɑ̃'tje:) *nm* path, footpath.
sentiment (sɑ̃ti:'mɑ̃) *nm* **1** feeling. **2** sensation. **3** opinion. **4** sentiment. **sentimental, -aux** *adj* sentimental.
sentinelle (sɑ̃ti:'nɛl) *nf* sentry.
sentir* (sɑ̃'ti:r) *vt* **1** feel. **2** be conscious of. **3** smell. *vi* **1** smell of. **2** taste of. **sentir mauvais** stink.

seoir* (swar) *vi* suit, become.
séparer (sɛpa're:) *vt* **1** separate. **2** divide. **séparation** *nf* separation. **séparé** *adj* **1** separate. **2** apart.
sept (sɛt) *adj,nm* seven. **septième** (sɛ'tjɛm) *adj* seventh.
septembre (sɛp'tɑ̃br) *nm* September.
septentrional, -aux (sɛptɑ̃ri:ɔ'nal, -'no) *adj* north, northern.
septique (sɛp'ti:k) *adj* septic.
séquence (sɛ'kɑ̃s) *nf* sequence.
sequin (sə'kɛ̃) *nm* sequin.
serai (sə'rɛ) *v* see **être.**
serais (sə'rɛ) *v* see **être.**
serein (sə'rɛ̃) *adj* serene, calm.
sérénade (se:rɛ'nad) *nf* serenade.
serf, serve (sɛrf, sɛrv) *nm,f* serf.
sergent (sɛr'ʒɑ̃) *nm* sergeant.
série (se:'ri:) *nf* **1** series, succession. **2** range. **3** set. **hors série 1** specially made. **2** outsize.
sérieux, -euse (se:'rjœ, -'rjœz) *adj* **1** serious. **2** grave. **3** earnest. **4** important. *nm* gravity.
serin (sə'rɛ̃) *nm* canary.
seringue (sə'rɛ̃g) *nf* syringe.
serment (sɛr'mɑ̃) *nm* oath.
sermon (sɛr'mɔ̃) *nm* sermon.
serpent (sɛr'pɑ̃) *nm* snake, serpent.
serpenter (sɛrpɑ̃'te:) *vi* meander, wind.
serrer (sɛ're:) *vt* **1** squeeze, clench. **2** put away. **3** tighten. **4** close (up). **serrer la main à** shake hands with. **se serrer** *vr* group together. **serre** *nf* **1** greenhouse, conservatory. **2** claw. **3** grip. **serre chaude** hothouse. **serré** *adj* **1** close. **2** tight. **3** concise. **4** *inf* mean. **serre-tête** *nm invar* crash-helmet.
serrure (sɛ'ryr) *nf* lock.
sers (sɛr) *v* see **servir.**
servante (sɛr'vɑ̃t) *nf* maid.
serveur, -euse (sɛr'vœr, -'vœz) *nm,f* **1** barman, barmaid. **2** waiter, waitress.
service (sɛr'vi:s) *nm* **1** service. **2** attendance. **3** department. **4** duty. **5** set.
serviette (sɛrv'jɛt) *nf* **1** napkin. **2** towel. **3** briefcase. **serviette hygiénique** sanitary towel.
servir* (sɛr'vi:r) *vt* **1** serve. **2** attend to. **3** help. *vi* be useful. **servir de** be used as. **se servir de** *vr* use. **serviteur** *nm* servant.
ses (se:) *poss adj* see **son.**
session (sɛ'sjɔ̃) *nf* session, sitting.
seuil (sœj) *nm* **1** threshold. **2** doorstep.
seul (sœl) *adj* **1** only. **2** single, sole. **3** alone. **seulement** *adv* only.
sève (sɛv) *nf* sap.
sévère (se:'vɛr) *adj* **1** harsh, hard. **2** strict. **3** severe. **sévérité** *nf* **1** severity. **2** strictness.
sévir (se:'vi:r) *vi* **1** punish severely. **2** rage.
sexe (sɛks) *nm* sex. **sexualité** *nf* sexuality. **sexuel, -elle** (sɛk'sɥɛl) *adj* sexual.
sextuor (sɛk'stɥɔr) *nm* sextet.
shampooing (ʃɑ̃pu:'i:ɲ) *nm* shampoo.
shérif (ʃɛ'ri:f) *nm* sheriff.
si[1] (si:) *conj* **1** if. **2** whether.
si[2] (si:) *adv* **1** so, so much. **2** such. **3** as. **4** yes. **si...que** however.
Sicile (si:'si:l) *nf* Sicily. **sicilien, -ienne** (si:-si:'ljɛ̃, -'ljɛn) *adj,n* Sicilian.
siècle (sjɛkl) *nm* **1** century. **2** age, time.
siéger (sjɛ'ʒe:) *vi* **1** *pol* sit. **2** be centred. **siège** *nm* **1** seat. **2** chair. **3** siege. **4** see. **siège central** *comm* head office.
sien, sienne (sjɛ̃, sjɛn) *poss pron 3rd pers s* **le sien, la sienne 1** his, hers, one's. **2** his, hers, one's or its own.
sieste (sjɛst) *nf* **1** siesta. **2** *inf* nap.
siffler (si:'fle:) *vi,vt* whistle, hiss. **sifflet** *nm* whistle.
signal, -aux (si:'ɲal, -'ɲo) *nm* signal.
signaler (si:ɲa'le:) *vt* **1** point out. **2** signal. **3** report. **4** give a description of. **se signaler** *vr* distinguish oneself. **signalement** *nm* description, particulars. **signalisateur anti-vol** *nm* burglar alarm.
signature (si:ɲa'tyr) *nf* **1** signature. **2** signing.
signe (si:ɲ) *nm* **1** sign. **2** mark. **3** gesture. **faire signe à** beckon. **signet** *nm* bookmark.
signer (si:'ɲe) *vt* sign.
signifier (si:ɲi:'fje:) *vt* signify, mean. **significatif, -ive** (si:ɲi:fi:ka'ti:f, -'ti:v) *adj* significant. **signification** *nf* meaning.
silence (si:'lɑ̃s) *nm* silence. **silencieux, -euse** (si:lɑ̃'sjœ, -'sjœz) *adj* silent.
silex (si:'lɛks) *nm* flint.
silhouette (si:l'wɛt) *nf* silhouette, outline.
sillon (si:'jɔ̃) *nm* **1** furrow. **2** trail. **3** groove.
sillonner (si:jɔ'ne:) *vt* **1** furrow. **2** streak. **3** wrinkle.
simagrée (si:ma'gre:) *nf* **1** pretence. **2** *pl* grimaces. **3** *pl* affectation.
simple (sɛ̃pl) *adj* **1** simple. **2** single. **3** ordinary. **4** plain. **simplicité** *nf* simplicity.
simplifier (sɛ̃pli:'fje:) *vt* simplify.
simulacre (si:my'lakr) *nm* **1** pretence, show. **2** image.
simuler (si:my'le:) *vt* feign, counterfeit.

simultané (si:mylta'ne:) *adj* simultaneous. **simultanément** *adv* simultaneously.

sincère (sɛ̃'sɛr) *adj* **1** sincere. **2** genuine. **3** true. **sincérité** *nf* **1** sincerity. **2** honesty. **3** candour.

singe (sɛ̃ʒ) *nm* monkey, ape.

singer (sɛ̃'ʒe:) *vt* ape, mimic. **singerie** *nf* grimace.

singulier, -ière (sɛ̃gy'lje:, -'ljɛr) *adj* **1** singular. **2** peculiar. **3** strange. *nm* singular. **singularité** *nf* **1** singularity. **2** peculiarity. **3** eccentricity.

sinistre (si:'ni:str) *adj* **1** sinister, ominous. **2** dangerous. **3** gloomy. *nm* disaster.

sinon (si:'nɔ̃) *conj* **1** otherwise, or else. **2** except.

sinueux, -euse (si:'nɥœ, -'nɥœz) *adj* winding.

sionisme (sjɔ'ni:sm) *nm* Zionism. **sioniste** *adj,n* Zionist.

siphon (si:'fɔ̃) *nm* siphon.

sirène (si:'rɛn) *nf* **1** siren, hooter. **2** mermaid.

sirop (si:'ro) *nm* syrup.

siroter (si:rɔ'te:) *vt inf* sip.

site (si:t) *nm* **1** beauty spot. **2** site.

sitôt (si:'to) *adv* as soon. **sitôt que** as soon as.

situer (si:'tɥe:) *vt* situate, place. **situation** *nf* **1** situation. **2** position. **3** condition. **4** appointment, job. **situation difficile** predicament.

six (si:s) *adj,nm* six. **sixième** *adj* sixth.

ski (ski:) *nm* **1** ski. **2** skiing. **faire du ski** ski. **ski-nautique** *nm* water-skiing.

slip (sli:p) *nm* underpants, briefs.

slogan (slɔ'gɑ̃) *nm* slogan.

smoking (smɔ'ki:ɲ) *nm* dinner jacket.

snob (snɔb) *adj invar* **1** *inf* smart. **2** snobbish. *nm* snob.

sobre (sɔbr) *adj* **1** temperate. **2** sober. **3** economical. **sobriété** *nf* **1** sobriety. **2** moderation.

sobriquet (sɔbri:'kɛ) *nm* nickname.

sociable (sɔ'sjabl) *adj* sociable.

social, -aux (sɔ'sjal, -'sjo) *adj* social. **socialisme** *nm* socialism. **socialiste** *adj,n* socialist.

société (sɔsje:'te:) *nf* **1** society. **2** community. **3** club. **4** company. **5** companionship. **sociétaire** *nm,f* **1** member. **2** shareholder.

sociologie (sɔsjɔlɔ'ʒi:) *nf* sociology. **sociologique** *adj* sociological. **sociologue** *nm,f* sociologist.

socle (sɔkl) *nm* **1** pedestal. **2** base.

socquette (sɔ'kɛt) *nf* ankle-sock.

sœur (sœr) *nf* **1** sister. **2** nun.

soi (swa) *pron 3rd pers m,f s* oneself, himself, herself, itself. **soi-disant** *adj invar* so-called. *adv* supposedly. **soi-même** *pron 3rd pers m,f s* oneself.

soie (swɑ) *nf* **1** silk. **2** bristle (of a badger, etc.). **soie artificielle** rayon.

soif (swaf) *nf* thirst. **avoir soif** be thirsty.

soigner (swa'ɲe) *vt* **1** look after. **2** nurse. **3** do carefully. **se soigner** *vr* look after oneself. **soigné** (swa'ɲe:) *adj* **1** neat, tidy. **2** carefully done. **soigneux, -euse** (swa'ɲœ, -'ɲœz) *adj* **1** careful. **2** painstaking. **3** tidy.

soin (swɛ̃) *nm* care.

soir (swar) *nm* **1** evening. **2** night. **ce soir** tonight. **hier soir** last night. **soirée** *nf* **1** evening. **2** party.

sois (swa) *v see* **être.**

soit (swa) *interj* agreed!. *conj* whether. **soit... soit** either...or.

soixante (swa'sɑ̃t) *adj,nm* sixty. **soixantième** *adj* sixtieth.

soixante-dix *adj,nm* seventy. **soixante-dixième** *adj* seventieth.

soja (sɔʒa) *nm* soya bean.

sol (sɔl) *nm* **1** ground, earth. **2** soil.

solaire (sɔ'lɛr) *adj* **1** solar. **2** sun.

soldat (sɔl'da) *nm* soldier.

solde[1] (sɔld) *nf mil* pay

solde[2] (sɔld) *nm* **1** *comm* balance. **2** surplus stock. **3** (clearance) sale.

sole (sɔl) *nf cul* sole.

soleil (sɔ'lɛj) *nm* **1** sun. **2** sunshine.

solennel, -elle (sɔla'nɛl) *adj* **1** solemn. **2** state, official.

solidarité (sɔli:dari:'te:) *nf* **1** solidarity. **2** fellowship.

solide (sɔ'li:d) *adj* **1** solid. **2** strong. **3** sound.

solidifier (sɔli:di:'fje:) *vt* solidify.

soliste (sɔ'li:st) *nm,f* soloist.

solitaire (sɔli:'tɛr) *adj* solitary, lonely. *nm* hermit.

solitude (sɔli:'tyd) *nf* solitude.

solive (sɔ'li:v) *nf* **1** joist. **2** beam.

solliciter (sɔlli:si:'te:) *vt* **1** request. **2** incite.

solo (sɔ'lo) *adj invar,nm* solo.

soluble (sɔ'lybl) *adj* soluble.

solution (sɔly'sjɔ̃) *nf* **1** solution. **2** answer, explanation.

solvable (sɔl'vabl) *adj* solvent.

sombre (sɔ̃br) *adj* **1** sombre, gloomy. **2** dark. **3** dejected.

sombrer (sɔ̃'bre:) *vi* sink.

sommaire (sɔm'mɛr) *adj* **1** concise. **2** elementary. **3** rapid. *nm* summary.

sommation (sɔma'sjɔ̃) *nf law* summons.

somme[1] (sɔm) *nm* nap, snooze.
somme[2] (sɔm) *nf* sum, amount. **en somme 1** on the whole. **2** in short.
somme[3] (sɔm) **bête de somme** *nf* beast of burden.
sommeil (sɔ'mɛj) *nm* **1** sleep. **2** sleepiness. **avoir sommeil** be sleepy.
sommeiller (sɔmɛ'je:) *vi* doze, sleep lightly.
sommelier (sɔmə'lje:) *nm* wine waiter.
sommer (sɔ'me:) *vt law* summon.
sommes (sɔm) *v* see **être.**
sommet (sɔ'mɛ) *nm* summit, top.
somnambule (sɔmnɑ̃'byl) *nm,f* sleepwalker. **somnambulisme** *nm* sleepwalking. **somnifère** *nm* sleeping-pill.
somnoler (sɔmnɔ'le:) *vi* doze, drowse. **somnolent** *adj* sleepy.
son[1]**, sa, ses** (sɔ̃, sa, se:) *poss adj 3rd pers s* his, her, its, one's.
son[2] (sɔ̃) *nm* sound.
son[3] (sɔ̃) *nm* bran.
sonate (sɔ'nat) *nf* sonata.
sonder (sɔ̃'de:) *vt* **1** sound. **2** probe, examine. **3** fathom. **sondage** *nm* **1** sounding. **2** *min* boring. **3** opinion poll.
songer (sɔ̃'ʒe:) *vi* **1** dream. **2** imagine. **3** muse. **songer à** think about. **songe** *nm* dream. **songerie** *nf* dreaming. **songeur, -euse** (sɔ̃'ʒœr, -'ʒœz) *nm,f* dreamer. *adj* pensive.
sonique (sɔ'ni:k) *adj* sonic.
sonner (sɔ'ne:) *vi,vt* **1** ring. **2** toll. *vi* **1** sound. **2** strike. **sonnerie** *nf* **1** ringing. **2** chimes. **3** bell. **4** trumpet call. **sonnette** *nf* **1** small bell. **2** doorbell.
sonnet (sɔ'nɛ) *nm* sonnet.
sonore (sɔ'nɔr) *adj* **1** resonant. **2** loud.
sont (sɔ̃) *v* see **être.**
soprano (sɔpra'no) *nm,f* soprano.
sorcier, -ière (sɔr'sje:, -'sjɛr) *nm,f* wizard, witch. **sorcellerie** *nf* witchcraft.
sordide (sɔr'di:d) *adj* **1** sordid, squalid. **2** base.
sors (sɔr) *v* see **sortir.**
sort (sɔr) *nm* **1** fate. **2** lot. **3** spell.
sorte (sɔrt) *nf* **1** sort, kind. **2** manner. **de sorte que** so that.
sortir* (sɔr'ti:r) *vi* **1** go out. **2** come up. **3** leave. *vt* take or bring out. **sortie** *nf* **1** way out, exit. **2** leaving. **3** outing. **4** *inf* outburst. **sortie de secours** emergency exit.
sot, sotte (so, sɔt) *adj* **1** stupid. **2** ridiculous. **3** sheepish. *nm,f* fool, idiot. **sottise** (sɔ'ti:z) *nf* **1** stupidity. **2** silly remark or action.
sou (su:) *nm* penny. **sans le sou** penniless.
soubresaut (su:brə'so) *nm* sudden start, jerk.
souche (su:ʃ) *nf* **1** stump. **2** stub. **3** counterfoil.
souci[1] (su:'si:) *nm* **1** worry. **2** anxiety. **3** care. **sans souci** carefree.
souci[2] (su:'si:) *nm* marigold.
se soucier (su:'sje:) *vr* **1** care, concern oneself. **2** be anxious. **soucieux, -euse** (su:'sjœ, -'sjœz) *adj* **1** anxious. **2** thoughtful. **3** preoccupied.
soucoupe (su:'ku:p) *nf* saucer.
soudain (su:'dɛ̃) *adj* **1** sudden. **2** unexpected. *adv* suddenly.
soude (su:d) *nf* soda.
souder (su:'de:) *vt* **1** solder. **2** weld. **se souder** *vr* **1** weld. **2** join together.
soudoyer (su:dwa'je:) *vt* **1** hire. **2** bribe.
souffler (su:'fle:) *vi* **1** blow. **2** pant. **3** breathe. *vt* **1** blow out or up. **2** utter. **3** *inf* trick. **souffler son rôle à** prompt. **souffle** *nm* **1** breath. **2** puff. **3** blast. **4** inspiration. **soufflet** *nm* **1** bellows. **2** box (the ears). **3** *inf* insult.
souffleter (su:flə'te:) *vt* **1** slap. **2** insult.
souffrir* (su:'fri:r) *vt* **1** endure. **2** permit. *vi* suffer, be in pain. **souffrance** *nf* **1** suspense. **2** pain. **souffrant** *adj* **1** suffering. **2** unwell. **souffre-douleur** *nm invar* **1** drudge. **2** butt (of jokes, etc.).
soufre (su:fr) *nm* sulphur.
souhait (swɛ) *nm* wish. **souhaiter** *vt* wish, desire.
souiller (su:'je:) *vt* **1** soil. **2** pollute. **3** tarnish. **souillure** *nf* **1** spot, stain. **2** blemish.
soûl (su:) *adj inf* **1** drunk. **2** full.
soulager (su:la'ʒe:) *vt* **1** relieve, ease. **2** soothe. **soulagement** *nm* **1** relief. **2** comfort.
se soûler (su:'le:) *vr* **1** get drunk. **2** gorge oneself. **soûlard** *nm sl* drunkard.
soulever (su:l've:) *vt* **1** lift. **2** raise. **3** rouse. **4** provoke. **soulèvement** *nm* **1** raising. **2** revolt. **3** protest.
soulier (su:'lje:) *nm* shoe.
souligner (su:li:'ɲe) *vt* **1** underline. **2** emphasize.
soumettre* (su:'mɛtr) *vt* **1** subdue. **2** subject. **3** submit, refer. **se soumettre** *vr* submit, yield. **soumis** *adj* obedient.
soumission (su:mi:'sjɔ̃) *nf* **1** submission. **2** obedience. **3** *comm* tender.
soupape (su:'pap) *nf* **1** valve. **2** plug.
soupçon (su:p'sɔ̃) *nm* **1** suspicion. **2** slight flavour, dash.
soupçonner (su:psɔ'ne:) *vt* **1** suspect. **2** guess.

soupçonneux, -euse (su:psɔ'nœ, -'nœz) *adj* suspicious.
soupe (su:p) *nf* soup.
soupente (su:'pɑ̃t) *nf* loft.
souper (su:'pe:) *vi* have supper. *nm* supper.
soupir (su:'pi:r) *nm* sigh. **soupirer** *vi* sigh.
soupirail, -aux (su:pi:'raj, -'ro) *nm* ventilator.
souple (su:pl) *adj* **1** supple. **2** flexible. **3** adaptable. **souplesse** *nf* **1** suppleness. **2** flexibility.
source (su:rs) *nf* **1** source. **2** spring, well. **3** origin.
sourcil (su:r'si:) *nm* eyebrow.
sourd (su:r) *adj* **1** deaf. **2** dull, muffled. **3** hollow. **4** secret. *nm* deaf person. **sourd-muet, sourde-muette** *adj,pl* **sourds-muets, sourdes-muettes** deaf-and-dumb. *nm,f* deaf-mute.
souricière (su:ri:'sjɛr) *nf* **1** mousetrap. **2** trap.
sourire* (su:'ri:r) *vi* smile. **sourire à belles dents** grin. ~*nm* smile. **large sourire** grin. **sourire affecté** smirk.
souris (su:'ri:) *nf* mouse.
sournois (su:r'nwa) *adj* **1** sly. **2** cunning. **3** underhand. *nm* sneak.
sous (su:) *prep* **1** under. **2** below. **3** within (time). **sous la pluie** in the rain. **sous terre** underground.
sous-alimentation *nf* malnutrition.
souscrire* (su:'skri:r) *vt* **1** subscribe. **2** sign. **souscription** *nf* **1** subscription. **2** signature. **3** contribution.
sous-développé *adj* underdeveloped.
sous-entendre *vt* **1** imply. **2** understand. **sous-entendu** *nm* implication.
sous-estimer *vt* underestimate.
sous-marin *adj* underwater.
sous-sol *nm* basement.
sous-titrer *vt* subtitle. **sous-titre** *nm* subtitle.
soustraire* (su:'strɛr) *vt* **1** take away. **2** withdraw. **3** subtract. **4** protect. **se soustraire** *vr* escape. **soustraction** *nf* **1** removal. **2** subtraction.
sous-traiter *vt* subcontract.
soutane (su:'tan) *nf* cassock.
soutenir* (su:t'ni:r) *vt* **1** support. **2** prop up. **3** maintain. **4** encourage. **5** withstand. **6** sustain. **se soutenir** *vr* **1** support oneself. **2** continue. **soutenu** *adj* **1** sustained. **2** elevated. **3** constant.
souterrain (su:tɛ'rɛ̃) *adj* underground. *nm* **1** underground passage. **2** vault.
soutien (su:'tjɛ̃) *nm* **1** support, prop. **2** supporter. **soutien-gorge** *nm invar* brassiere, bra.
souvenir* (su:v'ni:r) *v imp* come to mind. **se souvenir de** *vr* remember, recall. ~*nm* **1** memory. **2** remembrance, recollection. **3** memento. **4** souvenir.
souvent (su:'vɑ̃) *adv* often. **peu souvent** seldom.
souverain (su:v'rɛ̃) *adj* **1** sovereign. **2** supreme. *nm* sovereign. **souveraineté** *nf* sovereignty.
soyez (swa'je:) *v* see **être.**
soyons (swa'jɔ̃) *v* see **être.**
spacieux, -euse (spa'sjœ, -'sjœz) *adj* spacious.
spasme (spasm) *nm* spasm. **spasmodique** *adj* spasmodic.
spatial, -aux (spa'sjal, -'sjo) *adj* spatial.
spatule (spa'tyl) *nf* spatula.
spécial, -aux (spe:'sjal, -'sjo) *adj* **1** special. **2** especial. **3** particular.
spécialiser (spe:sjali:'ze:) *vt* specialize. **se spécialiser dans** *vr* specialize in. **spécialiste** *nm,f* **1** expert. **2** *med* specialist. **spécialité** *nf* speciality.
spécieux, -euse (spe:'sjœ, -'sjœz) *adj* plausible.
spécifier (spe:si:'fje:) *vt* specify. **spécifique** *adj* specific.
spécimen (spe:si:'mɛn) *nm* specimen.
spectacle (spɛk'takl) *nm* **1** sight, spectacle. **2** *Th* play. **3** show. **spectaculaire** *adj* spectacular.
spectateur, -trice (spɛkta'tœr, -'tri:s) *nm,f* **1** onlooker, spectator. **2** *pl* audience.
spectre (spɛktr) *nm* **1** ghost, apparition. **2** spectrum.
spéculer (spe:ky'le:) *vi* speculate. **spéculateur, -trice** (spe:kyla'tœr, -'tri:s) *nm,f* speculator. **spéculation** *nf* speculation.
spéléologie (spe:le:ɔlɔ'ʒi:) *nf* potholing. **spéléologue** *nm* potholer.
sperme (spɛrm) *nm* sperm.
sphère (sfɛr) *nf* **1** sphere. **2** globe. **3** field, area.
spiral, -aux (spi:'ral, -'ro) *adj* spiral. **spirale** *nf* spiral.
spirituel, -elle (spi:ri:'tɥɛl) *adj* **1** spiritual. **2** witty.
splendeur (splɑ̃'dœr) *nf* **1** splendour. **2** magnificence. **3** pomp. **splendide** *adj* **1** splendid, magnificent. **2** superb.
spolier (spɔ'lje:) *vt* rob, plunder.
spontané (spɔ̃ta'ne:) *adj* spontaneous.
sport (spɔr) *nm* sport, games. **sportif, -ive** (spɔr'ti:f, -'ti:v) *adj* sporting.

square (skwar) *nm* small square with a (public) garden.
squelette (skə'lɛt) *nm* **1** skeleton. **2** framework.
stabiliser (stabi:li:'ze:) *vt* stabilize, steady.
stable (stabl) *adj* stable, steady, firm.
stade (stad) *nm* **1** stadium. **2** stage, phase.
stage (staʒ) *nm* **1** probationary period. **2** training course.
stagnant (stag'nɑ̃) *adj* stagnant.
stalle (stal) *nf* stall, seat.
standard (stɑ̃'dar) *nm* **1** switchboard. **2** standard.
station (sta'sjɔ̃) *nf* **1** stop. **2** (tube) station. **3** standing. **station-service** *nf, pl* **stations-service** service station.
stationner (stasjɔ'ne:) *vi* **1** stop. **2** park. **stationnaire** *adj* stationary. **stationnement** *nm* parking.
statique (sta'ti:k) *adj* static.
statistique (stati:'sti:k) *nf* statistics. *adj* statistical.
statue (sta'ty) *nf* statue.
statuer (sta'tɥe:) *vi* decide. *vt* decree.
stature (sta'tyr) *nf* stature.
statut (sta'ty) *nm* **1** statute, rule. **2** status.
sténodactylographe (ste:nɔdakti:lɔ'graf) *nm,f* shorthand typist.
sténographie (ste:nɔgra'fi:) *nf* shorthand.
stéréophonique (ste:re:ɔfɔ'ni:k) *adj* stereophonic.
stéréotype (ste:re:ɔ'ti:p) *adj* stereotype.
stérile (ste:'ri:l) *adj* **1** sterile. **2** barren. **3** fruitless. **stérilité** *nf* sterility.
stériliser (ste:ri:li:'ze:) *vt* sterilize.
sterling (stɛr'lɛ̃) *adj invar* sterling.
stéthoscope (ste:tɔ'skɔp) *nm* stethoscope.
stigmate (sti:g'mat) *nm* **1** stigma. **2** scar. **3** brand, mark. **4** stain.
stimuler (sti:my'le:) *vt* **1** stimulate. **2** incite. **stimulant** *adj* stimulating. *nm* **1** stimulus. **2** tonic.
stipuler (sti:py'le:) *vt* stipulate.
stock (stɔk) *nm* stock (of goods, etc.).
stocker (stɔ'ke:) *vt* **1** stock. **2** stockpile.
stoïque (stɔ'i:k) *adj* stoical.
stop (stɔp) *nm* **faire du stop** hitch-hike.
store (stɔr) *nm* blind.
strabisme (stra'bi:sm) *nm* squint.
strapontin (strapɔ̃'tɛ̃) *nm* folding seat.
stratégie (strate:'ʒi:) *nf* strategy. **stratégique** *adj* strategic.
strict (stri:kt) *adj* **1** strict, severe. **2** exact.
strident (stri:'dɑ̃) *adj* **1** shrill. **2** piercing.
strié (stri:'e:) *adj* **1** streaked. **2** scratched.
strophe (strɔf) *nf* verse.
structure (stryk'tyr) *nf* structure.
studieux, -euse (sty'djœ, -'djœz) *adj* studious.
studio (sty'djo) *nm* **1** studio. **2** small or one-room flat.
stupéfier (stype:'fje:) *vt* astound, dumbfound. **stupéfaction** (stypɛfak'sjɔ̃) *nf* amazement. **stupéfait** *adj* astounded. **stupéfiant** *adj* amazing. *nm* narcotic, drug.
stupide (sty'pi:d) *adj* stupid, silly. **stupidité** *nf* stupidity.
style (sti:l) *nm* style.
stylo (sti:'lo) *nm* fountain pen. **stylo à bille** ball-point pen.
su (sy) *v* see **savoir.**
suaire (sɥɛr) *nm* shroud.
suant (sɥɑ̃) *adj* sweating, sweaty.
suave (sɥav) *adj* **1** sweet, mellow. **2** soft, delicate.
subconscient (sybkɔ̃'sjɑ̃) *adj,nm* subconscious.
subir (sy'bi:r) *vt* **1** undergo. **2** endure. **3** suffer.
subit (sy'bi:) *adj* sudden. **subitement** *adv also inf* **subito** suddenly.
subjectif, -ive (sybʒɛk'ti:f, -'ti:v) *adj* subjective.
subjonctif, -ive (sybʒɔ̃k'ti:f, -'ti:v) *adj,nm* subjunctive.
subjuguer (sybʒy'ge:) *vt* **1** subdue. **2** captivate.
sublime (sy'bli:m) *adj* sublime, exalted.
submerger (sybmɛr'ʒe:) *vt* **1** submerge. **2** immerse. **3** swamp.
subordonner (sybɔrdɔ'ne:) *vt* subordinate. **subordonné** *adj,n* subordinate.
subséquent (sybsɛ'kɑ̃) *adj* subsequent. **subséquemment** (sybsɛka'mɑ̃) *adv* subsequently.
subsister (sybsi:'ste:) *vi* remain, subsist.
substance (syb'stɑ̃s) *nf* **1** substance. **2** matter. **3** stuff. **substantiel, -elle** (sybstɑ̃'sjɛl) *adj* substantial. **substantif** *nm* substantive.
substituer (sybsti:'tɥe:) *vt* substitute. **substitut** *nm* substitute.
subtil (syp'ti:l) *adj* **1** subtle. **2** sharp, penetrating. **3** fine. **subtilité** *nf* subtlety.
suburbain (sybyr'bɛ̃) *adj* suburban.
subvenir* (sybvə'ni:r) *vt* provide, supply.
subvention (sybvɑ̃'sjɔ̃) *nv* subsidy, grant.
subventionner (sybvɑ̃sjɔ'ne:) *vt* subsidize.
suc (syk) *nm* **1** juice. **2** quintessence.
succédané (syksɛda'ne:) *nm* substitute.
succéder (sykse:'de:) *vt* **1** succeed, inherit. **2** follow. **succès** (syk'sɛ) *nm* **1** success. **2** result, issue. **succession** (syksɛ'sjɔ̃) *nf* suc-

cession. **successeur** *nm* successor. **successif, -ive** (syksɛ'si:f, -'si:v) *adj* successive.
succomber (sykɔ̃'be:) *vi* **1** succumb. **2** die.
succulent (syky'lɑ̃) *adj* succulent, tasty.
succursale (sykyr'sal) *nf comm* branch.
sucer (sy'se:) *vt* suck. **sucette** *nf* lollipop.
sucrer (sy'kre:) *vt* sugar, sweeten. **sucre** *nm* sugar. **sucre d'orge 1** barley-sugar. **2** lollipop.
sud (syd) *nm* south. *adj invar* south, southerly, southern. **au sud** in the south. **du sud** southern, southerly. **vers le sud** southward, southwards. **sud-est** *nm,adj invar* south-east. **du sud-est 1** south-eastern. **2** south-easterly. **sud-ouest** *nm,adj invar* south-west. **du sud-ouest** south-western, south-westerly.
Suède (sɥɛd) *nf* Sweden. **suède** *nf* suede. **suédois** *adj,n* Swedish. *nm* Swedish (language).
suer (sɥe:) *vi* sweat, perspire. **sueur** *nf* sweat, perspiration.
suffire* (sy'fi:r) *vi* be sufficient. **suffisant** *adj* **1** sufficient, adequate. **2** conceited.
suffixe (syf'fi:ks) *nm* suffix.
suffoquer (syfɔ'ke:) *vt* suffocate, stifle. *vi* choke.
suffrage (sy'fraʒ) *nm* **1** franchise. **2** vote.
suggérer (sygʒe:'re:) *vt* suggest. **suggestion** *nf* suggestion.
se suicider (sɥi:si:'de:) *vr* commit suicide. **suicide** *nm* suicide.
suie (sɥi:) *nf* soot.
suinter (sɥɛ̃'te:) *vi* **1** ooze, seep. **2** leak.
suis[1] (sɥi:) *v* see **être.**
suis[2] (sɥi:) *v* see **suivre.**
Suisse (sɥi:s) *nf* Switzerland. **suisse** *adj,n* Swiss.
suite (sɥi:t) *nf* **1** continuation. **2** sequel. **3** consistency. **4** sequence. **5** suite, train. **de suite** in succession. **par la suite 1** later on. **2** consequently. **tout de suite** immediately.
suivre* (sɥi:vr) *vt* **1** follow. **2** attend. **3** accompany. *v imp* result. **faire suivre** forward (a letter). **suivant** *adj* next, following. *prep* according to. **suivi** *adj* **1** consistent. **2** steady. **3** coherent.
sujet, -ette (sy'ʒɛ, -'ʒɛt) *adj* **1** subject. **2** dependent. **3** exposed. **4** liable. *nm,f* subject (person). *nm* **1** subject. **2** cause. **3** theme.
sultan (syl'tɑ̃) *nm* sultan.
superbe (sy'pɛrb) *adj* **1** superb, splendid. **2** stately. **3** arrogant.
supercherie (sypɛrʃə'ri:) *nf* **1** deceit. **2** fraud. **3** hoax.
superficie (sypɛrfi:'si:) *nf* **1** surface. **2** *math* area.
superficiel, -elle (sypɛrfi:'sjɛl) *adj* superficial.
superflu (sypɛr'fly) *adj* **1** superfluous. **2** useless.
supérieur (sype:'rjœr) *adj* **1** upper. **2** superior. **3** higher. *nm* superior. **supériorité** *nf* superiority.
superlatif, -ive (sypɛrla'ti:f, -'ti:v) *adj,nm* superlative.
supermarché (sypɛrmar'ʃe:) *nm* supermarket.
supersonique (sypɛrsɔ'ni:k) *adj* supersonic.
superstition (sypɛrsti:'sjɔ̃) *nf* superstition. **superstitieux, -euse** (sypɛrsti:'sjœ, -'sjœz) *adj* superstitious.
suppléer (syple:'e:) *vt* **1** make up or good. **2** deputize. **suppléer à 1** make up for. **2** fill. **suppléant** *adj* temporary. *nm* **1** substitute. **2** deputy. **supplément** *nm* **1** supplement. **2** addition. **3** extra charge. **supplémentaire** *adj* **1** supplementary. **2** additional.
supplice (sy'pli:s) *nm* **1** corporal punishment. **2** torture. **3** torment. **dernier supplice** death penalty.
supplier (sypli:'e:) *vt* implore, entreat.
support (sy'pɔr) *nm* **1** support, prop. **2** stand, rest.
supporter (sypɔr'te:) *vt* **1** support, prop up. **2** endure. **3** tolerate.
supposer (sypo'ze:) *vt* **1** suppose, imagine. **2** imply.
supprimer (sypri:'me:) *vt* **1** suppress. **2** abolish. **3** omit. **4** *inf* kill.
suprême (sy'prɛm) *adj* **1** supreme, highest. **2** last. **suprématie** (syprɛma'si:) *nf* supremacy.
sur (syr) *prep* **1** on. **2** upon. **3** after. **4** about. **5** out of. **6** by. **sur ce** whereupon. **sur-le-champ** *adv* immediately.
sûr (syr) *adj* **1** sure. **2** trustworthy. **3** certain. **à coup sûr** for certain. **bien sûr!** of course!
surabondance (syrabɔ̃'dɑ̃s) *nf* surfeit.
suranné (syra'ne:) *adj* **1** out of date. **2** old-fashioned.
surcharger (syrʃar'ʒe:) *vt* **1** overload. **2** overwork. **surcharge** *nf* **1** overload. **2** surcharge.
surchauffer (syrʃo'fe:) *vt* overheat.
surcroît (syr'krwa) *nm* increase. **par surcroît** in addition.
surdité (syrdi:'te:) *nf* deafness.
sureau, -aux (sy'ro) *nm* elder tree.
surélever (syre:l've:) *vt* **1** heighten. **2** raise.

surenchère (syrɑ̃'ʃɛr) *nf* higher bid.
surestimer (syrɛsti:'me:) *vt* overestimate.
sûreté (syr'te:) *nf* **1** safety, protection. **2** sureness. **3** guarantee.
surface (syr'fas) *nf* **1** surface. **2** outside.
surfaire* (syr'fɛr) *vt* **1** overcharge. **2** overestimate.
surgeler (syrʒə'le:) *vt* deep-freeze.
surgir (syr'ʒi:r) *vt* **1** rise. **2** loom, crop up.
surhumain (syry'mɛ̃) *adj* superhuman.
surimposer (syrɛ̃po'ze:) *vt* **1** superimpose. **2** increase the tax on.
surlendemain (syrlɑ̃d'mɛ̃) *nm* next day but one, two days later.
surmener (syrmə'ne:) *vt* overwork. **surmenage** *nm* overworking.
surmonter (syrmɔ̃'te) *vt* **1** surmount. **2** dominate, overcome.
surnaturel, -elle (syrnaty'rɛl) *adj* supernatural.
surnom (syr'nɔ̃) *nm* nickname.
surnombre (syr'nɔ̃br) *nm* excess.
surpasser (syrpɑ'se:) *vt* surpass, transcend.
surplomb (syr'plɔ̃) *nm* overhang.
surplomber (syrplɔ̃'be:) *vi,vt* overhang.
surplus (syr'ply) *nm* surplus, excess. **au surplus** besides.
surprendre* (syr'prɑ̃dr) *vt* **1** surprise, astonish. **2** catch in the act. **surprise** *nf* surprise.
surréalisme (syre:a'li:sm) *nm* surrealism. **surréaliste** *adj,n* surrealist.
sursaut (syr'so) *nm* start, jump.
surseoir* (syr'swar) *vt* suspend, put off. **sursis** *nm* **1** delay. **2** reprieve.
surtout (syr'tu:) *adv* **1** above all. **2** especially, particularly. **surtout que** especially as.
surveiller (syrvɛ'je:) *vt* **1** supervise. **2** inspect. **3** observe, watch. **4** look after. **surveillance** *nf* supervision. **surveillant** *nm* **1** supervisor. **2** superintendent. **3** master on duty.
survenir* (syrvə'ni:r) *vi* **1** happen, occur. **2** crop up.
survêtement (syrvɛt'mɑ̃) *nm* tracksuit.
survivre* (syr'vi:vr) *vi* **survivre à** outlive. **survivance** *nf* survival. **survivant** *nm* survivor.
sus (sys) **en sus** *adv* in addition.
susceptible (sysɛp'ti:bl) *adj* **1** susceptible. **2** capable. **3** sensitive. **4** thin-skinned. **peu susceptible** thick-skinned.
susciter (syssi:'te:) *vt* **1** rouse. **2** create.
susdit (syz'di:) *adj* aforesaid.
suspect (sy'spɛ) *adj* suspicious, dubious. *nm* suspect.
suspendre (sy'spɑ̃dr) *vt* **1** suspend. **2** hang up. **suspension** *nf* suspension.
suspens (sy'spɑ̃) **en suspens** *adv* **1** in suspense. **2** undecided.
susurrer (sysy're:) *vi* murmur, rustle.
suture (sy'tyr) *nf* join. **point de suture** *nm med* stitch.
svastika (svasti:'ka) *nm* swastika.
svelte (svɛlt) *adj* slim, slender.
sycomore (sikɔ'mɔr) *nm* sycamore.
syllabe (si:l'lab) *nf* syllable.
sylvestre (si:l'vɛstr) *adj* woodland.
symbole (sɛ̃'bɔl) *nm* symbol. **symbolique** *adj* symbolic.
symboliser (sɛ̃bɔli:'ze:) *vt* symbolize. **symbolisme** *nm* symbolism.
symétrie (si:me:'tri:) *nf* symmetry. **symétrique** *adj* symmetrical.
sympathie (sɛ̃pa'ti:) *nf* **1** liking, attraction. **2** sympathy. **sympathique** *adj* likeable, attractive.
symphonie (sɛ̃fɔ'ni:) *nf* symphony.
symposium (sɛ̃pɔ'zjɔm) *nm* symposium.
symptôme (sɛ̃p'tom) *nm* **1** symptom. **2** sign.
synagogue (si:na'gɔg) *nf* synagogue.
synchroniser (sɛ̃krɔni:'ze:) *vt* synchronize.
syndicat (sɛ̃di:'ka) *nm* **1** syndicate. **2** association. **3** trade union. **syndicat d'initiative** tourist information bureau. **syndical, -aux** (sɛ̃di:'kal, -'ko) *adj* trade-union. **syndicaliste** *nm,f* trade unionist. **syndiqué** *nm* trade-union member.
syndrome (sɛ̃'drom) *nm* syndrome.
synonyme (si:nɔ'ni:m) *adj* synonymous. *nm* synonym.
syntaxe (sɛ̃'taks) *nf* syntax.
synthèse (sɛ̃'tɛz) *nf* synthesis.
synthétique (sɛ̃te:'ti:k) *adj* synthetic.
syphilis (si:fi:'li:s) *nf* syphilis.
Syrie (si:'ri:) *nf* Syria. **syrien, -ienne** (si:'rjɛ̃, -'rjɛn) *adj,n* Syrian.
système (si:'stɛm) *nm* **1** system. **2** network. **3** device. **systématique** *adj* systematic.

T

ta (ta) *poss adj* see **ton.**
tabac (ta'ba) *nm* tobacco. **tabac à priser** snuff.
table (tabl) *nf* **1** table. **2** tablet, slab. **3** list. **table roulante** trolley. **tableau, -aux** (ta'blo) *nm* **1** picture. **2** board. **3** list. **tableau d'annonces** notice board. **tableau noir** black-

board. **tablette** *nf* **1** shelf. **2** slab. **tablier** *nm* apron.
tabou (ta'bu:) *adj,nm* taboo.
tabouret (tabu:'rɛ) *nm* stool.
tacher (ta'ʃe:) *vt* **1** stain, spot. **2** impair. **tache** *nf* **1** stain, spot. **2** blot. **tache de rousseur** freckle.
tâcher (tɑ'ʃe:) *vi* try, strive. **tâche** *nf* task, job.
tacheté (taʃ'te:) *adj* flecked, mottled.
tact (takt) *nm* **1** sense of touch. **2** tact. **avoir du tact** be tactful.
tactique (tak'ti:k) *adj* tactical. *nf* tactics.
taffetas (taf'tɑ) *nm* taffeta.
taie (tɛ) *nf* **taie d'oreiller** pillowcase.
tailler (ta'je:) *vt* **1** cut. **2** prune. **3** trim. **4** sharpen. **taillade** *nf* **1** slash. **2** gash. **taille** *nf* **1** cutting. **2** cut. **3** stature. **4** waist. **taille-crayon** *nm invar* pencil-sharpener. **taille de cheveux** haircut. **tailleur** *nm* **1** tailor. **2** cutter. **3** (woman's) suit.
tain (tɛ̃) *nm* tinfoil.
taire* (tɛr) *vt* conceal, hide. **faire taire** silence. **se taire** *vr* be quiet, hold one's tongue.
talc (talk) *nm* talcum powder.
talent (ta'lɑ̃) *nm* **1** talent, gift. **2** ability.
talon (ta'lɔ̃) *nm* **1** heel. **2** stock. **3** remainder. **4** voucher.
talonner (talɔ'ne:) *vt* **1** follow closely. **2** spur on.
tambour (tɑ̃'bu:r) *nm* **1** drum. **2** barrel. **tambour de basque** tambourine.
tamis (ta'mi:) *nm* sieve.
tamiser (tami:'ze:) *vt* **1** sieve. **2** strain, filter.
tampon (tɑ̃'pɔ̃) *nm* **1** plug. **2** *med* wad. **3** stamp, mark. **4** buffer.
tamponner (tɑ̃pɔ'ne:) *vt* **1** plug. **2** dab. **3** collide with. **tamponnement** *nm* **1** plugging. **2** collision.
tancer (tɑ̃'se:) *vt inf* scold.
tandis que (tɑ̃'di: kə) *conj* **1** whereas. **2** whilst.
tangent (tɑ̃'ʒɑ̃) *nf* tangent.
Tanger (tɑ̃'ʒe:) *nm* Tangier.
tanguer (tɑ̃'ge:) *vi naut* pitch.
tanière (ta'njɛr) *nf* den, earth, hole.
tan-sad (tɑ̃'sad) *nm mot* pillion.
tant (tɑ̃) *adv* **1** so much. **2** so many. **3** as much. **4** as many. **5** so. **en tant que** in so far as. **tant mieux/pis!** so much the better/too bad! **tant s'en faut** far from it.
tante (tɑ̃t) *nf* aunt.
tantôt (tɑ̃'to) *adv* **1** soon. **2** a little while ago. **tantôt...tantôt** sometimes....sometimes.
taon (tɑ̃) *nm* horsefly.
tapage (ta'paʒ) *nm* din, racket. **tapageur, -euse** (tapa'ʒœr, -'ʒœz) *adj* **1** rowdy, noisy. **2** showy.
taper (ta'pe:) *vt* **1** tap. **2** hit. **3** beat. **4** *inf* borrow. **ça tape** it's hot. **taper à la machine** type. **taper sur les nerfs** get on one's nerves. **tape** *nf* tap, pat.
se tapir (ta'pi:r) *vr* crouch.
tapis (ta'pi:) *nm* **1** carpet. **2** rug. **3** cover. **tapis de sol** groundsheet.
tapisser (tapi:'se:) *vt* paper (a room). **tapisserie** *nf* **1** tapestry. **2** wallpaper. **tapissier** *nm* upholsterer.
tapoter (tapɔ'te:) *vt inf* **1** pat. **2** strum.
taquin (ta'kɛ̃) *adj* teasing. **taquiner** *vt* tease. **taquinerie** *nf* teasing.
tard (tar) *adv* late.
tarder (tar'de:) *vi* delay. **tardif, -ive** (tar'di:f, -'di:v) *adj* **1** late. **2** backward.
tarif (ta'ri:f) *nm* **1** price-list. **2** tariff. **3** fare.
tarir (ta'ri:r) *vt,vi* dry up.
tarte (tart) *nf* **1** tart. **2** flan. **tartine** *nf* slice of bread and butter.
tas (tɑ) *nm* **1** pile. **2** *inf* group, crew. **3** *inf* lot.
tasse (tɑs) *nf* cup. **tasse à thé** teacup. **tassée** *nf* cupful.
tasser (tɑ'se:) *vt* **1** cram together. **2** press down. **se tasser** *vr* **1** settle. **2** huddle together.
tâter (tɑ'te:) *vt* **1** feel, handle. **2** sound. **3** try.
tâtonner (tɑtɔ'ne:) *vi* **1** grope. **2** feel one's way.
tâtons (tɑ'tɔ̃) **à tâtons** *adv* warily.
tatouer (ta'twe:) *vt* tattoo.
taudis (to'di:) *nm* slum.
taupe (top) *nf zool* mole.
taureau, -aux (tɔ'ro) *nm* **1** bull. **2** *cap* Taurus.
taux (to) *nm* rate, scale.
taverne (ta'vɛrn) *nf* **1** tavern. **2** restaurant.
taxer (tak'se:) *vt* **1** tax. **2** regulate the price. **3** accuse. **taxe** *nf* **1** fixed price. **2** charge. **3** tax.
taxi (tak'si:) *nm* taxi.
Tchécoslovaquie (tʃekɔslɔva'ki:) *nf* Czechoslovakia. **tchèque** (tʃɛk) *adj,n* Czech. *nm* Czech (language).
te, t' (tə) *pron 2nd pers m,f s fam* **1** you. **2** to you.
technique (tɛk'ni:k) *adj* technical. *nf* technique. **technicien** *nm* technician. **technologie** *nf* technology. **technologique** *adj* technological.
teck (tɛk) *nm also* **tek** teak.
teindre* (tɛ̃dr) *vt* **1** dye. **2** tinge. **3** colour.
teint (tɛ̃) *nm* **1** dye. **2** complexion.
teinter (tɛ̃'te:) *vt* tint. **teinte** *nf* **1** tint. **2** tinge. **teinture** *nf* **1** dyeing. **2** colour. **3** dye.

tel, telle (tɛl) *adj* **1** such. **2** as. **3** like. **tel que** such as. *pron* **1** such a one. **2** many a.
télégramme (te:le:ˈgram) *nm* telegram.
télégraphier (te:le:graˈfje:) *vt* telegraph. **télégraphe** *nm* telegraph.
téléphérique (te:le:fe:ˈri:k) *nm* cable car.
téléphoner (te:le:fɔˈne:) *vt,vi* telephone. **téléphone** *nm* telephone. **téléphoniste** *nm,f* operator.
télésiège (te:le:ˈsjɛʒ) *nm* chair-lift.
téléski (te:le:ˈski:) *nm* ski-lift.
téléviser (te:le:vi:ˈze:) *vt* televise. **télévision** *nf* television.
tellement (tɛlˈmɑ̃) *adv* **1** so. **2** in such a way.
téméraire (te:me:ˈrɛr) *adj* **1** rash. **2** reckless.
témoigner (te:mwaˈɲe:) *vi* give evidence. *vt* **1** testify. **2** show. **3** prove. **témoignage** *nm* **1** evidence. **2** *law* statement. **3** token, mark. **témoin** *nm* **1** witness. **2** *sport* baton.
tempe (tɑ̃p) *nf anat* temple.
tempérament (tɑ̃pɛraˈmɑ̃) *nm* **1** temperament. **2** *med* constitution. **3** *comm* instalment.
tempérant (tɑ̃pɛˈrɑ̃) *adj* temperate.
température (tɑ̃pɛraˈtyr) *nf* temperature.
tempérer (tɑ̃pe:ˈre:) *vt* moderate.
tempête (tɑ̃ˈpɛt) *nf* storm. **tempétueux, -euse** (tɑ̃pe:ˈtɥœ, -ˈtɥœz) *adj* stormy, tempestuous.
temple (tɑ̃pl) *nm* **1** *rel* temple. **2** church.
tempo (tɛ̃ˈpo) *nm* tempo.
temporaire (tɑ̃pɔˈrɛr) *adj* **1** temporary. **2** provisional.
temporel, -elle (tɑ̃pɔˈrɛl) *adj* temporal.
temps (tɑ̃) *nm* **1** time. **2** age, period. **3** weather. **4** tense. **5** *mus* beat. **à temps** on time. **de temps en temps** now and again. **quel temps fait-il?** what's the weather like?
tenace (təˈnas) *adj* **1** tenacious. **2** tough. **3** stubborn. **ténacité** *nf* tenacity.
tenailles (təˈnaj) *nf pl* pincers.
tendance (tɑ̃ˈdɑ̃s) *nf* tendency, trend.
tendon (tɑ̃ˈdɔ̃) *nm* **1** tendon. **2** sinew.
tendre[1] (tɑ̃dr) *adj* **1** tender. **2** affectionate. **3** delicate. **tendresse** *nf* **1** affection. **2** tenderness. **3** *pl* caress. **tendreté** *nf cul* tenderness.
tendre[2] (tɑ̃dr) *vt* **1** stretch. **2** strain. **3** tighten. **4** hold out. **5** set. **tendre à 1** tend to. **2** aim at. **se tendre** *vr* become taut or strained. **tendu** *adj* **1** taut. **2** strained. **3** tense.
ténèbres (te:ˈnɛbr) *nf pl* darkness, gloom. **ténébreux, -euse** (te:ne:ˈbrœ, -ˈbrœz) *adj* **1** dark, gloomy. **2** sinister. **3** mysterious.
tenir* (təˈni:r) *vt* **1** hold. **2** keep. **3** run. **4** restrain. **5** occupy. *vi* **1** hold. **2** stick. **3** remain. **4** last. **tenir à 1** value. **2** result from. **tenir bon** hold out. **tenir compte de** take into consideration. **tenir de** take after. **se tenir** *vr* **1** keep. **2** remain. **3** contain oneself. **se tenir à 1** hold on to. **2** abide by. **se tenir bien** behave.
tennis (tɛˈni:s) *nm* **1** tennis. **2** tennis court.
ténor (te:ˈnɔr) *nm* tenor.
tension (tɑ̃ˈsjɔ̃) *nf* **1** tension. **2** pressure. **3** voltage. **tension artérielle** blood pressure.
tente (tɑ̃t) *nf* **1** tent. **2** awning.
tenter (tɑ̃ˈte:) *vt* **1** tempt. **2** try. **3** attempt. **tentant** *adj* tempting. **tentation** *nf* temptation. **tentative** *nf* attempt.
tenture (tɑ̃ˈtyr) *nf* **1** tapestry. **2** wallpaper.
tenu (təˈny) *v see* **tenir.** *adj* **bien tenu** neat, tidy. **être tenu à** be bound to. **mal tenu 1** neglected. **2** untidy. **tenue** *nf* **1** holding. **2** bearing. **3** behaviour. **4** dress. **tenue de soirée** evening dress. **tenue des livres** bookkeeping.
ténu (te:ˈny) *adj* **1** fine. **2** thin. **3** tenuous. **4** subtle.
tenure (təˈnyr) **tenure à bail** *nf* leasehold.
térébenthine (te:re:bɑ̃ˈti:n) *nf* turpentine.
tergiverser (tɛrʒi:vɛrˈse:) *vi* **1** beat about the bush. **2** hesitate.
terme (tɛrm) *nm* **1** limit. **2** term, expression. **3** quarter's rent. **avant terme** prematurely. **mettre terme à** put an end to.
terminer (tɛrmi:ˈne:) *vt* end, terminate. **terminaison** *nf* ending.
terminologie (tɛrmi:nɔlɔˈʒi:) *nf* terminology.
terminus (tɛrmi:ˈnys) *nm* terminus, terminal.
ternir (tɛrˈni:r) *vt* **1** tarnish. **2** dull. **terne** *adj* **1** dull. **2** lifeless.
terrain (tɛˈrɛ̃) *nm* **1** ground. **2** plot of land. **terrain de jeux** playing field.
terrasse (tɛˈras) *nf* **1** terrace. **2** bank.
terre (tɛr) *nf* **1** earth. **2** world. **3** land, soil. **4** estate. **descendre à terre** go ashore. **par-terre** on the ground. **basses terres** *nf pl* lowlands. **hautes terres** *nf pl* highlands.
terrestre (tɛˈrɛstr) *adj* **1** terrestrial. **2** worldly.
terreur (tɛˈrœr) *nf* terror, fear.
terrible (tɛˈri:bl) *adj* **1** terrible, awful. **2** *inf* terrific.
terrier (tɛˈrje:) *nm* hole, burrow.
terrifier (tɛri:ˈfje:) *vt* terrify.
terrine (tɛˈri:n) *nf* **1** earthenware dish. **2** potted meat.
territoire (tɛri:ˈtwar) *nm* territory. **territorial, -aux** (tɛri:tɔˈrjal, -ˈrjo) *adj* territorial.

terroir (tɛr'war) *nm* soil.

terroriser (tɛrɔri:'ze:) *vt* terrorize. **terrorisme** *nm* terrorism. **terroriste** *nm,f* terrorist.

Térylène (te:ri:'lɛn) *nm Tdmk* Terylene.

tes (te:) *poss adj* see **ton.**

tesson (tɛ'sɔ̃) *nm* broken fragment (of glass, etc.).

testament (tɛsta'mɑ̃) *nm* **1** *law* will. **2** testament. **ancien Testament** Old Testament. **nouveau Testament** New Testament.

testicule (tɛsti:'kyl) *nm* testicle.

têtard (tɛ'tar) *nm* tadpole.

tête (tɛt) *nf* **1** head. **2** brains. **3** front. **4** top. **en tête** in front, ahead. **forte tête** strong-minded. **tenir tête à** resist. **tête-à-tête** *nm invar* private interview. **têtu** *adj* stubborn.

tétin (te:'tɛ̃) *nm* nipple, teat.

tétras (te:'trɑ) *nm zool* grouse.

texte (tɛkst) *nm* **1** text. **2** passage. **3** subject.

textile (tɛk'sti:l) *adj,nm* textile.

texture (tɛk'styr) *nf* texture.

thé (te:) *nm* tea. **théière** *nf* teapot.

théâtre (te:'ɑtr) *nm* **1** theatre. **2** stage. **3** drama. **théâtral, -aux** (te:ɑ'tral, -'tro) *adj* theatrical.

thème (tɛm) *nm* **1** theme, subject. **2** *educ* prose.

théologie (te:ɔlɔ'ʒi:) *nf* theology. **théologien** *nm* theologian. **théologique** *adj* theological.

théorème (te:ɔ'rɛm) *nm* theorem.

théorie (te:ɔ'ri:) *nf* theory. **théorique** *adj* theoretical.

théoriser (te:ɔri:'ze:) *vi* theorize.

thérapeutique (tɛrapœ'ti:k) *adj* therapeutic.

thérapie (te:ra'pi:) *nf* therapy.

thermal, -aux (tɛr'mal, -'mo) *adj* thermal.

thermodynamique (tɛrmɔdi:na'mi:k) *nf* thermodynamics.

thermomètre (tɛrmɔ'mɛtr) *nm* thermometer.

thermonucléaire (tɛrmonykle.'ɛr) *adj* thermonuclear.

thermoplongeur (termɔplɔ̃'ʒœr) *nm* immersion heater.

Thermos (tɛr'mɔs) *nm Tdmk* Thermos flask.

thermostat (tɛrmɔ'sta) *nm* thermostat.

thésauriser (te:zɔri:'ze:) *vt,vi* hoard.

thèse (tɛz) *nf* **1** proposition. **2** theory. **3** thesis.

thon (tɔ̃) *nm* tunny, tuna fish.

thym (tɛ̃) *nm* thyme.

tiare (tjar) *nf* tiara.

tic (ti:k) *nm* **1** *med* twitch. **2** mannerism.

ticket (ti:'kɛ) *nm* **1** ticket. **2** slip.

tiède (tjɛd) *adj* tepid, lukewarm.

tien, tienne (tjɛ̃, tjɛn) **le tien, la tienne** *poss pron 2nd pers s fam* **1** yours. **2** your own.

tiens[1] (tjɛ̃) *v* see **tenir.**

tiens[2] (tjɛ̃) *interj* **1** hello! **2** look!

tiers, tierce (tjɛr, tjɛrs) *adj* third. *nm* **1** third. **2** third person or party.

tige (ti:ʒ) *nf* **1** stem, stalk. **2** *bot* trunk. **3** rod.

tigre (ti:gr) *nm* tiger. **tigré** *adj* **1** spotted. **2** striped.

tilleul (ti:'jœl) *nm* linden or lime tree.

timbale (tɛ̃'bal) *nf* **1** kettledrum. **2** *pl* timpani. **3** metal mug.

timbrer (tɛ̃'bre:) *vt* **1** stamp. **2** postmark. **timbre** *nm* **1** stamp. **2** bell.

timide (ti:'mi:d) *adj* **1** timid. **2** shy.

tintamarre (tɛ̃ta'mar) *nm* din, racket.

tinter (tɛ̃'te:) *vt* ring, toll (a bell). *vi* **1** tinkle. **2** jingle. **3** clink.

tir (ti:r) *nm* **1** shooting. **2** firing. **tir à l'arc** archery.

tirelire (ti:r'li:r) *nf* moneybox.

tirer (ti:'re:) *vt* **1** pull. **2** draw (out). **3** drag. **4** take out. **5** shoot. *vi* **1** pull. **2** incline. **se tirer** *vr* extricate oneself. **tirage** *nm* **1** pulling. **2** draw (of a lottery). **3** *comm* circulation. **tire** *nf* pull. **tire-bouchon** *nm, pl* **tire-bouchons** corkscrew.

tiret (ti:'rɛ) *nm* **1** hyphen. **2** dash.

tiroir (ti'rwɑr) *nm, pl* drawer. **tiroir-caisse** *nm, pl* **tiroirs-caisses** till.

tisane (ti:'zan) *nf* infusion.

tisonner (ti:zɔ'ne:) *vt* poke, stir. **tisonnier** *nm* poker.

tisser (ti:'se:) *vt* weave. **tissu** *nm* **1** material. **2** fabric. **3** *zool* tissue.

titre (ti:tr) *nm* **1** title. **2** diploma. **3** claim. **4** *comm* bond. **à titre de** by virtue of.

tituber (ti:'ty'be:) *vi* stagger, lurch.

toast (tɔst) *nm* toast (drink).

toi (twa) *pron 2nd pers m,f s fam* you. **toi-même** *pron 2nd pers m,f s fam* yourself.

toile (twal) *nf* **1** linen. **2** canvas. **3** oil painting. **4** *Th* curtain. **toile cirée** oilskin. **toile d'araignée** cobweb.

toilette (twa'lɛt) *nf* **1** washing, toilet. **2** dressing-table. **3** lavatory. **4** dress.

toise (twaz) *nf* fathom.

toison (twa'zɔ̃) *nf* fleece.

toit (twa) *nm* **1** roof. **2** *inf* home.

tôle (to:l) *mf* metal sheet.

tolérer (tɔle:'re:) *vt* tolerate. **tolérance** *nf* tolerance. **tolérant** *adj* tolerant.

tomate (tɔ'mat) *nf* tomato.

tombe (tɔ̃b) *nf* **1** tomb. **2** tombstone. **tombeau, -aux** (tɔ̃'bo) *nm* **1** tomb. **2** monument (over a grave).

tomber (tɔ̃'be:) *vi* (*aux* être) **1** fall. **2** hang. **3** subside. **laisser tomber** drop. **tomber juste** **1** happen at the right moment. **2** guess right. **tombée** *nf* fall.

tome (tom) *nm* volume (of a book).

ton[1], **ta, tes** (tɔ̃, ta, te:) *poss adj 2nd pers s fam* your.

ton[2] (tɔ̃) *nm* **1** tone. **2** colour. **3** *mus* pitch. **4** *mus* key.

tondre (tɔ̃dr) *vt* shear, clip, mow. **tondeuse** *nf* **1** shears. **2** lawn-mower.

tonifier (tɔni:'fje:) *vt* invigorate, brace.

tonique (tɔ'ni:k) *nm* tonic.

tonne (tɔn) *nf* ton.

tonneau, -aux (tɔ'no) *nm* barrel.

tonner (tɔ'ne:) *vi* thunder. **tonnerre** *nm* thunder.

topaze (tɔ'paz) *nf* topaz.

toper (tɔ'pe:) *vi inf* agree. **tope!** *interj* done!

torche (tɔrʃ) *nf* torch.

torchon (tɔr'ʃɔ̃) *nm* **1** duster. **2** dishcloth.

tordre (tɔrdr) *vt* **1** twist. **2** wring. **3** distort. **se tordre** *vr* writhe.

tornade (tɔr'nad) *nf* tornado.

torpille (tɔr'pi:j) *nf* torpedo.

torréfier (tɔrre:'fje:) *vt* **1** roast. **2** scorch.

torrent (tɔ'rɑ̃) *nm* torrent. **torrentiel, -elle** (tɔrɑ̃'sjɛl) *adj* torrential.

tors (tɔr) *adj* **1** twisted. **2** crooked.

torse (tɔrs) *nm* torso.

tort (tɔr) *nm* **1** wrong. **2** fault. **3** harm. **avoir tort** be wrong.

torticolis (tɔrti:kɔ'li:) *nm* stiff neck.

tortiller (tɔrti:'je:) *vt* **1** twist. **2** twiddle. *vi* **1** wriggle. **2** quibble. **se tortiller** *vr* **1** writhe. **2** squirm.

tortu (tɔr'ty) *adj* crooked.

tortue (tɔr'ty) *nf* tortoise. **tortue de mer** turtle.

tortueux, -euse (tɔr'tɥœ, -'tɥœz) *adj* **1** winding. **2** underhand.

torturer (tɔrty're:) *vt* torture. **torture** *nf* torture.

Tory (tɔ'ri:) *adj* or *nm, pl* **Tories** Tory.

tôt (to) *adv* **1** soon. **2** early. **tôt ou tard** sooner or later.

total, -aux (tɔ'tal, -'to) *adj* **1** total, whole. **2** complete, absolute. *nm* total. **au total** on the whole. **totalitaire** *adj* totalitarian. **totalité** *nf* whole.

toucher (tu:'ʃe:) *vt* **1** touch. **2** hit. **3** cash. **4** receive. **5** move. **6** concern. **toucher à 1** be near to. **2** affect. **3** meddle with. **se toucher** *vr* adjoin. ~*nm* touch, feel. **touche** *nf* **1** touch. **2** *mus* key.

touffu (tu:'fy) *adj* **1** bushy. **2** thick. **3** complicated.

toujours (tu:'ʒu:r) *adv* **1** always, ever, forever. **2** still. **3** all the same.

toupet (tu:'pɛ) *nm* **1** tuft (of hair). **2** forelock. **3** *sl* cheek, nerve.

toupie (tu:'pi:) *nf* top (toy).

tour[1] (tu:r) *nf* tower.

tour[2] (tu:r) *nm* **1** turn. **2** revolution. **3** circumference. **4** lathe. **5** stroll. **6** trick. **à tour de rôle** in turn. **tour de main** knack.

tourbe (tu:rb) *nf* peat, turf.

tourbillon (tu:rbi:'jɔ̃) *nm* whirlwind.

tourelle (tu:'rɛl) *nf* turret.

tourisme (tu:'ri:sm) *nm* tourism. **touriste** *nm,f* tourist.

tourment (tu:r'mɑ̃) *nm* **1** torment. **2** anguish. **tourmenter** *vt* **1** torture. **2** harass. **3** pester.

tourmente (tu:r'mɑ̃) *nf* **1** storm. **2** upheaval.

tournedos (tu:rnə'do) *nm* fillet steak.

tourner (tu:r'ne:) *vt* **1** turn. **2** rotate. **3** dodge. **4** wind. *vi* **1** revolve. **2** result. **3** curdle. **tourner un film** shoot a film. **tournant** *adj* **1** turning. **2** winding. *nm* **1** bend, turning. **2** turning point. **tourne-disques** *nm invar* record-player. **tournée** *nf* **1** round, circuit. **2** tour. **tournevis** *nm* screwdriver.

tournesol (tu:rnə'sɔl) *nm* sunflower.

tourniquet (tu:rni:'kɛ) *nm* **1** turnstile. **2** tourniquet.

tournoi (tu:r'nwa) *nm* tournament.

tournoyer (tu:rnwa'je:) *vi* whirl.

tournure (tu:r'nyr) *nf* **1** shape, appearance. **2** form, figure.

tourte (tu:rt) *nf* **1** pie. **2** *inf* idiot.

tourterelle (tu:rtə'rɛl) *nf* turtle dove.

Toussaint (tu:'sɛ̃) *nf* All Saints' Day.

tousser (tu:'se:) *vi* cough.

tout (tu:) *adj, pl* **tous, toutes 1** all. **2** every. **3** any. **de toute importance** of utmost importance. **tous les deux** both. **toutes les fois que** whenever. ~*pron* **1** all. **2** anything. **3** everything. *nm* **1** whole. **2** total. *adv* **1** quite, completely. **2** while. **3** though. **tout à fait** completely. **tout au plus** at the very most. **tout fait** ready-made. **tout neuf** brand new. **toutefois** *adv* however, yet. **tout-puissant** *adj* omnipotent.

toux (tu:) *nf* cough.

toxique (tɔk'si:k) *adj* **1** toxic. **2** poisonous. *nm* poison.
trac (trak) *nm sl* fright.
tracas (tra'ka) *nm* **1** worry. **2** bother.
tracasser (traka'sje:) *vt* **1** worry. **2** plague. **3** annoy.
tracer (tra'se:) *vt* **1** trace. **2** outline. **3** mark out. **4** plot. **trace** *nf* trace, trail, track.
tract (trakt) *nm pol* leaflet.
tracteur (trak'tœr) *nm* tractor.
tradition (tradi:'sjɔ̃) *nf* **1** tradition. **2** legend. **tradition populaire** folklore. **traditionnel, -elle** (tradi:sjɔ'nɛl) *adj* traditional.
traduire* (tra'dɥi:r) *vt* **1** translate. **2** interpret. **traducteur, -trice** (tradyk'tœr, -'tri:s) *nm,f* translator. **traduction** *nf* translation.
trafiquer (trafi:'ke:) *vi* **trafiquer en** traffic or deal in.
tragédie (traʒe:'di:) *nf* tragedy. **tragique** *adj* tragic.
trahir (tra'i:r) *vt* **1** betray. **2** reveal. **trahison** *nf* **1** betrayal. **2** treachery.
train (trɛ̃) *nm* **1** train. **2** line. **3** movement. **4** pace. **5** mood. **être en train de** be in the middle of. **mettre en train** start, set going. **train de marchandises** goods train. **train-train** *nm inf* routine.
traîner (trɛ'ne:) *vt* **1** drag. **2** trail. **3** drawl. **4** drag on or out. *vi* **1** trail. **2** linger. **3** languish. **se traîner** *vr* crawl. **traînant** *adj* **1** dragging. **2** listless. **traîneau, -aux** (trɛ'no) *nm* sledge. **traînée** *nf* **1** train. **2** trail.
traire* (trɛr) *vt* milk.
trait (trɛ) *nm* **1** gulp. **2** dart. **3** flash. **4** line. **5** stroke. **6** *anat* feature. **d'un trait** at a stretch. **trait d'union** hyphen.
traiter (trɛ'te:) *vt* **1** treat. **2** call. **3** discuss. **4** handle. *vi* negotiate. **traité** *nm* **1** treatise. **2** treaty. **traitement** *nm* **1** treatment. **2** salary.
traître, traîtresse (trɛtr, trɛ'trɛs) *adj* treacherous. *nm* traitor.
trajet (tra'ʒɛ) *nm* **1** journey. **2** passage.
trame (tram) *nf* **1** thread. **2** conspiracy.
tramway (tram'wɛ) *nm* tram.
trancher (trɑ̃'ʃe:) *vt* **1** cut. **2** break off. **3** solve. *vi* contrast. **tranche** *nf* **1** slice, portion. **2** slab. **3** edge. **tranchée** *nf* trench.
tranquille (trɑ̃'ki:l) *adj* **1** tranquil. **2** calm. **3** peaceful. **tranquillisant** *nm* tranquillizer. **tranquillité** *nf* **1** quiet. **2** calm. **3** stillness.
transaction (trɑ̃zak'sjɔ̃) *nf* **1** transaction. **2** compromise.
transatlantique (trɑ̃zatlɑ̃'ti:k) *adj* transatlantic. *nm* **1** liner. **2** deckchair.
transcrire* (trɑ̃'skri:r) *vt* transcribe.
transe (trɑ̃s) *nf* **1** trance. **2** fear.
transférer (trɑ̃sfe:'re:) *vt* **1** transfer. **2** remove. **3** convey. **transfert** *nm* transfer.
transformer (trɑ̃sfɔr'me:) *vt* **1** transform. **2** convert. **transformateur** *nm* transformer.
transfuge (trɑ̃s'fyʒ) *nm* deserter.
transfuser (trɑ̃sfy'ze:) *vt* transfuse. **transfusion** *nf* transfusion.
transiger (trɑ̃zi:'ʒe:) *vi* come to a compromise.
transir (trɑ̃'si:r) *vt* **1** chill. **2** seize (with fear).
transistor (trɑ̃zi:'stɔr) *nm* transistor.
transition (trɑ̃zi:'sjɔ̃) *nf* transition.
transmettre* (trɑ̃s'mɛtr) *vt* **1** transmit. **2** *law* transfer. **3** hand down.
transparent (trɑ̃spa'rɑ̃) *adj* transparent.
transpirer (trɑ̃spi:'re:) *vi* perspire. **transpiration** *nf* perspiration.
transplanter (trɑ̃splɑ̃'te:) *vt* transplant.
transport (trɑ̃'spɔr) *nm* **1** transport, carriage. **2** outburst.
transporter (trɑ̃spɔr'te:) *vt* **1** transport, convey. **2** carry away, delight.
transposer (trɑ̃spo'ze:) *vt* transpose.
transvaser (trɑ̃svɑ'ze:) *vt* decant.
trapèze (tra'pɛz) *nm* trapeze.
trappe (trap) *nf* **1** pitfall. **2** trapdoor.
trapu (tra'py) *adj* **1** stocky. **2** squat.
traquer (tra'ke:) *vt* **1** surround. **2** track down. **traquenard** *nm* trap.
trauma (tro'ma) *nm* trauma. **traumatique** *adj* traumatic.
travail, -aux (tra'vaj, -'vo) *nm* work. **travail à l'aiguille** needlework.
travailler (trava'je:) *vt* **1** work. **2** work on. *vi* **1** work, toil. **2** ferment. **travaillé** *adj* **1** elaborate. **2** wrought. **travailleur, -euse** (trava'jœr, -'jœz) *nm* workman. *adj* industrious. **travailliste** *nm,f* member of the Labour Party. *adj pol* Labour.
travers (tra'vɛr) *nm* **1** breadth. **2** fault, defect. **à travers** across. **au travers de** across. **de travers** amiss, the wrong way.
traverser (travɛr'se:) *vt* **1** cross. **2** go through. **traverse** *nf* **1** short cut. **2** *tech* sleeper. **3** hitch. **traversée** *nf* passage, crossing.
traversin (travɛr'sɛ̃) *nm* bolster.
travestir (travɛ'sti:r) *vt* disguise, dress up. **travesti** *adj* disguised. *nm* fancy dress.
trébucher (tre:by'ʃe:) *vi* **1** stumble. **2** trip. **faire trébucher** trip up.

trèfle (trɛfl) *nm* **1** clover. **2** *game* club.
treillis (trɛˈjiː) *nm* trellis, lattice.
treize (trɛz) *adj,nm* thirteen. **treizième** *adj* thirteenth.
trembler (trɑ̃ˈbleː) *vi* **1** tremble. **2** flicker. **3** shake. **4** quake. **tremblement** *nm* **1** trembling. **2** tremor. **tremblement de terre** earthquake.
trémière (treːˈmjɛr) **rose trémière** *nf* hollyhock.
se trémousser (treːmuːˈseː) *vr* **1** fidget. **2** flutter.
tremper (trɑ̃ˈpeː) *vt,vi* soak, steep. *vt* **1** drench. **2** dip. **3** mix.
tremplin (trɑ̃ˈplɛ̃) *nm* **1** springboard. **2** diving board.
trente (trɑ̃t) *adj,nm* thirty. **trentième** *adj* thirtieth.
trépas (treːˈpɑ) *nm* death.
trépider (treːpiːˈdeː) *vi* vibrate.
trépied (treːˈpjeː) *nm* tripod.
trépigner (treːpiːˈɲeː) *vi* stamp, prance.
très (trɛ) *adv* **1** very. **2** most. **3** very much.
trésor (treːˈzɔr) *nm* **1** treasure. **2** *pl* riches. **3** treasury. **trésorerie** (treːzɔrˈriː) *nf* treasury. **trésorier, -ière** (treːzɔˈrjeː, -ˈrjɛr) *nm,f* treasurer.
tressaillir* (trɛsaˈjiːr) *vi* **1** start, jump. **2** quiver. **3** shudder. **tressaillir de douleur** wince. **tressaillement** *nm* **1** start, jump. **2** shudder. **3** wince.
tresser (trɛˈseː) *vt* **1** plait. **2** weave. **tresse** *nf* plait.
tréteau, -aux (treːˈto) *nm* **1** trestle. **2** support. **3** stage.
treuil (trœj) *nm* **1** winch. **2** windlass.
trêve (trɛv) *nf* truce.
tri (triː) *nm* sorting. **triage** *nm* sorting.
triangle (triːˈɑ̃gl) *nm* triangle. **triangulaire** *adj* triangular.
tribord (triːˈbɔr) *nm* starboard.
tribu (triːˈby) *nf* tribe.
tribunal, -aux (triːbyˈnal, -ˈno) *nm* **1** tribunal. **2** *law* court. **tribune** *nf* **1** platform. **2** grandstand. **3** forum.
tribut (triːˈby) *nm* tribute.
tributaire (triːbyˈtɛr) *adj,nm* tributary.
tricher (triːˈʃeː) *vt,vi* **1** cheat. **2** trick.
tricolore (triːkɔˈlɔr) *nm inf* French national flag, tricolour.
tricot (triːˈko) *nm* **1** knitting. **2** jersey, jumper.
tricoter (triːkɔˈteː) *vi* knit.
tricycle (triːˈsiːkl) *nm* tricycle.
trier (triːˈeː) *vt* sort. **trier à la main** hand-pick.
trille (triːj) *nm mus* trill.
trimestre (triːˈmɛstr) *nm* **1** *educ* term. **2** quarter, three months. **trimestriel, -elle** (triːmɛstriːˈɛl) *adj* quarterly.
tringle (trɛ̃gl) *nf* rod, bar.
trinquer (trɛ̃ˈkeː) *vi* clink glasses.
trio (triːˈo) *nm* trio.
triompher (triːɔ̃ˈfeː) *vi* **1** triumph. **2** overcome. **triomphant** *adj* triumphant. **triomphe** *nm* triumph.
tripaille (triːˈpɑj) *nf inf* offal.
tripe (triːp) *nf* **1** tripe. **2** *sl* guts.
tripler (triːˈpleː) *vt,vi* triple, treble. **triple** *adj* triple, treble. **triplés** *nm* triplets.
tripoter (triːpɔˈteː) *vt inf* **1** meddle with. **2** deal dishonestly with. *vi* **1** mess about. **2** tamper with.
triste (triːst) *adj* **1** sad. **2** melancholy. **3** dismal. **4** unfortunate. **tristesse** *nf* **1** sadness. **2** gloom. **3** bleakness.
triton (triːˈtɔ̃) *nm* newt.
trivial (triːˈvjal) *adj* **1** trite. **2** trivial. **3** vulgar. **4** obscene. **trivialité** *nf* **1** obscenity. **2** triviality.
troc (trɔk) *nm* **1** swop. **2** barter.
trognon (trɔˈɲɔ̃) *nm* **1** core (of an apple, etc.). **2** stump.
trois (trwɑ) *adj,nm* three. **troisième** *adj* third. **trois-quarts** *nm invar* three-quarters.
trombe (trɔ̃b) *nf* **1** waterspout. **2** whirlwind.
trombone (trɔ̃ˈbɔn) *nm* **1** trombone. **2** paper-clip.
tromper (trɔ̃ˈpeː) *vt* **1** deceive. **2** cheat. **3** mislead. **4** baffle. **se tromper** *vr* be mistaken, make a mistake. **tromperie** *nf* deceit.
trompette (trɔ̃ˈpɛt) *nf* trumpet.
tronc (trɔ̃) *nm bot* trunk.
tronçon (trɔ̃ˈsɔ̃) *nm* **1** fragment. **2** stump, stub.
trône (tron) *nm* throne.
tronquer (trɔ̃ˈkeː) *vt* cut up, mutilate.
trop (tro) *adv* **1** too. **2** too much. *nm* too much or many. **de trop** too much or many. **trop-plein** *nm, pl* **trop-pleins** overflow.
trophée (trɔˈfeː) *nm* trophy.
tropique (trɔˈpiːk) *nm* tropic. *adj* tropical. **tropical, -aux** (trɔpiːˈkal, -ˈko) *adj* tropical.
troquer (trɔˈkeː) *vt* **1** swop. **2** barter.
trot (tro) *nm* trot.
trotter (trɔˈteː) *vi* trot.
trottoir (trɔˈtwar) *nm* pavement.
trou (truː) *nm* **1** hole. **2** *inf* pothole. **trou de serrure** keyhole. **trou d'homme** manhole.
trouble[1] (truːbl) *adj* **1** cloudy. **2** confused.
trouble[2] (truːbl) *nm* **1** disorder. **2** agitation.

troubler (tru:'ble:) *vt* **1** disturb. **2** confuse. **3** agitate. **4** make muddy. **se troubler** *vr* **1** become cloudy or overcast. **2** get confused.

trouer (tru:'e:) *vt* make a hole in, pierce. **trouée** *nf* **1** gap. **2** *mil* breakthrough.

troupe (tru:p) *nf* **1** troop, gang. **2** troupe. **3** herd. **4** *pl* troops. **troupeau, -aux** *nm* herd, flock.

trousser (tru:'se:) *vt* **1** turn up. **2** *inf* get through. **3** *inf* turn out. **trousse** *nf* **1** bundle. **2** kit. **trousseau, -aux** *nm* **1** bunch. **2** bride's outfit.

trouver (tru:'ve:) *vt* **1** find. **2** discover. **3** think. **se trouver** *vr* **1** be. **2** feel. **3** happen. **trouvaille** *nf* **1** find. **2** discovery. **3** windfall.

truc (tryk) *nm inf* **1** thing, gadget. **2** knack.

truelle (try'ɛl) *nf* trowel.

truffe (tryf) *nf* truffle.

truie (trɥi:) *nf* sow.

truite (trɥi:t) *nf* trout.

trumeau, -aux (try'mo) *nm arch* pier.

truquer (try'ke:) *vt* fake.

tsar (tsar) *nm* tsar.

tu[1] (tu) *pron 2nd pers m,f s fam* you.

tu[2] (ty) *v see* **taire.**

tuba (ty'ba) *nm* tuba.

tube (tyb) *nm* **1** tube. **2** pipe.

tuberculose (tybɛrky'loz) *nf* tuberculosis.

tuer (tɥe:) *vt* **1** kill. **2** slaughter. **à tue-tête** at the top of one's voice. **tuerie** *nf* slaughter.

tuile (tɥi:l) *nf* **1** tile. **2** *inf* bother, trouble.

tulipe (ty'li:p) *nf* tulip.

tumeur (ty'mœr) *nf* tumour, growth.

tumulte (ty'mylt) *nm* tumult, uproar. **tumultueux, -euse** (tymyl'tɥœ, -'tɥœz) *adj* noisy, riotous.

tunique (ty'ni:k) *nf* tunic.

Tunisie (tyni:'zi:) *nf* Tunisia. **tunisien, -ienne** (tyni:'zjɛ̃, -'zjɛn) *adj,n* Tunisian.

tunnel (ty'nɛl) *nm* tunnel.

turbulent (tyrby'lɑ̃) *adj* **1** turbulent, restless. **2** unruly.

turf (tyrf) *nm* **1** racecourse. **2** racing.

Turquie (tyr'ki:) *nf* Turkey. **turc, turque** (tyrk) *adj* Turkish. *nm,f* Turk. *nm* Turkish (language).

turquoise (tyr'kwaz) *nf* turquoise. *nm* turquoise (colour). *adj invar* turquoise.

tutelle (ty'tɛl) *nf* **1** guardianship. **2** protection.

tuteur, -trice (ty'tœr, -'tri:s) *nm,f* guardian. *nm* prop.

tutoyer (tytwa'je:) *vt* address as **tu,** be on familiar terms with.

tuyau, -aux (tɥi:'jo) *nm* **1** pipe, hose. **2** *inf* tip, hint.

tympan (tɛ̃'pɑ̃) *nm* eardrum.

type (ti:p) *nm* **1** type, pattern. **2** *inf* chap, bloke.

typhoïde (ti:fɔ'i:d) *adj,nf* typhoid.

typhon (ti:'fɔ̃) *nm* typhoon.

typique (ti:'pi:k) *adj* typical.

tyran (ti:'rɑ̃) *nm* tyrant. **tyrannie** *nf* tyranny. **tyrannique** *adj* tyrannical.

U

ulcérer (ylse:'re:) *vt* **1** ulcerate. **2** wound, embitter. **ulcère** *nm* ulcer.

ultérieur (ylte:'rjœr) *adj* **1** ulterior. **2** subsequent.

ultimatum (yltima'tɔm) *nm* ultimatum.

ultime (yl'ti:m) *adj* ultimate, final.

ultrasonique (yltrasɔ'ni:k) *adj* supersonic.

ultra-violet, -ette (yltravjɔle, -'lɛt) *adj, pl* **ultra-violets, -ettes** ultraviolet.

un, une (œ̃, yn) *indef art* a, an. *indef pron* one. *nm,f* one. **les uns...les autres** some...others. ~ *adj* **1** one. **2** first. **unième** *adj* first.

unanime (yna'ni:m) *adj* unanimous.

uni (y'ni:) *adj* **1** united. **2** smooth. **3** plain.

unifier (yni:'fje:) *vt* **1** unify. **2** amalgamate. **3** standardize.

uniforme (yni:'fɔrm) *adj* uniform, unvarying. *nm* uniform. **uniformité** *nf* uniformity.

union (y'njɔ̃) *nf* **1** union. **2** society, association. **3** harmony, agreement.

unique (y'ni:k) *adj* **1** sole, only. **2** unique.

unir (y'ni:r) *vt* unite, join. **unité** *nf* **1** unity. **2** unit.

unisson (yni:'sɔ̃) *nf* unison.

univers (yni:'vɛr) *nm* universe. **universel, -elle** (yni:vɛr'sɛl) *adj* universal, worldwide.

université (yni:vɛrsi:'te:) *nf* university.

urbain (yr'bɛ̃) *adj* urban, town. **urbanisme** *nm* town-planning.

urgent (yr'ʒɑ̃) *adj* urgent, pressing. **urgence** *nf* **1** urgency. **2** emergency.

uriner (yri:'ne:) *vi* urinate. **urine** *nf* urine. **urinoir** *nm* urinal.

urne (yrn) *nf* **1** urn. **2** ballot-box.

user (y'ze:) *vt* **1** use, consume. **2** wear out. **user de** make use of. **s'user** *vr* wear away. **usage** *nm* **1** use. **2** custom. **3** practice. **4** wear. **5** breeding, manners. **usagé** *adj* second-hand. **usé** *adj* **1** worn. **2** threadbare. **3** hackneyed. **usité** *adj* current, in use.

usine (y'zi:n) *nf* factory, works.
ustensile (ytã'si:l) *nm* utensil, implement.
usuel, -elle (y'zɥɛl) *adj* **1** usual, customary. **2** current.
usurper (yzyr'pe:) *vt* usurp. **usurpateur, -trice** (yzyrpa'tœr, -'tri:s) *n* usurper.
utérus (yte:'rys) *nm* uterus.
utiliser (yti:li:'ze:) *vt* use, make use of. **utile** *adj* **1** useful, handy. **2** effective. **3** necessary. **utilité** *nf* use, utility.

V

va (va) *v* see **aller.**
vacance (va'kɑ̃s) *nf* **1** vacancy. **2** *pl* holidays. **vacant** *adj* vacant, empty.
vacarme (va'karm) *nm* din, racket.
vaccin (vak'sɛ̃) *nm* vaccine.
vacciner (vaksi:'ne:) *vt* vaccinate, inoculate. **vaccination** *nf* vaccination.
vache (vaʃ) *nf* **1** cow. **2** *sl* bitch. **vachement** *adv sl* terribly, very.
vaciller (vasi:'je:) *vi* **1** waver. **2** flicker. **3** wobble. **vacillant** *adj* **1** wobbly. **2** undecided.
va-et-vient *nm invar* **1** coming and going. **2** shuttle.
vagabond (vaga'bɔ̃) *adj* wandering. *nm* tramp, vagrant.
vagabonder (vagabɔ̃'de:) *vi* **1** roam. **2** wander.
vagin (va'ʒɛ̃) *nm* vagina.
vague[1] (vag) *nf* **1** wave. **2** generation, age-group. **vague de chaleur** heatwave.
vague[2] (vag) *adj* vague, hazy. *nm* vagueness.
vague[3] (vag) *adj* vacant, empty. *nm* empty space.
vaillant (va'jɑ̃) *adj* valiant, brave.
vain (vɛ̃) *adj* **1** vain, conceited. **2** empty, futile.
vaincre* (vɛ̃kr) *vt* **1** conquer. **2** beat, defeat. **vainqueur** *nm* **1** conqueror. **2** winner. *adj* victorious.
vaincu (vɛ̃'ky) *v* see **vaincre.**
vainquant (vɛ̃'kɑ̃) *v* see **vaincre.**
vais (vɛ) *v* see **aller.**
vaisseau, -aux (vɛ'so) *nm* **1** ship. **2** container.
vaisselle (vɛ'sɛl) *nf* crockery, plates and dishes. **faire la vaisselle** do the washing up.
val (val) *nm* valley.
valable (va'labl) *adj* valid.
valet (va'lɛ) *nm* **1** valet, servant. **2** *game* jack.
valeur (va'lœr) *nf* **1** value, worth. **2** courage. **3** *comm* assets.
valide (va'li:d) *adj* valid.
valise (va'li:z) *nf* suitcase.
vallée (va'le:) *nf* valley.
valoir* (val'war) *vt,vi* **1** be worth. **2** deserve. **3** yield. **faire valoir 1** make the most of. **2** put forward. **il vaut mieux** it is better.
valse (vals) *nf* waltz.
vandale (vɑ̃'dal) *nm* vandal. **vandalisme** *nm* vandalism.
vanille (va'ni:j) *nf* vanilla.
vanité (vani:'te:) *nf* **1** vanity, pride. **2** conceit. **vaniteux, -euse** (vani:'tœ, -'tœz) *adj* **1** vain. **2** conceited.
vantail, -aux (vɑ̃taj, -'to) *nm* leaf (of a table, etc.).
vanter (vɑ̃'te:) *vt* praise. **se vanter** *vr* boast. **se vanter de** pride oneself on.
vanterie (vɑ̃'tri:) *nf* **1** boasting. **2** boast.
vapeur (va'pœr) *nf* **1** vapour. **2** steam. *nm* steamer.
varicelle (vari:'sɛl) *nf* chickenpox.
varier (va'rje:) *vt,vi* vary. **variation** *nf* variation. **varié** *adj* **1** varied. **2** miscellaneous. **variété** *nf* variety.
variole (va'rjɔl) *nf* smallpox.
vase[1] (vɑz) *nm* **1** vase. **2** vessel.
vase[2] (vɑz) *nf* mud, slime.
vaste (vast) *adj* **1** vast, huge. **2** wide, spacious.
vau (vo) **à vau l'eau** *adv* **1** downstream. **2** to rack and ruin.
vaudou (vo'du:) *nm* voodoo.
vaudra (vo:'drɑ) *v* see **valoir.**
vaurien, -ienne (vo'rjɛ̃, -'rjɛn) *nm,f inf* scoundrel.
vautour (vo'tu:r) *nm* vulture.
vaux (vo:) *v* see **valoir.**
veau, veaux (vo) *nm* **1** *zool* calf. **2** veal. **3** calfskin.
vécu (ve:'ky) *v* see **vivre.**
vedette (və'dɛt) *nf* **1** motor boat. **2** *Th* star. **vedette de l'écran** filmstar.
végétal, -aux (ve:ʒɛ'tal, -'to) *adj* plant, vegetable. *nm* plant.
végétarien, -enne (ve:ʒɛta'rjɛ̃, -'rjɛn) *adj,n* vegetarian.
végétation (ve:zɛta'sjɔ̃) *nf* **1** vegetation. **2** *pl inf* adenoids.
véhément (ve:ɛ'mɑ̃) *adj* vehement, passionate, eager.
véhicule (ve:i:'kyl) *nm* vehicle.
veiller (vɛ'je:) *vi* **1** stay up. **2** watch. *vt* look after. **veiller à** see to. **veille** *nf* **1** wakefulness. **2** watch. **3** eve, day before. **veillée** *nf* **1** vigil. **2** party.

veine (vɛn) *nf* **1** vein. **2** *inf* luck.
vélo (ve:'lo:) *nm inf* bike.
vélocité (ve:lɔsi:'te:) *nf* speed, velocity.
velours (və'lu:r) *nm* **1** velvet. **2** corduroy.
velu (və'ly) *adj* hairy.
venaison (vənɛ'zɔ̃) *nf* venison.
vendange (vɑ̃'dɑ̃ʒ) *nf* **1** grape harvest. **2** vintage.
vendre (vɑ̃dr) *vt* **1** sell. **2** betray. **vendeur, -euse** (vɑ̃'dœr, -'dœz) *nm,f* **1** seller. **2** shop assistant.
vendredi (vɑ̃drə'di:) *nm* Friday. **vendredi saint** Good Friday.
vénéneux, -euse (ve:ne:'nœ, -'nœz) *adj* poisonous.
vénérer (ve:ne:'re:) *vt* **1** venerate. **2** worship.
vénérien, -ienne (ve:ne:'rjɛ̃, -'rjɛn) *adj* venereal.
venger (vɑ̃'ʒe:) *vt* avenge. **se venger** *vr* have one's revenge. **vengeance** *nf* revenge.
venin (və'nɛ̃) *nm* **1** poison. **2** spite. **venimeux, -euse** (vəni:'mœ, -'mœz) *adj* poisonous.
venir* (və'ni:r) *vi* (*aux* être) **1** come. **2** result. **3** occur. **4** grow. **venir de** have just.
vent (vɑ̃) *nm* **1** wind, breeze. **2** scent. **il fait du vent** it is windy.
vente (vɛ̃t) *nf* sale.
ventiler (vɛ̃ti:'le:) *vt* ventilate, air. **ventilateur** *nm* **1** ventilator. **2** fan.
ventre (vɛ̃tr) *nm* **1** abdomen. **2** stomach, belly. **3** paunch.
ventriloque (vɑ̃tri:'lɔk) *nm* ventriloquist.
venu (və'ny) *v* see **venir.**
venue (və'ny) *nf* **1** coming, arrival. **2** advent. **3** growth.
Vénus (ve:'nys) *nf* Venus.
ver (vɛr) *nm* **1** worm. **2** maggot. **ver à soie** silkworm.
véranda (verɑ̃'da) *nf* veranda.
verbe (vɛrb) *nm* verb. **verbal, -aux** (vɛr'bal, -'bo) *adj* verbal.
verdir (vɛr'di:r) *vi* turn green. *vt* make green. **verdeur** *nf* **1** greenness. **2** tartness, sourness. **3** heartiness. **verdure** *nf* **1** greenness. **2** greenery.
verge (vɛrʒ) *nf* **1** rod, cane. **2** penis.
verger (vɛr'ʒe:) *nm* orchard.
verglas (vɛr'gla) *nm* black ice.
vergogne (vɛr'gɔɲ) *nf* shame.
véridique (ve:ri:'di:k) *adj* truthful.
vérifier (ve:ri:'fje) *vt* **1** verify, check. **2** overhaul. **3** audit.
vérité (ve:ri:'te:) *nf* truth. **véritable** *adj* **1** true. **2** real, genuine.
vermeil, -eille (vɛr'mɛj) *adj* bright red, rosy.
vermine (vɛr'mi:n) *nf* vermin.
vermout (vɛr'mu:t) *nm* vermouth.
vernir (vɛr'ni:r) *vt* **1** varnish. **2** polish. **vernis** *nm* **1** varnish. **2** polish. **3** glaze.
vérole (ve:'rɔl) *nf* **petite vérole** smallpox.
verrai (vɛre) *v* see **voir.**
verre (vɛr) *nm* glass. **verre (de lunettes)** lens.
verrou, -oux (vɛ'ru.) *nm* bolt, bar.
verrouiller (vɛru:'je:) *vt* bolt, fasten.
verrue (vɛ'ru:) *nf* wart.
vers[1] (vɛr) *nm* **1** line. **2** *pl* poetry, verse.
vers[2] (vɛr) *prep* **1** towards, to. **2** about.
versant (vɛr'sɑ̃) *nm* **1** slope. **2** side, bank.
Verseau (vɛr'so) *nm* Aquarius.
verser (vɛr'se:) *vt* **1** pour. **2** shed. **3** pay in. **4** overturn. **à verse** in torrents. **versé** *adj* experienced. **versement** *nm* **1** payment. **2** *comm* instalment.
version (vɛr'sjɔ̃) *nf* **1** version, account. **2** *educ* translation, unseen.
verso (vɛr'so) *nm* back, reverse side.
vert (vɛr) *adj* **1** green. **2** unripe. **3** sharp, stern. **4** *inf* spicy. *nm* green (colour).
vertébré (vɛrte:'bre:) *adj,nm* vertebrate.
vertical, -aux (vɛrti:'kal, -'ko) *adj* vertical, upright.
vertige (vɛr'ti:ʒ) *nm* dizziness. **avoir le vertige** feel dizzy. **vertigineux, -euse** (vɛrti:ʒi:'nœ, -'nœz) *adj* dizzy, giddy.
vertu (vɛr'ty) *nf* **1** virtue. **2** chastity. **3** quality, property. **vertueux, -euse** (vɛr'tɥœ, -'tɥœz) *adj* virtuous.
verve (vɛrv) *nf* zest, vigour, go.
vessie (vɛ'si:) *nf* bladder.
veste (vɛst) *nf* jacket. **veston** *nm* jacket.
vestiaire (vɛ'stjɛr) *nm* **1** cloakroom. **2** changing room.
vestibule (vɛsti:'byl) *nm* **1** hall. **2** lobby.
vestige (vɛ'sti:ʒ) *nm* **1** mark, trace. **2** remnant, remains.
vêtement (vɛt'mɑ̃) *nm* **1** garment. **2** *pl* clothing. **3** *pl* clothes.
vétéran (ve:tɛ'rɑ̃) *nm* veteran.
vétérinaire (ve:te.ri:'nɛr) *nm* veterinary surgeon. *adj* veterinary.
vêtir* (vɛ'ti:r) *vt* **1** clothe. **2** dress.
veto (ve:'to) *nm* veto. **mettre son veto à** veto.
vêtu (vɛ'ty) *v* see **vêtir.**
vétusté (ve:ty'ste:) *nf* decay.
veuf, veuve (vœf, vœv) *nm,f* widower, widow. *adj* widowed.
veule (vœl) *adj* **1** weak, soft. **2** flabby. **3** drab.

veulent (vœl) *v* see **vouloir.**
veux (vœ) *v* see **vouloir.**
vexer (vɛk'se:) *vt* **1** vex, annoy. **2** harass.
viable[1] (vjabl) *adj* strong enough to live.
viable[2] (vjabl) *adj* fit for traffic.
viaduc (vja'dyk) *nm* viaduct.
viager, -ère (vja'ʒe:, -'ʒɛr) *adj* for life.
viande (vjɑ̃d) *nf* meat.
vibrer (vi:'bre:) *vi* vibrate. **vibrant** *adj* **1** vibrating. **2** resonant. **vibration** *nf* **1** vibration. **2** resonance.
vicaire (vi:'kɛr) *nm* curate.
vice (vi:s) *nm* **1** vice, corruption. **2** fault, flaw. **vice-président** *nm, pl* **vice-présidents** **1** vice-president. **2** vice-chairman.
vicié (vi:'sje:) *adj* corrupt.
vicieux, -euse (vi:'sjœ, -'sjœz) *adj* **1** vicious. **2** faulty. **3** perverted.
vicomte, -esse (vi:'kɔ̃t, -kɔ̃'tɛs) *nm,f* viscount, viscountess.
victime (vi:k'ti:m) *nf* victim.
victoire (vi:k'twar) *nf* victory. **victorieux, -euse** (vi:ktɔ'rjœ, -'rjœz) *adj* victorious.
vidange (vi:'dɑ̃ʒ) *nf* **1** emptying. **2** draining. **3** *mot* oil change.
vider (vi:'de:) *vt* **1** empty. **2** clear out. **3** drain. **4** settle (an argument). **vide** *adj* **1** empty. **2** vacant. *nm* **1** gap. **2** vacuum.
vie (vi:) *nf* **1** life. **2** existence. **3** living, livelihood.
vieillir (vjɛ'ji:r) *vi* grow old, age. **vieillard** *nm* old man. **vieillesse** *nf* old age.
viens (vjɛ̃) *v* see **venir.**
vierge (vjɛrʒ) *nf* **1** virgin. **2** *cap* Virgo. *adj* **1** virgin. **2** pure. **3** blank.
Viet-nam (vjɛt'nam) *nm* Vietnam. **vietnamien, -ienne** (vjɛtna'mjɛ̃, -'mjɛn) *adj,n* Vietnamese.
vieux, vieil, vieille (vjœ, vjɛj, vjɛj) *adj* old. **vieux** *nm* old man. **vieille** *nf* old woman.
vif, vive (vi:f, vi:v) *adj* **1** alive. **2** lively, vivacious. **3** brisk. **4** sharp, keen. **5** quick-tempered. **6** vivid. **7** bright. *nm* quick, core.
vigile (vi:'ʒi:l) *nf* vigil.
vigne (viɲ) *nf* **1** vine. **2** vineyard. **vigneron** *nm* vine-grower. **vignoble** *nm* vineyard.
vignette (vi:ɲɛt) *nf* **1** car tax label. **2** cigarette card.
vigoureux, -euse (vi:gu:'rœ, -'rœz) *adj* vigorous, strong.
vigueur (vi:'gœr) *nf* **1** vigour, strength. **2** effect, force.
vil (vi:l) *adj* **1** base, low, vile. **2** cheap.
vilain (vi:'lɛ̃) *adj* **1** unpleasant, nasty. **2** mean. **3** ugly. *nm* villain.
villa (vi:'la) *nf* villa, house.
village (vi:'laʒ) *nm* village.
ville (vi:l) *nf* town. **grande ville** city. **ville d'eau** spa.
villégiateur (vi:le:ʒja'tœr) *nm* holiday-maker.
vin (vɛ̃) *nm* wine. **vin du Rhin** hock. **vin ordinaire** table wine.
vinaigre (vi:'nɛgr) *nm* vinegar. **vinaigrette** *nf* French dressing.
vindicatif, -ive (vɛ̃di:ka'ti:f, -'ti:v) *adj* spiteful.
vingt (vɛ̃) *adj,nm* twenty. **vingtaine** *nf* about twenty, a score. **vingtième** *adj* twentieth.
viol (vjɔl) *nm* rape.
violence (vjɔ'lɑ̃s) *nf* violence, force. **violent** *adj* **1** violent. **2** intense. **3** strong.
violer (vjœ'le:) *vt* **1** violate, break. **2** rape.
violet, -ette (vjɔ'lɛ, -'lɛt) *adj,nm* violet (colour). *nf bot* violet.
violon (vjɔ'lɔ̃) *nm* **1** violin. **2** *sl* (prison) cell. **violoncelle** *nm* cello.
vipère (vi:'pɛr) *nf* adder, viper.
virage (vi:'raʒ) *nm* **1** turning. **2** sharp turn, bend.
virer (vi:'re:) *vi* turn. *vt comm* transfer.
virgule (vi:r'gyl) *nf* comma.
viril (vi:'ri:l) *adj* virile, manly. **virilité** *nf* **1** manliness. **2** manhood.
virtuel, -elle (vi:r'tɥɛl) *adj* virtual.
virus (vi:'rys) *nm* virus.
vis[1] (vi:) *v* see **vivre.**
vis[2] (vi:s) *nf* screw.
visa (vi:'za) *nm* **1** visa. **2** signature.
visage (vi:'zaʒ) *nm* **1** face. **2** countenance.
vis-à-vis (vi:za'vi:) *adv* opposite. **vis-à-vis de** **1** opposite. **2** with regard to.
viser (vi:'ze:) *vt* **1** aim. **2** relate to. **3** allude to. **visée** *nf* **1** aim. **2** design, plan.
visible (vi:'zi:bl) *adj* **1** visible. **2** obvious, evident. **visibilité** *nf* visibility.
visière (vi:'zjɛr) *nf* **1** visor. **2** peak (of a cap).
vision (vi:'zjɔ̃) *nf* **1** vision, sight. **2** eyesight. **3** apparition, phantom.
visiter (vi:zi:'te:) *vt* **1** visit. **2** examine. **3** search. **visite** *nf* **1** visit. **2** inspection. **3** search. **rendre visite à** call on. **visiteur, -euse** (vi:zi:'tœr, -'tœz) *nm,f* visitor.
vison (vi:'zɔ) *nm* mink.
visser (vi:'se:) *vt* screw in or up.
visuel, -elle (vi:'zɥɛl) *adj* visual.
vital, -aux (vi:'tal, -'to) *adj* vital. **vitalité** *nf* vitality.

vitamine (vi:ta'mi:n) *nf* vitamin.
vite (vi:t) *adj* quick, rapid, fast. *adv* **1** quickly, fast. **2** soon. **au plus vite** as quickly as possible. **vitesse** *nf* **1** speed. **2** quickness.
vitrer (vi:'tre:) *vt* glaze (a window, etc.). **vitrail, -aux** (vi:'traj, -'tro) *nm* stained-glass window. **vitre** *nf* pane of glass. **vitrine** *nf* **1** shopwindow. **2** showcase. **3** glass case.
vivace (vi:'vas) *adj* **1** hardy. **2** perennial. **vivacité** *nf* **1** vivacity. **2** outburst of temper.
vivier (vi:'vje:) *nm* fishpond.
vivifier (vi:vi:'fje:) *vt* enliven, invigorate.
vivre* (vi:vr) *vi* **1** live. **2** be alive. *nm* **1** food. **2** *pl* provisions. **vivant** *adj* **1** living, alive. **2** lively.
vocabulaire (vɔkaby'lɛr) *nm* vocabulary.
vocal, -aux (vɔ'kal, -'ko) *adj* vocal.
vocation (vɔka'sjɔ̃) *nf* **1** vocation. **2** bent, inclination.
vœu, vœux (vœ) *nm* **1** wish. **2** vow.
voguer (vɔ'ge:) *vi* sail. **vogue** *nf* vogue, fashion.
voici (vwa'si:) *prep* here is or are.
voie (vwa) *nf* way, road, track. **voie d'eau 1** *naut* leak. **2** canal. **voie ferrée** railway line. **voie publique** public highway.
voilà (vwa'la) *prep* there is or are.
voile[1] (vwal) *nf* sail. **voilier** *nm* sailing vessel.
voile[2] (vwal) *nm* veil.
voiler (vwa'le:) *vt* **1** veil. **2** obscure, dim. **3** muffle. **se voiler** *vr* cloud over.
voir* (vwar) *vt* **1** see. **2** visit. **3** understand. **4** notice. **faire voir** show. **n'avoir rien à voir avec** have nothing to do with.
voire (vwar) *adv* indeed. **voire même** and even.
voirie (vwa'ri:) *nf* **1** highways. **2** refuse dump.
voisin (vwa'zɛ̃) *adj* neighbouring, near. *nm* neighbour. **voisinage** *nm* **1** neighbourhood, district. **2** proximity.
voiture (vwa'tyr) *nf* **1** car. **2** van. **voiture d'enfant** pram.
voix (vwa) *nf* **1** voice. **2** vote. **à haute voix** aloud. **voix publique** public opinion.
vol[1] (vɔl) *nm* **1** flight. **2** flying. **3** flock, swarm. **vol à voile** *aviat* gliding.
vol[2] (vɔl) *nm* theft. **vol à l'étalage** shoplifting. **vol avec effraction** burglary.
volaille (vɔ'laj) *nf* poultry.
volatil (vɔla'ti:l) *adj* volatile.
volcan (vɔl'kɑ̃) *nm* volcano. **volcanique** *adj* volcanic.
voler[1] (vɔ'le:) *vi* fly. **volant** *nm* **1** steering wheel. **2** shuttlecock. **volée** *nf* **1** flight. **2** volley.
voler[2] (vɔ'le:) *vt* **1** steal. **2** rob. **voleur, -euse** (vɔ'lœr, -'lœz) *nm,f* thief, robber. **voleur à tire** *nm* pickpocket. ~*adj* thieving.
volet (vɔ'lɛ) *nm* shutter.
volière (vɔ'ljɛr) *nf* aviary.
volontaire (vɔlɔ̃'tɛr) *adj* **1** voluntary. **2** deliberate. **3** headstrong. *nm* volunteer.
volonté (vɔlɔ̃'te:) *nf* **1** will. **2** *pl* whims. **bonne volonté** goodwill. **volontiers** *adv* willingly, with pleasure.
volt (vɔlt) *nm* volt. **voltage** *nm* voltage.
volte-face *nf invar* about turn.
voltiger (vɔlti:'ʒe:) *vi* flit.
volume (vɔ'lym) *nm* **1** volume. **2** bulk, mass. **3** capacity.
volupté (vɔlyp'te:) *nf* sensual pleasure.
vomir (vɔ'mi:r) *vt* vomit.
vont (vɔ̃) *v* see **aller.**
vorace (vɔ'ras) *adj* ravenous.
vos (vo) *poss adj* see **votre.**
voter (vɔ'te:) *vi* vote. *vt* **1** pass. **2** vote (money). **vote** *nm* vote.
votre, vos (vɔtr, vo) *poss adj 2nd pers s,pl* your.
vôtre (votr) *poss pron 2nd pers s,pl* **le** or **la vôtre 1** yours. **2** your own.
voudrai (vu:'drɛ) *v* see **vouloir.**
vouer (vwe:) *vt* devote, consecrate.
vouloir* (vu:'lwar) *vt* **1** be willing. **2** want. **3** mean. **4** consent. **5** need. **6** try. **en vouloir à** have a grudge against. ~*nm* will.
vous (vu:) *pron 2nd pers m,f* **1** *s fml* you. **2** *pl* you. **vous-même** *pron 2nd pers m,f s fml* yourself. **vous-mêmes** *pron 2nd pers m,f pl* yourselves.
voûter (vu:'te:) *vt* arch. **voûte** *nf* arch, vault.
vouvoyer (vu:vwa'je:) *vt* address as **vous.**
voyager (vwaja'ʒe:) *vi* travel. **voyage** *nm* journey, trip, tour. **voyageur, -euse** (vwaja'ʒœr, -'ʒœz) *nm,f* **1** traveller. **2** passenger. *adj* travelling.
voyant (vwa'jɑ̃) *adj* **1** gaudy. **2** conspicuous.
voyelle (vwa'jɛl) *nf* vowel.
voyou, -oux (vwa'ju:) *nm inf* hooligan.
vrai (vrɛ) *adj* **1** true. **2** real, genuine. **3** downright. *adv* really, truly. **à vrai dire** as a matter of fact. ~*nm* truth. **vraiment** *adv* **1** really. **2** indeed.
vraisemblable (vrɛsɑ̃'blabl) *adj* **1** probable. **2** credible. **vraisemblance** *nf* **1** probability, likelihood. **2** credibility.

vrille (vri:j) *nf* tendril.
vrombir (vrɔ̃'bi:r) *vi* hum, throb. **vrombissement** *nm* **1** humming. **2** drone.
vu (vy) *v* see **voir.** *adj* **1** seen. **2** considered. *prep* considering, in view of. **vu que** *conj* seeing that. ~*nm* sight. **vue** *nf* **1** sight. **2** view. **3** intention, design.
vulgaire (vyl'gɛr) *adj* **1** vulgar **2** common.
vulnérable (vylnɛ'rabl) *adj* vulnerable.

W

wagon (va'gɔ̃) *nm* **1** (railway) carriage or coach. **2** waggon, truck. **wagon-lit** *nm, pl* **wagons-lits** sleeping-car.
watt (wat) *nm* watt. **wattage** *nm* wattage.
week-end (wi:k'ɛnd) *nm* weekend.
whist (wi:st) *nm* whist.

X

xénophobie (kse:nɔfɔ'bi:) *nf* xenophobia.
xérès (gze:'rɛs) *nm* sherry.

Y

y (i:) *adv* **1** there. **2** here. **ça y est!** that's it! **j'y suis** I've got it, I understand. **n'y être pour rien** have nothing to do with it. ~*pron invar* **1** at, by, or in it. **2** of them.
yacht (jɔt) *nm* yacht.
yaourt (ja'u:rt) *nm* yoghurt.
yeux (jœ) *nm pl* eyes.
yiddish (ji:'di:ʃ) *nm* Yiddish.
yoga (jɔ'ga) *nm* yoga.
Yougoslavie (ju:gɔ'sla'vi:) *nf* Yugoslavia. **yougoslave** *adj,n* Yugoslav.
youyou (ju:'ju:) *nm* dinghy.

Z

zèbre (zɛbr) *nm* zebra. **zébré** *adj* striped.
zèle (zɛl) *nm* zeal, ardour. **zélé** *adj* zealous.
zéro (ze:'ro) *nm* zero, nought.
zeste (zɛst) *nm cul* zest, outer skin.
zézayer (ze:zɛ'je:) *vi,vt* lisp. **zézaiement** *nm* **1** lisp. **2** lisping.
zigzag (zi:g'zag) *nm* zigzag. **zigzaguer** *vi* zigzag.
zinc (zɛ̃g) *nm* **1** zinc. **2** *sl* bar, counter (in a pub).
zodiaque (zɔ'djak) *nm* zodiac.
zone (zon) *nm* zone, area.
zoo (zo) *nm* zoo. **zoologie** (zɔɔlɔ'ʒi:) *nf* zoology. **zoologique** (zɔɔlɔ'ʒi:k) *adj* zoological. **zoologiste** (zɔɔlɔ'ʒi:st) *nm* zoologist.

A

a, an (ə, ən; *stressed* ei, æn) *indef art* un *m*. une *f*.

aback (ə'bæk) *adv* en arrière. **be taken aback** être déconcerté.

abandon (ə'bændən) *vt* **1** abandonner. **2** délaisser. **3** renoncer à. **abandoned** *adj* **1** abandonné. **2** dévergondé, dépravé. **abandonment** *n* **1** abandon *m*. **2** délaissement *m*.

abash (ə'bæʃ) *vt* confondre, déconcerter.

abate (ə'beit) *vt* diminuer, affaiblir. *vi* **1** s'affaiblir. **2** se calmer.

abattoir ('æbətwɑ:) *n* abattoir *m*.

abbess ('æbis) *n* abesse *f*.

abbey ('æbi) *n* abbaye *f*.

abbot ('æbət) *n* abbé *m*.

abbreviate (ə'bri:vieit) *vt* abréger, raccourcir. **abbreviation** *n* abréviation *f*.

abdicate ('æbdikeit) *vt,vi* abdiquer. *vt* renoncer à. **abdication** *n* abdication *f*.

abdomen ('æbdəmən) *n* abdomen *m*.

abduct (æb'dʌkt) *vt* enlever. **abduction** *n* enlèvement *m*. **abductor** *n* ravisseur *m*.

abet (ə'bet) *vt* encourager. **abettor** *n* complice *m,f*.

abhor (əb'hɔ:) *vt* abhorrer, avoir horreur de. **abhorrent** *adj* **1** répugnant. **2** contraire.

abide* (ə'baid) *vi* **1** demeurer. **2** *inf* supporter. **abide by** **1** rester fidèle à. **2** se conformer à.

ability (ə'biliti) *n* **1** capacité *f*. **2** pouvoir *m*. intelligence *f*. **to the best of one's ability** de son mieux.

abject ('æbdʒekt) *adj* **1** abject, misérable. **2** vil. **abjection** *n* **1** abjection *f*. **2** misère *f*.

ablaze (ə'bleiz) *adv,adj* en flammes. *adj* enflammé.

able ('eibəl) *adj* capable, compétent, habile. **be able** **1** pouvoir. **2** savoir. **able-bodied** *adj* fort, robuste.

abnormal (æb'nɔ:məl) *adj* anormal, -aux. **abnormality** *n* **1** anomalie *f*. **2** malformation *f*.

aboard (ə'bɔ:d) *adv* à bord. **all aboard!** embarquez! **go aboard** s'embarquer. ~*prep* à bord de.

abode (ə'boud) *n* **1** demeure, habitation *f*. **2** *law* domicile *m*.

abolish (ə'bɔliʃ) *vt* abolir, supprimer. **abolition** *n* abolition *f*.

abominable (ə'bɔminəbəl) *adj* **1** abominable, odieux, -euse. **2** exécrable.

Aborigine (æbə'ridʒini) *n* aborigène, indigène *m*. **aboriginal** *adj* **1** aborigène, indigène. **2** primitif, -ive.

abort (ə'bɔ:t) *vi* avorter. **abortion** *n* **1** avortement *m*. **2** avorton *m*.

abound (ə'baund) *vi* abonder.

about (ə'baut) *adv, prep* **1** autour (de). **2** de ci de là. **3** environ. **4** au sujet de. **be about to** être sur le point de. **what is it about?** de quoi s'agit-il?

above (ə'bʌv) *prep* **1** au-dessus (de). **2** plus de. **above all** surtout. ~*adv* **1** en haut. **2** ci-dessus. **3** au-dessus. **aboveboard** *adj* loyal, -aux.

abrasion (ə'breiʒən) *n* **1** frottement *m*. **2** *med* écorchure *f*. **abrasive** *adj,n* abrasif, -ive *m*.

abreast (ə'brest) *adv* de front, sur la même ligne.

abridge (ə'bridʒ) *vt* **1** abréger. **2** restreindre.

abroad (ə'brɔ:d) *adv* **1** à l'étranger. **2** au loin.

abrupt (ə'brʌpt) *adj* **1** abrupt. **2** brusque. **abruptly** *adv* **1** à pic. **2** brusquement.

abscess ('æbses) *n* abcès *m*.

abscond (əb'skɔnd) *vi* **1** s'évader. **2** *law* se soustraire à.

absent (*adj* 'æbsənt; *v* ab'sent) *adj* **1** absent. **2** manquant. **absent-minded** *adj* distrait. **absent-mindedness** *n* distraction *f*. ~*v* **absent oneself** s'absenter. **absence** *n* **1** absence *f*. **2** manque *m*. **absentee** *n* absent *m*.

absolute ('æbsəlu:t) *adj* **1** absolu. **2** parfait. **3** catégorique. **absolutely** *adv* **1** absolument. **2** complètement.

absolve (əb'zɔlv) *vt* **1** absoudre. **2** *law* acquitter.

absorb (əb'zɔ:b) *vt* absorber. **absorbent** *adj* absorbant. **absorption** *n* **1** absorption *f*. **2** concentration *f*.

abstain (əb'stein) *vi* s'abstenir. **abstention** *n* abstention *f*. **abstinence** *n* abstinence *f*.

abstract (*adj,n* 'æbstrækt; *v* əb'strækt) *adj,n* abstrait *m*. *n* résumé *m*. *vt* **1** soustraire. **2** extraire. **abstraction** *n* abstraction *f*.

absurd (əb'sə:d) *adj* absurde.

abundance (ə'bʌndəns) *n* abondance *f*. **abundant** *adj* abondant, copieux, -euse. **abundantly** *adv* abondamment.

abuse (*v* ə'bju:z; *n* ə'bju:s) *vt* **1** abuser de. **2** médire. **3** injurier. *n* **1** abus *m*. **2** insultes *f pl*. **abusive** *adj* **1** abusif, -ive. **2** injurieux, -euse.

abyss (ə'bis) *n* abîme *m*. **abysmal** *adj* **1** sans fond. **2** profond.

academy (ə'kædəmi) *n* académie *f*. **academic** *adj* **1** académique. **2** universitaire. **3** théorique.

accelerate (ək'seləreit) *vt* accélérer. *vi* s'accélérer. **acceleration** *n* accélération *f*. **accelerator** *n* accélérateur *m*.

accent ('æksənt) *n* **1** accent *m*. **2** ton *m*. **accentuate** *vt* accentuer.

accept (ək'sept) *vt* **1** accepter. **2** admettre. **acceptance** *n* **1** acceptation *f*. **2** réception *f*.

access ('ækses) *n* **1** accès *m*. **2** entrée *f*. **accessible** *adj* accessible, abordable. **accession** *n* **1** accès *m*. **2** accession *f*. **3** accroissement *m*.

accessory (ək'sesəri) *adj* accessoire, subsidiaire. *n* **1** accessoire *m*. **2** *pl* équipement *m*. **3** *law* complice *m,f*.

accident ('æksidn̩t) *n* accident *m*. **by accident** par hasard. **accidental** *adj* **1** accidentel, -elle. **2** accessoire.

acclaim (ə'kleim) *vt* acclamer.

acclimatize (ə'klaimətaiz) *vt* acclimater. **get acclimatized** s'acclimater, s'habituer.

accommodate (ə'kɔmədeit) *vt* **1** accommoder. **2** rendre service à. **3** loger. **accomodating** *adj* complaisant. **accommodation** *n* **1** adaptation *f*. **2** arrangement *m*. **3** logement *m*.

accompany (ə'kʌmpəni) *vt* accompagner. **accompaniment** *n* accompagnement *m*. **accompanist** *n mus* accompagnateur, -trice.

accomplice (ə'kʌmplis) *n* complice *m,f*.

accomplish (ə'kʌmpliʃ) *vt* **1** accomplir, aboutir. **2** achever. **accomplishment** *n* **1** accomplissement, achèvement *m*. **2** talent *m*. **3** *pl* arts d'agrément *m pl*.

accord (ə'kɔ:d) *n* accord *m*. **of one's own accord** de son plein gré. ~*vt* accorder. *vi* s'accorder. **accordance** *n* conformité *f*. **according to** suivant, d'après.

accordion (ə'kɔ:diən) *n* accordéon *m*.

accost (ə'kɔst) *vt* accoster, aborder.

account (ə'kaunt) *n* **1** compte *m*. **2** valeur *f*. profit *m*. **3** récit *m*. description *f*. **take into account** tenir compte de. ~*v* **account for** expliquer. **accountant** *n* comptable *m*. **chartered accountant** expert comptable *m*.

accumulate (ə'kju:mjuleit) *vt* accumuler. *vi* s'accumuler. **accumulation** *n* accumulation *f*.

accurate ('ækjurət) *adj* **1** exact, juste. **2** fidèle. **accuracy** *n* exactitude, précision *f*.

accuse (ə'kju:z) *vt* accuser. **accusation** *n* accusation *f*.

accustom (ə'kʌstəm) *vt* accoutumer, habituer.

ace (eis) *n* **1** *game* as *m*. **2** atout *m*.

ache (eik) *n* mal *m*. douleur *f*. *vi* faire mal.

achieve (ə'tʃi:v) *vt* **1** accomplir. **2** acquérir. **3** atteindre. **achievement** *n* **1** accomplissement *m*. **2** exploit *m*.

acid ('æsid) *adj* **1** acide. **2** aigre. *n* acide *m*.

acknowledge (ək'nɔlidʒ) *vt* reconnaître. **acknowledgement** *n* **1** reconnaissance *f*. **2** aveu, -eux *m*.

acne ('ækni) *n* acné *f*.

acorn ('eikɔ:n) *n* gland *m*.

acoustic (ə'ku:stik) *adj* acoustique. **acoustics** *n* acoustique *f*.

acquaint (ə'kweint) *vt* informer, faire savoir. **be acquainted with** connaître. **acquaintance** *n* connaissance *f*.

acquiesce (ækwi'es) *vi* acquiescer.

acquire (ə'kwaiə) *vt* acquérir. **acquisition** *n* acquisition *f*. **acquisitive** *adj* âpre au gain.

acquit (ə'kwit) *vt* acquitter. **acquittal** *n* **1** acquittement *m*. **2** exécution *f*.

acre ('eikə) *n* arpent *m*.

acrimony ('ækriməni) *n* acrimonie *f*. **acrimonious** *adj* acrimonieux, -euse.

acrobat ('ækrəbæt) *n* acrobate *m,f*. **acrobatic** *adj* acrobatique. **acrobatics** *n pl* acrobatie *f*.

across (ə'krɔs) *adv,prep* à *or* en travers. *adv* de l'autre côté.

acrylic (ə'krilik) *adj* acrylique.

act (ækt) *n* **1** acte *m*. action *f*. **2** décret *m*. **3** *Th* acte *m*. *vt* jouer. *vi* agir.

action ('ækʃən) *n* action *f*.

active ('æktiv) *adj,n* actif, -ive *m*. **activate** *vt* activer. **activity** *n* **1** activité *f*. **2** *pl* occupations *f pl*.

actor ('æktə) *n* **1** acteur *m*. **2** comédien *m*.

actress ('æktris) *n* **1** actrice *f*. **2** comédienne *f*.
actual ('æktʃuəl) *adj* **1** réel, -elle. **2** actuel, -elle. **in actual fact** en fait. **actually** *adv* **1** réellement. **2** à l'heure actuelle, maintenant.
actuary ('æktʃuəri) *n* actuaire *m*.
acupuncture ('ækjupʌŋktʃə) *n* acuponcture *f*.
acute (ə'kju:t) *adj* **1** aigu, -uë. **2** perspicace.
adamant ('ædəmənt) *adj* insensible.
Adam's apple ('ædəmz) *n* pomme d'Adam *f*.
adapt (ə'dæpt) *vt* adapter.
add (æd) *vt* **1** ajouter. **2** additionner. **add up 1** totaliser. **2** *inf* s'accorder. **addition** *n* addition *f*. **in addition** en outre. **additional** *adj* additionel, -elle, supplémentaire.
addendum (ə'dendəm) *n*, *pl* **addenda** addendum *m invar*. supplément *m*.
adder ('ædə) *n* vipère *f*.
addict (*n* 'ædikt; *v* ə'dikt) *n* **drug addict** toxicomane *m,f*. *v* **be addicted to** s'adonner à.
address (ə'dres) *n* **1** adresse *f*. **2** discours *m*. *vt* **1** adresser. **2** aborder.
adenoids ('ædinɔidz) *n pl* adénoïdes *f pl*.
adept ('ædept) *adj* habile, expert. *n* **1** adepte *m*. **2** expert *m*.
adequate ('ædikwət) *adj* **1** adéquat, suffisant. **2** proportionné.
adhere (əd'hiə) *vi* adhérer. **adherent** *adj,n* adhérent *m*. **adhesion** *n* **1** adhésion *f*. **2** approbation *f*. **adhesive** *adj,n* adhésif, -ive *m*.
adjacent (ə'dʒeisənt) *adj* adjacent, contigu, -uë.
adjective ('ædʒiktiv) *n* adjectif *m*.
adjoin (ə'dʒɔin) *vt* être contigu à, avoisiner.
adjourn (ə'dʒə:n) *vt* ajourner, différer. *vi* **1** s'ajourner. **2** lever la séance.
adjudicate (ə'dʒu:dikeit) *vt,vi* juger. **adjudication** *n* jugement *m*. **adjudicator** *n* arbitre *m*.
adjust (ə'dʒʌst) *vt* **1** concilier. **2** ajuster.
ad-lib (æd'lib) *adv* à volonté. *vt inf* improviser.
administer (əd'ministə) *vt* **1** administrer. **2** rendre. **administration** *n* administration *f*. **administrative** *adj* administratif, -ive. **administrator** *n* administrateur, gestionnaire *m*.
admiral ('ædmərəl) *n* amiral, -aux, *m*. **admiralty** *n* **1** amirauté *f*. **2** ministère de la marine *m*.
admire (əd'maiə) *vt* admirer. **admiration** *n* admiration *f*. **admirer** *n* soupirant *m*. **admiring** *adj* admiratif, -ive.
admission (əd'miʃən) *n* **1** admission *f*. **2** entrée *f*. **3** aveu, -eux *m*.
admit (əd'mit) *vt* **1** admettre. **2** laisser entrer. **3** avouer. **admittance** *n* admission *f*. **no admittance** entrée interdite.
adolescence (ædə'lesəns) *n* adolescence *f*. **adolescent** *adj,n* adolescent *m*.
adopt (ə'dɔpt) *vt* adopter. **adopted child** *n* enfant adoptif *m*. **adoption** *n* adoption *f*.
adore (ə'dɔ:) *vt* adorer. **adoration** *n* adoration *f*.
adorn (ə'dɔ:n) *vt* orner.
adrenaline (ə'drenəlin) *n* adrénaline *f*.
Adriatic (eidri'ætik) *adj* adriatique. **Adriatic (Sea)** *n* (Mer) Adriatique *f*.
adrift (ə'drift) *adv* à la dérive.
adroit (ə'drɔit) *adj* adroit, habile.
adulation (ædju'leiʃən) *n* flatterie *f*.
adult ('ædʌlt) *adj,n* adulte.
adulterate (ə'dʌltəreit) *vt* adultérer, falsifier. **adulteration** *n* adultération, falsification *f*.
adultery (ə'dʌltəri) *n* adultère *m*. **adulterer** *n* adultère *m,f*.
advance (əd'vɑ:ns) *vt* **1** avancer. **2** faire progresser. **3** augmenter. *vi* (s')avancer. *n* **1** avance *f*. **2** progrès *m*. **3** hausse *f*.
advantage (əd'vɑ:ntidʒ) *n* avantage *m*. **take advantage of** profiter de.
advent ('ædvent) *n* **1** venue *f*. **2** *cap rel* Avent *m*.
adventure (əd'ventʃə) *n* aventure *f*. **adventurer** *n* aventurier *m*. **adventurous** *adj* **1** aventureux, -euse. **2** entreprenant.
adverb ('ædvə:b) *n* adverbe *m*.
adverse ('ædvə:s) *adj* **1** adverse, opposé. **2** hostile. **3** défavorable. **adversary** *n* adversaire *m,f*. **adversity** *n* adversité *f*.
advertise ('ædvətaiz) *vi* **1** faire de la publicité. **2** insérer une annonce. *vt* annoncer. **advertisement** *n* **1** publicité *f*. **2** annonce *f*. **advertising** *n* publicité *f*.
advise (əd'vaiz) *vt* **1** conseiller. **2** avertir. **advise with** (se) consulter avec. **advice** *n* avis, conseil *m*. **advisable** *adj* **1** recommendable, judicieux, -euse. **2** convenable.
advocate (*n* 'ædvəkət; *v* 'ædvəkeit) *n* **1** avocat *m*. **2** défenseur *m*. *vt* **1** préconiser. **2** défendre.
Aegean (i'dʒi:ən) *adj* égée. **Aegean (Sea)** (Mer) Egée *f*.
aerate ('ɛəreit) *vt* **1** aérer. **2** gazéifier. **aerated** *adj* **1** aéré. **2** gazeux, -euse.
aerial ('ɛəriəl) *adj* aérien, -ienne. *n* antenne *f*.
aerodynamics (ɛəroudai'næmiks) *n* aérodynamique *f*.
aeronautics (ɛərə'nɔ:tiks) *n* aéronautique *f*.
aeroplane ('ɛərəplein) *n* avion *m*.

aerosol (ˈɛərəsɔl) *n* aérosol *m*.
aesthetic (isˈθetik) *adj* esthétique. **aesthetics** *n* esthétique *f*.
afar (əˈfɑː) *adv* **from afar** de loin.
affable (ˈæfəbəl) *adj* affable.
affair (əˈfɛə) *n* affaire *f*.
affect[1] (əˈfekt) *vt* **1** atteindre, affecter. **2** influer sur. **3** émouvoir. **affection** *n* affection *f*. **affectionate** *adj* affectueux, -euse.
affect[2] (əˈfekt) *vt* affecter, feindre. **affected** *adj* **1** affecté, maniéré. **2** simulé.
affiliate (əˈfilieit) *vt* affilier. **affiliated firm** *n* filiale *f*. **affiliation** *n* affiliation *f*.
affinity (əˈfiniti) *n* affinité *f*.
affirm (əˈfəːm) *vt* affirmer. **affirmative** *adj* affirmatif, -ive.
affix (*v* əˈfiks; *n* ˈæfiks) *vt* apposer. *n* **1** addition *f*. **2** *gram* affixe *m*.
afflict (əˈflikt) *vt* affliger. **affliction** *n* **1** affliction *f*. **2** infirmité *f*.
affluent (ˈæfluənt) *adj* **1** abondant. **2** riche. **affluence** *n* richesse *f*.
afford (əˈfɔːd) *vt* **1** avoir les moyens. **2** pouvoir. **3** fournir.
affront (əˈfrʌnt) *n* affront *m*. *vt* **1** insulter. **2** faire honte à.
Afghanistan (æfˈgænistɑːn, -stæn) *n* Afghanistan *m*. **Afghan** *adj,n* afghan.
afield (əˈfiːld) *adv* **far afield** très loin.
afloat (əˈflout) *adv* à flot.
afoot (əˈfut) *adv* à pied. **there's something afoot** il se prépare quelque chose.
aforesaid (əˈfɔːsed) *adj* susdit.
afraid (əˈfreid) *adj* **be afraid 1** avoir peur. **2** ne pas oser.
afresh (əˈfreʃ) *adv* de *or* à nouveau.
Africa (ˈæfrikə) *n* Afrique *f*. **African** *adj,n* africain.
aft (ɑːft) *adv* à *or* sur l'arrière.
after (ˈɑːftə) *adv* après, ensuite, d'après. *prep* **1** après. **2** suivant, selon. **after all** après tout. ~*conj* après que. **after-care** *n* surveillance *f*. **after-effects** *n pl* **1** suites *f pl*. **2** *med* reliquat *m*. **aftermath** *n* regain *m*. **afternoon** *n* après-midi *m*. **afterthought** *n* réflexion après coup, arrière-pensée *f*. **afterwards** *adv* ensuite, après.
again (əˈgen) *adv* de nouveau, encore. **again and again** à plusieurs reprises.
against (əˈgenst) *prep* **1** contre. **2** vis-à-vis. **3** à l'encontre de.
age (eidʒ) *n* **1** âge *m*. **2** époque *f*. **age-group** *n* classe *f*. **be of age** être majeur. ~*vt,vi* vieillir. **aged** *adj* vieux, vieille, âgé.
agency (ˈeidʒənsi) *n* **1** *comm* agence *f*, bureau, -aux *m*. **2** action *f*.
agenda (əˈdʒendə) *n* ordre du jour *m*.
agent (ˈeidʒənt) *n* agent, représentant *m*.
aggravate (ˈægrəveit) *vt* **1** aggraver. **2** *inf* exaspérer, agacer.
aggregate (*adj,n* ˈægrigit; *v* ˈægrigeit) *n* ensemble, total, -aux *m*. *adj* global, -aux, collectif, -ive. *vt* rassembler.
aggression (əˈgreʃən) *n* agression *f*. **aggressive** *adj* agressif, -ive.
aghast (əˈgɑːst) *adj* épouvanté, ébahi.
agile (ˈædʒail) *adj* agile, leste. **agility** *n* agilité *f*.
agitate (ˈædʒiteit) *vt* **1** agiter. **2** troubler. **agitated** *adj* ému, troublé. **agitation** *n* agitation *f*. **agitator** *n* agitateur, -trice.
agnostic (ægˈnɔstik) *adj,n* agnostique.
ago (əˈgou) *adj,adv* il y a. **long ago** il y a longtemps.
agog (əˈgɔg) *adj* impatient. **be all agog** brûler d'envie.
agony (ˈægəni) *n* **1** angoisse *f*. **2** *med* agonie *f*.
agrarian (əˈgrɛəriən) *adj* agraire.
agree (əˈgriː) *vi* **1** consentir. **2** s'accorder. **3** être d'accord. **4** convenir. **agreeable** *adj* **1** plaisant, agréable. **2** consentant. **agreement** *n* **1** accord *m*. **2** contrat *m*.
agriculture (ˈægrikʌltʃə) *n* agriculture *f*. **agricultural** *adj* agricole.
ahead (əˈhed) *adv* en avant, devant.
aid (eid) *vt* aider, assister. **aid and abet** être le complice de. ~*n* **1** aide *f*. **2** secours *m*, assistance *f*.
ailment (ˈeilmənt) *n* mal *m*, indisposition *f*.
aim (eim) *vt,vi* viser. *n* **1** but *m*. **2** objet *m*. **aimless** *adj* sans but.
air (ɛə) *n* **1** air *m*. **2** brise *f*. **3** apparence *f*. *vt* aérer.
airborne (ˈɛəbɔːn) *adj* aéroporté.
air-conditioning *n* climatisation *f*. **air-conditioned** *adj* climatisé.
aircraft (ˈɛəkrɑːft) *n* avion *m*. **aircraft carrier** *n* porte-avions *m invar*.
airfield (ˈɛəfiːld) *n* terrain d'aviation *m*.
airforce (ˈɛəfɔːs) *n* armée de l'air *f*.
airhostess (ˈɛəhoustis) *n* hôtesse de l'air *f*.
air lift *n* pont aérien *m*.
airline (ˈɛəlain) *n* ligne aérienne *f*.
airmail (ˈɛəmeil) *n* poste aérienne *f*. **by airmail** par avion.

airman ('ɛəmən) *n* aviateur *m*.
airport ('ɛəpɔ:t) *n* aéroport *m*.
air-raid *n* raid aérien *m*.
airtight ('ɛətait) *adj* hermétique.
airy ('ɛəri) *adj* **1** aéré. **2** léger, -ère. **3** sans consistance.
aisle (ail) *n* **1** *rel* nef latérale *f*. bas-côté *m*. **2** passage *m*.
ajar (ə'dʒɑ:) *adj,adv* entrouvert.
alabaster ('æləbɑ:stə) *n* albâtre *m*.
alarm (ə'lɑ:m) *n* alarme, alerte *f*. **alarm clock** *n* réveille-matin *m invar*. ~*vt* **1** alarmer. **2** effrayer.
alas (ə'læs) *interj* hélas!
albatross ('ælbətros) *n* albatros *m*.
albeit (ɔ:l'bi:it) *conj* quoique, bien que.
album ('ælbəm) *n* album *m*.
alchemy ('ælkəmi) *n* alchimie *f*.
alcohol ('ælkəhɔl) *n* alcool *m*. **alcoholic** *adj,n* alcoolique. **alcoholism** *n* alcoolisme *m*.
alcove ('ælkouv) *n* **1** alcôve *f*. **2** niche *f*.
alderman ('ɔ:ldəmən) *n* conseiller municipal *m*.
ale (eil) *n* bière *f*.
alert (ə'lə:t) *adj,n* alerte *f*.
algebra ('ældʒibrə) *n* algèbre *f*.
Algeria (æl'dʒiəriə) *n* Algérie *f*. **Algerian** *adj,n* algérien, -ienne.
alias ('eiliəs) *adv* autrement dit.
alibi ('ælibai) *n* alibi *m*.
alien ('eiliən) *adj,n* étranger, -ère. **alienate** *vt* aliéner. **alienation** *n* aliénation *f*.
alight[1] (ə'lait) *adj* en feu, allumé.
alight[2] (ə'lait) *vi* **1** descendre. **2** se poser.
align (ə'lain) *vt* aligner. *vi* s'aligner.
alike (ə'laik) *adj* semblable. *adv* pareillement, également.
alimentary (æli'mentəri) *adj* alimentaire.
alimony ('æliməni) *n* pension alimentaire *f*.
alive (ə'laiv) *adj* **1** vivant. **2** éveillé. **be alive with** grouiller de.
alkali ('ælkəlai) *n* alcali *m*.
all (ɔ:l) *pron,adj* tout, tous. **all of us** nous tous. ~*adv* tout, entièrement. **all but** presque. **all right** ça va. ~*n* totalité *f*. tout *m*.
allay (ə'lei) *vt* soulager, apaiser.
allege (ə'ledʒ) *vt* alléguer. **allegation** *n* allégation *f*.
allegiance (ə'li:dʒəns) *n* fidélité *f*.
allegory ('æligəri) *n* allégorie *f*. **allegorical** *adj* allégorique.
allergy ('ælədʒi) *n* allergie *f*. **allergic** *adj* allergique.
alleviate (ə'li:vieit) *vt* soulager.
alley ('æli) *n* **1** allée *f*. **2** passage *m*.
alliance (ə'laiəns) *n* alliance *f*. **allied** *adj* **1** allié. **2** apparenté.
alligator ('æligeitə) *n* alligator *m*.
alliteration (əlitə'reiʃən) *n* allitération *f*.
allocate ('æləkeit) *vt* allouer. **allocation** *n* allocation *f*.
allot (ə'lɔt) *vt* **1** attribuer. **2** distribuer. **allotment** *n* **1** répartition *f*. **2** jardin ouvrier *m*.
allow (ə'lau) *vt* **1** permettre. **2** admettre. **3** accorder. **allow for** tenir compte de. **allowance** *n* **1** allocation *f*. **2** pension *f*. **3** indemnité *f*. **4** *comm* remise *f*. **5** ration *f*.
alloy ('ælɔi) *n* alliage *m*. *vt* allier.
All Saints' Day *n* Toussaint *f*.
allude (ə'lu:d) *vi* faire allusion. **allusion** *n* allusion *f*.
allure (ə'luə) *vt* attirer, séduire. **alluring** *adj* attrayant.
ally (*n* 'ælai; *v* ə'lai) *n* allié *m*. *vt* allier. *vi* s'allier.
almanac ('ɔ:lmənæk) *n* almanach *m*.
almighty (ɔ:l'maiti) *adj* tout-puissant.
almond ('ɑ:mənd) *n* amande *f*.
almost ('ɔ:lmoust) *adv* presque, à peu près.
alms (ɑ:mz) *n pl* aumône *f*.
aloft (ə'lɔft) *adv* en haut.
alone (ə'loun) *adj* seul, solitaire. **leave alone** laisser tranquille.
along (ə'lɔŋ) *prep* le long de. **all along** tout le temps. **alongside** *adv* bord à bord.
aloof (ə'lu:f) *adv* à l'écart. *adj* **1** éloigné. **2** distant.
aloud (ə'laud) *adv* à haute voix, haut.
alphabet ('ælfəbet) *n* alphabet *m*. **alphabetical** *adj* alphabétique.
alpine ('ælpain) *adj* alpin, alpestre.
Alps (ælps) *n pl* Alpes *f pl*.
already (ɔ:l'redi) *adv* déjà.
Alsatian (æl'seiʃən) *n* chien-loup *m*.
also ('ɔ:lsou) *adv* aussi.
altar ('ɔ:ltə) *n* autel *m*.
alter ('ɔ:ltə) *vt,vi* changer. **alteration** *n* **1** changement *m*. **2** modification *f*.
alternate (*v* 'ɔ:ltəneit; *adj* ɔ:l'tə:nit) *vt,vi* alterner. *adj* alternatif, -ive. **alternative** *n* alternative *f*. choix *m*.
although (ɔ:l'ðou) *conj* quoique, bien que.
altitude ('æltitju:d) *n* altitude *f*.
alto ('æltou) *n* alto *m*.
altogether (ɔ:ltə'geðə) *adv* **1** entièrement, tout à fait. **2** tout compris.
aluminium (ælju'miniəm) *n* aluminium *m*.

always ('ɔ:lweiz) *adv* toujours.
am (əm; *stressed* æm) *v* see **be.**
amalgamate (ə'mælgəmeit) *vt* amalgamer, fusionner. *vi* s'amalgamer. **amalgamation** *n* **1** amalgamation *f*. **2** fusion *f*.
amass (ə'mæs) *vt* amasser.
amateur ('æmətə) *n* amateur *m*.
amaze (ə'meiz) *vt* stupéfier, étonner. **amazement** *n* stupéfaction *f*. étonnement *m*.
ambassador (æm'bæsədə) *n* ambassadeur *m*.
amber ('æmbə) *n* ambre *m*.
ambidextrous (æmbi'dekstrəs) *adj* ambidextre.
ambiguous (æm'bigjuəs) *adj* ambigu, -ue, équivoque. **ambiguity** *n* ambiguité *f*.
ambition (æm'biʃən) *n* ambition *f*. **ambitious** *adj* ambitieux, -euse.
ambivalent (æm'bivələnt) *adj* ambivalent.
amble ('æmbəl) *vi* **1** aller l'amble. **2** flâner. *n* **1** (of horse) amble *m*. **2** pas tranquille *m*.
ambulance ('æmbjuləns) *n* ambulance *f*.
ambush ('æmbuʃ) *n* embuscade *f*. *vt* attirer dans un piège.
amenable (ə'mi:nəbəl) *adj* **1** responsable. **2** soumis.
amend (ə'mend) *vt* amender, corriger. *vi* s'amender. **amendment** *n* **1** modification *f*. **2** *pol* amendement *m*.
amenity (ə'mi:niti) *n* **1** aménité *f*. agrément *m*. **2** *pl* commodités *f pl*.
America (ə'merikə) *n* Amérique *f*. **American** *adj,n* américain.
amethyst ('æmiθist) *n* améthyste *f*.
amiable ('eimiəbəl) *adj* aimable.
amicable ('æmikəbəl) *adj* **1** amical, -aux. **2** *law* à l'amiable.
amid (ə'mid) *prep also* **amidst** parmi, au milieu de.
amiss (ə'mis) *adv* **1** mal, de travers. **2** mal à propos. *adj* de travers, qui cloche.
ammonia (ə'mouniə) *n* ammoniaque *f*.
ammunition (æmju'niʃən) *n* munitions *f pl*.
amnesty ('æmnəsti) *n* amnistie *f*.
amoeba (ə'mi:bə) *n, pl* **-bae** *or* **-bas** amibe *f*.
among (ə'mʌŋ) *prep also* **amongst** parmi, entre.
amoral (ei'mɔrəl) *adj* amoral, -aux.
amorous ('æmərəs) *adj* amoureux, -euse.
amorphous (ə'mɔ:fəs) *adj* amorphe.
amount (ə'maunt) *n* **1** montant *m*. **2** quantité *f*. *vi* **1** s'élever. **2** revenir.
ampere ('æmpɛə) *n* ampère *m*.
amphetamine (æm'fetəmi:n) *n* amphétamine *f*.
amphibian (æm'fibiən) *n* amphibie *m*. **amphibious** *adj* amphibie.
amphitheatre ('æmfiθiətə) *n* amphithéâtre *m*.
ample ('æmpəl) *adj* **1** ample, vaste. **2** abondant.
amplify ('æmplifai) *vt* amplifier. **amplifier** *n* amplificateur *m*.
amputate ('æmpjuteit) *vt* amputer. **amputation** *n* amputation *f*.
amuse (ə'mju:z) *vt* amuser, divertir. **amusement** *n* divertissement *m*.
an (ən; *stressed* æn) *indef art* see **a.**
anachronism (ə'nækrənizəm) *n* anachronisme *m*.
anaemia (ə'ni:miə) *n* anémie *f*. **anaemic** *adj* anémique.
anaesthetic (ænis'θetik) *adj,n* anesthésique *m*. **anaesthetist** *n* anesthésiste *m,f*. **anaesthetize** *vt* anesthésier.
anagram ('ænəgræm) *n* anagramme *f*.
anal ('einl̩) *adj* anal, -aux.
analogy (ə'nælədʒi) *n* analogie *f*.
analysis (ə'nælisis) *n, pl* **analyses** analyse *f*. **analyse** *vt* analyser.
anarchy ('ænəki) *n* anarchie *f*. **anarchism** *n* anarchisme *m*. **anarchist** *n* anarchiste *m,f*.
anatomy (ə'nætəmi) *n* anatomie *f*.
ancestor ('ænsəstə) *n* ancêtre, aïeul, -eux *m*. **ancestral** *adj* héréditaire, de famille.
anchor ('æŋkə) *n* ancre *f*. *vt* ancrer. *vi* jeter l'ancre.
anchovy ('æntʃəvi) *n* anchois *m*.
ancient ('einʃənt) *adj* ancien, -ienne, antique.
ancillary (æn'siləri) *adj* **1** subordonné. **2** auxiliaire.
and (ən, ənd; *stressed* ænd) *conj* et. **and so on** et ainsi de suite.
Andorra (æn'dɔ:rə) *n* Andorre *f*.
anemone (ə'neməni) *n* anémone *f*.
anew (ə'nju:) *adv* de nouveau.
angel ('eindʒəl) *n* ange *m*. **angelic** *adj* angélique.
angelica (æn'dʒelikə) *n* angélique *f*.
anger ('æŋgə) *n* colère *f*. *vt* irriter, mettre en colère. **angry** *adj* fâché, en colère.
angle[1] ('æŋgəl) *n* angle *m*.
angle[2] ('æŋgəl) *vi* pêcher à la ligne. **angler** *n* pêcheur à la ligne *m*.
Anglican ('æŋglikən) *adj,n* anglican.
anguish ('æŋgwiʃ) *n* angoisse *f*.
angular ('æŋgjulə) *adj* **1** angulaire. **2** anguleux, -euse. **3** maigre.
animal ('æniməl) *adj,n* animal, -aux *m*.
animate (*adj* 'ænimət; *v* 'ænimeit) *adj* animé. *vt* animer. **animation** *n* animation, vivacité *f*.
aniseed ('ænisi:d) *n* graine d'anis *f*.

ankle ('æŋkəl) *n* cheville *f*.
annals ('ænļz) *n pl* annales *f pl*.
annex (ə'neks) *vt* annexer. **annexe** *n* annexe *f*.
annihilate (ə'naiəleit) *vt* anéantir. **annihilation** *n* anéantissement *m*.
anniversary (æni'və:səri) *n* anniversaire *m*.
annotate ('ænəteit) *vt* annoter.
announce (ə'nauns) *vt* annoncer. **announcement** *n* annonce *f*. avis *m*. **announcer** *n* **1** annonceur *m*. **2** speaker *m*.
annoy (ɔ'nɔi) *vt* **1** gêner, ennuyer. **2** contrarier. **annoyance** *n* désagrément, ennui *m*.
annual ('ænjuəl) *adj* annuel, -elle. *n* **1** annuaire *m*. **2** *bot* plante annuelle *f*.
annul (ə'nʌl) *vt* annuler.
anode ('ænoud) *n* anode *f*.
anoint (ə'nɔint) *vt* oindre.
anomaly (ə'nɔməli) *n* anomalie *f*. **anomalous** *adj* anormal, -aux, irregulier, -ière.
anonymous (ə'nɔniməs) *adj* anonyme.
another (ə'nʌðə) *pron,adj* **1** encore un. **2** un autre. **one another** l'un l'autre, les uns les autres.
answer ('ɑ:nsə) *n* **1** réponse *f*. **2** solution *f*. *vt,vi* répondre. **answerable** *adj* responsable.
ant (ænt) *n* fourmi *f*.
antagonize (æn'tægənaiz) *vt* contrarier. **antagonism** *n* antagonisme *m*. **antagonist** *n* antagoniste, adversaire *m,f*.
Antarctic (æn'tɑ:ktik) *adj,n* antarctique *m*.
antelope ('æntiloup) *n* antilope *f*.
antenatal (ænti'neitļ) *adj* prénatal, -aux.
antenna (æn'tenə) *n, pl* **antennae** antenne *f*.
anthem ('ænθəm) *n* hymne *m*.
anthology (æn'θɔlədʒi) *n* anthologie *f*.
anthropology (ænθrə'pɔlədʒi) *n* anthropologie *f*. **anthropologist** *n* anthropologiste *m,f*.
anti-aircraft *adj* antiaérien, -ienne.
antibiotic (æntibai'ɔtik) *n* antibiotique *m*.
antibody ('æntibɔdi) *n* anticorps *m*.
antic ('æntik) *n* singerie *f*.
anticipate (æn'tisipeit) *vt* **1** anticiper. **2** prévoir. **anticipation** *n* **1** anticipation *f*. **2** prévision *f*. **3** attente *f*.
anticlimax (ænti'klaimæks) *n* anticlimax *m*. chute, culbute *f*.
anticlockwise (ænti'klɔkwaiz) *adj* en sens inverse des aiguilles d'une montre.
anticyclone (ænti'saikloun) *n* anticyclone *m*.
antidote ('æntidout) *n* antidote *m*.
antifreeze ('æntifri:z) *n* antigel *m invar*.
antique (æn'ti:k) *adj* antique. *n* objet antique *m*. antiquité *f*. **antique dealer** *n* antiquaire *m*. **antique shop** *n* magasin d'antiquités *m*. **antiquated** *adj* **1** vieilli. **2** démodé. **antiquity** *n* antiquité *f*.
anti-Semitic *adj* antisémitique.
antiseptic (ænti'septik) *adj,n* antiseptique *m*.
antisocial (ænti'souʃəl) *adj* antisocial, -aux.
antithesis (æn'tiθəsis) *n, pl* **antitheses** antithèse *f*.
antler ('æntlə) *n* **1** andouiller *m*. **2** *pl* bois *m pl*.
antonym ('æntənim) *n* antonyme *m*.
anus ('einəs) *n* anus *m*.
anvil ('ænvil) *n* enclume *f*.
anxious ('æŋkʃəs) *adj* **1** soucieux, -euse. **2** désireux, -euse. **anxiety** *n* anxiété, angoisse *f*.
any ('eni) *adj,pron* **1** du, de la. **2** en. **3** aucun. **4** n'importe (le)quel. **5** tout. **any further** plus loin. **any more** encore. **anybody** *pron also* **anyone** n'importe qui, quelqu'un. **not anybody** personne. **anyhow** *conj also* **anyway** de toute façon. *adv* n'importe comment. **anything** *pron* **1** quelque chose. **2** n'importe quoi. **not anything** rien. **anywhere** *adv* n'importe où. **not anywhere** nulle part.
apart (ə'pɑ:t) *adv* de côté. **apart from** en dehors de. **apart from the fact that** hormis que.
apartheid (ə'pɑ:tait) *n* ségrégation *f*.
apartment (ə'pɑ:tmənt) *n* **1** pièce *f*. **2** appartement *m*. **3** *pl* logement *m*.
apathy ('æpəθi) *n* apathie *f*. **apathetic** *adj* apathique.
ape (eip) *n* singe *m*. *vt* singer.
aperitive (ə'peritiv) *n* apéritif *m*.
aperture ('æpətʃə) *n* ouverture *f*.
apex ('eipeks) *n* sommet *m*. apogée *f*.
apiece (ə'pi:s) *adv* chacun.
apology (ə'pɔlədʒi) *n* **1** excuses *f pl*. **2** apologie *f*. **apologetic** *adj* **1** d'excuse. **2** apologétique. **apologize** *vi* s'excuser, demander pardon.
apostle (ə'pɔsəl) *n* apôtre *m*.
apostrophe (ə'pɔstrəfi) *n* apostrophe *f*.
appal (ə'pɔ:l) *vt* épouvanter. **appalling** *adj* effroyable.
apparatus (æpə'reitəs) *n, pl* **-tus** or **-tuses** appareil *m*.
apparent (ə'pærənt) *adj* apparent, manifeste. **apparently** *adv* apparemment. **apparition** *n* apparition *f*.
appeal (ə'pi:l) *n* appel *m*. *vi* faire appel. **appeal to 1** plaire à. **2** s'adresser à.
appear (ə'piə) *vi* **1** paraître, sembler. **2** apparaître. **appearance** *n* **1** apparition *f*. **2** apparence *f*.

appease (ə'pi:z) *vt* apaiser.
appendix (ə'pendiks) *n, pl* **appendices** appendice *m.* **appendicitis** *n* appendicite *f.*
appetite ('æpətait) *n* **1** appétit *m.* **2** désir *m.* **appetizer** *n* apéritif *m.* **appetizing** *adj* appétissant.
applaud (ə'plɔ:d) *vt,vi* applaudir. **applause** *n* applaudissements *m pl.*
apple ('æpəl) *n* pomme *f.*
apply (ə'plai) *vt* appliquer. *vi* s'adresser. **appliance** *n* **1** dispositif *m.* **2** *pl* accessoires *m pl.* **applicable** *adj* applicable. **applicant** *n* candidat *m.* **application** *n* **1** application *f.* **2** demande *f.*
appoint (ə'pɔint) *vt* **1** nommer. **2** fixer. **3** équiper. **appointment** *n* **1** rendez-vous *m.* **2** désignation *f.*
appraise (ə'preiz) *vt* estimer, apprécier. **appraisal** *n* évaluation *f.*
appreciate (ə'pri:ʃieit) *vt* apprécier. *vi* augmenter de valeur. **appreciation** *n* **1** appréciation *f.* **2** hausse de valeur *f.*
apprehend (æpri'hend) *vt* **1** appréhender. **2** comprendre. **apprehension** *n* **1** appréhension *f.* **2** crainte *f.* **3** arrestation *f.* **apprehensive** *adj* anxieux, -euse.
apprentice (ə'prentis) *n* apprenti *m. vt* mettre en apprentissage. **apprenticeship** *n* apprentissage *m.*
approach (ə'proutʃ) *vi* (s')approcher. *vt* (s')approcher de. *n* **1** approche *f.* **2** accès *m.*
appropriate (*adj* ə'proupriət; *v* ə'prouprieit) *adj* approprié, convenable. *vt* (s')approprier.
approve (ə'pru:v) *vt* approuver. **approval** *n* approbation *f.*
approximate (*adj* ə'prɔksimət; *v* ə'prɔksimeit) *adj* approximatif, -ive. *vt* rapprocher.
apricot ('eiprikɔt) *n* abricot *m.* **apricot tree** *n* abricotier *m.*
April ('eiprəl) *n* avril *m.* **April Fools' Day** *n* premier avril *m.*
apron ('eiprən) *n* tablier *m.*
apse (æps) *n* abside *f.*
apt (æpt) *adj* **1** porté à. **2** juste. **3** doué. **aptly** *adv* à propos.
aptitude ('æptitju:d) *n* **1** tendance *f.* **2** aptitude, disposition *f.*
aquarium (ə'kwɛəriəm) *n* aquarium *m.*
Aquarius (ə'kwɛəriəs) *n* Verseau *m.*
aquatic (ə'kwætik) *adj* aquatique. **acquatics** *n pl* sports nautiques *m pl.*
Arabia (ə'reibiə) *n* Arabie *f.* **Arab** *adj,n* arabe. **Arabian** *adj* arabe. **Arabic** *adj* arabique, arabe. **Arabic** (language) *n* arabe *m.*
arable ('ærəbəl) *adj* arable.
arbitrary ('ɑ:bitrəri) *adj* arbitraire.
arbitrate ('ɑ:bitreit) *vt,vi* arbitrer. **arbitration** *n* arbitrage *m.*
arc (ɑ:k) *n* arc *m.*
arcade (ɑ:'keid) *n* **1** arcade *f.* **2** passage *m.*
arch (ɑ:tʃ) *n* **1** arche *f.* **2** arc *m.* **3** voûte *f. vt* arquer. *vi* former voûte.
archaeology (ɑ:ki'ɔlədʒi) *n* archéologie *f.* **archaeological** *adj* archéologique. **archaeologist** *n* archéologue *m,f.*
archaic (ɑ:'keiik) *adj* archaïque.
archbishop (ɑ:tʃ'biʃəp) *n* archevêque *m.*
archduke (ɑ:tʃ'dju:k) *n* archiduc *m.* **archduchess** *n* archiduchesse *f.*
archery ('ɑ:tʃəri) *n* tir à l'arc *m.*
archetype ('ɑ:kitaip) *n* archétype *m.*
archipelago (ɑ:ki'peləgou) *n* archipel *m.*
architect ('ɑ:kitekt) *n* architecte *m.* **architecture** *n* architecture *f.*
archives ('ɑ:kaivz) *n pl* archives *f pl.*
Arctic ('ɑ:ktik) *adj* arctique. **Arctic (Ocean)** *n* (Océan) Arctique *m.*
ardent ('ɑ:dnt) *adj* ardent.
ardour ('ɑ:də) *n* ardeur *f.*
arduous ('ɑ:djuəs) *adj* **1** ardu. **2** acharné.
are (ə; *stressed* ɑ:) *v* see **be.**
area ('ɛəriə) *n* **1** aire, surface *f.* **2** territoire *m.* région *f.*
arena (ə'ri:nə) *n* arène *f.*
argue ('ɑ:gju:) *vi* **1** discuter. **2** se disputer. *vt* **1** prouver. **2** soutenir. **argument** *n* **1** argument *m.* **2** discussion *f.* **argumentative** *adj* raisonneur, -euse.
arid ('ærid) *adj* aride.
Aries ('ɛəri:z) *n* Bélier *m.*
arise* (ə'raiz) *vi* **1** s'élever. **2** se lever. **3** provenir.
aristocracy (æri'stɔkrəsi) *n* aristocratie *f.* **aristocrat** *n* aristocrate *m,f.* **aristocratic** *adj* aristocratique.
arithmetic (ə'riθmətik) *n* arithmétique *f.*
arm[1] (ɑ:m) *n anat* bras *m.* **at arm's length** à distance. **armchair** *n* fauteuil *m.* **armhole** *n* emmanchure *f.* **armpit** *n* aisselle *f.* **armful** *n* brassée *f.*
arm[2] (ɑ:m) *n* **1** *mil* arme *f.* **2** *pl* armoiries *f pl.* **be up in arms** se gendarmer. ~*vt* armer. *vi* s'armer. **armament** *n* armement *m.*
armour ('ɑ:mə) *n* **1** armure *f.* **2** blindage *f. vt*

cuirasser, blinder. **armour-plated** *adj* cuirassé, blindé. **armoury** *n* arsenal, -aux *m*.

army ('ɑ:mi) *n* armée *f*.

aroma (ə'roumə) *n* arome *m*. **aromatic** *adj* aromatique.

arose (ə'rouz) *v see* **arise.**

around (ə'raund) *prep* autour de. *adv* autour, à l'entour.

arouse (ə'rauz) *vt* **1** réveiller. **2** provoquer.

arrange (ə'reindʒ) *vt* **1** arranger, organiser. **2** ranger. *vi* s'arranger. **arrangement** *n* disposition *f*. arrangement *m*.

array (ə'rei) *vt* **1** ranger. **2** orner. *n* **1** ordre *m*. **2** atours *m pl*.

arrears (ə'riəz) *n pl* arrérages *m pl*. **in arrears** en retard.

arrest (ə'rest) *vt* arrêter. *n* **1** arrestation *f*. **2** arrêt *m*.

arrive (ə'raiv) *vi* arriver. **arrival** *n* arrivée *f*.

arrogance ('ærəgəns) *n* arrogance *f*. **arrogant** *adj* arrogant.

arrow ('ærou) *n* flèche *f*.

arsenic ('ɑ:snik) *n* arsenic *m*.

arson ('ɑ:sən) *n* crime d'incendie *m*.

art (ɑ:t) *n* **1** art *m*. **2** habileté *f*. **3** artifice *m*. **art gallery** *n* musée d'art *m*. **art school** *n* école de beaux arts *f*. **artful** *adj* **1** astucieux, -euse, rusé. **2** adroit.

artery ('ɑ:təri) *n* artère *f*. **arterial** *adj* artériel, -elle.

arthritis (ɑ:'θraitis) *n* arthrite *f*.

artichoke ('ɑ:titʃouk) *n* artichaut *m*.

article ('ɑ:tikəl) *n* **1** article *m*. **2** *pl law* contrat *m*. *vt* engager par contrat.

articulate (*v* ɑ:'tikjuleit; *adj* ɑ:'tikjulət) *vt* articuler, énoncer. *vi* s'articuler. *adj* **1** articulé. **2** distinct. **articulation** *n* articulation *f*.

artificial (ɑ:ti'fiʃəl) *adj* artificiel, -elle.

artillery (ɑ:'tiləri) *n* artillerie *f*.

artist ('ɑ:tist) *n* artiste *m,f*. **artistic** *adj* artistique.

as (əz; *stressed* æz) *adv* **1** aussi, si. **2** comme, en. *conj* **1** comme. **2** puisque. **3** au moment où. **4** à mesure que. **5** que. **as for** quant à. **as if** comme si. **as well** aussi.

asbestos (æs'bestəs) *n* amiante *m*.

ascend (ə'send) *vt,vi* monter. *vi* remonter. **ascension** *n* ascension *f*. **ascent** *n* montée *f*.

ascertain (æsə'tein) *vt* **1** constater. **2** vérifier.

ash[1] (æʃ) *n* cendre *f*. **ashtray** *n* cendrier *m*.

ash[2] (æʃ) *n bot* frêne *m*.

ashamed (ə'ʃeimd) *adj* honteux, -euse. **be ashamed of** avoir honte de.

ashore (ə'ʃɔ:) *adv* à terre. **go ashore** débarquer.

Asia ('eiʃə) *n* Asie *f*. **Asian** *adj,n also* **Asiatic** asiatique.

aside (ə'said) *adv* **1** de côté. **2** à l'écart. *n* aparté *m*.

ask (ɑ:sk) *vt* **1** demander, prier. **2** inviter. **ask about** se renseigner sur. **ask a question** poser une question. **ask for** demander.

askew (ə'skju:) *adv* de côté.

asleep (ə'sli:p) *adv* endormi. **be asleep** dormir. **fall asleep** s'endormir.

asparagus (ə'spærəgəs) *n* asperge *f*.

aspect ('æspekt) *n* aspect *m*. point de vue *f*.

asphalt ('æsfælt) *n* asphalte *m*. *vt* asphalter.

aspire (ə'spaiə) *vi* aspirer. **aspiring** *adj* ambitieux, -euse.

aspirin ('æsprin) *n* aspirine *f*.

ass (æs) *n* **1** âne, ânesse. **2** sot, sotte.

assassin (ə'sæsin) *n* assassin *m*. **assassinate** *vt* assassiner. **assassination** *n* assassinat *m*.

assault (ə'sɔ:lt) *n* attaque *f*. assaut *m*. *vt* attaquer.

assemble (ə'sembəl) *vt* assembler. *vi* s'assembler. **assembly** *n* **1** assemblée *f*. **2** montage *m*. **assembly line** *n* chaîne de montage *f*.

assent (ə'sent) *n* assentiment *m*. *vi* consentir.

assert (ə'sə:t) *vt* **1** affirmer. **2** revendiquer. **assertion** *n* **1** assertion *f*. **2** revendication *f*.

assess (ə'ses) *vt* **1** estimer. **2** imposer. **assessment** *n* **1** estimation *f*. **2** impôt *m*.

asset ('æset) *n* **1** avantage *m*. **2** *pl comm* actif *m*. **3** *pl* biens *m pl*.

assign (ə'sain) *vt* assigner. **assignment** *n* assignation *f*. **2** *law* transfert *m*.

assimilate (ə'simileit) *vt* assimiler.

assist (ə'sist) *vt,vi* assister. **assistance** *n* aide *f*. **assistant** *adj* auxiliaire. *n* **1** assistant *m,f*. adjoint *m*. **2** *comm* commis *m*.

assizes (ə'saiziz) *n pl* assises *f pl*.

associate (ə'souʃieit) *adj,n* associé. *n* collègue *m*. *vt* associer. *vi* s'associer. **association** *n* association *f*.

assort (ə'sɔ:t) *vt* assortir. *vi* s'associer. **assortment** *n* assortiment *m*.

assume (ə'sju:m) *vt* **1** supposer. **2** assumer. **3** affecter. **assumption** *n* supposition, présomption *f*.

assure (ə'ʃuə) *vt* assurer. **assurance** *n* assurance *f*.

asterisk ('æstərisk) *n* astérisque *m*.

asthma ('æsmə) *n* asthme *m*. **asthmatic** *adj,n* asthmatique.

astonish (ə'stɔniʃ) *vt* étonner. **astonishment** *n* étonnement *m*.

astound (ə'staund) *vt* ébahir.

astray (ə'strei) *adv* égaré.

astride (ə'straid) *adv* à califourchon.

astrology (ə'strɔlədʒi) *n* astrologie *f*. **astrologer** *n* astrologue *m*. **astrological** *adj* astrologique.

astronaut ('æstrənɔ:t) *n* astronaute *m*. **astronautics** *n* astronautique *f*.

astronomy (ə'strɔnəmi) *n* astronomie *f*. **astronomer** *n* astronome *m*. **astronomical** *adj* astronomique.

astute (ə'stju:t) *adj* astucieux, -euse, avisé.

asunder (ə'sʌndə) *adv* en deux, à part.

asylum (ə'sailəm) *n* **1** asile *m*. **2** *med* hospice *m*.

at (ət; *stressed* æt) *prep* **1** à. **2** chez. **at first** d'abord. **at hand** sous la main. **at last** enfin. **at least** du moins. **at once** tout de suite.

ate (eit, et) *v* see **eat**.

atheism ('eiθiizəm) *n* athéisme *m*. **atheist** *n* athée *m,f*. **atheistic** *adj* athée.

Athens ('æθinz) *n* Athènes *f*.

athlete ('æθli:t) *n* athlète *m*. **athletic** *adj* athlétique. **athletics** *n* athlétisme *m*.

Atlantic (ət'læntik) *adj* atlantique. **Atlantic (Ocean)** *n* (Océan) Atlantique *m*.

atlas ('ætləs) *n* atlas *m*.

atmosphere ('ætməsfiə) *n* atmosphère *f*. **atmospheric** *adj* atmosphérique. **atmospherics** *n pl* parasites *m pl*.

atom ('ætəm) *n* atome *m*. **atom bomb** *n* bombe atomique *f*. **atomic** *adj* atomique.

atone (ə'toun) *vi* expier. **atonement** *n* expiation *f*.

atrocious (ə'trouʃəs) *adj* atroce. **atrocity** *n* atrocité *f*.

attach (ə'tætʃ) *vt* attacher, lier. *vi* s'attacher. **attachment** *n* **1** attache *f*. **2** attachement *m*.

attaché (ə'tæʃei) *n* attaché *m*.

attack (ə'tæk) *vt* attaquer. *n* **1** attaque *f*. **2** *med* crise *f*. accès *m*.

attain (ə'tein) *vt,vi* atteindre, parvenir à.

attempt (ə'tempt) *n* **1** tentative *f*. **2** *law* attentat *m*. *vt* tenter, tâcher.

attend (ə'tend) *vt* **1** assister à. **2** servir, accompagner. **3** s'occuper de. *vi* faire attention. **attend to** s'occuper de. **attendance** *n* **1** assistance *f*. **2** fréquentation *f*. **3** service *m*. **attendant** *n* **1** serviteur *m*. **2** employé *m*. **attention** *n* attention *f*. **attentive** *adj* **1** attentif, -ive. **2** prévenant.

attic ('ætik) *n* mansarde *f*. grenier *m*.

attire (ə'taiə) *vt* vêtir. *n* vêtements *m pl*.

attitude ('ætitju:d) *n* attitude *f*.

attorney (ə'tə:ni) *n* **1** avoué *m*. **2** mandataire *m*. **attorney general** *n* procureur général *m*.

attract (ə'trækt) *vt* attirer. **attraction** *n* **1** attraction *f*. **2** *pl* attraits *m pl*. **attractive** *adj* attrayant, séduisant.

attribute (*v* ə'tribju:t; *n* 'ætribju:t) *vt* attribuer, imputer. *n* attribut *m*.

aubergine ('oubəʒi:n) *n* aubergine *f*.

auburn ('ɔ:bən) *adj* châtain, roux, rousse.

auction ('ɔ:kʃən) *n* vente aux enchères *f*. **auctioneer** *n* commissaire-priseur *m*.

audacious (ɔ:'deiʃəs) *adj* audacieux, -euse. **audacity** *n* audace *f*.

audible ('ɔ:dibəl) *adj* **1** audible. **2** intelligible. **audibly** *adv* distinctement.

audience ('ɔ:diəns) *n* **1** audience *f*. **2** public *m*. spectateurs *m pl*.

audiovisual (ɔ:diou'viʒuəl) *adj* audio-visuel, -elle.

audit ('ɔ:dit) *n* vérification *f*. *vt* vérifier. **auditor** *n* expert comptable *m*.

audition (ɔ:'diʃən) *n* audition *f*.

auditorium (ɔdi'tɔ:riəm) *n*, *pl* **auditoria** *or* **auditoriums** auditorium *m*.

August ('ɔ:gəst) *n* août *m*.

aunt (ɑ:nt) *n* tante *f*.

au pair (ou 'pɛə) *n* (jeune fille) au pair *f*.

aura ('ɔ:rə) *n* aura *f*.

austere (ɔ:'stiə) *adj* austère. **austerity** *n* austérité *f*.

Australia (ɔ'streiliə) *n* Australie *f*. **Australian** *adj,n* australien, -ienne.

Austria ('ɔ:striə) *n* Autriche *f*. **Austrian** *adj,n* autrichien, -ienne.

authentic (ɔ:'θentik) *adj* authentique. **authenticity** authenticité *f*.

author ('ɔ:θə) *n* auteur *m*. **authoress** *n* femme auteur *f*.

authority (ɔ:'θɔriti) *n* autorité *f*. **authoritarian** *adj* autoritaire. **authoritative** *adj* **1** autoritaire. **2** impérieux, -ieuse. **3** autorisé.

authorize ('ɔ:θəraiz) *vt* autoriser. **authorization** *n* autorisation *f*.

autistic (ɔ:'tistik) *adj* autistique.

autobiography (ɔ:təbai'ɔgrəfi) *n* autobiographie *f*. **autobiographical** *adj* autobiographique.

autograph ('ɔ:təgrɑ:f) *n* autographe *m*. *vt* signer, dédicacer.

automatic (ɔ:tə'mætik) *adj* automatique.
automation (ɔ:tə'meiʃən) *n* automatisation *f*.
autonomous (ɔ:'tɔnəməs) *adj* autonome. **autonomy** *n* autonomie *f*.
autumn ('ɔ:təm) *n* automne *m*.
auxiliary (ɔ:g'ziliəri) *adj,n* auxiliaire *m*.
available (ə'veiləbəl) *adj* **1** disponible. **2** valable.
avalanche ('ævəla:nʃ) *n* avalanche *f*.
avenge (ə'vendʒ) *vt* venger.
avenue ('ævənju:) *n* avenue *f*.
average ('ævridʒ) *n* moyenne *f*. *adj* moyen, -enne. *vt* prendre la moyenne de. *vi* donner une moyenne.
aversion (ə'və:ʃən) *n* aversion *f*. **pet aversion** bête noire *f*.
aviary ('eiviəri) *n* volière *f*.
aviation (eivi'eiʃən) *n* aviation *f*.
avid ('ævid) *adj* avide. **avidity** *n* avidité *f*.
avocado (ævə'ka:dou) *n* avocat *m*.
avoid (ə'vɔid) *vt* éviter.
await (ə'weit) *vt* attendre.
awake* (ə'weik) *vt* **1** éveiller. **2** réveiller. *vi* s'éveiller, se réveiller. **awaken** *vt* **1** éveiller. **2** réveiller.
award (ə'wɔ:d) *n* **1** récompense *f*. **2** adjudication *f*. *vt* **1** décerner. **2** accorder.
aware (ə'wɛə) *adj* **1** conscient. **2** avisé. **be aware** savoir. **not be aware of** ignorer. **awareness** *n* conscience *f*.
away (ə'wei) *adv* **1** au loin, loin. **2** absent. **right away** tout de suite.
awe (ɔ:) *n* crainte *f*. **awe-inspiring** *adj* impressionnant. **awe-struck** *adj* trés impressionné.
awful ('ɔ:fəl) *adj* **1** redoutable. **2** imposant. **3** épouvantable.
awkward ('ɔ:kwəd) *adj* **1** maladroit. **2** gêné. **3** embarrassant. **4** incommode. **awkwardness** *n* **1** maladresse *f*. **2** embarras *m*. **3** inconvénient *m*.
awoke (ə'wouk) *v* see **awake.**
axe (æks) *n* hache *f*.
axis ('æksis) *n, pl* **axes** axe *m*.
axle ('æksəl) *n* essieu, -eux *m*.
azalea (ə'zeiliə) *n* azaleé *f*.

B

babble ('bæbəl) *vi* babiller. *n* babil, bavardage *m*.
baboon (bə'bu:n) *n* babouin *m*.
baby ('beibi) *n* bébé *m*. *adj* puéril. **baby-sit** *vi* garder des enfants. **baby-sitter** *n* garde d'enfants *m,f*.
baccarat ('bækəra:) *n* baccara *m*.
bachelor ('bætʃələ) *n* célibataire *m*. **bachelor of Arts/Science** licencié ès lettres/sciences *m*. **bachelorhood** *n* célibat *m*.
back (bæk) *n* **1** dos *m*. reins *m pl*. **2** arrière, derrière *m*. **3** verso *m*. **4** fond *m*. **5** dossier *m*. *adj* arrière. *adv* en arrière. **be back** être de retour. **come back** revenir.
backache ('bækeik) *n* maux de reins *m pl*. courbature *f*.
backbone ('bækboun) *n* epine dorsale *f*.
backdate ('bækdeit) *vt* antidater.
backfire ('bækfaiə) *n* retour de flamme *m*. *vi* **1** *mot* pétarader. **2** *sl* échouer.
backgammon ('bækgæmən) *n* jacquet *m*.
background ('bækgraund) *n* arrière-plan, fond *m*.
backhand ('bækhænd) *n* *sport* revers *m*. **backhanded** *adj* injuste, equivoque. **back hander** *n* *sl* pot-de-vin *m*.
backlash ('bæklæʃ) *n* **1** battement *m*. **2** contre-coup *m*.
backlog ('bæklɔg) *n* arriéré *m*.
backstage (bæk'steidʒ) *adv* dans les coulisses.
backstroke ('bækstrouk) *n* brasse sur le dos *f*.
backward ('bækwəd) *adj* arriéré, rétrograde, lent. **backwardness** *n* **1** retard *m*. **2** arriération mentale *f*. **backwards** *adv* en arrière, à reculons, à rebours.
backwater ('bækwɔtə) *n* eau stagnante *f*.
bacon ('beikən) *n* lard, bacon *m*.
bacteria (bæk'tiəriə) *n pl* bactéries *f pl*. **bacterial** *adj* bactérien, -ienne.
bad (bæd) *adj* **1** mauvais, mal. **2** méchant. **bad-tempered** *adj* acariâtre, de mauvaise humeur. **badly** *adv* **1** mal. **2** grièvement.
bade (bæd) *v* see **bid.**
badge (bædʒ) *n* **1** insigne *m*. **2** symbole *m*.
badger ('bædʒə) *n* blaireau, -aux *m*. *vt* harceler.
badminton ('bædmintən) *n* badminton, volant *m*.
baffle ('bæfəl) *vt* **1** déconcerter. **2** déjouer.
bag (bæg) *n* sac, sachet *m*. *vt* **1** mettre en sac. **2** *sl* chiper. **baggage** *n* bagages *m pl*. **baggy** *adj* bouffant. **bagpipes** *n pl* cornemuse *f*.
bail (beil) *n* **1** caution *f*. **2** répondant *m*. *vt* porter garant de.
bailiff ('beilif) *n* **1** huissier *m*. **2** régisseur *m*. **3** bailli *m*.
bait (beit) *n* **1** amorce *f*. **2** appât, leurre *m*. *vt* **1** amorcer. **2** *inf* harceler.

bake (beik) *vt,vi* cuire au four. **baker** *n* boulanger *m*. **bakery** *n* boulangerie *f*.
balance ('bæləns) *n* **1** balance *f*. **2** équilibre *m*. **3** solde *m*. *vt* **1** balancer, équilibrer. **2** solder. *vi* **1** se balancer, s'équilibrer. **2** se solder. **balance sheet** *n* bilan *m*.
balcony ('bælkəni) *n* balcon *m*.
bald (bɔ:ld) *adj* **1** chauve. **2** sec, sèche, plat.
bale[1] (beil) *vt* **bale out** écoper.
bale[2] (beil) *vt* empaqueter.
baleful ('beilfəl) *adj* sinistre, funeste.
ball[1] (bɔ:l) *n* **1** boule *f*. **2** balle *f*. ballon *m*. **3** boulet *m*. **4** pelote *f*. **5** *cul* boulette *f*. **ball-bearing** *n* roulement à bille *m*.
ball[2] (bɔ:l) *n* bal *m*. **ballroom** *n* salle de bal *or* de danse *f*.
ballad ('bæləd) *n* **1** *mus* romance *f*. **2** *lit* ballade *f*.
ballast ('bæləst) *n* **1** *naut* lest *m*. **2** ballast *m*. *vt* **1** lester. **2** empierrer, ballaster.
ballet ('bælei) *n* **1** ballet *m*. **2** corps de ballet *m*.
ballistic (bə'listik) *adj* balistique.
balloon (bə'lu:n) *n* **1** ballon à air *m*. **2** *aviat* ballon, aérostat *m*. *vi* se gonfler.
ballot ('bælət) *n* scrutin, vote *m*. *vi* voter au scrutin. **ballot-box** *n* urne électorale *f*.
Baltic ('bɔ:ltik) *adj* balte. **Baltic (Sea)** *n* (Mer) Baltique *f*.
bamboo (bæm'bu:) *n* bambou *m*.
ban (bæn) *n* **1** ban *m*. proscription *f*. **2** *rel* interdit *m*. *vt* interdire.
banal (bə'nɑ:l) *adj* banal, -aux.
banana (bə'nɑ:nə) *n* banane *f*.
band[1] (bænd) *n* **1** bande, troupe *f*. **2** orchestre *m*. *vt* liguer. *vi* se liguer.
band[2] (bænd) *n* **1** lien *m*. **2** bande *f*. **bandage** *n* bandage, pansement *m*. *vt* bander, panser.
bandit ('bændit) *n* bandit, brigand *m*.
bandy ('bændi) *vt* échanger. *adj* arqué. **bandy-legged** *adj* bancal.
bang (bæŋ) *n* **1** coup *m*. **2** détonation *f*. *interj* pan! *vi,vt* frapper. **bang the door** claquer la porte.
bangle ('bæŋgəl) *n* bracelet *m*.
banish ('bæniʃ) *vt* bannir, exiler. **banishment** *n* bannissement, exil *m*.
banister ('bænistə) *n* rampe *f*.
banjo ('bændʒou) *n* banjo *m*.
bank[1] (bæŋk) *n* **1** talus, remblai *m*. **2** *geog* berge, rive *f*. *vt* endiguer. **bank up** remblayer.
bank[2] (bæŋk) *n* *comm* banque *f*. **bank account** *n* compte en banque *m*. **bankbook** *n* carnet de banque *m*. **bank holiday** *n* jour férié légal *m*. **banknote** *n* billet de banque *m*. ~*vt* déposer en banque. **bank on** compter sur.
bankrupt ('bæŋkrʌpt) *n* banqueroutier *m*. *adj* en faillite, ruiné. **go bankrupt** faire faillite. ~*vt* mettre en faillite.
banner ('bænə) *n* bannière *f*.
banquet ('bæŋkwit) *n* banquet, festin *m*.
baptize (bæp'taiz) *vt* baptiser, surnommer. **baptism** *n* baptême *m*.
bar (bɑ:) *n* **1** bar *m*. **2** barre *f*. **3** *law* barreau, -aux *m*. **4** obstacle *m*. **5** *mus* mesure *f*. **6** tablette *f*. *vt* **1** barrer. **2** interdire. **barmaid** *n* serveuse *f*.
barbarian (bɑ:'bɛəriən) *adj,n* barbare. **barbaric** *adj* barbare, primitif, -ive. **barbarity** *n* barbarie, cruauté *f*. **barbarous** *adj* barbare.
barbecue ('bɑ:bikju:) *n* gril *m*. *vt* rôtir à la broche.
barbed wire (bɑ:bd) *n* fil de fer barbelé *m*.
barber ('bɑ:bə) *n* coiffeur *m*.
barbiturate (bɑ:'bitjurət) *n* barbiturique *m*.
bare (bɛə) *adj* **1** nu, dégarni. **2** sec, sèche, simple. *vt* mettre à nu, révéler. **barefoot** *adv* nu-pieds. **barely** *adv* à peine, tout juste.
bargain ('bɑ:gin) *n* affaire, occasion *f*.
barge (bɑ:dʒ) *n* péniche *f*. chaland *m*. *v* **barge into** bousculer, entrer en coup de vent.
baritone ('bæritoun) *n* baryton *m*.
bark[1] (bɑ:k) *n* aboiement *m*. *vi* aboyer.
bark[2] (bɑ:k) *n* *bot* écorce *f*.
barley ('bɑ:li) *n* orge *f*. **barley-sugar** *n* sucre d'orge *m*. **barley-water** *n* orgeat *m*.
barn (bɑ:n) *n* grange *f*.
barometer (bə'rɔmitə) *n* baromètre *m*.
baron ('bærən) *n* baron *m*. **baroness** *n* baronne *f*. **baronet** *n* baronnet *m*.
barracks ('bærəks) *n pl* caserne *f*.
barrel ('bærəl) *n* **1** tonneau, -aux *m*. **2** caque *f*. **3** cylindre *m*. **4** (of a gun) canon *m*.
barren ('bærən) *adj* stérile, aride.
barricade ('bærikeid) *n* barricade *f*. *vt* barricader.
barrier ('bæriə) *n* **1** barrière *f*. **2** obstacle *m*.
barrister ('bæristə) *n* avocat *m*.
barrow ('bærou) *n* brouette *f*.
barter ('bɑ:tə) *n* troc *m*. *vt* troquer.
base[1] (beis) *n* base *f*. fondement *m*. *vt* fonder. **baseball** *n* base-ball *m*. **basement** *n* **1** sous-sol *m*. **2** soubassement *m*.
base[2] (beis) *adj* vil, bas, basse.
bash (bæʃ) *n* coup *m*. *vt* *inf* taper sur, cogner.
bashful ('bæʃfəl) *adj* timide.

basic ('beisik) *adj* **1** fondamental, -aux. **2** basique.

basil ('bæzəl) *n* basilic *m*.

basin ('beisən) *n* **1** cuvette *f*. **2** *cul* bol *m*. **3** *geog* bassin *m*.

basis ('beisis) *n, pl* **bases** base *f*. fondement *m*.

bask (bɑ:sk) *vi* se chauffer.

basket ('bɑ:skit) *n* panier *m*. corbeille *f*. **basketball** *n* basket-ball *m*.

bass[1] (beis) *n mus* basse *f*.

bass[2] (bæs) *n zool* perche *f*.

bassoon (bə'su:n) *n* basson *m*.

bastard ('bɑ:stəd) *n* bâtard *m*. *adj* bâtard, faux, fausse.

baste ('beist) *vt* **1** arroser. **2** faufiler, bâtir.

bat[1] (bæt) *n* batte *f*. battoir *m*. **batsman** *n* batteur *m*.

bat[2] (bæt) *n zool* chauve-souris *f*.

batch (bætʃ) *n* **1** fournée *f*. **2** tas *m*.

bath (bɑ:θ) *n* **1** bain *m*. **2** baignoire *f*. *vt* baigner. *vi* prendre un bain. **bathrobe** *n* peignoir de bain *m*. **bathroom** *n* salle de bain *f*.

bathe (beið) *vt* baigner. *vi* se baigner. **bathing costume** *n* maillot de bain *m*. **bathing trunks** *n* caleçon de bain *m*.

baton ('bætɔn) *n* **1** bâton *m*. **2** matraque *f*.

battalion (bə'tæliən) *n* bataillon *m*.

batter[1] ('bætə) *vt* **1** battre, rouer de coups. **2** démolir. **battered** *adj* délabré.

batter[2] ('bætə) *n* pâte lisse *f*.

battery ('bætəri) *n* **1** pile *f*. **2** *mil* batterie *f*.

battle ('bætl̩) *n* bataille *f*. combat *m*. *vi* se battre, lutter. **battlefield** *n* champ de bataille *m*. **battleship** *n* cuirassé *m*.

bawl (bɔ:l) *vi,vt* brailler.

bay[1] (bei) *n geog* baie *f*.

bay[2] (bei) *n arch* travée *f*. **bay window** *n* fenêtre en saillie *f*.

bay[3] (bei) *n* abois *m pl*. **keep at bay** tenir en échec. ~*vi* aboyer.

bay[4] (bei) *n bot* laurier *m*.

bayonet ('beiənit) *n* baïonnette *f*.

be* (bi:) *vi* **1** être. **2** se trouver. **3** exister. *v aux* être. **there is** *or* **are** il y a.

beach (bi:tʃ) *n* plage *f*.

beacon ('bi:kən) *n* **1** feu, feux *m*. **2** balise *f*.

bead (bi:d) *n* **1** perle *f*. **2** grain *m*. **3** *pl* chapelet *m*.

beak (bi:k) *n* bec *m*.

beaker ('bi:kə) *n* gobelet *m*.

beam (bi:m) *n* **1** poutre *f*. **2** rayon, faisceau, -aux *m*. *vi* rayonner. **beaming** *adj* radieux, -euse.

bean (bi:n) *n* **1** grain *m*. **2** haricot *m*.

bear*[1] (bɛə) *vt* **1** porter, supporter. **2** produire. **3** donner naissance à. *vi* **1** souffrir. **2** peser. **3** avoir rapport. **bearable** *adj* supportable. **bearing** *n* **1** port, maintien *m*. conduite *f*. **2** rapport *m*. **lose one's bearings** perdre le nord.

bear[2] (bɛə) *n* ours *m*.

beard (biəd) *n* barbe *f*.

beast (bi:st) *n* **1** bête *f*. **2** animal, -aux *m*. brute *f*.

beat* (bi:t) *vt* **1** battre. **2** frapper. *n* **1** battement *m*. **2** ronde *f*. **3** *mus* mesure *f*. **beating** *n* **1** battement *m*. **2** *inf* rossée *f*.

beauty ('bju:ti) *n* beauté *f*. **beautiful** *adj* **1** beau, belle, beaux, magnifique. **2** admirable. **beauty queen** *n* reine de beauté *f*.

beaver ('bi:və) *n* castor *m*.

became (bi'keim) *v* see **become.**

because (bi'kɔ:z) *conj* parce que, car. **because of** à cause de.

beckon ('bekən) *vt* faire signe à. *vi* faire signe.

become* (bi'kʌm) *vi* devenir, se faire. *vt* convenir. **becoming** *adj* **1** convenable. **2** seyant.

bed (bed) *n* **1** lit *m*. **2** parterre *m*. **3** couche *f*. **go to bed** se coucher. **bedclothes** *n pl* couvertures et draps de lit. **bedding** *n* literie *f*. **bedridden** *adj* alité, cloué au lit. **bedroom** *n* chambre (à coucher) *f*. **bedside** *n* chevet *m*. **bed-sitter** *n* chambre-studio *f*. **bedspread** *n* dessus de lit *m*.

bedraggled (bi'drægəld) *adj* dépenaillé.

bee (bi:) *n* abeille *f*. **beehive** *n* ruche *f*. **beekeeper** *n* apiculteur *m*. **beeline** *n* ligne droite *f*.

beech (bi:tʃ) *n* hêtre *m*.

beef (bi:f) *n* bœuf *m*. **roast beef** rosbif *m*.

been (bi:n) *v* see **be.**

beer (biə) *n* bière *f*.

beet (bi:t) *n* betterave *f*. **beetroot** *n* betterave *f*.

beetle ('bi:tl̩) *n* scarabée, coléoptère *m*.

befall* (bi'fɔ:l) *vt* survenir, arriver.

before (bi'fɔ:) *adv* **1** avant, auparavant. **2** devant. *prep* **1** devant. **2** avant. *conj* avant que. **beforehand** *adv* au préalable.

befriend (bi'frend) *vt* venir en aide à.

beg (beg) *vt* demander, prier. *vt,vi* mendier. **I beg your pardon 1** plaît-il? **2** *inf* comment? **beggar** *n* mendiant *m*. **poor beggar!** pauvre type!

begin* (bi'gin) *vt* commencer, entamer. **begin**

to se mettre à. **beginner** *n* débutant, novice *m.* **beginning** *n* commencement, début *m.*
begrudge (biˈgrʌdʒ) *vt* envier. **begrudge doing something** faire quelque chose à contre-cœur.
behalf (biˈhɑːf) *n* **1** sujet *m.* **2** faveur *f.* **on behalf of** au nom de, pour le compte de.
behave (biˈheiv) *vi* se comporter. **behave yourself!** *inf* tiens-toi bien! **badly-behaved** mal élevé. **well-behaved** sage. **behaviour** *n* **1** conduite *f.* **2** tenue *f.* **3** manières *f pl.*
behind (biˈhaind) *adv* derrière, en arrière. *prep* derrière, en arrière de. *n* **1** derrière *m.* **2** *inf* cul *m.* **behindhand** *adj,adv* en retard, en arrière.
behold* (biˈhould) *vt* contempler, regarder.
beige (beiʒ) *adj,n* beige *m.*
being (ˈbiːiŋ) *n* **1** être *m.* **2** existence *f.* **for the time being** pour le moment.
belfry (ˈbelfri) *n* beffroi *m.*
Belgium (ˈbeldʒəm) *n* Belgique *f.* **Belgian** *adj,n* belge.
believe (biˈliːv) *vt,vi* croire. **I believe so** je crois que oui. **make believe** faire semblant. **belief** *n* **1** croyance *f.* **2** confiance *f.* **believable** *adj* croyable. **believer** *n* croyant *m.*
bell (bel) *n* **1** cloche *f.* **2** sonnette *f.* **bellringer** *n* sonneur, carillonneur *m.*
bellow (ˈbelou) *vt,vi* **1** beugler, mugir. **2** vociférer. *n* **1** mugissement *m.* **2** hurlement *m.*
bellows (ˈbelouz) *n pl* soufflet *m.*
belly (ˈbeli) *n* **1** ventre *m.* **2** panse *f.*
belong (biˈlɔŋ) *vi* **1** appartenir. **2** être propre. **belongings** *n pl* effets *m pl.* affaires *f pl.*
below (biˈlou) *adv* **1** en bas, (au-)dessous, ci-dessous. *prep* au-dessous de, sous.
belt (belt) *n* **1** ceinture *f.* **2** *tech* courroie *f.* **3** zone *m.*
bench (bentʃ) *n* **1** banc *m.* **2** établi *m.* **3** *law* tribunal, -aux *m.*
bend* (bend) *vt* plier, courber, fléchir. *vi* **1** se pencher. **2** se soumettre à. *n* **1** virage, tournant *m.* **2** coude *m.* courbe *f.*
beneath (biˈniːθ) *adv* au-dessous, en bas. *prep* sous, au-dessous de.
benefit (ˈbenifit) *n* **1** profit, avantage *m.* **2** bienfait *m.* **3** allocation *f.* *vt* profiter à, faire du bien à. **benefit by** profiter de. **beneficial** *adj* profitable, avantageux, -euse.
benevolent (biˈnevələnt) *adj* **1** bienveillant. **2** charitable.
bent (bent) *v* see **bend.** *adj* **1** courbé. **2** déterminé.
bequeath (biˈkwiːð) *vt* léguer.
bereave* (biˈriːv) *vt* priver. **bereavement** *n* deuil *m.* perte *f.*
berry (ˈberi) n baie *f.*
berth (bəːθ) *n* **1** couchette *f.* **2** *naut* emplacement *m.* *vt* amarrer. *vi* mouiller.
beside (biˈsaid) *prep* **1** à côté de. **2** hors de. **besides** *adv* en outre, de plus.
besiege (biˈsiːdʒ) *vt* assiéger.
best (best) *adj,pron* le meilleur *m.* *adv,n* le mieux *m.* **best man** *n* garçon d'honneur *m.* **best-seller** *n* livre à succès *m.* **do one's best** faire de son mieux. **make the best of** tirer le meilleur parti de.
bestow (biˈstou) *vt* accorder.
bet* (bet) *vt* parier. *n* pari *m.* **betting shop** *n* bureau de pari *m.*
betray (biˈtrei) *vt* **1** trahir. **2** révéler. **betrayal** *n* trahison *f.*
better (ˈbetə) *adj* meilleur. *adv* mieux. **be better 1** aller mieux. **2** valoir mieux. **get better 1** s'améliorer. **2** guérir. **so much the better!** tant mieux! **think better of** se raviser.
between (biˈtwiːn) *prep* entre.
beverage (ˈbevridʒ) *n* boisson *f.*
beware* (biˈwɛə) *vi* prendre garde. **beware of** se méfier de.
bewilder (biˈwildə) *vt* désorienter. **bewildered** *adj* **1** ahuri. **2** abasourdi.
beyond (biˈjɔnd) *adv* au-delà, plus loin. *prep* au-delà de, par-delà, outre. **that is beyond me** cela me dépasse.
bias (ˈbaiəs) *n* **1** parti pris *m.* **2** penchant *m.* **3** biais *m.* *vt* prédisposer. **biased** *adj* partial, -aux.
bib (bib) *n* bavette *f.*
Bible (ˈbaibəl) *n* Bible *f.* **biblical** *adj* biblique.
bibliography (bibliˈɔgrəfi) *n* bibliographie *f.* **bibliographer** *n* bibliographe *m.* **bibliographical** *adj* bibliographique.
biceps (ˈbaiseps) *n* biceps *m.*
bicker (ˈbikə) *vi* se chamailler, se quereller. **bickering** *n* prise de bec *f.* querelles *f pl.*
bicycle (ˈbaisikəl) *n* **1** bicyclette *f.* **2** *inf* vélo *m.*
bid* (bid) *n* **1** offre, soumission *f.* **2** enchère *f.* *vt* **1** ordonner. **2** inviter à. **3** souhaiter. *vi* faire une offre.
biennial (baiˈeniəl) *adj* biennal, -aux.
big (big) *adj* grand, gros, grosse.
bigamy (ˈbigəmi) *n* bigamie *f.*
bigot (bigət) *n* fanatique *m,f.* **bigoted** *adj* à l'esprit étroit.

bikini (bi'ki:ni) *n* bikini *m*.
bilingual (bai'liŋgwəl) *adj* bilingue.
bilious ('biliəs) *adj* **1** bilieux, -euse. **2** colérique.
bill[1] (bil) *n* **1** facture, note, addition *f*. **2** effet *m*. **3** affiche *f*. **4** *pol* projet de loi *m*. **bill-board** *n* panneau d'affichage *m*.
bill[2] (bil) *n zool* bec *m*.
billiards ('biliədz) *n pl* billard *m*.
billion ('biliən) *n* **1** billion *m*. **2** *US* milliard *m*.
bin (bin) *n* coffre *m*. poubelle *f*.
binary ('bainəri) *adj* binaire.
bind* (baind) *vt* **1** lier. **2** attacher. **3** relier. **binding** *n* **1** reliure *f*. **2** ligature *f*. **3** fixation *f*. *adj* obligatoire.
binoculars (bi'nɔkjuləz) *n pl* jumelles *f pl*.
biography (bai'ɔgrəfi) *n* biographie *f*. **biographer** *n* biographe *m*. **biographical** *adj* biographique.
biology (bai'ɔlədʒi) *n* biologie *f*. **biological** *adj* biologique. **biologist** *n* biologiste *m*.
birch (bə:tʃ) *n* bouleau, -aux *m*.
bird (bə:d) *n* **1** oiseau, -aux *m*. **2** *inf* fille *f*. **birdcage** *n* volière, cage d'oiseau *f*. **bird's-eye view** vue à vol d'oiseau *f*.
birth (bə:θ) *n* **1** naissance *f*. **2** *zool* mise bas *f*. **3** origine *f*. **birth certificate** *n* acte de naissance *m*. **birth control** *n* limitation des naissances *f*. **birthday** *n* anniversaire *m*. **birth mark** *n* tache de naissance *f*. **birth rate** *n* natalité *f*.
biscuit ('biskit) *n* biscuit *m*.
bishop ('biʃəp) *n* **1** évêque *m*. **2** *game* fou *m*.
bit[1] (bit) *n* **1** (of a bridle) mors *m*. **2** mèche *f*.
bit[2] (bit) *n* morceau, -aux, bout *m*. *adv* un peu. **bit by bit** petit à petit.
bitch (bitʃ) *n* **1** chienne *f*. **2** femelle *f*. **3** *sl* garce *f*.
bite* (bait) *n* **1** morsure, piqûre *f*. **2** bouchée *f*. *vt* mordre, piquer. **biting** *adj* **1** mordant. **2** perçant.
bitter ('bitə) *adj* amer, -ère, aigre. *n* bière amère *f*. **bitterness** *n* **1** amertume *f*. **2** rancune, rancœur *f*.
bizarre (bi'zɑ:) *adj* bizarre.
black (blæk) *adj,n* noir *m*. *n cap* Noir *m*. **blacken** *vt* noircir *vi* se noircir. **blackness** *n* **1** noirceur *f*. **2** obscurité *f*.
blackberry ('blækbəri) *n* mûre *f*. **blackberry bush** *n* ronce *f*. mûrier *m*.
blackbird ('blækbə:d) *n* merle *m*.
blackboard ('blækbɔ:d) *n* tableau noir *m*.
blackcurrant (blæk'kʌrənt) *n* cassis *m*.
black eye *n* œil poché *m*.
blackleg ('blæklεg) *n* jaune *m*.
blackmail ('blækmeil) *n* chantage *m*. *vt* faire chanter.
black market *n* marché noir *m*.
blackout ('blækaut) *n* **1** blackout *m*. **2** panne d'électricité *f*. **3** *med* évanouissement *m*. *vt* obscurcir. *vi* s'évanouir.
black pudding *n* boudin noir *m*.
blacksmith ('blæksmiθ) *n* forgeron, maréchal ferrant *m*.
bladder ('blædə) *n* vessie *f*. **gall-bladder** *n* vésicule biliaire *f*.
blade (bleid) *n* **1** brin *m*. **2** lame *f*. **3** pale *f*.
blame (bleim) *n* **1** reproches *m pl*. **2** faute *f*. *vt* blâmer.
blancmange (blə'mɔnʒ) *n* blanc-manger *m*.
blank (blæŋk) *adj* **1** blanc, -che, vierge. **2** vide. *n* vide *m*. lacune *f*.
blanket ('blæŋkit) *n* couverture *f*. **wet blanket** trouble-fête *m invar*.
blare (blεə) *vi* sonner. *n* **1** sonnerie *f*. **2** fracas *m*.
blaspheme (blæs'fi:m) *vi,vt* blasphémer. **blasphemy** *n* blasphème *m*.
blast (blɑ:st) *n* **1** bouffée *f*. coup de vent *m*. **2** explosion *f*. **3** coup *m*. *vt* **1** faire sauter. **2** détruire.
blatant ('bleitnt) *adj* **1** criard. **2** criant, flagrant.
blaze (bleiz) *n* **1** feu *m*. flamme *f*. **2** éclat *m*. *vi* **1** flamber. **2** étinceler.
bleach (bli:tʃ) *vt,vi* blanchir. *n* eau de javel *f*.
bleak (bli:k) *adj* **1** désolé, nu. **2** triste, morne.
bleat (bli:t) *vi* bêler. *n* bêlement *m*.
bleed* (bli:d) *vi,vt* saigner. **bleeding** *n* **1** écoulement de sang *m*. **2** *med* saignée *f*.
blemish ('blemiʃ) *n* **1** imperfection *f*. **2** souillure, tache *f*. *vt* **1** tacher. **2** abîmer.
blend (blend) *n* mélange *m*. *vt* mélanger, mêler. *vi* **1** se fondre. **2** aller bien ensemble.
bless (bles) *vt* bénir, consacrer. **blessed** *adj* bienheureux, -euse, saint. **blessing** *n* **1** *rel* bénédiction *f*. **2** bienfait *m*.
blew (blu:) *v* see **blow**[2].
blind (blaind) *adj* **1** aveugle. **2** sans issue. *n* store *m*. abat-jour *m invar*. *vt* aveugler, éblouir. **blindfold** *adj,adv* les yeux bandés. *vt* bander les yeux à. **blindness** *n* cécité *f*.
blink (bliŋk) *vi* clignoter. *n* battement de paupières *m*. **blinker** *n* œillère *f*.
bliss (blis) *n* félicité *f*. **blissful** *adj* heureux, -euse, serein.
blister ('blistə) *n* **1** *med* ampoule *f*. vésicatoire

m. **2** cloque *f.* *vi* **1** se couvrir d'ampoules. **2** se cloquer.

blizzard ('blizəd) *n* tempête de neige *f.*

blob (blɔb) *n* tache *f.* pâté *m.*

bloc (blɔk) *n* bloc *m.*

block (blɔk) *n* **1** bloc *m.* **2** billot *m.* **3** obstacle *m.* **block of flats** immeuble *m.* ~*vt* obstruer, bloquer. **block up** boucher.

blockade (blɔ'keid) *n* blocus *m.* *vt* bloquer.

bloke (blouk) *n inf* type, mec *m.*

blond (blɔnd) *adj* blond. **blonde** *adj,n* blonde *f.*

blood (blʌd) *n* sang *m.* **bloodcurdling** *adj* à vous figer le sang. **blood pressure** *n* tension artérielle *f.* **bloodshot** *adj* injecté de sang. **bloodstream** *n* sang, flot sanguin *m.* **bloodthirsty** *adj* sanguinaire, avide de sang. **bloody** *adj* **1** ensanglanté. **2** *sl* sacré.

bloom (blu:m) *n* fleur, floraison *f.* *vi* **1** fleurir. **2** resplendir. **blooming** *adj* **1** en fleur. **2** florissant.

blossom ('blɔsəm) *n* fleur *f.* *vi* fleurir.

blot (blɔt) *n* **1** tache *f.* **2** pâté *m.* *vt* **1** tacher. **2** sécher. **blotting paper** *n* papier buvard *m.*

blouse (blauz) *n* blouse *f.* chemisier *m.*

blow[1] (blou) *n* coup *m.*

blow*[2] (blou) *vt,vi* souffler. *vt* sonner. **blow away** emporter. **blow one's nose** se moucher. **blow up** **1** éclater. **2** faire sauter. **3** gonfler.

blubber ('blʌbə) *n* graisse de baleine *f.*

blue (blu:) *adj* **1** bleu. **2** triste. **3** grivois. *n* bleu *m.* **bluebell** *n* jacinthe des prés *f.*

bluff (blʌf) *n* bluff *m.* *vt* bluffer.

blunder ('blʌndə) *n* bévue *f.* *vi* gaffer, faire une gaffe.

blunt (blʌnt) *adj* **1** émoussé. **2** épointé. **3** obtus. **4** brusque. *vt* émousser.

blur (blə:) *vt* **1** brouiller. **2** obscurcir. *n* **1** tache *f.* **2** brouillard *m.* **blurred** *adj* flou, confus.

blush (blʌʃ) *n* rougeur *f.* *vi* rougir.

boar (bɔ:) *n* verrat *m.* **wild boar** *n* sanglier *m.*

board (bɔ:d) *n* **1** planche *f.* **2** tableau, -aux *m.* **3** table, pension *f.* **4** *naut* bord *m.* **5** conseil *m.* **6** carton *m.* *vi* être en pension. *vt* monter dans, aborder. **boarder** *n* pensionnaire *m,f.* **boarding house** *n* pension de famille *f.* **boarding school** *n* pensionnat *m.*

boast (boust) *vi* se vanter. *n* vanterie *f.*

boat (bout) *n* bateau, -aux *m.* barque *f.* navire *m.*

bob (bɔb) *vt* **1** écourter. **2** secouer. *vi* s'agiter.

bodice ('bɔdis) *n* corsage *m.*

body ('bɔdi) *n* **1** corps *m.* **2** carrosserie *f.* **3** organisme *m.* **4** consistance *f.* **bodyguard** *n* gorille, garde du corps *m.*

bog (bɔg) *n* marais *m.* fondrière *f.* **boggy** *adj* marécageux, -euse.

bohemian (bə'hi:miən) *adj,n* **1** bohémien, -ienne. **2** bohème.

boil[1] (bɔil) *vi* bouillir. *vt* **1** faire bouillir. **2** cuire à l'eau. **boil down** se réduire. **boil over** déborder. **boiler** *n* chaudière *f.* **boiling** *adj* bouillant, en ébullition.

boil[2] (bɔil) *n med* furoncle *m.*

boisterous ('bɔistərəs) *adj* **1** turbulent. **2** tumultueux, -euse.

bold (bould) *adj* **1** hardi, audacieux, -euse. **2** effronté. **boldness** *n* **1** hardiesse, audace *f.* **2** impudence *f.*

bolster ('boulstə) *n* traversin *m.* *vt* **1** rembourrer. **2** soutenir, étayer.

bolt (boult) *n* **1** verrou, -oux *m.* **2** boulon *m.* *vt* **1** verrouiller. **2** avaler. *vi* décamper.

bomb (bɔm) *n* bombe *f.* *vt* bombarder. **bombshell** *n* **1** obus *m.* **2** grande surprise *f.* **bombard** *vt* **1** bombarder. **2** assaillir.

bond (bɔnd) *n* **1** lien *m.* attache *f.* **2** obligation *f.* bon *m.* **3** dépôt, entrepôt douanier *m.* **bondage** *n* servitude *f.*

bone (boun) *n* **1** os *m.* **2** (of fish) arête *f.* **3** *pl* ossements *m pl.* *vt* désosser. **bone-dry** *adj* archisec, archisèche. **bony** *adj* **1** osseux, -euse. **2** plein d'os.

bonfire ('bɔnfaiə) *n* feu de joie *m.*

bonnet ('bɔnit) *n* **1** bonnet, béret *m.* **2** capot *m.*

bonus ('bounəs) *n* gratification, prime, indemnité *f.*

booby trap ('bu:bi) *n* attrape-nigaud *f.*

book (buk) *n* **1** livre *m.* **2** *inf* bouquin *m.* **3** registre *m.* **4** (of tickets) carnet *m.* *vt* **1** inscrire. **2** retenir. **3** *sl law* dresser procès-verbal. **bookcase** *n* bibliothèque *f.* **bookkeeping** comptabilité *f.* **bookmaker** *n* bookmaker *m.* **bookseller** *n* libraire *m.* **bookshop** *n* librairie *f.* **bookstall** *n* **1** étalage de librairie *m.* **2** kiosque à livres *m.* **booking** *n* **1** réservation *f.* **2** enregistrement *m.* **booking office** *n* **1** guichet *m.* **2** bureau de location *m.* **booklet** *n* livret, fascicule *m.*

boom (bu:m) *n* **1** grondement *m.* **2** *comm* essor *m.* hausse *f.* *vi* **1** gronder. **2** *comm* être en hausse.

boost (bu:st) *vt* **1** faire de la réclame. **2** augmenter. **3** survolter. *n* poussée *f.* coup de pouce *m.*

boot (bu:t) *n* **1** botte *f.* **2** bottine, chaussure *f.* **3** *mot* coffre *m.*
booth (bu:θ) *n* **1** loge *f.* **2** cabine *f.*
booze (bu:z) *n inf* boisson alcoolique *f.* *vi inf* picoler.
border ('bɔ:də) *n* **1** bordure *f.* bord *m.* **2** frontière *f.* *vt* border. **border on** confiner à. **borderline** *n* ligne de démarcation *f.* **borderline case** *n* cas limite *m.*
bore[1] (bɔ:) *vt* **1** forer, percer. **2** sonder. *n* **1** calibre *m.* **2** sondage *m.*
bore[2] (bɔ:) *vt* ennuyer. *n* **1** raseur *m.* **2** ennui *m.* **boredom** *n* ennui *m.* **boring** *adj* ennuyeux, -euse, assommant.
bore[3] (bɔ:) *v* see **bear.**
born (bɔ:n) *adj* né, de naissance. **be born** naître.
borough ('bʌrə) *n* **1** circonscription électorale *f.* **2** ville *f.*
borrow ('bɔrou) *vt* emprunter.
bosom ('buzəm) *n* **1** sein *m.* **2** giron, cœur *m.* **bosom friend** *n* ami intime *m.*
boss (bɔs) *n* patron, chef *m.* *vt* diriger, mener. **bossy** *adj* autoritaire.
botany ('bɔtəni) *n* botanique *f.* **botanical** *adj* botanique. **botanist** *n* botaniste *m,f.*
botch (bɔtʃ) *vt* bousiller, saboter. **botch up** rafistoler.
both (bouθ) *adj,pron* tous les deux, tous deux. *conj* à la fois.
bother ('bɔðə) *n* ennui, tracas *m.* *vt* **1** gêner, ennuyer. **2** soucier. *vi* se tracasser.
bottle ('bɔtl̩) *n* bouteille *f.* flacon *m.* **bottleneck** *n* **1** goulot d'étranglement *m.* **2** embouteillage *m.* ~*vt* mettre en bouteilles. **bottle up** ravaler, étouffer.
bottom ('bɔtəm) *n* **1** fond *m.* **2** bas *m.* **3** derrière *m.* **4** base *f.* *adj* **1** inférieur. **2** du bas. **bottomless** *adj* **1** insondable. **2** sans fond.
bought (bɔ:t) *v* see **buy.**
boulder ('bouldə) *n* galet *m.* grosse pierre *f.*
bounce (bauns) *vi* rebondir. *vt* faire rebondir. *n* bond *m.* **bouncing** *adj* rebondissant.
bound[1] (baund) *v* see **bind.**
bound[2] (baund) *n* bond, saut *m.* *vi* bondir.
bound[3] (baund) *n* limite, borne *f.* *vt* borner. **boundary** *n* bornes *f pl.* frontière *f.*
bound[4] (baund) *adj* **bound for** en partance pour, à destination de.
boundary ('baundri) *n* bornes *f pl.* frontière *f.*
bouquet (bu'kei) *n* bouquet *m.*
bourgeois ('buəʒwa:) *adj,n* bourgeois.
bout (baut) *n* **1** *med* accès *m.* attaque *f.* **2** coup *m.* **3** partie *f.* **4** assaut *m.*
bow[1] (bau) *vt* courber, incliner. *vi* s'incliner, baisser la tête. *n* salut *m.*
bow[2] (bou) *n* **1** *sport* arc *m.* **2** *mus* archet *m.* **3** nœud *m.* **bow-legged** *adj* bancal.
bow[3] (bau) *n naut* avant *m.* proue *f.*
bowels ('bauəlz) *n pl* **1** intestins *m pl.* **2** *inf* entrailles *f pl.*
bowl[1] (boul) *n* **1** bol *m.* **2** bassin *m.* **bowler hat** *n* chapeau melon *m.*
bowl[2] (boul) *vt* rouler. *vi* servir la balle. *n* **1** boule *f.* **2** *pl* boules *f pl.* pétanque *f.*
box[1] (bɔks) *n* **1** boîte, caisse *f.* coffret *m.* **2** *Th* cabine, loge *f.* **box number** *n* boîte postale *f.* **box office** *n* **1** bureau de location *m.* **2** guichet *m.*
box[2] (bɔks) *vt* gifler, boxer. *n* gifle *f.* **boxer** *n* boxeur, pugiliste *m.* **boxing** *n* boxe *f.*
Boxing Day *n* lendemain de Noël *m.*
boy (bɔi) *n* **1** garçon, fils *m.* **2** *inf* gars *m.* **3** élève *m.* **boyfriend** *n* (petit) ami *m.* **boyhood** *n* enfance, adolescence *f.*
boycott ('bɔikɔt) *vt* boycotter. *n* boycottage *m.*
bra (bra:) *n* soutien-gorge *m invar.*
brace (breis) *n* **1** paire, couple *f.* **2** attache *f.* **3** *pl* bretelles *f pl.* **4** *tech* vilebrequin *m.* *vt* **1** fortifier. **2** lier.
bracelet ('breislət) *n* bracelet *m.*
bracket ('brækit) *n* **1** support *m.* **2** applique *f.* **3** *gram* parenthèse *f.* *vt* **1** mettre entre parenthèses. **2** accolader.
brag (bræg) *vi* se vanter.
braid (breid) *n* tresse *f.* galon *m.*
Braille (breil) *n* Braille *m.*
brain (brein) *n* **1** cerveau, -aux *m.* **2** cervelle *f.* **brainwash** *vt* endoctriner. **brainwave** *n* idée lumineuse *f.* **brainy** *adj inf* intelligent.
braise (breiz) *vt* braiser.
brake (breik) *n* frein *m.* *vt* freiner, ralentir.
branch (bra:ntʃ) *n* **1** branche *f.* **2** embranchement *m.* **3** *comm* succursale *f.* **4** secteur *m.* *v* **branch off** bifurquer. **branch out** se ramifier, se diversifier.
brand (brænd) *n* **1** brandon *m.* **2** fer chaud *m.* **3** stigmate *m.* **4** *comm* marque *f.* *vt* **1** marquer. **2** graver. **3** stigmatiser. **brand-new** *adj* tout neuf.
brandish ('brændiʃ) *vt* brandir.
brandy ('brændi) *n* eau-de-vie *f.* cognac *m.*
brass (bra:s) *n* cuivre jaune, laiton *m.* *adj* de cuivre. **brass band** *n* fanfare *f.*
brassiere ('bræziə) *n* soutien-gorge *m invar.*

brat (bræt) *n sl* gosse, môme *m,f.*

brave (breiv) courageux, -euse, brave. *vt* braver, affronter.

brawl (brɔ:l) *n* rixe *f.* tapage *m. vi* **1** chamailler. **2** brailler.

bray (brei) *vi* braire. *n* braiment *m.*

brazen (ˈbreizən) *adj* **1** d'airain. **2** *inf* effronté, impudent.

Brazil (brəˈzil) *n* Brésil *m.* **Brazilian** *adj,n* brésilien, -ienne.

breach (bri:tʃ) *n* **1** infraction *f.* manque *m.* **2** rupture *f.* **3** brèche *f.* **breach of the peace** attentat contre l'ordre public *m.*

bread (bred) *n* **1** pain *m.* **2** *sl* du fric. **breadcrumb** *n* chapelure *f.* **breadknife** *n* couteau à pain *m.* **breadwinner** *n* chef de famille *m.* gagne-pain *m invar.* **loaf of bread** pain *m.* **wholemeal bread** pain complet.

breadth (bredθ) *n* largeur *f.*

break* (breik) *vt* **1** casser, rompre, briser. **2** amortir. **3** violer, manquer à. **4** ruiner. **break into** s'introduire par effraction. **break out 1** se déclarer. **2** s'échapper. **break up 1** se disperser. **2** morceler. ~*n* **1** rupture *f.* **2** brèche *f.* **3** altération *f.* **4** interruption *f.* **5** répit *m.* **breakage** *n* **1** casse *f.* **2** rupture *f.* **breakdown** *n* **1** *mot* panne *f.* **2** rupture *f.* **3** effondrement *m.* **4** *med* dépression nerveuse *f.* **breakthrough** *n* **1** découverte *f.* pas en avant *m.* **2** *mil* percée *f.*

breakfast (ˈbrekfəst) *n* petit déjeuner *m. vi* prendre le petit déjeuner.

breast (brest) *n* sein *m.* poitrine *f.* **breastbone** *n* sternum, bréchet *m.* **breaststroke** *n* brasse *f.*

breath (breθ) *n* haleine *f.* souffle *m.* **out of breath** essoufflé. **breathtaking** *adj* **1** à vous couper le souffle. **2** ahurissant.

breathe (bri:ð) *vt,vi* respirer. *vi* souffler. **breathe in/out** aspirer/exhaler. **breathing** *n* respiration *f.* **breathing space** *n* répit *m.*

breed* (bri:d) *n* race, espèce *f. vt* **1** produire, engendrer. **2** élever. *vi* se reproduire.

breeze (bri:z) *n* brise *f.*

Breton (ˈbretn̩) *adj,n* breton, -onne. **Breton** (language) *n* breton *m.*

brew (bru:) *vt* **1** brasser. **2** faire infuser. *vi* **1** s'infuser. **2** se préparer. *n* **1** infusion *f.* **2** brassage *m.* **brewery** *n* brasserie *f.*

bribe (braib) *n* **1** paiement illicite. **2** *inf* pot-de-vin *m. vt* corrompre, acheter. **bribery** *n* corruption *f.*

brick (brik) *n* **1** brique *f.* **2** *inf* chic type *m.* **bricklayer** *n* maçon *m.*

bride (braid) *n* fiancée, mariée *f.* **bridegroom** *n* nouveau marié *m.* **bridesmaid** *n* demoiselle d'honneur *f.*

bridge[1] (bridʒ) *n* **1** pont *m.* **2** *naut* passerelle *f.* **3** *anat* dos *m.* arête *f. v* **bridge a gap** combler une lacune.

bridge[2] (bridʒ) *n game* bridge *m.* **game of bridge** partie de bridge *f.*

bridle (ˈbraidl̩) *n* bridle *f.* **bridlepath** *n* sentier pour cavaliers *m.* piste cavalière *f.*

brief (bri:f) *adj* bref, brève, succinct. *n* **1** dossier *m.* **2** résumé *m. vt* documenter. **briefing** *n* instructions *f pl.* **briefcase** *n* serviette *f.*

brigade (briˈgeid) *n* brigade *f.* **brigadier** *n* général de brigade *m.*

bright (brait) *adj* **1** lumineux, -euse, brillant. **2** vif, vive, éveillé. **3** intelligent. **brighten** *vt* faire briller. *vi* **1** s'éclaircir. **2** s'épanouir. **brightness** *n* **1** éclat *m.* **2** clarté *f.* **3** vivacité *f.*

brilliant (ˈbriliənt) *adj* brillant. **brilliance** *n* éclat, lustre *m.*

brim (brim) *n* bord *m.* **to the brim** à ras bord. ~*v* **brim over** déborder.

bring* (briŋ) *vt* **1** amener, apporter. **2** mettre. **3** porter. **bring about** occasionner, aménager. **bring back** rapporter. **bring in 1** faire entrer. **2** *comm* rapporter. **bring out 1** faire sortir. **2** mettre en évidence, faire valoir. **bring round 1** ranimer. **2** rallier. **bring together** réunir. **bring up 1** élever. **2** soulever. **3** apporter. **4** vomir.

brink (briŋk) *n* bord *m.*

brisk (brisk) *adj* vif, vive, alerte, animé.

bristle (ˈbrisəl) *n* soie *f.* poil *m. vt* hérisser.

Britain (ˈbritn̩) *n* Grande-Bretagne *f.* **British** *adj* britannique. **British Isles** *n pl* Iles Britanniques *m pl.* **Briton** *n* anglais *m.*

Brittany (ˈbritəni) *n* Bretagne *f.*

brittle (ˈbritl̩) *adj* cassant, fragile.

broad (brɔ:d) *adj* **1** large. **2** (of an accent) prononcé. **3** hardi. **broad bean** *n* fève *f.* **broadcast** *n* émission, transmission radiodiffusée *f. vt* **1** radiodiffuser. **2** annoncer à la radio. **broad-minded** *adj* tolérant. **broaden** *vt* élargir. *vi* s'élargir. **broadness** *n* largeur *f.*

broccoli (ˈbrɔkəli) *n* brocoli *m.*

brochure (ˈbrouʃə) *n* brochure *f.*

broke (brouk) *v* see **break.** *adj inf* fauché, sans le sou.

broken (ˈbroukən) *v* see **break.**

broker ('broukə) *n* courtier *m.* **stock-broker** *n* agent de change *m.*
bronchitis (brɔŋ'kaitis) *n* bronchite *f.*
bronze (brɔnz) *n* bronze *m. adj* de bronze. *vt* bronzer. *vi* se bronzer.
brooch (broutʃ) *n* broche *f.*
brood (bru:d) *n* **1** couvée *f.* **2** *inf* marmaille. *vi* couver. **brood over** ressasser, ruminer.
brook (bruk) *n* ruisseau, -aux *m.*
broom (bru:m) *n* **1** balai *m.* **2** *bot* genêt *m.*
brothel ('brɔðəl) *n* bordel *m.*
brother ('brʌðə) *n* frère *m.* **brother-in-law** *n* beau-frère *m.* **brotherhood** *n* **1** fraternité *f.* **2** *rel* confrérie *f.*
brow (brau) *n* **1** sourcil *m.* **2** front *m.* **3** *geog* sommet *m.*
brown (braun) *adj* **1** brun, marron. **2** bronzé. *vt* **1** brunir. **2** *cul* faire roussir. *vi* (se) brunir. **be browned off** avoir le cafard.
browse (brauz) *vt* brouter. *vi* bouquiner.
bruise (bru:z) *n* contusion *f.* bleu *m. vt* meurtrir.
brunette (bru:'net) *n* brunette *f.*
brush (brʌʃ) *n* **1** brosse *f.* **2** *Art* pinceau, -aux *m.* **3** coup de brosse *m.* **4** escarmouche *f. vt* **1** brosser. **2** effleurer, frôler. **brush up 1** brosser. **2** rafraîchir, dérouiller.
brusque (bru:sk) *adj* brusque, bourru.
Brussels ('brʌsəlz) *n* Bruxelles *f.* **Brussels sprout** *n* chou de Bruxelles *m.*
brute (bru:t) *n* brute *f.* animal, -aux *m. adj* brut, brutal, -aux. **brutal** *adj* brutal, -aux, animal, -aux.
bubble ('bʌbəl) *n* bulle *f. vi* **1** bouillonner. **2** pétiller.
buck[1] (bʌk) *n* **1** daim, chevreuil *m.* **2** mâle *m.*
buck[2] (bʌk) *vi* se cabrer. **buck someone off** désarçonner quelqu'un.
bucket ('bʌkit) *n* **1** seau, -aux *m.* **2** godet *m.*
buckle ('bʌkəl) *n* boucle *f. vt* **1** boucler. **2** *tech* déjeter, voiler. *vi* se déformer.
bud (bʌd) *n* **1** bourgeon *m.* **2** bouton *m. vi* bourgeonner. **budding** *adj* **1** en bouton. **2** en herbe.
Buddhism ('budizəm) *n* bouddhisme *m.* **Buddhist** *n* bouddhiste *m,f. adj* bouddhique.
budget ('bʌdʒit) *n* budget *m.*
buffalo ('bʌfəlou) *n pl* **-os** *or* **-oes** buffle *m.*
buffer ('bʌfə) *n* **1** tampon. **2** amortisseur *m.*
buffet[1] ('bʌfit) *n* coup *m vt* souffleter. *vi* se battre à coups de poing.
buffet[2] ('bufei)) *n* buffet *m.*
bug (bʌg) *n* punaise *f.*
bugle ('bju:gəl) *n* clairon *m.*
build* (bild) *vt* **1** bâtir, construire. **2** échafauder. **3** fonder. *n* carrure, stature *f.* **builder** *n* entrepreneur *m.* **building** *n* **1** construction *f.* **2** bâtiment *m. adj* de construction, à bâtir. **building society** *n* société immobilière *f.*
bulb (bʌlb) *n* **1** *bot* bulbe, oignon *m.* **2** ampoule, lampe *f.*
Bulgaria (bʌl'gɛəriə) *n.* Bulgarie *f.* **Bulgarian** *adj,n* bulgare.
bulge (bʌldʒ) *n* renflement *m.* bosse *f. vi* faire saillie, ballonner.
bulk (bʌlk) *n* **1** charge *f.* **2** grosseur *f.* volume *m.* **in bulk** en gros, en vrac.
bull (bul) *n* **1** taureau, -aux *m.* **2** mâle *m.* **bulldog** *n* bouledogue *m.* **bulldoze** *vt* **1** intimider, menacer. **2** passer au bulldozer. **bulldozer** *n* bulldozer *m.* **bullfight** *n* corrida *f.* **bullring** *n* arène *f.* **bull's eye** *n* mouche *f.* noir *m.*
bullet ('bulit) *n* balle *f.* **bullet-proof** *adj* à l'épreuve des balles, blindé.
bulletin ('bulətin) *n* bulletin, communiqué *m.* **news bulletin** informations *f pl.*
bully ('buli) *n* **1** brute *f.* tyran *m.* **2** bravache *m. vt* malmener.
bumble bee ('bʌmbəl) *n* bourdon *m.*
bump (bʌmp) *n* **1** choc *m.* secousse *f.* **2** bosse *f. vt* cogner. **bump into 1** entrer en collision avec. **2** *inf* rencontrer. **bumper** *n* pare-chocs *m invar. adj inf* magnifique, comble.
bun (bʌn) *n* **1** *cul* petit pain *m.* brioche *f.* **2** chignon *m*
bunch (bʌntʃ) *n* **1** bouquet *m.* grappe *f.* **2** touffe *f.* **3** groupe *m. vt* réunir.
bundle ('bʌndḷ) *n* **1** ballot, paquet *m.* **2** liasse *f. vt* botteler, entasser.
bungalow ('bʌŋgəlou) *n* bungalow *m.*
bungle ('bʌŋgəl) *n* gâchis *m. vt* bousiller, gâcher. **bungling** *adj* maladroit.
bunk (bʌŋk) *n* couchette *f.*
bunker ('bʌŋkə) *n* **1** soute *f.* **2** *sport* banquette *f.*
buoy (bɔi) *n* bouée, balise flottante *f.* **buoyancy** *n* **1** flottabilité *f.* **2** *inf* entrain *m.* **buoyant** *adj* **1** flottable, léger, -ère. **2** vif, vive.
burden ('bə:dṇ) *n* fardeau, -aux *m.* charge *f. vt* **1** charger. **2** être un fardeau pour.
bureau ('bjuərou) *n* **1** bureau, -aux *m.* **2** secrétaire *m.*
bureaucracy (bju'rɔkrəsi) *n* bureaucratie *f.* **bureaucrat** *n* **1** bureaucrate *m,f.* **2** *inf* rond-de-cuir *m.*
burglar ('bə:glə) *n* cambrioleur *m.* **burglar**

alarm *n* sonnerie d'alarme *f*. **burglary** *n* vol avec effraction, cambriolage *m*. **burgle** *vt* cambrioler, dévaliser.

burn* (bə:n) *vt* **1** brûler. **2** incendier. *vi* flamber. *n* brûlure *f*. **burning** *adj* brûlant, ardent.

burrow ('bʌrou) *n* terrier *m*. *vt* creuser. *vi* se terrer.

burst* (bə:st) *vi* éclater, crever. *vt* faire éclater, fendre. **burst in** faire irruption. ~*n* **1** éclatement *m*. explosion *f*. **2** élan *m*. **bursting** *adj* **1** sur le point d'éclater. **2** débordant.

bury ('beri) *vt* enterrer. **burial** *n* enterrement *m*. **burial ground** *n* cimetière *m*.

bus (bʌs) *n* autobus, bus, car *m*. **bus-stop** *n* arrêt du bus *m*.

bush (buʃ) *n* **1** buisson *m*. **2** arbuste *m*. **3** brousse *f*.

bushy ('buʃi:) *adj* **1** touffu. **2** broussailleux, -euse.

business ('biznis) *n* **1** affaire, occupation *f*. **2** affaires *f pl*. **3** commerce *m*. **set up in business** s'établir. **businessman** *n* homme d'affaires *m*.

bust[1] (bʌst) *n* **1** *Art* buste *m*. **2** *anat* poitrine *f*.

bust[2] (bʌst) *vi inf* éclater. **go bust** faire faillite.

bustle ('bʌsəl) *n* agitation *f*. mouvement *m*. *vi* se remuer, s'affairer. *vt* faire dépêcher.

busy ('bizi) *adj* affairé, occupé. **busybody** *n* officieux, -euse. **busy oneself with** s'occuper à.

but (bət; *stressed* bʌt) *conj* **1** mais. **2** sauf que. *adv* ne...que, seulement. *prep* excepté, sinon. **but for** sans.

butcher ('butʃə) *n* boucher *m*. *vt* égorger. **butcher's shop** *n* boucherie *f*. **butchery** *n* carnage *m*.

butler ('bʌtlə) *n* **1** maître d'hôtel *m*. **2** sommelier *m*.

butt[1] (bʌt) *n* **1** bout *m*. **2** crosse *f*. **3** mégot *m*.

butt[2] (bʌt) *n* souffre-douleur *m invar*.

butt[3] (bʌt) *vt* donner des coups de corne à, buter. **butt in** *inf* intervenir sans façon, s'ingérer. ~*n* coup de tête *or* corne *m*.

butter ('bʌtə) *n* beurre *m*. *vt* beurrer. **buttercup** *n* **1** renoncule *f*. **2** *inf* bouton d'or *m*. **butter-fingers** *n inf* maladroit. **butterfly** *n* papillon *m*. **butterscotch** *n* caramel dur au beurre *m*.

buttocks ('bʌtəks) *n pl* **1** *anat* derrière *m*. fesses *f pl*. **2** *zool* croupe *f*.

button ('bʌtn̩) *n* bouton *m*. *vt* boutonner. **buttonhole** *n* boutonnière *f*. *vt inf* attraper, cramponner.

buttress ('bʌtrəs) *n* arc-boutant *m*.

buy* (bai) *vt* acheter. **buy up** accaparer. ~*n* affaire *f*. achat *m*. **buyer** *n* **1** acheteur, -euse. **2** *comm* chef de rayon *m*.

buzz (bʌz) *n* **1** bourdonnement, vrombissement *m*. **2** bruit confus, brouhaha *m*. *vi* bourdonner.

by (bai) *prep* **1** près de, à côté de. **2** au bord de. **3** par. **4** de. **5** à. **6** sur. *adv* **1** près. **2** de côté. **by and by** tout à l'heure. **by-election** *n* élection partielle *f*. **bylaw** *n* arrêté municipal, -aux *m*. **bypass** *n* route d'évitement *f*. détour *m*. *vt* contourner, éviter. **bystander** *n* spectateur, -trice.

Byzantine (bi'zæntain, bai-) *adj,n* byzantin.

C

cab (kæb) **1** fiacre *m*. **2** taxi *m*. **3** (of a lorry, etc.) cabine *f*.

cabaret ('kæbərei) *n* **1** cabaret, café-concert *m*. **2** spectacle au cabaret *m*.

cabbage ('kæbidʒ) *n* chou, choux *m*.

cabin ('kæbin) *n* **1** cabine *f*. **2** cabane *f*. **cabin cruiser** *n* yacht à moteur *m*.

cabinet ('kæbinət) *n* cabinet *m*. **cabinet-maker** *n* ébéniste *m*. **cabinet minister** *n* ministre d'état.

cable ('keibəl) *n* câble *m*. *vt* câbler.

cackle ('kækəl) *n* caquet *m*. *vt* **1** caqueter. **2** ricaner.

cactus ('kæktəs) *n*, *pl* **-ti** *or* **-tuses** cactus *m*.

cadence ('keidn̩s) *n* cadence *f*.

cadet (kə'det) *n* cadet *m*.

cafe ('kæfei) *n* café(-restaurant) *m*.

cafeteria (kæfi'tiəriə) *n* cafétéria *f*. libre-service *m*.

caffeine ('kæfi:n) *n* caféine *f*.

cage (keidʒ) *n* cage *f*.

cake (keik) *n* **1** *cul* gâteau, -aux *m*. **2** pain, bloc, morceau, -aux *m*. *vi* se cailler.

calamity (kə'læməti) *n* calamité *f*. désastre *m*.

calcium ('kælsiəm) *n* calcium *m*.

calculate ('kælkjuleit) *vt,vi* calculer. *vt* combiner. *vi* compter. **calculation** *n* calcul *m*. **calculator** *n* machine à calculer *f*.

calendar ('kælində) *n* calendrier *m*.

calf[1] (kɑ:f) *n*, *pl* **calves** *zool* veau, -aux *m*.

calf[2] (kɑ:f) *n*, *pl* **calves** *anat* mollet *m*.

calibre ('kælibə) *n* calibre *m*.

call (kɔ:l) *vt* **1** appeler. **2** convoquer. **call for** demander. **call on** passer chez. **call off** décommander. **call out** appeler. ~*n* **1** appel, cri *m*. **2** visite *f*. **3** demande *f*. **4** *naut* escale *f*. **callbox** *n* taxiphone *m*. cabine téléphonique *f*.

callous ('kæləs) *adj* endurci, insensible.

calm (kɑ:m) *adj,n* calme *m*. *vt* calmer. **calm down** se calmer.

calorie ('kæləri) *n* calorie *f*.

Cambodia (kæm'boudiə) *n* Cambodge *m*. **Cambodian** *adj,n* cambodgien, -ienne.

came (keim) *v* see **come.**

camel ('kæməl) *n* chameau, -aux *m*. chamelle *f*. **camelhair** *n* poil de chameau *m*.

camera ('kæmrə) *n* appareil photographique *m*. **cameraman** *n* **1** photographe *m*. **2** opérateur *m*.

camouflage ('kæməflɑ:ʒ) *n* camouflage *m*. *vt* camoufler.

camp[1] (kæmp) *vt,vi* camper. *n* camp *m*. **camp-bed** *n* lit de camp *m*. **camping** *n* camping *m*. **camping site** *n* terrain de camping *m*.

camp[2] (kæmp) *adj* **1** exagéré, affecté. **2** efféminé. **3** *inf* homosexuel, -elle.

campaign (kæm'pein) *n* campagne *f*. *vi* faire campagne.

campus ('kæmpəs) *n* campus *m*.

can*[1] (kæn) *v mod aux* **1** pouvoir. **2** savoir.

can[2] (kæn) *n* **1** bidon, pot *m*. **2** boîte *f*. *vt* mettre en boîte.

Canada ('kænədə) *n* Canada *m*. **Canadian** *adj,n* canadien, -ienne.

canal (kə'næl) *n* canal, -aux *m*.

canary (kə'nɛəri) *n* serin *m*.

Canary Islands *n* îles Canaries *f pl*.

cancel ('kænsəl) *vt* annuler. **cancellation** *n* **1** annulation *f*. **2** contre-ordre *m*.

cancer ('kænsə) *n* **1** cancer *m*. **2** *cap* Cancer *m*.

candid ('kændid) *adj* **1** franc, franche. **2** impartial, -aux.

candidate ('kændidət) *n* candidat *m*.

candle ('kændḷ) *n* bougie *f*. **candlelight** *n* lumière d'une chandelle *f*. **candlestick** *n* chandelier, bougeoir *m*.

candour ('kændə) *n* **1** franchise *f*. **2** impartialité *f*.

cane ('kein) *n* canne *f*. *vt* **1** fouetter. **2** canner.

canine ('keinain) *adj* canin. *n* (tooth) canine *f*.

cannabis ('kænəbis) *n* chanvre indien *m*.

cannibal ('kænəbəl) *adj,n* cannibale. **cannibalism** *n* cannibalisme *m*.

cannon ('kænən) *n* canon *m*. **cannonball** *n* boulet de canon *m*.

cannot ('kænət) contraction of **can not.**

canoe (kə'nu:) *n* canoë *m*. périssoire *f*.

canon[1] ('kænən) *n* (law) canon *m*. règle *f*. **canonical** *adj* canonique, canonial, -aux. **canonize** *vt* canoniser. **canonization** *n* canonisation *f*.

canon[2] ('kænən) *n* (title) chanoine *m*.

canopy ('kænəpi) *n* dais *m*.

canteen (kæn'ti:n) *n* **1** cantine *f*. **2** *mil* bidon *m*. **canteen (of cutlery)** ménagère *f*.

canter ('kæntə) *n* petit galop *m*. *vi* aller au petit galop.

canton ('kæntɔn) *n* canton *m*.

canvas ('kænvəs) *n* toile *f*.

canvass ('kænvəs) *vi* faire une campagne électorale. *vt* **1** solliciter. **2** discuter. **canvasser** *n* **1** *pol* agent électoral *m*. **2** *comm* demarcheur *m*.

canyon ('kænjən) *n* cañon *m*.

cap (kæp) *n* bonnet *m*. toque, casquette *f*. *vt* **1** coiffer. **2** couvrir. **3** surpasser.

capable ('keipəbəl) *adj* **1** capable, compétent. **2** susceptible. **capability** *n* **1** capacité *f*. **2** faculté *f*.

capacity (kə'pæsiti) *n* capacité *f*.

cape[1] (keip) *n* cape, pèlerine *f*.

cape[2] (keip) *n geog* cap *m*.

caper ('keipə) *n cul* câpre *f*.

capital ('kæpitḷ) *n* **1** capitale *f*. **2** *comm* capital, -aux *m*. *adj* **1** capital, -aux. **2** essentiel, -elle. **capital letter** *n* lettre majuscule *f*. **capitalism** *n* capitalisme *m*. **capitalist** *adj,n* capitaliste. **capitalize** *vt* **1** capitaliser. **2** exploiter.

capricious (kə'priʃəs) *adj* capricieux, -euse.

Capricorn ('kæprikɔ:n) *n* Capricorne *m*.

capsicum ('kæpsikəm) *n* piment *m*.

capsize ('kæpsaiz) *vi* chavirer. *vt* faire chavirer.

capsule ('kæpsju:l) *n* capsule f.

captain ('kæptin) *n* capitaine *m*.

caption ('kæpʃən) *n* **1** rubrique *f*. **2** légende *f*. **3** sous-titre *m*.

captivate ('kæptiveit) *vt* captiver.

captive ('kæptiv) *adj,n* captif, -ive. **captivity** *n* captivité *f*.

capture ('kæptʃə) *n* capture, prise *f*. *vt* capturer, prendre.

car (kɑ:) *n* **1** automobile, voiture *f*. **2** (of a train) wagon *m*. **car park** *n* parking *m*.

caramel ('kærəməl) *n* caramel *m*.

carat ('kærət) *n* carat *m*.

caravan ('kærəvæn) *n* caravane *f*.

caraway ('kærəwei) *n* cumin *m*.

carbohydrate (kɑ:bou'haidreit) *n* hydrate de carbone *m*.

carbon ('kɑ:bən) *n* carbone *m*. **carbon dioxide**

n anhydride carbonique *m*. **carbon paper** *n* papier carbone *m*.
carburettor (kɑ:bju'retə) *n* carburateur *m*.
carcass ('kɑ:kəs) *n* cadavre *m*. carcasse *f*.
card (kɑ:d) *n* carte *f*. **cardboard** *n* carton *m*.
cardigan ('kɑ:digən) *n* cardigan, gilet de tricot *m*.
cardinal ('kɑ:dinl̩) *adj,n* cardinal, -aux *m*.
care (kɛə) *n* **1** soin *m*. **2** attention *f*. **3** souci *m*. **care of** chez. **take care** prendre garde. ~*vi* se soucier. **care for 1** aimer. **2** soigner. **carefree** *adj* insouciant. **careful** *adj* **1** soigneux, -euse. **2** attentif, -ive. **3** prudent. **4** économe. **careless** *adj* **1** insouciant. **2** négligent. **caretaker** *n* gardien, -ienne, concierge *m,f*.
career (kə'riə) *n* carrière, course *f*. *vi* courir rapidement.
caress (kə'res) *n* caresse *f*. *vt* caresser, câliner.
cargo ('kɑ:gou) *n, pl* **cargoes** cargaison *f*.
Caribbean (kæri'biən) *adj* des Caraïbes. **Caribbean Islands** *n* Antilles *f pl*. **Caribbean (Sea)** *n* Mer des Antilles *f*.
caricature ('kærikətjuə) *n* caricature *f*. *vt* caricaturer. **caricaturist** *n* caricaturiste *m*.
carnal ('kɑ:nl̩) *adj* charnel, -elle.
carnation (kɑ:'neiʃən) *n* œillet *m*.
carnival ('kɑ:nivəl) *n* carnaval *m*.
carnivorous (kɑ:'nivərəs) *adj* carnivore.
carol ('kærəl) *n* chant *m*. **Christmas carol** *n* noël *m*.
carpenter ('kɑ:pintə) *n* charpentier, menuisier *m*. **carpentry** *n* charpenterie *f*.
carpet ('kɑ:pit) *n* tapis *m*. **carpet-sweeper** *n* balai mécanique *m*.
carriage ('kæridʒ) *n* **1** voiture *f*. **2** port, transport *m*. **3** maintien *m*. **dual carriageway** *n* route à double voie *f*.
carrier ('kæriə) *n* porteur, -euse. **carrier bag** *n* (grand) sac *m*.
carrot ('kærət) *n* carotte *f*.
carry ('kæri) *vt* **1** porter. **2** transporter. **3** entraîner. **4** adopter. **5** retenir. *vi* porter. **carry on** continuer. **carry out** exercer. **carry-cot** *n* porte-bébé *m invar*.
cart (kɑ:t) *n* charrette *f*. *vt* transporter. **carthorse** *n* cheval de trait *m*. **cartwheel** *n* roue de charrette *f*. **turn cartwheels** faire la roue.
cartilage ('kɑ:tlidʒ) *n* cartilage *m*.
carton ('kɑ:tn̩) *n* carton *m*.
cartoon (kɑ:'tu:n) *n* **1** carton *m*. caricature *f*. **2** dessin animé *m*.
cartridge ('kɑ:tridʒ) *n* cartouche *f*.
carve (kɑ:v) *vt* **1** *Art* sculpter. **2** découper. **carving** *n* sculpture *f*. **carving-knife** *n* couteau à découper *m*.
cascade (kæ'skeid) *n* cascade *f*.
case[1] (keis) *n* **1** cas *m*. **2** *law* affaire *f*.
case[2] (keis) *n* **1** caisse *f*. **2** boîte *f*. **3** étui *m*. *vt* envelopper, encaisser.
cash (kæʃ) *n* espèces *f pl*. monnaie *f*. *vt* toucher. **cash desk** *n* caisse *f*. **cash register** *n* caisse enregistreuse *f*.
cashier[1] (kæ'ʃiə) *n* caissier, -ière.
cashier[2] (kæ'ʃiə) *vt* casser.
cashmere (kæʃ'miə) *n* cachemire *m*.
casino (kə'si:nou) *n* casino *m*.
casket ('kɑ:skit) *n* coffret *m*.
casserole ('kæsəroul) *n* **1** cocotte en terre *f*. **2** ragoût *m*.
cassette (kə'set) *n* cassette *f*. chargeur *m*.
cassock ('kæsək) *n* soutane *f*.
cast* (kɑ:st) *vt* **1** lancer. **2** projeter. **3** *tech* couler. **cast off** rejeter ~*n* **1** coup *m*. **2** *Th* distribution *f*. **3** moule *m*.
castanets (kæstə'nets) *n pl* castagnettes *f pl*.
caste (kɑ:st) *n* caste *f*.
castle ('kɑ:səl) *n* **1** château, -aux *m*. **2** *game* tour *f*.
castrate (kæ'streit) *vt* châtrer. **castration** *n* castration *f*.
casual ('kæʒuəl) *adj* **1** fortuit. **2** insouciant. **casualty** *n* **1** accident *m*. **2** *pl* pertes *f pl*.
cat (kæt) *n* chat, chatte. **cat's eye** *n mot* cataphote *m*.
catalogue ('kætəlɔg) *n* catalogue *m*. *vt* cataloguer.
catamaran (kætəmə'ræn) *n* catamaran *m*.
catapult ('kætəpʌlt) *n* lance-pierre *m invar*. catapulte *f*. *vt* catapulter, lancer.
cataract ('kætərækt) *n* cataracte *f*.
catarrh (kə'tɑ:) *n* catarrhe *m*.
catastrophe (kə'tæstrəfi) *n* catastrophe *f*. **catastrophic** *adj* désastreux, -euse.
catch* (kætʃ) *vt* **1** attraper. **2** surprendre. **3** accrocher. **4** comprendre. *vi* s'accrocher. **catch up** rattraper ~*n* **1** prise *f*. **2** loquet *m*. **3** attrape *f*.
catechism ('kætikizəm) *n* catéchisme *m*.
category ('kætigəri) *n* catégorie *f*. **categorical** *adj* catégorique. **categorize** *vt* classer.
cater ('keitə) *vi* **cater for 1** approvisionner. **2** pourvoir à. **caterer** *n* fournisseur, traiteur *m*.
caterpillar ('kætəpilə) *n* chenille *f*.
cathedral (kə'θi:drəl) *n* cathédrale *f*.

cathode (ˈkæθoud) *n* cathode *f.*
catholic (ˈkæθlik) *n* catholique *m,f.* *adj* **1** universel, -elle. **2** catholique. **catholicism** *n* catholicisme *m.*
catkin (ˈkætkin) *n* chaton *m.*
cattle (ˈkætl̩) *n* bétail, bestiaux *m.*
caught (kɔ:t) *v* see **catch.**
cauliflower (ˈkɔliflauə) *n* chou-fleur *m.*
cause (kɔ:z) *n* **1** cause *f.* **2** motif *m.* *vt* causer, occasionner.
causeway (ˈkɔ:zwei) *n* chaussée *f.*
caustic (ˈkɔ:stik) *adj* caustique.
caution (ˈkɔ:ʃən) *n* **1** prudence *f.* **2** *law* caution *f.* **3** avis *m.* *vt* avertir. **cautious** *adj* prudent.
cavalry (ˈkævəlri) *n* cavalerie *f.*
cave (keiv) *n* caverne, grotte *f.* *v* **cave in 1** s'effondrer. **2** céder.
caviar (ˈkævia:) *n* caviar *m.*
cavity (ˈkæviti) *n* cavité *f.*
cayenne (keiˈen) *n* *also* **cayenne pepper** cayenne, poivre de Cayenne *m.*
cease (si:s) *vt,vi* cesser. **cease-fire** *n* cessez-le-feu *m.* **ceaseless** *adj* incessant.
cedar (ˈsi:də) *n* cèdre *m.*
cedilla (siˈdilə) *n* cédille *f.*
ceiling (ˈsi:liŋ) *n* plafond *m.*
celebrate (ˈseləbreit) *vt* célébrer. **celebration** *n* célébration *f.* **celebrity** *n* célébrité *f.*
celery (ˈseləri) *n* céleri *m.*
celestial (siˈlestiəl) *adj* céleste.
celibate (ˈselibət) *adj,n* célibataire. **celibacy** *n* célibat *m.*
cell (sel) *n* **1** cellule *f.* **2** (of a prison) cachot *m.*
cellar (ˈselə) *n* cave *f.*
cello (ˈtʃelou) *n* violoncelle *m.*
Cellophane (ˈseləfein) *n* *Tdmk* Cellophane *f.*
Celt (kelt) *n* Celte *m,f.* **Celtic** *adj,n* celtique. **Celtic** (language) *n* celtique *m.*
cement (siˈment) *n* ciment *m.* *vt* cimenter.
cemetery (ˈsemətri) *n* cimetière *m.*
censor (ˈsensə) *n* censeur *m.* *vt* censurer, interdire. **censorship** *n* censure *f.*
censure (ˈsenʃə) *n* blâme *m.* *vt* blâmer, censurer.
census (ˈsensəs) *n* recensement *m.*
cent (sent) *n* **1** cent *m.* **2** *inf* sou *m.* **per cent** pour cent.
centenary (senˈti:nəri) *adj,n* centenaire *m.*
centigrade (ˈsentigreid) *adj* centigrade.
centime (sɔnˈti:m) *n* centime *m.*
centimetre (ˈsentimi:tə) *n* centimètre *m.*
centipede (ˈsentipi:d) *n* mille-pattes *m.*
centre (ˈsentə) *n* centre *m.* *vt* placer au centre. *vi* se concentrer. **centre-forward** *n* avant-centre *m.* **centre-half** *n* demi-centre *m.* **central** *adj* central, -aux. **central heating** *n* chaffage central *m.* **centralization** *n* centralisation *f.* **centralize** *vt* centraliser.
century (ˈsentʃəri) *n* siècle *m.*
ceramic (siˈræmik) *adj* céramique. *n pl* céramique *f.*
cereal (ˈsiəriəl) *adj,n* céréale *f.*
ceremony (ˈserəməni) *n* cérémonie *f.* **without ceremony** sans façon. **ceremonial** *adj* de cérémonie. *n* cérémonial, -aux *m.* **ceremonious** *adj* cérémonieux, -euse.
certain (ˈsə:tn̩) *adj* certain, sûr. **make certain** s'assurer. **certainly** *adv* assurément. **certainty** *n* certitude *f.*
certify (ˈsɔ:tifai) *vt* certifier, attester. **certificate** *n* **1** certificat *m.* **2** acte *m.*
Ceylon (siˈlɔn) *n* Ceylan *m.* **Ceylonese** *adj,n* cingalais.
chaffinch (ˈtʃæfintʃ) *n* pinson *m.*
chain (tʃein) *n* chaîne *f.* **chain-smoke** *vi* fumer des cigarettes à la file. **chain-store** *n* succursale de grand magasin *f.*
chair (tʃɛə) *n* **1** chaise *f.* **2** *educ* chaire *f.* **chair-lift** *n* télésiège *m.* **chairman** *n* président *m.*
chalet (ˈʃælei) *n* chalet *m.*
chalk (tʃɔ:k) *n* **1** craie *f.* **2** calcaire *m.* **chalky** *adj* **1** crayeux, -euse. **2** calcaire.
challenge (ˈtʃæləndʒ) *n* défi *m.* *vt* **1** défier. **2** contester.
chamber (ˈtʃeimbə) *n* **1** chambre *f.* **2** *pl* cabinet *m.* étude *f.* **chambermaid** *n* femme de chambre *f.* **chamber music** *n* musique de chambre *f.*
chamberlain (ˈtʃeimbəlin) *n* chambellan *m.*
chameleon (kəˈmi:liən) *n* caméléon *m.*
chamois (ˈʃæmwa:) *n* chamois *m.*
champagne (ʃæmˈpein) *n* champagne *m.*
champion (ˈtʃæmpiən) *n* champion, -ionne. *vt* défendre. **championship** *n* championnat *m.*
chance (tʃa:ns) *n* **1** chance *f.* hasard *m.* **2** occasion *f.* *vt* risquer. *vi* arriver par hasard. *adj* fortuit.
chancellor (ˈtʃa:nsələ) *n* chancelier *m.*
chandelier (ʃændəˈliə) *n* lustre *m.*
change (tʃeindʒ) *n* **1** changement *m.* **2** monnaie *f.* **3** *comm* change *m.* *vt* changer. *vi* se changer.
channel (ˈtʃænl̩) *n* **1** canal, -aux *m.* **2** voie *f.* **3** (television) chaîne *f.* **4** *cap* Manche *f.* *vt* **1** creuser. **2** diriger.

Channel Islands *n pl* îles Anglo-Normandes *f pl*.
chant (tʃɑ:nt) *n* chant *m*. *vt* psalmodier.
chaos ('keiɔs) *n* chaos *m invar*. **chaotic** *adj* chaotique.
chap[1] (tʃæp) *n* gerçure *f*. *vt* gercer, crevasser. *vi* se gercer.
chap[2] (tʃæp) *n inf* garçon, type *m*.
chapel ('tʃæpəl) *n* chapelle *f*.
chaperon ('ʃæpəroun) *n* chaperon *m*. *vt* chaperonner.
chaplain ('tʃæplin) *n* aumônier *m*.
chapter ('tʃæptə) *n* chapitre *m*.
char[1] (tʃɑ:) *vt* carboniser. *vi* se carboniser.
char[2] (tʃɑ:) *vi* faire des ménages. **charwoman** *n* femme de ménage *f*.
character ('kæriktə) *n* **1** caractère *m*. **2** réputation *f*. **3** *Th* personnage *m*. **characteristic** *adj,n* caractéristique *f*. **characterize** *vt* caractériser.
charcoal ('tʃɑ:koul) *n* charbon (de bois) *m*.
charge (tʃɑ:dʒ) *n* **1** charge *f*. **2** devoir *m*. **3** prix *m*. frais *m pl*. **4** recommandation *f*. *vt,vi* charger. *vt* **1** ordonner de faire. **2** payer. **3** *law* accuser.
chariot ('tʃæriət) *n* char *m*.
charisma (kə'rizmə) *n* charisme *m*.
charity ('tʃæriti) *n* **1** charité *f*. **2** œuvre de bienfaisance *f*. **charitable** *adj* charitable.
charm (tʃɑ:m) *n* **1** charme *m*. **2** porte-bonheur *m invar*. *vt* charmer, enchanter. **charming** *adj* ravissant, charmant.
chart (tʃɑ:t) *n* **1** *naut* carte *f*. **2** tableau, -aux *m*. *vt* porter sur une carte.
charter ('tʃɑ:tə) *n* **1** charte *f*. **2** *comm* affrètement *m*. *vt* affréter.
chase (tʃeis) *n* chasse *f*. *vt* chasser, poursuivre.
chasm ('kæzəm) *n* abîme *m*.
chassis ('ʃæsi) *n* châssis *m*.
chaste (tʃeist) *adj* **1** chaste. **2** pur. **chastity** *n* **1** chasteté *f*. **2** pureté *f*.
chastise (tʃæ'staiz) *vt* châtier, corriger. **chastisement** *n* châtiment *m*.
chat (tʃæt) *n inf* causerie *f*. *vi* bavarder, causer.
chatter ('tʃætə) *n* bavardage *m*. *vi* **1** bavarder. **2** (of teeth) claquer. **chatterbox** *n inf* jacasse *f*. moulin à paroles *m*.
chauffeur ('ʃoufə) *n* chauffeur *m*.
chauvinism ('ʃouvinizəm) *n* chauvinisme *m*. **chauvinist** *adj,n* chauvin *m*.
cheap (tʃi:p) *adj* **1** bon marché *invar*. **2** sans grande valeur. **cheapen** *vt* rabaisser le prix de.
cheat (tʃi:t) *vt* **1** tromper. **2** tricher. *n* **1** tricheur, escroc *m*. **2** fraude *f*.
check (tʃek) *vt* **1** vérifier. **2** retenir. **3** *game* faire échec à. *n* **1** contrôle *m*. **2** frein *m*. **3** *game* échec *m*. **4** chèque *m*. **5** carreau, -aux *m*. **checkmate** *n* échec et mat *m*. *vt* faire échec et mat. **checkpoint** *n* contrôle routier *m*. **check-up** *n* **1** vérification *f*. **2** examen medical, -aux *m*.
cheek (tʃi:k) *n* **1** *anat* joue *f*. **2** impudence *f*. **cheekbone** *n* pommette *f*. **cheeky** *adj* effronté.
cheer (tʃiə) *n* **1** gaieté *f*. **2** *pl* acclamations *f*. **cheers!** *interj* à la vôtre! ~*vt* **1** réconforter. **2** acclamer. **cheer up** prendre courage. **cheerful** *adj* gai, joyeux, -euse.
cheese (tʃi:z) *n* fromage *m*. **cheesecake** *n* tarte à la frangipane *f*.
cheetah ('tʃi:tə) *n* guépard *m*.
chef (ʃef) *n* chef de cuisine *m*.
chemical ('kemikəl) *adj* chimique. **chemicals** *n pl* produits chimiques *m pl*.
chemist ('kemist) *n* **1** *med* pharmacien, -ienne. **2** *sci* chimiste *m*. **chemist's shop** *n* pharmacie *f*.
chemistry ('kemistri) *n* chimie *f*.
cheque (tʃek) *n* chèque *m*. **chequebook** *n* carnet de chèques *m*. **cheque card** *n* carte bancaire *f*.
cherish ('tʃeriʃ) *vt* **1** soigner tendrement. **2** caresser.
cherry ('tʃeri) *n* cerise *f*. **cherry tree** *n* cerisier *m*.
cherub ('tʃerəb) *n* chérubin *m*.
chess (tʃes) *n* échecs *m pl*. **chess-board** *n* échiquier *m*. **chess set** *n* échecs *m pl*.
chest (tʃest) *n* poitrine *f*. **chest of drawers** *n* commode *f*.
chestnut ('tʃesnʌt) *n* châtaigne *f*. marron *m*. *adj* châtain, marron. **chestnut tree** *n* châtaignier *m*.
chew (tʃu:) *vt* mâcher. **chew over** ruminer. **chewing gum** *n* chewing-gum *m*.
chick (tʃik) *n* poussin *m*.
chicken ('tʃikən) *n* poulet *m*. **chickenpox** *n* varicelle *f*.
chicory ('tʃikəri) *n* chicorée *f*.
chief (tʃi:f) *n* chef *m*. *adj* principal, -aux, premier, -ière. **chiefly** *adv* surtout.
chilblain ('tʃilblein) *n* engelure *f*.
child (tʃaild) *n, pl* **children** enfant m,f. **childbirth** *n* accouchement *m*. **childhood** *n*

enfance *f.* **childish** *adj* **1** enfantin. **2** puéril. **childlike** *adj* enfantin, candide.

Chile (ˈtʃili) *n* Chili *m.* **Chilean** *adj,n* chilien, -ienne.

chill (tʃil) *n* **1** froid *m.* **2** frisson *m.* **catch a chill** prendre froid. ~*adj* froid. *vt* refroidir, réfrigérer. *vi* se refroidir.

chilli (ˈtʃili) *n* piment *m.*

chilly *adj* **1** frais, fraîche. **2** (of a person) frileux, -euse.

chime (tʃaim) *n* carillon *m.* *vt,vi* carillonner.

chimney (ˈtʃimni) *n* cheminée *f.* **chimneypot** *n* mitre *f.* pot de cheminée *m.* **chimneysweep** *n* ramoneur *m.*

chimpanzee (tʃimpænˈzi:) *n* chimpanzé *m.*

chin (tʃin) *n* menton *m.*

china (ˈtʃainə) *n* porcelaine *f.*

China (ˈtʃainə) *n* Chine *f.* **Chinese** *adj,n* chinois. **Chinese** (language) *n* chinois *m.*

chink[1] (tʃiŋk) *n* fissure, lézarde *f.* *vi* se fendiller.

chink[2] (tʃiŋk) *n* tintement *m.* *vt* tinter. *vi* faire tinter.

chip (tʃip) *n* **1** éclat, fragment *m.* **2** *pl* frites *f pl.* *vt* ébrécher. *vi* s'ébrécher, s'écailler.

chiropody (kiˈrɔpədi) *n* soins du pédicure *m pl.* **chiropodist** *n* pédicure *m,f.*

chirp (tʃə:p) *n* gazouillement *m.* *vi* gazouiller.

chisel (ˈtʃizəl) *n* ciseau, -aux. *vt* ciseler.

chivalry (ˈʃivəlri) *n* **1** chevalerie *f.* **2** courtoisie *f.* **chivalrous** *adj* chevaleresque.

chive (tʃaiv) *n* ciboulette *f.*

chlorine (ˈklɔ:ri:n) *n* chlore *m.*

chlorophyll (ˈklɔrəfil) *n* chlorophylle *f.*

chocolate (ˈtʃɔklit) *n* chocolat *m.*

choice (tʃɔis) *n* choix *m invar.* *adj* (bien) choisi, de choix *invar.*

choir (kwaiə) *n* chœur *m.* **choirboy** *n* enfant de chœur *m.* **choirmaster** *n* maître de chapelle *m.*

choke (tʃouk) *vt* **1** étouffer. **2** boucher. *vi* **1** s'étrangler. **2** se boucher. *n mot* starter *m.*

cholera (ˈkɔlərə) *n* choléra *m.*

choose* (tʃu:z) *vt* **1** choisir. **2** élire. *vi* vouloir.

chop[1] (tʃɔp) *vt* couper, hacher. *n* **1** coup de hache *m.* **2** *cul* côtelette *f.*

chop[2] (tʃɔp) *vi* changer. **chop and change** changer à chaque instant.

chopstick (ˈtʃɔpstik) *n* baguette *f.*

chord (kɔ:d) *n* **1** corde *f.* **2** *mus* accord *m.*

chore (tʃɔ:) *n* corvée *f.*

choreography (kɔriˈɔgrəfi) *n* chorégraphie *f.* **choreographer** *n* chorégraphe *m,f.*

chorus (ˈkɔ:rəs) *n* **1** chœur *m.* **2** refrain *m.* **choral** *adj* choral.

chose (tʃouz) *v see* **choose.**

chosen (ˈtʃouzən) *v see* **choose.**

Christ (kraist) *n* Christ *m.*

christen (ˈkrisən) *vt* baptiser. **christening** *n* baptême *m.*

Christian (ˈkristʃən) *adj,n* chrétien, -ienne. **Christian name** *n* prénom *m.* **Christianity** *n* christianisme *m.*

Christmas (ˈkrisməs) *n* Noël *m.* **Christmas tree** *n* arbre de Noël *m.*

chromatic (krəˈmætik) *adj* chromatique.

chrome (kroum) *n* chrome *m.* *adj* chromé. *vt* chromer.

chromium (ˈkroumiəm) *n* chrome *m.*

chromosome (ˈkrouməsoum) *n* chromosome *m.*

chronic (ˈkrɔnik) *adj* chronique.

chronicle (ˈkrɔnikəl) *n* chronique *f.*

chronological (krɔnəˈlɔdʒikəl) *adj* chronologique.

chrysalis (ˈkrisəlis) *n* chrysalide *f.*

chrysanthemum (kriˈzænθiməm) *n* chrysanthème *m.*

chubby (ˈtʃʌbi) *adj* potelé, joufflu.

chuck (tʃʌk) *vt* **1** lancer. **2** lâcher. **chuck out** expulser.

chuckle (ˈtʃʌkəl) *n* rire étouffé *m.* *vi* rire tout bas.

chunk (tʃʌŋk) *n* **1** gros morceau, -aux *m.* **2** (of bread) quignon *m.*

church (tʃə:tʃ) *n* **1** église *f.* **2** temple *m.* **churchyard** *n* cimetière *m.*

churn (tʃə:n) *n* baratte *f.* *vt* baratter.

chute (ʃu:t) *n* glissière, piste *f.*

chutney (ˈtʃʌtni) *n* chutney *m.*

cicada (siˈka:də) *n* cigale *f.*

cider (ˈsaidə) *n* cidre *m.*

cigar (siˈga:) *n* cigare *m.* **cigarette** *n* cigarette *f.*

cinder (ˈsində) *n* **1** cendre *f.* **2** *pl* escarbilles *f pl.*

cinecamera (ˈsinikæmrə) *n* caméra *f.*

cinema (ˈsinəmə) *n* cinéma *m.*

cinnamon (ˈsinəmən) *n* cannelle *f.*

circle (ˈsə:kəl) *n* **1** cercle *m.* **2** milieu, -eux *m.* *vt* **1** entourer. **2** faire le tour de. *vi* tourner. **circular** *adj,n* circulaire *f.* **circulate** *vi* circuler. *vt* faire circuler, répandre. **circulation** *n* **1** circulation *f.* **2** (of a newspaper) tirage *m.*

circuit (ˈsə:kit) *n* **1** circuit *m.* **2** *law* tournée *f.* **circuitous** *adj* indirect, détourné.

circumcise (ˈsəkəmsaiz) *vt* circoncire. **circumcision** *n* circoncision *f.*

circumference (sə'kʌmfərəns) *n* circonférence *f.*

circumflex ('sə:kəmfleks) *n* accent circonflexe *m. adj* circonflexe.

circumscribe ('sə:kəmskraib) *vt* circonscrire. **circumscription** *n* circonscription *f.*

circumstance ('sə:kəmstæns) *n* **1** circonstance *f.* **2** *pl* moyens *m pl.*

circus ('sə:kəs) *n* cirque *m.*

cistern ('sistən) *n* réservoir *m.* citerne *f.*

cite (sait) *vt* citer.

citizen ('sitizən) *n* **1** citoyen, -enne. **2** bourgeois, habitant *m.* **citizenship** *n* nationalité *f.*

citrus ('sitrəs) *n* citron *m.* **citrus fruits** agrumes *m pl.*

city ('siti) *n* ville, cité *f.*

civic ('sivik) *adj* civique.

civil ('sivəl) *adj* civil. **civil engineering** *n* génie civil *m.* **civil servant** *n* fonctionnaire *m.* **civil service** *n* administration *f.* **civil war** *n* guerre civile *f.*

civilian (si'viliən) *adj,n* civil *m.*

civilization (sivilai'zeiʃən) *n* civilization *f.* **civilize** *vt* civiliser.

claim (kleim) *n* **1** demande, réclamation *f.* **2** droit *m. vt* **1** réclamer, revendiquer. **2** prétendre à.

clam (klæm) *n* palourde *f.*

clamber ('klæmbə) *vt* grimper.

clammy ('klæmi) *adj* moite, humide, pâteux, -euse.

clamour ('klæmə) *n* clameur *f. vi* vociférer.

clamp (klæmp) *n* **1** serre-joint *m.* **2** crampon *m. vt* **1** cramponner. **2** presser.

clan (klæn) *n* clan *m.*

clandestine (klæn'destin) *adj* clandestin.

clang (klæŋ) *n* bruit métallique *m. vi* retentir.

clank (klæŋk) *n* cliquetis *m. vi* résonner. *vt* faire résonner.

clap (klæp) *n* **1** battement (of hands) *m.* **2** coup (of thunder) *m. vt,vi* applaudir.

claret ('klærət) *n* bordeaux *m.*

clarify ('klærifai) *vt* clarifier, éclaircir. *vi* se clarifier. **clarity** *n* clarté *f.*

clarinet (klæri'net) *n* clarinette *f.*

clash (klæʃ) *n* **1** choc *m.* **2** conflit *m.* **3** cliquetis *m. vi* **1** s'entre-choquer. **2** (of colours) jurer. *vt* heurter.

clasp (klɑ:sp) *n* **1** agrafe *f.* **2** fermoir *m.* **3** étreinte *f. vt* **1** agrafer. **2** étreindre.

class (klɑ:s) *n* **1** classe *f.* **2** *educ* cours *m.* **3** catégorie *f. vt* classer. **classification** *n* classification *m.* **classify** *vt* classifier. **classroom** *n* salle de classe *f.*

classic ('klæsik) *adj,n* classique *m.* **classical** *adj* classique.

clatter ('klætə) *n* vacarme, bruit *m. vi* claquer. *vt* faire résonner.

clause (klɔ:z) *n* **1** clause *f.* **2** *gram* membre de phrase *m.* proposition *f.*

claustrophobia (klɔstrə'foubiə) *n* claustrophobie *f.*

claw (klɔ:) *n* griffe, serre, pince *f. vt* griffer.

clay (klei) *n* argile *f.*

clean (kli:n) *adj* **1** propre. **2** net, nette. *vt* nettoyer. **cleaning** *n* nettoyage *m.* **cleanliness** *n* propreté *f.*

cleanse (klenz) *vt* **1** nettoyer. **2** démaquiller.

clear (kliə) *adj* **1** clair. **2** net, nette. **3** libre. **4** certain. *vt* **1** débarrasser, déblayer. **2** évacuer. **3** franchir. **4** acquitter. **5** desservir. *vi* s'éclaircir. **clear up 1** ranger. **2** éclaircir. **clearance** *n* **1** dégagement *m.* **2** *comm* (sale) solde *m.* **clear-headed** *adj* lucide. **clearing** *n* **1** défrichement *m.* **2** acquittement *m.* **3** éclaircie *f.* **clearness** *n* clarté *f.*

clef (klef) *n* clef *f.*

clench (klentʃ) *vt* serrer.

clergy ('klə:dʒi) *n* clergé *m.* **clergyman** *n* pasteur, prêtre *m.*

clerical ('klerikəl) *adj* **1** *rel* ecclésiastique. **2** *comm* de bureau, -aux.

clerk (klɑ:k) *n* **1** employé *m.* **2** clerc *m.*

clever ('klevə) *adj* **1** habile. **2** intelligent.

cliché ('kli:ʃei) *n* cliché *m.*

click (klik) *n* bruit sec *m. vt,vi* cliqueter.

client ('klaiənt) *n* client *m.*

cliff (klif) *n* falaise *f.*

climate ('klaimit) *n* climat *m.*

climax ('klaimæks) *n* **1** apogée, comble *m.* **2** gradation *f.*

climb (klaim) *vt,vi* **1** monter. **2** grimper. *vt* gravir, franchir. *n* **1** montée *f.* **2** ascension *f.*

cling* (kliŋ) *vi* s'accrocher, adhérer. **clinging** *adj* collant.

clinic ('klinik) *n* clinique *f.* **clinical** *adj* clinique.

clip[1] (klip) *vt* tondre, couper.

clip[2] (klip) *n* pince, attache *f. vt* pincer.

clitoris ('klitəris) *n* clitoris *m.*

cloak (klouk) *n* manteau, -aux *m. vt* masquer. **cloakroom** *n* vestiaire *m.* consigne *f.*

clock (klɔk) *n* horloge *f.* **it is two o'clock** il est deux heures. **clocktower** *n* tour d'horloge *f.* **clockwise** *adj* dans le sens des aiguilles d'une montre. **clockwork** *n* mouvement d'horlogerie *m.* **like clockwork** comme sur des roulettes.

clog (klɔg) *n* **1** sabot *m.* **2** entrave *f. vt* **1** entraver. **2** boucher. *vi* se boucher, s'obstruer.

cloister ('klɔistə) *n* cloître *m. vt* cloîtrer.

close *(adj,adv* klous; *v* klouz) *adj* **1** proche. **2** lourd. **3** serré. **4** fermé. **close fitting** *adj* ajusté. ~*n* **1** (klous) enclos *m.* **2** (klous) cul-de-sac *m.* **3** (klouz) fin *f. vt* **1** fermer. **2** conclure. **3** serrer. *vi* **1** se fermer. **2** se terminer. *adv* (de) près. **closing** *n* fermeture *f.*

closet ('klɔzit) *n* **1** cabinet *m.* **2** placard *m.*

clot (klɔt) *n* caillot *m. vi* se cailler, se figer.

cloth (klɔθ) *n* **1** étoffe *f.* **2** toile *f.* **3** nappe *f.*

clothe (klouð) *vt* vêtir, habiller. **clothes** *n pl* vêtements *m pl.* **clothes brush** *n* brosse à habits *f.* **clothes line** *n* corde à linge *f.* **clothes peg** *n* pince à linge *f.* **clothing** *n* habillement *m.*

cloud (klaud) *n* nuage *m. vt* couvrir. **cloudburst** *n* rafale de pluie *f.* **cloudy** *adj* nuageux, -euse.

clove[1] (klouv) *n* (of garlic, etc.) gousse *f.*

clove[2] (klouv) *n* clou de girofle *m.*

clover ('klouvə) *n* trèfle *m.*

clown (klaun) *n* clown, pitre, rustre *m.*

club (klʌb) *n* **1** club *m.* **2** *game* trèfle *m.* **3** *sport* crosse *f.* **club foot** *n* pied bot *m.*

clue (klu:) *n* fil, indice *m.*

clump (klʌmp) *n* **1** masse *f.* **2** bouquet, massif *m.*

clumsy ('klʌmzi) *adj* maladroit, gauche.

clung (klʌŋ) *v* see **cling.**

cluster ('klʌstə) *n* groupe, bouquet *m. vi* se grouper.

clutch (klʌtʃ) *vt* empoigner, saisir *n* **1** griffe *f.* **2** étreinte *f.* **3** *mot* embrayage *m.*

clutter ('klʌtə) *n* encombrement *m. v* **clutter up** encombrer.

coach (koutʃ) *n* **1** *mot* (auto)car *m.* **2** (railway) wagon *m.* **3** *educ* répétiteur *m.* **4** *sport* entraîneur *m. vt* **1** préparer. **2** entraîner. **coaching** *n* **1** répétitions *f pl.* **2** entraînement *m.*

coal (koul) *n* charbon *m.* houille *f.* **coalmine** *n* mine de charbon *f.* houillère *f.*

coalition (kouə'liʃən) *n* coalition *f.*

coarse (kɔ:s) *adj* **1** grossier, -ière. **2** rude.

coast (koust) *n* côte *f. vi naut* côtoyer. **coastguard** *n* garde-côte, gardes-côte *m.* **coastline** *n* littoral, -aux *m.*

coat (kout) *n* **1** habit, manteau, -aux *m.* **2** (of an animal) pelage *m.* **3** robe *f.* **4** (of paint) couche *f. vt* couvrir, enduire. **coat-hanger** *n* cintre *m.*

coax (kouks) *vt* cajoler.

cobble ('kɔbəl) *n* galet *m. vt* carreler.

cobbler ('kɔblə) *n* cordonnier *m.*

cobra ('koubrə) *n* cobra *m.*

cobweb ('kɔbweb) *n* toile d'araignée *f.*

cock[1] (kɔk) *n* **1** coq *m.* **2** mâle *m.*

cock[2] (kɔk) *vt* **1** dresser. **2** retrousser.

cockle ('kɔkəl) *n* **1** *zool* clovisse *f.* **2** *bot* ivraie *f.*

cockpit ('kɔkpit) *n* carlingue *f.*

cockroach ('kɔkroutʃ) *n* blatte *f.*

cocktail ('kɔkteil) *n* cocktail *m.* **cocktail party** *n* cocktail *m.*

cocky ('kɔki) *adj inf* impertinent.

cocoa ('koukou) *n* cacao *m.*

coconut ('koukənʌt) *n* noix de coco *f.* **coconut palm** *n* cocotier *m.*

cocoon (kə'ku:n) *n* cocon *m.*

cod (kɔd) *n* morue *f.*

code (koud) *n* code *m. vt* chiffrer.

codeine ('koudi:n) *n* codéine *f.*

co-education (kouedju'keiʃən) *n* enseignement mixte *m.* **co-educational** *adj* mixte.

coerce (kou'ə:s) *vt* contraindre. **coercion** *n* contrainte *f.*

coexist (kouig'zist) *vi* coexister.

coffee ('kɔfi) *n* café *m.* **coffee bar** *n* café *m.* **coffee bean** *n* grain de café *m.* **coffee table** *n* table de salon *f.*

coffin ('kɔfin) *n* cercueil *m.* bière *f.*

cog (kɔg) *n* dent *f.*

cognac ('kɔnjæk) *n* cognac *m.*

cohabit (kou'hæbit) *vi* cohabiter.

cohere (kou'hiə) *vi* **1** adhérer. **2** s'agglomérer. **3** se tenir. **coherence** *n* cohérence *f.* **coherent** *adj* cohérent.

coil (kɔil) *n* **1** rouleau, -aux *m.* **2** (electric) bobine *f. vt* enrouler. *vi* s'enrouler.

coin (kɔin) *n* pièce de monnaie *f. vt* **1** frapper. **2** inventer.

coincide (kouin'said) *vi* coïncider. **coincidence** *n* coïncidence *f.*

colander ('kʌləndə) *n* passoire *f.*

cold (kould) *adj* froid. **be cold** **1** (of a person) avoir froid. **2** (of the weather) faire froid. ~*n* **1** froid *m.* **2** *med* rhume *m.* **have a cold** être enrhumé. **cold-blooded** *adj* **1** (of a person) insensible. **2** (of an animal) à sang froid.

collaborate (kə'læbəreit) *vi* collaborer. **collaboration** *n* collaboration *f.*

collapse (kə'læps) *vi* s'effondrer. *n* effondrement, écroulement *m*. **collapsible** *adj* pliant.

collar ('kɔlə) *n* **1** (of a shirt, etc.) col *m*. **2** collier *m*. **collarbone** *n* clavicule *f*.

colleague ('kɔli:g) *n* collègue *m,f*.

collect (kə'lekt) *vt* **1** rassembler. **2** collectionner. **3** percevoir. *vi* se grouper. **collected** *adj* calme. **collection** *n* **1** collection *f*. **2** quête *f*. **3** levée *f*. **collective** *adj* collectif, -ive.

college ('kɔlidʒ) *n* collège *m*.

collide (kə'laid) *vi* se heurter, entrer en collision. **collision** *n* collision *f*. choc *m*.

colloquial (kə'loukwiəl) *adj* familier, -ière, parlé.

colon ('koulən) *n gram* deux points *m pl*.

colonel ('kə:nl̩) *n* colonel *m*.

colony ('kɔləni) *n* colonie *f*. **colonial** *adj* colonial, -aux. **colonization** *n* colonisation *f*. **colonize** *vt* coloniser.

colossal (kə'lɔsəl) *adj* colossal, -aux.

colour ('kʌlə) *n* **1** couleur *f*. **2** *mil* drapeau, -aux *m*. *vt* colorer. *vi* **1** se colorer. **2** rougir. **colour-bar** *n* ségrégation raciale *f*. **colour-blind** *adj* daltonien, -ienne. **coloured** *adj* de couleur, coloré. **colourless** *adj* incolore.

column ('kɔləm) *n* colonne *f*.

coma ('koumə) *n* coma *m*.

comb (koum) *n* **1** peigne *m*. **2** *zool* crête *f*. *vt* peigner.

combat ('kɔmbæt) *n* combat *m*. lutte *f*. *vt,vi* combattre. **combatant** *n* combattant *m*.

combine (*v* kəm'bain; *n* 'kɔmbain) *vt* combiner. *vi* s'unir. *n* cartel *m*. **combination** *n* combinaison *f*.

combustion (kəm'bʌstʃən) *n* combustion *f*.

come* (kʌm) *vi* venir, arriver. **come about** arriver. **come across** recontrer. **come back** revenir, rentrer. **comeback** *n* retour *m*. **come down** descendre. **come in** entrer. **come off** se détacher. **come out** sortir.

comedy ('kɔmədi) *n* comédie *f*. **comedian** *n* comédien, -ienne. **comic** *adj* comique, drôle. *n* **1** comique *m*. **2** journal de bandes illustrées *m*. **comical** *adj* comique.

comet ('kɔmit) *n* comète *f*.

comfort ('kʌmfət) *n* réconfort *m*. consolation *f*. *vt* réconforter. **comfortable** *adj* **1** confortable, commode. **2** à l'aise.

comical ('kɔmikəl) *adj* comique.

comma ('kɔmə) *n* virgule *f*. **inverted commas** *n pl* guillemets *m pl*.

command (kə'mɑ:nd) *vt* **1** ordonner, commander. **2** posséder. *n* **1** commandement, ordre *m*. **2** maîtrise *f*. **commandment** *n* commandement *m*.

commemorate (kə'meməreit) *vt* commémorer. **commemoration** *n* commémoration *f*. **commemorative** *adj* commémoratif, -ive.

commence (kə'mens) *vt,vi* commencer. **commencement** *n* commencement, début *m*.

commend (kə'mend) *vt* **1** recommander. **2** louer. **3** confier. **commendation** *n* louange *f*. éloge *m*.

comment ('kɔment) *n* commentaire *m*. observation *f*. *vi* commenter. **commentary** *n* commentaire *m*. **commentator** *n* commentateur, -trice.

commerce ('kɔmə:s) *n* commerce *m*. affaires *f pl*. **commercial** *adj* commercial, -aux. **commercial vehicle** *n* véhicule utilitaire *m*.

commission (kə'miʃən) *n* **1** commission *f*. **2** *mil* brevet *m*. *vt* **1** charger. **2** déléguer. **commissioner** *n* commissaire *m*.

commit (kə'mit) *vt* **1** commettre. **2** confier. **3** engager. **commitment** *n* engagement *m*.

committee (kə'miti) *n* **1** comité *m*. **2** *pol* commission *f*.

commodity (kə'mɔditi) *n* marchandise, denrée *f*.

common ('kɔmən) *adj* **1** commun, ordinaire. **2** vulgaire. **3** public. *n* lieu commun *m*. **commonplace** *adj* banal, -aux, terre à terre. *n* banalité *f*. **commonsense** *n* sens commun *m*. **commonwealth** *n* **1** fédération, république *f*. **2** *cap* Commonwealth *m*.

Common Market *n* Marché Commun *m*.

commotion (kə'mouʃən) *n* tumulte *m*. commotion *f*.

commune[1] (kə'mju:n) *vi* converser intimement. **communion** *n* communion *f*.

commune[2] ('kɔmju:n) *n* commune *f*. **communal** *adj* communal, -aux.

communicant (kə'mju:nikənt) *n* communiant *m*.

communicate (kə'mju:nikeit) *vt,vi* communiquer. **communication** *n* communication *f*. **communicative** *adj* communicatif, -ive.

communism ('kɔmjunizəm) *n* communisme *m*. **communist** *adj,n* communiste.

community (kə'mju:niti) *n* communauté *f*.

commute (kə'mju:t) *vt* échanger. *vi* faire un trajet journalier de sa résidence à son lieu de travail et vice-versa. **commuter** *n* abonné *m*.

compact[1] (kəm'pækt) *adj* compact, serré. *vt* condenser.

compact[2] ('kɔmpækt) *n* contrat *m*.

companion (kəm'pæniən) *n* compagnon *m*. compagne *f*. **companionship** *n* camaraderie *f*.

company ('kʌmpəni) *n* **1** compagnie *f*. **2** société *f*. **3** *naut* équipage *m*. **4** *Th* troupe *f*.

compare (kəm'pɛə) *vt* comparer. *vi* se comparer. **compared with** par rapport à, auprès de. **comparable** *adj* comparable. **comparative** *adj* comparatif, -ive, relatif, -ive. *n* comparatif *m*. **comparison** *n* comparaison *f*.

compartment (kəm'pɑːtmənt) *n* compartiment *m*.

compass ('kʌmpəs) *n* boussole *f*. **(pair of) compasses** *n* compas *m*.

compassion (kəm'pæʃən) *n* compassion *f*. **compassionate** *adj* compatissant.

compatible (kəm'pætibəl) *adj* compatible.

compel (kəm'pel) *vt* contraindre, obliger.

compensate ('kɔmpənseit) *vt* dédommager, rémunérer. *vi* compenser. **compensation** *n* compensation *f*.

compete (kəm'piːt) *vi* concourir, rivaliser. **competition** *n* **1** compétition *f*. concours *m*. **2** concurrence *f*. **competitive** *adj* compétitif, -ive. **competitor** *n* **1** concurrent *m*. **2** compétiteur *m*.

competent ('kɔmpitənt) *adj* compétent, capable.

compile (kəm'pail) *vt* compiler.

complacent (kəm'pleisənt) *adj* satisfait de soi. **complacency** *n* suffisance *f*.

complain (kəm'plein) *vi* se plaindre. **complaint** *n* **1** plainte *f*. **2** *med* maladie *f*.

complement ('kɔmplimənt) *n* complément *m*. **complementary** *adj* complémentaire.

complete (kəm'pliːt) *adj* **1** complet, -ète. **2** achevé. *vt* **1** achever. **2** accomplir. **completion** *n* achèvement *m*.

complex ('kɔmpleks) *adj,n* complexe *m*. **complexity** *n* complexité *f*.

complexion (kəm'plekʃən) *n* **1** teint *m*. **2** aspect *m*.

complicate ('kɔmplikeit) *vt* compliquer. **complication** *n* complication *f*.

compliment ('kɔmplimənt) *n* compliment *m*. *vt* complimenter. **complimentary** *adj* **1** flatteur, -euse. **2** gracieux, -euse, gratuit.

comply (kəm'plai) *vi* se conformer, accéder.

component (kəm'pounənt) *adj* constituant. *n* composant *m*.

compose (kəm'pouz) *vt* **1** composer. **2** apaiser. **composed** *adj* calme. **composer** *n* compositeur *m*. **composition** *n* **1** composition *f*. arrangement *m*. **2** *educ* rédaction *f*.

composure (kəm'pouʒə) *n* calme, sang-froid *m*.

compound[1] (*adj,n* 'kɔmpaund; *v* kəm'paund) *n* composé *m*. *adj* composé. *vt* composer, mélanger. *vi* s'arranger.

compound[2] ('kɔmpaund) *n* enclos fortifié *m*.

comprehend (kɔmpri'hend) *vt* comprendre. **comprehensible** *adj* compréhensible. **comprehension** *n* compréhension *f*. **comprehensive** *adj* compréhensif, -ive, étendu. **comprehensive school** *n* centre d'études secondaires *m*.

compress (*v* kəm'pres; *n* 'kɔmpres) *vt* comprimer. *n* compresse *f*.

comprise (kəm'praiz) *vt* comprendre, contenir.

compromise ('kɔmprəmaiz) *n* compromis *m*. *vt,vi* compromettre.

compulsion (kəm'pʌlʃən) *n* contrainte *f*. **compulsive** *adj* forcé. **compulsory** *adj* obligatoire.

computer (kəm'pjuːtə) *n* ordinateur *m*.

comrade ('kɔmrəd, -reid) *n* camarade *m,f*.

concave ('kɔŋkeiv) *adj* concave.

conceal (kən'siːl) *vt* **1** cacher. **2** dissimuler. **concealment** *n* dissimulation *f*.

concede (kən'siːd) *vt* **1** accorder. **2** admettre. *vi* faire des concessions.

conceit (kən'siːt) *n* vanité *f*. **conceited** *adj* prétentieux, -euse, suffisant.

conceive (kən'siːv) *vt,vi* concevoir. *vt* comprendre. **conceivable** *adj* concevable.

concentrate ('kɔnsəntreit) *vt* concentrer. *vi* se concentrer. **concentration** *n* concentration *f*. **concentration camp** *n* camp de concentration *m*.

concentric (kɔn'sentrik) *adj* concentrique.

concept ('kɔnsept) *n* concept *m*. **conception** *n* conception, idée *f*.

concern (kən'səːn) *vt* **1** concerner, regarder. **2** inquiéter. *n* **1** rapport *m*. **2** intérêt *m*. **3** inquiétude *f*. **4** *comm* entreprise *f*. **concerning** *prep* en ce qui concerne.

concert ('kɔnsət) *n* concert *m*.

concertina (kɔnsə'tiːnə) *n* concertina *f*.

concerto (kən'tʃɛətou) *n* concerto *m*.

concession (kən'seʃən) *n* concession *f*.

concise (kən'sais) *adj* concis.

conclude (kən'kluːd) *vt,vi* conclure. **conclusion** *n* conclusion *f*.

concoct (kən'kɔkt) *vt* **1** *cul* préparer. **2** inventer. **concoction** *n* **1** confectionnement *m*. **2** machination *f*.

concrete (ˈkɔŋkriːt) *n* béton *m*. *adj* concret. *vt* bétonner. *vi* se solidifier.

concussion (kənˈkʌʃən) *n* **1** choc *m*. **2** *med* commotion (cérébrale) *f*.

condemn (kənˈdem) *vt* condamner. **condemnation** *n* condamnation, censure *f*.

condense (kənˈdens) *vt* **1** condenser. **2** abréger. *vi* se condenser. **condensation** *n* condensation *f*.

condescend (kɔndiˈsend) *vi* condescendre, daigner. **condescension** *n* condescendance *f*.

condition (kənˈdiʃən) *n* condition *f*. état *m*. *vt* conditionner. **conditional** *adj,n* conditionnel, -elle *m*.

condolence (kənˈdouləns) *n* condoléance *f*.

condone (kənˈdoun) *vt* pardonner.

conduct (*v* kənˈdʌkt; *n* ˈkɔndʌkt) *vt* **1** conduire. **2** *mus* diriger. *n* conduite *f*.

conductor (kənˈdʌktə) *n* **1** conducteur *m*. **2** (on a bus) receveur *m*. **3** chef d'orchestre *m*.

cone (koun) *n* cône *m*.

confectioner (kənˈfekʃənə) *n* confiseur *m*. **confectionery** *n* confiserie *f*.

confederate (*adj,n* kənˈfedərət; *v* kənˈfedəreit) *adj,n* confédéré *m*. *vt* confédérer. *vi* se confédérer. **confederation** *n* confédération *f*.

confer (kənˈfəː) *vt,vi* conférer. **conference** *n* conférence *f*.

confess (kənˈfes) *vt* confesser, avouer. *vi* se confesser. **confession** *n* confession *f*. aveu, -eux *m*.

confetti (kənˈfeti) *n pl* confetti *m*.

confide (kənˈfaid) *vt* confier. *vi* se fier. **confidence** *n* **1** confiance *f*. **2** confidence *f*. **confident** *adj* sûr, confiant, assuré. **confidently** *adv* avec confiance. **confidential** *adj* confidentiel, -elle, de confiance. **confidentially** *adv* de confiance.

confine (kənˈfain) *vt* **1** limiter, restreindre. **2** enfermer. **confinement** *n* **1** emprisonnement *m*. **2** *med* accouchement *m*. couches *f pl*.

confirm (kənˈfəːm) *vt* confirmer. **confirmation** *n* confirmation *f*.

confiscate (ˈkɔnfiskeit) *vt* confisquer. **confiscation** *n* confiscation *f*.

conflict (*n* ˈkɔnflikt; *v* kənˈflikt) *n* conflit *m*. *vi* s'opposer. **conflicting** *adj* incompatible, contradictoire.

conform (kənˈfɔːm) *vt* conformer. *vi* se conformer. **conformity** *n* conformité *f*.

confound (kənˈfaund) *vt* **1** confondre. **2** embarrasser.

confront (kənˈfrʌnt) *vt* **1** affronter. **2** confronter. **confrontation** *n* confrontation *f*.

confuse (kənˈfjuːz) *vt* **1** embrouiller. **2** confondre, déconcerter. **confusion** *n* **1** confusion *f*. **2** désordre *m*.

congeal (kənˈdʒiːl) *vt* congeler, figer. *vi* se congeler.

congenial (kənˈdʒiːniəl) *adj* **1** approprié. **2** agréable, sympathique.

congested (kənˈdʒestid) *adj* congestionné, embouteillé. **congestion** *n* **1** *med* congestion *f*. **2** encombrement *m*.

congratulate (kənˈgrætjuleit) *vt* féliciter. **congratulation** *n* félicitation *f*.

congregate (ˈkɔŋgrigeit) *vt* rassembler. *vi* s'assembler. **congregation** *n* assemblée *f*.

congress (ˈkɔŋgres) *n* congrès *m*.

conical (ˈkɔnikəl) *adj* conique.

conifer (ˈkɔnifə) *n* conifère *m*.

conjugal (ˈkɔndʒugəl) *adj* conjugal, -aux.

conjugate (ˈkɔndʒugeit) *vt* conjuguer. **conjugation** *n* conjugaison *f*.

conjunction (kənˈdʒʌŋkʃən) *n* conjonction *f*.

conjure (ˈkʌndʒə) *vt,vi* conjurer. *vt* faire apparaître. **conjurer** *n* prestidigitateur *m*.

connect (kəˈnekt) *vt* relier, joindre. *vi* se lier, se joindre. **connection** *n* **1** rapport *m*. liaison *f*. **2** (train, bus, etc.) correspondance *f*.

connoisseur (kɔnəˈsəː) *n* connaisseur *m*.

connotation (kɔnəˈteiʃən) *n* signification *f*.

conquer (ˈkɔŋkə) *vt* conquérir, vaincre. **conqueror** *n* conquérant, vainqueur *m*. **conquest** *n* conquête *f*.

conscience (ˈkɔnʃəns) *n* conscience *f*. **conscientious** *adj* consciencieux, -euse.

conscious (ˈkɔnʃəs) *adj* conscient. **consciously** *adv* sciemment. **consciousness** *n* **1** conscience *f*. **2** *med* connaissance *f*.

conscript (ˈkɔnskript) *n* conscrit *m*. **conscription** *n* conscription *f*.

consecrate (ˈkɔnsikreit) *vt* consacrer. **consecration** *n* consécration *f*.

consecutive (kənˈsekjutiv) *adj* consécutif, -ive.

consent (kənˈsent) *n* consentement *m*. *vi* consentir.

consequence (ˈkɔnsikwəns) *n* **1** conséquence, suite *f*. **2** importance *f*. **consequent** *adj* résultant.

conserve (kənˈsəːv) *vt* conserver. **conservation** *n* conservation *f*. **conservative** *adj,n* conservateur, -trice. *n cap* Conservateur, -trice. **conservatory** *n* serre *f*.

consider (kənˈsidə) *vt* **1** considérer. **2** regarder.

considerable *adj* considérable. **considerate** *adj* attentionné, attentif, -ive. **consideration** *n* **1** considération *f*. **2** rémunération *f*. **3** importance *f*.

consign (kən'sain) *vt* **1** consigner. **2** expédier. **consignment** *n* envoi, expédition *m*.

consist (kən'sist) *vi* **consist of** consister en, se composer de. **consistency** *n* **1** consistance *f*. **2** logique *f*. **consistent** *adj* **1** conséquent. **2** en accord.

console (kən'soul) *vt* consoler.

consolidate (kən'sɔlideit) *vt* consolider. *vi* se consolider.

consonant ('kɔnsənənt) *n* consonne *f*.

conspicuous (kən'spikjuəs) *adj* en vue, remarquable.

conspire (kən'spaiə) *vt* comploter. *vi* conspirer. **conspiracy** *n* conspiration *f*.

constable ('kɔnstəbəl) *n* agent de police *m*. **constabulary** *n* police, gendarmerie *f*.

constant ('kɔnstənt) *adj* **1** constant. **2** continuel. *n* constante *f*.

constellation (kɔnstə'leiʃən) *n* constellation *f*.

constipation (kɔnsti'peiʃən) *n* constipation *f*.

constitute ('kɔnstitju:t) *vt* constituer. **constituency** *n* circonscription électorale *f*. **constituent** *n* électeur, -trice. *adj* constituant, essentiel, -elle. **constitution** *n* constitution *f*. **constitutional** *adj* constitutionnel, -elle.

constraint (kən'streint) *n* contrainte *f*.

constrict (kən'strikt) *vt* resserrer.

construct (kən'strʌkt) *vt* construire. **construction** *n* construction *f*. **constructive** *adj* constructif, -ive.

consul ('kɔnsəl) *n* consul *m*. **consular** *adj* consulaire. **consulate** *n* consulat *m*.

consult (kən'sʌlt) *vt* consulter. *vi* délibérer. **consultant** *n* médecin consultant *m*.

consume (kən'sju:m) *vt* **1** consumer. **2** consommer, épuiser. **consumer** *n* consommateur, -trice. **consumption** *n* consommation *f*.

contact ('kɔntækt) *vt* contacter. *n* contact, rapport *m*. **contact lenses** *n* verres de contact *m pl*.

contagious (kən'teidʒəs) *adj* contagieux, -euse.

contain (kən'tein) *vt* contenir. **container** *n* récipient *m*.

contaminate (kən'tæmineit) *vt* contaminer.

contemplate ('kɔntəmpleit) *vt* **1** contempler. **2** envisager. *vi* réfléchir. **contemplation** *n* **1** contemplation *f*. **2** projet *m*.

contemporary (kən'temprəri) *adj,n* contemporain.

contempt (kən'tempt) *n* mépris *m*. **contemptible** *adj* méprisable.

content[1] ('kɔntent) *n* contenu *m*.

content[2] (kən'tent) *adj* satisfait. *vt* satisfaire. **be content with** se contenter de.

contest (*n* 'kɔntest; *v* kən'test) *n* **1** conflict *m*. **2** compétition *f*. *vt* contester. **contestant** *n* contestant, concurrent *m*.

context ('kɔntekst) *n* contexte *m*.

continent ('kɔntinənt) *n* continent *m*. **continental** *adj* continental, -aux.

contingency (kən'tindʒənsi) *n* éventualité *f*. **contingent** *adj* contingent, fortuit.

continue (kən'tinju:) *vt* continuer. **continual** *adj* continuel, -elle. **continuation** *n* **1** continuation *f*. **2** suite *f*. **continuity** *n* continuité *f*. **continuous** *adj* continu.

contour ('kɔntuə) *n* contour, profil *m*.

contraband ('kɔntrəbænd) *n* contrebande *f*.

contraception (kɔntrə'sepʃən) *n* contraception *f*. **contraceptive** *adj* anticonceptionnel, -elle. *n* **1** contraceptif *m*. **2** préservatif *m*.

contract (*n* 'kɔntrækt; *v* kən'trækt) *n* contrat *m*. entreprise *f*. *vt* contracter. *vi* **1** se contracter. **2** s'engager. **contraction** *n* contraction *f*. **contractor** *n* entrepreneur *m*.

contradict (kɔntrə'dikt) *vt* contredire. **contradiction** *n* contradiction *f*. **contradictory** *adj* contradictoire.

contralto (kən'træltou) *n* contralto *m*.

contraption (kən'træpʃən) *n* machin, truc *m*.

contrary ('kɔntrəri) *adj,n* contraire *m*.

contrast (*n* 'kɔntra:st; *v* kən'tra:st) *n* contraste *m*. *vt* mettre en contraste. *vi* contraster.

contravene (kɔntrə'vi:n) *vt* **1** transgresser, enfreindre. **2** s'opposer à.

contribute (kən'tribju:t) *vt,vi* contribuer. **contribution** *n* contribution *f*. **contributor** *n* **1** collaborateur, -trice. **2** souscripteur *m*.

contrive (kən'traiv) *vt* **1** inventer. **2** arranger. *vi* s'arranger.

control (kən'troul) *n* **1** autorité, maîtrise *f*. **2** contrôle *m*. *vt* **1** contrôler. **2** diriger.

controversy ('kɔntrəvə:si, kən'trɔvəsi) *n* controverse *f*. **controversial** *adj* controversable.

convalesce (kɔnvə'les) *vi* relever de maladie. **convalescence** *n* convalescence *f*. **convalescent** *adj,n* convalescent.

convenience (kən'vi:niəns) *n* commodité, convenance *f*. **convenient** *adj* commode, approprié.

convent ('kɔnvənt) *n* couvent *m*.

convention (kən'venʃən) *n* **1** convention *f*. **2**

assemblée *f*. **conventional** *adj* conventionnel, -elle.

converge (kən'və:dʒ) *vi* converger.

converse[1] (kən'və:s) *vi* causer. **conversation** *n* conversation *f*. entretien *m*.

converse[2] ('kɔnvə:s) *adj* **1** contraire. **2** *math* réciproque.

convert (*v* kən'və:t; *n* 'kɔnvə:t) *vt* convertir, transformer. *n* converti *m*.

convex ('kɔnveks) *adj* convexe.

convey (kən'vei) *vt* **1** transporter. **2** transmettre. **conveyor belt** *n* chaîne de montage *f*.

convict (*n* 'kɔnvikt; *v* kən'vikt) *n* forçat *m*. *vt* condamner, convaincre.

conviction (kən'vikʃən) *n* **1** condamnation *f*. **2** conviction *f*.

convince (kən'vins) *vt* convaincre.

convoy ('kɔnvɔi) *n* convoi *m*.

cook (kuk) *vt* **1** faire cuire. **2** *comm inf* falsifier. *vi* cuire. *n* cuisinier, -ière. **cooker** *n* cuisinière *f*. **cookery** *n* cuisine *f*. **cookery book** *n* livre de cuisine *m*. **cooking** *n* cuisine *f*.

cool (ku:l) *adj* **1** frais, fraîche. **2** calme. *vt* rafraîchir, refroidir. *vi* se refroidir. **cool down** s'apaiser. **coolness** *n* **1** fraîcheur *f*. **2** sang-froid *m*.

coop (ku:p) *n* mue *f*.

cooperate (kou'ɔpəreit) *vi* coopérer. **cooperation** *n* coopération *f*. **cooperative** *adj* coopératif, -ive.

coordinate (*v* kou'ɔ:dineit; *adj* kou'ɔ:dinət) *vt* coordonner. *adj* coordonné.

cope[1] (koup) *vi* venir à bout, se débrouiller.

cope[2] (koup) *n* chape *f*.

Copenhagen (koupən'heigən) *n* Copenhague *f*.

copper[1] ('kɔpə) *n* cuivre *m*. *adj* de cuivre. **copper beech** *n* hêtre rouge *m*.

copper[2] ('kɔpə) *n inf* flic *m*.

copy ('kɔpi) *n* **1** copie *f*. **2** exemplaire *m*. *vt* copier. **copyright** *n* droit d'auteur *m*.

coral ('kɔrəl) *n* corail, -aux *m*.

cord (kɔ:d) *n* corde *f*. *vt* corder.

cordial ('kɔ:diəl) *adj,n* cordial, -aux *m*.

cordon ('kɔ:dn̩) *n* cordon *m*.

corduroy ('kɔ:dərɔi) *n* velours côtelé *m*.

core (kɔ:) *n* **1** centre *m*. **2** (of an apple, etc.)trognon *m*.

cork (kɔ:k) *n* **1** liège *m*. **2** bouchon *m*. *vt* boucher. **corkscrew** *n* tire-bouchon *m*.

corn[1] (kɔ:n) *n* blé, grain *m*. **cornflour** *n* farine de maïs *f*. **cornflower** *n* bleuet *m*.

corn[2] (kɔ:n) *n med* cor *m*.

corner ('kɔ:nə) *n* **1** coin, angle *m*. **2** virage *m*. *vt* **1** *inf* mettre au pied du mur. **2** *comm* accaparer.

cornet ('kɔ:nit) *n* cornet (à piston) *m*.

coronary ('kɔrənəri) *adj* coronaire *f*. **coronary thrombosis** *n* infarctus *m*.

coronation (kɔrə'neiʃən) *n* couronnement *m*.

corporal[1] ('kɔ:prəl) *adj* corporel, -elle.

corporal[2] ('kɔ:prəl) *n* caporal, -aux *m*.

corporation (kɔ:pə'reiʃən) *n* **1** corporation *f*. **2** conseil municipal, -aux *m*.

corps (kɔ:) *n invar* corps *m invar*.

corpse (kɔ:ps) *n* cadavre *m*.

correct (kə'rekt) *adj* correct, exact. *vt* corriger.

correction *n* correction *f*.

correlate ('kɔrəleit) *vi* correspondre. *vt* mettre en corrélation. **correlation** *n* corrélation *f*.

correspond (kɔri'spɔnd) *vi* correspondre. **correspondence** *n* correspondance *f*. courrier *m*. **correspondent** *n* correspondant *m*.

corridor ('kɔridɔ:) *n* corridor *m*.

corrode (kə'roud) *vt* corroder. *vi* se corroder. **corrosion** *n* corrosion *f*. **corrosive** *adj,n* corrosif, -ive *m*.

corrupt (kə'rʌpt) *vt* corrompre, altérer. *vi* se corrompre. *adj* corrompu. **corruption** *n* corruption *f*.

corset ('kɔ:sit) *n* corset *m*.

Corsica ('kɔ:sikə) *n* Corse *f*. **Corsican** *adj,n* corse.

cosmetic (kɔz'metik) *adj,n* cosmétique *m*.

cosmopolitan (kɔzmə'pɔlitən) *adj,n* cosmopolite.

cosmos ('kɔzmɔs) *n* cosmos *m*. **cosmic** *adj* cosmique.

cost* (kɔst) *n* coût *m*. frais *m pl*. *vi* coûter. **costly** *adj* coûteux, -euse.

costume ('kɔstju:m) *n* costume *m*.

cosy ('kouzi) *adj* confortable.

cot (kɔt) *n* lit d'enfant *m*.

cottage ('kɔtidʒ) *n* **1** chaumière *f*. **2** villa *f*.

cotton ('kɔtn̩) *n* coton *m*. **cotton-wool** *n* ouate *f*. coton hydrophile *m*.

couch (kautʃ) *n* canapé *m*. *vt* coucher.

cough (kɔf) *n* toux *f*. *vi* tousser.

council ('kaunsəl) *n* conseil *m*. **councillor** *n* conseiller *m*.

counsel ('kaunsəl) *n* conseil, avis *m*. *vt* conseiller.

count[1] (kaunt) *vt,vi* compter. *n* compte, calcul *m*. **countdown** *n* compte à rebours *m*.

count[2] (kaunt) *n* (title) comte *m*.

counter[1] ('kauntə) *n* **1** comptoir, guichet *m*. **2** *game* jeton *m*.

counter[2] ('kauntə) *adj* contraire. *adv* en sens inverse, contre.
counterattack ('kauntərətæk) *n* contre-attaque *f*.
counterfeit ('kauntəfit) *adj* faux, fausse. *n* contrefaçon *f*. *vt* contrefaire.
counterfoil ('kauntəfɔil) *n* souche *f*. talon *m*.
counterpart ('kauntəpɑ:t) *n* contrepartie *f*.
countess ('kauntis) *n* comtesse *f*.
country ('kʌntri) *n* **1** pays *m*. **2** campagne *f*. **countryside** *n* campagne *f*.
county ('kaunti) *n* comté *m*. **county council** *n* conseil général *m*.
coup (ku:) *n* coup *m*.
couple ('kʌpəl) *n* couple *m*. *vt* coupler.
coupon ('ku:pɔn) *n* coupon *m*.
courage ('kʌridʒ) *n* courage *m*. **courageous** *adj* courageux, -euse.
courgette (kuə'ʒet) *n* courgette *f*.
courier ('kuriə) *n* **1** courrier *m*. **2** guide *m*.
course (kɔ:s) *n* **1** cours *m*. **2** route *f*. **3** *cul* plat *m*. **4** champ de courses *m*. **of course** bien entendu.
court (kɔ:t) *n* **1** cour *f*. **2** *law* tribunal, -aux *m*. *vt* **1** courtiser. **2** solliciter. **court martial** *n* conseil de guerre *m*. **courtship** *n* cour *f*. **courtyard** *n* cour *f*
courteous ('kə:tiəs) *adj* courtois. **courtesy** *n* courtoisie *f*.
cousin ('kʌzən) *n* cousin *m*.
cove (kouv) *n* crique *f*.
covenant ('kʌvənənt) *n* contrat, pacte *m*. *vt* accorder. *vi* convenir de.
cover ('kʌvə) *vt* couvrir. *n* **1** couverture *f*. **2** couvercle *m*. **3** abri *m*.
cow (kau) *n* vache *f*. **cowboy** *n* cowboy *m*.
coward ('kauəd) *adj,n* lâche *m*. **cowardice** *n* lâcheté *f*.
cower ('kauə) *vi* se blottir.
coy (kɔi) *adj* farouche, timide.
crab (kræb) *n* crabe *m*. **crab-apple** pomme sauvage *f*.
crack (kræk) *n* **1** craquement *m*. **2** fissure *f*. *adj* de premier ordre. *vt* **1** faire claquer. **2** fêler. **3** casser. *vi* **1** claquer. **2** se fêler. **3** se casser.
cracker ('krækə) *n* pétard *m*.
crackle ('krækəl) *n* crépitement *m*. *vi* crépiter.
cradle ('kreidl) *n* berceau, -aux *m*.
craft (krɑ:ft) *n* **1** métier (manuel) *m*. **2** ruse *f*. **3** bateau, -aux *m*. **craftsman** *n* artisan *m*. **craftsmanship** *n* habileté d'exécution *f*. **crafty** *adj* rusé.
cram (kræm) *vt* bourrer. *vi* s'entasser.
cramp[1] (kræmp) *n med* crampe *f*.
cramp[2] (kræmp) *n* crampon *m*.
crane (krein) *n* grue *f*.
crash (kræʃ) *n* **1** fracas *m*. **2** catastrophe *f*. *vt* fracasser. *vi* **1** retentir. **2** se tamponner. **crash-helmet** *n* casque protecteur *m*.
crate (kreit) *n* caisse à claire-voie *f*.
crater ('kreitə) *n* cratère *m*.
crave (kreiv) *vt* **1** implorer. **2** demander. **crave for** désirer ardemment.
crawl (krɔ:l) *vi* **1** ramper. **2** se traîner. *n sport* crawl *m*.
crayfish ('kreifiʃ) *n* écrevisse *f*.
crayon ('kreiən) *n* pastel *m*. *vt* crayonner.
craze (kreiz) *n inf* manie *f*. **crazy** *adj* fou, folle, insensé.
creak (kri:k) *n* grincement *m*. *vi* grincer.
cream (kri:m) *n* crème *f*. **creamy** *adj* crémeux, -euse.
crease (kri:s) *n* (faux) pli *m*. *vt* froisser. *vi* se plisser. **crease-resistant** *adj* infroissable.
create (kri'eit) *vt* créer. **creation** *n* création *f*. **creative** *adj* créateur, -trice.
creature ('kri:tʃə) *n* créature *f*.
creche (kreʃ) *n* crèche *f*.
credible ('kredibəl) *adj* croyable. **credibility** *n* crédibilité *f*.
credit ('kredit) *n* **1** crédit *m*. **2** mérite *m*. **3** croyance *f*. **credit card** *n* carte de crédit *f*. ~*vt* **1** croire. **2** reconnaître. **3** *comm* créditer. **creditable** *adj* estimable. **creditor** *n* créancier *m*.
creep* (kri:p) *vi* ramper, se glisser, grimper.
cremate (kri'meit) *vt* incinérer. **cremation** *n* incinération *f*. **crematorium** *n* four crématoire *m*.
crept (krept) *v see* **creep**.
crescent ('kresənt) *n* croissant *m*.
cress (kres) *n* cresson *m*.
crest (krest) *n* crête *f*.
crevice ('krevis) *n* fissure *f*.
crew (kru:) *n* équipage *m*. équipe *f*.
crib (krib) *n* **1** mangeoire *f*. **2** berceau, -aux *m*.
cricket[1] ('krikit) *n zool* grillon *m*.
cricket[2] ('krikit) *n sport* cricket *m*.
crime (kraim) *n* crime *m*. **criminal** *adj,n* criminel, -elle.
crimson ('krimzən) *adj,n* pourpre *m*.
cringe (krindʒ) *vi* **1** se faire tout petit. **2** s'humilier. *n* courbette servile *f*.
crinkle ('kriŋkəl) *vt* froisser. *vi* se chiffonner. *n* fronce, ride *f*.
cripple ('kripəl) *n* infirme *m,f*. *vt* estropier.

crisis ('kraisis) *n, pl* **crises** crise *f.*
crisp (krisp) *adj* **1** croquant, croustillant. **2** vif, vive. **3** tranchant, net, nette.
criterion (krai'tiəriən) *n, pl* **criteria** *or* **criterions** critérium, critère *m.*
criticize ('kritisaiz) *vt* **1** critiquer. **2** blâmer, censurer. **critic** *n* **1** critique. **2** censeur *m.* **critical** *adj* critique. **criticism** *n* critique *f.*
croak (krouk) *n* coassement, croassement *m. vi* **1** coasser, croasser. **2** *inf* grogner.
crochet ('krouʃei) *n* crochet *m. vt* faire au crochet. *vi* faire du crochet.
crockery ('krɔkəri) *n* faïence, poterie *f.*
crocodile ('krɔkədail) *n* crocodile *m.*
crocus ('kroukəs) *n* crocus *m.*
crook (kruk) *n* **1** croc, crochet *m.* **2** angle *m.* **3** *inf* escroc *m.*
crooked ('krukid) *adj* **1** courbé, tordu. **2** tortueux, -euse. **3** malhonnête.
crop (krɔp) *n* **1** récolte, moisson *f.* **2** (of hair) coupe *f. vt* couper, tondre.
croquet ('kroukei) *n* croquet *m.*
cross (krɔs) *n* **1** croix *f.* **2** contrariété *f.* **3** croisement *m. adj* **1** en colère, fâché. **2** transversal, -aux, oblique. *vt* **1** croiser. **2** traverser. **3** (a cheque) barrer. **cross-examine** *vt* contre-interroger. **cross-examination** *n* contre-interrogatoire. *m.* **cross-eyed** *adj* louche. **cross-fire** *n* feu croisé *m.* **crossing** *n* **1** croisement *m.* **2** traversée *f.* passage *m.* **cross-question** *vt* interroger contradictoirement. **cross-reference** *n* renvoi *m.* **crossroads** *n* carrefour *m.* **crossword** *n* mots croisés *m pl.*
crotchet ('krɔtʃit) *n mus* noire *f.*
crouch (krautʃ) *vi* se blottir, s'accroupir.
crow[1] (krou) *n* corbeau, -aux *m.*
crow[2] (krou) *n* chant du coq, coquerico *m. vi* chanter.
crowd (kraud) *n* foule, bande *f.* rassemblement *m. vt* **1** serrer, entasser. **2** remplir. **crowded** *adj* bondé, encombré.
crown (kraun) *n* **1** couronne *f.* **2** sommet *m. vt* couronner. **crown prince** *n* prince héritier *m.*
crucial ('kru:ʃəl) *adj* critique, décisif, -ive.
crucify ('kru:sifai) *vt* crucifier, mettre en croix. **crucifix** *n* crucifix *m.* **crucifixion** *n* crucifixion *f.*
crude (kru:d) *adj* **1** brut. **2** cru. **3** grossier, -ère. **crude oil** *n* mazout *m.* **crudely** *adv* crûment, grossièrement.
cruel ('kruəl) *adj* cruel, -elle. **cruelty** *n* cruauté *f.*
cruise (kru:z) *n* croisière *f. vi* croiser.
crumb (krʌm) *n* miette *f.*
crumble ('krʌmbəl) *vt* émietter, effriter. *vi* **1** s'émietter. **2** s'écrouler.
crumple ('krʌmpəl) *vt* friper, froisser. **crumple up** se friper, se froisser.
crunch (krʌntʃ) *vt* croquer. *vi* craquer. *n* bruit de broiement *m.*
crusade (kru:'seid) *n* croisade *f.*
crush (krʌʃ) *n* presse, foule *f. vt* **1** écraser. **2** froisser. *vi* se presser en foule.
crust (krʌst) *n* croûte *f. vt* encroûter.
crustacean (krʌs'teiʃən) *n* crustacé *m.*
crutch (krʌtʃ) *n* béquille *f.*
cry* (krai) *n* cri *m. vt,vi* **1** crier. **2** pleurer. **cry off** se récuser. **cry out** s'écrier.
crypt (kript) *n* crypte *f.*
crystal ('kristḷ) *n* cristal, -aux *m.* **crystallize** *vt* cristalliser. *vi* se cristalliser.
cub (kʌb) *n* petit *m.*
cube (kju:b) *n* cube *m. vt* cuber. **cubic** *adj* cubique. **cubicle** *n* **1** alcôve *f.* **2** cabine *f.*
cuckoo ('kuku:) *n* coucou *m.*
cucumber ('kju:kʌmbə) *n* concombre *m.*
cuddle ('kʌdḷ) *vt* serrer dans les bras. *vi* se pelotonner. *n* étreinte, embrassade *f.*
cue[1] (kju:) *n* **1** *Th* réplique *f.* **2** avis *m.* indication *f.*
cue[2] (kju:) *n* queue (de billard) *f.*
cuff[1] (kʌf) *n* manchette *f.* **cufflink** *n* bouton de manchette *f.*
cuff[2] (kʌf) *n* taloche *f. vt* talocher.
culinary ('kʌlinri) *adj* culinaire.
culprit ('kʌlprit) *n* **1** coupable *m,f.* **2** *law* accusé, prévenu *m.*
cult (kʌlt) *n* culte *m.*
cultivate (kʌltiveit) *vt* cultiver. **cultivation** *n* culture *f.*
culture ('kʌltʃə) *n* culture *f.*
cultural *adj* culturel, -elle. **cultured** *adj* cultivé, instruit.
cumbersome ('kʌmbəsəm) *adj* encombrant, incommode.
cunning ('kʌniŋ) *adj* malin, -igne, rusé. *n* ruse, fourberie *f.*
cup (kʌp) *n* **1** tasse *f.* **2** *sport* coupe *f.* **cupful** *n* pleine coupe *f.*
cupboard ('kʌbəd) *n* armoire *f.* placard *m.*
curate ('kjuəreit) *n* vicaire *m.*
curator (kju'reitə) *n* conservateur *m.*
curb (kə:b) *n* **1** bordure *f.* **2** frein *m. vt* réprimer, brider.

curdle ('kə:dḷ) *vt* **1** cailler. **2** glacer. *vi* **1** se cailler. **2** se figer.

cure (kjuə) *n* **1** *med* guérison *f*. **2** remède *m*. *vt* **1** guérir. **2** *cul* saler, fumer.

curfew ('kə:fju:) *n* couvre-feu *m invar*.

curious ('kjuəriəs) *adj* **1** curieux, -euse. **2** singulier, -ière. **curiosity** *n* curiosité *f*.

curl (kə:l) *n* boucle *f*. *vt,vi* **1** boucler, friser. **2** enrouler. **curly** *adj* bouclé.

currant ('kʌrənt) *n* **1** groseille *f*. **2** raisin de Corinthe *m*. **currant bush** *n* groseillier *m*.

current ('kʌrənt) *adj* courant, en cours. *n* courant *m*. **currency** *n* **1** circulation *f*. cours *m*. **2** unité monétaire *f*. **currently** *adv* couramment. **current account** *n* compte courant *m*.

curry ('kʌri) *n* cari *m*. **curry powder** *n* cari *m*.

curse (kə:s) *n* **1** malédiction *f*. **2** juron *m*. **3** fléau, -aux *m*. *vt* maudire. *vi* blasphémer.

curt (kə:t) *adj* brusque, sec, sèche.

curtail (kə:'teil) *vt* **1** raccourcir. **2** diminuer.

curtain ('kə:tn̩) *n* rideau, -aux *m*.

curtsy ('kə:tsi) *n* révérence *f*. *vi* faire une révérence.

curve (kə:v) *n* **1** courbe *f*. **2** tournant *m*. *vt* courber, cintrer. *vi* se courber.

cushion ('kuʃən) *n* coussin *m*. *vt* amortir.

custard ('kʌstəd) *n* crème anglaise *f*.

custody ('kʌstədi) *n* **1** garde *f*. **2** emprisonnement *m*.

custom ('kʌstəm) *n* **1** coutume, habitude *f*. **2** clientèle *f*. **3** *pl* douane *f*. **customary** *adj* habituel, -elle, d'usage. **customer** *n* **1** client *m*. **2** *inf* type *m*.

cut* (kʌt) *vt,vi* couper. **cut down** réduire. **cut off** trancher. **cut out 1** enlever. **2** supprimer. **cut glass** *n* cristal taillé *m*. **cut-price** *adj* à prix réduit. ~*n* **1** coupe *f*. **2** coupure *f*. **3** tranche. *f*. **4** réduction *f*. **cutting** *n* **1** coupage *m*. **2** coupure *f*. *adj* mordant.

cute (kju:t) *adj inf* **1** mignon, -onne. **2** rusé.

cuticle ('kju:tikəl) *n* cuticule *f*.

cutlery ('kʌtləri) *n* coutellerie *f*.

cutlet ('kʌtlit) *n* côtelette *f*.

cycle ('saikəl) *n* **1** cycle *m*. **2** vélo *m*. *vi* faire de la bicyclette, aller à bicyclette. **cycling** *n* cyclisme *m*. **cyclist** *n* cycliste *m,f*.

cyclone ('saikloun) *n* cyclone *m*.

cygnet ('signit) *n* jeune cygne *m*.

cylinder ('silində) *n* cylindre *m*. **cylindrical** *adj* cylindrique.

cymbal ('simbəl) *n* cymbale *f*.

cynic ('sinik) *n* sceptique, cynique *m*. **cynical** *adj* sceptique, cynique.

cypress ('saiprəs) *n* cyprès *m*.

Cyprus ('saiprəs) *n* Chypre *f*. **Cypriot** *adj,n* cypriote.

czar (za:) *n* tsar *m*.

Czechoslovakia (tʃekəslə'vækiə) *n* Tchécoslovaquie *f*. **Czech** *adj,n* tchèque. **Czechoslovakian** *adj* tchécoslovaque.

D

dab (dæb) *n* **1** coup léger *m*. **2** tache *f*. *vt* tamponner, tapoter.

dabble ('dæbəl) *vt* mouiller. *vi* barboter. **dabble in** se mêler de.

dad (dæd) *n inf* papa *m*.

daffodil ('dæfədil) *n* narcisse des bois *m*. jonquille *f*.

daft (da:ft) *adj* écervelé, toqué.

dagger ('dægə) *n* poignard *m*. dague *f*.

daily ('deili) *adj* quotidien, -ienne, journalier, -ière. *n* **1** (newspaper) quotidien *m*. **2** *inf* femme de ménage *f*. *adv* tous les jours.

dainty ('deinti) *adj* délicat, friand.

dairy ('dɛəri) *n* laiterie *f*. ferme laitière *f*.

daisy ('deizi) *n* marguerite, pâquerette *f*.

dam[1] (dæm) *n* barrage. *vt* contenir, endiguer.

dam[2] (dæm) *n zool* mère *f*.

damage ('dæmidʒ) *n* **1** dégâts, dommages *m pl*. **2** préjudice *m*. **3** *law* dommages-intérêts *m pl*. *vt* **1** abîmer, endommager. **2** nuire à.

damn (dæm) *vt* **1** condamner. **2** ruiner. **3** damner. *interj* zut! **damnable** *adj* maudit. **damnation** *n* damnation *f*.

damp (dæmp) *adj* humide, moite. *n* humidité *f*. *vt* **1** mouiller. **2** étouffer. **3** décourager. **dampen** *vt* humidifier.

damson ('dæmzən) *n* prune de Damas *f*.

dance (da:ns) *n* **1** danse *f*. **2** bal *m*. *vt,vi* danser. **dancing** *n* danse *f*.

dandelion ('dændilaiən) *n* pissenlit *m*.

dandruff ('dændrʌf) *n* pellicules *f pl*.

Dane (dein) *n* danois *m*. **Danish** *adj,n* danois. **Danish** (language) *n* danois *m*.

danger ('deindʒə) *n* danger, péril *m*. **dangerous** *adj* dangereux, -euse, périlleux, -euse.

dangle ('dæŋgəl) *vi* pendiller, se balancer. *vt* faire pendiller.

dare* (dɛə) *vt* **1** oser, risquer. **2** défier. **daring** *adj* hardi, audacieux, -euse. *n* témérité, audace *f*.

dark (da:k) *adj* **1** noir, obscur. **2** foncé. **3** brun. **4** secret, -ète. *n also* **darkness** obscurité *f*.

ténèbres *f pl.* **darken** *vt* obscurcir, assombrir. *vi* s'obscurcir, s'assombrir.

darling ('dɑ:liŋ) *adj,n* chéri.

darn (dɑ:n) *vt* repriser, raccommoder. *n* reprise *f.* **darning** *n* reprise *f.*

dart (dɑ:t) *n* **1** dard *m.* **2** *sport* fléchette *f.* **3** (in sewing) pince *f.* *vi* s'élancer, se précipiter. **dartboard** *n* cible *f.*

dash (dæʃ) *n* **1** coup *m.* **2** goutte *f.* **3** trait *m.* **4** élan *m.* *vt* **1** jeter. **2** anéantir. *vi* s'élancer. **dashboard** *n* tablier *m.* **dashing** *adj* plein d'élan.

data ('deitə) *n* données *f pl.* **data processing** *n* traitement d'informatique *m.*

date[1] (deit) *n* **1** date *f.* **2** rendez-vous *m.* **date line** *n* ligne de changement de date *f.* **out of date** démodé. **up to date** à la page.

date[2] (deit) *n bot* datte *f.* **date palm** *n* dattier *m.*

daughter ('dɔ:tə) *n* fille *f.* **daughter-in-law** *n* belle-fille, bru *f.*

dawdle ('dɔ:dl̩) *vi* flâner, lambiner.

dawn (dɔ:n) *n* aube *f.* **at dawn** au point du jour.

day (dei) *n* jour *m.* journée *f.* **day after** lendemain *m.* **day before** veille *f.* **in those days** à ce moment-là. **daybreak** *n* point du jour *m.* **daydream** *n* rêverie *f.* *vi* rêvasser. **daylight** *n* jour *m.*

daze (deiz) *vt* **1** hébéter. **2** étourdir. *n* étourdissement *m.*

dazzle ('dæzəl) *vt* éblouir, aveugler. *n* éblouissement *m.*

dead (ded) *adj* mort, décédé. **deadline** *n* date limite *f.* **deadlock** *n* impasse *f.* **deaden** *vt* amortir, assourdir, assoupir. **deadly** *adj* mortel, -elle.

deaf (def) *adj* sourd. **deaf-aid** *n* appareil de correction auditive pour sourds *m.* **deaf-mute** *n* sourd-muet, sourde-muette. **deafness** *n* surdité *f.* **deafen** *vt* assourdir.

deal* (di:l) *n* **1** *comm* affaire *f.* **2** quantité *f.* **3** *game* donne *f.* *vt* distribuer, donner. *vi* **1** s'occuper. **2** faire des affaires. **dealer** *n* **1** fournisseur, marchand *m.* **2** *game* donneur *m.*

dean (di:n) *n* doyen *m.*

dear (diə) *adj* **1** cher, chère. **2** coûteux, -euse. *n* cher, chère. **dearly** *adv* cher, chèrement.

death (deθ) *n* mort *f.* **death certificate** *n* acte de décès *m.* **death rate** *n* mortalité *f.*

debate (di'beit) *n* débat *m.* discussion *f.* *vt* discuter, débattre. *vi* disputer.

debit ('debit) *n* débit *m.* *vt* débiter.

debris ('deibri) *n* débris *m pl.*

debt (det) *n* dette *f.* créance *f.* **debtor** *n* débiteur *m.*

decade ('dekeid) *n* décade *f.*

decadent ('dekədənt) *adj* décadent. **decadence** *n* décadence *f.*

decant (di'kænt) *vt* décanter. **decanter** *n* carafe *f.*

decay (di'kei) *n* **1** pourriture *f.* **2** décadence *f.* *vi* **1** pourrir. **2** tomber en ruine.

decease (di'si:s) *n* décès *m.* *vi* décéder.

deceit (di'si:t) *n* tromperie *f.* **deceitful** *adj* trompeur, -euse, fourbe. **deceitfulness** *n* fausseté *f.*

deceive (di'si:v) *vt* tromper, décevoir.

December (di'sembə) *n* décembre *m.*

decent ('di:sənt) *adj* **1** honnête, bienséant. **2** assez bon. **decency** *n* décence *f.*

deceptive (di'septiv) *adj* trompeur, -euse.

decibel ('desibel) *n* décibel *m.*

decide (di'said) *vt* décider. *vi* se décider. **decided** *adj* décidé, arrêté. **decidedly** *adv* résolument. **deciding** *adj* décisif, -ive.

deciduous (di'sidjuəs) *adj* caduc, caduque.

decimal ('desiməl) *adj* décimal, -aux. *n* décimale *f.* **decimalization** *n* décimalisation *f.*

decipher (di'saifə) *vt* déchiffrer.

decision (di'siʒən) *n* **1** décision *f.* **2** résolution *f.* **decisive** *adj* décisif, -ive.

deck (dek) *n* **1** *naut* pont *m.* **2** (of a bus) impériale *f.* *vt* orner. **deckchair** *n* transatlantique *m.*

declaration (dekla'reiʃən) *n* déclaration, annonce *f.*

declare (di'klɛə) *vt* déclarer, annoncer. *vi* se déclarer. **declared** *adj* avoué, ouvert.

decline (di'klain) *n* **1** déclin *m.* **2** baisse *f.* **3** pente *f.* *vt,vi* décliner. *vt* refuser poliment. *vi* **1** décliner, repousser. **2** baisser. **declension** *n* déclinaison *f.*

decorate ('dekəreit) *vt* décorer, orner. **decoration** *n* **1** décoration *f.* **2** décor *m.* **decorative** *adj* décoratif, -ive. **decorator** *n* décorateur *m.*

decoy (*n* 'di:kɔi; *v* di'kɔi) *n* appât, leurre *m.* amorce *f.* *vt* **1** piper. **2** leurrer.

decrease (di'kri:s) *n* diminution *f.* *vt,vi* diminuer. *vt* amoindrir. *vi* décroître.

decree (di'kri:) *n* décret, édit *m.* *vt* ordonner, décréter.

decrepit (di'krepit) *adj* décrépit *m.*

dedicate ('dedikeit) *vt* dédier. **dedication** *n* dedicace *f.*

deduce (di'dju:s) *vt* déduire, conclure.

deduct (di'dʌkt) *vt* déduire, retrancher. **deduction** *n* déduction *f*.

deed (di:d) *n* **1** action *f*. acte *m*. **2** exploit *m*.

deep (di:p) *adj* **1** profond. **2** (of colour) foncé. *n* **1** profondeur *f*. **2** abîme *m*. **deepen** *vt* approfondir. *vi* devenir plus profond. **deeply** *adv* profondément. **deep-freeze*** *n* congélateur *m*. *vt* congeler. **deep-seated** *adj* profond, enraciné.

deer (diə) *n* cerf, daim *m*.

deface (di'feis) *vt* mutiler, défigurer, lacérer.

default (di'fɔ:lt) *n* défaut *m*. contumace *f*. *vi* faire défaut.

defeat (di'fi:t) *n* défaite *f*. *vt* **1** vaincre. **2** renverser.

defect (*n* 'di:fekt; *v* di'fekt) *n* défaut *m*. *vi* déserter. **defection** *n* défection *f*. **defective** *adj* **1** défectueux, -euse. **2** *gram* défectif, -ive.

defence (di'fens) *n* défense, protection, justification *f*. **defend** *vt* défendre. **defendant** *n* défendeur, -eresse. **defensive** *adj* défensif, -ive.

defer (di'fə:) *vt* ajourner, différer. *vi* déférer. **deference** *n* déférence *f*. **deferential** *adj* déférent.

defiant (di'faiənt) *adj* rebelle, provocant. **defiance** *n* défi *m*. **defiantly** *adv* d'un air de défi.

deficient (di'fiʃənt) *adj* insuffisant, défectueux, -euse. **deficiency** *n* **1** manque *m*. **2** défaut *m*.

deficit ('defisit) *n* déficit *m*.

define (di'fain) *vt* **1** définir. **2** déterminer. **definition** *n* définition *f*.

definite ('defənit) *adj* **1** défini. **2** bien déterminé. *adv* décidément.

deflate (di'fleit) *vt* dégonfler. **deflation** *n* **1** dégonflement *m*. **2** *comm* déflation *f*.

deform (di'fɔ:m) *vt* déformer. **deformed** *adj* difforme. **deformity** *n* difformité *f*.

defraud (di'frɔ:d) *vt* frauder.

defrost (di'frɔst) *vt* déglacer, décongeler.

deft (deft) *adj* habile, adroit. **deftness** *n* habileté, dextérité *f*.

defunct (di'fʌŋkt) *adj* défunt, décédé.

defy (di'fai) *vt* défier.

degenerate (*adj,n* di'dʒenərit; *v* di'dʒenəreit) *adj,n* dégénéré. *vi* dégénérer.

degrade (di'greid) *vt* dégrader, avilir. **degradation** *n* dégradation *f*.

degree (di'gri:) *n* **1** degré *m*. **2** *educ* licence *f*. **by degrees** petit à petit. **in some degree** dans une certaine mesure. **to some degree** à un certain degré.

dehydrate (di'haidreit) *vt* déshydrater. **dehydration** *n* déshydratation *f*.

deity ('deiiti) *n* **1** dieu *m*. déesse *f*. **2** déité *f*.

dejected (di'dʒektid) *adj* triste, abattu.

delay (di'lei) *n* délai, retard *m*. *vt* traîner, retarder, arriérer. *vi* s'attarder.

delegate (*n* 'deligət; *v* 'deligeit) *n* délégué *m*. *vt* déléguer. **delegation** *n* délégation *f*.

delete (di'li:t) *vt* effacer, rayer.

deliberate (*adj* di'libərət; *v* di'libəreit) *adj* **1** intentionnel, -elle, prémédité. **2** réfléchi. *vt,vi* délibérer. **deliberately** *adv* exprès.

delicate ('delikət) *adj* délicat. **delicacy** *n* **1** délicatesse. **2** *cul* friandise *f*.

delicatessen (delikə'tesən) *n* charcuterie *f*.

delicious (di'liʃəs) *adj* délicieux, -euse, exquis.

delight (di'lait) *n* délices *f pl*. joie *f*. *vt* enchanter, réjouir. **delightful** *adv* délicieux, -euse, ravissant.

delinquency (di'liŋkwənsi) *n* **1** délinquance *f*. **2** délit *m*. **delinquent** *n* délinquant *m*.

deliver (di'livə) *vt* **1** livrer, distribuer. **2** (a speech) faire. **delivery** *n* **1** livraison *f*. **2** distribution *f*.

delta ('deltə) *n* delta *m*.

delude (di'lu:d) *vt* tromper, abuser, duper. **delusion** *n* erreur, illusion *f*.

delve (delv) *vt* fouiller.

demand (di'ma:nd) *vt* exiger, demander, réclamer. *n* demande *f*.

democracy (di'mɔkrəsi) *n* démocratie *f*. **democratic** *adj* démocratique.

demolish (di'mɔliʃ) *vt* démolir. **demolition** *n* démolition *f*.

demon ('di:mən) *n* démon *m*.

demonstrate ('demənstreit) *vt* **1** démontrer. **2** *pol* manifester. **demonstration** *n* **1** démonstration *f*. **2** *pol* manifestation *f*. **demonstrator** *n* **1** démonstrateur *m*. **2** manifestant *m*. **demonstrative** *adj* démonstratif, -ive.

demoralize (di'mɔrəlaiz) *vt* démoraliser.

demure (di'mjuə) *adj* réservé, composé.

den (den) *n* **1** tanière *f*. **2** repaire *m*.

denial (di'naiəl) *n* déni *m*. dénégation *f*.

denim ('denim) *n* **1** serge de coton *f*. **2** *pl* blue-jean *m*.

Denmark ('denma:k) *n* Danemark *m*.

denomination (dinɔmi'neiʃən) *n* **1** dénomination *f*. **2** *rel* secte *f*. **denominator** *n* dénominateur *m*.

denote (di'nout) *vt* **1** dénoter. **2** signifier.

denounce (di'nauns) *vt* dénoncer.

dense (dens) *adj* **1** dense, épais, -aisse. **2** *inf* stupide, bête. **density** *n* 1 densité *f*. 2 *inf* stupidité *f*.

dent (dent) *n* bosselure *f*. renfoncement *m*. *vt* bosseler.

dental ('dentḷ) *adj* dentaire. **dentist** *n* dentiste *m*. **dentistry** *n* art dentaire *m*. **denture** *n* dentier *m*.

deny (di'nai) *vt* 1 nier, démentir. 2 refuser.

deodorant (di'oudərənt) *n* déodorant *m*.

depart (di'pɑ:t) *vi* partir, s'en aller. *vt* quitter. **departed** *adj* passé, mort. **departure** *n* départ *m*.

department (di'pɑ:tmənt) *n* 1 département *m*. 2 (of a shop) rayon *m*.

depend (di'pend) *vi* dépendre. **depend on** compter sur. **dependant** *n* charge de famille *f*. **dependence** *n* dépendance *f*.

depict (di'pikt) *vt* peindre.

deplete (di'pli:t) *vt* épuiser.

deplore (di'plɔ:) *vi* déplorer, regretter fort.

deport (di'pɔ:t) *vt* déporter. **deportment** *n* tenue *f*.

depose (di'pouz) *vt* déposer.

deposit (di'pɔzit) *n* 1 *comm* dépôt, versement *m*. 2 sédiment *m*. *vt* déposer.

depot ('depou) *n* dépôt, entrepôt *m*.

deprave (di'preiv) *vt* dépraver, corrompre.

depreciate (di'pri:ʃieit) *vt* déprécier. *vi* se déprécier, baisser.

depress (di'pres) *vt* 1 abaisser. 2 décourager. 3 *comm* faire languir. **depressed** *adj* 1 abattu. 2 *comm* languissant. **depression** *n* 1 abattement *m*. 2 dépression *f*. **depressive** *adj* déprimant.

deprive (di'praiv) *vt* priver.

depth (depθ) *n* profondeur *f*.

deputize ('depjutaiz) *vi* remplacer. **deputation** *n* délégation *f*. **deputy** *n* délégué, suppléant *m*.

derail (di'reil) *vt* faire dérailler.

derelict ('derəlikt) *adj* abandonné, délaissé.

deride (di'raid) *vt* se moquer de, railler. **derision** *n* dérision *f*. **derisive** *adj* railleur, -euse.

derive (di'raiv) *vt,vi* tirer. *vi* provenir. **derivation** *n* dérivation *f*.

derogatory (di'rɔgətri) *adj* dérogatoire.

descend (di'send) *vt,vi* descendre. **descendant** *n* descendant *m*.

descent (di'sent) *n* descente *f*.

describe (di'skraib) *vt* décrire. **description** *n* description *f*.

desert[1] ('dezət) *n* désert *m*.

desert[2] (di'zə:t) *vt* abandonner, laisser. *vi* déserter. **deserter** *n* déserteur *m*.

deserve (di'zə:v) *vt* mériter.

design (di'zain) *n* 1 dessein *m*. 2 dessin *m*. 3 intention *f*. 4 modèle *m*. *vt* 1 projeter. 2 créer. 3 destiner. **designing** *adj* intrigant.

designate ('dezigneit) *vt* désigner, nommer. 2 indiquer.

desire (di'zaiə) *n* désir, souhait *m*. *vt* désirer, vouloir.

desk (desk) *n* 1 (school) pupitre *m*. 2 (office) bureau, -aux *m*. 3 caisse *f*.

desolate ('desələt) *adj* 1 désert, abandonné. 2 affligé.

despair (di'spɛə) *n* désespoir *m*.

desperate ('desprət) *adj* désespéré. **desperation** *n* désespoir *m*.

despise (di'spaiz) *vt* mépriser.

despite (di'spait) *prep* malgré.

despondent (di'spɔndənt) *adj* découragé, abattu.

dessert (di'zə:t) *n* dessert *m*. **dessertspoon** *n* cuiller à dessert *f*.

destine ('destin) *vt* destiner. **destination** *n* destination *f*. **destiny** *n* destin, sort *m*.

destitute ('destitju:t) *adj* 1 dépourvu, dénué. 2 sans ressources.

destroy (di'strɔi) *vt* 1 détruire, anéantir. 2 tuer. **destruction** *n* destruction *f*. **destructive** *adj* destructeur, -trice, destructif, -ive. **destroyer** *n* contre-torpilleur *m*.

detach (di'tætʃ) *vt* détacher, séparer. **detachment** *n* 1 détachement *m*. 2 indifférence *f*.

detail ('di:teil) *n* détail *m*. *vt* 1 détailler. 2 affecter.

detain (di'tein) *vt* 1 *law* détenir. 2 retenir. **detention** *n* 1 détention *f*. 2 *educ* retenue *f*.

detect (di'tekt) *vt* 1 découvrir. 2 apercevoir. **detective** *n* détective *m*. **detective story** roman policier *m*.

deter (di'tə:) *vt* décourager, détourner. **deterrent** *n* force préventive *f*.

detergent (di'tə:dʒənt) *n* détergent *m*.

deteriorate (di'tiəriəreit) *vi* se détériorer. **deterioration** *n* détérioration *f*.

determine (di'tə:min) *vt,vi* déterminer, décider. **determination** *n* détermination, résolution *f*. **determined** *adj* résolu.

detest (di'test) *vt* détester.

detonate ('detəneit) *vt* faire détoner. *vi* détoner. **detonator** *n* amorce *f*.

detour ('di:tuə) *n* détour *m*.

detract (di'trækt) *vi* **detract from** diminuer de, déprécier de.
devalue (di'vælju:) *vt* dévaluer. **devaluation** *n* dévaluation *f*.
devastate ('devəsteit) *vt* ravager, dévaster.
develop (di'veləp) *vt* développer. *vi* se développer, se manifester. **development** *n* **1** développement *m*. **2** exploitation *f*. **3** fait *m*.
deviate ('di:vieit) *vi* dévier, s'écarter. **deviation** *n* déviation *f*. **devious** *adj* tortueux, -euse, détourné.
device (di'vais) *n* **1** moyen *m*. **2** ruse *f*. **3** truc *m*.
devil ('devəl) *n* diable *m*.
devise (di'vaiz) *vt* inventer, combiner.
devoid (di'vɔid) *adj* dépourvu, dénué.
devote (di'vout) *vt* consacrer, vouer, accorder.
devotion (di'vouʃən) *n* dévouement *m*.
devour (di'vauə) *vt* dévorer.
devout (di'vaut) *adj* pieux, -euse, dévot.
dew (dju:) *n* rosée *f*.
dexterous ('dekstrəs) *adj* habile, adroit. **dexterity** *n* dextérité, habileté *f*.
diabetes (daiə'bi:tiz) *n* diabète *m*. **diabetic** *adj,n* diabétique.
diagonal (dai'agənḷ) *adj* diagonal, -aux. *n* diagonale *f*.
diagram ('daiəgræm) *n* diagramme, schéma *m*.
dial (dail) *n* cadran *m*. *vt* **1** appeler. **2** (a number) composer.
dialect ('daiəlekt) *n* dialecte, patois *m*.
dialogue ('daiəlɔg) *n* dialogue *m*.
diameter (dai'æmitə) *n* diamètre *m*.
diamond ('daiəmənd) *n* **1** diamant *m*. **2** *game* carreau, -aux *m*.
diaphragm ('daiəfræm) *n* diaphragme *m*.
diarrhoea (daiə'riə) *n* diarrhée *f*.
diary ('daiəri) *n* **1** (personal) journal, -aux *m*. **2** agenda *m*.
dice (dais) *n pl or s* dé *m*. *vt* couper en cubes.
dictate (*v* dik'teit; *n* 'dikteit) *vt* dicter. *vi* faire la loi. *n* commandement *m*. **dictation** *n* dictée *f*. **dictator** *n* dictateur *m*. **dictatorship** *n* dictature *f*.
dictionary ('dikʃənri) *n* dictionnaire *m*.
did (did) *v* see **do.**
die (dai) *vi* mourir. **die down** s'apaiser.
diesel ('di:zəl) *n* diesel *m*.
diet ('daiət) *n* régime *m*. *vi* être au régime.
differ ('difə) *vi* différer. **difference** *n* **1** différence *f*. **2** dispute *f*. **different** *adj* différent, divers, autre. **differential** *adj* différentiel, -elle. *n* **1** *mot* différentiel *m*. **2** différentielle *f*. **differentiate** *vt* différencier.
difficult ('difikəlt) *adj* difficile. **difficulty** *n* **1** difficulté *f*. **2** obstacle, ennui *m*.
dig* (dig) *vt* bêcher, creuser. *n* **1** fouille *f*. **2** *inf* coup de patte *m*.
digest (dai'dʒest) *vt* digérer. *vi* se digérer. **digestion** *n* digestion *f*.
digit ('didʒit) *n* **1** chiffre *m*. **2** *anat* doigt *m*.
dignity ('digniti) *n* dignité *f*. **dignified** *adj* digne.
dilapidated (di'læpideitid) *adj* délabré, décrépit.
dilemma (di'lemə) *n* dilemme *f*.
diligent ('dilidʒənt) *adj* diligent, assidu. **diligently** *adv* diligemment.
dilute (dai'lu:t) *vt* diluer, arroser.
dim (dim) *adj* faible, pâle. *vt* obscurcir, ternir. *vi* s'effacer, baisser.
dimension (di'menʃən) *n* dimension *f*.
diminish (di'miniʃ) *vt,vi* diminuer, réduire.
diminutive (di'minjutiv) *adj,n* diminutif, -ive *m*.
dimple ('dimpəl) *n* fossette *f*.
din (din) *n* fracas, tapage *m*.
dine (dain) *vt* dîner. **dining car** *n* wagon-restaurant. **dining room** *n* salle à manger *f*.
dinghy ('diŋgi) *n* canot *m*.
dingy ('dindʒi) *adj* terne, sombre.
dinner ('dinə) *n* dîner *m*. **dinner jacket** *n* smoking *m*.
dinosaur ('dainəsɔ:) *n* dinosaure *m*.
diocese ('daiəsis) *n* diocèse *m*.
dip (dip) *vt,vi* **1** plonger. **2** baisser. *vi* incliner. *n* **1** plongée *f*. **2** *inf* baignade *f*.
diphthong ('difθɔŋ) *n* diphtongue *f*.
diploma (di'ploumə) *n* diplôme *m*.
diplomacy (di'ploumәsi) *n* diplomatie *f*. *n* diplomate *m*. **diplomatic** *adj* **1** diplomatique. **2** prudent.
direct (di'rekt) *vt* **1** diriger. **2** ordonner. **3** indiquer. *adj* **1** direct. **2** franc, -che. **3** absolu. **direct object** *n* objet direct *m*. **direction** *n* **1** direction *f*. sens *m*. **2** *pl* instructions *f pl*. **director** *n* administrateur, directeur *m*. **directory** *n* annuaire. **directly** *adv* tout de suite.
dirt (də:t) *n* **1** saleté *f*. **2** ordure *f*. **dirty** *adj* **1** sale, crasseux, -euse. **2** *inf* vulgaire. **3** *inf* vilain. *vt* salir, crotter.
disability (disə'biliti) *n* **1** incapacité *f*. **2** infirmité *f*. **disabled** *adj* invalide, estropié.
disadvantage (disəd'va:ntidʒ) *n* désavantage, inconvénient *m*.
disagree (disə'gri:) *vi* **1** être en désaccord. **2** se

brouiller. **disagreeable** *adj* désagréable. **disagreement** *n* **1** différence *f.* **2** querelle *f.*

disappear (disə'piə) *vi* disparaître. **disappearance** *n* disparition *f.*

disappoint (disə'pɔint) *vt* désappointer, décevoir. **disappointment** *n* déception *f.*

disapprove (disə'pru:v) *vi* désapprouver. **disapproval** *n* désapprobation *f.* **disapproving** *adj* désapprobateur, -trice.

disarm (dis'ɑ:m) *vt,vi* désarmer. **disarmament** *n* désarmement *m.*

disaster (di'zɑ:stə) *n* désastre *m.* **disastrous** *adj* désastreux, -euse.

disband (dis'bænd) *vt* licencier. *vi* se débander.

disc (disk) *n* disque *m.* **disc jockey** *n* présentateur de disques *m.*

discard (di'skɑ:d) *vt* rejeter, se défausser de.

discern (di'sə:n) *vt* discerner, distinguer. **discerning** *adj* judicieux, -euse.

discharge (dis'tʃɑ:dʒ) *vt* **1** décharger. **2** congédier. **3** renvoyer. **4** *law* libérer, acquitter. *n* **1** décharge *f.* **2** renvoi *m.* **3** acquittement *m.*

disciple (di'saipəl) *n* disciple *m.*

discipline ('disəplin) *n* discipline *f.* *vt* discipliner.

disclose (dis'klouz) *vt* révéler, divulguer.

disconnect (diskə'nekt) *vt* couper, décrocher, disjoindre.

disconsolate (dis'kɔnsələt) *adj* désolé, triste.

discontinue (diskən'tinju:) *vt* discontinuer. *vi* cesser.

discord ('diskɔ:d) *n* **1** discorde *f.* **2** *mus* dissonance *f.* **discordant** *adj* **1** discordant. **2** *mus* dissonant.

discotheque ('diskətek) *n* discothèque *f.*

discount (*n* 'diskaunt; *v* dis'kaunt) *n* rabais *m.* remise *f.* *vt* ne pas tenir compte de.

discourage (dis'kʌridʒ) *vt* décourager, abattre.

discover (dis'kʌvə) *vt* découvrir. **discovery** *n* découverte *f.*

discreet (dis'kri:t) *adj* discret, -ète, prudent. **discretion** *n* **1** discrétion *f.* **2** jugement *m.*

discrepancy (dis'krepənsi) *n* désaccord *m.*

discrete (dis'kri:t) *adj* discret, -ète.

discriminate (dis'krimineit) *vt* distinguer, discerner. *vi* faire des distinctions. **discrimination** *n* **1** discernement *m.* **2** jugement *m.* **3** distinction *f.*

discus ('diskəs) *n* disque *m.*

discuss (dis'kʌs) *vt* discuter, débattre. **discussion** *n* discussion *f.* débat *m.*

disease (di'zi:z) *n* maladie *f.* mal *m.*

disembark (disim'bɑ:k) *vt,vi* débarquer. **disembarkation** *n* débarquement *m.*

disfigure (dis'figə) *vt* défigurer. **disfigurement** *n* défiguration *f.*

disgrace (dis'greis) *n* **1** disgrâce *f.* **2** honte *f.* *vt* déshonorer. **disgraceful** *adj* honteux, -euse.

disgruntled (dis'grʌntəld) *adj* mécontent, contrarié.

disguise (dis'gaiz) *vt* déguiser, travestir. *n* déguisement *m.*

disgust (dis'gʌst) *n* dégoût *m.* *vt* dégoûter, écœurer.

dish (diʃ) *n* **1** plat *m.* **2** *cul* mets *m.* **dishcloth** *n* torchon *m.*

dishearten (dis'hɑ:tn̩) *vt* décourager.

dishevelled (di'ʃevəld) *adj* échevelé, en désordre.

dishonest (dis'ɔnist) *adj* malhonnête. **dishonesty** *n* malhonnêteté *f.*

dishonour (dis'ɔnə) *n* déshonneur *m.* *vt* déshonorer. **dishonourable** *adj* déshonorant, honteux, -euse.

disillusion (disi'lu:ʒən) *n* désillusion *f.* désenchantement *m.*

disinfect (disin'fekt) *vt* désinfecter. **disinfectant** *adj,n* désinfectant *m.*

disinherit (disin'herit) *vt* déshériter.

disintegrate (dis'intigreit) *vt* désintégrer, désagréger. *vi* se désintégrer, se désagréger. **disintegration** *n* désagrégation *f.*

disinterested (dis'intrəstid) *adj* désintéressé, impartial, -aux.

disjointed (dis'dʒɔintid) *adj* **1** désarticulé. **2** décousu, sans suite.

dislike (dis'laik) *vt* détester, avoir de l'aversion pour. *n* aversion *f.* dégoût *m.* **take a dislike to** prendre en aversion.

dislocate ('disləkeit) *vt* **1** disloquer. **2** *med* déboîter.

disloyal (dis'lɔiəl) *adj* infidèle, déloyal, -aux.

dismal ('dizməl) *adj* **1** sombre. **2** lugubre. **3** triste.

dismantle (dis'mæntl̩) *vt* **1** démonter. **2** dégarnir.

dismay (dismei) *vt* effrayer, consterner. *n* consternation *f.*

dismiss (dis'mis) *vt* **1** renvoyer, congédier. **2** écarter (a thought, etc.).

dismount (dis'maunt) *vi* descendre. *vt* désarçonner, démonter.

disobey (disə'bei) *vt* désobéir à. **disobedience** *n* désobéissance *f.* **disobedient** *adj* désobéissant.

disorder (dis'ɔ:də) *n* désordre *m*. confusion *f*.
disorganized (dis'ɔ:gənaizd) *adj* désorganisé.
disown (dis'oun) *vt* **1** renier. **2** désavouer.
disparage (dis'pæridʒ) *vt* **1** dénigrer. **2** discréditer.
dispassionate (dis'pæʃənət) *adj* **1** impassible. **2** impartial, -aux. **dispassionately** *adv* **1** sans parti pris. **2** avec calme.
dispatch (dis'pætʃ) *vt* expédier. *n* **1** envoi *m*. **2** expédition *f*.
dispel (dis'pel) *vt* dissiper.
dispense (dis'pens) *vt* **1** distribuer, dispenser. **2** *law* administrer. **3** *med* préparer. **dispense with** se passer de. **dispensary** *n* **1** dispensaire *m*. **2** pharmacie *f*.
disperse (dis'pə:s) *vt* **1** disperser, éparpiller. **2** dissiper. *vi* **1** se disperser, s'éparpiller. **dispersal** *n* dispersion *f*.
displace (dis'pleis) *vt* déplacer.
display (dis'plei) *vt* **1** exposer, exhiber. **2** manifester. *n* **1** exposition. **2** *comm* étalage *m*.
displease (dis'pli:z) *vt* **1** déplaire à. **2** contrarier.
dispose (dis'pouz) *vt* disposer, arranger. *vi* disposer, se débarrasser. **be ill-/well-disposed** être mal/bien disposé. **disposal** *n* **1** disposition *f*. **2** *comm* vente *f*. **disposition** *n* **1** disposition *f*. **2** tempérament, caractère *m*. **3** penchant *m*.
disprove (dis'pru:v) *vt* réfuter.
dispute (dis'pju:t) *vi* **1** discuter. **2** se disputer. *vt* **1** débattre. **2** contester. *n* **1** dispute *f*. **2** contestation *f*. **beyond dispute** incontestable.
disqualify (dis'kwɔlifai) *vt* disqualifier.
disregard (disri'ga:d) *vt* négliger, ne pas faire attention à. *n* indifférence, insouciance *f*.
disreputable (dis'repjutəbəl) *adj* **1** de mauvaise réputation. **2** louche. **3** minable.
disrespect (disri'spekt) *n* manque de respect *m*. irrévérence *f*. **disrespectful** *adj* irrespectueux, -euse.
disrupt (dis'rʌpt) *vt* rompre, briser.
dissatisfy (di'sætisfai) *vt* mécontenter. **dissatisfied** *adj* mécontent.
dissect (di'sekt) *vt* disséquer. **dissection** *n* dissection *f*.
dissent (di'sent) *vi* différer. *n* dissentiment *m*. **dissenting** *adj* dissident.
dissimilar (di'similə) *adj* dissemblable, différent.
dissociate (di'souʃieit) *vt* désassocier.
dissolve (di'zɔlv) *vt* dissoudre. *vi* **1** se dissoudre. **2** fondre.
dissuade (di'sweid) *vt* dissuader.
distance ('distəns) *n* **1** distance *f*. **2** éloignement *m*. **3** lointain *m*. **in the distance** au loin. **distant** *adj* **1** éloigné, lointain. **2** distant, froid.
distaste (dis'teist) *n* dégoût *m*. **distasteful** *adj* déplaisant.
distil (dis'til) *vt* distiller.
distinct (dis'tiŋkt) *adj* **1** distinct, différent. **2** net, clair. **3** bien défini, marqué. **distinction** *n* distinction *f*. **distinctive** *adj* distinctif, -ive.
distinguish (dis'tiŋgwiʃ) *vt* **1** distinguer. **2** caractériser. *vi* faire une distinction. **distinguished** *adj* distingué.
distort (dis'tɔ:t) *vt* **1** déformer. **2** fausser.
distract (dis'trækt) *vt* **1** distraire, détourner. **2** troubler. **distraction** *n* **1** distraction *f*. **2** folie *f*.
distraught (dis'trɔ:t) *adj* affolé, fou, folle.
distress (dis'tres) *n* **1** détresse, angoisse *f*. **2** (poverty) misère *f*. *vt* désoler. **distressing** *adj* **1** affligeant. **2** douloureux, -euse.
distribute (dis'tribju:t) *vt* distribuer. **distribution** *n* distribution, répartition *f*.
district ('distrikt) *n* **1** région. **2** (of a town) quartier *m*. **3** arrondissement *m*.
distrust (dis'trʌst) *vi* se méfier de. *n* méfiance *f*.
disturb (dis'tə:b) *vt* **1** déranger. **2** troubler. **disturbance** *n* **1** dérangement *m*. **2** tapage *m*. **3** agitation *f*.
ditch (ditʃ) *n* fossé *m*.
ditto ('ditou) *adv* idem, de même.
divan (di'væn) *n* divan *m*.
dive (daiv) *vi* plonger. *n* **1** plongeon *m*. **2** *sl* cabaret *m*. **diving board** *n* plongeoir *m*.
diverge (dai'və:dʒ) *vi* diverger, s'écarter.
diverse (dai'və:s) *adj* divers, varié.
divert (dai'və:t) *vt* **1** détourner, dévier. **2** distraire. **diversion** *n* **1** (of a road, etc.) déviation *f*. **2** distraction *f*.
divide (di'vaid) *vt* **1** diviser, séparer. **2** répartir. **3** désunir. *vi* se diviser. **divisible** *adj* divisible. **division** *n* **1** division *f*. **2** partage *m*. discorde *f*.
dividend ('dividend) *n* dividende *m*.
divine (di'vain) *adj* divin, sacré. **divinity** *n* **1** divinité *f*. **2** théologie *f*.
divorce (di'vɔ:s) *n* divorce *m*. *vi* divorcer. *vt* divorcer d'avec.
divulge (di'vʌldʒ) *vt* divulguer, révéler.
dizzy ('dizi) *adj* **1** étourdi. **2** vertigineux, -euse. **dizziness** *n* vertige, étourdissement *m*.
do* (du:) *vt* **1** faire. **2** rendre. **3** finir. **4** *sl* duper. **do again** **1** refaire. **2** recommencer. **do one's best** faire de son mieux. **do up 1**

empaqueter. **2** *inf* réparer. **do without** se passer de. **how do you do?** comment allez-vous? **that will do** cela suffit.

docile ('dousail) *adj* docile.

dock[1] (dɔk) *n naut* bassin *m*. **dockyard** *n* chantier de constructions navales *m*.

dock[2] (dɔk) *vt* **1** retrancher. **2** couper la queue à.

dock[3] (dɔk) *n law* banc des accusés *m*.

doctor ('dɔktə) *n* **1** *med* médecin *m*. **2** *educ* docteur *m*.

doctrine ('dɔktrin) *n* doctrine *f*.

document ('dɔkjumənt) *n* document *m*. pièce *f*. *vt* documenter. **documentary** *adj,n* documentaire *m*.

dodge (dɔdʒ) *vi* **1** s'esquiver. **2** biaiser. *vt* **1** esquiver. **2** éviter. *n* **1** détour *m*. **2** esquive *f*. **3** *inf* ruse *f*. **dodgy** *adj inf* roublard.

dog (dɔg) *n* chien *m*. *vt* **1** suivre à la piste. **2** harceler. **dogged** *adj* tenace. **dog-collar** *n* **1** collier de chien *m*. **2** *rel* col droit *m*. **dogfish** *n* roussette *f*.

dogma ('dɔgmə) *n* dogme *m*. **dogmatic** *adj* **1** dogmatique. **2** autoritaire.

dole (doul) *n* allocation de chômage *f*.

doll (dɔl) *n* poupée *f*.

dollar ('dɔlə) *n* dollar *m*.

dolphin ('dɔlfin) *n* dauphin *m*.

domain (də'mein) *n* domaine *m*.

dome (doum) *n* dôme *m*.

domestic (də'mestik) *adj* **1** domestique. **2** de famille. **3** *comm* intérieur. *n* domestique *m,f*. **domesticate** *vt* domestiquer.

dominate ('dɔmineit) *vt,vi* dominer. **dominant** *adj* dominant.

domineer (dɔmi'niə) *vi* dominer. **domineering** *adj* autoritaire.

dominion (də'miniən) *n* **1** dominion *m*. **2** autorité *f*.

domino ('dɔminou) *n, pl* **dominoes** domino *m*.

donate (dou'neit) *vt* faire don de. **donation** *n* donation *f*.

done (dʌn) *v* see **do.**

donkey ('dɔŋki) *n* âne *m*.

donor ('dounə) *n* donateur, -trice.

doom (du:m) *n* destin *m*. *vt* **1** condamner. **2** vouer.

door (dɔ:) *n* **1** porte *f*. **2** *mot* portière *f*. **out of doors** dehors. **doorbell** *n* sonnette *f*. **doorhandle** *n* poignée de porte *f*. **doorknob** *n* bouton de porte *m*. **doorknocker** *n* marteau, -aux *m*. **doormat** *n* paillasson *m*. **doorstep** *n* pas, seuil *m*. **doorway** *n* encadrement de la porte *m*.

dope (doup) *vt* doper, droguer. *n* **1** *inf* drogue, narcotique *f*. **2** *inf* imbécile *m,f*.

dormant ('dɔ:mənt) *adj* assoupi, endormi.

dormitory ('dɔ:mitri) *n* dortoir *m*.

dormouse ('dɔ:maus) *n* loir *m*.

dose (dous) *n* dose *f*. *vt* médicamenter. **dosage** *n* dosage *m*.

dot (dɔt) *n* point *m*. *vt* **1** mettre un point sur. **2** *Art* pointiller.

dote (dout) *vi* **dote on** raffoler de.

double ('dʌbəl) *adj* double, en deux. *n* **1** double *m*. **2** sosie *m*. *vt* **1** doubler. **2** plier en deux. *vi* (se) doubler. **double back** revenir sur ses pas. **double bass** *n* contrebasse *f*. **double bed** *n* grand lit *m*. **double-cross** *vt inf* duper, tromper. **double-decker bus** *n* autobus à impériale *m*. **double-dutch** *n* chinois, hébreu *m*. **talk double-dutch** baragouiner. **double glazing** *n* double vitrage *m*.

doubt (daut) *n* doute *m*. *vt,vi* douter. *vi* **1** soupçonner. **2** hésiter. **doubtful** *adj* **1** douteux, -euse. **2** incertain. **3** *inf* louche.

dough (dou) *n* **1** pâte *f*. **2** *sl* galette *f*. **doughnut** *n* beignet *m*.

dove (dʌv) *n* colombe *f*. **dovecote** *n* colombier *m*.

Dover ('douvə) *n* Douvres *m*.

dowdy ('daudi) *adj* mal vêtu.

down[1] (daun) *adv* **1** en bas. **2** par terre. **3** à bas. *prep* **1** en bas de. **2** le long de. **down there** là-bas.

down[2] (daun) *n* duvet *m*.

downcast ('daunka:st) *adj* abattu, découragé.

downfall ('daunfɔ:l) *n* chute *f*.

downhearted (daun'ha:tid) *adj* découragé.

downhill ('daunhil) *adj* en pente. *adv* en descendant.

downpour ('daunpɔ:) *n* pluie torrentielle *f*. déluge *m*.

downright ('daunrait) *adj* **1** franc. **2** véritable. *adv* **1** tout à fait. **2** carrément.

downstairs (daun'stɛəz) *adv* en bas.

downstream (daun'stri:m) *adv* en aval, à l'aval.

downtrodden ('dauntrɔdn̩) *adj* opprimé.

downward ('daunwəd) *adj* descendant.

downwards ('daunwədz) *adv* **1** en bas. **2** en descendant. **3** en aval.

dowry ('dauəri) *n* dot *f*.

doze (douz) *vi* somnoler, sommeiller. *n* petit somme *m*.

dozen (ˈdʌzən) *n* douzaine *f*.
drab (dræb) *adj* terne.
drachma (ˈdrækmə) *n* drachme *m*.
draft (drɑːft) *n* **1** *mil* détachement *m*. **2** *Art* dessin *m*. **3** brouillon *m*. **4** *comm* traite *f*. *vt* **1** *mil* détacher. **2** rédiger.
drag (dræg) *vt* **1** traîner. **2** *naut* draguer. *vi* se traîner. *n* **1** drague *f*. **2** *inf* obstacle *m*.
dragon (ˈdrægən) *n* dragon *m*. **dragonfly** *n* libellule *f*.
drain (drein) *n* égoût *m*. *vt* **1** assécher. **2** faire écouler. **3** vider. *vi* s'écouler. **drainage** *n* système d'égouts *m*. **draining board** *n* égouttoir *m*. **drainpipe** *n* tuyau d'écoulement *m*.
drake (dreik) *n* canard *m*.
dram (dræm) *n* goutte *f*.
drama (ˈdrɑːmə) *n* drame *m*. **dramatic** *adj* dramatique. **dramatist** *n* dramaturge *m*. **dramatize** *vt* dramatiser.
drank (dræŋk) *v* see **drink.**
drape (dreip) *n* rideau *m*. *vt* draper. **draper** *n* drapier *m*. **draper's shop** *n* magasin de nouveautés *m*. mercerie *f*. **drapery** *n* draperie *f*.
drastic (ˈdræstik) *adj* **1** énergique. **2** rigoureux, -euse.
draught (drɑːft) *n* **1** courant d'air *m*. **2** tirage *m*. **3** *med* potion *f*. **4** coup *m*. **5** *pl* jeu de dames *m*. **draught beer** *n* bière à la pression *f*. **draughtboard** *n* damier *m*. **draughtsman** *n* dessinateur *m*.
draw* (drɔː) *vt* **1** tirer. **2** dessiner. **3** attirer. *vi* tirer. **draw back** reculer. **draw near** se rapprocher. ~*n* **1** loterie *f*. tirage *m*. **2** partie nulle *f*. **3** attraction *f*. **drawback** *n* obstacle, inconvénient *m*. **drawbridge** *n* pont-levis *m*. **drawer** *n* tiroir *m*. **drawing** *n* dessin *m*. **drawing board** *n* planche à dessin *f*. **drawing pin** *n* punaise *f*. **drawing room** *n* salon *m*.
drawl (drɔːl) *vi* parler d'une voix traînante. *n* voix traînante *f*.
dread (dred) *n* crainte, terreur *f*. *vt* redouter. **dreadful** *adj* affreux, -euse. **dreadfully** *adv* terriblement.
dream* (driːm) *n* rêve, songe *m*. *vi* **1** rêver. **2** rêvasser. *vt* **1** rêver. **2** imaginer. **dreamy** *adj* **1** rêveur, -euse. **2** chimérique.
dreary (ˈdriəri) *adj* morne, lugubre.
dredge (dredʒ) *n* drague *f*. *vt* **1** draguer. **2** *cul* saupoudrer.
dregs (dregz) *n pl* **1** lie *f*. **2** rebut *m*
drench (drentʃ) *vt* **1** tremper, mouiller. **2** (an animal) purger.
dress (dres) *vt* **1** habiller, vêtir. **2** parer, orner. **3** *med* panser. **4** *cul* apprêter. *vi* s'habiller. *n* **1** vêtement *m*. **2** robe *f*. **3** tenue *f*. **4** toilette *f*. **dress circle** *n* premier balcon *m*. **dressmaker** *n* couturière *f*. **dress rehearsal** *n* répétition générale *f*. **dressing** *n* **1** toilette *f*. **2** *cul* assaisonnement *m*. **3** *med* pansement *m*. **dressing-gown** *n* robe de chambre *f*. peignoir *m*. **dressing-room** *n* **1** cabinet de toilette *m*. **2** *Th* loge. **dressing-table** *n* coiffeuse *f*. **dressy** *adj* élégant.
dresser[1] (ˈdresə) *n* habilleur, -euse.
dresser[2] (ˈdresə) *n* dressoir, buffet *m*.
drew (druː) *v* see **draw.**
dribble (ˈdribəl) *vi* **1** dégoutter. **2** (of a child) baver. *vt sport* dribbler. *n* **1** goutte *f*. **2** bave *f*.
drier (ˈdraiə) *n* séchoir *m*.
drift (drift) *n* **1** (of snow) monceau, -aux *m*. **2** *naut* dérive *f*. **3** portée *f*. *vi* **1** dériver, aller à la dérive. **2** se laisser aller.
drill (dril) *n* **1** foret *m*. foreuse *f*. **2** *mil* exercise *m*. *vt* **1** percer, forer. **2** instruire.
drink* (driŋk) *n* boisson *f*. *vt* boire. **drinking water** *n* eau potable *f*.
drip (drip) *n* **1** égouttement *m*. **2** goutte *f*. **3** *inf* nouille *f*. *vi* dégoutter. **drip-dry** *adj* ne nécessitant aucun repassage. **dripping** *n* **1** *cul* graisse de rôti *f*. **2** égouttement *m*.
drive* (draiv) *vt* **1** conduire. **2** enfoncer. **3** pousser. **4** forcer. *vi* **1** se promener. **2** conduire. *n* **1** promenade en voiture *f*. **2** énergie *f*. **3** allée *f*. **driver** *n* chauffeur, conducteur *m*. **driving licence** *n* permis de conduire *m*. **driving school** *n* auto-école *f*. **driving test** *n* examen de permis de conduire *m*.
drivel (ˈdrivəl) *vi* **1** baver. **2** *inf* radoter. *n* **1** bave *f*. **2** radotage *m*.
drizzle (ˈdrizəl) *v imp* bruiner. *n* bruine *f*.
dromedary (ˈdrʌmədəri) *n* dromadaire *m*.
drone[1] (droun) *n zool* faux-bourdon *m*.
drone[2] (droun) *n* bourdonnement *m*. *vi* bourdonner.
droop (druːp) *vi* **1** languir. **2** s'affaiblir. **3** se pencher.
drop (drɔp) *vt* **1** laisser tomber. **2** abandonner. *vi* tomber. **drop in** entrer en passant. *n* **1** goutte *f*. **2** chute *f*. **3** baisse *f*. **dropout** *n* raté *m*.
drought (draut) *n* sécheresse *f*.
drove (drouv) *v* see **drive.**
drown (draun) *vt* noyer. *vi* se noyer.
drowsy (drauzi) *adj* somnolent, assoupi.

drudge (drʌdʒ) *vi* peiner, trimer. *n* souffre-douleur *m,f.* **drudgery** *n* corvée *f.*
drug (drʌg) *vt* droguer. *n* **1** drogue *f.* **2** *inf* stupéfiant *m.* **drug addict** *n* toxicomane *m,f.*
drum (drʌm) *n* **1** *mus* tambour *m.* **2** tonneau, -aux *m. vi* tambouriner. **drummer** *n* tambour *m.* **drumstick** *n* baguette de tambour *f.*
drunk (drʌŋk) *v* see **drink.** *adj* ivre, soûl. **drunkard** *n* ivrogne *m.* **drunken** *adj* ivre.
dry (drai) *vt* **1** sécher, essuyer. *vi* (se) sécher. *adj* sec, sèche. **dry-clean** *vt* nettoyer à sec. **dry-cleaning** *n* nettoyage à sec *m.*
dual ('djuəl) *adj* double. **dual carriageway** *n* route à double voie *f.*
dubious ('dju:biəs) *adj* douteux, -euse.
duchess ('dʌtʃis) *n* duchesse *f.*
duck[1] (dʌk) *n* canard m. **duckling** *n* caneton *m.*
duck[2] (dʌk) *vi* **1** plonger. **2** baisser la tête.
duct (dʌkt) *n* conduit *m.*
dud (dʌd) *adj* **1** raté. **2** *inf* moche.
due (dju:) *adj* **1** dû. **2** voulu. **3** attendu. *n* **1** dû *m.* **2** *pl* droits *m pl. adv* droit. **due to** à cause de, par suite à.
duel ('djuəl) *n* duel *m. vi* se battre en duel.
duet (dju'et) *n* duo *m.*
dug (dʌg) *v* see **dig.**
duke (dju:k) *n* duc *m.*
dulcimer ('dʌlsimə) *n* tympanon *m.*
dull (dʌl) *adj* **1** sombre. **2** ennuyeux, -euse. **3** terne, stupide. *vt* **1** émousser. **2** amortir.
duly ('dju:li) *adv* **1** dûment. **2** en temps voulu.
dumb (dʌm) *adj* **1** muet, -ette. **2** *inf* stupide. **dumbfound** *vi* abasourdir, confondre.
dummy ('dʌmi) *n* **1** mannequin *m.* **2** *game* mort. **3** (for a baby) sucette *f.* **4** *comm* simulacre *m.*
dump (dʌmp) *vt* décharger, vider. **2** *inf* trou *m. n* dépôt *m.*
dumpling ('dʌmpliŋ) *n* chausson *m.*
dunce (dʌns) *n* ignorant, âne *m.*
dune (dju:n) *n* dune *f.*
dung (dʌŋ) *n* fiente, crotte *f.* fumier *m.*
dungeon ('dʌndʒən) *m* cachot *m.*
Dunkirk (dʌn'kə:k) *n* Dunkerque *m.*
duplicate (*adj,n* 'dju:plikət; *v* 'dju:plikeit) *adj,n* double *m. vt* faire en double, copier.
durable ('djuərəbəl) *adj* durable. **duration** *n* durée *f.*
during ('djuəriŋ) *prep* pendant.
dusk (dʌsk) *n* crépuscule *m.* **dusky** *adj* **1** sombre. **2** noirâtre.
dust (dʌst) *n* poussière *f. vt* épousseter. **dustbin** *n* poubelle *f.* **dustman** *n* boueur *m.* **dustpan** *n* pelle à poussière *f.* **duster** *n* torchon *m.* **dusty** *adj* poussiéreux, -euse.
Dutch (dʌtʃ) *adj* hollandais. **Dutchman** *n* hollandais *m.*
duty ('dju:ti) *n* **1** devoir *m.* **2** *comm* droit *m.* **3** fonction *f.* **on duty** de service. **duty-free** *adj* **1** exempt de droits. **2** en franchise. **dutiful** *adj* obéissant, soumis.
duvet ('dju:vei) *n* duvet *m.*
dwarf (dwɔ:f) *adj,n* nain. *vt* rapetisser.
dwell* (dwel) *vi* habiter, demeurer. **dwell on** s'étendre sur. **dwelling** *n* demeure, résidence *f.*
dwindle ('dwindl̩) *vi* **1** diminuer. **2** se réduire.
dye (dai) *n* teinte *f. vt* teindre.
dyke (daik) *n* digue *f.*
dynamic (dai'næmik) *adj* dynamique.
dynamite ('dainəmait) *n* dynamite *f.*
dynasty ('dinəsti) *n* dynastie *f.*
dysentery ('disəntri) *n* dysenterie *f.*
dyslexia (dis'leksiə) *n* dyslexie *f.*

E

each (i:tʃ) *adj* chaque. *pron* chacun. **each other** l'un l'autre, les uns les autres.
eager ('i:gə) *adj* **1** passionné, ardent. **2** avide. **3** impatient. **eagerness** *n* **1** ardeur *f.* **2** avidité. **3** empressement *m.*
eagle ('i:gəl) *n* aigle *m.*
ear[1] (iə) *n anat* oreille *f.* **earache** *n* mal d'oreille *m.* **eardrum** *n* tympan *m.* **earmark** *n* marque distinctive *f. vt* mettre de côté. **earphone** *n* casque *m.* **earring** *n* boucle d'oreille *f.* **earwig** *n* perce-oreille *m.*
ear[2] (iə) *n bot* épi *m.*
earl (ə:l) *n* comte *m.*
early ('ə:li) *adv* de bonne heure, tôt. *adj* **1** matinal, -aux. **2** précoce.
earn (ə:n) *vt* **1** gagner. **2** mériter.
earnest ('ə:nist) *adj* **1** sérieux, -euse. **2** sincère.
earth (ə:θ) *n* **1** terre *f.* **2** (of animal) terrier *m.* **down to earth** terre à terre, réaliste. **earthenware** *n* poterie, faïence *f.* **earthquake** *n* tremblement de terre *m.* **earthworm** *n* ver de terre, lombric *m.*
ease (i:z) *n* **1** aise *f.* **2** tranquillité *f.* **3** facilité *f. vt* **1** adoucir. **2** soulager. **easy** *adj* **1** facile. **2** tranquille. **3** libre. *adv* doucement.
easel ('i:zəl) *n* chevalet *m.*
east (i:st) *n* **1** est *m.* **2** *cap* Orient *m. adj* est

invar. adv à *or* vers l'est. **easterly** *adj* d'est. **eastern** *adj* de l'est, oriental, -aux. **eastward** *adj* à l'est, dans l'est. **eastwards** *adv* vers l'est.

Easter ('i:stə) *n* Pâques *f pl.*

eat* (i:t) *vt* manger. **eatable** *adj* mangeable.

eavesdrop ('i:vzdrɔp) *vi* écouter aux portes.

ebb (eb) *n* **1** reflux *m.* **2** déclin *m.*

ebony ('ebəni) *n* ébène *f.*

eccentric (ik'sentrik) *adj* excentrique.

ecclesiastical (ikli:zi'æstikəl) *adj* ecclésiastique.

echo ('ekou) *n, pl* **echoes** écho *m. vi* **1** faire écho. **2** retentir. *vt* répéter (en écho).

eclair (ei'klɛə) *n* éclair *m.*

eclipse (i'klips) *n* éclipse *f. vt* éclipser.

ecology (i:'kɔlədʒi) *n* écologie *f.*

economize (i'kɔnəmaiz) *vt* économiser.

economy (i'kɔnəmi) *n* économie *f.* **economic** *adj* économique. **economical** *adj* **1** économe. **2** économique. **economics** *n* sciences économiques *f pl.*

ecstasy ('ekstəsi) *n* **1** extase *f.* **2** ravissement *m.* **ecstatic** *adj* extatique.

edelweiss ('eidļvais) *n* edelweiss *m.*

edge (edʒ) *n* **1** bord *m.* **2** lisière, bordure *f.* **3** (of a blade) tranchant *m.* **on edge** énervé. ~*vt* border.

edible ('edibəl) *adj* comestible.

Edinburgh ('edinbərə) *n* Edimbourg *m.*

edit ('edit) *vt* **1** éditer. **2** rédiger. **edition** *n* édition *f.* **editor** *n* **1** éditeur *m.* **2** (of a paper) rédacteur en chef *m.* **editorial** *adj* éditorial, -aux. *n* article de fond *m.*

educate ('edjukeit) *vt* **1** élever. **2** instruire. **educated** *adj* instruit, cultivé. **education** *n* éducation *f.* enseignement *m.* instruction *f.*

eel (i:l) *n* anguille *f.*

eerie ('iəri) *adj* étrange, mystérieux, -euse.

effect (i'fekt) *n* **1** effet *m.* influence *f.* **2** *pl* biens *m pl.* **in effect** en réalité. ~*vt* effectuer. **effective** *adj* efficace. **effectiveness** *n* efficacité *f.*

effeminate (i'feminət) *adj* efféminé.

effervesce (efə'ves) *vi* **1** être en effervescence. **2** mousser. **effervescence** *n* effervescence *f.* **effervescent** *adj* effervescent.

efficient (i'fiʃənt) *adj* **1** capable, compétent. **2** efficace. **efficiency** *n* efficacité *f.*

effigy ('efidʒi) *n* effigie *f.*

effort ('efət) *n* effort *m.*

egg[1] (eg) *n* œuf *m.* **boiled egg** œuf à la coque. **fried egg** œuf sur le plat. **hard-boiled/poached egg** œuf dur/poché. **scrambled eggs** œufs brouillés. **egg-cup** *n* coquetier *m.* **egg-shell** *n* coquille d'œuf *f.* **egg-whisk** *n* batteur *or* fouet à œufs *m.*

egg[2] (eg) *vt* **egg on** encourager, inciter.

ego ('i:gou) *n* moi *m.* **egocentric** *adj* égocentrique. **egoism** *n* égoïsme *m.*

Egypt ('i:dʒipt) *n* Egypte *f.* **Egyptian** *adj,n* égyptien, -ienne.

eiderdown ('aidədaun) *n* édredon *m.*

eight (eit) *adj,n* huit *m.* **eighth** *adj* huitième.

eighteen (ei'ti:n) *adj,n* dix-huit *m.* **eighteenth** *adj* dix-huitième.

eighty ('eiti) *adj,n* quatre-vingts *m.* **eightieth** *adj* quatre-vingtième.

either ('aiðə) *adj,pron* **1** l'un et *or* ou l'autre. **2** chaque. **3** chacun. *conj* ou, soit. **either...or** ou...ou, soit...soit. ~*adv* non plus.

ejaculate (i'dʒækjuleit) *vt* **1** éjaculer. **2** pousser.

eject (i'dʒekt) *vt* expulser, émettre.

eke (i:k) *vt* **1** allonger, suppléer. **2** faire durer.

elaborate (*adj* i'læbrət; *v* i'læbəreit) *adj* **1** compliqué. **2** soigné. *vt* élaborer.

elapse (i'læps) *vi* s'écouler.

elastic (i'læstik) *adj* élastique. **elastic band** *n* élastique *m.* **elasticity** élasticité *f.*

elated (i'leitid) *adj* transporté, exalté.

elbow ('elbou) *n* coude *m. vt* coudoyer.

elder[1] ('eldə) *adj,n* aîné. **elderly** *adj* d'un certain âge, âgé.

elder[2] ('eldə) *n bot* sureau *m.* **elderberry** *n* baie de sureau *f.*

eldest ('eldist) *adj,n* aîné.

elect (i'lekt) *vt* élire, choisir. **election** *n* élection *f.* **electoral** *adj* électoral, -aux. **electorate** *n* corps électoral *m.*

electricity (ilek'trisiti) *n* électricité *f.* **electric** *adj* électrique. **electrician** *n* électricien *m.* **electrify** *vt* électrifier, électriser. **electrocute** *vt* électrocuter. **electrode** *n* électrode *f.* **electron** *n* électron *m.* **electronic** *adj* électronique. **electronics** *n pl* électronique *f.*

elegant ('eligənt) *adj* **1** élégant. **2** *inf* chic. **elegance** *n* élégance *f.*

element ('eləmənt) *n* élément *m.* **elemental** *adj* **1** des éléments. **2** élémentaire. **elementary** *adj* élémentaire.

elephant ('eləfənt) *n* éléphant *m.*

elevate ('eləveit) *vt* **1** élever, hausser. **2** exalter. **elevation** *n* élévation *m.* **elevator** *n* ascenseur, élévateur, monte-charge *m.*

eleven (i'levən) *adj,n* onze *m.* **eleventh** *adj* onzième.

elf (elf) *n, pl* **elves** elfe, lutin *m.*

eligible ('elidʒəbəl) *adj* éligible.
eliminate (i'limineit) *vt* **1** éliminer. **2** supprimer. **elimination** *n* élimination *f*.
elite (ei'li:t) *n* élite *f*.
ellipse (i'lips) *n* ellipse *f*.
elm (elm) *n* orme *m*.
elocution (elə'kju:ʃən) *n* élocution, diction *f*.
elope (i'loup) *vi* s'enfuir.
eloquent ('eləkwənt) *adj* éloquent.
else (els) *adv* autrement, ou bien. *adj* autre. **elsewhere** *adv* ailleurs.
elucidate (i'lu:sideit) *vt* élucider, éclaircir.
elude (i'lu:d) *vt* éluder, échapper à.
emaciate (i'meiʃieit) *vt* amaigrir. **emaciated** *adj* émacié, étique.
emanate ('eməneit) *vi* émaner.
emancipate (i'mænsipeit) *vt* émanciper. **emancipation** *n* émancipation *f*.
embalm (im'bɑ:m) *vt* embaumer.
embankment (im'bæŋkmənt) *n* **1** levée *f*. **2** (of a river) quai *m*. **3** (of a road) remblai *m*.
embargo (im'bɑ:gou) *n, pl* **embargoes** embargo *m*.
embark (im'bɑ:k) *vt* embarquer. *vi* s'embarquer.
embarrass (im'bærəs) *vt* embarrasser, gêner. **embarrassment** *n* embarras *m*.
embassy ('embəsi) *n* ambassade *f*.
embellish (im'beliʃ) *vt* embellir, orner.
ember ('embə) *n* braise *f*.
embezzle (im'bezəl) *vt* détourner. **embezzlement** *n* détournement de fonds *m*.
embitter (im'bitə) *vt* **1** aigrir. **2** envenimer.
emblem ('embləm) *n* emblème, insigne *m*.
embody (im'bɔdi) *vt* **1** incarner. **2** personnifier. **embodiment** *n* personnification *f*.
emboss (im'bɔs) *vt* **1** graver en relief. **2** repousser.
embrace (im'breis) *vt* embrasser, étreindre. *n* étreinte *f*.
embroider (im'brɔidə) *vt* broder. **embroidery** *n* broderie *f*.
embryo ('embriou) *n* embryon *m*.
emerald ('emrəld) *n* émeraude *f*.
emerge (i'mə:dʒ) *vi* émerger, sortir.
emergency (i'mə:dʒənsi) *n* **1** circonstance critique *f*. cas urgent *m*. **2** *med* urgence *f*. **emergency exit** *n* sortie de secours *f*.
emigrate ('emigreit) *vi* émigrer. **emigrant** *adj,n* émigrant. **emigration** *n* émigration *f*.
eminent ('eminənt) *adj* éminent. **eminence** *n* éminence *f*.
emit (i'mit) *vt* **1** émettre. **2** dégager.
emotion (i'mouʃən) *n* émotion *f*. **emotional** *adj* émotif, -ive.
empathy ('empəθi) *n* identification *f*.
emperor ('empərə) *n* empereur *m*.
emphasis ('emfəsis) *n, pl* **emphases** emphase *f*. **emphasize** *vt* accentuer, souligner. **emphatic** *adj* emphatique, énergique.
empire ('empaiə) *n* empire *m*.
empirical (im'pirikəl) *adj* empirique.
employ (im'plɔi) *vt* employer. **employee** *n* employé. **employer** *n* patron, employeur *m*. **employment** *n* emploi *m*. **employment agency** *n* bureau de placement *m*.
empower (im'pauə) *vt* autoriser.
empress ('emprəs) *n* impératrice *f*.
empty ('empti) *adj* vide. *vt* vider. **empty-handed** *adj* bredouille.
emu ('i:mju:) *n* émeu *m*.
emulate ('emjuleit) *vt* rivaliser avec, imiter. **emulation** *n* émulation *f*.
emulsion (i'mʌlʃən) *n* émulsion *f*.
enable (i'neibəl) *vt* permettre, rendre capable.
enact (i'nækt) *vt* décréter, ordonner.
enamel (i'næməl) *vt* émailler. *n* émail, -aux *m*.
encapsulate (in'kæpsjuleit) *vt* incorporer.
enchant (in'tʃɑ:nt) *vt* enchanter. **enchantment** *n* enchantement *m*.
encircle (in'sə:kəl) *vt* entourer, cerner.
enclose (in'klouz) *vt* **1** enclore. **2** enfermer, joindre. **enclosed** *adj* ci-inclus, ci-joint.
encore ('ɔŋkɔ:) *interj,n* bis *m*. *vt* bisser.
encounter (in'kauntə) *vt* rencontrer. *n* rencontre *f*.
encourage (in'kʌridʒ) *vt* encourager. **encouragement** *n* encouragement *m*.
encroach (in'kroutʃ) *vi* **encroach on 1** empiéter sur. **2** abuser de. **encroachment** *n* empiétement *m*.
encumber (in'kʌmbə) *vt* encombrer. **encumbrance** *n* embarras *m*. charge *f*.
encyclopedia (insaklə'pi:diə) *n* encyclopédie *f*.
end (end) *n* fin *f*. bout *m*. **make ends meet** joindre les deux bouts. ~*vt* terminer, finir, achever. *vi* finir, se terminer. **ending** *n* **1** fin *f*. **2** *gram* terminaison *f*. **3** dénouement *m*. **endless** *adj* sans fin, incessant.
endanger (in'deindʒə) *vt* **1** mettre en danger. **2** risquer.
endeavour (in'devə) *vi* s'efforcer, tâcher. *n* effort *m*.
endemic (en'demik) *adj* endémique. *n* endémie *f*.
endive ('endaiv) *n* chicorée *f*.

endorse (in'dɔ:s) *vt* **1** endosser, viser. **2** appuyer. **endorsement** *n* **1** endossement *m*. **2** sanction *f*.
endow (in'dau) *vt* doter.
endure (in'djuə) *vt* supporter. *vi* durer. **endurance** *n* résistance *f*.
enemy ('enəmi) *adj,n* ennemi.
energy ('enədʒi) *n* énergie *f*. **energetic** *adj* énergique.
enfold (in'fould) *vt* envelopper.
enforce (in'fɔ:s) *vt* **1** faire observer. **2** imposer.
engage (in'geidʒ) *vt* **1** engager. **2** embaucher. *vi* **1** s'engager. **2** s'embarquer. **engaged** *adj* **1** occupé, pris. **2** fiancé. **engaging** *adj* attirant. **engagement** *n* **1** engagement *m*. promesse f. **2** fiançailles *f pl*. **3** *mil* combat *m*.
engine ('endʒin) *n* **1** machine *f*. **2** moteur *m*.
engineer (endʒi'niə) *n* ingénieur *m*. *vt inf* machiner. **engineering** *n* technique de l'ingénieur *f*. **civil engineering** *n* génie civil *m*.
England ('iŋglənd) *n* Angleterre *f*. **English** *adj,n* anglais. **English** (language) *n* anglais *m*.
engrave (in'greiv) *vt* graver.
engross (in'grous) *vt* **1** rédiger. **2** absorber.
engulf (in'gʌlf) *vt* engouffrer.
enhance (in'ha:ns) *vt* **1** rehausser. **2** mettre en valeur.
enigma (i'nigmə) *n* énigme *f*. **enigmatic** *adj* énigmatique.
enjoy (in'dʒɔi) *vt* **1** aimer, prendre plaisir à. **2** jouir de. **enjoy oneself** s'amuser. **enjoyable** *adj* agréable. **enjoyment** *n* plaisir *m*.
enlarge (in'la:dʒ) *vt* **1** agrandir. **2** élargir. **enlargement** *n* agrandissement *m*.
enlighten (in'laitn̩) *vt* éclairer.
enlist (in'list) *vt* enrôler, recruter. *vi* s'enrôler, s'engager.
enormous (i'nɔ:məs) *adj* énorme. **enormously** *adv* énormément.
enough (i'nʌf) *adv,adj* assez. **be enough** suffire.
enquire (in'kwaiə) *vi* se renseigner, s'informer. **enquiry** *n* **1** enquête *f*. **2** demande de renseignements *f*.
enrage (in'reidʒ) *vt* faire enrager, exaspérer.
enrich (in'ritʃ) *vt* enrichir.
enrol (in'roul) *vt* enrôler, immatriculer. *vi* se faire inscrire.
ensign ('ensain) *n* **1** (flag) enseigne *f*. **2** *naut* pavillon *m*. **3** (rank) enseigne *m*.
enslave (in'sleiv) *vt* asservir.
ensure (in'ʃuə) *vt* assurer.
entail (in'teil) *vt* **1** substituer. **2** occasionner.
entangle (in'tæŋgəl) *vt* empêtrer, emmêler.
enter ('entə) *vt* **1** entrer dans. **2** prendre part à. **3** inscrire. *vi* entrer.
enterprise ('entəpraiz) *n* entreprise *f*. **enterprising** *adj* entreprenant.
entertain (entə'tein) *vt* **1** amuser, divertir. **2** (guests) recevoir. **3** (an idea) concevoir. *vi* recevoir. **entertaining** *adj* amusant. **entertainment** *n* divertissement *m*.
enthral (in'θrɔ:l) *vt* captiver.
enthusiasm (in'θju:ziæzəm) *n* enthousiasme *m*. **enthusiast** *n* enthousiaste *m,f*. **enthusiastic** *adj* enthousiaste.
entice (in'tais) *vt* attirer, séduire.
entire (in'taiə) *adj* entier, -ière, complet, -ète.
entitle (in'taitl̩) *vt* **1** intituler. **2** donner droit à.
entity ('entiti) *n* entité *f*.
entrails ('entreilz) *n pl* entrailles *f pl*.
entrance[1] ('entrəns) *n* entreé *f*.
entrance[2] (in'tra:ns) *vt* extasier, ravir.
entreat (in'tri:t) *vt* supplier. **entreaty** *n* supplication *f*.
entrench (in'trentʃ) *vt* retrancher.
entrepreneur (ɔntrəprə'nə:) *n* entrepreneur *m*.
entrust (in'trʌst) *vt* confier, charger.
entry ('entri) *n* entrée *f*. **no entry 1** *mot* sens interdit. **2** interdit au public.
entwine (in'twain) *vt* entrelacer. *vi* s'entrelacer.
enunciate (i'nʌnsieit) *vt* **1** énoncer. **2** articuler.
envelop (in'veləp) *vt* envelopper.
envelope ('envəloup) *n* enveloppe *f*.
environment (in'vairənmənt) *n* milieu, -eux, environnement *m*
envisage (in'vizidʒ) *vt* envisager.
envoy ('envɔi) *n* envoyé *m*.
envy ('envi) *n* envie *f*. *vt* envier.
enzyme ('enzaim) *n* enzyme *f*
epaulet ('epəlet) *n* épaulette *f*.
ephemeral (i'femərəl) *adj* éphémère.
epic ('epik) *adj* épique. *n* poème épique *m* épopée *f*.
epidemic (epi'demik) *n* épidémie *f*. *adj* épidémique.
epilepsy ('epilepsi) *n* épilepsie *f*. **epileptic** *adj,n* épileptique.
epilogue ('epilɔg) *n* épilogue *m*.
Epiphany (i'pifəni) *n* Epiphanie *f*. la fête des Rois.
episcopal (i'piskəpəl) *adj* épiscopal, -aux.
episode ('episoud) *n* épisode *m*.
epitaph ('epita:f) *n* épitaphe *f*.

epitome (i'pitəmi) *n* **1** épitomé, abrégé *m*. **2** quintessence *f*.
epoch ('i:pɔk) *n* époque *f*.
equable ('ekwəbəl) *adj* uniforme, egal, -aux.
equal ('i:kwəl) *adj,n* égal, -aux. *vt* égaler. **equality** *n* égalité *f*. **equalize** *vt* **1** égaliser. **2** compenser. *vi* s'égaliser.
equate (i'kweit) *vt* égaler. **equation** *n* équation *f*. **equator** *n* équateur *m*. **equatorial** *adj* équatorial, -aux.
equestrian (i'kwestriən) *adj* équestre.
equilateral (i:kwi'lætərəl) *adj* équilatéral, -aux.
equilibrium (i:kwi'libriəm) *n* équilibre *m*.
equinox ('i:kwinɔks) *n* équinoxe *m*.
equip (i'kwip) *vt* **1** équiper, munir. **2** *tech* outiller. **equipment** *n* **1** équipement *m*. **2** outillage *m*. **3** matériel *m*.
equity ('ekwiti) *n* équité *f*.
equivalent (i'kwivələnt) *adj,n* équivalent *m*.
era ('iərə) *n* ère *f*.
eradicate (i'rædikeit) *vt* déraciner, extirper.
erase (i'reiz) *vt* **1** effacer, gommer. **2** rayer.
erect (i'rekt) *vt* **1** dresser. **2** ériger. *adj* droit, debout. **erection** *n* construction *f*.
ermine ('ə:min) *n* hermine *f*.
erode (i'roud) *vt* éroder, corroder. **erosion** *n* érosion *f*.
erotic (i'rɔtik) *adj* érotique.
err (ə:) *vi* **1** s'égarer, errer. **2** se tromper.
errand ('erənd) *n* commission, course *f*.
erratic (i'rætik) *adj* **1** irrégulier, -ière. **2** fantasque.
error ('erə) *n* erreur, faute *f*.
erupt (i'rʌpt) *vi* faire éruption. **eruption** *n* éruption *f*.
escalate ('eskəleit) *vt* (a war) élargir. **escalator** *n* escalier roulant *m*.
escalope (i'skæləp) *n* escalope *f*.
escape (i'skeip) *vt* échapper à. *vi* s'échapper. *n* fuite, évasion *f*.
escort ('eskɔ:t) *n* escorte *f*. *vt* escorter.
Eskimo ('eskimou) *n* esquimau, -aude, -aux.
esoteric (esə'terik) *adj* ésotérique.
especial (i'speʃəl) *adj* spécial, -aux. **especially** *adv* surtout.
espionage ('espiənɑ:ʒ) *n* espionnage *m*.
esplanade ('espləneid) *n* esplanade *f*.
essay ('esei) *n* **1** tentative, épreuve *f*. **2** *lit* essai *m*. **3** *educ* dissertation *f*.
essence ('esəns) *n* essence *f*. **essential** *adj* essentiel, -elle, indispensable.
establish (i'stæbliʃ) *vt* fonder. **establishment** *n* **1** établissement *m*. fondation *f*. **2** maison (de commerce) *f*. **3** *cap* ordre établi *m*.
estate (i'steit) *n* **1** état *m*. **2** *law* biens *m pl*. **estate car** *n* break *m*.
esteem (i'sti:m) *n* estime *f*. *vt* estimer.
estimate (*n* 'estimət; *v* 'estimeit) *n* **1** évaluation *f*. **2** devis *m*. *vt* estimer, évaluer, apprécier.
estuary ('estʃuəri) *n* estuaire *m*.
etching ('etʃiŋ) *n* gravure à l'eau-forte *f*.
eternal (i'tə:nl̩) *adj* éternel, -elle. **eternity** *n* éternité *f*.
ether ('i:θə) *n* éther *m*.
ethereal (i'θiəriəl) *adj* éthéré.
ethical ('eθikəl) *adj* moral, -aux. **ethics** *n pl* éthique, morale *f*.
ethnic ('eθnik) *adj* ethnique.
etiquette ('etikit) *n* étiquette *f*. convenances *f pl*. protocole *m*.
etymology (eti'mɔlədʒi) *n* étymologie *f*.
eucalyptus (ju:kə'liptəs) *n* eucalyptus *m*.
Eucharist ('ju:kərist) *n* Eucharistie *f*.
eunuch ('ju:nək) *n* eunuque *m*.
euphemism ('ju:fəmizəm) *n* euphémisme *m*. **euphemistic** *adj* euphémique.
euphoria (ju:'fɔ:riə) *n* euphorie *f*.
Europe ('juərəp) *n* Europe *f*. **European** *adj,n* européen, -enne.
European Economic Community *n* Communauté Economique Européenne *f*.
euthanasia (ju:θə'neiziə) *n* euthanasie *f*.
evacuate (i'vækjueit) *vt* évacuer. **evacuation** *n* évacuation *f*.
evade (i'veid) *vt* éviter, esquiver. **evasive** *adj* évasif, -ive.
evaluate (i'væljueit) *vt* évaluer.
evangelical (i:væn'dʒelikəl) *adj* évangélique. **evangelist** *n* évangéliste *m*.
evaporate (i'væpəreit) *vt* faire évaporer. *vi* s'évaporer, se volatiliser. **evaporation** *n* évaporation *f*.
evasive (i'veisiv) *adj* evasif, -ive.
eve (i:v) *n* veille *f*.
even ('i:vən) *adj* **1** égal, -aux. **2** uni. **3** pair. **4** quitte. *adv* **1** même. **2** encore. **even so** quand même. ~*vt* aplanir, égaliser. **even-tempered** *adj* d'humeur égale, placide.
evening ('i:vəniŋ) *n* soir *m*. soireé *f*. **evening class** *n* cours du soir *m*. **evening dress** *n* tenue de soireé *f*.
event (i'vent) *n* **1** événement *m*. **2** cas *m*. **in the event of** au cas où. **eventful** *adj* mouvementé. **eventual** *adj* **1** éventuel, -elle. **2** définitif, -ive. **eventually** *adv* finalement.

ever ('evə) *adv* **1** toujours. **2** jamais. **evergreen** *adj* toujours vert. *n* arbre vert *m*. **everlasting** *adj* éternel, -elle.

every ('evri) *adj* **1** chaque. **2** tout. **everybody** *pron* tout le monde, chacun. **everyday** *adj* quotidien, -enne. *adv* tous les jours. **everyone** *pron* tout le monde, chacun. **every other day** tous les deux jours, un jour sur deux. **everything** *pron* tout. **everywhere** *adv* partout.

evict (i'vikt) *vt* expulser.

evidence ('evidəns) *n* **1** évidence *f*. **2** témoignage *m*. **give évidence** témoigner. **evident** *adj* évident. **evidently** *adv* évidemment.

evil ('i:vəl) *adj* mauvais, méchant. *n* mal, maux *m*.

evoke (i'vouk) *vt* évoquer.

evolution (i:və'lu:ʃən) *n* **1** développement *m*. **2** évolution *f*.

evolve (i'vɔlv) *vt* développer, dérouler. *vi* se dérouler, évoluer. **evolution** *n* évolution *f*.

ewe (ju:) *n* brebis *f*.

exact (ig'zækt) *adj* exact, précis. *vt* exiger. **exacting** *adj* exigeant. **exactly** précisément, justement, tout juste.

exaggerate (ig'zædʒəreit) *vt* exagérer. **exaggeration** *n* exagération *f*.

exalt (ig'zɔ:lt) *vt* **1** exalter. **2** louer.

examine (ig'zæmin) *vt* examiner, inspecter. **examination** *n* examen *m*. **fail/pass an examination** échouer/réussir à un examen. **take an examination** passer un examen.

example (ig'zɑ:mpəl) *n* exemple *m*. **for example** par exemple.

exasperate (ig'zɑ:spəreit) *vt* exaspérer, irriter.

excavate ('ekskəveit) *vt* creuser, fouiller. **excavation** *n* fouille, excavation *f*.

exceed (ik'si:d) *vt* excéder, dépasser.

excel (ik'sel) *vt,vi* surpasser. **excellence** *n* excellence *f*. **excellent** *adj* excellent.

Excellency ('eksələnsi) *n* Excellence *f*.

except (ik'sept) *prep* excepté, sauf. **except that** sauf que. **exception** *n* exception *f*. **exceptional** *adj* exceptionnel, -elle.

excerpt ('eksə:pt) *n* extrait *m*.

excess (ik'ses) *n* excès, excédent *m*. **excessive** *adj* excessif, -ive.

exchange (iks'tʃeindʒ) *vt* échanger. *vi* faire un échange. *n* **1** échange *m*. **2** *comm* change *m*.

exchequer (eks'tʃekə) *n* trésorerie *f*.

excise ('eksaiz) *n* **1** contributions indirectes *f pl*. **2** régie *f*.

excite (ik'sait) *vt* exciter. **excited** *adj* excité, agité. **excitement** *n* surexcitation, émotion *f*. **exciting** *adj* captivant, passionnant.

exclaim (ik'skleim) *vi* s'écrier, s'exclamer.

exclamation (eksklə'meiʃən) *n* exclamation *f*. **exclamation mark** *n* point d'exclamation *m*.

exclude (ik'sklu:d) *vt* exclure. **exclusive** *adj* exclusif, -ive.

excommunicate (ekskə'mju:nikeit) *vt* excommunier. **excommunication** *n* excommunication *f*.

excruciating (ik'skru:ʃieitiŋ) *adj* atroce, affreux, -euse.

excursion (ik'skə:ʒən) *n* excursion, partie de plaisir *f*.

excuse (*n* ik'skju:s; *v* ik'skju:z) *n* excuse *f*. prétexte *m*. *vt* excuser, pardonner. **excuse me!** pardon!

execute ('eksikju:t) *vt* exécuter. **execution** *n* exécution *f*. **executioner** *n* bourreau, -aux *m*.

executive (ig'zekjutiv) *n* cadre (supérieur) *m*.

exempt (ig'zempt) *vt* exempter, dispenser. *adj* exempt, dispensé. **exemption** *n* exemption *f*.

exercise ('eksəsaiz) *n* exercice *m*. *vt* exercer, pratiquer. *vi* s'entrainer. **exercise book** *n* cahier *m*.

exert (ig'zə:t) *vt* employer, exercer. **exertion** *n* effort, emploi *m*.

exhale (eks'heil) *vt* exhaler.

exhaust (ig'zɔ:st) *vt* épuiser. *n* échappement *m*. **exhaust pipe** *n* tuyau d'échappement *m*.

exhibit (ig'zibit) *vt* exhiber, montrer, exposer. *n* objet exposé *m*. **exhibition** *n* exposition *f*. **exhibitionism** *n* exhibitionisme *m*.

exhilarate (ig'ziləreit) *vt* rejouir, ranimer. **exhilaration** *n* joie de vivre *f*.

exile ('egzail) *n* **1** exil *m*. **2** exilé, banni *m*. *vt* exiler, bannir.

exist (ig'zist) *vi* exister, être. **existence** *n* existence *f*. **existentialism** *n* existentialisme *m*. **existing** *adj* actuel, -elle.

exit ('eksit) *n* sortie *f*.

exorbitant (ig'zɔ:bitənt) *adj* exorbitant, excessif, -ive.

exorcize ('eksɔ:saiz) *vt* exorciser.

exotic (ig'zɔtik) *adj* exotique.

expand (ik'spænd) *vt* élargir, dilater, développer. *vi* se développer, se dilater. **expanding** *adj* extensible. **expansion** *n* développement *m*. dilatation *f*.

expanse (ik'spæns) *n* étendue *f*.

expatriate (*v* iks'peitrieit; *n* iks'peitriit) *vt* expatrier. *n* expatrié *m*.

expect (ik'spekt) *vt* attendre, s'attendre à. **expectation** *n* espérance, attente *f*.
expedient (ik'spi:diənt) *n* expédient, moyen *m*. *adj* expédient, convenable.
expedition (ekspi'diʃən) *n* expédition, excursion *f*.
expel (ik'spel) *vt* expulser, bannir.
expenditure (ik'spenditʃə) *n* dépense *f*.
expense (ik'spens) *n* **1** dépense *f*. frais *m pl*. **2** dépens *m*. **expensive** *adj* cher, chère, coûteux, -euse.
experience (ik'spiəriəns) *n* **1** expérience *f*. **2** épreuve *f*. *vt* éprouver. **experienced** *adj* expérimenté.
experiment (ik'sperimənt) *n* expérience *f*. essai *m*. *vi* faire une expérience, expérimenter. **experimental** *adj* expérimental, -aux.
expert ('ekspə:t) *n* expert, spécialiste *m*. *adj* habile, expert. **expertise** *n* expertise *f*.
expire (ik'spaiə) *vi* expirer.
explain (ik'splein) *vt* expliquer, éclaircir. **explanation** *n* explication *f*.
expletive (ik'spli:tiv) *adj,n* explétif, -ive.
explicit (ik'splisit) *adj* explicite, catégorique.
explode (ik'sploud) *vt* faire sauter. *vi* sauter, éclater. **explosive** *adj,n* explosif, -ive *m*.
exploit[1] ('eksplɔit) *n* exploit *m*.
exploit[2] (ik'splɔit) *vt* exploiter.
explore (ik'splɔ:) *vt* explorer. **explorer** *n* explorateur *m*.
exponent (ik'spounənt) *n* interprète *m,f*.
export (*v* ik'spɔ:t, 'ekspɔ:t; *n* 'ekspɔ:t) *vt* exporter. *n* exportation *f*.
expose (ik'spouz) *vt* **1** exposer. **2** révéler. **exposure** *n* **1** exposition *f*. **2** dévoilement *m*.
express (ik'spres) *vt* exprimer. *n* rapide *m*. *adj* exprès. **expression** *n* expression *f*.
exquisite (ek'skwizit) *adj* **1** exquis. **2** vif, vive.
extend (ik'stend) *vt* étendre, prolonger. *vi* s'étendre. **extension** *n* extension *f*. prolongement *m*. **extensive** *adj* **1** vaste, ample. **2** approfondi.
extent (ik'stent) *n* **1** étendue *f*. **2** point *m*. mesure *f*.
exterior (ek'stiəriə) *adj,n* extérieur *m*.
exterminate (ik'stə:mineit) *vt* exterminer.
external (ek'stə:nl̩) *adj* externe, extérieur.
extinct (ik'stiŋkt) *adj* disparu, éteint.
extinguish (ik'stiŋgwiʃ) *vt* éteindre.
extra ('ekstrə) *adj* de plus, en sus, supplémentaire. *n* **1** supplément *m* **2** *pl inf* à-côtés *m pl*.
extract (*n* 'ekstrakt; *v* ik'strækt) *n* extrait *m*. *vt* extraire.
extramural (ekstrə'mjuərəl) *adj* extramuros *invar*.
extraordinary (ik'strɔ:dənri) *adj* extraordinaire, remarquable.
extravagant (ik'strævəgənt) *adj* extravagant, dépensier, -ière. **extravagance** *n* extravagance *f*.
extreme (ik'stri:m) *adj,n* extrême *m*. **extremity** *n* extrémité *f*.
extricate ('ekstrikeit) *vt* dégager.
extrovert ('ekstrəvə:t) *n* extroverti *m*.
exuberant (ig'zju:bərənt) *adj* exubérant.
eye (ai) *n* œil *m pl* yeux. vt regarder, lorgner.
eyeball ('aibɔ:l) *n* globe de l'oeil *m*.
eyebrow ('aibrau) *n* sourcil *m*.
eye-catching *adj* accrocheur, -euse.
eyelash ('ailæʃ) *n* cil *m*.
eyelid ('ailid) *n* paupière *f*.
eye-opener *n* révélation *f*.
eye shadow *n* fard à paupières *m*.
eyesight ('aisait) *n* vue *f*.
eyestrain ('aistrein) *n* mal aux yeux *m*.
eye-witness (ai'witnis) *n* témoin oculaire *m*.

F

fable ('feibəl) *n* conte *m*. fable *f*.
fabric ('fæbrik) *n* **1** tissu *m*. étoffe *f*. **2** fabrique *f*. **fabricate** *vt* fabriquer, inventer.
fabulous ('fæbjuləs) *adj* fabuleux, -euse.
facade (fə'sɑ:d) *n* façade *f*.
face (feis) *n* **1** *anat* visage *m*. figure *f*. **2** face *f*. **3** *inf* toupet *m*. **4** mine *f*. *vt* faire face à. **facecloth** *n* gant de toilette *m*. **facelift** *n* ridectomie *f*. **face-pack** *n* masque anti-rides *m*. **face value** *n* valeur nominale *f*.
facet ('fæsit) *n* aspect *m*.
facetious (fə'si:ʃəs) *adj* plaisant, facétieux, -euse.
facile ('fæsail) *adj* facile. **facilitate** *vt* faciliter. **facility** *n* facilité *f*.
facing ('feisiŋ) *n* parement *m*.
facsimile (fæk'siməli) *n* fac-similé *m*.
fact (fækt) *n* fait *m*. **as a matter of fact** à vrai dire. **factual** *adj* positif, -ive.
faction ('fækʃən) *n* faction *f*.
factor ('fæktə) *n* **1** facteur, diviseur *m*. **2** élément *m*.
factory ('fæktri) *n* usine, fabrique *f*.
faculty ('fækəlti) *n* **1** faculté *f*. **2** talent *m*.
fad (fæd) *n* dada *m*. manie *f*.

fade (feid) *vi* se faner, se déteindre, passer. *vt* décolorer. **fade away** s'évanouir.

fag (fæg) *n* **1** corvée *f*. **2** *sl* sèche *f*.

Fahrenheit ('færənhait) *adj* Fahrenheit.

fail (feil) *vi* **1** manquer. **2** échouer. **3** baisser. *vt* refuser. **failing** *n* défaut *m*. *prep* faute de. **failure** *n* **1** défaut *m*. **2** échec *m*. **3** raté *m*.

faint (feint) *vi* s'évanouir. *n* évanouissement *m*. *adj* faible, pâle, léger, -ère. **faint-hearted** *adj* timide, pusillanime.

fair[1] (fεə) *adj* **1** juste. **2** passable. **3** beau, belle. **4** blond. **fair-minded** *adj* impartial, -aux. **fairly** *adv* **1** honnêtement. **2** assez. **fairness** *n* **1** justice *f*. **2** blondeur *f*.

fair[2] (fεə) *n* foire *f*. **fairground** *n* champ de foire *m*.

fairy ('fεəri) *n* fée *f*. *adj* féerique. **fairytale** *n* conte de fées *m*.

faith (feiθ) *n* **1** foi *f*. **2** confiance *f*. **faithful** *adj* fidèle, loyal, -aux. **faithfulness** *n* fidélité *f*.

fake (feik) *n* article truqué *m*. *vt* truquer.

falcon ('fɔ:lkən) *n* faucon *m*.

fall* (fɔ:l) *n* **1** chute, tombée *f*. **2** baisse *f*. *vi* **1** tomber. **2** baisser.

fallacy ('fæləsi) *n* erreur *f*. **fallacious** *adj* trompeur, -euse.

fallible ('fæləbəl) *adj* faillible.

fallow ('fælou) *adj* en friche.

false (fɔ:ls) *adj* **1** faux, fausse. **2** artificiel, -elle. **3** perfide. **false alarm** *n* fausse alerte *f*. **falsehood** *n* mensonge *m*. **false pretences** *n pl* faux semblant *m*. **under false pretences** par fraude. **false teeth** *n pl* fausses dents *f pl*. **falseness** *n* **1** fausseté *f*. **2** infidélité *f*. **falsify** *vt* fausser, dénaturer.

falter ('fɔ:ltə) *vi* **1** vaciller, chanceler. **2** hésiter.

fame (feim) *n* renommée *f*.

familiar (fə'miliə) *adj* intime, familier, -ière. **familiarize** *vt* familiariser.

family ('fæmili) *n* famille *f*.

famine ('fæmin) *n* famine *f*. **famished** *adj* affamé.

famous ('feiməs) *adj* célèbre, fameux, -euse.

fan[1] (fæn) *n* **1** éventail *m*. **2** ventilateur *m*. *vt* éventer, vanner. **fanbelt** *n* courroie de ventilateur *m*.

fan[2] (fæn) *n* passionné, fervent, fan *m*. **fan club** *n* club de fans *m*.

fanatic (fə'nætik) *n* fanatique *m,f*.

fancy ('fænsi) *n* **1** imagination *f*. **2** caprice *f*. **3** envie *f*. *vt* **1** imaginer. **2** avoir envie de. **fancy oneself** se gober. ~*adj* de fantaisie. **fancy dress** *n* déguisement, travesti *m*.

fanfare ('fænfεə) *n* fanfare *f*.

fang (fæŋ) *n* croc, crochet *m*.

fantastic (fæn'tæstik) *adj* **1** *inf* fantastique. **2** bizarre, excentrique.

fantasy ('fæntəsi) *n* fantaisie *f*.

far (fɑ:) *adj* éloigné. *adv* **1** loin. **2** beaucoup. **far and wide** partout. **so far** jusqu'ici. **faraway** *adj* lointain, éloigné. **far-fetched** *adj* outré, tiré par les cheveux. **far-off** *adj* éloigné. **far-reaching** *adj* d'une grande portée.

farce (fɑ:s) *n* farce *f*. **farcical** *adj* risible.

fare (fεə) *n* prix du voyage *m*.

Far East *n* Extrême-Orient *m*.

farewell (fεə'wel) *interj* adieu! *n* au revoir, adieu, -eux *m*.

farm (fɑ:m) *n* ferme *f*. *vt* exploiter, cultiver. *vi* être cultivateur. **farmer** *n* agriculteur *m*. **farmhouse** *n* ferme *f*. **farming** *n* exploitation agricole *f*. **farmland** *n* ferme *f*. **farmyard** *n* basse-cour *f*.

farther ('fɑ:ðə) *adv* plus loin. *adj* **1** plus lointain. **2** supplémentaire. **farthest** *adj* **1** le plus éloigné. **2** le plus long. *adv* le plus loin.

fascinate ('fæsineit) *vt* fasciner, charmer. **fascinating** *adj* séduisant. **fascination** *n* fascination *f*. charme *m*.

fascism ('fæʃizəm) *n* fascisme *m*. **fascist** *adj,n* fasciste.

fashion ('fæʃən) *n* **1** mode *f*. **2** façon *f*. **3** manière *f*. **in fashion** à la mode. ~*vt* façonner, former. **fashionable** *adj* à la mode.

fast[1] (fɑ:st) *adj* **1** vite, rapide. **2** (of colour) bon teint *invar*. **3** ferme. **4** en avance. *adv* **1** fort, ferme. **2** vite.

fast[2] (fɑ:st) *vi* jeûner. *n* jeûne *m*.

fasten ('fɑ:sən) *vt* **1** attacher. **2** fermer. *vi* s'attacher. **fastener** *n* attache *f*.

fastidious (fə'stidiəs) *adj* **1** difficile. **2** délicat.

fat (fæt) *n* graisse *f*. gras *m*. *adj* gras, grasse, gros, grosse. **get fat** grossir. **fatten** *vi,vt* engraisser.

fatal ('feitl̩) *adj* fatal. **fatality** *n* fatalité *f*.

fate (feit) *n* destin, sort *m*.

father ('fɑ:ðə) *n* père *m*. *vt* engendrer. **father-in-law** *n* beau-père *m*. **fatherland** *n* patrie *f*.

fathom ('fæðəm) *n* brasse *f*. *vt* sonder.

fatigue (fə'ti:g) *n* fatigue *f*. *vt* fatiguer.

fatuous ('fætjuəs) *adj* imbécile, sot, sotte.

fault (fɔ:lt) *n* **1** défaut *m*. **2** faute *f*. **faultless** *adj* impeccable. **faulty** *adj* défectueux, -euse.

fauna ('fɔ:nə) *n* faune *f*.

favour ('feivə) *n* faveur *f*. *vt* favoriser.

favourable *adj* favorable, avantageux, -euse. **favourite** *adj,n* préféré, favori, -ite.
fawn[1] (fɔ:n) *n* faon *m. adj* fauve.
fawn[2] (fɔ:n) *vt* se coucher servilement.
fear (fiə) *n* peur, crainte *f. vt* craindre, redouter. **fearful** *adj* craintif, -ive, effroyable. **fearless** *adj* intrépide.
feasible ('fi:zibəl) *adj* **1** faisable, possible. **2** probable.
feast (fi:st) *n* fête *f.* banquet *m.*
feat (fi:t) *n* **1** exploit *m.* **2** tour de force *m.*
feather ('feðə) *n* plume *f. vt* emplumer. **featherbed** *n* lit de plume *m.* **featherweight** *n* poids plume *m.*
feature ('fi:tʃə) *n* trait *m.* caractéristique *f. vt* **1** caractériser. **2** mettre en manchette.
February ('februəri) *n* février *m.*
feckless ('fekləs) *adj* incapable.
fed (fed) *v* see **feed.**
federal ('fedərəl) *adj* fédéral, -aux. **federate** *vt* fédérer. *vi* se fédérer. *adj* fédéré. **federation** *n* fédération *f.*
fee (fi:) *n* honoraires *m pl.* droit *m.*
feeble ('fi:bəl) *adj* faible.
feed* (fi:d) *vt* nourrir, alimenter. *vi* manger, se nourrir. **be fed up** en avoir assez. *n* nourriture *f.* fourrage *m.* **feedback** *n* rétroaction *f.*
feel* (fi:l) *n* **1** toucher *m.* **2** sensation *f. vt* **1** toucher, palper. **2** sentir. *vi* **1** tâtonner. **2** se sentir. **feeler** *n* antenne *f.* **feeling** *n* **1** sensation *f.* **2** sentiment *m.* **3** impression *f.* **4** toucher *m. adj* sensible.
feign (fein) *vt* simuler, affecter.
feint[1] (feint) *vi* feindre. *n* feinte *f.*
feint[2] (feint) **feint-ruled paper** *n* papier réglé *m.*
feline ('fi:lain) *adj* félin.
fell[1] (fel) *v* see **fall.**
fell[2] (fel) *vt* abattre, assommer.
fellow ('felou) *n* **1** compagnon *m.* **2** membre *m.* **3** type *m.* **4** pareil *m.* **fellowship** *n* **1** amitié *f.* **2** association *f.* **3** fraternité *f.*
felony ('feləni) *n* crime *m.*
felt[1] (felt) *v* see **feel.**
felt[2] (felt) *n* feutre *m.*
female ('fi:meil) *adj* féminin. *n* femelle, femme *f.*
feminine ('feminin) *adj* féminin.
fence (fens) *n* clôture, palissade *f. vi* faire de l'escrime. *vt* renfermer. **fencing** *n* **1** *sport* escrime *f.* **2** clôture, barrière *f.*
fend (fend) *vt* **fend off** parer. **fend for oneself** se débrouiller. **fender** *n* garde-feu *m invar.*
fennel ('fenl̩) *n* fenouil *m.*
ferment (*n* 'fə:ment; *v* fə'ment) *n* **1** ferment *m.* **2** agitation *f. vi* fermenter.
fern (fə:n) *n* fougère *f.*
ferocious (fə'rouʃəs) *adj* féroce.
ferret ('ferit) *n* furet *m. vi* fureter.
ferry ('feri) *n* bac *m. vt* transborder. **ferryboat** *n* navire transporteur *m.*
fertile ('fə:tail) *adj* fécond, fertile. **fertility** *n* fertilité, fécondité *f.* **fertilize** *vt* fertiliser, féconder. **fertilizer** *n* engrais *m.*
fervent ('fə:vənt) *adj* fervent.
fervour ('fə:və) *n* ferveur, passion *f.*
fester ('festə) *vi* suppurer, pourrir.
festival ('festivəl) *n* fête *f.* festival *m.*
fetch (fetʃ) *vt* aller chercher, apporter. **fetching** *adj* séduisant.
fete (feit) *n* fête *f.*
fetid ('fetid) *adj* fétide.
fetish ('fetiʃ) *n* fétiche *m.*
fetlock ('fetlɔk) *n* fanon *m.*
fetter ('fetə) *n* **1** lien *m.* entrave *f.* **2** *pl* chaînes *f pl. vt* enchaîner, entraver.
feud (fju:d) *n* inimitié, vendetta *f.* **feudal** *adj* féodal, -aux.
fever ('fi:və) *n* fièvre *f.* **feverish** *adj* fiévreux, -euse.
few (fju:) *adj* peu de. **a few** quelques, quelques-uns, quelques-unes.
fiancé (fi'ɔnsei) *n* fiancé *m.*
fiasco (fi'æskou) *n* fiasco *m.*
fib (fib) *n* petit mensonge *m. vi* en conter.
fibre ('faibə) *n* fibre *f.* **fibreglass** *n* fibre de verre *f.*
fickle ('fikəl) *adj* inconstant.
fiction ('fikʃən) *n* fiction *f.* **fictitious** *adj* **1** fictif, -ive. **2** simulé.
fiddle ('fidl̩) *n* **1** violon *m.* **2** *inf* combine *f. vi* **1** jouer du violon. **2** tripoter. *vt* truquer.
fidelity (fi'deliti) *n* fidélité, loyauté *f.*
fidget ('fidʒit) *vi* se trémousser. *vt* agacer.
field (fi:ld) *n* **1** champ *m.* **2** *sport* terrain *m.* **3** domaine *m. vi* tenir le champ. *vt* arrêter.
fiend (fi:nd) *n* démon *m.* **fiendish** *adj* diabolique.
fierce (fiəs) *adj* féroce, acharné, ardent.
fiery ('faiəri) *adj* **1** brûlant, ardent. **2** emporté, irascible.
fifteen (fif'ti:n) *adj,n* quinze *m.* **fifteenth** *adj* quinzième.
fifth (fifθ) *adj* cinquième.
fifty ('fifti) *adj,n* cinquante *m.* **fifty-fifty** moitié-moitié. **fiftieth** *adj* cinquantième.

fig (fig) *n* figue *f*. **fig tree** figuier *m*.

fight* (fait) *n* bataille, lutte *f*. combat *m*. *vi* se battre. *vt,vi* combattre.

figment ('figmənt) *n* invention *f*.

figure ('figə) *n* **1** figure *f*. **2** forme *f*. **3** taille *f*. **4** chiffre *m*. *vt* **1** figurer, représenter. **2** *inf* estimer. *vi* calculer. **figurehead** *n* prête-nom *m*. **figurative** *adj* **1** figuratif, -ive. **2** *gram* figuré.

filament ('filəmənt) *n* filament, fil *m*.

file[1] (fail) *n* **1** (in an office) classeur *m*. **2** dossier *m*. *vt* classer, ranger. **filing cabinet** *n* classeur *m*.

file[2] (fail) *n* lime *f*. *vt* limer. **filing** *n* **1** limage *m*. **2** *pl* limaille *f*.

filial ('filiəl) *adj* filial, -aux.

fill (fil) *vt* **1** remplir, combler. **2** (a tooth) plomber. *vi* se remplir. **fill up** faire le plein. ~*n* **1** plein *m*. **2** suffisance *f*. **filling** *n* plombage *m*. **filling station** *n* poste d'essence *m*.

fillet ('filit) *n* filet *m*. *vt* détacher les filets.

filly ('fili) *n* pouliche *f*.

film (film) *n* **1** film *m*. **2** *phot* pelliçule *f*. **3** couche *f*. *vt* filmer, tourner. **film star** *n* vedette de cinéma *f*.

filter ('filtə) *n* filtre *m*. *vt* filtrer, épurer. *vi* s'infiltrer.

filth (filθ) *n* ordure, saleté *f*. **filthy** *adj* sale, infecte.

fin (fin) *n* nageoire *f*. aileron *m*.

final ('fainḷ) *adj* **1** final, dernier, -ière. **2** définitif, -ive. **finalize** *vt* finaliser.

finance ('fainæns) *n* **1** finance *f*. **2** fonds *m*. *vt* financer. **financial** *adj* financier, -ière. **financier** *n* financier *m*.

finch (fintʃ) *n* pinson *m*.

find* (faind) *n* **1** découverte *f* **2** trouvaille *f*. *vt* trouver, découvrir. **find out** découvrir.

fine[1] (fain) *adj* **1** fin, raffiné. **2** beau, belle. **3** excellent. **4** menu. **fine arts** *n pl* beaux arts *m pl*. **finery** *n* parure *f*.

fine[2] (fain) *n* amende *f*. *vt* condamner à une amende.

finger ('fiŋgə) *n* doigt *m*. *vt* tâter, manier. **fingermark** *n* empreinte digitale *f*. **fingernail** *n* ongle *m*. **fingerprint** *n* empreinte digitale *f*. **fingertip** *n* bout du doigt *m*.

finish ('finiʃ) *vt* finir, terminer, achever. *vi* se terminer. *n* **1** fin *f*. **2** arrivée *f*.

finite ('fainait) *adj* fini. **finite verb** *n* verbe à un mode fini *m*.

Finland ('finlənd) *n* Finlande *f*. **Finn** *n* finlandais, finnois. *m*. **Finnish** *adj* finlandais. **Finnish** (language) *n* finnois *m*.

fiord (fjɔ:d) *n also* **fjord** fiord *m*.

fir (fə:) *n* sapin *m*. **fir cone** *n* pomme de pin *f*.

fire (faiə) *n* **1** feu *m pl* feux. **2** incendie *m*. *vt* **1** mettre le feu à. **2** enflammer. **3** tirer.

fire alarm *n* avertisseur d'incendie *m*.

fire brigade *n* corps de sapeurs-pompiers *m*.

fire drill *n* exercices de sauvetage *m pl*.

fire engine *n* pompe à incendie *f*.

fire-escape *n* échelle de sauvetage *f*.

fireguard ('faiəgɑ:d) *n* garde-feu *m invar*.

firelight ('faiəlait) *n* lumière du feu *f*.

fireman ('faiəmən) *n* (sapeur-)pompier *m*.

fireplace ('faiəpleis) *n* cheminée *f*. foyer *m*.

fireside ('faiəsaid) *n* coin du feu *m*.

fire station *n* caserne de pompiers *f*. poste d'incendie *m*.

firework ('faiəwə:k) *n* **1** pièce d'artifice *f*. **2** *pl* feu d'artifice *m*.

firing squad *n* peloton d'exécution *m*.

firm[1] (fə:m) *adj* **1** ferme, solide, constant. **2** résolu. **firmness** *n* fermeté *f*.

firm[2] (fə:m) *n* maison de commerce *f*.

first (fə:st) *adj,n* premier, -ière. *adv* premièrement. **at first** d'abord. **first aid** *n* premiers secours *m pl*. **first-class** *adj* **1** de première classe. **2** de premier ordre. **first-hand** *adj* de première main. **first name** *n* prénom *m*. **first person** *n* première personne *f*. **first-rate** *adj* excellent, de première classe.

fiscal ('fiskəl) *adj* fiscal, -aux.

fish (fiʃ) *n,pl* **fish** *or* **fishes** poisson *m*. *vt,vi* pêcher. **fisherman** *n* pêcheur *m*. **fish finger** *n* carre de poisson pané *m*. **fishing** *n* pêche *f*. **go fishing** aller à la peche. **fishing rod** *n* canne à pêche *f* **fishmonger** *n* marchand de poisson *m*. **fishslice** *n* truelle à poisson *f*.

fission ('fiʃən) *n* fission *f*.

fist (fist) *n* poing *m*.

fit[1] (fit) *adj* **1** propre, convenable. **2** capable. **3** en forme. *vt* **1** ajuster. **2** aller à. **3** garnir. *n* ajustement *m*. **fitting** *n* **1** essayage, ajustage *m*. **2** *pl* accessoires *m pl*. **fitness 1** aptitude *f*. **2** bonne forme *f*.

fit[2] (fit) *n* accès *m*. attaque *f*.

five (faiv) *adj,n* cinq *m*.

fix (fiks) *vt* fixer. *n inf* difficulté *f*. embarras *m*. **fixation** *n* fixation *f*. **fixture** *n* **1** appareil fixe *m*. **2** *sport* engagement *m*. **fixture list** programme *m*.

fizz (fiz) *vi* pétiller, siffler. *n* pétillement, sifflement *m*. **fizzy** *adj* gaseux, -euse.

flabbergast (ˈflæbəgɑ:st) *vt* épater, ahurir.
flabby (ˈflæbi) *adj* mou, molle, flasque.
flag[1] (flæg) *n* drapeau, -aux *m.* **flagpole** *n* mât *m.*
flag[2] (flæg) *vi* languir, pendre.
flagon (ˈflægən) *n* flacon *m.*
flagrant (ˈfleigrənt) *adj* flagrant, scandaleux, -euse.
flair (ˈflɛə) *n* flair *m.*
flake (fleik) *n* flocon *m.* écaille, paillette *f.* *vi* tomber en flocons. **flake off** écailler. **flaky** *adj* **1** écailleux, -euse. **2** feuilleté.
flamboyant (flæmˈbɔiənt) *adj* flamboyant.
flame (fleim) *n* flamme *f.* *vi* flamber.
flamingo (fləˈmiŋgou) *n, pl* **-gos** *or* **-goes** flamant *m.*
flan (flæn) *n* flan *m.* tarte *f.*
flank (flæŋk) *n* flanc *m.* *vt* flanquer.
flannel (ˈflænl̩) *n* **1** flanelle *f.* **2** gant de toilette *m.*
flap (flæp) *n* **1** rabat *m.* **2** battement *m.* **3** battant *m.* **4** affolement *m.* *vt* battre. *vi* **1** claquer. **2** s'affoler. **3** battre.
flare (flɛə) *n* **1** feu de signal *m.* **2** godet *m.* *vi* **1** flamboyer. **2** s'évaser. **flare up** s'émporter.
flash (flæʃ) *n* éclair, éclat *m.* *vi* jeter des éclairs. *vt* projeter. **flashback** *n* retour en arrière *m.* **flashbulb** *n* ampoule flash *f.* **flashlight** *n* flash *m.* **flashy** *adj* tapageur, -euse.
flask (flɑ:sk) *n* flacon *m.*
flat[1] (flæt) *adj* **1** plat. **2** catégorique. **3** fade. **4** *mus* faux. *n* *mus* bémol *m.* **flatfish** *n* poisson plat *m.* **flat-footed** *adj* à pied plat, aux pieds plats. **flatten** *vt* aplatir. *vi* s'aplatir.
flat[2] (flæt) *n* appartement *m.*
flatter (ˈflætə) *vt* flatter. **flattering** *adj* flatteur, -euse. **flattery** *n* flatterie *f.*
flaunt (flɔ:nt) *vi* s'afficher. *vt* faire étalage de.
flautist (ˈflɔ:tist) *n* flûtiste *m,f.*
flavour (ˈfleivə) *n* **1** saveur *m.* **2** parfum *m.* *vt* assaisonner. **flavouring** *n* assaisonnement *m.*
flaw (flɔ:) *n* défaut *m.* **flawed** *adj* défectueux, -euse.
flax (flæks) *n* lin *m.*
flea (fli:) *n* puce *f.* **fleabite** *n* **1** morsure de puce *f.* **2** rien *m.*
fleck (flek) *n* **1** petite tache *f.* **2** particule *f.* *vt* tacheter.
fled (fled) *v* see **flee.**
flee* (fli:) *vt* fuir. *vi* s'enfuir, fuire.
fleece (fli:s) *n* toison *f.* *vt* *inf* tondre, rouler.
fleet (fli:t) *n* flotte *f.*
fleeting (ˈfli:tiŋ) *adj* fugace, passager, -ère.
Fleming (ˈflemiŋ) *n* flamand *m.*
Flemish (ˈflemiʃ) *adj* flamand. **Flemish** (language) *n* flamand *m.*
flesh (fleʃ) *n* chair *f.*
flew (flu:) *v* see **fly.**
flex (fleks) *n* câble souple *m.* *vt* fléchir. **flexible** *adj* flexible, souple.
flick (flik) *n* **1** petit coup *m.* **2** *pl inf* ciné *m.* *vt* effleurer.
flicker (ˈflikə) *n* battement, clignement *m.* *vi* trembloter, vaciller.
flight[1] (flait) *n* **1** vol *m.* volée *f.* **2** trajectoire *m.*
flight[2] (flait) *n* fuite *f.*
flimsy (ˈflimzi) *adj* peu solide, léger, -ère.
flinch (flintʃ) *vi* **1** reculer. **2** tressaillir. **without flinching** sans broncher.
fling* (fliŋ) *vi* jeter. *n* **1** jet *m.* **2** tentative *f.*
flint (flint) *n* **1** silex *m.* **2** pierre à briquet *f.*
flip (flip) *n* secousse, chiquenaude *f.* *vt* tapoter. **flip through** feuilleter. **flipper** *n* nageoire *m.*
flippant (ˈflipənt) *adj* désinvolte. **flippantly** *adv* légèrement.
flirt (flə:t) *n* coquette *f.* *vi* flirter.
flit (flit) *vi* **1** passer légèrement. **2** voleter. **3** déménager. *n* déménagement *m.*
float (flout) *vi* **1** flotter, nager. **2** faire la planche. *vt* flotter. *n* flotteur *m.*
flock[1] (flɔk) *n* (of sheep, etc.) troupeau, -aux *m.* troupe *f.* *vi* s'attrouper.
flock[2] (flɔk) *n* bourre de laine *f.*
flog (flɔg) *vt* flageller, fouetter.
flood (flʌd) *n* inondation *f.* déluge *m.* *vt* inonder. *vi* déborder. **floodlight** *n* phare d'éclairage *m.* *vt* illuminer par projecteurs.
floor (flɔ:) *n* **1** plancher *m.* **2** (of a building) étage *m.* *vt* terrasser. **floorboard** *n* planche *f.*
flop (flɔp) *vi* **1** faire faillite. **2** se laisser tomber. *n* fiasco *m.*
flora (ˈflɔ:rə) *n* flore *f.*
floral (ˈflɔ:rəl) *adj* floral, -aux. **florist** *n* fleuriste *m,f.*
flounce[1] (flauns) *n* mouvement vif *m.* *vi* se démener.
flounce[2] (flauns) *n* (of a dress) volant *m.*
flounder[1] (ˈflaundə) *vi* patauger.
flounder[2] (ˈflaundə) *n* flet *m.*
flour (ˈflauə) *n* farine *f.*
flourish (ˈflʌriʃ) *n* trait de plume *m.* *vt* brandir. *vi* prospérer.
flout (flaut) *vt* railler, narguer.
flow (flou) *n* écoulement, flot *m.* *vi* couler.
flower (ˈflauə) *n* fleur *f.* *vi* fleurir. **flowerbed** *n* plate-bande *f.* **flowery** *adj* fleuri.

flown (floun) *v* see **fly.**
fluctuate ('flʌktʃueit) *vi* fluctuer, vaciller. **fluctuation** *n* fluctuation *f.*
flue (flu:) *n* tuyau de cheminée *m.*
fluent ('flu:ənt) *adj* coulant. **fluently** *adv* couramment.
fluff (flʌf) *n* peluches *f pl.* duvet *m.*
fluid ('flu:id) *adj,n* fluide *m.*
flung (flʌŋ) *v* see **fling.**
fluorescent (flu'resənt) *adj* fluorescent. **fluorescence** *n* fluorescence *f.*
fluoride ('fluəraid) *n* fluorure *f.*
flush[1] (flʌʃ) *vi* rougir. *vt* inonder, balayer à grande eau. *n* **1** éclat *m.* **2** accès *m.* **3** rougeur *f.*
flush[2] (flʌʃ) *adj* **1** ras, de niveau. **2** abondant.
fluster ('flʌstə) *n* agitation *f.* *vt* agiter. *vi* s'énerver.
flute (flu:t) *n* flûte *f.*
flutter ('flʌtə) *n* **1** battement *m.* **2** trouble *m.* *vi* trembler, s'agiter. *vt* agiter.
flux (flʌks) *n* flux *m.*
fly*[1] (flai) *vi* voler. **fly away** s'envoler. **flyover** *n mot* saut-de-mouton *m.*
fly[2] (flai) *n* mouche *f.*
foal (foul) *n* poulain *m.*
foam (foum) *n* écume *f.* *vi* écumer.
focal ('foukəl) *adj* focal, -aux. **focus** *n, pl* **-ci** *or* **-cuses** foyer *m.* *vt* concentrer. *vi* converger.
fodder ('fɔdə) *n* fourrage *m*
foe (fou) *n* ennemi *m.*
foetus ('fi:təs) *n* fœtus *m.*
fog (fɔg) *n* **1** brouillard *m.* **2** brume *f.* **foggy** *adj* brumeux, -euse. **foghorn** *n* sirène de brume *f.*
foible ('fɔibəl) *n* faible *m.* faiblesse *f.*
foil[1] (fɔil) *vt* faire échouer.
foil[2] (fɔil) *n* tain *m.*
foil[3] (fɔil) *n sport* fleuret *m.*
foist (fɔist) *vt* refiler.
fold[1] (fould) *n* pli *m.* *vt,vi* plier. **fold one's arms** se croiser les bras. **folder** *n* classeur *m.*
fold[2] (fould) *n* parc à moutons *m.*
foliage ('fouliidʒ) *n* feuillage *m.*
folk (fouk) *n pl* gens *m,f pl.* **folkdance** *n* danse rustique *f.* **folklore** *n* folklore *m.* **folksong** *n* chanson populaire *or* folklorique *f.* **folktale** *n* histoire traditionnelle *f.*
follicle ('fɔlikəl) *n* follicule *m.*
follow ('fɔlou) *vt* **1** suivre. **2** poursuivre. **3** succéder à. *vi* **1** suivre. **2** s'ensuivre. **following** *n* suite *f.* *adj* suivant. **follower** *n* disciple *m.*
folly ('fɔli) *n* folie, sottise *f.*
fond (fɔnd) *adj* affectueux, -euse, aimant.
fondant ('fɔndənt) *n* fondant *m.*
fondle ('fɔndl) *vt* caresser, câliner.
font (fɔnt) *n* fonts baptismaux *m pl.*
food (fu:d) *n* **1** nourriture *f.* aliments, vivres *m pl.* **2** pâture *f.* **food poisoning** *n* intoxication alimentaire *f.*
fool (fu:l) *n* imbécile *m,f.* *vt* berner, mystifier. *vi* faire l'idiot. **foolhardy** *adj* téméraire. **foolish** *adj* sot, sotte. **foolproof** *adj* indéréglable, indétraquable.
foolscap ('fu:lzkæp) *n* papier ministre *m.*
foot (fut) *n, pl* **feet 1** pied *m.* **2** *zool* patte *f.* **3** base *f.* **put one's foot in it** mettre les pieds dans le plat. **football** *n* **1** football *m.* **2** ballon *m.* **footbridge** *n* passerelle *f.* **foothold** *n* **1** prise pour le pied *f.* **2** position *f.* **footing** *n* pied *m.* **footlights** *n pl* rampe *f.* **footnote** *n* note (au bas de la page) *f.* renvoi *m.* **footprint** *n* empreinte de pas *f.* **footstep** *n* pas *m.* **footwear** *n* chaussures *f pl.*
for (fə; *stressed* fɔ:) *prep* pour, comme, pendant. *conj* car.
forage ('fɔridʒ) *vi* fourrager, fouiller. *vt* saccager. *n* fourrage *m.*
forbear* (fə'bɛə) *vt* s'abstenir de. *vi* s'abstenir.
forbid* (fə'bid) *vt* défendre, interdire. **forbidding** *adj* rébarbatif, -ive.
force (fɔ:s) *n* **1** force, violence *f.* **2** puissance *f.* **3** corps *m.* *vt* **1** forcer. **2** contraindre. **force-feed** *vt* alimenter de force. **forceful** *adj* vigoureux, -euse, fort.
forceps ('fɔ:seps) *n pl* pince *f.* forceps *m.*
ford (fɔ:d) *n* gué *m.* *vt* passer à gué.
fore (fɔ:) *adj* de devant, antérieur. *n* avant, premier plan *m.* *adv* à l'avant.
forearm[1] ('fɔ:ra:m) *n anat* avant-bras *m invar.*
forearm[2] (fɔ:'ra:m) *vt* prévenir, avertir.
forecast* ('fɔ:ka:st) *n* prévision *f.* *vt* prévoir.
forecourt ('fɔ:kɔ:t) *n* avant-cour *f.*
forefather ('fɔ:fa:ðə) *n* aïeul, -eux, ancêtre *m.*
forefinger ('fɔ:fiŋgə) *n* index *m.*
forefront ('fɔ:frʌnt) *n* premier plan *or* rang *m.*
foreground ('fɔ:graund) *n* premier plan, avant-plan *m.*
forehand ('fɔ:hænd) *adj* d'avant-main. **forehand stroke** *n* coup droit *m.*
forehead ('fɔrid) *n* front *m.*
foreign ('fɔrin) *adj* étranger, -ère. **foreigner** *n* étranger, -ère.
foreleg ('fɔ:leg) *n* jambe *or* patte de devant *f.*
forelock ('fɔ:lɔk) *n* mèche *f.* toupet *m.*

foreman ('fɔ:mən) *n* contremaître, chef d'équipe *m*.

foremost ('fɔ:moust) *adj* premier, en tête. *adv* en premier.

forensic (fə'rensik) *adj* judiciaire, légale.

forerunner ('fɔ:rʌnə) *n* précurseur *m*.

foresee* (fɔ:'si:) *vt* prévoir, entrevoir. **foreseeable** *adj* prévisible.

foresight ('fɔ:sait) *n* prévoyance *f*.

forest ('fɔrist) *n* fôret *f*. **forestry** *n* sylviculture *f*.

forestall (fɔ:'stɔ:l) *vt* anticiper, devancer.

foretaste ('fɔ:teist) *n* avant-goût *m*.

foretell* (fɔ:'tel) *vt* prédire, présager.

forethought ('fɔ:θɔ:t) *n* **1** préméditation *f*. **2** prévoyance *f*.

forfeit ('fɔ:fit) *n* **1** amende *f*. **2** *sport* gage *m*. punition *f*. *vt* perdre, forfaire.

forge[1] (fɔ:dʒ) *vt* **1** forger. **2** contrefaire. *n* forge *f*.

forge[2] (fɔ:dʒ) *vi* **forge ahead** pousser de l'avant.

forgery ('fɔ:dʒəri) *n* contrefaçon *f*. faux *m*.

forget* (fə'get) *vt* **1** oublier. **2** omettre. **forgetful** *adj* oublieux, -euse.

forgive* (fə'giv) *vt* pardonner. **forgiving** *adj* indulgent. **forgiveness** *n* **1** pardon *m*. **2** clémence *f*.

forgo* (fɔ:'gou) *vt* renoncer à, s'abstenir de.

fork (fɔ:k) *n* **1** fourche *f*. **2** *cul* fourchette *f*. **3** (of a road) bifurcation. *vi* bifurquer, fourcher.

forlorn (fə'lɔ:n) *adj* **1** abandonné. **2** désespéré.

form (fɔ:m) *n* **1** forme *f*. **2** figure *f*. **3** formule *f*. **4** *educ* classe *f*. **5** banc *m*. *vt* former, façonner. *vi* se former, se faire. **formal** *adj* formel, -elle. **formality** *n* formalité *f*. **formation** *n* formation *f*. **formative** *adj* formatif, -ive, de formation.

former ('fɔ:mə) *adj* précédent, ancien, -enne, premier, -ière. *pron* celui-là, celle-là. **formerly** *adj* autrefois, jadis.

formidable ('fɔ:midəbəl) *adj* formidable, redoutable.

formula ('fɔ:mjulə) *n, pl* **-las** *or* **-lae** formule *f*.

formulate ('fɔ:mjuleit) *vt* formuler.

forsake* (fə'seik) *vt* abandonner, délaisser.

fort (fɔ:t) *n* fort *m*.

forth (fɔ:θ) *adv* en avant. **and so forth** et ainsi de suite. **forthcoming** *adj* **1** à venir. **2** (of a person) ouvert.

fortify ('fɔ:tifai) *vt* **1** fortifier. **2** affermir. **fortification** *n* fortification *f*. **fortitude** *n* courage *m*.

fortnight ('fɔ:tnait) *n* quinzaine *f*. **fortnightly** *adj* bimensuel, -elle. *adv* tous les quinze jours.

fortress ('fɔ:trəs) *n* forteresse *f*.

fortune ('fɔ:tʃən) *n* **1** hasard *m*. chance *f*. **2** fortune, richesse *f*. **fortune-teller** *n* diseur de bonne aventure *m*. **fortune-telling** *n* bonne aventure *f*. **fortunate** *adj* **1** heureux, -euse, fortuné. **2** propice. **fortunately** *adv* **1** heureusement. **2** par bonheur.

forty ('fɔ:ti) *adj,n* quarante *m*. **fortieth** *adj* quarantième.

forum ('fɔ:rəm) *n* forum *m*.

forward ('fɔ:wəd) *adj* **1** de devant. **2** avancé. **3** précoce. *adv* en avant. *n sport* avant *m*. *vt* **1** avancer. **2** expédier. **please forward** prière de faire suivre. **forwardness** *n* précocité *f*. **forwards** *adv* en avant.

fossil ('fɔsəl) *adj,n* fossile *m*.

foster ('fɔstə) *vt* **1** nourrir. **2** encourager. **fosterchild** *n* enfant adoptif *m*. **fostermother** *n* mère adoptive.

fought (fɔ:t) *v* see **fight.**

foul (faul) *adj* **1** infect, nauséabond. **2** sale. **3** obscène. **4** déloyal, -aux. *n* coup déloyal *m*. *vt* **1** salir. **2** enchevêtrer. *vi* s'encrasser. *adv* déloyalement. **foul play** *n* **1** *sport* jeu déloyal *m*. **2** malveillance *f*.

found[1] (faund) *v* see **find.**

found[2] (faund) *vt* fonder. **foundation** *n* **1** fondation *f*. **2** institution *f*. **3** fondement *m*. **founder** *n* fondateur *m*.

foundry ('faundri) *n* fonderie *f*.

fountain ('fauntin) *n* **1** fontaine *f*. **2** source *f*.

four (fɔ:) *adj,n* quatre *m*. **four-poster** *n* lit à colonnes *m*. **fourth** *adj* quatrième. **foursome** *n* partie double *f*. *adj* à quatre.

fourteen (fɔ:'ti:n) *adj,n* quatorze *m*. **fourteenth** *adj* quatorzième.

fowl (faul) *n* **1** oiseau, -aux *m*. volaille *f*. **2** *cul* poule *f*.

fox (fɔks) *n* renard *m*. *vt inf* mystifier. **foxglove** *n* digitale *f*. **foxhound** *n* chien courant *m*. **foxhunting** *n* chasse au renard *f*.

foyer ('fɔiei) *n* foyer *m*.

fraction ('frækʃən) *n* **1** fragment *m*. **2** fraction *f*.

fracture ('fræktʃə) *n* fracture *f*. *vt* casser, fracturer. *vi* se casser, se fracturer.

fragile ('frædʒail) *adj* fragile.

fragment ('frægmənt) *n* fragment, morceau, -aux *m*.

fragrant ('freigrənt) *adj* embaumé, parfumé. **fragrance** *n* parfum *m*.

frail (freil) *adj* fragile, frêle.

frame (freim) *n* **1** cadre *m*. **2** structure *f*. **3** charpente *f*. **4** châssis *m*. **5** monture *f*. *vt* **1** former. **2** encadrer. **framework** *n* **1** construction, charpente *f*. **2** cadre *m*.

franc (fræŋk) *n* franc *m*.

France (frɑ:ns) *n* France *f*.

franchise ('fræntʃaiz) *n* franchise *f*. droit de vote *m*.

frank (fræŋk) *adj* franc, franche, sincère. **frankness** *n* sincérité *f*.

frantic ('fræntik) *adj* frénétique, forcené.

fraternal (frə'tə:nḷ) *adj* fraternel, -elle. **fraternity** *n* fraternité, confrérie *f*. **fraternize** *vi* fraterniser.

fraud (frɔ:d) *n* **1** supercherie, fraude *f*. **2** imposteur *m*.

fraught (frɔ:t) *adj* **fraught with** plein de.

fray[1] (frei) *n* bagarre, rixe *f*.

fray[2] (frei) *vt* érailler, effiler. *vi* s'érailler, s'effiler.

freak (fri:k) *n* **1** fantaisie *f*. **2** curiosité *f*. phénomène *m*. *adj* extraordinaire.

freckle ('frekəl) *n* tache de rousseur *f*.

free (fri:) *adj* **1** libre. **2** gratuit. **free and easy** sans façons. ~*vt* **1** libérer, affranchir. **2** dégager. **freedom** *n* liberté *f*. **freehand** *adj* à main levée. **freehold** *n* propriété libre *f*. **freelance** *adj* indépendant. **freemason** *n* franc-maçon *m*. **free will** *n* libre arbitre *m*.

freeze* (fri:z) *v imp* geler. *vt* **1** congeler, glacer. **2** bloquer. *vi* se congeler. *n* gel *m*. **freezing** *n* congélation *f*.

freight (freit) *n* **1** fret, transport *m*. **2** cargaison *f*. *vt* fréter, affréter. **freight train** *n* train de marchandises *m*.

French (frentʃ) *adj* français. **French** (language) *n* français *m*. **French bean** *n* haricot vert *m*. **French dressing** *n* vinaigrette *f*. **French horn** *n* cor d'harmonie *m*. **Frenchman** *n* français *m*. **French window** *n* porte-fenêtre *f*.

frenzy ('frenzi) *n* frénésie *f*.

frequency ('fri:kwənsi) *n* fréquence *f*. **frequent** *adj* fréquent. *vt* fréquenter, hanter. **frequently** *adv* fréquemment.

fresco ('freskou) *n, pl* **-oes** *or* **-os** fresque *f*.

fresh (freʃ) *adj* **1** frais, fraîche, nouveau, -elle. **2** novice. **3** alerte. **freshness** *n* fraîcheur *f*. **freshwater** *n* eau douce *f*.

fret (fret) *vi* se tourmenter, se tracasser. *vt* ronger.

friar ('fraiə) *n* moine *m*. **friary** *n* monastère *m*.

friction ('frikʃən) *n* **1** friction *f*. **2** frottement *m*. **3** conflit *m*.

Friday ('fraidi) *n* vendredi *m*.

fridge (fridʒ) *n inf* réfrigérateur, frigo *m*.

friend (frend) *n* ami *m*. **make friends with** se lier d'amitié avec. **friendliness** *n* bienveillance *f*. bonté *f*. **friendly** *adj* amical, -aux, sympathique. **friendship** *n* amitié *f*.

frieze (fri:z) *n* frise *f*.

fright (frait) *n* peur *f*. effroi *m*. **frighten** *vt* effrayer, faire peur. **frightful** *adj* terrible, épouvantable.

frigid ('fridʒid) *adj* **1** glacial, froid. **2** *med* frigide.

frill (fril) *n* volant *m*. ruche *f*. *vt* plisser, froncer.

fringe ('frindʒ) *n* **1** frange *f*. **2** bord *m*. bordure *f*.

frisk (frisk) *vi* gambader. **frisky** *adj* folâtre.

fritter[1] ('fritə) *vt* morceler. **fritter away** gaspiller.

fritter[2] ('fritə) *n* beignet *m*.

frivolity (fri'vɔliti) *n* frivolité *f*. **frivolous** *adj* frivole, futile.

frizz (friz) *vt* friser, crêper. *vi* se friser. **frizzy** *adj* crépu.

frizzle[1] ('frizḷ) *vt* (hair) friser.

frizzle[2] ('frizəl) *vt* grésiller, crépiter.

fro (frou) *adv* **to and fro** de long en large.

frock (frɔk) *n* robe *f*.

frog (frɔg) *n* grenouille *f*. **frogs' legs** *n pl* cuisses de grenouille *f pl*.

frolic ('frɔlik) *n* cabriole *f*. ébats *m pl*. *vi* batifoler, folâtrer.

from (frəm; *stressed* frɔm) *prep* **1** de. **2** à partir de. **3** à. **4** d'après. **5** de la part de.

front (frʌnt) *n* front, devant *m*. façade *f*. **in front of** devant. ~*adj* de devant, d'avant. **frontal** *adj* de devant.

frontier ('frʌntiə) *n* frontière *f*.

frost (frɔst) *n* gelée *f*. *vt* geler, givrer. **frosty** *adj* gelé, glacial. **frostbite** *n* gelure *f*.

froth (frɔθ) *n* écume, mousse *f*. **frothy** *adj* mousseux, -euse.

frown (fraun) *vi* froncer les sourcils. **frown upon** regarder de travers. ~*n* froncement de sourcils *m*.

froze (frouz) *v* see **freeze.**

frozen ('frouzṇ) *v* see **freeze.** *adj* gelé, glacé.

frugal ('fru:gəl) *adj* frugal, -aux.

fruit (fru:t) *n* fruit *m*. **fruit machine** *n* machine à sous *f*. **fruitful** *adj* fructueux, -euse, fécond. **fruition** *n* **1** jouissance *f*. **2** réalisation *f*. **fruitless** *adj* stérile.

frustrate (frʌs'treit) *vt* frustrer.

fry (frai) *vt* faire frire. *vi* frire. **frying pan** *n* poêle (à frire) *f*.
fudge (fʌdʒ) *n* fondant *m*.
fuel ('fju:əl) *n* combustible, carburant *m*.
fugitive ('fju:dʒitiv) *adj,n* fugitif, -ive.
fulcrum ('fʌlkrəm) *n, pl* **-crums** *or* **-cra 1** *tech* point d'appui *m*. **2** centre *m*.
fulfil (ful'fil) *vt* **1** accomplir. **2** satisfaire. **3** achever. **fulfilment** *n* **1** accomplissement *m*. **2** achèvement *m*.
full (ful) *adj* **1** plein, rempli, complet, -ète. **2** ample. **full-length** *adj* **1** *Art* en pied. **2** long, longue. **full moon** *n* pleine lune *f*. **full stop** *n* point *m*. **full-time** *adj* à temps complet. **fullness** *n* **1** plénitude *f*. **2** ampleur *f*. **fully** *adv* pleinement, entièrement.
fumble ('fʌmbəl) *vi* fouiller, farfouiller.
fume (fju:m) *n* fumée, vapeur *f*. *vi* fumer.
fun (fʌn) *n* **1** amusement *m*. **2** plaisanterie *f*. **for fun** pour rire. **make fun of** se moquer de. **funfair** *n* fête foraine *f*.
function ('fʌŋkʃən) *n* **1** fonction *f*. **2** réception *f*. *vi* fonctionner, marcher.
fund (fʌnd) *n* fonds *m*. caisse *f*.
fundamental (fʌndə'mentl̩) *adj* fondamental, -aux, essentiel, -elle.
funeral ('fju:nərəl) *n* funérailles, obsèques *f pl*. *adj* funéraire, funèbre.
fungus ('fʌŋgəs) *n, pl* **-gi** *or* **-guses** champignon (vénéneux) *m*.
funnel ('fʌnl̩) *n* **1** entonnoir *m*. **2** cheminée *f*.
funny ('fʌni) *adj* **1** drôle, comique, marrant. **2** étrange, bizarre.
fur (fə:) *n* **1** fourrure *f*. poil *m*. **2** tartre *m*. *vt* incruster. *vi* s'incruster. **furrier** *n* fourreur *m*.
furious ('fjuəriəs) *adj* furieux, -euse, furibond.
furnace ('fə:nis) *n* fourneau, -aux, four *m*.
furnish ('fə:niʃ) *vt* **1** fournir, munir. **2** (a room, etc.) meubler.
furniture ('fə:nitʃə) *n* meubles *m pl*. mobilier *m*. **antique furniture** meubles d'époque. **piece of furniture** meuble *m*.
furrow ('fʌrou) *n* **1** sillon *m*. **2** rainure *f*. *vt* sillonner.
further ('fə:ðə) *adv* **1** plus loin. **2** d'avantage. *adj* supplémentaire. *vt* avancer, favoriser. **furthermore** *adv* en outre. **furthest** *adj* **1** le plus éloigné. **2** le plus long. *adv* le plus loin.
furtive ('fə:tiv) *adj* furtif, -ive, sournois.
fury ('fjuəri) *n* furie, fureur *f*.
fuse[1] (fju:z) *n* fusible, plomb *m*.
fuse[2] (fju:z) *vt,vi* **1** fondre. **2** fusionner.
fuselage ('fju:zəlɑ:ʒ) *n* fuselage *m*.
fusion ('fju:ʒən) *n* fusion *f*.
fuss (fʌs) *n* **1** bruit exagéré *m*. **2** embarras *m pl*. *vi* faire des histoires. *vt* tracasser. **fussy** *adj* tatillon, -onne, méticuleux, -euse.
futile ('fju:tail) *adj* futile, vain.
future ('fju:tʃə) *adj* future, à venir. *n* **1** avenir *m*. **2** *gram* futur *m*.
fuzz (fʌz) *n* peluches *m pl*. *vt* faire bouffer. *vi* bouffer, frisotter. **fuzzy** *adj* **1** frisotté. **2** flou.

G

gabble ('gæbəl) *n* bredouillement *m*. jacasserie *f*. *vi* bredouiller, jacasser. *vt* débiter très vite.
gable ('geibəl) *n* pignon *m*.
gadget ('gædʒit) *n inf* dispositif, truc *m*.
gag[1] (gæg) *n* bâillon *m*. *vt* bâillonner.
gag[2] (gæg) *inf vt* tromper. *vi* blaguer. *n* blague *f*.
gaiety ('geiəti) *n* gaieté *f*.
gaily ('geili) *adv* gaiement, allègrement.
gain (gein) *vt* **1** gagner, acquérir. **2** (of a clock) avancer. *n* gain, profit *m*.
gait (geit) *n* allure, démarche *f*.
gala ('gɑ:lə) *n* fête *f*. gala *m*.
galaxy ('gæləksi) *n* galaxie *f*.
gale (geil) *n* tempête *f*. coup de vent *m*.
gallant ('gælənt) *adj* **1** brave, vaillant. **2** galant. **gallantly** *adv* **1** bravement. **2** galamment. **gallantry** *n* **1** vaillance *f*. **2** galanterie *f*.
gallery ('gæləri) *n* **1** galerie *f*. **2** *pol* tribune *f*. **3** *Art* musée *m*.
galley ('gæli) *n naut* cuisine *f*.
gallon ('gælən) *n* gallon *m*.
gallop ('gæləp) *n* galop *m*. *vi* galoper. *vt* faire galoper.
gallows ('gælouz) *n* potence *f*. gibet *m*.
galore (gə'lɔ:) *adv* en abondance, à gogo.
galvanize ('gælvənaiz) *vt* galvaniser.
gamble ('gæmbəl) *vt,vi* jouer, miser. *vt* risquer. *n* jeu, jeux *m*. spéculation *f*. **gambling** *n* jeu, jeux *m*.
game (geim) *n* **1** amusement, jeu, jeux *m*. **2** (hunting) gibier *m*. **gamekeeper** *n* garde-chasse *m*.
gammon ('gæmən) *n* **1** quartier de lard fumé *m*. **2** jambon fumé *m*.
gander ('gændə) *n* jars *m*.
gang (gæŋ) *n* troupe, bande *f*. *v* **gang up**

s'allier. **gangster** *n* bandit, gangster *m*. **gangway** *n* **1** passage *m*. **2** *naut* passerelle *f*.

gangrene (gæŋ'gri:n) *n* gangrène *f*.

gap (gæp) *n* **1** trou *m*. ouverture, brèche *f*. **2** écart *m*.

gape (geip) *vi* **1** regarder bouche bée. **2** bâiller. **gaping** *adj* **1** bouche bée. **2** béant.

garage ('gærɑ:ʒ) *n* garage *m*.

garble ('gɑ:bəl) *vt* fausser, mutiler.

garden ('gɑ:dn̩) *n* jardin *m*. *vi* jardiner. **gardening** *n* jardinage *m*.

gargle ('gɑ:gəl) *vt* se gargariser. *n* gargarisme *m*.

gargoyle ('gɑ:gɔil) *n* gargouille *f*.

garland ('gɑ:lənd) *n* guirlande *f*. *vt* enguirlander.

garlic ('gɑ:lik) *n* ail *m,pl* aulx. **clove of garlic** *n* gousse d'ail *f*.

garment ('gɑ:mənt) *n* vêtement *m*.

garnish ('gɑ:niʃ) *n* garniture *f*. *vt* garnir, orner.

garrison ('gærisən) *n* garnison *f*. *vt* mettre en garnison.

garter ('gɑ:tə) *n* jarretière *f*.

gas (gæs) *n* gaz *m invar*. *vt* asphyxier.

gash (gæʃ) *n* coupure, entaille *f*. *vt* entailler, couper, balafrer.

gasket ('gæskit) *n* joint *m*.

gasp (gɑ:sp) *n* hoquet, sursaut *m*. *vi* **1** haleter, suffoquer. **2** sursauter.

gastric ('gæstrik) *adj* gastrique. **gastronomic** *adj* gastronomique.

gate (geit) *n* porte, grille, barrière *f*. **gatecrash** *vi* resquiller.

gateau ('gætou) *n,pl* **-teaux** gâteau, -aux *m*.

gather ('gæðə) *vt* **1** rassembler, recueillir. **2** prendre. **3** comprendre, déduire. *vi* se rassembler. **gathering** *n* rassemblement *m*.

gauche (gouʃ) *adj* gauche.

gaudy ('gɔ:di) *adj* voyant, criard. **gaudily** *adv* de manière voyante.

gauge (geidʒ) *n* calibre, indicateur *m*. jauge *f*. *vt* calibrer, jauger, mesurer.

gaunt (gɔ:nt) *adj* maigre, decharné.

gauze (gɔ:z) *n* gaze *f*.

gave (geiv) *v* see **give.**

gay (gei) *adj* **1** gai, allègre. **2** *sl* homosexuel, -elle.

gaze (geiz) *n* regard fixe *m*. *vi* regarder fixement.

gazelle (gə'zel) *n* gazelle *f*.

gear (giə) *n* **1** équipement *m*. effets *m pl*. **2** *mot* vitesse *f*. **put into/out of gear** embrayer/débrayer. **gearbox** *n* boîte de vitesses *f*. **gear lever** *n* levier de changement de vitesse *m*.

gelatine ('dʒeləti:n) *n* gélatine *f*.

gelignite ('dʒelignait) *n* gélignite *f*.

gem (dʒem) *n* pierre précieuse, gemme *f*. joyau, -aux *m*.

Gemini ('dʒɛminai) *n pl* Gémeaux *m pl*.

gender ('dʒendə) *n* **1** *gram* genre *m*. **2** sexe *m*.

gene (dʒi:n) *n* gène *m*.

genealogy (dʒini'ælədʒi) *n* généalogie *f*.

general ('dʒenərəl) *adj,n* général, -aux *m*. **general practitioner** *n* médecin généraliste *m*. **generalization** *n* généralisation *f*. **generalize** *vt* généraliser.

generate ('dʒenəreit) *vt* engendrer, produire. **generation** *n* génération *f*. **generator** *n* générateur *m*.

generic (dʒi'nerik) *adj* générique.

generous ('dʒenərəs) *adj* généreux, -euse, magnanime. **generosity** *n* générosité *f*.

genetic (dʒi'netik) *adj* génétique. **genetics** *n* génétique *f*.

Geneva (dʒi'ni:və) *n* Genève *f*. **Lake Geneva** lac Léman *m*.

genial ('dʒi:niəl) *adj* doux, clément, bienveillant.

genital ('dʒenitl̩) *adj* génital, -aux. **genitals** *n pl* organes génitaux *m pl*.

genius ('dʒi:niəs) *n* **1** génie *m*. **2** démon *m*. **3** aptitude *f*.

genteel (dʒen'ti:l) *adj* de bon ton.

gentile ('dʒentail) *adj,n* gentil.

gentle ('dʒentl̩) *adj* doux, douce. **gentleman** *n* **1** monsieur. **2** homme comme il faut *m*. **gentleness** *n* douceur *f*.

genuflect ('dʒenjuflekt) *vi* faire une génuflexion.

genuine ('dʒenjuin) *adj* **1** authentique, véritable. **2** sincère.

genus ('dʒi:nəs) *n, pl* **genera** genre *m*.

geography (dʒi'ɔgrəfi) *n* géographie *f*. **geographic** *adj also* **geographical** géographique.

geology (dʒi'ɔlədʒi) *n* géologie *f*. **geological** *adj* géologique. **geologist** *n* géologue *m*.

geometry (dʒi'ɔmətri) *n* géométrie *f*. **geometric** *adj also* **geometrical** géométrique.

geriatrics (dʒeri'ætriks) *n* gériatrie *f*.

germ (dʒə:m) *n* germe, microbe *m*.

Germany ('dʒə:məni) *n* Allemagne *f*. **German** *adj,n* allemand. **German** (language) *n* allemand *m*. **German measles** *n* rubéole *f*. **Germanic** *adj* germanique.

germinate ('dʒə:mineit) *vi* germer. *vt* faire germer.

gerund ('dʒerənd) *n* gérondif *m*.
gesticulate (dʒis'tikuleit) *vt* gesticuler.
gesture ('dʒestʃə) *n* geste, signe *m*.
get* (get) *vt* **1** obtenir. **2** gagner. **3** aller chercher. **4** *inf* comprendre. **5** faire. **6** avoir. *vi* **1** devenir. **2** arriver. **get back** revenir. **get down** descendre. **get in 1** entrer. **2** arriver. **get off** descendre. **get on** monter. **get out** sortir. **get up** se lever.
geyser ('gi:zə) *n* geyser *m*.
ghastly ('gɑ:stli) *adj* **1** horrible, effroyable. **2** blême. *adv* horriblement, effroyablement.
gherkin ('gə:kin) *n* cornichon *m*.
ghetto ('getou) *n, pl* **-os** *or* **-oes** ghetto *m*.
ghost (goust) *n* fantôme *f*. spectre *m*.
giant ('dʒaiənt) *adj,n* géant.
giddy ('gidi) *adj* **1** étourdi, vertigineux, -euse. **2** frivole. **giddiness** *n* vertige *m*.
gift (gift) *n* don, cadeau, -aux *m*. **gifted** *adj* doué.
gigantic (dʒai'gæntik) *adj* gigantesque, géant.
giggle ('gigəl) *n* petit rire, gloussement *m*. *vi* rire nerveusement, glousser.
gild (gild) *vt* dorer. **gilded** *adj* doré.
gill (gil) *n* *zool* branchie *f*.
gilt (gilt) *n* dorure *f*.
gimmick ('gimik) *n* machin, truc *m*. trouvaille *f*.
gin (dʒin) *n* gin, genièvre *m*.
ginger ('dʒindʒə) *n* gingembre *m*. *adj* roux, rousse. **gingerbread** *n* pain d'épice *m*. **gingerly** *adv* avec précaution.
gingham ('giŋəm) *n* guingan *m*.
Gipsy ('dʒipsi) *n* bohemien, -ienne.
giraffe (dʒi'rɑ:f) *n* girafe *f*.
girder ('gə:də) *n* support *m*. poutre *f*.
girdle ('gə:dl̩) *n* ceinture, cordelière *f*. *vt* ceindre.
girl (gə:l) *n* (jeune) fille *f*. **girlfriend** *n* (petite) amie *f*. **girlhood** *n* jeunesse *f*.
girth (gə:θ) *n* sangle *f*.
give* (giv) *vt,vi* donner. *vt* faire. **give away 1** donner. **2** *inf* trahir. **give in** céder. **give out 1** distribuer. **2** annoncer. **give up** renoncer, abandonner. **give way 1** céder. **2** s'affaisser.
glacier ('glæsiə) *n* glacier *m*.
glad (glæd) *adj* heureux, -euse, content. **gladly** *adv* avec plaisir, volontiers.
glamour ('glæmə) *n* **1** charme *m*. **2** fascination *f*. prestige *m*. **glamorize** *vt* donner un prestige factice. **glamorous** *adj* enchanteur, -eresse.
glance (glɑ:ns) *n* regard, coup d'œil *m*. *vi* jeter un coup d'œil. **glance through** feuilleter.
gland (glænd) *n* glande *f*.
glare (glɛə) *n* **1** lumière aveuglante *f*. éclat *m*. **2** regard farouche *m*. *vi* éblouir. **glare at** regarder d'un air furieux.
glass (glɑ:s) *n* **1** verre *m*. **2** *pl* lunettes *f pl*. **pane of glass** vitre *f*.
glaze (gleiz) *n* glace *f*. lustre, vernis *m*. *vi* **1** vitrer. **2** vernir. **3** *cul* glacer.
gleam (gli:m) *n* lueur *f*. rayon *m*. *vi* luire, miroiter.
glean (gli:n) *vt* glaner.
glee (gli:) *n* joie, allégresse *f*. *adj* joyeux, -euse, allègre.
glib (glib) *adj* spécieux, -euse.
glide (glaid) *vi* **1** glisser, couler. **2** *aviat* planer. *n* **1** glissement *m*. **2** vol plané *m*. **glider** *n* planeur *m*.
glimmer ('glimə) *n* lueur (faible) *f*. *vi* luire faiblement.
glimpse (glimps) *n* aperçu *m*. **catch a glimpse** entrevoir, apercevoir.
glint (glint) *n* trait de lumière *m*. *vi* étinceler.
glisten ('glisən) *vi* étinceler, reluire.
glitter ('glitə) *n* étincellement *m*. *vi* étinceler.
gloat (glout) *vi* **gloat over** couver du regard, se réjouir.
globe (gloub) *n* globe *m*. sphère *f*.
gloom[1] (glu:m) *n* (darkness) obscurité *f*. ténèbres *f pl*. **gloomy** *adj* sombre, ténébreux, -euse.
gloom[2] (glu:m) *n* mélancolie *f*. **gloomy** *adj* lugubre, morne.
glory ('glɔ:ri) *n* gloire *f*. honneur *m*. *v* **glory in** se glorifier de, se faire gloire de. **glorify** *vt* glorifier. **glorious** *adj* glorieux, -euse.
gloss[1] (glɔs) *n* (shine) lustre *m*. *vt* lustrer, glacer. **gloss over** farder. **glossy** *adj* lustré, brillant.
gloss[2] (glɔs) *n* glose *f*. commentaire *m*. *vt* gloser.
glossary ('glɔsəri) *n* glossaire, lexique *m*.
glove (glʌv) *n* gant *m*.
glow (glou) *n* rougeur, ardeur *f*. *vi* briller, rayonner. **glowing** *adj* **1** rayonnant. **2** chaleureux, -euse.
glower ('glauə) *vi* **glower at** regarder d'un air fâché.
glucose ('glu:kous) *n* glucose *m*.
glue (glu:) *n* colle *f*. *vt* coller.
glum (glʌm) *adj* renfrogné, maussade.
glut (glʌt) *n* surabondance *f*. **glutton** *n* gourmand *m*. **gluttony** *n* gloutonnerie *f*.
gnarled (nɑ:ld) *adj* noueux, -euse, tordu.

gnash (næʃ) *vt* grincer.
gnat (næt) *n* moustique, cousin *m*.
gnaw (nɔ:) *vt* ronger. **gnawing** *n* rongement *m*.
gnome (noum) *n* gnome *m*.
go* (gou) *vi* **1** aller, partir. **2** (of a machine) marcher. **3** passer. **go away** s'en aller. **go back** retourner. **go down** descendre. **go on** continuer. **go out** sortir. **go through** traverser. **go up** monter. **go without** se passer de. ~*n, pl* **goes 1** coup *m*. **2** entrain *m*.
goad (goud) *vt* aiguillonner. *n* aiguillon *m*.
goal (goul) *n* **1** but *m*. **2** objectif *m*. **goalkeeper** *n* gardien de but *m*. **goalpost** *n* montant de but *m*.
goat (gout) *n* chèvre *f*. **he-goat** *n* bouc *m*.
gobble ('gɔbəl) *vt* avaler goulûment.
goblin ('gɔblin) *n* lutin *m*.
god (gɔd) *n* dieu, -eux *m*. **godchild** *n* filleul *m*. **goddaughter** *n* filleule *f*. **godfather** *n* parrain *m*. **godmother** *n* marraine *f*. **godson** *n* filleul *m*. **goddess** *n* déesse *f*.
goggles ('gɔgəlz) *n* lunettes protectrices *f pl*.
gold (gould) *n* or *m*. **golden** *adj* doré, d'or. **golden syrup** *n* mélasse raffinée *f*. **goldfinch** *n* chardonneret *m*. **goldfish** *n* poisson rouge *m*. **goldmine** *n* **1** mine d'or *f*. **2** *inf* affaire d'or *f*. **goldsmith** *n* orfèvre *m*.
golf (gɔlf) *n* golf *m*. **golfcourse** *n* terrain de golf *m*.
gondola ('gɔndələ) *n* gondole *f*. **gondolier** *n* gondolier *m*.
gone (gɔn) *v* see **go.**
gong (gɔŋ) *n* gong *m*.
good (gud) *adj* **1** bon, bonne. **2** sage. **good for nothing** bon à rien. ~*n* **1** bien *m*. **2** *pl* effets *m pl*. marchandises *f pl*. **for good** pour de bon. **good afternoon** *interj* bonjour! **goodbye** *interj,n* au revoir, adieu, -eux *m*. **good evening** *interj* bonsoir! **good-looking** *adj* beau, belle. **good morning** *interj* bonjour! **good night** *interj* bonne nuit! **goods train** *n* train de marchandises *m*. **good will** *n* bonne volonté, bienveillance *f*.
Good Friday *n* vendredi saint *m*.
goose (gu:s) *n, pl* **geese** oie *f*. **gooseberry** *n* groseille à maquereau *f*. **gooseberry bush** groseillier (à maquereau) *m*.
gore[1] (gɔ:) *n* sang caillé *m*.
gore[2] (gɔ:) *vt* encorner.
gorge (gɔ:dʒ) *n* gorge *f*. *vi* se gorger, s'empiffrer. *vt* gorger, rassasier.
gorgeous ('gɔ:dʒəs) *adj* magnifique, splendide.
gorilla (gə'rilə) *n* gorille *m*.
gorse (gɔ:s) *n* ajonc *m*.
gory ('gɔ:ri) *adj* ensanglanté.
gosh (gɔʃ) *interj* sapristi!
gosling ('gɔzliŋ) *n* oison *m*.
gospel ('gɔspəl) *n* évangile *m*.
gossip ('gɔsip) *vi* bavarder, faire des cancans. *n* **1** commérage *m*. **2** commère, bavarde *f*.
got (gɔt) *v* see **get.**
Gothic ('gɔθik) *adj* gothique.
goulash ('gu:læʃ) *n* gulache *m*.
gourd (guəd) *n* courge, gourde *f*.
gourmet (guə'mei) *n* gourmet, gastronome *m*.
govern ('gʌvən) *vt* gouverner, régir, administrer. **government** *n* gouvernement *m*. **governor** *n* **1** gouverneur *m*. **2** *inf* patron *m*.
gown (gaun) *n* robe *f*.
grab (græb) *n* mouvement vif pour saisir *m*. étreinte *f*. *vi* saisir brusquement, empoigner.
grace (greis) *n* **1** grâce *f*. **2** bénédicité *m*. **Her/His Grace** Madame/Monseigneur. **Your Grace** votre Grandeur. **graceful** *adj* grâcieux, -euse. **gracefully** *adv* avec grâce. **gracious** *adj* bienveillant.
grade (greid) *n* grade, rang, degré *m*. *vt* **1** grader, classer. **2** graduer. **gradient** *n* dénivellation, pente, rampe *f*. **gradual** *adj* graduel, -elle. **graduate** *n* diplômé. *vi* recevoir ses diplômes. *vt* graduer.
graffiti (grə'fi:ti) *n pl* graffiti *n pl*.
graft (grɑ:ft) *n* greffe *f*. *vt* greffer.
grain (grein) *n* **1** grain *m*. **2** texture *f*.
gram (græm) *n* gramme *m*.
grammar ('græmə) *n* grammaire *f*. **grammar school** *n* lycée *m*. **grammatical** *adj* grammatical, -aux.
gramophone ('græməfoun) *n* phonographe *m*.
granary ('grænəri) *n* grenier *m*.
grand (grænd) *adj* grandiose, magnifique. **grandeur** *n* grandeur, splendeur *f*.
grandad ('grændæd) *n inf also* **grandpa** *n* grand-papa *m*.
grandchild ('græntʃaild) *n* petit-enfant *m*.
granddaughter ('grændɔ:tə) *n* petite-fille *f*.
grandfather ('grænfɑ:ðə) *n* grand-père *m*.
grandma ('grænmɑ:) *n inf also* **granny** bonne-maman, mémé *f*.
grandmother ('grændmʌðə) *n* grand-mère *f*.
grandparent ('grænpɛərənt) *n* grand-parent *m*.
grand piano *n* piano à queue *m*.
grandson (grænsʌn) *n* petit-fils *m*.
grandstand ('grændstænd) *n* tribune (d'honneur) *f*.

granite ('grænit) *n* granit *m*.

grant (grɑ:nt) *n* subvention, bourse *f*. *vt* accorder, concéder.

grape (greip) *n* raisin *m*. **bunch of grapes** grappe de raisins *f*. **grapefruit** *n* pamplemousse *m*. **grapevine** *n* **1** vigne *f*. **2** source d'informations *f*.

graph (græf) *n* graphique *n*. courbe *f*.

grapple ('græpəl) *vi* **grapple with** en venir aux prises avec.

grasp (grɑ:sp) *n* prise, étreinte *f*. *vt* **1** saisir, empoigner. **2** comprendre. **grasping** *adj* rapace, avide.

grass (grɑ:s) *n* herbe *f*. **grassroots** *n* base, source *f*.

grate[1] (greit) *n* grille *f*.

grate[2] (greit) *vt* râper. *vi* grincer.

grateful ('greitfəl) *adj* reconnaissant. **gratify** *vt* **1** faire plaisir. **2** satisfaire. **gratifying** *adj* agréable.

gratitude ('grætitju:d) *n* gratitude, reconnaissance *f*.

grave[1] (greiv) *n* tombe *f*. tombeau, -aux *m*. **gravestone** *n* pierre tombale *f*. **graveyard** *n* cimetière *m*.

grave[2] (greiv) *adj* sérieux, -euse, grave.

gravel ('grævəl) *n* gravier *m*.

gravity ('græviti) *n* gravité *f*.

gravy ('greivi) *n* jus *m*. sauce *f*.

graze[1] (greiz) *vi* (of animals) paître, brouter. *vt* faire paître.

graze[2] (greiz) *n* éraflure, écorchure *f*. *vt* **1** érafler, écorcher. **2** frôler.

grease (gri:s) *n* graisse *f*. *vt* graisser. **greasepaint** *n* fard *m*. **greaseproof** *adj* sulfurisé, parcheminé. **greasy** *adj* graisseux, -euse.

great (greit) *adj* grand, fort. **greatly** *adv* beaucoup. **greatness** *n* grandeur *f*.

Great Britain *n* Grande-Bretagne *f*.

Greece (gri:s) *n* Grèce *f*. **Grecian** *adj* grec, grecque. **Greek** *adj,n* grec, grecque. **Greek** (language) *n* grec *m*.

greed (gri:d) *n* cupidité, avidité *f*. **greedy** *adj* **1** gourmand. **2** avide. **greedily** *adv* avidement, goulûment.

green (gri:n) *adj* **1** vert. **2** *inf* naif, naïve. *n* **1** vert *m*. **2** *pl* légumes verts *m pl*. **greenery** *n* verdure *f*. feuillage *m*. **greenfly** *n* puceron *m*. **greengage** *n* reine-claude *f*. **greengrocer** *n* marchand de légumes *m*. fruitier, -ière. **greenhouse** *n* serre *f*.

Greenland ('gri:nlənd) *n* Groenland *m*. **Greenlander** *n* groenlandais *m*.

greet (gri:t) *vt* saluer, accueillir. **greeting** *n* salutation *f*.

gregarious (gri'gɛəriəs) *adj* grégaire.

grenade (gri'neid) *n* grenade *f*.

grew (gru:) *v* see **grow.**

grey (grei) *adj,n* gris *m*. **greyhound** *n* lévrier *m*.

grid (grid) *n* grille *f*. grillage *m*.

grief (gri:f) *n* chagrin *m*. douleur *f*.

grieve (gri:v) *vt* chagriner, peiner. *vi* se chagriner, s'affliger. **grievance** *n* grief *m*. injustice *f*. **grieved** *adj* désolé. **grievous** *adj* douloureux, -euse, pénible.

grill (gril) *n* **1** *cul* grillade *f*. **2** gril *m*. *vt cul* griller.

grille (gril) *n* grille *f*.

grim (grim) *adj* **1** menaçant, sinistre. **2** sévère.

grimace (gri'meis) *n* grimace *f*. *vi* grimacer.

grime (graim) *n* saleté, crasse *f*. **grimy** *adj* crasseux, -euse.

grin (grin) *n* large sourire *m*. *vi* sourire à belles dents.

grind* (graind) *vt* **1** moudre, broyer. **2** aiguiser. *vi* grincer. *n* **1** grincement *m*. **2** *sl* corvée *f*.

grip (grip) *n* prise, étreinte *f*. **come to grips with** en venir aux mains avec. ~*vt* **1** saisir. **2** serrer. **gripping** *adj inf* passionnant.

gripe (graip) *vt* affliger. *vi inf* rouspéter. *n* colique *f*.

gristle ('grisəl) *n* cartilage *m*.

grit (grit) *n* **1** grès *m*. **2** *sl* cran, courage *m*. *vi,vt* grincer. *vt* sabler.

groan (groun) *n* gémissement *m*. *vi* gémir, se plaindre.

grocer ('grousə) *n* épicier, -ière. **grocery** *n* épicerie *f*.

groin (grɔin) *n anat* aine *f*.

groom (gru:m) *n* palefrenier *m*. *vt* panser.

groove (gru:v) *n* rainure, cannelure *f*. *vt* rayer, canneler.

grope (group) *vi* tâtonner. **grope for** chercher à tâtons.

gross (grous) *adj* **1** gros, grosse. **2** grossier, -ière. **3** flagrant. *n* grosse *f*.

grotesque (grou'tesk) *adj,n* grotesque *m*.

grotto ('grɔtou) *n, pl* **-os** *or* **-oes** grotte *f*.

ground[1] (graund) *n* **1** sol, terrain *m*. **2** raison *f*. **3** fond *m*. *vt* fonder, baser. *vi* s'échouer. **ground floor** *n* rez-de-chaussée *m*. **groundsheet** *n* tapis de sol *m*. **groundsman** *n* préposé à l'entretien d'un terrain de jeux *m.* **groundwork** *n* assise *f.* plan *m.*

ground[2] (graund) *v* see **grind.**

group (gru:p) *n* groupe *m.* *vt* grouper. *vi* se grouper.

grouse[1] (graus) *n zool* tétras *m.*

grouse[2] (graus) *vi inf* grogner, rouspéter.

grove (grouv) *n* bocage *m.*

grovel ('grɔvəl) *vi* ramper.

grow* (grou) *vi* pousser, grandir, croître. *vt* cultiver. **grown-up** *n* adulte *m,f.* **growth** *n* croissance *f.*

growl (graul) *vi* grogner, gronder. *n* grognement *m.*

grub (grʌb) *n* **1** larve *f.* **2** *sl* boustifaille *f.*

grubby ('grʌbi) *adj* sale, malpropre.

grudge (grʌdʒ) *n* rancune *f.* *vt* donner à contre-cœur. **grudgingly** *adv* à contre-cœur.

gruelling ('gru:əliŋ) *adj* épuisant, éreintant.

gruesome ('gru:səm) *adj* macabre.

gruff (grʌf) *adj* bourru, brusque.

grumble ('grʌmbəl) *vt,vi* grommeler, grogner. *n* grognement *m.*

grumpy ('grʌmpi) *adj* maussade, grincheux, -euse.

grunt (grʌnt) *n* grognement *m.* *vi* grogner.

guarantee (gærən'ti:) *n* garantie *f.* *vt* garantir, cautionner. **guarantor** *n* garant *m.*

guard (gɑ:d) *n* **1** garde *m.* **2** chef de train *m.* *vt* garder, protéger. **guard's van** *n* fourgon *m.* **guarded** *adj* prudent, mesuré. **guardian** *n* **1** gardien, -ienne. **2** *law* tuteur, -trice. **guardianship** *n* tutelle *f.*

Guernsey ('gə:nzi) *n* Guernesey *m.*

guerrilla (gə'rilə) *n* guérillero *m.*

guess (ges) *vt,vi* deviner, conjecturer. *n* conjecture *f.* **at a guess** au jugé. **guesswork** *n* conjecture, hypothèse *f.*

guest (gest) *n* **1** invité *m.* convive *m,f.* **2** (in a hotel, etc.) pensionnaire *m,f.* **guesthouse** *n* pension de famille *f.*

guide (gaid) *n* guide *m.* *vt* guider, diriger. **guidebook** *n* guide *m.* **guide-dog** *n* chien d'aveugles *m.* **guidance** *n* direction, conduite *f.*

guild (gild) *n* corporation, confrérie *f.*

guillotine (gilə'ti:n) *n* guillotine *f* *vt* guillotiner.

guilt (gilt) *n* culpabilité *f.* **guilty** *adj* coupable.

guinea ('gini) *n* guinée *f.* **guinea pig** *n* cobaye, cochon d'Inde *m.*

guitar (gi'tɑ:) *n* guitare *f.*

gulf (gʌlf) *n* **1** *geog* golfe *m.* **2** abîme *m.*

gull (gʌl) *n* mouette *f.* goéland *m.*

gullet ('gʌlit) *n* **1** œsophage *m.* **2** *inf* gosier *m.*

gulp (gʌlp) *n* trait *m.* lampée *f.* *vt* avaler.

gum[1] (gʌm) *n* gomme *f.* *vt* gommer.

gum[2] (gʌm) *n anat* gencive *f.*

gun (gʌn) *n* fusil, canon *m.* **gunman** *n* bandit (armé) *m.* **gunpowder** *n* poudre (à canon) *f.* **gunrunning** *n* trafic d'armes *m.* **gunshot** *n* coup de fusil *m.*

gurgle ('gə:gəl) *n* glouglou, gloussement *m.* *vi* gargouiller.

gush (gʌʃ) *n* jet, flot *m.* *vi* jaillir, déborder.

gust (gʌst) *n* ondée, giboulée, rafale *f.*

gut (gʌt) *n* **1** *anat* boyau, -aux, intestin *m.* **2** *pl inf* cran *m.* *vt* étriper, vider.

gutter ('gʌtə) *n* **1** gouttière *f.* **2** ruisseau, -aux *m.*

guy[1] (gai) *n* **1** épouvantail *m.* **2** type *m.*

guy[2] (gai) *n* cable, hauban *m.*

gymnasium (dʒim'neiziəm) *n* gymnase *m.* **gymnast** *n* gymnaste *m,f.* **gymnastic** *adj* gymnastique. **gymnastics** *n* gymnastique *f.*

gynaecology (gaini'kɔlədʒi) *n* gynécologie *f.* **gynaecologist** *n* gynécologue *m,f.*

gypsum ('dʒipsəm) *n* gypse *m.*

H

haberdasher ('hæbədæʃə) *n* mercier *m.* **haberdashery** *n* mercerie *f.*

habit ('hæbit) *n* **1** coutume, habitude *f.* **2** habit *m.* **3** *pl* mœurs *f pl.* **habitable** *adj* habitable. **habitual** *adj* habituel, -elle.

hack[1] (hæk) *vt* hacher, taillader. *vi* toussoter. *n* entaille *f.* **hacksaw** *n* scie à métaux *f.*

hack[2] (hæk) *n* **1** cheval de louage *m.* **2** *inf* rosse *f.* **3** homme de peine *m.*

hackneyed ('hæknid) *adj* banal, -aux, rebattu.

had (hæd) *v* see **have.**

haddock ('hædək) *n* aiglefin *m.*

haemorrhage ('hemərid3) *n* hémorragie *f.*

hag (hæg) *n* sorcière *f.*

haggard ('hægəd) *adj* hagard, hâve.

haggle ('hægḷ) *vi* **1** marchander. **2** chicaner.

Hague, The (heig) *n* La Haye *f.*

hail[1] (heil) *n* grêle *f.* *v imp* grêler. **hailstone** *n* grêlon *m.* **hailstorm** *n* averse de grêle *f.*

hail[2] (heil) *interj* salut! *vt* **1** saluer, acclamer. **2** héler.

hair (hɛə) *n* **1** (of the head) cheveu, -eux *m.* **2** (of the head) chevelure *f.* **3** poil *m.* **4** (of a horse) crin *m.* **hairbrush** *n* brosse à cheveux *f.* **haircut** *n* coupe de cheveux *f.* **hairdresser**

n coiffeur *m.* **hairdressing** *n* coiffure *f.* **hairgrip** *n* épingle à cheveux *f.* **hairnet** *n* résille *f.* **hairpiece** *n* postiche *m.* **hair-raising** *adj* horripilant. **hairstyle** *n* coiffure *f.*

half (hɑ:f) *n, pl* **halves** moitié *f.* demi *m.* demie *f. adj* demi. *adv* à moitié, à demi.

half-a-dozen *n* demi-douzaine *f.*

half-and-half *adv* moitié l'un moitié l'autre.

half-back *n* demi m.

half-baked *adj inf* **1** qui ne tient pas debout, bâclé. **2** niais.

half-breed *n* **1** métis, -isse. **2** cheval demi-sang *m.*

half-brother *n* demi-frère *m.*

half-caste *n* métis, -isse.

half-hearted *adj* peu enthousiaste, tiède.

half-hour *n* demi-heure *f.*

half-mast *adv* **at half-mast** en berne.

halfpenny ('heipni) *n* **1** *pl* **halfpence** demi-penny *m.* **2** *pl* **halfpennies** pièce d'un demi-penny *f.*

half-pint *n* demi-pinte, chopine *f.*

half-sister *n* demi-sœur *f.*

half-term *n* congé de mi-trimestre *m.*

half-time *n* mi-temps *f.*

halftone ('hɑ:ftoun) *n* **1** *Art* demi-teinte *f.* **2** *mus* demi-ton *m.*

halfway (hɑ:f'wei) *adv* à mi-chemin.

halfwit ('hɑ:fwit) *n* faible d'esprit, idiot *m.*

half-year *n* semestre *m.*

halibut ('hælibət) *n* flétan *m.*

hall (hɔ:l) *n* salle *f.* vestibule, hall *m.*

hallelujah (hæli'lu:jə) *interj,n* alléluia *m.*

hallmark ('hɔ:lmɑ:k) *n* **1** poinçon *m.* **2** empreinte *f.* cachet *m. vt* poinçonner.

hallo (hə'lou) *interj* see **hello.**

hallowed ('hæloud) *adj* saint, sanctifié.

Hallowe'en (hælou'i:n) *n* veille de la Toussaint *f.*

hallucination (həlu:si'neiʃən) *n* hallucination *f.*

halo ('heilou) *n, pl* **-os** *or* **oes** halo *m.* auréole *f.*

halt (hɔ:lt) *n* arrêt *m.* halte *f. vi* faire halte, s'arrêter. *vt* arrêter.

halter ('hɔ:ltə) *n* licou *m.*

halve (hɑ:v) *vt* partager en deux, réduire de moitié.

ham (hæm) *n* jambon *m.*

hamburger ('hæmbə:gə) *n* steak haché grillé *m.*

hammer ('hæmə) *n* marteau, -aux *m. vt* marteler.

hammock ('hæmək) *n* hamac *m.*

hamper[1] ('hæmpə) *vt* gêner.

hamper[2] ('hæmpə) *n* manne *f.* panier *m.*

hamster ('hæmstə) *n* hamster *m.*

hand (hænd) *n* **1** main *f.* **2** (of a clock) aiguille *f.* **3** *game* jeu *m.* **4** *inf* coup de main *m. vt* remettre, passer. **handful** *n* poignée *f.*

handbag ('hændbæg) *n* sac à main *m.*

handbook ('hændbuk) *n* **1** manuel *m.* **2** guide *m.*

handbrake ('hændbreik) *n* frein à main *m.*

handcart ('hændkɑ:t) *n* charrette à bras *f.*

handcuffs ('hændkʌfs) *n pl* menottes *f pl.*

hand grenade *n* grenade à main *f.*

handicap ('hændikæp) *n* handicap, désavantage *m. vt* handicaper.

handicraft ('hændikrɑ:ft) *n* **1** travail manuel *m.* **2** artisanat *m.*

handiwork ('hændiwə:k) *n* ouvrage *m.*

handkerchief ('hæŋkətʃif) *n* mouchoir *m.*

handle ('hændḷ) *n* manche *m.* poignée, anse, manivelle *f. vt* manipuler, manier. **handlebars** *n pl* guidon *m.*

handmade (hænd'meid) *adj* fait à la main.

hand-out *n* communiqué *m.*

hand-pick *vt* trier à la main.

handrail ('hændreil) *n* balustrade, rampe *f.*

handshake ('hændʃeik) *n* poignée de main *f.*

handsome ('hænsəm) *adj* **1** beau, belle. **2** généreux, -euse.

handstand ('hændstænd) *m* poirier *m.* **do a handstand** faire l'arbre droit.

handwriting ('hændraitiŋ) *n* écriture *f.*

handy ('hændi) *adj* **1** adroit. **2** commode. **3** sous la main.

hang* (hæŋ) *vt* pendre, suspendre. *vi* **1** pendre. **2** peser. **hang around** flâner. **hang up** accrocher. **hanger** *n* cintre *m.* **hangman** *n* bourreau, -aux *m.* **hangover** *n* gueule de bois *f.*

hanker ('hæŋkə) *vi* **hanker after** désirer ardemment. **hankering** *n* aspiration, grande envie *f.*

haphazard (hæp'hæzəd) *adj* fortuit. *adv* au hasard.

happen ('hæpən) *vi* arriver, se passer.

happy ('hæpi) *adj* heureux, -euse. **happiness** *n* bonheur *m.*

harass ('hærəs) *vt* **1** *mil* harceler. **2** tourmenter.

harbour ('hɑ:bə) *n* port *m. vt* héberger, receler.

hard (hɑ:d) *adj* **1** dur. **2** difficile. **3** sévère. **hard up** à court d'argent. ~*adv* **1** fort. **2** difficilement. **hardback** *n* livre relié *m.* **hard-boiled** *adj* dur. **hard-headed** *adj* positif, -ive, pratique. **hard-hearted** *adj* insensible, impitoyable. **hardware** *n* quincaillerie *f.* **harden**

vt,vi durcir. **hardness** *n* **1** dureté *f.* **2** difficulté *f.* **hardship** *n* épreuve, privation *f.*

hardly (ˈhɑ:dli) *adv* à peine, ne...guère. **hardly ever** presque jamais.

hardy (ˈhɑ:di) *adj* **1** hardi. **2** robuste. **3** *bot* vivace.

hare (ˈhɛə) *n* lièvre *m.*

haricot (ˈhærikou) *n* haricot blanc *m.*

hark (hɑ:k) *vi* écouter.

harm (hɑ:m) *n* mal, tort *m.* *vt* faire du mal à, nuire à. **harmful** *adj* nuisible. **harmless** *adj* inoffensif, -ive, anodin.

harmonic (hɑ:ˈmɔnik) *adj,n* harmonique *m.* **harmonica** *n* harmonica *m.* **harmonize** *vt* harmoniser. *vi* s'assortir. **harmony** *n* **1** *mus* harmonie *f.* **2** entente *f.* accord *m.*

harness (ˈhɑ:nis) *n* harnais *m.* *vt* **1** harnacher. **2** aménager.

harp (hɑ:p) *n* harp *f.* *v* **harp on about** rabâcher.

harpoon (hɑ:ˈpu:n) *n* harpon *m.* *vt* harponner.

harpsichord (ˈhɑ:psikɔ:d) *n* clavecin *m.*

harsh (hɑ:ʃ) *adj* **1** dur. **2** âpre. **3** aigre. **harshly** *adv* rudement, sévèrement.

harvest (ˈhɑ:vist) *n* récolte *f.* *vt* récolter.

has (hæz) *v* see **have.**

hashish (ˈhæʃiʃ) *n* hachisch *m*

haste (heist) *n* hâte *f.* **hasten** *vi* se presser, s'empresser. *vt* accélérer, hâter, presser.

hat (hæt) *n* chapeau, -aux *m.*

hatch[1] (hætʃ) *n* couvée *f.* *vt* faire éclore, incuber. **hatch out** éclore.

hatch[2] (hætʃ) *n* **1** *naut* écoutille *f.* **2** trappe *f.* passe-plats *m.*

hatchet (ˈhætʃit) *n* cognée, hachette *f.*

hate (heit) *vt* haïr, détester. *n* haine *f.* **hateful** *adj* odieux, -euse.

haughty (ˈhɔ:ti) *adj* hautain, arrogant.

haul (hɔ:l) *vt* **1** traîner. **2** transporter. *vt,vi* haler. *n* **1** coup de filet *m.* **2** charge *f.* **haulage** *n* **1** roulage *m.* **2** remorquage *m.*

haunch (hɔ:ntʃ) *n* **1** hanche *f.* **2** *cul* cuissot *m.*

haunt (hɔ:nt) *vt* hanter, obséder. *n* repaire *m.*

have* (hæv) *vt* **1** avoir, posséder. **2** obtenir. **3** prendre. **4** faire. *v aux* avoir. **have to** devoir.

haven (ˈheivən) *n* **1** havre *m.* **2** abri *m.*

haversack (ˈhævəsæk) *n* haversac *m.*

havoc (ˈhævək) *n* ravage *m.*

hawk (hɔ:k) *n* faucon, épervier *m.*

hawthorn (ˈhɔ:θɔ:n) *n* aubépine *f.*

hay (hei) *n* foin *m.* **hayfever** *n* rhume des foins *m.* **haystack** *n* meule de foin *f.* **haywire** *adj* loupé.

hazard (ˈhæzəd) *n* hasard, risque *m.* *vt* hasarder. **hazardous** *adj* périlleux, -euse.

haze (heiz) *n* **1** brume *f.* **2** incertitude *f.* *vt* embrumer. **hazy** *adj* **1** brumeux, -euse. **2** nébuleux, -euse.

hazel (ˈheizəl) *n* noisetier *m.* **hazelnut** *n* noisette *f.*

he (hi:) *pron 3rd pers s* **1** il. **2** lui. **he who** celui qui.

head (hed) *n* **1** tête *f.* **2** chef, directeur *m.* **3** principal, -aux *m.* *adj* principal, -aux, premier, -ière. *vt* **1** conduire. **2** intituler. **heading** *n* titre, en-tête *m.*

headache (ˈhedeik) *n* mal de tête *m.*

headfirst (hedˈfə:st) *adv* la tête la première.

headlight (ˈhedlait) *n* phare *m.*

headline (ˈhedlain) *n* manchette *f.*

headlong (ˈhedlɔŋ) *adv* **1** la tête la première. **2** témérairement.

headmaster (hedˈmɑ:stə) *n* directeur (d'école) *m.* **headmistress** *n* directrice (d'école) *f.*

headphone (ˈhedfoun) *n* écouteur, casque *m.*

headquarters (ˈhedkwɔ:təz) *n pl* **1** siège social *m.* **2** *mil* quartier général *m.*

headscarf (ˈhedskɑ:f) *n* foulard *m.*

headstrong (ˈhedstrɔŋ) *adj* têtu, obstiné.

headway (ˈhedwei) *n* avance *f.* progrès *m.*

heal (hi:l) *vt,vi* guérir.

health (helθ) *n* santé *f.* **healthy** *adj* **1** en bonne santé. **2** robuste.

heap (hi:p) *n* tas *m.* *vt* entasser, amasser, combler.

hear* (hiə) *vi* entendre. *vt* **1** entendre. **2** écouter. **3** apprendre. **hear from** recevoir des nouvelles de. **hear of** entendre parler de. **hearing** *n* **1** ouïe *f.* **2** audience *f.* **3** audition *f.* **hearing aid** *n* appareil auditif *m.* **hearsay** *n* ouï-dire *m invar.*

hearse (hə:s) *n* corbillard *m.*

heart (hɑ:t) *n* **1** cœur *m.* **2** courage *m.* **heart attack** *n* crise cardiaque *f.* **heartbeat** *n* battement de cœur *m.* **heartbroken** *adj* accablé, navré. **heartily** *adv* **1** de bon cœur. **2** avec appétit. **heartless** *adj* insensible, cruel, -elle. **hearty** *adj* **1** chaleureux, -euse. **2** robuste.

hearth (hɑ:θ) *n* âtre *m.*

heat (hi:t) *n* **1** chaleur *f.* **2** épreuve *f.* *vt* chauffer. **heater** *n* appareil de chauffage, radiateur *m.* **heatwave** *n* vague de chaleur *f.*

heath (hi:θ) *n* bruyère, lande *f.*

heathen (ˈhi:ðən) *adj,n* païen, -enne.

heather (ˈheðə) *n* bruyère *f.*

heave (hi:v) *vt* **1** lever. **2** porter. **3** pousser. *vi* **1** se soulever. **2** avoir des haut-le-cœur. *n* **1** effort *m*. **2** soulèvement *m*.
heaven ('hevən) *n* ciel, cieux *m*. **heavenly** *adj* céleste.
heavy ('hevi) *adj* **1** lourd, gros, grosse. **2** profond. **3** pénible. **heaviness** *n* **1** lourdeur *f*. **2** lassitude *f*. **heavyweight** *n* poids lourd *m*. *adj* lourd.
Hebrew ('hi:bru:) *n* hébreu, -eux *m*. *adj* hébreu, -eux, hébraïque. **Hebrew** (language) *n* hébreu *m*.
heckle ('hekəl) *vt* interpeller.
hectic ('hektik) *adj* agité.
hedge (hedʒ) *n* **1** haie *f*. **2** protection *f*. *vt* entourer d'une haie. *vi* chercher des faux-fuyants. **hedgehog** *n* hérisson *m*.
heed (hi:d) *n* attention *f*. *vt* faire attention à. **heedless** *adj* étourdi, peu soucieux, -euse.
heel (hi:l) *n* talon *m*.
hefty ('hefti) *adj* solide, costaud.
height (hait) *n* **1** hauteur *f*. **2** élévation *f*. **3** apogée *f*. **heighten** *vt* **1** surélever. **2** accroître, rehausser.
heir (εə) *n* héritier *m*. **heiress** *n* héritière *f*. **heirloom** *n* meuble *or* bijou de famille *m*.
held (held) *v* see **hold.**
helicopter ('helikɔptə) *n* hélicoptère *m*.
hell (hel) *n* enfer *m*. **hellish** *adj* infernal, -aux.
hello (hə'lou) *interj* **1** bonjour! **2** salut! **3** allô! holà!
helm (helm) *n naut* barre *f*. gouvernail *m*.
helmet ('helmit) *n* casque *m*.
help (help) *n* **1** aide *f*. secours *m*. **2** *inf* domestique *f*. *interj* au secours! *vt* **1** secourir, aider. **2** servir. **it can't be helped!** tant pis! **helpful** *adj* utile. **helpless** *adj* impuissant.
hem (hem) *n* ourlet, bord *m*.
hemisphere ('hemisfiə) *n* hémisphère *m*.
hemp (hemp) *n* chanvre *m*.
hen (hen) *n* **1** poule *f*. **2** femelle *f*. **henpecked** *adj* mené par le bout du nez.
hence (hens) *adv* **1** en conséquence. **2** dorénavant. **3** d'ici. **henceforth** *adv* désormais.
henna ('henə) *n* henné *m*.
her (hə:) *pron 3rd pers s* **1** elle. **2** la. **3** lui. *poss adj 3rd pers s* son, sa, ses.
herald ('herəld) *n* **1** héraut *m*. **2** avant-coureur *m*. *vt* annoncer. **heraldry** *n* blason *m*.
herb (hə:b) *n* herbe *f*.
herd (hə:d) *n* troupeau, -aux *m*. bande *f*. *vi* s'attrouper. **herdsman** *m* gardien *m*.
here (hiə) *adv* ici. **here and there** par-ci par-là. **here, there, and everywhere** un peu partout. **hereafter** *adv* **1** ci-après. **2** désormais. **hereby** *adv* par là. **herein** *adv* ci-inclus.
hereditary (hi'reditri) *adj* héréditaire.
heredity (hi'rediti) *n* hérédité *f*.
heresy ('herəsi) *n* hérésie *f*. **heretic** *n* hérétique *m,f*.
heritage ('heritidʒ) *n* héritage *m*.
hermit ('hə:mit) *n* ermite *m*.
hero ('hiərou) *n, pl* **-oes** héros *m*. **heroine** *n* héroïne *f*.
heroin ('herouin) *n* héroïne *f*.
heron ('herən) *n* héron *m*.
herring ('heriŋ) *n* hareng *m*. **red herring** *n inf* diversion *f*.
hers (hə:z) *poss pron 3rd pers s* **1** le sien, la sienne. **2** à elle. **herself** *pron 3rd pers s* **1** elle-même. **2** se. **by herself** toute seule.
hesitate ('heziteit) *vi* hésiter. **hesitation** *n* hésitation *f*.
hexagon ('heksəgən) *n* hexagone *m*. **hexagonal** *adj* hexagone.
hibernate ('haibəneit) *vi* hiberner.
hiccup ('hikʌp) *n* hoquet *m*. *vi* avoir le hoquet.
hide*[1] (haid) *vt* cacher. *vi* se cacher. **hide-and-seek** *n* cache-cache *m*.
hide[2] (haid) *n* peau, peaux *f*. cuir *m*.
hideous ('hidiəs) *adj* hideux, -euse.
hiding[1] ('haidiŋ) *n* **1** cachette *f*. **2** dissimulation *f*.
hiding[2] ('haidiŋ) *n inf* raclée *f*.
hierarchy ('haiərɑ:ki) *n* hiérarchie *f*.
high (hai) *adj* **1** haut. **2** élevé. **3** grand. **4** faisandé. **5** *sl* parti. **highbrow** *adj* intellectuel, -elle. **high frequency** *adj* à haute fréquence. **highland** *adj* montagnard. *n* **1** haute terre *f*. **2** *cap pl* Haute Ecosse *f*. **highlight** *vt* mettre en évidence. *n* point culminant *m*. **highly** *adv* **1** hautement. **2** fort, très. **highpitched** *adj* aigu, -uë, criard. **high-rise** *adj* élevé. **high-rise block** *n* tour *f*. **high-spirited** *adj* **1** exubérant. **2** fougueux, -euse. **highway** *n* **1** grand-route *f*. **2** voie publique *f*.
Highness ('hainəs) *n* Altesse *f*.
hijack ('haidʒæk) *vt* détourner.
hike (haik) *n* excursion à pied *f*. *vi* faire de la marche.
hilarious (hi'lεəriəs) *adj* hilare. **hilarity** *n* hilarité *f*.
hill (hil) *n* **1** colline *f*. **2** côte *f*. **hillside** *n* versant, flanc de coteau *m*. **hilltop** *n* cime *f*.
him (him) *pron 3rd pers s* **1** le. **2** lui. **himself**

pron 3rd pers s **1** lui-même. **2** se. **by himself** tout seul.

hind (haind) *adj* de derrierè, postérieur. **hindleg** *n* patte de derrière *f.* **hindsight** *n* sagesse d'après coup *f.*

hinder ('hində) *vt* **1** gêner. **2** empêcher. **hindrance** *n* empêchement *m.*

Hindu ('hindu:) *adj,n* hindou.

hinge (hindʒ) *n* **1** gond *m.* **2** pivot *m.* **3** charnière *f.* *v* **hinge on** être axé sur, dépendre de.

hint (hint) *n* **1** insinuation, allusion *f.* **2** conseil *m.* *vi* insinuer.

hip (hip) *n* hanche *f.*

hippopotamus (hipə'pɔtəməs) *n pl* **-mi** *or* **-muses** hippopotame *m.*

hire (haiə) *vt* louer, engager. **hire out** donner en location. ~*n* location *f.* louage *m.* **hire-purchase** *n* vente à tempérament *f.*

his (hiz) *poss adj 3rd pers s* son, sa, ses. *poss pron 3rd pers s* **1** le sien, la sienne. **2** à lui.

hiss (his) *vi* siffler. *n* sifflement *m.*

history ('histri) *n* histoire *f.* **historian** *n* historien *m.* **historic** *adj* historique.

hit* (hit) *vt* **1** frapper. **2** atteindre, toucher. *n* coup *m.*

hitch *n* **1** saccade, secousse *f.* **2** contretemps *m.* *vt* **1** accrocher. **2** remuer par saccades. **hitch-hike** *vi* faire du stop.

hive (haiv) *n* ruche *f.*

hoard (hɔ:d) *vt* amasser, accumuler. *vi* thésauriser. *n* **1** amas *m.* **2** trésor *m.*

hoarding ('hɔ:diŋ) *n* **1** palissade *f.* panneau-réclame *m.* **2** resserre, cache *f.*

hoarfrost ('hɔ:frɔst) *n* givre *m.*

hoarse (hɔ:s) *adj* enroué, rauque.

hoax (houks) *n* mystification *f.* mauvais tour *m.*

hobble ('hɔbəl) *vi* boitiller. *vt* entraver. *n* boitillement *m.*

hobby ('hɔbi) *n* passe-temps *m.*

hock[1] (hɔk) *n* jarret *m.*

hock[2] (hɔk) *n* vin du Rhin *m.*

hockey ('hɔki) *n* hockey *m.*

hoe (hou) *n* houe *f.* *vt* sarcler.

hog (hɔg) *n* **1** porc *m.* **2** *inf* goinfre *m.* *vt inf* monopoliser.

hoist (hɔist) *n* treuil *m.* *vt* hisser.

hold*[1] (hould) *vt,vi* tenir. *vt* **1** contenir. **2** avoir, posséder. **3** retenir. **hold back** retenir. **hold on** tenir ferme, s'accrocher. **hold out** tendre. ~*n* prise *f.* **holdall** *n* fourre-tout *m invar.* **holder** *n* **1** détenteur *m.* **2** propriétaire *m.* **3** récipient *m.*

hold[2] (hould) *n naut* cale *f.*

hole (houl) *n* **1** trou, creux *m.* **2** orifice *m.* *vt* trouer. *vi* se trouer.

holiday ('hɔlidi) *n* **1** jour férié, congé *m.* **2** *pl* vacances *f pl.* **holiday-maker** *n* estivant *m.*

Holland ('hɔlənd) *n* Hollande *f.*

hollow ('hɔlou) *adj* **1** creux, creuse. **2** sourd. *adv* creux. *n* **1** creux *m.* **2** vallon *m.* *vt* creuser.

holly ('hɔli) *n* houx *m.* **hollyhock** *n* rose trémière *f.*

holster ('houlstə) *n* étui *m.*

holy ('houli) *adj* saint, sacré.

Holy Ghost *n* Saint-Esprit *m.*

homage ('hɔmidʒ) *n* hommage *m.*

home (houm) *n* **1** logis, foyer *m.* maison *f.* **2** patrie *f.* **3** hospice *m.* *adv* à la maison, de retour. *adj* **1** familial, -aux, domestique. **2** *pol* intérieur. **homecoming** *n* retour *m.* **home help** *n* aide ménagère *f.* **homeland** *n* patrie *f.* **homesick** *adj* nostalgique. **homesickness** *n* mal du pays *m.* nostalgie *f.* **homework** *n* devoirs (du soir) *m pl.*

homonym ('hɔmənim) *n* homonyme *m.*

homosexual (houmə'sekʃuəl) *adj,n* homosexuel, -elle.

honest ('ɔnist) *adj* **1** honnête. **2** sincère. **honesty** *n* honnêteté, probité *f.*

honey ('hʌni) *n* miel *m.* **honeycomb** *n* rayon de miel *m.* **honeymoon** *n* lune de miel *f.* **honeysuckle** *n* chèvrefeuille *m.*

honour ('ɔnə) *vt* **1** honorer. **2** faire honneur à. *n* **1** honneur *m.* **2** distinction *f.* **His** *or* **Your Honour** Monsieur le juge, Monsieur le président. **honorary** *adj* **1** honoraire. **2** honorifique.

hood (hud) *n* **1** capuchon *m.* **2** *mot* capote *f.*

hoof (hu:f) *n, pl* **hooves** sabot *m.*

hook (huk) *n* **1** crochet, croc *m.* agrafe *f.* **2** (in angling) hameçon *m.* *vt* **1** accrocher. **2** agrafer. **3** attraper.

hooligan ('hu:ligən) *n* voyou *m.*

hoop (hu:p) *n* **1** cercle, cerceau, -aux *m.* **2** *sport* arceau, -aux *m.*

hoot (hu:t) *vi* **1** huer. **2** *mot* klaxonner. *n* **1** huée *f.* **2** klaxonnement *m.* **hooter** *n* klaxon *m.*

hop[1] (hɔp) *n* saut, sautillement *m.* *vi* sautiller, sauter.

hop[2] (hɔp) *n bot* houblon *m.*

hope (houp) *n* **1** espérance *f.* **2** espoir *m.* *vi,vt* espérer. *vt* s'attendre à. **hopeful** *adj* plein d'espoir. **hopeless** *adj* **1** sans espoir. **2** vain.

horde (hɔ:d) *n* horde *f.*

horizon (hə'raizən) *n* horizon *m*. **horizontal** *adj* horizontal, -aux.
hormone ('hɔ:moun) *n* hormone *f*.
horn (hɔ:n) *n* **1** corne *f*. **2** *mus* cor *m*. trompe *f*.
hornet ('hɔ:nit) *n* frelon *m*.
horoscope ('hɔrəskoup) *n* horoscope *m*.
horrible ('hɔrəbl̩) *adj* horrible, épouvantable.
horrid ('hɔrid) *adj* horrible, affreux, -euse.
horrify ('hɔrifai) *vt* horrifier.
horror ('hɔrə) *n* horreur *f*.
hors d'oeuvres (ɔ: 'də:v) *n pl* hors d'œuvre *m invar*.
horse (hɔ:s) *n* cheval, -aux *m*. *adj* hippique. **on horseback** *adv* à cheval. **horse chestnut** *n* marron d'Inde *m*. **horse chestnut tree** *n* marronnier d'Inde *m*. **horsefly** *n* taon *m*. **horseman** *n* cavalier, chevalier *m*. **horsepower** *n* cheval-vapeur *m*. **horseradish** *n* raifort *m*. **horseshoe** *n* fer à cheval *m*.
horticulture ('hɔ:tikʌltʃə) *n* horticulture *f*. **horticultural** *adj* horticole.
hose (houz) *n* **1** tuyau, -aux *m*. **2** bas *m*.
hosiery ('houziəri) *n* bonneterie *f*.
hospitable ('hɔspitəbəl) *adj* accueillant, hospitalier, -ière.
hospital ('hɔspitl̩) *n* hôpital, -aux *m*.
hospitality (hɔspi'tæliti) *n* hospitalité *f*.
host[1] (houst) *n* **1** hôte *m*. **2** hôtelier *m*.
host[2] (houst) *n* foule, armée *f*.
hostage ('hɔstidʒ) *n* otage *m*.
hostel ('hɔstl̩) *n* pension *f*. foyer *m*.
hostess ('houstis) *n* hôtesse *f*.
hostile ('hɔstail) *adj* hostile, opposé. **hostility** *n* hostilité, animosité *f*.
hot (hɔt) *adj* **1** chaud. **2** ardent. **3** violent. **4** *cul* épicé. **5** *inf* intenable. **hotplate** *n* chauffe-plat *m*. **hotpot** *n* ragoût *m*. **hot-tempered** *adj* emporté, vif, vive. **hot-water bottle** *n* bouillotte *f*.
hotel (hou'tel) *n* hôtel *m*.
hound (haund) *n* **1** chien de chasse *m*. **2** *pl* meute *f*. équipage *m*. *vt* chasser, poursuivre.
hour (auə) *n* heure *f*. **hourly** *adj* à chaque heure. *adv* toutes les heures.
house (*n* haus; *v* hauz) *n* **1** maison *f*. **2** *Th* salle *f*. *vt* loger, héberger.
houseboat ('hausbout) *n* péniche (aménagée en habitation) *f*.
housebound ('hausbaund) *adj* reclus.
household ('haushould) *n* famille *f*. ménage *m*. *adj* domestique.
housekeeper ('hauski:pə) *n* concierge, ménagère *f*. **housekeeping** *n* ménage *m*.
housemaid ('hausmeid) *n* bonne *f*.
House of Commons *n* Chambre des Communes *f*.
House of Lords *n* Chambre des Lords *f*.
houseproud ('hauspraud) *adj* fier de son intérieur.
housewife ('hauswaif) *n* ménagère *f*.
housework ('hauswə:k) *n* travaux domestiques *m pl*.
housing (hauziŋ) *n* logement *m*. **housing estate** *n* cité *f*.
hover ('hɔvə) *vi* **1** planer. **2** rôder. **hovercraft** *n* aéroglisseur *m*.
how (hau) *adv* comment, comme. **how do you do?** comment allez-vous? **how much** *or* **many?** combien? **however** *conj* cependant. *adv* de quelque manière que.
howl (haul) *n* hurlement *m*. *vi* hurler.
hub (hʌb) *n* **1** moyeu, -eux *m*. **2** centre *m*.
huddle ('hʌdl̩) *n* ramassis *m*. *vt* **1** entasser, fourrer. **2** confondre. *vi* se presser.
huff (hʌf) *vt* souffler. **be in a huff** être fâché.
hug (hʌg) *n* étreinte *f*. *vt* embrasser.
huge (hju:dʒ) *adj* énorme, vaste.
hulk (hʌlk) *n* **1** *naut* carcasse *f*. **2** *inf* lourdaud *m*. **hulking** *adj* lourd, gros, grosse.
hull[1] (hʌl) *n* cosse, gousse *f*. *vt* écosser.
hull[2] (hʌl) *n* *naut* coque *f*.
hullo (hə'lou) *interj* see **hello.**
hum (hʌm) *n* bourdonnement *m*. *vi* bourdonner. *vt* fredonner.
human ('hju:mən) *n* être humain *m*. *adj* humain. **human nature** *n* nature humaine *f*. **humane** *adj* humain, compatissant. **humanism** *n* humanisme *m*.
humanity (hju:'mæniti) *n* humanité *f*. **humanitarian** *adj,n* humanitaire.
humble ('hʌmbəl) *adj* **1** humble. **2** modeste. *vt* humilier. **humbly** *adv* avec humilité, pauvrement.
humdrum ('hʌmdrʌm) *adj* monotone.
humid ('hju:mid) *adj* humide.
humiliate (hju:'milieit) *vt* humilier. **humiliation** *n* affront *m*.
humility (hju:'militi) *n* humilité *f*.
humour ('hju:mə) *n* **1** humeur, disposition *f*. **2** humour *m*. *vt* ménager. **humorist** *n* comique, humoriste *m*. **humorous** *adj* humoristique, comique.
hump (hʌmp) *n* bosse *f*. *vt* arquer.
hunch (hʌntʃ) *n* **1** bosse *f*. **2** *inf* pressentiment *m*. *vt* arrondir. **hunchback** *n* bossu *m*.
hundred ('hʌndrəd) *adj* cent. *n* **1** cent *m*. **2**

centaine *f.* **hundredth** *adj* centième. **hundredweight** *n* quintal, -aux *m.*

hung (hʌŋ) *v see* **hang.**

Hungary (ˈhʌŋgəri) *n* Hongrie *f.* **Hungarian** *adj,n* hongrois. **Hungarian** (language) *n* hongrois *m.*

hunger (ˈhʌŋgə) *n* faim *f. vi* avoir faim. **hunger for** désirer. **hunger-strike** *n* grève de la faim *f.* **hungrily** *adv* voracement. **hungry** *adj* **1** affamé. **2** avide. **be hungry** avoir faim.

hunt (hʌnt) *n* **1** chasse *f.* **2** recherche *f. vt* chasser. **hunting** *n* chasse *f.* **huntsman** *n* chasseur, veneur *m.*

hurdle (ˈhəːdl̩) *n* **1** *sport* claie *f.* **2** obstacle *m. vt,vi* sauter.

hurl (həːl) *vt* jeter, lancer.

hurrah (huˈrɑː) *interj* hourra!

hurricane (ˈhʌrikein) *n* ouragan *m.*

hurry (ˈhʌri) *vi* se dépêcher, se hâter. *vt* presser. *n* hâte. **be in a hurry** être pressé. **hurried** *adj* précipité.

hurt* (həːt) *vt* **1** faire mal à. **2** blesser. *vi* faire mal. *n* **1** mal *m.* **2** tort *m.*

husband (ˈhʌzbənd) *n* mari *m.*

hush (hʌʃ) *vt* **1** calmer. **2** étouffer. *vi* se taire. *interj* chut! *n* calme *m.*

husk (hʌsk) *n* cosse, gousse *f. vt* décortiquer.

husky (ˈhʌski) *adj* enroué.

hussar (huˈzɑː) *n* hussard *m.*

hustle (ˈhʌsəl) *vt* bousculer. *vi* se dépêcher. *n* **1** activité *f.* **2** bousculade *f.*

hut (hʌt) *n* hutte *f.*

hutch (hʌtʃ) *n* **1** huche *f.* **2** clapier *m.*

hyacinth (ˈhaiəsinθ) *n* jacinthe *f.*

hybrid (ˈhaibrid) *adj,n* hybride *m.*

hydraulic (haiˈdrɔːlik) *adj* hydraulique.

hydro-electric (haidrouiˈlektrik) *adj* hydroélectrique. **hydro-electric power** *n* énergie hydroélectrique *f.*

hydrogen (ˈhaidrədʒən) *n* hydrogène *m.*

hyena (haiˈiːnə) *n* hyène *f.*

hygiene (ˈhaidʒiːn) *n* hygiène *f.* **hygienic** *adj* hygiénique.

hymn (him) *n* hymne *f,* cantique *m.* **hymnbook** *n* hymnaire *m.*

hyphen (ˈhaifən) *n* trait d'union *m.*

hypnosis (hipˈnousis) *n, pl* **-ses** hypnose *f.* **hypnotism** *n* hypnotisme *m.*

hypochondria (haipəˈkɔndriə) *n* hypocondrie *f.* **hypochondriac** *adj,n* hypocondriaque.

hypocrisy (hiˈpɔkrəsi) *n* hypocrisie *f.* **hypocrite** *n* hypocrite *m,f.* **hypocritical** *adj* hypocrite.

hypodermic (haipəˈdəːmik) *adj* hypodermique.

hypothesis (haiˈpɔθəsis) *n, pl* **-ses** hyp *f.* **hypothetical** *adj* hypothétique.

hysterectomy (histəˈrektəmi) *n* hystérectomi

hysteria (hisˈtiəriə) *n* hystérie *f.* **hysterical** *a* **1** *med* hystérique. **2** énervé. **hysterics** *n pl* crise de nerfs *f.*

I

I (ai) *pron 1st pers s* **1** je. **2** moi.

Iberia (aiˈbiəriə) *n* Ibérie *f.* **Iberian** *adj,n* ibérien, -ienne.

ice (ais) *n* glace *f. vt* **1** geler. **2** *cul* glacer. **3** (champagne, etc.) frapper. **iceberg** *n* iceberg *m.* **ice-cream** *n* glace *f.* **ice-cube** *n* glaçon *m.* **ice hockey** *n* hockey sur glace *m.* **ice rink** *n* patinoire *f.* **ice-skate** *n* patin (à glace) *m.* **icicle** *n* glaçon *m.* **icing** *n* **1** *cul* glacé *m.* **2** glaçage *m.* **icy** *adj* **1** glacial. **2** verglacé.

Iceland (ˈaislənd) *n* Islande *f.* **Icelander** *n* islandais *m.* **Icelandic** *adj* islandais. **Icelandic** (language) *n* islandais *m.*

icon (ˈaikɔn) *n* icone *f.*

idea (aiˈdiə) *n* idée *f.*

ideal (aiˈdiəl) *adj,n* idéal, -aux *m.* **idealistic** *adj* idéaliste. **idealize** *vt* idealiser.

identify (aiˈdentifai) *vt* identifier.

identity (aiˈdentiti) *n* identité *f.* **identity card** *n* carte d'identité *f.* **identical** *adj* identique. **identical twins** *n pl* vrais jumeaux *m pl.*

ideology (aidiˈɔlədʒi) *n* idéologie *f.*

idiom (ˈidiəm) *n* idiome *m.*

idiosyncrasy (idiəˈsiŋkrəsi) *n* idiosyncrasie *f.*

idiot (ˈidiət) *n* idiot *m.* **idiotic** *adj* idiot, bête.

idle (ˈaidl̩) *adj* **1** oisif, -ive, paresseux, -euse. **2** futile. *vi* fainéanter. **idleness** *n* oisiveté *f.*

idol (ˈaidl̩) *n* idole *f.* **idolatry** *n* idolâtrie *f.* **idolize** *vt* idolâtrer.

idyllic (iˈdilik) *adj* idyllique.

if (if) *conj* si. **as if** comme si. **if not** sinon.

ignite (igˈnait) *vt* allumer. *vi* prendre feu. **ignition** *n* **1** allumage *m.* **2** *mot* contact *m.*

ignorant (ˈignərənt) *adj* ignorant.

ignore (igˈnɔː) *vt* ne tenir aucun compte de.

ill (il) *adj* **1** malade. **2** mauvais. *n* **1** mal, ma *m.* **2** tort *m. adv* mal. **ill-bred** *adj* mal él **illness** *n* maladie *f.*

illegal (iˈliːgəl) *adj* illégal, -aux.

illegible (iˈledʒəbəl) *adj* illisible.

illegitimate (iliˈdʒitimət) *adj* illégitime

illicit (iˈlisit) *adj* illicite.

illiterate (iˈlitərət) *adj,n* illettré, ana

al (iˈlɔdʒikəl) *adj* illogique.

inate (iˈlu:mineit) *vt* **1** illuminer. **2** éclair-cir. **illumination** *n* illumination *f.* éclairage *m.*

usion (iˈlu:ʒən) *n* illusion *f.*

illustrate (ˈiləstreit) *vt* **1** illustrer. **2** expliquer. **illustration** *n* **1** illustration *f.* **2** exemple *m.*

illustrious (iˈlʌstriəs) *adj* illustre.

image (ˈimidʒ) *n* image *f.* **imagery** *n* images *f pl.*

imagine (iˈmædʒin) *vt* **1** s'imaginer. **2** croire. **imaginary** *adj* imaginaire. **imagination** *n* imagination *f.* **imaginative** *adj* imaginatif, -ive.

imitate (ˈimiteit) *vt* imiter. **imitation** *n* **1** imitation *f.* **2** *comm* contrefaçon *f.*

immaculate (iˈmækjulət) *adj* **1** immaculé. **2** impeccable.

immature (iməˈtjuə) *adj* **1** pas mûr. **2** prématuré.

immediate (iˈmi:diət) *adj* immédiat, direct, proche.

immense (iˈmens) *adj* immense, énorme.

immerse (iˈmə:s) *vt* immerger.

immigrate (ˈimigreit) *vi* immigrer. **immigrant** *adj,n* immigrant. **immigration** *n* immigration *f.*

imminent (ˈiminənt) *adj* imminent.

immobile (iˈmoubail) *adj* **1** immobile. **2** fixe.

immoral (iˈmɔrəl) *adj* **1** immoral, -aux. **2** (of a person) dissolu. **immorality** *n* **1** immoralité *f.* **2** débauche *f.*

immortal (iˈmɔ:tl̩) *adj* immortel, -elle. **immortality** *n* immortalité *f.*

immovable (iˈmu:vəbəl) *adj* **1** fixe. **2** immuable.

immune (iˈmju:n) *adj* immunisé, vacciné. **immune from** à l'abri de. **immunity** *n* **1** exemption *f.* **2** immunité *f.* **immunization** *n* immunisation *f.* **immunize** *vt* immuniser.

imp (imp) *n* diablotin *m.*

impact (ˈimpækt) *n* **1** impact, choc *m.* **2** effet *m.*

impair (imˈpɛə) *vt* affaiblir, abîmer.

impart (imˈpɑ:t) *vt* **1** communiquer. **2** faire part de.

mpartial (imˈpɑ:ʃəl) *adj* impartial, -aux.

impatient (imˈpeiʃənt) *adj* impatient. **get impatient** s'impatienter.

mpeach (imˈpi:tʃ) *vt* **1** accuser. **2** contester. **impeachment** *n* accusation *f.*

pediment (imˈpedimənt) *n* empêchement *m.*

el (imˈpel) *vt* pousser, forcer.

rative (imˈperativ) *adj* **1** impérieux, -euse. gent. *n gram* impératif *m.*

ect (imˈpə:fikt) *adj,n* imparfait *m.*

imperial (imˈpiəriəl) *adj* impérial, -aux. **imperialism** *n* impérialisme *m.*

impersonal (imˈpə:sənl̩) *adj* impersonnel, -elle.

impersonate (imˈpə:səneit) *vt* **1** personnifier. **2** *Th* représenter.

impertinent (imˈpə:tinənt) *adj* impertinent, insolent. **impertinence** *n* impertinence *f.*

impetuous (imˈpetʃuəs) *adj* impétueux, -euse, fougueux, -euse.

impetus (ˈimpitəs) *n* élan *m.* impulsion *f.*

impinge (imˈpindʒ) *vi* **impinge on** empiéter sur.

implement (*n* ˈimpləmənt; *v* ˈimpləment) *n* instrument, outil *m.* *vt* exécuter.

implicit (imˈplisit) *adj* **1** implicite. **2** sans réserve.

implore (imˈplɔ:) *vt* implorer.

imply (imˈplai) *vt* **1** impliquer, supposer. **2** insinuer. **implied** *adj* tacite, sous-entendu.

import (*v* imˈpɔ:t; *n* ˈimpɔ:t) *vt* **1** *comm* importer. **2** signifier. *n* **1** sens *m.* **2** importance *f.* **3** *pl* importations *f pl.*

importance (imˈpɔ:tn̩s) *n* importance *f.* **important** *adj* important.

impose (imˈpouz) *vt* imposer. **impose upon** en imposer à. **imposing** *adj* imposant. **imposition** *n* **1** imposition *f.* **2** abus *m.*

impossible (imˈposəbəl) *adj* impossible.

impostor (imˈpɔstə) *n* imposteur *m.*

impotent (ˈimpətənt) *adj* impuissant. **impotence** *n* impuissance *f.*

impound (imˈpaund) *vt* **1** enfermer. **2** confisquer.

impoverish (imˈpɔvəriʃ) *vt* appauvrir.

impress (imˈpres) *vt* **1** imprimer. **2** impressionner. *n* empreinte *f.* **impression** *n* impression *f.* **impressive** *adj* impressionnant.

imprint (*n* ˈimprint; *v* imˈprint) *n* empreinte *f.* *vt* imprimer.

imprison (imˈprizən) *vt* emprisonner. **imprisonment** *n* emprisonnement *m.*

improbable (imˈprɔbəbəl) *adj* invraisemblable.

impromptu (imˈprɔmptju:) *adj* improvisé. *adv* impromptu.

improper (imˈprɔpə) *adj* **1** malséant. **2** impropre.

improve (imˈpru:v) *vt* améliorer, perfectionner. *vi* s'améliorer, se perfectionner. **improvement** *n* amélioration *f.* progrès *m.*

improvise (ˈimprəvaiz) *vt,vi* improviser. **improvisation** *n* improvisation *f.*

impudent (ˈimpjudənt) *adj* insolent, impudent. **impudence** *n* impudence *f.*

impulse ('impʌls) *n* **1** impulsion *f*. **2** poussée *f*. **impulsive** *adj* impulsif, -ive.
impure (im'pjuə) *adj* impur. **impurity** *n* impureté *f*.
in (in) *prep* **1** en, à, dans, de. **2** sur, par. *adv* **1** chez soi, y, là. **2** dedans.
inability (inə'biliti) *n* incapacité *f*.
inaccurate (in'ækjurət) *adj* inexact, incorrect.
inadequate (in'ædikwit) *adj* inadéquat, insuffisant. **inadequacy** *n* insuffisance *f*.
inadvertent (inəd'və:tnt) *adj* **1** involontaire. **2** inattentif, -ive. **inadvertently** *adv* par inadvertance.
inane (i'nein) *adj* inepte, niais.
inarticulate (inɑ:'tikjulət) *adj* inarticulé.
inasmuch (inəz'mʌtʃ) *conj* **inasmuch as** attendu *or* vu que.
inaudible (in'ɔ:dəbəl) *adj* imperceptible.
inaugurate (i'nɔ:gjureit) *vt* inaugurer. **inauguration** *n* inauguration *f*.
incapable (in'keipəbəl) *adj* incapable, incompétent.
incendiary (in'sendiəri) *adj* incendiaire.
incense[1] ('insens) *n* encens *m*. *vt* encenser.
incense[2] (in'sens) *vt* exaspérer, courroucer.
incessant (in'sesənt) *adj* incessant.
incest ('insest) *n* inceste *m*. **incestuous** *adj* incestueux, -euse.
inch (intʃ) *n* pouce *m*. **inch by inch** petit à petit. ~*vi* avancer petit à petit.
incident ('insidənt) *n* incident *m*. **incidental** *adj* **1** fortuit. **2** accessoire.
incite (in'sait) *vt* inciter.
incline (in'klain) *vt* incliner, pencher. *vi* s'incliner. *n* pente *f*. **inclination** *n* **1** pente *f*. **2** penchant *m*. tendance *f*.
include (in'klu:d) *vt* inclure, comprendre. **inclusive** *adj* **1** global, -aux. **2** inclus.
incognito (inkɔg'ni:tou) *adv* incognito.
incoherent (inkou'hiərənt) *adj* incohérent.
income ('inkʌm) *n* revenu *m*. **income tax** *n* impôt sur le revenu *m*. **income tax return** déclaration de revenu *f*. **private income** rente *f*.
incompatible (inkəm'pætibəl) *adj* incompatible.
incompetent (in'kɔmpətənt) *adj* incompétent.
incomprehensible (inkɔmpri'hensibəl) *adj* incompréhensible.
inconclusive (inkən'klu:siv) *adj* peu concluant.
incongruous (in'kɔŋgruəs) *adj* incongru, déplacé.
inconsiderate (inkən'sidərit) *adj* **1** irréfléchi. **2** sans égards.

inconsistent (inkən'sistənt) *adj* **1** incompatible. **2** illogique. **3** incongru. **inconsistency** *n* **1** disparité *f*. **2** contradiction *f*.
inconspicuous (inkənspikjuəs) *adj* effacé, discret, -ète.
inconvenient (inkən'vi:niənt) *adj* incommode, inopportun.
incorporate (in'kɔ:pəreit) *vt* **1** incorporer. **2** *comm* réunir. *vi* s'incorporer.
incorrect (inkə'rekt) *adj* inexact, incorrect.
increase (*v* in'kri:s; *n* 'inkri:s) *vi* **1** augmenter. **2** s'accroître. *vt* accroître, augmenter. *n* augmentation *f*. **increasing** *adj* croissant.
incredible (in'kredəbəl) *adj* incroyable.
incubate ('inkjubeit) *vt,vi* couver. **incubator** *n* couveuse *f*.
incur (in'kə:) *vt* **1** (expenses) courir, faire. **2** encourir.
indecent (in'di:sənt) *adj* indécent.
indeed (in'di:d) *adv* en effet, vraiment, à vrai dire.
indefinite (in'defənit) *adj* **1** indéfini. **2** illimité.
indent (in'dent) *vt* denteler.
independent (indi'pendənt) *adj* indépendant. **independence** *n* indépendance *f*.
index ('indeks) *n pl* **-dexes** *or* **-dices** **1** (of a book) répertoire *m*. **2** indice, signe *m* *vt* classer. **index finger** *n* index *m*.
India ('indiə) *n* Inde *f*. **Indian** *adj,n* indien, -ienne.
indicate ('indikeit) *vt* indiquer. **indication** *n* signe *m*. **indicator** *n* indicateur *m*.
indifferent (in'difrənt) *adj* **1** indifférent. **2** médiocre.
indigestion (indi'dʒestʃən) *n* indigestion *f*. **in-**
indignant (in'dignənt) *adj* indigné.
dignant s'indigner. ...né.
indirect (indi'rekt) *adj* **1** indirect. **2** ...gle.
indiscriminate (indi'skriminit) a... ...m. *adj* **1**
individual (indi'vidʒuəl) *n* in...
particulier, -ière. **2** original, ...triner.
indoctrinate (in'dɔktrineit) ... paresseux,
indolent ('indələnt) *adj*
-euse. ...r. **2** de société
indoor ('indɔ:) *adj* **1** ...intérieur.
indoors *adv* à la m... ...uire. **2** causer
induce (in'dju:s) ... encouragemen...
provoquer. **indu**... ...atisfaire. **indul**...
indulge (in'dʌl... ...ce *n* indulgence
s'adonner à. ... industrie *f*. **2** ...
industry ('in... ...dustriel, -elle. **in**...
f. **industri**... ...eux, -euse. ...7
adj assidu...

inefficient (ini'fiʃənt) *adj* **1** inefficace. **2** incapable.
inept (i'nept) *adj* **1** inepte. **2** déplacé.
inequality (ini'kwɔliti) *n* inégalité *f*.
inert (i'nə:t) *adj* inerte. **inertia** *n* inertie *f*.
inevitable (in'evitəbəl) *adj* inévitable, fatal.
infallible (in'fæləbəl) *adj* infaillible.
infamous ('infəməs) *adj* infâme.
infancy ('infənsi) *n* **1** enfance *f*. bas âge *m*. **2** débuts *m pl*.
infant ('infənt) *n* **1** enfant (en bas âge) *m,f*. **2** *law* mineur *m*. **infantile** *adj* enfantin.
infantry ('infəntri) *n* infanterie *f*.
infatuate (in'fætʃueit) *vt* **1** enticher. **2** affoler. **be infatuated with** s'enticher de. **infatuation** *n* engouement *m*.
infect (in'fekt) *vt* **1** *med* contaminer. **2** infecter. **infection** *n* **1** *med* contamination *f*. **2** infection *f*.
infer (in'fə:) *vt* **1** impliquer. **2** déduire.
inferior (in'fiəriə) *adj,n* inférieur *m*. **inferiority** *n* infériorité *f*.
infernal (in'fə:nl̩) *adj* infernal, -aux.
infest (in'fest) *vt* infester.
infidelity (infi'deliti) *n* infidélité, déloyauté *f*.
infiltrate ('infiltreit) *vt* infiltrer. *vi* s'infiltrer.
infinite ('infinit) *adj* infini. **infinitely** *adv* infiniment. **infinity** *n* infinité *f*.
infinitive (in'finitiv) *adj,n* infinitif, -ive *m*.
infirm (in'fə:m) *adj* infirme.
inflame (in'fleim) *vt* enflammer. *vi* s'enflammer.
inflammable (in'flæməbəl) *adj* inflammable.
[...]flate (in'fleit) *vt* **1** gonfler. **2** *comm* faire [...]onter. **inflation** *n* inflation *f*.
in[...]tion (in'flekʃən) *n* inflexion *f*.
infl[...] (in'flikt) *vt* **1** infliger. **2** occasionner.
in[...]e ('influəns) *n* influence *f*. *vt* **1** infl[...]er. **2** influer sur. **influential** *adj*
influen[...]
influx ([...]lu'enzə) *n* grippe *f*.
inform (i[...] *n* affluence *f*.
mation [...] *vt* informer, renseigner. **infor-**
of inform[...][...]nements *m pl*. avis *m*. **piece**
mouchard, [...]nseignement *m*. **informer** *n*
informal (in[...]teur *m*.
familier, -ère. [...] *adj* sans cérémonie,
[...]fringe (in'frin[...]
[...]nfringement *n* [...]freindre. *vi* empiéter.
[...]riate (in'fjuərie[...] *f*.
[...]er. [...] furieux, [...]as-
[...]ious (in'dʒi:niəs) [...] -euse.

ingredient (in'gri:diənt) *n* ingrédient, élément *m*.
inhabit (in'hæbit) *vt* habiter. **inhabitant** *n* habitant *m*.
inhale (in'heil) *vt* **1** inhaler. **2** inspirer.
inherent (in'hiərənt) *adj* inhérent, propre.
inherit (in'herit) *vt* hériter de. **inheritance** *n* **1** héritage *m*. **2** succession *f*.
inhibit (in'hibit) *vt* **1** inhiber, empêcher. **2** prohiber. **inhibition** *n* **1** inhibition *f*. **2** prohibition *f*.
inhuman (in'hju:mən) *adj* inhumain. **inhumanity** *n* cruauté *f*.
initial (i'niʃəl) *adj* premier, initial, -aux. *n* initiale *f*. *vt* parafer.
initiate (i'niʃieit) *vt* **1** commencer, lancer. **2** initier. **initiation** *n* **1** début *m*. **2** initiation *f*.
initiative (i'niʃətiv) *n* initiative *f*.
inject (in'dʒekt) *vt* injecter. **injection** *n* injection, piqûre *f*.
injure ('indʒə) *vt* **1** blesser. **2** endommager. **injury** *n* **1** blessure *f*. **2** tort *m*.
injustice (in'dʒʌstis) *n* injustice *f*.
ink (iŋk) *n* encre *f*.
inkling ('iŋkliŋ) *n* soupçon *m*.
inland (*adj* 'inlənd; *n,adv* 'inlænd) *adj,n* intérieur *m*. *adv* à l'intérieur.
Inland Revenue *n* fisc *m*.
inmate ('inmeit) *n* **1** pensionnaire *m*. **2** prisonnier, -ière.
inn (in) *n* auberge *f*.
innate (i'neit) *adj* inné.
inner ('inə) *adj* intérieur, interne.
innocent ('inəsənt) *adj* **1** innocent. **2** naïf, -ïve. **innocence** *n* **1** innocence *f*. **2** naïveté *f*.
innocuous (i'nɔkjuəs) *adj* inoffensif, -ive.
innovation (inə'veiʃən) *n* innovation *f*.
innuendo (inju'endou) *n* insinuation *f*.
inoculate (i'nɔkjuleit) *vt* inoculer, vacciner. **inoculation** *n* inoculation *f*.
input ('input) *n* entrée, consommation *f*.
inquest ('inkwest) *n* enquête *f*.
inquire (in'kwaiə) *vt* demander. *vi* s'enquérir, se renseigner. **inquiry** *n* **1** demande de renseignements *f*. **2** enquête *f*.
inquisition (inkwi'ziʃən) *n* **1** investigation *f*. **2** *cap* Inquisition *f*.
inquisitive (in'kwizitiv) *adj* curieux, -euse.
insane (in'sein) *adj* **1** fou, folle. **2** insensé. **insanity** *n* folie, démence *f*.
insatiable (in'seiʃəbəl) *adj* insatiable.
inscribe (in'skraib) *vt* inscrire, graver. **inscription** *n* inscription *f*.

insect ('insekt) *n* insecte *m*.
insecure (insi'kjuə) *adj* **1** incertain. **2** peu solide.
inseminate (in'semineit) *vt* inséminer. **insemination** *n* insémination *f*.
insert (in'sə:t) *vt* **1** insérer. **2** introduire. **insertion** *n* insertion *f*.
inside (in'said) *adj* intérieur. *adv* à l'intérieur. *prep* à l'intérieur de. *n* dedans, intérieur *m*. **on the inside** au dedans.
insidious (in'sidiəs) *adj* insidieux, -euse.
insight ('insait) *n* **1** perspicacité *f*. **2** aperçu *m*.
insinuate (in'sinjueit) *vt* insinuer.
insist (in'sist) *vi* insister. **insistence** *n* insistance *f*.
insolent ('insələnt) *adj* insolent.
insomnia (in'sɔmniə) *n* insomnie *f*.
inspect (in'spekt) *vt* inspecter, examiner. **inspection** *n* inspection *f*. contrôle *m*. **inspector** *n* inspecteur *m*.
inspire (in'spaiə) *vt* inspirer. **inspiration** *n* inspiration *f*.
instability (instə'biliti) *n* instabilité *f*.
install (in'stɔ:l) *vt* installer.
instalment (in'stɔ:lmənt) *n* **1** versement partiel *m*. **2** (of a serial) épisode *m*.
instance ('instəns) *n* **1** exemple, cas *m*. **2** instance *f*. **for instance** par exemple. **instant** *n* instant *m*. *adj* **1** immédiat. **2** courant. **3** urgent. **instantaneous** *adj* instantané.
instead (in'sted) **instead of** *prep* au lieu de. *adv* à la place.
instep ('instep) *n* **1** *anat* cou-de-pied *m*. **2** cambrure *f*.
instigate ('instigeit) *vt* inciter, provoquer.
instil (in'stil) *vt* inculquer.
instinct ('instiŋkt) *n* instinct *m*. **instinctive** *adj* instinctif, -ive.
institute ('institju:t) *n* institut *m*. *vt* instituer. **institution** *n* institution *f*. établissement *m*.
instruct (in'strʌkt) *vt* **1** instruire. **2** charger. **instruction** *n* **1** instruction *f*. **2** *pl* ordres *m pl*.
instrument ('instrumənt) *n* instrument *m*. **instrumental** *adj* **1** contributif, -ive. **2** *mus* instrumental, -aux.
insubordinate (insə'bɔ:dinət) *adj* insubordonné.
insular ('insjulə) *adj* **1** insulaire. **2** borné.
insulate ('insjuleit) *vt* **1** isoler. **2** calorifuger. **insulation** *n* isolement *m*.
insulin ('insjulin) *n* insuline *f*.
insult (*v* in'sʌlt; *n* 'insʌlt) *vt* insulter. *n* insulte *f*. affront *m*.
insure (in'ʃuə) *vt* assurer. **insurance** *n* assurance *f*.
intact (in'tækt) *adj* intact, indemne.
intake ('inteik) *n* **1** consommation *f*. **2** prise *f*. **3** admission *f*.
integral ('intigrəl) *adj* intégrant.
integrate ('intigreit) *vt* intégrer, compléter.
integrity (in'tegriti) *n* intégrité *f*.
intellect ('intəlekt) *n* intelligence *f*. esprit *m*. **intellectual** *adj,n* intellectuel, -elle.
intelligent (in'telidʒənt) *adj* intelligent. **intelligence** *n* **1** intelligence *f*. **2** renseignements *m pl*.
intelligible (in'telidʒəbəl) *adj* intelligible.
intend (in'tend) *vt* **1** avoir l'intention. **2** destiner.
intense (in'tens) *adj* intense, profond. **intensify** *vt* intensifier. *vi* s'accroître. **intensity** *n* intensité *f*. **intensive** *adj* intensif, -ive.
intent[1] (in'tent) *n* intention *f*. dessein *m*.
intent[2] (in'tent) *adj* **1** absorbé. **2** résolu. **3** acharné. **4** sérieux, -euse.
intention (in'tenʃən) *n* intention *f*. **intentional** *adj* voulu. **intentionally** *adv* exprès.
inter (in'tə:) *vt* enterrer.
interact (intə'rækt) *vi* agir l'un sur l'autre.
intercept (intə'sept) *vt* intercepter, arrêter en passage.
interchange (intə'tʃeindʒ) *vt* échanger. *vi* s'interchanger. *n* **1** échange *m*. **2** succession *f*.
intercourse ('intəkɔ:s) *n* commerce *m*. rapports *m pl*.
interest ('intrəst) *n* **1** intérêt *m*. **2** avantage *m*. *vt* intéresser. **be interested in** s'intéresser à.
interfere (intə'fiə) *vi* s'ingérer, s'immiscer. **interference** *n* **1** intervention *f*. **2** *tech* parasites *m pl*. **interfering** *adj* importun.
interim ('intərim) *adj* intérimaire. *n* intérim *m*.
interior (in'tiəriə) *adj,n* intérieur *m*.
interjection (intə'dʒekʃn̩) *n* interjection *f*.
interlude ('intəlu:d) *n* intermède *m*.
intermediate (intə'mi:diət) *adj* intermédiaire. **intermediary** *adj,n* intermédiaire *m*.
intermission (intə'miʃən) *n* **1** interruption *f*. **2** (cinema) entracte *m*.
intermittent (intə'mitn̩t) *adj* intermittent.
intern (in'tə:n) *vt* interner.
internal (in'tə:nl̩) *adj* intérieur, interne.
international (intə'næʃn̩l̩) *adj* international, -aux.
internment (in'tə:nmənt) *n* internement *m*.
interpose (intə'pouz) *vt* interposer. *vi* s'interposer.
interpret (in'tə:prit) *vt* interpréter. **interpretation** *n* interprétation *f*. **interpreter** *n* interprète *m,f*.

interrogate (in'terəgeit) *vt* questionner, interroger. **interrogation** *n* **1** interrogation *f*. **2** *law* interrogatoire *m*. **interrogative** *adj* **1** interrogateur, -trice. **2** *gram* interrogatif, -ive.

interrupt (intə'rʌpt) *vt* interrompre. **interruption** *n* interruption *f*.

intersect (intə'sekt) *vt* entrecouper. *vi* se couper. **intersection 1** intersection *f*. **2** *mot* carrefour *m*.

interval ('intəvəl) *n* **1** intervalle *m*. **2** *Th* entracte *m*.

intervene (intə'vi:n) *vi* **1** intervenir. **2** survenir. **intervention** *n* intervention *f*.

interview ('intəvju:) *n* entrevue, interview *f*. *vt* interviewer.

intestine (in'testin) *n* intestin *m*.

intimate[1] ('intimit) *adj* intime. **intimacy** *n* intimité *f*.

intimate[2] ('intimeit) *vt* suggérer, intimer.

intimidate (in'timideit) *vt* intimider. **intimidation** *n* **1** intimidation *f*. **2** *law* menaces *f pl*.

into ('intə; *stressed* 'intu:) *prep* dans, en, à.

intolerable (in'tɔlərəbəl) *adj* intolérable, insupportable. **intolerant** *adj* intolérant.

intonation (intə'neiʃən) *n* **1** intonation *f*. **2** ton *m*.

intoxicate (in'tɔksikeit) *vt* enivrer. **intoxicated** *adj* ivre. **intoxication** *n* **1** intoxication *f*. **2** ivresse *f*.

intransitive (in'trænsitiv) *adj* intransitif, -ive.

intrepid (in'trepid) *adj* intrépide.

intricate ('intrikət) *adj* **1** compliqué. **2** confus. **intricacy** *n* complexité *f*.

intrigue (in'tri:g) *n* intrigue *f*. *vt,vi* intriguer.

intrinsic (in'trinsik) *adj* intrinsèque.

introduce (intrə'dju:s) *vt* **1** introduire. **2** présenter. **introduction** *n* **1** introduction *f*. **2** présentation *f*. **3** *lit* avant-propos *m invar*.

introspective (intrə'spektiv) *adj* introspectif, -ive.

introvert ('intrəvə:t) *n* introverti *m*.

intrude (in'tru:d) *vi* faire intrusion. **intruder** *n* intrus *m*.

intuition (intju'iʃən) *n* intuition *f*. **intuitive** *adj* intuitif, -ive.

inundate ('inʌndeit) *vt* inonder.

invade (in'veid) *vt* envahir.

invalid[1] ('invəli:d) *adj,n* infirme, malade.

invalid[2] (in'vælid) *adj* nul et non avenu, périmé.

invaluable (in'væljubəl) *adj* inestimable.

invariable (in'vɛəriəbəl) *adj* invariable. **invariably** *adv* immanquablement.

invent (in'vent) *vt* inventer. **invention** *n* invention *f*. **inventor** *n* inventeur *m*.

inventory ('invəntəri) *n* inventaire *m*.

invert (in'və:t) *vt* **1** renverser. **2** intervertir. **inverted commas** *n pl* guillemets *m pl*.

invertebrate (in'və:təbreit) *adj,n* invertébré *m*.

invest (in'vest) *vt* **1** investir. **2** revêtir. **investment** *n* placement *m*.

investigate (in'vestigeit) *vt* **1** examiner. **2** enquêter sur.

invincible (in'vinsəbəl) *adj* invincible.

invisible (in'vizəbəl) *adj* invisible.

invite (in'vait) *vt* inviter. **invitation** *n* invitation *f*. **inviting** *adj* tentant, engageant.

invoice ('invɔis) *n* facture *f*. *vt* facturer.

invoke (in'vouk) *vt* **1** invoquer. **2** évoquer.

involve (in'vɔlv) *vt* **1** impliquer. **2** comporter. **involved** *adj* compliqué. **involvement** *n* implication *f*.

inward ('inwəd) *adj* **1** intérieur, interne. **2** vers l'intérieur. **inwards** *adv* vers l'intérieur.

iodine ('aiədi:n) *n* iode *m*.

Iran (i'rɑ:n) *n* Iran *m*. **Iranian** *adj,n* iranien, -ienne.

Iraq (i'rɑ:k) *n* Irak *m*. **Iraqi** *adj,n* irakien, -ienne.

Ireland ('aiələnd) *n* Irlande *f*. **Irish** *adj* irlandais. **Irishman** *n* irlandais *m*.

iris ('airis) *n anat, bot* iris *m*.

iron ('aiən) *n* **1** fer *m*. **2** *dom* fer à repasser *m*. *adj* de fer. *vt* repasser. **ironing board** *n* planche à repasser *f*. **ironmonger** *n* quincaillier *m*. **Iron Curtain** *n* Rideau de Fer *m*.

irony ('airəni) *n* ironie *f*. **ironic** *adj* ironique.

irrational (i'ræʃən|) *adj* absurde, déraisonnable.

irregular (i'regjulə) *adj* irrégulier, -ière.

irrelevant (i'reləvənt) *adj* hors de propos.

irresistible (iri'zistəbəl) *adj* irrésistible.

irrespective (iri'spektiv) *adj* indépendant. *adv* indépendamment.

irresponsible (iri'spɔnsəbəl) *adj* irresponsable.

irrevocable (i'revəkəbəl) *adj* irrévocable.

irrigate ('irigeit) *vt* irriguer. **irrigation** *n* irrigation *f*.

irritate ('iriteit) *vt* irriter. **irritating** *adj* irritant, agaçant. **irritation** *n* irritation *f*.

is (iz) *v* see **be.**

Islam ('izlɑ:m) *n* Islam *m*. **Islamic** *adj* Islamique.

island ('ailənd) *n* **1** île *f*. **2** îlot *m*.

isle (ail) *n* île *f*.

isolate ('aisəleit) *vt* isoler. **isolation** *n* isolement *m*.

kid[2] (kid) *vt inf* faire marcher. **kid oneself** se faire accroire, se leurrer.
kidnap ('kidnæp) *vt* enlever, kidnapper. **kidnapper** *n* ravisseur *m.* **kidnapping** *n* enlèvement *m.*
kidney ('kidni) *n* **1** *anat* rein *m.* **2** (of animals) rognon *m.* **kidney bean** *n* haricot nain *m.*
kill (kil) *vt* **1** tuer. **2** (an animal) abattre. **killing** *adj* **1** meurtrier, -ière. **2** *inf* crevant. *n* tuerie *f.*
kiln (kiln) *n* four *m.*
kilo ('ki:lou) *n* kilo *m.*
kilogram ('kiləgræm) *n* kilogramme *m.*
kilometre (ki'lɔmitə) *n* kilomètre *m.*
kilowatt ('kiləwɔt) *n* kilowatt *m.*
kilt (kilt) *n* kilt *m.*
kin (kin) *n* **1** parenté *f.* **2** parents *m pl.*
kind[1] (kaind) *adj* bon, bonne, aimable, gentil, -ille, bienveillant. **kindness** *n* bonté, bienveillance *f.*
kind[2] (kaind) *n* espèce, sorte *f.* genre *m.*
kindergarten ('kindəgɑ:tn̩) *n* école maternelle *f.*
kindle ('kindl̩) *vt* **1** allumer, enflammer. **2** éveiller, exciter. *vi* **1** s'allumer. **2** s'éveiller.
kinetic (ki'netik) *adj* cinétique.
king (kiŋ) *n* **1** roi *m.* **2** (draughts) dame *f.* **kingdom** *n* **1** royaume *m.* **2** règne *m.* **kingfisher** *n* martin-pêcheur *m.*
kink (kiŋk) *n* nœud, tortillement *m.* *vi* se nouer, se tortiller.
kiosk ('kiɔsk) *n* kiosque *m.*
kipper ('kipə) *n* hareng fumé *m.*
kiss (kis) *n* baiser *m.* *vt* embrasser.
kit (kit) *n* **1** trousse *f.* fourniment *m.* **2** *inf* effets *m pl.*
kitchen ('kitʃin) *n* cuisine *f.* *adj* de cuisine, cuisinier, -ière. **kitchen garden** *n* jardin potager *m.*
kite (kait) *n* **1** cerf-volant *m.* **2** *zool* milan *m.*
kitten ('kitn̩) *n* chaton *m.*
kitty ('kiti) *n* cagnotte *f.*
kiwi ('ki:wi) *n* kiwi, aptéryx *m.*
kleptomania (kleptə'meiniə) *n* kleptomanie *f.* **kleptomaniac** *adj,n* kleptomane.
knack (næk) *n* tour de main, truc *m.*
knave (neiv) *n* **1** coquin *m.* **2** *game* valet *m.*
knead (ni:d) *vt* pétrir, travailler.
knee (ni:) *n* genou, -oux *m.* **kneecap** *n* rotule *f.*
kneel* (ni:l) *vi* s'agenouiller.
knew (nu:) *v* see **know.**
knickers ('nikəz) *n pl* culotte *f.*
knife (naif) *n, pl* **knives** couteau, -aux *m.* *vt* donner un coup de couteau à, poignarder.
knight (nait) *n* **1** chevalier *m.* **2** *game* cavalier *m.* *vt* créer chevalier.
knit* (nit) *vt* **1** tricoter. **2** joindre. *vi* se souder. **knitting** *n* tricot *m.* **knitting needle** aiguille à tricoter *f.* **knitwear** *n* tricot *m.*
knob (nɔb) *n* **1** bouton *m.* bosse *f.* **2** morceau, -aux *m.*
knock (nɔk) *n* coup, heurt *m.* *vt,vi* frapper, heurter. **knock down** renverser. **knock over** renverser. **knocker** *n* marteau, -aux *m.*
knot (nɔt) *n* nœud *m.* *vt* nouer.
know* (nou) *vt* **1** savoir, connaître. **2** reconnaître. **get to know** **1** apprendre. **2** faire la connaissance de. **knowing** *adj* fin, rusé.
knowledge ('nɔlidʒ) *n* **1** connaissance *f.* **2** savoir *m.* science *f.*
knuckle ('nʌkəl) *n* articulation, jointure *f.*
Korea (kə'riə) *n* Corée *f.* **Korean** *adj,n* coréen, -enne.
kosher ('kouʃə) *adj* cachir *invar.*

L

label ('leibəl) *n* étiquette *f.* *vt* étiqueter.
laboratory (lə'bɔrətri) *n* laboratoire *m.*
labour ('leibə) *n* **1** travail, -aux, labeur *m.* **2** main-d'œuvre *f.* *vi* travailler, peiner. **labour-saving** *adj* qui allège le travail. **laborious** *adj* laborieux, -euse, pénible. **Labour Party** *n* parti travailliste *m.*
laburnum (lə'bə:nəm) *n* cytise *m.*
labyrinth ('læbərinθ) *n* labyrinthe, dédale *m.*
lace (leis) *n* **1** dentelle *f.* **2** (of a shoe, etc.) lacet *m.* *vt* lacer.
lack (læk) *n* manque, défaut *m.* **for lack of** faute de. ~*vt,vi* manquer.
lacquer ('lækə) *n* vernis *m.* laque *f.* *vt* laquer.
lad (læd) *n* gars, garçon *m.*
ladder ('lædə) *n* **1** échelle *f.* **2** (in a stocking) maille filée *f.*
laden ('leidn̩) *adj* chargé.
ladle ('leidl̩) *n* louche *f.*
lady ('leidi) *n* dame *f.* **ladies and gentlemen** mesdames, mesdemoiselles, messieurs. **ladybird** *n* coccinelle, *inf* bête à bon Dieu *f.*
lag[1] (læg) *vi* traîner, rester en arrière. *n* retard *m.*
lag[2] (læg) *vt* calorifuger. **lagging** *n* revêtement calorifuge *m.*
lager ('lɑ:gə) *n* bière blonde allemande *f.*
laid (leid) *v* see **lay.**
lain (lein) *v* see **lie.**

laity (ˈleiəti) *n* laïques *m pl.*
lake (leik) *n* lac *m.*
lamb (læm) *n* agneau, -aux *m.*
lame (leim) *adj* **1** boiteux, -euse, estropié. **2** pauvre, faible. *vt* estropier.
lament (ləˈment) *n* lamentation *f. vt* pleurer. *vi* se lamenter.
lamp (læmp) *n* lampe *f.* **standard lamp** lampadaire *m.* **lamppost** *n* réverbère *m.* **lampshade** *n* abat-jour *m invar.*
lance (lɑ:ns) *n* lance *f.*
land (lænd) *n* **1** terre *f.* **2** pays *m. vt,vi* **1** *naut* débarquer. **2** *aviat* atterrir. **landing** *n* **1** palier *m.* **2** *aviat* atterrissage *m.* **3** *naut* débarquement *m.* **landlady** *n* propriétaire, patronne *f.* **landlord** *n* propriétaire, patron *m.* **landmark** *n* **1** point de repère *m.* **2** événement marquant *m.* **landscape** *n* paysage *m.*
lane (lein) *n* **1** chemin, sentier *m.* ruelle *f.* **2** (on a motorway) voie f.
language (ˈlæŋgwidʒ) *n* **1** (of a people) langue *f.* **2** langage *m.*
lanky (ˈlæŋki) *adj* maigre, décharné.
lantern (ˈlæntən) *n* lanterne *f.* fanal, -aux *m.*
lap[1] (læp) *n anat* genoux *m pl.* giron *m.*
lap[2] (læp) *n sport* tour, circuit *m. vt* **1** assembler. **2** ourler.
lap[3] (læp) *vt* laper. *vi* (of waves) clapoter. *n* clapotement *m.*
lapel (ləˈpel) *n* revers *m.*
Lapland (ˈlæplænd) *n* Laponie *f.* **Lapp** *adj,n* lapon. **Lapp** (language) *n* lapon *m.*
lapse (læps) *n* **1** cours *m.* **2** faute, erreur *f. vi* s'écouler. **2** manquer.
larceny (ˈlɑ:səni) *n* larcin *m.*
larch (lɑ:tʃ) *n* mélèze *m.*
lard (lɑ:d) *n* saindoux *m.*
larder (ˈlɑ:də) *n* garde-manger *m invar.*
large (lɑ:dʒ) *adj* grand, fort, gros, grosse. **at large** en liberté.
lark[1] (lɑ:k) *n zool* alouette *f.*
lark[2] (lɑ:k) *n inf* farce, blague *f.*
larva (ˈlɑ:və) *n, pl* **larvae** larve *f.*
larynx (ˈlæriŋks) *n* larynx *m.* **laryngitis** *n* laryngite *f.*
laser (ˈleizə) *n* laser *m.*
lash (læʃ) *n* **1** coup de fouet m. **2** lanière *f.* **3** cil *m. vt,vi* fouetter, cingler. **lash out 1** lâcher un coup. **2** ruer.
lass (læs) *n* jeune fille *f.*
lasso (læˈsu:) *n* lasso *m.*
last[1] (lɑ:st) *adj* dernier, -ière. **at last** enfin. **last but one** avant-dernier. **last night** cette nuit *f.*
last[2] (lɑ:st) *vi* durer. **lasting** *adj* durable.
latch (lætʃ) *n* loquet *m.* clenche *f. vt* fermer au loquet.
late (leit) *adv* **1** tard. **2** en retard. *adj* **1** tard. **2** tardif, -ive. **3** feu. **4** dernier, -ière. **5** ancien, -ienne. **lately** *adv* dernièrement, récemment. **latecomer** *n* retardataire *m,f.* **later** *adv* plus tard. *adj* ultérieur.
latent (ˈleitnt) *adj* latent, caché.
lateral (ˈlætərəl) *adj* latéral, -aux.
latest (ˈleitist) *adj* récent, dernier, -ière. **at the latest** au plus tard.
lathe (leið) *n* tour *m.*
lather (ˈlɑ:ðə) *n* mousse *f. vt* savonner. *vi* mousser.
Latin (ˈlætin) *adj,n* latin *m.* **Latin America** *n* Amérique latine *f.*
latitude (ˈlætitju:d) *n* **1** latitude *f.* **2** largeur, étendue *f.*
latter (ˈlætə) *adj* **1** dernier, -ière. **2** celui-ci, celle-ci.
lattice (ˈlætis) *n* treillage, treillis *m.*
laugh (lɑ:f) *n* rire *m. vi* rire. **laugh at** se moquer de. **laughter** *n* rire *m.*
launch[1] (lɔ:ntʃ) *n* chaloupe *f.*
launch[2] (lɔ:ntʃ) *vt* lancer. **launch out** se lancer. **launching** *n* lancement *m.*
launder (ˈlɔ:ndə) *vt* blanchir. **launderette** *n* laverie *f.* **laundry** *n* **1** blanchisserie *f.* **2** linge *m.*
laurel (ˈlɔrəl) *n* laurier *m.*
lava (ˈlɑ:və) *n* lave *f.*
lavatory (ˈlævətri) *n* lavabo *m.* toilette *f.* cabinets *m pl.*
lavender (ˈlævində) *n* lavande *f.*
lavish (ˈlæviʃ) *adj* **1** prodigue. **2** somptueux, -euse, abondant. *vt* prodiguer.
law (lɔ:) *n* **1** loi *f.* **2** droit *m.* **law-abiding** *adj* respectueux des lois. **lawful** *adj* **1** légal, -aux. **2** légitime. **lawyer** *n* avocat, avoué *m.*
lawn (lɔ:n) *n* pelouse *f.* gazon *m.* **lawn-mower** *n* tondeuse à gazon *f.*
lax (læks) *adj* **1** mou, molle, lâche. **2** vague.
laxative (ˈlæksətiv) *adj,n* laxatif, -ive *m.*
lay[*1] (lei) *vt* **1** placer, mettre, poser. **2** (an egg) pondre. **3** coucher. **lay down 1** déposer. **2** stipuler. **lay out** étaler. **lay the table** mettre le couvert. **layer** *n* couche *f.*
lay[2] (lei) *v* see **lie.**
lay[3] (lei) *adj rel* lai, laïe, laïque. **layman** *n* laïque *m.*
laze (leiz) *vi* **laze about** fainéanter. **lazy** *adj* paresseux, -euse. **laziness** *n* paresse *f.*

lead*[1] (li:d) *vt* **1** mener, conduire. **2** diriger. **3** *game* jouer. *vi* mener, conduire. *n* **1** exemple *m*. **2** laisse *f*. **3** *game* main *f*. **4** *Th* premier rôle *m*. **5** câble *m*. *adj* principal, -aux. **leader** *n* **1** directeur, -trice, chef *m*. **2** guide *m*. **3** article de fond *m*. **leadership** *n* conduite *f*. commandement *m*.

lead[2] (led) *n* **1** plomb *m*. **2** (of a pencil) mine *f*. *vt* plomber.

leaf (li:f) *n, pl* **leaves** **1** *bot* feuille *f*. **2** rallonge *f*. **leaflet** *n* tract, prospectus *m*.

league (li:g) *n* ligue *f*.

leak (li:k) *n* fuite *f*. écoulement *m*. *vi* **1** fuir. **2** faire eau. **leak out** s'ébruiter.

lean*[1] (li:n) *vi* s'appuyer, s'incliner. *vt* incliner, appuyer. **lean out** se pencher. ~*n* inclinaison *f*.

lean[2] (li:n) *adj* maigre.

leap* (li:p) *n* saut, bond *m*. *vi* sauter, bondir. *vt* franchir. **leapfrog** *n* saute-mouton *m*. **leap year** *n* année bissextile *f*.

learn* (lə:n) *vi,vt* apprendre. **learned** *adj* savant, érudit. **learner** *n* débutant.

lease (li:s) *n* bail *m, pl* baulx. *vt* louer, donner à bail. **leasehold** *n* location à bail *f*.

leash (li:ʃ) *n* laisse, attache *f*. *vt* attacher.

least (li:st) *adj* le *or* la moindre. *n* moins *m*. **at least** au moins. *adv* le moins.

leather ('leðə) *n* cuir *m*.

leave*[1] (li:v) *vt* **1** laisser. **2** quitter. **3** abandonner. **4** léguer. *vi* partir, s'en aller. **leave out** omettre, oublier.

leave[2] (li:v) *n* **1** permission *f*. **2** congé *m*.

Lebanon ('lebənən) *n* Liban *m*. **Lebanese** *adj,n* libanais.

lecherous ('letʃərəs) *adj* lascif -ive, débauché.

lectern ('lektən) *n* lutrin *m*.

lecture ('lektʃə) *n* **1** conférence *f*. cours *m*. **2** *inf* semonce *f*. *vi* donner une conférence. *vt* réprimander. **lecturer** *n* conférencier, chargé de cours *m*.

led (led) *v see* **lead.**

ledge (ledʒ) *n* rebord *m*. saillie *f*.

ledger ('ledʒə) *n* grand livre *m*.

lee (li:) *n* **1** abri *m*. **2** *naut* côté sous le vent *m*.

leech (li:tʃ) *n* sangsue *f*.

leek (li:k) *n* poireau, -aux *m*.

leer (liə) *n* œillade (en dessous) *f*. regard polisson *m*. *vi* lorgner, guigner.

left[1] (left) *adj,n* gauche *f*. **left-hand** *adj* à gauche. **left-handed** *adj* gaucher, -ère. **left-wing** *adj* gauchiste, de gauche.

left[2] (left) *v see* **leave. left-luggage office** *n* consigne *m*.

leg (leg) *n* **1** jambe *f*. **2** (of an animal) patte *f*. **3** (of furniture) pied *m*. **4** *cul* cuisse *f*. gigot *m*.

legacy ('legəsi) *n* legs *m*.

legal ('li:gəl) *adj* licite, judiciaire, légal, -aux. **legalize** *vt* légaliser.

legend ('ledʒənd) *n* légende, fable *f*. **legendary** *adj* légendaire.

legible ('ledʒibl) *adj* lisible.

legion ('li:dʒən) *n* légion *f*.

legislate ('ledʒisleit) *vi* faire les lois, légiférer. **legislation** *n* législation *f*.

legitimate (li'dʒitimət) *adj* légitime.

leisure ('leʒə) *n* loisir *m*.

lemon ('lemən) *n* citron *m*. **lemonade** *n* limonade *f*. **lemon tree** *n* citronnier *m*.

lend* (lend) *vt* prêter.

length (leŋθ) *n* **1** longueur *f*. **2** durée *f*. **3** morceau, -aux *m*. **lengthen** *vt* allonger. *vi* s'allonger. **lengthy** *adj* long, longue.

lenient ('li:niənt) *adj* clément, indulgent. **leniently** *adv* avec clémence.

lens (lenz) *n* **1** lentille *f*. verre *m*. **2** *phot* objectif *m*.

lent (lent) *v see* **lend.**

Lent (lent) *n* Carême *m*.

lentil ('lentl) *n* lentille *f*.

Leo ('li:ou) *n* Lion *m*.

leopard ('lepəd) *n* léopard *m*.

leper ('lepə) *n* lépreux, -euse. **leprosy** *n* lèpre *f*. **leprous** *adj* lépreux, -euse.

lesbian ('lezbiən) *n* lesbienne *f*.

less (les) *adj* moindre. *adv,prep* moins. **less and less** de moins en moins. ~*n* moins *m*. **lessen** *vi* s'amoindrir. *vt* diminuer.

lesson ('lesən) *n* leçon *f*.

lest (lest) *conj* de peur que.

let* (let) *vt* **1** permettre, laisser. **2** louer. **let down** **1** baisser. **2** allonger. **let in** laisser entrer. **let out** laisser sortir.

lethal ('li:θəl) *adj* mortel, -elle.

lethargy ('leθədʒi) *n* léthargie *f*.

letter ('letə) *n* lettre *f*. **letterbox** *n* boîte aux lettres *f*.

lettuce ('letis) *n* laitue *f*.

leukaemia (lu:'ki:miə) *n* leucémie *f*.

level ('levəl) *n* niveau, -aux *m*. *adj* de niveau, égal, -aux, en palier. *vt* **1** niveler, aplanir. **2** viser. **level crossing** *n* passage à niveau *m*. **level-headed** *adj* d'aplomb, pondéré.

lever ('li:və) *n* levier *m*.

levy ('levi) *n* impôt *m*. *vt* lever, imposer.

lewd (lu:d) *adj* impudique.
liable ('laiəbəl) *adj* **1** *law* responsable. **2** sujet, -ette, exposé. **liability** *n* **1** responsabilité. **2** *pl* engagements *m pl.*
liaison (li'eizɔn) *n* liaison *f.*
liar ('laiə) *n* menteur, -euse.
libel ('laibəl) *n* diffamation, libelle *f.*
liberal ('libərəl) *adj,n* libéral -aux.
liberate ('libəreit) *vt* libérer.
liberty ('libəti) *n* liberté *f.*
Libra ('li:brə) *n* Balance *f.*
library ('laibrəri) *n* bibliothèque *f.* **librarian** *n* bibliothécaire *m,f.*
libretto (li'bretou) *n, pl* **-tos** *or* **-ti** *n* libretto, livret *m.*
Libya ('libiə) *n* Libye *f.* **Libyan** *adj,n* libyen, -enne.
licence ('laisəns) *n* **1** permis *m.* **2** autorisation *f.* **license** *vt* autoriser, patenter. **licensee** *n* patenté, gérant *m.*
lick (lik) *vt* lécher. **lick into shape** dégrossir. ~*n* coup de langue *m.*
lid (lid) *n* couvercle *m.*
lie[1] (lai) *n* mensonge *m.* *vi* mentir.
lie*[2] (lai) *vi* **1** être couché. **2** se trouver. **lie down** se coucher.
lieutenant (lef'tenənt) *n* lieutenant *m.* **lieutenant colonel** *n* lieutenant-colonel *m.*
life (laif) *n, pl* **lives** **1** vie *f.* **2** vivacité *f.* entrain *m.* **lifebelt** *n* ceinture de sauvetage *f.* **lifeboat** *n* canot de sauvetage *m.* **lifebuoy** *n* bouée de sauvetage *f.* **lifeguard** *n* garde du corps *m.* **lifeline** *n* ligne de sauvetage, sauvegarde *f.* **lifetime** *n* vie *f.*
lift (lift) *vt* **1** lever, soulever. **2** voler. *vi* se lever. *n* ascenseur *m.* **give someone a lift** emmener quelqu'un dans sa voiture.
light*[1] (lait) *n* lumière, clarté *f.* jour *m.* *vt* **1** allumer. **2** éclairer. **lighthouse** *n* phare *m.* **lighting** *n* éclairage *m.*
light[2] (lait) *adj* **1** léger, -ère. **2** (of colour, etc.) clair. **light-hearted** *adj* allègre. **lightweight** *n* poids léger *m.* *adj* léger, -ère.
light*[3] (lait) *vi* **light upon** tomber sur.
lighten[1] ('laitn̩) *vt* éclairer. *vi* s'éclairer, s'illuminer.
lighten[2] ('laitn̩) *vt* alléger, réduire.
lightning ('laitniŋ) *n* éclair *m.* foudre *f.*
like[1] (laik) *adj* pareil, -eille, semblable. *prep* comme. **likelihood** *n* probabilité *f.* **likewise** *adv* également, de même.
like[2] (laik) *vt* **1** aimer. **2** vouloir. **liking** *n* goût, gré *m.*
likely ('laikli) *adj* **1** probable. **2** susceptible. *adv* probablement.
lilac ('lailək) *n* lilas *m.*
lily ('lili) *n* lis *m.* **lily-of-the-valley** *n* muguet *m.*
limb (lim) *n* membre *m.*
limbo ('limbou) *n* limbes *m pl.*
lime[1] (laim) *n* chaux *f.* **in the limelight** *adv* en vedette. **limestone** *n* pierre à chaux *f.*
lime[2] (laim) *n* *bot* limon. **lime tree** *n* **1** limonier *m.* **2** tilleul *m.*
limerick ('limərik) *n* poème comique *m.*
limit ('limit) *n* limite, borne *f.* **that's the limit!** ça c'est le comble! ~*vt* limiter, borner, restreindre. **limitation** *n* limitation, restriction *f.*
limp[1] (limp) *vi* boiter. *n* boitement *m.*
limp[2] (limp) *adj* flasque, mou, molle.
limpet ('limpit) *n* patelle, bernique *f.*
linden ('lindn̩) *n* tilleul *m.*
line[1] (lain) *n* **1** ligne *f.* **2** corde *f.* **3** trait *m.* **4** compagnie *f.* **5** (railway) voie *f.* *vt* ligner, régler. **lineage** *n* lignée *f.* **linear** *adj* linéaire.
line[2] (lain) *vt* (of clothes, etc.) doubler.
linen ('linin) *n* **1** toile *f.* **2** linge *m.* **linen basket** *n* panier à linge, corbeille *f.*
liner ('lainə) *n* paquebot, transatlantique *m.*
linger ('liŋgə) *vi* traîner, lambiner.
lingerie ('lɔnʒəri:) *n* lingerie *f.*
linguist ('liŋgwist) *n* linguiste *m,f.* **linguistic** *adj* linguistique. **linguistics** *n* linguistique *f.*
lining ('lainiŋ) *n* doublure *f.*
link (liŋk) *n* **1** chaînon, maillon *m.* **2** lien *m.* *vt* **1** attacher. **2** lier.
linoleum (li'nouliəm) *n* linoléum *m.* **lino** *n inf* lino *m.*
linseed ('linsi:d) *n* graine de lin *f.* **linseed oil** *n* huile de lin *f.*
lion ('laiən) *n* lion *m.*
lip (lip) *n* **1** *anat* lèvre *f.* **2** (of animals) babine *f.* **3** bord *m.* **lip-read** *vi* lire sur les lèvres. **lipstick** *n* rouge à lèvres *m.*
liqueur (li'kjuə) *n* liqueur *f.*
liquid ('likwid) *adj,n* liquide *m.* **liquidate** *vt* liquider. **liquidize** *vt* liquéfier.
liquor ('likə) *n* boisson alcoolique *f.*
liquorice ('likəris) *n* réglisse *f.*
lira ('liərə) *n* lire *f.*
lisp (lisp) *n* zézaiement *m.* *vi,vt* zézayer.
list[1] (list) *n* liste *f.* *vt* cataloguer.
list[2] (list) *n* *naut* bande *f.* faux bord *m.* *vi* donner de la bande.
listen ('lisən) *vi* écouter.
listless ('listləs) *adj* nonchalant, apathique.
lit (lit) *v* see **light.**

litany ('litəni) *n* litanies *f pl.*
literal ('litərəl) *adj* littéral, -aux.
literary ('litərəri) *adj* littéraire.
literate ('litərət) *adj* qui sait lire et écrire.
literature ('litərətʃə) *n* littérature *f.*
litre ('li:tə) *n* litre *m.*
litter ('litə) *n* **1** fouillis *m.* **2** *zool* portée *f.* *vt* mettre en désordre. **litter-bin** *n* poubelle *f.*
little ('litl̩) *adj* **1** petit. **2** peu de. *n* peu *m.* **little by little** petit à petit. ~*adv* peu. **little finger** *n* petit doigt *m.* **little toe** *n* petit orteil *m.*
liturgy ('litədʒi) *n* liturgie *f.*
live[1] (liv) *vi* **1** vivre. **2** demeurer, habiter. *vt* mener. **live down** faire oublier.
live[2] (laiv) *adj* **1** vivant. **2** (of a wire, etc.) en charge. **livestock** *n* bétail *m, pl* bestiaux.
livelihood ('laivlihud) *n* vie *f.* gagne-pain *m invar.*
lively ('laivli) *adj* animé, plein d'entrain. **liveliness** *n* vivacité *f.* entrain *m.*
liver ('livə) *n* foie *m.*
livid ('livid) *adj* **1** blême. **2** enragé, emporté.
living ('liviŋ) *n* **1** vie *f.* **2** *rel* bénéfice *m.* *adj* vivant. **living room** *n* salle de séjour *f.*
lizard ('lizəd) *n* lézard *m.*
llama ('la:mə) *n* lama *m.*
load (loud) *n* **1** charge *f.* **2** *inf* quantité *f.* tas *m.* *vt* charger.
loaf[1] (louf) *n, pl* **loaves** pain *m.* miche *f.*
loaf[2] (louf) *vi* **loaf about** flâner, fainéanter.
loan (loun) *n* **1** prêt *m.* avance *f.* **2** emprunt *m.* *vt* prêter.
loathe (louð) *vt* haïr, détester.
lob (lɔb) *n* chandelle *f.* *vt* envoyer en chandelle.
lobby ('lɔbi) *n* **1** vestibule *m.* **2** groupe de pression *m.* **3** *pol* couloirs *m pl.* *vi* faire les couloirs.
lobe (loub) *n* lobe *m.*
lobster ('lɔbstə) *n* homard *m.*
local ('loukəl) *adj* local, -aux, du pays. **locals** *n pl* gens du pays *m pl.* **locality** *n* localité *f.* parages *m pl.* **localize** *vt* localiser. **locate** *vt* situer, localiser. **location** *n* emplacement, repérage *m.*
loch (lɔx) *n* lac *m.*
lock[1] (lɔk) *n* **1** serrure *f.* **2** (of a canal) écluse *f.* *vt* fermér à clef.
lock[2] (lɔk) *n* (of hair) mèche, boucle *f.*
locker ('lɔkə) *n* armoire *f.* coffre *m.*
locket ('lɔkit) *n* médaillon *m.*
locomotive (loukə'moutiv) *adj,n* locomotif, -ive *m.*
locust ('loukəst) *n* criquet *m.* sauterelle *f.*
lodge (lɔdʒ) *n* loge *f.* *vt* **1** loger. **2** déposer. *vi* se loger. **lodger** *n* pensionnaire *m,f.* **lodgings** *n pl* logis, logement *m.*
loft (lɔft) *n* grenier *m.* soupente *f.* **lofty** *adj* **1** haut. **2** élevé.
log (lɔg) *n* bûche *f.* **logbook** *n* **1** *naut* journal de bord *m.* **2** *mot* carnet de route *m.* *vt* enregistrer.
logarithm ('lɔgəriðəm) *n* logarithme *m.*
logic ('lɔdʒik) *n* logique *f.* **logical** *adj* logique.
loins (lɔinz) *n pl* reins *m pl.*
loiter ('lɔitə) *vi* flâner, traîner.
lollipop ('lɔlipɔp) *n* sucette *f.*
London ('lʌndən) *n* Londres *m.*
lonely ('lounli) *adj* solitaire, isolé. **loneliness** *n* solitude *f.* isolement *m.*
long[1] (lɔŋ) *adj* long, longue. *adv* longtemps. **long-distance** *adj* **1** à longue distance. **2** (of a telephone) interurbain. **long-playing record** *n* microsillon *m.* **long-range** *adj* à longue portée. **long-sighted** *adj* **1** presbyte, hypermétrope. **2** prévoyant. **longstanding** *adj* de longue date. **long wave** *n* onde longue *f.* **longwinded** *adj* **1** interminable. **2** verbeux, -euse.
long[2] (lɔŋ) *vi* **long for** désirer ardemment. **longing** *n* désir ardent *m.*
longevity (lɔn'dʒevɪtɪ) *n* longévité *f.*
longitude ('lɔndʒitju:d) *n* longitude *f.*
loo (lu:) *n inf* cabinets *m pl.*
look (luk) *n* **1** regard *m.* **2** apparence, mine *f.* *vi* **1** regarder. **2** avoir l'air. **look after** soigner, s'occuper de. **look for** chercher. **look forward to** s'attendre à. **look out** faire attention. **look out of** regarder par.
loom[1] (lu:m) *n* métier à tisser *m.*
loom[2] (lu:m) *vi* apparaître indistinctement, se dessiner.
loop (lu:p) *n* boucle *f.* *vt,vi* boucler.
loophole ('lu:phoul) *n* **1** trou *m.* ouverture *f.* **2** échappatoire *f.*
loose (lu:s) *vt* détacher, délier. **2** relâcher. *adj* **1** lâche. **2** branlant. **3** détaché. **4** dissolu. **loosen** *vt* **1** relâcher. **2** desserrer. **3** défaire. *vi* **1** se défaire. **2** se délier.
loot (lu:t) *vt* piller, saccager. *n* butin *m.*
lop (lɔp) *vt* élaguer. **lop off** couper.
lopsided (lɔp'saidid) *adj* de guingois, déjeté.
lord (lɔ:d) *n* **1** maître *m.* **2** *cap rel* Seigneur *m.* **3** *cap* (title) Lord *m.* *v* **lord it** faire l'important. **lordship** *n* **1** suzeraineté *f.* **2** *cap* Seigneurie *f.* Monseigneur *m.*
lorry ('lɔri) *n* camion *m.*

lose* (lu:z) *vt,vi* perdre.
loss (lɔs) *n* perte *f.* **be at a loss** être désorienté.
lost (lɔst) *v* see **lose.**
lot (lɔt) *n* **1** sort *m.* **2** tas *m.* **3** tout *m.* **a lot (of)** beaucoup (de).
lotion ('louʃən) *n* lotion *f.*
lottery ('lɔtəri) *n* lotterie *f.*
loud (laud) *adj* **1** haut, fort. **2** (of a person, etc.) bruyant. **3** *inf* (of a colour) criard. **loud-mouthed** *adj inf* fort en gueule, braillard. **loudspeaker** *n* haut-parleur *m.*
lounge (laundʒ) *n* salon *m.* *vi* **1** flâner. **2** s'étendre.
louse (laus) *n, pl* **lice** pou, poux *m.* **lousy** *adj* **1** pouilleux, -euse. **2** *inf* sale. **3** *inf* môche.
love (lʌv) *n* **1** amour *m.* affection *f.* **2** *sport* rien *m.* **fall in love with** s'éprendre de. ~*vt* aimer. **lover** *n* amant *m.* **lovely** *adj* beau, belle. **loveliness** *n* **1** beauté *f.* **2** charme *m.*
low[1] (lou) *adj* **1** bas, basse, peu élevé. **2** vulgaire. **3** vil. **4** abattu. *adv* bas. **lowbrow** *adj* terre à terre *invar.* **lower-case** *adj* minuscule, bas de casse. **low-grade** *adj* de qualité inférieure. **lowland** *n* plaine basse *f.* **low-necked** *adj* décolleté. **low-pitched** *adj* grave.
low[2] (lou) *vi* meugler. *n* meuglement *m.*
lower ('louə) *vt* baisser, abaisser.
loyal ('lɔiəl) *adj* fidèle, loyal, -aux. **loyalty** *n* fidélité *f.*
lozenge ('lɔzindʒ) *n med* pastille *f.*
LSD *n* LSD, drogue hallucinogène *f.*
lubricate ('lu:brikeit) *vt* lubrifier, graisser.
lucid ('lu:sid) *adj* lucide, clair.
luck (lʌk) *n* **1** hasard *m.* **2** bonheur *m.* chance *f.* **lucky** *adj* heureux, -euse, fortuné.
lucrative ('lu:krətiv) *adj* lucratif, -ive.
ludicrous ('lu:dikrəs) *adj* risible, grotesque.
lug (lʌg) *vt* traîner, tirer.
luggage ('lʌgidʒ) *n* bagages *m pl.* **luggage rack** *n* porte-bagages *m invar*
lukewarm (lu:k'wɔ:m) *adj* tiède.
lull (lʌl) *n* calme *m.* trève *f.* *vt* **1** bercer. **2** endormir. *vi* se calmer. **lullaby** *n* berceuse *f.*
lumbago (ləm'beigou) *n* lumbago *m.*
lumber[1] ('lʌmbə) *n* **1** bois de charpente *m.* **2** fatras *m.* *vt* encombrer. **lumberjack** *n* bûcheron *m.*
lumber[2] ('lʌmbə) *vi* se trainer lourdement.
luminous ('lu:minəs) *adj* lumineux, -euse.
lump (lʌmp) *n* **1** bloc *m.* **2** grumeau, -aux *m.* **3** bosse *f.* **4** *sl* pataud *m.* *vt* mettre en tas. **lumpy** *adj* grumeleux, -euse.
lunacy ('lu:nəsi) *n* folie, démence *f.*
lunar ('lu:nə) *adj* lunaire.
lunatic ('lu:nətik) *n* fou, folle. *adj* aliéné.
lunch (lʌntʃ) *n* déjeuner *m.* *vi* déjeuner.
lung (lʌŋ) *n* poumon *m.*
lunge (lʌndʒ) *n* **1** *sport* botte *f.* **2** ruée *f.* *v* **lunge forward** se jeter en avant.
lurch[1] (lə:tʃ) *n* **1** embardée *f.* **2** cahot *m.* *vi* **1** faire une embardée. **2** tituber.
lurch[2] (lə:tʃ) *n* **leave in the lurch** laisser le bec dans l'eau.
lure (luə) *n* **1** leurre *m.* **2** piège *m.* *vt* **1** leurrer. **2** attirer, séduire.
lurid ('luərid) *adj* blafard.
lurk (lə:k) *vi* se cacher, rester tapis.
luscious ('lʌʃəs) *adj* succulent.
lush (lʌʃ) *adj* plein de sève.
lust (lʌst) *n* désir *m.* convoitise *f.*
lustre ('lʌstə) *n* lustre, éclat *m.* *vt* lustrer.
lute (lu:t) *n* luth *m.*
Luxembourg ('lʌksəmbə:g) *n* Luxembourg *m.*
luxury ('lʌkʃəri) *n* luxe *m.* **luxurious** *adj* somptueux, -euse.
lynch (lintʃ) *vt* lyncher.
lynx (liŋks) *n* lynx, loup-cervier *m.*
Lyons ('laiənz) *n* Lyon *m.*
lyre ('laiə) *n* lyre *f.*
lyrics ('liriks) *n* paroles *m pl.* **lyrical** *adj* lyrique.

M

mac (mæk) *n inf* imper *m.*
macabre (mə'kɑ:b) *adj* macabre.
mace[1] (meis) *n* masse *f.*
mace[2] (meis) *n cul* muscade *f.*
machine (mə'ʃi:n) *n* machine *f.* appareil *m.* **machine-gun** *n* mitrailleuse *f.* **machinery** *n* machines *f pl.* mécanisme *m.* **machinist** *n* **1** machiniste *m.* **2** mécanicienne *f.*
mackerel ('mækrəl) *n* maquereau, -aux *m.*
mackintosh ('mækintɔʃ) *n* imperméable *m.*
mad (mæd) *adj* fou, folle. **madness** *n* folie, démence *f.*
madam ('mædəm) *n* madame, mesdames *f.*
made (meid) *v* see **make.**
Madonna (mə'dɔnə) *n* Madone *f.*
madrigal ('mædrigəl) *n* madrigal, -aux *m.*
magazine (mægə'zi:n) *n* **1** magazine *m.* revue *f.* **2** *mil* magasin *m.*
maggot ('mægət) *n* ver, asticot *m.*
magic ('mædʒik) *n* magie *f.* *adj* magique, enchanté. **magician** *n* magicien, -ienne.

magistrate (ˈmædʒistreit) *n* magistrat *m*.

magnanimous (mægˈnænimәs) *adj* magnanime.

magnate (ˈmægneit) *n* magnat *m*.

magnet (ˈmægnit) *n* aimant *m*. **magnetic** *adj* magnétique. **magnetism** *n* **1** magnétisme *m*. **2** aimantation *f*. **magnetize** *vt* **1** magnétiser. **2** aimanter.

magnificent (mægˈnifisәnt) *adj* magnifique.

magnify (ˈmægnifai) *vt* grossir, agrandir. **magnifying glass** *n* loupe *f*.

magnitude (ˈmægnitju:d) *n* **1** grandeur *f*. **2** importance *f*.

magpie (ˈmægpai) *n* pie *f*.

mahogany (mәˈhɔgәni) *n* acajou *m*.

maid (meid) *n* **1** domestique *f*. **2** jeune fille *f*. **maiden** *n* jeune fille *f*. *adj* **1** non mariée. **2** premier, -ière, inaugural, -aux. **maiden name** *n* nom de jeune fille *m*.

mail (meil) *n* courrier *m*. poste *f*. *vt* envoyer par la poste, expédier. **mail order** *n* commande par correspondance *f*. **mailing list** *n* liste des abonnés *f*.

maim (meim) *vt* mutiler.

main (mein) *adj* principal, -aux, essentiel, -elle. *n* (pipe, wire, etc.) conduite principale *f*. **mainland** *n* continent *m*. **mainly** *adv* surtout. **mainsail** *n* grand-voile *f*.

maintain (meinˈtein) *vt* **1** maintenir. **2** soutenir. **3** garder. **maintenance** *n* **1** entretien *m*. **2** *law* pension alimentaire *f*.

maize (meiz) *n* maïs *m*.

majesty (ˈmædʒisti) *n* majesté *f*. **majestic** *adj* majestueux, -euse.

major (ˈmeidʒә) *adj* majeur, principal, -aux. *n mil* commandant *m*. **major general** *n* général de division *m*. **majority** *n* majorité *f*.

Majorca (mәˈdʒɔ:kә) *n* Majorque *f*.

make* (meik) *n* **1** marque *f*. **2** fabrication *f*. *vt* **1** faire. **2** fabriquer, confectionner. **3** rendre. **make for** se diriger vers. **make off** filer. **make over** céder. **make up 1** compléter. **2** rattraper. **3** inventer. **4** se maquiller. **make-up** *n* maquillage *m*. **make up one's mind** se décider. **make-believe** *n* semblant *m*. feinte *f*. *adj* fictif, -ive. **maker** *n* fabricant *m*. **makeshift** *n* pis-aller *m invar*. *adj* de fortune.

maladjusted (mælәˈdʒʌstid) *adj* inadapté.

malaria (mәˈlɛәriә) *n* malaria *f*.

Malaya (mәˈleiә) *n* Malaisie *f*. **Malay** *adj,n* malais. **Malay** (language) *n* malais *m*.

Malaysia (mәˈleiziә) *n* Malaysia *f*. **Malaysian** *adj,n* malais.

male (meil) *adj,n* mâle *m*.

malice (ˈmælis) *n* malveillance, rancune *f*. **malicious** *adj* malveillant, malicieux, -euse.

malignant (mәˈlignәnt) *adj* **1** malin, maligne. **2** méchant.

mallet (ˈmælәt) *n* maillet *m*.

malt (mɔ:lt) *n* malt *m*.

Malta (ˈmɔ:ltә) *n* Malte *f*. **Maltese** *adj,n* maltais.

maltreat (mælˈtri:t) *vt* maltraiter.

mammal (ˈmæmәl) *n* mammifère *m*.

mammoth (ˈmæmәθ) *n* mammouth *m*. *adj* énorme.

man (mæn) *n, pl* **men 1** homme *m*. **2** employé *m*. **3** *game* pièce *f*. pion *m*. *vt* armer, garnir. **manhandle** *vt* **1** manutentionner. **2** maltraiter. **manhole** *n* regard *m*. **manhood** *n* maturité, virilité *f*. **man-made** *adj* artificiel, -elle. **manpower** *n* main-d'œuvre *f*. **manslaughter** *n* homicide *m*.

Man, Isle of (mæn) *n* île de Man *f*.

manage (ˈmænidʒ) *vt* **1** diriger, administrer, gérer. **2** venir à bout de. **3** manœuvrer. *vi* se débrouiller. **manageable** *adj* maniable. **management** *n* **1** direction, gestion *f*. **2** administration *f*. **manager** *n* directeur, gérant *m*. **manageress** *n* directrice, gérante *f*. **managing director** *n* administrateur gérant *m*.

mandarin (ˈmændәrin) *n* **1** mandarin *m*. **2** *bot* mandarine *f*.

mandate (ˈmændeit) *n* mandat *m*. **mandatory** *adj* obligatoire.

mandolin (ˈmændәlin) *n* mandoline *f*.

mane (mein) *n* crinière *f*.

mange (meindʒ) *n* gale *f*. **mangy** *adj* galeux, -euse.

mangle[1] (ˈmæŋgәl) *vt* **1** taillader. **2** dénaturer.

mangle[2] (ˈmæŋgәl) *n* calandre *f*. *vt* calandrer.

mango (ˈmæŋgou) *n, pl* **-oes** *or* **-os** mangue *f*.

mania (ˈmeiniә) *n* **1** manie, passion *f*. **2** *med* folie *f*. **maniac** *adj,n* fou, folle, furieux, -euse. **manic** *adj* qui tient de la folie.

manicure (ˈmænikjuә) *n* soins des mains *m pl*. *vt* soigner les mains.

manifest (ˈmænifest) *vt,vi* manifester. *adj* manifeste, évident.

manifesto (mæniˈfestou) *n* manifeste *m*.

manifold (ˈmænifould) *adj* multiple, varié.

manipulate (mәˈnipjuleit) *vt* manipuler, actionner. **manipulation** *n* manipulation *f*.

mankind (ˈmænkaind) *n* genre humain *m*.

manner (ˈmænә) *n* **1** manière, façon *f*. **2** *pl*

mœurs *f pl.* **3** *pl* manières *f pl.* savoir-vivre *m.* **mannerism** *n* maniérisme *m.*

manoeuvre (məˈnu:və) *vt,vi* manœuvrer. *n* manœuvre *f.*

manor (ˈmænə) *n* manoir *m.*

mansion (ˈmænʃən) *n* château, -aux, hôtel particulier *m.*

mantelpiece (ˈmæntəlpi:s) *n* dessus de cheminée *m.*

mantle (ˈmæntḷ) *n* **1** cape *f.* **2** manteau, -aux *m.* *vt* couvrir.

manual (ˈmænjuəl) *adj,n* manuel, -elle *m.*

manufacture (mænjuˈfæktʃə) *vt* manufacturer, fabriquer. *n* **1** fabrication *f.* **2** produit manufacturé *m.* **manufacturer** *n* fabricant, industriel *m.*

manure (məˈnjuə) *n* fumier *m.* *vt* fumer.

manuscript (ˈmænjuskript) *adj,n* manuscrit *m.*

Manx (mæŋks) *adj* de l'île de Man.

many (ˈmeni) *adj* beaucoup (de), bien des, nombreux, -euse. *n* multitude, foule *f.* **as many as** autant que. **how many?** combien? **many a** maint. **so many** tant (de). **too many** trop (de).

Maori (ˈmauri) *adj,n* maori.

map (mæp) *n* **1** carte *f.* **2** (of a town) plan *m.*

maple (ˈmeipəl) *n* érable *m.*

mar (mɑ:) *vt* gâcher, troubler.

marathon (ˈmærəθən) *n* marathon *m.*

marble (ˈmɑ:bəl) *n* **1** marbre *m.* **2** *game* bille *f.*

march (mɑ:tʃ) *n* marche *f.* *vi* marcher. *vt* faire marcher. **march past** défiler.

March (mɑ:tʃ) *n* mars *m.*

marchioness (ˈmɑ:ʃənis) *n* marquise *f.*

mare (mɛə) *n* jument *f.*

margarine (mɑ:dʒəˈri:n) *n* margarine *f.*

margin (ˈmɑ:dʒin) *n* **1** marge *f.* **2** bord *m.* **marginal** *adj* marginal, -aux.

marigold (ˈmærigould) *n* souci *m.*

marijuana (mæriˈwɑ:nə) *n* marijuana *f.*

marinade (mæriˈneid) *n* marinade *f.* **marinate** *vt* mariner.

marine (məˈri:n) *adj* **1** marin, maritime. **2** de marine. *n* marine *f.*

marital (ˈmæritḷ) *adj* **1** marital, -aux. **2** matrimonial, -aux.

maritime (ˈmæritaim) *adj* maritime.

marjoram (ˈmɑ:dʒərəm) *n* marjolaine *f.*

mark[1] (mɑ:k) *n* **1** marque *f.* **2** but *m.* **3** note *f.* *vt* **1** marquer. **2** noter. **3** corriger. **markedly** *adv* nettement. **marksman** *n* tireur d'élite *m.*

mark[2] (mɑ:k) *n comm* mark *m.*

market (ˈmɑ:kit) *n* **1** marché *m.* **2** débouché *m.* *vt* lancer sur le marché. **market garden** *n* jardin maraîcher *m.* **marketplace** *n* marché *m.* **market research** *n* étude du marché *f.* **market town** *n* bourg *m.*

marmalade (ˈmɑ:məleid) *n* confiture d'oranges *f.*

maroon[1] (məˈru:n) *adj,n* marron *m.*

maroon[2] (məˈru:n) *vt* abandonner.

marquee (mɑ:ˈki:) *n* marquise, grande tente *f.*

marquess (ˈmɑ:kwis) *n* marquis *m.*

marriage (ˈmæridʒ) *n* mariage *m.* **marriage certificate** *n* acte de mariage *m.*

marrow (ˈmærou) *n* **1** moelle *f.* **2** *bot* courge *f.* **marrowbone** *n* os à moelle *m.*

marry (ˈmæri) *vt* marier, épouser. *vi* se marier avec.

Mars (mɑ:z) *n* Mars *m.*

Marseillaise (mɑ:səˈleiz) *n* Marseillaise *f.*

Marseilles (mɑ:ˈsei) *n* Marseille *f.*

marsh (mɑ:ʃ) *n* marécage, marais *m.* **marshy** *adj* marécageux, -euse. **marshmallow** *n* guimauve *f.*

marshal (ˈmɑ:ʃəl) *n* **1** maréchal, -aux *m.* **2** maître des cérémonies *m.* *vt* ranger.

marsupial (mɑ:ˈsju:piəl) *adj,n* marsupial, -aux *m.*

martial (ˈmɑ:ʃəl) *adj* martial, -aux.

martin (ˈmɑ:tin) *n* martinet *m.*

martini (mɑ:ˈti:ni) *n* martini *m.*

martyr (ˈmɑ:tə) *n* martyr *m.* *vt* martyriser. **martyrdom** *n* martyre *m.*

marvel (ˈmɑ:vəl) *n* merveille *f.* *vi* s'étonner. **marvellous** *adj* merveilleux, -euse.

Marxism (ˈmɑ:ksizəm) *n* marxisme *m.* **marxist** *adj,n* marxiste.

marzipan (ˈmɑ:zipæn) *n* massepain *m.*

mascara (mæˈskɑ:rə) *n* mascara *m.*

mascot (ˈmæskɔt) *n* mascotte *f.* porte-bonheur *m invar.*

masculine (ˈmæskjulin) *adj* masculin, mâle. *n* masculin *m.*

mash (mæʃ) *n* **1** pâtée *f.* **2** *cul* purée *f.* *vt* écraser.

mask (mɑ:sk) *n* masque *m.* *vt* **1** masquer. **2** cacher, voiler.

masochism (ˈmæsəkizəm) *n* masochisme *m.* **masochist** *adj,n* masochiste.

mason (ˈmeisən) *n* maçon *m.* **masonry** *n* maçonnerie *f.*

masquerade (mæskəˈreid) *n* mascarade *f.* *vi* se déguiser.

mass[1] (mæs) *n* **1** masse *f.* **2** foule *f.* *vt* masser. *vi* se masser. **mass media** *n pl* moyens publicitaires de masse *m pl.* **mass-produce** *vt* fabriquer en série.

mass[2] (mæs) *n rel* messe *f.*

massacre ('mæsəkə) *n* massacre *m. vt* massacrer.

massage ('mæsɑ:ʒ) *n* massage *m. vt* masser.

massive ('mæsiv) *adj* massif, -ive.

mast (mɑ:st) *n* **1** *naut* mât *m.* **2** pylône *m.* **masthead** *n* tête de mât *f.*

mastectomy (mæs'tektəmi) *n* mastectomie *f.*

master ('mɑstə) *n* **1** maître *m.* **2** patron, chef *m.* **3** professeur *m.* **Master of Arts/Science** licencié ès lettres/sciences *m.* ~*vt* **1** maîtriser. **2** surmonter. *adj* **1** principal, -aux. **2** de maître. **masterful** *adj* autoritaire. **mastermind** *n* esprit supérieur *m.* **masterpiece** *n* chef-d'œuvre *m.*

masturbate ('mæstəbeit) *vi* se masturber. **masturbation** *n* masturbation *f.*

mat (mæt) *n* **1** natte *f.* **2** tapis *m.* **3** dessous de plat *m. vt* emmêler, tresser. *vi* s'emmêler.

match[1] (mætʃ) *n* allumette *f.* **matchbox** *n* boîte d'allumettes *f.* **matchstick** *n* allumette *f.*

match[2] (mætʃ) *n* **1** match *m.* lutte, partie *f.* **2** égal, -aux *m.* **3** mariage *m.* **4** assortiment *m. vt* **1** égaler. **2** assortir. *vi* s'assortir, s'harmoniser. **matchless** *adj* incomparable.

mate (meit) *n* **1** compagnon, compagne. **2** *naut* officier *m. vt* accoupler. *vi* s'accoupler.

material (mə'tiəriəl) *n* **1** matière *f.* **2** (for building, etc.) matériaux *m pl.* **3** étoffe, tissu *m. adj* **1** matériel, -aux. **2** essentiel, -elle. **raw material** *n* matière première *f.* **materialism** *n* matérialisme *m.* **materialist** *n* matérialiste *m,f.* **materialistic** *adj* matérialiste. **materialize** *vi* se réaliser.

maternal (mə'tə:nl̩) *adj* maternel, -elle. **maternity** *n* maternité *f.*

mathematics (mæθə'mætiks) *n* mathématiques *f pl.* **mathematical** *adj* mathématique.

matins ('mætinz) *n pl* matines *f pl.*

matinee ('mætinei) *n* matinée *f.*

matriarchal ('meitriɑ:kəl) *adj* matriarcal, -aux.

matrimony ('mætriməni) *n* mariage *m.* **matrimonial** *adj* matrimonial, -aux.

matrix ('meitriks) *n, pl* **-rices** matrice *f.*

matron ('meitrən) *n* **1** intendante *f.* **2** infirmière en chef *f.* **3** matrone *f.*

matter ('mætə) *n* **1** matière *f.* **2** affaire *f.* **3** sujet *m.* **4** *med* pus *m.* **what's the matter?** qu'y a-t-il? ~*vi* importer. **matter-of-fact** *adj* pratique.

Matterhorn ('mætəhɔ:n) *n* Mont Cervin *m.*

mattress ('mætrəs) *n* matelas *m.*

mature (mə'tjuə) *adj* **1** mûr. **2** *comm* échu. *vt,vi* mûrir. **maturity** *n* **1** maturité *f.* **2** *comm* échéance *f.*

maudlin ('mɔ:dlin) *adj* larmoyant, pleurard.

maul (mɔ:l) *vt* malmener, meurtrir.

Maundy Thursday ('mɔ:ndi) *n* jeudi saint *m.*

mausoleum (mɔ:sə'liəm) *n* mausolée *m.*

mauve (mouv) *adj,n* mauve *m.*

maxim ('mæksim) *n* maxime *f.* dicton *m.*

maximum ('mæksiməm) *adj* maximum, limite. *n, pl* **-ums** *or* **-a** maximum *m.* **maximize** *vt* maximiser.

may* (mei) *v mod aux* pouvoir. **that may be** cela se peut. **maybe** *adv* peut-être.

May (mei) *n* mai *m.* **May Day** *n* premier mai *m.* **maypole** *n* mai *m.*

mayonnaise (meiə'neiz) *n* mayonnaise *f.*

mayor ('mɛə) *n* maire *m.* **mayoress** *n* mairesse *f.*

maze (meiz) *n* labyrinthe *m.*

me (mi:) *pron 1st pers s* **1** me. **2** moi.

meadow ('medou) *n* prairie *f.*

meagre ('mi:gə) *adj* maigre.

meal[1] (mi:l) *n* repas *m.*

meal[2] (mi:l) *n* farine *f.* **mealy** *adj* farineux, -euse.

mean*[1] (mi:n) *vt* **1** vouloir dire, signifier. **2** avoir l'intention de. **meaning** *n* signification *f.* sens *m.* **meaningful** *adj* significatif, -ive.

mean[2] (mi:n) *adj* **1** avare, mesquin **2** méprisable.

meander (mi'ændə) *n* méandre *m. vi* serpenter.

means (mi:nz) *n pl* **1** moyen *m.* **2** ressources *f pl.* moyens *m pl.* **by means of** au moyen de.

meantime ('mi:ntaim) *adv* **in the meantime** dans l'intervalle.

meanwhile ('mi:nwail) *adv* dans l'intervalle.

measles ('mi:zəlz) *n pl* rougeole *f.*

measure ('meʒə) *n* mesure *f. vt* mesurer. **measurement** *n* mesure, dimension *f.*

meat (mi:t) *n* viande *f.*

mechanic (mi'kænik) *n* mécanicien *m.* **mechanical** *adj* mécanique. **mechanical engineering** *n* construction mécanique *f.* **mechanics** *n* **1** mécanique *f.* **2** *pl* mécanisme *m.* **mechanism** *n* mécanisme *m.* **mechanize** *vt* mécaniser. **mechanization** *n* mécanisation *f.*

medal ('medl̩) *n* médaille *f.* **medallion** *n* médaillon *m.*

meddle ('medl̩) *vi* **meddle in** s'immiscer dans.

media (ˈmi:diə) *n pl* voie *f.* moyen *m.*
medial (ˈmi:diəl) *adj* moyen, -enne, intermédiaire.
median (ˈmi:diən) *adj* médian. *n math* médiane *f.*
mediate (ˈmi:dieit) *vi* s'entremettre, intervenir. **mediation** *n* médiation *f.* **mediator** *n* médiateur *m.*
medical (ˈmedikəl) *adj* médical, -aux. **medication** *n* médication *f.* **medicine** *n* **1** (science) médecine *f.* **2** médicament *m.*
medieval (mediˈi:vəl) *adj* médiéval, -aux.
mediocre (mi:diˈoukə) *adj* médiocre.
meditate (ˈmediteit) *vt,vi* méditer. **meditation** *n* méditation *f.* **meditative** *adj* méditatif, -ive.
Mediterranean (meditəˈreiniən) *adj* méditerranéen, -enne. **Mediterranean (Sea)** *n* (Mer) Mediterranée *f.*
medium (ˈmi:diəm) *n, pl* **media** **1** moyen *m.* **2** milieu, -eux *m.* **3** intermédiaire *m.* **4** médium *m.* **happy medium** juste milieu. ~*adj* moyen, -enne.
meek (mi:k) *adj* doux, douce, humble. **meekly** *adv* avec douceur.
meet* (mi:t) *vt* **1** rencontrer. **2** faire la connaissance de. **3** satisfaire. *vt* **1** se rencontrer. **2** se réunir. **meet with** éprouver, trouver. **meeting** *n* **1** rencontre *f.* **2** assemblée, réunion *f.*
megaphone (ˈmegəfoun) *n* porte-voix *m invar.*
melancholy (ˈmelənkəli) *n* mélancolie *f. adj* mélancolique.
mellow (ˈmelou) *adj* **1** doux, douce. **2** moelleux, -euse. *vt,vi* mûrir.
melodrama (ˈmelədrɑ:mə) *n* mélodrame *m.* **melodramatic** *adj* mélodramatique.
melody (ˈmelədi) *n* mélodie *f.* air *m.* **melodious** *adj* mélodieux, -euse.
melon (ˈmelən) *n* melon *m.*
melt (melt) *vt,vi* fondre. *vt* attendrir. **melting** *n* fusion *f.*
member (ˈmembə) *n* membre *m.* **member of Parliament** député *m.* **membership** *n* **1** cotisation *f.* **2** qualité de membre *f.*
membrane (ˈmembrein) *n* membrane *f.*
memento (məˈmentou) *n, pl* **-os** *or* **-oes** mémento, souvenir *m.*
memo (ˈmemou) *n* mémo *m.* note *f.*
memoir (ˈmemwɑ:) *n* mémoire *m.*
memorandum (meməˈrændəm) *n, pl* **-dums** *or* **-da** mémorandum *m.*
memory (ˈmeməri) *n* **1** mémoire *f.* **2** souvenir *m.* **memorable** *adj* mémorable. **memorial** *n* monument commémoratif *m. adj* commémoratif, -ive. **memorize** *vt* apprendre par cœur.
menace (ˈmenəs) *n* menace *f. vt* menacer.
menagerie (məˈnædʒəri) *n* ménagerie *f.*
mend (mend) *vt* **1** raccommoder. **2** réparer. **3** arranger. *vi* s'améliorer. *n* reprise *f.* **mending** *n* raccommodage *m.*
menial (ˈmi:niəl) *adj* servile.
menopause (ˈmenəpɔ:z) *n* ménopause *f.*
menstrual (ˈmenstruəl) *adj* menstruel, -elle. **menstruate** *vi* avoir ses règles.
mental (ˈmentl̩) *adj* **1** mental, -aux. **2** *inf* fou, folle. **mental hospital** *n* hôpital psychiatrique *m.* **mentality** *n* mentalité *f.*
menthol (ˈmenθɔl) *n* menthol *m.*
mention (ˈmenʃən) *n* mention *f. vt* mentionner.
menu (ˈmenju:) *n* menu *m.*
mercantile (ˈmə:kəntail) *adj* commercial, -aux.
mercenary (ˈmə:sənəri) *adj,n* mercenaire *m.*
merchant (ˈmə:tʃənt) *n* négociant, commerçant *m. adj* marchand, de commerce. **merchant bank** *n* banque commerciale *f.* **merchant navy** *n* marine marchande *f.* **merchandise** *n* marchandise *f.*
mercury (ˈmə:kjuri) *n* **1** mercure *m.* **2** *cap* Mercure *m.*
mercy (ˈmə:si) *n* **1** grâce, pitié *f.* **2** bienfait *m.* **merciful** *adj* clément. **merciless** *adj* impitoyable.
mere (miə) *adj* simple, pur.
merge (mə:dʒ) *vt* fusionner, fondre. *vi* **1** se fondre. **2** *comm* fusionner. **merger** *n* fusion *f.*
meridian (məˈridiən) *adj,n* méridien, -ienne *m.*
meringue (məˈræŋ) *n* meringue *f.*
merit (ˈmerit) *n* **1** mérite *m.* **2** valeur *f. vt* mériter.
mermaid (ˈmə:meid) *n* sirène *f.*
merry (ˈmeri) *adj* **1** joyeux, -euse, gai. **2** *inf* gris. **merry-go-round** *n* manège (de chevaux de bois) *m.*
mesh (meʃ) *n* maille *f. vt* engrener. *vi* être en prise.
mesmerize (ˈmezməraiz) *vt* hypnotiser.
mess (mes) *n* **1** saleté *f.* **2** gâchis *m.* confusion *f.* **3** *mil* mess *m.* **make a mess of** gâcher. ~*v* **mess up** **1** gâcher. **2** salir.
message (ˈmesidʒ) *n* message *m.* **messenger** *n* messager, -ère.
met (met) *v* see **meet.**
metabolism (miˈtæbəlizəm) *n* métabolisme *m.*
metal (ˈmetl̩) *n* métal, -aux *m.* **metallic** *adj* métallique. **metallurgy** *n* métallurgie *f.* **metallurgical** *adj* métallurgique.

metamorphosis (metəˈmɔːfəsis) *n, pl* **-ses** métamorphose *f.*

metaphor (ˈmetəfə) *n* métaphore *f.* **metaphorical** *adj* métaphorique.

metaphysics (metəˈfiziks) *n* métaphysique *f.* **metaphysical** *adj* métaphysique.

meteor (ˈmiːtiə) *n* météore *m.* **meteorological** *adj* météorologique. **meteorologist** *n* météorologiste, météorologue *m,f.* **meteorology** *n* météorologie *f.*

meter (ˈmiːtə) *n* compteur *m.*

methane (ˈmiːθein) *n* méthane *m.*

method (ˈmeθəd) *n* méthode *f.* procédé *m.* **methodical** *adj* méthodique.

Methodist (ˈmeθədist) *adj,n* méthodiste.

meticulous (miˈtikjuləs) *adj* méticuleux, -euse.

metre (ˈmiːtə) *n* mètre *m.* **metric** *adj* métrique.

metropolis (məˈtrɔpəlis) *n* métropole *f.* **metropolitan** *adj* métropolitain.

miaow (miˈau) *vi* miauler. *n* miaulement *m.*

microbe (ˈmaikroub) *n* microbe *m.*

microphone (ˈmaikrəfoun) *n* microphone *m.*

microscope (ˈmaikrəskoup) *n* microscope *m.* **microscopic** *adj* microscopique.

mid (mid) *adj* mi, moyen, -enne. **midday** *n* midi *m.* **midland** *adj* du centre. **midmorning** *n* mi matin *m.* **midnight** *n* minuit *m.* **in midstream** *adv* au milieu de la rivière. **midsummer** *n* cœur de l'été *m.* **midway** *adv,adj* à mi-chemin. **midweek** *adj* du milieu de la semaine.

middle (ˈmidl̩) *n* centre, milieu, -eux *m.* *adj* du milieu, moyen -enne. **middle-aged** *adj* d'un certain âge. **middle class** *n* bourgeoisie *f.* **middle-class** *adj* bourgeois. **middleman** *n* intermédiaire *m.*

Middle Ages *n* moyen âge *m.*

Middle East *n* Moyen Orient *m.*

midget (ˈmidʒit) *n* nain *m.*

midst (midst) **in the midst of** *prep* parmi, au milieu de.

midwife (ˈmidwaif) *n* sage-femme *f.*

might[1] (mait) *v* see **may.**

might[2] (mait) *n* force, puissance *f.* **mighty** *adj* **1** puissant. **2** vaste, énorme.

migraine (ˈmiːgrein) *n* migraine *f.*

migrate (maiˈgreit) *vi* émigrer. **migration** *n* **1** migration *f.* **2** émigration *f.* **migratory** *adj* migrateur, -trice.

mike (maik) *n inf* micro *m.*

mild (maild) *adj* doux, douce. **mildness** *n* douceur *f.*

mildew (ˈmildjuː) *n* **1** (on a plant) rouille *f.* **2** moisissure *f.*

mile (mail) *n* mille *m.* **mileage** *n* distance en milles *f.* **mileometer** *n* compteur kilométrique *m.* **milestone** *n* borne kilométrique *f.*

militant (ˈmilitənt) *adj,n* militant *m.* **military** *adj* militaire.

milk (milk) *n* lait *m.* *vt* traire. **milking** *n* traite *f.* **milkman** *n* laitier *m.*

Milky Way *n* Voie lactée *f.*

mill (mil) *n* **1** moulin *m.* **2** usine, fabrique *f.* *vt* moudre. *vi* fourmiller. **millstone** *n* meule *f.*

millennium (miˈleniəm) *n, pl* **-niums** *or* **-nia** millénaire *m.*

millet (ˈmilit) *n* millet *m.*

milligram (ˈmiligræm) *n* milligramme *m.*

millilitre (ˈmililiːtə) *n* millilitre *m.*

millimetre (ˈmilimiːtə) *n* millimètre *m.*

million (ˈmiliən) *adj,n* million *m.* **millionaire** *n* millionnaire *m,f.* **millionth** *adj* millionième.

mime (maim) *n* mime *m.* *vt* mimer. *vi* imiter par gestes. **mimic** *n* mime *m.* *adj* **1** imitateur, -trice. **2** mimique. *vt* imiter, singer. **mimicry** *n* mimique, imitation *f.*

mince (mins) *vt* hacher. *vi* minauder. *n* hachis *m.* **mincer** *n* hachoir *m.*

mind (maind) *n* **1** esprit *m.* **2** mémoire *f.* **3** avis *m.* **4** envie *f.* *vt* **1** faire attention à. **2** surveiller. **I don't mind 1** cela m'est égal. **2** je veux bien. **never mind!** peu importe!

mine[1] (main) *poss pron 1st pers s* **1** le mien, la mienne. **2** à moi.

mine[2] (main) *n* mine *f.* *vt* **1** exploiter. **2** *mil* miner. **miner** *n* mineur *m.*

mineral (ˈminərəl) *adj* minéral, -aux. *n* **1** minéral, -aux *m.* **2** *min* minerai *m.* **mineral water** *n* eau minérale *f.*

mingle (ˈmiŋgəl) *vt* mêler. *vi* se mêler.

miniature (ˈminiətʃə) *n* miniature *f.* *adj* minuscule, en miniature.

minim (ˈminim) *n* blanche *f.*

minimum (ˈminiməm) *n, pl* **-mums** *or* **-ma** minimum *m.* **minimal** *adj* minimal, -aux, minime.

mining (ˈmainiŋ) *n* exploitation des mines *f.*

minister (ˈministə) *n* ministre *m.* **ministerial** *adj* ministériel, -elle. **ministry** *n* ministère *m.*

mink (miŋk) *n* vison *m.*

minor (ˈmainə) *adj,n* mineur. **minority** *n* minorité *f.*

Minorca (miˈnɔːkə) *n* Minorque *f.*

minstrel (ˈminstrəl) *n* ménestrel *m.*

mint[1] (mint) *n bot* menthe *f.*

mint[2] (mint) *n* Hôtel de la Monnaie *m.* *vt* **1** (a coin, etc.) battre, frapper. **2** forger.
minuet (minju'et) *n* menuet *m.*
minus ('mainəs) *prep* moins, sans. *adj* **1** moins. **2** négatif, -ive.
minute[1] ('minit) *n* **1** minute *f.* **2** instant *m.* **3** *pl* procès-verbal *m.*
minute[2] (mai'nju:t) *adj* **1** menu, minuscule. **2** minutieux, -euse.
miracle ('mirəkəl) *n* miracle *m.* **miraculous** *adj* miraculeux, -euse.
mirage ('mirɑ:ʒ) *n* mirage *m.*
mirror ('mirə) *n* miroir *m.*
mirth (mə:θ) *n* gaieté *f.*
misbehave (misbi'heiv) *vi* se conduire mal.
miscarriage (mis'kæridʒ) *n* **1** echec, insuccès *m.* **2** *med* fausse couche *f.* **miscarry** *vi* **1** échouer. **2** *med* avorter.
miscellaneous (misə'leiniəs) *adj* divers, varié. **miscellany** *n* mélange *m.*
mischance (mis'tʃɑ:ns) *n* malheur *m.* mésaventure *f.*
mischief ('mistʃif) *n* **1** mal *m,pl* maux. **2** malice *f.* **3** sottises *f pl.* **mischievous** *adj* **1** malfaisant. **2** espiègle.
misconceive (miskən'si:v) *vt* mal comprendre. **misconception** *n* **1** idée fausse *f.* **2** malentendu *m.*
misconduct (*n* mis'kɔndʌkt; *v* miskən'dʌkt) *n* **1** (of a person) inconduite *f.* **2** mauvaise gestion *f.* *vt* mal gérer.
misdeed (mis'di:d) *n* méfait *m.*
miser ('maizə) *n* avare *m,f.* **miserly** *adj* avare. **miserliness** *n* avarice *f.*
miserable ('mizərəbəl) *adj* **1** triste, malheureux, -euse. **2** misérable, pitoyable.
misery ('mizəri) *n* **1** souffrance *f.* **2** misère, détresse *f.*
misfire (mis'faiə) *vi* **1** rater. **2** tomber à plat.
misfit ('misfit) *n* **1** malfaçon *f.* **2** inadapté *m.*
misfortune (mis'fɔ:tʃən) *n* malheur *m.*
misgiving (mis'giviŋ) *n* doute, pressentiment *m.* crainte *f.*
misguided (mis'gaidid) *adj* **1** égaré. **2** hors de propos.
mishap ('mishæp) *n* mésaventure *f.*
mislay* (mis'lei) *vt* égarer.
mislead* (mis'li:d) *vt* **1** tromper. **2** fourvoyer.
misprint ('misprint) *n* faute d'impression *f.*
miss[1] (mis) *vt,vi* manquer, rater. **miss out** passer, omettre. *n* coup manqué *m.* **missing** *adj* **1** manquant, absent. **2** perdu.
miss[2] (mis) *n* **1** mademoiselle *f.* **2** *cap* (title of address) Mlle.
missile ('misail) *n* projectile *m.*
mission ('miʃən) *n* mission *f.* **missionary** *adj,n* missionnaire *m.*
mist (mist) *n* brume *f.*
mistake* (mis'teik) *n* erreur, faute *f.* **by mistake** par mégarde. ~*vt* **1** se méprendre (sur), se tromper de. **2** prendre. **mistaken** *adj* faux, fausse. **be mistaken** se tromper.
mister ('mistə) *n* monsieur *m.*
mistletoe ('misəltou) *n* gui *m.*
mistress ('mistrəs) *n* **1** maîtresse *f.* **2** *educ* professeur *m.*
mistrust (mis'trʌst) *vt* se méfier de. *n* méfiance *f.* **mistrustful** *adj* méfiant.
misunderstand* (misʌndə'stænd) *vt* mal comprendre. **misunderstanding** *n* **1** malentendu *m.* **2** mésentente *f.*
misuse (*v* mis'ju:z; *n* mis'ju:s) *vt* **1** faire mauvais usage de. **2** maltraiter. *n* abus, mauvais usage *m.*
mitre ('maitə) *n* mitre *f.*
mitten ('mitn̩) *n* mitaine *f.*
mix (miks) *vt* mélanger, mêler. *vi* se mélanger. **mix up 1** embrouiller. **2** confondre. **mixed** *adj* mixte. **mixed grill** *n* grillade variée *f.* **mixture** *n* **1** mélange *m.* **2** *med* potion *f.*
moan (moun) *vi* gémir. *n* plainte *f.*
moat (mout) *n* fossé *m.* douve *f.*
mob (mɔb) *n* cohue, foule *f.* *vt* **1** molester. **2** s'attrouper.
mobile ('moubail) *adj* mobile. **mobility** *n* mobilité *f.* **mobilize** *vt* mobiliser.
mock (mɔk) *vt,vi* se moquer de. *vt* imiter. *adj* simulé, faux, fausse. **mockery** *n* raillerie, moquerie *f.*
mode (moud) *n* **1** manière *f.* **2** mode *f.*
model ('mɔdl̩) *adj* modèle. *n* **1** modèle *m.* **2** (fashion) mannequin *m.* *vt* modeler. *vi* être mannequin.
moderate ('mɔdərət) *adj* **1** modéré, raisonnable. **2** médiocre. **3** moyen, -enne. *vt* modérer. *vi* se modérer. **moderation** *n* modération *f.* **in moderation** modérément.
modern ('mɔdən) *adj* moderne. **modernity** *n* modernité *f.* **modernize** *vt* moderniser.
modest ('mɔdist) *adj* **1** modeste. **2** pudique. **modesty** *n* **1** modestie *f.* **2** pudeur *f.* **3** modération *f.*
modify ('mɔdifai) *vt* modifier. **modification** *n* modification *f.* **modifier** *n* modificateur *m.*
modulate ('mɔdjuleit) *vt,vi* moduler.

module (ˈmɔdjuːl) *n* module *m*.
mohair (ˈmouhɛə) *n* mohair *m*.
moist (mɔist) *adj* **1** humide. **2** moite. **moisten** *vt* humecter, mouiller.
moisture (ˈmɔistʃə) *n* humidité *f*. **moisturize** *vt* humidifier.
mole[1] (moul) *n* grain de beauté *m*.
mole[2] (moul) *n zool* taupe *f*.
molecule (ˈmɔlikjuːl) *n* molécule *f*. **molecular** *adj* moléculaire.
molest (məˈlest) *vt* molester, rudoyer.
mollusc (ˈmɔləsk) *n* mollusque *m*.
molten (ˈmoultən) *adj* fondu.
moment (ˈmoumənt) *n* moment, instant *m*. **momentary** *adj* momentané. **momentous** *adj* important, capital, -aux. **momentum** *n*, *pl* **-ta** **1** *sci* force vive *f*. **2** vitesse acquise *f*.
monarch (ˈmɔnək) *n* monarque *m*. **monarchism** *n* monarchisme *m*. **monarchist** *n* monarchiste *m,f*. **monarchy** *n* monarchie *f*.
monastery (ˈmɔnəstri) *n* monastère *m*. **monastic** *adj* monastique.
Monday (ˈmʌndi) *n* lundi *m*.
money (ˈmʌni) *n* **1** argent *m*. **2** (coin) monnaie *f*. **ready money** argent comptant. **moneybox** *n* tirelire *f*. **money order** *n* mandat-poste *m*. **monetary** *adj* monétaire.
mongrel (ˈmʌngrəl) *n* métis, -isse. *adj* métis, -isse, hybride.
monitor (ˈmɔnitə) *n* moniteur, -trice. *vt* contrôler.
monk (mʌŋk) *n* moine *m*.
monkey (ˈmʌŋki) *n* **1** singe *m*. **2** *inf* polisson, -onne.
monochrome (ˈmɔnəkroum) *adj,n* monochrome *m*.
monogamy (məˈnɔgəmi) *n* monogamie *f*. **monogamist** *n* monogame *m,f*. **monogamous** *adj* monogame.
monologue (ˈmɔnəlɔg) *n* monologue *m*.
monopoly (məˈnɔpəli) *n* monopole *m*. **monopolize** *vt* **1** monopoliser. **2** accaparer.
monosyllable (ˈmɔnəsiləbəl) *n* monosyllabe *m*. **monosyllabic** *adj* monosyllabique.
monotone (ˈmɔnətoun) *n* voix monotone *f*. **monotonous** *adj* monotone. **monotony** *n* monotonie *f*.
monsoon (mɔnˈsuːn) *n* mousson *f*.
monster (ˈmɔnstə) *n* monstre *m*. **monstrous** *adj* monstrueux, -euse. **monstrosity** *n* monstruosité *f*.
month (mʌnθ) *n* mois *m*. **monthly** *adj* mensuel, -elle. *adv* mensuellement. *n* publication mensuelle *f*.
monument (ˈmɔnjumənt) *n* monument *m*. **monumental** *adj* monumental, -aux.
moo (muː) *vi* meugler. *n* meuglement *m*.
mood[1] (muːd) *n* humeur *f*. **moody** *adj* d'humeur changeante, maussade.
mood[2] (muːd) *n gram* mode *m*.
moon (muːn) *n* lune *f*. **moonlight** *n* clair de lune *m*.
moor[1] (muə) *n* lande *f*. **moorhen** *n* poule d'eau *f*.
moor[2] (muə) *vt* amarrer. **moorings** *n pl* amarres *f pl*.
Moor (muə) *n* maure *m*. mauresque *f*. **Moorish** *adj* mauresque.
mop (mɔp) *n* balai à laver *m*. **mop of hair** tignasse *f*. ~*vt* éponger.
mope (moup) *vi* s'ennuyer, avoir le cafard.
moped (ˈmouped) *n* cyclomoteur *m*.
moral (ˈmɔrəl) *adj* moral, -aux. *n* **1** morale *f*. **2** *pl* mœurs *f pl*. **moralist** *n* moraliste *m*. **morale** *n* moral *m*. **morality** *n* moralité *f*. **moralize** *vi,vt* moraliser.
morbid (ˈmɔːbid) *adj* morbide, malsain.
more (mɔː) *adj* plus. *adv* **1** plus. **2** davantage, encore. **more and more** de plus en plus. **once more** encore une fois. **more than** plus que, plus de. **some more** encore, davantage. **moreover** *adv* de plus, en outre.
morgue (mɔːg) *n* morgue *f*.
morning (ˈmɔːniŋ) *n* matin *m*. matinée *f*. **morning coat** *n* jaquette *f*.
Morocco (məˈrɔkou) *n* Maroc *m*. **Moroccan** *adj,n* marocain.
moron (ˈmɔːrɔn) *n* **1** *med* arriéré *m*. **2** *sl* idiot, moron *m*.
morose (məˈrous) *adj* morose, maussade.
morphine (ˈmɔːfiːn) *n* morphine *f*.
morse code (mɔːs) *n* (alphabet) morse *m*.
mortal (ˈmɔːtl) *adj,n* mortel, -elle. **mortality** *n* mortalité *f*.
mortar[1] (ˈmɔːtə) *n cul,mil* mortier *m*.
mortar[2] (ˈmɔːtə) *n* (for building) mortier *m*.
mortgage (ˈmɔːgidʒ) *n* hypothèque *f*. *vt* hypothéquer.
mortify (ˈmɔːtifai) *vt* mortifier.
mortuary (ˈmɔːtjuəri) *n* **1** morgue *f*. **2** salle mortuaire *f*. *adj* mortuaire.
mosaic (mouˈzeiik) *n* mosaïque *f*.
mosque (mɔsk) *n* mosquée *f*.
mosquito (məˈskiːtou) *n*, *pl* **-oes** *or* **-os** moustique *m*.

moss (mɔs) *n* mousse *f.* **mossy** *adj* moussu.

most (moust) *adj* le *or* la plus, la plupart. *n* plus *m.* plupart *f.* **at most** au maximum. ~*adv* **1** très, fort. **2** plus. **mostly** *adv* **1** principalement. **2** le plus souvent.

motel (mou'tel) *n* motel *m.*

moth (mɔθ) *n* papillon de nuit *m.* **clothes moth** *n* mite *f.*

mother ('mʌðə) *n* mère *f. vt* dorloter. **motherhood** *n* maternité *f.* **mother-in-law** *n* belle-mère *f.* **mother superior** *n* mère supérieure *f.* **mother tongue** *n* langue maternelle *f.* **motherly** *adj* maternel, -elle.

motion ('mouʃən) *n* **1** mouvement *m.* **2** signe *m.* **3** *pol* motion *f. vt* faire signe. **motionless** *adj* immobile.

motive ('moutiv) *n* motif *m. adj* moteur, -trice. **motivate** *vt* motiver.

motor ('moutə) *n* moteur *m. adj* moteur, -trice. **motor car** *n* automobile *f.* **motor cycle** *n* motocyclette *f.* **motorist** *n* automobiliste *m,f.* **motorway** *n* autoroute *f.*

mottle ('mɔtḷ) *vt* tacheter, moucheter.

motto ('mɔtou) *n, pl* **-oes** *or* **-os** devise *f.*

mould[1] (mould) *n* moule *m. vt* mouler, pétrir.

mould[2] (mould) *n* (mildew) moisi *m.* moissure *f. vi* se moisir. **mouldy** *adj* moisi.

moult (moult) *vi* muer. **moulting** *n* mue *f.*

mound (maund) *n* tertre *m.*

mount[1] (maunt) *vt,vi* monter. **mount up** augmenter. ~*n* monture *f.*

mount[2] (maunt) *n geog* mont *m.*

mountain ('mauntin) *n* montagne *f.* **mountainous** *adj* montagneux, -euse. **mountaineer** *n* alpiniste *m,f.* **mountaineering** *n* alpinisme *m.*

mourn (mɔ:n) *vt,vi* pleurer. **mournful** *adj* lugubre, funèbre. **mourning** *n* deuil *m.*

mouse (maus) *n, pl* **mice** souris *f.* **mousetrap** *n* souricière *f.* **mousy** *adj* (of hair) terne.

mousse (mu:s) *n* mousse *f.*

moustache (mə'stɑ:ʃ) *n* moustache *f.*

mouth (mauθ) *n* **1** *anat* bouche *f.* **2** (of animals) geule *f.* **3** ouverture *f.* **4** (of rivers) embouchure *f.* **mouthful** *n* bouchée *f.* **mouthpiece** *n* **1** embouchure *f.* **2** porte-parole *m invar.*

move (mu:v) *vt* **1** déplacer. **2** animer. **3** émouvoir. **4** proposer. *vi* **1** se déplacer, bouger. **2** agir. **move in** emménager. **move on** s'avancer, circuler. **move out** déménager. ~*n* **1** mouvement *m.* **2** *game* tour, coup *m.* **3** déménagement *m.* **movable** *adj* mobile. **movement** *n* mouvement *m.* **moving** *adj* **1** en marche. **2** émouvant.

mow* (mou) *vt* **1** faucher. **2** tondre.

Mr ('mistə) (title of address) M.

Mrs ('misiz) (title of address) Mme.

much (mʌtʃ) *adj* beaucoup (de). adv **1** beaucoup. **2** bien. **as much** autant. **how much?** combien de? **much more** bien plus. **very much** beaucoup.

muck (mʌk) *n* **1** fumier *m.* **2** saleté *f. v* **muck up** gâcher. **mucky** *adj* sale.

mud (mʌd) *n* boue *f.* **mudguard** *n* garde-boue *m invar.* **muddy** *adj* boueux, -euse.

muddle ('mʌdḷ) *n* confusion *f. vt* embrouiller.

muff (mʌf) *n* manchon *m.*

muffle ('mʌfəl) *vt* **1** emmitoufler. **2** assourdir. *n* mufle *m.*

mug (mʌg) *n* timbale *f.* pot *m.*

muggy ('mʌgi) *adj* lourd.

mulberry ('mʌlbəri) *n* mûre *f.* **mulberry bush** *n* mûrier *m.*

mule[1] (mju:l) *n zool* mule *f.* mulet *m.*

mule[2] (mju:l) *n* mule *f.*

mullet ('mʌlit) *n* muge *m.*

multiple ('mʌltipəl) *adj,n* multiple *m.*

multiply ('mʌltiplai) *vt* multiplier. *vi* se multiplier. **multiplication** *n* multiplication *f.*

multitude ('mʌltitju:d) *n* multitude *f.*

mum (mʌm) *n inf* maman *f.*

mumble ('mʌmbəl) *vt,vi* marmonner.

mummy[1] ('mʌmi) *n* momie *f.* **mummify** *vt* momifier.

mummy[2] ('mʌmi) *n inf* maman *f.*

mumps (mʌmps) *n* oreillons *m pl.*

munch (mʌntʃ) *vt* mâcher, mâchonner.

mundane ('mʌndein) *adj* mondain.

municipal (mju'nisipəl) *adj* municipal, -aux.

mural ('mjuərəl) *adj* mural, -aux.

murder ('mə:də) *n* meurtre *m. vt* assassiner. **murderer** *n* assassin, meurtrier *m.* **murderous** *adj* meurtrier, -ière.

murmur ('mə:mə) *vi,vt* murmurer. *n* murmure *m.*

muscle ('mʌsəl) *n* muscle *m.* **muscular** *adj* **1** musculaire. **2** musclé.

muse (mju:z) *n* muse *f. vi* méditer, rêver.

museum (mju:'ziəm) *n* musée *m.*

mushroom ('mʌʃrum) *n* champignon *m.*

music ('mu:zik) *n* musique *f.* **musical** *n* **1** musical, -aux. **2** (of a person) musicien, -ienne. **musician** *n* musicien, -ienne.

musk (mʌsk) *n* musc *m.*

musket ('mʌskit) *n* mousquet *m*. **musketeer** *n* mousquetaire *m*.
Muslim ('muzlim) *adj,n* musulman.
muslin ('mʌzlin) *n* mousseline *f*.
mussel ('mʌsəl) *n* moule *f*.
must* (mʌst) *v mod aux* falloir, devoir. *n* nécessité *f*.
mustard ('mʌstəd) *n* moutarde *f*.
mute (mju:t) *adj,n* muet, -ette. *vt* amortir, assourdir. **muteness** *n* mutisme *m*.
mutilate ('mju:tileit) *vt* mutiler. **mutilation** *n* mutilation *f*.
mutiny ('mju:tini) *n* mutinerie, révolte *f*. *vi* se révolter. **mutinous** *adj* rebelle.
mutter ('mʌtə) *vi* marmotter.
mutton ('mʌtn̩) *n* mouton *m*. **leg of mutton** *n* gigot *m*.
mutual ('mju:tjuəl) *adj* mutuel, -elle, commun.
muzzle ('mʌzəl) *n* **1** *zool* mouseau, -aux *m*. **2** *mil* gueule *f*. **3** muselière *f*. *vt* museler.
my (mai) *poss adj 1st pers s* mon, ma, mes. **myself** *pron 1st pers s* **1** moi-même. **2** me. **by myself** tout seul.
myrrh (mə:) *n* myrrhe *f*.
myrtle ('mə:tl̩) *n* myrte *m*.
mystery ('mistəri) *n* mystère *m*. **mysterious** *adj* mystérieux, -euse.
mystic ('mistik) *adj,n* mystique. **mysticism** *n* mysticisme *m*. **mystified** *adj* intrigué. **mystify** *vt* **1** mystifier. **2** désorienter.
mystique (mi'sti:k) *n* mystique *f*.
myth (miθ) *n* mythe *m*. **mythical** *adj* mythique. **mythological** *adj* mythologique. **mythology** *n* mythologie.

N

nag[1] (næg) *vt* gronder, criailler. *vi* être toujours après.
nag[2] (næg) *n inf* bidet *m*.
nail (neil) *n* **1** *anat* ongle *m*. **2** clou *m*. *vt* clouer. **nailbrush** *n* brosse à ongles *f*. **nailfile** *n* lime à ongles *f*. **nail varnish** *n* vernis à ongles *m*.
naive (nai'i:v) *adj* naïf, -ïve, ingénu.
naked ('neikid) *adj* nu. **nakedness** *n* nudité *f*.
name (neim) *n* **1** nom *m*. **2** réputation *f*. *vt* nommer. **namely** *adv* à savoir, c'est-à-dire.
nanny ('næni) *n* **1** bonne d'enfant *f*. **2** *inf* nounou *f*.
nap (næp) *n* somme *m*. sieste *f*. *vi* sommeiller.
napalm ('neipɑ:m) *n* napalm *m*.
napkin ('næpkin) *n* serviette *f*.
nappy ('næpi) *n* couche *f*.
narcotic (nɑ:'kɔtik) *adj,n* narcotique *m*.
narrate (nə'reit) *vt* raconter. **narration** *n* narration *f*. **narrative** *n* récit *m*. *adj* narratif, -ive. **narrator** *n* narrateur, -trice.
narrow ('nærou) *adj* étroit, serré. *vt* restreindre. *vi* se rétrécir. **narrow-minded** *adj* borné. **narrowness** *n* étroitesse *f*.
nasal ('neizəl) *adj* nasal, -aux.
nasturtium (nə'stə:ʃəm) *n* capucine *f*.
nasty ('nɑ:sti) *adj* **1** mauvais, méchant. **2** désagréable. **3** dangereux, -euse. **nastiness** *n* **1** méchanceté *f*. **2** saleté *f*.
nation ('neiʃən) *n* nation *f*. **national** *adj* national, -aux. **national anthem** *n* hymne national *m*. **national insurance** *n* assurances sociales *f pl*. **national service** *n* service militaire *m*. **nationality** *n* nationalité *f*. **nationalization** *n* nationalisation *f*. **nationalize** *vt* nationaliser. **nationwide** *adj* sur le plan national.
native ('neitiv) *n* originaire, indigène *m,f*. *adj* **1** natal. **2** naturel, -elle.
nativity (nə'tiviti) *n* nativité *f*.
natural ('nætʃərəl) *adj* naturel, -elle. **natural gas** *n* gaz naturel *m*. **natural history** *n* histoire naturelle *f*. **natural science** *n* sciences naturelles *f pl*. **naturalization** *n* naturalisation *f*. **naturalize** *vt* naturaliser.
nature ('neitʃə) *n* **1** nature *f*. **2** sorte *f*.
naughty ('nɔ:ti) *adj* méchant, vilain.
nausea ('nɔ:siə, -ziə) *n* nausée *f*. **nauseate** *vt* dégoûter. **nauseating** *adj* ecœurant.
nautical ('nɔ:tikəl) *adj* nautique, marin.
naval ('neivəl) *adj* de marine, maritime.
nave (neiv) *n* nef *f*.
navel ('neivəl) *n* nombril *m*.
navigate ('nævigeit) *vi* naviguer. *vt* diriger, gouverner. **navigation** *n* navigation *f*. **navigator** *n* navigateur *m*.
navy ('neivi) *n* marine de guerre *f*. **navy blue** *n* bleu marine *m*.
near (niə) *adj* proche. *adv* près. *prep* près or auprès de. *vt* approcher de. **nearby** *adv* tout près (de). *adj* avoisinant. **nearly** *adv* presque, à peu près. **nearside** *n* côté gauche *m*. *adj* gauche.
Near East *n* Proche Orient *m*.
neat (ni:t) *adj* **1** net, nette, soigné. **2** élégant. **3** pur. **neatness** *n* **1** netteté *f*. **2** ordre *m*.
nebulous ('nebjuləs) *adj* nébuleux, -euse.
necessary ('nesəsəri) *adj* nécessaire. **if**

necessary au besoin. **necessity** *n* nécessité *f.*

neck (nek) *n* **1** *anat* cou *m.* **2** (of a bottle) goulot *m.* **3** (of clothing) col *m.* encolure *f.* **neckband** *n* encolure *f.* **necklace** *n* collier *m.* **neckline** *n* encolure *f.*

nectar ('nektə) *n* nectar *m.*

need (ni:d) *vt* **1** avoir besoin de. **2** exiger, demander. *vi* **1** être obligé. **2** falloir. **needy** *adj* indigent.

needle ('ni:dl̩) *n* aiguille *f.* **needlework** *n* travail à l'aiguille *m.*

negate (ni'geit) *vt* nier. **negation** *n* négation *f.* **negative** *adj* négatif, -ive. *n* **1** négative *f.* **2** *phot* négatif *m.*

neglect (ni'glekt) *vt* négliger. *n* négligence *f.*

negligent ('neglidʒənt) *adj* négligent. **negligence** *n* négligence *f.*

negotiate (ni'gouʃieit) *vi,vt* négocier. *vt* franchir, surmonter. **negotiation** *n* négociation *f.*

Negro ('ni:grou) *n, pl* **-oes** nègre *m.* **Negress** *n* négresse *f.*

neigh (nei) *vi* hennir. *n* hennissement *m.*

neighbour ('neibə) *n* voisin *m.* **neighbourhood** *n* voisinage *m.* alentours *m pl.* **neighbourly** *adj* (de) bon voisin.

neither ('naiðə) *adj,pron* ni l'un ni l'autre. *conj* ni, non plus. **neither...nor** ni...ni.

neon ('ni:ən) *n* néon *m.*

nephew ('nevju:) *n* neveu, -eux *m.*

Neptune ('neptju:n) *n* Neptune *m.*

nerve (nə:v) *n* **1** *anat* nerf *m.* **2** *inf* aplomb, toupet *m.* **3** courage *m.***nerve-racking** *adj* énervant. **nervous** *adj* **1** nerveux, -euse. **2** intimidé. **nervous breakdown** *n* crise de nerfs *f.* **nervousness** *n* nervosité *f.*

nest (nest) *n* nid *m.* *vi* nicher.

nestle ('nesəl) *vi* se nicher.

net[1] (net) *n* filet *m.* **netball** *n* netball *m.* **network** *n* réseau, -aux *m.*

net[2] (net) *adj* net, nette. *vt* toucher *or* rapporter net.

Netherlands ('neðələndz) *n pl* Pays Bas *m pl.*

nettle ('netl̩) *n* ortie *f.* *vt* agacer, piquer. **nettle rash** *n* urticaire *f.*

neurosis (njuə'rousis) *n pl* **-ses** névrose *f.* **neurotic** *adj,n* névrosé.

neuter ('nju:tə) *adj,n* neutre *m.*

neutral ('nju:trəl) *adj* neutre. **neutrality** *n* neutralité *f.* **neutralize** *vt* neutraliser.

neutron ('nju:trɔn) *n* neutron *m.*

never ('nevə) *adv* (ne...)jamais. *interj* pas possible! **never mind!** peu importe! **nevertheless** *adv* pourtant, quand-même.

new (nju:) *adj* **1** neuf, neuve. **2** nouveau, -elle. **3** frais, fraîche. **newcomer** *n* nouveau venu *m.* **news** *n pl* **1** nouvelle *f pl.* **2** (radio, etc.) informations *f pl.* **newsagent** *n* marchand de journaux *m.* **newspaper** *n* journal, -aux *m.* **newsreel** *n* bande d'actualités *f.*

newt (nju:t) *n* salamandre *f.*

New Testament *n* Nouveau Testament *m.*

New Year *n* Nouvel An *m.* **New Year's Day** *n* jour de l'an *m.*

New Zealand ('zi:lənd) *n* Nouvelle-Zélande *f.* **New Zealander** *n* néo-zélandais *m.*

next (nekst) *adj* **1** prochain. **2** suivant. **3** voisin. *adv* ensuite. **next to** à côté de. **next-door** *adj* d'à côté. *adv* à côté.

nib (nib) *n* plume *f.*

nibble ('nibəl) *vt,vi* grignoter.

nice (nais) *adj* **1** agréable, bon, bonne. **2** gentil, -ille. **3** délicat. **nicety** *n* **1** délicatesse *f.* **2** précision *f.*

niche (nitʃ) *n* niche *f.*

nick (nik) *n* **1** encoche *f.* **2** *sl* prison *f.*

nickel ('nikəl) *n* nickel *m.*

nickname ('nikneim) *n* sobriquet *m.* *vt* surnommer.

nicotine ('nikəti:n) *n* nicotine *f.*

niece (ni:s) *n* nièce *f.*

Nigeria (nai'dʒiəriə) *n* Nigéria *m.* **Nigerian** *adj,n* nigérien, -ienne.

nigger ('nigə) *n derog* nègre *m.* négresse *f.*

niggle ('nigəl) *vi* tatillonner.

night (nait) *n* **1** nuit *f.* **2** soir *m.* **nightclub** *n* boîte de nuit *f.* **nightdress** *n also* **nightgown** chemise de nuit *f.* **nightmare** *n* cauchemar *m.* **night-time** *n* nuit *f.* **night-watchman** *n* veilleur de nuit *m.*

nightingale ('naitiŋgeil) *n* rossignol *m.*

nil (nil) *n* zéro, rien *m.*

Nile (nail) *n* Nil *m.*

nimble ('nimbəl) *adj* agile. **nimbleness** *n* agileté *f.*

nine (nain) *adj,n* neuf *m.* **ninth** *adj* neuvième.

nineteen (nain'ti:n) *adj,n* dix-neuf *m.* **nineteenth** *adj* dix-neuvième.

ninety ('nainti) *adj,n* quatre-vingt-dix *m.* **ninetieth** *adj* quatre-vingt-dixième.

nip[1] (nip) *vt* pincer. **nip off** filer. ~*n* pincement *m.*

nip[2] (nip) *n* goutte *f.* doigt *m.*

nipple ('nipəl) *n anat* mamelon *m.*

nit (nit) *n* **1** lente *f.* **2** *inf* crétin *m.*

nitrogen ('naitrədʒən) *n* azote *m*.
no[1] (nou) *adv* **1** non. **2** ne... pas. *n, pl* **noes** non *m invar*.
no[2] (nou) *adj* **1** pas un, pas de, aucun, nul, nulle. **2** peu, ne...pas. **no longer** ne...plus. **no more** ne...plus. **no smoking** défense de fumer.
noble ('noubəl) *adj,n* noble *m*. **nobility** *n* noblesse *f*. **nobleman** *n* noble *m*.
nobody ('noubədi) *pron* personne. *n inf* zéro, rien *m*.
nocturnal (nɔk'tə:nḷ) *adj* nocturne.
nod (nɔd) *n* signe de tête *m*. *vi* **1** faire un signe de tête. **2** somnoler.
node (noud) *n* nœud *m*.
noise (nɔiz) *n* **1** bruit *m*. **2** tapage, fracas *m*. **noisily** *adv* bruyamment. **noisy** *adj* tumultueux, -euse.
nomad ('noumæd) *n* nomade *m,f*. **nomadic** *adj* nomade.
nominal ('nɔminḷ) *adj* nominal, -aux.
nominate ('nɔmineit) *vt* désigner, nommer. **nomination** *n* nomination *f*.
non- *pref* **1** non-. **2** in-. **3** sans.
nonchalant ('nɔnʃələnt) *adj* nonchalant. **nonchalance** *n* nonchalance *f*.
nondescript ('nɔndiskript) *adj* **1** indéfinissable. **2** quelconque.
none (nʌn) *pron* **1** aucun. **2** personne. *adv* pas, point.
nonentity (nɔn'entiti) *n* non-être *m*. nullité *f*.
nonsense ('nɔnsəns) *n* absurdité *f*.
noodles ('nu:dḷz) *n pl* nouilles *f pl*.
noon (nu:n) *n* midi *m*.
no-one *pron* personne.
noose (nu:s) *n* nœud coulant, collet *m*.
nor (nɔ:) *conj* ni, ni...ne.
norm (nɔ:m) *n* norme *f*. **normal** *adj* normal, -aux.
Norman ('nɔ:mən) *adj,n* normand.
Normandy ('nɔ:məndi) *n* Normandie *f*.
Norse (nɔ:s) *adj* nordique. **Norse** (language) *n* norvégien *m*.
north (nɔ:θ) *n* nord *m*. *adj* septentrional, -aux, nord *invar*. *adv* au *or* vers le nord. **northeast** *n* nord-est *m*. *adv* vers le nord-est. *adj* du nord-est. **northeasterly** *adj* du nord-est. **northeastern** *adj* du nord-est. **northerly** *adj* du nord. **northern** *adj* du nord. **northwards** vers le nord. **northwest** *n* nord-ouest *m*. *adv* vers le nord-ouest. *adj* du nord-ouest. **northwesterly** *adj* du nord-ouest. **northwestern** *adj* du nord-ouest.
North America *n* Amérique du Nord *f*.
Northern Ireland *n* Irlande du Nord *f*.
Norway ('nɔ:wei) *n* Norvège *f*. **Norwegian** *adj,n* norvégien, -ienne. **Norwegian** (language) *n* norvégien *m*.
nose (nouz) *n* **1** nez *m*. **2** (of animals) museau, -aux *m*. *vt* flairer. **nosy** *adj inf* fouinard, indiscret, -ète.
nostalgia (nɔ'stældʒiə) *n* nostalgie *f*. **nostalgic** *adj* nostalgique.
nostril ('nɔstril) *n* **1** narine *f*. **2** (of an animal) naseau, -aux *m*.
not (nɔt) *adv* ne...pas, ne...point, pas.
notch (nɔtʃ) *n* encoche *f*. cran *m*. *vt* entailler, encocher.
note (nout) *n* **1** note *f*. **2** remarque *f*. **3** *comm* billet *m*. *vt* noter, remarquer. **notable** *adj* notable. **notation** *n* notation *f*. **notebook** *n* carnet *m*. **notepaper** *n* papier à lettres *m*. **noteworthy** *adj* remarquable.
nothing ('nʌθiŋ) *pron,n* rien *m*. **for nothing** en vain. ~*adv* pas du tout. **nothingness** *n* néant *m*.
notice ('noutis) *n* **1** avis *m*. notification *f*. **2** affiche *f*. **3** congé *m*. *vt* remarquer, apercevoir. **noticeable** *adj* perceptible. **notice board** *n* tableau d'affichage *m*.
notify ('noutifai) *vt* notifier, aviser. **notification** *n* avis *m*.
notion ('nouʃən) *n* notion, idée *f*.
notorious (nou'tɔ:riəs) *adj* notoire, mal famé. **notoriety** *n* notoriété *f*.
notwithstanding (nɔtwiθ'stændiŋ) *prep* malgré. *adv* néanmoins. *conj* bien que.
nougat ('nu:ga:) *n* nougat *m*.
nought (nɔ:t) *n* zéro, rien *m*.
noun (naun) *n* nom *m*.
nourish ('nʌriʃ) *vt* nourrir. **nourishment** *n* nourriture *f*.
novel[1] ('nɔvəl) *n* roman *m*. **novelist** *n* romancier, -ière.
novel[2] ('nɔvəl) *adj* original, -aux, singulier, -ière. **novelty** *n* nouveauté *f*.
November (nou'vembə) *n* novembre *m*.
novice ('nɔvis) *n* novice *m,f*.
now (nau) *adv* **1** maintenant, à l'heure actuelle. **2** tout de suite. **now and then** de temps en temps. **nowadays** *adv* de nos jours.
nowhere ('nouwɛə) *adv* nulle part.
noxious ('nɔkʃəs) *adj* nuisible.
nozzle ('nɔzəl) *n* lance *f*.
nuance ('nju:əns) *n* nuance *f*.

nucleus (ˈnjuːkliəs) *n, pl* **-clei** noyau, -aux *m.* **nuclear** *adj* nucléaire.
nude (njuːd) *adj,n* nu *m.* **nudity** *n* nudité *f.*
nudge (nʌdʒ) *vt* pousser du coude. *n* coup de coude *m.*
nugget (ˈnʌgit) *n* pépite *f.*
nuisance (ˈnjuːsəns) *n* **1** ennui *m.* **2** *inf* peste *f.*
null (nʌl) *adj* nul, nulle. **null and void** nul et non avenu. **nullify** *vt* annuler.
numb (nʌm) *adj* engourdi. *vt* engourdir.
number (ˈnʌmbə) *n* **1** nombre *m.* **2** (of a house, etc.) numéro *m.* **3** quantité *f. vt* **1** compter. **2** numéroter. **numeral** *n* chiffre *m. adj* numéral, -aux. **numerate** *adj* possédant les mathématiques de base. **numerical** *adj* numérique. **numerous** *adj* nombreux, -euse.
nun (nʌn) *n* religieuse *f.* **nunnery** *n* couvent *m.*
nurse (nəːs) *n* **1** infirmière *f.* **2** nourrice *f.* **3** (for children) bonne *f.* **nursing home** *n* clinique *f.*
nursery (ˈnəːsəri) *n* **1** chambre d'enfants *f.* **2** garderie *f.* **3** *bot* pépinière *f.* **nursery man** *n* pépinièriste *m.* **nursery rhyme** *n* chanson enfantine *f.* **nursery school** *n* école maternelle *f.*
nurture (ˈnəːtʃə) *vt* **1** élever. **2** nourrir. *n* **1** éducation *f.* **2** nourriture *f.*
nut (nʌt) *n* **1** noix *f.* **2** *tech* écrou *m.* **nutcrackers** *n pl* casse-noisettes *m invar.* **nutmeg** *n* muscade *f.* **nutshell** *n* coquille de noix *f.* **in a nutshell** en un mot.
nutrition (njuːˈtriʃən) *n* nutrition *f.* **nutritious** *adj* nourrissant.
nuzzle (ˈnʌzəl) *vi* fouiller. *vt* fourrer son nez contre.
nylon (ˈnailən) *n* **1** nylon *m.* **2** *pl inf* bas *m pl.*
nymph (nimf) *n* nymphe *f.*

O

oak (ouk) *n* chêne *m.*
oar (ɔː) *n* rame *f.* aviron *m.* **oarsman** *n* rameur *m.*
oasis (ouˈeisis) *n, pl* **oases** oasis *f.*
oath (ouθ) *n* **1** serment *m.* **2** juron *m.*
oats (outs) *n pl* avoine *f.*
oatmeal (ˈoutmiːl) *n* farine d'avoine *f.*
obedient (əˈbiːdiənt) *adj* obéissant. **obedience** *n* obéissance *f.*
obese (ouˈbiːs) *adj* obèse. **obesity** *n* obésité *f.*
obey (əˈbei) *vt* obéir à. *vi* obéir.
obituary (əˈbitjuəri) *n* nécrologie *f. adj* nécrologique.
object (*n* ˈɔbdʒikt; *v* əbˈdʒekt) *n* **1** objet *m.* **2** but *m.* **3** *gram* complément *m. vt* objecter. **object to** trouver à redire à, s'opposer à. **objection** *n* **1** objection *f.* **2** inconvénient *m.* **objectionable** *adj* **1** répréhensible. **2** désagréable. **objective** *adj,n* objectif, -ive *m.* **objectivity** *n* objectivité *f.*
oblige (əˈblaidʒ) *vt* **1** obliger, contraindre. **2** rendre service à. **obligation** *n* obligation *f.* **obligatory** *adj* obligatoire, de rigueur.
oblique (əˈbliːk) *adj* oblique, indirect.
obliterate (əˈblitəreit) *vt* **1** effacer. **2** oblitérer.
oblivion (əˈbliviən) *n* oubli *m.* **oblivious** *adj* oublieux, -euse.
oblong (ˈɔblɔŋ) *n* rectangle *m. adj* oblong, -gue.
obnoxious (əbˈnɔkʃəs) *adj* exécrable, odieux, -euse.
oboe (ˈoubou) *n* hautbois *m.*
obscene (əbˈsiːn) *adj* obscène. **obscenity** *n* obscénité *f.*
obscure (əbˈskjuə) *adj* obscur. *vt* obscurcir. **obscurity** *n* obscurité *f.*
observe (əbˈzəːv) *vt* **1** observer. **2** remarquer. **3** faire remarquer. **observance** *n* observance *f.* **observant** *adj* observateur, -trice. **observation** *n* observation *f.* **observatory** *n* observatoire *m.*
obsess (əbˈses) *vt* obséder. **obsession** *n* obsession, idée fixe *f.*
obsolete (ˈɔbsəliːt) *adj* hors d'usage, suranné.
obstacle (ˈɔbstəkəl) *n* obstacle *m.*
obstinate (ˈɔbstinət) *adj* opiniâtre, têtu. **obstinacy** *n* obstination *f.*
obstruct (əbˈstrʌkt) *vt* **1** obstruer, boucher. **2** gêner. **obstruction** *n* **1** obstruction *f.* **2** obstacle *m.*
obtain (əbˈtein) *vt* obtenir, se procurer.
obtrusive (əbˈtruːsiv) *adj* importun.
obtuse (əbˈtjuːs) *adj* obtus.
obverse (ˈɔbvəːs) *n* face *f.*
obvious (ˈɔbviəs) *adj* évident, manifeste. **obviously** *adv* évidemment.
occasion (əˈkeiʒən) *n* occasion *f. vt* occasionner. **occasional** *adj* **1** occasionel, -elle. **2** de circonstance. **occasionally** *adv* de temps en temps.
Occident (ˈɔksidənt) *n* Occident *m.* **occidental** *adj* occidental, -aux.
occult (ɔˈkʌlt) *adj* occulte. **occultism** *n* occultisme *m.*
occupy (ˈɔkjupai) *vt* **1** occuper. **2** habiter. **occupant** *n* locataire *m,f.* **occupation** *n* **1**

occupation *f.* **2** métier *m.* **occupational** *adj* professionnel, -elle. **occupier** *n* occupant *m.*

occur (ə'kə:) *vi* **1** arriver. **2** se trouver. **3** venir à l'esprit. **occurrence** *n* fait, événement *m.*

ocean ('ouʃən) *n* océan *m.* **oceanic** *adj* océanique.

ochre ('oukə) *n* ocre *f.*

octagon ('ɔktəgən) *n* octogone *m.* **octagonal** *adj* octogonal, -aux.

octane ('ɔktein) *n* octane *m.*

octave ('ɔktiv) *n* octave *f.*

October (ɔk'toubə) *n* octobre *m.*

octopus ('ɔktəpəs) *n, pl* **-puses** *or* **-pi** pieuvre *f.*

oculist ('ɔkjulist) *n* oculiste *m,f.*

odd (ɔd) *adj* **1** (of a number) impair. **2** dépareillé. **3** quelconque. **4** étrange. **oddity** *n* **1** étrangeté *f.* **2** (of a person) original, -aux *m.* **oddly** *adv* singulièrement. **oddment** *n* article dépareillé *m.* fin de série *f.* **odds** *n pl* **1** chances *f pl.* **2** inégalités *f pl.* **odds and ends** restes *m pl.*

ode (oud) *n* ode *f.*

odious ('oudiəs) *adj* odieux, -euse.

odour ('oudə) *n* odeur *f.* **odourless** *adj* inodore.

oesophagus (i'sɔfəgəs) *n* œsophage *m.*

oestrogen ('i:strədʒən) *n* œstrogène *m.*

oestrus ('i:strəs) *n* œstro *m.*

of (əv; stressed ɔv) *prep* **1** de. **2** parmi, d'entre. **3** à, en. **4** par.

off (ɔf) *adv* **1** au loin. **2** fermé. *prep* de.

offal ('ɔfəl) *n* abats *m pl.*

offend (ə'fend) *vt* offenser, froisser. **offence** *n* **1** offense *f.* **2** *law* délit *m.* **take offence** s'offenser. **offender** *n* coupable *m,f.* **offensive** *adj* désagréable. *n* offensive *f.*

offer ('ɔfə) *n* offre *f.* **on offer** en vente. ~*vt* **1** offrir. **2** tenter. *vi* se présenter. **offering** *n* offre *f.*

offhand (ɔf'hænd) *adj* **1** improvisé. **2** désinvolte.

office ('ɔfis) *n* **1** bureau, -aux *m.* **2** *pol* ministère *m.* **3** fonction *f.* **officer** *n* **1** officier *m.* **2** agent *m.* **official** *adj* officiel, -elle. *n* fonctionnaire *m.*

officious (ə'fiʃəs) *adj* **1** empressé. **2** officieux, -euse. **officiousness** *n* excès de zèle *m.*

offing ('ɔfiŋ) **in the offing** *adv* au large.

off-licence *n* débit de boissons à emporter *m.*

off-peak *adj* **1** creux, creuse. **2** de nuit.

off-putting *adj inf* déconcertant.

off-season *n* morte-saison *f.*

offset ('ɔfset) *vt* compenser.

offshore (ɔf'ʃɔ:) *adv* au large. *adj* éloigné de la côte.

offside (ɔf'said) *n* **1** côté droit *m.* **2** *sport* hors-jeu *m invar. adj* droit.

offspring ('ɔfspriŋ) *n* rejeton *m.*

offstage (ɔf'steidʒ) *adv* à la cantonade.

often ('ɔfən) *adv* souvent. **how often?** combien de fois? **more often than not** le plus souvent.

ogre ('ougə) *n* ogre *m.*

oil (ɔil) *n* huile *f.* *vt* graisser. **oilfield** *n* gisement pétrolifère *m.* **oil painting** *n* peinture à l'huile *f.* **oilskin** *n* ciré *m.*

ointment ('ɔintmənt) *n* onguent *m.* pommade *f.*

old (ould) *adj* **1** vieux, vieil, vieille. **2** ancien, -ienne. **how old are you?** quel âge avez-vous? **I am twelve years old** j'ai douze ans. **old-fashioned** *adj* démodé.

Old Testament *n* Ancien Testament *m.*

olive ('ɔliv) *n* olive *f.* **olive oil** *n* huile d'olive *f.* **olive tree** *n* olivier *m.*

omelette ('ɔmlət) *n* omelette *f.*

omen ('oumen) *n* augure *m.*

ominous ('ɔminəs) *adj* de mauvais augure, inquiétant. **ominously** *adv* d'une façon menaçante.

omit (ə'mit) *vt* omettre. **omission** *n* omission *f.*

omnibus ('ɔmnibəs) *adj,n* omnibus *m.*

omnipotent (ɔm'nipətənt) *adj* tout puissant.

on (ɔn) *prep* **1** sur. **2** à. **3** de. **4** en. *adv* **1** en avant. **2** dessus. **3** ouvert.

once (wʌns) *adv* **1** une fois. **2** autrefois. **at once** immédiatement.

one (wʌn) *adj* **1** un. **2** seul, unique. **3** certain. *n* un *m.* *pron 3rd pers s* on. **one another** l'un, l'autre. **one's** *poss adj 3rd pers s* son, sa, ses. **oneself** *pron 3rd pers s* **1** soi-même. **2** se. **one-sided** *adj* **1** unilatéral, -aux. **2** injuste. **one-sidedness** *n* partialité *f.* **one-way** *adj* **1** à sens unique. **2** (of a ticket) simple.

onion ('ʌniən) *n* oignon *m.*

onlooker ('ɔnlukə) *n* spectateur, -trice.

only ('ounli) *adj* seul, unique. *adv* seulement, ne...que. *conj* mais.

onset ('ɔnset) *n* attaque *f.* **at the onset** d'emblée.

onslaught ('ɔnslɔ:t) *n* attaque *f.*

onus ('ounəs) *n* responsabilité *f.*

onwards ('ɔnwədz) *adv also* **onwards** **1** en avant. **2** à partir de.

ooze (u:z) *vi,vt* suinter, filtrer.

opal ('oupəl) *n* opale *f.*

opaque (ou'peik) *adj* opaque.

open ('oupən) *adj* ouvert. *vt* ouvrir. *vi* s'ouvrir. **open air** *adj* en plein air. **open-ended** *adj* pendant. **open-handed** *adj* généreux, -euse. **open-hearted** *adj* franc, franche. **open minded** *adj* sans parti pris. **open-mouthed** *adj* bouche bée. **open-plan** *adj* sans cloisons. **opening** *n* ouverture *f*.

opera ('ɔprə) *n* opéra *m*. **opera house** *m* opéra *m*. **operetta** *n* opérette *f*.

operate ('ɔpəreit) *vt,vi* opérer. *vt tech* faire manœuvrer. **operation** *n* opération *f*. **come into operation** entrer en vigueur. **operative** *adj* actif, -ive.

opinion (ə'piniən) *n* opinion *f*. avis *m*. **opinion poll** *n* sondage *m*.

opium ('oupiəm) *n* opium *m*.

opponent (ə'pounənt) *n* adversaire *m,f*.

opportune (ɔpə'tju:n) *adj* opportun.

opportunity (ɔpə'tju:niti) *n* occasion *f*. **take the opportunity** profiter de l'occasion.

oppose (ɔ'pouz) *vt* **1** opposer. **2** s'opposer à, contrecarrer. **opposed** *adj* hostile. **as opposed to** par opposition à.

opposite ('ɔpəzit) *adj* **1** opposé, en face. **2** inverse. *n* contraire *m*. *adv* vis-à-vis. *prep* en face de. **opposition** *n* **1** opposition *f*. **2** résistance *f*. **3** obstacle *m*.

oppress (ə'pres) *vt* opprimer. **oppression** *n* oppression *f*. **oppressive** *adj* **1** opprimant. **2** étouffant, accablant.

opt (ɔpt) *vi* opter.

optical ('ɔptikəl) *adj* **1** optique. **2** d'optique. **optician** *n* opticien, -ienne.

optimism ('ɔptimizəm) *n* optimisme *m*. **optimist** *n* optimiste *m,f*. **optimistic** *adj* optimiste. **optimistically** *adv* avec optimisme.

option ('ɔpʃən) *n* option *f*. choix *m*. **optional** *adj* facultatif, -ive.

opulent ('ɔpjulənt) *adj* opulent, abondant.

or (ɔ:) *conj* ou. **or else** sinon. **or so** environ.

oral ('ɔ:rəl) *adj* **1** oral, -aux. **2** *anat* buccal. **orally** *adv* de vive voix.

orange ('ɔrindʒ) *n* **1** *bot* orange *f*. **2** (colour) orange, orangé *m*. *adj* orangé, orange. **orange tree** *n* oranger *m*.

oration (ɔ'reiʃən) *n* allocution *f*. discours *m*. **orator** *n* orateur *m*.

orbit ('ɔ:bit) *n* orbite *f*. *vt* tourner autour de.

orchard ('ɔ:tʃəd) *n* verger *m*.

orchestra ('ɔ:kistrə) *n* orchestre *m*. **orchestral** *adj* orchestral, -aux. **orchestrate** *vt* orchestrer.

orchid ('ɔ:kid) *n* orchidée *f*.

ordain (ɔ:'dein) *vt* **1** *rel* ordonner. **2** décréter.

ordeal (ɔ:'di:l) *n* épreuve *f*.

order ('ɔ:də) *n* **1** ordre *m*. **2** *comm* commande *f*. **in order to** afin de, pour. **in order that** afin *or* pour que. **out of order** en panne. ~*vt* **1** ordonner. **2** commander. **orderly** *adj* **1** ordonné. **2** posé. *n* planton *m*.

ordinal ('ɔ:dinl̩) *adj* ordinal, -aux.

ordinary ('ɔ:dənri) *adj* **1** ordinaire, normal, -aux. **2** quelconque. **out of the ordinary** exceptionnel, -elle.

ore (ɔ:) *n* minerai *m*.

oregano (ɔri'gɑ:nou) *n* marjolaine *f*.

organ ('ɔ:gən) *n* **1** *mus* orgue *m*. **2** organe *m*. **organist** *n* organiste *m,f*.

organism ('ɔ:gənizəm) *n* organisme *m*. **organic** *adj* organique.

organize ('ɔ:gənaiz) *vt* **1** organiser. **2** arranger. **organization** *n* **1** organisation *f*. **2** organisme, mouvement *m*. **organizer** *n* organisateur, -trice. **organizing** *n* organisation *f*. aménagement *m*.

orgasm ('ɔ:gæzəm) *n* orgasme *m*.

orgy ('ɔ:dʒi) *n* orgie *f*.

Orient ('ɔ:riənt) *n* Orient *m*. **oriental** *adj,n* oriental, -aux.

orientate ('ɔ:rienteit) *vt* orienter.

origin ('ɔridʒin) *n* origine *f*. **original** *adj,n* original, -aux *m*. **originality** *n* originalité *f*. **originate** *vi* prendre naissance, provenir. *vt* créer, amorcer. **origination** *n* source *f*.

Orkneys ('ɔ:kniz) *n* Orcades *f*.

Orlon ('ɔ:lɔn) *n Tdmk* Orlon *m*.

ornament ('ɔ:nəmənt) *n* ornement *m*. parure *f*. *vt* orner, agrémenter. **ornamental** *adj* ornemental, -aux.

ornate (ɔ:'neit) *adj* orné, surchargé.

ornithology (ɔ:ni'θɔlədʒi) *n* ornithologie *f*.

orphan ('ɔ:fən) *n* orphelin *m*. **orphanage** *n* orphelinat *m*.

orthodox ('ɔ:θədɔks) *adj* orthodoxe. **orthodoxy** *n* orthodoxie *f*.

orthography (ɔ:'θɔgrəfi) *n* orthographe *f*.

orthopaedic (ɔ:θə'pi:dik) *adj* orthopédique.

oscillate ('ɔsəleit) *vi* osciller.

ostensible (ɔ'stensəbəl) *adj* prétendu, soi-distant. **ostensibly** *adv* censément.

ostentatious (ɔsten'teiʃəs) *adj* ostentatoire.

osteopath ('ɔstiəpæθ) *n* chiropracteur *m*. **osteopathy** *n* ostéopathie *f*.

ostracize ('ɔstrəsaiz) *vt* ostraciser, exiler. **ostracism** *n* ostracisme *m*.

ostrich ('ɔ:stritʃ) *n* autruche *f*.

other ('ʌðə) *adj* autre. **every other day** tous les deux jours. ~*pron* autre, autrui. *adv* autrement. **otherwise** *adv* autrement.
otter ('ɔtə) *n* loutre *f*.
ought* (ɔ:t) *v mod aux* devoir, falloir.
ounce (auns) *n* once *f*.
our (auə) *poss adj 1st pers pl* notre, nos. **ours** *poss pron 1st pers pl* le *or* la nôtre. **ourselves** *pron 1st pers pl* **1** nous-mêmes. **2** nous.
oust (aust) *vt* **1** supplanter. **2** *law* déposséder.
out (aut) *adv* **1** hors, dehors. **2** sorti. **3** éteint. **4** *sport* hors jeu. **out of 1** hors de, au dehors de. **2** dans. **3** par. **4** parmi.
outboard ('autbɔ:d) *adj* extérieur.
outbreak ('autbreik) *n* éruption, ouverture *f*.
outburst ('autbə:st) *n* accès, éclat *m*.
outcast ('autkɑ:st) *adj,n* proscrit.
outcome ('autkʌm) *n* résultat *m*. issue *f*.
outcry ('autkrai) *n* cri *m*. clameur *f*.
outdo* (aut'du:) *vt* surpasser.
outdoor ('autdɔ:) *adj* extérieur, de plein air. **outdoors** *adv* dehors, en plein air.
outer ('autə) *adj* extérieur, externe.
outfit ('autfit) *n* **1** attirail, équipement *m*. **2** costume *m*.
outgoing ('autgouiŋ) *adj* **1** ouvert. **2** sortant. **3** démissionnaire.
outgrow* (aut'grou) *vt* **1** dépasser. **2** devenir trop grand pour.
outhouse ('authaus) *n* dépendance *f*.
outing ('autiŋ) *n* sortie *f*.
outlandish (aut'lændiʃ) *adj* extravagant, bizarre.
outlaw ('autlɔ:) *n* hors-la-loi *m invar*. *vt* proscrire.
outlay ('autlei) *n* débours *m pl*. mise de fonds *f*.
outlet ('autlet) *n* **1** sortie *f*. **2** débouché *m*.
outline ('autlain) *n* **1** contour *m*. **2** ébauche *f*. *vt* **1** esquisser. **2** silhouetter.
outlive (aut'liv) *vt* survivre à.
outlook ('autluk) *n* perspective *f*. point de vue *m*.
outlying ('autlaiiŋ) *adj* isolé, écarté.
outnumber (aut'nʌmbə) *vt* surpasser en nombre.
outpatient ('autpeiʃənt) *n* malade venant consulter à l'hôpital *m*
outpost ('autpoust) *n* avant-poste *m*.
output ('autput) *n* production *f*. rendement *m*.
outrage (aut'reidʒ) *n* outrage *m*. *vt* outrager, violenter. **outrageous** *adj* **1** outrageux, -euse. **2** indigne, exorbitant.
outright ('autrait) *adv* **1** franchement. **2** complètement. **3** du premier coup. *adj* **1** carré. **2** pur et simple.
outside (aut'said) *adj* extérieur, externe. *prep* en dehors de. *adv* dehors, à l'extérieur. *n* dehors, extérieur *m*. **on the outside** à l'extérieur. **outsider** *n* **1** étranger *m*. **2** *sport* ailier *m*.
outsize ('autsaiz) *n* taille hors série *f*. *adj* **1** de taille hors série. **2** énorme.
outskirts ('autskə:ts) *n pl* banlieue *f*. abords *m pl*.
outspoken (aut'spoukən) *adj* franc, franche. **outspokenness** *n* franc-parler *m invar*.
outstanding (aut'stændiŋ) *adj* **1** saillant, marquant. **2** excellent. **3** *comm* en souffrance, arriéré.
outstrip (aut'strip) *vt* **1** devancer. **2** surpasser.
outward ('autwəd) *adj* **1** extérieur, externe. **2** apparent. *adv* au dehors. **outwards** *adv* au dehors, vers l'extérieur.
outweigh (aut'wei) *vt* **1** peser plus que. **2** l'emporter sur.
outwit (aut'wit) *vt* **1** circonvenir. **2** dépister.
oval ('ouvəl) *adj,n* ovale *m*.
ovary ('ouvəri) *n* ovaire *m*.
ovation (ou'veiʃən) *n* ovation *f*.
oven ('ʌvən) *n* four *m*.
over ('ouvə) *prep* **1** sur, au-dessus de. **2** au cours de. **3** de l'autre côté de. **over and above** en outre. **over there** là-bas.
overall ('ɔvərɔ:l) *adj* global, -aux. *n* **1** blouse *f*. **2** *pl* salopette *f*.
overbalance (ouvə'bæləns) *vt* renverser. *vi* tomber.
overboard ('ouvəbɔ:d) *adv* par-dessus bord.
overcast (ouvə'kɑ:st) *adj* couvert, assombri.
overcharge (ouvə'tʃɑ:dʒ) *vt* surcharger.
overcoat ('ouvəkout) *n* pardessus *m*.
overcome* (ouvə'kʌm) *vt* surmonter, triompher de. **be overcome by** être accablé de, succomber à.
overdo* (ouvə'du:) *vt* **1** exagérer. **2** surmener. **3** *cul* trop cuire.
overdose ('ouvədous) *n* dose mortelle *f*.
overdraft ('ouvədrɑ:ft) *n* découvert *m*.
overdraw* (ouvə'drɔ:) *vt* tirer à découvert.
overdue (ouvə'dju:) *adj* échu, en retard.
overestimate (ouvər'estimeit) *vt* surestimer.
overfill (ouvə'fil) *vt* remplir trop.
overflow (*v* ouvə'flou; *n* 'ouvəflou) *vi* déborder. *n* trop-plein *m invar*.
overhang* (*v* ouvə'hæŋ; *n* 'ouvəhæŋ) *vt* surplomber, faire saillie. *n* porte-à-faux *m*. saillie *f*. **overhanging** *adj* en porte-à-faux.

overhaul (ouvə'hɔ:l) *n* révision *f*. *vt* examiner, réviser.
overhead (*adv* ouvə'hed; *adj*, *n* 'ouvəhed) *adv* en haut, en l'air. *adj* aérien, -ienne. **overheads** *n pl* frais généraux *m pl*.
overhear* (ouvə'hiə) *vt* surprendre.
overheat (ouvə'hi:t) *vt* surchauffer. *vi* chauffer.
overjoyed (ouvə'dʒɔid) *adj* transporté de joie.
overland (ouvə'lænd) *adv* par voie de terre.
overlap (*v* ouvə'læp; *n* 'ouvəlæp) *vt* recouvrir, chevaucher. *n* recouvrement, chevauchement *m*.
overlay (*v* ouvə'lei; *n* 'ouvəlei) *vt* recouvrir. *n* matelas *m*.
overleaf (ouvə'li:f) *adv* au verso.
overload (*v* ouvə'loud; *n* 'ouvəloud) *vt* **1** surcharger. **2** surmener. *n* surcharge *f*.
overlook (ouvə'luk) *vt* **1** oublier. **2** donner sur. **3** laisser passer.
overnight (*adv* ouvə'nait; *adj* œuvənait) *adv* **1** la nuit, jusqu'au lendemain. **2** du jour au lendemain. *adj* de nuit.
overpower (ouvə'pauə) *vt* maîtriser. **overpowering** *adj* **1** accablant. **2** écrasant.
overrate (ouvə'reit) *vt* surestimer, surfaire.
overreach (ouvə'ri:tʃ) *vt* dépasser.
overrule (ouvə'ru:l) *vt* **1** diriger. **2** rejeter.
overrun* (ouvə'rʌn) *vt* **1** envahir, se répandre. **2** dépasser.
overseas (ouvə'si:z) *adv* outre-mer. *adj* d'outre-mer.
overshadow (ouvə'ʃædou) *vt* **1** ombrager. **2** éclipser.
overshoot* (ouvə'ʃu:t) *vt* dépasser.
oversight ('ouvəsait) *n* oubli *m*. **through an oversight** par inadvertance.
oversleep* (ouvə'sli:p) *vi* dormir trop longtemps.
overspill* (*v* ouvə'spil; *n* 'ouvəspil) *vi* déborder. *n* déversement de population *m*.
overt ('ouvə:t) *adj* manifeste, évident.
overtake* (ouvə'teik) *vt* **1** rattraper. **2** (a car, etc.) doubler.
overthrow* (*v* ouvə'θrou; *n* 'ouvəθrou) *vt* vaincre. *n* chute *f*.
overtime ('ouvətaim) *n* heures supplémentaires *f pl*.
overtone ('ouvətoun) *n* nuance *f*.
overture ('ouvətʃə) *n* ouverture *f*.
overturn (ouvə'tə:n) *vt* renverser. *vi* verser, se retourner.
overweight (*n* 'ouvəweit; *adj* ouvə'weit) *n* surpoids *m*. *adj* trop lourd.
overwhelm (ouvə'welm) *vt* **1** écraser, accabler. **2** combler.
overwork (*v* ouvə'wə:k; *n* 'ouvəwə:k) *vt* surmener. *n* surmenage *m*.
overwrought (ouvə'rɔ:t) *adj* excédé.
ovulate ('ɔvjuleit) *vi* ovuler. **ovulation** *n* ovulation *f*.
owe (ou) *vt* devoir. **owing** *adj* dû, due. **owing to** en raison de.
owl (aul) *n* hibou, -oux *m*.
own (oun) *vt* posséder. **own up to** avouer. ~*adj* propre. **owner** *n* propriétaire *m,f*. **ownership** *n* propriété, possession *f*.
ox (ɔks) *n*, *pl* **oxen** bœuf *m*. **oxtail** *n* queue de bœuf *f*.
oxygen ('ɔksidʒən) *n* oxygène *m*.
oyster ('ɔistə) *n* huître *f*. **oyster-bed** *n* banc d'huîtres *m*.

P

pace (peis) *n* **1** pas *m*. **2** allure *f*. *vt* arpenter. **pace up and down** faire les cent pas.
Pacific (pə'sifik) *adj* pacifique. **Pacific (Ocean)** *n* (Océan) Pacifique *m*.
pacify ('pæsifai) *vt* pacifier, apaiser. **pacifism** *n* pacifisme *m*.
pack (pæk) *n* **1** paquet *m*. **2** bande *f*. **3** *game* jeu, jeux *m*. **4** (of hounds) meute *f*. *vt* **1** emballer. **2** tasser, empiler. **3** bourrer. **package** *n* **1** paquet *m*. **2** emballage *m*. **packet** *n* **1** paquet *m*. **2** colis *m*. **packhorse** *n* cheval de somme *m*.
pact (pækt) *n* pacte *m*. convention *f*.
pad[1] (pæd) *n* **1** coussinet *m*. **2** tampon *m*. **3** (of paper) bloc *m*. *vt* **1** rembourrer, matelasser. **2** délayer. **padding** *n* rembourrage *m*.
pad[2] (pæd) *n* bruit de pas feutrés *m*.
paddle[1] ('pædl̩) *n* **1** pagaie *f*. **2** aube *f*. *vt* pagayer.
paddle[2] ('pædl̩) *vi* patauger.
paddock ('pædɔk) *n* **1** enclos *m*. **2** paddock *m*.
paddyfield ('pædifi:ld) *n* champ de riz *m*.
padlock ('pædlɔk) *n* cadenas *m*. *vt* cadenasser.
paediatric (pi:di'ætrik) *adj* pédiatrique. **paediatrician** *n* pédiatre *m*.
pagan ('peigən) *adj,n* païen, -ïenne.
page[1] (peidʒ) *n* (of a book) page *f*.
page[2] (peidʒ) *n* (boy) page *m*.
pageant ('pædʒənt) *n* cortège historique *m*.
pagoda (pə'goudə) *n* pagode *f*.
paid (peid) *v* see **pay**.

pain (pein) *n* **1** douleur, souffrance *f.* **2** *pl* peine *f.* **painful** *adj* douloureux, -euse. **painless** *adj* sans douleur. **painstaking** *adj* soigneux, -euse, appliqué.

paint (peint) *n* **1** peinture *f.* **2** *Art* couleur *f. vt* **1** peindre. **2** dépeindre. *vi* faire de la peinture. **paintbrush** *n* pinceau, -aux *m.* **painter** *n* peintre *m.* **painting** *n* **1** peinture *f.* **2** tableau, -aux *m.*

pair (pɛə) *n* **1** paire *f.* **2** couple *m. vt* assortir. **pair off 1** disposer deux par deux. **2** s'en aller à deux.

Pakistan (pɑ:ki'stɑ:n) *n* Pakistan *m.* **Pakistani** *adj,n* pakistanais.

pal (pæl) *n inf* camarade *m.*

palace ('pælis) *n* palais *m.*

palate ('pælət) *n* palais *m.* **palatable** *adj* savoureux, -euse.

pale (peil) *adj* pâle, blême. **turn pale** pâlir. **paleness** *n* pâleur *f.*

Palestine ('pælistain) *n* Palestine *f.* **Palestinian** *adj,n* palestinien, -ienne.

palette ('pælit) *n* palette *f.*

palm[1] (pɑ:m) *n anat* paume *f. v* **palm off** refiler. **palmist** *n* chiromancien *m.* **palmistry** *n* chiromancie *f.*

palm[2] (pɑ:m) *n bot* palmier *m.*

Palm Sunday *n* dimanche des Rameaux *m.*

pamper ('pæmpə) *vt* dorloter.

pamphlet ('pæmflət) *n* **1** brochure *f.* **2** pamphlet *m.* **pamphleteer** *n* **1** auteur de brochures *m.* **2** pamphlétaire *m.*

pan (pæn) *n* **1** casserole *f.* **2** bac *m.* **pancake** *n* crêpe *f.*

Panama ('pænəmɑ:) *n* Panama *m.*

pancreas ('pæŋkriəs) *n* pancréas *m.*

panda ('pændə) *n* panda *m.*

pander ('pændə) *vi* **pander to** encourager.

pane (pein) *n* vitre *f.* carreau, -aux *m.*

panel ('pænḷ) *n* **1** panneau, -aux *m.* **2** (of people) liste *f.* jury *m. vt* lambrisser.

pang (pæŋ) *n* angoisse *f.*

panic* ('pænik) *n* panique *f. vi* paniquer. **panic-stricken** *adj* pris de panique.

pannier ('pæniə) *n* panier *m.* hotte *f.*

panorama (pænə'rɑ:mə) *n* panorama *m.* **panoramic** *adj* panoramique.

pansy ('pænzi) *n bot* pensée *f.*

pant (pænt) *vi* panteler, haleter. *n* halètement *m.*

panther ('pænθə) *n* panthère *f.*

pantomime ('pæntəmaim) *n* pantomime *f.*

pantry ('pæntri) *n* garde-manger *m invar.*

pants (pænts) *n pl* caleçon, slip *m.*

papal ('peipəl) *adj* papal, -aux.

paper ('peipə) *n* **1** papier *m.* **2** document, rapport *m.* **3** journal, -aux *m.* **4** épreuve *f. adj* de papier. *vt* tapisser. **paperback** *n* livre de poche *m.* **paperclip** *n* attache-papiers *m invar.* trombone *f.* **paperwork** *n* écritures *f pl.*

papier-mâché (,pæpiei'mæʃei) *n* carton-pâte *m.*

papist ('peipist) *n* papiste *m,f.*

paprika ('pæprikə) *n* paprika *m.*

par (pɑ:) *n* pair *m.* moyenne *f.* **be on a par with** être au niveau de.

parable ('pærəbəl) *n* parabole *f.*

parachute ('pærəʃu:t) *n* parachute *m. vi* descendre en parachute. **parachutist** *n* parachutiste *m,f.*

parade (pə'reid) *n* **1** parade *f.* **2** *mil* exercice, rassemblement *m.* **3** défilé *m. vt* faire parade de. *vi* **1** *mil* parader. **2** se pavaner.

paradise ('pærədais) *n* paradis *m.*

paradox ('pærədɔks) *n* paradoxe *m.* **paradoxical** *adj* paradoxal, -aux.

paraffin ('pærəfin) *n* **1** paraffine *f.* **2** *comm* pétrole *m.*

paragraph ('pærəgrɑ:f) *n* paragraphe *m.*

parallel ('pærəlel) *adj* **1** parallèle. **2** semblable. *n* parallèle *f. vt* **1** placer parellèlement. **2** comparer. **3** égaler.

paralyse ('pærəlaiz) *vt* paralyser. **paralysed** *adj* **1** *med* paralysé. **2** transi. **paralysis** *n* paralysie *f.* **paralytic** *adj* **1** paralytique. **2** *sl* soûl.

paramount ('pærəmaunt) *adj* **1** éminent. **2** suprême.

paranoia (pærə'nɔiə) *n* paranoïa *f.*

parapet ('pærəpit) *n* parapet *m.*

paraphernalia (pærəfə'neiliə) *n pl* attirail *m.*

paraphrase ('pærəfreiz) *n* paraphrase *f. vt* paraphraser.

parasite ('pærəsait) *n* **1** parasite *m.* **2** (person) pique-assiette *m,f invar.*

paratrooper ('pærətru:pə) *n* parachutiste *m.*

parcel ('pɑ:səl) *n* **1** colis *m.* **2** portion, parcelle *f. vt* **1** empaqueter. **2** morceler.

parch (pɑ:tʃ) *vt* **1** rôtir. **2** dessécher. *vi* se dessécher. **parched** *adj* sec, aride.

parchment ('pɑ:tʃmənt) *n* parchemin *m.*

pardon ('pɑ:dṇ) *vt* **1** excuser. **2** absoudre. **3** gracier. **pardon me!** excusez-moi! ~*n* **1** pardon *m.* **2** grâce *f.* **I beg your pardon 1** excusez-moi! **2** pardon? comment?

pare (pɛə) *vt* **1** rogner. **2** éplucher. **paring** *n* **1** ébarbage *m*. **2** épluchures *f pl*.

parent (ˈpɛərənt) *n* **1** père *m*. mère *f*. **2** *pl* parents *m pl*. *adj* mère. **parenthood** *n* paternité, maternité *f*.

parenthesis (pəˈrenθəsis) *n pl* **-eses** parenthèse *f*.

Paris (ˈpæris) *n* Paris *m*. **Parisian** *adj,n* parisien, -ienne.

parish (ˈpæriʃ) *n* **1** paroisse *f*. **2** commune *f*. **parishioner** *n* paroissien, -ienne.

parity (ˈpæriti) *n* **1** égalité *f*. **2** *comm* parité *f*. pair *m*.

park (pɑ:k) *n* parc *m*. *vt* garer. *vi* stationner. **parking** *n* stationnement *m*. **parking meter** *n* parcomètre *m*.

parliament (ˈpɑ:ləmənt) *n* parlement *m*. **parliamentary** *adj* parlementaire.

parlour (ˈpɑ:lə) *n* salon *m*.

parochial (pəˈroukiəl) *adj* **1** paroissial, -aux. **2** de clocher. **parochialism** *n* esprit de clocher *m*.

parody (ˈpærədi) *n* parodie *f*. *vt* parodier.

parole (pəˈroul) *n* parole, foi *f*.

parquet (ˈpɑ:kei) *n* parquet *m*.

parrot (ˈpærət) *n* perroquet *m*.

parsley (ˈpɑ:sli) *n* persil *m*.

parsnip (ˈpɑ:snip) *n* panais *m*.

parson (ˈpɑ:sən) *n* pasteur *m*. **parsonage** *n* presbytère *m*.

part (pɑ:t) *n* **1** partie *f*. **2** part *f*. **3** pièce *f*. **4** région *f*. **5** *Th* rôle *m*. *vt* **1** diviser. **2** séparer. *vi* **1** se quitter. **2** se diviser. **part with** céder.

partake* (pɑ:ˈteik) *vt* partager. *vi* **1** prendre part. **2** manger.

partial (ˈpɑ:ʃəl) *adj* **1** partial, -aux. **2** partiel, -elle. **be partial to** avoir un faible pour. **partiality** *n* **1** partialité *f*. **2** prédilection *f*.

participate (pɑ:ˈtisipeit) *vi* participer. **participant** *n* participant *m*. **participation** *n* participation *f*.

participle (ˈpɑ:tisəpəl) *n* participe *m*. **present/past participle** participe présent/passé.

particle (ˈpɑ:tikəl) *n* particule *f*.

particular (pəˈtikjulə) *adj* **1** particulier, -ière, spécial, -aux. **2** détaillé. **3** méticuleux, -euse. **4** exigeant. *n* détail *m*.

parting (ˈpɑ:tiŋ) *n* **1** séparation *f*. **2** (of the hair) raie *f*.

partisan (pɑ:tiˈzæn) *n* partisan *m*.

partition (pɑ:ˈtiʃən) *n* **1** partage *m*. **2** cloison *f*. *vt* **1** morceler. **2** partager. **3** cloisonner.

partner (ˈpɑ:tnə) *n* **1** *comm* associé *m*. **2** *sport* partenaire *m,f*. **3** danseur *m*. *vt* être associé à. **partnership** *n* **1** association *f*. **2** *comm* société *f*. **go into partnership with** s'associer avec.

partridge (ˈpɑ:tridʒ) *n* **1** perdrix *f*. **2** *cul* perdreau, -aux.

part-time *adj,adv* à mi-temps.

party (ˈpɑ:ti) *n* **1** parti *m*. **2** groupe *m*. **3** réception, soirée *f*. **4** *law* partie *f*. **party line** *n* **1** ligne à poste groupés *f*. **2** *pol* ligne du parti *f*.

pass* (pɑ:s) *n* **1** col, défilé *m*. **2** *educ* réussite sans mention *f*. **3** permis *m*. laissez-passer *m invar*. *vt* **1** passer devant. **2** transmettre. **3** *educ* être reçu à. **4** approuver. **5** *law* voter. vi passer. **pass out** s'évanouir. **password** *n* mot de passe *m*.

passage (ˈpæsidʒ) *n* **1** passage *m*. **2** couloir *m*. **3** traversée *f*. **passageway** *n* ruelle *f*.

passenger (ˈpæsindʒə) *n* voyageur, -euse, passager, -ère.

passion (ˈpæʃən) *n* passion *f*. **passionate** *adj* **1** passionné. **2** emporté.

passive (ˈpæsiv) *adj,n* passif, -ive *m*.

Passover (ˈpɑ:souvə) *n* Pâque *f*.

passport (ˈpɑ:spɔ:t) *n* passeport *m*.

past (pɑ:st) *adj,n* passé *m*. **in the past** autrefois. ~*prep* au delà de. **twenty past two** deux heures vingt. ~*adv* **go past** passer.

pasta (ˈpæstə) *n* pâtes *f pl*.

paste (peist) *n* **1** pâte *f*. **2** colle *f*. *vt* coller.

pastel (ˈpæstəl) *n* pastel *m*.

pasteurize (ˈpæstəraiz) *vt* pasteuriser.

pastime (ˈpɑ:staim) *n* passe-temps *m invar*. délassement *m*.

pastoral (ˈpæstərəl) *adj* pastoral, -aux.

pastry (ˈpeistri) *n* **1** pâtisserie *f*. **2** pâte *f*. **puff pastry** *n* pâte feuilletée *f*.

pasture (ˈpɑ:stʃə) *n* pâturage *m*. *vt,vi* paître.

pasty[1] (ˈpeisti) *adj* **1** pâteux, -euse. **2** terreux, -euse.

pasty[2] (ˈpæsti) *n* pâté (en croûte) *m*.

pat[1] (pæt) *n* **1** caresse *f*. **2** (of butter) rondelle *f*. *vt* **1** tapoter. **2** caresser.

pat[2] (pæt) *adv* à propos. **off pat** par cœur. ~*adj* apte.

patch (pætʃ) *n* **1** pièce *f*. **2** tache *f*. **3** lopin *m*. **4** emplâtre *f*. *vt* rapiécer. **patch up** ravauder. **patchwork** *n* rapiéçage *m*.

patent (ˈpeitn̩t) *n* brevet *m*. patente *f*. *vt* breveter. *adj* **1** manifeste. **2** breveté. **patent leather** *n* cuir verni *m*.

paternal (pəˈtə:nl̩) *adj* paternel, -elle. **paternity** *n* paternité *f*.

path (pɑ:θ) *n* **1** chemin, sentier *m.* **2** cours *m.*
pathetic (pə'θetik) *adj* pathétique.
pathology (pə'θɔlədʒi) *n* pathologie *f.* **pathologist** *n* pathologiste *m,f.*
patience ('peiʃəns) *n* **1** patience *f.* **2** *game* réussite *f.* **patient** *adj* patient. *n* malade *m,f.*
patio ('pætiou) *n* patio *m.*
patriarchal (peitri'ɑ:kəl) *adj* patriarcal, -aux.
patriot ('peitriət) *n* patriote *m,f.* **patriotic** *adj* **1** patriote. **2** patriotique. **patriotism** *n* patriotisme *m.*
patrol (pə'troul) *vi* patrouiller. *vt* faire la patrouille dans. *n* patrouille *f.*
patron ('peitrən) *n* **1** protecteur *m.* **2** client *m.* **patronage** *n* **1** protection *f.* patronage *m.* **2** clientèle *f.* **patronize** *vt* **1** patronner. **2** fréquenter.
patter[1] ('pætə) *n* tapotement *m. vi* **1** trottiner. **2** crépiter.
patter[2] ('pætə) *n* boniment, bavardage *m.*
pattern ('pætən) *n* **1** modèle *m.* **2** motif *m.* **3** patron *m.* **4** échantillon *m.*
paunch (pɔ:ntʃ) *n* panse *f.* ventre *m.*
pauper ('pɔ:pə) *n* indigent, mendiant *m.*
pause (pɔ:z) *n* **1** pause *f.* **2** silence *m. vi* **1** s'arrêter un instant. **2** hésiter.
pave (peiv) *vt* paver. **pave the way** préparer le terrain. **pavement** *n* trottoir *m.* **paving** *n* dallage *m.*
pavilion (pə'viliən) *n* pavillon *m.*
paw (pɔ:) *n* patte *f. vt* donner des coups de patte à.
pawn[1] (pɔ:n) *n* gage *m. vt* mettre en gage. **pawnbroker** *n* prêteur sur gage *m.*
pawn[2] (pɔ:n) *n game* pion *m.*
pay* (pei) *n* paie *f.* traitement *m. vt* **1** payer, verser. **2** rétribuer. **payroll** *n* état des paiements *m.*
pea (pi:) *n* **1** pois *m.* **2** *cul* petit pois *m.*
peace (pi:s) *n* **1** paix *f.* **2** tranquillité *f.* **peaceful** *adj* **1** paisible. **2** pacifique. **peacemaker** *n* pacificateur, -trice.
peach (pi:tʃ) *n* pêche *f.* **peach tree** *n* pêcher *m.*
peacock ('pi:kɔk) *n* paon *m.*
peak (pi:k) *n* **1** cime *f.* **2** pointe *f.* **3** visière *f.*
peal (pi:l) *n* **1** carillon *m.* **2** grondement *m. vi* **1** carillonner. **2** gronder. *vt* sonner.
peanut ('pi:nʌt) *n* arachide, cacahuète *f.*
pear (pɛə) *n* poire *f.* **pear tree** *n* poirier *m.*
pearl ('pə:l) *n* perle *f.* **mother of pearl** *n* nacre *f.* **pearly** *adj* perlé, nacré.
peasant ('pezənt) *n* paysan, -anne.
peat (pi:t) *n* tourbe *f.*
pebble ('pebəl) *n* caillou, -oux, galet *m.* **pebbly** *adj* caillouteux, -euse.
peck (pek) *n* **1** coup de bec *m.* **2** *inf* bécot *m. vt* **1** becqueter. **2** bécoter. *vi inf* manger du bout des dents.
peckish ('pekiʃ) *adj* **feel peckish** avoir le ventre creux.
peculiar (pi'kju:liə) *adj* **1** particulier, -ière. **2** bizarre. **peculiarity** *n* **1** particularité *f.* **2** singularité *f.*
pedal ('pedl̩) *n* pédale *f. vi* pédaler.
peddle ('pedl̩) *vt* colporter.
pedestal ('pedistəl) *n* **1** piédestal, -aux *m.* **2** socle *m.*
pedestrian (pi'destriən) *n* piéton *m.* **pedestrian crossing** passage clouté *m.* ~*adj* **1** à pied. **2** prosaïque.
pedigree ('pedigri:) *n* **1** pedigree *m.* **2** ascendance *f.*
peel (pi:l) *n* **1** pelure, écorce *f.* **2** *cul* zeste *m. vt* **1** éplucher, peler. **2** dépouiller. *vi* **1** se peler. **2** se décrépir.
peep (pi:p) *n* coup d'œil *m. v* **peep at** regarder à la dérobée. **peep out** se montrer.
peer[1] (piə) *n* **1** (title) pair *m.* **2** égal, -aux *m.* **peerage** *n* pairie *f.*
peer[2] (piə) *vi* risquer un coup d'œil. **peer at** scruter.
peevish ('pi:viʃ) *adj* maussade.
peg (peg) *n* **1** cheville *f.* **2** fiche *f.* **3** patère *f. vt* **1** cheviller, accrocher. **2** *game* marquer.
pejorative (pi'dʒɔrətiv) *adj* péjoratif, -ive.
pelican ('pelikən) *n* pélican *m.*
pellet ('pelit) *n* **1** boulette *f.* **2** plomb *m.*
pelmet ('pelmit) *n* lambrequin *m.*
pelt[1] (pelt) *vt* **1** assaillir. **2** cribler. *vi* tomber à verse. **at full pelt** à toute vitesse.
pelt[2] (pelt) *n* peau, -aux *f.*
pelvis ('pelvis) *n* bassin *m.*
pen[1] (pen) *n* plume *f.* **penfriend** *n* correspondant *m.* **penknife** *n* canif *m.* **pen-nib** *n* bec de plume *m.*
pen[2] (pen) *n* enclos *m. v* **pen in** parquer.
penal ('pi:nl̩) *adj* pénal, -aux. **penalize** *vt* **1** sanctionner. **2** *sport* pénaliser. **penalty** *n* **1** peine *f.* **2** *sport* pénalisation *f.*
penance ('penəns) *n* pénitence *f.*
pencil ('pensəl) *n* crayon *m.* **pencil-sharpener** *n* taille-crayon *m.*
pendant ('pendənt) *n* pendentif *m.*
pending ('pendiŋ) *prep* **1** en attendant. **2** durant. *adj* pendant.

pendulum ('pendjuləm) *n* pendule *m*.
penetrate ('penitreit) *vt,vi* pénétrer. **penetrating** *adj* **1** pénétrant. **2** perspicace. **penetration** *n* pénétration *f*.
penguin ('peŋgwin) *n* manchot, pingouin *m*.
penicillin (peni'silin) *n* pénicilline *f*.
peninsula (pə'ninsjulə) *n* péninsule *f*. **peninsular** *adj* péninsulaire.
penis ('pi:nis) *n* pénis *m*.
penitent ('penitənt) *adj,n* pénitent.
pennant ('penənt) *n* banderole *f*.
penny ('peni) *n* **1** *pl* **pence** British unit of currency. **2** *pl* **pennies** sou *m*. **penniless** *adj* sans le sou.
pension ('penʃən) *n* **1** pension *f*. **2** pension de famille *f*. **old age pension** retraite *f*. ~*vt* pensionner. **pension off** mettre à la retraite. **pensioner** *n* retraité *m*.
pensive ('pensiv) *adj* pensif, -ive.
pent (pent) *adj* **pent up 1** renfermé. **2** refoulé.
pentagon ('pentəgən) *n* pentagone *m*.
Pentecost ('pentikɔst) *n* Pentecôte *f*.
penthouse ('penthaus) *n* appentis *m*.
people ('pi:pəl) *n* **1** peuple *m*. **2** nation *f*. **3** gens *m or f pl*. **4** *inf* parents *m pl*. *vt* peupler.
pepper ('pepə) *n* poivre *m*. *vt* **1** poivrer. **2** cribler. **peppercorn** *n* grain de poivre *m*. **peppermill** *n* moulin à poivre *m*. **peppermint** *n* menthe poivrée *f*. **pepper-pot** *n* poivrière *f*.
per (pə:) *prep* par. **as per** selon.
perambulator (pə'ræmbjuleitə) *n* voiture d'enfant *f*.
perceive (pə'si:v) *vt* **1** percevoir. **2** s'apercevoir de. **3** apercevoir. **perceivable** *adj* perceptible, sensible.
per cent (pə'sent) *n* pour cent *m*.
percentage (pə'sentidʒ) *n* **1** pourcentage *m*. **2** proportion *f*.
perception (pə'sepʃən) *n* **1** perception *f*. **2** sensibilité *f*. **perceptive** *adj* perceptif, -ive.
perch (pə:tʃ) *n* perchoir *m*. *vi* (se) percher. *vt* jucher.
percolate ('pə:kəleit) *vi* s'infiltrer, filtrer. *vt* passer. **percolator** *n* percolateur *m*.
percussion (pə'kʌʃən) *n* percussion *f*.
perennial (pə'reniəl) *adj* **1** éternel, -elle. **2** *bot* vivace. *n* plante vivace *f*.
perfect (*adj,n* 'pə:fikt; *v* pə'fekt) *adj* **1** parfait. **2** complet, -ète. *n* parfait *m*. *vt* **1** achever. **2** perfectionner, mettre au point. **perfection** *n* **1** perfection *f*. **2** achèvement *m*.
perforate ('pə:fəreit) *vt,vi* perforer. **perforation** *n* perforation *f*.
perform (pə'fɔ:m) *vt* **1** exécuter. **2** *Th* jouer. **performance** *n* **1** exécution *f*. **2** exploit *m*. **3** *Th* représentation *f*.
perfume (pə'fju:m) *n* parfum *m*. odeur *f*. *vt* parfumer.
perhaps (pə'hæps) *adv* peut-être.
peril ('perəl) *n* péril *m*. **perilous** *adj* périlleux, -euse.
perimeter (pə'rimitə) *n* périmètre *m*.
period ('piəriəd) *n* **1** période *f*. **2** durée *f*. **3** époque *f*. **4** *med* règles *f pl*. **periodical** *adj,n* périodique *m*.
peripheral (pə'rifərəl) *adj* périphérique.
periscope ('periskoup) *n* périscope *m*.
perish ('periʃ) *vi* **1** périr. **2** se détériorer. *vt* altérer, gâter. **perishable** *adj* périssable.
perjury ('pə:dʒəri) *n* **1** parjure *m*. **2** *law* faux témoignage *m*.
perk (pə:k) **perk up** *vi* se ranimer. *vt* redresser.
perm (pə:m) *n* *also* **permanent wave** permanente *f*.
permanent ('pə:mənənt) *adj* permanent. **permanence** *n* permanence *f*. **permanently** *adv* en permanence, à titre définitif.
permeate ('pə:mieit) *vt* s'infiltrer.
permit (*v* pə'mit; *n* 'pə:mit) *vt* **1** permettre. **2** autoriser. *n* **1** permis *m*. **2** autorisation *f*. **permission** *n* **1** permission *f*. **2** permis *m*. **permissible** *adj* admissible. **permissive** *adj* **1** libertin. **2** toléré.
permutation (pə:mju'teiʃən) *n* permutation *f*.
peroxide (pə'rɔksaid) *n* peroxyde *m*. *vt* *inf* décolorer.
perpendicular (pə:pən'dikjulə) *adj,n* perpendiculaire *f*.
perpetual (pə'petʃuəl) *adj* **1** perpétuel, -elle. **2** incessant.
perpetuate (pə'petʃueit) *vt* perpétuer.
perplex (pə'pleks) *vt* embarrasser, troubler. **perplexed** *adj* perplexe. **perplexity** *n* perplexité *f*.
persecute ('pə:sikju:t) *vt* **1** persécuter. **2** tourmenter. **persecution** *n* persécution *f*.
persevere (pə:si'viə) *vi* persévérer. **perseverance** *n* persévérance *f*.
Persia ('pə:ʃə) *n* Perse *f*. **Persian** *adj,n* persan. **Persian** (language) *n* persan *m*.
persist (pə'sist) *vi* **1** persister, s'obstiner. **2** continuer. **persistence** *n* persistance *f*. **persistent** *adj* **1** persistant, tenace. **2** continu.
person ('pə:sən) *n* personne *f*. **personal** *adj*

personnel, -elle. **personality** *n* **1** personnalité *f.* **2** caractère personnel *m.*
personify (pə'sɔnifai) *vt* personnifier. **personification** *n* personnification *f.*
personnel (pə:sə'nel) *n* personnel *m.*
perspective (pə'spektiv) *n* perspective *f.*
Perspex ('pə:speks) *n Tdmk* Perspex *m.*
perspire (pə'spaiə) *vi* transpirer. **perspiration** *n* transpiration, sueur *f.* **perspiring** *adj* en sueur.
persuade (pə'sweid) *vt* persuader. **persuasion** *n* persuasion *f.* **persuasive** *adj* persuasif, -ive.
pert (pə:t) *adj* mutin, effronté.
pertain (pə'tein) *vi* appartenir, se rapporter. **pertinent** *adj* pertinent, à propos.
perturb (pə'tə:b) *vt* perturber, troubler.
Peru (pə'ru:) *n* Pérou *m.* **Peruvian** *adj,n* péruvien, -ienne.
pervade (pə'veid) *vt* s'infiltrer *or* pénétrer dans. **pervading** *adj* dominant.
perverse (pə'və:s) *adj* **1** pervers. **2** contrariant. **perversity** *n* perversité *f.*
pervert (*v* pə'və:t *n* 'pə:və:t) *vt* **1** pervertir. **2** détourner. *n* perverti *m.*
peseta (pə'seitə) *n* peseta *f.*
peso ('peisou) *n* peso *m.*
pessimism ('pesimizəm) *n* pessimisme *m.* **pessimist** *n* pessimiste *m,f.* **pessimistic** *adj* pessimiste.
pest (pest) *n* peste *f.* fléau, -aux *m.* **pesticide** *n* pesticide *m.*
pester ('pestə) *vt* importuner.
pet[1] (pet) *n* **1** animal familier *m.* **2** *inf* chouchou *m. adj* favori, -ite. *vt* choyer.
pet[2] (pet) *n* accès de mauvaise humeur *m.*
petal ('petl) *n* pétale *m.*
peter ('pi:tə) *vi* **peter out 1** s'épuiser. **2** flancher, s'arrêter.
petition (pi'tiʃən) *n* **1** pétition, requête *f.* **2** *law* recours *m. vt* **1** adresser une pétition. **2** réclamer.
petrify ('petrifai) *vt* pétrifier. *vi* se pétrifier.
petroleum (pi'trouliəm) *n* pétrole *m.* **petrol** *n* essence *f.*
petticoat ('petikout) *n* jupon *m.*
petty ('peti) *adj* **1** insignifiant. **2** mesquin. **petty cash** *n* petite caisse *f.* **petty officer** *n* sous-officier *m.*
petulant ('petjulənt) *adj* irritable. **petulance** *n* irritabilité *f.*
pew (pju:) *n* banc d'église *m.*
pewter ('pju:tə) *n* étain *m.*
phantom ('fæntəm) *n* fantôme *m.*
pharmacy ('fɑ:məsi) *n* pharmacie *f.*
pharynx ('færiŋks) *n* pharynx *m.*
phase (feiz) *n* phase *f.*
pheasant ('fezənt) *n* faisan *m.*
phenomenon (fi'nɔminən) *n pl* **-ena** phénomène *m.* **phenomenal** *adj* phénoménal, -aux.
philanthropy (fi'lænθrəpi) *n* philanthropie *f.* **philanthropist** *n* philanthrope *m,f.*
philately (fi'lætəli) *n* philatélie *f.* **philatelist** *n* philatéliste *m,f.*
Philippines ('filipi:nz) *n pl* Philippines *f pl.*
Philistine ('filistain) *adj,n* philistin.
philosophy (fi'lɔsəfi) *n* philosophie *f.* **philosopher** *n* philosophe *m.* **philosophical** *adj* **1** philosophique. **2** philosophe.
phlegm (flem) *n* flegme *m.*
phlegmatic (fleg'mætik) *adj* flegmatique.
phobia ('foubiə) *n* phobie *f.*
phoenix ('fi:niks) *n* phénix *m.*
phone (foun) *n inf* téléphone *m. vt* téléphoner à. **phone for** appeler.
phonetic (fə'netik) *adj* phonétique. **phonetics** *n* phonétique *f.*
phoney ('founi) *adj* faux, fausse.
phosphate ('fɔsfeit) *n* phosphate *m.*
phosphorescence (fɔsfə'resəns) *n* phosphorescence *f.* **phosphorescent** *adj* phosphorescent.
phosphorus ('fɔsfərəs) *n* phosphore *m.* **phosphorous** *adj* phosphoreux, -euse.
photo ('foutou) *n inf* photo *f.*
photocopy ('foutoukɔpi) *vt* photocopier. *n* photocopie *f.*
photogenic (foutə'dʒenik) *adj* photogénique.
photograph ('foutəgrɑ:f) *n* photographie *f. vt* photographier. **photographer** *n* photographe *m,f.* **photography** *n* photographie *f.*
phrase (freiz) *n* locution, expression *f. vt* exprimer. **phrasebook** *n* recueil de locutions *m.*
physical ('fizikəl) *adj* physique. **physical education** *n* culture physique *f.*
physician (fi'ziʃən) *n* médecin *m.*
physics ('fiziks) *n* physique *f.*
physiology (fizi'ɔlədʒi) *n* physiologie *f.*
physiotherapy (fiziou'θerəpi) *n* physiothérapie *f.* **physiotherapist** *n* physiothérapeute *m,f.*
physique (fi'zi:k) *n* physique *m.*
piano (pi'ænou) *n* piano *m.* **grand piano** *n* piano à queue *m.* **pianist** *n* pianiste *m,f.*
pick[1] (pik) *vt* **1** choisir. **2** cueillir. **3** (a lock) crocheter. **pick a quarrel with** chercher querelle. **pick out** faire le tri de, choisir. **pick**

over trier. **pick up 1** ramasser. **2** apprendre. **3** prendre. **pick-up** *n* **1** reprise *f.* **2** pick-up *m.* **3** connaissance de rencontre *f.* ~*n* choix *m.* élite *f.* **pickpocket** *n* voleur à la tire *m.*
pick[2] (pik) *n* pic *m.*
picket ('pikit) *n* piquet *m.* *vi* se tenir en faction. *vt* piqueter.
pickle ('pikəl) *n* **1** marinade *f.* **2** *pl* conserves au vinaigre *f pl.* *vt* **1** mariner. **2** conserver au vinaigre.
picnic* ('piknik) *n* pique-nique *m.* *vi* pique-niquer.
pictorial (pik'tɔ:riəl) *adj* **1** en images. **2** illustré.
picture ('piktʃə) *n* **1** image *f.* **2** tableau, -aux *m.* **3** *pl inf* ciné *m.* *vt* représenter, dépeindre.
picturesque (piktʃə'resk) *adj* pittoresque.
pidgin ('pidʒən) *n* pidgin *m.* **speak pidgin** parler petit nègre.
pie (pai) *n* **1** pâté (en croûte) *m.* **2** tourte *f.*
piece (pi:s) *n* **1** morceau, -aux *m.* **2** pièce *f.* **3** partie *f.* **piecemeal** *adv* par morceaux. *adj* fragmentaire. **piecework** *n* travail à la pièce *m.* ~*vt* joindre, assembler. **piece together** rassembler.
pied (paid) *adj* bigarré.
pier (piə) *n* **1** jetée *f.* **2** *arch* pilier *m.*
pierce (piəs) *vt* percer, transpercer. **piercing** *adj* **1** perçant. **2** (of cold) pénétrant.
piety ('paiəti) *n* piété *f.*
pig (pig) *n* porc, cochon *m.* **pig-headed** *adj* têtu, buté. **pig-iron** *n* gueuse de fer *f.* **piglet** *n* porcelet *m.* **pigskin** *n* cuir de porc *m.* **pigsty** *n* porcherie *f.* **pigtail** *n* queue, natte *f.*
pigeon ('pidʒən) *n* pigeon *m.* **pigeonhole** *n* alvéole *f.* casier *m.* *vt* caser.
piggyback ('pigibæk) *n* **give someone a piggyback** porter quelqu'un sur le dos.
pigment ('pigmənt) *n* **1** *sci* pigment *m.* **2** matière colorante *f.* **pigmentation** *n* pigmentation *f.*
pike (paik) *n zool* brochet *m.*
pilchard ('piltʃəd) *n* pilchard *m.*
pile[1] (pail) *n* tas, monceau, -aux. *v* **pile up 1** entasser. **2** amasser.
pile[2] (pail) *n* pieu, pieux *m.* *vt* soutenir avec des pieux.
pile[3] (pail) *n* (of carpet, etc.) poil *m.*
pile[4] (pail) *n med* hémorroïde *f.*
pilfer ('pilfə) *vt* dérober, chaparder. **pilferage** *n* larcins *m pl.*
pilgrim ('pilgrim) *n* pèlerin *m.* **pilgrimage** *n* pèlerinage *m.*
pill (pil) *n* pilule *f.*
pillage ('pilidʒ) *n* pillage *m.* *vt* piller, saccager.
pillar ('pilə) *n* pilier *m.* colonne *f.* **pillar-box** *n* boîte aux lettres *f.*
pillion ('piliən) *n* siège arrière *m.* **ride pillion** monter en croupe.
pillow ('pilou) *n* oreiller *m.* **pillowcase** *n* taie d'oreiller *f.*
pilot ('pailət) *n* pilote *m.* *vt* piloter, guider.
pimento (pi'mentou) *n* piment *m.*
pimple ('pimpəl) *n* bouton *m.* *adj* boutonneux, -euse.
pin (pin) *n* épingle *f.* **pins and needles** fourmillements *m.* **pinball** *n* billard automatique *m.* **pincushion** *n* pelote à épingles *f.* **pinpoint** *vt* indiquer. **pinstripe** *n* rayure *f.* **pin-up** *n* pin-up *f invar.* ~*vt* **1** épingler. **2** clouer. **pin down** engager.
pinafore ('pinəfɔ:) *n* tablier *m.*
pincers ('pinsəz) *n pl* tenaille, pince *f.*
pinch (pintʃ) *vt* **1** pincer. **2** *inf* chiper. *n* **1** pincée *f.* **2** pincement *m.* **at a pinch** au besoin.
pine[1] (pain) *n* pin *m.*
pine[2] (pain) *vi* languir.
pineapple ('painæpəl) *n* ananas *m.*
Ping-pong ('piŋpɔŋ) *n Tdmk* Ping-pong *m.*
pinion ('piniən) *n* aileron *m.* *vt* **1** rogner les ailes à. **2** lier, ligoter.
pink (piŋk) *n* **1** rose *m.* **2** *bot* œillet *m.* *adj* rose.
pinnacle ('pinəkəl) *n* **1** *arch* pinacle *m.* **2** cime *f.* **3** apogée *f.*
pint (paint) *n* pinte *f.*
pioneer (paiə'niə) *n* **1** pionnier *m.* **2** précurseur *m.* *vt* défricher. *vi* frayer le chemin.
pious ('paiəs) *adj* pieux, -euse.
pip (pip) *n* pépin *m.*
pipe (paip) *n* **1** tuyau, -aux *m.* **2** pipe *f.* **pipedream** *n* rêvasserie *f.* **pipeline** *n* canalisation, conduite *f.* **pipette** *n* pipette *f.* compte-gouttes *m invar.*
piquant ('pi:kənt) *adj* piquant. **piquancy** *n* **1** piquant *m.* **2** goût relevé *m.*
pique (pi:k) *n* pique *f.* *vt* piquer, vexer.
pirate ('pairət) *n* pirate *m.* *vt* **1** contrefaire. **2** s'approprier de.
pirouette (piru'et) *n* pirouette *f.* *vi* pirouetter.
Pisces ('pisi:z) *n pl* Poissons *m pl.*
piss (pis) *tab vi* uriner. *n* urine *f.*
pistachio (pis'tæʃiou) *n* pistache *f.*
pistol ('pistəl) *n* pistolet *m.*

piston ('pistən) *n* piston *m.*

pit (pit) *n* **1** fosse *f.* **2** puits *m.* **pitfall** *n* embûche *f.* piège *m.*

pitch[1] (pitʃ) *vt* **1** dresser. **2** placer. **3** lancer. *n* **1** niveau, -aux *m.* **2** *mus* diapason *m.* **3** *sport* terrain *m.* **pitchfork** *n* fourche *f.*

pitch[2] (pitʃ) *n* poix *f.* *vt* enduire de poix.

pith (piθ) *n* **1** moelle *f.* **2** sève, vigueur *f.*

pittance ('pitn̩s) *n* pitance *f.*

pity ('piti) *n* pitié, compassion *f.* **what a pity!** quel dommage! ~*vt* plaindre.

pivot ('pivət) *n* pivot m. vi pivoter.

pizza ('pi:tsə) *n* pizza *f.*

placard ('plækɑ:d) *n* affiche *f.* *vt* afficher.

placate (plə'keit) *vt* apaiser.

place (pleis) *n* **1** lieu, -eux *m.* **2** localité *f.* **3** place *f.* **out of place** hors de propos. **placename** *n* nom de lieu *m.* **take place** se passer. ~*vt* **1** mettre. **2** situer. **place an order** passer commande.

placenta (plə'sentə) *n* placenta *m.*

placid ('plæsid) *adj* placide.

plagiarize ('pleidʒəraiz) *vt* plagier. **plagiarist** *n* plagiaire *m.*

plague (pleig) *n* **1** peste *f.* **2** fléau, -aux *m.* *vt* harceler.

plaice (pleis) *n* plie *f.*

plaid (plæd) *n* **1** plaid *m.* **2** tartan *m.*

plain (plein) *adj* **1** clair. **2** simple. **3** plat. **4** quelconque. *n* plaine *f.* **plain-clothes** *adj* en civil.

plaintiff ('pleintif) *n* *law* demandeur, plaignant *m.*

plaintive ('pleintiv) *adj* plaintif, -ive.

plait (plæt) *n* natte, tresse *f.* *vt* tresser.

plan (plæn) *n* **1** plan *m.* **2** projet *m.* *vt* **1** projeter. **2** planifier. **planning** *n* **1** conception *f.* **2** planification *f.*

plane[1] (plein) *n* **1** plan *m.* **2** *inf* avion *m.* **3** niveau, -aux *m.* *adj* plat.

plane[2] (plein) *n* rabot *m.* *vt* raboter.

planet ('plænit) *n* planète *f.*

plank (plæŋk) *n* planche *f.*

plankton ('plæŋktən) *n* plancton, plankton *m.*

plant (plɑ:nt) *n* **1** *bot* plante *f.* **2** *tech* usine *f.* *vt* **1** planter. **2** poser, asséner. **plantation** *n* plantation *f.*

plaque (plɑ:k) *n* plaque *f.*

plasma ('plæzmə) *n* plasma *m.*

plaster ('plɑ:stə) *n* **1** *med* emplâtre *m.* **2** plâtre *m.* **plaster of Paris** plâtre de moulage *m.* **sticking plaster** sparadrap *m.* ~*vt* **1** plâtrer. **2** couvrir.

plastic ('plæstik) *adj,n* plastique *m.* **plastic surgery** *n* chirurgie esthétique *f.*

Plasticine ('plæstisi:n) *n* *Tdmk* pâte à modeler *f.*

plate (pleit) *n* **1** plaque *f.* **2** assiette *f.* **3** *Art* gravure, estampe *f.* **dinner/soup plate** assiette plate/creuse *f.* **number plate** plaque d'immatriculation *f.* **platelayer** *n* poseur de rails *m.* ~*vt* plaquer.

plateau ('plætou) *n* plateau, -aux *m.*

platform ('plætfɔ:m) *n* **1** estrade, tribune *f.* **2** (railway) quai *m.* **3** plate-forme *f.*

platinum ('plætnəm) *n* platine *m.*

platonic (plə'tɔnik) *adj* platonique.

plausible ('plɔ:zəbəl) *adj* **1** plausible, vraisemblable. **2** enjoleur, -euse.

play (plei) *vi,vt* jouer *n* **1** *Th* pièce *f.* **2** jeu *m.* **playboy** *n* gaillard *m.* **player** *n* jouer *m.* **playful** *adj* folâtre, enjoué. **playfulness** *n* badinage *m.* **playground** *n cour de récréation f.* **playhouse** *n* théâtre *m.* **playing card** *n* carte à jouer *f.* **playing field** *n* terrain de jeux *m.* **playmate** *n* camarade (de jeu) *m,f.* **playschool** *n* jardin d'enfants *m.* **playwright** *n* dramaturge *m.*

plea (pli:) *n* **1** prétexte *m.* **2** appel *m.*

plead (pli:d) *vi,vt* plaider. *vt* prétexter, alléguer. **plead guilty** s'avouer coupable. **plead not guilty** nier sa culpabilité.

please (pli:z) *vt* plaire à, faire plaisir à. *vi* plaire. *adv* s'il vous plaît. **please do!** je vous en prie! **pleasant** *adj* **1** agréable, charmant. **2** aimable. **pleased** *adj* satisfait, content. **pleasing** *adj* agréable. **pleasure** *n* **1** plaisir *m.* **2** gré *m.*

pleat (pli:t) *n* pli *m.* *vt* plisser.

plectrum ('plektrəm) *n* médiator *m.*

pledge (pledʒ) *n* **1** gage *m.* **2** promesse *f.* *vt* **1** mettre en gage. **2** engager.

plenty ('plenti) *n* abondance *f.* *adv* *inf* largement, bien. **plentiful** *adj* abondant, copieux, -euse.

pliable ('plaiəbəl) *adj* **1** flexible, souple. **2** docile.

pliers ('plaiəz) *n pl* pince, tenaille *f.*

plight (plait) *n* état *m.* condition *f.*

plimsoll ('plimsəl) *n* sandale de gymnastique *f.*

plod (plɔd) *vi* marcher lourdement. **plod on** persévérer. **plodder** *n* bûcheur, -euse.

plonk (plɔŋk) *n* bruit sourd *m.* *v* **plonk down** poser sans façons.

plot[1] (plɔt) *n* **1** *lit* intrigue *f.* **2** complot *m.* conspiration *f.* *vt,vi* comploter, conspirer.

plot[2] (plɔt) *n* terrain *m.* **building plot** lotissement *m.*

plough (plau) *n* charrue *f*. *vt* labourer. **plough through** avancer péniblement dans.

pluck (plʌk) *vt* **1** arracher, cueillir. **2** plumer. **pluck up courage** prendre courage. ~*n* courage, cran *m*.

plug (plʌg) *n* **1** boucher *m*. **2** (electric) prise *f*. *vt* boucher, tamponner.

plum (plʌm) *n* prune *f*. **plum tree** prunier *m*.

plumage (ˈplu:midʒ) *n* plumage *f*.

plumb (plʌm) *n* plomb *m*. *adj* d'aplomb, vertical, -aux. *adv* **1** d'aplomb. **2** juste. *vt* sonder. **plumber** *n* plombier *m*. **plumbing** *n* plomberie *f*.

plume (plu:m) *n* plume *f*. *vt* orner de plumes.

plump[1] (plʌmp) *adj* grassouillet, -ette, dodu.

plump[2] (plʌmp) *vi* tomber lourdement. *vt* jeter brusquement. **plump for** choisir.

plunder (ˈplʌndə) *n* **1** pillage *m*. **2** butin *m*. *vt* piller.

plunge (plʌndʒ) *n* plongeon *m*. *vt* plonger, immerger. *vi* **1** jeter. **2** tanguer.

pluperfect (plu:ˈpə:fikt) *n* plus-que-parfait *m*.

plural (ˈpluərəl) *adj,n* pluriel, -elle *m*.

plus (plʌs) *prep* plus. *adj* positif, -ive.

plush (plʌʃ) *n* peluche *f*.

Pluto (ˈplu:tou) *n* Pluton *f*.

ply[1] (plai) *vt* **1** manier. **2** exercer. **3** assaillir. *vi* faire la navette.

ply[2] (plai) *n* **1** épaisseur *f*. **2** pli *m*. **plywood** *n* contre-plaqué *m*.

pneumatic (nju:ˈmætik) *adj* pneumatique. **pneumatic drill** *n* marteau piqueur *m*.

pneumonia (nju:ˈmouniə) *n* pneumonie *f*.

poach[1] (poutʃ) *vi* braconner. **poacher** *n* braconnier *m*.

poach[2] (poutʃ) *vt cul* pocher.

pocket (ˈpɔkit) *n* poche *f*. *vt* empocher. **pocket-knife** *n* couteau de poche, canif *m*. **pocket-money** *n* argent de poche *m*.

pod (pɔd) *n* cosse, gousse *f*. *vt* écosser.

poem (ˈpouim) *n* poème *m*. poésie *f*.

poet (ˈpouit) *n* poète *m*. **poetic** *adj* poétique. **poetry** *n* poésie *f*.

poignant (ˈpɔinjənt) *adj* **1** poignant. **2** vif, vive.

point (pɔint) *n* **1** point *m*. **2** question *f*. sujet *m*. **3** idée *f*. **4** pointe *f*. **beside the point** hors de propos. **come to the point** en venir au fait. **point-blank** *adj* **1** à bout portant. **2** direct, catégorique. *adv* **1** à bout portant. **2** catégoriquement. ~*vt* **1** indiquer, signaler. **2** aiguiser. **point out** faire remarquer. **point to** annoncer. **pointed** *adj* **1** pointu. **2** mordant.

poise (pɔiz) *n* **1** équilibre *m*. **2** port *m*. *vt* équilibrer, balancer.

poison (ˈpɔizən) *n* poison *m*. *vt* empoisonner. **poisonous** *adj* **1** empoisonné. **2** (of an animal) venimeux, -euse. **3** (of a plant) vénéneux, -euse.

poke (pouk) *vt* **1** pousser du coude. **2** attiser. **3** passer. **poke fun at** se moquer de. ~*n* **1** coup de coude m. **2** coup de tisonnier *m*.

poker[1] (ˈpoukə) *n* tisonnier *m*.

poker[2] (ˈpoukə) *n game* poker *m*.

Poland (ˈpoulənd) *n* Pologne *f*.

polar (ˈpoulə) *adj* polaire. **polar bear** *n* ours blanc *m*. **polarize** *vt* polariser. *vi* se polariser.

pole[1] (poul) *n* perche *f*. mât *m*. **pole-vault** *vi* sauter à la perche. **pole-vaulting** *n* saut à la perche *m*.

pole[2] (poul) *n geog* pôle *m*.

Pole (poul) *n* polonais *m*.

polemic (pəˈlemik) *adj,n* polémique *f*.

Pole Star *n* étoile polaire *f*.

police (pəˈli:s) *n* police *f*. **policeman** *n* agent de police, gendarme *m*. **police station** *n* commissariat de police *m*.

policy[1] (ˈpɔlisi) *n* politique, ligne de conduite *f*.

policy[2] (ˈpɔlisi) *n* police *f*. **insurance policy** police d'assurance.

polish (ˈpɔliʃ) *n* **1** poli, lustre *m*. **2** cire *f*. cirage *m*. **3** raffinement *m*. *vt* **1** polir. **2** cirer.

Polish (ˈpouliʃ) *adj* polonais. **Polish** (language) *n* polonais *m*.

polite (pəˈlait) *adj* poli, courtois. **politeness** *n* politesse, courtoisie *f*.

politics (ˈpɔlitiks) *n* politique *f*. **political** *adj* politique. **politician** *n* homme politique *m*.

polka (ˈpɔlkə) *n* polka *f*.

poll (poul) *n* vote, scrutin *m*. *vi* voter. **polling booth** isoloir *m*.

pollen (ˈpɔlən) *n* pollen *m*. **pollinate** *vt* polliniser.

pollute (pəˈlu:t) *vt* polluer, souiller. **pollution** *n* pollution *f*.

polygamy (pəˈligəmi) *n* polygamie *f*.

polygon (ˈpɔligən) *n* polygone *m*.

polytechnic (pɔliˈteknik) *adj* polytechnique. *n* institut de technologie *m*.

polythene (ˈpɔliθi:n) *n* polyéthylène *m*.

pomegranate (ˈpɔmigrænət) *n* grenade *f*. **pomegranate tree** *n* grenadier *m*.

pommel (ˈpʌməl) *n* pommeau, -aux *m*. *vt* rouer de coups.

pomp (pɔmp) *n* faste, apparat *m*. pompe *f*.

pompous *adj* **1** fastueux, -euse. **2** suffisant. **3** ampoulé.
pond (pɔnd) *n* étang *m*. mare *f*.
ponder ('pɔndə) *vi* méditer. *vt* considérer, peser, ruminer.
pony ('pouni) *n* poney *m*.
poodle ('pu:dḷ) *n* caniche *m*.
pool[1] (pu:l) *n* flaque, mare *f*.
pool[2] (pu:l) *n* **1** *game* cagnotte, poule *f*. **2** fonds commun *m*. *vt* mettre en commun.
poor (puə, pɔ:) *adj* **1** pauvre. **2** de mauvaise qualité, médiocre.
pop[1] (pɔp) *n* bruit sec *m*. *vi* **1** éclater, sauter. **2** crever. *vt* **1** faire sauter. **2** *inf* mettre au clou. **3** fourrer. **pop in** entrer en passant. ~*interj* crac! **popcorn** *n* maïs grillé *m*.
pop[2] (pɔp) *adj* pop. **pop music** *n* musique pop *f*.
pope (poup) *n* pape *m*.
poplar ('pɔplə) *n* peuplier *m*.
poppy ('pɔpi) *n* coquelicot, pavot *m*.
popular ('pɔpjulə) *adj* **1** populaire. **2** à la mode. **3** courant. **popularity** *n* popularité *f*.
population (pɔpju'leiʃən) *n* population *f*.
porcelain ('pɔ:slin) *n* porcelaine *f*.
porch (pɔ:tʃ) *n* porche *m*. marquise *f*.
porcupine ('pɔ:kjupain) *n* porc-épic *m*.
pore[1] (pɔ:) *vi* **pore over** s'absorber dans, méditer.
pore[2] (pɔ:) *n* pore *m*.
pork (pɔ:k) *n* porc *m*.
pornography (pɔ:'nɔgrəfi) *n* pornographie *f*. **pornographic** *adj* pornographique.
porous ('pɔ:rəs) *adj* poreux, -euse, perméable.
porpoise ('pɔ:pəs) *n* marsouin *m*.
porridge ('pɔridʒ) *n* porridge *m*.
port[1] (pɔ:t) *n* (harbour) port *m*.
port[2] (pɔ:t) *n naut* bâbord *m*.
port[3] (pɔ:t) *n* (wine) porto *m*.
portable ('pɔ:təbəl) *adj* portatif, -ive.
porter[1] ('pɔ:tə) *n* (luggage) porteur, garçon *m*.
porter[2] ('pɔ:tə) *n* concierge, portier *m*.
portfolio (pɔ:t'fouliou) *n* **1** serviette *f*. porte-documents *m*. **2** *Art* chemise *f*. **3** *pol* portefeuille *f*.
porthole ('pɔ:thoul) *n* hublot *m*.
portion ('pɔ:ʃən) *n* **1** partie, part *f*. **2** portion, ration *f*.
portrait ('pɔ:trit) *n* portrait *m*.
portray (pɔ:'trei) *vt* **1** peindre. **2** dépeindre.
Portugal ('pɔ:tjugəl) *n* Portugal *m*. **Portuguese** *adj,n* portugais *invar*. **Portuguese** (language) *n* portugais *m*.
pose (pouz) *vt,vi* poser. **pose as** se faire passer pour. ~*n* pose *f*.
posh (pɔʃ) *adj* chic.
position (pə'ziʃən) *n* **1** position *f*. **2** situation *f*. **3** place *f*. **4** rang *m*. **position closed** guichet fermé. ~*vt* **1** situer. **2** orienter.
positive ('pɔzitiv) *adj* **1** positif, -ive. **2** convaincu, assuré. *n* positif *m*.
possess (pə'zes) *vt* **1** posséder. **2** s'approprier. **possession** *n* possession, jouissance *f*. **possessive** *adj* possessif, -ive.
possible ('pɔsəbəl) *adj* possible. **it is possible that** il se peut que. **possibility** *n* **1** possibilité *f*. **2** éventualite *f*. **possibly** *adv* peut-être.
post[1] (poust) *n* poteau, -aux *m*. *vt* afficher, placarder.
post[2] (poust) *n* **1** *mil* poste *m*. **2** situation *f*. emploi *m*. *vt* mettre en faction, affecter.
post[3] (poust) *n* **1** courrier *m*. **2** poste *f*. *vt* mettre à la poste. **postage** *n* affranchissement, port *m*. **postal order** *n* mandat-poste *m*. **postbox** *n* boîte aux lettres *f*. **postcard** *n* carte postale *f*. **postcode** *n* code postal *m*. **postman** *n* facteur *m*. **postmark** *n* cachet de la poste *m*. **post office** *n* bureau de poste *m*.
poster ('poustə) *n* affiche *f*.
posterior (pɔs'tiəriə) *adj* postérieur. *n inf* postérieur, derrière *m*.
posterity (pɔs'teriti) *n* postérité *f*.
postgraduate (poust'grædjuət) *adj* de troisième cycle. *n* étudiant de troisième cycle *m*.
posthumous ('pɔstjuməs) *adj* posthume.
post-mortem (poust'mɔ:təm) *n* autopsie *f*.
postpone (pəs'poun) *vt* ajourner, différer. **postponement** *n* ajournement *m*.
postscript ('pousskript) *n* post-scriptum *m invar*.
postulate (*v* 'pɔstjuleit; *n* 'pɔstjulət) *vt* **1** postuler, demander. **2** supposer. *n* postulat *m*.
posture ('pɔstʃə) *n* **1** posture, attitude *f*. **2** état *m*.
pot (pɔt) *n* **1** pot *m*. **2** marmite *f*. **pots and pans** batterie de cuisine *f*.
potato (pə'teitou) *n, pl* **-oes** pomme de terre *f*.
potent ('poutnt) *adj* fort, puissant.
potential (pə'tenʃəl) *adj* **1** possible, latent. **2** potentiel, -elle. *n* potentiel *m*.
pothole ('pɔthoul) *n* **1** (in a road) trou, nid de poule *m*. **2** marmite torentielle *f*. **potholer** *n* spéléologue *m,f*. **potholing** *n* spéléologie *f*.
potion ('pouʃən) *n* potion *f*.

potter (ˈpɔtə) *n* potier *m.* *vi* s'occuper de bagatelles. **potter about** bricoler.
pottery (ˈpɔtəri) *n* poterie *f.*
pouch (pautʃ) *n* **1** poche *f.* petit sac *m.* **2** *zool* poche ventrale *f.* **3** (for tobacco) blague *f.*
poultice (ˈpoultis) *n* cataplasme *m.*
poultry (ˈpoultri) *n* volaille *f.*
pounce (pauns) *vi* **pounce on** fondre *or* s'abattre sur. ~*n* attaque, griffe *f.*
pound[1] (paund) *vt* **1** cogner, battre. **2** piler, broyer.
pound[2] (paund) *n, pl* **pounds** *or* **pound** **1** (currency) livre sterling *f.* **2** (weight) livre *f.*
pour (pɔ:) *vt* verser, couler. *vi* tomber à verse. **pour in** entrer à flots. **pour out** **1** verser. **2** sortir en foule.
pout (paut) *vi* faire la moue, bouder. *n* moue *f.*
poverty (ˈpɔvəti) *n* **1** misère, pauvreté *f.* **2** manque *m.* **poverty-stricken** *adj* indigent.
powder (ˈpaudə) *n* poudre *f.* *vt* **1** pulvériser. **2** saupoudrer. **3** poudrer. **powder room** *n* toilette pour dames *f.*
power (ˈpauə) *n* **1** pouvoir *m.* **2** faculté *f.* **3** puissance *f.* **4** force *f.* **power station** *n* centrale électrique *f.* **powerful** *adj* puissant, fort. **powerless** *adj* impuissant.
practicable (ˈpræktikəbəl) *adj* faisable, praticable.
practical (ˈpræktikəl) *adj* pratique. **practical joke** *n* mauvaise plaisanterie *f.*
practice (ˈpræktis) *n* **1** pratique *f.* **2** coutume *f.* **3** clientèle *f.* **4** *sport* exercice *m.* **out of practice** rouillé.
practise (ˈpræktis) *vt* **1** pratiquer, exercer. **2** étudier, s'exercer. *vi* s'entrainer, faire des exercices.
practitioner (prækˈtiʃənə) *n* praticien *m.*
pragmatic (prægˈmætik) *adj* pragmatique.
prairie (ˈprɛəri) *n* prairie *f.*
praise (preiz) *n* éloge *m.* louange *f.* *vt* faire l'éloge de, louer. **praiseworthy** *adj* louable, méritoire.
pram (præm) *n* landau *m.* voiture d'enfant *f.*
prance (prɑ:ns) *vi* **1** piaffer. **2** se pavaner.
prank (præŋk) *n* **1** escapade, fredaine *f.* **2** tour *m.* farce *f.*
prattle (ˈprætḷ) *vi* babiller, bavarder. *n* babillage *m.*
prawn (prɔ:n) *n* crevette *f.*
pray (prei) *vi,vt* **1** prier. **2** implorer. **prayer** *n* prière *f.* **prayerbook** *n* livre de prières *m.*
preach (pri:tʃ) *vi,vt* prêcher.
precarious (priˈkɛəriəs) *adj* **1** précaire. **2** incertain. **precariousness** *n* **1** précarité *f.* **2** incertitude *f.*
precaution (priˈkɔ:ʃən) *n* précaution *f.*
precede (priˈsi:d) *vt* précéder. **precedence** *n* préséance, priorité *f.* **precedent** *n* précédent *m.*
precinct (ˈpri:siŋkt) *n* enceinte *f.* **pedestrian precinct** zone piétonnière *f.*
precious (ˈpreʃəs) *adj* **1** précieux, -euse. **2** recherché, affecté.
precipice (ˈpresipis) *n* précipice *m.*
precipitate (prəˈsipiteit) *vt* **1** hâter. **2** précipiter. *vi* (se) précipiter. *adj* **1** précipité. **2** irréfléchi. **precipitation** *n* précipitation *f.*
precis (ˈpreisi) *n* résumé, précis *m.*
precise (priˈsais) *adj* **1** précis, exact. **2** méticuleux, -euse. **precision** *n* précision *f.*
precocious (priˈkouʃəs) *adj* précoce. **precociousness** *n* précocité *f.*
preconceive (pri:kənˈsi:v) *vt* préconcevoir. **preconception** *n* **1** idée préconçue. **2** préjugé *m.*
predatory (ˈpredətəri) *adj* prédateur, -trice, rapace.
predecessor (ˈpri:disesə) *n* prédécesseur *m.*
predestine (pri:ˈdestin) *vt* prédestiner. **predestination** *n* prédestination *f.*
predicament (priˈdikəmənt) *n* situation difficile, mauvaise passe *f.*
predicate (*n* ˈpredikit; *v* ˈpredikeit) *n* prédicat *m.* *vt* affirmer.
predict (priˈdikt) *vt* prédire. **predictable** *adj* prévisible. **prediction** *n* prédiction *f.*
predominate (priˈdɔmineit) *vi* prédominer. **predominance** *n* prédominance *f.* **predominant** *adj* prédominant.
pre-eminent *adj* **1** prééminent. **2** remarquable.
preen (pri:n) *vt* lisser, nettoyer. **preen oneself** se bichonner, faire des grâces.
prefabricate (priˈfæbrikeit) *vt* préfabriquer.
preface (ˈprefis) *n* **1** *lit* préface *f.* avant-propos *m invar.* **2** préambule *m.* *vt* **1** *lit* préfacer. **2** préluder à.
prefect (ˈpri:fekt) *n* préfet *m.*
prefer (priˈfə:) *vt* préférer, aimer mieux. **preference** *n* préférence *f.* **preferential** *adj* préférentiel, -elle.
prefix (ˈpri:fiks) *n* préfixe *m.* *vt* mettre en tête.
pregnant (ˈpregnənt) *adj* **1** (of a woman) enceinte, grosse. **2** (of an animal) pleine. **3** chargé, lourd.
prehistoric (pri:hisˈtɔrik) *adj* préhistorique.
prejudice (ˈpredʒədis) *n* **1** préjugé, parti pris *m.* **2** tort *m.* *vt* **1** prévenir, prédisposer. **2** nuire à.

preliminary (pri'liminəri) *adj* préliminaire, préalable.
prelude ('prelju:d) *n* prélude *m*.
premarital (pri:'mæritḷ) *adj* prénuptial.
premature ('premətʃuə) *adj* prématuré.
premeditate (pri:'mediteit) *vt* préméditer.
premise ('premis) *n* **1** prémisse *f*. **2** *pl* lieux *m pl*. *vt* poser en prémisse.
premium ('pri:miəm) *n* **1** prime *f*. **2** prix, récompense *f*. **premium bond** *n* bon du trésor *m*.
preoccupied (pri:'ɔkjupaid) *adj* préoccupé. **preoccupation** *n* préoccupation *f*.
prepare (pri'pɛə) *vt* préparer. *vi* se préparer, s'apprêter. **preparation** *n* **1** préparation *f*. **2** *pl* préparatifs *m pl*. **preparatory** *adj* préparatoire.
preposition (prepə'ziʃən) *n* préposition *f*.
preposterous (pri'pɔstərəs) *adj* absurde.
prerogative (pri'rɔgətiv) *n* prérogative *f*. privilège *m*.
prescribe (pri'skraib) *vt* prescrire, ordonner. **prescription** *n* **1** *med* ordonnance *f*. **2** prescription *f*.
presence ('prezəns) *n* **1** présence *f*. **2** prestance *f*. air *m*. **presence of mind** sang-froid *m*.
present[1] ('prezənt) *adj* présent, actuel, -elle. *n* présent *m*. **presently** *adv* dans un instant, tout à l'heure.
present[2] (*v* pri'zent; *n* 'prezənt) *vt* **1** présenter. **2** offrir. *n* cadeau, -aux *m*. **presentable** *adj* présentable, portable. **presentation** *n* **1** présentation *f*. **2** remise *f*.
preserve (pri'zə:v) *vt* **1** conserver. **2** préserver. **preserves** *n pl* conserves *f pl*.
preside (pri'zaid) *vi* présider.
president ('prezidənt) *n* président *m*. **presidency** *n* présidence *f*. **presidential** *adj* présidentiel, -elle.
press (pres) *vt* **1** appuyer sur. **2** presser. **3** repasser. *vi* se serrer, se presser. *n* presse *f*. **press conference** *n* conférence de presse *f*. **press-gang** *n* presse *f*. **press-stud** *n* bouton pression *m*. **press-up** *n* exercice musculaire *m*. **pressing** *adj* urgent.
pressure ('preʃə) *n* **1** pression *f*. **2** urgence *f*. **pressure cooker** *n* marmite à pression, cocotte minute *f*. **pressurize** *vt* pressuriser.
prestige (pres'ti:ʒ) *n* prestige *m*.
presume (pri'zju:m) *vt,vi* présumer, supposer. *vt* oser.
pretend (pri'tend) *vt* **1** feindre, simuler. **2** prétendre. *vi* faire semblant. **pretence** *n* **1** simulation *f*. prétexte *m*. **2** prétention *f*. **pretension** *n* prétention *f*. **pretentious** *adj* prétentieux, -euse.
pretext ('pri:tekst) *n* prétexte *m*.
pretty ('priti) *adj* joli, beau, belle. *adv inf* assez, passablement.
prevail (pri'veil) *vi* **1** prévaloir. **2** régner. **prevail upon** persuader. **prevalent** *adj* prédominant, répandu.
prevent (pri'vent) *vt* **1** empêcher. **2** détourner. **prevention** *n* prévention *f*. empêchement *m*. **preventive** *adj* préventif, -ive.
preview ('pri:vju:) *n* **1** exhibition préalable. **2** (cinema, etc.) avant-première *f*.
previous ('pri:viəs) *adj* précédent, antérieur, préalable. **previously** *adv* auparavant.
prey (prei) *n* proie *f*. *v* **prey on** tourmenter, ronger.
price (prais) *n* prix *m*. *vt* mettre un prix à. **price-list** *n* tarif *m*.
prick (prik) *n* piqûre *f*. *vt* piquer, crever. *vi* picoter. **prick up one's ears** dresser l'oreille. **prickle** *n* piquant *m*. épine *f*. *vi* picoter, fourmiller. *vt* piquer. **prickly** *adj* épineux, -euse.
pride (praid) *n* orgueil *m*. fierté *f*. **pride oneself on** se vanter de.
priest (pri:st) *n* prêtre *m*. **priesthood** *n* prêtrise *f*.
prim (prim) *adj* guindé, pincé, collet monté *invar*.
primary ('praiməri) *adj* **1** premier, -ière. **2** originel, -elle. **3** primaire. **primary school** *n* école primaire *f*.
primate *n* **1** ('praimit) *rel* primat *m*. **2** ('praimeit) *zool* primate *m*.
prime (praim) *adj* **1** premier, -ière. **2** de premier ordre. **3** principal, -aux. *vt* préparer. **prime minister** *n* premier ministre *m*.
primitive ('primitiv) *adj* primitif, -ive.
primrose ('primrouz) *n* primevère *f*.
prince (prins) *n* prince *m*.
princess (prin'ses) *n* princesse *f*.
principal ('prinsəpəl) *adj* principal, -aux. *n* directeur, patron *m*.
principality (prinsi'pæliti) *n* principauté *f*.
principle ('prinsəpəl) *n* principe *m*.
print (print) *n* **1** empreinte, trace *f*. **2** impression *f*. **3** *phot* épreuve *f*. **in/out of print** disponible/épuisé. ~*vt* imprimer, tirer. **printed matter** *n* imprimés *m pl*. **printing** *n* impression *f*.

prior (ˈpraiə) *adj* précédent, antérieur. **priority** *n* priorité *f*.

prise (praiz) *vt* **prise open** ouvrir de force.

prism (ˈprizəm) *n* prisme *m*.

prison (ˈprizən) *n* prison *f*. **prisoner** *n* prisonnier, -ière.

private (ˈpraivit) *adj* **1** privé, particulier, -ière. **2** intime, confidentiel, -elle. *n* simple soldat *m*. **privacy** *n* intimité *f*. **privately** *adv* en particulier.

privet (ˈprivit) *n* troène *m*.

privilege (ˈprivilidʒ) *n* privilège *m*. prérogative *f*. *vt* privilégier.

prize[1] (praiz) *n* prix *m*.

prize[2] (praiz) *vt* évaluer, estimer.

probable (ˈprɔbəbəl) *adj* probable, vraisemblable. **probability** *n* probabilité *f*.

probation (prəˈbeiʃən) *n* **1** épreuve *f*. **2** *law* liberté surveillée *f*. **probation officer** *n* délégué à la liberté surveillée *m*. **probationer** *n* stagiaire *m,f*.

probe (proub) *vt* sonder.

problem (ˈprɔbləm) *n* problème *m*. **problematic** *adj* problématique, douteux, -euse.

proceed (prəˈsi:d) *vi* **1** continuer. **2** procéder. **3** provenir. **proceedings** *n pl* **1** débats *m pl*. **2** *law* poursuites *f pl*. **procedure** *n* **1** procédé *m*. **2** *law* procédure *f*.

process (ˈprouses) *n* **1** processus *m*. **2** cours *m*. **3** procédé *m*. méthode *f*. *vt* traiter. **procession** *n* cortège, défilé *m*.

proclaim (prəˈkleim) *vt* proclamer, annonçer. **proclamation** *n* proclamation, déclaration *f*.

procreate (ˈproukrieit) *vt* procréer, engendrer.

procure (prəˈkjuə) *vt* procurer.

prod (prɔd) *vt* **1** pousser du doigt. **2** aiguillonner. *n* coup de pointe *m*.

prodigal (ˈprɔdigəl) *adj* prodigue.

prodigy (ˈprɔdidʒi) *n* prodige *m*.

produce (*v* prəˈdju:s; *n* ˈprɔdju:s) *vt* **1** produire. **2** présenter, montrer. **3** *Th* mettre en scène. *n* produit *m*. denrées *f pl*. **producer** *n* **1** producteur, -trice. **2** *Th* metteur en scène *m*. **product** *n* **1** produit *m*. **2** résultat *m*. **production** *n* **1** production *f*. **2** *comm* fabrique *f*. **3** *Th* mise en scène *f*. **productive** *adj* productif, -ive.

profane (prəˈfein) *adj* profane. *vt* profaner.

profess (prəˈfes) *vt* **1** professer. **2** prétendre. **profession** *n* **1** profession *f*. **2** métier *m*. **professional** *adj* professionnel, -elle. **professor** *n* professeur *m*.

proficient (prəˈfiʃənt) *adj* compétent, capable. **proficiency** *n* compétence *f*.

profile (ˈproufail) *n* profil *m*. silhouette *f*.

profit (ˈprɔfit) *n* bénéfice, profit *m*. *vi* bénéficier *or* profiter de. *vt* bénéficier *or* profiter à.

profound (prəˈfaund) *adj* **1** profond. **2** approfondi. **profoundly** *adv* profondément.

profuse (prəˈfju:s) *adj* abondant, excessif, -ive.

programme (ˈprougræm) *n* **1** programme *m*. **2** (radio, etc.) émission *f*. **program** (in computers) *n* programme *m*. *vt* programmer.

progress (*n* ˈprougres; *v* prəˈgres) *n* **1** progrès *m*. **2** cours *m*. marche *f*. **make progress** faire des progrès. ~*vi* s'avancer, progresser. **progression** *n* progression *f*. **progressive** *adj* progressif, -ive.

prohibit (prəˈhibit) *vt* défendre, interdire. **smoking prohibited** défense de fumer. **prohibition** *n* interdiction, défense *f*.

project (*n* ˈprɔdʒekt; *v* prəˈdʒekt) *n* projet *m*. *vi* dépasser, faire saillie. *vt* projeter. **projectile** *n* projectile *m*. **projection** *n* **1** projection *f*. **2** lancement *m*. **3** saillie *f*. **projector** *n* projecteur *m*.

proletariat (prouliˈtɛəriət) *n* prolétariat *m*.

proliferate (prəˈlifəreit) *vi,vt* proliférer.

prolific (prəˈlifik) *adj* prolifique, fécond.

prologue (ˈproulɔg) *n* prologue *m*.

prolong (prəˈlɔŋ) *vt* prolonger.

promenade (prɔməˈnɑ:d) *n* promenade, esplanade *f*. *vi* se promener.

prominent (ˈprɔminənt) *adj* **1** éminent, remarquable. **2** saillant, proéminent. **prominence** *n* **1** proéminence *f*. **2** importance *f*.

promiscuous (prəˈmiskjuəs) *adj* **1** casuel, -elle. **2** confus. **promiscuity** *n* promiscuité *f*.

promise (ˈprɔmis) *n* promesse *f*. **break one's promise** manquer de parole. ~*vt,vi* promettre. **promising** *adj* plein de promesses.

promote (prəˈmout) *vt* **1** donner de l'avancement à. **2** encourager. **be promoted** monter en grade. **promotion** *n* promotion *f*.

prompt (prɔmpt) *adj* prompt. *vt* **1** *Th* souffler. **2** suggérer à, inciter. **prompter** *n* souffleur, -euse.

prone (proun) *adj* enclin, porté.

prong (prɔŋ) *n* **1** fourche *f*. **2** dent de fourche *f*.

pronoun (ˈprounaun) *n* pronom *m*.

pronounce (prəˈnauns) *vt* **1** articuler. **2** déclarer. **pronounced** *adj* marqué. **pronunciation** *n* prononciation *f*.

proof (pru:f) *n* **1** preuve *f*. **2** épreuve *f*. *adj* à l'épreuve de, résistant. **proofread** *vt* faire des corrections sur épreuves.

prop[1] (prɔp) *n* appui, soutien *m*. *vt* soutenir, appuyer.

prop[2] (prɔp) *n Th* accessoire *m*.

propaganda (prɔpə'gændə) *n* propagande *f*.

propagate ('prɔpəgeit) *vt* propager.

propel (prə'pel) *vt* propulser. **propeller** *n* hélice *f*.

proper ('prɔpə) *adj* **1** propre. **2** approprié, juste. **3** convenable, comme il faut. **properly** *adv* **1** correctement. **2** comme il faut. **proper noun** *n* nom propre *m*.

property ('prɔpəti) *n* **1** propriété *f*. **2** biens *m pl*. **3** immeuble *m*. **4** qualité *f*. **lost property** objets trouvés *m pl*.

prophecy ('prɔfisi) *n* prophétie *f*. **prophesy** *vt* prophétiser, prédire. *vi* parler en prophète.

prophet ('prɔfit) *n* prophète *m*. **prophetic** *adj* prophétique.

proportion (prə'pɔ:ʃən) *n* **1** part, partie *f*. **2** rapport *m*. proportion *f*. **out of proportion** mal proportionné. ~*vt* proportionner. **proportional** *adj* proportionnel, -elle, proportionné à.

propose (prə'pouz) *vt* proposer. *vi* faire une demande en mariage. **proposal** *n* **1** proposition *f*. **2** projet *m*. **3** demande en mariage *f*. **proposition** *n* **1** proposition *f*. **2** affaire *f*.

proprietor (prə'praiətə) *n* propriétaire *m,f*.

propriety (prə'praiəti) *n* **1** bienséance *f*, convenances *f pl*. **2** propriété *f*.

propulsion (prə'pʌlʃən) *n* propulsion *f*.

prose (prouz) *n* **1** prose *f*. **2** *educ* thème *m*.

prosecute ('prɔsikju:t) *vt* poursuivre. **prosecution** *n* poursuites *f pl*. **prosecutor** *n* plaignant *m*.

prospect ('prɔspekt) *n* **1** perspective *f*. **2** vue *f*. **3** *pl* avenir *m*. *vt* prospecter. **prospective** *adj* à venir, futur. **prospectus** *n* prospectus *m*.

prosper ('prɔspə) *vi* prospérer, réussir. **prosperity** *n* prospérité *f*. **prosperous** *adj* prospère.

prostitute ('prɔstitju:t) *n* prostituée *f*. *vt* prostituer. **prostitution** *n* prostitution *f*.

prostrate (*v* prɔs'treit; *adj* 'prɔstreit) *vt* coucher, étendre. **prostrate oneself** se prosterner. ~*adj* **1** prosterné, étendu. **2** accablé.

protagonist (prə'tægənist) *n* protagoniste *m*.

protect (prə'tekt) *vt* **1** protéger. **2** sauvegarder. **protection** *n* **1** protection, défense *f*. **2** abri *m*. **protective** *adj* protecteur, -trice.

protein ('prouti:n) *n* protéine *f*.

protest (*n* 'proutest; *v* prə'test) *n* protestation *f*. *vt,vi* protester.

Protestant ('prɔtistənt) *adj,n* protestant.

protocol ('proutəkɔl) *n* protocole *m*.

proton ('proutɔn) *n* proton *m*.

prototype ('proutətaip) *n* prototype *m*.

protrude (prə'tru:d) *vi* déborder, faire saillie. **protruding** *adj* saillant.

proud (praud) *adj* orgueilleux, -euse, fier, -ère.

prove (pru:v) *vt* démontrer, prouver. *vi* se montrer, se trouver. **proven** *adj* avéré.

proverb ('prɔvə:b) *n* proverbe *m*. **proverbial** *adj* proverbial, -aux.

provide (prə'vaid) *vt* fournir, munir, pourvoir. **provide for** pourvoir à. **provided** *conj* pourvu que. **provision** *n* **1** provision *f*. **2** stipulation *f*. **3** *pl* comestibles *m pl*. **make provision for** pourvoir à. **provisional** *adj* provisoire.

province ('prɔvins) *n* **1** province *f*. **2** ressort, domaine *m*. **provincial** *adj* provincial, -aux.

proviso (prə'vaizou) *n* condition, clause conditionnelle *f*.

provoke (prə'vouk) *vt* **1** provoquer, exaspérer. **2** exciter. **provocation** *n* provocation *f*. **provocative** *adj* provocateur, -trice.

prow (prau) *n* proue *f*.

prowess ('prauis) *n* prouesse *f*.

prowl (praul) *vi* rôder.

proximity (prɔk'simiti) *n* proximité *f*.

prude (pru:d) *n* prude *f*. **prudish** *adj* prude, bégueule.

prudent ('pru:dn̩t) *adj* prudent, sage. **prudence** *n* prudence *f*.

prune[1] (pru:n) *n* pruneau, -aux *m*.

prune[2] (pru:n) *vt* tailler, émonder.

pry (prai) *vt* fureter, fourrer le nez.

psalm (sɑ:m) *n* psaume *m*.

pseudonym ('sju:dənim) *n* pseudonyme *m*.

psychedelic (saiki'delik) *adj* psychédélique.

psychiatry (sai'kaiətri) *n* psychiatrie *f*. **psychiatric** *adj* psychiatrique. **psychiatrist** *n* psychiatre *m*.

psychic ('saikik) *adj* psychique, métaphysique.

psychoanalysis (saikouə'nælisis) *n* psychanalyse *f*. **psychoanalysist** *n* psychanalyste *m*.

psychology (sai'kɔlədʒi) *n* psychologie *f*. **psychological** *adj* psychologique. **psychologist** *n* psychologue *m*.

psychopathic (saikə'pæθik) *adj* psychopathe.

psychosomatic (saikousə'mætik) *adj* psychosomatique.

pub (pʌb) *n inf* bistrot, bar *m*. **pub crawl** *n* tournée des bistrots *f*.

puberty ('pju:bəti) *n* puberté *f*.
public ('pʌblik) *adj,n* public, -ique *m*. **general public** grand public. **public house** *n* auberge *f*. **public relations** *n* rapports exterieurs *m pl*. **public school** *n* grande école privée d'enseignement secondaire *f*. **publican** *n* propriétaire de bistrot *m*.
publication (pʌbli'keiʃən) *n* publication *f*.
publicity (pʌb'lisiti) *n* publicité, réclame *f*.
publicize ('pʌblisaiz) *vt* faire connaître au public.
publish ('pʌbliʃ) *vt* publier, faire paraître. **publisher** *n* éditeur *m*. **publishing** *n* publication *f*. **publishing house** *n* maison d'édition *f*.
pucker ('pʌkə) *vt* **1** rider. **2** froncer. *vi* faire des plis, se froncer. *n* **1** ride *f*. **2** fronce *f*.
pudding ('pudiŋ) *n* pouding, pudding *m*.
puddle ('pʌdl̩) *n* flaque d'eau *f*.
puff (pʌf) *n* souffle *m*. bouffée *f*. *vi* souffler, haleter. *vt* gonfler. **puff pastry** *n* pâte feuilletée *f*. **puffy** *adj* boursouflé.
pull (pul) *n* coup *m*. *vt,vi* tirer. **pull a face** faire une grimace. **pull down** démolir. **pull off** enlever. **pull oneself together** se reprendre. **pull out 1** arracher. **2** sortir. **pull up 1** remonter. **2** arrêter. **pullover** *n* pull *m*.
pulley ('puli) *n* poulie *f*.
pulp (pʌlp) *n* pulpe *f*. *vt* réduire en pulpe, décortiquer.
pulpit ('pʌlpit) *n* chaire *f*.
pulsate (pʌl'seit) *vi* **1** (of the heart) battre. **2** palpiter.
pulse (pʌls) *n* pouls *m*. *vi* battre, vibrer.
pulverize ('pʌlvəraiz) *vt* pulvériser.
pump (pʌmp) *n* pompe *f*. *vt* **1** pomper. **2** *sl* tirer les vers du nez de.
pumpkin ('pʌmpkin) *n* citrouille *f*.
pun (pʌn) *n* jeu de mots *m*.
punch[1] (pʌntʃ) *n* coup de poing *m*. *vt* donner un coup de poing à.
punch[2] (pʌntʃ) *n* (drink) punch *m*.
punch[3] (pʌntʃ) *vt* percer. *n* poinçon *m*.
punctual ('pʌŋktʃuəl) *adj* ponctuel, -elle, exact. **punctuality** *n* ponctualité *f*.
punctuate ('pʌŋktʃueit) *vt* ponctuer. **punctuation** *n* ponctuation *f*.
puncture ('pʌŋktʃə) *n* crevaison, perforation *f*. *vt* **1** crever. **2** ponctionner.
pungent ('pʌndʒənt) *adj* **1** âcre, fort. **2** mordant. **pungency** *n* **1** aigreur *f*. **2** saveur *f*.
punish ('pʌniʃ) *vt* punir, châtier. **punishment** *n* punition *f*. châtiment *m*. **capital punishment** *n* peine capitale *f*.
punt[1] (pʌnt) *n* bateau plat *m*. *vt* conduire à la perche.
punt[2] (pʌnt) *vi game* ponter. **punter** *n* joueur *m*.
pupil[1] ('pju:pəl) *n* élève *m,f*. écolier, -ière.
pupil[2] ('pju:pəl) *n anat* pupille *f*.
puppet ('pʌpit) *n* **1** marionnette *f*. **2** (person) pantin *m*.
puppy ('pʌpi) *n* jeune chien, chiot *m*.
purchase ('pə:tʃis) *vt* acheter. *n* achat *m*.
pure (pjuə) *adj* pur. **purity** *n* pureté *f*.
purgatory ('pə:gətri) *n* purgatoire *m*.
purge (pə:dʒ) *vt* purger, purifier. *n* purge *f*.
purify ('pjuərifai) *vt* purifier, épurer.
Puritan ('pjuəritən) *adj,n* puritain.
purl (pə:l) *vt* faire des mailles à l'envers.
purple ('pə:pəl) *adj,n* pourpre *f*.
purpose ('pə:pəs) *n* dessein, but *m*. fin *f*. **on purpose** exprès. **purposely** *adv* **1** à dessein. **2** exprès.
purr (pə:) *vi* ronronner. *n* ronron *m*.
purse (pə:s) *n* porte-monnaie *m invar*. bourse *f*.
pursue (pə'sju:) *vt,vi* poursuivre. **pursuit** *n* **1** poursuite *f*. **2** recherche *f*.
pus (pʌs) *n* pus *m*. sanie *f*.
push (puʃ) *vt,vi* pousser. *vt* **1** appuyer. **2** bousculer. *n* poussée *f*. **at a push** au besoin. **pushchair** *n* poussette *f*.
pussy ('pusi) *n* minet, chaton *m*.
put* (put) *vt* mettre, poser, placer. **put back 1** remettre. **2** retarder. **put down 1** déposer. **2** noter. **3** attribuer. **put forward** avancer. **put off** différer. **put on** mettre. **put out 1** éteindre. **2** déconcerter. **3** tendre. **put up 1** construire. **2** hausser. **put up with** supporter.
putrid ('pju:trid) *adj* putride.
putt (pʌt) *n* coup roulé *m*. *vt* poter. **putting green** *n* vert *m*.
putty ('pʌti) *n* mastic *m*.
puzzle ('pʌzəl) *n* **1** devinette, énigme *f*. **2** puzzle *m*. *vt* intriguer.
PVC *n* PCV *m*.
Pygmy ('pigmi) *n* pygmée *m*.
pyjamas (pə'dʒɑ:məz) *n pl* pyjama *m*.
pylon ('pailən) *n* pylône *m*.
pyramid ('pirəmid) *n* pyramide *f*.
Pyrenees (pirə'ni:z) *n pl* Pyrénées *f pl*.
Pyrex ('paireks) *n Tdmk* pyrex *m*.
python ('paiθən) *n* python *m*.

Q

quack[1] (kwæk) *n* couin-couin *m*. *vi* faire couin-couin.
quack[2] (kwæk) *n* charlatan *m*.
quadrangle ('kwɔdræŋgəl) *n* **1** *math* quadrilatère *m*. **2** cour *f*.
quadrant ('kwɔdrənt) *n* quadrant *m*.
quadrilateral (kwɔdri'lætərəl) *adj,n* quadrilatère *m*.
quadruped ('kwɔdruped) *adj,n* quadrupède *m*.
quadruple ('kwɔdrupəl) *adj* quadruple. *vt* quadrupler.
quadruplet ('kwɔdruplit) *n* quadruplé *m*.
quail[1] (kweil) *n* caille *f*.
quail[2] (kweil) *vi* fléchir, faiblir.
quaint (kweint) *adj* **1** étrange, bizarre. **2** pittoresque, de l'ancienne mode.
quake (kweik) *vi* **1** trembler. **2** frémir.
Quaker ('kweikə) *n* quaker *m*.
qualify ('kwɔlifai) *vt* **1** qualifier. **2** modifier. *vi* se qualifier, acquérir les connaissances nécessaires. **qualification** *n* **1** capacité *f*. **2** restriction *f*. **3** *pl* titres *m pl*.
quality ('kwɔliti) *n* qualité *f*
qualm (kwa:m) *n* remords, scrupule *m*.
quandary ('kwɔndəri) *n* embarras *m*. **be in a quandary** se trouver dans une impasse.
quantify ('kwɔntifai) *vt* quantifier.
quantity ('kwɔntiti) *n* quantité *f*.
quarantine ('kwɔrənti:n) *n* quarantaine *f*. *vt* mettre en quarantaine.
quarrel ('kwɔrəl) *vi* se disputer. *n* querelle, dispute *f*. **quarrelsome** *adj* querelleur, -euse.
quarry[1] ('kwɔri) *n min* carrière *f*. *vt* extraire.
quarry[2] ('kwɔri) *n* proie *f*. gibier *m*.
quart (kwɔ:t) *n* quart de gallon *m*.
quarter ('kwɔ:tə) *n* **1** quart *m*. **2** quartier *m*. **3** trimestre *m*. **quarter past four** quatre heures et quart. **quarter to four** quatre heures moins le quart. ~*vt* **1** diviser en quatre. **2** *mil* caserner. **quarterdeck** *n* gaillard d'arrière *m*. *m*. **quartermaster** *n* maître de timonerie *m*. **quarterly** *adj* trimestriel, -elle.
quartet (kwɔ:'tet) *n* quatuor *m*.
quartz (kwɔ:ts) *n* quartz *m*.
quash[1] (kwɔʃ) *vt* étouffer.
quash[2] (kwɔʃ) *vt law* annuler.
quaver ('kweivə) *n* **1** *mus* croche *f*. **2** tremblement *m*. *vi* trembloter.
quay (ki:) *n* quai *m*.
queasy ('kwi:zi) *adj* délicat, barbouillé.
queen (kwi:n) *n* **1** reine *f*. **2** *game* dame *f*. **queen mother** *n* reine-mère *f*.
queer (kwiə) *adj* **1** bizarre, singulier, -ière. **2** suspect. **3** *sl* homosexuel, -elle. *n sl* homosexuel *m*.
quell (kwel) *vt* **1** étouffer. **2** vaincre. **3** calmer.
quench (kwentʃ) *vt* apaiser, éteindre.
query ('kwiəri) *n* **1** question *f*. **2** point d'interrogation *m*. *vt* mettre en question. **query whether** s'informer si.
quest (kwest) *n* quête, recherche *f*.
question ('kwestʃən) *n* question *f*. *vt* questionner. **question mark** *n* point d'interrogation *m*. **questionable** *adj* discutable. **questionnaire** *n* questionnaire *m*.
queue (kju:) *n* queue *f*. *vi* faire la queue.
quibble ('kwibəl) *n* chicane. *vi* chicaner.
quick (kwik) *adj* **1** vite, rapide. **2** vif, vive. *n* vif *m*. **quicksand** *n* sable mouvant *m*. **quicksilver** *n* mercure, vif-argent *m*. **quickstep** *n* pas redoublé *m*. **quick-tempered** *adj* emporté, prompt à la colère. **quick-witted** *adj* d'un esprit vif. **quicken** *vt* **1** stimuler. **2** accélerer. *vi* s'animer. **quickly** *adv* vite, rapidement.
quid (kwid) *n invar inf* livre sterling *f*.
quiet[1] ('kwaiət) *n* tranquillité *f*. repos *m*.
quiet[2] ('kwaiət) *adj* **1** tranquille. **2** (of behaviour, etc.) discret, -ète. **quieten** *vt* **1** apaiser, calmer. **2** faire taire. **quieten down** se calmer. **quietly** *adv* silencieusement, doucement. **quietness** *n* tranquillité *f*.
quill (kwil) *n* tuyau, -aux *m*. plume *f*.
quilt (kwilt) *n* couverture piquée *f*. *vt* piquer, ouater. **quilting** *n* piquage *m*.
quince (kwins) *n* coing *m*.
quinine (kwi'ni:n) *n* quinine *f*.
quintessence (kwin'tesəns) *n* quintessence *f*.
quintet (kwin'tet) *n* quintette *m*.
quirk (kwə:k) *n* faux-fuyant *m*.
quit* (kwit) *vt* **1** quitter. **2** cesser. *vi* **1** démissionner. **2** s'en aller. **quits** *adj* quitte.
quite (kwait) *adv* **1** tout à fait, bien. **2** assez.
quiver[1] ('kwivə) *vi* trembler, tressaillir. *n* tremblement, frisson *m*.
quiver[2] ('kwivə) *n* (for arrows) carquois *m*.
quiz (kwiz) *n, pl* **quizzes** devinette *f*. *vt* interroger, poser des colles à.
quizzical ('kwizikəl) *adj* railleur, -euse.
quoit (kɔit) *n* palet *m*.
quota ('kwoutə) *n* quote-part, quotité *f*.
quote (kwout) *vt* **1** citer. **2** *comm* établir. *n*

citation *f.* **quotation** *n* citation *f.* **quotation marks** *n pl* guillemets *m pl.*

R

rabbi ('ræbai) *n* rabbin *m.*
rabbit ('ræbit) *n* lapin *m.*
rabble ('ræbəl) *n* cohue, foule *f.*
rabies ('reibi:z) *n* rage *f.* **rabid** *adj* enragé, féroce.
race[1] (reis) *n* course *f.* *vt* faire courir. *vi* faire une course. **racecourse** *n* champ de courses *m.* **racehorse** *n* cheval de course *m.*
race[2] (reis) *n* (of people) race *f.* **race relations** *n pl* relations raciales *f pl.* **racial** *adj* de race. **racialism** *n* racisme *m.*
rack (ræk) *n* **1** râtelier *m.* **2** classeur *m.* **3** filet *m.* **4** roue *f.* **be on the rack** être au supplice. ~*vt* tourmenter. **rack one's brains** se creuser la tête.
racket[1] ('rækit) *n inf* **1** vacarme, tapage *m.* **2** combine, escroquerie *f.*
racket[2] ('rækit) *n sport* raquette *f.*
radar ('reidɑ:) *n* radar *m.*
radial ('reidiəl) *adj* radial, -aux.
radiant ('reidiənt) *adj* rayonnant, radieux, -euse. **radiance** *n* rayonnement *m.* splendeur *f.*
radiate ('reidieit) *vt,vi* émettre. *vi* rayonner. **radiation** *n* irradiation *f.* **radiator** *n* radiateur *m.*
radical ('rædikəl) *adj,n* radical, -aux.
radio ('reidiou) *n* radio *f.* *vt* envoyer par radio.
radioactivity (reidiouæk'tiviti) *n* radio-activité *f.* **radioactive** *adj* radio-actif, -ive.
radish ('rædiʃ) *n* radis *m.*
radium ('reidiəm) *n* radium *m.*
radius ('reidiəs) *n pl* **-dii** *or* **-diuses** rayon *m.*
raffia ('ræfiə) *n* raphia *m.*
raffle ('ræfəl) *n* loterie *f.* *vt* mettre en loterie.
raft (rɑ:ft) *n* radeau, -aux *m.*
rafter ('rɑ:ftə) *n* chevron *m.*
rag[1] (ræg) *n* **1** chiffon, lambeau, -aux *m.* **2** *pl* haillons *m pl.* **ragged** *adj* en lambeaux, en loques.
rag[2] (ræg) *vt inf* chahuter, brimer.
rage (reidʒ) *n* **1** rage, fureur *f.* **2** manie *f.* **be all the rage** être du dernier cri. ~*vi* rager, être furieux.
raid (reid) *n* rafle *f.* *vt* faire une rafle, marauder.
rail (reil) *n* **1** barre, rampe *f.* barreau, -aux *m.* **2** (railway) rail *m.* **railing** *n* grille *f.* garde-fou *m.* **railway** *n* chemin de fer *m.* **railway station** *n* gare *f.*
rain (rein) *n* pluie *f.* *vt,vi* pleuvoir. **rainbow** *n* arc-en-ciel *m.* **raindrop** *n* goutte de pluie *f.* **rainfall** *n* chute de pluie, précipitation *f.*
raise (reiz) *vt* **1** dresser. **2** lever. **3** hausser. **4** soulever.
raisin ('reizən) *n* raisin sec *m.*
rajah ('rɑ:dʒə) *n* raja *m.*
rake (reik) *n* râteau, -aux *m.* *vt* ratisser, râteler.
rally ('ræli) *n* **1** ralliement *m.* **2** *mot* rallye *m.* *vt* rallier. *vi* se rallier, se reprendre.
ram (ræm) *n* bélier *m.* *vt* pilonner, battre. éperonner.
ramble ('ræmbəl) *vi* **1** flâner, errer. **2** parler sans suite. *n* **1** promenade *f.* **2** randonnée *f.*
ramp (ræmp) *n* rampe *f.*
rampage ('ræmpeidʒ) *n* **be on the rampage** en avoir après tout le monde.
rampant ('ræmpənt) *adj* rampant, forcené. **be rampant** sévir.
rampart ('ræmpɑ:t) *n* rempart *m.*
ramshackle ('ræmʃækəl) *adj* délabré.
ran (ræn) *v* see **run.**
ranch (rɑ:ntʃ) *n* ranch *m.* ferme d'élevage *f.*
rancid ('rænsid) *adj* rance. **turn rancid** rancir.
rancour ('ræŋkə) *n* rancune *f.*
random ('rændəm) *adj* fait au hasard. **at random** au hasard, à tort et à travers.
rang (ræŋ) *v* see **ring**[2]**.**
range (reindʒ) *n* **1** gamme *f.* **2** étendue *f.* **3** distance *f.* **4** *geog* chaîne *f.* **5** champ de tir *m.* **6** *cul* fourneau, -aux *m.* *vt* ranger. *vi* **1** parcourir. **2** s'étendre.
rank[1] (ræŋk) *n* rang *m.* *vt* compter. *vi* se classer, se ranger. **rank and file** *n* hommes de troupe *m pl.*
rank[2] (ræŋk) *adj* **1** (trop) luxuriant. **2** rance, fétide.
rankle ('ræŋkəl) *vi* s'envenimer, s'irriter.
ransack ('rænsæk) *vt* **1** fouiller. **2** saccager.
ransom ('rænsəm) *n* rançon *f.* *vt* racheter, rançonner.
rap (ræp) *vt,vi* frapper. *n* petit coup sec *m.*
rape (reip) *n* viol *m.* *vt* violer.
rapid ('ræpid) *adj,n* rapide *m.* **rapidity** *n* rapidité *f.*
rapier ('reipiə) *n* rapière *f.*
rapture ('ræptʃə) *n* extase *m.*
rare[1] (rɛə) *adj* rare, peu commun. **rareness** *n* rareté *f.*
rare[2] (rɛə) *adj cul* saignant.
rascal ('rɑ:skəl) *n* polisson *m.*

rash[1] (ræʃ) *adj* téméraire. **rashness** *n* témérité *f*.
rash[2] (ræʃ) *n med* éruption *f*.
rasher ('ræʃə) *n* tranche *f*.
raspberry ('rɑ:zbri) *n* framboise *f*. **raspberry cane** *n* framboisier *m*.
rat (ræt) *n* rat *m*.
rate (reit) *n* **1** taux *f*. **2** cours *m*. **3** proportion *f*. **4** vitesse *f*. **5** *pl* impôts locaux *m pl*. **at any rate** en tout cas. ~*vt* évaluer, classer. **ratepayer** *n* contribuable *m*.
rather ('rɑ:ðə) *adv* **1** plutôt. **2** un peu, assez.
ratio ('reiʃiou) *n* rapport *m*. proportion *f*.
ration ('ræʃən) *n* ration *f*. *vt* rationner. **rationing** *n* rationnement *m*.
rational ('ræʃənəl) *adj* raisonnable, raisonné. **rationalize** *vt* rationaliser.
rattle ('rætl) *vi* cliqueter, faire du bruit. *vt* agiter, faire cliqueter. *n* **1** fracas, cliquetis *m*. **2** (toy) hochet *m*.
raucous ('rɔ:kəs) *adj* rauque.
ravage ('rævidʒ) *vt* ravager, dévaster.
rave (reiv) *vi* être en délire. **rave about** s'extasier sur. **raving** *adj* furieux, -euse. *n* délire *m*.
raven ('reivən) *n* corbeau, -aux *m*.
ravenous ('rævənəs) *adj* vorace.
ravine (rə'vi:n) *n* ravin *m*. ravine *f*.
ravish ('ræviʃ) *vt* ravir, enlever.
raw (rɔ:) *adj* **1** cru, brut. **2** sans expérience. **3** *med* à vif.
ray (rei) *n* rayon *m*. lueur *f*.
rayon ('reiɔn) *n* rayonne *f*.
razor ('reizə) *n* rasoir *m*. **razor blade** *n* lame de rasoir *f*.
reach (ri:tʃ) *vt* **1** arriver à. **2** atteindre. **3** tendre. *vi* s'élever. **reach out** s'étendre. ~*n* **1** portée *f*. **2** *sport* allonge *f*.
react (ri'ækt) *vi* réagir. **reaction** *n* réaction *f*. **reactionary** *adj,n* réactionnaire.
read* (ri:d) *vt* **1** lire. **2** *educ* étudier. **reading** *n* lecture *f*.
readjust (ri:ə'dʒʌst) *vt* rajuster. **readjustment** *n* rajustement *m*. rectification *f*.
ready ('redi) *adj* **1** prêt. **2** prompt. **get ready** se préparer. **ready-made** *adj* tout fait. **readily** *adv* volontiers.
real (riəl) *adj* **1** réel, -elle. **2** authentique. **realism** *n* réalisme *m*. **realist** *n* réaliste *m,f*. **realistic** *adj* réaliste. **reality** *n* réalité *f*. **really** *adv* vraiment.
realize ('riəlaiz) *vi* se rendre compte de. *vt* réaliser.
realm (relm) *n* royaume *m*.
reap (ri:p) *vt* moissonner, recueillir.
reappear (ri:ə'piə) *vi* reparaître. **reappearance** *n* réapparition *f*.
rear[1] (riə) *adj* d'arrière, postérieur. *n* arrière, derrière *m*. **rear admiral** *n* contre-amiral *m*. **rearguard** *n* arrière-garde *f*.
rear[2] (riə) *vt* élever, cultiver. *vi* se cabrer.
rearrange (riə'reindʒ) *vt* arranger de nouveau.
reason ('ri:zən) *n* **1** raison *f*. **2** cause *f*. *vi* raisonner. **reasonable** *adj* **1** raisonnable. **2** modéré, abordable. **reasoning** *n* raisonnement *m*.
reassure (ri:ə'ʃuə) *vt* rassurer.
rebate ('ri:beit) *n* **1** *comm* rabais *m*. **2** ristourne *f*.
rebel (*adj,n* 'rebəl; *v* ri'bel) *adj,n* rebelle. *vi* se révolter. **rebellion** *n* révolte *f*. **rebellious** *adj* rebelle.
rebuff (ri'bʌf) *n* rebuffade *f*. échec *m*. *vt* repousser.
rebuild* (ri:'bild) *vt* rebâtir, reconstruire.
rebuke (ri'bju:k) *vt* réprimander. *n* réprimande *f*.
recall (ri'kɔ:l) *vt* **1** rappeler. **2** se souvenir de. *n* **1** mémoire *m*. **2** rappel *m*.
recede (ri'si:d) *vi* **1** reculer, s'éloigner. **2** fuir.
receipt (ri'si:t) *n* **1** *comm* quittance *f*. **2** reçu *m*. *vt* acquitter.
receive (ri'si:v) *vt* recevoir. **receiver** *n* **1** destinataire *m,f*. **2** *law* administrateur judiciaire *m*. **3** (of a telephone) récepteur *m*.
recent ('ri:sənt) *adj* récent. **recently** *adv* récemment.
receptacle (ri'septəkəl) *n* récipient *m*.
reception (ri'sepʃən) *n* **1** réception *f*. **2** accueil *m*. **3** soirée *f*. **receptionist** *n* préposée à la réception *f*. **receptive** *adj* réceptif, -ive.
recess (ri'ses) *n* **1** recoin, renfoncement *m*. **2** alcôve *f*. **3** *pol* vacances *f pl*.
recession (ri'seʃən) *n* **1** recul *m*. régression *f*. **2** *pol* récession *f*.
recipe ('resipi) *n* recette *f*.
recipient (ri'sipiənt) *n* bénéficiaire *m,f*.
reciprocate (ri'siprəkeit) *vt* **1** rendre. **2** payer de retour. *vi* rendre la pareille. **reciprocal** *adj* **1** réciproque, mutuel, -elle. **2** *math* inverse.
recite (ri'sait) *vt* réciter, réclamer. **recital** *n* **1** *mus* audition *f*. récital *m*. **2** narration *f*.
reckless ('rekləs) *adj* insouciant, téméraire, imprudent.
reckon ('rekən) *vt,vi* compter, calculer.
reclaim (ri'kleim) *vt* **1** récupérer. **2** défricher, assécher. **3** corriger.

recline (ri'klain) *vt* reposer, appuyer. *vi* être couché, se reposer.
recluse (ri'klu:s) *n* reclus *m*.
recognize ('rekəgnaiz) *vt* **1** reconnaître. **2** avouer, admettre. **recognition** *n* reconnaissance *f*.
recoil (ri'kɔil) *vi* **1** reculer. **2** se détendre. *n* **1** recul *m*. **2** mouvement de dégoût *m*.
recollect (rekə'lekt) *vt* se rappeler, se souvenir de. **recollection** *n* souvenir *m*. mémoire *f*.
recommence (ri:kə'mens) *vt,vi* recommencer.
recommend (rekə'mend) *vt* recommander, conseiller. **recommendation** *n* recommandation *f*.
recompense ('rekəmpəns) *n* **1** récompense *f*. **2** dédommagement *m* *vt* **1** récompenser. **2** réparer. **3** dédommager.
reconcile ('rekənsail) *vt* **1** réconcilier. **2** concilier.
reconstruct (ri:kən'strʌkt) *vt* reconstruire.
record (*n* 'rekɔ:d; *v* ri'kɔ:d) *n* **1** registre *m*. **2** dossier *m*. **3** disque *m*. **4** *sport* record *m*. *vt* **1** enregistrer. **2** rapporter. **record-player** *n* électrophone *m*. tourne-disques *m invar*.
recount (ri'kaunt) *vt* raconter.
recover (ri'kʌvə) *vt* **1** recouvrer, retrouver. **2** rattraper. **3** récupérer. *vi* se rétablir, se remettre. **recovery** *n* **1** guérison *f*. **2** redressement *m*. **3** recouvrement *m*.
recreation (rekri'eiʃən) *n* récréation *f*. divertissement *m*.
recruit (ri'kru:t) *vt* recruter. *n* recrue *f*. conscrit *m*.
rectangle ('rektæŋgəl) *n* rectangle *m*. **rectangular** *adj* rectangulaire.
rectify ('rektifai) *vt* rectifier, réparer.
recuperate (ri'kju:pəreit) *vt* remettre, récupérer. *vi* se remettre.
recur (ri'kə:) *vi* revenir. **recurrence** *n* **1** réapparition *f*. **2** *med* récidive *f*. **recurring** *adj* récidive.
red (red) *adj,n* rouge *m*. **turn red** rougir. **redcurrant** *n* groseille rouge *f*. **red-handed** *adj* sur le fait, en flagrant délit. **red herring** *n* **1** hareng saur *m*. **2** diversion *f*.
redeem (ri'di:m) *vt* **1** racheter. **2** rembourser. **3** dégager.
redevelop (ri:di'veləp) *vt* redévelopper.
Red Indian *n* peau rouge *m*.
redress (ri'dres) *n* redressement *m*. réparation *f*. *vt* **1** rétablir. **2** réparer.
reduce (ri'dju:s) *vt* **1** réduire. **2** rabaisser. **reduction** *n* **1** réduction *f*. **2** baisse *f*. **3** rabais *m*.
redundant (ri'dʌndənt) *adj* **1** surabondant, superflu. **2** en surnombre.
reed (ri:d) *n* roseau, -aux *m*.
reef (ri:f) *n* récif, banc *m*.
reek (ri:k) *vt* exhaler une mauvaise odeur, puer. *n* odeur âcre *f*.
reel[1] (ri:l) *n* **1** bobine *f*. **2** moulinet *m*.
reel[2] (ri:l) *vi* chanceler, tituber.
re-establish (ri:i'stæbliʃ) *vt* rétablir.
refectory (ri'fektəri) *n* réfectoire *m*.
refer (ri'fə:) *vt* **1** rapporter. **2** renvoyer. **3** s'en référer. *vi* **1** s'en rapporter. **2** se référer, faire allusion. **referee** *n* arbitre *m*. **reference** *n* **1** renvoi *m*. référence *f*. **2** rapport *m*. **3** allusion *f*. **4** recommandation *f*. **referendum** *n* référendum *m*.
refill (*v* ri:'fil; *n* 'ri:fil) *vt* remplir, regarnir. *n* recharge, cartouche *f*.
refine (ri'fain) *vt* raffiner, affiner. *vi* se raffiner. **refinement** *n* **1** affinage, raffinage *m*. **2** raffinement *m*. **refinery** *n* raffinerie *f*.
reflation (ri'fleiʃən) *n pol* nouvelle inflation, reprise *f*.
reflect (ri'flekt) *vt* réfléchir, refléter. *vi* méditer. **reflection** *n* **1** réflexion *f*. **2** reflet *m*. **reflector** *n* réflecteur *m*.
reflex ('ri:fleks) *n* **1** reflet *m*. **2** réflexe *m*. **reflexive** *adj* réfléchi.
reform (ri'fɔ:m) *n* réforme *f*. *vt* réformer. *vi* se réformer. **reformation** *n* réformation, réforme *f*.
refract (ri'frækt) *vt* réfracter.
refrain[1] (ri'frein) *vi* s'abstenir, s'empêcher.
refrain[2] (ri'frein) *n* refrain *m*.
refresh (ri'freʃ) *vt* rafraîchir. *vi* se rafraîchir, se restaurer. **refreshment** *n* rafraîchissement *m*.
refrigerator (ri'fridʒəreitə) *n* réfrigérateur *m*.
refuel (ri:'fju:əl) *vi* se réapprovisionner, faire le plein d'essence.
refuge ('refju:dʒ) *n* **1** refuge, abri *m*. **2** asile *m*. **take refuge** se réfugier. **refugee** *n* réfugié *m*.
refund (*v* ri'fʌnd; *n* 'ri:fʌnd) *vt* rembourser, rendre. *n* remboursement *m*.
refuse[1] (ri'fju:z) *vt* **1** refuser. **2** rejeter. **refusal** *n* refus *m*.
refuse[2] ('refju:s) *n* déchets *m pl*. ordures *f pl*. rebut *m*. *adj* de rebut.
refute (ri'fju:t) *vt* réfuter.
regain (ri'gein) *vt* **1** regagner, reconquérir. **2** reprendre.

regal ('ri:gəl) *adj* royal, -aux.
regard (ri'gɑ:d) *n* **1** égard *m*. **2** considération *f*. respect *m*. **3** *pl* amitiés *f pl*. *vt* **1** considérer. **2** concerner. **regarding** *prep* quant à. **regardless** *adj* **1** insouciant. **2** inattentif,-ive. **regardless of** sans regarder à.
regatta (ri'gɑ:tə) *n* régates *f pl*.
regent ('ri:dʒənt) *adj,n* régent *m*.
regime (rei'ʒi:m) *n* régime *m*.
regiment ('redʒimənt) *n* régiment *m*. *vt* **1** enrégimenter. **2** organiser. **regimental** *adj* régimentaire.
region ('ri:dʒən) *n* région *f*.
register ('redʒistə) *n* **1** registre *m*. **2** compteur *m*. *vt* **1** enregistrer, inscrire. **2** (a letter) recommander. **registrar** *n* **1** officier d'etat civil *m*. **2** *educ* secrétaire *m*. **registration** *n* enregistrement *m*. inscription, immatriculation *f*.
regress (ri'gres) *vi* régresser. *n* retour en arrière *m*. **regression** *n* retour *m*.
regret (ri'gret) *n* regret *m*. *vt* regretter.
regular ('regjulə) *adj* **1** régulier, -ière. **2** rangé. **3** réglementaire. **4** habituel, -elle. **5** véritable. **regularity** *n* régularité *f*.
regulate ('regjuleit) *vt* régler. **regulation** *n* règlement *m*. *adj* réglementaire.
rehabilitate (ri:ə'biliteit) *vt* **1** réhabiliter. **2** réadapter. **rehabilitation** *n* **1** réhabilitation *f*. **2** rééducation *f*.
rehearse (ri'hɔ:s) *vt* répéter. **rehearsal** *n* répétition *f*.
reheat (ri:'hi:t) *vt* réchauffer.
reign (rein) *vi* régner. *n* règne.
reimburse (ri:im'bɔ:s) *vt* rembourser.
rein (rein) *n* rêne, guide *f*.
reincarnation (ri:inkɑ:'neiʃən) *n* réincarnation *f*.
reindeer ('reindiə) *n* renne *m*.
reinforce (ri:in'fɔ:s) *vt* **1** renforcer. **2** consolider. **reinforcement** *n* **1** renforcement *m*. **2** *pl* renforts *m pl*.
reinstate (ri:in'steit) *vt* **1** réintégrer. **2** rétablir.
reinvest (ri:in'vest) *vt* replacer.
reissue (ri:'iʃu:) *n* **1** nouvelle émission *f*. **2** (of a book) nouvelle édition *f*. *vt* **1** émettre de nouveau. **2** donner une nouvelle édition.
reject (*v* ri'dʒekt; *n* 'ri:dʒekt) *n* pièce de rebut *f*. *vt* **1** rejeter, repousser. **2** refuser. **rejection** *n* **1** rejet *m*. **2** refus *m*.
rejoice (ri'dʒɔis) *vt* réjouir. *vi* se réjouir.
rejuvenate (ri'dʒu:vəneit) *vt* rajeunir.
relapse (ri'læps) *n* **1** récidive *f*. **2** *med* rechute *f*. *vi* **1** retomber, récidiver. **2** *med* faire une rechute.
relate (ri'leit) *vt* raconter. *vi* se rapporter, avoir rapport. **related** *adj* apparenté.
relation (ri'leiʃən) *n* **1** relation *f*. récit *m*. **2** rapport *m*. **3** parent *m*. **relationship** *n* **1** parenté *f*. **2** rapport *m*.
relative ('relətiv) *adj* relatif, -ive. *n* parent *m*. **relativity** *n* relativité *f*.
relax (ri'læks) *vt* **1** relâcher, détendre. **2** mitiger. *vi* se relâcher, se décontracter. **relaxation** *n* **1** relâchement *m*. **2** mitigation *f*. **3** détente *f*.
relay (*n* 'ri:lei; *v* ri'lei) *n* relais *m*. *vt* **1** relayer. **2** transmettre.
release (ri'li:s) *n* **1** décharge, libération *f*. **2** échappement, dégagement *m*. **3** relâche *f*. *vt* **1** acquitter, libérer. **2** dégager, émettre.
relent (ri'lent) *vi* se radoucir, céder.
relevant ('reləvənt) *adj* pertinent, à propos, en rapport. **relevance** *n* pertinence *f*. rapport *m*.
reliable (ri'laiəbəl) *adj* **1** sûr, sérieux, -euse. **2** solide. **reliability** *n* sûreté, régularité *f*.
relic ('relik) *n* **1** relique *f*. **2** *pl* vestiges, restes *m pl*.
relief (ri'li:f) *n* **1** soulagement *m*. **2** secours *m*. **3** *Art* relief *m*.
relieve (ri'li:v) *vt* **1** soulager, alléger. **2** secourir, aider. **3** débarrasser. **4** faire ressortir.
religion (ri'lidʒən) *n* religion *f*. culte *m*. **religious** *adj* **1** religieux, -euse. **2** scrupuleux, -euse.
relinquish (ri'liŋkwish) *vt* **1** abandonner, renoncer. **2** lâcher.
relish ('reliʃ) *n* gôut *m*. saveur *f*. *vt* **1** relever. **2** savourer, aimer.
relive (ri:'liv) *vt* revivre.
reluctant (ri'lʌktənt) *adj* peu disposé. **reluctance** *n* répugnance *f*. **reluctantly** *adv* à contre-cœur.
rely (ri'lai) *vi* **rely on** compter sur, se fier à.
remain (ri'mein) *vi* **1** rester. **2** demeurer. **remainder** *n* reste, restant *m*. **remains** *n pl* restes, vestiges *m pl*.
remand (ri'mɑ:nd) *vt* renvoyer à une autre audience. *n* renvoi *m*.
remark (ri'mɑ:k) *n* **1** observation *f*. commentaire *m*. **2** remarque *f*. *vt* observer, remarquer. *vi* faire une remarque. **remarkable** *adj* remarquable, frappant.
remarry (ri:'mæri) *vi* se remarier.
remedy ('remədi) *n* remède *m*. *vt* remédier à.
remember (ri'membə) *vt* se rappeler, se sou-

venir de. **remembrance** *n* souvenir *m*. mémoire *f*.

remind (ri'maind) *vt* rappeler, faire penser. **reminder** *n* 1 mémento *m*. 2 *comm* rappel *m*.

reminiscence (remi'nisəns) *n* réminiscence *f*. souvenir *m*. **reminiscent** *adj* 1 qui se souvient. 2 qui rapelle.

remiss (ri'mis) *adj* 1 négligent, insouciant. 2 inexact, lâche.

remission (ri'miʃən) *n* pardon *m*. rémission *f*.

remit (ri'mit) *vt* remettre. **remittance** *n* remise *f*. envoi de fonds *m*.

remnant ('remnənt) *n* 1 reste, restant *m*. 2 (of material) coupon *m*.

remorse (ri'mɔ:s) *n* remords *m*.

remote (ri'mout) *adj* 1 éloigné, reculé. 2 loin, lointain. 3 vague. 4 distant.

remove (ri'mu:v) *vt* 1 enlever, écarter. 2 déplacer. 3 déménager. **removal** *n* 1 enlèvement *m*. 2 déplacement *m*. 3 déménagement *m*.

remunerate (ri'mju:nəreit) *vt* rémunérer. **remuneration** *n* rémunération *f*. **remunerative** *adj* rémunérateur, -trice.

renaissance (ri'neisəns) *n* renaissance *f*.

rename (ri:'neim) *vt* débaptiser.

render ('rendə) *vt* 1 rendre. 2 remettre. 3 *cul* fondre.

renew (ri'nju:) *vt* 1 renouveler. 2 remplacer. *vi* se renouveler. **renewal** *n* 1 renouvellement *m*. 2 remplacement *m*.

renounce (ri'nauns) *vt* 1 renoncer. 2 renier, dénoncer. **renunciation** *n* renoncement *m*. renonciation *f*.

renovate ('renəveit) *vt* rénover, remettre à neuf. **renovation** *n* rénovation *f*.

renown (ri'naun) *n* renommée *f*. renom *m*. **renowned** *adj* célèbre.

rent (rent) *n* loyer *m*. location *f*. *vt* louer, affermer. **rental** *n* loyer *m*. location *f*.

reopen (ri:'oupən) *vt* 1 rouvrir. 2 reprendre. *vi* 1 se rouvrir. 2 rentrer.

reorganize (ri:'ɔ:gənaiz) *vt* réorganiser. *vi* se réorganiser. **reorganization** *n* réorganisation *f*.

repair (ri'pɛə) *vt* réparer, réfectionner. *n* réparation *f*. rétablissement *m*.

repartee (repə'ti:) *n* répartie, riposte *f*.

repatriate (ri'pætrieit) *vt* rapatrier. *n* rapatrié *m*. **repatriation** *n* rapatriement *m*.

repay* (ri'pei) *vt* 1 rendre, rembourser. 2 récompenser, s'acquitter envers. **repayment** *n* 1 remboursement *m*. 2 récompense *f*.

repeal (ri'pi:l) *vt* 1 rapporter, abroger. 2 révoquer. *n* abrogation, révocation *f*.

repeat (ri'pi:t) *vt* répéter, réitérer. *vi* 1 se répéter. 2 donner des renvois. *n* 1 répétition *f*. 2 *mus* reprise *f*.

repel (ri'pel) *vt* 1 repousser. 2 répugner à. **repellent** *adj* 1 répulsif, -ive. 2 repoussant.

repent (ri'pent) *vi* se repentir. *vt* se repentir de. **repentance** *n* repentir *m*.

repercussion (ri:pə'kʌʃən) *n* 1 répercussion *f*. 2 résonnance *f*.

repertoire ('repətwa:) *n* répertoire *m*.

repertory ('repətri) *n* répertoire *m*. **repertory theatre** *n* théâtre de province *m*.

repetition (repə'tiʃən) *n* répétition *f*.

replace (ri'pleis) *vt* 1 replacer, remettre. 2 remplacer.

replay (*v* ri:'plei; *n* 'ri:plei) *v* rejouer. *n* match rejoué *m*.

replenish (ri'pleniʃ) *vt* remplir, se réapprovisionner.

replica ('replikə) *n* 1 reproduction, copie *f*. 2 double *m*.

reply (ri'plai) *n* réponse *f*. *vt,vi* répondre.

report (re'pɔ:t) *n* 1 rapport, compte rendu *m*. 2 nouvelle *f*. 3 *educ* bulletin *m*. 4 *mil* détonation *f*. *vt* 1 rapporter, rendre compte de. 2 signaler. **reporter** *n* journaliste *m,f*.

repose (ri'pouz) *n* repos, calme *m*. *vi* se délasser.

represent (repri'zent) *vt* représenter. **representation** *n* représentation *f*. **representative** *adj* représentatif, -ive. *n* représentant *m*.

repress (ri'pres) *vt* 1 réprimer. 2 étouffer. **repression** *n* répression *f*.

reprieve (ri'pri:v) *vt* 1 grâcier. 2 donner un répit à. *n* 1 grâce *f*. 2 sursis, répit *m*.

reprimand ('reprima:nd) *n* réprimande *f*. *vt* réprimander.

reprint (*v* ri:'print; *n* 'ri:print) *vt* réimprimer. *n* réimpression *f*. nouveau tirage *m*.

reprisal (ri'praizəl) *n* représaille *f*.

reproach (ri'proutʃ) *n* reproche, blâme *m*. *vt* reprocher à.

reproduce (ri:prə'dju:s) *vt* reproduire. *vi* se reproduire. **reproduction** *n* 1 reproduction *f*. 2 copie, imitation *f*.

reptile ('reptail) *n* reptile *m*.

republic (ri'pʌblik) *n* république *f*. **republican** *adj,n* républicain.

repudiate (ri'pju:dieit) *vt* répudier. **repudiation** *n* répudiation *f*.

repugnant (ri'pʌgnənt) *adj* répugnant.

repulsion (ri'pʌlʃən) *n* répulsion, répugnance *f*. **repulsive** *adj* repoussant, répugnant.

repute (ri'pjuːt) *n* réputation, renommée *f*. *vt* estimer. **reputable** *adj* honorable, estimable. **reputation** *n* réputation *f*. renom *m*. **reputed** *adj* censé, supposé.

request (ri'kwest) *n* demande, requête *f*. *vt* demander, prier.

requiem ('rekwiəm) *n* **1** requiem *m*. **2** chant funèbre *m*.

require (ri'kwaiə) *vt* **1** demander, exiger. **2** avoir besoin de, falloir. **requirement** *n* **1** besoin *m*. **2** demande *f*.

re-read (riː'riːd) *vt* relire.

re-run (riː'rʌn) *vt* **1** recourir. **2** recommencer. *n* répétition d'un film *f*.

resale ('riːseil) *n* revente *f*.

rescue ('reskjuː) *n* délivrance *f*. sauvetage *m*. *vt* sauver, delivrer, secourir.

research (ri'səːtʃ) *n* recherche *f*. *vi* faire des recherches.

resell* (riː'sel) *vt* revendre.

resemble (ri'zembəl) *vt* ressembler à. **resemblance** *n* ressemblance, similarité *f*.

resent (ri'zent) *vt* s'offenser de, ressentir. **resentful** *adj* rancunier, -ière. **resentment** *n* ressentiment *m*.

reserve (ri'zəːv) *n* **1** réserve *f*. **2** prix minimum *m*. **3** terrain réservé *m*. *vt* réserver. **reservation** *n* **1** réserve *f*. **2** location, place retenue *f*. **reserved** *adj* **1** réservé. **2** renfermé.

reservoir ('rezəvwɑː) *n* réservoir *m*.

reside (ri'zaid) *vi* résider. **residence** *n* résidence, demeure *f*. **resident** *n* **1** pensionnaire *m,f*. habitant *m*. **2** résident *m*. *adj* résidant.

residue ('rezidjuː) *n* résidu *m*.

resign (ri'zain) *vt* donner sa démission de, résigner. *vi* démissionner. **resignation** *n* **1** démission *f*. **2** résignation *f*.

resilient (ri'ziliənt) *adj* **1** rebondissant, élastique. **2** qui a du ressort. **resilience** *n* **1** élasticité *f*. **2** ressort *m*.

resin ('rezin) *n* résine *f*. *vt* résiner.

resist (ri'zist) *vt* résister à. **resistance** *n* résistance *f*.

resit (riː'sit) *vi* doubler, retenter.

resolute ('rezəluːt) *adj* résolu, déterminé, ferme. **resolutely** *adv* résolument. **resolution** *n* **1** résolution *f*. **2** fermeté *f*.

resolve (ri'zɔlv) *vt* **1** résoudre. **2** décider. *vi* se résoudre. *n* résolution *f*.

resonant ('rezənənt) *adj* résonnant, sonore.

resort (ri'zɔːt) *n* **1** station *f*. séjour *m*. **2** ressource *f*. recours *m*. *vi* avoir recours, user.

resound (ri'zaund) *vi* résonner, retentir.

resource (ri'zɔ's) *n* ressource *f*.

respect (ri'spekt) *n* **1** respect *m*. **2** rapport, égard *m*. **3** *pl* respects, hommages *m pl*. *vt* respecter. **respectable** *adj* **1** convenable. **2** honnête. **3** passable. **respectful** *adj* respectueux, -euse. **respective** *adj* respectif, -ive.

respite ('respit) *n* répit *m*. relâche *f*.

respond (ri'spɔnd) *vi* répondre. **response** *n* réponse *f*. **responsibility** *n* responsabilité *f*. **responsible** *adj* **1** responsable, chargé. **2** compétent, capable. **responsive** *adj* impressionnable, sensible.

rest¹ (rest) *n* **1** repos *m*. **2** support *m*. **3** *mus* pause *f*. *vi* **1** se reposer. **2** se poser, s'appuyer. *vt* **1** reposer. **2** appuyer. **restful** *adj* calme, tranquille. **restive** *adj* **1** rétif, -ive, quinteux, -euse. **2** inquiet, -ète.

rest² (rest) *n* **1** reste, restant *m*. **2** autres *m,f pl*. *vi* rester. **restive** *adj* rétif, ivc.

restaurant ('restərɔnt) *n* restaurant *m*.

restless ('restləs) *adj* agité, inquiet, ète.

restore (ri'stɔː) *vt* **1** restituer. **2** restaurer, réparer. **3** rétablir. **restoration** *n* **1** restitution *f*. **2** restauration *f*.

restrain (ri'strein) *vt* **1** retenir, empêcher. **2** contenir. **restrain oneself** se contraindre. **restraint** *n* **1** contrainte, entrave *f*. **2** réserve *f*.

restrict (ri'strikt) *vt* restreindre, limiter. **restriction** *n* restriction *f*. **restrictive** *adj* restrictif, -ive.

result (ri'zʌlt) *n* **1** résultat *m*. **2** conséquence *f*. *vi* **1** résulter, s'ensuivre. **2** aboutir.

resume (ri'zjuːm) *vt* reprendre. **resumption** *n* reprise *f*.

resurrect (rezə'rekt) *vt* ressusciter. **resurrection** *n* résurrection *f*.

retail ('riːteil) *n* détail *m*. *vt* détailler, vendre au détail.

retain (ri'tein) *vt* **1** retenir, maintenir. **2** conserver. **3** garder.

retaliate (ri'tælieit) *vi* user de représailles. **retaliation** *n* revanche *f*. représailles *f*. *pl*.

retard (ri'tɑːd) *vt* retarder. **retarded** *adj* attardé, arriéré.

reticent ('retisənt) *adj* réticent, taciturne.

retina ('retinə) *n* rétine *f*.

retire (ri'taiə) *vi* **1** se retirer. **2** prendre sa retraite. **3** reculer. *vt* mettre à la retraite. **retirement** *n* **1** retraite *f*. **2** retrait *m*.

retort[1] (ri'tɔ:t) *n* réplique, riposte *f*. *vt* répliquer, riposter.
retort[2] (ri'tɔ:t) *n sci* cornue *f*.
retrace (ri'treis) *vt* **1** reconstituer. **2** revenir sur.
retract (ri'trækt) *vt* **1** rétracter. **2** rentrer. *vi* se rétracter.
retreat (ri'tri:t) *n* retraite *f*. *vi* **1** se retirer, s'éloigner. **2** *mil* battre en retraite.
retrieve (ri'tri:v) *vt* **1** rapporter, retrouver. **2** relever.
retrograde ('retrəgreid) *adj* **1** rétrograde. **2** inverse.
retrogress (retrə'gres) *vi* rétrograder.
retrospect ('retrəspekt) *n* coup d'œil rétrospectif *m*.
return (ri'tə:n) *vi* **1** revenir, rentrer. **2** retourner. *vt* **1** rendre. **2** renvoyer. **3** *pol* élire. *n* **1** retour *m*. **2** renvoi *m*. **3** récompense *f*. **4** échange *f*. **5** profit *m*. **6** *pl* recettes *f pl*. **return ticket** *n* billet d'aller et retour *m*.
reunite (ri:ju:'nait) *vt* réunir. *vi* se réunir.
reveal (ri'vi:l) *vt* **1** révéler. **2** déceler. **revealing** *adj* révélateur, -trice. **revelation** *n* révélation *f*.
revel ('revəl) *vi* se réjouir, se délecter.
revenge (ri'vendʒ) *vt* venger. *n* vengeance *f*.
revenue ('revənju:) *n* revenu, rapport *m*.
reverberate (ri'və:bəreit) *vt* renvoyer, répercuter. *vi* résonner, retentir. **reverberation** *n* **1** renvoi *m*. **2** réverbération *f*.
reverence ('revərəns) *n* révérence, vénération *f*.
reverse (ri'və:s) *adj* inverse, contraire. *n* **1** inverse *m*. **2** revers *m*. **3** marche arrière *f*. *vt* renverser, invertir. *vi* faire marche arrière.
revert (ri'və:t) *vi* revenir, retourner.
review (ri'vju:) *n* **1** revue *f*. **2** examen *m*. **3** revue périodique *f*. **4** critique *f*. *vt* **1** passer en revue. **2** faire la critique de.
revise (ri'vaiz) *vt* **1** revoir, corriger. **2** réviser. **revision** *n* révision *f*.
revive (ri'vaiv) *vi* ressusciter, se ranimer, reprendre. *vt* faire revivre, ranimer. **revival** *n* reprise *f*.
revoke (ri'vouk) *vt* révoquer, retirer.
revolt (ri'voult) *n* révolte *f*. *vi* se révolter, se soulever. *vt* révolter. **revolting** *adj* écœurant, dégoûtant. **revolution** *n* révolution *f*. **revolutionary** *adj* révolutionnaire.
revolve (ri'vɔlv) *vt* tourner. *vt* faire tourner. **revolver** *n* revolver *m*.
revue (ri'vju:) *n* revue *f*.
revulsion (ri'vʌlʃən) *n* **1** revirement *m*. **2** écœurement *m*.
reward (ri'wɔ:d) *n* récompense *f*. *vt* récompenser.
rhetoric ('retərik) *n* rhétorique *f*. **rhetorical** *adj* **1** de rhétorique. **2** ampoulé. **rhetorical question** *n* question pour la forme *f*.
rheumatism ('ru:mətizəm) *n* rhumatisme *m*.
Rhine (rain) *n* Rhin *m*.
rhinoceros (rai'nɔsərəs) *n* rhinocéros *m*.
Rhodesia (rou'di:ʃə) *n* Rhodésie *f*. **Rhodesian** *adj,n* rhodésien, -ienne.
rhododendron (roudə'dendrən) *n* rhododendron *m*.
Rhone (roun) *n* Rhône *m*.
rhubarb ('ru:bɑ:b) *n* rhubarbe *f*.
rhyme (raim) *n* rime *f*. *vi* rimer.
rhythm ('riðəm) *n* rythme *m*.
rib (rib) *n* côte *f*.
ribbon ('ribən) *n* ruban *m*.
rice (rais) *n* riz *m*. **rice pudding** riz au lait *m*.
rich (ritʃ) *adj* **1** riche. **2** fertile. **3** somptueux, -euse. **richness** *n* **1** richesse *f*. **2** somptuosité *f*.
rickety ('rikiti) *adj* branlant, chancelant.
rickshaw ('rikʃɔ:) *n* pousse-pousse *m invar*.
rid* (rid) *vt* débarrasser, délivrer. **get rid of** se débarrasser de. **riddance** *n* débarras *m*.
riddle[1] ('ridḷ) *n* (puzzle) énigme *f*.
riddle[2] ('ridḷ) *n* crible *m*. claie *f*. *vt* cribler, tamiser.
ride* (raid) *vi* **1** monter à cheval. **2** voguer. *vt* **1** monter. **2** diriger. *n* promenade, course *f*. **rider** *n* cavalier, -ière.
ridge (ridʒ) *n* **1** crête, cime *f*. **2** faîte *m*. **3** strie *f*.
ridicule ('ridikju:l) *vt* se moquer de. *n* moquerie, raillerie *f*. **ridiculous** *adj* ridicule.
rife (raif) *adj* abondant, répandu. **be rife** régner.
rifle[1] ('raifəl) *n* fusil *m*. carabine *f*.
rifle[2] ('raifəl) *vt* piller, vider.
rift (rift) *n* **1** fente, dechirure *f*. **2** fissure *f*.
rig (rig) *n* **1** *naut* gréement *m*. **2** équipement *m*. *vt* gréer. **rig out** accoutrer, equiper. **rigging** *n* gréement *m*. agrès *m pl*.
right (rait) *adj* **1** droit. **2** bon, bonne. **3** juste. **be right** avoir raison. ~*adv* droit, juste, bien. *n* **1** droit *m*. **2** droite *f*. **right of way** priorité *f*. droit de passage *m*. ~*vt* **1** redresser, remettre. **2** rectifier. **right angle** *n* angle droit *m*. **right-hand** *adj* de *or* à droite. **right handed** *adj* droitier, -ière. **right-wing** *adj* de droite.
righteous ('raitʃəs) *adj* droit, vertueux, -euse.
rigid ('ridʒid) *adj* **1** rigide, raide. **2** sévère, strict.

rigour (ˈrigə) *n* rigueur *f*. **rigorous** *adj* rigoureux, -euse.

rim (rim) *n* **1** bord *m*. **2** (of a wheel) jante *f*.

rind (raind) *n* peau, -aux, croûte, couenne *f*.

ring[1] (riŋ) *n* **1** cercle *m*. **2** bague *f*. **3** anneau, -aux *m*. **4** arène *f*. **ringleader** *n* meneur *m*. **ring-road** *n* boulevard périphérique *m*. **ringside** *adj* au premier rang.

ring*[2] (riŋ) *n* **1** tintement *m*. **2** coup de sonnette *m*. *vt* sonner, faire sonner. *vi* **1** sonner. **2** retentir. **ring off** raccrocher. **ring up** téléphoner.

rink (riŋk) *n* patinoire *f*.

rinse (rins) *vt* rincer. *n* rinçage *m*.

riot (ˈraiət) *n* émeute, bagarre *f*. *vi* s'ameuter.

rip (rip) *n* déchirure, fente *f*. *vt* déchirer, fendre. *vi* se déchirer. **rip out** arracher.

ripe (raip) *adj* **1** mûr. **2** prêt, à point. **ripen** *vt,vi* mûrir.

ripple (ˈripəl) *n* **1** ride, ondulation *f*. **2** murmure *m*. *vi* se rider, onduler.

rise* (raiz) *vi* **1** se lever. **2** monter, s'élever. **3** hausser. **4** se soulever. *n* **1** lever *m*. **2** montée *f*. **3** hausse *f*. **4** avancement *m*. **give rise to** occasionner.

risk (risk) *n* risque, péril *m*. *vt* risquer, hasarder. **risky** *adj* hasardeux, -euse.

rissole (ˈrisoul) *n* croquette *f*.

rite (rait) *n* rite *m*.

ritual (ˈritjuəl) *adj,n* rituel, -elle *m*.

rival (ˈraivəl) *n* **1** rival, -aux *m*. **2** *comm* concurrent *m*. *adj* rival, -aux. *vt* rivaliser avec. **rivalry** *n* rivalité *f*.

river (ˈrivə) *n* fleuve *m*. rivière *f*. **riverbed** *n* lit de rivière *m*. **riverside** *n* bord de l'eau *m*. *adj* situé au bord de la rivière.

rivet (ˈrivit) *n* rivet, clou *m*. *vt* **1** river. **2** capter, fixer.

road (roud) *n* route, voie *f*. chemin *m*. **roadblock** *n* barrage *m*. **roadside** *n* bord de la route *m*. *adj* situé au bord de la route.

roam (roum) *vi* errer, rôder. *vt* parcourir.

roar (rɔ:) *n* hurlement, rugissement *m*. *vi* hurler, rugir.

roast (roust) *vt,vi* rôtir. *adj,n* rôti *m*.

rob (rɔb) *vt* voler, dérober. **robber** *n* voleur, -euse. **robbery** *n* vol *m*.

robe (roub) *n* robe *f*. *vt,vi* revêtir.

robin (ˈrɔbin) *n* rouge-gorge *m*.

robot (ˈroubɔt) *n* robot *m*.

robust (rouˈbʌst) *adj* robuste, vigoureux, -euse.

rock[1] (rɔk) *n* rocher, roc *m*. **rock-bottom** *adj* le plus bas. **rockery** *n* jardin de rocaille *m*.

rock[2] (rɔk) *vt* bercer, balancer, basculer. *vi* (se) balancer, osciller. **rocker** *n* bascule *f*. **rocking-chair** *n* fauteuil à bascule *m*. **rocking-horse** *n* cheval à bascule *m*.

rocket (ˈrɔkit) *n* fusée *f*.

rod (rɔd) *n* **1** baguette, verge *f*. **2** tringle *f*.

rode (roud) *v* see **ride**.

rodent (ˈroudnt) *adj,n* rongeur, -euse *m*.

roe (rou) *n* œufs de poisson *m pl*. laitance *f*.

rogue (roug) *n* coquin, fripon *m*.

role (roul) *n* rôle *m*.

roll (roul) *n* **1** rouleau, -aux *m*. **2** petit pain *m*. **3** roulement *m*. *vt,vi* rouler. **roll over** se retourner. **roll up** s'enrouler. **rollcall** *n* appel *m*. **roller** *n* **1** rouleau, -aux *m*. **2** cylindre *m*. **roller-skate** *vi* patiner sur roulettes. *n* patin à roulettes *m*. **rolling pin** *n* rouleau, -aux *m*.

Roman Catholic *adj,n* catholique.

romance (*n,adj* ˈroumæns; *v* rəˈmæns) *n* **1** idylle *f*. **2** romanesque *m*. *adj* roman. *vi* exagérer, broder.

romantic (rəˈmæntik) *adj* **1** romantique. **2** romanesque.

romanticize (rəˈmæntisaiz) *vt* romancer. *vi* donner dans le romantique.

romp (rɔmp) *vi* s'ébattre. *n* gambades *f pl*. **rompers** *n pl* barboteuse *f*.

roof (ru:f) *n* **1** toit *m*. **2** *anat* palais *m*.

rook (ruk) *n zool* corneille *f*. *vt sl* filouter, rouler.

room (ru:m) *n* **1** salle, pièce *f*. **2** place *f*.

roost (ru:st) *n* juchoir, perchoir *m*. *vi* se jucher, se percher.

root[1] (ru:t) *n* **1** racine *f*. **2** source *f*. *vt* enraciner. *vi* s'enraciner.

root[2] (ru:t) *vi* **1** fouiller avec le groin. **2** fouiller.

rope (roup) *n* corde *f*. cordage *m*. *vt* corder, lier.

rosary (ˈrouzəri) *n* rosaire *m*.

rose[1] (rouz) *n* rose *f*. **rose bush** *n* rosier *m*. **rosette** *n* **1** cocarde *f*. **2** *arch* rosace *f*. **rosy** *adj* rose, rosé, vermeil, -eille.

rose[2] (rouz) *v* see **rise**.

rosemary (ˈrouzməri) *n* romarin *m*.

rot (rɔt) *n* **1** pourriture, carie *f*. **2** démoralisation *f*. **3** *sl* bêtises *f pl*. *vi,vt* pourrir. *vi* se décomposer. **rotten** *adj* **1** pourri, carié. **2** fichu, patraque.

rota (ˈroutə) *n* liste de roulement *f*. **rotary** *adj* rotatoire, rotatif, -ive. **rotate** *vi* tourner, pivoter. *vt* **1** faire tourner. **2** alterner, varier. **rotation** *n* **1** succession *f*. **2** rotation *f*. **in rotation** à tour de rôle.

rotor (ˈroutə) *n* rotor *m*.

rouble (ˈru:bəl) *n* rouble *m*.

rouge (ruːʒ) *n* rouge, fard *m*.

rough (rʌf) *adj* **1** rugueux, -euse, rude. **2** grossier, -ière. **3** tempêtueux, -euse. **4** approximatif, -ive. **5** rauque. **roughly** *adv* **1** brutalement. **2** à peu près. **roughness 1** rudesse *f*. **2** grossièreté *f*.

roulette (ruːˈlet) *n* roulette *f*.

round (raund) *adj* rond, circulaire. *n* **1** rond, cercle *m*. **2** tour, circuit *m*. **3** tournée *f*. *prep* autour de. *vt* arrondir. **roundabout** *n* rond-point *m*. *adj* détourné, indirect.

rouse (rauz) *vt* **1** réveiller. **2** susciter.

route (ruːt) *n* itinéraire, chemin *m*. route *f*.

routine (ruːˈtiːn) *n* routine *f*. *adj* routinier, -ière.

rove (rouv) *vi* rôder. *vt* parcourir.

row[1] (rou) *n* rang *m*. ligne *f*.

row[2] (rou) *vi naut* ramer. *vt naut* conduire à l'aviron. *n* promenade en bateau *f*. **rowing** *n* canotage *m*.

row[3] (rau) *n* **1** querelle, dispute *f*. **2** chahut, tapage *m*.

rowdy (ˈraudi) *adj* tapageur, -euse.

royal (ˈrɔiəl) *adj* royal, -aux. **royal blue** *n* bleu roi *m*. **royalty** *n* **1** royauté *f*. **2** pl droits d'auteur *m pl*.

rub (rʌb) *vt,vi* frotter. *vt* enduire, frictionner. **rub in** faire pénétrer. **rub out** effacer. ~*n* **1** frottement *m*. **2** friction *f*.

rubber (ˈrʌbə) *n* **1** gomme *f*. **2** caoutchouc *m*. **rubber band** *n* élastique *m*.

rubbish (ˈrʌbiʃ) *n* **1** détritus *m*. déchets *m pl*. **2** *inf* camelote *f*. **3** *inf* bêtises *f pl*.

rubble (ˈrʌbəl) *n* **1** moellon *m*. **2** décombres *m pl*.

ruby (ˈruːbi) *n* rubis *m*.

rucksack (ˈrʌksæk) *n* sac à dos *m*.

rudder (ˈrʌdə) *n* gouvernail *m*.

rude (ruːd) *adj* **1** impoli, grossier, -ière. **2** primitif, -ive. **3** violent. **4** brut. **rudeness** *n* impolitesse *f*.

rudiment (ˈruːdimənt) *n* rudiment *m*. **rudimentary** *adj* rudimentaire.

rueful (ˈruːfəl) *adj* triste, lugubre.

ruff (rʌf) *n* fraise *f*.

ruffian (ˈrʌfiən) *n* bandit, polisson *m*.

ruffle (ˈrʌfəl) *n* **1** agitation *f*. **2** volant *m*. *vt* **1** troubler. **2** plisser.

rug (rʌg) *n* **1** couverture *f*. **2** (mat) tapis *m*.

rugby (ˈrʌgbi) *n* rugby *m*.

rugged (ˈrʌgid) *adj* **1** accidenté, rugueux, -euse. **2** bourru, rude.

ruin (ˈruːin) *n* ruine *f*. *vt* ruiner.

rule (ruːl) *n* **1** règle *f*. **2** autorité *f*. *vt* **1** gouverner. **2** rayer, régler. **rule out 1** écarter. **2** biffer. **ruler** *n* **1** souverain *m*. **2** règle *f*. **ruling** *adj* dominant. *n* ordonnance *f*.

rum (rʌm) *n* rhum *m*.

Rumania (ruːˈmeiniə) *n* Roumanie *f*. **Rumanian** *adj,n* roumain.

rumble (ˈrʌmbəl) *n* grondement, roulement *m*. *vi* gronder.

rummage (ˈrʌmidʒ) *vi* fouiller.

rumour (ˈruːmə) *n* rumeur *f*. bruit *m*.

rump (rʌmp) *n* croupe *f*.

run* (rʌn) *vi* **1** courir. **2** fuir. **3** marcher, circuler. **4** couler. **5** déteindre. *vt* **1** tenir, diriger, gerer. **2** courir. **3** entretenir. **4** promener. **run away** s'enfuir. **run out 1** expirer. **2** s'épuiser. ~*n* **1** course *f*. **2** tour *m*. promenade *f*. **3** suite *f*. **4** vogue *f*. **5** enclos *m*. **in the long run** à la longue. **runner** *n* coureur, -euse. **runner bean** *n* haricot vert *m*. **runner-up** *n* second *m*. **running** *adj* **1** courant. **2** continu. **3** de suite. *n* **1** course *f*. **2** marche *f*. fonctionnement *m*. **3** direction *f*. **runway** *n* piste d'envol *f*.

rung[1] (rʌŋ) *v* see **ring.**

rung[2] (rʌŋ) *n* échelon, barreau, -aux *m*.

rupee (ruːˈpiː) *n* roupie *f*.

rupture (ˈrʌptʃə) *n* rupture *f*. *vt* rompre. *vi* se rompre.

rural (ˈruərəl) *adj* rural, -aux, champêtre.

rush[1] (rʌʃ) *vi* **1** se dépêcher. se précipiter. **2** faire irruption. *vt* bousculer, dépêcher, précipiter. *n* hâte, course précipitée *f*.

rush[2] (rʌʃ) *n bot* jonc *m*. paille *f*.

Russia (ˈrʌʃə) *n* Russie *f*. **Russian** *adj,n* russe. **Russian** (language) *n* russe *m*.

rust (rʌst) *n* rouille *f*. *vi* se rouiller. **rusty** *adj* rouillé.

rustic (ˈrʌstik) *adj* rustique.

rustle (ˈrʌsəl) *vi* bruire. *vt* froisser. *n* bruissement *m*.

rut (rʌt) *n* ornière *f*. **get into a rut** s'encroûter.

ruthless (ˈruːθləs) *adj* impitoyable, sans pitié.

rye (rai) *n* seigle *m*.

S

Sabbath (ˈsæbəθ) *n* sabbat *m*.

sable (ˈseibəl) *n* zibeline *f*.

sabotage (ˈsæbətɑːʒ) *n* sabotage *m*. *vt* saboter.

sabre (ˈseibə) *n* sabre *m*.

saccharin (ˈsækərin) *n* saccharine *f*.

sachet (ˈsæʃei) *n* sachet *m*.

sack (sæk) *n* sac *m*. **get the sack** recevoir son congé. ~*vt inf* congédier.

sacrament ('sækrəmənt) *n* sacrement *m*.

sacred ('seikrid) *adj* sacré, saint.

sacrifice ('sækrifais) *n* sacrifice *m*. *vt* sacrifier, immoler.

sacrilege ('sækrilidʒ) *n* sacrilège *m*. **sacrilegious** *adj* sacrilège.

sad (sæd) *adj* **1** triste. **2** cruel, -elle. **3** déplorable. **sadden** *vt* attrister, affliger. *vi* s'attrister. **sadness** *n* tristesse *f*.

saddle ('sædḷ) *n* selle *f*. *vt* **1** seller. **2** *inf* encombrer. **saddler** *n* sellier *m*.

sadism ('seidizəm) *n* sadisme *m*. **sadist** *n* sadique *m,f*. **sadistic** *adj* sadique.

safari (sə'fɑ:ri) *n* safari *m*.

safe (seif) *adj* **1** en sûreté, à l'abri, sauf, sauve. **2** solide, sûr. **3** prudent. **safe and sound** sain et sauf. ~*n* coffre-fort *m*. **safeguard** *n* sauvegarde *f*. *vt* sauvegarder, protéger. **safety** *n* sûreté, sécurité *f*. **safety belt** *n* ceinture de sécurité *f*. **safety pin** *n* épingle de sûreté *f*. **safety valve** *n* soupape de sûreté *f*.

saffron ('sæfrən) *n* safran *m*.

sag (sæg) *vi* s'affaisser, fléchir. *n* affaissement *m*.

saga ('sɑ:gə) *n* saga *f*.

sage[1] (seidʒ) *adj,n* sage.

sage[2] (seidʒ) *n bot* sauge *f*.

Sagittarius (sædʒi'tɛəriəs) *n* Sagittaire *m*.

sago ('seigou) *n* sagou *m*.

said (sed) *v* see **say**.

sail (seil) *n* **1** voile *f*. **2** promenade en bateau *f*. *vi* **1** naviguer. **2** faire de la voile. **sailing** *n* navigation *f*. **sailor** *n* matelot, marin *m*.

saint (seint) *n* saint *m*.

sake (seik) *n* **for the sake of 1** pour, par égard pour. **2** à cause de. **3** pour l'amour de.

salad ('sæləd) *n* salade *f*. **salad dressing** *n* vinaigrette *f*. assaisonnement *m*.

salamander ('sæləmændə) *n* salamandre *f*.

salami (sə'lɑ:mi) *n* salami *m*.

salary ('sæləri) *n* traitement, salaire *m*. appointements *m pl*.

sale (seil) *n* **1** vente *f*. **2** solde *f*. **salesman** *n* vendeur *m*. **travelling salesman** commis voyageur *m*. **salesmanship** *n* art de vendre *m*.

saliva (sə'laivə) *n* salive *f*. **salivate** *vi* saliver.

sallow ('sælou) *adj* jaunâtre, blême.

salmon ('sæmən) *n* saumon *m*.

salon ('sælɔn) *n* salon *m*.

saloon (sə'lu:n) *n* salle *f*. salon *m*. **saloon car** *n* conduite intérieure *f*.

salt (sɔ:lt) *n* sel *m*. *adj* salé. *vt* saler. **saltcellar** *n* salière *f*. **salty** *adj* salé.

salute (sə'lu:t) *n* **1** salut *m*. salutation *f*. **2** (of guns) salve *f*. *vt* saluer.

salvage ('sælvidʒ) *n* sauvetage *m*. récupération *f*. *vt* sauver.

salvation (sæl'veiʃən) *n* salut *m*.

salve (sælv) *n* onguent *m*. pommade *f*.

same (seim) *adj,pron* même. **all the same** tout de même.

sample ('sɑ:mpəl) *n* échantillon *m*. *vt* goûter, essayer.

sanatorium (sænə'tɔ:riəm) *n*, *pl* **-oriums** *or* **-oria** sanatorium *m*.

sanction ('sæŋkʃən) *n* **1** sanction *f*. **2** consentement *m*. *vt* **1** sanctionner. **2** approuver.

sanctity ('sæŋktiti) *n* **1** sainteté *f*. **2** inviolabilité *f*.

sanctuary ('sæŋktʃuəri) *n* **1** sanctuaire *m*. **2** asile, refuge *m*.

sand (sænd) *n* sable *m*. *vt* sabler. **sandpaper** *n* papier de verre *m*. **sandpit** *n* sablière *f*. **sandy** *adj* sablonneux, -euse.

sandal ('sændḷ) *n* sandale *f*.

sandwich ('sænwidʒ) *n* sandwich *m*.

sane (sein) *adj* sain d'esprit, sensé. **sanity** *n* santé d'esprit, raison *f*.

sang (sæŋ) *v* see **sing**.

sanitary ('sænitri) *adj* sanitaire, hygiénique. **sanitary towel** *n* serviette hygiénique *f*.

sank (sæŋk) *v* see **sink**.

sap (sæp) *n* sève *f*.

sapphire ('sæfaiə) *n* saphir *m*.

sarcasm ('sɑ:kæzəm) *n* sarcasme *m*. ironie *f*. **sarcastic** *adj* sarcastique, mordant.

sardine (sɑ:'di:n) *n* sardine *f*.

Sardinia (sɑ:'diniə) *n* Sardaigne *f*. **Sardinian** *adj,n* sarde.

sardonic (sɑ:'dɔnik) *adj* sardonique.

sari ('sɑ:ri) *n* sari *m*.

sash[1] (sæʃ) *n* écharpe, ceinture *f*.

sash[2] (sæʃ) *n arch* châssis, cadre *m*. **sash-window** *n* fenêtre à guillotine *f*.

sat (sæt) *v* see **sit**.

Satan ('seitṇ) *n* Satan *m*.

satchel ('sætʃəl) *n* cartable *m*. sacoche *f*.

satellite ('sætəlait) *n* satellite *m*.

satin ('sætin) *n* satin *m*.

satire ('sætaiə) *n* satire *f*. **satirical** *adj* satirique.

satisfy ('sætisfai) *vt* **1** satisfaire, contenter. **2**

convaincre. **satisfaction** *n* satisfaction *f.* **satisfactory** *adj* satisfaisant.

saturate ('sætʃəreit) *vt* saturer, imprégner.

Saturday ('sætədi) *n* samedi *m.*

Saturn ('sætən) *n* Saturne *m.*

sauce (sɔ:s) *n* sauce *f.* **saucepan** *n* casserole *f.* **saucer** *n* soucoupe *f.* **saucy** *adj* impertinent, effronté.

Saudi Arabia ('saudi) *n* Arabie Séoudite *f.*

sauerkraut ('sauəkraut) *n* choucroute *f.*

sauna ('sɔ:nə) *n* sauna *m.*

saunter ('sɔ:ntə) *vi* flâner, se balader.

sausage ('sɔsidʒ) *n* saucisse *f.* **sausage meat** *n* chair à saucisse *f.*

savage ('sævidʒ) *adj* sauvage, féroce. *n* sauvage *m,f.* *vt* attaquer.

save[1] (seiv) *vt* **1** sauver. **2** économiser, épargner. **3** éviter. **4** garder. **savings** *n pl* économies *f pl.* épargne *f.*

save[2] (seiv) *prep* sauf.

saviour ('seiviə) *n* sauveur *m.*

savoury ('seivəri) *adj* savoureux -euse, appétissant. *n* entremets non sucré *m.*

saw*[1] (sɔ:) *n* scie *f.* *vt* scier. **sawdust** *n* sciure *f.*

saw[2] (sɔ:) *v* see **see**[1].

Saxon ('sæksən) *adj,n* saxon, -onne.

saxophone ('sæksəfoun) *n* saxophone *m.*

say* (sei) *vt,vi* dire. **saying** *n* proverbe, dicton *m.*

scab (skæb) *n* croûte *f.* *vi* se cicatriser, former une croûte.

scaffold ('skæfəld) *n* échafaud *m.* **scaffolding** *n* échafaudage *m.*

scald (skɔ:ld) *vt* échauder, ébouillanter. *n* échaudure *f.*

scale[1] (skeil) *n* (of a fish, etc.) écaille *f.* *vt* écailler. *vi* s'écailler.

scale[2] (skeil) *n* **1** plateau, -aux *m.* **2** *pl* balance *f.*

scale[3] (skeil) *n* échelle, graduation *f.* *vt* escalader.

scallop ('skɔləp) *n* **1** coquille Saint-Jacques *f.* **2** (in sewing) feston *m.*

scalp (skælp) *n* épicrâne, cuir chevelu *m.* *vt* scalper.

scalpel ('skælpəl) *n* scalpel *m.*

scampi ('skæmpi) *n pl* langoustines *f pl.*

scan (skæn) *vt* **1** examiner, scruter. **2** parcourir. **3** *lit* scander. *n* regard scrutateur *m.*

scandal ('skændḷ) *n* scandale *m.* médisance *f.* **scandalous** *adj* scandaleux, -euse.

Scandinavia (skændi'neiviə) *n* Scandinavie *f.* **Scandinavian** *adj,n* scandinave.

scant (skænt) *adj* insuffisant, sommaire.

scapegoat ('skeipgout) *n* bouc émissaire *m.*

scar (skɑ:) *n* cicatrice *f.* *vt* balafrer. *vi* se cicatriser.

scarce (skɛəs) *adj* rare. **scarcely** *adv* à peine, ne...guère.

scare (skɛə) *vt* effrayer. *n* panique, alarme *f.* **scarecrow** *n* épouvantail *m.*

scarf (skɑ:f) *n, pl* **scarfs** *or* **scarves** écharpe *f.*

scarlet ('skɑ:lit) *adj,n* écarlate *f.* **scarlet fever** *n* fièvre scarlatine *f.*

scathing ('skeiðiŋ) *adj* acerbe, cinglant.

scatter ('skætə) *vt* éparpiller, semer. *vi* se disperser.

scavenge ('skævindʒ) *vt* **1** nettoyer. **2** balayer.

scene (si:n) *n* scène *f.*

scenery ('si:nəri) *n* **1** paysage *m.* **2** *Th* décors *m pl.*

scent (sent) *n* **1** parfum *m.* odeur *f.* **2** odorat, flair *m.* *vt* **1** parfumer. **2** flairer.

sceptic ('skeptik) *n* sceptique *m,f.* **sceptical** *adj* sceptique. **scepticism** *adj* sceptique.

sceptre ('septə) *n* sceptre *m.*

schedule ('ʃedju:l) *n* plan *m.* *vt* ajouter.

scheme (ski:m) *n* **1** arrangement *m.* **2** projet *m.* *vi* comploter, intriguer.

schizophrenia (skitsou'fri:niə) *n* schizophrénie *f.* **schizophrenic** *adj,n* schizophrène.

scholar ('skɔlə) *n* **1** savant *m.* **2** écolier, -ière. **scholarship** *n* **1** érudition *f.* **2** bourse *f.*

scholastic (skə'læstik) *adj* **1** scolastique. **2** scolaire.

school[1] (sku:l) *n* école *f.* *vt* instruire, entrainer. **schoolboy** *n* élève, écolier *m.* **schoolgirl** *n* élève, écolière *f.* **schoolmaster** *n* instituteur *m.* **schoolmistress** *n* institutrice *f.* **schoolteacher** *n* professeur *m,f.*

school[2] (sku:l) *n* bande *f.*

schooner ('sku:nə) *n* schooner *m.* goélette *f.*

science ('saiəns) *n* science *f.* **science fiction** *n* science-fiction *f.* **scientific** *adj* scientifique. **scientist** *n* homme de science *m.*

scissors ('sizəz) *n pl* ciseaux *m pl.*

scoff[1] (skɔf) *vi* railler.

scoff[2] (skɔf) *vt inf* manger gloutonnement, bouffer.

scold (skould) *vt* gronder.

scone (skoun) *n* pain au lait *m.*

scoop (sku:p) *n* **1** pelle, écope *f.* **2** *tech* cuiller *f.* *vt* creuser, écoper.

scooter ('sku:tə) *n* scooter *m.*

scope (skoup) *n* **1** portée *f*. **2** étendue *f*.
scorch (skɔ:tʃ) *vt* roussir, dessécher. *n* brûlure *f*.
score (skɔ:) *n* **1** *sport* marque *f*. **2** sujet *m*. **3** vingtaine *f*. *vt* **1** marquer, compter. **2** entailler. **scoreboard** *n* tableau, -aux *m*.
scorn (skɔ:n) *n* mépris, dédain *m*. *vt* mépriser.
Scorpio ('skɔ:piou) *n* Scorpion *m*.
scorpion ('skɔ:piən) *n* scorpion *m*.
Scotland ('skɔtlənd) *n* Écosse *f*. **Scot** *n* écossais *m*. **Scotch** *adj* écossais. *n* whisky *m*. **Scots** *adj,n* écossais. **Scottish** *adj* écossais.
scoundrel ('skaundrəl) *n* scélérat, gredin *m*.
scour[1] ('skauə) *vt* (clean) récurer.
scour[2] ('skauə) *vt* parcourir, battre.
scout (skaut) *n* éclaireur *m*.
scowl (skaul) *n* froncement des sourcils *m*. *vi* se renfrogner.
scramble ('skræmbəl) *vt* brouiller. *vi* se bousculer.
scrap (skræp) *n* **1** bout, fragment *m*. **2** *pl* restes *m pl*. *vt* mettre au rebut. **scrapbook** *n* album de découpures *m*. **scrap iron** *n* ferraille *f*.
scrape (skreip) *vt* **1** érafler. **2** racler. *vi* gratter. *n* **1** grincement *m*. **2** *inf* embarras *m*.
scratch (skrætʃ) *vt* **1** égratigner, griffer. **2** gratter. *vi* **1** se gratter, griffer. **2** *sport inf* se retirer. *n* **1** égratignure *f*. **2** grincement *m*.
scrawl (skrɔ:l) *vt* griffonner. *n* griffonnage *m*.
scream (skri:m) *vi* crier. *n* cri perçant *m*.
screech (skri:tʃ) *vi* pousser un cri rauque. *n* cri rauque *m*.
screen (skri:n) *n* écran *m*. *vt* protéger, cacher.
screw (skru:) *n* vis *f*. *vt* visser. *vi* tourner. **screwdriver** *n* tournevis *m*.
scribble ('skribəl) *n* griffonnage *m*. *vt* griffonner.
script (skript) *n* manuscrit *m*.
Scripture ('skriptʃə) *n* Ecriture sainte *f*.
scroll (skroul) *n* rouleau, -aux *m*.
scrounge (skraundʒ) *vt inf* chiper, écornifler.
scrub[1] (skrʌb) *vt* frotter, récurer. *n* friction *f*. nettoyage *m*. **scrubbing brush** *n* brosse dure *f*.
scrub[2] (skrʌb) *n bot* brousse *f*. broussailles *m pl*.
scruffy ('skrʌfi) *adj inf* peu soigné.
scrunch (skrʌntʃ) *vt* **1** croquer. **2** écraser.
scruple ('skru:pəl) *n* scrupule *m*. **scrupulous** *adj* **1** scrupuleux, -euse. **2** méticuleux, -euse.
scrutiny ('skru:tini) *n* examen minutieux *m*. **scrutinize** *vt* scruter.
scuffle ('skʌfəl) *n* mêlée *f*. *vi* se bousculer.
scullery ('skʌləri) *n* arrière-cuisine *f*.
sculpt (skʌlpt) *vt* sculpter. **sculptor** *n* sculpteur *m*. **sculpture** *n* sculpture *f*.
scum (skʌm) *n* **1** écume, mousse *f*. **2** rebut *m*.
scurf (skə:f) *n* pellicule *f*.
scythe (saið) *n* faux *f*. *vt* faucher.
sea (si:) *n* mer *f*. **by the sea** au bord de la mer. ~*adj* marin, maritime.
seabed ('si:bed) *n* fond marin *m*.
seafaring ('si:fɛəriŋ) *adj* marin, de mer.
seafront ('si:frʌnt) *n* esplanade de mer *f*.
seagull ('si:gʌl) *n* mouette *f*.
seahorse ('si:hɔ:s) *n* hippocampe *m*.
seal[1] (si:l) *n* sceau, -aux, cachet *m*. *vt* sceller, cacheter.
seal[2] (si:l) *n zool* phoque *m*. **sealskin** *n* peau de phoque *f*.
sea-level *n* niveau de la mer *m*.
sea-lion *n* otarie *f*.
seam (si:m) *n* **1** couture *f*. **2** *min* veine *f*.
seaman ('si:mən) *n* marin *m*. **seamanship** *n* matelotage *m*.
search (sə:tʃ) *vt* **1** fouiller. **2** chercher. *n* recherche *f*. **searchlight** *n* projecteur *m*.
seashore ('si:ʃɔ:) *n* **1** rivage *m*. **2** plage *f*.
seasick ('si:sik) *adj* **be seasick** avoir le mal de mer.
seaside ('si:said) *n* bord de la mer *m*. **seaside resort** *n* station balnéaire *f*.
season ('si:zən) *n* **1** saison *f*. **2** période *f*. *vt* assaisonner. *vi* sécher. **seasoning** *n* assaisonnement *m*. **season ticket** *n* carte d'abonnement *f*.
seat (si:t) *n* **1** siège *m*. **2** place *f*. *vt* (faire) asseoir. **seat-belt** *n* ceinture de sécurité *f*.
seaweed ('si:wi:d) *n* algue *f*.
secluded (si'klu:did) *adj* retiré, écarté.
second[1] ('sekənd) *adj* second, deuxième. *n* deuxième *m,f*. *vt* seconder, appuyer. **second-best** *adj* numéro deux. **second-class** *adj* de qualité inférieure. **second-hand** *adj* d'occasion. **second nature** *n* seconde nature *f*. **second-rate** *adj* médiocre, inférieur. **secondary** *adj* secondaire. **secondary school** *n* école secondaire *f*. lycée *m*.
second[2] ('sekənd) *n* seconde *f*.
secret ('si:krət) *n* secret *m*. *adj* secret, -ète, caché. **secrecy** *n* discrétion *f*. **secretive** *adj* réservé, cachottier, -ière.
secretary ('sekrətri) *n* **1** secrétaire *m,f*. **2** *pol* ministre *m*.
secrete (si'kri:t) *vt* **1** sécréter. **2** cacher.
sect (sekt) *n* secte *f*. **sectarian** *adj* sectaire.

section (ˈsekʃən) *n* section *f.*
sector (ˈsektə) *n* secteur *m.*
secular (ˈsekjulə) *adj* **1** séculier, -ère, laïque. **2** séculaire.
secure (siˈkjuə) *adj* **1** sûr, assuré. **2** en sûreté. **3** ferme, solide. *vt* **1** mettre en sûreté. **2** assujettir, maintenir. **3** obtenir, se procurer. **security** *n* sécurité, sûreté *f.*
sedate (siˈdeit) *adj* posé. **sedation** *n* sédation *f.* **sedative** *adj,n* sédatif, -ive *m.*
sediment (ˈsedimənt) *n* sédiment *m.* lie *f.*
seduce (siˈdjuːs) *vt* séduire. **seduction** *n* séduction *f.*
see*[1] (siː) *vt* **1** voir. **2** comprendre. **3** examiner. **see to** s'occuper de.
see[2] (siː) *n rel* siège *m.*
seed (siːd) *n* graine, semence *f.*
seedy (ˈsiːdi) *adj* **1** minable, râpé. **2** patraque.
seek* (siːk) *vt* **1** chercher, rechercher. **2** demander.
seem (siːm) *vi* sembler, paraître, avoir l'air. **seeming** *adj* apparent, soi -disant. **seemingly** *adv* apparemment.
seep (siːp) *vi* suinter, s'infiltrer.
seesaw (ˈsiːsɔː) *n* balançoire *f.* *vi* osciller.
seethe (siːð) *vi* grouiller, bouillonner.
segment (ˈsegmənt) *n* segment *m.* tranche *f.*
segregate (ˈsegrigeit) *vt* isoler, séparer. **segregation** *n* ségrégation *f.*
seize (siːz) *vt* **1** saisir. **2** s'emparer de.
seldom (ˈseldəm) *adv* rarement.
select (siˈlekt) *vt* choisir, trier. *adj* choisi. **selection** *n* sélection *f.* choix *m.* **selective** *adj* sélectif, -ive.
self (self) *n, pl* **selves** moi *m.* *pron* soi-même, se.
self-assured *adj* sûr de soi.
self-aware *adj* conscient de soi.
self-centred *adj* égocentrique.
self-confident *adj* plein d'assurance.
self-conscious *adj* intimidé, gêné.
self-contained *adj* **1** indépendant. **2** renfermé.
self-defence *n* légitime défense *f.*
self-discipline *n* maîtrise de soi *f.*
self-employed *adj* indépendant.
self-expression *n* expression personnelle *f.*
self-government *n* autonomie *f.*
self-indulgent *adj* sybarite, qui se dorlote.
self-interest *n* intérêt personnel, égoïsme *m.*
selfish (ˈselfiʃ) *adj* égoïste. **selfishness** *n* égoïsme *m.*
self-made *adj* arrivé par soi-même.
self-pity *n* pitié de soi-même *f.*
self-portrait *n* autoportrait *m.*
self-respect *n* respect de soi, amour propre *m.*
self-righteous *adj* pharisaïque.
self-sacrifice *n* abnégation *f.*
selfsame (ˈselfseim) *adj* identique.
self-satisfied *adj* content de soi.
self-service *n* libre-service *m.*
self-sufficient *adj* indépendant, suffisant.
self-will *n* obstination *f.* entêtement *m.*
sell* (sel) *vt* vendre. **sell off** solder, liquider. **sell up** vendre.
Sellotape (ˈselәteip) *n Tdmk* Scotch *Tdmk m.*
semantic (siˈmæntik) *adj* sémantique. **semantics** *n* sémantique *f.*
semaphore (ˈseməfɔː) *n* sémaphore *m.*
semibreve (ˈsemibriːv) *n* ronde *f.*
semicircle (ˈsemisəːkəl) *n* demi-cercle *m.*
semicolon (semiˈkoulən) *n* point-virgule *m.*
semidetached (semidiˈtætʃt) *adj* accolé, jumeau, -elle.
semifinal (semiˈfainl̩) *n* demi-finale *f.*
seminar (ˈseminɑː) *n* séminaire *m.*
semiprecious (semiˈpreʃəs) *adj* fin.
semiquaver (semiˈkweivə) *n* double croche *f.*
semivowel (ˈsemivauəl) *n* semi-voyelle *f.*
semolina (seməliːnə) *n* semoule *f.*
senate (ˈsenət) *n* sénat *m.* **senator** *n* sénateur *m.*
send* (send) *vt* envoyer. **send back** renvoyer. **send for** envoyer chercher.
Senegal (seniˈgɔːl) *n* Sénégal *m.* **Senegalese** *adj,n* sénégalais.
senile (ˈsiːnail) *adj* sénile.
senior (ˈsiːniə) *adj,n* aîné, doyen, -enne.
sensation (senˈseiʃən) *n* sensation *f.* **sensational** *adj* sensationnel, -elle.
sense (sens) *n* **1** sens *m.* **2** bon sens *m.* *vt* sentir, pressentir. **senseless** *adj* **1** déraisonnable. **2** inanimé.
sensible (ˈsensəbəl) *adj* **1** sensé. **2** sensible. **3** conscient. **sensibility** *n* sensibilité, émotivité *f.*
sensitive (ˈsensitiv) *adj* sensible, susceptible.
sensual (ˈsenʃuəl) *adj* sensuel, -elle.
sensuous (ˈsenʃuəs) *adj* voluptueux, -euse, susceptible. **sensual** *adj* sensuel, -elle. **sensuous** *adj* voluptueux, -euse.
sentence (ˈsentəns) *n* **1** *gram* phrase *f.* **2** jugement *m.* sentence *f.* *vt* condamner.
sentiment (ˈsentimənt) *n* sentiment *m.* opinion *f.*. **sentimental** *adj* sentimental, -aux.
sentry (ˈsentri) *n* sentinelle *f.*
separate (ˈsepəreit) *vt* séparer, détacher. *vi* se

séparer, se désunir. *adj* séparé, distinct, indépendant. **separation** *n* séparation *f*.

September (sep'tembə) *n* septembre *m*.

septet (sep'tet) *n* septuor *m*.

septic ('septik) *adj* septique.

sequel ('si:kwəl) *n* **1** suite *f*. **2** conséquence *f*.

sequence ('si:kwəns) *n* **1** succession *f*. **2** séquence *f*.

sequin ('si:kwin) *n* sequin *m*.

serenade (serə'neid) *n* sérénade *f*.

serene (si'ri:n) *adj* serein. **serenity** *n* sérénité *f*.

serf (sə:f) *n* serf, serve.

sergeant ('sɑ:dʒənt) *n* sergent *m*. **sergeant major** *n* sergent-major, adjudant *m*.

serial ('siəriəl) *adj* de série. *n* feuilleton *m*. **serialize** *vt* publier *or* présenter en feuilleton.

series ('siəri:z) *n invar* série, suite *f*.

serious ('siəriəs) *adj* grave, sérieux, -euse. **seriousness** *n* gravité *f*.

sermon ('sə:mən) *n* sermon *m*.

serpent ('sə:pənt) *n* serpent *m*.

serrated (sə'reitid) *adj* dentelé.

serve (sə:v) *vt* **1** servir. **2** être utile à. **3** desservir. *vi* servir. **serve out** distribuer. **servant** *n* domestique *m,f*.

service ('sə:vis) *n* **1** service *m*. **2** entretien *m*. **3** *rel* office *m*. *vt* entretenir, réparer. **service station** *n* station-service *f*.

serviette (sə:vi'et) *n* serviette *f*.

servile ('səvail) *adj* servile.

session ('seʃən) *n* session, séance *f*.

set* (set) *n* **1** ensemble, jeu, jeux *m*. **2** collection *f*. **3** groupe *f*. **4** mise en pli *f*. **5** *Th* décors *m pl*. *adj* **1** figé, immobile. **2** fixe. *vt* **1** mettre, poser. **2** régler. **3** composer. **4** donner. **5** poser. **6** sertir. **7** fixer. **8** dresser. *vi* **1** se coucher. **2** se coaguler, prendre. **3** *med* se ressouder. **set about** se mettre à. **set off** partir. **set out 1** arranger. **2** se mettre en route. **set up 1** établir. **2** ériger. **setback** *n* revers de fortune *m*. **setting** *n* **1** montage *m*. **2** monture *f*. cadre *m*. **3** disposition *f*. **4** coucher *m*.

settee (se'ti:) *n* canapé *m*.

settle ('setl̩) *vt* **1** installer. **2** conclure, résoudre. **3** régler. **4** déterminer. *vi* **1** s'installer. **2** s'arranger. **settlement** *n* **1** établissement *m*. colonie *f*. **2** règlement *m*.

seven ('sevən) *adj,n* sept *m*. **seventh** *adj* septième.

seventeen (sevən'ti:n) *adj,n* dix-sept *m*. **seventeenth** *adj* dix-septième.

seventy ('sevənti) *adj,n* soixante-dix *m*. **seventieth** *adj* soixante-dixième.

several ('sevrəl) *adj* **1** plusieurs, quelques. **2** différent.

severe (si'viə) *adj* **1** sévère, rigoureux, -euse. **2** dur. **severity** *n* sévérité, rigueur *f*.

sew* (sou) *vt* coudre. **sewing machine** *n* machine à coudre *f*.

sewage ('su:idʒ) *n* eau d'égout *f*.

sewer ('su:ə) *n* égout *m*. **sewerage** *n* système d'égout *m*.

sex (seks) *n* sexe *m*. **sexual** *adj* sexuel, -elle. **sexual intercourse** *n* rapports sexuels *m pl*. **sexuality** *n* sexualité *f*. **sexy** *adj* excitant, affriolant.

sextet (seks'tet) *n* sextuor *m*.

shabby ('ʃæbi) *adj* râpé, usé, minable.

shack (ʃæk) *n* cabane *f*.

shade (ʃeid) *n* **1** ombre *f*. **2** nuance *f*. *vt* **1** ombrager. **2** nuancer.

shadow ('ʃædou) *n* ombre *f*. *vt* filer. **shadow cabinet** *n* cabinet fantôme *m*.

shaft (ʃɑ:ft) *n* **1** hampe *f*. **2** flèche *f*. trait *m*.

shaggy ('ʃægi) *adj* hirsute.

shake* (ʃeik) *vt* **1** secouer, agiter. **2** hocher. *vi* trembler, chanceler. **shake hands** serrer la main. ~*n* **1** secousse *f*. **2** hochement *m*.

shall* (ʃəl; *stressed* ʃæl) *v mod aux* **1** devoir. **2** vouloir.

shallot (ʃə'lɔt) *n* échalote *f*.

shallow ('ʃælou) *adj* **1** peu profond. **2** frivole.

sham (ʃæm) *adj* simulé, feint. *n* feinte *f*. *vt* feindre, simuler.

shame (ʃeim) *n* honte *f*. *vt* faire honte à. **shamefaced** *adj* penaud, timide.

shampoo (ʃæm'pu:) *n* shampooing *m*. *vt* se laver la tête.

shamrock ('ʃæmrɔk) *n* trèfle d'Irlande *m*.

shandy ('ʃændi) *n* panaché *m*.

shanty[1] ('ʃænti) *n* cabane, baraque *f*. **shantytown** *n* bidonville *m*.

shanty[2] ('ʃænti) *n* chanson de marin *f*.

shape (ʃeip) *n* **1** forme *f*. **2** coupe, tournure *f*. *vt* modeler, former.

share (ʃɛə) *n* **1** part, portion *f*. **2** *comm* action *f*. *vt,vi* partager. **shareholder** *n* actionnaire *m,f*.

shark (ʃɑ:k) *n* requin *m*.

sharp (ʃɑ:p) *adj* **1** aigu, -uë, pointu. **2** fin. **3** aigre. **4** *sl* rusé. *n mus* dièse *m*. **sharp-sighted** *adj* à la vue perçante. **sharpen** *vt* aiguiser, affûter. *vi* s'aiguiser. **sharpness** *n* acuité *f*.

shatter ('ʃætə) *vt* fracasser, briser. *vi* se fracasser, se briser.
shave (ʃeiv) *vt* raser. *vi* se raser.
shawl (ʃɔ:l) *n* châle *m*.
she (ʃi:) *pron 3rd pers s* elle.
sheaf (ʃi:f) *n, pl* **sheaves** gerbe *f*.
shear* (ʃiə) *vt* tondre. **shears** *n pl* cisailles *f pl*.
sheath (ʃi:θ) *n* fourreau, -aux, étui *m*. **sheathe** *vt* rengainer, recouvrir.
shed[1] (ʃed) *n* hangar *m*. remise *f*.
shed*[2] (ʃed) *vt* jeter, répandre.
sheen (ʃi:n) *n* lustre, chatoiement *m*.
sheep (ʃi:p) *n invar* mouton *m*. **sheepdog** *n* chien de berger *m*. **sheepskin** *n* peau de mouton *f*.
sheer[1] (ʃiə) *adj* **1** pur, véritable. **2** perpendiculaire, à pic. **3** transparent.
sheer[2] (ʃiə) *vi* embarder.
sheet (ʃi:t) *n* **1** drap *m*. **2** (of paper, etc.) feuille *f*.
sheikh (ʃeik) *n* cheik *m*.
shelf (ʃelf) *n, pl* **shelves** rayon *m*. étagère *f*.
shell (ʃel) *n* **1** coquille, carapace, écaille *f*. **2** *mil* obus *m*. *vt* **1** écosser. **2** *mil* bombarder. **shellfish** *n* coquillage *m*. fruits de mer *m pl*.
shelter ('ʃeltə) *n* **1** abri *m*. **2** refuge *m*. *vt* abriter, protéger. *vi* s'abriter.
shelve (ʃelv) *vt* **1** mettre sur un rayon. **2** mettre au rancart. **3** ajourner.
shepherd ('ʃepəd) *n* berger *m*.
sherbet ('ʃə:bət) *n* sorbet *m*.
sheriff ('ʃerif) *n* sherif *m*.
sherry ('ʃeri) *n* xérès *m*.
shield (ʃi:ld) *n* bouclier *m*. carapace *f*. *vt* protéger, couvrir.
shift (ʃift) *n* **1** changement de place *m*. **2** équipe *f*. poste *m*. *vt* **1** remuer. **2** changer. *vi* se changer, se déplacer. **shiftwork** *n* travail par équipes *m*.
shilling ('ʃiliŋ) *n* shilling *m*.
shimmer ('ʃimə) *vi* luire, miroiter. *n* lueur *f*. chatoiement *m*.
shin (ʃin) *n* tibia *m*.
shine* (ʃain) *vi* briller, reluire, rayonner. *vt* polir. *n* **1** éclat *m*. **2** brillant *m*.
ship (ʃip) *n* bateau, -aux, navire *m*. *vt* embarquer, expédier. *vi* s'embarquer. **shipwreck** *n* naufrage *m*. *vt* faire naufrager. **be shipwrecked** faire naufrage. **shipyard** *n* chantier naval *m*.
shirk (ʃə:k) *vt* se dérober à, esquiver. **shirker** *n* carotteur, -euse.
shirt (ʃə:t) *n* chemise *f*.

shiver ('ʃivə) *vi* frissonner, grelotter. *n* frisson *m*.
shock[1] (ʃɔk) *n* **1** choc, heurt, coup *m*. **2** secousse *f*. *vt* choquer, scandaliser. **shock absorber** *n* amortisseur *m*. **shocking** *adj* **1** choquant. **2** abominable.
shock[2] (ʃɔk) *n* (of hair) tignasse *f*.
shoddy ('ʃɔdi) *adj* de camelote.
shoe* (ʃu:) *n* soulier *m*. chaussure *f*. *vt* **1** chausser. **2** ferrer. **shoelace** *n* lacet *m*. **shoemaker** *n* cordonnier *m*.
shone (ʃɔn) *v* see **shine.**
shook (ʃuk) *v* see **shake.**
shoot* (ʃu:t) *vi* **1** s'élancer, se précipiter. **2** pousser, jaillir. **3** tirer. *vt* **1** précipiter, lancer. **2** fusiller. **3** abattre. *n* **1** *bot* pousse *f*. **2** goulotte *f*. **3** *sport* chasse *f*. **shooting** *n* **1** tir *m*. **2** chasse *f*.
shop (ʃɔp) *n* magasin *m*. boutique *f*. *vi* faire des achats. **shop assistant** *n* vendeur, -euse. **shop floor** *n* **1** atelier *m*. **2** ouvriers *m pl*. **shopkeeper** *n* commerçant *m*. **shoplifter** *n* voleur à l'étalage *m*. **shopping** *n* achats *m pl*. emplettes *f pl*. **shop steward** *n* délégué syndicale *m*. **shopwindow** *n* vitrine *f*.
shore[1] (ʃɔ:) *n* rivage, littoral, -aux *m*.
shore[2] (ʃɔ:) *vt* **shore up** étayer, étançonner.
shorn (ʃɔ:n) *v* see **shear.**
short (ʃɔ:t) *adj* **1** court, bref, brève. **2** petit. **3** insuffisant. **4** à court de. **shortage** *n* insuffisance, crise *f*. **shorten** *vt* raccourcir, rapetisser, abréger.
shortbread ('ʃɔ:tbred) *n* sablé *m*.
shortcoming ('ʃɔ:tkʌmiŋ) *n* défaut *m*. imperfection *f*.
short cut *n* raccourci *m*.
shorthand ('ʃɔ:thænd) *n* sténographie *f*. **shorthand typist** *n* sténodactylographe *m,f*.
shortlived ('ʃɔ:tlivd) *adj* de courte durée, éphémère.
short-sighted *adj* myope.
short-term *adj* à court terme.
short wave *n* onde courte *f*.
shot[1] (ʃɔt) *n* **1** coup de feu *m*. **2** boulet *m*. **3** *inf* coup *m*. **4** *phot* prise de vue *f*.
shot[2] (ʃɔt) *v* see **shoot.** *adj* **1** chatoyant. **2** moiré.
should (ʃəd; *stressed* ʃud) *v* see **shall.**
shoulder ('ʃouldə) *n* épaule *f*. *vt* endosser. **shoulder-blade** *n* omoplate *f*.
shout (ʃaut) *vi,vt* crier. *n* cri *m*.

shove (ʃʌv) *n* coup d'épaule *m*. poussée *f*. *vt,vi* pousser.

shovel ('ʃʌvəl) *n* pelle *f*. *vt* entasser à la pelle.

show* (ʃou) *vt* **1** montrer, exhiber. **2** indiquer. **3** témoigner. *vi* apparaître, se montrer. **show off** parader, se pavaner. ~*n* **1** exposition *f*. spectacle *m*. **2** étalage *m*. **3** apparence *f*. **show business** *n* monde du spectacle *m*. **showcase** *n* vitrine *f*. **showdown** *n* règlement de compte *m*. **show-jumping** *n* saut à cheval *m*. **showmanship** *n* art de la mise en scène *m*. **showroom** *n* salle d'exposition *f*.

shower ('ʃauə) *n* **1** averse *f*. **2** (bath) douche *f*. *vt* **1** verser. **2** accabler, combler. **showerproof** *adj* caoutchouté, imperméable.

shrank (ʃræŋk) *v* see **shrink.**

shred (ʃred) *n* brin, lambeau, -aux *m*. *vt* déchiqueter.

shrew (ʃru:) *n* mégère *f*.

shrewd (ʃru:d) *adj* sagace, perspicace.

shriek (ʃri:k) *vi* pousser des cris perçants. *n* cri perçant *m*.

shrill (ʃril) *adj* aigu, -uë, strident.

shrimp (ʃrimp) *n* crevette *f*.

shrine (ʃrain) *n* **1** châsse *f*. **2** tombeau, -aux *m*. **3** sanctuaire *m*.

shrink* (ʃriŋk) *vi* se rétrécir, se contracter. *vt* rétrécir, faire se contracter.

shrivel ('ʃrivəl) *vt* rider. *vi* se rider, se ratatiner.

shroud (ʃraud) *n* linceul *m*. *vt* ensevelir, voiler.

Shrove Tuesday (ʃrouv) *n* mardi gras *m*.

shrub (ʃrʌb) *n* arbuste *m*. **shrubbery** *n* bosquet *m*.

shrug (ʃrʌg) *vt* hausser. *vi* hausser les épaules. *n* haussement d'épaules *m*.

shrunk (ʃrʌŋk) *v* see **shrink.**

shudder ('ʃʌdə) *vi* frissonner, frémir. *n* frisson, frémissement *m*.

shuffle ('ʃʌfəl) *vt* **1** *game* battre. **2** traîner. *vi* traîner les pieds. *n* **1** traînement de pieds *m*. **2** *game* mélange *m*.

shun (ʃʌn) *vt* fuir, éviter.

shunt (ʃʌnt) *vt* manœuvrer, garer. *n* manœuvre *f*.

shut* (ʃʌt) *vt,vi* fermer. **shut down** fermer. **shut in** enfermer. **shut off** **1** couper. **2** isoler. **shut out** exclure. **shut up!** ta gueule!

shutter ('ʃʌtə) *n* **1** volet *m*. **2** *phot* obturateur *m*.

shuttlecock ('ʃʌtəlkɔk) *n* volant *m*.

shy (ʃai) *adj* timide, farouche.

Sicily ('sisəli) *n* Sicile *f*. **Sicilian** *adj,n* sicilien, -ienne.

sick (sik) *adj* malade. **be sick** vomir. **be sick of** en avoir marre de. **sicken** *vi* tomber malade. *vt* dégoûter. **sickening** *adj* navrant, écœurant. **sickness** *n* maladie *f*.

side (said) *n* **1** côté *m*. **2** flanc *m*. **3** versant *m*. **4** parti, camp *m*. **5** face *f*. **6** bord *m*. *adj* **1** de côté, latéral, -aux. **2** secondaire. **sideboard** *n* buffet *m*. **side effect** *n* répercussion *f*. **sidelight** *n* feu de position *m*. **sideline** *n* violon d'Ingres *m*. **sideshow** *n* spectacle forain *m*. **sidestep** *n* pas de côté *m*. *vi* faire un pas de côté. *vt* éviter. **sidetrack** *vt* détourner l'attention de. **sideways** *adv* de côté, latéralement. *adj* latéral, -aux. **siding** *n* voie de garage *f*.

sidle ('saidl̩) *vi* **sidle up to** s'approcher de biais.

siege (si:dʒ) *n* siège *m*.

siesta (si'estə) *n* sieste *f*.

sieve (siv) *n* crible, tamis *m*. *vt* tamiser.

sift (sift) *vt* **1** tamiser, cribler. **2** dégager, démêler.

sigh (sai) *n* soupir *m*. *vi* soupirer.

sight (sait) *n* **1** vue, vision *f*. **2** spectacle *m*. *vt* apercevoir, aviser. **sightread** *vt* déchiffrer à vue. **sightseeing** *n* visite touristique *f*.

sign (sain) *n* **1** signe, indice *m*. trace *f*. **2** enseigne *f*. *vt* signer. **signpost** *n* poteau indicateur *m*.

signal ('signl̩) *n* signal, -aux *m*. *vi,vt* signaler.

signature ('signətʃə) *n* signature *f*.

signify ('signifai) *vt* signifier. *vi* importer. **significance** *n* **1** signification *f*. **2** conséquence *f*. **significant** *adj* **1** significatif, -ive. **2** important.

silence ('sailəns) *n* silence *m*. *vt* faire taire, réduire au silence. **silencer** *n* silencieux, pot d'échappement *m*. **silent** *adj* silencieux, -euse.

silhouette (silu:'et) *n* silhouette *f*. *vt* silhouetter.

silk (silk) *n* soie *f*. **silkworm** *n* vers à soie *m*.

sill (sil) *n* **1** seuil *m*. **2** appui *m*.

silly ('sili) *adj* sot, sotte, stupide.

silt (silt) *n* vase *f*. *v* **silt up** envaser.

silver ('silvə) *n* argent *m*. *adj* argenté, d'argent. *vt* argenter.

similar ('similə) *adj* semblable. **similarity** *n* ressemblance *f*.

simile ('simili) *n* image, comparaison *f*.

simmer ('simə) *vi* mijoter, cuire à petit feu. *vt* faire mijoter.

simple ('simpəl) *adj* **1** simple. **2** niais. **simplicity** *n* simplicité *f*. **simplify** *vt* simplifier.
simultaneous (siməl'teiniəs) *adj* simultané.
sin (sin) *n* péché *m*. *vi* pécher.
since (sins) *adv,prep* depuis. *conj* **1** depuis que. **2** puisque.
sincere (sin'siə) *adj* sincère. **sincerity** *n* sincérité *f*.
sinew ('sinju:) *n* tendon *m*.
sing* (siŋ) *vt,vi* chanter. **singer** *n* chanteur, -euse.
singe (sindʒ) *vt* brûler légèrement, roussir. *n* légère brûlure *f*.
single ('siŋgəl) *adj* **1** seul, unique. **2** célibataire. **3** simple. **single-handed** *adj* seul. **single-minded** *adj* sincère, loyal, -aux.
singular ('siŋgjulə) *adj* singulier, -ère. **2** unique. *n* singulier *m*.
sinister ('sinistə) *adj* sinistre.
sink* (siŋk) *vi* **1** couler, sombrer. **2** s'enfoncer. **3** baisser. *vt* **1** faire sombrer. **2** creuser. *n* évier *m*.
sinner ('sinə) *n* pécheur, -eresse.
sinus ('sainəs) *n* **1** sinus *m*. **2** *med* fistule *f*.
sip (sip) *vt* boire à petites gorgées. *n* petite gorgée *f*.
siphon ('saifən) *n* siphon *m*. *vt* siphonner.
sir (sə:) *n* **1** monsieur *m*. **2** *cap* Sir *m*.
siren ('sairən) *n* sirène *f*.
sirloin ('sə:lɔin) *n* aloyau, -aux, faux-filet *m*.
sister ('sistə) *n* **1** sœur *f*. **2** *rel* religieuse *f*. **sisterhood** *n* communauté religieuse *f*. **sister-in-law** *n* belle-sœur *f*.
sit* (sit) *vi* **1** s'asseoir, se tenir. **2** siéger. **3** couver. *vt* asseoir. **sit down** s'asseoir. **sit up** se redresser. **sit-in** *n* occupation *f*. **sitting** *n* séance *f*. *adj* assis. **sitting room** *n* salle de séjour *f*.
site (sait) *n* site, emplacement *m*.
situation (sitju'eiʃən) *n* **1** situation *f*. **2** emploi *m*.
six (siks) *adj,n* six *m*. **sixth** *adj* sixième.
sixteen (siks'ti:n) *adj,n* seize *m*. **sixteenth** *adj* seizième.
sixty ('siksti) *adj,n* soixante *m*. **sixtieth** *adj* soixantième.
size (saiz) *n* **1** grandeur, dimension *f*. **2** taille, pointure *f*.
sizzle ('sizəl) *vi* grésiller. *n* grésillement *m*.
skate[1] (skeit) *n* patin *m*. *vi* patiner.
skate[2] (skeit) *n* *zool* raie *f*.
skeleton ('skelətn̩) *n* squelette *m*.
sketch (sketʃ) *n* croquis *m*. esquisse *f*. *vt* esquisser.
skewer ('skjuə) *n* brochette *f*.
ski (ski:) *n* ski *m*. *vi* faire du ski. **ski-lift** *n* remonte-pente *m invar*. téléski *m*.
skid (skid) *vi* déraper, glisser. *n* dérapage *m*.
skill (skil) *n* habileté, adresse *f*. **skilful** *adj* adroit, habile. **skilled** *adj* qualifié.
skim (skim) *vt,vi* **1** écumer. **2** raser, effleurer. **skim through** parcourir rapidement.
skimp (skimp) *vt* **1** mesurer, lésiner sur. **2** bâcler. **skimpy** *adj* étriqué.
skin (skin) *n* **1** peau, -aux *f*. **2** (of an animal) dépouille *f*. cuir *m*. **3** écorce, pelure *f*. *vt* **1** peler. **2** écorcher. **3** *sl* plumer. **skin-diving** *n* plongée autonome *f*. **skin-tight** *adj* collant. **skinny** *adj inf* maigre.
skip (skip) *n* petit saut *m*. gambade *f*. *vi* **1** sauter, gambader. **2** sauter à la corde.
skipper ('skipə) *n* patron (de bateau) *m*.
skirmish ('skə:miʃ) *n* escarmouche *f*.
skirt (skə:t) *n* jupe *f*. *vt* contourner, longer.
skittle ('skitl̩) *n* **1** quille *f*. **2** *pl* jeu de quilles *m*.
skull (skʌl) *n* crâne *m*.
skunk (skʌŋk) *n* mouffette *f*.
sky (skai) *n* ciel, cieux *m*. **sky-high** *adv* jusqu'aux nues. **skylark** *n* alouette *f*. **skyline** *n* ligne d'horizon *f*. **skyscraper** *n* gratte-ciel *m invar*.
slab (slæb) *n* **1** plaque, dalle *f*. **2** tablette *f*.
slack (slæk) *adj* **1** lâche, flasque. **2** négligent. **3** faible. *n* mou *m*. **slacken** *vt* **1** ralentir. **2** détendre. *vi* se relâcher.
slacks (slæks) *n pl* pantalon *m*.
slalom ('slɑ:ləm) *n* slalom *m*.
slam (slæm) *vt,vi* claquer.
slander ('slændə) *n* calomnie *f*. *vt* **1** calomnier. **2** *law* diffamer.
slang (slæŋ) *n* argot *m*. *vt* **1** injurier. **2** engueuler.
slant (slɑ:nt) *n* **1** pente, inclinaison *f*. **2** biais *m*. *vt* incliner. *vi* s'incliner. **slanting** *adj* oblique.
slap (slæp) *n* claque, gifle *f*. *vt* claquer, gifler. **slapdash** *adj* sans soin, bâclé. *adv* sans soin. **slapstick** *n* bouffonnerie *f*.
slash (slæʃ) *vt* entailler, balâfrer, taillader. *n* entaille, balâfre *f*.
slat (slæt) *n* lame *f*.
slate (sleit) *n* ardoise *f*. *vt* ardoiser.
slaughter ('slɔ:tə) *n* **1** abattage *m*. **2** carnage *m*. *vt* **1** abattre. **2** massacrer.
slave (sleiv) *n* esclave *m,f*. **slavery** *n* esclavage *m*.

sledge (sledʒ) *n* traîneau, -aux *m.*
sledgehammer ('sledʒhæmə) *n* marteau de forgeron *m.*
sleek (sli:k) *adj* lisse, luisant.
sleep* (sli:p) *vi* dormir, coucher. *n* sommeil *m.* **go to sleep** s'endormir. **sleeper** *n* (railway) poutre horizontale *f.* **sleeping-bag** *n* sac de couchage *m.* **sleeping car** *n* wagon-lit *m.* **sleeping-pill** *n* somnifère *m.* **sleepwalk** *vi* être noctambule.
sleet (sli:t) *n* grésil *m. v imp* grésiller.
sleeve (sli:v) *n* manche *f.*
sleigh (slei) *n* traîneau, -aux *m.*
slender ('slendə) *adj* **1** svelte. **2** mince.
slept (slept) *v* see **sleep.**
slice (slais) *n* tranche *f.* rond *m. vt* découper en tranches.
slick (slik) *adj* **1** habile, adroit. **2** lisse.
slide* (slaid) *n* **1** glissade *f.* **2** *phot* diapositive *f. vi,vt* glisser. **slide-rule** *n* règle à calculer *f.*
slight (slait) *adj* **1** mince, ténu. **2** léger, -ère. *vt* manquer d'égards envers. *n* affront *m.*
slim (slim) *adj* svelte, mince. *vt* amincir. *vi* suivre un régime.
slime (slaim) *n* vase *f.* limon *m.*
sling* (sliŋ) *n* **1** *med* écharpe *f.* **2** fronde *f. vt* **1** lancer, jeter. **2** suspendre.
slink* (sliŋk) *vi* **slink off** partir furtivement.
slip[1] (slip) *vi* glisser. *vt* **1** échapper. **2** filer. **3** décrocher. *n* **1** glissade *f.* **2** erreur *f.* faux-pas *m.* **slippery** *adj* **1** glissant. **2** incertain.
slip[2] (slip) *n* bout *m.* bande *f.*
slipper ('slipə) *n* pantoufle *f.*
slit* (slit) *n* fente, fissure *f. vt* fendre, couper.
sloe (slou) *n* prunelle *f.*
slog (slɔg) *vt inf* **1** cogner violemment. **2** bûcher. *n* coup violent *m.*
slogan ('slougən) *n* slogan *m.*
slop (slɔp) *vt* répandre.
slope (sloup) *n* pente *f. vi* incliner, pencher.
sloppy ('slɔpi) *adj inf* **1** bâclé. **2** flasque. **3** mal ajusté.
slot (slɔt) *vt* mettre. *n* **1** entaille, encoche *f.* **2** fente *f.* **3** ouverture *f.* **slot machine** *n* distributeur automatique *m.*
slouch (slautʃ) *vi* pencher, se tenir mal.
slovenly ('slʌvənli) *adj* mal peigné *or* soigné.
slow (slou) *adj* **1** lent. **2** en retard. *v* **slow down** ralentir.
slug[1] (slʌg) *n* limace *f.* **sluggish** *adj* **1** paresseux, -euse. **2** lent. **3** lourd.
slug[2] (slʌg) *vt* cogner(violemment).
sluice (slu:s) *n* écluse *f.*
slum (slʌm) *n* taudis *m.*
slumber (slʌmbə) *vi* sommeiller, être assoupi. *n* assoupissement *m.*
slump (slʌmp) *n* dépression économique, baisse des cours *f. vi* tomber lourdement.
slung (slʌŋ) *v* see **sling.**
slur (slə:) *n* **1** affront *m.* flétrissure *f.* **2** *mus* liaison *f. vt* **1** bredouiller. **2** lier.
slush (slʌʃ) *n* neige à demi fondue *f.*
sly (slai) *adj* matois, rusé.
smack[1] (smæk) *n* léger goût *m.* saveur *f.*
smack[2] (smæk) *n* claquement *m.* claque *f. vt* donner une gifle à.
small (smɔ:l) *adj* **1** petit, menu. **2** mesquin. **3** peu de. **smallholding** *n* petite ferme *f.* **smallpox** *n* petite vérole *f.*
smart (smɑ:t) *vi* cuire, brûler. *adj* **1** vif, vive. **2** fin, malin. **3** élégant, chic. *n* cinglant *m.* **smarten** *vt* animer. **smarten up** dégourdir.
smash (smæʃ) *n* **1** accident *m.* **2** coup écrasant *m. vt* briser en morceaux.
smear (smiə) *n* tache, souillure *f. vt* souiller, barbouiller.
smell* (smel) *n* **1** odorat, flair *m.* **2** odeur *f.* parfum *m. vt,vi* sentir. *vt* flairer.
smile (smail) *n* sourire *m. vi* sourire.
smirk (smə:k) *vi* minauder. *n* sourire affecté *m.*
smock (smɔk) *n* chemise, blouse *f.*
smog (smɔg) *n* purée de pois *f.* brouillard épais *m.*
smoke (smouk) *n* fumée *f. vi,vt* fumer.
smooth (smu:ð) *adj* lisse, aplani, uni. *vt* lisser, aplanir. **smoothen** *vt* lisser.
smother ('smʌðə) *vt* étouffer, suffoquer.
smoulder ('smouldə) *vi* couver, brûler lentement.
smudge (smʌdʒ) *vt* barbouiller, maculer. *n* tache *f.*
smug (smʌg) *adj* suffisant, béat.
smuggle ('smʌgəl) *vt* passer en contrebande.
snack (snæk) *n* casse-croûte *m invar.* **snack-bar** *n* snack-bar *m.*
snag (snæg) *n* **1** écueil, obstacle *m.* **2** accroc *m. vt* accrocher.
snail (sneil) *n* escargot *m.*
snake (sneik) *n* serpent *m.*
snap (snæp) *n* **1** claquement *m.* **2** coup de dents *m. adj* immédiat, instantané. *vt* **1** faire claquer. **2** casser net. **3** happer. **snapshot** *n* instantané *m.*
snarl (snɑ:l) *vi* gronder, grogner. *n* grondement, grognement *m.*

snatch (snætʃ) *vt* saisir brusquement, arracher. *n* mouvement brusque pour saisir *m*.
sneak (sni:k) *n inf* cafard *m*. *v* **sneak in** se faufiler dans. **sneak off** partir furtivement.
sneer (sniə) *n* sourire de mépris *m*. *vi* ricaner.
sneeze (sni:z) *n* éternuement *m*. *vi* éternuer.
sniff (snif) *n* reniflement *m*. *vi,vt* renifler.
snipe (snaip) *n* bécassine *f*.
snivel ('snivəl) *vi* pleurnicher.
snob (snɔb) *n* snob, prétentieux *m*.
snooker ('snu:kə) *n* jeu de billard *m*.
snoop (snu:p) *vi* fureter, fouiner.
snooty ('snu:ti) *adj* prétentieux, -euse.
snooze (snu:z) *n* somme, roupillon *m*. *vi* sommeiller.
snore (snɔ:) *vi* ronfler. *n* ronflement *m*.
snort (snɔ:t) *n* renâclement, ébrouement *m*. *vi* renâcler, s'ébrouer.
snout (snaut) *n* museau, -aux, mufle *m*.
snow (snou) *n* neige *f*. *v imp* neiger. **snowball** *n* boule de neige *f*. **snowdrift** *n* congère *f*. **snowdrop** *n* perce-neige *m or f invar*. **snowflake** *n* flocon de neige *m*. **snowman** *n* bonhomme de neige *m*. **snowplough** *n* chasse-neige *m invar*. **snowstorm** *n* tempête de neige *f*.
snub (snʌb) *n* mortification, rebuffade *f*. *vt* rabrouer, faire affront à.
snuff (snʌf) *n* tabac à priser *m*.
snug (snʌg) *adj* confortable, douillet, -ette.
snuggle ('snʌgəl) *vt* serrer. *vi* se blottir.
so (sou) *adv* **1** si, tellement. **2** ainsi. **3** le. **so much** *or* **many** autant de. ~*conj* donc. **so as to** afin de. **so that** pour que. **so-and-so** *n* **1** *inf* individu *m*. **2** ceci et cela. **3** *inf* machin *m*. **Mr So-and-so** Monsieur un tel. **so-called** *adj* soi-disant. **so-so** *adj,adv* comme ci comme ça.
soak (souk) *vt,vi* tremper.
soap (soup) *n* savon *m*. **soap-powder** *n* savon en poudre *m*.
soar (sɔ:) *vi* s'élever, monter.
sob (sɔb) *n* sanglot *m*. *vi* sangloter.
sober ('soubə) *adj* **1** sobre, modéré. **2** pas ivre.
social ('souʃəl) *adj* social, -aux. **sociable** *adj* sociable. **socialism** *n* socialisme *m*. **socialist** *adj,n* socialiste.
society (sə'saiəti) *n* société *f*.
sociology (sousi'ɔlədʒi) *n* sociologie *f*. **sociological** *adj* sociologique. **sociologist** *n* sociologue *m,f*.
sock[1] (sɔk) *n* chaussette *f*.
sock[2] (sɔk) *vt inf* donner une beigne à.
socket ('sɔkit) *n* **1** emboîture *f*. **2** *anat* alvéole, jointure *f*.
soda ('soudə) *n* soude *f*. **soda-water** *n* eau de Seltz *f*. soda *m*.
sofa ('soufə) *n* canapé *m*.
soft (sɔft) *adj* **1** mou, molle. **2** doux, douce. **soften** *vt* **1** amollir. **2** assouplir. **3** adoucir. *vi* **1** s'amollir. **2** s'attendrir.
soggy ('sɔgi) *adj* détrempé, saturé.
soil[1] (sɔil) *n* sol, terrain *m*.
soil[2] (sɔil) *vt* salir, souiller.
solar ('soulə) *adj* solaire.
sold (sould) *v* see **sell.**
solder ('sɔldə) *vt* souder. *n* soudure *f*.
soldier ('souldʒə) *n* soldat *m*.
sole[1] (soul) *adj* **1** seul, unique. **2** exclusif, -ive.
sole[2] (soul) *n* **1** *anat* plante *f*. **2** semelle *f*.
sole[3] (soul) *n zool* sole *f*.
solemn ('sɔləm) *adj* solennel, -elle.
solicitor (sə'lisitə) *n* avoué *m*.
solid ('sɔlid) *adj* solide. **solidify** *vt* solidifier. *vi* se solidifier, se figer.
solitary ('sɔlitri) *adj* solitaire.
solitude ('sɔlitju:d) *n* solitude *f*.
solo ('soulou) *n* solo *m*. **soloist** *n* soliste *m,f*.
solstice ('sɔlstis) *n* solstice *m*.
soluble ('sɔljubəl) *adj* soluble.
solution (sə'lu:ʃən) *n* solution *f*.
solve (sɔlv) *vt* résoudre. **solvent** *adj* **1** solvable. **2** dissolvant. *n* dissolvant *m*.
sombre ('sɔmbə) *adj* sombre, morne.
some (sʌm) *adj* **1** quelque, quelconque. **2** de. **3** environ. *pron* **1** certains. **2** en. **somebody** *pron* quelqu'un. **somehow** *adv* d'une façon ou d'une autre. **someone** *pron* quelqu'un. **something** *pron* quelquechose. **sometime** *adv* tôt ou tard. **sometimes** *adv* quelquefois, parfois. **somewhat** *adv* quelque peu, un peu. **somewhere** *adv* quelque part. **somewhere else** ailleurs.
somersault ('sʌməsɔ:lt) *n* saut périlleux *m*. culbute *f*. *vi* faire la culbute.
son (sʌn) *n* fils *m*. **son-in-law** *n* beau-fils, gendre *m*.
sonata (sə'nɑ:tə) *n* sonate *f*.
song (sɔŋ) *n* chant *m*. chanson *f*.
sonic ('sɔnik) *adj* sonique.
sonnet ('sɔnit) *n* sonnet *m*.
soon (su:n) *adv* bientôt, tôt. **as soon as** aussitôt que, dès que.
soot (sut) *n* suie *f*.
soothe (su:ð) *vt* calmer, apaiser.

sophisticated (sə'fistikeitid) *adj* blasé, sophistiqué.
soprano (sə'prɑ:nou) *n* soprano *m*.
sordid ('sɔ:did) *adj* sordide.
sore (sɔ:) *adj* **1** douloureux, -euse, irrité. **2** sensible. *n* **1** plaie *f*. **2** mal *m*.
sorrow ('sɔrou) *n* peine *f*. chagrin *m*. *vi* s'affliger.
sorry ('sɔri) *adj* **1** désolé. **2** fâché, peiné. *interj* pardon!
sort (sɔ:t) *n* sorte, espèce *f*. genre *m*. *vt* assortir, trier, classifier.
sou (su:) *n* sou *m*.
souffle ('su:flei) *n* soufflé *m*.
sought (sɔ:t) *v* see **seek.**
soul (soul) *n* âme *f*.
sound[1] (saund) *n* son, bruit *m*. *vi* **1** sonner, retentir. **2** paraître. **soundproof** *adj* isolé, insonore.
sound[2] (saund) *adj* **1** sain, robuste. **2** solide. **3** profond.
sound[3] (saund) *vt* sonder.
soup (su:p) *n* soupe *f*. potage *m*.
sour (sauə) *adj* **1** aigre, acide. **2** revêche. *vt* aigrir. *vi* s'aigrir.
source (sɔ:s) *n* source, origine *f*.
south (sauθ) *n* sud *m*. **south of France** midi *m*. *adj* méridional, -aux, sud *invar*. *adv* au *or* vers le sud. **south-east** *n* sud-est *m*. *adv* vers le sud-est. *adj* du sud-est. **southerly** *adj* du sud. **southern** *adj* du sud, méridional, -aux. **southward** *adj* du côté du sud. **southwards** *adv* vers le sud. **south-west** *n* sud-ouest *m*. *adv* vers le sud-ouest. *adj* du sud-ouest.
South Africa *n* Afrique du Sud *f*. **South African** *adj,n* sud-africain.
South America *n* Amérique du Sud *f*. **South American** *adj,n* sud-américain.
South Pole *n* pôle sud *m*.
souvenir (su:və'niə) *n* souvenir *m*.
sovereign ('sɔvrin) *n* souverain *m*. *adj* souverain, suprême.
Soviet Union ('souviət) *n* Union soviétique *f*.
sow*[1] (sou) *vt* semer, ensemencer.
sow[2] (sau) *n* truie *f*.
soya bean ('sɔiə) *n* soja *m*.
spa (spɑ:) *n* station thermale *f*.
space (speis) *n* espace *m*. *vt* espacer.
spade[1] (speid) *n* bêche *f*.
spade[2] (speid) *n game* pique *m*.
Spain (spein) *n* Espagne *f*. **Spaniard** *n* espagnol *m*. **Spanish** *adj* espagnol. **Spanish** (language) *n* espagnol *m*.
span (spæn) *n* **1** empan *m*. envergure *f*. **2** portée *f*. écartement *m*. **3** durée *f*. *vt* **1** enjamber. **2** embrasser.
spaniel ('spæniəl) *n* épagneul *m*.
spank (spæŋk) *vt* fesser. *n* fessée, claque *f*.
spanner ('spænə) *n* clef (à écrous) *f*.
spare (spɛə) *adj* **1** disponible. **2** de rechange. *vt* **1** épargner, ménager. **2** se passer de. **sparing** *adj* **1** économe, chiche. **2** modéré.
spark (spɑ:k) *n* étincelle *f*. trait *m*. *vi* émettre des étincelles. **spark plug** *n* bougie d'allumage *f*.
sparkle ('spɑ:kəl) *vi* étinceler, scintiller, pétiller. *n* étincellement, pétillement *m*.
sparrow ('spærou) *n* moineau, -aux *m*.
sparse (spɑ:s) *adj* clairsemé, épars.
spasm ('spæzəm) *n* spasme *m*. **spasmodic** *adj* **1** spasmodique. **2** fait par à-coups. **spastic** *adj* spasmodique. *n* malade de paralysie spasmodique *m,f*.
spat (spæt) *v* see **spit.**
spatial ('speiʃəl) *adj* spatial, -aux.
spatula ('spætjulə) *n* spatule *f*.
spawn (spɔ:n) *n* frai *m*. œufs (de poisson) *m pl*. *vi* frayer.
speak* (spi:k) *vi,vt* parler, dire. **speaker** *n* orateur *m*.
spear (spiə) *n* lance *f*. javelot *m*.
special ('speʃəl) *adj* spécial, -aux, particulier, -ière. **specialist** *n* spécialiste *m,f*. **speciality** *n* spécialité *f*. **specialize** *vt* particulariser. *vi* se spécialiser.
species ('spi:ʃi:z) *n* espèce *f*.
specify ('spesifai) *vt* spécifier, préciser. **specific** *adj* spécifique.
specimen ('spesimən) *n* spécimen, échantillon *m*.
speck (spek) *n* **1** petite tache *f*. **2** grain *m*.
spectacle ('spektəkəl) *n* **1** spectacle *m*. **2** *pl* lunettes *f pl*. **spectacular** *adj* spectaculaire.
spectator (spek'teitə) *n* spectateur, -trice.
spectrum ('spektrəm) *n pl* **-tra** *or* **-trums** spectre *m*.
speculate ('spekjuleit) *vi* **1** spéculer. **2** méditer.
speech (spi:tʃ) *n* **1** parole *f*. **2** discours *m*. **speechless** *adj* interdit, muet, -ette.
speed (spi:d) *n* vitesse *f*. *vi* se hâter. **speedboat** *n* canot automobile *m*.
spell[1] (spel) *vt* épeler, s'écrire. **spelling** *n* orthographe *f*.
spell[2] (spel) *n* charme *m*. formule magique *f*. **spellbound** *adj* ensorcelé, charmé.
spell[3] (spel) *n* **1** période *f*. **2** tour *m*.

spend* (spend) *vt* **1** dépenser. **2** passer. **3** consacrer. **spendthrift** *adj,n* dépensier, -ière.
sperm (spə:m) *n* sperme *m*.
sphere (sfiə) *n* sphère *f*. **spherical** *adj* sphérique.
spice (spais) *n* épice *f*.
spider ('spaidə) *n* araignée *f*.
spike (spaik) *n* pointe *f*. piquant *m*. *vt* clouer.
spill* (spil) *vt* répandre, verser. *vi* se répandre.
spin* (spin) *n* rotation *f*. *vt* **1** filer. **2** faire tourner. *vi* tourner. **spin-dry** *vt* essorer.
spinach ('spinidʒ) *n* épinards *m pl*.
spine (spain) *n* colonne vertébrale *f*.
spinster ('spinstə) *n* femme non mariée *f*.
spiral ('spairəl) *n* spirale, hélice *f*. *adj* spiral, -aux.
spire (spaiə) *n* flèche *f*.
spirit ('spirit) *n* **1** esprit *m*. **2** alcool *m*. **spiritual** *adj* spirituel, -elle.
spit* [1] (spit) *vi* **1** cracher. **2** (with rain) bruiner. *n* crachat *m*. salive *f*.
spit [2] (spit) *n* broche *f*.
spite (spait) *n* rancune *f*. dépit *m*. **in spite of** malgré. **spiteful** *adj* rancunier, -ière, méchant.
splash (splæʃ) *n* éclaboussure, tache *f*. *vt* éclabousser.
splendid ('splendid) *adj* splendide. **splendour** *n* splendeur *f*.
splint (splint) *n* éclisse, attelle *f*. **splinter** *n* éclat *m*. écharde *f*. *vi* voler en éclats.
split* (split) *vt* **1** fendre. **2** diviser. *vi* se fendre. *n* **1** fente *f*. **2** division *f*.
splutter ('splʌtə) *n* bredouillement, crachement *m*. *vi* bredouiller, crochoter.
spoil* (spɔil) *vt* gâter, abîmer, endommager. *vi* s'abîmer. **spoil-sport** *n* rabat-joie *m,f invar*.
spoke [1] (spouk) *n* rayon *m*.
spoke [2] (spouk) *v see* **speak.**
spoken ('spoukən) *v see* **speak.**
spokesman ('spouksmən) *n* porte-parole *m invar*.
sponge (spʌndʒ) *n* éponge *f*. *vt* éponger. **sponge on** vivre aux crochets de.
sponsor ('spɔnsə) *n* garant *m*. *vt* subventionner. **sponsorship** *n* parrainage *m*.
spontaneous (spɔn'teiniəs) *adj* spontané, automatique. **spontaneously** *adv* spontanément.
spool (spu:l) *n* bobine *f*.
spoon (spu:n) *n* cuiller, cuillère *f*. **spoonful** *n* cuillerée *f*.
sport (spɔ:t) *n* sport *m*. **sportive** *adj* badin. **sportsman** *n* sportif *m*.

spot (spɔt) *n* **1** endroit *m*. **2** tache *f*. **3** pois *m*. **4** goutte *f*. **on the spot** sur-le-champ. ~*vt* **1** tacher. **2** apercevoir. **spotless** *adj* immaculé. **spotlight** *n* projecteur *m*.
spouse (spaus) *n* époux, -ouse.
spout (spaut) *n* **1** bec *m*. **2** gouttière *f*. *vi* **1** jaillir. **2** pérorer. *vt* déclamer.
sprain (sprein) *n* entorse, foulure *f*. *vt* se fouler.
sprang (spræŋ) *v see* **spring.**
sprawl (sprɔ:l) *vi* s'étaler, se vautrer.
spray [1] (sprei) *vt* **1** pulvériser. **2** asperger. *n* **1** atomiseur *m*. **2** jet *m*. **3** embrun *m*.
spray [2] (sprei) *n* (of flowers, etc.) brin *m*.
spread* (spred) *vt* **1** étendre. **2** répandre. **3** déployer. *vi* **1** s'étendre. **2** se répandre. *n* **1** étendue *f*. **2** diffusion *f*. **3** *inf* festin *m*.
spree (spri:) *n* fête, rigolade *f*.
sprig (sprig) *n* brindille *f*.
sprightly ('spraitli) *adj* éveillé, sémillant.
spring* (spriŋ) *n* **1** printemps *m*. **2** source *f*. **3** saut *m*. **4** ressort *m*. *vi* **1** bondir, sauter. **2** jaillir. **springboard** *n* tremplin *m*. **spring-clean** *vt* nettoyer à fond. **springtime** *n* printemps *m*.
sprinkle ('spriŋkəl) *vt* saupoudrer, arroser. *n* pincée *f*.
sprint (sprint) *n* course de vitesse *f*. sprint *m*. *vi* faire une course de vitesse.
sprout (spraut) *n* pousse *f*. germe *m*. *vi* pousser, germer, bourgeonner.
sprung (sprʌŋ) *v see* **spring.**
spun (spʌn) *v see* **spin.**
spur (spə:) *n* **1** éperon *m*. **2** stimulant *m*. **3** éperon *m*. ~*vt* éperonner. **spur on** stimuler.
spurt (spə:t) *n* **1** giclée *f*. **2** coup de collier, sursaut *m*. *vi* jaillir.
spy (spai) *n* espion, -onne. *vi* espionner. *vt* épier.
squabble ('skwɔbəl) *vi* se chamailler. *n* prise de bec *f*.
squad (skwɔd) *n* **1** *mil* peloton *m*. **2** brigade *f*.
squadron ('skwɔdrən) *n* **1** *mil* escadron *m*. **2** *naut* escadre *f*.
squalid ('skwɔlid) *adj* sale, crasseux, -euse.
squander ('skwɔndə) *vt* gaspiller.
square (skwɛə) *n* **1** carré *m*. **2** carreau, -aux *m*. **3** place *f*. *adj* **1** carré. **2** en ordre. **3** quitte. *vt* **1** carrer. **2** régler. **3** accorder.
squash (skwɔʃ) *n* **1** écrasement *m*. cohue *f*. **2** *sport* squash *m*. *vt* écraser. *vi* s'écraser.
squat (skwɔt) *vi* **1** s'accroupir. **2** occuper sans titre de possession. *adj* trapu, accroupi.

squawk (skwɔ:k) *vi* pousser des cris rauques. *n* cri rauque *m*.
squeak (skwi:k) *vi* **1** pousser des cris aigus, crier. **2** grincer, crisser. *n* **1** petit cri aigu *m*. **2** crissement *m*.
squeal (skwi:l) *vi* pousser des cris aigus. *n* cri aigu *m*.
squeamish ('skwi:miʃ) *adj* **1** délicat, difficile. **2** nauséeux, -euse.
squeeze (skwi:z) *vt* **1** presser, serrer. **2** extorquer.
squid (skwid) *n* calmar *m*.
squiggle ('skwigəl) *n* tortillement *m*. fioriture *f*.
squint (skwint) *n* strabisme *m*. *vi* loucher.
squirm (skwə:m) *vi* **1** se tordre. **2** être au supplice.
squirrel ('skwirl) *n* écureuil *m*.
squirt (skwə:t) *vt* faire jaillir. *vi* gicler. *n* jet *m*. giclée *f*.
stab (stæb) *n* coup de couteau *m*. *vt* poignarder.
stabilize ('steibəlaiz) *vt* stabiliser.
stable[1] ('steibəl) *n* écurie *f*.
stable[2] ('steibəl) *adj* **1** stable, solide. **2** permanent. **3** constant.
stack (stæk) *n* **1** meule *f*. **2** tas *m*. **3** cheminée *f*. *vt* **1** empiler. **2** entasser.
stadium ('steidiəm) *n*, *pl* **-ia** *or* **-iums** stade *m*.
staff (sta:f) *n* **1** personnel *m*. **2** bâton *m*.
stag (stæg) *n* cerf *m*.
stage (steidʒ) *n* **1** *Th* scène *f*. **2** estrade *f*. **3** phase *f*. **4** étape *f*. *vt* monter. **stage manager** *n* régisseur *m*.
stagger ('stægə) *vi* chanceler. *vt* **1** échelonner, étaler. **2** *inf* renverser, étonner. **3** faire chanceler.
stagnant ('stægnənt) *adj* **1** stagnant. **2** inactif, -ive. **stagnate** *vi* croupir.
stain (stein) *n* **1** tache *f*. **2** couleur *f*. colorant *m*. *vt* **1** souiller. **2** teindre, teinter. **stained-glass window** *n* vitrail, -aux *m*. **stainless** *adj* inoxydable.
stair (stɛə) *n* **1** marche *f*. **2** *pl* escalier *m*. **staircase** *n* escalier *m*.
stake[1] (steik) *n* **1** pieu, -eux, jalon *m*. **2** bûcher *m*. *vt* jalonner.
stake[2] (steik) *n* *game* enjeu, -eux *m*. mise *f*. **at stake** en jeu. ~*vt* jouer, risquer.
stale (steil) *adj* **1** rassis, vicié. **2** passé, rebattu. **3** défraîchi.
stalemate ('steilmeit) *n* **1** *game* pat *m*. **2** impasse *m*.
stalk[1] (stɔ:k) *n* tige *f*. trognon *m*.
stalk[2] (stɔ:k) *vt* traquer. *vi* marcher à grands pas.
stall[1] (stɔ:l) *n* **1** stalle *f*. **2** étalage *m*. **3** *pl* *Th* fauteuils d'orchestre *m pl*. *vt,vi* caler.
stall[2] (stɔ:l) *vt* (evade) repousser, berner.
stallion ('stæliən) *n* étalon *m*.
stamina ('stæminə) *n* vigueur, énergie *f*.
stammer ('stæmə) *vi,vt* bégayer, balbutier. *n* bégaiement *m*.
stamp (stæmp) *n* **1** timbre *m*. **2** poinçon *m*. **3** trépignement *m*. *vt* **1** timbrer. **2** poinçonner. **3** frapper. **4** trépigner.
stampede (stæm'pi:d) *n* débandade *f*. *vi* fuir en désordre.
stand* (stænd) *vi* **1** être *or* se tenir debout. **2** se trouver. **3** se maintenir. **4** représenter, signifier. **5** durer. *vt* **1** mettre. **2** supporter. *n* **1** situation *f*. **2** support *m*. **3** étalage *m*. **4** stand *m*. **stand-by** *n* **1** appui *m*. **2** ressource *f*. **standing** *n* **1** situation *f*. **2** rang *m*. **3** durée *f*. *adj* **1** debout. **2** stagnant. **3** sur pied. **4** fixe. **standstill** *n* arrêt *m*.
standard ('stændəd) *n* **1** norme *f*. **2** bannière *f*. **3** degré *m*. étalon *m*. *adj* **1** type. **2** classique. **3** courant.
stank (stæŋk) *v see* **stink**
stanza ('stænzə) *n* stance, strophe *f*.
staple[1] ('steipəl) *n* **1** crampon *m*. **2** agrafe *f*. *vt* **1** cramponner. **2** agrafer.
staple[2] ('steipəl) *adj* principal, -aux.
star (sta:) *n* **1** étoile *f*. astre *m*. **2** (films, etc.) star, vedette *f*. *vi* être en vedette. **starfish** *n* étoile de mer *f*.
starboard ('sta:bəd) *n* tribord *m*.
starch (sta:tʃ) *n* amidon *m*. *vt* empeser.
stare (stɛə) *vi* regarder fixement. *n* regard fixe *m*.
stark (sta:k) *adj* **1** raide. **2** absolu. *adv* entièrement, tout.
starling ('sta:liŋ) *n* étourneau, -aux, sansonnet *m*.
start (sta:t) *n* **1** commencement *m*. **2** départ *m*. **3** sursaut *m*. *vi* **1** commencer. **2** sursauter. *vt* **1** entamer, se mettre à. **2** mettre en marche. **3** lancer. **starter** *n* *mot* démarreur *m*.
startle ('sta:tl̩) *vt* faire sursauter, effrayer.
starve (sta:v) *vi* mourir de faim. *vt* **1** faire mourir de faim, affamer. **2** priver.
state (steit) *n* **1** état *m*. **2** position *f*. **3** pompe *f*. *adj* **1** d'état. **2** d'apparat. *vt* **1** déclarer. **2** fixer. **stately** *adj* majestueux, -euse. **statement** *n* **1** déclaration *f*. compte rendu *m*. **2**

law déposition *f.* **3** *comm* relevé *m.* **statesman** *n* homme d'Etat *m.*

static ('stætik) *adj,n* statique *f.*

station ('steiʃən) **1** (railway) gare *f.* **2** poste *m.* **3** position *f.* rang *m.* **station-master** *n* chef de gare *m.*

stationary ('steiʃənri) *adj* stationnaire.

stationer ('steiʃənə) *n* libraire *m.* **stationer's shop** *n* papeterie *f.* **stationery** *n* papeterie *f.*

statistics (stə'tistiks) *n* statistique *f.*

statue ('stætju:) *n* statue *f.*

stature ('stætʃə) *n* stature, taille *f.*

status ('steitəs) *n* position *f.* rang *m.*

statute ('stætju:t) *n* loi *f.* statut *m.* **statutory** *adj* réglementaire.

stay[1] (stei) *n* séjour *m.* *vi* **1** rester, se tenir. **2** séjourner. **3** attendre.

stay[2] (stei) *n* support *m.* *vt* étayer.

steadfast ('stedfɑ:st) *adj* **1** constant. **2** stable, ferme.

steady ('stedi) *adj* **1** ferme. **2** soutenu, régulier, -ière. **3** rangé. *vt* raffermir. *vi* reprendre son aplomb.

steak (steik) *n* bifteck *m.* entrecôte *f.*

steal* (sti:l) *vt* **1** voler. **2** dérober. **stealing** *n* vol *m.*

steam (sti:m) *n* vapeur *f.* *vt* cuire à la vapeur. *vi* fumer. **steam-roller** *n* rouleau compresseur *m.*

steel (sti:l) *n* acier *m.* *adj* d'acier.

steep[1] (sti:p) *adj* escarpé, raide.

steep[2] (sti:p) *vt,vi* tremper.

steeple ('sti:pəl) *n* clocher *m.* **steeplechase** *n* steeple-chase *m.*

steer (stiə) *vt* diriger, conduire. **steering-wheel** *n* volant *m.*

stem[1] (stem) *n* tige *f.* *v* **stem from** provenir de.

stem[2] (stem) *vt* **1** arrêter, endiguer. **2** refouler.

stencil ('stensəl) *n* **1** pochoir *m.* **2** stencil *m.*

step (step) *n* **1** pas *m.* **2** démarche *f.* **3** marche *f.* échelon *m.* *vi* faire un pas, aller. **step-ladder** *n* marchepied *m.*

stepbrother ('stepbrʌðə) *n* demi-frère *m.*

stepdaughter ('stepdɔ:tə) *n* belle-fille *f.*

stepfather ('stepfɑ:ðə) *n* beau-père *m.*

stepmother ('stepmʌðə) *n* belle-mère *f.*

stepsister ('stepsistə) *n* demi-soeur *f.*

stepson ('stepsʌn) *n* beau-fils *m.*

stereo ('steriou) *adj,n* stéréo *m.*

stereophonic (steriə'fɔnik) *adj* stéréophonique.

stereotype ('steriətaip) *n* cliché *m.* *vt* stéréotyper.

sterile ('sterail) *adj* stérile. **sterilize** *vt* stériliser.

sterling ('stə:liŋ) *n* sterling *m.* *adj* **1** de bon aloi. **2** sterling.

stern[1] (stə:n) *adj* sévère, rigide, austère.

stern[2] (stə:n) *n naut* arrière *m.* poupe *f.*

stethoscope ('steθəskoup) *n* stéthoscope *m.*

stew (stju:) *n* ragoût *m.* *vt* faire cuire à la casserole. *vi* mijoter.

steward ('stju:əd) *n* **1** intendant *m.* **2** économe *m.* **3** commissaire *m.* **stewardess** *n* femme de chambre, stewardess *f.*

stick[1] (stik) *n* **1** bâton *m.* **2** canne *f.* **3** morceau de bois *m.*

stick*[2] (stik) *vt* **1** coller. **2** enfoncer. **3** *inf* mettre. **4** *sl* supporter. *vi* **1** adhérer. **2** s'embourber. **3** se coincer. **stick at** s'arrêter devant. **stick out** saillir. **stick to** **1** s'en tenir à. **2** rester fidèle à.

sticky ('stiki) *adj* **1** collant. **2** *inf* difficile.

stiff (stif) *adj* **1** raide, dur. **2** pénible, difficile. **stiffen** *vt* raidir. *vi* se saidir, se guinder. **stiffly** *adv* avec raideur.

stifle ('staifəl) *vt* **1** étouffer. **2** réprimer. *vi* suffoquer.

stigma ('stigmə) *n, pl* **-mata** *or* **-as** stigmate *m.*

stile (stail) *n* échalier *m.*

still[1] (stil) *adj* **1** tranquille, calme. **2** immobile. *adv* toujours, encore. *conj* cependant, pourtant. **stillborn** *adj* mort-né. **still life** *n* nature morte *f.*

still[2] (stil) *n* alambic *m.*

stilt (stilt) *n* échasse *f.* **stilted** *adj* guindé, tendu.

stimulate ('stimjuleit) *vt* stimuler, activer.

stimulus ('stimjuləs) *n, pl* **-li** stimulant *m.* impulsion *f.*

sting* (stiŋ) *vt* piquer. *vi* cuire. *n* **1** piqûre *f.* dard *m.* **2** pointe *f.*

stink* (stiŋk) *vi* puer. *n* puanteur *f.*

stipulate ('stipjuleit) *vt,vi* stipuler.

stir (stə:) *n* **1** remuement *m.* **2** mouvement *m.* **3** *inf* remue-ménage *m invar.* *vt* **1** remuer. **2** agiter, susciter. *vi* remuer, bouger.

stirrup ('stirəp) *n* étrier *m.*

stitch (stitʃ) *n* **1** point *m.* maille *f.* **2** *med* suture *f.* *vt* **1** coudre. **2** *med* suturer.

stoat (stout) *n* hermine d'été *f.*

stock (stɔk) *n* **1** provision *f.* **2** stock *m.* **3** souche *f.* **4** *pl comm* titres *m pl.* actions *f pl.* **5** *cul* bouillon *m.* *adj* courant. *vt* **1** approvisionner. **2** stocker. **stockbreeding** *n* élevage *m.* **stockbroker** *n* agent de change *m.* **stock exchange** *n* bourse *f.* **stockpile** *n* stocks de

réserve *m pl.* *vt,vi* stocker. **stocktaking** *n* inventaire *m.*
stocking ('stɔkiŋ) *n* bas *m.*
stocky ('stɔki) *adj* trapu.
stodge (stɔdʒ) *n inf* aliment bourratif *m.*
stoical ('stouikḷ) *adj* stoïque.
stoke (stouk) *vt* chauffer, entretenir.
stole[1] (stoul) *v* see **steal.**
stole[2] (stoul) *n* étole *f.*
stolen ('stoulən) *v* see **steal.**
stomach ('stʌmək) *n* **1** estomac *m.* **2** ventre *m.* *vt inf* supporter. **stomach-ache** *n* mal de ventre *m.*
stone (stoun) *n* **1** pierre *f.* **2** (of a fruit) noyau, -aux *m.* **3** (weight) stone *m.* *adj* de pierre. *vt* **1** lapider. **2** dénoyauter.
stood (stud) *v* see **stand.**
stool (stu:l) *n* tabouret *m.*
stoop (stu:p) *vi* **1** se pencher. **2** s'abaisser. **3** être voûté.
stop (stɔp) *vt* **1** arrêter. **2** boucher. **3** cesser. **4** retenir. *vi* s'arrêter. *n* arrêt *m.* **stoppage** *n* **1** suspension *f.* **2** obstruction *f.* **stopper** *n* bouchon *m.* **stopwatch** *n* chronomètre *m.*
store (stɔ:) *n* **1** provision, réserve *f.* **2** magasin *m.* *vt* **1** approvisionner. **2** amasser. **3** emmagasiner. **storage** *n* emmagasinage *m.*
storey ('stɔ:ri) *n* étage *m.*
stork (stɔ:k) *n* cigogne *f.*
storm (stɔ:m) *n* orage *m.* tempête *f.* *vi* faire rage. *vt* donner l'assaut à. **stormy** *adj* orageux, -euse.
story ('stɔ:ri) *n* histoire *f.* conte, récit *m.*
stout (staut) *adj* **1** fort. **2** costaud, vaillant. **3** corpulent. *n* stout *m.* bière brune forte *f.*
stove (stouv) *n* poêle, fourneau, -aux *m.*
stow (stou) *vt* arrimer. **stowaway** *n* passager clandestin *m.*
straddle (strædḷ) *vi* se tenir *or* marcher les jambes ecartées. *vt* chevaucher, s'affourcher sur, enfourcher.
straggle ('strægəl) *vi* **1** s'éparpiller. **2** traîner. **straggler** *n* traînard *m.*
straight (streit) *adj* **1** droit, raide. **2** franc, -che. **3** en ordre. *adv* **1** droit. **2** juste. **3** directement. **4** tout droit. **straignten** *vt* **1** redresser. **2** mettre en ordre. *vi* se redresser. **straightforward** *adj* loyal, -aux, franc, -che.
strain[1] (strein) *vt* **1** tendre. **2** *med* se fouler. **3** filtrer. *vi* peiner, fatiguer. *n* **1** tension *f.* **2** *med* entorse *f.*
strain[2] (strein) *n* lignée, race *f.*
strand[1] (strænd) *vt,vi* échouer.
strand[2] (strænd) *n* brin *m.* fibre *f.*
strange (streindʒ) *adj* étrange, bizarre, singulier, -ière. **strangeness** *n* étrangeté *f.* **stranger** *n* inconnu *m.*
strangle ('stræŋgəl) *vt* étrangler.
strap (stræp) *n* **1** courroie *f.* **2** bande *f.* *vt* lier avec une courroie.
strategy ('strætidʒi) *n* stratégie *f.* **strategic** *adj* stratégique.
straw (strɔ:) *n* paille *f.* **that's the last straw!** ça, c'est le comble! *~adj* de paille. **strawberry** *n* fraise *f.* **strawberry plant** fraisier *m.*
stray (strei) *vi* **1** s'égarer. **2** s'éloigner, errer.
streak (stri:k) *n* **1** rayure *f.* **2** trait *m.* *vt* rayer, strier.
stream (stri:m) *n* **1** ruisseau, -aux *m.* **2** flux *m.* **3** courant *m.* *vi* couler. **streamline** *vt* **1** profiler. **2** moderniser.
street (stri:t) *n* rue *f.*
strength (streŋθ) *n* **1** force *f.* **2** nombre *m.* **strengthen** *vt* consolider, renforcer.
strenuous ('strenjuəs) *adj* **1** énergique. **2** acharné. **3** fatiguant.
stress (stres) *n* **1** tension *f.* **2** force *f.* **3** accent *m.* *vt* insister sur, souligner.
stretch (stretʃ) *n* **1** étendue *f.* **2** section *f.* **3** extension *f.* *vt* tendre. *vi* **1** s'élargir. **2** s'étendre. **stretcher** *n* brancard *m.*
strict (strikt) *adj* **1** strict. **2** rigide. **3** sévère.
stride* (straid) *vi* marcher à grandes enjambées. *n* enjambée *f.*
strike* (straik) *n* **1** grève *f.* **2** coup *m.* *vt* **1** frapper. **2** frotter. **3** heurter. *vi* **1** sonner. **2** se mettre en grève. **striking** *adj* remarquable.
string* (striŋ) *n* **1** corde *f.* **2** ficelle *f.* **3** cordon *m.* **4** chapelet *m.* **5** train *m.* *vt* enfiler.
stringent ('strindʒənt) *adj* rigoureux, -euse.
strip[1] (strip) *vt* **1** mettre à nu, dépouiller. **2** dégarnir. *vi* se dévêtir. **striptease** *n* striptease *m.*
strip[2] (strip) *n* **1** bande *f.* **2** lambeau, -aux *m.*
stripe (straip) *n* **1** raie *f.* **2** bande *f.* *vt* rayer, barrer.
strive* (straiv) *vi* **1** s'efforcer. **2** se débattre.
strode (stroud) *v* see **stride.**
stroke[1] (strouk) *n* **1** coup *m.* **2** trait *m.* **3** brassée *f.* **4** *med* apoplexie *f.*
stroke[2] (strouk) *vt* caresser. *n* caresse *f.*
stroll (stroul) *n* promenade *f.* tour *m.* *vi* flâner.
strong (strɔŋ) *adj* **1** fort. **2** solide. **3** prononcé. *adv* fort. **stronghold** *n* forteresse *f.* **strong-minded** *adj* résolu, décidé.
strove (strouv) *v* see **strive.**

struck (strʌk) *v* see **strike.**
structure (ˈstrʌktʃə) *n* **1** structure *f.* **2** édifice *m.*
struggle (ˈstrʌgəl) *n* lutte *f. vi* lutter, se débattre.
strum (strʌm) *vi* pianoter, tapoter.
strung (strʌŋ) *v* see **string.**
strut[1] (strʌt) *vi* se pavaner.
strut[2] (strʌt) *n* entretoise *f.*
stub (stʌb) *n* **1** souche *f.* **2** bout, mégot *m. vt* cogner, heurter. **stub out** éteindre.
stubborn (ˈstʌbən) *adj* obstiné, têtu, opiniâtre. **stubbornness** *n* entêtement *m.*
stud[1] (stʌd) *n* **1** clou à grosse tête *m.* **2** bouton *m.* **3** poteau, -aux *m. vt* **1** clouter. **2** parsemer.
stud[2] (stʌd) *n* écurie *f.* haras *m.*
student (ˈstju:dn̩t) *n* étudiant *m.*
studio (ˈstju:diou) *n* **1** *Art* atelier *m.* **2** studio *m.*
study (ˈstʌdi) *n* **1** étude *f.* **2** cabinet de travail *m. vt* étudier. **studious** *adj* studieux, -euse.
stuff (stʌf) *n* matière *f. vt* **1** rembourrer. **2** *cul* farcir. **3** empailler. **stuffing** *n* **1** *cul* farce *f.* **2** bourre *f.* **stuffy** *adj* **1** renfermé, mal aéré. **2** *inf* collet monté.
stumble (ˈstʌmbəl) *vi* trébucher.
stump (stʌmp) *n* **1** tronçon *m.* souche *f.* **2** bout *m.* **3** moignon *m. vt inf* coller.
stun (stʌn) *vt* **1** étourdir. **2** abasourdir. **stunning** *adj* **1** *inf* épatant. **2** étourdissant.
stung (stʌŋ) *v* see **sting.**
stunk (stʌŋk) *v* see **stink.**
stunt[1] (stʌnt) *vt* empêcher de croître, rabougrir.
stunt[2] (stʌnt) *n* **1** tour de force *m.* acrobatie *f.* **2** affaire publicitaire *f.*
stupid (ˈstju:pid) *adj* stupide, bête.
sturdy (ˈstə:di) *adj* **1** robuste. **2** hardi.
sturgeon (ˈstə:dʒən) *n* esturgeon *m.*
stutter (ˈstʌtə) *vt,vi* bégayer. *n* bégaiement *m.*
sty (stai) *n* étable *f.*
style (stail) *n* **1** style *m.* **2** manière *f.* **3** chic *m. vt* dénommer. **stylish** *adj* élégant, chic.
stylus (ˈstailəs) *n* stylet *m.*
subconscious (sʌbˈkɔnʃəs) *adj,n* subconscient *m.* **subconsciously** *adv* inconsciemment.
subcontract (sʌbkənˈtrækt) *vt* sous-traiter. **subcontractor** *n* sous-entrepreneur, sous-traitant *m.*
subdue (səbˈdju:) *vt* **1** subjuguer, soumettre. **2** atténuer.
subject (*n,adj* ˈsʌbdʒikt; *v* səbˈdʒekt) *n* **1** sujet *m.* **2** matière *f. adj* **1** assujetti. **2** sujet, -ette. *vt* assujettir. **subjective** *adj* subjectif, -ive.
subjunctive (səbˈdʒʌŋktiv) *adj,n* subjonctif, -ive *m.*
sublime (səˈblaim) *adj* sublime, suprême.
submachine-gun (səbməˈʃi:ngʌn) *n* mitraillette *f.*
submarine (sʌbməˈri:n) *n* sous-marin *m.*
submerge (səbˈmə:dʒ) *vt* submerger. *vi* plonger.
submit (səbˈmit) *vi* se soumettre. *vt* soumettre, présenter. **submission** *n* soumission *m.* **submissive** *adj* soumis, docile.
subnormal (sʌbˈnɔ:məl) *adj* au-dessous de la normale.
subordinate (səˈbɔ:dinət) *adj* inférieur, accessoire. *n* subordonné *m. vt* subordonner.
subscribe (səbˈskraib) *vt* souscrire. *vi* s'abonner à. **subscription** *n* **1** souscription *f.* **2** adhésion *f.* **3** abonnement *m.*
subsequent (ˈsʌbsikwint) *adj* subséquent. **subsequently** *adv* plus tard.
subservient (səbˈsə:viənt) *adj* **1** obséquieux, -euse. **2** subordonné. **3** utile.
subside (səbˈsaid) *vi* **1** s'affaisser. **2** baisser. **3** s'apaiser.
subsidiary (səbˈsidiəri) *n* filiale *f. adj* auxiliaire, subsidiaire.
subsidize (ˈsʌbsidaiz) *vt* subventionner. **subsidy** *n* subvention *f.*
subsist (səbˈsist) *vi* subsister.
substance (ˈsʌbstəns) *n* **1** substance *f.* **2** solidité *f.* **substantial** *adj* **1** substantiel, -elle. **2** important. **substantive** *n* substantif *m.*
substitute (ˈsʌbstitju:t) *n* **1** remplaçant *m.* **2** succédané *m. vt* substituer. *vi* remplacer. **substitution** *n* substitution *f.* remplacement *m.*
subtitle (ˈsʌbtaitl̩) *n* sous-titre *m. vt* sous-titrer.
subtle (ˈsʌtl̩) *adj* **1** subtil. **2** fin.
subtract (səbˈtrækt) *vt* soustraire. **subtraction** *n* soustraction *f.*
suburb (ˈsʌbə:b) *n* **1** faubourg *m.* **2** *pl* banlieue *f.* **suburban** *adj* suburbain.
subvert (sʌbˈvə:t) *vt* subvertir. **subversion** *n* subversion *f.* **subversive** *adj* subversif, -ive.
subway (ˈsʌbwei) *n* passage souterrain *m.*
succeed (səkˈsi:d) *vt* succéder. *vi* réussir. **success** *n* succès *m.* réussite *f.* **successful** *adj* heureux, -euse, réussi. **succession** *n* **1** succession *f.* **2** suite, série *f.* **successive** *adj* successif, -ive.
succulent (ˈsʌkjulənt) *adj* succulent.
succumb (səˈkʌm) *vi* succomber, céder.
such (sʌtʃ) *adj* **1** tel, telle, semblable. **2** si. **such as** tel que, comme. ~*pron* tel, telle.
suck (sʌk) *vt,vi* sucer. *vt* téter.

sucker ('sʌkə) *n* **1** *inf* gobeur, niais *m*. **2** *bot* rejeton *m*.
suction ('sʌkʃən) *n* succion, aspiration *f*.
sudden ('sʌdn̩) *adj* soudain, subit. **all of a sudden** tout à coup.
suds (sʌdz) *n pl* **1** mousse de savon *f*. **2** lessive *f*.
sue (su:) *vt* poursuivre en justice.
suede (sweid) *n* daim *m*.
suet ('su:it) *n* graisse de rognon *f*.
suffer ('sʌfə) *vt* **1** souffrir, éprouver. **2** supporter. *vi* souffrir. **suffering** *n* souffrance *f*.
sufficient (sə'fiʃənt) *adj* suffisant, assez de. **sufficiently** *adv* suffisamment, assez.
suffix ('sʌfiks) *n* suffixe *m*.
suffocate ('sʌfəkeit) *vt,vi* suffoquer, étouffer. **suffocation** *n* asphyxie *f*.
sugar ('ʃugə) *n* sucre. *vt* sucrer. **sugarbeet** *n* betterave à sucre *f*. **sugar cane** *n* canne à sucre *f*.
suggest (sə'dʒest) *vt* **1** suggérer. **2** inspirer. **suggestion** *n* **1** suggestion *f*. **2** trace *f*. **suggestive** *adj* suggestif, -ive, évocateur, -trice.
suicide ('su:isaid) *n* **1** suicide *m*. **2** (person) suicidé *m*. **commit suicide** se suicider.
suit (su:t) *n* **1** costume *m*. **2** poursuites *f pl*. **3** *game* couleur *f*. **4** requête *f*. *vt* **1** convenir à, aller bien. **2** accommoder. **suitable** *adj* **1** convenable. **2** approprié. **suitcase** *n* valise *f*.
suite (swi:t) *n* **1** suite *f*. **2** appartement *m*. **3** mobilier *m*.
sulk (sʌlk) *vi* bouder. *n* bouderie *f*. **sulky** *adj* maussade, boudeur, -euse.
sullen ('sʌlən) *adj* morose, morne.
sulphur ('sʌlfə) *n* soufre *m*.
sultan ('sʌltən) *n* sultan *m*.
sultana (sʌl'tɑ:nə) *n* raisin sec (de Smyrne) *m*.
sultry ('sʌltri) *adj* étouffant.
sum (sʌm) *n* **1** somme *f*. total, -aux *m*. **2** calcul *m*. *v* **sum up** **1** résumer. **2** classer.
summarize ('sʌməraiz) *vt* résumer. **summary** *n* sommaire, résumé *m*. *adj* sommaire.
summer ('sʌmə) *n* été *m*. **summerhouse** *n* pavillon *m*. **summertime** *n* été *m*.
summit ('sʌmit) *n* sommet, faîte *m*.
summon ('sʌmən) *vt* **1** convoquer. **2** sommer. **3** faire appel à. **summons** *n* **1** *law* citation *f*. **2** appel *m*. *vt* citer en justice.
sun (sʌn) *n* soleil *m*. *vt* exposer au soleil.
sunbathe ('sʌnbeið) *vi* prendre un bain de soleil.
sunburn ('sʌnbə:n) *n* hâle *m*.
Sunday ('sʌndi) *n* dimanche *m*.
sundial ('sʌndaiəl) *n* cadran solaire *m*.
sundry ('sʌndri) *adj* divers. **all and sundry** tout le monde. **sundries** *n pl* frais divers *m pl*.
sunflower ('sʌnflauə) *n* tournesol *m*.
sung (sʌŋ) *v see* **sing.**
sunglasses ('sʌnglɑ:siz) *n pl* lunettes de soleil *f pl*.
sunk (sʌŋk) *v see* **sink.**
sunlight ('sʌnlait) *n* lumière solaire *f*. soleil *m*.
sunny ('sʌni) *adj* ensoleillé.
sunrise ('sʌnraiz) *n* lever du soleil *m*.
sunset ('sʌnset) *n* coucher du soleil *m*.
sunshine ('sʌnʃain) *n* soleil *m*.
sunstroke ('sʌnstrouk) *n* insolation *f*. coup de soleil *m*.
suntan ('sʌntæn) *n* hâle *m*.
super ('su:pə) *adj inf* superbe, magnifique.
superannuation (su:pərænju'eiʃən) *n* retraite par limite d'âge *f*.
superb (su:'pə:b) *adj* superbe, magnifique.
superficial (su:pə'fiʃəl) *adj* superficiel, -elle.
superfluous (su:'pə:fluəs) *adj* superflu, de trop.
superhuman (su:pə'hju:mən) *adj* surhumain.
superimpose (su:pərim'pouz) *vt* superposer, surimposer.
superintendent (su:pərin'tendənt) *n* directeur, surveillant *m*.
superior (su'piəriə) *adj,n* supérieur *m*.
superlative (su'pə:lətiv) *n* superlatif *m*. *adj* **1** suprême. **2** superlatif, -ive.
supermarket ('su:pəmɑ:kit) *n* supermarché *m*.
supernatural (su:pə'nætʃrəl) *adj,n* surnaturel, -elle *m*.
supersede (su:pə'si:d) *vt* remplacer, supplanter.
supersonic (su:pə'sɔnik) *adj* supersonique.
superstition (su:pə'stiʃən) *n* superstition *f*. **superstitious** *adj* superstitieux, -euse.
supervise ('su:pəvaiz) *vt* **1** surveiller. **2** diriger. **supervision** *n* **1** surveillance *f*. **2** direction *f*.
supper ('sʌpə) *n* souper *m*.
supple ('sʌpəl) *adj* souple, pliant, maniable.
supplement (*n* 'sʌplimənt; *v* sʌpli'ment) *n* supplément *m*. *vt* compléter, ajouter à. **supplementary** *adj* supplémentaire.
supply (sə'plai) *vt* fournir, munir. *n* **1** fourniture, offre *f*. **2** *pl* vivres *f pl*. approvisionnements *m pl*.
support (sə'pɔ:t) *n* appui, soutien *m*. *vt* **1** soutenir, appuyer, entretenir. **supporter** *n* **1** partisan, adhérent *m*. **2** *sport* supporter *m*.
suppose (sə'pouz) *vt* supposer. **supposed** *adj* prétendu. **supposedly** *adv* soi-disant, censément.

suppress (sə'pres) *vt* **1** réprimer, refouler. **2** dissimuler. **suppression** *n* **1** répression *f*. **2** étouffement *m*.

supreme (sə'pri:m) *adj* suprême. **supremacy** *n* suprématie *f*.

surcharge ('sə:tʃɑ:dʒ) *n* surcharge, surtaxe *f*.

sure (ʃuə) *adj* sûr, certain. *adv* certainement. **surely** *adv* assurément, bien sûr. **surety** *n* **1** garant *m*. caution *f*. **2** certitude *f*.

surf (sə:f) *n* ressac *m*.

surface ('sə:fis) *n* **1** surface *f*. **2** apparence *f*. *vi* remonter à la surface.

surfeit ('sə:fit) *n* surabondance *f*.

surge (sə:dʒ) *n* **1** vague, lame *f*. **2** *naut* houle *f*. *vi* se soulever.

surgeon ('sə:dʒən) *n* chirurgien *m*. **surgery** *n* **1** chirurgie *f*. **2** cabinet de consultation, dispensaire *m*. **surgical** *adj* chirurgical, -aux.

surly ('sə:li) *adj* bourru, revêche, hargneux, -euse.

surmount (sə'maunt) *vt* surmonter, maîtriser.

surname ('sə:neim) *n* nom de famille *m*.

surpass (sə'pɑ:s) *vt* **1** surpasser. **2** l'emporter sur.

surplus ('sə:plis) *n* surplus, excédent *m*. *adj* excédentaire.

surprise (sə'praiz) *n* surprise *f*. *vt* surprendre, étonner.

surrealism (sə'riəlizəm) *n* surréalisme *m*. **surrealist** *adj,n* surréaliste *m*.

surrender (sə'rendə) *vi* se rendre. *vt* rendre, céder. *n* reddition *f*.

surreptitious (sʌrəp'tiʃəs) *adj* subreptice, clandestin.

surround (sə'raund) *vt* entourer, cerner. *n* bordure *f*. **surroundings** *n pl* milieu *m*.

survey (*n* 'sə:vei; *v* sə:'vei) *n* **1** étude . **2** levé *m*. **3** enquête *f*. *vt* **1** examiner. **2** arpenter.

surveyor (sə'veiə) *n* **1** arpenteur *m*. **2** surveillant *m*.

survive (sə'vaiv) *vi* survivre. *vt* survivre à. **survival** *n* survivance *f*. **survivor** *n* survivant *m*.

susceptible (sə'septəbəl) *adj* **1** susceptible. **2** sensible.

suspect (*v* sə'spekt; *n,adj* 'sʌspekt) *vt* **1** soupçonner. **2** se douter de. *adj,n* suspect.

suspend (sə'spend) *vt* suspendre. **suspense** *n* suspens *m*. **suspension** *n* suspension *f*.

suspicion (sə'spiʃən) *n* soupçon *m*. **suspicious** *adj* **1** méfiant, soupçonneux, -euse. **2** suspect, louche.

sustain (sə'stein) *vt* **1** soutenir. **2** éprouver.

swab (swɔb) *n* tampon, torchon *m*. *vt* nettoyer, essuyer.

swagger ('swægə) *n* **1** air important *m*. **2** crânerie *f*. *vi* crâner.

swallow[1] ('swɔlou) *vt* avaler, gober. *n* **1** gosier *m*. **2** gorgée *f*.

swallow[2] ('swɔlou) *n zool* hirondelle *f*.

swam (swæm) *v* see **swim.**

swamp (swɔmp) *n* marais *m*. *vt* inonder, submerger.

swan (swɔn) *n* cygne *m*.

swank (swæŋk) *vi* crâner. *n inf* prétention *f*.

swap (swɔp) *vt* troquer, échanger. *n* troc, échange *m*.

swarm (swɔ:m) *n* essaim *m*. nuée *f*. *vi* **1** essaimer. **2** fourmiller.

swastika ('swɔstikə) *n* croix gammée *f*.

swat (swɔt) *vt inf* écraser.

sway (swei) *vi* osciller, se balancer. *vt* **1** agiter. **2** influencer.

swear* (swɛə) *vt,vi* jurer. **swearword** *n* juron *m*.

sweat (swet) *n* sueur, transpiration *f*. *vi,vt* suer **sweater** *n* chandail *m*.

swede (swi:d) *n* rutabaga *m*.

Sweden ('swi:dn̩) *n* Suède *f*. **Swede** *n* suédois *m*. **Swedish** *adj* suédois. **Swedish (language)** *n* suédois *m*.

sweep* (swi:p) *vt* **1** balayer, ramoner. **2** enlever. *vi* **1** passer rapidement. **2** s'étendre. *n* **1** coup de balai *m*. **2** ramoneur *m*. **3** mouvement circulaire *m*. **sweeping** *adj* **1** large. **2** rapide. **3** radical, -aux. **4** complet, -ète.

sweet (swi:t) *adj* **1** doux, douce. **2** sucré. **3** charmant. *n* **1** bonbon *m*. **2** dessert *m*. **sweetbread** *n* ris de veau *or* d'agneau *m*. **sweet corn** *n* maïs *m*. **sweetheart** *n* amoureux, -euse. **sweet pea** *n* pois de senteur *m*. **sweeten** *vt* sucrer.

swell* (swel) *vi* s'enfler, se gonfler. *vt* gonfler. *n naut* houle *f*. **swelling** *n* enflure *f*.

swept (swept) *v* see **sweep.**

swerve (swə:v) *n* écart *m*. embardée *f*. *vi* faire un écart *or* une embardée.

swift (swift) *adj* rapide. *n* martinet *m*.

swig (swig) *n inf* lampée *f*. *vt* boire à grands traits.

swill (swil) *vt* laver à grande eau. **swill out** rincer. ~*n* **1** pâtee pour les porcs *f*. **2** lavage *m*. **3** lampée *f*.

swim* (swim) *vi* **1** nager. **2** tourner. **3** être inondé. *vt* traverser à la nage. *n* nage *f*. **swimming** *n* natation *f*. **swimming cos-**

tume *n* maillot de bain *m*. **swimming pool** *n* piscine *f*.
swindle ('swindl̩) *vt* escroquer. *n* escroquerie *f*. **swindler** *n* escroc *m*.
swine (swain) *n invar* cochon *m*.
swing* (swiŋ) *vi* **1** se balancer. **2** changer de direction. *vt* **1** balancer. **2** tourner. *n* **1** balançoire *f*. **2** oscillation *f*. **3** revirement *m*.
swipe (swaip) *inf vt* **1** cogner. **2** chiper. *n* coup *m*.
swirl (swə:l) *vi* tourbillonner. *vt* faire tournoyer. *n* remous *m*.
swish (swiʃ) *vi* siffler, bruire. *vt* fouetter, battre, faire siffler. *n* sifflement, bruissement *m*.
switch (switʃ) *n* **1** interrupteur, commutateur *m*. **2** cravache *f*. *vt* **1** aiguiller. **2** battre. **switch off/on** éteindre/allumer. **switchboard** *n* standard téléphonique *m*.
Switzerland ('switsələnd) *n* Suisse *f*. **Swiss** *adj,n* suisse.
swivel ('swivəl) *vi* pivoter. *n* pivot *m*.
swollen ('swoulən) *v* see **swell.** *adj* enflé, gonflé.
swoop (swu:p) *vi* fondre, foncer. *n* descente *f*.
swop (swɔp) *n* troc *m*. *vt* échanger.
sword (sɔ:d) *n* épée *f*. **swordfish** *n* espadon *m*.
swore (swɔ:) *v* see **swear.**
sworn (swɔ:n) *v* see **swear.**
swot (swɔt) *vi inf* bûcher.
swum (swʌm) *v* see **swim.**
swung (swʌŋ) *v* see **swing.**
sycamore ('sikəmɔ:) *n* sycomore *m*.
syllable ('siləbəl) *n* syllabe *f*.
syllabus ('siləbəs) *n, pl* **-buses** *or* **-bi** programme *m*.
symbol ('simbəl) *n* symbole *m*. **symbolic** *adj* symbolique. **symbolism** *n* symbolisme *m*. **symbolize** *vt* symboliser.
symmetry ('simitri) *n* symétrie *f*. **symmetrical** *adj* symétrique.
sympathy ('simpəθi) *n* **1** sympathie *f*. **2** condoléances *f pl*. **sympathetic** *adj* sympathique, compatissant. **sympathize** *vi* sympathiser, avoir de la compassion.
symphony ('simfəni) *n* symphonie *f*.
symposium (sim'pouziəm) *n, pl* **-iums** *or* **-ia** conférence *f*. recueil *m*.
symptom ('simptəm) *n* symptôme *m*.
synagogue ('sinəgɔg) *n* synagogue *f*.
synchronize ('siŋkrənaiz) *vt* synchroniser.
syndicate ('sindikət) *n* syndicat *m*.
syndrome ('sindroum) *n* syndrome *m*.
synonym ('sinənim) *n* synonyme *m*. **synonymous** *adj* synonyme.
synopsis (si'nɔpsis) *n, pl* **-ses** sommaire, résumé *m*.
syntax ('sintæks) *n* syntaxe *f*.
synthesis ('sinθəsis) *n, pl* **-ses** synthèse *f*.
synthetic (sin'θetik) *adj* synthétique.
syphilis ('sifəlis) *n* syphilis *f*.
Syria ('siriə) *n* Syrie *f*. **Syrian** *adj,n* syrien, -ienne.
syringe (si'rindʒ) *n* seringue *f*. *vt* seringuer.
syrup ('sirəp) *n* sirop *m*.
system ('sistəm) *n* **1** système, réseau, -aux *m*. **2** méthode *f*. **systematic** *adj* systématique, méthodique.

T

tab (tæb) *n* **1** étiquette *f*. **2** patte *f*.
tabby ('tæbi) *adj* tacheté, moucheté. *n* chat tigré *m*
table ('teibəl) *n* **1** table *f*. **2** plaque *f*. **3** tableau, -aux *m*. *vt* déposer. **tablecloth** *n* nappe *f*. **tablemat** *n* rond de table *m*. **tablespoon** *n* cuiller à dessert *f*. **table tennis** *n* tennis de table *m*.
tablet ('tæblət) *n* **1** tablette *f*. **2** comprimé *m*.
taboo (tə'bu:) *n* tabou *m*. *adj* interdit, proscrit. *vt* proscrire.
tack (tæk) *n* **1** petit clou *m*. pointe *f*. **2** *dom* point de bâti *m*. **3** *naut* bordée *f*. *vt* **1** clouer. **2** *dom* faufiler. *vi* virer.
tackle ('tækəl) *n* attirail, appareil *m*. *vt* s'attaquer à, aborder.
tact (tækt) *n* tact *m*. **tactful** *adj* délicat, de tact.
tactic ('tæktik) *n* tactique *f*.
tadpole ('tædpoul) *n* têtard *m*.
taffeta ('tæfitə) *n* taffetas *m*.
tag (tæg) *n* fiche *f*. ferret *m*.
Tahiti (tə:'hi:ti) *n* Tahiti *m*.
tail (teil) *n* **1** queue *f*. **2** arrière *m*. **3** pile *f*. **4** pan *m*. *vt* pister.
tailor ('teilə) *n* tailleur *m*. *vt* façonner.
taint (teint) *n* **1** corruption, souillure *f*. **2** trace *f*. *vt* vicier, corrompre, gâter.
take* (teik) *vt,vi* prendre. *vt* **1** conduire. **2** emporter. **3** saisir. **4** falloir. **take away** emmener. **take off 1** enlever. **2** décoller. **take-off** *n* **1** envol *m*. **2** *inf* caricature *f*. **take on** entreprendre. **take place** se passer. **take up** relever. **take-over** *n* reprise *f*. *adj* de rachat.

talcum powder ('tælkəm) *n* talc *m*.
tale (teil) *n* conte, récit *m*.
talent ('tælənt) *n* talent *m*.
talk (tɔ:k) *vt,vi* parler. *vi* jaser, causer. *n* paroles *f pl*. bavardage *m*. conversation *f*. **talkative** *adj* bavard.
tall (tɔ:l) *adj* **1** grand. **2** haut. **3** *inf* incroyable.
tally ('tæli) *vt* pointer, contrôler. *vi* correspondre. *n* pointage *m*.
talon ('tælən) *n* serre, griffe *f*.
tambourine (tæmbə'ri:n) *n* tambourin *m*.
tame (teim) *adj* **1** domestique, apprivoisé. **2** soumis. *vt* apprivoiser.
tamper ('tæmpə) *vi* **tamper with** tripoter.
tampon ('tæmpɔn) *n* tampon *m*.
tan (tæn) *vt* tanner. *vi* se bronzer. *n* hâle *m*.
tangent ('tændʒənt) *n* tangente *f*.
tangerine (tændʒə'ri:n) *n* mandarine *f*.
tangible ('tændʒəbəl) *adj* **1** tangible. **2** sensible.
Tangier (tæn'dʒiə) *n* Tanger *m*.
tangle ('tæŋgəl) *n* enchevêtrement, emmêlement *m*. *vt* embrouiller. *vi* s'embrouiller.
tango ('tæŋgou) *n* tango *m*.
tank (tæŋk) *n* **1** réservoir *m*. **2** *mil* char de combat *m*. **tanker** *n* **1** *naut* pétrolier *m*. **2** *mot* camion-citerne *m*.
tankard ('tæŋkəd) *n* pot *m*. chope *f*.
tantalize ('tæntəlaiz) *vt* tourmenter, taquiner.
tantrum ('tæntrəm) *n* accès de colère *m*.
tap[1] (tæp) *vt* taper. *n* tape *f*. petit coup *m*.
tap[2] (tæp) *n* robinet *m*. *vt* **1** percer. **2** vider. **3** capter.
tape (teip) *n* **1** ruban *m*. **2** *tech* bande magnétique *f*. *vt* **1** attacher. **2** enregistrer. **tape-measure** *n* mètre à ruban *m*. **tape-recorder** *n* magnétophone *m*.
taper ('teipə) *n* cierge *m*. *vi* s'effiler. *vt* effiler.
tapestry ('tæpistri) *n* tapisserie *f*.
tapioca (tæpi'oukə) *n* tapioca *m*.
tar (tɑ:) *n* goudron *m*. *vt* goudronner.
Tarmac ('tɑ:mæk) *n* *Tdmk* bitume *m*.
tarantula (tə'ræntjulə) *n* tarentule *f*.
target ('tɑ:git) *n* but *m*. cible *f*.
tariff ('tærif) *n* tarif *m*.
tarnish ('tɑ:niʃ) *vt* ternir. *vi* se ternir. *n* ternissure *f*.
tarragon ('tærəgən) *n* estragon *m*.
tart[1] (tɑ:t) *adj* **1** âpre, acerbe. **2** mordant, caustique.
tart[2] (tɑ:t) *n* **1** tarte *f*. **2** *sl* poule *f*.
tartan ('tɑ:tn̩) *n* tartan *m*.
task (tɑ:sk) *n* tâche, besogne *f*.
tassel ('tæsəl) *n* gland *m*.
taste (teist) *n* **1** goût *m*. saveur *f*. **2** prédilection *f*. penchant *m*. ~*vt* goûter, déguster. **taste of** avoir un goût de. **tasteless** *adj* insipide, fade. **tasty** *adj* savoureux, -euse.
tattoo[1] (tə'tu:) *n* *mil* retraite du soir *f*.
tattoo[2] (tə'tu:) *n* tatouage *m*. *vt* tatouer.
taught (tɔ:t) *v* see **teach.**
taunt (tɔ:nt) *vt* se gausser de, accabler de sarcasmes. *n* reproche *m*.
Taurus ('tɔ:rəs) *n* Taureau *m*.
taut (tɔ:t) *adj* raide, tendu.
tautology (tɔ:'tɔlədʒi) *n* tautologie *f*.
tavern ('tævən) *n* taverne *f*.
tax (tæks) *n* **1** impôt *m*. contribution *f*. **2** charge *f*. *vt* **1** taxer. **2** imposer. **3** mettre à l'épreuve. **taxation** *n* impôts *m*. **taxpayer** *n* contribuable *m*.
taxi ('tæksi) *n* taxi *m*.
tea (ti:) *n* **1** thé *m*. **2** goûter *m*. **tea-bag** *n* sachet de thé *m*. **tea-break** *n* pause café *f*. **tea-cloth** *n* torchon *m*. **teacup** *n* tasse à thé *f*. **tealeaf** *n* feuille de thé *f*. **teapot** *n* théière *f*. **teaspoon** *n* cuiller à thé *f*.
teach* (ti:tʃ) *vt* enseigner, instruire, apprendre. **teacher** *n* **1** professeur *m,f*. **2** instituteur, -trice. **teacher training college** école normale.
teak (ti:k) *n* teck *m*.
team (ti:m) *n* **1** équipe *f*. **2** (of horses, etc.) attelage *m*.
tear[1] (tiə) *n* larme *f*. pleur *m*. **teardrop** *n* larme *f*. **tearful** *adj* en pleurs, larmoyant. **tear-gas** *n* gaz lacrymogène *m*.
tear*[2] (tɛə) *vt* **1** déchirer. **2** arracher. *vi* **1** se déchirer. **2** *inf* aller très rapidement. *n* déchirure *f*.
tease (ti:z) *vt* taquiner.
teat (ti:t) *n* **1** mamelon *m*. **2** (of a bottle) tétine *f*.
technical ('teknikəl) *adj* technique. **technician** *n* technicien *m*. **technique** *n* technique *f*. **technology** *n* technologie *f*. **technological** *adj* technologique.
teddy bear ('tedi) *n* ours en peluche, nounours *m*.
tedious ('ti:diəs) *adj* fastidieux, -euse, pénible.
tee (ti:) *n* but *m*. *vt* surélever.
teenage ('ti:neidʒ) *adj* adolescent. **teenager** *n* adolescent *m*.
teetotal (ti:'toutl̩) *adj* antialcoolique. **teetotaller** *n* abstinent *m*.
telegram ('teligræm) *n* télégramme *m*.
telegraph ('teligrɑ:f) *n* télégraphe *m*. *vt* télé-

graphier. **telegraph pole** *n* poteau télégraphique *m*.
telepathy (ti'lepəθi) *n* télépathie *f*.
telephone ('telifoun) *n* téléphone *m*. *vt,vi* téléphoner.
telescope ('teliskoup) *n* télescope *m*. longue-vue *f*.
television ('teləviʒən) *n* télévision *f*. **televise** *vt* téléviser.
telex ('teleks) *n* télex *m*.
tell* (tel) *vt* **1** dire, raconter. **2** discerner. *vi* porter. **tell off** réprimander.
temper ('tempə) *n* **1** tempérament *m*. humeur *f*. **2** sang-froid *m*. **3** colère *f*. **4** *tech* trempe *f*. *vt* **1** modérer. **2** délayer. **3** *tech* tremper. **temperament** *n* tempérament *m*. **temperamental** *adj* capricieux, -euse. **temperate** *adj* **1** modéré, sobre. **2** tempéré. **temperature** *n* température *f*.
tempestuous (tem'pestjuəs) *adj* tempétueux, -euse.
temple[1] ('tempəl) *n* *rel* temple *m*.
temple[2] ('tempəl) *n* *anat* tempe *f*.
tempo ('tempou) *n* tempo *m*.
temporal ('tempərəl) *adj* temporel, -elle. **temporary** *adj* temporaire, provisoire.
tempt (tempt) *vt* tenter. **temptation** *n* tentation *f*.
ten (ten) *adj,n* dix *m*. **tenth** *adj* dixième.
tenacious (tə'neiʃəs) *adj* tenace.
tenant ('tenənt) *n* locataire *m,f*. **tenancy** *n* location *f*.
tend[1] (tend) *vi* **1** tendre. **2** être sujet.
tend[2] (tend) *vt* surveiller, garder, soigner.
tendency ('tendənsi) *n* tendance *f*.
tender[1] ('tendə) *adj* **1** tendre. **2** sensible.
tender[2] ('tendə) *vt* offrir. **tender for** soumissionner pour. ~*n* offre, soumission *f*.
tendon ('tendən) *n* tendon *m*.
tendril ('tendril) *n* vrille *f*.
tenement ('tenəmənt) *n* appartement, logement *m*.
tennis ('tenis) *n* tennis *m*. **tennis court** *n* court de tennis *m*.
tenor ('tenə) *n* **1** *mus* ténor *m*. **2** teneur, marche *f*.
tense[1] (tens) *adj* **1** tendu. **2** raide. **tension** *n* tension *f*.
tense[2] (tens) *n* temps *m*.
tent (tent) *n* tente *f*.
tentacle ('tentəkəl) *n* tentacule *f*.
tentative ('tentətiv) *adj* **1** expérimental, -aux. **2** hésitant.
tenuous ('tenjuəs) *adj* ténu, mince.
tepid ('tepid) *adj* tiède.
term (tə:m) *n* **1** terme *m*. **2** période *f*. **3** *educ* trimestre *m*. **4** *pl* conditions *f pl*. **5** *pl* rapports *m pl*. **6** *pl* facilités de paiement *f pl*. *vt* désigner, nommer.
terminal ('tə:minḷ) *n* **1** terminus *m*. **2** *tech* borne *f*.
terminate ('tə:mineit) *vt* achever. *vi* se terminer.
terminology (tə:mi'nɔlədʒi) *n* terminologie *f*.
terminus ('tə:minəs) *n* terminus *m*.
terrace ('terəs) *n* terrasse *f*.
terrestrial (tə'restriəl) *adj* terrestre.
terrible ('teribəl) *adj* terrible, épouvantable.
terrier ('teriə) *n* terrier *m*.
terrify ('terifai) *vt* épouvanter, effrayer. **terrific** *adj* formidable.
territory ('teritri) *n* territoire *m*.
terror ('terə) *n* terreur, épouvante *f*. **terrorism** *n* terrorisme *m*. **terrorist** *n* terroriste *m,f*. **terrorize** *vt* terroriser.
Terylene ('terili:n) *n* *Tdmk* Térylène *m*.
test (test) *n* **1** essai *m*. épreuve *f*. **2** examen *m*. *vt* essayer, mettre à l'épreuve. **test-tube** *n* éprouvette *f*.
testament ('testəmənt) *n* testament *m*.
testicle ('testikəl) *n* testicule *f*.
testify ('testifai) *vt* témoigner, déclarer. *vi* déposer.
testimony ('testiməni) *n* témoignage *m* déposition *f*. **testimonial** *n* attestation *f*.
tether ('teθə) *vt* mettre à l'attache. *n* longe *f*.
text (tekst) *n* texte *m*. **textbook** *n* manuel *m*.
textile ('tekstail) *n* **1** tissu *m*. étoffe *f*. **2** textile *m*. *adj* textile.
texture ('tekstʃə) *n* texture *f*. grain *m*.
Thames (temz) *n* Tamise *f*.
than (ðən; *stressed* ðæn) *conj* que, de.
thank (θæŋk) *vt* remercier. **thanks!** *interj* merci! **thanks to** grâce à. **thank you!** merci! **thankful** *adj* reconnaissant.
that (ðæt) *adj* **1** ce, cet, cette. **2** ce...là. *conj* que, afin que. *pron* **1** cela, *inf* ça, ce. **2** celui-là, celle-là. **3** qui, que. **4** lequel, laquelle. **5** où. **6** dont. **that's all** voilà tout.
thatch (θætʃ) *n* chaume *m*. *vt* couvrir de chaume.
thaw (θɔ:) *vt* dégeler, décongeler, faire fondre. *vi* fondre, se décongeler. *v imp* dégeler. *n* dégel *m*.
the (ðə; *stressed* ði:) *def art* **1** le, l' *ms*. la, l' *fs*. **2** *pl* les *m,f pl*. *adv* d'autant.

theatre ('θiətə) *n* **1** théâtre *m*. **2** *med* salle d'opération *f*. **theatrical** *adj* théâtrical, -aux.
theft (θeft) *n* **1** vol *m*. **2** larcin *m*.
their (ðɛə) *poss adj 3rd pers pl* leur *m,f s*. leurs *m,f pl*. **theirs** *poss pron 3rd pers pl* le *or* la leur.
them (ðəm; *stressed* ðem) *pron 3rd pers pl* **1** les. **2** eux *m*. elles *f*. **3** leur. **themselves** *pron 3rd pers pl* **1** eux-mêmes *m*. elles-mêmes *f*. **2** se.
theme (θi:m) *n* thème, sujet, motif *m*.
then (ðən; *stressed* ðen) *adv* **1** alors, en ce temps-là, à cette époque. **2** puis, ensuite. *conj* en ce cas, donc, alors.
theology (θi'ɔlədʒi) *n* théologie *f*. **theologian** *n* théologien *m*. **theological** *adj* théologique.
theorem ('θiərəm) *n* théorème *m*.
theory ('θiəri) *n* théorie *f*. **theoretical** *adj* théorique. **theorize** *vi* théoriser.
therapy ('θerəpi) *n* thérapie *f*. **therapeutic** *adj* thérapeutique.
there (ðɛə) *adv* là, y. **thereabouts** *adv* **1** par là, dans les environs. **2** à peu près, environ. **thereafter** *adv* après, ensuite, par la suite. **thereby** *adv* par ce moyen, de cette façon. **therefore** *adv* donc, par conséquent. **thereupon** *adv* là dessus, sur ce. **therewith** *adv* **1** avec cela. **2** en outre.
thermal ('θə:məl) *adj* thermal, -aux, thermique.
thermodynamics (θə:moudai'næmiks) *n* thermodynamique *f*.
thermometer (θə'mɔmitə) *n* thermomètre *m*.
thermonuclear (θə:mou'nju:kliə) *adj* thermonucléaire.
Thermos ('θə:məs) *n Tdmk* bouteille Thermos, bouteille isolante *f*.
thermostat ('θə:məstæt) *n* thermostat *m*.
these (ði:z) *adj pl* **1** ces. **2** ces...ci. *pron pl* ceux-ci *m pl*. celles-ci *f pl*.
thesis ('θi:sis) *n, pl* **-sec** thèse *f*.
they (ðei) *pron 3rd pers pl* **1** ils *m pl*. elles *f pl*. **2** eux *m pl*. elles *f pl*. **they say** on dit.
thick (θik) *adj* **1** épais, épaisse, gros, grosse. **2** touffu, dru. **3** *inf* stupide, bête. **thicken** *vt* épaissir, lier. *vi* **1** s'épaissir, se lier. **2** se compliquer. **thickness** *n* épaisseur *f*. **thick-skinned** *adj* peu susceptible.
thief (θi:f) *n, pl* **thieves** voleur *m*.
thigh (θai) *n* cuisse *f*. **thigh-bone** *n* fémur *m*.
thimble ('θimbəl) *n* dé (à coudre) *m*.
thin (θin) *adj* **1** mince, maigre, léger, -ère. **2** rare, clairsemé. *vt* **1** amincir. **2** éclaircir. *vi* **1** s'amincir. **2** s'éclaircir. **3** amincir. **thinness** *n* maigreur, minceur *f*. **thin-skinned** *adj* susceptible, sensible.
thing (θiŋ) *n* **1** chose *f*. objet *m*. **2** *pl* affaires *f pl*. effets *m pl*. **3** *inf* machin, truc *m*. **for one thing...for another** en premier lieu...d'autre part.
think* (θiŋk) *vi* penser, réfléchir. *vt* croire, songer. **think about/of** penser à/de. **think over** réfléchir.
third (θə:d) *adj* troisième. **third party** *n* tiers *m*. **third-party** *adj* au tiers. **third person** *n* tiers *m*. troisième personne *f*. **third-rate** *adj* de qualité inférieure.
thirst (θə:st) *n* soif *f*. **thirsty** *adj* assoiffé. **be thirsty** avoir soif.
thirteen (θə:'ti:n) *adj,n* treize *m*. **thirteenth** *adj* treizième.
thirty ('θə:ti) *adj,n* trente *m*. **thirtieth** *adj* trentième.
this (ðis) ce, cet, cette. *pron* **1** ceci, ce. **2** celui-ci *m*. celle-ci *f*. **this way and that** de-ci, de-là.
thistle ('θisəl) *n* chardon *m*.
thorn (θɔ:n) *n* épine *f*.
thorough ('θʌrə) *adj* **1** complet, -ète, parfait. **2** profond, minutieux, -euse. **thoroughbred** *adj* pur sang *invar*, de race. *n* cheval pur sang *m*. **thoroughfare** *n* voie *f*.
those (ðouz) *adj pl* **1** ces *m,f pl*. **2** ces...là *m,f pl*. *pron* **1** ceux-là *m pl*. celles-là *f pl*. **2** ceux *m pl*. celles *f pl*.
though (ðou) *conj* quoique, bien que. **as though** comme si. ~*adv* cependant, pourtant.
thought[1] (θɔ:t) *n* **1** pensée, idée *f*. **2** réflexion *f*. **thoughtful** *adj* **1** pensif, -ive. **2** prévenant. **thoughtless** *adj* **1** irréfléchi. **2** sans égards.
thought[2] (θɔ:t) *v see* **think.**
thousand ('θauzənd) *adj,n* mille *m invar*. **a thousand** millier *m*. **thousandth** *adj* millième.
thrash (θræʃ) *vt* battre, rosser.
thread (θred) *n* **1** fil *m*. trame *f*. **2** *tech* filet, pas *m*. *vt* enfiler. **threadbare** *adj* usé, râpé.
threat (θret) *n* menace *f*. **threaten** *vt* menacer.
three (θri:) *adj,n* trois *m*. **three-dimensional** *adj* tridimensionnel, -elle, à trois dimensions. **three-quarters** *n* trois-quarts *invar*. **threesome** *n* ménage à trois *m*.
thresh (θreʃ) *vt* battre.
threshold ('θreʃhould) *n* seuil, pas de porte *m*.
threw (θru:) *v see* **throw.**
thrift (θrift) *n* économie, épargne *f*. **thrifty** *adj* économe, ménager, -ère.
thrill (θril) *n* frisson *m*. sensation *f*. *vt* faire

frissonner, émouvoir. *vi* frissonner. **thriller** *n* roman *or* film à sensation *m*.

thrive (θraiv) *vi* **1** pousser, se développer. **2** prospérer.

throat (θrout) *n* gorge *f*. **clear one's throat** s'éclaircir la voix.

throb (θrɔb) *vi* palpiter, battre. *n* palpitation *f*. battement *m*.

throne (θroun) *n* trône *m*.

throng (θrɔŋ) *n* **1** foule, populace *f*. **2** cohue *f*. *vi* faire foule, affluer. *vt* encombrer.

throttle ('θrɔtl̩) *vt* étrangler. *n tech* papillon *m*.

through (θru:) *prep* **1** à travers. **2** pendant. **3** par. **4** à cause de. *adj* direct. *adv* **1** à travers. **2** d'un bout à autre. **throughout** *prep* **1** d'un bout à l'autre. **2** partout. *adv* de fond en comble.

throw* (θrou) *vt* jeter, lancer. **throw away 1** rejeter. **2** gaspiller. ~*n* jet, lancement *m*.

thrush (θrʌʃ) *n* grive *f*.

thrust* (θrʌst) *vt* pousser violemment, enfoncer. *n* **1** poussée *f*. **2** coup de pointe *m*.

thud (θʌd) *n* bruit sourd *m*.

thumb (θʌm) *n* pouce *m*. *vt* feuilleter.

thump (θʌmp) *n* **1** coup sourd *m*. **2** bourrade *f*. *vt* frapper du poing.

thunder ('θʌndə) *n* tonnerre *m*. *vi* tonner. **thunderstorm** *n* orage *m*.

Thursday ('θə:zdi) *n* jeudi *m*.

thus (ðʌs) *adv* **1** ainsi, de cette manière. **2** donc, par conséquent.

thwart (θwɔ:t) *vt* contrecarrer, déjouer.

thyme (taim) *n* thym *m*.

thyroid ('θairɔid) *adj* thyroïde.

tiara (ti'ɑ:rə) *n* tiare *f*.

tick[1] (tik) *n* **1** tic-tac *m*. **2** *inf* instant *m*. **3** marque *f*. trait *m*. *vi* faire tic-tac. *vt* pointer, marquer.

tick[2] (tik) *n zool* tique *f*.

ticket ('tikit) *n* **1** billet *m*. **2** étiquette *f*. **ticket collector** *n* contrôleur *m*. **ticket office** *n* guichet *m*.

tickle ('tikəl) *vt* chatouiller. *vi* démanger. *n* chatouillement *m*. **ticklish** *adj* **1** chatouilleux, -euse. **2** susceptible, délicat.

tide (taid) *n* marée *f* courant *m*. **high/low tide** marée haute/basse. **tidemark** *n* ligne de marée haute *f*.

tidy ('taidi) *adj* bien rangé, en ordre, ordonné. *vt* ranger, mettre en ordre.

tie (tai) *vt* lier, nouer, attacher. *vi* faire match nul. *n* **1** lien *m*. attache *f*. **2** cravate *f*. **3** match nul *m*.

tier (tiə) *n* rangée *f*. étage, gradin *m*.

tiger ('taigə) *n* tigre *m*.

tight (tait) *adj* **1** tendu, raide. **2** imperméable, étanche, hermétique. **3** *inf* serré, radin. **4** *inf* ivre. *adv* **1** fermement. **2** serré. **3** hermétiquement. **tighten** *vt* serrer, reserrer, tendre. *vi* se reserrer, se tendre. **tight-fisted** *adj inf* radin, près de ses sous. **tightrope** *n* corde raide *f*. **tightrope walker** funambule *m,f*. **tights** *n pl* collant *m*.

tile (tail) *n* **1** tuile *f*. **2** carreau, -aux *m*. *vt* **1** couvrir de tuiles. **2** carreler.

till[1] (til) *prep* **1** jusqu'à. **2** que. **till now** jusqu'à présent. **till then** jusque-là. ~*conj* jusqu'à ce que.

till[2] (til) *n* caisse *f*. guichet *m*.

till[3] (til) *vt* labourer, cultiver.

tiller ('tilə) *n* barre du gouvernail *f*.

tilt (tilt) *vt* faire pencher. *vi* pencher, s'incliner. *n* pente, inclinaison *f*.

timber ('timbə) *n* bois de charpente *m*.

time (taim) *n* **1** temps *m*. **2** fois *f*. **3** heure *f*. **4** époque *f*. âge *m*. **5** mesure *f*. **in time** à temps. **on time** à l'heure. ~*vt* **1** fixer l'heure de. **2** chronométrer. **3** régler. **time bomb** *n* bombe à retardement *f*. **timekeeper** *n* chronométreur *m*. **timetable** *n* emploi du temps, horaire *m*.

timid ('timid) *adj* timide, craintif, -ive.

timpani ('timpəni) *n pl* timbales *f pl*.

tin (tin) *n* **1** étain, fer blanc *m*. **2** boîte *f*. *vt* **1** étamer. **2** mettre en boîtes. **tin-opener** *n* ouvre-boîtes *m invar*.

tinge (tindʒ) *n* teinte, nuance *f*. *vt* teinter, nuancer.

tingle ('tiŋgəl) *vi* picoter, tinter. *n* tintement, picotement *m*.

tinker ('tiŋkə) *n* chaudronnier ambulant *m*. *vi* bricoler.

tinkle ('tiŋkəl) *vi* tinter. *vt* faire tinter. *n* tintement, drelin *m*.

tinsel ('tinsəl) *n* clinquant *m*.

tint (tint) *n* teinte, nuance *f*. *vt* teinter, nuancer.

tiny ('taini) *adj* minuscule, tout petit.

tip[1] (tip) *n* extrémité *f*. bout *m*. **tiptoe** *n* pointe des pieds *f*. *vi* marcher sur la pointe des pieds.

tip[2] (tip) *vt* renverser, faire basculer. *vi* se renverser, basculer, chavirer. *n* pente, inclinaison *f*.

tip[3] (tip) *n* **1** pourboire *m*. **2** tuyau, -aux *m*. *vt* donner un pourboire. **tip-off** *n* tuyau, -aux, indice *m*.

tipsy ('tipsi) *adj inf* gris, éméché.

tire ('taiə) *vt* fatiguer, lasser. *vi* se fatiguer. **tired** *adj* fatigué. **tired out** épuisé.

tissue ('tiʃu:) *n* **1** tissu *m*. étoffe *f*. **2** mouchoir en papier *m*.

title ('taitl̩) *n* **1** titre *m*. **2** droit *m*. *vt* intituler.

to (tə; *stressed* tu:) *prep* **1** à, en, vers. **2** chez. **3** pour, envers. **4** sur. **5** contre. *conj* pour, afin de. **to-do** *n* remue-ménage *m*.

toad (toud) *n* crapaud *m*. **toadstool** *n* champignon vénéneux *m*.

toast[1] (toust) *n* pain grillé *m*. *vt,vi* griller.

toast[2] (toust) *n* toast *m*. *vt* boire à la santé de.

tobacco (tə'bækou) *n* tabac *m*. **tobacconist** *n* marchand de tabac *m*.

toboggan (tə'bɔgən) *n* toboggan *m*. luge *f*.

today (tə'dei) *adv,n* aujourd'hui *m*. **a week today** aujourd'hui en huit.

toddler ('tɔdlə) *n* tout petit enfant *m*.

toe (tou) *n* orteil, doigt de pied *m*. **toenail** *n* ongle de pied *m*.

toffee ('tɔfi) *n* caramel *m*.

toga ('tougə) *n* toge *f*.

together (tə'geðə) *adv* ensemble.

toil (tɔil) *n* travail dur, labeur *m*. *vi* travailler durement.

toilet ('tɔilət) *n* **1** toilette *f*. **2** *pl* toilettes *f pl*. cabinets *m pl*. **toilet paper** *n* papier hygiénique *m*. **toilet roll** *n* rouleau de papier hygiénique *m*. **toilet water** *n* eau de toilette *f*.

token ('toukən) *n* **1** signe *m*. marque *f*. **2** jeton, bon *m*.

told (tould) *v see* **tell.**

tolerate ('tɔləreit) *vt* tolérer, supporter. **tolerance** *n* tolérance *f*. **tolerant** *adj* tolérant.

toll[1] (toul) *n* péage, droit de passage *m*. **tollgate** *n* barrière de péage *f*.

toll[2] (toul) *n* glas *m*. *vt* sonner, tinter. *vi* sonner le glas.

tomato (tə'mɑ:tou) *n, pl* **-oes** tomate *f*.

tomb (tu:m) *n* tombe *f*. tombeau, -aux *m*.

tomorrow (tə'mɔrou) *adv,n* demain *m*. **day after tomorrow** après-demain *m*.

ton (tʌn) *n* tonne *f*.

tone (toun) *n* **1** ton *m*. **2** voix *f*. timbre *m*. **3** nuance *f*. *vt* tonifier. **tone down** adoucir.

tongs (tɔŋz) *n* pincettes, pinces *f pl*.

tongue (tʌŋ) *n* langue *f*. **tongue-tied** *adj* muet, muette.

tonic ('tɔnik) *n* fortifiant *m*. *adj* tonique. **tonic water** *n* eau minérale *f*.

tonight (tə'nait) *adv,n* ce soir *m*. cette nuit *f*.

tonsil ('tɔnsəl) *n* amygdale *f*. **tonsilitis** *n* amygdalite *f*.

too (tu:) *adv* **1** trop. **2** aussi. **3** d'ailleurs, de plus.

took (tuk) *v see* **take.**

tool (tu:l) *n* outil, ustensile *m*.

tooth (tu:θ) *n, pl* **teeth** dent *f*. **toothache** *n* mal de dents *m*. **have toothache** avoir mal aux dents. **toothbrush** *n* brosse à dents *f*. **toothpaste** *n* dentifrice *m*. **toothpick** *n* cure-dents *m invar*.

top[1] (tɔp) *n* **1** haut, sommet *m*. cime *f*. **2** surface *f*. **3** dessus *m*. *adj* **1** supérieur, d'en haut. **2** principal, -aux. *vt* **1** coiffer. **2** dépasser. **top up** remplir. **top hat** *n* haut de forme *m*. **top-heavy** *adj* trop lourd du haut.

top[2] (tɔp) *n* (toy) toupie *f*.

topaz ('toupæz) *n* topaze *f*.

topic ('tɔpik) *n* sujet, thème *m*. matière *f*. **topical** *adj* topique, d'actualité.

topography (tə'pɔgrəfi) *n* topographie *f*.

topple ('tɔpəl) *vi* tomber, s'écrouler. *vt* faire tomber, culbuter.

topsoil ('tɔpsɔil) *n* terre du dessus *f*.

topsy-turvy (tɔpsi'tə:vi) *adv,adj* sens dessus dessous.

torch (tɔ:tʃ) *n* **1** torche *f*. **2** lampe électrique *f*.

tore (tɔ:) *v see* **tear.**

torment (*v* tɔ:'ment; *n* 'tɔ:ment) *vt* tourmenter. *n* tourment, supplice *m*.

torn (tɔ:n) *v see* **tear.**

tornado (tɔ:'neidou) *n, pl* **-oes** or **-os** tornade *f*. ouragan *m*.

torpedo (tɔ:'pi:dou) *n, pl* **-oes** torpille *f*. *vt* torpiller.

torrent ('tɔrənt) *n* torrent *m*.

torso ('tɔ:sou) *n* torse *m*.

tortoise ('tɔ:təs) *n* tortue *f*.

tortuous ('tɔ:tʃuəs) *adj* tortueux, -euse, sinueux, -euse.

torture ('tɔ:tʃə) *n* torture *f*. supplice *m*. *vt* torturer, mettre au supplice.

Tory ('tɔ:ri) *adj,n* Tory *m*.

toss (tɔs) *vt* **1** lancer en l'air. **2** tirer à pile ou face. **3** hocher, agiter. *vi* s'agiter. *n* lancement, jet *m*.

tot[1] (tɔt) *n* **1** petit enfant, bambin *m*. **2** goutte *f*.

tot[2] (tɔt) *vt* **tot up** additionner.

total ('toutl̩) *adj* total, -aux, complet, -ète. *n* montant, total, tout *m*. **totalitarian** *adj* totalitaire.

totter ('tɔtə) *vi* chanceler, tituber.

touch (tʌtʃ) *vt* **1** toucher. **2** émouvoir. *vi* se toucher. *n* **1** toucher, tact *m*. **2** attouchement *m*. **3** touche *f*. **touchy** *adj* susceptible.

tough (tʌf) *adj* **1** dur, coriace. **2** fort. **3** raide. **toughen** *vt* durcir. *vi* s'endurcir.
toupee ('tu:pei) *n* toupet *m.* perruque *f.*
tour (tuə) *n* **1** voyage, tour *m.* **2** tournée *f.* *vt,vi* voyager. **tourism** *n* tourisme *m.* **tourist** *n* touriste *m,f.*
tournament ('tuənəmənt) *n* tournoi, concours *m.*
tow (tou) *vt* remorquer. *n.* remorque *f.* **towrope** *n* corde de remorque *f.*
towards (təwɔ:dz) *prep also* **toward** **1** vers. **2** envers, à l'égard de. **3** pour.
towel ('tauəl) *n* serviette *f.* essuie-mains *m invar.*
tower ('tauə) *n* tour *f.* *vi* dominer, planer. **tower-block** *n* tour d'habitation *f.*
town (taun) *n* ville *f.* **town hall** *n* hôtel de ville *m.* **town-planning** *n* urbanisme *m.*
toxic ('tɔksik) *adj* toxique.
toy (tɔi) *n* jouet *m.* *adj* de jouet. *vi* jouer, s'amuser.
trace (treis) *n* trace *f.* *vt* **1** tracer. **2** suivre. **3** calquer.
track (træk) *n* **1** trace *f.* **2** piste *f.* **3** chemin, sentier *m.* *vt* traquer. **tracksuit** *n* survêtement *m.*
tract (trækt) *n* étendue *f.*
tractor ('træktə) *n* tracteur *m.*
trade (treid) *n* **1** commerce *m.* affaires *f pl.* **2** métier *m.* *vt* échanger, troquer. *vi* faire le commerce. **trademark** *n* marque de fabrique *f.* **tradesman** *n* fournisseur *m.* **trade union** *n* syndicat *m.* **trade unionist** *n* syndiqué *m.*
tradition (trə'diʃən) *n* tradition *f.* **traditional** *adj* traditionnel, -elle.
traffic ('træfik) *n* **1** circulation *f.* **2** trafic, commerce *m.* **traffic jam** *n* embouteillage *m.* **traffic lights** *n pl* feu de circulation *m pl.* **traffic warden** *n* contractuel, -elle.
tragedy ('trædʒədi) *n* **1** tragédie *f.* **2** drame *m.* **tragic** *adj* tragique.
trail (treil) *n* **1** traînée *f.* **2** piste, trace *f.* **3** route *f.* *vt* **1** suivre à la piste. **2** traîner. *vi* traîner. **trailer** *n* **1** remorque *f.* **2** (for a film) bande publicitaire *f.*
train (trein) *n* **1** train *m.* **2** suite *f.* **3** convoi *m.* **4** traîne *f.* **5** série *f.* *vt* entraîner, dresser, former. *vi* s'entraîner, s'exercer. **trainee** *n* stagiaire *m,f.* **training** *n* **1** formation *f.* **2** *sport* entraînement *m.*
traitor ('treitə) *n* traître, perfide *m.*
tram (træm) *n* tramway *m.*
tramp (træmp) *n* **1** vagabond, clochard *m.* **2** bruit de piétinement *m.* *vi* vagabonder. *vt* faire à pied.
trample ('træmpəl) *vi,vt* piétiner, fouler.
trampoline ('træmpəli:n) *n* trampolino *m.*
trance (trɑ:ns) *n* trance, extase *f.*
tranquil ('træŋkwil) *adj* tranquille, serein, calme. **tranquillity** *n* tranquillité *f.* calme *m.* **tranquillizer** *n* tranquillisant, calmant *m.*
transact (træn'zækt) *vt* traiter, faire, passer. **transaction** *n* **1** conduite *f.* **2** opération *f.*
transatlantic (trænzət'læntik) *adj* transatlantique.
transcend (træn'send) *vt* dépasser, surpasser.
transcribe (træn'skraib) *vt* transcrire.
transfer (*v* træns'fə:; *n* 'trænsfə:) *vt* transférer, déplacer, virer. *n* transfert, déplacement *m.*
transform (træns'fɔ:m) *vt* transformer, métamorphoser. **transformation** *n* métamorphose *f.*
transfuse (træns'fju:z) *vt* transfuser. **transfusion** *n* transfusion *f.*
transistor (træn'zistə) *n* transistor *m.*
transit ('trænsit) *n* **1** passage *m.* **2** transport, transit *m.*
transition (træn'ziʃən) *n* transition *f.* passage *m.*
transitive ('trænsitiv) *adj* transitif, -ive.
translate (trænz'leit) *vt* traduire. **translation** *n* traduction *f.*
translucent (trɒnz'lu:sənt) *adj* translucide.
transmit (trænz'mit) *vt* transmettre. **transmitter** *n* transmetteur, émetteur *m.*
transparent (træns'pærənt) *adj* **1** transparent, limpide. **2** clair.
transplant (*v* træns'plɑ:nt; *n* 'trænsplɑ:nt) *vt* transplanter, greffer. *n* greffe *f.*
transport (*v* træns'pɔ:t; *n* 'trænspɔ:t) *vt* transporter. *n* transport *m.*
transpose (træns'pouz) *vt* transposer.
trap (træp) *n* trappe *f.* piège *m.* *vt* attraper, prendre au piège. *vi* trapper. **trapdoor** *n* trappe *f.*
trapeze (trə'pi:z) *n* trapèze *m.*
trash (træʃ) *n* camelote *f.*
trauma ('trɔ:mə) *n* traumatisme *m.* **traumatic** *adj* traumatique.
travel ('trævəl) *vi* **1** voyager. **2** aller. *vt* parcourir. *n* voyage *m.* **travel agency** *n* agence de voyages *f.* bureau de tourisme *m.* **traveller's cheque** *n* chèque de voyage *m.*
trawl (trɔ:l) *vi* chaluter. **trawler** *n* chalutier *m.*
tray (trei) *n* plateau, -aux *m.*
treachery ('tretʃəri) *n* trahison, perfidie *f.* **treacherous** *adj* perfide, déloyal.

treacle ('tri:kəl) *n* mélasse *f*.
tread* (tred) *vi* marcher. *vt* écraser, fouler. *n* **1** pas *m*. **2** *mot* chape *f*.
treason ('tri:zən) *n* trahison *f*.
treasure ('treʒə) *n* trésor *m*. *vt* tenir beaucoup à. **treasurer** *n* trésorier *m*. **treasury** *n* trésorerie *f*.
treat (tri:t) *vt,vi* traiter. *vt* régaler. *n* plaisir, régal *m*. **treatment** *n* traitement *m*.
treatise ('tri:tiz) *n* traité *m*.
treaty ('tri:ti) *n* traité, accord *m*.
treble ('trebəl) *adj* **1** triple. **2** *mus* aigu -uë, de soprano. *adv* trois fois plus. *vt* tripler. *vi* se tripler.
tree (tri:) *n* arbre *m*.
trek (trek) *vi* **1** faire route. **2** changer de pays. *n* étape *f*.
trellis ('trelis) *n* treillis, treillage *m*. *vt* treillisser.
tremble ('trembəl) *vi* trembler, frissonner. *n* frisson *m*.
tremendous (tri'mendəs) *adj* **1** terrible. **2** *inf* énorme, immense.
tremor ('tremə) *n* tremblement *m*. secousse *f*.
trench (trentʃ) *n* tranchée *f*. fossé *m*.
trend (trend) *n* tendance *f*. **trendy** *adj* à la mode, dans le vent.
trespass ('trespəs) *n* infraction, violation *f*. *vi* enfreindre, violer.
trestle ('tresəl) *n* tréteau, -aux *m*. chevalet *m*.
trial ('traiəl) *n* **1** *law* jugement, procès *m*. **2** essai *m*. épreuve *f*. *adj* d'essai.
triangle ('traiæŋgəl) *n* triangle *m*. **triangular** *adj* triangulaire.
tribe (traib) *n* tribu *f*. **tribal** *adj* de tribu, tribal, -aux. **tribesman** *n* membre de la tribu *m*.
tribunal (trai'bju:nl) *n* tribunal, -aux *m*.
tributary ('tribju:təri) *adj* tributaire. *n* tributaire, affluent *m*.
tribute ('tribju:t) *n* tribut *m*.
trick (trik) *n* **1** tour *m*. **2** ruse *f*. **3** *game* levée *f*. *vt* attraper, duper. **tricky** *adj* compliqué, délicat.
trickle ('trikəl) *vi* couler, suinter. *n* filet *m*.
tricycle ('traisikəl) *n* tricycle *m*.
trifle ('traifəl) *n* **1** bagatelle *f*. **2** *cul* diplomate *m*. *vi* jouer, badiner.
trigger ('trigə) *n* détente, gâchette *f*.
trill (tril) *n* trille *m*. *vt* triller, rouler. *vi* faire des trilles.
trim (trim) *vt* **1** parer, tailler. **2** orner. *n* **1** bon ordre *m*. **2** coupe *f*. *adj* soigné, ordonné.
trio ('triou) *n* trio *m*.
trip (trip) *n* **1** excursion *f*. **2** faux-pas, croc-en-jambe *m*. *vi* faire un faux-pas, trébucher. **trip up** donner un croc-en-jambe à.
tripe (traip) *n* **1** tripe *f*. **2** *inf* camelote *f*.
triple ('tripəl) *adj* triple. *vt* tripler. *vi* se tripler. **triplet** *n* **1** trio *m*. **2** *pl* triplés *m pl*.
tripod ('traipɔd) *n* trépied *m*.
trite (trait) *adj* banal, trivial.
triumph ('traiʌmf) *n* triomphe *m*. victoire *f*. *vi* triompher, remporter un succès. **triumphant** *adj* triomphant.
trivial ('triviəl) *adj* **1** insignifiant, superficiel, -elle. **2** banal.
trod (trɔd) *v* see **tread.**
trodden ('trɔdn̩) *v* see **tread.**
trolley ('trɔli) *n* **1** chariot *m*. **2** table roulante *f*.
trombone (trɔm'boun) *n* trombone *m*.
troop (tru:p) *n* troupe *f*.
trophy ('troufi) *n* trophée *m*.
tropic ('trɔpik) *n* tropique *m*. **tropical** *adj* tropical, -aux.
trot (trɔt) *n* trot *m*. *vi* aller au trot, trottiner. **trotter** *n* pied de cochon *m*.
trouble ('trʌbəl) *n* **1** ennui *m*. difficulté *f*. **2** peine *f*. malheur *m*. **3** dérangement *m*. *vt* **1** affliger, inquiéter. **2** déranger. *vi* **1** s'inquiéter. **2** se donner de la peine. **troublemaker** *n* trublion *m*.
trough (trɔf) *n* auge *f*.
troupe (tru:p) *n* troupe *f*.
trousers ('trauzəz) *n pl* pantalon *m*.
trout (traut) *n* truite *f*.
trowel ('trauəl) *n* truelle *f*.
truant ('truənt) *n* **play truant** faire l'école buissonnière *f*.
truce (tru:s) *n* trêve *f*.
truck (trʌk) *n* wagon, camion *m*.
trudge (trʌdʒ) *vi* marcher péniblement.
true (tru:) *adj* **1** vrai, exact. **2** authentique. **3** fidèle, loyal, -aux. **truly** *adv* sincèrement, vraiment.
truffle ('trʌfəl) *n* truffe *f*.
trump (trʌmp) *n* atout *m*. *vt* couper. *vi* jouer atout.
trumpet ('trʌmpit) *n* trompette *f*.
truncheon ('trʌntʃən) *n* bâton *m*. matraque *f*.
trunk (trʌŋk) *n* **1** tronc *m*. **2** (luggage) malle *f*. **3** *zool* trompe *f*. **trunk call** *n* appel interurbain *m*.
trust (trʌst) *n* **1** confiance *f*. **2** espoir *m*. **3** *comm* trust *m*. *vt* **1** se fier à, faire confiance à. *vi* **1** se confier. **2** espérer. **trustee** *n* fidéicommissaire *m*. **trustworthy** *adj* digne de confiance, honnête.

truth (tru:θ) *n* vérité *f.* **truthful** *adj* 1 véridique. 2 vrai, fidèle.

try (trai) *vt* 1 essayer, tenter. 2 *law* juger. 3 éprouver. **try on** essayer. **try out** essayer à fond. ~*n* essai *m.* **trying** *adj* vexant, contrariant.

tsar (tsɑ:) *n* tsar *m.*

T-shirt *n* maillot à manches courtes *m.*

tub (tʌb) *n* bac, baquet *m.*

tuba (ˈtju:bə) *n* tuba *m.*

tube (tju:b) *n* 1 tube, tuyau, -aux *m.* 2 métro *m.*

tuber (ˈtju:bə) *n* tubercule *f.*

tuberculosis (tju:bə:kjuˈlousis) *n* tuberculose *f.*

tuck (tʌk) *vt* 1 remplir. 2 relever, retrousser. **tuck in** *vt* border. *vi* manger à belles dents. ~*n* pli, rempli *m.*

Tuesday (ˈtju:zdi) *n* mardi *m.*

tuft (tʌft) *n* touffe, houppe, huppe *f.*

tug (tʌg) *vt,vi* tirer avec effort. *vt* 1 tirer, traîner. 2 remorquer. *n* 1 traction, saccade *f.* 2 *naut* remorqueur *m.*

tuition (tju:ˈiʃən) *n* instruction *f.*

tulip (ˈtu:lip) *n* tulipe *f.*

tumble (ˈtʌmbəl) *n* chute, culbute, dégringolade *f.* *vi* chuter, culbuter, dégringoler. *vt* culbuter, faire tomber, renverser. **tumbler** *n* grand verre *m.*

tummy (ˈtʌmi) *n* *inf* ventre *m.*

tumour (ˈtju:mə) *n* tumeur *f.*

tumult (ˈtumʌlt) *n* tumulte *m.*

tuna (ˈtju:nə) *n* thon *m.*

tune (tju:n) *n* 1 air *m.* 2 mélodie, harmonie *f.* 3 accord *m.* *vt* accorder. **tuneful** *adj* mélodieux, -euse, harmonieux, -euse.

tunic (ˈtju:nik) *n* tunique *f.*

Tunisia (tju:ˈniziə) *n* Tunisie *f.* **Tunisian** *adj,n* tunisien, -ienne.

tunnel (ˈtʌnl̩) *n* tunnel *m.* galerie *f.*

tunny (ˈtʌni) *n* thon *m.*

turban (ˈtə:bən) *n* turban *m.*

turbine (ˈtə:bain) *n* turbine *f.*

turbot (ˈtə:bət) *n* turbot *m.*

turbulent (ˈtə:bjulənt) *adj* turbulent, tumultueux, -euse.

turf (tə:f) *n* 1 gazon *m.* 2 *sport* turf *m.* **turf accountant** *n* bookmaker *m.*

turkey (ˈtə:ki) *n* 1 dindon *m.* 2 *cul* dinde *f.*

Turkey (ˈtə:ki) *n* Turquie *f.* **Turk** *n* turc, turque. **Turkish** *adj* turc, turque, de Turquie. **Turkish** (language) *n* turc *m.*

turmeric (ˈtə:mərik) *n* curcuma *m.*

turmoil (ˈtə:mɔil) *n* trouble, tumulte *m.* agitation *f.*

turn (tə:n) *vt* 1 tourner. 2 retourner. 3 changer. 4 diriger. *vi* 1 tourner. 2 se retourner. 3 se changer. **turn down** refuser. **turn off** éteindre, couper. **turn on** allumer, ouvrir. **turn out** 1 mettre à la porte. 2 éteindre. 3 s'arranger. **turn up** 1 se relever. 2 arriver. ~*n* 1 tour *m.* 2 virage, tournant *m.* 3 service *m.* **to a turn** à point. **turning** *n* tournant, virage *m.* *adj* tournant. **turning point** *n* point décisif *m.* **turntable** *n* 1 plaque tournante *f.* 2 platine *f.*

turnip (ˈtə:nip) *n* navet *m.*

turnover (ˈtə:nouvə) *n* 1 chiffre d'affaires *m.* 2 *cul* chausson *m.*

turpentine (ˈtə:pəntain) *n* térébenthine *f.*

turquoise (ˈtə:kwɔiz) *n* 1 turquoise *f.* 2 (colour) turquoise *m invar.* *adj* turquoise *invar.*

turret (ˈtʌrət) *n* tourelle *f.*

turtle (ˈtə:tl̩) *n* tortue de mer *f.*

tusk (tʌsk) *n* défense *f.* croc *m.*

tussle (ˈtʌsəl) *n* lutte, bagarre *f.* *vi* lutter, se bagarrer.

tutor (ˈtju:tə) *n* précepteur *m.* *vt* instruire, donner des leçons particulières.

tweed (twi:d) *n* tweed *m.*

tweezers (ˈtwi:zəz) *n* pince à épiler *f.*

twelve (twelv) *adj,n* douze *m.* **twelfth** *adj* douzième.

twenty (ˈtwenti) *adj,n* vingt *m.* **twentieth** *adj* vingtième.

twice (twais) *adv* deux fois.

twiddle (ˈtwidl̩) *vt,vi* tourner, tortiller.

twig (twig) *n* brindille, ramille *f.*

twilight (ˈtwailait) *n* crépuscule *m.*

twin (twin) *n* jumeau, -elle. *adj* jumelé, jumeau, -aux.

twine (twain) *vt* tordre, enrouler. *vi* 1 se tordre, s'enrouler. 2 serpenter. *n* ficelle *f.*

twinge (twindʒ) *n* élancement *m.* *vt,vi* torturer, élancer.

twinkle (ˈtwiŋkəl) *vi* scintiller. *n* scintillement *m.*

twirl (twə:l) *vt* faire tournoyer, tortiller. *vi* tournoyer, pirouetter. *n* 1 tournoiement *m.* 2 pirouette *f.*

twist (twist) *vt* 1 tordre, tortiller. 2 se tordre. 3 déformer. *vi* 1 se tordre, se tortiller. 2 tourner. *n* 1 fil retors, cordon *m.* 2 torsion *f.*

twitch (twitʃ) *vt* donner une saccade, tirer. *vi* se contracter, se crisper. *n* 1 saccade *f.* 2 convulsion *f.*

twitter (ˈtwitə) *vi* gazouiller. *n* gazouillement *m.*

two (tu:) *adj,n* deux *m.* **two-faced** *adj* 1 à deux visages, hypocrite. 2 sans envers. **twosome** *n*

partie à deux *f.* couple *m.* **two-way** *adj* à deux sens.
tycoon (tai'ku:n) *n* magnat *m.*
type (taip) *n* **1** type, genre *m.* **2** caractère *m.* *vt* taper à la machine. **typewriter** *n* machine à écrire *f.* **typical** *adj* typique. **typist** *n* dactylographe *m,f.*
typhoid ('taifɔid) *n* typhoïde *f.*
typhoon (tai'fu:n) *n* typhon *m.*
tyrant ('tairənt) *n* tyran *m.* **tyranny** *n* tyrannie *f.*
tyre ('taiə) *n* pneu *m.*

U

ubiquitous (ju:'bikwitəs) *adj* présent partout.
udder ('ʌdə) *n* mamelle *f.* pis *m.*
ugly ('ʌgli) *adj* laid, moche. **ugliness** *n* laideur *f.*
ukulele (ju:kə'le:li) *n* ukulele *m.*
ulcer ('ʌlsə) *n* ulcère *m.*
ulterior (ʌl'tiəriə) *adj* **1** ultérieur. **2** caché. **ulterior motive** *n* motif caché *m.*
ultimate ('ʌltimət) *adj* **1** final. **2** définitif, -ive, dernier, -ère. **3** ultime. **ultimately** *adv* en fin de compte. **ultimatum** *n, pl* **-tums** *or* **-ta** ultimatum *m.*
ultraviolet (ʌltrə'vaiələt) *adj* ultraviolet, -ette.
umbrella (ʌm'brelə) *n* parapluie *m.*
umpire ('ʌmpaiə) *n* arbitre *m.*
umpteen (ʌmp'ti:n) *adj* je ne sais combien.
unable (ʌn'eibəl) *adj* incapable.
unacceptable (ʌnək'septəbəl) *adj* inacceptable.
unaccompanied (ʌnə'kʌmpnid) *adj* seul, non accompagné.
unanimous (ju:'nanimas) *adj* unanime.
unarmed (ʌn'ɑ:md) *adj* sans arme.
unattractive (ʌnə'træktiv) *adj* peu attrayant.
unaware (ʌnə'wɛə) *adj* pas au courant, ignorant. **unawares** *adv* inconsciemment, au dépourvu.
unbalanced (ʌn'bælənst) *adj* **1** mal équilibré. **2** déséquilibré.
unbearable (ʌn'bɛərəbəl) *adj* insupportable.
unbelievable (ʌnbi'li:vəbəl) *adj* incroyable.
unbend* (ʌn'bend) *vt* **1** détendre. **2** redresser. *vi* se détendre. **unbending** *adj* inflexible.
unbreakable (ʌn'breikəbəl) *adj* incassable.
unbutton (ʌn'bʌtn̩) *vt* déboutonner.
uncalled-for *adj* déplacé, injustifié.
uncanny (ʌn'kæni) *adj* mystérieux, -euse, inquiétant.
uncertain (ʌn'sə:tn̩) *adj* incertain.
uncle ('ʌŋkəl) *n* oncle *m.*
unclear (ʌn'kliə) *adj* peu clair, obscur.
uncomfortable (ʌn'kʌmftəbəl) *adj* **1** inconfortable, incommode. **2** mal à l'aise.
unconscious (ʌn'kɔnʃəs) *adj* inconscient.
unconventional (ʌnkən'venʃnəl) *adj* non-conformiste.
uncooked (ʌn'kukt) *adj* cru.
uncouth (ʌn'ku:θ) *adj* grossier, -ière, rude.
uncover (ʌn'kʌvə) *vt* découvrir.
uncut (ʌn'kʌt) *adj* **1** non-coupé. **2** sur pied, non taillé. **3** brut.
undecided (ʌndi'saidid) *adj* indécis.
undeniable (ʌndi'naiəbəl) *adj* indéniable, incontestable.
under ('ʌndə) *prep* sous, au dessous de. *adv* (au) dessous. *adj* de dessous, subalterne.
undercharge (ʌndə'tʃɑ:dʒ) *vt* faire payer un prix trop bas.
undercoat ('ʌndəkout) *n* première couche *f.*
undercover ('ʌndəkʌvə) *adj* secret, -ète.
undercut (ʌndə'kʌt) *vt* vendre à meilleur marché que.
underdeveloped (ʌndədi'veləpd) *adj* sous-développé.
underdone (ʌndə'dʌn) *adj* **1** pas assez cuit. **2** (of meat) saignant.
underestimate (ʌndər'estimeit) *vt* sous-estimer.
underfoot (ʌndə'fut) *adv* sous les pieds.
undergo* (ʌndə'gou) *vt* subir, éprouver.
undergraduate (ʌndə'grædjuət) *n* étudiant *m.*
underground (*adv* ʌndə'graund; *adj,n* 'ʌndəgraund) *adv* **1** sous terre. **2** secrètement. *adj* **1** souterrain. **2** secret, -ète. *n* métro *m.*
undergrowth ('ʌndəgrouθ) *n* sous-bois *m.* broussailles *f pl.*
underhand (ʌndə'hænd) *adj* sournois, clandestin. *adv* **1** sous main, sournoisement. **2** *sport* par en dessous.
underline (ʌndə'lain) *vt* souligner.
undermine (ʌndə'main) *vt* miner, saper.
underneath (ʌndə'ni:θ) *prep* au dessous de, sous. *adv* au-dessous, par-dessous, dessous. *adj* inférieur, de dessous.
underpants ('ʌndəpænts) *n pl* caleçon, slip *m.*
underpass ('ʌndəpɑ:s) *n* passage inférieur *m.*
underrate (ʌndə'reit) *vt* mésestimer, sous-estimer.
understand* (ʌndə'stænd) *vt* **1** comprendre. **2** s'entendre à. **3** sous-entendre. **understanding** *n* entendement *m.* compréhension *f.*
understate (ʌndə'steit) *vt* minimiser. **under-**

statement *n* **1** amoindrissement *m*. **2** euphémisme *m*.
understudy ('ʌndəstʌdi) *n* doublure *f*. *vt* doubler.
undertake* (ʌndə'teik) *vt* entreprendre, assumer. **undertaker** *n* entrepreneur de pompes funèbres *m*.
undertone ('ʌndətoun) *n* demi-ton *m*. demi-voix *f*.
underwater (ʌndə'wɔ:tə) *adj* sous-marin.
underwear ('ʌndəwɛə) *n* sous-vêtements *m pl*.
underworld ('ʌndəwə:ld) *n* **1** bas-fonds *m pl*.milieu *m*. pègre *f*. **2** enfers *m pl*.
underwrite* ('ʌndərait) *vt* garantir, souscrire.
undesirable (ʌndi'zaiərəbəl) *adj* indésirable, importun.
undo* (ʌn'du:) *vt* **1** détruire, réparer. **2** défaire.
undoubted (ʌn'dautid) *adj* indubitable, incontestable.
undress (ʌn'dres) *vt* déshabiller, dévêtir. *vi* déshabiller, se dévêtir.
undue ('ʌndju:) *adj* injuste, illégitime.
undulate ('ʌndʒəleit) *vi,vt* onduler.
unearth (ʌn'ə:θ) *vt* déterrer, exhumer. **unearthly** *adj* surnaturel, -elle, sinistre.
uneasy (ʌn'i:zi) *adj* mal à l'aise, gêné.
unemployed (ʌnim'plɔid) *adj* désœuvré en chômage. *n* chômeurs *m pl*. **unemployment** *n* chômage *m*.
unequal (ʌn'i:kwəl) *adj* inégal, -aux.
uneven (ʌn'i:vən) *adj* inégal, -aux, accidenté.
unfair (ʌn'fɛə) *adj* injuste.
unfaithful (ʌn'feiθfəl) *adj* infidèle, déloyal, -aux.
unfamiliar (ʌnfə'miliə) *adj* peu familier, -ière, inconnu.
unfit (ʌn'fit) *adj* impropre, inapte.
unfold (ʌn'fould) *vt* déplier, déployer. *vi* se dérouler.
unfortunate (ʌn'fɔ:tʃunət) *adj* infortuné, malheureux,-euse.
unfurnished (ʌn'fə:niʃt) *adj* non meublé.
ungrateful (ʌn'greitfəl) *adj* ingrat.
unhappy (ʌn'hæpi) *adj* malheureux, -euse.
unhealthy (ʌn'helθi) *adj* malsain, insalubre.
unicorn ('ju:nikɔ:n) *n* licorne *f*.
uniform ('ju:nifɔ:m) *adj* uniforme, constant. *n* uniforme *m*.
unify ('ju:nifai) *vt* unifier.
uninterested (ʌn'intrəstid) *adj* non intéressé, indifférent.
union ('ju:niən) *n* union *f*.
Union Jack *n* pavillon britannique *m*.
unique (ju:'ni:k) *adj* unique.
unison ('ju:nizən) *n* unisson *m*.
unit ('ju:nit) *n* unité *f*.
unite (ju:'nait) *vt* unir. *vi* s'unir, se joindre. **unity** *n* unité *f*.
United Kingdom *n* Royaume-Uni *m*.
United States of America *n* Etats-Unis d'Amérique *m pl*.
universe ('ju:nivə:s) *n* univers *m*. **universal** *adj* universel, -elle.
university (ju:ni'və:siti) *n* université *f*. *adj* universitaire.
unkempt (ʌn'kempt) *adj* dépeigné, mal soigné.
unkind (ʌn'kaind) *adj* dur, cruel, -elle.
unknown (ʌn'noun) *adj* inconnu, étranger.
unlawful (ʌn'lɔ:fəl) *adj* illégal, -aux.
unless (ən'les) *conj* à moins que.
unlike (ʌn'laik) *adj* différent, peu ressemblant. **unlikely** *adj* invraisemblable, peu probable.
unload (ʌn'loud) *vt* décharger.
unlucky (ʌn'lʌki) *adj* **1** malheureux, -euse, infortuné. **2** maléfique.
unnatural (ʌn'nætʃərəl) *adj* **1** anormal, -aux, monstrueux, -euse. **2** contre nature.
unnecessary (ʌn'nesəsri) *adj* inutile, superflu.
unofficial (ʌnə'fiʃəl) *adj* non officiel, -elle, officieux, -euse.
unorthodox (ʌn'ɔ:θədɔks) *adj* peu orthodoxe.
unpack (ʌn'pæk) *vt* **1** déballer, dépaqueter. **2** défaire. *vi* défaire.
unpleasant (ʌn'plezənt) *adj* désagréable, déplaisant.
unpopular (ʌn'pɔpjulə) *adj* impopulaire.
unravel (ʌnrævəl) *vt* effiler, effilocher. *vi* s'effiler, se démêler.
unreasonable (ʌn'ri:zənəbəl) *adj* déraisonnable.
unreliable (ʌnri'laiəbəl) *adj* sur lequel on ne peut pas compter, sujet à caution.
unrest (ʌn'rest) *n* **1** inquiétude *f*. **2** agitation *f*. malaise *m*.
unruly (ʌn'ru:li) *adj* indiscipliné, insoumis.
unscrew (ʌn'skru:) *vt* dévisser.
unsettle (ʌn'setl̩) *vt* ébranler, troubler.
unsightly (ʌn'saitli) *adj* laid.
unsound (ʌn'saund) *adj* défectueux, -euse.
unsteady (ʌn'stedi) *adj* peu stable, inconstant.
unsuccessful (ʌnsək'sesfəl) *adj* infructueux, -euse, sans succès.
untangle (ʌn'tæŋgəl) *vt* démêler, dépêtrer.
untidy (ʌn'taidi) *adj* mal tenu, en désordre.
untie (ʌn'tai) *vt* dénouer, déficeler.
until (ʌn'til) *conj* jusqu'à ce que. *prep* jusqu'à. **not until** pas avant.

untrue (ʌn'tru:) *adj* faux, fausse.
unusual (ʌn'ju:ʒuəl) *adj* inhabituel, -elle, insolite.
unwanted (ʌn'wɔntid) *adj* indésirable.
unwell (ʌn'wel) *adj* indisposé.
unwind* (ʌn'waind) *vt* dérouler.
unwrap (ʌn'ræp) *vt* désenvelopper.
up (ʌp) *adj* **1** debout, levé. **2** fini, expiré. **3** droit. *adv* **1** en haut, au haut. **2** en l'air. **3** en avance. **4** droit, debout. **up there** là-haut. **up to** jusqu'à, jusque. ~*prep* en haut de, en montant. **up and down** de haut en bas.
upbringing ('ʌpbriŋiŋ) *n* éducation *f*.
upheaval (ʌp'hi:vəl) *n* bouleversement *m*. agitation *f*.
uphill (ʌp'hil) *adv* en montant. *adj* **1** en rampe. **2** ardu.
uphold* (ʌp'hould) *vt* supporter, soutenir.
upholstery (ʌp'houlstəri) *n* capitonnage *m*. tapisserie *f*.
upkeep ('ʌpki:p) *n* entretien *m*.
uplift (ʌp'lift) *vt* soulever, élever. *n* élévation *f*.
upon (ə'pɔn) *prep* sur.
upper ('ʌpə) *adj* **1** plus haut, d'au-dessus, de dessus. **2** supérieur. **upper-class** *adj* de la classe supérieure. **uppermost** *adj* le plus haut, premier, -ière.
upright ('ʌprait) *adj* **1** vertical, -aux, perpendiculaire. **2** droit.
uprising ('ʌpraiziŋ) *n* insurrection *f*. soulèvement *m*.
uproar ('ʌprɔ:) *n* vacarme, tapage *m*.
uproot (ʌp'ru:t) *vt* déraciner, arracher.
upset* (*v,adj* ʌp'set; *n* 'ʌpset) *vt* **1** renverser, culbuter. **2** déranger. **3** bouleverser. *vi* se renverser. *adj* bouleversé, ému. *n* **1** renversement *m*. **2** désordre *m*.
upshot ('ʌpʃɔt) *n* résultat *m*. conséquence *f*.
upside down (ʌpsaid 'daun) *adv* sens dessus dessous, la tête en bas.
upstairs (ʌp'stɛəz) *adv* en haut.
upstream (ʌp'stri:m) *adv* en amont. *adj* d'amont.
upward ('ʌpwəd) *adj* ascendant, montant. **upwards** *adv* vers le haut, en montant.
uranium (ju 'reiniəm) *n* uranium *m*.
Uranus (ju'reinəs) *n* Uranus *f*.
urban ('ə:bən) *adj* urbain.
urge (ə:dʒ) *vt* **1** encourager, exciter. **2** conseiller. *n* incitation, impulsion *f*.
urgent ('ə:dʒənt) *adj* urgent, pressant.
urine ('juərin) *n* urine *f*. **urinate** *vi* uriner.
urn (ə:n) *n* urne *f*.
us (ʌs) *pron Ist pers pl* nous.
use (*v* ju:z; *n* ju:s) *vt* utiliser, employer, se servir de. **use up** épuiser, consommer. ~*n* **1** emploi, usage *m*. **2** jouissance *f*. **usage** *n* usage *m*. **used** *adj* **1** usagé. **2** d'occasion. **useful** *adj* utile, pratique. **useless** *adj* inutile, bon à rien.
usher ('ʌʃə) *n* **1** (at a wedding) garçon d'honneur *m*. **2** introducteur *m*. *v* **usher in** inaugurer, introduire. **usherette** *n* ouvreuse *f*.
usual ('ju:ʒuəl) *adj* usuel, -elle, habituel, -elle. **usually** *adv* d'habitude.
usurp (ju'zə:p) *vt* usurper.
utensil (ju:'tensəl) *n* ustensile, outil *m*.
uterus ('ju:tərəs) *n, pl* **uteri** utérus *m*.
utility (ju:'tiliti) *n* utilité *f*.
utmost ('ʌtmoust) *adj also* **uttermost** extrême, dernier, -ière. *n* dernière limite *f*. **do one's utmost** faire tout son possible.
utter[1] ('ʌtə) *vt* dire, pousser, proférer.
utter[2] ('ʌtə) *adj* complet, -ète, absolu.

V

vacant ('veikənt) *adj* **1** vacant, libre, vide. **2** vague, distant. **vacancy** *n* **1** vacance *f*. **2** vide *m*.
vacate (və'keit) *vt* quitter, évacuer.
vacation (və'keiʃən) *n* vacances *f pl*.
vaccine ('væksi:n) *n* vaccin *m*. **vaccinate** *vt* vacciner. **vaccination** *n* vaccination *f*.
vacillate ('væsəleit) *vi* vaciller, chanceler.
vacuum ('vækjuəm) *n* vide *m*. **vacuum cleaner** *n* aspirateur *m*. **vacuum flask** *n* bouteille Thermos *f*.
vagina (və'dʒainə) *n* vagin *m*.
vagrant ('veigrənt) *n* vagabond *m*. *adj* vagabond, errant.
vague (veig) *adj* vague, imprécis, flou.
vain (vein) *adj* **1** vain, creux, creuse. **2** inutile. **3** vaniteux, -euse.
valiant ('væliənt) *adj* vaillant, brave.
valid ('vælid) *adj* valide, valable. **validity** *n* validité, justesse *f*.
valley ('væli) *n* vallée *f*.
value ('vælju:) *n* valeur *f*. *vt* **1** estimer, priser. **2** tenir à, faire grand cas de. **valuable** *adj* précieux, -euse, de valeur.
valve ('vælv) *n* soupape, valve *f*.
vampire ('væmpaiə) *n* vampire *m*.
van (væn) *n* fourgon *m*. camionnette *f*.

vandal ('vændḷ) *n* vandale *m.* **vandalism** *n* vandalisme *m.*
vanilla (və'nilə) *n* vanille *f.*
vanish ('væniʃ) *vi* disparaître, s'évanouir.
vanity ('væniti) *n* vanité *f.*
vapour ('veipə) *n* vapeur, buée *f.*
variety (və'raiəti) *n* variété, diversité *f.*
various ('vɛəriəs) *adj* varié, divers.
varnish ('vɑ:niʃ) *n* vernis *m.* *vt* vernir.
vary ('vɛəri) *vt* varier, diversifier. *vi* varier, différer. **variant** *n* variante *f.* **variation** *n* variation, différence *f.*
vase (vɑ:z) *n* vase *m.*
vasectomy (væ'sektəmi) *n* vasectomie *f.*
vast (vɑ:st) *adj* vaste, immense.
vat (væt) *n* cuve *f.*
Vatican ('vætikən) *n* Vatican *m.*
vault[1] (vɔ:lt) *n arch* **1** voûte *f.* **2** caveau, -aux *m.*
vault[2] (vɔ:lt) *vt,vi* sauter. *n* saut *m.*
veal (vi:l) *n* veau *m.*
veer (viə) *vi* tourner, changer de direction.
vegetable ('vedʒtəbəl) *n* légume *m.* *adj* végétal, -aux. **vegetarian** *adj,n* végétarien, -ienne. **vegetation** *n* végétation *f.*
vehement ('viəmənt) *adj* **1** véhément. **2** passionné.
vehicle ('vi:ikəl) *n* véhicule *m.*
veil (veil) *n* voile *m.* *vt* voiler, cacher.
vein (vein) *n* veine *f.*
velocity (və'lɔsiti) *n* vitesse *f.*
velvet ('velvit) *n* velours *m.*
veneer (vi'niə) *n* **1** placage *m.* **2** vernis *m.* *vt* plaquer.
venerate ('venəreit) *vt* vénérer.
venereal disease (vi'niəriəl) *n* maladie vénérienne *f.*
Venetian (vi'ni:ʃən) *adj,n* vénitien, -ienne. **Venetian blind** *n* jalousie *f.*
vengeance ('vendʒəns) *n* vengeance *f.*
Venice ('venis) *n* Venise *f.*
venison ('venisən) *n* venaison *f.*
venom ('venəm) *n* venin *m.*
vent[1] (vent) *n* trou, orifice *m.* ouverture *f.*
vent[2] (vent) *vt* donner libre cours à.
ventilate ('ventileit) *vt* aérer, ventiler. **ventilation** *n* aération, ventilation *f.*
venture ('ventʃə) *n* entreprise risquée *f.* *vt* oser, se risquer à. *vi* risquer de.
Venus ('vi:nəs) *n* Vénus *f.*
veranda (və'rændə) *n* véranda *f.*
verb (və:b) *n* verbe *m.* **verbal** *adj* verbal, -aux.
verdict ('və:dikt) *n* verdict *m.*
verge (və:dʒ) *n* bord *m.* bordure *f.* *v* **verge on** toucher à, friser.
verify ('verifai) *vt* vérifier, confirmer.
vermin ('və:min) *n* vermine *f.*
vermouth ('və:məθ) *n* vermout *m.*
vernacular (və'nækjulə) *adj* vernaculaire, indigène. *n* **1** langue du pays *f.* **2** langage *m.*
versatile ('və:sətail) *adj* souple, apte à tout.
verse (və:s) *n* **1** vers *m.* **2** strophe *f.*
version ('və:ʃən) *n* version, interprétation *f.*
vertebrate ('və:tibreit) *adj,n* vertébré *m.*
vertical ('və:tikəl) *adj* vertical, -aux.
verve (və:v) *n* verve *f.*
very ('veri) *adv* **1** très. **2** fort, bien. **3** tout. *adj* **1** vrai, véritable. **2** même.
vessel ('vesəl) *n* **1** *naut* navire *m.* **2** récipient *m.*
vest (vest) *n* gilet, maillot (de corps) *m.* *vt* revêtir, confier. **vested** *adj* acquis.
vestment ('vestmənt) *n* vêtement *m.*
vestry ('vestri) *n* sacristie *f.*
vet (vet) *n inf* vétérinaire *m.* *vt inf* examiner.
veteran ('vetərən) *n* vétéran *m.* *adj* aguerri, expérimenté.
veterinary surgeon ('vetrinəri) *n* vétérinaire *m.*
veto ('vi:tou) *n, pl* **-oes** veto *m.* *vt* mettre son veto à, interdire.
vex (veks) *vt* vexer, fâcher.
via ('vaiə) *prep* via, par.
viable ('vaiəbəl) *adj* viable.
viaduct ('vaiədʌkt) *n* viaduc *m.*
vibrate (vai'breit) *vi* vibrer. *vt* faire vibrer. **vibration** *n* vibration *f.*
vicar ('vikə) *n* curé *m.*
vicarious (vi'kɛəriəs) *adj* **1** pour *or* par un autre. **2** délégué, par substitution.
vice[1] (vais) *n* vice, défaut *m.*
vice[2] (vais) *n tech* étau, -aux *m.*
vice-chancellor *n* **1** vice-chancelier *m.* **2** *educ* recteur *m.*
vice-president *n* vice-président *m.*
vice-versa ('və:sə) *adv* vice versa.
vicinity (vi'sinəti) *n* voisinage *m.* alentours *m pl.*
vicious ('viʃəs) *adj* vicieux, -euse, méchant.
victim ('viktim) *n* victime *f.* **victimize** *vt* prendre comme victime.
victory ('viktri) *n* victoire *f.* **victorious** *adj* victorieux, -euse.
video-tape ('vidiouteip) *n* bande magnétique vidéo *f.*
Vietnam (viet'næm) *n* Viet-nam *m.* **Vietnamese** *adj,n* vietnamien, -ienne.
view (vju.) *n* **1** vue, perspective *f.* **2** opinion *f.* *vt,vi* regarder. **view-finder** *n* viseur *m.*

vigil ('vidʒil) *n* veille *f*. **vigilant** *adj* vigilant, éveillé.
vigour ('vigə) *n* vigueur *f*.
vile (vail) *adj* **1** vil, infâme. **2** *inf* exécrable.
villa ('vilə) *n* villa *f*.
village ('vilidʒ) *n* village *m*.
villain ('vilən) *n* scélérat, gredin *m*.
vindictive (vin'diktiv) *adj* vindicatif, -ive.
vine (vain) *n* vigne *f*. **vineyard** *n* vignoble *m*.
vinegar ('vinigə) *n* vinaigre *m*.
vintage ('vintidʒ) *n* **1** vendanges *f pl*. **2** année *f*.
vinyl ('vainil) *n* vinyl *m*.
viola (vi'oulə) *n* alto *m*.
violate ('vaiəleit) *vt* violer, profaner. **violation** *n* violation, infraction *f*.
violence ('vaiələns) *n* violence *f*. **violent** *adj* violent.
violet ('vaiələt) *n* **1** *bot* violette *f*. **2** (colour) violet *m*. *adj* violet, -ette.
violin (vaiə'lin) *n* violon *m*.
viper ('vaipə) *n* vipère *f*.
virgin ('və:dʒin) *n* vierge *f*. *adj* de vierge, virginal, -aux.
Virgo ('və:gou) *n* Vierge *f*.
virile ('virail) *adj* viril, mâle.
virtue ('və:tju:) *n* **1** vertu *f*. **2** qualité *f*. **virtual** *adj* **1** de *or* en fait. **2** virtuel, -elle. **virtuous** *adj* vertueux, -euse.
virus ('vairəs) *n* virus *m*.
visa ('vi:zə) *n* visa *m*.
viscount ('vaikaunt) *n* vicomte *m*. **viscountess** *n* vicomtesse *f*.
vision ('viʒən) *n* **1** vision, vue *f*. **2** apparition *f*. **visible** *adj* visible. **visibility** *n* visibilité *f*. **visionary** *adj,n* visionnaire.
visit ('vizit) *n* visite *f*. *vt* visiter, rendre visite à. **visitor** *n* visiteur, -euse.
visual ('vizjuəl) *adj* visuel, -elle. **visualize** *vi* se représenter. *vt* envisager.
vital ('vaitḷ) *adj* vital, -aux. **vitality** *n* vitalité *f*.
vitamin ('vitəmin) *n* vitamine *f*.
vivacious (vi'veiʃəs) *adj* vif, vive, enjoué.
vivid ('vivid) *adj* vif, vive, éclatant.
vixen ('viksən) *n* renarde *f*.
vocabulary (və'kæbjuləri) *n* vocabulaire *m*.
vocal ('voukəl) *adj* vocal, -aux.
vocation (vou'keiʃən) *n* vocation *f*. **vocational** *adj* professionnel, -elle.
vodka ('vɔdkə) *n* vodka *f*.
voice (vɔis) *n* voix *f*. *vt* exprimer.
void (vɔid) *adj* **1** vide. **2** *law* nul, nulle. **3** dépourvu. *n* vide *m*.
volatile ('vɔlətail) *adj* volatile.
volcano (vɔl'keinou) *n, pl* **-oes** *or* **-os** volcan *m*.
vole (voul) *n* compagnol *m*.
volley ('vɔli) *n* volée, salve *f*. *vi* reprendre la balle de volée.
volt (voult) *n* volt *m*.
volume ('vɔlju:m) *n* **1** volume *m*. **2** *lit* tôme *m*.
volunteer (vɔlən'tiə) *n* volontaire *m*. *vt* offrir volontairement. *vi* s'offrir. **voluntary** *adj* volontaire, spontané.
voluptuous (və'lʌptʃuəs) *adj* voluptueux, -euse.
vomit ('vɔmit) *vt,vi* vomir. *n* vomissement *m*.
voodoo ('vu:du:) *n* vaudou *m*.
vote (vout) *n* vote, scrutin *m*. *vt,vi* voter.
vouch (vautʃ) *vt* affirmer, garantir. **vouch for** répondre de.
voucher ('vautʃə) *n* bon, reçu *m*.
vow (vau) *n* vœu, vœux, serment *m*. *vt* vouer, jurer.
vowel ('vauəl) *n* voyelle *f*.
voyage ('vɔiidʒ) *n* voyage sur mer *m*.
vulgar ('vʌlgə) *adj* vulgaire, commun. **vulgarity** *n* vulgarité *f*.
vulnerable ('vʌlnərəbəl) *adj* vulnérable.
vulture ('vʌltʃə) *n* vautour *m*.

W

wad (wɔd) *n* tampon, bouchon *m*. bourre *f*. *vt* capitonner, ouater. **wadding** *n* ouatage, rembourrage *m*.
waddle ('wɔdḷ) *vi* se dandiner. *n* dandinement *m*.
wade (weid) *vi* marcher dans l'eau. *vt* passer à gué. **wade through** venir péniblement à bout de.
wafer ('weifə) *n* gaufrette *f*.
waft (wɔft) *n* bouffée *f*. souffle *m*. *vt* porter. *vi* flotter.
wag (wæg) *n* agitation *f*. frétillement *m*. *vt* agiter, remuer. *vi* s'agiter, se remuer.
wage (weidʒ) *n* gages *m pl*. salaire *m*. *v* **wage war** faire la guerre.
waggle ('wægəl) *vt* frétiller.
wagon ('wægən) *n* chariot, wagon *m*.
waif (weif) *n* épave *f*. enfant abandonné *m*.
wail (weil) *vi* gémir, vagir. *n* cri plaintif *m*. plainte *f*.
waist (weist) *n* taille, ceinture *f*. **waistband** *n* ceinture *f*. **waistcoat** *n* gilet *m*. **waistline** *n* taille *f*.
wait (weit) *vi,vt* attendre. *n* attente *f*. **waiter** *n* garçon *m*. **waiting list** *n* liste d'attente

f. **waiting room** *n* salle d'attente *f.* **waitress** *n* serveuse *f.*

waive (weiv) *vt* renoncer à, abandonner, écarter.

wake* (weik) *vi* se réveiller. *vt* réveiller. **waken** *vt* **1** réveiller. **2** éveiller. *vi* se réveiller.

Wales (weilz) *n* pays de Galles *m.*

walk (wɔ:k) *vi* **1** marcher. **2** se promener. **3** aller à pied. *vt* faire marcher, promener. *n* **1** promenade *f.* **2** marche *f.* **walking stick** *n* canne *f.* **walkout** *n* grève spontanée *f.* **walkover** *n* victoire facile *f.*

wall (wɔ:l) *n* **1** mur *m.* **2** muraille *f.* **wallflower** *n* giroflée des murailles *f.* **be a wallflower** faire tapisserie. **wallpaper** *n* papier peint *m.*

wallet ('wɔlit) *n* portefeuille *m.*

wallop ('wɔləp) *vt inf* rosser, flanquer une volée à. *n* coup vigoureux *m.*

wallow ('wɔlou) *vi* se vautrer, croupir.

walnut ('wɔ:lnʌt) *n* noix *f.* **walnut tree** *n* noyer *m.*

walrus ('wɔ:lrəs) *n* morse *m.*

waltz (wɔ:ls) *n* valse *f. vi* valser.

wand (wɔnd) *n* baguette *f.*

wander ('wɔndə) *vi* errer, vaguer.

wane (wein) *n* déclin *m. vi* décliner, décroître.

wangle ('wæŋgəl) *vt inf* obtenir par subterfuge, resquiller. *n* intrigue *f.*

want (wɔnt) *vt* **1** vouloir. **2** manquer de, avoir besoin de. *vi* manquer. *n* **1** manque, défaut *m.* **2** besoin *m.* **for want of** faute de. **wanted** *adj* **1** on demande. **2** recherché (par la police).

war (wɔ:) *n* guerre *f. vi* lutter, faire la guerre. **warfare** *n* guerre *f.*

warble ('wɔ:bəl) *n* gazouillement *m. vi* gazouiller.

ward (wɔ:d) *n* **1** salle *f.* **2** cellule *f.* **3** pupille *m,f. v* **ward off** parer. **warden** *n* directeur, gardien, conservateur *m.* **warder** *n* gardien de prison *m.* **wardrobe** *n* garde-robe *f.*

warehouse ('wɑəhaus) *n* entrepôt *m. vt* emmagasiner.

warm (wɔ:m) *adj* **1** chaud. **2** chaleureux, -euse. *vt* chauffer. *vi* se chauffer. **warmth** *n* chaleur *f.*

warn (wɔ:n) *vt* avertir, prévenir. **warning** *n* avertissement, préavis *m.*

warp (wɔ:p) *vt* fausser, pervertir. *vi* gauchir, se déformer, jouer. *n* **1** chaîne *f.* **2** voilure *f.*

warrant ('wɔrənt) *n* **1** garantie *f.* **2** autorisation *f.* **3** mandat *m. vt* **1** garantir, certifier. **2** justifier.

warren ('wɔrən) *n* garenne *f.*

warrior ('wɔriə) *n* guerrier *m.*

wart (wɔ:t) *n* verrue *f.*

wary ('wɛəri) *adj* avisé, prudent.

was (wəz; *stressed* wɔz) *v* see **be.**

wash (wɔʃ) *vt* laver. *vi* se laver. **wash down** arroser. **wash out 1** enlever. **2** rincer. **washout** *n sl* fiasco, four *m.* **wash up** faire la vaisselle. ~*n* **1** lavage *m.* **2** lessive *f.* **washbasin** *n* lavabo *m.* **washer** *n* rondelle *f.* **washing** *n* **1** lavage *m.* **2** linge *m.* **washing machine** *n* machine à laver *f.* **washing powder** *n* lessive *f.* **washroom** *n* cabinet de toilette *m.*

wasp (wɔsp) *n* guêpe *f.*

waste (weist) *adj* **1** de rebut. **2** inculte. *n* **1** gaspillage *m.* perte *f.* **2** rebut *m.* déchets *m pl. vt* **1** gaspiller. **2** épuiser. *vi* s'user. **wasteful** *adj* prodigue, gaspilleur, -euse. **wastepaper basket** *n* corbeille à papier *f.*

watch (wɔtʃ) *vt* **1** observer, regarder. **2** surveiller. *vi* veiller. *n* **1** garde *f.* **2** montre *f.* **3** *naut* quart *m.* **watchdog** *n* chien de garde *m.* **watchful** *adj* vigilant, attentif, -ive.

water ('wɔ:tə) *n* eau, eaux *f. vt* **1** arroser. **2** abreuver. *vi* se mouiller. **water down** diluer.

water-closet *n* cabinet *m.*

watercolour ('wɔ:təkʌlə) *n* aquarelle *f.*

watercress ('wɔ:təkres) *n* cresson *m.*

waterfall ('wɔ:təfɔ:l) *n* chute d'eau, cascade *f.*

watering-can *n* arrosoir *m.*

waterlily ('wɔ:təlili) *n* nénuphar *m.*

waterlogged ('wɔ:təlɔgd) *adj* imbibé d'eau.

watermark ('wɔ:təmɑ:k) *n* filigrane *m.*

watermelon ('wɔ:təmelən) *n* pastèque *f.*

waterproof ('wɔ:təpru:f) *adj* imperméable. *vt* caoutchouter.

water-ski *vi* faire du ski nautique.

watertight ('wɔ:tətait) *adj* étanche.

waterway ('wɔ:təwei) *n* voie navigable *f.*

watery ('wɔ:təri) *adj* aqueux, -euse.

watt (wɔt) *n* watt *m.*

wave (weiv) *n* **1** vague *f.* **2** geste *m.* **3** ondulation *f. vi* **1** s'agiter. **2** onduler. **3** faire signe à. *vt* **1** agiter. **2** faire signe de. **waveband** *n* longueur d'onde *f.* **wavelength** *n* longueur d'onde *f.* **wavy** *adj* onduleux, -euse.

waver ('weivə) *vi* **1** vaciller. **2** hésiter, fléchir.

wax[1] (wæks) *n* cire *f. vt* cirer, encaustiquer.

wax[2] (wæks) *vi* croître.

way (wei) *n* **1** voie, route *f.* chemin *m.* **2** moyen *m.* façon, manière *f.* **3** direction *f.* **4** sens *m.* **5** point de vue *f.* **by the way** à propos. **this way** par ici. **under way** en train. **wayside** *n* bas-côté, bord de la route *m*. *adj* du bord de la route.

waylay* (wei'lei) *vt* arrêter au passage.

wayward ('weiwəd) *adj* entêté, fantasque.

we (wi:) *pron 1st pers pl* nous.

weak (wi:k) *adj* **1** faible. **2** infirme. **weaken** *vt* affaiblir. *vi* s'affaiblir. **weak-minded** *adj* faible d'esprit. **weakness** *n* **1** faiblesse *f*. **2** faible *m*. **weak-willed** *adj* sans volonté.

wealth (welΘ) *n* **1** richesse *f*. **2** abondance *f*. **wealthy** *adj* riche.

weapon ('wepən) *n* arme *f*.

wear* (wɛə) *vt* **1** porter, mettre. **2** user. *vi* s'user. **wear out 1** user. **2** épuiser. ~*n* **1** usage *m*. **2** usure *f*. **wear and tear** usage *m*.

weary ('wiəri) *adj* las, lasse. *vt* lasser, fatiguer. *vi* se lasser.

weasel ('wi:zəl) *n* belette *f*.

weather ('weðə) *n* temps *m*. *vt* survivre. **weather-beaten** *adj* basané. **weather forecast** *n* bulletin météorologique *m*.

weave* (wi:v) *vt* tisser. *n* tissage *m*.

web (web) *n* **1** toile *f*. **2** tissu *m*.

wedding ('wediŋ) *n* mariage *m*. noces *f pl*. **wedding ring** *n* alliance *f*.

wedge (wedʒ) *n* coin *m*. cale *f*. *vt* **1** coincer, assujettir. **2** serrer.

Wednesday ('wenzdi) *n* mercredi *m*.

wee (wi:) *adj inf* tout petit.

weed (wi:d) *n* mauvaise herbe *f*. *vt* désherber.

week (wi:k) *n* semaine *f*. **weekday** *n* jour de semaine *m*. **weekend** *n* fin de semaine *f*. week-end *m*. **weekly** *adj,n* hebdomadaire. *adv* tous les huit jours.

weep* (wi:p) *vi* pleurer.

weigh (wei) *vt,vi* peser. **weighbridge** *n* bascule *f*. **weight** *n* poids *m*. pesanteur *f*. **weight-lifting** *n* haltérophilie *f*.

weird ('wiəd) *adj* étrange, mystérieux, -euse.

welcome ('welkəm) *adj* bienvenu. *n* bienvenue *f*. *vt* souhaiter la bienvenue à.

weld (weld) *n* soudure *f*. *vt* souder.

welfare ('welfɛə) *n* bien-être *m*. prospérité *f*.

well[1] (wel) *n* puits *m*.

well[2] (wel) *adv* bien. **as well** aussi. ~*adj* bien, bon, bonne. **well-behaved** *adj* sage, bien élevé.

well-bred *adj* **1** bien élevé. **2** de race.

well-built *adj* costaud.

well-known *adj* bien connu, célèbre.

well-off *adj* à l'aise, riche.

well-paid *adj* bien payé.

well-spoken *adj* au langage cultivé.

well-worn *adj* usagé.

Welsh (welʃ) *adj* gallois. *n* (language) gallois *m*. **Welshman** *n* gallois *m*.

went (went) *v* see **go.**

wept (wept) *v* see **weep.**

were (wə:) *v* see **be.**

west (west) *n* **1** ouest *m*. **2** *cap* Occident *m*. *adj* occidental, -aux, ouest *invar*. *adv* à *or* vers l'ouest. **westerly** *adj* d'ouest. **western** *adj* de l'ouest, occidental, -aux. *n* western *m*. **westward** *adj* à l'ouest, de l'ouest. **westwards** *adv* vers l'ouest.

West Indies ('indiz) *n* Antilles *f pl*. **West Indian** *adj,n* antillais.

wet (wet) *adj* **1** mouillé, humide. **2** pluvieux, -euse. *n* pluie *f*. *vt* mouiller.

whack (wæk) *n* coup violent *m*. *vt* donner des coups à, rosser.

whale (weil) *n* baleine *f*.

wharf (wɔ:f) *n* débarcadère *m*.

what (wɔt) *pron* **1** qu'est-ce qui? qu'est-ce que? que? quoi? **2** ce qui, ce que, ce dont. *adj* **1** quel? quelle? **2** que, qui. *interj* quoi! comment! **whatever** *pron* tout ce qui, tout ce que, quoi, qui, quoi que. *adj* **1** quelque... qui, quelque... que. **2** aucun, quelconque.

wheat (wi:t) *n* blé *m*.

wheedle ('wi:dl̩) *vt* cajoler, câliner.

wheel (wi:l) *n* roue *f*. **wheelbarrow** *n* brouette *f*. **wheelchair** *n* fauteuil roulant *m*.

wheeze (wi:z) *vi* respirer péniblement.

whelk (welk) *n* buccin *m*.

when (wen) *adv* quand? *conj* **1** quand, lorsque. **2** où, que. **whenever** *adv* toutes les fois que, chaque fois que.

where (wɛə) *adv* **1** où? **2** où. *conj,pron* où. **whereabouts** *adv* où? *n* situation *f*. **whereas** *conj* **1** attendu que. **2** tandis que. **whereby** *adv* par lequel. **whereupon** *adv* sur quoi, sur ce. **wherever** *adv* **1** partout où, n'importe où. **2** où que.

whether ('weðə) *conj* si.

which (witʃ) *adj* **1** quel? quelle? **2** lequel, laquelle. *pron* **1** lequel? laquelle? **2** qui, que, dont, lequel, laquelle. **3** ce qui, ce que. **whichever** *pron* celui qui, celui que, n'importe lequel. *adj* n'importe quel, quelque...que.

whiff (wif) *n* bouffée *f*.

while (wail) *conj* pendant que, tandis que. *n* temps *m*. **be worth one's while** valoir la peine.

whim (wim) *n* caprice *m*.

whimper ('wimpə) *vi* pleurnicher, geindre. *n* pleurnichement, geignement *m*.
whimsical ('wimzikəl) *adj* capricieux, -euse.
whine (wain) *vi* se plaindre, pleurnicher, geindre. *n* geignement *m*.
whip (wip) *n* fouet *m*. *vt* fouetter.
whippet ('wipit) *n* whippet, lévrier *m*.
whir (wə:) *vi* vrombir, siffler, ronronner. *n* bruissement, ronronnement *m*.
whirl (wə:l) *n* tourbillon, tournoiement *m*. *vi* tourbillonner, tournoyer. **whirlwind** *n* trombe *f*.
whisk[1] (wisk) *vt* **1** agiter. **2** enlever, escamoter. *vi* s'élancer.
whisk[2] (wisk) *vt* fouetter, battre. *n* fouet *m*.
whisker ('wiskə) *n* **1** (of a cat, etc.) moustache *f*. **2** *pl* favoris *m pl*.
whisky ('wiski) *n* whisky *m*.
whisper ('wispə) *n* chuchotement *m*. *vi,vt* chuchoter.
whist (wist) *n* whist *m*.
whistle ('wisəl) *n* sifflement *m*. *vi,vt* siffler.
white (wait) *adj* blanc, -che. *n* **1** blanc *m*. **2** *cap* Blanc, -che. **whiten** *vt* blanchir. *vi* pâlir. **whitewash** *vt* badigeonner à la chaux, blanchir. *n* blanc de chaux *m*. **whiting** *n* merlan *m*.
Whitsun ('witsən) *n* Pentecôte *f*.
whiz (wiz) *vi* siffler.
who (hu:) *pron* **1** qui? qui est-ce qui? **2** qui, lequel, laquelle, celui qui. **whoever** *pron* **1** celui qui, quiconque. **2** qui, que.
whole (houl) *adj* **1** sain, intact. **2** entier, -ière. *n* tout *m*. totalité *f*. **on the whole** en somme. **wholehearted** *adj* de tout cœur, sincère. **wholemeal** *adj* complet, -ète. **wholesale** *n* vente en gros *f*. *adj* **1** de *or* en gros. **2** général, -aux. *adv* en gros. **wholesome** *adj* sain, salubre. **wholly** *adv* **1** tout à fait. **2** intégralement.
whom (hu:m) *pron* **1** qui? qui est-ce que? **2** que, lequel, laquelle, qui.
whooping cough ('hu:piŋ) *n* coqueluche *f*.
whore (hɔ:) *n* prostituée, putain *f*.
whose (hu:z) *pron* **1** de qui? à qui? **2** dont, de qui.
why (wai) *adv* pourquoi? *conj,n* pourquoi *m*. *interj* tiens!
wick (wik) *n* mèche *f*.
wicked ('wikid) *adj* mauvais, méchant.
wide (waid) *adj* **1** large. **2** vaste. **3** loin. *adv* **1** loin. **2** (tout) grand. **widely** *adv* largement, très. **widen** *vt* élargir, étendre. *vi* s'élargir. **widespread** *adj* étendu, répandu.
widow ('widou) *n* veuve *f*. **widower** *n* veuf *m*.
width (widθ) *n* largeur *f*.
wield (wi:ld) *vt* manier.
wife (waif) *n, pl* **wives** femme, épouse *f*.
wig (wig) *n* perruque *f*.
wiggle ('wigəl) *vt* tortiller, remuer. *vi* se tortiller.
wigwam ('wigwæm) *n* wigwam *m*.
wild (waild) *adj* **1** sauvage, farouche. **2** affolé. **3** furieux, -euse. **wildlife** *n* faune *f*.
wilderness ('wildənəs) *n* lieu sauvage, inculte *m*.
wilful ('wilfəl) *adj* entêté, volontaire.
will*[1] (wil) *v mod aux* **1** translated by the future tense. **2** aller.
will[2] (wil) *n* **1** volonté *f*. vouloir *m*. **2** testament *m*. *vt* **1** vouloir, désirer. **2** léguer. **willpower** *n* volonté *f*.
willing ('wiliŋ) *adj* de bonne volonté, consentant.
willow ('wilou) *n* saule *m*.
wilt (wilt) *vi* se flétrir, dépérir.
win* (win) *vi,vt* gagner, remporter.
wince (wins) *n* crispation *f*. tressaillement *m*. *vi* grimacer, tressaillir de douleur.
winch (wintʃ) *n* manivelle *f*. treuil *m*.
wind[1] (wind) *n* vent *m*. **windfall** *n* **1** fruit tombé *m*. **2** aubaine *f*. **windmill** *n* moulin à vent *m*. **windpipe** *n* gosier *m*. **windscreen** *n* pare-brise *m invar*. **windscreen wipers** *n pl* essuie-glace *m*. **windswept** *adj* venteux, -euse, balayé par le vent. **windy** *adj* venteux, -euse.
wind*[2] (waind) *vt* tourner, enrouler. **wind up** remonter.
windlass ('windləs) *n* treuil *m*.
window ('windou) *n* fenêtre *f*. **window box** *n* caisse à fleurs, jardinière *f*. **window-dressing** *n* art de l'étalage *m*. **window-shop** *vi* faire du lèche-vitrines.
wine (wain) *n* vin *m*. **wineglass** *n* verre à vin *m*.
wing (wiŋ) *n* **1** aile *f*. **2** *pl Th* coulisses *f pl*. **wing commander** *n* lieutenant-colonel d'aviation *m*. **wingspan** *n* envergure *f*.
wink (wiŋk) *vi* cligner les yeux, faire de l'œil. *vt* cligner. *n* clignement, clin d'œil *m*.
winkle ('wiŋkəl) *n* bigorneau, -aux *m*.
winter ('wintə) *n* hiver *m*.
wipe (waip) *vt* essuyer. *n* coup de torchon *or* d'éponge *m*.

wire (ˈwaiə) *n* **1** fil de fer *m*. **2** dépêche *f*. *vt* **1** clôturer. **2** télégraphier. *vi* télégraphier.

wise (waiz) *adj* sage, prudent. **wisdom** *n* sagesse *f*.

wish (wiʃ) *vt* **1** désirer. **2** souhaiter. **3** vouloir. *n* désir, souhait *m*.

wisp (wisp) *n* bouchon *m*. poignée, mèche *f*.

wisteria (wisˈtiəriə) *n* glycine *f*.

wit (wit) *n* **1** esprit *m*. **2** intelligence *f*.

witch (witʃ) *n* sorcière *f*. **witchcraft** *n* sorcellerie *f*.

with (wið) *prep* **1** avec. **2** de, à. **3** chez. **4** malgré.

withdraw* (wiðˈdrɔ:) *vt* retirer, enlever. *vi* se retirer. **withdrawal** *n* **1** retrait *m*. **2** retraite *f*.

wither (ˈwiðə) *vt* **1** dessécher, faner. **2** foudroyer. *vi* se dessécher, se faner.

withhold* (wiðˈhould) *vt* **1** refuser. **2** dissimuler.

within (wiðˈin) *adv* à l'intérieur. *prep* **1** à l'intérieur de. **2** dans. **3** en. **4** en moins de.

without (wiðˈaut) *prep* **1** sans. **2** en dehors de. *adv* à l'extérieur.

withstand* (wiðˈstænd) *vt* résister, supporter.

witness (ˈwitnəs) *vt* être témoin de, assister à. *vi* témoigner. *n* **1** témoin *m*. **2** témoignage *m*.

witty (ˈwiti) *adj* spirituel, -elle, piquant.

wizard (ˈwizəd) *n* sorcier, magicien *m*.

wobble (ˈwɔbəl) *vi* ballotter, branler. *n* oscillation *f*. branlement *m*.

woke (wouk) *v* see **wake.**

woken (ˈwoukən) *v* see **wake.**

wolf (wulf) *n, pl* **wolves** loup *m*.

woman (ˈwumən) *n, pl* **women** femme *f*. **womanhood** *n* état de femme *m*. feminité *f*.

womb (wu:m) *n* matrice *f*. sein *m*.

won (wʌn) *v* see **win.**

wonder (ˈwʌndə) *vi* s'étonner, s'émerveiller. *vt* **1** se demander. **2** s'étonner. *n* **1** merveille *f*. prodige *m*. **2** étonnement *m*. **wonderful** *adj* merveilleux, -euse, épatant.

wonky (ˈwɔŋki) *adj inf* branlant, patraque.

wood (wud) *n* bois *m*. **woodcock** *n* bécasse *f*. **wooden** *adj* **1** de *or* en bois. **2** raide. **woodland** *n* pays boisé, bois *m*. *adj* des bois, sylvestre. **woodpecker** *n* pic *m*. **wood-pigeon** *n* ramier *m*. palombe *f*. **woodwind** *n* bois *m pl*. **woodwork** *n* **1** menuiserie, ébénisterie *f*. **2** bois travaillé *m*. **woodworm** *n* ver du bois *m*.

wool (wul) *n* laine *f*. **woollen** *adj* de laine. **woolly** *adj* **1** laineux, -euse. **2** flou.

word (wə:d) *n* **1** mot *m*. **2** parole *f*. *vt* formuler, énoncer. **word-perfect** *adj* qui connaît parfaitement son rôle.

wore (wɔ:) *v* see **wear.**

work (wɔ:k) *n* **1** travail, -aux, ouvrage *m*. **2** œuvre *f*. *vi* **1** travailler. **2** exploiter. **3** fonctionner, marcher. **working class** *n* classe ouvrière *f*. **workman** *n* ouvrier *m*. **workmanship** *n* façon *f*. fini de l'exécution *m*. **workshop** *n* atelier *m*.

world (wə:ld) *n* monde *m*. **worldly** *adj* **1** du monde. **2** mondain. **worldwide** *adj* universel, -elle, répandu partout.

worm (wə:m) *n* ver *m*.

wormwood (ˈwə:mwud) *n* absinthe *f*.

worn (wɔ:n) *v* see **wear.** *adj* usagé. **worn out** *adj* **1** épuisé. **2** usé.

worry (ˈwʌri) *vi* se tracasser, s'inquiéter. *vt* **1** tourmenter, tracasser. **2** harceler. **don't worry!** ne vous en faites pas! ~*n* ennui, souci, tracas *m*.

worse (ˈwə:s) *adj* pire, plus mauvais. *n* pire *m*. *adv* pis, plus mal. **worsen** *vt* empirer, aggraver. *vi* s'empirer, s'aggraver.

worship (ˈwə:ʃip) *vt* adorer. *n* **1** culte *m*. adoration *f*. **2** *cap* Honneur *m*.

worst (wə:st) *adj* le *or* la pire. *n* pire *m*. **at the worst** au pis aller. ~*adv* le pis, le plus mal.

worth (wə:θ) *adj* valant, digne de. **be worth** valoir. ~*n* valeur *f*. **worthwhile** *adj* qui en vaut la peine. **worthy** *adj* digne *f*.

would (wəd; *stressed* wud) *v* see **will**[1].

wound[1] (wu:nd) *n* blessure *f*. *vt* blesser, froisser.

wound[2] (waund) *v* see **wind**[2].

wove (wouv) *v* see **weave.**

woven (ˈwouvn̩) *v* see **weave.**

wrangle (ˈræŋgəl) *vi* se disputer, se quereller. *n* dispute *f*.

wrap (ræp) *vt* envelopper. **wrap oneself up** s'emmitoufler. **wrapping** *n* emballage *m*.

wreath (ri:θ) *n* couronne mortuaire *f*.

wreathe (ri:ð) *vt* enguirlander. *vi* tourbillonner.

wreck (rek) *n* épave, ruine *f*. *vt* faire naufrage, faire ruiner. **wreckage** *n* débris *m*. épave *f*.

wren (ren) *n* roitelet *m*.

wrench (rentʃ) *n* mouvement de torsion *m*. *vt* tordre, forcer, arracher.

wrestle (ˈresəl) *vi,vt* lutter. *n* lutte *f*.

wretch (retʃ) *n* **1** malheureux *m*. **2** scélérat *m*. **wretched** *adj* **1** misérable. **2** pitoyable.

wriggle (ˈrigəl) *vi* se tortiller, se remuer. *vt* tortiller. *n* tortillement *m*.

wring* (riŋ) *vt* tordre. *n* torsion *f*.
wrinkle ('riŋkəl) *n* ride *f*. *vt* rider, froncer. *vi* se rider.
wrist (rist) *n* poignet *m*. **wristwatch** *n* montre-bracelet *f*.
writ (rit) *n* acte judiciaire *m*.
write* (rait) *vt,vi* écrire. **writer** *n* auteur, écrivain *m*. **writing paper** *n* papier à lettres *m*.
writhe (raið) *vi* se tordre.
wrong (rɔŋ) *adj* **1** mauvais, mal *invar*. **2** incorrect, faux, fausse. **be wrong 1** avoir tort. **2** se tromper. ~*n* mal, tort *m*. *adv* mal, de travers, à tort. *vt* faire tort à.
wrote (rout) *v* see **write.**
wrought iron (rɔ:t) *n* fer forgé *m*.
wrung (rʌŋ) *v* see **wring.**
wry (rai) *adj* tordu, de travers.

X

xenophobia (zenə'foubiə) *n* xénophobie *f*.
Xerox ('ziərɔks) *n Tdmk* machine à photocopier *f*. *vt* photocopier.
X-ray *n* rayon X *m*. *vt* radiographier.
xylophone ('zailəfoun) *n* xylophone *m*

Y

yacht (jɔt) *n* yacht *m*. **yachtsman** *n* plaisancier *m*.
yank (jæŋk) *vt* tirer brusquement. *n* secousse, saccade *f*.
yap (jæp) *vi* japper. *n* jappement *m*.
yard[1] (jɑ:d) *n* (measurement) yard *m*. **yardstick** *n* **1** yard *m*. **2** mesure *f*. aune *m*.
yard[2] (jɑ:d) *n* **1** cour *f*. **2** chantier *m*.
yarn (jɑ:n) *n* **1** fil *m*. **2** histoire *f*.
yawn (jɔ:n) *vi* bâiller. *n* bâillement *m*.
year (jiə) *n* an *m*. année *f*.
yearn (jə:n) *vi* languir, soupirer. **yearning** *n* désir *m*. envie *f*.
yeast (ji:st) *n* levure *f*.
yell (jel) *n* hurlement *m*. *vi,vt* hurler.
yellow ('jelou) *adj,n* jaune *m*.
yelp (jelp) *vi* glapir, japper. *n* glapissement *m*.
yes (jes) *adv,n* oui *m*.
yesterday ('jestədi) *adv,n* hier *m*. **the day before yesterday** avant-hier *m*.
yet (jet) *adv* **1** encore. **2** déjà, jusqu'ici. *conj* cependant, malgré tout.
yew (ju:) *n* if *m*.
Yiddish ('jidiʃ) *adj,n* yiddish *m*.
yield (ji:ld) *vt* **1** donner, rapporter. **2** céder. *vi* céder, fléchir. *n* production *f*. rendement *m*.
yodel ('joudl̩) *vi* iouler.
yoga ('jougə) *n* yoga *m*.
yoghurt ('jɔgət) *n* yaourt *m*.
yoke (jouk) *n* joug *m*. *vt* accoupler.
yolk (jouk) *n* jaune d'œuf *m*.
yonder ('jɔndə) *adv* là-bas.
you (ju:) *pron 2nd pers s* **1** *fam* tu. **2** *fam* te. **3** *fam* toi. **4** *fml* vous. **5** *pl* vous.
young (jʌŋ) *adj* **1** jeune. **2** (of an animal) petit. **youngster** *n* jeune personne *f*. gosse *m,f*.
your (jɔ:; juə) *poss adj 2nd pers s* **1** *fam* ton, ta, tes. **2** *fml* votre, vos. **3** *pl* votre, vos. **yours** *poss pron 2nd pers s* **1** *fam* le tien, la tienne, à toi. **2** *fml* le *or* la vôtre, à vous. **3** *pl* le *or* la vôtre, à vous. **yourself** *pron 2nd pers s* **1** *fam* toi-même. **2** *fam* te. **3** *fml* vous-même. **4** *fml* vous. **5** *pl* vous-mêmes. **6** *pl* vous.
youth (ju:θ) *n* jeunesse *f*. **youth hostel** *n* auberge de la jeunesse *f*.
Yugoslavia (ju:gou'slɑ:viə) *n* Yougoslavie *f*. **Yugoslav** *adj,n* yougoslave.

Z

zeal (zi:l) *n* zèle *m*. **zealous** *adj* zélé, empressé.
zebra ('zebrə) *n* zèbre *m*. **zebra crossing** *n* passage clouté *m*.
zero ('ziərou) *n* zéro *m*.
zest (zest) *n* **1** enthousiasme, entrain *m*. **2** saveur *f*. piquant *m*.
zigzag ('zigzæg) *n* zigzag *m*. *vi* zigzaguer.
zinc (ziŋk) *n* zinc *m*.
Zionism ('zaiənizəm) *n* sionisme *m*.
zip (zip) *n* **1** Fermeture Éclair *Tdmk f invar*. **2** *inf* énergie *f*.
zither ('ziðə) *n* cithare *f*.
zodiac ('zoudiæk) *n* zodiaque *m*.
zone (zoun) *n* zone *f*.
zoo (zu:) *n* zoo *m*.
zoology (zou'ɔlədʒi) *n* zoologie *f*. **zoological** *adj* zoologique. **zoologist** *n* zoologiste *m,f*.
zoom (zu:m) *vi* vrombir. *n* bourdonnement *m*.